Fodor's 94
USA

Fodor's Travel Publications, Inc.
New York • Toronto • London • Sydney • Auckland

Fodor's USA

Editor: Nancy van Itallie
Associate Editor: Andrew Collins
Contributors: Stephen Allen, Marcia Andrews, Richard Bak, Tom Barr, Brenda Blagg, Robert Blake, Kevin Bonham, John Branston, Ellen E. Browne, Janet Clark, Stacey Clark, Doug Cunningham, Karen Cure, Don Davenport, Diana Dickinson, Mary Engel, John Filiatreau, Nigel Fisher, Mary Frakes, Ed Frost, Roon Frost, Mitzi Gammon, Elizabeth Gardner, Tom Gauntt, Candice Gianetti, Mark Hein, Sylvia Higginbotham, Alan Hines, Barbara Hodgin, Ann Hughes, Holly Hughes, Edie Jarolim, Christopher Johnston, John Kelly, Jeff Kuechle, David Laskin, Dale Leatherman, Andrea Lehman, Konnie Le May, Julia Lisella, Jillian Magalaner, Janet Majure, Michael McPhee, Ellen Meloy, Rathe Miller, Honey Naylor, Mary Norris, Geoffrey O'Gara, Barbara Palmer, Conrad Paulus, Dick Pivetz, Mark Porter, Mark Potok, Carolyn Price, Marcy Pritchard, Gene Rebek, Judy Ringel, Bill Roberts, Francis X. Rocca, Lori Dodge Rose, Melanie Roth, Helayne Schiff, Matt Schofield, Mary Ellen Schultz, Donna Singer, Craig Seligman, Aaron Shurin, Mike Spring, Carol Timblin, Ron Welch, Loralee Wenger, Marty Wentzel, Sandra Widener, Delta Willis, Bobbi Zane
Creative Director: Fabrizio LaRocca
Cartographer: David Lindroth
Illustrator: Karl Tanner
Cover Photograph: Nicholas Devore III/Photographers/Aspen

Design: Vignelli Associates

Special Sales

Contents

Maps

Maps

Foreword

While every care has been taken to ensure the accuracy of the information in this guide, the passage of time will always bring change, and consequently the publisher cannot accept responsibility for errors that may occur.

All prices and opening times quoted here are based on information supplied to us at press time. Hours and admission fees may change, however, and the prudent traveler will avoid inconvenience by calling ahead.

Fodor's wants to hear about your travel experiences, both pleasant and unpleasant. When a hotel or restaurant fails to live up to its billing, let us know and we will investigate the complaint and revise our entries where the facts warrant it.

Send your letters to the editors of Fodor's Travel Publications, 201 E. 50th Street, New York, NY 10022.

Highlights'94 and Fodor's Choice

Highlights '94

The United States in 1994 greets travelers with world-class sports events, government-mandated improvements in access for people with disabilities, and a tentatively more hopeful economic outlook. What doesn't change is the country's delight in celebrating anniversaries, harvests, history, and itself.

For a glimpse of down-home all-American life, nothing beats the annual **state and county fairs,** farm shows, and special festivals that effervesce around the country each year. From the New York State Fair to the Midwest Farm Show in Wisconsin to the Georgia Apple Festival and Arts and Crafts Fair, attractions include exhibitions of livestock and local artists' works, pie baking and eating contests, and much more. State tourism boards can supply schedules of events.

At press time the waters of the Mississippi River and its tributaries were at flood stage in many parts of Illinois, Iowa, Missouri, Nebraska, and South Dakota, and damage was still being estimated. Visitors to these states in 1994 may find that some places of interest did not survive or are still under repair; check with local tourist offices before you go.

The stellar event in the U.S.A. in 1994 is the **World Cup Soccer** championship. From June 17 to July 17, 24 teams from around the world will compete in 52 games played in nine cities across the country: Boston, Chicago, Dallas, Detroit, Los Angeles (Pasadena), New York (Meadowlands, New Jersey), Orlando (Florida), San Francisco, and Washington, D.C. The matches are expected to draw up to a million international visitors by the final event at the Rose Bowl. Also in sports, the four major professional leagues—baseball, basketball, hockey, and football—are expanding; many cities, such as Miami, Denver, and Dallas/Fort Worth, have new teams to root for.

Zoos across the country may follow the lead of New York's institutions, renamed **"wildlife conservation parks"** to avoid the negative connotations attached to the word *zoo* in popular speech and to place emphasis on conservation rather than on confinement.

If you plan to travel by **car** in unfamiliar urban areas in 1994, you should be aware of the latest trend in crime—carjackings. Use discretion, and when it seems prudent, keep your car doors locked. When leaving a freeway in a major city, be sure you know where the exit ramp leads; if possible, call ahead to your destination to get detailed, clear directions for your route from the highway.

On a more pleasant note, National Forest **Scenic Byways** are auto-touring routes that are often as appealing as your destination. Begun in 1988, when National Forest Service employees were invited to choose the roads they thought most beautiful, the Scenic Byways program has expanded from the original 50 selections to 115 roads that cover 6,176 mi in 33 states, and new routes continue to be designated. Regional Forest Service offices or the U.S. Forest Service Public Affairs office can provide listings.

With the administration in Washington seemingly more attuned to environmental concerns than its predecessors, ecotourism within the country is growing. Local environmental groups are sponsoring service outings—cleanups, trail maintenance, tree planting—and nature preserves are welcoming visitors in order to educate them in the role of wilderness areas in the greater environment and the conflicts and problems that threaten local ecosystems. The Sierra Club (*see* Appendix) and the Nature Conservancy (tel. 703/841–5300) are among the national organizations that arrange field trips and other activities.

Train travel in the United States took a revolutionary step on April 4, 1993, when **Amtrak** began the country's first regularly scheduled **transcontinental** passenger service, from Los Angeles to Miami. Amtrak is also testing high-speed equipment from around the world on its Northeast Corridor lines in preparation for the inauguration of high-speed electrified train service between Boston and Washington, D.C., in 1996. Be on the lookout for special children's rates when making your Amtrak reservations.

Travel by bus is also taking a step forward as **Greyhound** introduces its new **computerized reservations** system city by city across the nation. This will make it possible to book schedule-specific trips in advance, using a toll-free number. Greyhound is also continuing to add new buses to its fleet and equip both new and old buses with radar to improve highway safety.

Six new domestic **airlines** started up in late 1992 and early 1993: Family, Kiwi, Morris, Reno, Skybus, and UltrAir. The first five offer various low-fare options based on one-class, high-density seating and/or high-volume or underserved routes. UltrAir aims for the business traveler with superior service and seating at prices comparable to full fares charged by the major airlines. The challenge for these new operations will be to ride out the majors' fare cuts and frequent-flier lures.

Hotels in the United States are increasingly focusing on families and on the fitness-conscious traveler, offering special organized programs for children and teens and expanding or installing health clubs and spas, as well as providing parklands for "light adventure" and group activities such as bicycling, in-line skating, motorcross, rodeos, and team sports. Many also offer special rates for families and a choice of packages for a variety of meal plans and sports and fitness activities. Booking your stay in advance is a cost cutter at several hotel chains. Be sure to check your options when reserving.

The American Hotel and Motel Association has launched a campaign to make travelers conscious of **security** when they're away from home; peepholes and dead bolts on room doors are becoming increasingly common, and in-hotel television channels highlight safety measures.

The 1990 **Americans with Disabilities Act,** which established national access standards for public facilities, continues to be put into effect. Throughout the country you'll see lower public telephones, lower control panels with Braille indicators on elevators, fire alarms that flash as well as sound, ramps or elevators at restaurant and hotel entrances, more parking for the disabled, specially equipped hotel rooms and baths, and other much-needed changes.

Restaurant owners in major U.S. cities have responded to the sluggish economy and to half-empty dining rooms by maintaining or, in many cases, lowering prices. In addition, a number of expensive restaurants, such as Le Bec-Fin in Philadelphia and Spiaggia in Chicago, have opened spin-off cafés and grills (often by converting a room of the existing restaurant), featuring more casual decor and less-expensive fare. Taking this attitude of value for money one step further, many restaurants now serve portions ranging from hefty to gargantuan. At such places as Carmine's in New York City, entrées are so large that diners commonly share a single order. U.S. visitors from rural and suburban areas will find dining in cities more affordable and relaxed than they may have feared; visitors from major European and Asian cities will find it a downright bargain. Ethnic restaurants draw devoted hordes in every American city.

In the galleries, New York City's **Museum of Modern Art** hosts a major show from February to May 1994: "Frank Lloyd Wright—Architect." The important retrospective includes 400 original drawings, 30 scale models, several full-scale constructions, photographs, and decorative artwork and furniture by Wright. Also in New York, the **Metropolitan Museum of Art** in May presents "American Impressionism and Realism," with paintings by Cassatt, Chase, and Twachtman, which will also appear at Fort Worth's **Kimbell Art Museum,** the **Denver Art Museum,** and the **Los Angeles County Museum of Art.** The **National Gallery of Art** in Washington, D.C., presents a major retrospective of the works of Willem de Kooning in May, which will travel to New York's Musuem of Modern Art in September. In Pittsburgh, the **Andy Warhol Museum,** a comprehensive collection of the works of the pop artist, opens this year.

Fodor's Choice

No two people will agree on what makes a perfect vacation, but it's fun and helpful to know what others think. We hope you'll have a chance to experience some of Fodor's Choices yourself while traveling in the United States. Because we wish to provide a range of cost options, hotels and restaurants are recommended within price categories only. For detailed information about each entry, refer to the appropriate chapters in this guidebook.

Historic Sites and Monuments

The Northeast Bunker Hill (Boston, MA)
Plimouth Plantation, (Plymouth, MA)
Ellis Island (New York, NY)
Statue of Liberty (New York, NY)

The Middle Independence National Historical Park (Philadelphia, PA)
Atlantic States Gettysburg National Military Park (Gettysburg, PA)
Washington Monument (Washington, DC)
Frederick Douglass National Historic Site (Washington, DC)

The Southeast Civil Rights Memorial (Montgomery, AL)
Martin Luther King, Jr., National Historic District (Atlanta, GA)
Ft. Sumter National Monument (Charleston, SC)

The Great Plains Scotts Bluff National Monument (NE)
Mt. Rushmore National Memorial (SD)

The Southwest Canyon de Chelly (Chinle, AZ)
Mission Ysleta (near El Paso, TX)

The West Coast Olvera Street (Los Angeles, CA)

Historic Buildings

The Northeast African Meeting House (Boston, MA)
Faneuil Hall (Boston, MA)
Old North Church (Boston, MA)
Mansions (Newport, RI)
United Nations Building (New York, NY)

The Middle Edgar Allan Poe House (Baltimore, MD)
Atlantic States Monticello (Charlottesville, VA)
The White House (Washington, DC)

The Southeast Sixteenth Street Baptist Church (Birmingham, AL)

The Mississippi Rosalie (Natchez, MS)
Valley The Pontalba Buildings (New Orleans, LA)

The Great Plains Laura Ingalls Wilder Home (Mansfield, MO)

The Southwest	Betatakin Cliff Dwellings (Tonalea, AZ)
The West Coast	Hearst Castle (San Simeon, CA)
	Sutter's Mill (Coloma, CA)
The Pacific	Iolani Palace (Honolulu, HI)

Natural Wonders

The Northeast	Niagara Falls (NY)
The Southeast	Okefenokee (GA)
The Mississippi Valley	Hot Springs (AR)
	Bayou Teche (Acadiana, LA)
	Mammoth Cave (KY)
The Midwest and Great Lakes	Boundary Waters (MN)
	Starved Rock State Park (Utica, IL)
The Great Plains	Badlands (ND/SD)
The Southwest	Grand Canyon (AZ)
	Carlsbad Caverns (NM)
	Lake Tahoe (NV/CA)
	Bryce Canyon (UT)
	Zion Canyon (UT)
The Rockies	Old Faithful Geyser (Yellowstone, WY)
The West Coast	La Brea Tar Pits (Los Angeles, CA)
	Joshua Tree National Monument (CA)
	Muir Woods (Mill Valley, CA)
	Crater Lake (OR)
	Rain Forest (Olympic Peninsula, WA)
The Pacific	Mt. McKinley (AK)
	Kilauea Volcano (Hawaii, HI)

Viewpoints

The Northeast	John Hancock Tower (Boston, MA)
	World Trade Center Tower (New York, NY)
The Mississippi Valley	Sabine Wildlife Refuge Tower (LA)
	Newfound Gap (near Gatlinburg, TN)
The Midwest and Great Lakes	Chicago from a boat on the river (IL)
	Wyalusing State Park (Bagley, WI)
The Great Plains	Mississippi River from Lansing Municipal Park (Lansing, IA)
	Theodore Roosevelt National Park from Painted Canyon Overlook (ND)
The Southwest	Sandia Crest (near Albuquerque, NM)
	Dead Horse Point (near Moab, UT)
The Rockies	Trail Ridge Road, Rocky Mountain National Park (CO)
The West Coast	Golden Gate Bridge and San Francisco from Marin Headlands (CA)

Napa Valley from a hot-air balloon (CA)
Bixby Creek Bridge (Big Sur, CA)
Los Angeles from Griffith Park (CA)

The Pacific Glacier-clad coastline from a boat on the Inside Passage (AK)
Mt. Haleakala (Maui, HI)

Museums

The Northeast Museum of Fine Arts (Boston, MA)
Metropolitan Museum of Art (New York, NY)
Museum of Modern Art (New York, NY)
Frick Collection (New York, NY)
Museum of Natural History (New York, NY)

The Middle Atlantic States Winterthur (Wilmington, DE)
Smithsonian Institution (Washington, DC)

The Midwest and Great Lakes Art Institute (Chicago, IL)
Museum of Science and Industry (Chicago, IL)
American Geographical Society Collection (Milwaukee, WI)

The Great Plains Nelson-Atkins Museum of Art (Kansas City, MO)

The Southwest Navajo Nation Museum (Window Rock, AZ)
Kimbell Art Museum (Fort Worth, TX)

The West Coast San Francisco Museum of Contemporary Art (CA)
Los Angeles County Museum of Art (CA)
Los Angeles Museum of Contemporary Art (CA)
Seattle Art Museum (Seattle, WA)

The Pacific Alaska State Museum (Juneau, AK)

Noteworthy Architecture

The Northeast Nook Farm (Hartford, CT)
Round Shaker barn (Hancock, MA)
Guggenheim Museum (New York, NY)
Radio City Music Hall (New York, NY)
Brooklyn Bridge (New York, NY)

The Middle Atlantic States Fallingwater (Mill Run, PA)
Old Town (Alexandria, VA)
University of Virginia (Charlottesville, VA)

The Southeast Art Deco District (Miami Beach, FL)

The Mississippi Valley American Life and Accident Building (Louisville, KY)
New Capitol Building (Jackson, MS)

The Midwest and Great Lakes 333 West Wacker Drive (Chicago, IL)
The Rookery (Chicago, IL)
Columbus (IN)

The Great Plains Gateway Arch (St. Louis, MO)

The Southwest	First Interstate Bank Building (Dallas, TX) Taliesin West (Scottsdale, AZ)
The West Coast	Victorian houses (San Francisco, CA) Capitol Records Building (Los Angeles, CA) Gamble House (Pasadena, CA)

Towns

The Northeast	Nantucket, MA Provincetown, MA Hanover, NH Middlebury, VT
The Middle Atlantic States	New Hope, PA Solomons, MD
The Southeast	Key West, FL Charleston, SC
The Midwest and Great Lakes	New Harmony, IN Mackinaw City, MI
The Great Plains	Amana Colonies, IA Lindsborg, KS Nebraska City, NE
The Southwest	Acoma, NM Jefferson, TX
The Rockies	Aspen, CO Steamboat Springs, CO
The West Coast	Laguna Beach, CA
The Pacific	Homer, AK

Neighborhoods

The Northeast	Beacon Hill (Boston, MA) Greenwich Village (New York, NY)
The Middle Atlantic States	Society Hill (Philadelphia, PA) Georgetown (Washington, DC)
The Southeast	Old Salem (Winston-Salem, NC)
The Mississippi Valley	French Quarter (New Orleans, LA) Old Louisville (Louisville, KY)
The Midwest and Great Lakes	German Village (Columbus, OH)
The Southwest	Plaza (Santa Fe, NM) Deep Ellum (Dallas, TX)
The West Coast	Nob Hill (San Francisco, CA) Rodeo Drive (Beverly Hills, CA) Pioneer Square (Seattle, WA)

Parks and Gardens

The Northeast	Back Bay Fens (Boston, MA)
	Central Park (New York, NY)
The Middle Atlantic States	Longwood Gardens (Brandywine Valley, PA)
	Dumbarton Oaks (Washington, DC)
The Southeast	Bellingrath Gardens (Mobile, AL)
	Town squares (Savannah, GA)
	Biltmore Estate Gardens (Asheville, NC)
	Magnolia Plantation (Charleston, SC)
The Mississippi Valley	Tyler Park (Louisville, KY)
	Tennessee Botanical Gardens at Cheekwood (Nashville, TN)
The Great Plains	International Peace Garden (ND)
The Southwest	Arizona–Sonora Desert Museum (Tucson, AZ)
	Water Gardens Park (Fort Worth, TX)
The West Coast	Golden Gate Park (San Francisco, CA)
	Balboa Park (San Diego, CA)

Beaches

The Northeast	Cape Cod National Seashore (MA)
	Jones Beach (Long Island, NY)
The Middle Atlantic States	Island Beach State Park (NJ)
	Assateague Island (MD/VA)
The Southeast	Miami Beach (FL)
	Sarasota County Beaches (Sarasota, FL)
	Cumberland Island National Seashore (GA)
	Hilton Head Island (SC)
Mississippi Valley	Gulf Islands National Seashore (Ocean Springs, MS)
The Great Plains	Lake McConaughy State Recreation Area (NE)
The Southwest	Padre Island National Seashore (TX)
The West Coast	Point Reyes National Seashore (CA)
	Corona del Mar (CA)
	Pismo Beach (CA)
The Pacific	Kauanoa Beach (Hawaii, HI)
	Wailea's five crescent beaches (Maui, HI)

Amusement and Theme Parks

The Northeast	Coney Island (NY)
The Middle Atlantic States	Sesame Place (Langhorne, PA)
	Trimper's Amusement Park (Ocean City, MD)
The Southeast	Walt Disney World (Orlando, FL)
Mississippi Valley	Opryland USA (Nashville, TN)

The Midwest and Great Lakes	Boblo Island (Detroit, MI) Cedar Point Amusement Park (Sandusky, OH)
The Great Plains	Silver Dollar City (Branson, MO) Worlds of Fun (Kansas City, MO)
The Southwest	Astroworld/Waterworld (Houston, TX)
The West Coast	Disneyland (Anaheim, CA)
The Pacific	Alaskaland Park (Fairbanks, AK)

Hotels

The Northeast	Copley Plaza (Boston, MA; Very Expensive) Red Lion Inn (Stockbridge, MA; Expensive) The Pierre (New York, NY; Very Expensive) Royalton (New York, NY; Expensive)
The Middle Atlantic States	Hay-Adams Hotel (Washington, DC; Very Expensive) The Greenbrier (White Sulphur Springs, WV; Very Expensive) The Homestead (Hot Springs, WV; Expensive)
The Southeast	The Breakers (Palm Beach, FL; Very Expensive) Hotel Place St. Michel (Coral Gables, FL; Moderate) The Gastonian (Savannah, GA; Expensive)
The Mississippi Valley	The Seelbach (Louisville, KY; Expensive) Pontchartrain Hotel (New Orleans, LA; Moderate)
The Midwest and Great Lakes	The Drake (Chicago, IL; Very Expensive) Lafayette Hotel (Marietta, OH; Moderate)
The Great Plains	Inn of the Six-Toed Cat (Allerton, IA; Moderate) Island Guest Ranch (Ames, OK; Expensive)
The Southwest	Hopi Cultural Center Motel (Second Mesa, AZ; Moderate) The Menger Hotel (San Antonio, TX; Expensive)
The Rockies	The Oxford (Denver, CO; Expensive) Coeur d'Alene Resort (Coeur d'Alene, ID; Very Expensive) The Old Faithful Inn (Yellowstone, WY; Moderate)
The West Coast	Four Seasons Clift (San Francisco, CA; Very Expensive) Ritz-Carlton Laguna Niguel (Dana Point, CA; Very Expensive) Hollywood Roosevelt (Hollywood, CA; Expensive) The Timberline Lodge (Mt. Hood, OR; Moderate–Expensive)
The Pacific	Camp Denali (Denali National Park, AK; Very Expensive) Hotel Hana-Maui (Maui, HI; Expensive)

Restaurants

The Northeast	Bertrand (Greenwich, CT; Expensive) Durgin Park (Boston, MA; Inexpensive–Moderate)

Harraseeket Lunch & Lobster Co. (S. Freeport, ME; Inexpensive)
Lutèce (New York, NY; Very Expensive)
Union Square Cafe (New York, NY; Moderate)

The Middle Atlantic States
Crab Claw (St. Michael's, MD; Moderate)
Le Bec-Fin (Philadelphia, PA; Very Expensive)
Jean-Louis at the Watergate (Washington, DC; Very Expensive)

The Southeast
Louie's Backyard (Key West, FL; Very Expensive)
Unicorn Village Restaurant & Marketplace (Miami, FL; Moderate)
Mrs. Wilkes Boarding House (Savannah, GA; Inexpensive)

The Mississippi Valley
Antoine's (New Orleans, LA; Very Expensive)
Galatoire's (New Orleans, LA; Moderate)
The Praline Connection (New Orleans, LA; Inexpensive)

The Midwest and Great Lakes
Printer's Row (Chicago, IL; Expensive)
Maxie's Left Field Deli (Detroit, MI; Inexpensive)

The Great Plains
Arthur Bryant's (Kansas City, MO; Inexpensive)
Mandan Drug (Mandan, ND; Inexpensive)
The Cattleman's Cafe (Oklahoma City, OK; Inexpensive)

The Southwest
Maria's New Mexico Kitchen (Santa Fe; Inexpensive)
Calle Doce (Dallas, TX; Moderate)

The Rockies
String's (Denver, CO; Expensive)

The West Coast
Stars (San Francisco, CA; Expensive)
Chez Panisse (Berkeley, CA; Moderate–Expensive)
Spago (West Hollywood, CA; Moderate–Expensive)
Ray's Boathouse (Seattle, WA; Moderate–Expensive)

The Pacific
Double Musky (Anchorage, AK; Moderate)
Ka Ohelo Room (Hawaii Volcanoes National Park, Hawaii, HI; Inexpensive)

Performing Arts

The Northeast
Tanglewood (Lenox, MA)
JVC Jazz Festival (Newport, RI)
Lincoln Center for the Performing Arts (New York, NY)
Broadway (New York, NY)
Carnegie Hall (New York, NY)

The Middle Atlantic States
Philadelphia Symphony Orchestra (PA)
Wolf Trap Farm Park (Vienna, VA)

The Southeast
Spoleto USA (Charleston, SC)

The Mississippi Valley
Actors Theatre of Louisville (KY)
Grand Ole Opry (Nashville, TN)

The Midwest and Great Lakes
Lyric Opera of Chicago (IL)
Steppenwolf (theater) (Chicago, IL)
Guthrie Theater (Minneapolis, MN)

St. Paul Chamber Orchestra (MN)
Cleveland Orchestra (OH)

The Southwest Santa Fe Opera (NM)
Morton H. Meyerson Symphony Center (Dallas, TX)
Mormon Tabernacle Choir (Salt Lake City, UT)

The West Coast Hollywood Bowl (CA)
The Music Center (Los Angeles, CA)
Monterey Jazz Festival (CA)
San Francisco Opera (CA)
Seattle Repertory Theater (WA)

Nightlife

The Northeast East Village, New York, NY (club of the moment)

The Middle Atlantic States Atlantic City, NJ (casinos and shows)
Georgetown, Washington, DC (political satire)

The Southeast Key West, FL (evening street performers)
Miami Beach, FL (dance clubs)

The Mississippi Valley New Orleans, LA (jazz, R&B, Cajun music)
Nashville, TN (country music)

The Midwest and Great Lakes Chicago, IL (blues)
Detroit, MI (blues)

The Great Plains Branson, MO (country music)

The Southwest Las Vegas, NV (casinos, shows)
Reno, NV (casinos, shows)

The Rockies Montana and Wyoming (cowboy bars)
Colorado (resorts' après-ski)

The West Coast Los Angeles (comedy clubs)
South of Market, San Francisco, CA (dance clubs)
Pacific Northwest (brew pubs)

The United States

Amtrak Rail Passenger System

CANADA

MAINE

MINNESOTA
Detroit Lakes

Montréal
St. Albans
Plattsburgh
Montpelier
Fort Edward/Glens Falls
VT.
N.H.
Brattleboro
NEW
YORK
Pittsfield
Boston
MASS.
Providence
R.I.
Syracuse
Albany
Hartford
New Haven
New London
CONN.

St. Cloud
WISCONSIN
Red Wing
LaCrosse
Toronto
Buffalo
Rochester

neapolis/
St. Paul

Grand
Rapids
Detroit

Milwaukee
Chicago
Toledo
Cleveland
PENNSYLVANIA
New York City
N.J.
Philadelphia
Atlantic City
Harrisburg
Wilmington

IOWA
South
Bend
Pittsburgh
Johnstown
MD.
Baltimore
DEL.
Omaha
Ottumwa
ILLINOIS
Indianapolis
OHIO
Cumberland
Washington, D.C.
Burlington
Galesburg
Springfield
Cincinnati
W. VA.
Charleston
Staunton
Charlottesville
Richmond
St. Louis
INDIANA
Maysville
Huntington
VA.
Petersburg
Lynchburg
Norfolk
Virginia Beach
opeka
Centralia
Jefferson
City
White
Sulphur
Springs
Danville
Kansas
City
Carbondale
KENTUCKY
Greensboro
Durham
Raleigh
Selma
MISSOURI
Salisbury
NORTH
CAROLINA
Poplar Bluff
TENNESSEE
Charlotte
Newport
Dyersburg
Spartanburg
Greenville
ARKANSAS
Memphis
Gainesville
Columbia
SOUTH
CAROLINA
Florence
Little Rock
Atlanta
Charleston
ATLANTIC
OCEAN
Arkadelphia
Birmingham
Anniston
GEORGIA
Grenada
Tuscaloosa
MISSISSIPPI
Texarkana
Montgomery
Savannah
allas
Jackson
Meridian
ALABAMA
Longview
Jessup
Corsicana
Laurel
Greenville
College
Station/
Bryan
McComb
Atmore
Jacksonville
Beaumont
Mobile
Pensacola
Tallahassee
Lafayette
Ocala
DeLand
Houston
Lake
Charles
New Orleans
FLORIDA
Orlando
LOUISIANA
Walt Disney World
Tampa
Okeechobee
St. Petersburg
West Palm Beach
Fort Lauderdale
Miami

Gulf of Mexico

MICHIGAN

N

0   200 miles

0   300 km

World Time Zones

Numbers below vertical bands relate each zone to Greenwich Mean Time (0 hrs.).
Local times frequently differ from these general indications,
as indicated by light-face numbers on map.

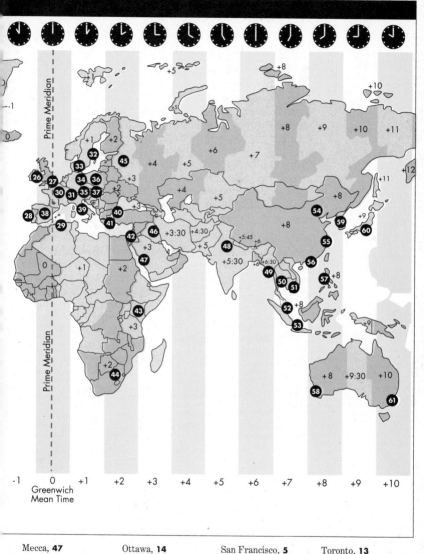

Mecca, **47**	Ottawa, **14**	San Francisco, **5**	Toronto, **13**
Mexico City, **12**	Paris, **30**	Santiago, **21**	Vancouver, **4**
Miami, **18**	Perth, **58**	Seoul, **59**	Vienna, **35**
Montréal, **15**	Reykjavík, **25**	Shanghai, **55**	Warsaw, **36**
Moscow, **45**	Rio de Janeiro, **23**	Singapore, **52**	Washington, D.C., **17**
Nairobi, **43**	Rome, **39**	Stockholm, **32**	Yangon, **49**
New Orleans, **11**	Saigon (Ho Chi Minh	Sydney, **61**	Zürich, **31**
New York City, **16**	City), **51**	Tokyo, **60**	

Introduction

With the 500th anniversary of Columbus's voyages to the New World, it's a good time to remember how much of our landscape remains essentially unchanged from the days when the earliest explorers stepped ashore. Flowers continue to bloom each spring in the deserts of the Southwest, the oceans go on pounding the coasts of Oregon and Maine, and the Great Plains still stretch as far as the eye can see beneath endless arches of sky. From the Grand Canyon to the Hudson Highlands, from Yellowstone to the Smokies, you can still see much of what the early settlers saw, and with the same sense of wonder and awe.

What amazes almost all foreign visitors, and many Americans as well, is the huge distances—(ever heard of an Italian driving 100 mi for dinner? Texans do it all the time)—as well as all those open spaces. To travel through America is to experience its vastness, its timelessness, and its possibilities. Arizona is larger than Great Britain, California is larger than Italy, Texas is larger than France, and Alaska is larger than Egypt. There's no way to conquer or even comprehend it all—the distances are too great, the scenery too varied. But you can always keep coming back for more.

Visitors are also wowed and sometimes overwhelmed by our greatest cities. As Sartre once pointed out, European streets tend to turn in on themselves with the logic of dreams, while American streets seem to go on forever. Stand on 34th Street in New York and you have a sense that if only you kept walking in a straight line you'd wind up in Los Angeles someday.

European visitors, accustomed to cities as collections of neighborhoods that root them to the past, are surprised to find themselves set loose among soaring spaces, confronting the present or future—a frightening or exhilarating experience, depending on who you are, where you're coming from, and what you had for lunch. Visitors also discover that while European cities are rich in detail and therefore become more beautiful the closer you get, American cities dazzle with their lights, their energy, and their towering heights, and are often best seen from a distance and at night.

There are as many ways to tour the United States as there are people experiencing it, and *Fodor's USA* helps you discover them all. We show you the ins and outs of all the major cities, from Anchorage to Miami; we lead you to the country's natural wonders, from Alaska's glaciers to Florida's Everglades; and we take you around the most popular regions, from California's wine country to the beaches of Cape Cod. All the best-known spots are covered, from the Statue of Liberty to Disney World. But we also lead you to the small towns in the heart of the country that so many visitors identify with the "real," unspoiled America.

We recommend some wonderful driving tours, but since the United States is not a place to see framed through a car window, we invite you to get out and poke around and become discoverers, explorers, too. Travel guides are a great place to begin, but as we all know, every sight, every attraction, deserves three stars if the slant of the sun is right, or the mood, or the company.

Fodor's recipe for a great vacation? Try to visit in the off-season, often the spring or fall. Pack light. Try to stay put for a night or two—happiness on the road is coming home to the same room, the same closet full of clothes. Head down at least one back road. Take a step or two off the beaten track. National parks get crowded, yes, but they have millions of acres, and you don't have to go far from the pavement to be alone and enjoy a wilderness experience. Experience the beauty—and photograph it—at dawn or dusk.

A few words about how this guide is organized. The first chapter, "Visiting the USA," gives you all the information you'll need to plan and enjoy your trip. The 10 regional chapters that follow begin with the Northeast and zigzag across the country to the Pacific. Within each region, states are listed alphabetically; within each state are sections on the major cities, the most popular tourist areas, and worthwhile but less-known destinations grouped together under the heading "Elsewhere in the State." In the book's Appendix, the special-interest vacations section tells you the best places in the country to pursue your favorite hobby or sport.

Because this is a guide to the entire country, it's by necessity selective. If we included every wonderful park, forest, historic site, and town, you'd need a suitcase just for this guide, and you'd be dragging along more information than you could ever need. What *Fodor's USA '94* does is point you to the very best and tell you how to find out more. If you want to read about an area in more depth, we encourage you to buy one of Fodor's city, state, regional, or special-interest guides. All are listed at the back of this book.

Michael Spring
Editorial Director

1 Visiting the USA

Planning Your Trip

Visitor Information

By Holly Hughes

Updated by Marcy Pritchard

State tourism offices, city tourist bureaus, and local chambers of commerce, which are usually the best source of information about their communities, are listed throughout this book at the beginning of each state, city, or regional section.

On the national level, the United States does not do as good a job as most other countries in providing centralized information about country-wide travel. British visitors seeking general information about the United States can contact the **U.S. Travel and Tourism Administration** (Box 1EN, London W1A 1EN, tel. 071/439–7433, fax 071/439–1152). Canadian travelers can contact **Travel USA** (480 University Ave., Suite 602, Toronto, Ont., M5G IV2, tel. 416/595–0335).

Passports and Visas

U.K. Citizens You need a valid 10-year passport to enter the United States. A British Visitor's Passport is not acceptable.

A visa is not necessary unless (1) you are planning to stay more than 90 days; (2) your trip is for purposes other than vacation; (3) you have at some time been refused a visa, or refused admission, to the United States, or have been required to leave by the U.S. Immigration and Naturalization Service; or (4) you do not have a return or onward ticket. You will need to fill out the Visa Waiver Form, 1–94W, supplied by the airline.

To apply for a visa or for more information, call the U.S. Embassy's Visa Information Line (tel. 0891/200–290; calls cost 48p per minute or 36p per minute cheap rate). If you qualify for the visa-free travel but want a visa anyway, you must apply in writing, enclosing a self-addressed envelope, to the U.S. Embassy's Visa Branch (5 Upper Grosvenor St., London W1A 2JB), or, for residents of Northern Ireland, to the U.S. Consulate General (Queen's House, Queen St., Belfast BT1 6EO). Submit a completed Nonimmigrant Visa Application (Form 156), a valid passport, a photograph, and evidence of your intended departure from the United States after a temporary visit. If you require a visa, call 0891/234–224 to schedule an interview.

For additional information while visiting the United States, contact the **British Embassy** (3100 Massachusetts Ave. NW, Washington, DC 20036, tel. 202/462–1340). Consulates are located in Atlanta, Chicago, Houston, Los Angeles, and New York.

Canadian Citizens Canadian citizens are required to have proof of citizenship and identity to enter the United States (a passport, birth certificate with raised seal, or voter registration card are preferred). For additional information while in the United States, contact the **Canadian Embassy** (501 Pennsylvania Ave. NW, Washington, DC 20001, tel. 202/682–1740). Consulates are located in Atlanta, Boston, Chicago, Cleveland, Dallas, Detroit, Los Angeles, Minneapolis, New York City, San Francisco, and Seattle.

Australian Citizens Australian citizens are required to have a valid passport and visa to enter the United States. Passport applications are available at any post office or at passport offices located in every major city. In addition, details on applying for a passport are listed in public telephone books. A birth or citizenship certificate and photo I.D. are required. For information on obtaining a visa, contact the American Embassy or Consulate nearest you. While in the United States, Australians may obtain additional information from the **Embassy of Australia** (1601 Massachusetts Ave. NW, Washington, DC 20036, tel. 202/797–3000). Consulates are located in Chicago, Honolulu, Los Angeles, and New York City.

Tours and Packages

Should you buy your travel arrangements to the United States packaged or do it yourself? There are advantages either way. Buying packaged arrangements saves you money, particularly if can find a program that includes exactly the features you want. You also get a pretty good idea of what your trip will cost from the outset.

Generally, two types of packaged travel arrangements are available. Escorted tours are one option if you don't mind having limited free time and traveling with strangers. Escorted tours are most often via motorcoach, with a tour director in charge. Your baggage is handled, your time rigorously scheduled, and most meals planned. Escorted tours are therefore the most hassle-free way to see a destination, as well as generally the least expensive. Independent packages allow plenty of flexibility. They generally include airline travel and hotels, with certain options available, such as sightseeing, car rental, and excursions. Independent packages are usually more expensive than escorted tours, but your time is your own.

While you can book directly through tour operators, you will pay no more to go through a travel agent, who will be able to tell you about tours and packages from a number of operators. Whatever program you ultimately choose, be sure to find out exactly what is included: taxes, tips, transfers, meals, baggage handling, ground transportation, entertainment, excursions, sports or recreation (and rental equipment if necessary). Ask about the level of hotel used, its location, the size of its rooms, the kind of beds, and its facilities and amenities, such as pool, room service, or programs for children, if they're important to you. Find out the operator's cancellation penalties. Nearly everyone charges them, and the only way to avoid them is to buy trip-cancellation insurance (*see* Trip Insurance, *below*). Also ask about the single supplement, a surcharge assessed to solo travelers. Some operators do not make you pay it if you agree to be matched up with a roommate of the same sex, even if one is not found by departure time. Remember that a program that has features you won't use may not be the most cost-wise choice.

At the beginning of each regional chapter of this book, you'll find additional listings of tours highlighting the best of that region. For tour operators and packagers specializing in various special-interest tours, see the Appendix.

Fully Escorted Escorted tours are usually sold in three categories: deluxe, **Tours** first-class, and tourist or budget class. The most important differences are the price, of course, and the level of accommodations. Some operators specialize in one category, while others offer a range.

Most itineraries are jam-packed with sightseeing, so you see a lot in a short amount of time (usually one place per day). To judge just how fast-paced the tour is, review the itinerary carefully. If you are in a different hotel each night, you will be getting up early each day to head out, travel to your next destination, do some sightseeing, have dinner, and go to bed, then you'll start all over again. If you want some free time, make sure it's mentioned in the tour brochure; if you want to be escorted to every meal, confirm that any tour you consider does that. Also, when comparing programs, be sure to find out if the motorcoach is air-conditioned and has a rest room on board. Make your selection based on price and stops on the itinerary.

U.S. Operators For deluxe tours, look into **Maupintour** (Box 807, Lawrence, KS 66044, tel. 913/255–4266, 913/843–1211, or 800/255–4266) and **Tauck Tours** (11 Wilton Rd., Westport, CT 06881, tel. 800/ 468–2825). In the first-class category, try **Globus-Gateway** (95- 25 Queens Blvd., Rego Park, NY 11374, tel. 800/221–0090) or **Mayflower Tours** (1225 Warren Ave., Downers Grove, IL 60515, tel. 708/960–3430 or 800/323–7604 outside IL). Globus's sister company, **Cosmos** (*see above*; and in the U.K., Ground Floor, Dale House, Tiviot Dale, Stockport, Cheshire SK1 1TB, tel. 061/480–5799)) has budget programs. **Tours** (751 Broadway, Bayonne, NJ 07002, tel. 800/554–8687) has both first-class and deluxe programs.

U.K. Operators Contact **Jetsave Travel Ltd.** (Sussex House, London Rd., East Grinstead, W. Sussex RH19 1LD, tel. 0342/312033), **North American Vacations** (Acorn House, 172/174 Albert Rd., Jarrow, Tyne & Wear NE32 5JA, tel. 091/483–6226), or **Travelsphere Ltd.** (Compass House, Rockingham Rd., Market Harborough, Leicestershire LE16 7QD, tel. 0858/410818).

Independent Packages Independent packages are offered by airlines, tour operators who may also do escorted programs, and any number of other companies from large, established firms to small, new entrepreneurs. Their programs come in a wide range of prices based on levels of luxury and options—in addition to hotel and airfare, sightseeing, car rental, transfers, admission to local attractions, and other extras.

Note that when pricing different packages, it sometimes pays to purchase the same arrangements separately, as when a rock-bottom promotional airfare is being offered, for example. Again, base your choice what's available at your budget for the destinations you want to visit.

U.S. Operators Look into **American Airlines Fly AAway Vacations** (tel. 800/321– 2121), **American Express Vacations** (300 Pinnacle Way, Norcross, GA 30093, tel. 800/241–1700), **Continental Airlines' Grand Destinations** (tel. 800/634–5555), **Delta Dream Vacations** (tel. 800/872–7786), **Supercities** (Box 1789, Minneapolis, MN 55400, tel. 800/333–1234), and **United Airlines' Vacation Planning Center** (tel. 800/328–6877). Most of their packages can be booked through a travel agent overseas before you arrive in the United States.

U.K. Operators A good range of offerings is available from **British Airways Holidays** (Atlantic House, Hazelwick Ave., 3 Bridges, Crawley,

W. Sussex RH10 1NP, tel. 0293/518022) and **Kuoni Travel**
(Kuoni House, Dorking, Surrey RH5 4AZ, tel. 0306/742222).

What to Pack

Clothing The American lifestyle is generally casual, meaning that wom-
en may wear slacks and men can go without a jacket and tie virtually anywhere, except in expensive restaurants in the larger
cities. If you prefer to dress up for dinner or the theater,
though, go right ahead. As a rule of thumb, the northeast part
of the country dresses more formally, while such places as Florida, Texas, and southern California are more informal. In beach
towns, many hotels and restaurants may post signs announcing
that they will not serve customers who are shoeless, shirtless,
or dressed in bathing suits or other skimpy attire, so tote along
some shoes and cover-ups.

The United States is a big country, with a wide range of cli-
mates. When deciding what weather to dress for, read the
"When to Go" section in this book's introductions to each region
you'll be visiting. One caveat: Even in warm destinations, you
may want an extra layer of clothing to compensate for overact-
ive air-conditioning or to protect against brisk ocean breezes.
Although you can count on all modern buildings being well
heated in winter, historic inns and hunting lodges in rugged cli-
mates—New England, the Great Lakes states, the Rockies, or
the Pacific Northwest—may be poorly insulated, drafty, or
heated only by wood-burning fireplaces. It's charming, but
you'll need warmer clothing.

If you'll be sightseeing in historic cities, you'll spend a lot of
time walking, so bring sturdy, well-fitting, flat-heeled shoes.
Don't forget deck shoes if you want to go sailing, and sandals
for walking across the burning-hot sand of southern beaches. If
you plan to hike in the country, pack shoes or boots with strong
flexible soles, and wear long pants to protect your legs from
brambles and insect bites.

Miscellaneous Overseas visitors will need to bring adapters to convert their
personal appliances to the U.S. standard: AC, 110 volts/60 cycles, with a plug of two flat pins set parallel to one another.

If you wear eyeglasses or contact lenses, bring a spare pair.
Pack an ample supply of any medication you take regularly (or a
prescription from your own doctor for an emergency refill).

Bring sunscreen lotion if you expect to be out in the sun, because prices may be high at beachside stores. Most upscale hotels these days provide a basket of toiletries—soaps, shampoo,
conditioner, bath gel—but if you are picky about the brand you
use, bring your own. Hand-held hair driers are sometimes
provided, but don't rely on this. You can generally request an
iron and ironing board from the front desk.

Arriving and Departing by Plane

From the U.K. The range of air service from Great Britain to the United
States has improved remarkably over the past couple of years,
with more destinations in the heart of the United States served
directly from the United Kingdom. Airlines include **American
Airlines** (tel. 0800/010151), **British Airways** (tel. 081/897–4000
or 0345/222111), **Continental** (tel. 0293/776464), **Delta Airlines**

(tel. 0800/414767), **Northwest** (tel. 0293/28822), **TWA** (tel. 0800/222222), **United Airlines** (tel. 0800/888555), **USAir** (tel. 0800/777333), and **Virgin Atlantic** (tel. 0293/562000). Most serve at least the New York area, plus their own U.S. hubs. British Airways serves the largest number of U.S. cities—an impressive 18 destinations, including Anchorage; Atlanta; Boston; Chicago; Dallas; Detroit; Houston; Los Angeles; Miami; New York; Newark; Orlando; Philadelphia; Pittsburgh; San Francisco; Seattle; Tampa; and Washington, DC. A few cities not served by British Airways can be reached by other carriers: Continental flies to Denver; Delta to Cincinnati; Northwest to Minneapolis; TWA to Baltimore and St. Louis; and USAir to Charlotte, North Carolina.

Flying Times   Approximate times from London are: to New York, 7 hours; to Miami, 9 hours, 45 minutes; to Chicago, 8 hours, 40 minutes; to Los Angeles, 11 hours.

Discount Flights   Fares vary enormously. Fares from consolidators are usually the cheapest, followed by promotional fares such as APEX. A few phone calls should reveal the current picture. When comparing fares, don't forget to figure airport taxes and weekend supplements. Once you know which airline is going your way at the right time for the least money, book immediately, since seats at the lowest prices often sell out quickly. Travel agents will generally hold a reservation for up to five days, especially if you give a credit card number.

Generally, low season runs November 1–March 31, excluding the two weeks before Christmas. Shoulder season is April 1–May 31 and October. Peak season is June 1–September 30 and the pre-Christmas period.

Some travel agents that offer cheap fares to the United States include **Trailfinders** (42–50 Earl's Court Rd., London W8 6EJ, tel. 071/937–5400), specialists in Round-The-World fares and independent travel; **Travel Cuts** (295a Regent St., London W1R 7YA, tel. 071/637–3161), the Canadian Students' travel service; **Flightfile** (49 Tottenham Court Rd., London W1P 9RE, tel. 071/700–2722), a flight-only agency.

From Australia   Airlines flying from Australia include **Air New Zealand** (tel. 008/221–111), **Continental** (tel. 02/249–0111 in Sydney or 03/602–4899 in Melbourne), **Northwest** (tel. 008/221–714), **Qantas** (tel. 02/957–0111 in Sydney or 03/602–6111 in Melbourne), and **United** (tel. 008/230–322).

Flying time from Sydney to Los Angeles is 13 hours, 25 minutes, on a direct flight; to New York, 21–22 hours. Flights from Melbourne add about 3 hours of flying time.

From Canada   Every major U.S. airline flies between the United States and Canada, as does **Air Canada** (tel. 800/776–3000).

Flying time from Toronto is 1½ hours to New York, 4½ hours to Los Angeles. Flying time from Vancouver is 2½ hours to Los Angeles, 4 hours to Chicago.

Traveling in the USA

By Plane

The U.S. domestic air route system is based on a pattern of hubs and spokes—each airline concentrates its services at certain hub cities and sends out spokes of connecting flights to other cities in the region. That's why, for example, many USAir flights are routed through Pittsburgh and Northwest flights through Minneapolis, even if those routes are not the most direct way to reach your final destination. Because of this system, it's wise to choose your airline according to which carrier has a hub closest to your destination. For major routes, however, such as New York–Los Angeles, you should have a range of options so you can shop around for the best available fare and the most convenient departure/arrival times.

On flights within the United States, most airlines offer non-U.S. residents discounted Visit USA fares, with savings of 25%–30%, provided the arrangements are made outside the United States. Many airlines, including **America West, American, Delta, Hawaiian, Northwest, TWA,** and **United,** also have air-pass programs that give you a fixed number of domestic flights for a flat fee (these also must be booked before you come to America). Check details with the airline or a travel agent (*see* the Appendix for a list of airlines' toll-free numbers).

Flights are either nonstop, direct, or connecting. A **nonstop** flight requires no change of plane and makes no stops. A **direct** flight stops at least once and can involve a change of plane, although the flight number remains the same; if the first leg is late, the second waits. This is not the case with a **connecting** flight, which involves a different plane and a different flight number.

If you want to book the flight yourself, call the airlines' toll-free reservation numbers (*see* Appendix). In order to qualify for an APEX fare, you may be asked to buy your ticket at a local ticket office or travel agent a certain number of days before departure. Otherwise, you can buy your ticket at the airport on the day of departure. In either case, try to arrive at the airport an hour before takeoff (the exception being hourly shuttle flights between neighboring major cities such as New York and Washington, DC). This will give you time to check your luggage, select your seat, and pass through the security metal-detectors. Flights usually begin boarding a half-hour or so before the scheduled departure time.

Smoking Since February 1990, smoking has been banned on all domestic flights of less than six hours' duration; the ban also applies to domestic segments of international flights aboard U.S. and foreign carriers. On U.S. carriers flying abroad, a seat in a no-smoking section must be provided for every passenger who requests one, and the section must be enlarged to accommodate such passengers if necessary as long as they have complied with the airline's deadline for check-in and seat assignment. If smoking bothers you, request a seat far from the smoking section.

Foreign airlines are exempt from these rules but do provide no-smoking sections, and as of July 1, 1993, some nations, including Canada, have gone as far as to ban smoking on all domestic flights; other countries may ban smoking on flights of less than a specified duration. The International Civil Aviation Organization has set July 1, 1996, as the date to ban smoking aboard airlines worldwide, but the organization has no power to enforce its decisions.

Luggage
Regulations Free baggage allowances on an airline depend on the airline, the route, and the class of your ticket. In general, on domestic flights and on international flights between the United States and foreign destinations, you are entitled to check two bags—neither exceeding 62 inches, or 158 centimeters (length + width + height), or weighing more than 70 pounds (32 kilograms). A third piece may be brought aboard as a carryon; its total dimensions are generally limited to less than 45 inches (114 centimeters), so it will fit easily under the seat in front of you or in the overhead compartment. There are variations, so ask in advance. The single rule, a Federal Aviation Administration safety regulation that pertains to carry-on baggage on U.S. airlines, requires only that carryons be properly stowed and allows the airline to limit allowances and tailor them to different aircraft and operational conditions. Charges for excess, oversize, or overweight pieces vary, so inquire before you pack.

Safeguarding Your
Luggage Before leaving home, itemize your bags' contents and their worth; this list will help you estimate the extent of your loss if your bags go astray. To minimize that risk, tag them inside and out with your name, address, and phone number. (If you use your home address, cover it so potential thieves can't see it.) At check-in, make sure that the tag attached by baggage handlers bears the correct three-letter code for your destination. If your bags do not arrive with you, or if you detect damage, do not leave the airport until you've filed a written report with the airline.

In the event of loss, damage, or theft on international flights, airlines limit their liability to $20 per kilogram for checked baggage (roughly about $640 per 70-pound bag) and $400 per passenger for unchecked baggage. On domestic flights, the ceiling is $1,250 per passenger. Excess-valuation insurance can be bought directly from the airline at check-in but leaves your bags vulnerable on the ground. Your own homeowner's policy may fill the gap; or you may want special luggage insurance. Sources include **The Travelers Companies** (1 Tower Sq., Hartford, CT 06183, tel. 203/277–0111 or 800/243–3174) and **Wallach and Company, Inc.** (107 W. Federal St., Box 480, Middleburg, VA 22117, tel. 703/687–3166 or 800/237–6615), underwritten by Lloyds, London. For information in Britain, contact the **Association of British Insurers** (51 Gresham St., London EC2V 7HQ, tel. 071/600–3333; 30 Gordon St., Glasgow G1 3PU, tel. 041/226–3905; Scottish Provincial Bldg., Donegall Sq. W, Belfast BT1 6JE, tel. 0232/249176; call for other locations).

Flying with
Children
Airfares On international flights, the fare for infants under 2 not occupying a seat is generally 10% of the accompanying adult's fare; children ages 2–11 usually pay half to two-thirds of the adult fare. On domestic flights, children under 2 not occupying a seat travel free, and older children currently travel on the "lowest applicable" adult fare.

Baggage In general, infants paying 10% of the adult fare are allowed one carry-on bag, not to exceed 70 pounds or 45 inches (length +

width + height). The adult baggage allowance applies for children paying half or more of the adult fare. Check with the airline for particulars.

Safety Seats The FAA recommends the use of safety seats aloft and details approved models in the free leaflet "**Child/Infant Safety Seats Recommended for Use in Aircraft**" (available from the Federal Aviation Administration, APA–200, 800 Independence Ave. SW, Washington, DC 20591, tel. 202/267–3479). Airline policy varies. U.S. carriers must allow FAA-approved models, but because these seats are strapped into a regular passenger seat, they may require that parents buy a ticket even for an infant under 2 who would otherwise ride free. Foreign carriers may not allow infant seats, may charge the child's rather than the infant's fare for their use, or may require you to hold your baby during takeoff and landing, thus defeating the seat's purpose.

Facilities Aloft Airlines do provide other facilities and services for children, such as children's meals and freestanding bassinets (to those sitting in seats on the bulkhead, where there's enough legroom to accommodate them). Make your request when reserving. The annual February/March issue of ***Family Travel Times*** ($10 from Travel With Your Children, 45 W. 18th St., 7th Floor Tower, New York, NY 10011, tel. 212/206–0688) gives details of the children's services of dozens of airlines. "Kids and Teens in Flight" (free from the U.S. Department of Transportation, tel. 202/366–2220) offers tips for children flying alone.

Passengers with Disabilities *New Horizons*, a free brochure available on request from the U.S. Department of Consumer Affairs (tel. 202/366–2220), gives airline access information for the disabled.

By Car

Rules of the Road Highway speed limits are 55 miles per hour or 65 miles per hour. Watch for lower speed limits on smaller back roads. Except for limited-access roads, highways usually post a lower speed limit in towns, so slow down when houses and buildings start to appear. Most states require front-seat passengers to wear seat belts, and in all states children under age 4 must ride in approved child-safety seats.

In some communities, it is permissible to make a right turn at a red light once the car has come to a full stop and there is no oncoming traffic. When in doubt about local laws, however, wait for the green light.

Beware of weekday rush-hour traffic—anywhere from 7 to 10 AM and 4 to 7 PM—around major cities. To encourage car-sharing, some crowded expressways may reserve an express lane for cars carrying more than one passenger. In downtown areas, watch signs carefully—there are lots of one-way streets, "no left turn" intersections, and blocks closed to car traffic, all in the name of easing congestion.

Highways The fastest routes are usually the interstate highways, each numbered with a prefix "I–". Even numbers (I–80, I–40, and so on) are east–west roads, odd numbers (I–91, I–55, and so on) run north–south. These are fully signposted, limited-access highways with at least two lanes in each direction. In some cases they are toll roads (the Pennsylvania Turnpike is I–76; the Massachusetts Turnpike is I–90). Near large cities, interstates usually intersect with a circumferential loop high-way (I–295, and so on) that carries traffic around the city.

The next level of highway—not necessarily limited access, but well paved and usually multilane—is the U.S. highways (designated U.S. 1, and so on). State highways are also well paved and often have more than one lane in each direction. Large cities usually have a number of limited-access expressways, freeways, and parkways, referred to by names rather than numbers (the Merritt Parkway, the Kennedy Expressway, the Santa Monica Freeway).

Car Rentals Major U.S. companies such as **Avis, Budget, Dollar, Hertz, National,** and **Thrifty** maintain airport and city locations throughout the United States. Other national companies, which may offer lower rates, include **Alamo, General, Rent-A-Wreck,** and **Ugly Duckling.** For a list of toll-free reservation numbers for these car-rental companies, see the Appendix.

Shop around for the best rates and make reservations well in advance if you can. Costs vary greatly among companies, depending on the season, the number of days you expect to use the car, whether you need it for weekend or weekday use, and whether you expect to do a lot of driving or a little. In metropolitan areas, rates can range from $37 plus tax per day for an economy car to as high as $240 per day for a large car, with unlimited free mileage. Many companies have tempting promotional packages for weekly rentals, but there may be only a few cars available at that rate, and you may have to pay twice as much if you keep the car for fewer days. Some companies make you pay extra for crossing state lines, and they are quick to charge for an extra day when you return a vehicle a few hours late.

Most companies require renters to be at least 25 years of age, although some will rent to drivers as young as 21, and there may be restrictions for drivers over age 60. You will need to show the rental clerk a valid driver's license, and it is quite helpful to have a major credit card to insure payment—otherwise you will probably be asked to leave a substantial sum of money as a deposit.

Be sure to ask about add-on charges for gasoline (some companies include gas in their daily rate, others in their mileage fees, others make a separate charge for gas, and still others leave the gas up to you) and charges for dropping the car off at a location other than the one where you picked it up (surcharges here can be substantial). Child seats are compulsory for children under age 5 (about $3 per day), and there are usual extra charges for additional drivers (around $1.50 per day).

Find out what is covered by the collision-damage waiver (CDW), usually an $8–$12 daily surcharge, and whether your corporate or personal insurance already covers damage to a rental car (if so, bring a photocopy of the benefits section along). More and more companies are now holding renters responsible for theft and vandalism damages if they don't buy the CDW; in response, some credit-card and insurance companies are extending *their* coverage to rental cars, and New York and Illinois have outlawed the sale of CDW altogether. With so many renters opting not to buy the CDW, some rental companies have countered by automatically including the cost in the rate. Be sure to ask what you are getting.

When you've decided on the company and reserved a car, *be sure to get a reservation number*. Remember, if the company doesn't have the car you reserved when you arrive to pick it up, the company must provide a comparable or better car at the price you reserved.

Auto Clubs The **American Automobile Association (AAA)** is a federation of state auto clubs that offers maps, route planning, and emergency road service to its members; members of Britain's Automobile Association (AA) are granted reciprocal privileges. To join AAA, check local phone directories under AAA for the nearest club, or contact the national organization (1000 AAA Dr., Heathrow, FL 32746–5063, tel. 407/444–7000).

Other auto clubs that offer roadside assistance and trip-planning services include **Allstate Motor Club** (Customer Service Center, Box 3093, Arlington Heights, IL 60004, tel. 800/347–8880); **AMOCO Motor Club** (Box 9046, Des Moines, IA 50369, tel. 800/334–3300), which also handles the **AARP Motor Club,** a service of the American Association of Retired Persons; **Exxon Travel Club** (4550 Dacoma St., Houston, TX 77092, tel. 800/833–9966); **Ford Auto Club** (Ford Motor Company Customer Service Division, 300 Renaissance Center, Box 43360, Detroit MI 48243, tel. 800/348–5220); and **United States Auto Club (USAC)** (Box 660460, Dallas, TX 75266–0460, tel. 800/348–2761).

By Train

Amtrak (tel. 800/872–7245, TDD 800/523–6590) is the national passenger rail service. Amtrak runs a limited number of routes; the northeast coast from Boston down to Washington, DC, is generally well served. Chicago is a major rail terminus as well.

Some trains travel overnight, and you can sleep in your seat or book a roomette at additional cost. Most trains have diner cars with acceptable food, but you may prefer to bring your own. Excursion fares, when available, may save you nearly half the round-trip fare.

Children Children under 2 ride for free (one child per adult) if they don't occupy a seat; children 2–15 accompanied by a fare-paying adult pay half-price (two children per adult); children 15 and over pay the full adult fare.

Older Travelers Senior citizens (over 62) are entitled to a 15% discount on the lowest available fares Monday–Thursday only.

Travelers with Amtrak requests 48 hours' advance notice to provide redcap
Disabilities service, special seats, or wheelchair assistance at stations equipped to provide these services.

Passengers with disabilities receive a 25% discount. A special fare for children with disabilities is also available. For a free copy of *Access Amtrak*, which outlines all its services for the elderly and the disabled, contact Amtrak (National Railroad Corp., 60 Massachusetts Ave. NE, Washington, DC 20002).

Rail Passes The **USA Railpass** allows overseas visitors 15 or 30 days of unlimited travel for $308 or $389, respectively; you can purchase this in the United States at any Amtrak station, but to qualify you must show a valid non-U.S. passport. U.S. citizens can buy

All Aboard America tickets, which allow a coast-to-coast trip with up to three stopovers in a 45-day period for $339.

By Bus

Once you get away from the two coasts and the major cities, long-distance buses (motorcoaches) serve much more of the United States than trains do. Various regional bus companies serve their areas of the country; the most extensive long-haul service is provided by **Greyhound Lines**, (tel. 800/231–2222). Generally no reservations are needed—buy your tickets before boarding (allow 15 minutes in advance in small towns, up to 45 minutes in larger cities). Usually you check in your baggage while boarding, and it is stowed in a large compartment at the bottom of the bus. Long-distance buses often feature reclining seats, individually controlled reading lights, rest rooms, and air-conditioning and heating.

Travelers with Disabilities Greyhound offers no special fares or facilities for disabled passengers, but an attendant is entitled to ride for free. If you will be traveling alone and need special assistance, call Greyhound (TDD 800/752–4841) at least 48 hours before departure.

Older Travelers Greyhound offers a 5% discount on regular fares for passengers 64 and older; there are restrictions, so be sure to call local numbers for specific information.

Children On Greyhound buses, one child under age 2 travels free on an adult's lap, children 2–4 accompanied by an adult pay 10% of the adult fare, and children 5–11 pay half-fare. Again, call ahead for specifics, as special fares have restrictions.

Bus Passes Visitors from overseas obtain unlimited travel on Greyhound by presenting the **International Ameripass** at the ticket counter. The cost is $175 for a 7-day pass, $250 for 15 days, and $325 for 30 days. The pass can be obtained only in New York City (Greyhound International, 625 8th Ave., New York, NY 10018, tel. 212/971–0492) or Los Angeles (USA Travel West, c/o Central Holidays, 5777 W. Century Blvd., Suite 300, Los Angeles, CA 90045, tel. 213/216–4940); you must show a valid non-U.S. passport. U.S. citizens can buy Greyhound's **Ameripass** for unlimited travel; the cost is $229 for 7 days, $319 for 15 days, and $429 for 30 days.

Staying in the USA

Customs

Entering the United States, a visitor 21 or older can bring in 200 cigarettes or 50 cigars or 2 kilograms of tobacco, 1 liter of alcohol, and duty-free gifts to a value of $100. You may not bring in meat or meat products, seeds, plants, or fruit. Absolutely avoid carrying illegal drugs.

Money

Currency The basic unit of U.S. currency is the dollar, which is subdivided into 100 cents. Coins are the copper penny (1¢) and four silver coins, the nickel (5¢), the dime (10¢), the quarter (25¢), and the half-dollar (50¢). Silver $1 coins are rarely seen in circulation. Paper money comes in denominations of $1, $5, $10, $20, $50, and $100. All these bills are the same size and green color; they are distinguishable only by the dollar amount quoted on them and by different pictures of famous American men. At press time the exchange rate was $1.38 to the pound sterling, $1.30 to the Canadian dollar, and $1.51 to the Australian dollar.

Exchanging Money In the United States, it is not as easy to find places to exchange currency as it is in European cities. In major international cities, such as New York and Los Angeles, currency may be exchanged at some bank branches, as well as at currency-exchange booths in airports and at foreign-currency offices such as **American Express Travel Service** and **Thomas Cook** (check local directories for addresses and phone numbers). The best strategy is to buy traveler's checks in U.S. dollars before you come to the United States; while the rates may not be as good abroad, the time saved by not having to search constantly for exchange facilities far outweighs any financial loss.

Banks In general, U.S. banks will not cash a personal check for you unless you have an account at that bank (it doesn't have to be at that branch). Only in major cities are large bank branches equipped to exchange foreign currencies. Therefore, it's best to rely on credit cards, cash machines, and traveler's checks to handle expenses while you're traveling.

Credit Cards Credit-card abbreviations in this book refer to the most commonly accepted credit cards in the United States: American Express (AE), Discover (D), Diners Club (DC), MasterCard (MC), and Visa (V). It's always a good idea to call ahead to confirm an establishment's credit-card policy.

MasterCard is the U.S. equivalent of the Access card in Britain, or the EuroCard in other European countries. Visa is the equivalent of the BarclayCard in Britain or the ChargeEx card in Canada. Charges incurred in the United States will appear on your regular monthly bill, converted to your own currency at the exchange rate applicable on the day the charge was entered.

Traveler's Checks Most stores, restaurants, hotels, and other businesses in the United States accept traveler's checks in U.S. dollars; hardly any will accept them in foreign currency. You can purchase traveler's checks at your home bank branch; you may be charged a transaction fee of 1% of the amount you purchase. Be sure to keep a record of the check numbers as you cash them so you can claim a refund for any lost or stolen checks. Major traveler's checks companies maintain toll-free numbers for people to report lost or stolen checks: **American Express** (tel. 800/221-7282); **Bank of America** (tel. 800/227-3460); **Citicorp** (tel. 800/645-6556); **MasterCard** or **Thomas Cook** (tel. 800/223-7373); Visa (tel. 800/227-6811).

Cash Machines Virtually all U.S. banks belong to a network of ATMs (Automated Teller Machines) that dispense cash 24 hours a day in cities throughout the country. These cash machines are usually found at bank branches along major local streets; in downtown areas, they are walk-up windows, but in suburban areas they may be drive-up windows. In many parts of the country, cash machines are also located in supermarkets. You can usually find a couple at airports, train stations, and bus terminals as well. There are some eight major networks in the United States, the largest of which are Cirrus, owned by MasterCard, and Plus, which is affiliated with Visa. Some banks belong to more than one network.

You can use your bank card at ATMs away from home to withdraw money from an account and get cash advances on a credit-card account (providing your card has been programmed with a personal identification number, or PIN). Check in advance on limits on withdrawals and cash advances within specified periods. Ask whether your bank-card or credit-card PIN number will need to be reprogrammed for use in the area you'll be visiting—a possibility if the number has more than four digits. Remember that you are charged interest from day you get the money from ATMs as well as from tellers. And note that transaction fees for ATM withdrawals outside your home turf will probably be higher than for withdrawals at home.

For specific Cirrus locations in the United States and Canada, call 800/424–7787 (for U.S. Plus locations, 800/843–7587), and press the area code and first three digits of the number you're calling from (or the calling area where you want an ATM).

American Express Cardholder Services The company's **Express Cash** system lets you withdraw cash and/or traveler's checks from a worldwide network of 57,000 American Express dispensers and participating bank ATMs. You must *enroll first* (call 800/CASH–NOW for a form and allow two weeks for processing). Withdrawals are charged not to your card but to a designated bank account. You can withdraw up to $1,000 per seven-day period on the basic card, more if your card is gold or platinum. There is a 2% fee (minimum $2.50, maximum $10) for each cash transaction, and a 1% fee for traveler's checks (except for the platinum card), which are available only from American Express dispensers.

At AmEx offices, cardholders can also cash personal checks for up to $1,000 in any seven-day period; of this, $200 can be in cash, more if available, with the balance paid in traveler's checks, for which all but platinum cardholders pay a 1% fee. Higher limits apply to the gold and platinum cards.

Wiring Money You don't have to be a cardholder to send or receive an **American Express MoneyGram** for up to $10,000. To send one, go to an American Express MoneyGram agent, pay up to $1,000 with a credit card and anything over that in cash, and phone a transaction reference number to your intended recipient, who needs only present identification and the reference number to the nearest MoneyGram agent to pick up the cash. There are MoneyGram agents in more than 60 countries (call 800/543–4080 for locations). Fees range from 5% to 10%, depending on the amount and how you pay. You can't use American Express, which is really a convenience card—only Discover, Master-Card, and Visa credit cards.

You can also use **Western Union.** To wire money, take either cash or a check to the nearest office. (Or you can call and use a credit card.) Fees are roughly 5%–10%. Money sent from the United States or Canada will be available for pick up within minutes. (Note that once the money is in the system it can be picked up at *any* location. You don't have to miss your train waiting for it to arrive in City A, because if there's an agent in City B, where you're headed, you can pick it up there, too.) There are approximately 20,000 agents worldwide (call 800/325–6000 for locations).

Money Orders, Funds Transfers With prior arrangement, any U.S. bank is equipped to accept transfers of funds from foreign banks. It helps if you can plan specific dates to pick up money at specific bank branches. Your home bank can supply you with a list of its correspondent banks in the United States.

If you have more time, and you have a U.S. address where you can receive mail, you can have someone send you a **certified check,** which you can cash at any bank, or a **postal money order** (for up to $700, obtained for a fee of up to $1 at any U.S. post office, and redeemable at any other post office). From overseas, you can have someone go to a bank to send to you an **international money order** (also called a bank draft), which will cost a $15–$20 commission plus air-mail postage. Always bring two valid pieces of identification, preferably with photos, to claim your money.

Tipping Tipping is a way of life in America, and some individuals may even be rude if you don't give them the size of tip they expect. At restaurants, a 15% tip is standard for waiters, up to 20% at more expensive establishments. The same goes for taxi drivers, bartenders, and hairdressers. Coat-check facilities usually expect $1; bellhops and porters should get about 50¢ per bag; hotel maids in upscale hotels should get about $1 per day of your stay. On package tours, conductors and drivers usually get $10 per day from the group as a whole; check whether this has already been figured into your cost. For local sightseeing tours, you may individually tip the driver-guide $1 if he or she has been helpful or informative. Ushers in theaters do not expect tips.

Sales Taxes There is no U.S. value-added tax, but sales taxes are set by most individual states, and they can vary anywhere from 3% to 8¼%. In some states, localities are permitted to add their own sales taxes as well. Exactly what is taxable, however, varies from place to place. In some, food and other essentials are not taxable, although you might pay tax for restaurant food. Luxury items such as cigarettes and alcohol are sometimes taxed extra (known colloquially as a "sin tax"), as is gasoline, on the theory that car users should pay funds used to improve local roads.

Money-Saving Tips

- Use a **travel agent** to book your plane tickets, as well as tour packages—they don't charge you a fee, but they can get you the lowest airfares and, often, discounts on hotels. For reliability, make sure they are accredited members of the American Society of Travel Agents.

- Although there is no country-wide tourist "season," various regions may have **high** and **low seasons** that are reflected in airfares and hotel rates. Unless the weather is a real drawback (as in Alaska in the winter, or Miami in August) visit areas during their off-season, both to save money and to avoid crowds.

- Lower airfares may be available at **off-peak flying times**— weekends, some mid-day flights on short routes (not as popular with business travelers), or late-night flights on coast-to-coast routes, otherwise known as the "red-eye" flights because passengers lose a night's sleep.

- **Round-trip plane tickets** are significantly cheaper than two corresponding one-way fares—so much so, in fact, that if you need a one-way ticket, you may be able to fly cheaper by buying the round-trip fare and throwing away the second half.

- Sometimes **air/hotel packages** are so cheap that it's worth booking it just for the airfare, even if you don't plan to use the hotel portion.

- Even after booking a plane ticket, call back a few days before takeoff to see if additional **seats** have been **discounted** in order to fill the plane.

- In cities, **hotel rates** are often lower on weekends, when business travelers have gone home. Conversely, in weekend resort areas, mid-week may be a cheaper time to visit.

- If you're a corporate professional, even if you're not traveling on business, ask for a **corporate rate discount** when you book your hotel room.

- If you travel relatively often and can be flexible in your plans, join a **half-price hotel program,** which helps members get up to 50% discounts on rooms at participating hotels, subject to availability. The names of some prominent groups: **Entertainment Publications** (300 W. Schrock Rd., Westerville, OH 43081, tel. 800/285–5525), **International Travel Card** (6001 N. Clark St., Chicago, IL 60660, tel. 800/342–0558), **Privilege Card** (3400 Peachtree Rd., Suite 615, Atlanta, GA 30326, tel. 404/623–0066), and **Quest International** (402 E. Yakima Ave., Suite 1200, Yakima, WA 98901, tel. 509/248–7512).

- If a hotel quotes you a special low rate, for instance as part of a promotion, get **written confirmation** of it to ensure that that's what you'll be charged upon arrival.

- Across America, look for signs outside restaurants advertising **"early-bird specials"**—some real bargains for travelers who don't mind eating dinner at 5 or 6 PM.

- To sample some big-city gourmet restaurants, try **lunch** instead of dinner—the same menu is often offered for a good deal less.

- Even if their room rates are slightly higher than those of regular hotels, **all-suite hotels** can save you money in the long run if you fix your own breakfasts, quick lunches, or even dinner in their kitchenettes.

- If you plan to rent a car at your destination, check into **fly/drive packages,** which offer good savings compared to the separate costs of plane travel and car rental.

- If you make a call from your hotel room, be aware that many hotels tack on exorbitant charges for **telephone calls;** ask about the charges in advance, or use an alternative method of calling.

- Families should always check how much is charged for **kids** to sleep in the same room as their parents. Some chains charge nothing, which can represent substantial savings.

Dining

The restaurants listed in this guide are grouped by price categories. Prices may vary greatly from region to region, or between a city and the surrounding countryside. Highly recommended restaurants are indicated by a star (★).

Chart 1	(A)	(B)
Category	Cost: Major City or Resort	Cost: Other *Areas*
Very Expensive	over $50	
Expensive	$30–$50	over $25
Moderate	$15–$30	$10–$25
Inexpensive	under $15	under $10

Rates are per person for a 3-course meal excluding drinks, tips, and taxes

Part of the experience of visiting cities such as Chicago, Los Angeles, New York, New Orleans, or San Francisco lies in sampling their famous gourmet restaurants, gastronomic shrines presided over by such celebrity chefs as Daniel Boulud, Charles Palmer, Paul Prudhomme, or Wolfgang Puck. At fine **steak houses** and **seafood restaurants,** you'll pay a premium not for fancy cooking but for fresh, top-quality beef or fish. The American habit of eating out frequently, especially strong among young professionals, has given most cities a roster of **bistros, wine bars,** nostalgically decorated **diners,** and other trendy eating spots where the emphasis is as much on the theme and the scene as on the food. **Bars** may offer a few simple foods— notably during "happy hour," roughly 5–7 PM—but many drinking spots serve nothing more than peanuts and pretzels. Tucked away in residential neighborhoods you can find some reasonably priced **coffee shops, delicatessens,** or **cafés** where the food may be good and the atmosphere friendly. In cities with strong ethnic populations, some of your best bets for an inexpensive, memorable meal may be in **ethnic restaurants** that serve up authentic homeland cooking. Try to get a knowledgeable recommendation, however, as they may be run by immigrants who never cooked until they came to the United States.

Away from the cities, some fine **country inns** hold their own against the city chefs in serving top-flight gourmet meals; follow recommendations from this book or from locals. Small towns may harbor delightful small restaurants, either **family-style restaurants** serving substantial, if somewhat conventional, meals, or basic **soup-and-sandwich restaurants** with an emphasis on healthy, even vegetarian, cooking.

Fast-food restaurants are not hard to find, as their success depends on being in handy locations. Among the biggest and most dependable chains are hamburger restaurants (McDonald's, Burger King, Wendy's, Jack in the Box), chicken restaurants (Kentucky Fried Chicken, Roy Rogers), and pizza joints (Pizza Hut, Domino's). With the addition of salads, the menus are not as narrow as they once were. Youngsters like the food, and many restaurants have compact but innovative playgrounds out front.

Along the interstates, chain restaurants, many of them fast-food outlets, advertise their locations prominently; most are quite close to the highway, or even at a special stopoff plaza at the side of the highway itself. **Truck stops** are a special breed of highway restaurant, usually open 24 hours a day, catering to long-haul truck drivers. Service is quick, portions hearty, and the gift shops full of quirky (sometimes obscene) items.

Hotel restaurants have improved markedly in quality over the past several years; it's not unusual these days for some of the top gourmet restaurants in a city to be in hotels, attracting local people as well as guests from other hotels. Large hotels and resorts often have a number of restaurants, ranging from quick coffee shops and lobby lounges to elegant dining rooms.

Breakfast is served anywhere from 6 to 11 AM, lunch 11–2, dinner from 5 until late. Like business hours in general, mealtimes tend to become earlier when you leave the cities and as you go farther west. At very expensive restaurants in some cities, men may be required to wear a jacket and tie at dinner (we've noted such policies in our reviews in this book); otherwise, you can generally wear what you wish, as long as you are clean and neat. We've also noted restaurants that require reservations or that won't take any reservations at all, but except for the more inexpensive places, it's always a good idea to call ahead and reserve a table so you won't be disappointed.

Liquor Laws   Liquor laws vary from state to state, affecting such matters as bar and liquor store opening times and whether restaurants can sell liquor by the glass or only by the bottle. A few states—mostly in the South or Midwest—allow each county to choose its own policy, resulting in so-called dry counties, where no alcoholic beverages are sold, next to counties where the bars do a roaring business. If you are traveling through several states, inquire about local restrictions at your hotel or restaurant.

The drinking age is 21 in all states, and you should be prepared to show identification in order to be served. Restaurants must obtain a license to sell alcoholic beverages on the premises, so some inexpensive establishments, or places that have just recently opened, may not sell drinks at all, or may sell only beer or wine. In most of these restaurants, however, you can bring your own beer or wine in with you to drink with your meal. In this book, we note such a policy as BYOB (bring your own bottle).

Local laws against driving while intoxicated are growing stricter. Many bars now serve nonalcoholic drinks for the "designated driver" so at least one person in a group is sober enough to drive everyone else safely home.

Lodging

The hotels, motels, inns, and resorts listed in this guide are grouped according to the price categories shown below. Prices may vary greatly from region to region, or between a city and the surrounding countryside.

Highly recommended lodgings are indicated by a star (★).

Chart 2	(A)	(B)
Category	Cost: Major city or Resort	Cost: Other *Areas*
Very Expensive	over $200	
Expensive	$125–$200	over $85

Moderate	$75–$125	$50–$85
Inexpensive	under $75	under $50

*rates are for a standard double room for two, excluding tax and service charges

Various rate categories define what you're getting for your room rate: the so-called American Plan (AP) includes three meals a day, Modified American Plan (MAP) includes breakfast and dinner, and European Plan (EP) includes no meals. These categories are used mostly at resorts; most other hotels quote a rate for a room, and any meals you eat there cost extra.

Motels are geared to motorists, with locations close to highways and convenient parking. **Airport hotels,** located within a few minutes' drive of major airports, are geared to plane travelers in transit, with a strong business-travel clientele; noise may be a problem, although the best ones are excellently soundproofed. **Convention hotels,** located in large cities near convention centers, have hundreds of guest rooms, warrens of meeting rooms (usually on separate floors), and big ballrooms used for exhibits and banquets; when a large convention is staying at one, other guests sometimes feel overwhelmed. Other **downtown hotels** cater more to individual guests and may offer more in the way of health facilities and à la carte restaurants, but some may emphasize their attraction to business travelers with extensive office services. **Suburban hotels** in many cities attract travelers who want to be close to the circumferential highway and to suburban office parks, shopping malls, or theme parks; they may be larger and more upscale than motels, offering more restaurants, health facilities, and other amenities. **Resorts** tend to be destinations in and of themselves—complete with golf courses, tennis courts, beaches, several restaurants, on-site entertainment, and so on. Sometimes a resort features one large hotel building surrounded by landscape, while others are designed with clusters of smaller buildings, down to individual cottages or huts. The setting usually emphasizes one particular outdoor activity, whether skiing, water sports, or golf. One variation on this is the **dude ranch,** where paying guests sample horseback riding, hiking, lake fishing, cookouts, and such western-style activities as rodeos. **Country inns** and **bed-and-breakfasts** are generally charming older properties that, unlike European B&Bs, tend to be pricey and upscale. They may not have private bathrooms, in-room phone, or TVs, and as they are frequently meticulously furnished with antiques, they may not be the best place to take young children. Breakfast is usually included in the room rate, but verify this when you make a reservation. For recommendations, see *Fodor's Bed & Breakfasts and Country Inns* books for various regions of the country. At the budget end of the scale, **YMCAs** and **youth hostels** offer somewhat more spartan accommodations, often dormitory-style, and limited amenities.

The United States has several reputable chains of hotels. Some of the large chains, such as **Holiday Inn, Hilton, Hyatt, Marriott,** and **Ramada,** are even further subdivided into chains of budget properties, all-suite properties, downtown hotels, or luxury resorts, each with different names. While some chain hotels may have a standardized look to them, this "cookie-cutter" approach also means that you can rely on the same level of comfort and efficiency at all properties in a well-managed chain, and at a chain's premier properties—its so-called flagship hotels—decor and services may be outstanding. Toll-free reservation numbers for the major hotel and motel chains are listed in the back of this book (*see* Appendix). Local tourist bureaus and chambers of commerce listed in the city and region sections of this book can often refer you to hotels.

Most hotels will hold your reservation until 6 PM; if you know you're going to arrive later than that, call ahead. Hotels will be more willing to hold a late reservation for you if you reserve with a credit-card number.

When you call to make a reservation, ask all the necessary questions up front. If you are arriving with a car, ask if the hotel has a parking lot or covered garage, and whether there is an extra fee for parking. If you like to eat your meals in, ask if the hotel has a restaurant, or whether it has room service (most do, but not necessarily 24 hours a day—and be forewarned that it can be expensive). Most hotels have in-room telephones, but double-check this at inexpensive properties and bed-and-breakfasts. Most hotels and motels have in-room TV, often with cable movies (usually pay-per-view), but verify this if you like to watch TV. If you want a crib for your child to stay in the room with you, there will probably be an additional charge.

Hotel Taxes Many states and cities levy hotel taxes, usually as a percentage of the room rate. For example, in New York City, which already has an 8¼% sales tax, the progressive hotel tax can raise the tariff as much as 13% more, to 21¼%. When you make room reservations, ask how much tax will be added to the basic rate.

Youth Hostels An **International Youth Hostel Federation** (IYHF) membership card is the key to sex-segregated, dormitory-style sleeping quarters, including some for families, priced at $7–$20 a night per person. Membership is available in the United States through **American Youth Hostels** (AYH, 733 15th St. NW, Washington, DC 20005, tel. 202/783–6161), the American link in the worldwide chain, and costs $25 for adults 18–54, $10 for those under 18, $15 for those 55 and older, and $35 for families. *Hostelling North America*, a guide to hostels in the United States and and Canada, is free to members ($8 to nonmembers, postage included). Volume 2 of the two-volume *Guide to Budget Accommodation* also lists hostels in the United States and Canada, as well as those in Asia and Australasia ($13.95 including postage). IYHF membership is available in Canada through the **Canadian Hostelling Association** (CHA, 1600 James Naismith Dr., Suite 608, Gloucester, Ont. K1B 5N4, tel. 613/748–5638) for $26.75, and in the United Kingdom through the **Youth Hostel Association of England and Wales** (Trevelyan House, 8 St. Stephen's Hill, St. Albans, Herts. AL1 2DY, tel. 0727/55215) for £9.

YMCAs are another source of clean, respectable low-cost accommodations. Contact **Sloane House YMCA** (356 W. 34th St., New York, NY 10001, tel. 212/760–5860 or 212/760–5856) for reservations at other Ys around the country.

Home Exchange This is obviously an inexpensive solution to the lodging problem, because house-swapping means living rent-free. You find a house, apartment, or other vacation property to exchange for your own by becoming a member of a home-exchange organization, which then sends you its annual directories listing available exchanges and includes your own listing in at least one of them. Arrangements for the actual exchange are made by the two parties to it, not by the organization. Principal clearinghouses include **Intervac U.S./International Home Exchange** (Box 590504, San Francisco, CA 94159, tel. 415/435–3497), the oldest, with thousands of foreign and domestic homes for exchange in its three annual directories; membership is $62, or $72 if you want to receive the directories but remain unlisted. The **Vacation Exchange Club** (Box 650, Key West, FL 33041, tel. 800/638–3841), also with thousands of foreign and domestic listings, publishes four annual directories plus updates; the $50 membership includes your listing in one book. **Loan-a-Home** (2 Park La., Apt. 6E, Mount Vernon, NY 10552, tel. 914/664–7640) specializes in long-term exchanges; there is no charge to list your home, but the directories cost $35 or $45 depending on the number you receive.

National Parklands and Forests

For information on the extensive U.S. system of national parks, battlefields, and recreational areas, write to the **National Park Service** (Department of the Interior, Washington, DC 20240) or call the regional offices: North Atlantic (tel. 617/223–5199); Mid-Atlantic (tel. 215/597–3679); National Capital Region (tel. 202/619–7222 or 202/619–7226); Southeast (tel. 404/331–4998); Midwest (tel. 402/221–3448); Rocky Mountains (tel. 303/969–2503); Southwest (tel. 505/988–6012); Western (tel. 415/744–3929); Pacific Northwest (tel. 206/553–5622); and Alaska (tel. 907/257–2696).

Children 16 and younger are admitted free to all national parks and recreational areas; U.S. residents age 62 or older can pick up a **Golden Age Passport,** a free lifetime pass to all national parks, at any park that charges admission. Non-U.S. citizens of all ages can buy a 12-month **Golden Eagle Pass,** which provides free admission to all national parks, for $25 at any national park facility.

For information on recreational opportunities in national forests, write to the **U.S. Forest Service** (Department of Agriculture, 201 14th St. SW, Washington, DC 20250).

Telecommunications

Telephones All U.S. telephone numbers consist of 10 digits—the three-digit area code, followed by a seven-digit local number. If you're calling a number from another area code region, dial "1" then all 10 digits. If you're calling from a distance but within the same area code, dial "1" then the last seven digits. For calls within the same local calling area, just dial the seven-digit number. A map of U.S. area codes is printed in the front of most local telephone directories; throughout this book, we have listed each phone number in full, including its area code.

Two special prefixes, "800" and "900," are not area codes but indicators of particular kinds of service. "800" numbers can be dialed free from anywhere in the country—usually they are prepaid commercial lines that make it easier for consumers to obtain information, products, or services. "900" numbers charge a special (often high) rate for the privilege of calling and generally offer some kind of entertainment, such as horoscope readings, sports scores, or sexually suggestive conversations. Know what you're getting into before you dial a "900" number.

Public Phones Instructions for **pay telephones** should be posted on the phone, but generally you insert your coins—anywhere from 10¢ to 30¢ for a local call—in a slot and wait for the steady hum of a dial tone before dialing the number you wish to reach. If you dial a long-distance number, the operator will come on the line and tell you how much more money you must insert in order for your call to go through.

Credit-Card Calls U.S. telephone credit cards are not like the magnetic cards used in some European countries, which pay for calls in advance; they simply represent an account that lets you charge a call to your home or business phone. On any phone, you can make a credit-card call by punching in your individual account number, or by telling the operator that number. Certain specially marked pay phones (usually found in airports, hotel lobbies, and so on) can be used only for credit-card calls. To get a credit card, contact your long-distance telephone carrier, such as AT&T, MCI, or Sprint.

Operator Assistance For assistance from an operator, dial 0. To find out a telephone number, call directory assistance, 555–1212 in every locality. These calls are free even from a pay phone. If you want to charge a long-distance call to the person you're calling, you can call collect by dialing 0 instead of 1 before the 10-digit number, and an operator will come on the line to assist you (the party you're calling, however, has the right to refuse the call).

International Calls International calls can be direct-dialed from most phones; dial 011, followed by the country code and then the local number (the front pages of many local telephone directories include a list of overseas country codes). To have an operator assist you, dial 0 and ask for the overseas operator.

Telegrams To send a telegram, stop by a **Western Union** office, or call Western Union (tel. 800/325–6000) to order a telegram billed to your home phone or major credit card. Rates vary with the length or your message, and how quickly you need it delivered.

Fax Machines Fax transmission has become a mainstay of American communications. You can usually make hotel reservations via fax, and you can probably send a fax on the hotel's machine while staying there, especially if the hotel caters to business travelers. If your hotel isn't helpful or charges exorbitantly for this service, look for fax service at local photocopying stores; the charge may be as much as $2 a page, more for overseas.

Mail

Every address in the United States belongs to a specific zip-code district, and each zip code has five digits. Some addresses include a second sequence of four numbers following the first five numbers, but while this speeds mail delivery for large organizations, it is not necessary to use it. Each zip-code district has at least one post office, where you can buy stamps and aerogrammes, send parcels, or conduct other postal business. Occasionally you may find small stamp-dispensing machines in airports, train stations, bus terminals, large office buildings, drugstores, or grocery stores, but don't count on it. Most Americans go to the post office to buy their stamps, and the lines can be long.

Official mail boxes are either the stout royal-blue steel bins located on city sidewalks or mail chutes on the walls of post offices or in large office buildings. A schedule posted on mailboxes and mail slots should indicate when the mail is picked up.

Postal Rates First-class letters weighing up to 1 ounce can be sent anywhere within the United States with a 29¢ stamp; each additional ounce costs 23¢. Postcards need a 19¢ stamp. A half-ounce airmail letter overseas takes 50¢, an airmail postcard 40¢, and a surface-rate postcard 35¢. For Canada, you'll need a 40¢ stamp for a one-ounce letter, 30¢ for a postcard. For Mexico, you'll need 35¢ for a half-ounce letter, 30¢ for a postcard. For 45¢, you can buy an aerogramme—a single sheet of light-weight blue paper that folds into its own envelope, already stamped for overseas airmail delivery.

Receiving Mail Travelers can have mail sent to them **c/o General Delivery** at the city's main post office (be sure to use the right zip code). It should be held there for up to 30 days. You must pick it up in person, and bring identification with you. American Express offices in the United States do not hold mail.

Opening and Closing Times

Banks are generally open weekdays 9 AM–2 or 3 PM, post offices weekdays 8 AM–5 PM; many branches operate Saturday morning hours. Business hours tend to be weekdays 9–5, a little later on the East Coast and earlier the farther west you go. Many stores may not open until 10 or 11, but they remain open until 6 or 7; most carry on brisk business on Saturdays as well. Large suburban shopping malls, the focus of most Americans' shopping activity, are generally open seven days a week, with evening hours every day except Sunday. All across the country, so-called convenience stores sell food and sundries until about 11 PM. Along the highways and in major cities you can usually find all-night diners, supermarkets, drugstores, and convenience stores, as Americans gravitate toward a 24-hour society.

National Holidays

Some U.S. holidays fall on specific dates, but most of them fall on designated Mondays, to ensure three-day weekends for workers. Banks, post offices, and government offices, as well as many shops and restaurants, are closed on the following dates in 1994: New Year's Day (January 1), Martin Luther King, Jr. Day (January 17), President's Day (February 21), Memorial Day (May 30), Independence Day (July 4), Labor Day (September 5), Columbus Day (October 10), Veteran's Day (November 11), Thanksgiving (November 24), Christmas (December 25).

Emergencies

In most local communities you can call **police, fire,** or **ambulance** services by dialing 911. If your car breaks down on an interstate highway, try to pull over onto the shoulder of the road and either wait for the state police to find you or, if you have other passengers who can wait in the car, walk to the nearest emergency roadside phone and call the state police. If you are calling for help, note your location according to the small green mileage markers posted along the highway. Other highways are also patrolled but may not have emergency phones or mileage markers. If you are a member of the AAA auto club (*see* Auto Clubs, *above*), look in the local phone book for the AAA emergency road-service number, or call 800/222–4357.

Great American Itineraries

Highlights of New England

Begin in **Boston** (2–3 days), unofficial capital of the New England states. Drive west on I–90 to the scenic Berkshire hills (1–2 days), then north on Rte. 7 to **Vermont** (1–2 days), going through the Green Mountains with their many ski-resort towns. At Rutland, go east on U.S. 4 to **New Hampshire** (1–3 days). Stop in Hanover to see Dartmouth College, then continue east to either the White Mountains or the Lake Winnipesaukee area. Drive east on either U.S. 302 (from the White Mountains) or Rte. 25 (from Winnipesaukee) to **Maine** (2 days). From Portland, Maine, hug the coast on U.S. 1 south, stopping off as desired in the Kennebunks, the Yorks, or Portsmouth, New Hampshire, continuing down the North Shore and back to Boston.

Length of Trip 7–12 days

Civil War Landmarks

After touring **Washington, DC** (1–3 days), devote a day to these major Civil War battlefields, each only a couple of hours' drive from the others. Head west on I–66 to **Manassas,** Virginia, also known as Bull Run, site of two battles (July 1861 and August 1862). Continue west on I–66 to U.S. 340, which takes you north to West Virginia, to see **Harpers Ferry,** site of John Brown's raid and many Civil War clashes. Cross the Potomac River into Maryland and follow Rte. 65, then Rte. 34, north to **Antietam,** also called Sharpsburg, site of a bloody battle in September 1862. Return to U.S. 340, go to Frederick, and pick up U.S. 15 for the drive north to **Gettysburg,** Pennsylvania, where a July 1863 battle marked the turning point of the war. To pick up the next cluster of Virginia battlefields, backtrack on U.S. 15 to Frederick, take I–270 south to skirt Washington, then pick up I–95 south to **Fredericksburg/Spotsylvania Battlefield,** site of four major battles throughout the Civil War. Continue on I–95 through Richmond to **Petersburg,** besieged for 10 months from June 1864 to April 1865. Return to **Richmond,** capital of the Confederacy and a major battle site in April 1865. Take U.S. 360, then U.S. 460, west from Richmond to **Appomattox Courthouse,** where Confederate commander Robert E. Lee finally surrendered to Union commander Ulysses S. Grant on April 9, 1865. Returning to **Washington,** visit Ford's Theater, where President Abraham Lincoln was assassinated a few days after the peace was signed.

Length of Trip 10–12 days

The Mighty Mississippi River

This tour varies in length according to how much of the river's majestic course you want to follow. For an extensive trip, begin in Minneapolis; you can also pick up the tour from St. Louis or Memphis. From Minneapolis, head northwest to the river's source in **Lake Itasca** (1–3 days), near Bemidji, the heart of Paul Bunyan country. Even novice canoers can paddle along the river here, nearly all the way to **Minneapolis/St. Paul** (1–3 days). From there, U.S. 61 traces the river on dramatic bluffs along the Minnesota/Wisconsin border (stop off in charming **Red Wing**). Cross the river at **LaCrosse**, Wisconsin, and follow Rte. 35 along the river as it marks the Wisconsin/Iowa border (stop off in historic **Prairie du Chien**, where you may be able to pick up a steamboat to continue downriver). At **Dubuque**, Iowa, you may want to cross the river for the view, but get back on the Illinois shore for the best views driving south. Follow Rte. 84, then Rte. 92, then Rte. 96; watch along the way for a series of locks and dams as the river gets wider. Stop off in the major river city **St. Louis** (1–3 days), then follow scenic Rte. 3 south through Illinois, or I–55 on the Missouri side for a faster drive straight to Memphis. At **Cairo**, Illinois, is the major confluence of the Mississippi with the Ohio River. Cross the Ohio south into Kentucky on U.S. 51/62, then take Rte. 239 to Rte. 94, which will take you into Tennessee. Pick up Rte. 78 to U.S. 51, which continues south to another major river city, **Memphis** (1–3 days). From Memphis, U.S. 61 is the main route, Rte. 1 the slower riverside road, south to **Vicksburg**, Mississippi (1–2 days), site of a major Civil War battle. Stay on U.S. 61 to **Natchez** (1–2 days), a town full of glorious antebellum mansions, then on to **Baton Rouge** (1–2 days), capital of Louisiana. Rte. 1 meanders along the river through plantation country, or I–10 will lead you straight to **New Orleans** (2–4 days), the great city at the mouth of Mississippi.

Length of Trip 6 days–3 weeks

Canyons of the West

Starting in **Las Vegas** (1–3 days), it's a short drive east on U.S. 93 to **Hoover Dam** and the recreational area it created, **Lake Mead** (1–2 days). Continue on U.S. 93 to I–40, which shoots east to **Flagstaff**, Arizona, from which U.S. 180 north will take you to the **Grand Canyon National Park** (1–3 days), one of America's most awesome landscapes. U.S. 89 will take you north to **Glen Canyon** (1 day), another large recreational area built around the dam creating Lake Powell. Now in Utah, you can head west on U.S. 89, with an optional turnoff west on Rte. 9 to **Zion National Park** (1–4 days). U.S. 89 will eventually take you to Rte. 12, where you turn east for **Bryce Canyon National Park** (1–4 days). Take Rte. 14 west from U.S. 89 to I–15, which you can either take north to **Salt Lake City** (1–2 days), home of the Mormon church, or south back to Las Vegas.

Length of Trip 6–20 days

Pacific Coast Drive

Between **San Francisco** (2–4 days) and **Los Angeles** (2–5 days), the fastest routes are I–5 or U.S. 101, but travelers who have the time should take the coastal road, Highway 1, which offers some of the country's most beautiful scenery. Because of the coastline's easterly curve, the drive is most spectacular when taken from north to south. Allow for a full day's driving time from San Francisco to Los Angeles, two days if you make some stops (recommended: **Monterey** and the 17-Mile Drive around the Monterey Peninsula; **San Simeon,** home of Hearst Castle; **Santa Barbara;** and **Malibu**). After you visit Los Angeles, you may want to continue to **San Diego** (2–3 days), following Rte. 1 from Long Beach to San Juan Capistrano, and I–5 from there on into San Diego, a total drive of a couple of hours.

Length of Trip   5 days–2 weeks

Cross-Country Drives

Northern Route   Take I–90 west from **Boston** or I–87 from **New York City** to I–90. You'll drive along Lake Erie's southern shore through New York and Ohio, around the tip of Lake Michigan into **Chicago.** I–90 continues through southern Wisconsin and Minnesota into the Great Plains. In western South Dakota, detour south to see the Badlands, the Black Hills, and **Mount Rushmore;** in Wyoming, you'll pass near **Devil's Tower** and, later, **Yellowstone** and **Grand Teton national parks.** I–90 crosses the Rocky Mountains in northern Idaho and ends up in **Seattle,** Washington.

Middle Route   From **Washington, DC,** go west on I–66 to I–81, which runs down the Shenandoah Valley. At **Lexington,** Virginia, pick I–64 west through West Virginia. You'll visit **Lexington** and **Louisville,** Kentucky, southern Indiana and Illinois, and cross the Mississippi River at **St. Louis.** From there, take I–70 through **Kansas City** and cross the Great Plains to **Denver,** Colorado. After crossing the Rocky Mountains, in Utah pick up I–15, which you can take either all the way to **Los Angeles** or north to I–80 to head west to **San Francisco.**

Southern Route   Start in **Miami,** Florida, and drive north on I–95 to **Jacksonville.** From there, I–10 cuts straight west across the southern United States, passing through **New Orleans; Houston** and **San Antonio,** Texas; **Tucson** and **Phoenix,** Arizona; and ending up in **Los Angeles.**

2 The Northeast

The Northeast

CANADA

QUÉBEC

Montréal

ONTARIO

Ottawa ★

Massena

Potsdam

Plattsburgh

Saranac Lake

`11`

Lake Placid

Watertown

ADIRONDACK FOREST PRESERVE

`87`

Toronto

Lake Ontario

NEW YORK

Oswego

`81`

Rome

Utica

Glens Falls

Niagara Falls

Rochester

Oneida

Saratoga Sprs

Tonawanda

`90`

Auburn

Syracuse

`90`

Mohawk R.

Schenectady

Batavia

Geneva

Albany ★

Buffalo

Five Fingers Lakes

Cortland

Lake Erie

Dunkirk

`90`

Hornell

`17`

Ithaca

`81`

Oneonta

`88`

CATSKILL FOREST PRESERVE

Hudson River

Jamestown

`17`

Elmira

Binghamton

Kingston

Olean

Wellsville

`17`

Poughkeepsie

Monticello

Litc

Scranton

Middletown

`87`

PENNSYLVANIA

West Point

Yonkers

0 100 miles

0 150 km

NEW JERSEY

New

Newark

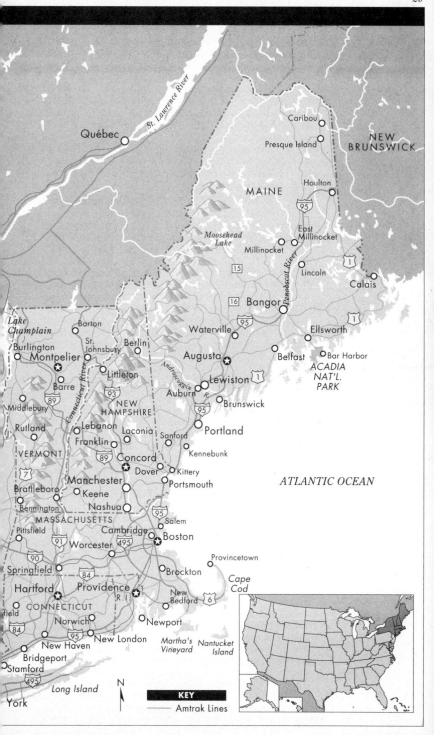

Introduction

The two major metropolitan areas of the Northeast—New
York and Boston—offer the best and worst extremes of modern
city life. As a financial and cultural capital, New York City belongs to the world as much as to the country. Boston, the
country's oldest (and still leading) college town, has been trying to redefine itself as a hub of new service and high-tech industries. Both cities are struggling to come to terms with
shifts in the economy and infrastructures badly in need of repair. Neither metropolis really defines the region, though:
Captured in a single wide-angle lens, the six states of New England and the massive bulk of New York State are decidedly un-
urban, offering more variety in terms of landscape and outdoor
diversions per square mile than any other part of the country.

Beyond the hustle and bustle, glitz and grime of New York
City, the Northeast fans out in waves of increasingly soothing
vistas, from the placid charms of the Connecticut River Valley
through the forests of Vermont and New Hampshire's Green
and White mountains to the pristine hinterland of Maine's remote Allagash Wilderness Waterway. Similarly, the "wilderness" of upstate New York begins within an hour's drive of the
Bronx: The Hudson River Valley lures frazzled urban dwellers
northward past the Catskill resorts to vast Adirondack Park—
at 6.2 million acres, almost three times as large as Yellowstone
National Park. At the western end of the state, the hydroelectric wonder of Niagara Falls continues to attract droves of
nature-loving, photo-snapping tourists and misty-eyed honey-
mooners.

The region was historically defined by the coastline, where the
Pilgrims first established a toehold in the New World. Until it
veers inland north of Yarmouth, Maine, I-95 skirts the inlets
and harbors that sheltered the whaling and trading vessels of
17th- to 19th-century settlers—Mystic, Connecticut; Providence, Rhode Island; Cape Cod, Nantucket, and Plymouth in
Massachusetts; and Portland, Maine. Beyond the interstate's
exits, in between the living museums and tourist centers, is a
region that offers a broad spectrum of diversions cerebral, spiritual, and athletic. Nowhere else in the country are the seasons
as clearly defined, and each time of year brings with it its own
recreations, such as fishing in New York and Vermont's Lake
Champlain, skiing in the White Mountains, camping on the Appalachian Trail, biking along Maine's rocky coast, sailing Long
Island Sound, applauding world-class musicians in the Berkshires, or watching whales cavort off Cape Cod.

Tour Groups

Many tour companies offer three- to seven-day tours of this region. A few extend their tours to 15 days, adding French-
speaking Canada. Most tours are in the autumn for the foliage,
though the companies listed also organize tours in summer.
Some of the leading companies: **Domenico Tours** (751 Broadway, Bayonne, NJ 07002, tel. 201/823–8687 or 800/554–8687)
offers a variety of three-day tours to the Berkshires, Boston,
Cape Cod, the Catskills, coastal Maine, New York City, and Niagara Falls; a five-day "New England Special"; and an 11-day
tour of East Coast highlights. **Gadabout Tours** (700 E. Tahquitz
Way, Palm Springs, CA 92262, tel. 619/325–5556 or 800/952–

5068) leads week-long tours of New York City and the Hudson River Valley, 11-day tours to New England and Cape Cod, and 18-day fall foliage tours. **Globus** (5301 S. Federal Circle, Littleton, CO 80123, tel. 303/797–2800 or 800/221–0090) offers eight-day fall foliage tours of New England from New York City, with stops in Stowe, Vermont; Kennebunkport, Maine; Newport, Rhode Island; and Boston, Massachusetts. A week-long fall tour from Boston includes Arcadia National Park in Maine; Lake Placid, New York; and Killington, Vermont. Also check out Globus's budget-minded affiliate, **Cosmos Tourama** (same address). **Maupintour** (Box 807, Lawrence, KS 66044, tel. 913/843–1211 or 800/255–4266) offers a 13-day tour of historic New England and French Canada and a six-day tour of Cape Cod, Martha's Vineyard, and Nantucket. **Talmage Tours** (1223 Walnut St., Philadelphia, PA 19107, tel. 215/923–7100) features four- and five-day tours of New England, Lake George, and Saratoga Springs. A week-long excursion to Maine is also available. **Tauck Tours** (11 Wilton Rd., Box 5027, Westport, CT 06881, tel. 203/226–6911 or 800/468–2825) offers a tour of seven to 11 days highlighting New England's fall foliage, an eight-day tour of Cape Cod and the islands, and a seven-day summer tour of the region.

When to Go

Each of the four seasons in the Northeast is distinct, and each has its own beauty. Spring blooms start in April along the south-coastal regions, later the farther north you go. This tends to be the quietest period throughout the region because of rains and melting snows. Summer, a hot 85°F in the southern region to a low of 59°F in the north, attracts beach lovers to the islands and coastal regions, while those preferring cooler climes make for the lakes in New York State, the mountains of Massachusetts, Vermont, and New Hampshire, or the mists of Maine. Autumn, the end of September in the north to the end of October in the south, is a kaleidoscope of colors as trees change their leaves from green to burning gold. Temperatures will still be around 55°F. Winter brings snow and skiers to the mountain slopes in every state of the region, Vermont being the most popular, while the coastal areas hibernate.

Prices during an area's peak season climb accordingly—Newport hotels in the summer, for example, are nearly double the late-autumn prices. Festivals also raise prices, such as the outdoor music festival at Tanglewood in Massachusetts's Berkshire Mountains. Reservations for hotels during peak seasons should be made well in advance, and traveling during summer weekends, especially on the overburdened Route 6 to Cape Cod, is best avoided.

Festivals and Seasonal Events

Mid-Jan.: Stowe Winter Carnival, among the country's oldest such celebrations, features winter-sports competitions in Vermont. *Tel. 802/253–7321.*

Late June–Aug.: Jacob's Pillow Dance Festival, at Becket, Massachusetts, in the Berkshires, hosts performers from various dance traditions. *Tel. 413/243–0745.*

July–Aug.: Tanglewood Music Festival at Lenox, Massachusetts, the summer home of the Boston Symphony Orchestra, schedules other top performers as well. *Tel. 413/637–1600 or 617/266–1492.*

Mid-July: Newport (RI) Music Festival brings together celebrated musicians for two weeks of morning, afternoon, and evening concerts in Newport mansions. *Tel. 401/846–1133.*

Early Aug.: Maine Lobster Festival is a public feast held on the first weekend of the month in Rockland. *Tel. 207/596–0376.*

Mid-Aug.: The JVC Jazz Festival brings renowned performers to Ft. Adams State Park in Newport, Rhode Island. *Tel. 401/847–3700.*

Getting Around the Northeast

By Plane New York City has three major airports served by major domestic and international airlines: **John F. Kennedy International Airport** (tel. 718/656–4520), **La Guardia Airport** (tel. 718/476–5000), and **Newark Airport.** Upper New York State has **Albany-Schenectady County Airport** (tel. 518/869–9611), which is served by 10 major airlines. Connecticut's **Bradley International Airport** (tel. 203/292–2000), in Hartford, is served by most major U.S. carriers. Massachusetts's **Logan International Airport** (tel. 617/567–5400), in Boston, is served by all major domestic airlines as well as several international carriers, such as British Airways. Vermont's main airport is **Burlington International Airport** (tel. 802/863–2874), served by six major airlines. For New Hampshire, the major airport is **Portland International Airport** (tel. 603/774–7301), served by most major U.S. airlines. Maine's major airport is **Bangor International Airport** (tel. 207/947–0384), served by several major U.S. airlines.

By Car The chief interstate through New England is I–95, which travels out of New York and along the Connecticut coast to Providence, Rhode Island, into Boston, Massachusetts, before continuing up through New Hampshire and along the coast of Maine. The New York State Thruway connects New York City to Albany and then veers northwest to Buffalo. I–87 runs between Albany and Montréal in Canada and passes by Lake Champlain. Crossing the eastern region between Albany and Boston is the Massachusetts Turnpike (I–90). I–84E connects I–684, which runs north from the New York metropolitan area to Hartford. Passing through Hartford is I–91, which links coastal Connecticut with New Hampshire and Eastern Vermont.

By Train **Amtrak** (tel. 800/872–7245) is the major long-distance train service for the region. Frequent trains make the run between New York, Stamford, New Haven, New London, Providence, and Boston. Fewer trains run between New York and Hartford. From Boston the *Lakeshore Limited* has train service west, stopping in Springfield and the Berkshires before continuing west to Chicago. On summer weekends, the *Cape Codder* runs between Hyannis and Washington, DC. The *Montrealer*, between Montreal and New York City, makes several stops in Vermont and has connections to Albany and Glens Falls, New York.

Local trains of the region: **Metro North** (tel. 212/532–4900 or 800/638–7646 outside NYC) connects New York City and New Haven with stops along the coast. The **Massachusetts Bay Transportation Authority** (tel. 617/722–5000) connects Boston with the north and south shores. Canada's **Via Rail** (tel. 800/361–3677) crosses northern Maine on its service between Montréal and Halifax. The **Long Island Railroad** (tel. 800/828–5540) runs from New York City to Montauk on its south-fork route and Greenport on its north fork.

By Bus   The major bus lines are **Greyhound** (tel. 800/231–2222) and **Bonanza** (tel. 800/556–3815). **Peter Pan** (tel. 413/781–3320) serves western Massachusetts and southern Connecticut.

By Boat   In Rhode Island, ferries leave Providence for Newport and Block Island from the **India Street Pier** (tel. 401/483–4613); ferries from Point Judith to Block Island depart from **Galilee State Pier** (tel. 401/783–4613). **Marine Atlantic** (tel. 800/341–7981) operates ferry service between Yarmouth, Nova Scotia, and Bar Harbor, Maine. **Prince of Fundy Cruises** (tel. 800/341–7540) operates ferry service between Yarmouth, Nova Scotia, and Portland, Maine (May–October only). **Casco Bay Lines** (tel. 207/774–7871) has ferries from Portland to the islands of Casco Bay. **Maine State Ferry Service** (tel. 207/594–5543) has ferry service from Rockland to Penobscot Bay. For information about ferry service to Martha's Vineyard and Nantucket, *see* Massachusetts. **The Bridgeport and Port Jefferson Steamboat Company** (tel. 203/367–3043) has ferries connecting the north shore of New York's Long Island to Bridgeport, Connecticut. **Cross Sound Ferry** (tel. 203/443–5281) connects New London, Connecticut, with Orient Point, New York, in northeastern Long Island.

CONNECTICUT

By Nigel Fisher

*Updated by
Andrew Collins*

Capital	Hartford
Population	3,277,980
Motto	He Who Transplanted Still Sustains
State Bird	American robin
State Flower	Mountain laurel

Visitor Information

Connecticut Department of Economic Development (865 Brook St., Rocky Hill 06067, tel. 203/258–4200 or 800/282–6863).

Scenic Drives

The narrow roads that wind through the **Litchfield Hills** in northwestern Connecticut offer scenic delights, especially in the spring and autumn. Each road bridge crossing the beautiful and historic **Merritt Parkway** (Rte. 15) between **Greenwich** and **Stratford** has its own architecturally significant design. Rtes. 57 to 53 to 107 to 302, connecting Exit 42 of the Merritt Parkway in **Westport** to Exit 10 of I–84 in **Newtown,** take you by Colonial homesteads, over steep ridges, and alongside the **Saugatuck Reservoir.** In northeastern Connecticut, Rte. 169 from **Norwich** to **North Woodstock** is one of the most outstanding scenic byways in the country.

National and State Parks

National Parks The **Weir Farm National Historic Site** (735 Nod Hill Rd., off Rte. 33, Wilton 06897, tel. 203/761–9945 or 203/834–1896) is the first national park in the United States dedicated to the legacy of an American artist. Hikers and picnickers can take advantage of trails traversing the property's 60 wooded acres and tour J. Alden Weir's former studios.

State Parks The largest of Connecticut's 91 state parks is the 4,000-acre **White Memorial Foundation** (Rte. 202, Litchfield 06759, tel. 203/567–0857), with its nature center, wildlife sanctuary, and 35 mi of hiking and horseback-riding trails. For information on state parks, contact the **Department of Economic Development** (*see* Visitor Information, *above*) or the **Bureau of Parks and Forests** (165 Capitol Ave., Hartford 06106, tel. 203/566–2304).

Coastal Connecticut

The state's 253-mi coast comprises a series of bedroom communities serving New York City and smaller towns linked to Connecticut's major cities of Stamford, Bridgeport, New Haven, and New London. Along with its Colonial heritage and 20th-century urban sprawl, the region offers numerous nature centers and wilderness preserves for hiking and bird-watching, as well as restored 18th- and 19th-century townships and a wealth of marine and other museums dedicated to keeping alive Connecticut's past.

Tourist Information

Southeastern Connecticut: Tourism District (27 Masonic St., Box 89, New London 06320, tel. 203/444–2206 or 800/222–6783 outside CT). **Yankee Heritage District** (297 West Ave., The Gate Lodge-Mathews Park, Norwalk 06850, tel. 203/854–7825). **New Haven:** Convention and Visitors Bureau (195 Church St., 06510, tel. 203/777–8550).

Getting There

By Plane The state's chief airport is **Bradley International Airport** (tel. 203/292–2000), 12 mi north of Hartford, with scheduled daily flights by most major U.S. airlines. Smaller airports along the coast are **Igor Sikorsky Memorial Airport** (tel. 203/576–7498), 4 mi south of Stratford, served by Business Express, Continental, and USAir; and **Tweed/New Haven Airport** (tel. 203/787–8283), 5 mi southeast of New Haven, served by USAir and Continental.

By Car The Merritt Parkway and I–95 are the principal highways on the coast between New York and New Haven. I–95 continues beyond New Haven into Rhode Island. From Hartford, I–91 goes south to New Haven. U.S. 7 is the major state road to the Litchfield Hills and the northwest.

By Train **Amtrak** stops at Greenwich, Stamford, Bridgeport, New Haven, Hartford, and New London. **Metro North** (tel. 212/532–4900 or 800/638–7646 outside NYC) runs between New York and New Haven, with stops at all towns along the coast.

By Bus **Greyhound** (tel. 203/772–2470) and **Bonanza Bus Lines** (tel. 800/556–3815) join Hartford, Middletown, New London, Stamford, Bridgeport, New Haven, and smaller towns with major cities of the eastern United States. **Connecticut Transit** (tel. 203/327–7433) provides bus service in the Stamford, Hartford, and New Haven areas. **Southeastern Area Rapid Transit** (tel. 203/886–2631) has local bus service in the eastern half of the area, between East Lyme and Stonington.

By Boat The **Bridgeport and Port Jefferson Steamboat Company** (tel. 203/367–3043) has ferries connecting Bridgeport with the north shore of New York's Long Island. **Cross Sound Ferry** (tel. 203/443–5281) connects New London with northeastern Long Island's Orient Point.

Exploring Coastal Connecticut

Greenwich, which borders New York state, is the epitome of affluent Fairfield County, with gourmet restaurants and chic boutiques. In the northern part of town the 485-acre **Audubon Center** (613 Riversville Rd., tel. 203/869–0376; donation suggested; closed Mon.) offers 8 mi of secluded hiking trails and exhibits on the local environment. The **Bruce Museum** (1 Museum Dr., tel. 203/869–0376; donation suggested; closed Mon.) has wildlife dioramas, a worthwhile small collection of American Impressionist paintings, and many exhibits on the area. The small, barn-red **Putnam Cottage,** (248 E. Putnam Ave., Rte. 1, tel. 203/869–9697; admission charged; closed Mon.–Tues., Thurs., Sat.) was built about 1690 and operated as Knapp's Tavern during the Revolutionary War. Inside are charts of battles, Colonial-era furnishings, and a huge stone fireplace.

In **Cos Cob,** the **Bush-Holley House,** built in 1732, is now the headquarters of the Greenwich Historical Society. Exhibits include paintings by Hassam, Twachtman, and Elmer Livingston MacRae, sculpture by John Rogers, and pottery by Leon Volkmar. *39 Strickland Rd., tel. 203/869–6899. Admission charged. Closed Mon., Sat., Jan.*

Stamford's shoreline may be given over primarily to industry and commerce, but to the north is the 118-acre **Stamford Museum and Nature Center** (39 Scofield Town Rd., tel. 203/322–1646; admission charged; closed Sun.), a 19th-century working farm and country store with exhibits of farm tools and local Native American life. Shows are offered at the center's observatory and planetarium. In the Champion International Corporation building, close to the center of Stamford, is the **Whitney Museum of American Art Champion.** Exhibits of primarily 20th-century American painting and photography change every 10 to 12 weeks, often featuring works from the Whitney's permanent collection in New York City. *Atlantic St. and Tresser Blvd., tel. 203/358–7652. Admission free. Free gallery talks at 12:30 Tues., Thurs., Sat. Closed Sun.–Mon.*

Beyond Stamford, I–95's Exit 15 leads to **South Norwalk.** Just steps away from a restored avenue of art galleries, restaurants, and boutiques is the **Maritime Center,** with a huge aquarium, marine vessels such as the steam tender *Glory Days* and the oyster sloop *Hope,* and an IMAX theater. *10 N. Water St., tel. 203/852–0700 or 800/243–2280. Admission charged. Closed major holidays.*

A brief detour away from the coast, up U.S. 7 and Rte. 33, traverses the wooded countryside of **Wilton** and **Ridgefield,** two well-preserved communities with good antiques shopping. Wilton has Connecticut's first national park, the **Weir Farm National Historical Site** (*see* National and State Parks, *above*). Ridgefield, with its sweeping lawns and stately mansions, is home to the **Aldrich Museum of Contemporary Art** (258 Main St., tel. 203/438–4519; admission charged; closed Mon.), offering changing exhibits, one of the finest sculpture gardens in the Northeast, and lectures, concerts, and films.

East of Norwalk is **Westport,** long an artistic and literary community and now a trendy hub of shops and eateries. In summer, the **Westport Playhouse** (*see* The Arts and Nightlife, *below*) presents a series of first-rate plays—many of which make their way to Broadway. At the **Levitt Pavilion** (tel. 203/226–7600), folk, jazz, and classical artists perform under evening skies. Nearby **Sherwood Island State Park** (I–95 Exit 18, tel. 203/226–6983) has the only beach accessible year-round between Greenwich and New Haven.

From Sherwood Island, drive east along Greens Farms Road, dubbed Connecticut's "Gold Coast," where grand mansions built in the days of conspicuous consumption are hidden behind high walls. The road leads into the exclusive Colonial village of **Southport,** on the Pequot River, and continues into **Fairfield,** where, in the northern part of town, the **Connecticut Audubon Society** (2325 Burr St., tel. 203/259–6305; admission charged) maintains a 160-acre wildlife sanctuary.

Bridgeport, a city that has fallen on hard times lately, is unsafe at night and rather unappealing even during the day. Two attractions here, however, bear visiting. The **Barnum Museum**

Southwestern Connecticut

(820 Main St., tel. 203/331–1104; admission charged; closed
Mon.), associated with onetime resident and mayor P. T. Barnum, has exhibits depicting the great showman's career and
a scaled-down model of his famous creation, the three-ring
circus. To the north, **Beardsley Park and Zoological Gardens**
(Noble Ave., tel. 203/576–8082; admission charged) is Connecticut's largest zoo. Its more than 200 animals range from North
American mammals, such as mountain lions, elks, and bison, to
the exotic Siberian tiger.

New Haven is a city of extremes: Though the area around the
common—encompassing the elite campus of **Yale University**
and the numerous shops, museums, and restaurants of **Chapel
Street**—prospers, one-fifth of the city's residents live below
the poverty level. Stay near the campus and city common, especially at night, and get a good map of the city. Knowledgeable
guides give free one-hour walking tours of the campus (344 College St., Phelps Gateway, tel. 203/432–2300). The **Yale Art Gallery,** the country's oldest college art museum, contains
Renaissance paintings; American, African, Near and Far Eastern art; and European art of the 20th century. Across the
street, the **Yale Center for British Art** (1080 Chapel St., tel. 203/
432–2800; admission free; closed Mon.) has the most extensive
collection of British paintings, drawings, prints, sculpture,
and rare books outside the United Kingdom. The **Peabody Museum of Natural History** (170 Whitney Ave., tel. 203/432–5050
or 203/432–5799; admission charged except Tues.) is the largest
of its kind in New England. Along with exhibits of dinosaur
fossils and meteorites, emphasis is placed on Connecticut's environment, including early Native American life and birds.

The urban buildup that characterizes the Connecticut coast
west of New Haven dissipates as you drive east on I–95 toward
New London. In **East Haven,** the **Shore Line Trolley Museum**
houses more than 100 classic trolleys, among them the oldest
rapid-transit car and the world's first electric freight locomotive. *17 River St., tel. 203/467–6927. Admission charged.
Closed Jan.–Mar.; weekdays Sept.–Oct., Dec.; Mon.–Sat.
Apr., Nov.*

On the western side of the mouth of the Connecticut River is
Old Saybrook, once a lively shipbuilding and fishing town. Today the bustle comes mostly from its many summer vacationers. On the other side of the river mouth is **Old Lyme.** Here
the **Florence Griswold Museum** (96 Lyme St., tel. 203/434–

Southeastern Connecticut

5542; admission charged), built in 1817, once housed an art colony that included Willard Metcalfe, Clark Voorhees, and Childe Hassam. Today the mansion displays many of these artists' works, along with early furnishings and decorative items.

A few steps away is the **Lyme Academy of Fine Arts** (84 Lyme St., tel. 203/434–5232; donation suggested). Housed in a Federal-style former private home built in 1817, the popular gallery features works by contemporary artists.

New London is widely known as the home of the **U.S. Coast Guard Academy.** The 100-acre cluster of traditional redbrick buildings includes a museum and a visitors' pavilion with a gift shop. When the three-masted training bark the *Eagle* is in port, you may board from Friday to Sunday, noon to 5 PM. *15 Mohegan Ave., tel. 203/444–8270. Admission free.*

Across the Thames River at **Groton** is the **U.S. submarine base** and, just outside the entrance, the **U.S. Nautilus Memorial/ Submarine Force Library and Museum.** The world's first nuclear,pnvered submarine, the *Nautilus*, was launched from here in 1954 and is now permanently berthed and open to visitors. The adjacent library and museum contains submarine memorabilia, artifacts, and displays, including working periscopes and controls. *Rte. 12, tel. 203/449–3174 or 203/449–3558. Admission free. Closed Tues.*

A few miles east is **Mystic,** the celebrated whaling seaport. **Mystic Seaport** (50 Greenmanville Ave., tel. 203/572–0711; admission charged)—the nation's largest maritime museum, on 17 riverfront acres—features 19th-century sailing vessels you can board; a maritime village with historic homes; craftspeople who give demonstrations; steamboat cruises; and small-boat rentals. Just off I–95, on Mystic's Coogan Boulevard, are **Olde Mistick Village** (tel. 203/536–1641; admission free)—a recreation of an early 18th-century American village—and the **Mystic Marinelife Aquarium** (tel. 203/536–3323; admission charged). The latter offers more than 6,000 specimens and 49 live exhibits of sea life, as well as dolphin and sea lion shows every hour on the half hour.

Little **Stonington Village** is your final peek at Connecticut's coastline, and some say the most memorable. Poking out into Fishers Island Sound, this quiet fishing community clustered around white-spired churches remains far less commercial than neighboring Mystic. Past the historic buildings that surround the town green and border both sides of Water Street is the imposing **Old Lighthouse Museum** (7 Water St., tel. 203/535–1440; admission charged; closed Mon. and Nov.–Apr.) Inside you'll find a wealth of shipping, whaling, and early village memorabilia and displays. Climb to the top of the granite tower for a spectacular view of the sound and the ocean.

What to See and Do with Children

Most nature centers (*see* Greenwich's **Audubon Center, Stamford Museum and Nature Center,** and Fairfield's **Connecticut Audubon Society** in Exploring Coastal Connecticut, *above*) feature special attractions for children, including hands-on exhibits. Other places with particular appeal (*see* Exploring Coastal Connecticut, *above*) are the **Maritime Center** in South Norwalk, the **Barnum Museum** in Bridgeport, the **Shore Line Trolley Museum** in East Haven, the **Peabody Museum of Natural History** in New Haven, **Mystic Seaport** and the **Mystic Marinelife Aquarium** in Mystic, and the **Children's Museum of Southeastern Connecticut** (409 Main St., Niantic, tel. 203/691–1255; closed Mon.–Wed.).

Shopping

Greenwich has one of the most exciting crafts galleries in the state, **The Elements Gallery** (14 Liberty Way, tel. 203/661–0014). A must for lovers of Southeast Asian art is the vast collection at the **Coastal & Peninsula Trading Co.** (85 Water St., South Norwalk, tel. 203/854–5090). In Stamford, **United House Wrecking** (535 Hope St., tel. 203/348–5371) has acres of architectural artifacts, collectibles, and junk. On **Westport's** tony Main Street you'll find an array of upscale clothiers and boutiques. Downtown **Mystic** boasts a collection of shops and art galleries, and **Mystic Factory Outlets** (Coogan Blvd., tel. 203/443–4788) has nearly two dozen stores offering discounts on famous-name clothing and other merchandise. Antiquers are rewarded throughout the region, especially in **Ridgefield, Wilton, Westport, Guilford, Old Lyme,** and **Stonington Village.**

Sports and Outdoor Activities

Fishing Saltwater fishing is best from June through October; bass, bluefish, and flounder are popular catches. Open boats are available from **Hel-Cat Dock** (Groton, tel. 203/445–5991) and **Yacht Haven** (Stamford, tel. 203/359–4500). For private charters, contact **Brewer Yacht Yard** (Mystic, tel. 203/536–2293), **Niantic Bay Marina** (Waterford, tel. 203/444–1999), and **Norwalk Cove Marina** (tel. 203/838–2326).

Golf Danbury's 18-hole **Richter Park Golf Course** (Aunt Hack Rd., tel. 203/792–2550) is one of the top 100 public courses in the country. Also try the 18-hole **H. Smith Richardson Golf Course** (Morehouse Hwy., Fairfield, tel. 203/255–5016), the Robert Trent Jones–designed **Lyman Meadow Golf Club** (Rte. 147, Middlefield, tel. 203/349–8055; 18 holes), and **Shennecosset Golf Course** (Plant St., Groton, tel. 203/445–0262; 18 holes).

Water Sports **Action Sports** (324 W. Main St., Branford, tel. 203/481–5511) and **Rick's Surf City** (570 Boston Post Rd., Milford, tel. 203/877–4257) rent sailboards and surfboards. **Dodson Boat Yard** (184 Water St., Stonington, tel. 203/535–1507), **Longshore Sail-**

ing School (Westport, tel. 203/226–4646), and **Shaffer's Boat Livery** (Mason's Island Rd., Mystic, tel. 203/536–8713) rent sailboats and motorboats.

Spectator Sports

Jai-alai   **Bridgeport Jai-Alai** (255 Kossuth St., tel. 203/576–1976, 800/243–9490, or 800/972–9471 in CT; Dec.–May). **Milford Jai-Alai** (311 Old Gate La., tel. 203/877–4242 or 800/243–9660; June–Nov.).

Dining and Lodging

Connecticut has undergone a gastronomic revolution in recent years: Preparation and ingredients now reflect the healthy New American trends of nearby Manhattan and Boston. Though a few traditional favorites remain, expect to be bombarded by heads of radicchio, slabs of chèvre, and bulbs of fennel. The drawback of this shift in cuisine is that finding an under-$10 entrée (or even an under-$10 14″ pizza) is proving increasingly difficult.

Connecticut offers a variety of accommodations. For help in finding a rustic B&B, contact **Bed & Breakfast, Ltd.** (Box 216, New Haven 06513, tel. 203/469–3260) or **Covered Bridge Bed & Breakfast** (Box 447, Norfolk 06058, tel. 203/542–5944). Rooms are costliest in summer and autumn. For safety's sake, do not stay in Bridgeport and avoid staying in New Haven, downtown Groton, and downtown New London. A 12% lodging tax is added to each bill.

For price ranges, see Charts 1 (B) and 2 (B) in Chapter 1.

Greenwich   **Bertrand.** The brick-vault interior of this former bank building
Dining   provides the setting for a menu of classic and nouvelle French
★   cuisine. Salmon in puff pastry and confit of duck with sorrel sauce are just two of Christian Bertrand's delightful creations. *253 Greenwich Ave., tel. 203/661–4618. Reservations advised. Jacket and tie required. AE, DC, MC, V. No lunch weekends; closed Sun. Expensive.*

Dining and Lodging   **Homestead Inn.** Each bedroom is decorated with attractive fur-
★   niture and period reproductions. The La Grange restaurant serves outstanding classic French cuisine. *420 Field Point Rd., 06830, tel. and fax 203/869–7500. 23 rooms. Facilities: restaurant. AE, DC, MC, V. Expensive.*

Lodging   **Stanton House Inn.** This large, Federal-period mansion within walking distance of downtown underwent considerable redesign by architect Stanford White in 1899. It has been carefully refurbished and redecorated with a turn-of-the-century flavor, mixing antiques and tasteful reproductions. *76 Maple Ave., 06830, tel. 203/869–2110; fax 203/629–2116. 25 rooms (2 share bath). AE, MC, V. Moderate.*

Mystic   **The Inn at Mystic.** The Corinthian-columned main inn and the
Dining and Lodging   gate house have guest rooms furnished in traditional Colonial style, some with four-poster or canopy beds. The best views are in the main inn, but the individually decorated rooms in the motor lodge are a better value. The sunlit Floodtide Restaurant serves traditional, if uninteresting, New England fare, such as Yankee pot roast and rainbow trout *meunière. Junction U.S. 1 and Rte. 27, 06355, tel. 203/536–9604 or 800/237–2415;*

fax 203/572–1635. 68 rooms. Facilities: restaurant, private dock with canoes and sailboats, outdoor pool and whirlpool. AE, D, DC, MC, V. Moderate–Expensive.

The Whaler's Inn and Motor Court. In the heart of downtown, this group of white clapboard buildings comprises the original Victorian guest house, the sprawling main building, and the motor court across the parking lot. Decor is modern with nautical touches; there are some canopy beds, but mostly it's department-stnre maple. *20 E. Main St., 06355, tel. 203/536–1506 or 800/243–2588 outside CT; fax 203/572–7697. 45 rooms. Facilities: 2 restaurants. AE, D, DC, MC, V. Moderate.*

New Haven
Dining

Azteca's. This restaurant offers an elegant presentation of Mexican and southwestern dishes. Among the favorites are the shellfish quesadilla and the tortilla filled with roasted chili, smoked turkey, and chèvre. *14 Mechanic St., tel. 203/624–2454. Reservations advised. Dress: neat but casual. MC, V. No lunch; closed Sun., major holidays. Moderate.*

Frank Pepe's. The big ovens on the back wall bake pizzas that are served by smart-mouthed waitresses. On weekend evenings the wait for a table can be more than an hour, but the pizza—the sole item on the menu—is worth it. *157 Wooster St., tel. 203/865–5762. No reservations. No credit cards. No lunch Mon., Wed., Thurs.; closed Tues. Inexpensive.*

Lodging
★

The Inn at Chapel West. Though it borders a questionable neighborhood, this 1847 Victorian mansion is one of the most polished small inns in the state. Luxurious rooms are furnished individually, from Victorian to country home to contemporary. The staff knows all the great eateries and points of interest in town, and the inn is steps away from Yale's campus and New Haven's theater district. *1201 Chapel St., 06511, tel. 203/777–1201; fax 203/776–7363. 10 rooms. AE, D, DC, MC, V. Expensive.*

Colony Inn. In the center of the Yale-area hotel district, this inn also offers sidewalk dining in the glass-enclosed Greenhouse Restaurant. The guest rooms have Colonial-reproduction furnishings and modern baths. Some rooms on the higher floors have excellent views of the campus. *1157 Chapel St., 06511, tel. 203/776–1234 or 800/458–8810 outside CT; fax 203/772–3929. 80 rooms, 6 suites. Facilities: restaurant, lounge. AE, DC, MC, V. Moderate.*

New London
Lodging

Queene Anne Inne and Antiques Gallery. This B&B in a 1903 turreted three-story mansion is decorated in keeping with its origins: floral wallpapers, stained-glass windows, fireplaces, and antique furniture. *265 Williams St., 06320, tel. 203/447–2600 or 800/347–8818. 9 rooms. V. Moderate.*

Noank
Dining
★

Abbott's Lobster in the Rough. If you want the best lobster, clams on the half-shell, mussels, and crab in the state, pick up a bottle of wine (it's BYOB) and head for this unassuming seaside lobster shack in sleepy Noank. Seating, which is indoors or on the dock, can be hard to come by, but the water views and mouth-watering lobster rolls are worth the wait. *117 Pearl St., tel. 203/536–7719. No reservations. MC, V. Closed Columbus Day–Memorial Day; weekdays Labor Day–Columbus Day. Inexpensive–Moderate.*

North Stonington
Dining and Lodging
★

Randall's Ordinary. Famed for its open-hearth cooking of authentic Colonial dishes, the Ordinary offers three-course fixed-price meals, served by staff in period costume. Accommodations are available in the John Randall House, where rooms are furnished simply, with a smattering of antiques, or in the converted barn, whose rooms have fireplaces and Jacuzzis. *Rte. 2, Box 243, 06359, tel. 203/599–4540. Facilities: restaurant (reservations required). AE, MC, V. Moderate–Expensive.*

Norwalk
Dining and Lodging

Silvermine Tavern. Parts of the lodgings date back to 1642, but the tavern is best known for its extraordinary restaurant. It's enormous, but a low ceiling, Colonial decor, glowing candles, and many windows make this landmark restaurant an intimate setting for traditional New England favorites. The cozy rooms have wide-plank floors, and many have hooked rugs. *194 Perry Ave. (on the Wilton/New Canaan border), 06850, tel. 203/847–4558; fax 203/847–9171. 10 rooms. Facilities: restaurant. AE, DC, MC, V. Closed Tues. Moderate.*

Old Lyme
Dining and Lodging

Bee & Thistle Inn. Innkeepers Bob and Penny Nelson have furnished this two-story 1756 Colonial on the Lieutenant River with period antiques and plenty of warm touches. Most rooms have canopy or four-poster beds. Outstanding American cuisine is served in one of the most romantic dining rooms around. *100 Old Lyme St., 06371, tel. 203/434–1667 or 800/622–4946 outside CT; fax 203/434–3402. 11 rooms (2 share a bath). AE, DC, MC, V. Closed 1st half Jan. Moderate–Expensive.*

Stamford
Dining

Il Forno Ristorante. Within walking distance of the city's theaters is this dining room with a two-story ceiling and decorated like a Venetian piazza. The list of specials always seems more extensive than the menu itself. Choose from among dozens of seafood and veal dishes or the crisp-crusted brick-oven gourmet pizzas. *45 Atlantic St., tel. 203/357–8882. Reservations advised. AE, MC, V. Moderate.*

Westport
Dining

Da Pietro's. At this tiny eatery, high-back chairs and banquettes upholstered in floral prints set the mood for fine northern Italian and southern French cuisine. Entrées include loin lamb chops with a sauce of capers, butter, lemon, and white wine, or Norwegian salmon with mushrooms, leeks, scallions, and Chablis. The *tiramisu* (espresso-soaked lady fingers, mascarpone cheese, and grated chocolate) is a delightful ending. *36 Riverside Ave., tel. 203/454–1213. Reservations advised. AE, DC, MC, V. Expensive.*

Lodging

The Inn at Longshore. This charming, restored throwback to the turn of the century, situated where the Saugatuck River meets Long Island Sound, offers some resort facilities and rooms decorated with Colonial reproductions. *260 Compo Rd. S, 06880, tel. 203/226–3316; fax 203/226–5723. 12 rooms. Facilities: restaurant, golf, swimming, boating. AE, DC, MC, V. Expensive.*

Motels

Along U.S. 1, paralleling I–95 up the coast, there are motels galore—the safest and cleanest are in Stamford and Mystic—with **Holiday Inn, Day's Inns,** and **Howard Johnson's** dominant. There are also smaller and less expensive spots: **Comfort Inn** (50 Ledge Rd., Darien 06820, tel. 203/655–8211), 99 rooms; moderate. **Niantic Inn** (345 Main St., 06357, tel. 203/739–5451 or 800/722–6582), 27 rooms; inexpensive–moderate. **Stamford Super 8 Motel** (32 Grenhart Rd., 06902, tel. 203/324–8887 or 800/843–1991), 92 rooms, coffee shop; inexpensive.

Campgrounds

Along Connecticut's shore, **Riverdale Farm Campsites** (111 River Rd., Clinton, tel. 203/669–2238) has 250 tent and RV sites, is open April 15–September, and has water, electricity, showers, toilets, and a river for swimming. **Seaport Campground** (Rte. 184, Old Mystic, tel. 203/536–4044) has 130 tent and RV sites, water, electricity, toilets, hot showers, and a laundry. It is open late March–October.

The Arts and Nightlife

The Arts   The Connecticut coast's wealth of successful repertory and Broadway-style theaters include **The Eugene O'Neill Theatre Center** (Waterford, tel. 203/443–5378), **Goodspeed Opera House** (East Haddam, tel. 203/873–8668), **Long Wharf Theatre** (New Haven, tel. 203/787–4282), **Schubert Performing Arts Center** (New Haven, tel. 203/562–5666), **Stamford Center for the Arts** (tel. 203/323–2131), **Westport Playhouse** (tel. 203/227–4177), and **Yale Repertory Theatre** (New Haven, tel. 203/432–1234).

Most towns along the coast have outdoor summer concerts and music festivals, and some have smaller regional theaters. Call tourist boards for details (*see* Tourist Information, *above*).

Nightlife   Bars and clubs are sprinkled liberally throughout southern Connecticut. The best of them are concentrated in **Westport, South Norwalk, New Haven's Chapel West** area, and along **New London's Bank Street.**

In 1992, **Foxwoods** (tel. 203/885–3000), an enormous gambling and entertainment complex, opened on the Mashantucket Pequots Reservation near Ledyard (8 mi north of Groton). Here you can try your hand at poker, baccarat, slot machines, blackjack, and bingo.

Elsewhere in the State

Litchfield Hills

Getting There   The Litchfield Hills are at the western end of Connecticut, about 1½ hours from New York City and less than an hour from Hartford. Rtes. 8 and 4 and U.S. 7, 44, and 202 are the primary routes through the region.

What to See   This is an area of rolling countryside, wooded hills, and charm-
and Do   ing Colonial towns renowned for antiquing. The **Litchfield Hills Travel Council** (Box 1776, Marbledale 06777, tel. 203/868–2214) can offer assistance and information.

The mountainous northern towns of **Sharon, Lakeville, Salisbury,** and **Norfolk** are crisscrossed by scenic winding roads. Auto-racing fans come in summer to **Lime Rock Park** (Rte. 112, Lakeville, tel. 203/435–2571 or 203/435–0896), home to the best road racing in the Northeast. This is also terrific hiking terrain, with **Haystack Mountain** (U.S. 44, Norfolk), **Dennis Hill** (Rte. 272, Norfolk), and the 684-acre **Northeast Audubon Center** (Rte. 4, Sharon, tel. 203/364–0520) offering the region's best opportunities.

Everything seems to exist on a larger scale in **Litchfield** than in neighboring towns: Enormous white Colonials line broad streets shaded by majestic elms, and serene **Litchfield Green** is surrounded by lovely shops and restaurants. Near the green is the **Tapping Reeve House and Law School** (South St., tel. 203/567–4501; admission charged; closed mid-Oct.–mid-Apr.), America's first law school, which was founded in 1773. Alumni include six U.S. cabinet members, 26 U.S. senators, more than 100 U.S. congressmen, and numerous other politicians, justices, and college presidents. The **Litchfield Historical Society Museum** (corner of Rtes. 63 and 118, tel. 203/567–4501; admission charged; closed mid-Dec.–mid-Mar.) has several well-laid-out galleries, an extensive reference library, and information on the town's many historic buildings. **White Flower Farm** (Rte. 63, 3 mi south of the green, tel. 800/888–7756; closed Nov.–Mar.), where much of America shops in person or by mail for perennials and bulbs, is a restful stop, whether to buy or to browse.

To the south, the quiet villages of **Washington, Roxbury,** and **Bridgewater** offer a gentler landscape, in which numerous actors and writers seek refuge from the din of Manhattan and Hollywood. Here you can buy the ingredients for a gourmet picnic lunch—try the **Pantry** (Titus Sq., Washington, tel. 203/868–0258)—then laze on the shores of sparkling **Lake Waramaug** or enjoy a leisurely country drive along precipitous ridges, passing gracious farmsteads and meadows alive with wildflowers.

The best antiques and crafts shopping is along Rte. 6 in **Woodbury** and **Southbury,** Rte. 45 in **New Preston,** U.S. 7 in **Kent**—which is also known for its estimable art galleries—Rte. 128 in **West Cornwall,** and U.S. 202 in **Bantam.**

The Connecticut River and Hartford

Getting There **Bradley International Airport** is the main airport; **Amtrak, Greyhound, Bonanza,** and **Connecticut Transit** provide service to the Hartford area (*see* Coastal Connecticut, *above*). By car, take I–91N from New Haven or I–84, which cuts diagonally southwest–northeast through the state. Head north along Rte. 9 from Old Saybrook for a scenic drive through this historic area.

What to See and Do The Connecticut River valley meanders through rolling hills, offering a taste of Colonial history and sophisticated inns. The **Connecticut Valley Tourism Commission** (393 Main St., Middletown 06457, tel. 203/347–6924) and the **Greater Hartford CVB** (1 Civic Center Plaza, 06103, tel. 203/728–6789) can provide information.

Essex, on the west bank of the Connecticut River, is where the first submarine, the *Turtle,* was built; a full-size reproduction is at the **Connecticut River Museum** (Steamboat Dock, tel. 203/767–8269). In **Hadlyme** is the region's leading oddity, **Gillette Castle State Park** (67 River Rd., off Rte. 82, tel. 203/526–2336), a 24-room oak-and-granite hilltop castle built by the actor William Gillette between 1914 and 1919.

East Haddam is the home of the **Goodspeed Opera House** (Rte. 82, tel. 203/873–8668). The upper floors of this elaborate 1876 structure have served as a venue for theatrical performances for more than a century. On Main Street you'll find the **school-**

house where Nathan Hale taught (Rte. 149, rear of St. Stephen's Church, tel. 203/873–9547).

Hartford, known as the "Insurance Capital of America," is the state capital as well. Mark Twain made his home here, in the extravagant Victorian mansion at **Nook Farm** (351 Farmington Ave., tel. 203/525–9317). The neighboring cottage, built in 1871, was the home of Harriet Beecher Stowe, the author of *Uncle Tom's Cabin.* Personal memorabilia and original furnishings of both writers are displayed at a joint visitor center. Hartford was also the home and birthplace of Noah Webster, author of the *American Dictionary.* His 18th-century farmhouse, now the **Noah Webster House and Museum** (227 S. Main St., tel. 203/521–5362), contains Webster memorabilia and period furnishings, along with changing exhibits. Hartford's most noteworthy attraction is the **Wadsworth Athenaeum** (600 Main St., tel. 203/247–9111 or 203/278–2670), the country's first public art museum. Along with changing exhibits, its more than 40,000 works span 5,000 years of art, including paintings by the Hudson River School, the Impressionists, and 20th-century artists.

MAINE

By Ed and
Roon Frost

Capital	Augusta
Population	1,227,928
Motto	I Direct
State Bird	Chickadee
State Flower	White pinecone and tassel

Visitor Information

Maine Publicity Bureau (Box 2300, Hallowell 04347, tel. 207/582–9300 or 800/533–9595). **Maine Innkeepers Association** (305 Commercial St., Portland 04101, tel. 207/773–7670).

Scenic Drives

Any road that offers views of Maine's dramatic **coastline** is usually worth exploring (see Exploring sections below for recommended coastal routes). For a leisurely inland excursion, try Rtes. 37 and 35 from Bridgton north through the Waterfords to the charming resort village of Bethel, continuing north on Rte. 26 past the Sunday River ski resort to Grafton Notch State Park and into northern New Hampshire.

National and State Parks

National Parks
Acadia National Park (Box 177, Bar Harbor 04609, tel. 207/288–3338), with fine stretches of shoreline and the highest mountains along the East Coast, offers camping, hiking, biking, and boating.

State Parks
More than two dozen state parks offer outdoor recreation along the coast and in less-traveled interior sections. Some coastal parks feature historic lighthouses. For more information, contact the **Bureau of Parks and Recreation** (State House Station 22, Augusta 04333, tel. 207/289–3821).

The Coast: From Kittery to Pemaquid Point

Maine's southern coast offers sandy beaches, historic towns, fine restaurants, and factory-outlet malls within an easy day trip from many points in New England. Maine's largest city, Portland, is small enough to be seen in a day or two. In easy striking distance of Portland are Freeport, a mecca for shoppers, and Boothbay Harbor, the state's boating capital.

Tourist Information

Boothbay Harbor Region: Chamber of Commerce (Box 356, Boothbay Harbor 04538, tel. 207/633–2353). **Freeport:** Merchants Association (Box 452, 04032, tel. 207/865–1212). **Kennebunk-Kennebunkport:** Chamber of Commerce (Cooper's Corner, Rtes. 9 and 35, Box 740, Kennebunk 04043, tel. 207/

967–0857). **Portland:** Convention and Visitors Bureau (305 Commercial St., 04101, tel. 207/772–5800). Additional information is available at the **Maine Tourist Information Center** (Rte. 1 and I–95, Box 396, Kittery 03904, tel. 207/439–1319).

Getting There

By Plane **Portland International Jetport** (tel. 207/774–7301), 5 mi from Portland, has scheduled daily flights by major U.S. carriers.

By Car From Boston take U.S. 1N to I–95N, passing through the short New Hampshire seacoast to Kittery, the first town in Maine. I–95 continues past Portland (I–295 gives access to the city) and Freeport (Exit 20 for the outlet stores). Pick up U.S. 1 in Brunswick to reach the coastal communities of Downeast.

By Bus **Vermont Transit** (tel. 207/772–6587), part of Greyhound, links Portsmouth, New Hampshire, with Portland, Maine.

Exploring from Kittery to Pemaquid Point

Paralleling I–95, U.S. 1 runs past more than 100 outlet stores between Kittery and the Yorks. Rtes. 103 and 1A hug the coastline and offer maritime scenery.

Rte. 1A north (reached from I–95 Exit 4) passes through fashionable **York Harbor** and the midriff-to-elbow summer cottages of **York Beach. Ogunquit,** a few miles north, is famed for its long white-sand beach and attractive galleries, shops, restaurants, and homes.

Rte. 35 (Summer St.) takes you past the Victorian Wedding Cake House into **Kennebunkport. Dock Square,** the busy town center, is lined with shops and galleries. Ocean Avenue follows the Kennebunk River to the sea, then winds around Cape Arundel.

Return to I–95 for the short drive to **Portland.** Just off Congress Street, the city's main artery, the distinguished **Portland Museum of Art** has a strong collection of seascapes and landscapes by such masters as Winslow Homer, John Marin, Andrew Wyeth, and Marsden Hartley. *7 Congress Sq., tel. 207/ 775–6148 or 207/773–2787 for recorded information. Admission charged. Closed Mon.*

Portland's **Old Port Exchange,** built following the Great Fire of 1866, was revitalized in the 1960s by artists and craftspeople. Now it is the city's shopping and dining hub, with boutiques, cafés, restaurants, and easy access to the waterfront. Allow a couple of hours to stroll on Market, Exchange, Middle, and Fore streets.

Continue north on I–95 or U.S. 1 to **Freeport,** the home of **L. L. Bean** (open 24 hours a day, including Christmas), which attracts some 3.5 million shoppers a year. Nearby, like seedlings under a mighty spruce, some 100 other outlets have sprouted, offering designer clothes, shoes, housewares, and toys at marked-down prices (*see* Shopping, *below*).

Farther up the coast, in **Bath,** the **Maine Maritime Museum** (take the Bath Business District exit from U.S. 1, turn right on Washington St., and follow the signs) has a collection to stir the nautical dreams of old salts and young. You can watch apprentice boatbuilders wield their tools on classic Maine boats at the

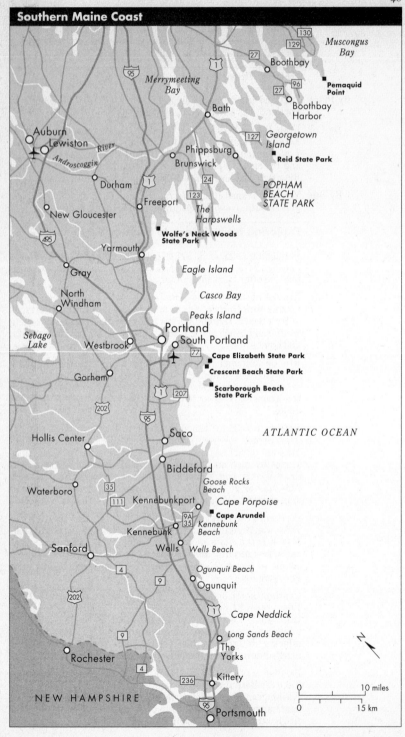

Southern Maine Coast

Muscongus Bay

130
129
27
Boothbay
27
96
Pemaquid Point
1
Boothbay Harbor
Merrymeeting Bay
95
Bath
127
Georgetown Island
Auburn
Lewiston
River
Androscoggin
Phippsburg
Brunswick
Reid State Park
Durham
24
POPHAM BEACH STATE PARK
123
Freeport
The Harpswells
495
New Gloucester
Wolfe's Neck Woods State Park
Yarmouth
Eagle Island
Gray
Casco Bay
North Windham
Peaks Island
Sebago Lake
Portland
Westbrook
South Portland
77
Cape Elizabeth State Park
Gorham
Crescent Beach State Park
1
207
Scarborough Beach State Park
202
95
Hollis Center
Saco
ATLANTIC OCEAN
Biddeford
Goose Rocks Beach
35
Cape Porpoise
111
Kennebunkport
Cape Arundel
Waterboro
9A
35
Kennebunk Beach
Kennebunk
Sanford
Wells
Wells Beach
4
Ogunquit Beach
9
Ogunquit
202
Cape Neddick
1
9
Long Sands Beach
Rochester
The Yorks
4
Kittery
236
0   10 miles
NEW HAMPSHIRE
0   15 km
95
Portsmouth

restored shipyard. *243 Washington St., tel. 207/443–1316. Admission charged.*

Continue northeast on U.S. 1 and drop south on Rte. 27 to **Boothbay Harbor,** a town for wandering, shopping, or hopping on an excursion boat. Rte. 129/130 leads to **Bristol** and ends at **Pemaquid Point,** where a much-photographed lighthouse fronts the sea. About 5 mi south of Bristol on Rte. 130, look for the turnoff to the **Colonial Pemaquid Restoration** (tel. 207/677–2423; admission charged; closed Oct.–May), where excavations have turned up thousands of artifacts from an early 17th-century English fishing and trading settlement and from even earlier Native American settlements.

What to See and Do with Children

The old-fashioned pinball machines and hand-cranked moving pictures at the **Wells Antique Auto Museum** (U.S. 1, Wells, tel. 207/646–9064) fascinate kids of all ages. Trolley rides are the order of the day at the **Seashore Trolley Museum** (Log Cabin Rd., Kennebunkport, tel. 207/967–2800). Touching is encouraged at the **Children's Museum of Maine** (142 Free St., Portland, tel. 207/797–5483), where little ones can pretend they are lobstermen, shopkeepers, or computer experts.

Shopping

More than 100 **factory outlets** along U.S. 1 in Kittery offer clothing, shoes, glassware, and other products from top manufacturers. **Freeport**'s name is synonymous with shopping at L. L. Bean and another 100 factory outlets. **The Freeport Visitors Guide** (Freeport Merchants Association, Box 452, 04032) is a free complete listing. In Portland's **Old Port Exchange** (*see* Exploring from Kittery to Pemaquid Point, *above*) the better shops are concentrated along Fore and Exchange streets.

Sports and Outdoor Activities

Boat Trips From Perkins Cove in Ogunquit, **Finestkind** (tel. 207/646–5227) runs boats to Nubble Light and lobstering trips. Boats offering whale-watching cruises and other excursions out of Kennebunkport include the *Elizabeth II,* the *Nautilus* (tel. 207/967–5595), and the *Indian* (tel. 207/967–5912).

In Portland, for tours of the harbor, Casco Bay, and the islands, try **Bay View Cruises** (tel. 207/761–0496), *The Buccaneer* (tel. 207/799–8188), or **Old Port Mariner Fleet** (tel. 207/775–0727). From Boothbay Harbor, choose between lobster boats and windjammers: The 66-foot *Appledore* (tel. 207/633–6598) runs trips to the outer islands, *Balmy Days II* (tel. 207/633–2284) does day trips to Monhegan Island, *Bay Lady* (tel. 207/633–6990) offers two-hour sails, and **Argo Cruises** (tel. 207/633–2500) has a variety of offerings.

Canoeing The Maine Audubon Society offers daily guided canoe trips in **Scarborough Marsh** (Rte. 9, Scarborough, tel. 207/781–2330), the largest salt marsh in Maine.

Deep-sea Fishing Departing from Perkins Cove is the *Bunny Clark* (tel. 207/646–5565). Half- and full-day fishing charters out of Portland include *Anjin-San* (tel. 207/772–7168), *Devils Den* (tel. 207/761–4466), and *Lazy Day* (tel. 207/883–3430). In Boothbay Harbor, try **Cap'n Fish's Deep Sea Fishing** (tel. 207/633–3244), **Lucky Star Charters** (tel. 207/633–4624), or the *Breakaway* (tel. 207/633–6990).

Beaches

Kennebunk Beach consists of three beaches with cottages and old Victorian boardinghouses nearby; for parking permits, go to the Kennebunk Town Office (1 Summer St., tel. 207/985–3675). **Goose Rocks**, north of Kennebunkport, is the largest area beach and a favorite with families with small children; the Kennebunkport Town Office (Elm St., tel. 207/967–4244) sells parking permits.

Old Orchard Beach, with an amusement park reminiscent of Coney Island, is only a few miles north of Biddeford on Rte. 9; there is no free parking anywhere in town.

At the end of Rte. 209 south of Bath, **Popham Beach State Park** (Phippsburg, tel. 207/389–1335) has a good sand beach and picnic tables. **Reid State Park** (tel. 207/371–2303), on Georgetown Island, off Rte. 127, has three beaches, bathhouses, picnic tables, and a snack bar.

Dining and Lodging

For most visitors Maine means lobster, and lobster can be found on the menus of a majority of Maine restaurants. Aficionados prefer to eat them "in the rough" at classic lobster pounds, where you choose your lobster in a pool and enjoy it at a waterside picnic table. B&Bs and Victorian inns have joined the family-oriented motels of the coastal towns. For price ranges, see Charts 1 (B) and 2 (B) in Chapter 1.

Bath
Dining
Kristina's Restaurant & Bakery. This frame house turned restaurant, with a deck built around a huge oak tree, turns out some of the finest pies, pastries, and cakes on the coast. A satisfying dinner menu features New American cuisine. *160 Centre St., tel. 207/442–8577. D, MC, V. No dinner Sun.; closed Mon. Moderate.*

Boothbay Harbor
Dining
Black Orchid. Classic Italian fare is featured in a trattoria atmosphere. In summer, cocktails and a raw bar are served outdoors. *5 By-Way, tel. 207/633–6659. AE, MC, V. No lunch. Moderate.*

Lodging
Fisherman's Wharf Inn. All rooms overlook the water at this modern motel built 200 feet out over the harbor. The large dining room has floor-to-ceiling windows, and several day cruises leave from here. *40 Commercial St., 04538, tel. 207/633–5090 or 800/628–6872. 54 rooms. AE, D, DC, MC, V. Closed Nov.–mid-May. Expensive.*

Brunswick
Dining
The Great Impasta. Whether it's lunch, tea, or dinner, this small storefront restaurant is determined to please. Try the seafood lasagna, or match your favorite pasta and sauce to create a new dish. *42 Maine St., tel. 207/729–5858. No reservations. AE, D, DC, MC, V. Closed Sun. Moderate.*

Lodging
Captain Daniel Stone Inn. This Federal-style inn furnishes no two rooms identically, but many have whirlpool baths and pull-out sofas in addition to queen-size beds. *10 Water St., 04011,*

tel. 207/725–9898. 28 rooms, 4 suites. Facilities: breakfast, restaurant. AE, DC, MC, V. Expensive.

Freeport
Dining
Harraseeket Lunch & Lobster Co. At this bare-bones lobster pound beside the town landing, fried-seafood baskets and lobster dinners are what it's all about. There are picnic tables outside and a dining room inside. *Main St., South Freeport, tel. 207/865–4888. No reservations. No credit cards. Inexpensive.*

Dining and Lodging
Harraseeket Inn. Two white clapboard houses join a three-story building that looks like an old New England inn but is actually a steel-and-concrete structure with elevators and whirlpools. Antique furniture and fireplaces in the common rooms give the inn a countrified feel; guest rooms have reproductions of Federal-period canopy beds and bright, coordinated fabrics. In the formal dining room waiters prepare fettuccine Alfredo and flaming desserts tableside. *162 Main St., 04032, tel. 207/865–9377 or 800/342–6423. 46 rooms, 6 suites. Facilities: restaurant, tavern. Reservations advised. AE, D, DC, MC, V. Expensive.*

Kennebunkport
Lodging
The Captain Lord Mansion. A long and distinguished history, a three-story elliptical staircase, and a cupola with a widow's walk make the Captain Lord something more than the standard bed-and-breakfast. The guest rooms, named after old clipper ships, are large and stately, and the refined Gathering Room would look like a period room (Chippendale) in a museum but for the lounging guests. *Box 800, 04046, tel. 207/967–3141. 16 rooms, 11 with fireplace. Facilities: full breakfast. D, MC, V. Expensive.*

Dining and Lodging
★
White Barn Inn. Rooms at this luxurious inn boast period antiques and king-size four-posters. In the elegant dining room, a stylish three-story barn complete with gilt-framed oils and a baby grand piano, an informed staff presents dishes that look like *Gourmet* magazine covers. *Beach St., Box 560C, 04046, tel. 207/967–2321. 25 rooms, 7 suites. Facilities: Continental breakfast, afternoon tea, bicycles. AE, MC, V. Expensive.*

Ogunquit
Dining
★
Hurricane. Don't let the unpretentious, weather-beaten exterior mislead you—this small, comfortable seafood bar and grill has spectacular views of the crashing surf as well as first-rate cooking. *Perkins Cove, tel. 207/646–6348. AE, MC, V. Moderate–Expensive.*

Portland
Dining
★
Back Bay Grill. Simply but elegantly restored, the grill is popular for its mellow jazz, the mural of Portland reflected by mirrors throughout, an impressive wine list, and carefully prepared food. *65 Portland St., tel. 207/772–8833. Reservations advised. Jackets advised. AE, D, MC, V. Closed Sun. Expensive.*

★
Street & Co. At what may be the best seafood restaurant in Maine, you enter through the kitchen, with all its wonderful aromas, and dine amid dried herbs and shelves of grocery staples. *33 Wharf St., tel. 207/775–0887. Reservations advised. AE, MC, V. No lunch. Moderate.*

Lodging
Portland Regency Inn. The only major hotel in the center of the Old Port Exchange, this luxurious renovation of a 19th-century armory has Victorian-style rooms, many complete with four-poster beds. *20 Milk St., 04101, tel. 207/774–4200 or 800/727–3436. 95 rooms, 8 suites. Facilities: restaurant, nightclub, health club, banquet rooms. AE, D, DC, MC, V. Expensive.*

Scarborough
Lodging

Black Point Inn. At the tip of a peninsula 10 mi south of Portland stands one of Maine's great old-time resorts. The 115-year-old inn is decorated with Early American Colonial and cherrywood furniture, and the pastel colors of the rooms create a light and relaxed air throughout. The grounds offer beaches, hiking, a bird sanctuary, and sports. The dining room, with pale Renaissance-style wallpaper and water-stained pine paneling, offers a menu strong in seafood. *510 Black Point Rd., 04074, tel. 207/883–4126 or 800/258–0003. 80 rooms, 6 suites. Facilities: restaurant, bar, tennis courts, golf course, salt- and freshwater pools. MC, V. Closed Nov.–Apr. Expensive.*

Spruce Head

Miller's Lobster Co. For lobster-in-the-rough, you won't find a more quintessential Maine setting than Miller's, located south of Rockland off the Spruce Head Road, midway between St. George and Spruce Head. Watch lobster boats unload their catch while you dine on the wharf at wood picnic tables overlooking a cove dotted with boats. The setting is rustic, and the fare is simple: lobster, mussels, clams, corn-on-the-cob, and homemade pies. *Wheeler's Bay, Spruce Head, tel. 207/594–7406. No credit cards. Inexpensive.*

The Yorks
Dining
★

Dockside Dining Room. Seclusion, gardens, and water views are the attractions of this inn dining room on a private island in York Harbor. Entrées may include scallop-stuffed shrimp and stuffed roast duckling. *Off Rte. 103, York Harbor, tel. 207/363–2722. Reservations advised. MC, V. Closed Mon.; late Oct.–late May. Moderate.*

Dining and Lodging

Stage Neck Inn. This attractive resort hugs the rocky shoreline. Accommodations are luxurious, with beach or ocean views, and the formal dining room offers American fare such as baked lobster and duckling in elegant surroundings. *Off Rte. 1A, Box 97, York Harbor 03911, tel. 207/363–3850 or 800/222–3238. Facilities: 2 dining rooms, beachside lounge with live music, whirlpool/sauna, indoor and outdoor pools, tennis courts, golf privileges. AE, MC, V. Expensive.*

★

York Harbor Inn. Historic country charm coupled with ocean views makes this a special spot. Guest rooms have a Colonial theme, as do the public areas. The cuisine runs to well-prepared Mediterranean French–style seafood specialties. *Rte. 1A, Box 573, York Harbor 03911, tel. 207/363–5119. 32 rooms (5 share baths), some with fireplaces. Facilities: restaurant, pub, beach, golf privileges. AE, DC, MC, V. Expensive.*

The Arts and Nightlife

The Arts

Ogunquit Playhouse (Rte. 1, tel. 207/646–5511), one of America's oldest summer theaters, mounts plays and musicals from late June to Labor Day. **Portland Performing Arts Center** (25A Forest Ave., tel. 207/761–0591) hosts music, dance, and theater. **Cumberland County Civic Center** (1 Civic Center Sq., Portland, tel. 207/775–3458) has concerts in a 9,000-seat auditorium.

Nightlife

Gritty McDuff's Brew Pub (396 Fore St., Portland, tel. 207/772–2739) attracts the young and lively, as well as connoisseurs of the ales and bitters brewed on the premises. **Three Dollar Dewey's** (446 Fore St., Portland, tel. 207/772–3310) is an English-style alehouse, long a popular local night spot.

The Coast: Penobscot Bay and Acadia

Purists hold that the Maine coast begins at Penobscot Bay, where water vistas are wider and bluer, the shore a jumble of broken granite boulders, cobblestones, and gravel. East of Penobscot Bay, Acadia is the informal name for Mount Desert (pronounced like *dessert*) Island and environs. Mount Desert, Maine's largest island, harbors most of Acadia National Park, the state's principal tourist attraction. Camden on Penobscot Bay and Bar Harbor on Mount Desert both offer a range of accommodations and restaurants.

Tourist Information

Bar Harbor: Chamber of Commerce (Box BC, Cottage St., 04609, tel. 207/288–3393, 207/288–5103, or 800/288–5103). **Rockport-Camden-Lincolnville:** Chamber of Commerce (Box 919, Camden 04843, tel. 207/236–4404).

Getting There

By Plane **Bangor International Airport** (tel. 207/947–0384), 30 mi north of Penobscot Bay, has daily flights by major U.S. carriers. **Knox County Regional Airport** (tel. 207/594–4131), 3 mi south of Rockland, has frequent flights to Boston. **Hancock County Airport** (tel. 207/667–7329), 8 mi northwest of Bar Harbor, is served by Continental Express.

By Car U.S. 1 follows the west coast of Penobscot Bay, linking Rockland, Camden, and Ellsworth. From Ellsworth, Rte. 3 will take you onto Mount Desert Island.

Exploring Penobscot Bay and Acadia

An easy detour off U.S. 1 onto Rte. 131S brings you to **Tenants Harbor.** This is a quintessential Maine fishing town, its harbor dominated by squat, serviceable lobster boats, its shores rocky and slippery, its town a scattering of clapboard houses, a church, a general store. South of here is the fishing town of **Port Clyde,** point of departure for the mailboat that serves **Monhegan Island** (*see also* The Coast: From Kittery to Pemaquid Point, Sports and Outdoor Activities, Boat Trips, *above*). The tiny, remote island, high cliffs fronting the open sea, was discovered by some of America's finest painters a century ago. Day-trippers now flock here for the scenery, the boat ride, and the artists' studios, which are occasionally open to visitors.

Return to U.S. 1 and proceed to **Rockland,** the coast's commercial hub, with fishing boats moored alongside a growing flotilla of cruise schooners. The **William A. Farnsworth Library and Art Museum** displays oil and watercolor landscapes of the coast you have just seen, among them Andrew Wyeth's *Eight Bells* and N. C. Wyeth's *Her Room. 19 Elm St., tel. 207/596–6457. Admission charged. Closed Mon. Oct.–May.*

From Rockland it's 8 mi north on U.S. 1 to **Camden,** where the mountains tower over the harbor and the fashionable waterfront. Camden is famous for the nation's largest windjammer fleet; such cruises are a superb way to explore the ports and islands of Penobscot Bay. The 6,000-acre **Camden Hills State Park** (tel. 207/236–3109), 2 mi north of town on U.S. 1, contains 25 mi of trails and a toll road up Mt. Battie.

Farther north on U.S. 1, **Searsport**—Maine's second-largest deepwater port—claims to be the antiques capital of Maine, with shops and a seasonal weekend flea market. Turn south onto Rtes. 175 and 166A, which terminate at **Castine.** Historic Castine, over which the French, the British, and the Americans fought, has two museums and the ruins of a British fort, but the finest thing about Castine is the town itself: the lively, welcoming town landing, the serene Federal and Greek Revival houses, and the town common.

Return to U.S. 1 and proceed to Ellsworth, where you pick up Rte. 3 to **Mount Desert Island.** Although most of **Bar Harbor's** grand mansions were destroyed in the fire of 1947, this busy resort town on the island's Frenchman Bay has retained its beauty. Shops, restaurants, and hotels are clustered along Main, Mount Desert, and Cottage streets.

The Hulls Cove approach to **Acadia National Park** (*see* National and State Parks, *above*) is northwest of Bar Harbor on Rte. 3. Though it is often clogged with traffic, the 27-mi Park Loop Road provides the best introduction to the park. The visitor center shows a free 15-minute film and has trail maps. The **Ocean Trail** is an easily accessible walk with some of Maine's most spectacular scenery. For a mountaintop experience without the effort of hiking, drive to the summit of Cadillac Mountain, the highest point on the eastern coast. The view from the bald summit is spectacular, especially at sunset.

What to See and Do with Children

The **Owls Head Transportation Museum** (Rte. 73, Owls Head, tel. 207/594–4418; closed Nov.–Apr.) has antique aircraft and cars, and stages weekend air shows. **Acadia Zoo** (Rte. 3, Trenton, tel. 207/667–3244; closed mid-Oct.–Apr.) has wild and domestic animals.

Shopping

The best shopping streets are Main and Bayview in **Camden.** Antiques shops (abundant in **Searsport**) are scattered around the outskirts of villages; yard sales abound in summer. **Bar Harbor** is a good place to browse for gifts. For bargains, head for the outlets along Rte. 3 in **Ellsworth.**

Sports and Outdoor Activities

Biking The carriage paths that wind through **Acadia National Park** are ideal for biking; pick up a map from the Hulls Cove visitor center. Bikes can be rented in Bar Harbor from **Acadia Bike & Canoe** (48 Cottage St., tel. 207/288–9605) and **Bar Harbor Bicycle Shop** (141 Cottage St., tel. 207/288–3886).

Boat Trips From Bar Harbor, **Acadia Boat Tours & Charters** (tel. 207/288–9505) has lobster-fishing trips, **Acadian Whale Watcher** (tel.

207/288–9794) runs whale-watching cruises, and the **Natalie Todd** (tel. 207/288–4585) offers weekend windjammer cruises. Camden is the East Coast windjammer headquarters (call or write Maine Windjammer Assoc., Box 317P, Rockport 04856, tel. 800/624–6380); the local chamber of commerce also has current listings (*see* Tourist Information, *above*).

Hiking **Acadia National Park** maintains nearly 200 mi of paths. Among the more rewarding hikes are the Precipice Trail to Champlain Mountain, the Great Head Loop, the Gorham Mountain Trail, and the path around Eagle Lake.

Sailing In Bar Harbor, **Harbor Boat Rentals** (Harbor Pl., 1 West St., tel. 207/288–3757) has Boston whalers and sailboats. In Southwest Harbor, **Manset Boat Rental** (Manset Boatyard, tel. 207/244–9233) rents sailboats.

Dining and Lodging

For price ranges, see Charts 1 (B) and 2 (B) in Chapter 1.

Bar Harbor **George's.** Candles, flowers, and linens decorate the tables in
Dining four small dining rooms in a romantic old house. The menu
★ shows a distinct Mediterranean influence. *7 Stephen's La., tel. 207/288–4505. Reservations advised. AE, D, DC, MC, V. No lunch; closed late Oct.–mid-June. Expensive.*

Jordan Pond House. Popovers and tea are a tradition at this rustic restaurant in Acadia National Park, where you can sit on the terrace and admire the views. The dinner menu offers lobster stew, seafood thermidor, and fisherman's stew. *Park Loop Rd., tel. 207/276–3316. Reservations advised. AE, D, MC, V. Closed late Oct.–late May. Moderate.*

Dining and Lodging **The Bar Harbor Inn.** Varied lodgings are set on 8 landscaped acres in the heart of town. The Main Inn overlooks Frenchman Bay; the Oceanfront Lodge affords spectacular views of the Porcupine Islands; the motel is comfortable—and more moderately priced. The Reading Room Restaurant, built as a clubhouse for the Morgans and Vanderbilts, offers first-class food such as salmon with pesto or a creamy lobster bisque. *Newport Dr., 04609, tel. 207/288–3351 or 800/248–3351. 130 rooms. Facilities: afternoon tea, pool, pier, sightseeing cruises, rental boats. AE, D, MC, V. Main Inn and Reading Room closed Nov.–Apr. Expensive.*

Camden **The Belmont.** In a spacious, well-lit room painted a pale laven-
Dining der, the relaxed atmosphere is enhanced with muted classical music or jazz. The New American menu changes daily and features five to eight entrées. *6 Belmont Ave., tel. 207/236–8053. Reservations advised. MC, V. No lunch; closed Jan.–Apr. Expensive.*

The Waterfront Restaurant. Come for a ringside seat on Camden Harbor; the best view is from the outdoor deck, open in warm weather. The fare is seafood. *Bayview St., tel. 207/236–3747. No reservations. MC, V. Moderate.*

Lodging **Norumbega.** The public rooms in this elegant stone castle have oak and mahogany paneling and Empire furnishings. The guest rooms, named after various castles and palaces, are airy and spacious, with hardwood floors; many offer views of the water. *61 High St., 04843, tel. 207/236–4646. 13 rooms with bath. AE, MC, V. Expensive.*

Dining and Lodging **Whitehall Inn.** Camden's best-known inn preserves memorabilia of the poet Edna St. Vincent Millay, who grew up in nearby Rockland. The inn, down to the faded Oriental rugs and old-fashioned phones, evokes an image of the past. The rooms are small and sparsely furnished, with dark-wood bedsteads and claw-foot bathtubs. The dining room, open to the public for dinner and breakfast, offers traditional and creative American cuisine. *Box 558, 04843, tel. 207/236–3391. 50 rooms (8 share baths). Facilities: tennis court, golf privileges. AE, MC, V. Closed mid-Oct.–mid-May. Expensive.*

Castine **The Castine Inn.** This stately, 100-year-old yellow clapboard
Dining and Lodging mixes Victorian antiques with sturdily traditional new furniture. Guest rooms typically feature four-poster beds and oil paintings. The dining room is open to the public for breakfast and dinner featuring traditional New England fare. *Main St., 04421, tel. 207/326–4365. 27 rooms, 3 suites. MC, V. Closed Nov.–mid-Apr. Expensive.*

Hancock **Le Domaine.** On a rural stretch of U.S. 1, 9 mi east of
Dining Ellsworth, a French chef prepares *lapin pruneaux* (rabbit in a rich brown prune sauce), sweetbreads with lemon and capers, and *coquilles St. Jacques*. The elegant but unintimidating dining room has polished wood floors, hanging copper pots, and tables set with silver, crystal, and linen. *U.S. 1, tel. 207/422–3395 or 207/422–3916. Reservations advised. AE, D, MC, V. No lunch; closed Nov.–Apr. Expensive.*

Lincolnville **Chez Michel.** This tiny, informal restaurant with windows
Dining overlooking the beach across the street could ornament the Riviera as easily as Ducktrap Beach. Chef Michel Hetuin creates bouillabaisse as deftly as New England chowder. *Rte. 1, tel. 207/789–5600. MC, V. Closed Mon.; Nov.–Mar. Moderate.*

Northeast Harbor **Asticou Inn.** At night, guests at this grand turn-of-the-century
Dining and Lodging inn trade Topsiders and polo shirts for jackets and ties. The formal dining room is open to the public for a prix-fixe dinner by reservation only. Guest rooms have a country feel, with bright fabrics, white lace curtains, and white painted furniture. Modern cottages are scattered on the grounds, and a Victorian-style lodge across the street also has rooms. *04662, tel. 207/276–3344. 27 rooms, 23 suites, 6 cottages. Facilities: restaurant, tennis court, heated pool. MC, V. Inn and restaurant closed mid-Sept.–mid-June; cottages and lodge closed Jan.–Mar. Expensive.*

Campgrounds

The two campgrounds in Acadia National Park—**Blackwoods** (tel. 207/288–3274) and **Seawall** (tel. 207/244–3600)—fill up quickly in summer. Nearby **Lamoine State Park** (tel. 207/667–4778) has a great location on Frenchman Bay.

The Arts

Bay Chamber Concerts (Rockport Opera House, tel. 207/236–2823) offers chamber music twice weekly in July and August, plus monthly concerts October through May. **Arcady Music Festival** (tel. 207/288–3151) schedules concerts around Mount Desert Island from late July through August. **Bar Harbor Festival** (59 Cottage St., tel. 207/288–5744) programs concerts in summer.

Western Lakes and Mountains

Less than 20 mi northwest of Portland, the lakes and mountains of western Maine stretch along the New Hampshire border to Quebec. The Sebago–Long Lake region has antiques stores and lake cruises on a 42-mi waterway. Kezar Lake, tucked away in a fold of the White Mountains, has long been a hideaway of the wealthy. Bethel, in the Androscoggin River valley, is a classic New England town, while the less-developed Rangeley Lakes area is a fishing paradise; both become ski country in winter.

Tourist Information

Bethel Area: Chamber of Commerce (Box 121, 04217, tel. 207/824–2282). **Bridgton–Lakes Region:** Chamber of Commerce (Box 236, Bridgton 04009, tel. 207/647–3472). **Rangeley Lakes Region:** Chamber of Commerce (Box 317, Rangeley 04970, tel. 207/864–5571).

Getting There

By Car U.S. 302 provides access to the region from I–95. U.S. 2, which runs east–west, links Bangor to Bethel.

Exploring the Western Lakes and Mountains

Sebago Lake State Park (tel. 207/693–6613 mid-June–Sept., 207/693–6231 Oct.–mid-June) offers opportunities for swimming, picnicking, camping, boating, and fishing. To the north is **Naples,** with cruises and boat rentals on Long Lake. **Bridgton,** near Highland Lake, has antiques shops in and around town. U.S. 302/Rte. 5 through **Lovell** or Rte. 37 through the **Waterfords** are scenic routes to **Bethel,** a town with white clapboard houses and a mountain vista at the end of every street.

The area from Bethel to **Rangeley Lake** is beautiful, particularly in the autumn. In **Grafton Notch State Park** (tel. 207/824–2912) you can hike to stunning gorges and waterfalls and into the Baldpate Mountains. For a century **Rangeley** has lured fishermen and hunters to its more than 40 lakes and ponds. The town has a rough, wilderness feel to it; the best parts are tucked away in the woods and around the lake. **Rangeley Lake State Park** (tel. 207/289–3824) offers superb scenery, swimming, picnicking, and boating. Campsites are set well apart in a spruce grove.

In the shadow of Sugarloaf Mountain, **Kingfield** is prime ski country. The picture-postcard town boasts a general store, historic inns, and a white clapboard church.

What to See and Do with Children

Sandy River & Rangeley Lakes Railroad (Phillips, tel. 207/639–3352; open June–Oct., 1st and 3rd Sun. of month) offers rides through the woods on a century-old train. The stern-wheeler *Songo River Queen II* (Rte. 302, Naples Causeway, tel. 207/

693–6861) cruises Long Lake or paddles down through Songo
Lock June–September.

Shopping

Bridgton and **Bethel** have lots of antiques and crafts shops. Otherwise, the pickings are slim.

Sports and Outdoor Activities

Canoeing   The **Saco River** and **Rangeley and Mooselookmeguntic lakes** are favorites. For rentals, try **Canal Bridge Canoes** (Rte. 302, Fryeburg Village, tel. 207/935–2605), **Mooselookmeguntic House** (Haines Landing, Oquossoc, tel. 207/864–2470), **Rangeley Region Sport Shop** (Main St., Rangeley, tel. 207/864–5615), or **Saco River Canoe and Kayak** (Rte. 5, Fryeburg, tel. 207/935–2369).

Hunting and   Required hunting and fishing licenses can be obtained at many
Fishing   sporting-goods and hardware stores and at local town offices. The **Department of Inland Fisheries and Wildlife** (284 State St., Augusta 04333, tel. 207/289–2043) has further information.

Skiing   **Sugarloaf/USA** (Kingfield 04947, tel. 207/237–2000) has 91 downhill trails, a gondola, 12 lifts, a 2,837-foot vertical drop, and 53 mi of cross-country trails. **Sunday River** (Box 450, Bethel 04217, tel. 207/824–3000) has 72 downhill trails, 12 lifts, and a 2,001-foot drop.

Water Sports   Sebago, Long, Rangeley, and Mooselookmeguntic are the most popular lakes for boating. Contact tourist offices for rentals.

Dining and Lodging

Bethel has the largest concentration of inns and bed-and-breakfasts, and its chamber of commerce (*see* Tourist Information, *above*) has a lodging reservations service (tel. 207/824–3585). For price ranges, see Charts 1 (B) and 2 (B) in Chapter 1.

Bethel   **Bethel Inn and Country Club.** Choice rooms in the old-fashioned
Dining and Lodging   hotel, sparsely furnished with Colonial reproductions and George Washington bedspreads, have fireplaces and face the golf course and the mountains beyond. Condos on the fairway are clean and a bit sterile. The formal dining room serves roast duck and prime rib. *Village Common, Box 49, 04217, tel. 207/824–2175 or 800/654–0125. 57 rooms, 40 condo units. Facilities: restaurant, health club, tennis court, golf course. AE, D, DC, MC, V. Expensive.*

Four Seasons Inn. This Victorian white elephant has ornate guest rooms complete with velvet Victorian sofas and canopy beds. The classic French restaurant is tops in the area. *63 Upper Main St., 04217, tel. 207/824–2755 or 800/227–7458. 15 rooms (10 share baths). Facilities: restaurant (reservations advised; no lunch; closed Mon.; expensive). AE, MC, V. Closed May, Nov.–Dec. Moderate.*

Kingfield   **The Inn on Winter's Hill.** Designed in 1895 by the Stanley
Lodging   brothers (of Stanley Steamer automobile fame), this Georgian mansion is renowned for rich Sunday brunches and seven-course New England dinners. The rooms of the renovated barn are simply and brightly furnished. *RR 1, Box 1272, tel. 207/265–5421 or 800/233–9687. 20 rooms. Facilities: restaurant,*

tennis court, pool, ice skating, cross-country skiing. AE, D, DC, MC, V. Expensive.

Elsewhere in the State

The North Woods

Getting There Charter planes can be arranged from Bangor. Rte. 6 wends its way from I–95 to Greenville; Rte. 11 provides access from I–95 to Millinocket.

What to See and Do **Moosehead Lake,** Maine's largest, offers rustic camps, restaurants, guides, and outfitters. Its 420 mi of shorefront are virtually uninhabited and mostly accessible only by floatplane or boat. Greenville is the largest town on the lake and the spot for canoe rentals, outfitters, and basic lodging. For information, contact **Moosehead Lake Region Chamber of Commerce** (Box 581MI, Greenville 04441, tel. 207/695–2702).

Baxter State Park (64 Balsam Dr., Millinocket 04462, tel. 207/723–5140) is a 200,000-acre wooded wilderness surrounding Katahdin, Maine's highest mountain and the northern terminus of the Appalachian Trail. There are 45 other mountains in the park, all accessible from a 150-mi trail network.

Even more remote is the **Allagash Wilderness Waterway,** a 92-mi corridor of lakes and rivers. **Ripogenus Dam,** 30 mi northwest of Millinocket on lumbering roads, is the most popular jumping-off point for Allagash trips. The **Maine Department of Conservation, Bureau of Parks and Recreation** (State House Station 22, Augusta 04333, tel. 207/289–3821) has information on camping and canoeing.

MASSACHUSETTS

By Julia Lisella and Candice Gianetti

Capital	Boston
Population	6,016,425
Motto	By the Sword We Seek Peace, but Peace Only under Liberty
State Bird	Chickadee
State Flower	Mayflower

Visitor Information

Massachusetts Office of Travel and Tourism (100 Cambridge St., 13th floor, Boston 02202, tel. 617/727–3201 or 800/447–6277).

Scenic Drives

Much of Cape Cod's **Rte. 6A,** from Sandwich to Orleans, is a National Historic District preserving traditional New England seacoast towns. **Rtes. 133 and 1A** on the North Shore, from Gloucester to Newburyport, cover some of the earliest settlements in the United States, established in the 1630s. In the Berkshires, the **Mohawk Trail,** 63 mi of Rte. 2, between Greenfield and North Adams, is famous for its fall foliage, which peaks in late September and early October; and in the southwest, **Rte. 23** from Great Barrington to Westfield yields wooded hills and rural towns.

National and State Parks

National Parks **Cape Cod National Seashore** (*see* Cape Cod and the Islands, *below*), a 40-mi stretch of dune-backed beach between Eastham and Provincetown, offers excellent swimming, bike riding, bird-watching, and nature walks.

State Parks The **Department of Environmental Management** (Division of Forests and Parks, 100 Cambridge St., Boston 02202, tel. 617/727–3180) has information on all state parks, including the Heritage State Parks, which feature exhibits on the state's industrial history.

Mt. Greylock State Reservation (Rockwell Rd., off Rte. 7, Lanesborough, tel. 413/499–4262) and **Tolland State Forest** (off Rte. 23, Otis, tel. 413/269–6002) in the Berkshires have camping facilities and hiking trails. **Nickerson State Park** (Rte. 6A, Brewster, tel. 508/896–3491) on Cape Cod has nearly 2,000 acres of forest, eight trout-stocked ponds, and camping.

Boston

New England's largest and most important city, and the cradle of American independence, Boston is just over 360 years old. Its most famous buildings are not merely civic landmarks but national icons; its great citizens, the Adamses, Reveres, and Hancocks who live at the crossroads of history and myth.

Boston is also New England's center of high finance and higher technology, a place of granite-and-glass towers rising along what were once rutted village lanes. Its enormous population of students, academics, artists, and young professionals makes the town a haven for the arts, foreign movies, late-night bookstores, new-wave music, and unconventional politics.

Tourist Information

Boston: Boston Common Information Kiosk (147 Tremont St., where Freedom Trail begins, tel. 617/536–4100). Chamber of Commerce (600 Atlantic Ave., 02210, tel. 617/227–4500). Convention and Visitors Information Bureau (Prudential Tower, Box 490, 02199, tel. 617/536–4100). National Park Service Visitor Center (15 State St., across from Old State House, tel. 617/242–5642). **Cambridge:** Cambridge Discovery (near MBTA station entrance, Harvard Sq.; Box 1987, 02238, tel. 617/497–1630).

Boston magazine (on newsstands) and *Where: Boston* and *Panorama* (both free in hotels and visitor information offices) list arts and entertainment events.

Arriving and Departing

By Plane **Logan International Airport** (tel. 617/567–5400 for 24-hour information) has scheduled flights by most major domestic and foreign carriers. Only 3 mi—and Boston Harbor—separate the airport from downtown, but traffic is heavy. Cab fare downtown is about $15, including tip. A 24-hour number (tel. 800/235–6426) provides schedules for **Logan Express buses** and the **Airport Water Shuttle,** which goes downtown to Rowes Wharf. The **MBTA Blue Line** subway from Airport Station (85¢) goes downtown; free shuttle buses connect the station with airline terminals and run every 8–12 minutes from 5:30 AM to 1 AM.

By Car Boston is the traffic hub of New England: I–95 skirts the city along the coast, while I–90 heads west.

Train Station **South Station** (Summer St. at Atlantic Ave., tel. 617/345–7451).

Bus Stations **Bonanza** (145 Dartmouth St., tel. 617/720–4110 or 800/556–3815). **Greyhound** (at South Station, tel. 617/292–4702 or 617/423–5810). **Peter Pan Bus Lines** (555 Atlantic Ave., tel. 617/426–7838). **Plymouth & Brockton** (at Peter Pan Terminal, tel. 508/746–0378).

Getting Around Boston

Boston is meant for walking; its historic and architectural attractions are found in compact areas.

By Car Avoid bringing a car into Boston if you can; streets are narrow and twisting, drivers rude and unpredictable. Major public parking lots are at Government Center and Quincy Market; beneath Boston Common (entrance on Charles St.); beneath Post Office Square; at the Prudential Center; at Copley Place; and off Clarendon Street near the John Hancock Tower. Rush hours are 6:30–9 AM and 3:30–6 PM; traffic becomes especially congested at the Callahan Tunnel and Tobin Bridge.

By Public
Transportation
The **MBTA** (tel. 617/722–3200; TDD 617/722–5146), or T, operates subways, elevated trains, and trolleys along four connecting lines. Trains run from 5:30 AM to about 12:30 AM daily. Base
fares are 85¢ adults, 20¢ senior citizens, 40¢ children 6–11, free 5
and under. Tourist passes are available for $9 for three days and
$18 for seven days.

By Taxi
Cabs are not easily hailed; if you're in a hurry, try a hotel taxi
stand or telephone for a cab. Companies offering 24-hour service include **Checker** (tel. 617/536–7000), **Independent Taxi Operators Association** (tel. 617/426–8700), and **Cambridge Taxi**
(tel. 617/876–5000).

Orientation Tours

By Bus and Trolley
Brush Hill Tours and Beantown Trolley (tel. 617/236–2148 or
617/986–6100) offers tours of Boston and Cambridge. **The Gray
Line** (Tel. 617/426–8805) offers tours of Greater Boston, and
Lexington, Concord, and Cambridge.

By Boat
Bay State Cruise Co. (ticket office at 67 Long Wharf, tel. 617/
723–7800) offers 3½-hour excursions to Provincetown.

Walking Tours
The 1½-mi **Freedom Trail** tour is marked on the sidewalk by a
red line that winds past 16 of Boston's most important historic
sites, beginning at the Information Center at Boston Common.
Harborwalk is a self-guided tour (beginning at the Old State
House) that traces Boston's maritime history. Maps for both
walks are available at the Boston Common Information Kiosk.

Exploring Boston

Boston Common
and Beacon Hill
Boston Common is the oldest public park in the United States
and undoubtedly the largest and most famous of the town commons around which all New England settlements were once arranged. The nearby Congregationalist **Park Street Church** (at
Park and Tremont Sts., tel. 617/523–3383) was built in 1809–10
and is where, in 1831, Samuel Smith's hymn "America" was
first sung. Next to the church is the **Old Granary Burial
Ground,** where lie the Revolutionary heroes Samuel Adams,
John Hancock, and Paul Revere.

At the summit of Beacon Hill is the magnificent neoclassical
State House, its dome sheathed in copper from the foundry of
Paul Revere. Tours are given weekdays. *Tel. 617/727–3676. Ad-
mission free. Closed weekends.*

With its brick row houses, most built between 1800 and 1850,
the classic face of **Beacon Hill** is in a style never far from the
early Federal norm. **Chestnut** and **Mt. Vernon streets** are distinguished not only for their individual houses but for their general atmosphere and character as well. Mt. Vernon opens out on
Louisburg Square, an 1840s model for town-house development.

On the north slope of Beacon Hill is the 1806 **African Meeting
House** (8 Smith Ct.), the oldest standing African-American
church building in the United States and where the New England Anti-Slavery Society was formed in 1832. Today the site
marks the beginning of the **Black Heritage Trail,** a walking
tour. Information is available at the **Museum of Afro-American
History.** *46 Joy St., tel. 617/742–1854. Admission charged.
Closed weekends.*

Across the Charles River, the **Museum of Science** has more than 400 exhibits covering astronomy, anthropology, medicine, computers, earth sciences, and more. The interactive exhibits are fun for both children and adults. The **Hayden Planetarium** and the **Mugar Omni Theater** are also here. *Science Park (Charles River Dam), tel. 617/723–2500. Admission charged. Closed Mon., Thanksgiving, and Christmas.*

The North End and Charlestown
In the 17th century the **North End** *was* Boston, as much of the rest of the peninsula was still under water. During most of this century the North End has been Italian Boston, full of Italian restaurants, groceries, bakeries, churches, social clubs, cafés, and festivals honoring saints and food.

Off Hanover Street, the North End's main thoroughfare, is North Square and the **Paul Revere House,** the oldest house in Boston, built nearly a century before its illustrious tenant's midnight ride. The restored rooms exemplify Colonial Boston dwellings. *19 North Sq., tel. 617/523–1676. Admission charged. Closed Mon. Jan.–Mar., Thanksgiving, Christmas, and New Year's Day.*

Past North Square on Hanover Street is **St. Stephen's,** the only one of Charles Bulfinch's churches still standing in Boston. Nearby on Tileston Street you can see the steeple of Christ Church, the **Old North Church** (193 Salem St., tel. 617/523–6676), where the two lanterns were hung as a signal to Paul Revere on the night of April 18, 1775. The oldest church building in Boston, it was designed by William Price from a study of Christopher Wren's London churches.

Cross the Charlestown Bridge to reach the USS *Constitution,* nicknamed "Old Ironsides" for the strength of its oaken hull, not because of any iron plating. The oldest commissioned ship in the U.S. Navy, launched in 1797, it is moored at the **Charlestown Navy Yard.** During its service against the Barbary pirates and in the War of 1812, the ship never lost an engagement. *Constitution Wharf, tel. 617/426–1812. Admission to the* Constitution *free. Admission charged to the museum. Closed Thanksgiving, Christmas, and New Year's Day.*

The phrase "Battle of Bunker Hill" is one of America's most famous misnomers. The battle was fought on Breed's Hill, and that is where Solomon Willard's **Bunker Hill Monument**—a 220-foot shaft of Quincy granite—stands. It rises from the spot where, on June 17, 1775, a citizens' militia—commanded not to fire "till you see the whites of their eyes"—inflicted more than 1,100 casualties on British regulars (who eventually did seize the hill). The views from the top are worth the 295-step ascent. *Main St. to Monument St., then straight uphill; tel. 617/242–5641. Admission free. Closed Thanksgiving, Christmas, and New Year's Day.*

Downtown Boston
To the east of Boston Common is **Downtown.** There is little logic to the streets here; they were once village lanes but are now lined with 40-story office towers. The granite **King's Chapel** (Tremont and School Sts.), built in 1754, houses Paul Revere's largest bell and, in his opinion, his sweetest-sounding.

The **Old South Meeting House** (corner of Washington and Milk Sts.), built in 1729, is Boston's second-oldest church. Unlike the older Old North, the Old South is no longer active. Some of the fieriest of the town meetings that led to the Revolution

Boston

CAMBRIDGE

Hampshire St.
Norfolk St.
Union St.
Elm St.
Market St.
Windsor St.
Webster Ave.
Willow St.
Berkshire St.
Portland St.
Cambridge St.
8th St.
7th St.
Otis St.
Thorndike St.
Sciarappa St.
McGrath Hwy.
6th St.
5th St.
Spring St.
Hurley St.
3rd St.
Fulkerson St.
Charles St.
Bent St.
Rogers St.
Binney St.
Munroe St.
2nd St.
1st St.
Commercial St.
Washington St.
Harvard St.
Portland St.
Broadway
St.
Main St.
Vassar St.
Ames
Carleton
St.
Wadsworth St.
Amherst St.
State St.
Massachusetts Ave.
TO HARVARD SQUARE
Albany St.
Longfellow Br.

Massachusetts Institute of Technology

3

Memorial Drive

2A

Harvard Br.

Charles River Basin

James J. Storrow Memorial Dr.

1

Gibson House

Back St.
Dartmouth
Marlborough St.
Berkeley St.

Beacon St.
Fairfield
St.
Clarendon St.

BACK BAY

Hereford
St.
Gloucester St.
Commonwealth Ave.
Newbury St.
Exeter St.
Boylston St.
Blagden St.

John Hancock Tower

Back St.

Kenmore Sq.

Mass Tpke.
Lansdowne St.
Brookline Ave.

1

Ipswich

90

90

Copley Place

Fenway Park

Van Ness St.
Boylston St.
Petersborough St.
Queensberry St.
Park Dr.
Ipswich St.
Hemenway St.
Fenway
Burbank St.
Westland Ave.
St. Stephen St.
St. Gainsborough St.

BACK BAY FENS

Belvidere
St.
Dalton St.
Massachusetts Ave.
9
Christian Science Church
Huntington Ave.
St. Botolph St.
28
Columbus Ave.
Appleton St.
Warren Ave.
Canton
St.
Pembroke
St.
Newton St.
Tremont St.

PRUDENTIAL CENTER

Symphony Hall

TO MUSEUM OF FINE ARTS, ISABELLA STEWART GARDNER MUSEUM

N

CHARLESTOWN

Bunker Hill
Monument

USS
Constitution

93

Copp's Hill
Burying
Ground

Museum
of Science

Sumner
Tunnel

NORTH
END

Callahan
Tunnel

TO
AIRPORT

North
Station

Charlestown Br.

Washington St.

Snowhill St.

Charter St.

Hull St.

Tileston St.

Prince St.

Margin St.

Old
North
Church

Paul
Revere
House

Commercial St.

North St.

Commercial St.

OLD
WEST
END

Charles St.

Blossom St.

Nashua St.

Causeway St.

Canal St.

Friend St.

Merrimac St.

New Chardon St.

Sudbury St.

African
Meeting House

Museum of
Afro-American
History

Fruit St.

Parkman
St.

Cambridge St.

Phillips
St.

Grove St.

Irving St.

Hancock St.

Joy St.

Temple St.

Bowdoin St.

GOVERNMENT
CENTER

Somerset St.

Clinton St.

Quincy
Market

Faneuil
Hall

Chatham St.

State St.

Congress St.

North St.

John F. Fitzgerald Expwy.

India St.

New
England
Aquarium

BEACON
HILL

Revere St.

Pinckney

Mt. Vernon
St.

Chestnut St.

Beacon St.

River St.

Brimmer St.

Chestnut St.

State
House

King's
Chapel

School St.

Old
State
House

Old
South
Meeting
House

Park St.

Old Granary
Burial Ground

Park
Street
Church

Milk St.

Broad St.

Franklin St.

High St.

Inner
Harbor

Public Garden

Charles St.

Arlington St.

Visitor
Information
Booth

Boston
Common

Temple Pl.

Washington St.

Avon St.

West St.

Bedford St.

Summer St.

Arch St.

Snow
Pl.

Federal St.

Purchase St.

Public
Garden

Boylston St.

DOWNTOWN

Essex St.

Eliot St.

James Ave.

Stuart St.

Church St.

Broadway

Melrose
St.

Stuart St.

Oak St.

Washington St.

Beach St.

Kneeland St.

Tyler St.

Hudson St.

Atlantic Ave.

Beaver II

Computer
Museum

Boston
Children's
Museum

Northern
Ave.

Congress St.

Summer St.

Cortes St.

Chandler St.

Gray St.

Tremont St.

E. Berkeley St.

Dwight St.

Milford St.

Waltham St.

Shawmut St.

Washington St.

SOUTH
END

Harrison Ave.

Marginal Rd.

Herald St.

Thayer St.

Randolph St.

93

Broadway Bridge

Dorchester Ave.

Fort Point Channel

A St.

SOUTH
BOSTON

B St.

W. 1st St.

W. 2nd St.

W. 3rd St.

C St.

D St.

Bullock St.

Cypher St.

W. 4th St.

W. Broadway

0   1/4 mile

0   250 meters

were held here, including the one Samuel Adams called concerning some dutiable tea that activists wanted returned to England.

A brightly colored lion and unicorn, symbols of British imperial power, adorn the facade of the **Old State House** (Washington and Court Sts.). This was the seat of the Colonial government from 1713 until the Revolution, and thereafter served the independent commonwealth until the new State House on Beacon Hill was completed. John Hancock was inaugurated here as the state's first governor, and in the 1830s the Old State House served as Boston City Hall. In 1992, after a two-year, $4 million federal preservation and renovation project, the Old State House reopened and changed the focus of its exhibits. The permanent collection traces Boston's Revolutionary War history, while changing exhibits on the second floor address contemporary issues, such as "Urban Renewal and Boston's West End." *206 Washington St., tel. 617/720–3290. Admission charged.*

On Congress Street is **Faneuil Hall** (pronounced "Fan'l"), erected in 1742 to serve as both a place for town meetings and a public market. It was here, in 1772, that Samuel Adams first suggested that Massachusetts and the other colonies organize a Committee of Correspondence to maintain semiclandestine lines of communication in the face of hardening British repression. In later years, Wendell Phillips and Charles Sumner spoke out for the abolition of slavery at the hall's podium, and in national election years the hall is usually host to debates featuring contenders in the Massachusetts presidential primary. Though it has been rebuilt, enlarged, and remodeled over the years, the great balconied hall is still made available to citizens' groups. Inside are the great mural *Webster's Reply to Hayne*, Gilbert Stuart's portrait of Washington at Dorchester Heights, and dozens of other paintings of famous Americans. On the top floors are the headquarters and museum of the **Ancient and Honorable Artillery Company of Massachusetts,** the oldest militia in the nation (1638). Its status is now ceremonial, but it proudly displays its arms, uniforms, and other artifacts.

Nearby **Quincy Market** has served as a retail and wholesale distribution center for meat and produce for 150 years. Thanks to creative urban renewal in the mid-1970s, it now houses a mix of retail shops, restaurants, and offices, all usually packed with shoppers, tourists, street performers, and locals. The central structure still has a traditional market-stall layout, but most of the businesses on the first floor offer international and specialty foods, interspersed with the stalls of provisioners who have been in the market for a century or more. Upstairs are restaurants, and along the arcades on either side, shops and bars. The north and south buildings, separated from the central market by pedestrian malls with trees and benches, house more substantial retail establishments, offices, and additional restaurants. Some people consider it all hopelessly trendy, but the 50,000 visitors who come here each day seem to enjoy it.

At the end of Quincy Market opposite Faneuil Hall, the newly constructed **Marketplace Center,** between the market buildings and the expressway, is filled with shops and boutiques. Beyond is Columbus Park, bordering on the harbor and on several of Boston's restored wharves. **Lewis Wharf** and **Commercial Wharf,** which long lay nearly derelict, had by the mid-1970s been transformed into condominiums, apartments, restaurants, and upscale shops. **Long Wharf's** Marriott hotel was designed to be compatible with the old seaside warehouses. Sailboats and power yachts ride here at anchor; Boston's workaday waterfront is now located along the docks of South Boston, in East Boston (directly opposite Columbus Park), and in the huge containerized shipping facilities at the mouth of the Mystic River.

Central Wharf, immediately to the right of Long Wharf as you face the harbor, is the home of one of Boston's most popular attractions, the **New England Aquarium.** Here you'll find seals, penguins, a variety of sharks and other sea creatures—more than 2,000 species in all, some of which make their home in the aquarium's four-story, 187,000-gallon observation tank. Ramps wind around the tank, allowing you to view the inhabitants from many vantage points. There are also dolphin and sea lion shows aboard *Discovery*, a floating marine mammal pavilion.

Thanks to landfill, the exact site of the **Boston Tea Party** is marked by a plaque set into the wall of a commercial building on Atlantic Avenue at the foot of Pearl Street. When you cross Fort Point Channel on the Congress Street Bridge, you encounter the *Beaver II,* a faithful replica of one of the Tea Party ships that were forcibly boarded and unloaded on the night Boston Harbor became a teapot. *Tel. 617/338–1773. Admission charged. Closed mid-Dec.–Feb.*

Back Bay and the South End Southwest of Boston Common is **Back Bay,** once a tidal flat that formed the south bank of a distended Charles River until it was filled as far as the Fens in the 19th century.

Back Bay is a living museum of urban Victorian residential architecture. The **Gibson House** (1859) offers a representative look at how life was arranged in—and by—these tall, narrow, formal buildings. The house has been preserved with all its Victorian fixtures and furniture intact: A conservative Gibson family scion lived here until the 1950s and left things as they were. *137 Beacon St., tel. 617/267–6338. Admission charged. Tours Wed.–Sun. at 1, 2, and 3 May–Oct.; weekends at 1, 2, and 3 Nov.–Apr.*

Newbury Street is lined with sidewalk cafés and dozens of upscale specialty shops offering clothing, china, antiques, and art.

The 60th-floor observatory of the tallest building in New England, the 62-story **John Hancock Tower,** is one of the best vantage points in the city. *Trinity Pl. and St. James Ave., tel. 617/ 247–1977. Admission charged. Closed Thanksgiving and Christmas.*

Copley Square is a civic space defined by three monumental buildings: the stately, bowfront **Copley Plaza Hotel; Trinity Church,** Henry Hobson Richardson's Romanesque Revival masterwork of 1877; and the **Boston Public Library** (tel. 617/ 536–5400), which confirmed in 1895 the status of McKim, Mead, and White as apostles of the Renaissance Revival. With a modern, assertive presence, **Copley Place** comprises two major hotels (the Westin and the Marriott) and dozens of shops and restaurants, grouped on several levels around bright, open indoor spaces.

On Huntington Avenue is the headquarters of the **Christian Science Church** (175 Huntington Ave. at Massachusetts Ave., tel. 617/450–3790). Mary Baker Eddy's original granite First Church of Christ, Scientist (1894) and the domed Renaissance basilica added to the site in 1906 are now surrounded by the offices of the *Christian Science Monitor* and by I. M. Pei's 1973 complex of church administration buildings. The best views of the precise, abstract geometry of the complex are from the **Prudential Center Skywalk** (800 Boylston St., tel. 617/236–3318), a 50th-floor observatory that overlooks Boston, Cambridge, and the suburbs to the west and south.

Symphony Hall (Massachusetts and Huntington Aves., tel. 617/266–1492), since 1900 the home of the Boston Symphony Orchestra, is another contribution of McKim, Mead, and White, though acoustics, rather than exterior design, make this a special place.

The **South End** was eclipsed by the Back Bay more than a century ago but is now back in fashion, with upscale galleries and restaurants catering to young professionals. An anomaly of planning and architecture in Boston, the South End neither grew up haphazardly along cowpaths and village lanes, like the old sections, nor followed a strict, uniform grid like that of the Back Bay. It is more a sum of random blocks and park-centered squares than of boulevards and long, clear vistas. The houses around here continue the pattern established on Beacon Hill (in a uniformly bowfront style) but have more florid decoration.

There is a substantial black presence in the South End, particularly along Columbus Avenue and Massachusetts Avenue, which marks the beginning of the neighborhood of Roxbury. The early integration of the South End set the stage for its eventual transformation into a remarkable polyglot of ethnic groups. You are likely to hear Spanish spoken along Tremont Street, and there are Middle Eastern groceries along Shawmut Avenue. At the northeastern extreme of the South End, Harrison Avenue and Washington Street connect the area with **Chinatown,** and consequently there is a growing Asian influence. Still another minority presence among the neighborhood's ethnic groups, and sometimes belonging to one or more of them, is the largest concentration of Boston's gay population. To see elegant house restorations, go to **Rutland Square** (between Columbus Avenue and Tremont Street) or **Union Park** (between Tremont Street and Shawmut Avenue). These oases seem miles distant from the city around them.

The Fens After all the work that had gone into filling in the bay, it would have been little extra trouble to march row houses straight through to Brookline. Instead, planners hired Frederick Law Olmsted to make the Fens into a park. Today's park consists of still, irregular reed-bound pools surrounded by broad meadows, trees, and flower gardens.

The **Museum of Fine Arts,** between Huntington Avenue and the Fenway, has holdings of American art that surpass those of all but two or three other U.S. museums; an extensive collection of Asian art; and European artworks from the 11th through the 20th century. Count on staying for a while if you have any hope of even beginning to see what is here. In the West Wing is a restaurant and a cafeteria. *465 Huntington Ave., tel. 617/267–9300. Admission charged; free Wed. 4–10 PM, reduced price to West Wing Thurs. and Fri. 5–10 PM. Closed Mon. and New Year's Day.*

On the Fenway Park side of the museum, the **Tenshin Garden,** the "garden at the heart of heaven," is a landscape-as-a-work-of-art. A stone wall separates the formal garden from the nearby park, and a path of Mexican river stones leads to a bench surrounded by white gravel. A combination of Japanese and American trees and shrubs fuses the concept of the Japanese garden with features of the New England landscape.

The Boston shrine known as **Fenway Park** is one of the smallest and oldest baseball parks in the major leagues. Built in 1912, it still has real grass on the field. **Kenmore Square** is home to fast-food parlors, new-wave rock clubs, an abundance of students from nearby Boston University, and the enormous, landmark neon Citgo Sign.

Cambridge In 1636 the country's first college was established across the Charles River from Boston, in **Cambridge.** Named in 1638 for John Harvard, a young Charlestown clergyman who died that year, leaving the college his entire library and half his estate, **Harvard** remained the only college in the New World until 1693. The information office, in Holyoke Center (1350 Massachusetts Ave., tel. 617/495–1573), offers area maps and a free hour-long walking tour of Harvard Yard most days. North of Cambridge Common is **Radcliffe College,** founded in 1897 "to furnish instruction and the opportunities of collegiate life to women and to promote their higher education"; since 1975 Radcliffe students have shared classes and degrees with Harvard students.

Harvard University has two celebrated art museums, each a treasure in itself. The more famous is the **Fogg Art Museum.** Founded in 1895, it now owns 80,000 works of art from every major period and from every corner of the world. Its focus is primarily on European, American, and East Asian works; it has notable collections of 19th-century French Impressionist and medieval Italian paintings. *32 Quincy St., tel. 617/495–5573. Admission charged except free Sat. AM. Closed Mon.*

Fogg admission also gets you into the **Arthur M. Sackler Museum** (tel. 617/459–9400; closed Mon.) across the street, which concentrates on ancient Greek and Roman, Egyptian, Islamic, Chinese, and other Eastern art.

A ticket to the Fogg further gains you admission to Harvard's **Busch-Reisinger Museum** (tel. 617/495–2317; closed Mon.), in the new Werner Otto Hall and entered through the Fogg. The collection specializes in Central and Northern European art.

The **Massachusetts Institute of Technology** sits on the banks of the Charles River south of Harvard Square. The West Campus, devoted to student leisure life, has buildings designed by Eero Saarinen and the Finnish architect Alvar Aalto. The Information Center (Bldg. 7, 77 Massachusetts Ave., tel. 617/253–4795) offers free tours of the campus weekdays at 10 and 2.

Other Attractions The world's first **Computer Museum** chronicles the spectacular development of machines that calculate and process information. Exhibits include "vintage" robots and computers. *300 Congress St., Museum Wharf, tel. 617/426–2800. Admission charged. Closed Mon. except during school vacations and holidays.*

The **Harvard University Museums of Cultural and Natural History** are within a vast brick building that contains four distinct collections. The most famous exhibit is the display of glass flowers in the **Botanical Museum.** The **Peabody Museum of Archae-ology and Ethnology** holds exhibits of Native American and Central and South American cultures. The **Museum of Comparative Zoology** traces the evolution of animals and man. The **Mineralogical Museum** has a collection of exotic crystals and meteorites, and scale models of volcanoes and famous mountains. *26 Oxford St., Cambridge, tel. 617/495–1910. Admission charged.*

The **Isabella Stewart Gardner Museum** is a monument to one woman's taste—and a trove of some 2,000 spectacular paintings, sculptures, furniture, and textiles, with an emphasis on Italian Renaissance and 17th-century Dutch masters. At the center of the building is a magnificent courtyard, enclosed beneath a glass roof. *280 The Fenway, tel. 617/566–1401. Admission charged. Closed Mon.*

Parks and Gardens

The **Back Bay Fens** mark the beginning of Boston's Emerald Necklace, a loosely connected chain of parks designed by Frederick Law Olmsted that extends along the Fenway, Riverway, and Jamaicaway to Jamaica Pond, the 265-acre **Arnold Arboretum** (125 Arborway, Jamaica Plain, tel. 617/524–1718), and the **Zoo** at **Franklin Park** (Columbia Rd. and Blue Hill Ave., Dorchester, tel. 617/442–2002).

The **Public Garden,** next to Boston Common, is the oldest botanical garden in the United States. Its pond has been famous since 1877 for its **swan boats,** which make leisurely cruises during the warm months of the year.

The **Dr. Paul Dudley White Bikeway,** approximately 18 mi long, runs along both sides of the Charles River. The river's banks are also popular with joggers.

Boston for Free—or Almost

The "Boston Travel Planner," available from the Convention and Visitors Information Bureau (*see* Tourist Information, *above*), contains a calendar of events, sports and regional activities, and hotel weekend packages.

The **Hatch Memorial Shell,** on the esplanade along the Charles River, is the site of numerous free concerts in summer.

What to See and Do with Children

Boston Children's Museum contains a multitude of hands-on exhibits, many designed to help children understand cultural diversity, their bodies, and disabilities. *300 Congress St., tel. 617/426–6500. Admission charged. Closed Mon. except during school vacations and holidays.*

The calendar of events in the ***Boston Parents Paper*** (tel. 617/522–1515), published monthly and distributed free throughout the city, is an excellent resource for parents and children.

Shopping

Most of Boston's stores are in the area bounded by Quincy Market, the Back Bay, downtown, and Copley Square. There are

few outlet stores but plenty of bargains, particularly in Filene's
Basement and Chinatown's fabric district. Boston's two daily
newspapers, the *Globe* and the *Herald*, are the best places to
learn about sales.

Shopping Districts **Copley Place,** an indoor shopping mall connecting two hotels,
has 87 stores, restaurants, and cinemas that blend the elegant,
the glitzy, and the overpriced. **Downtown Crossing,** between
Summer and Washington streets, is a pedestrian mall with outdoor food and merchandise kiosks, street performers, and
benches for people-watchers. **Faneuil Hall Marketplace** has
crowds, small shops, kiosks of every description, and one of the
all-time great food experiences: **Quincy Market. Newbury
Street** is where the trendy gives way to the chic and the expensive. **Charles Street** in Beacon Hill is a mecca for antiques lovers
from all over the country.

Harvard Square in Cambridge has more than 150 stores within
a few blocks; it is a book lover's paradise. **Cambridgeside Galleria,** between Kendall Square and the Museum of Science in
Cambridge, has over 60 shops.

Department Stores **Filene's** (426 Washington St.) is best-known for its outstanding
two-level bargain basement, filled with an ever-changing array
of high-quality overstock and irregulars from upstairs and other stores. Cambridge's **Harvard Coop Society** (1400 Massachusetts Ave., Harvard Sq.; 3 Cambridge Center), begun in 1882
as a service for students and faculty, is now a full-service department store known for its wide selection of records and
books.

Food Markets Every Friday and Saturday, **Haymarket** (near Faneuil Hall
Marketplace) is a crowded jumble of outdoor produce, meat,
and fish vendors.

Specialty Stores **Shreve, Crump & Low** (330 Boylston St., tel. 617/267–9100) is an
Jewelry old and most respected store carrying the finest in jewelry, china, crystal, and silver.

Clothing **Louis** (234 Berkeley St., tel. 617/262–6100) is Boston's signature clothier, carrying elegantly tailored designs and subtly
updated classics in everything from linen to tweeds.

Spectator Sports

Baseball **Boston Red Sox** (Fenway Park, tel. 617/267–8661 or 617/267–
1700; early Apr.–early Oct.).

Basketball **Boston Celtics** (Boston Garden, Causeway St., tel. 617/523–
3030 or 617/931–2000; Oct.–May).

Football **New England Patriots** (Sullivan Stadium, Foxboro [45 min
south of Boston], tel. 800/543–1776; Aug.–Dec.).

Hockey **Boston Bruins** (Boston Garden, tel. 617/227–3223; Oct.–Apr.).

Dining

The choice of restaurants in Boston is wide and cosmopolitan,
with nationally recognized spots featuring innovative young
chefs as well as bastions of tradition. No matter what the style
or cuisine, though, the main ingredient is still the bounty of the
North Atlantic; the daily catch of fish and shellfish appears

somewhere on virtually every menu. For price ranges, see Chart 1 (A) in Chapter 1.

Very Expensive
★ **L'Espalier.** Owner-chef Frank McClellan serves contemporary French and American cuisines in three small-but-elegant dining rooms. His fixed-price, three-course dinner ($56) might include roast native partridge with chanterelles, a salad of peas and radishes, and for dessert figs and peaches with wild strawberry sauce and mascarpone cheese. *30 Gloucester St. (Back Bay), tel. 617/262–3023. Reservations required. Jacket and tie advised. AE, D, MC, V. No lunch; closed Sun.*

Seasons. At this solariumlike restaurant in the Bostonian Hotel, overlooking Faneuil Hall, the cuisine of chef Anthony Ambrose is eclectic American with international influences. A summer menu might include steamed halibut with oriental spices and apple paper. *North and Blackstone Sts., tel. 617/523–3600. Reservations advised. Dress: neat but casual. AE, DC, MC, V.*

Expensive
★ **Hamersley's Bistro.** Fiona and Gordon Hamersley "warmed up" their French-American bistro with goldenrod-painted walls that accent the red, black, and yellow decor. Specialties include a garlic-and-seasonal-mushroom sandwich served as an appetizer, and roast chicken. *578 Tremont St. (South End), tel. 617/267–6068. Reservations advised. D, MC, V.*

The Harvest. This black-and-white nouvelle American restaurant hosts a game festival in early winter that features such rarities as elk and antelope. The leafy patio (no reservations) is a good choice for an outdoor meal in summer. *44 Brattle St., Cambridge, tel. 617/492–1115. Jacket and tie advised. AE, DC, MC, V.*

★ **Restaurant Jasper.** Jasper White has acquired a national reputation for his new American cuisine. Low-key decor, spacious seating, and good service complement a respectable wine list and innovative dishes, such as salad of grilled duck with cranberries and spiced nuts, as well as a traditional New England boiled dinner. *240 Commercial St. (North End), tel. 617/523–1126. Reservations advised, required on weekends. Jacket and tie advised. D, MC, V. No lunch except Fri.; closed Sun.–Mon.*

Moderate–Expensive
Ristorante Lucia. Some aficionados consider Lucia's the best Italian restaurant in the North End. Its specialties from the Abruzzi region include batter-fried artichoke hearts as appetizer and chicken alla Lucia (chicken breast sautéed with a spicy tomato sauce). *415 Hanover St., tel. 617/523–9148. Reservations advised. AE, D, MC, V. No lunch Mon.–Thurs.*

Union Oyster House. At Boston's oldest restaurant, where Daniel Webster used to devour dozens of oysters at one sitting, the upstairs rooms are dark, low-ceilinged, and Ye-Olde-New-Englandy; the bar has a lighter feel. The food here tends to be broiled, fried, or heavy on the cream sauce, and topped with breadcrumbs. *41 Union St. (near Faneuil Hall), tel. 617/227–2750. AE, D, DC, MC, V.*

Moderate
Daily Catch. Shoulder-crowding small, this storefront restaurant specializes in calamari dishes, lobster *fra diavolo*, and linguine with clam sauce—at extremely reasonable prices. A second branch is at 261 Northern Avenue. *323 Hanover St. (North End), tel. 617/523–8567. No reservations. No credit cards.*

East Coast Grill. The specialty is New American and American (in particular, North Carolina) barbecue, plus such ethnic dishes as whole rainbow trout with Hajicki seaweed, grilled sweetbreads, or jerk chicken. The dining room is small, bright, and very busy. Lunch is takeout only. *1271 Cambridge St., Cambridge, tel. 617/491–6568. Reservations advised for parties of 5 or more Thurs.–Sun. MC, V.*

Iruna. This Spanish restaurant, popular with students for years, specializes in paellas and seafoods and has great salads. Dine outdoors on a private patio in warm weather. *56 John F. Kennedy St., Cambridge, tel. 617/868–5633. AE, D, MC, V. Closed Sun.*

★ **Legal Sea Foods.** What began as a tiny adjunct to a fish market has grown to include branches in Cambridge, Chestnut Hill, and Worcester. Whatever seafood is available each day is presented straightforwardly—raw, broiled, fried, steamed, or baked. *Boston Park Plaza Hotel, 35 Columbus Ave. (Back Bay), tel. 617/426–4444. No reservations for dinner or weekend lunch. Dress: neat but casual. AE, D, DC, MC, V.*

Inexpensive–Moderate **Durgin Park.** Opened in the 1830s, this simple upstairs hall seats diners family style, elbow to elbow. The floor is worn plank, the ceiling embossed tin, and red-checkered cloths cover the long tables. Traditional New England prime rib, pot roast, and baked beans are served in generous portions; the strawberry shortcake is mountainous. *340 Faneuil Hall Marketplace (North Market Bldg.), tel. 617/227–2038. No reservations. AE, MC, V.*

★ **Ho Yuen Ting.** A line forms nightly outside this Chinatown hole-in-the-wall. The house specialty is a sole-and-vegetable stir-fry served in a spectacular crisply fried whole fish. *13A Hudson St. (downtown), tel. 617/426–2316. Reservations only for parties of 6 or more. No credit cards.*

Lodging

Many of the city's most costly lodging places offer attractively priced weekend packages. Consult the "Boston Travel Planner" (*see* Boston for Free—or Almost, *above*) for current rates. At many hotels, children may stay free in their parents' room, or breakfast may be included in the rate.

Although Boston does not have a large number of B&Bs, there are several, with daily rates between $55 and $120 per room. Reservations may be made through **Bed and Breakfast Associates Bay Colony** (Box 57166, Babson Park Branch, Boston 02157, tel. 617/449–5302).

For price ranges, see Chart 2 (A) in Chapter 1.

Very Expensive **Boston Harbor Hotel at Rowes Wharf.** This luxury hotel provides a dramatic entryway to the city for travelers arriving from Logan Airport on the water shuttle that docks at the hotel. The guest rooms begin on the eighth floor and have city or water views; the lobby features lots of marble, and the furnishings tend toward mahogany armchairs and plush sofas. *70 Rowes Wharf, 02110, tel. 617/439–7000 or 800/752–7077. 204 rooms, 26 suites. Facilities: restaurant, health club, marina, parking. AE, DC, MC, V.*

★ **Copley Plaza.** The stately, bowfront classic among Boston hotels was built in 1912 and completely refurbished in 1989. Guest rooms have carpeting from England, custom furniture from Italy, and new bathroom fixtures surrounded by marble tile. *138 St. James Ave., 02116, tel. 617/267–5300 or 800/826–7539. 319* *rooms, 51 suites. Facilities: 2 restaurants, 2 bars. AE, DC, MC, V.*

Ritz-Carlton. Since 1927 this has been one of the most luxurious and elegant hotels in Boston. The rooms are traditionally furnished; the suites in the older section have working fireplaces and views of the Public Garden. *15 Arlington St., 02117, tel. 617/536–5700 or 800/241–3333. 230 rooms, 48 suites. Facilities: restaurant, café, 2 bars, exercise room, multilingual staff. AE, DC, MC, V.*

Expensive **Hilton.** The Hilton is the only hotel at the airport, and the airport's proximity to downtown means that the hotel is close to the action, too. The rooms are modern and soundproof. *75 Service Rd., Logan International Airport, East Boston 02128, tel. 617/569–9300 or 800/445–8667. 542 rooms. Facilities: pool, parking, airport shuttle. AE, DC, MC, V.*

★ **Lenox Hotel.** Constructed in 1900, the Lenox has a low-key elegance. In the soundproof guest rooms, the decor is Early American or Chinese on the lower floors, French Provincial on the top floor. The ornate and handsome lobby is set off by a large, welcoming fireplace. *710 Boylston St., 02116, tel. 617/536–5300 or 800/225–7676. 222 rooms. Facilities: 2 restaurants, parking. AE, DC, MC, V.*

Moderate **Cambridge House Bed and Breakfast.** This gracious old home on the National Register of Historic Places offers seven antiques-filled guest rooms and five more in its Carriage House. Convenient to the T and buses, it also serves as a reservations center for host homes in metropolitan Boston. *2218 Massachusetts Ave., 02140, tel. 617/491–6300 or 800/232–9989. 12 rooms. Facilities: parking. AE, MC, V.*

Copley Square Hotel. One of Boston's oldest hotels (1891), the Copley Square has recently undergone an extensive restoration. It is popular with Europeans and is European in flavor. The rooms, set off long, circuitous hallways, vary from very small to spacious. *47 Huntington Ave., 02116, tel. 617/536–9000 or 800/225–7062. 143 rooms. Facilities: airport limo service, coffee shop, parking. AE, DC, MC, V.*

Eliot Hotel. An ambitious renovation in 1990 and 1991 brought a new elegance and lots of marble to a formerly modest nine-floor, European-style, family-run hotel. The one- and two-bedroom suites have marble baths and period furnishings. *370 Commonwealth Ave., 02215, tel. 617/267–1607. 12 rooms, 82 suites. Facilities: bar, valet. AE, DC, MC, V.*

Inexpensive **Boston International Hostel.** At this youth-oriented hostel, guests sleep in three- to five-person dormitories and must provide their own linens or sleep sacks (sleeping bags are not permitted). The maximum stay is three nights in summer, seven nights off-season. Reservations (only members may make them) are highly recommended. *12 Hemenway St., 02115, tel. 617/536–9455. 190 beds in summer, 100 in winter. Facilities: 2 kitchens, 2 dining rooms. MC, V.*

Susse Chalet Inn. Typical of this chain, the inn is clean, economical, and sparse. It's a 10-minute drive from Harvard Square but within walking distance of the Red Line terminus, offering T access to Boston and Harvard Square. *211 Concord Turnpike, Cambridge, 02140, tel. 617/661–7800 or 800/258–1980. 79 rooms. Facilities: parking. AE, DC, MC, V.*

Motels **Best Western Homestead Inn** (220 Alewife Brook Pkwy., Cambridge 01238, tel. 617/491–8000), 69 rooms, indoor pool, whirlpool; inexpensive–moderate. **Harvard Manor House** (110 Mt. Auburn St., Cambridge 02138, tel. 617/864–5200 or 800/458–5886), 72 rooms, parking, cable TV; inexpensive. **Ramada Hotel** (225 McClellan Hwy., East Boston 02128, tel. 617/569–5250), 350 rooms, restaurant, outdoor pool, parking; moderate.

The Arts and Nightlife

Thursday's *Boston Globe* Calendar and the weekly *Boston Phoenix* provide comprehensive listings of events for the coming week.

The Arts **Bostix** (Faneuil Hall Marketplace, tel. 617/723–5181; closed major holidays) sells half-price tickets for same-day performances. **Concert Charge, TheaterCharge, SportsCharge** (tel. 617/497–1118), and **Ticketmaster** (tel. 617/931–2000) sell tickets by phone.

Theater First-rate Broadway tryout theaters are clustered in the theater district (near the intersection of Tremont and Stuart streets) and include the **Colonial,** the **Shubert,** the **Wang Center for the Performing Arts,** and the **Wilbur.** Harvard's **American Repertory Theatre** (Loeb Drama Center, 64 Brattle St., Cambridge, tel. 617/495–2668) produces classic and experimental works. **The Huntington Theatre Company** (264 Huntington Ave., tel. 617/266–3913) is affiliated with Boston University.

Music Boston's churches offer outstanding, often free music programs; check the Saturday listings in the *Globe*. **Symphony Hall** (301 Massachusetts Ave., tel. 617/266–1492) is home to the Boston Symphony Orchestra and the Boston Pops.

Opera **Opera Company of Boston** (539 Washington St., tel. 617/426–5300), under the direction of Sarah Caldwell, has become a world force in opera.

Dance **Dance Umbrella** (tel. 617/492–7578) offers information on all dance performances. The **Boston Ballet** (19 Clarendon St., tel. 617/695–6950) performs at the Wang Center.

Film **The Brattle Theater** (40 Brattle St., Cambridge, tel. 617/876–6837) is a restored landmark cinema for classic-movie buffs. **Nickelodeon Cinema** (606 Commonwealth Ave., tel. 617/424–1500) shows first-run independent and foreign films and revivals.

Nightlife **Quincy Market, Copley Square,** and **Kenmore Square** in Boston and **Harvard Square** in Cambridge are centers of nightlife.

Café and Coffeehouse **Cafe Algiers** (40 Brattle St., Cambridge, tel. 617/492–1557) is a good place for serious conversation and strong Middle Eastern coffees and teas. **Passim's** (47 Palmer St., Cambridge, tel. 617/492–7679), by day a quiet basement café, is by night a renowned coffeehouse, offering folk, bluegrass, or poetry.

Comedy **Comedy Connection at the Charles Playhouse** (76 Warrenton St., tel. 617/426–6339) features local comedians at a popular cabaret-style club in the theater district.

Jazz **Regattabar** (Bennett and Eliot Sts., tel. 617/864–1200; tickets, tel. 617/876–7777) is an elegant club in the Charles Hotel that attracts top names.

Rock **Axis** (15 Lansdowne St., tel. 617/262–2424) attracts a funky mixed crowd for dancing to urban underground music.

Excursions from Boston

Lexington and Concord The events of April 19, 1775—the first military encounters of the American War of Independence—are very much a part of present-day **Lexington** and **Concord.** These two quintessential New England towns are also rich in literary history: Concord, for example, is the site of Walden Pond, immortalized by Thoreau. Several historic houses have been preserved and can be visited; the **Visitors Center** in Lexington (1875 Massachusetts Ave., 02173, tel. 617/862–1450) and the **Concord Chamber of Commerce tourist kiosk** (Heywood St., tel. 508/369–3120) can direct you.

Getting There To reach Lexington and Concord by car from Boston, take Rte. 2A (Massachusetts Ave.) west from Cambridge, or I–95/Rte. 128 north to the Lexington exit. Rte. 2A west will take you on to Concord. Both towns are about a half-hour drive from Metropolitan Boston. The MBTA (*see* Getting Around Boston, *above*) operates buses to Lexington.

The South Shore Southeastern Massachusetts between Boston and the Cape is a region with strong historical associations. The great seafaring towns of **Fall River** and **New Bedford** offer marine museums and reminders of the area's industrial past. The **Plimoth Plantation** living-history museum (Rte. 3A, Exit 4, tel. 508/746–1622; closed Dec.–Mar.) re-creates the Pilgrims' 1627 village. At the waterfront is the *Mayflower II,* an exact replica of the ship that brought the Pilgrims over from England, and nearby is **Plymouth Rock,** believed to be the very spot on which they first set foot in 1620 after unsuccessfully scouting the Provincetown area as a potential settlement.

Getting There The most direct way to Fall River and New Bedford (themselves connected by I–195) is via Rte. 24N, about a 45-minute drive; I–93 and Rte. 3 connect Boston with Plymouth, which is about an hour's drive. From Boston, the **American Eagle** bus line (tel. 508/993–5040) provides service to New Bedford and **H&L Bloom Bus** (tel. 508/822–1991) serves Fall River; **Plymouth & Brockton Street Railway** (tel. 508/746–0378) calls at Plymouth en route to Cape Cod.

The North Shore The North Shore extends from northern suburbs to the Cape Ann region and beyond to the New Hampshire border. It takes in **Salem,** which thrives on a history of witches, millionaires, and maritime trade; **Rockport,** crammed with crafts shops and artists' studios; **Gloucester,** the oldest seaport in America; and **Newburyport,** with its redbrick center and rows of clapboard Federal mansions. For information, contact the **North of Boston Tourist Council** (13 Washington Sq., Salem 01970, tel. 508/ 745–2268).

Getting There Boston to Gloucester is about 40 mi. The primary link between Boston and the North Shore is I–93 north to Rte. 128 east, which then follows the line of the coast just inland as far north as Gloucester. The more scenic route is along coastal Rte. 1A (which leaves Boston via the Callahan Tunnel) to Rte. 127.

Cape Cod and the Islands

Separated from the "mainland" by the 17.4-mi Cape Cod Canal, the Cape curves 70 mi from end to end. Its charming villages of weathered-shingle houses and white steepled churches, as well as its pine woods, grassy marshes, and beaches backed by rolling dunes, attract crowds every summer. To the south, Martha's Vineyard and Nantucket are resort islands ringed with beautiful sandy beaches, and Nantucket preserves a near-pristine whaling-era town.

Tourist Information

Cape Cod: Chamber of Commerce (junction of Rtes. 6 and 132, Hyannis 02601, tel. 508/362–3225. Information booths: Sagamore Bridge Rotary, tel. 508/888–2438; Bourne Bridge on Rte. 28, tel. 508/759–3814). **Martha's Vineyard:** Chamber of Commerce (Box 1698, Beach Rd., Vineyard Haven 02568, tel. 508/693–0085). **Nantucket:** Chamber of Commerce (Pacific Club, Main St., Nantucket 02554, tel. 508/228–1700).

Getting There

By Plane **Barnstable Municipal Airport,** in Hyannis, is served by Business Express/Delta Connection, and Cape Air (tel. 800/352–0714). The latter also serves **Provincetown Municipal Airport, Martha's Vineyard Airport,** and **Nantucket Memorial Airport,** which is also served by Business Express and Northwest Airlink.

By Car From Boston take I–93S to Rte. 3S to the Sagamore Bridge. From New York take I–95N to Providence; change to I–195E and follow signs to the Cape.

Ferries connect Martha's Vineyard and Nantucket to the mainland from New Bedford, Falmouth, Woods Hole, and Hyannis. The **Steamship Authority** (tel. 508/540–2022), **Hy-Line Cruises** (tel. 508/778–2600), and the *Island Queen* (tel. 508/548–4800) serve Martha's Vineyard; the Steamship Authority and Hy-Line serve Nantucket.

By Train **Amtrak** offers limited service in summer to Hyannis, with bus connections to Woods Hole.

By Bus **Plymouth & Brockton Street Railway** (tel. 508/775–7588 or 800/746–0378 in MA) has service from Boston and Logan Airport. **Bonanza** (tel. 508/548–7588 or 800/556–3815) connects Bourne, Falmouth, Woods Hole, and Hyannis with New York and points between.

Exploring Cape Cod and the Islands

U.S. 6, the Mid-Cape Highway, traverses the relatively unpopulated center of the Cape. Paralleling U.S. 6 but following the north coast is Rte. 6A, the Old King's Highway, which passes through some of the Cape's best-preserved old New England towns. The south shore, traced by Rte. 28, is heavily populated and the major center for tourism, encompassing Falmouth, Hyannis, and Chatham. The sparse outer portion of the Cape, from Orleans to Provincetown, is edged with white-sand beaches and nature preserves. At the Cape's southwestern cor-

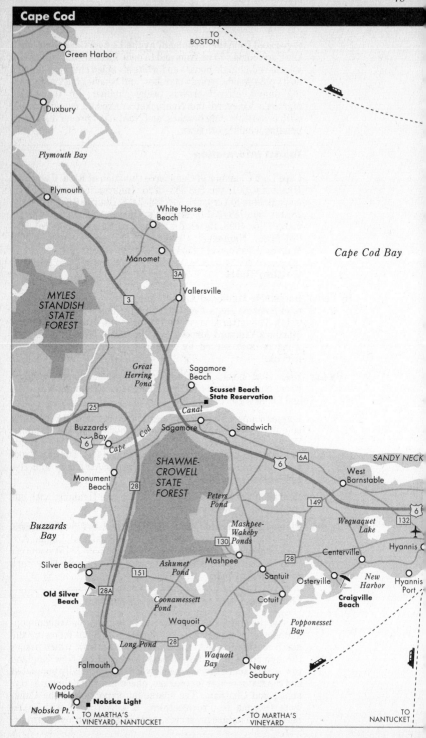

Cape Cod

TO BOSTON

Green Harbor

Duxbury

Plymouth Bay

Plymouth

White Horse Beach

Manomet

3A

Vallersville

Cape Cod Bay

MYLES STANDISH STATE FOREST

3

Great Herring Pond

Sagamore Beach

Scusset Beach State Reservation

25

Canal

Buzzards Bay

6

Cape Cod

Sagamore

Sandwich

SANDY NECK

SHAWME-CROWELL STATE FOREST

6A

6

West Barnstable

Monument Beach

28

Peters Pond

149

132

6

Buzzards Bay

Mashpee-Wakeby Ponds

Wequaquet Lake

Hyannis

130

Centerville

Silver Beach

151

Ashumet Pond

Mashpee

28

Santuit

Osterville

New Harbor

Hyannis Port

Old Silver Beach

28A

Coonamessett Pond

Cotuit

Craigville Beach

Waquoit

28

Long Pond

Waquoit Bay

New Seabury

Popponesset Bay

Falmouth

Woods Hole

Nobska Light

Nobska Pt.

TO MARTHA'S VINEYARD, NANTUCKET

TO MARTHA'S VINEYARD

TO NANTUCKET

0   6 miles

0   9 km

N

Provincetown

6A

Beach
Point

North
Truro

CAPE

COD

Truro

6

Wellfleet

NATIONAL

South
Wellfleet

*Wellfleet
Harbor*

SEASHORE

North
Eastham

Eastham

**Coast Guard
Beach**

Rock
Harbor

East
Brewster

6

Orleans

**Nauset
Beach**

Brewster

28

NICKERSON
STATE PARK

Dennis

6A

124

39

*Pleasant
Bay*

Yarmouth

134

Barnstable

6

Harwich

39

137

Chatham

South
Yarmouth

Bass R.

Harwich Port

28

28

West
Dennis

*Monomoy
Island*

Nantucket Sound

ner is **Woods Hole,** an international center for marine research. The **Marine Biological Laboratory** (tel. 508/548–3705, ext. 423) offers tours by reservation, or you can visit the **Woods Hole Oceanographic Institute Exhibit Center** (15 School St., tel. 508/457–2000, ext. 2663). Before leaving Woods Hole, stop at **Nobska Light** for a great view of the Elizabeth Islands and the sea beyond.

Ferries connect Woods Hole with **Martha's Vineyard** year-round (in summer, boats also leave from Hyannis, Falmouth, and New Bedford). On the island, the town of **Oak Bluffs** has a warren of some 300 candy-colored Victorian cottages. The main port of **Vineyard Haven** has a street of shops and a back street preserved from whaling days. Tidy and polished **Edgartown** has upscale boutiques, elegant sea-captains' houses, flower gardens, and a ferry to **Chappaquiddick Island,** laced with nature preserves. Rural **West Tisbury** and **Chilmark** offer good biking past sheep, llama, and other farms. The dramatically striated red-clay **Gay Head Cliffs,** the major tourist site, lie in a Wampanoag Indian township on the island's western tip.

Back on Cape Cod, the village green in **Falmouth,** a military training field in the 18th century, is today flanked by attractive old homes, some fine inns, and the **Congregational Church,** with a bell made by Paul Revere. The Falmouth Historical Society (Palmer Ave. at the Village Green, tel. 508/548–4857) maintains two museums and conducts free walking tours of the town in season.

Quietly wealthy **Hyannis Port** is the site of the **Kennedy family compound.** In **Hyannis,** the Cape's year-round commercial hub, the first stage of a projected **John F. Kennedy Memorial Museum**—an exhibit of photographs from the presidential years focusing on JFK's ties to the Cape—has been set up at the Old Town Hall on busy Main Street (tel. 508/775–2201).

From Hyannis, ferries travel year-round to **Nantucket,** 30 mi out in the open Atlantic Ocean. **Nantucket town,** an exquisitely preserved National Historic District, encapsulates the island's whaling past in over a dozen historical museums along its cobblestone streets. The beach community of **Siasconset** began as an actors' colony and today offers a peaceful, unhurried lifestyle in beautiful surroundings including tiny rose-covered cottages and white-clamshell drives. Most of the 12- by 3-mi island is covered with moors, scented with bayberry, wild roses, and cranberries; ringing it are miles of clean, white-sand beaches.

At the southeast tip of Cape Cod, **Chatham** is a seaside town relatively free of the development and commercialism found elsewhere, though offering a downtown of traditional shops and fine inns. The view from **Chatham Lighthouse** is spectacular.

At the beginning of the Cape's north shore is **Sandwich,** founded in 1637. This picturesque town, centered by a pond with a waterwheel-powered gristmill, remains famous for the colored glass produced here in the 19th century. A large collection is exhibited at the **Sandwich Glass Museum** (129 Main St., tel. 508/888–0251). Nearby are the **Hoxie House** (Rte. 130, tel. 508/888–1173), a restored 1637 saltbox unique in that it was never modernized, and **Yesteryears Doll Museum** (143 Main St., tel. 508/888–1711).

Off Rte. 130 is **Heritage Plantation,** a complex of museum buildings displaying classic and historic cars, antique military-re-
lated items, Currier & Ives prints, and other Americana—all
set amid extensive gardens. *Grove and Pine Sts., Sandwich,
tel. 508/888–3300. Admission charged. Closed Nov.–mid-
May.*

East on Rte. 6A, past fine views of meadows and the bay, is
Barnstable, a lovely town of large old houses. In **Yarmouth,
Hallet's Store,** a working drugstore and soda fountain, is preserved as it was 100 years ago. In **Dennis** is **Scargo Hill,** offering
a spectacular view of Cape Cod Bay and Scargo Lake, below.

Brewster has numerous mansions built for sea captains in the
1800s. The **Cape Cod Museum of Natural History** has environmental and marine exhibits and trails through 80 acres rich in
wildlife. *Rte. 6A, Brewster, tel. 508/896–3867. Admission
charged. Closed Mon. mid-Oct.–mid-Apr.*

Nauset Beach in **Orleans** begins a virtually unbroken stretch of
sand extending to Provincetown. The **Cape Cod National Seashore** preserves 30 mi of it, including superb beaches and lighthouses. Just past **Eastham** off U.S. 6, the national seashore's
Salt Pond Visitor Center (tel. 508/255–3421; closed weekdays
Jan.–mid-Feb.) offers displays, tours, lectures, and films.

Wellfleet was a Colonial whaling and codfishing port and is now
home to fishermen, artists, and craftsmen. At the national seashore's **Pilgrim Heights Area,** trails take you through terrain
the *Mayflower* crew explored before moving on to Plymouth.

The national seashore's **Province Lands** (visitor center, tel. 508/
487–1256; closed Jan.–Mar.) embrace **Provincetown's** spectacular beaches and dunes, as well as walking, biking, and horse
trails. In the town, which is filled with first-rate shops and galleries, Portuguese and American fishermen mix with painters,
poets, writers, whale-watchers, and, especially in high season,
a large gay and lesbian community. The **Pilgrim Monument and
Provincetown Museum,** on a hill above the town center, commemorates the landing of the Pilgrims in 1620. From atop the
252-foot tower you have a panoramic view of the entire Cape.
High Pole Hill, tel. 508/487–1310. Admission charged.

What to See and Do with Children

Aqua Circus of Cape Cod (Rte. 28, West Yarmouth, tel. 508/
775–8883) offers dolphin and sea-lion shows, a petting zoo,
pony rides, and aquariums. **Bassett Wild Animal Farm** (Tub-
man Rd., between Rtes. 124 and 137, Brewster, tel. 508/896–
3224; closed mid-Sept.–mid-May) has tigers, birds, and more
on 20 acres, plus hayrides and pony rides. In Martha's Vineyard's Oak Bluffs, the historic **Flying Horses Carousel** (tel. 508/
693–9481; closed in winter) delights youngsters.

Shopping

Provincetown has many fine galleries, and **Wellfleet** has
emerged as a vibrant center for art and crafts, as well as hosting a giant **flea market** (U.S. 6, Eastham-Wellfleet town line,
tel. 508/349–2520; weekends Apr.–Oct., also Wed.–Thurs.
July–Aug.). **Hyannis's** Main Street is lined with shops of every
sort. **Chatham's** Main Street has upscale and conservative mer-

chandise, and a few good antiques shops. **Cape Cod Mall** (Rte.
132, Hyannis, tel. 508/771–0200) is the Cape's largest, with 95
shops.

Edgartown is the Vineyard's chief shopping town, with the island's only department store, as well as antiques and crafts
shops. **Nantucket's** specialty is lightship baskets—expensive
woven baskets, often decorated with scrimshaw or rosewood.

Sports and Outdoor Activities

Biking   **Cape Cod Rail Trail,** a 20-mi paved railroad right-of-way from
Dennis to Eastham, is the Cape's premier bike path. On either
side of the **Cape Cod Canal** is an easy 7-mi straight trail. The
Cape Cod National Seashore and **Nickerson State Park** also
maintain bicycle trails.

Fishing   Tuna, mako and blue sharks, swordfish, bluefish, bass, and
marlin are the main ocean catches. The necessary license to fish
the Cape's freshwater ponds is available at tackle shops, such
as **Eastman's Sport & Tackle** (150 Main St., Falmouth, tel. 508/
548–6900) and **Truman's** (Rte. 28, West Yarmouth, tel. 508/
771–3470), which rent gear. Rental boats are available from
Cape Cod Boats (Rte. 28 at Bass River Bridge, West Dennis,
tel. 508/394–9268).

Deep-sea fishing trips are operated by **Cap'n Bill & Cee Jay**
(MacMillan Wharf, Provincetown, tel. 508/487–4330), **Hy-Line**
(Ocean St. Dock, Hyannis, tel. 508/778–2600), and **Patriot Par-
ty Boats** (Falmouth Harbor, tel. 508/548–2626). On Martha's
Vineyard, the party boat *Skipper* (tel. 508/693–1238) leaves
from Oak Bluffs Harbor. On Nantucket, charters sail out of
Straight Wharf.

Horseback Riding   **Deer Meadow Riding Stables** (Rte. 137, East Harwich, tel. 508/
432–6580). **Haland Stables** (Rte. 28A, West Falmouth, tel. 508/
540–2552). **Misty Meadows Horse Farm** (Old County Rd., West
Tisbury, Martha's Vineyard, tel. 508/693–1870). **Martha's
Vineyard Riding Center** (across from airport, off Edgartown
Rd., West Tisbury, tel. 508/693–3770).

Sailing and   **Arey's Pond Boat Yard** (off Rte. 28, Orleans, tel. 508/255–0994)
Water Sports   has a sailing school. **Cape Water Sports** (tel. 508/432–7079) has
locations on several beaches for sailboat, canoe, and other rentals and lessons. Lessons and rentals are available at **Wind's
Up!** (Beach Rd., Vineyard Haven, tel. 508/693–4252) on
Martha's Vineyard and at **Force 5** (Jetties Beach, tel. 508/228–
5358; Main St., tel. 508/228–0700) on Nantucket.

Beaches

Beaches fronting on **Cape Cod Bay** generally have cold water
and gentle waves. Southside beaches, on **Nantucket Sound,**
have rolling surf and are warmer. Open-ocean beaches on the
Cape Cod National Seashore have serious surf, are contiguous,
and have lifeguards and rest rooms. In summer, parking lots
can be full by 10 AM.

Dining and Lodging

Hearty meat-and-potatoes fare is the cuisine of choice on the
Cape, along with the ubiquitous New England clam chowder

and fresh fish and seafood. Extraordinary gourmet restaurants can be found—on Rte. 6A in Brewster and on Nantucket especially—along with occasional ethnic specialties. On Martha's Vineyard only Edgartown and Oak Bluffs allow the sale of liquor.

For summer, lodgings should be booked as far in advance as possible. Assistance with last-minute reservations is available from the Cape Cod and island chambers of commerce (*see* Tourist Information, *above*). Off-season rates are much reduced, and service may be more personalized. The rates for many inns include full breakfast.

B&B reservations services include **House Guests Cape Cod and the Islands** (Box 1881, Orleans 02653, tel. 800/666–4678) and **Bed and Breakfast Cape Cod** (Box 341, West Hyannis Port 02672, tel. 508/775–2772). **Provincetown Reservations System** (293 Commercial St., Provincetown 02657, tel. 508/487–2400 or 800/648–0364) makes reservations for accommodations and more. **Martha's Vineyard and Nantucket Reservations** (Box 1322, Lagoon Pond Rd., Vineyard Haven 02568, tel. 508/693–7200) and **Accommodations Plus** (RFD 273, Edgartown 02539, tel. 508/627–7374) book B&Bs, hotels, and cottages.

For price ranges, see Charts 1 (A) and 2 (A) in Chapter 1.

Brewster
Dining
★
Chillingsworth. The Cape's best restaurant, this elegant and elaborately decorated spot offers award-winning French and nouvelle cuisine and an outstanding wine cellar. The changing dinner menu features such entrées as venison with celery-root puree and fried pumpkin. *Rte. 6A, tel. 508/896–3640. Reservations required. Jacket advised at dinner. Closed Thanksgiving–Memorial Day; also some weekdays (call). AE, DC, MC, V. Very Expensive.*

Lodging
Captain Freeman Inn. This 1866 Victorian has 12-foot ceilings and windows and a spacious wraparound veranda. Guest rooms feature antiques; suites include fireplaces and porches with private spas. A fitness room is planned for '94. *15 Breakwater Rd., Brewster 02631, tel. 508/896–7481. 12 rooms (3 share a bath). Facilities: full breakfast, heated pool, bikes. AE, MC, V. No smoking. Moderate–Expensive.*

Chatham
Lodging
★
Captain's House Inn. This inn's tasteful Colonial decor and quiet comfort makes it one of the Cape's finest. Each room of the three buildings has its own distinct personality; the Hiram Harding Room has 200-year-old hand-hewn ceiling beams, a wall of raised walnut paneling, a working fireplace, and a rich red Oriental carpet. *371 Old Harbor Rd., 02633, tel. 508/945–0127. 16 rooms. Facilities: Continental breakfast, afternoon tea. No smoking. AE, MC, V. Closed mid-Nov.–mid-Feb. Expensive–Very Expensive.*

Dining and Lodging
★
Chatham Bars Inn. An oceanfront resort in the old style (MAP available), this renovated Chatham landmark comprises the main building—with its grand lobby—and cottages on 20 landscaped acres. Many rooms have private porches, some with lovely ocean views. *Shore Rd., 02633, tel. 508/945–0096 or 800/527–4884. 152 rooms, 26 cottages. Facilities: 3 restaurants, private beach, 4 tennis courts, pool, children's program. AE, DC, MC, V. Very Expensive.*

Falmouth
Lodging
Mostly Hall. Set in a landscaped yard, this imposing 1849 house has a wraparound porch and a cupola. Corner rooms have leafy

views, reading areas, antique pieces, and reproduction canopy
beds. Full breakfasts are complimentary and delicious. *27
Main St., 02540, tel. 508/548–3786. 6 rooms. MC, V. No smoking. Closed Jan.–mid-Feb. Moderate.*

Hyannis
Dining

Three Thirty One Main. This sophisticated northern Italian
restaurant focuses on seafood and homemade pastas. A signature dish is the veal chops Pasetto, stuffed with prosciutto and
Fontina, lightly breaded, panfried, and served with a sauce of
shallots, capers, prosciutto, and fresh tomatoes. On the walls,
mirrors alternate with warm wood paneling and exposed brick.
*331 Main St., Hyannis, tel. 508/775–2023. Reservations ad-
vised. Dress: neat but casual. AE, DC, MC, V. No lunch weekends. Moderate–Expensive.*

Lodging

Tara Hyannis Hotel & Resort. It's hard to beat the Tara's combination of landscaping, services, resort facilities, and location.
Although the lobby is elegant, the rooms are bland, with pale
colors and nondescript furnishings. All rooms have color TV
and a private balcony or patio. *West End Circle, 02601, tel. 508/
775–7775 or 800/843–8272. 224 rooms. Facilities: restaurant, 2
pools, tennis, health club (fee), children's programs. AE, D,
DC, MC, V. Expensive.*

Capt. Gosnold Village. An easy walk to the beach and town, this
colony of motel rooms and cottages is ideal for families. The decor ranges from light and airy new to pine and Colonial reproductions. *Gosnold St., 02601, tel. 508/775–9111. 8 motel rooms,
18 cottage units. Facilities: pool, playground. MC, V. Closed
Nov.–Apr. Moderate.*

Provincetown
Dining
★

Ciro and Sal's. After 30 years, this stage-set Italian
restaurant—raffia-covered Chianti bottles hanging from the
rafters, Italian opera in the air—is still a star. Veal and pasta
dishes are specialties. *4 Kiley Ct., tel. 508/487–0049. Reservations required in summer; Sat. dinner. MC, V. Closed
Mon.–Thurs. Christmas–Memorial Day. Moderate–Expensive.*

Lodging

Hargood House. This apartment complex on the water a walk
from the town center is a great option for longer stays and families. Most units have decks and large water-view windows; all
have kitchens and modern baths. *493 Commercial St., 02657,
tel. 508/487–9133. 19 apartments. Facilities: private beach.
AE, MC, V. Expensive.*

Martha's Vineyard
Dining

Black Dog Tavern. This island landmark serves basic chowders,
pastas, fish, and steak, as well as more elaborate dishes. The
glassed-in porch, lighted by ship's lanterns, looks onto the harbor. *Beach St. Ext., Vineyard Haven, tel. 508/693–9223. No
reservations. BYOB. AE, D, MC, V. Inexpensive–Expensive.*

Lodging
★

The Charlotte Inn. The original 1865 house has grown into a
complex of meticulously maintained accommodations and the
excellent L'étoile restaurant. The inn is exquisitely furnished
with English antiques, and artwork hangs in the hallways.
Some rooms have fireplaces, some porches or verandas. *27 S.
Summer St., 02539, tel. 508/627–4751. 26 rooms. Facilities:
Continental breakfast, restaurant, art gallery, gift shop. AE,
MC, V. Very Expensive.*

Nantucket
Dining
★

The Brotherhood of Thieves. Long queues are a fixture outside
this very old-English pub restaurant. Much of the seating is at
long, tightly packed tables where you can dine on good chowder

and soups, fried fish and seafood, and burgers. *23 Broad St., no tel. No reservations. No credit cards. Moderate.*

★ **Chanticleer.** Within this rose-covered cottage is what may be the best restaurant on the island. For more than 20 years Jean-Charles Berruet has created classic French fare, such as sautéed boneless loin of lamb with port-and-tarragon sauce, and grilled sea bass with roasted peppers and aïoli. The meals are complemented by the award-winning wine list. The main dining room is formal, with pearl-gray and faux-marble walls, a fireplace, and a garden view. Upstairs is more casual, and lunch in the rose garden is heavenly. *9 New St., Siasconset, tel. 508/ 257–6231. Reservations required, well in advance for dinner. Jacket required at dinner. AE, MC, V. Closed Wed. and Columbus Day–Mother's Day. Very Expensive.*

Lodging **White Elephant.** This hotel is right on the harbor. Rooms in the
★ Breakers, the hotel's ultraluxury arm, open onto private harborfront decks. Main-inn rooms are done in English country style, with stenciled-pine armoires and florals. *Easton St., Box 359, Nantucket 02554, tel. 508/228–2500 or 800/475–2637. 48 rooms, 32 cottages. Facilities: restaurant, lounge, heated outdoor pool, putting green, concierge, room service, business services, boat slips. AE, D, DC, MC, V. Closed mid-Sept.–May. Very Expensive.*

Campgrounds **Nickerson State Park** (Rte. 6A, Brewster 02631, tel. 508/896–3491), 420 sites, hot showers, convenience store, trails (walking, biking, jogging), fishing, boating, swimming, cross-country skiing (*see also* National and State Parks, *above*). **Shawme-Crowell State Forest** (Rte. 130, Sandwich, tel. 508/ 888–0351), 260 campsites, showers, interpretive programs, walking trails, day use of nearby beach.

The Arts and Nightlife

The Arts The Equity **Cape Playhouse** (Rte. 6A, Dennis, tel. 508/385–3911) and the **Falmouth Playhouse** (off Rte. 151, North Falmouth, tel. 508/563–5922) present summer stock. The **Vineyard Playhouse** (10 Church St., Vineyard Haven, tel. 508/693–6450) offers Broadway-vintage works year-round and summer Shakespeare. **Actor's Theatre of Nantucket** (Folger Hotel, 89 Easton St., tel. 508/228–6325) presents several plays each summer, including children's matinees.

Nightlife The Cape has all manner of nightlife, from the rowdiest college-crowd clubs to quiet folky coffeehouses, from Irish and country bars to ballrooms. Hyannis has the busiest, with many nightclubs and bars featuring live rock and jazz (Jazz Hot Line: tel. 508/394–5277). Oak Bluffs is the center of Vineyard nightlife, with rowdy bars and a year-round dance club. Nantucket town offers rock clubs, as well as restaurants with sedate piano bars or rocking live bands. For listings of events, see local papers.

The Berkshires

Though only about a 2½-hour drive west from Boston or north from New York City, the Berkshires lives up to storybook images of rural New England, with wooded hills, narrow winding roads, and compact charming villages. Summer offers a variety of cultural events, not the least of which is the Tanglewood classical-music festival in Lenox. Fall brings a blaze of brilliant foliage. In winter, the Berkshires is a popular ski area. Springtime visitors can enjoy maple-sugaring. The region can be crowded any weekend.

Tourist Information

Mohawk Trail Association (Box 722, Charlemont 01339, tel. 413/664–6256). **Berkshire Hills Visitor's Bureau** (Berkshire Common Plaza, Pittsfield 01201, tel. 413/443–9186 or 800/237–5747). **Lenox:** Chamber of Commerce (Lenox Academy Bldg., 75 Main St., 01240, tel. 413/637–3646 or 800/255–3669).

Getting There

By Plane The closest airports are in Boston (*see* Boston, *above*); Albany and New York City (*see* New York, *below*); and Hartford (*see* Connecticut, *above*). Small airports in Pittsfield and Great Barrington serve private planes.

By Car The Massachusetts Turnpike (I–90) connects Boston with Lee and Stockbridge. The scenic Mohawk Trail (Rte. 2) parallels the northern border of Massachusetts. To reach the Berkshires from New York City, take either the New York Thruway (I–87) or the Taconic State Parkway. Within the Berkshires the main north–south road is Rte. 7.

By Bus **Peter Pan Bus Lines** serves Lee (tel. 413/243–0135) and Pittsfield (tel. 413/442–4451) from Boston and Albany. **Bonanza Bus Lines** (tel. 800/343–9330) connects the Berkshires with Albany, New York City, and Providence.

Exploring the Berkshires

Williamstown is the northernmost Berkshires town, at the junction of Rte. 2 and U.S. 7. Williams College opened here in 1793, and the town still revolves around it. Gracious campus buildings lining the wide main street are open to visitors.

Formerly a private collection, the **Sterling and Francine Clark Art Institute** is now an outstanding small museum, featuring paintings by Renoir, Monet, and Degas. *225 South St., Williamstown, tel. 413/458–9545. Admission free. Closed Mon., Thanksgiving, Christmas, and New Year's Day.*

For a fine scenic drive (especially in autumn), head east on the **Mohawk Trail**, a 63-mi stretch of Rte. 2 that follows a former Native American path from Williamstown. The first stop is **North Adams.** Once a railroad and industrial boomtown, North Adams is home to the **Western Gateway Heritage State Park** (tel. 413/663–6312), which exhibits photographs and artifacts of the town's industrial history in a restored freightyard and warehouse.

South of Williamstown off Rte. 7 is **Mt. Greylock**, at 3,491 feet the highest point in the state. **Pittsfield,** county seat and geographic center of the region, has a lively small-town atmosphere. In 1850, outside of town, Herman Melville purchased a house he named **Arrowhead** (780 Holmes Rd., tel. 413/442–1793). The house, including the writer's desk, personal effects, and whaling trinkets, is open on a limited basis. In town, at the **Berkshire Athenaeum** (Pittsfield Public Library, 1 Wendell

Ave.), the **Herman Melville Memorial Room** (tel. 413/499–9486) houses memorabilia of the author of *Moby-Dick*.

Hancock Shaker Village, 5 mi west of Pittsfield on Rte. 20, was founded in the 1790s as the third Shaker community in America. The religious community closed in 1960, and the site, complete with living quarters, round stone barn, and working crafts shops, is now a museum. *Tel. 413/443–0188. Admission charged. Closed Dec.–Mar.*

South of Pittsfield 5 mi on Rte. 7, the village of **Lenox** epitomizes the Berkshires for many visitors. In the thick of the "summer cottage" region, it's rich with old inns and majestic mansions, including **The Mount,** summer home of novelist Edith Wharton, and now the site of outdoor theater. *Plunkett St., tel. 413/637–1899. Admission charged. Closed Nov.–Apr.*

Outside the village is **Tanglewood,** summer headquarters of the Boston Symphony. Thousands flock to the 200-acre estate every summer weekend to picnic on the lawns as musicians perform on the open-air stage (*see* The Arts, *below*).

The archetypal New England small town of **Stockbridge** has a history of literary and artistic inhabitants, including the painter Norman Rockwell and the writers Norman Mailer and Robert Sherwood. The town's **Norman Rockwell Museum** (tel. 413/298–4100) boasts the world's largest collection of his original paintings. Nearby is **Chesterwood,** for 33 years the summer home of Daniel Chester French, best known for his statues of the Minute Man in Concord and of Abraham Lincoln at the Lincoln Memorial in Washington, D.C. *Williamsville Rd. (off Rte. 183), tel. 413/298–3579. Admission charged. Closed Nov.–Apr. except Veteran's Day weekend (special programs).*

Great Barrington is the largest town in the southern Berkshires and a mecca for antiques hunters.

What to See and Do with Children

The **Jiminy Peak** ski resort (Corey Rd., Hancock 01237, tel. 413/738–5500) offers an alpine slide and trout fishing in summer. **The Robbins-Zust Family Marionettes** (East Rd., Richmond, tel. 413/698–2591) perform puppet shows in summer.

Shopping

Antiques   There are antiques stores throughout the Berkshires, but the greatest concentration is around Great Barrington, South Egremont, and Sheffield. For a list of storekeepers who belong to the **Berkshire County Antiques Dealers Association** and guarantee the authenticity of their merchandise, send a self-addressed, stamped envelope to RD 1, Box 1, Sheffield 01257.

Outlet Stores   Along Rte. 7 just north of Lenox are two factory-outlet malls, **Lenox House Country Shops** and **Brushwood Farms.** A number of outlet stores are concentrated at **The Buggy Whip Factory** (tel. 413/229–3576), some distance from the main tourist routes, on Rte. 272 in Southfield.

Sports and Outdoor Activities

Biking   The back roads of Berkshire County can be hilly, but the views and the countryside are incomparable. Bikes can be rented from **Plaine's Cycling Center** (55 W. Housatonic St., Pittsfield, tel. 413/499–0294).

Boating and Canoeing The **Housatonic River** flows south from Pittsfield between the Berkshire hills and the Taconic range toward Connecticut. Canoes and boats can be rented from the **Onota Boat Livery** (455 Pecks Rd., Pittsfield, tel. 413/442–1724) on Onota Lake.

Fishing The area's rivers, lakes, and streams abound with bass, pike, perch, and trout. **Points North Fishing and Hunting Outfitters** (Rte. 8, Adams, tel. 413/743–4030) organizes summer fly-fishing schools.

Golf Golf equipment can be rented from **Plaine's Cycling Center** (55 W. Housatonic St., Pittsfield, tel. 413/499–0294). **Greenock Country Club** (W. Park St., Lee, tel. 413/243–3323) has a nine-hole course; **Pontoosuc Lake Country Club** (Kirkwood Dr., Pittsfield, tel. 413/445–4217) and **Waubeeka Golf Links** (Rte. 7, Williamstown, tel. 413/458–5869) have 18-hole courses.

Hiking The **Appalachian Trail** goes through Berkshire County. Hiking is particularly rewarding in the higher elevations of **Mt. Greylock State Reservation** (*see* National and State Parks, *above*).

Ski Areas

Cross-country **Brodie** (Rte. 7, New Ashford 01237, tel. 413/443–4752 or 413/443–6597) has 16 mi of trails. **Butternut Basin** (Rte. 23, Great Barrington 01230, tel. 413/528–2000) has 4 mi of groomed trails.

Downhill **Berkshire East** (S. River Rd., Charlemont 01339, tel. 413/339–6617) has a 1,200-foot vertical drop, 25 trails, four double chair lifts, and two surface lifts. **Bousquet Ski Area** (Tamarack Rd., Pittsfield 01201, tel. 413/442–8316 or 413/442–2436) has a 750-foot drop, 21 trails, two double chair lifts, and two surface lifts. **Brodie** (*see* Cross-country, *above*) has a 1,250-foot drop, 26 trails, four double chair lifts, and two surface lifts. **Butternut Basin** (*see* Cross-country, *above*) has a 1,000-foot drop, 22 trails, one triple and five double chair lifts, and one surface lift. **Jiminy Peak** (*see* What to See and Do with Children, *above*) has a 1,140-foot drop, 24 trails, one quad, one triple, and three double chair lifts, and one surface lift.

Dining and Lodging

Lodging rates may include full or Continental breakfast. For price ranges, see Charts 1 (B) and 2 (B) in Chapter 1.

Great Barrington **Boiler Room Café.** In a turn-of-the-century clapboard house, *Dining* three comfortable dining rooms are painted in warm colors ac-
★ cented by arches with white moldings and whimsical wood sculptures. The eclectic, sophisticated menu may include delicious, light New England seafood stew, mouthwatering grilled baby back ribs, or osso buco Piedmontese. Desserts range from straightforward cherry pie to complex pecan tart. *405 Stockbridge Rd., tel. 413/528–4280. Reservations advised. Dress: casual. MC, V. Closed Mon., Tues. Expensive.*

20 Railroad St. The exposed brick and subdued lighting lend atmosphere to this bustling restaurant, which features a 28-foot-long mahogany bar. Specialties include sausage pie, burgers, and sandwiches. *20 Railroad St., tel. 413/528–9345. MC, V. Inexpensive.*

Lee
Lodging

The Morgan House. Most guest rooms at this inn, which dates to 1817, are small, but the rates reflect that. The furniture is Colonial style; some rooms have four-poster beds and stenciled walls. The lobby is papered with pages from old guest registers; among the signatures are those of George Bernard Shaw and Ulysses S. Grant. *31 Main St., 01238, tel. 413/243–0181. 14 rooms (12 share baths). Facilities: 3 dining rooms, bar. AE, D, DC, MC, V. Inexpensive.*

Lenox
Dining

Gateways Inn. Four dining rooms are hung with chandeliers and tapestries; working fireplaces soften the formal tone. Continental and American cuisine includes veal, pheasant, salmon, and rack of lamb. *71 Walker St., tel. 413/637–2532. Reservations advised. Dress: neat but casual. AE, D, DC, MC, V. Closed Sun. Nov.–May. Expensive.*

Church St. Cafe. In this popular restaurant, the walls are covered with original artwork, tables are surrounded by ficus trees, and classical music plays in the background. Specialties include roast duckling with thyme and Madeira sauce, and crab cakes. *69 Church St., tel. 413/637–2745. MC, V. Closed Sun.–Mon. Oct.–May. Moderate.*

Lodging

Blantyre. The castlelike Tudor architecture, vast public rooms, and 85 acres of beautiful grounds are impressive enough, but the guest rooms in the main house are also fabulous: huge and lavishly decorated. The stylishly prepared, five-course evening meal is wonderful. *Box 995, 01240, tel. 413/637–3556 or 413/298–3806. 13 rooms, 10 suites. Facilities: restaurant, pool, 4 tennis courts. AE, DC, MC, V. Expensive.*

Eastover. This resort was opened by an ex-circus roustabout, and the tradition of noisy fun and informality continues. Guest rooms are functional and vary only slightly from dormitory to motel style. Nondescript but comfortable decor and furnishings temper the informality of the vast dining rooms. *East St. (off Rte. 7), Box 2160, 01240, tel. 413/637–0625. 165 rooms (45 share baths). Facilities: dining rooms (breakfast and dinner), 6 tennis courts, 2 pools, exercise room, skiing, canoeing, dancing, local transport, horseback riding. AE, D, DC, MC, V. Closed weekdays Sept.–May. Moderate.*

Pittsfield Area
Dining

Dakota. Moose and elk heads eye diners at this large restaurant with a rustic hunting-lodge atmosphere. A broiler stocked with Texas mesquite wood is used for swordfish, shrimp, sirloin, and chicken. *Rtes. 7 and 20, tel. 413/499–7900. AE, DC, MC, V. No lunch Mon.–Sat. Moderate.*

Lodging

Berkshire Hilton Inn. A spacious hall features wing chairs, glass, and brass. Guest rooms have reproduction furnishings and floral-print drapes; rooms on the top floors have the best views over the town and surrounding mountains. *Berkshire Common, South St., 01201, tel. 413/499–2000 or 800/445–8667. 175 rooms. Facilities: restaurant, pool, sauna, whirlpool. AE, DC, MC, V. Expensive.*

Dalton House. This B&B, built in the 1800s, has a sunny dining room with pine furniture and cheerful bedrooms with floral-print drapes and wallpaper. The carriage house has spacious deluxe rooms featuring period furnishings. *955 Main St., Dalton 01226, tel. 413/684–3854. 9 rooms, 2 suites. Facilities: outdoor pool. AE, MC, V. Moderate–Expensive.*

Sheffield
Dining

Stagecoach Hill Inn. Constructed in the early 1800s as a stagecoach stop, the restaurant cultivates an English tone with such touches as pictures of the British royal family, hunting scenes, steak-and-kidney pie, roast beef and Yorkshire pudding, and British ale on tap. *Rte. 41, tel. 413/229–8585. AE, DC, MC, V. Closed Tues.–Wed.; Dec.–Apr. Expensive.*

Lodging

Ivanhoe Country House. The Appalachian Trail runs across the property of this B&B, built in 1780; the antiques-furnished guest rooms are generally spacious. *Undermountain Rd. (Rte. 41), 01257, tel. 413/229–2143. 9 rooms, 1 suite with kitchen. Facilities: pool. No credit cards. Moderate.*

South Egremont
Dining and Lodging

The Egremont Inn. The public rooms in this 1780 inn are enormous; the main lounge, with its vast open fireplace, is alone worth a visit. Bedrooms are small, with wide-board floors, uneven ceilings, four-poster beds, and claw-foot baths. The sunny dining room serves Continental fare. *Old Sheffield Rd., Box 418, 01258, tel. 413/528–2111. 22 rooms. Facilities: 3 dining rooms, lounge, pool, 2 tennis courts. AE, MC, V. Expensive.*

Stockbridge Area
Dining and Lodging

The Red Lion Inn. An inn since 1773, and rebuilt after a fire in 1896, this landmark is now massive, with guest rooms in the main building and several annexes. Annex rooms are individually decorated and furnished with antiques. New England specialties are served in the elegant dining room. *Main St., 02162, tel. 413/298–5545. 108 rooms (33 share baths), 10 suites. Facilities: dining room, pool, exercise room. AE, D, DC, MC, V. Expensive.*

★ **Merrell Tavern Inn.** Built between 1794 and 1800, this old New England inn on the National Register of Historic Places has some good-size bedrooms furnished with antiques and pencil-post beds. The breakfast room, with an open fireplace, contains the only complete "birdcage" Colonial bar in America. *Rte. 102, South Lee 01260, tel. 413/243–1794. 10 rooms. AE, MC, V. Moderate–Expensive.*

Williamstown
Dining

Four Acres. This restaurant has two dining rooms: One is decorated with street signs, paneling, and mirrors; the other features collegiate insignias and modern paintings. The American and Continental cuisine includes sautéed calf's liver with applejack glaze. *Rte. 2, tel. 413/458–5436. Reservations advised. AE, MC, V. Closed Sun. Moderate.*

Lodging

River Bend Farm. Listed on the National Register of Historic Places, River Bend was constructed in 1770 by one of the founders of Williamstown. Some bedrooms have wide-plank walls, curtains of unbleached muslin, and four-poster beds with canopies; all are sprinkled with antique pieces. *643 Simonds Rd., 01267, tel. 413/458–5504. 5 rooms share baths. Facilities: lounge, river swimming. No credit cards. Closed Nov.–Apr. Moderate.*

The Arts and Nightlife

Listings appear daily in the *Berkshire Eagle* and weekly in the *Williamstown Advocate;* major concerts are listed in the Thursday *Boston Globe.* The quarterly *Berkshire Magazine* contains "The Berkshire Guide," covering events from theater to sports.

The Arts **Jacob's Pillow Dance Festival,** the oldest in the nation, mounts a
Dance 10-week summer program every year. *Rte. 20, Becket (Box 287, Lee 01238), tel. 413/243–0745 in season or 413/637–1322.*

Music The best-known music festival in New England is at **Tanglewood** in Lenox (tel. 413/637–1940 June–Sept.; in the off-season, Boston Symphony Hall, Boston, MA 02115, tel. 617/266–1492), where the Boston Symphony Orchestra has its summer season (*see* Exploring the Berkshires, *above*). The **Berkshire Performing Arts Center** (Kemble St., Lenox, tel. 413/637–4088) attracts top-name artists in jazz, folk, rock, and blues each summer.

Theater The **Berkshire Theatre Festival** (Rte. 102, Box 797, Stockbridge 01262, tel. 413/298–5536) stages nightly performances in summer at a century-old theater. The **Williamstown Theatre Festival** (Adams Memorial Theatre, 1000 Main St., Box 517, Williamstown 01267, tel. 413/458–9545 or 413/597–3377) presents classics and contemporary works each summer.

Nightlife The most popular local night spot is **The Lion's Den** (tel. 413/298–5545), at the Red Lion Inn in Stockbridge (*see* Dining and Lodging, *above*), with nightly folk music and some contemporary local bands.

Elsewhere in the State

The Pioneer Valley

Getting There I–91 runs north–south the entire length of the Pioneer Valley, from Greenfield to Springfield; I–90 links Springfield to Boston; and Rte. 2 connects Boston with Greenfield in the north. Amtrak stops in Springfield on routes from Boston and New York.

What to See The **Greater Springfield Convention and Visitors Bureau** (34
and Do Boland Way, Springfield 01103, tel. 413/787–1548) provides information about the Pioneer Valley area.

Home to a number of educational institutions, the valley is filled with cultural and historic attractions. **Historic Deerfield** (Rte. 5, tel. 413/774–5581) in the north is a museum as well as the site of the prestigious Deerfield Academy. In **Amherst** are three of the valley's five major colleges—the University of Massachusetts, Amherst College, and Hampshire College—as well as the **Emily Dickinson Homestead** (280 Main St., tel. 413/542–8161). **Northampton** is the site of Smith College, as well as the onetime home of the 30th U.S. president, Calvin Coolidge. The village of **South Hadley** is best known for Mount Holyoke, founded in 1837 as the country's first women's college.

East of the southern end of the valley is **Old Sturbridge Village,** a living, working model of an early 1800s New England town, with more than 40 buildings on a 200-acre site. *1 Old Sturbridge Village Rd., tel. 508/347–3362. Admission charged. Closed Christmas and New Year's Day.*

NEW HAMPSHIRE

By Ed and
Roon Frost

Capital	Concord
Population	1,109,252
Motto	Live Free or Die
State Bird	Purple finch
State Flower	Purple lilac

Visitor Information

New Hampshire Office of Travel and Tourism Development (Box 856, Concord 03302, tel. 603/271–2343 or 800/944–1117). **Foliage hotline** (tel. 800/258–3608 or 800/262–6660).

Scenic Drives

The **Kancamagus Highway** (Rte. 112) rolls through 32 mi of the White Mountains between Lincoln and Conway. **Rte. 113** between Holderness and South Tamworth, also 32 mi, is full of hills and curves, and winds between mountains and plains with open views of both.

National and State Parks

National Forest The **White Mountain National Forest** (Box 63, Laconia 03247, tel. 603/528–8721 or 800/283–2267) occupies 770,000 acres of northern New Hampshire (*see* The White Mountains, *below*).

State Parks The **Division of Parks and Recreation** (172 Pembroke Rd., Concord 03302, tel. 603/271–3254) maintains 74 state parks, beaches, and historic sites. Surrounded by privately held forests, **Monadnock State Park** (Box 181, Jaffrey 03451, tel. 603/532–8035) seems larger than its 1,000 acres. **Bearbrook State Park** (RFD 1, Box 507, Allenstown 03275, tel. 603/485–9874) has 9,500 acres.

The Seacoast

The southern end of New Hampshire's 18-mi coastline is dominated by Hampton Beach—5 mi of sand, midriff-to-elbow sunbathers, motels, arcades, carryouts, and a boardwalk. At the northern end is Portsmouth, with its beautifully restored historic area, a slew of one-of-a-kind restaurants, and the state's only working port. In between are dunes, beaches, salt marshes, and state parks where you can picnic, hike, swim, boat, and fish.

Tourist Information

Seacoast Council on Tourism (235 West Rd. #10, Portsmouth 03801, tel. 603/436–7678 or 800/221–5623). **Greater Portsmouth:** Chamber of Commerce (500 Market St., Portsmouth 03801, tel. 603/436–1118). **Hampton Beach Area:** Chamber of Commerce (836 Lafayette Rd., Hampton 03842, tel. 603/926–8717).

Getting There

By Car I–95 accesses the Hamptons (Exit 2), central Portsmouth (Exits 3–6), and Portsmouth harbor and historic district (Exit 7).

By Bus **C & J Trailways** (tel. 603/431–2424 or 800/258–7111) runs between Boston and Portsmouth, Dover, and Durham. **Greyhound** (tel. 603/436–0163) and **Vermont Transit Lines** (tel. 603/228–3300 or 800/451–3292) link Portsmouth with major eastern cities. **Concord Trailways** (tel. 603/228–3300 or 800/639–3317 in New England) and **Peter Pan Bus Lines** (tel. 603/889–2121) operate in-state.

Exploring the Seacoast

From Rte. 1A, the Atlantic is rarely out of sight, and there are plenty of spots for pulling over. In **North Hampton,** enjoy the crashing surf on the rocky shore of **Little Boars Head Beach;** take a leisurely drive past the cottages of "Millionaire's Row"; or, in the summer, stop to see the 1,500 rosebushes at **Fuller Gardens** (10 Willow Ave., tel. 603/964–5414; admission charged). From granite-bound **Rye Harbor** inlet, **New Hampshire Seacoast Cruises** (tel. 603/382–6743) takes whale-watchers near the Isles of Shoals, a Colonial fishing settlement. **Odiorne Point State Park,** site of the area's first English settlement, is now 230 acres of tidal pools and footpaths punctuated by the **Seacoast Science Center** (570 Ocean Blvd., Rye, tel. 603/436–8043).

Portsmouth is both a working port—full of huge freighters, little tugboats, and piles of scrap metal—and a walkable city beloved of Boston trendsetters. Showcasing its architectural diversity is **Strawbery Banke,** a 10-acre village-museum whose 40 buildings date from 1695 to 1820. The gardens are splendid. *Marcy St., tel. 603/433–1100 or 603/433–1106. Admission charged. Closed Nov.–Apr.*

Prescott Park, across the street, has the **Sheafe Warehouse Museum** (tel. 603/431–8748; admission free), displaying decoys, ship models, and ship mastheads. The **Portsmouth Historical Society** (Middle and State Sts., tel. 603/436–1118; admission charged) has a self-guided walking tour that includes six historic houses.

What to See and Do with Children

In Portsmouth, start with the lively, hands-on **Children's Museum** (280 Marcy St., tel. 603/436–3853) or the USS *Albacore* (500 Market St., tel. 603/436–3680), a vintage submarine, then treat them to **Water Country** (Rte. 1, tel. 603/436–3556).

Shopping

Portsmouth is chockablock with crafts shops, galleries, and clothing boutiques. Stop at the **North Hampton Factory Outlet Center** (Rte. 1, tel. 603/964–9050) for bargains.

Sports and Outdoor Activities

Boating and Fishing Rentals and charters are available from **Atlantic Fishing Fleet** in Rye Harbor (tel. 603/964–5220) or **Al Gauron** (tel. 603/926–2469) and **Smith & Gilmore** (tel. 603/926–3503) in Hampton Beach.

Beaches

New Hampshire's wide strands have hard white sand, moderate surf, and brisk but still swimmable waters; the more northerly have smaller crowds. The state runs **Hampton Beach, North Hampton Beach, Jenness Beach,** and **Wallis Sands State Park,** the most northerly and a local favorite.

Dining and Lodging

Portsmouth shines in warm weather, when restaurants along Bow and Ceres streets open their decks for sea breezes and harbor views. Make lodging reservations well in advance for summer stays in the area. For price ranges, see Charts 1 (B) and 2 (B) in Chapter 1.

Hampton
Dining

Ron's Beach House. Imaginative fish dishes, such as sautéed scallops and shellfish gratinée, have made this restaurant popular year-round. *965 Ocean Blvd., tel. 603/926–1870. Reservations advised. AE, D, MC, V. Moderate–Expensive.*

Hampton Beach
Dining and Lodging

Ashworth by the Sea. At this centrally located favorite of generations of beach goers, most rooms have decks. Go for one of the queen rooms, dominated by a four-poster bed and glowing cherrywood furnishings. *295 Ocean Blvd., 03842, tel. 603/926–6762 or 800/345–6736. 105 rooms. Facilities: 3 restaurants, pool. AE, D, DC, MC, V. Moderate–Expensive.*

Portsmouth
Dining
★

Guido's Trattoria. Because the honest Tuscan fare at this harbor-view spot is so light, it's easy to polish off four generous courses without feeling stuffed. *67 Bow St., tel. 603/431–2989. Reservations advised. AE, MC, V. No lunch; closed Mon. Moderate–Expensive.*

The Oar House and Deck. The river-view deck is fun for drinks and dinner in summer; the main building, a massively beamed old stone warehouse across the parking lot, delights year-round. Try the bouillabaisse. *55 Ceres St., tel. 603/436–4025. Reservations advised for dinner. AE, MC, V. Moderate–Expensive.*

Lodging
★

Sise Inn. This elegant Queen Anne town house, full of chintz and gleaming armoires, is convenient for waterfront strolls. No two rooms are alike; some have whirlpools. *40 Court St., 03801, tel. 603/433–1200 or 800/267–0525. 34 rooms. AE, DC, MC, V. Expensive.*

The Arts and Nightlife

Summer concerts draw crowds at the **Hampton Beach Casino Ballroom** (Ocean Beach Blvd., tel. 603/926–4541). Media folk catch sea chanties and Celtic ballads at the **Press Room** (77 Daniel St., Portsmouth, tel. 603/431–5186).

The Lakes Region

The eastern half of central New Hampshire is scattered with beautifully preserved 18th- and 19th-century villages and with sparkling lakes—Winnipesaukee ("Smiling Water") is the largest—that echo with squeals and splashes all summer long.

Tourist Information

Lakes Region Chamber of Commerce (11 Veterans Sq., Laconia 03246, tel. 603/524–5531 or 800/531–2347). **Lakes Region Association** (Center Harbor 03226, tel. 603/569–1117).

Getting There

By Car I–93 is the principal north–south artery. From the coast, Rte. 11 goes to southern Lake Winnipesaukee; en route to the White Mountains, north–south Rte. 16 accesses spurs to the lake.

By Bus **Concord Trailways** (tel. 603/228–3300 or 800/639–3317 in New England) serves Meredith, Center Harbor, Moultonborough, and West Ossipee.

Exploring the Lakes Region

Alton Bay, at Winnipesaukee's southernmost tip, has the lake's cruise-boat dock and a Victorian bandstand. In affluent Colonial **Gilford** there's a large state beach, as well as the **Gunstock Recreation Area** (Rte. 11A, tel. 603/293–4341), with swimming, hiking, and camping. In honky-tonk **Weirs Beach,** fireworks light up summer nights; here you can board lake cruisers (tel. 603/366–2628) or the **Winnipesaukee Railroad** (tel. 603/279–5253 or 800/852–3311) for shore tours.

Commercial **Meredith,** on the northern tip of the most westerly of three bays on the north shore, has restaurants and shops. Rte. 25 passes through **Center Harbor,** a modest version of Meredith at the end of the middle bay, en route to **Moultonborough,** at the tip of the easternmost bay, and the viewful 5,000-acre **Castle in the Clouds** estate (tel. 603/476–2352 or 800/729–2468), anchored by an eccentric millionaire's former home.

Contrasting with the busy Winnipesaukee towns are pristine, historic **Center Sandwich; Tamworth,** whose birch-edged Chocorua Lake has been photographed so often that you may feel you've seen it before; and **Ossipee,** three lakeside villages with lots of antiquing. Scenic, lake-hugging Rte. 109 leads to **Wolfeboro,** an old-line resort. At **Canterbury Shaker Village** (Canterbury, tel. 603/783–9511), southwest of Winnipesaukee, guided tours and crafts demonstrations depict 19th-century Shaker life.

What to See and Do with Children

Try Center Harbor's hands-on **Children's Museum** (Senter's Market, tel. 603/253–8697); Holderness's **Science Center of New Hampshire** (Rte. 113, tel. 603/968–7194); and, on Rte. 3 in Weirs Beach, the **Funspot** (tel. 603/366–4377), **Surf Coaster** (tel. 603/366–4991), and **Water Slide** (tel. 603/366–5161) amusement centers.

New Hampshire Lakes

Shopping

Summer folk prowl area galleries and boutiques, such as those at the **Millworks Marketplace** (Rte. 3, Meredith, tel. 603/279–4116) and at the **League of New Hampshire Craftsmen** shops in Meredith (Rte. 3, tel. 603/279–7920) and Center Sandwich (Main St., tel. 603/284–6831). The **Old Country Store** in Moultonborough (Rte. 25, tel. 603/476–5750) has been purveying pickles and penny candy since 1781. Look for **antiques** in Wolfeboro, the Ossipees, and Center Sandwich.

Sports and Outdoor Activities

Biking Not too hilly, the Lakes Region is fun for even inexperienced bikers—though summer's heavy traffic can be a bit much. Lake's-edge roads make for good pedaling.

Boating and Canoeing Rent at **Thurston's** in Weirs Beach (tel. 603/366–4811) or the Meredith Marina and Boating Center (tel. 603/279–7921).

Fishing Local waters yield trout; Winnipesaukee also has salmon. Hardy anglers fish from "ice bob" huts in winter. The state fish and game department's local office (New Hampton, tel. 603/744–5470) can tell you where the action is.

Beaches

Most are private, so it's good to know about **Ellacoya State Beach** (Gilford, tel. 603/293–7821), a smallish man-made beach that's the area's major public strand. **Wentworth State Beach** is at Wolfeboro.

Dining and Lodging

This is steak-and-prime-rib country, though there are exceptions. Reserve ahead for both meals and rooms; summer and fall are crowded, and many businesses close in winter. For price ranges, see Charts 1 (B) and 2 (B) in Chapter 1.

Center Sandwich
Dining and Lodging

The Corner House Inn. This quaint Victorian inn with comfortable, old-fashioned guest rooms upstairs serves home-cooked meals in dining rooms cozy with local arts and crafts. Storytellers hold forth by the potbellied stove one night a week. *Rte. 113, 03227, tel. 603/284–6219 or 800/832–7829. 4 rooms (3 share bath). Facilities: restaurant, beach permits. AE, MC, V. Inexpensive–Moderate.*

Tamworth
Dining and Lodging
★

Tamworth Inn. This friendly B&B with romantic charm seems straight from an old movie. Guest rooms are decorated with 19th-century American pieces. The dining room serves American cuisine with a French twist, such as sautéed prime beef with mushrooms and artichokes, or roast duck with apricot sauce. In summer you can dine on the river-view porch. *Main St., Box 189, 03886, tel. 603/323–7721 or 800/642–7352. 15 rooms. Facilities: breakfast, restaurant, pub, pool. MC, V. Moderate–Expensive.*

Wolfeboro
Dining and Lodging
★

The Wolfeboro Inn. This landmark waterfront resort, partly dating from the 19th century, is furnished with polished cherry and pine pieces and abloom with flowered chintz; armoires hide TVs. Old Wolfe's Tavern, anchored by a huge old fireplace, pours 45 brands of beer. *44 N. Main St., 03894, tel. 603/569–3016 or 800/451–2389. 38 rooms, 5 suites. Facilities: 2 restaurants, tavern, private beach, excursion boat. AE, D, MC, V. Moderate–Very Expensive.*

Campgrounds

Gunstock (Laconia, tel. 603/293–4344), **Yogi Bear's Jellystone Park** (Ashland, tel. 603/968–3654), and **White Lake State Park** (Tamworth, tel. 603/323–7350) have both tent and RV sites.

The Arts and Nightlife

The **Belknap Mill Society** (Mill Plaza, Laconia, tel. 603/524–8813) has year-round concerts in an early 19th-century brick mill building. **Barnstormers** (Main St., Tamworth, tel. 603/323–8500), New Hampshire's oldest professional theater, performs in July and August. The **M/S *Mount Washington*** (Weirs Beach, tel. 603/366–2628) has moonlight cruises with dinner and dancing; it docks in Weirs Beach, Alton Bay, and Wolfeboro.

The White Mountains

Northern New Hampshire is the home of New England's highest mountains and the 750,000-acre White Mountain National Forest; the wilderness stretches to the Canadian border. Rivers are born here, gorges slash the forests, and hikers, climbers, and Sunday drivers marvel. Meanwhile, shoppers cheer for the bargain hunting in valley towns. Summers are busy, but foliage season draws the biggest crowds.

Tourist Information

Mt. Washington Valley: Visitors Bureau (Box 2300, North Conway 03860, tel. 603/356–3171 or 800/367–3364).

Getting There

By Car   North–south routes include I–93 and Rte. 3 in the west, Rte. 16 in the east. Rte. 112, the Kancamagus Highway, is the main east–west thoroughfare.

By Bus   **Concord Trailways** (tel. 603/228–3300 or 800/639–3317 in New England) serves Littleton, Colbrook, Berlin, Conway, Meredith, Plymouth, and other towns.

Exploring the White Mountains

One-street **North Conway** overflows with shops, restaurants, and inns. Trails from nearby **Echo Lake State Park** (off Rte. 302, North Conway, tel. 603/356–2672 in summer) lead up to **White Horse** and **Cathedral ledges**, 1,000-foot cliffs overlooking the town in the west. The mountain lakes are good for swimming, and the park road for New England woodland scenery; the picnicking is great.

Mountain-rimmed **Jackson** is picture-perfect, with its clapboard inns and shops. Dramatic **Pinkham Notch** is the departure point for hikes to the top of the Northeast's highest mountain, 6,288-foot **Mt. Washington** (be sure to carry warm clothing in case of sudden, nasty storms). In summer and fall, you can corkscrew up via the **Mt. Washington Auto Road** (Glen House, tel. 603/466–3988; admission charged) or, as sightseers have done since 1869, ride the steam-powered **Mt. Washington Cog Railway** (off Rte. 302, Bretton Woods, tel. 603/846–5404 or 800/922–8825, ext. 7; admission charged; reserve ahead).

Crawford Notch State Park (Rte. 302 at Twin Mountain, tel. 603/374–2272) is good for a picnic and a hike to a waterfall. The **Mount Washington Hotel** (Rte. 302, Bretton Woods, tel. 603/278–1000) was the site of the 1944 International Monetary Fund Conference, which established the American dollar as the basic medium of international exchange. The view of the lawns and the mountains beyond makes the vast veranda a pleasant place to sojourn; you can also have a drink in the Princess Lounge, a formal, intricately decorated club with a fireplace and live music. In **Franconia,** you can visit poet Robert Frost's home (Ridge Rd., tel. 603/823–5510). **Franconia Notch** is known for the **Old Man of the Mountains,** a rock formation that looks like a human profile, and the 800-foot-long natural chasm known as **The Flume** (tel. 603/823–5563).

The **Kancamagus Highway,** 32 mi of mountain scenery to the south (with bumper-to-bumper traffic during foliage season), starts in the resort town of **Lincoln** and passes campgrounds, picnic spots, scenic overlooks, and trailheads en route to Conway.

What to See and Do with Children

Youngsters love the antique steam- and diesel-powered **Conway Scenic Railroad** (Rtes. 16/302, North Conway, tel. 603/356–5251 or 800/232–5251), the water slides at the **Whale's Tale** (Rte. 3, Lincoln, tel. 603/745–8810), and two attractions on Rte. 16 in Glen: **Storyland** (tel. 603/383–4293), which has life-size nursery-rhyme characters and an African safari, and **Heritage New Hampshire** (tel. 603/383–9776), a simulated journey into New England history.

Shopping

More than 150 outlets and shops line **Rte. 16** north of Conway; **Lincoln** offers more of the same. Galleries throughout the region display local artisans' work.

Sports and Outdoor Activities

Fishing Clear White Mountain streams yield trout and salmon; lakes and ponds have trout and bass. The state fish and game department's regional office (tel. 603/788–3164) has the latest.

Hiking The White Mountains are crisscrossed with footpaths. The Maine-to-Georgia **Appalachian Trail** crosses the state; the **Appalachian Mountain Club** (Pinkham Notch, tel. 603/466–2725) operates Spartan hikers' huts along the way. The club also provides information and suggests routes, as does the **U.S. Forest Service** (tel. 603/528–8721). **New England Hiking Holidays–White Mountains** (Box 1648, North Conway 03860, tel. 603/356–9696) has guided inn-to-inn hikes.

Ski Areas

New Hampshire's best skiing is in the White Mountains. For the latest conditions statewide, call 800/262–6660 (cross-country) or 800/258–3608 (downhill).

Cross-country In **Jackson,** 100 mi of trails maintained by the **Jackson Ski Touring Foundation** (tel. 603/383–9355 for conditions or 603/383–9356 for lodging) string together inns, restaurants, and woodlands, and connect to another 40 mi of trails maintained by the Appalachian Mountain Club (*see* Hiking, *above*). There are 35 mi of trails at the grand **Balsams** hotel in Dixville Notch (*see* Dining and Lodging, *below*), 64 mi at **Bretton Woods** (Rte. 302, tel. 603/278–5000), 30 mi at the **Franconia Inn** (Easton Rd., Franconia, tel. 603/823–5542), and 45 mi at sprawling **Waterville Valley** (Rte. 49, Waterville Valley, tel. 603/236–8311; 603/236–4144 for conditions).

Downhill New Hampshire's biggest ski areas are pint-sized compared with those in neighboring Vermont; their charm is in their low-key atmosphere. **Waterville Valley** (*see* Cross-country, *above*) has 53 trails, 13 lifts, and a 2,020-foot vertical drop. **Loon Mountain** (Kancamagus Hwy., Lincoln, tel. 603/745–8111; 603/745–8100 for conditions) has 41 trails, 9 lifts, and a 2,100-foot drop.

In the **Mt. Washington Valley** are **Attitash** (Rte. 302, Bartlett, tel. 603/374–2369; 603/374–0946 for conditions), with 28 trails, 6 lifts, and a 1,750-foot vertical drop; **Mt. Cranmore** (Box 1640, North Conway, tel. 603/356–5543; 800/786–6754 for conditions), with 28 trails, 5 lifts, and a 1,200-foot drop; and **Wildcat**

(Rte. 16, Pinkham Notch, tel. 603/466–3326; 800/552–8952 or 617/965–7991 in MA for conditions), with 30 trails, 6 lifts, and a 2,100-foot drop.

State-run **Cannon** (Franconia, tel. 603/823–5563; 603/823–7771 or 800/552–1234 for conditions) has 32 steep-and-narrow trails, 6 lifts, and a 2,142-foot vertical drop. **Balsams/Wilderness,** with 13 trails, 4 lifts, and a 1,000-foot drop, and **Bretton Woods,** with 26 trails, five lifts, and a 1,500-foot drop, are small areas at grand old resort hotels (*see* Cross-country, *above*).

Dining and Lodging

Reservations are essential in fall and during winter vacations. For price ranges, see Charts 1 (B) and 2 (B) in Chapter 1.

Dixville Notch
Dining and Lodging

The Balsams. This elegant turn-of-the-century resort hotel on 15,000 acres is a real Victorian, even today. Accommodations are spare, bright, and homey, with floral-print wallpaper and lace curtains, and the array of facilities gives you no reason to leave the grounds. At the famous formal brunch (jacket and tie advised), the huge dining room overflows with elegantly presented bounty. *Rte. 26, 03576, tel. 603/255–3400 or 800/255–0600. 232 rooms. Facilities: restaurant, pool, golf, tennis, winter sports, boating, children's program, dancing. AE, MC, V. Closed Apr.–mid-May, mid-Oct.–mid-Dec. Expensive.*

Franconia
Dining and Lodging

Franconia Inn. Families like this resort: It's easy to get a baby-sitter, and the restaurant serves such fare as "Young Epicurean Cheeseburgers" to make mealtimes as pleasant for children as for parents. Guest rooms feature chintz and canopy beds; some have whirlpools or fireplaces. *Easton Rd., 03580, tel. 603/823–5542 or 800/473–5299. 34 rooms. Facilities: restaurant, pool, hot tub, tennis, riding, soaring. Smoking limited. AE, MC, V. Closed Apr.–mid-May. Moderate–Expensive.*

Jackson
Dining

T.H.E. Thompson House Eatery. This rustic restaurant with a farm stand and soda fountain serves hearty fare that draws raves from skiers and hikers alike. *Rte. 16A, tel. 603/383–9341. D, MC, V. Closed Nov., Apr. Inexpensive–Moderate.*

Dining and Lodging

The Inn at Thorn Hill. Dark furniture and rose-motif wallpapers recall the inn's origins as a home designed by Stanford White in 1895. Yet the comforts are strictly up-to-date, and the food—New England fare with a Continental touch—is some of the area's best. Try the lobster loaf or the hazelnutty chicken breasts. Rates are MAP. *Thorn Hill Rd., 03846, tel. 603/383–4242. 20 rooms. Facilities: restaurant, pub, pool, winter sports. No smoking. AE, MC, V. Closed Apr. Expensive.*

North Conway
Dining and Lodging
★

The 1785 Inn. Smoked-salmon ravioli and maple-marinated venison tenderloins strike a Continental note in this cozily beamed, quintessentially Early American dining room in one of the valley's oldest buildings. Attractive guest quarters in the same style as those at The Inn at Thorn Hill, if perhaps less charming, have spectacular views. *Box 1785, Rte. 16, 03860, tel. 603/356–9025. 16 rooms (5 share 2 baths). Facilities: dining room, lounge, pool. Inexpensive–Expensive.*

The Arts and Nightlife

Look into the **Mt. Washington Valley Theater Company** (Main St., North Conway, tel. 603/356–5776 or 603/356–5425). Catch some music at the **North Country Center for the Arts** (Rte. 112, Lincoln, tel. 603/745–2141). Or sample the bars: the **Red Parka Pub** (Rte. 302, Glen, tel. 603/383–4344), favored by under-30s; **Barnaby's** (Rte. 16, North Conway, tel. 603/356–5781), with live rock on weekends; and, especially après-ski, the **Wildcat Inn & Tavern** (Rte. 16A, Jackson, tel. 603/383–4245).

Western New Hampshire

The countryside east of the Connecticut River between the Massachusetts border and the White Mountains' foothills is a land of covered bridges and calendar-page villages, hardwood forests, jewellike lakes, and lonely mountains. Cultural centers enliven workaday urban centers such as Manchester, Nashua, and the capital, Concord.

Tourist Information

Lake Sunapee: Business Association (Box 400, Sunapee 03782, tel. 603/763–2495 or 800/258–3530 in New England). **Monadnock:** Travel Council (8 Central Sq., Keene 03431, tel. 603/352–1303). **Concord:** Chamber of Commerce (244 N. Main St., 03301, tel. 603/224–2508). **Hanover:** Chamber of Commerce (Box A–105, 03755, tel. 603/643–3115). **Manchester:** Chamber of Commerce (889 Elm St., 03101, tel. 603/666–6600). **Nashua:** Chamber of Commerce (188 Main St., 03060, tel. 603/881–8333). **Peterborough:** Chamber of Commerce (03458, tel. 603/924–7234).

Getting There

By Car I–89 cuts southeast–northwest into Vermont. North–south, I–93 provides often scenic travel while I–91 follows the river on its Vermont shore; in New Hampshire, Rtes. 12 and 12A are slow but beautiful. Rte. 4 winds between Lebanon and the coast.

By Bus **Concord Trailways** (tel. 603/228–3300 or 800/639–3317 in New England) operates within the state, **Advance Transit** (tel. 603/448–2815) within the area.

Exploring Western New Hampshire

Mountains and parks set off bright, clear **Lake Sunapee.** You can cruise it on the **MV *Mt. Sunapee II*** (Sunapee Harbor, tel. 603/763–4030). Or you can rise above it on a chair lift, or picnic on a beach, at quiet, woodsy **Mt. Sunapee State Park** (Rte. 103, 2 mi west of Newbury, tel. 603/763–2356).

Dartmouth College, to the north in **Hanover,** is a picture of red brick and white clapboard around a village green. On Wheelock Street, its **Hood Museum** (tel. 603/646–2808; admission free) houses works from Africa, Asia, Europe, and America, while the modern **Hopkins Center** (tel. 603/646–2422) is a focal point for the local arts scene.

In modest **Cornish,** to the south via Rte. 12A, you can cross four covered bridges, including the longest in the country, and tour 19th-century sculptor Augustus Saint-Gaudens's studio complex. The **Saint-Gaudens National Historic Site** displays some of the artist's heroic, sensitive sculptures. *Off Rte. 12A, tel. 603/675–2175. Admission charged. Closed late Oct.–late May.*

In **Charlestown** is **The Fort at No. 4** (Rte. 11, tel. 603/826–5700; admission charged), a frontier outpost in Colonial times, where today costumed guides demonstrate crafts and occasionally stage militia musters. Eighteenth-century villages punctuate the riverbanks farther south. **Keene,** to the east, has fine old trees, a wide main street, and many stately 19th-century mill-owners' homes; the **Arts Center on Brickyard Pond** at Keene State College (229 Main St., tel. 603/358–2168) has theaters, art and dance studios, and a gallery.

In **Monadnock State Park** (Rte. 124, Jaffrey, tel. 603/532–8035), 20 trails ascend to the bald summit of 3,165-foot **Mt. Monadnock,** one of the world's most-climbed mountains. You can exit the park onto Rte. 101 near **Dublin,** where proper Bostonians summer and locals publish the *Old Farmer's Almanac*. **Peterborough,** the model for Thornton Wilder's *Our Town*, is now a computer-magazine publishing center.

Beautifully preserved **Fitzwilliam,** spreading from the edges of an oval common, warrants a detour. About 2 mi north, you can picnic in a pine grove at 294-acre **Rhododendron State Park** (Rhododendron Rd., tel. 603/239–8153), washed with color in early July. The **Cathedral of the Pines** (off Rte. 119, Rindge, tel. 603/899–3300), an outdoor place of worship, has a view of Mt. Monadnock; early afternoon organ meditations are held Tuesday through Thursday. **Amherst,** a bedroom community for Nashua, has a beautiful village green edged with antique houses on the National Register of Historic Places.

What to See and Do with Children

Explore caverns and tunnels at Grafton's **Ruggles Mine** (off Rte. 4, tel. 603/448–6911). Reserve seats for shows at Concord's high-tech **Christa McAuliffe Planetarium** (3 Institute Dr., tel. 603/271–7827).

Shopping

Look for church fairs and artisans' studios marked by neat state signs. Antiques dealers sell "by chance or by appointment"; keep an eye peeled along Rte. 119 west of Fitzwilliam and along Rte. 101 east of Marlborough. Keene has malls and **Colony Mill Marketplace** (222 West St., tel. 603/357–1240) in a restored mill. In Peterborough, buy gadgets at the **Brookstone** factory outlet (Rte. 202N, tel. 603/924–7181) or outdoor gear at **Eastern Mountain Sports** (Vose Farm Rd., tel. 603/924–7231).

Sports and Outdoor Activities

Biking Try **Rte. 10** along the Ashuelot River south of Keene; spurs lead to covered bridges. Contact the **Granite State Wheelmen** (Salem, tel. 603/898–9926) for group rides, **Monadnock Bicycle Touring** (Harrisville, tel. 603/827–3925) for inn-to-inn tours.

Boating and The Connecticut River, while usually safe after June 15, is not
Canoeing for beginners. Rent gear at **North Star Canoe & Mountain Bike Rentals** (Rte. 12A, Cornish, tel. 603/542–5802).

Fishing To find out where the action is on the area's 200 lakes and ponds, contact the **Department of Fish and Game**'s regional office (tel. 603/271–3421).

Hiking Networks of trails can be found in many state parks and forests, among them **Mt. Sunapee** (Newbury, tel. 603/763–2356) and rugged **Pillsbury** (Washington, tel. 603/863–2860) state parks, and **Fox State Forest** (Hillsboro, tel. 603/464–3453).

Dining and Lodging

For price ranges, see Charts 1 (B) and 2 (B) in Chapter 1.

Bedford **Bedford Village Inn.** This former farm, minutes from Manches-
Lodging ter, is now a luxury inn. Antique four-posters recrafted to hold king-size mattresses, and Italian marble in whirlpool baths bespeak the latest in elegance; some rooms have fireplaces. *2 Old Bedford Rd., 03110, tel. 603/472–2602 or 800/852–1166. 12 rooms, 2 apartments. Facilities: restaurant. AE, DC, MC, V. Moderate–Expensive.*

Concord **Hermanos Cocina Mexicana.** Diners come from Boston for the
Dining Mexican fare served here; expect to queue. Don't eat too many
★ nachos supreme on blue-corn chips; you'll want room for Miguel's Dream (chocolate, cinnamon, pecans, and honey in a warm tortilla). *6 Pleasant St. Ext., tel. 603/224–5669. No reservations. MC, V. Inexpensive–Moderate.*

Hanover **Hanover Inn.** Three stories of white-trimmed brick, this em-
Dining and bodiment of American traditional architecture is the state's
Lodging oldest operating business. Now owned by Dartmouth College,
★ it's handsomely furnished with 19th-century antiques and reproductions. You can get classic New England fare in the Daniel Webster Room, lighter bites in the Ivy Grill. *Box 151, 03755, tel. 603/643–4300 or 800/443–7024. 92 rooms, 16 junior suites. AE, D, DC, MC, V. Expensive–Very Expensive.*

Peterborough **The Boilerhouse Restaurant.** Overlooking Noone Falls, this res-
Dining toration of an old textile mill serves great gravlax of Norwegian salmon, and creatively sauced dishes like veal with forest mushrooms and venison with apricots and currants. Weight watchers applaud the spa fare. *Rte. 202S, tel. 603/924–9486. D, MC, V. Moderate–Expensive.*

The Arts and Nightlife

The Arts In addition to the offerings of Keene's **Arts Center on Brickyard Pond** and Hanover's **Hopkins Center** (*see* Exploring Western New Hampshire, *above*), the arts flourish at the **Claremont Opera House** (City Hall, Tremont Sq., tel. 603/542–4433), the **Nashua Center for the Arts** (14 Court St., tel. 603/883–1506), and the **Palace Theatre** (80 Hanover St., Manchester, tel. 603/668–5588), the state performing-arts center. **Monadnock Music** (Peterborough Library, Main and Concord Sts., Peterborough, tel. 603/924–7610) has concerts in July and August. Milford is home to the state's largest professional theater, the **American Stage Festival** (Rte. 13N, tel. 603/673–4005).

Nightlife **The Folkway** (85 Grove St., Peterborough, tel. 603/924–7484) is a regional tradition. **Del Rossi's Trattoria** (junction of Rtes. 137 and 101, Dublin, tel. 603/563–7195) presents big names in jazz, bluegrass, folk, and blues. The **Colonial Theater** (95 Main St., Keene, tel. 603/352–2033) has folk, rock, jazz, and movies.

NEW YORK

By David Laskin

Capital	Albany
Population	18,057,598
Motto	Excelsior
State Bird	Bluebird
State Flower	Rose

Visitor Information

New York State Division of Tourism (1 Commerce Plaza, Albany 12245, tel. 518/474–4116 or 800/225–5697).

Scenic Drives

The **Taconic Parkway,** particularly the stretch from Hopewell Junction to East Chatham, passes through rolling hills, orchards, woods, and pastures reminiscent of the English countryside. To make a dramatic loop around the Adirondacks' **High Peaks** region, pick up Rte. 73 off the Northway at Exit 30, drive northwest through Lake Placid, proceed on Rte. 86 through Saranac Lake, then head southwest on Rte. 3 to Tupper Lake, due south on Rte. 30 to Long Lake, and east on Rte. 28N to North Hudson. For information on the dozen officially designated scenic drives, call 800/225–5697.

National and State Parks

National Parks The **Gateway National Recreation Area** (Floyd Bennett Field, Bldg. 69, Brooklyn 11234, tel. 718/338–3338) extends through Brooklyn, Queens, Staten Island, and New Jersey. It includes the **Jamaica Bay Wildlife Refuge,** where nature trails around ponds, marshes, and wooded uplands offer glimpses of migrating birds; **Jacob Riis Park,** where a boardwalk stretches along the surfy Atlantic; plus various beaches, parklands, and facilities for outdoor and indoor festivals. **Fire Island National Seashore** (120 Laurel St., Patchogue 11772, tel. 516/289–4810) offers Atlantic surf and beaches on a popular resort island with a strong gay population.

State Parks New York has 150 state parks, many offering outstanding recreational facilities. An **Empire State Passport,** permitting unlimited free entrance to the parks for a year (Apr.–Mar.), is available for $30 at most of the parks; you can also contact the **State Office of Parks and Recreation** (tel. 518/474–0456) or write for an application (Passport, State Parks, Albany 12238).

New York City

Whatever you're looking for in a big-city vacation, you'll find in New York. The city has a rich history, from early Dutch settlers and the swearing-in of George Washington as the first U.S. president to the arrival of millions of immigrants in the late 19th and early 20th centuries. The city today is known for its world-famous skyline, its world-class museums and performing-arts companies, and its status as the capital of finance, fashion, art, publishing, broadcasting, theater, and advertising. And of course New Yorkers themselves are world-famous, if not for their charm, at least for their panache, ethnic diversity, street smarts, and accents.

Beyond the laundry list of must-see sights, from the Statue of Liberty to Times Square, from the United Nations to Macy's, New York has an indefinable aura that exists nowhere else. It's a kind of energy level that has something to do with being in the big league, where everybody's watching and keeping score. Paraphrasing a slogan coined for The Plaza hotel, you get the feeling that "nothing unimportant ever happens in New York," and that gives an edge to everything that goes on here.

Tourist Information

New York: Convention and Visitors Bureau (2 Columbus Circle, at 58th St. and 8th Ave., 10019, tel. 212/397–8222).

Arriving and Departing

By Plane Virtually every major U.S. and foreign airline serves one or more of New York's three airports. **LaGuardia** (8 mi northeast of midtown) and **John F. Kennedy International Airport** (15 mi southeast of midtown) are in Queens. **Newark International Airport** is 16 mi southwest of midtown, in New Jersey. Cab fare to midtown Manhattan runs $14–$20 from LaGuardia, $24–$30 from JFK, and $30–$40 from Newark. **Carey Airport Express** (tel. 718/632–0500) runs buses to midtown every 20 minutes from LaGuardia and every 30 minutes from JFK. The **Gray Line Air Shuttle Minibus** (tel. 212/757–6840) also connects both airports to Manhattan. **NJ Transit Airport Express** (tel. 201/460–8444) runs between Newark airport and Manhattan's Port Authority Terminal. By public transportation, the A subway line to Howard Beach connects with a free airport shuttle bus to JFK.

By Car A complex network of bridges and tunnels provides access to Manhattan. I–95 enters upper Manhattan via the **George Washington Bridge,** and I–495 enters from Long Island via the **Midtown Tunnel.** From upstate New York, the city is accessible via the **New York (Dewey) Thruway** (I–87).

Train Station **Pennsylvania Station** (31st to 33rd Sts., between 7th and 8th Aves., tel. 212/532–4900).

Bus Station The **Port Authority Terminal** (40th to 42nd Sts., between 8th and 9th Aves., tel. 212/564–8484) handles all long-haul and commuter bus lines. Check local information for the **Greyhound** number in your area. Other lines that serve New York City are **Bonanza Bus Lines** (New England; tel. 800/556–3815) and **New Jersey Transit** (New Jersey; tel. 201/460–8444).

Getting Around New York

New York is a city of neighborhoods best explored at a leisurely pace, up close, and on foot. Extensive public transportation easily bridges gaps between areas of interest.

By Car If you drive into Manhattan, don't plan to use your car much to get around. Driving in the city can be a nightmare of gridlocked streets and predatory fellow motorists. Free parking is almost nonexistent in midtown, and parking lots everywhere are exorbitant ($16 for three hours is not unusual in midtown).

By Public Transportation The 300-mi **subway** system, the fastest and cheapest way to get around the city, serves Manhattan, Brooklyn, Queens, and the Bronx and operates 24 hours a day. Tokens cost $1.25 each, with reduced fares for the disabled and senior citizens, and are purchased in subway stations; transfers among subway lines are free at designated interchanges. Most **buses** follow easy-to-understand routes along the Manhattan grid, and some run 24 hours. Routes go up or down the north–south avenues, east and west on the major two-way crosstown streets: 96th, 86th, 79th, 59th, 42nd, 34th, 23rd, and 14th. Bus fare is $1.25 in change (no pennies or bills) or a subway token; for free transfer to a connecting bus line, ask for a transfer when paying the fare. For 24-hour bus and subway information, call 718/330–1234.

For subway or bus maps, ask at token booths or write to the Customer Service Department (NYCTA, 130 Livingston St., Rm. 9011D, Brooklyn 11201).

By Taxi Taxis (officially licensed ones are yellow) are usually easy to hail on the street, in front of major hotels, and by bus and train stations. The fare is $1.50 for the first ⅛ mi, 25¢ for each ⅛ mi thereafter, and 25¢ for each minute not in motion. A 50¢ surcharge is added to rides begun between 8 PM and 6 AM. Bridge and tunnel tolls are extra, and there is a surcharge for luggage.

Orientation Tours

Bus Tours **Gray Line** (900 8th Ave. at 53rd St., tel. 212/397–2600) offers a number of city bus tours, plus day trips to Brooklyn and Atlantic City. **Manhattan Sightseeing Bus Tours** (150 W. 49th St., tel. 212/354–5122) has 10 different tours.

Boat Tour **Circle Line** (Pier 83, west end of 42nd St., tel. 212/563–3200) offers a three-hour, 35-mi circumnavigation of Manhattan from March to December.

Walking Tours **Sidewalks of New York** (33 Alan Terr., Suite 2, Jersey City, NJ 07306, tel. 212/517–0201) offers day and evening theme tours—Historic Churches, Ye Old Taverns, Celebrity Homes—on weekends. **The Municipal Art Society** (tel. 212/935–3960) operates a series of bus and walking tours.

Exploring New York City

Midtown is the heart of New York City, so it makes sense to start your exploration there, moving on to the museum-rich Upper West and Upper East sides, then downtown to the funky neighborhoods of Greenwich Village, SoHo, Little Italy, and Chinatown, and finally to Lower Manhattan, the city's financial center.

Midtown The heart of midtown is **Rockefeller Center,** a complex of 19 buildings occupying nearly 22 acres of prime real estate between 5th and 7th avenues and 47th and 52nd streets. The outdoor **ice rink,** on Lower Plaza between 49th and 50th streets, is a great people-watching spot—in summer, from the café tables at restaurants surrounding it, and in winter, when retired skating stars, romantic couples, and flop-happy neophytes circle to the music. The rink is the site of the huge Christmas tree ceremoniously lit each year in December. The **Channel Gardens**

connecting the rink to 5th Avenue is a promenade with six pools surrounded by flower beds.

Across 50th Street from the RCA Building at Rockefeller Center is America's largest indoor theater, the 6,000-seat art deco **Radio City Music Hall** (tel. 212/632–4041). Home of the fabulous Rockettes chorus line, Radio City was built as a movie theater with live shows; today it produces major concerts, Christmas and Easter extravaganzas, awards presentations, and other special events. Its interior and bathrooms are worth a look even without a show.

The stretch of 5th Avenue between Rockefeller Center and 59th Street glitters with world-famous shops, including **Saks Fifth Avenue, Gucci, Steuben Glass,** and **Tiffany & Co.** Also here is the Gothic-style **St. Patrick's,** the Roman Catholic cathedral of New York. Dedicated to the patron saint of the Irish— then and now one of New York's principal ethnic groups—the white-marble-and-stone structure was begun in 1858, consecrated in 1879, and completed in 1906.

On 53rd Street between 5th and 6th avenues is the **Museum of Modern Art** (MOMA), a bright and airy four-story structure built around a secluded sculpture garden. All the most famous modern artists, from van Gogh to Picasso, Matisse to Andy Warhol, are represented. Afternoon and evening film showings are free with the price of admission. *11 W. 53rd St., tel. 212/708–9500. Admission charged. Closed Wed.*

A little farther west, the **American Craft Museum** shows the work of contemporary American and other craftspersons working in clay, glass, fiber, wood, metal, and paper. *40 W. 53rd St., tel. 212/956–3535. Admission charged. Closed Mon.*

Southwest of here is **Times Square,** bounded by Broadway, 7th Avenue, and 42nd Street and one of New York's main energy centers. Known as the Crossroads of the World, the Great White Way, and the New Year's Eve Capital of America, it is perhaps best known as the Broadway Theater District. Most of the so-called Broadway theaters are actually on the streets west of Broadway, between 43rd and 52nd streets.

Two pink Tennessee-marble lions guard the entrance to the distinguished Beaux-Arts building that houses the **New York Public Library's** central research facility (5th Ave. and 42nd St., tel. 212/930–0800), one of the largest research libraries in the world. Farther east is **United Nations Headquarters** (tel. 212/963–7713), occupying a lushly landscaped riverside tract along 1st Avenue between 42nd and 48th streets. A line of flagpoles with banners representing the current roster of 180 member nations stands before the striking 550-foot slab of the Secretariat Building. Tours (admission charged) depart from the General Assembly lobby, where you can pick up free tickets to most sessions.

At the southern end of midtown is the **Empire State Building.** Though no longer the world's tallest skyscraper, the pointy-towered art deco structure remains the best loved. More than 2.5 million people visit the 86th- and 102nd-floor observatories each year. *5th Ave. and 34th St., tel. 212/736–3100. Admission charged.*

Upper West Side   Once one of New York's most rundown neighborhoods, the Upper West Side is now chic, with boutiques and cafés lining Co-

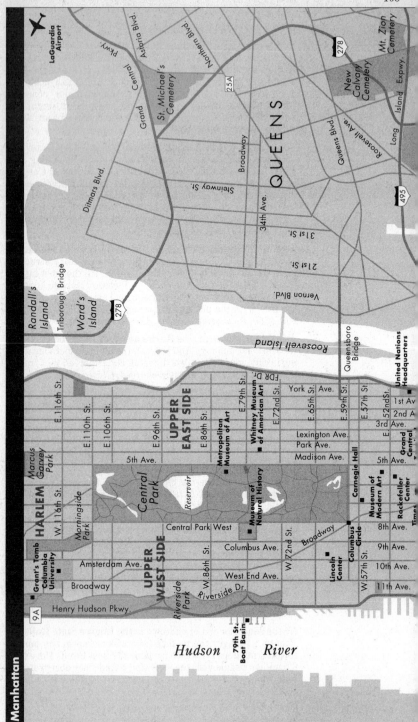

Manhattan

LaGuardia Airport

Grand Central Pkwy.

Astoria Blvd.

Northern Blvd.

St. Michael's Cemetery

25A

278

Mt. Zion Cemetery

New Calvary Cemetery

Long Island Expwy.

Roosevelt Ave.

Queens Blvd.

QUEENS

Broadway

Ditmars Blvd.

Steinway St.

34th Ave.

31st St.

21st St.

495

Vernon Blvd.

Randall's Island

Triborough Bridge

Ward's Island

278

Roosevelt Island

Queensboro Bridge

United Nations Headquarters

FDR Dr.

UPPER EAST SIDE

E.116th St.

E.110th St.

E.106th St.

E.96th St.

E.86th St.

E.79th St.

Whitney Museum of American Art

E.72nd St.

E.65th St.

E.59th St.

E.57th St.

E.52nd St.

York Ave.

1st Av

2nd Ave.

3rd Ave.

Lexington Ave.

Park Ave.

Madison Ave.

E.

Grand Central

Metropolitan Museum of Art

5th Ave.

HARLEM

Marcus Garvey Park

5th Ave.

Central Park

Reservoir

Museum of Natural History

Carnegie Hall

Museum of Modern Art

Rockefeller Center

Times

W.116th St.

Morningside Park

Central Park West

Columbus Ave.

Broadway

8th Ave.

9th Ave.

Columbus Circle

UPPER WEST SIDE

Grant's Tomb

Columbia University

Amsterdam Ave.

Broadway

W.86th St.

West End Ave.

Riverside Dr.

W.72nd St.

W.57th St.

Lincoln Center

10th Ave.

11th Ave.

9A

Henry Hudson Pkwy.

Riverside Park

79th St. Boat Basin

Hudson River

Newtown Creek

Grand Ave.

Flushing Ave.

Bushwick Ave.

Broadway

Lafayette Ave.

Bedford Ave.

Fulton St.

Cemetery

Humboldt Ave.

Expwy.

Brooklyn-Queens

BROOKLYN

Flatbush Ave.

Atlantic Ave.

East River

Williamsburg Bridge

FDR Dr.

Midtown Tunnel

E. 125th St.

GRAMERCY

EAST VILLAGE

E. 23rd St.

E. 14th St.

E. 4th St.

E. Houston St.

Delancy St.

LITTLE ITALY

E. Broadway

Manhattan Bridge

Brooklyn Bridge

South Street Seaport

Staten Island Ferry

2nd Ave.

Madison Square Gramercy Park

Union Square

Bowery

Lafayette St.

CHINA-TOWN

Fulton St.

Wall St.

Brooklyn-Battery Tunnel

Lexington Ave.

Public Library

Empire State Building

Broadway

Washington Square

Broadway

SOHO

LOWER MANHATTAN

Battery Park

MIDTOWN

(Ave.)

Madison Ave.

Ave. of the Americas

Sheridan Square

Hudson St.

W. Houston St.

W. Broadway

W. Chambers St.

World Trade Center

Trinity Church

NY Stock Exchange

Port Authority Bus Terminal

W. 34th St.

7th Ave.

GREENWICH VILLAGE

Canal St.

TRIBECA

West St.

Madison Square Garden/ Pennsylvania Station

CHELSEA

W. 23rd St.

W. 14th St.

Hudson St.

West Side Hwy.

Hudson River

Javits Convention Center

Lincoln Tunnel

Holland Tunnel

NEW JERSEY

N

0 440 yards

0 400 meters

lumbus Avenue and renovated brownstones standing proudly on the side streets. **Lincoln Center** (Broadway, between 62nd and 66th Sts., tel. 212/875–5000 for tour information), which spearheaded the area's revitalization, is today the West Side's cultural anchor. Flanking the central fountain are three major concert halls: **Avery Fisher Hall,** where the New York Philharmonic Orchestra performs; the glass-fronted **Metropolitan Opera House,** home of the Metropolitan Opera and the American Ballet Theatre; and the **New York State Theater,** home of the New York City Ballet and the New York City Opera.

The **American Museum of Natural History** (tel. 212/769–5100; admission charged) is set on a four-block tract bounded by Central Park West, Columbus Avenue, and 77th and 81st streets. Its collection of 36 million items includes a stuffed 94-foot blue whale, the 563-carat Star of India sapphire, and lots of dinosaur skeletons. The adjacent **Hayden Planetarium** (on 81st St., tel. 212/769–5920; admission charged) offers two stories of exhibits and sky and laser shows projected on 22 wraparound screens.

Columbia University (founded in 1754) is a large and wealthy private institution and New York City's Ivy League campus. Bounded by 114th and 121st streets, Broadway, and Amsterdam Avenue, the campus is so effectively walled off from the city by buildings that it's easy to believe you're in a more rustic setting. Enter at 116th Street for a look around.

Harlem Harlem has been the mecca of black American culture for nearly a century. In the 1920s, in an astonishing confluence of talent known as the Harlem Renaissance, black novelists, playwrights, musicians, and artists gathered here. By the 1960s, crowded housing, poverty, and crime had turned the neighborhood into a simmering ghetto. Today, Harlem is on the way to restoring itself. Mixed in with some seedy remains of the past are old jewels like the refurbished **Apollo Theatre** (253 W. 125th St., tel. 212/749–5838), where such music greats as Ella Fitzgerald and Duke Ellington brought black musicians into the limelight, and the **Studio Museum** (144 W. 125th St., tel. 212/864–4500), dedicated to collecting and exhibiting artworks of the African diaspora and black America in the form of paintings, sculpture, and photographs.

Upper East Side East of Central Park between 60th and 96th streets is the Upper East Side, long the city's most expensive and desirable residential area. The home of money, old and new, the neighborhood boasts singles bars and high-rise apartment buildings on 1st Avenue, sedate town houses in the East 60s, and an outstanding concentration of art museums and galleries. Along the **Madison Mile,** Madison Avenue between 59th and 79th streets, are patrician art galleries, unique specialty stores, and the boutiques of many of the world's major fashion designers. **Museum Mile** is a strip of cultural institutions, representing a broad spectrum of subjects and styles, located on or near 5th Avenue between 82nd and 104th streets.

The **Frick Collection,** housed in a Louis XVIII–style palace built by the Pittsburgh coke-and-steel baron Henry Clay Frick, is the city's finest small art museum. Specializing in European works from the late 13th to the late 19th century, it has masterpieces by Rembrandt, Fragonard, Bellini, and Vermeer, among others. *1 E. 70th St. at 5th Ave., tel. 212/288–0700. Admission charged. Closed Mon.*

The **Whitney Museum of American Art,** a gray granite vault with cantilevering and startling trapezoidal windows that project out, is devoted exclusively to 20th-century American work, from naturalism and impressionism to pop art, abstractionism, and whatever comes next. *945 Madison Ave. at 75th St., tel. 212/570–3676. Admission charged. Closed Mon.*

Nearby is the **Metropolitan Museum of Art,** the largest art museum in the Western Hemisphere. Major displays cover prehistoric to modern times and all areas of the world, including impressive Greek and Egyptian collections and an entire wing devoted to tribal arts. The museum has the world's most comprehensive collection of American art, and its holdings of European art are unequaled outside Europe. Also here are the Temple of Dendur, an Egyptian temple reassembled in a dramatic setting, and galleries devoted to musical instruments and arms and armor. Walking tours and lectures are free with admission. *5th Ave. at 82nd St., tel. 212/535–7710. Admission charged. Closed Mon.*

Frank Lloyd Wright's landmark **Guggenheim Museum,** expanded and restored in 1992, is a six-story spiral rotunda through which you wind down past mobiles, stabiles, and other exemplars of modern art. Displays alternate new artists and modern masters; the permanent collection includes more than 20 Picassos. *1071 5th Ave. at 89th St., tel. 212/423–3500. Admission charged. Closed Thurs.*

A former residence of the industrialist and philanthropist Andrew Carnegie now houses the **Cooper-Hewitt Museum,** officially the Smithsonian Institution's National Museum of Design. Exhibitions, which change regularly, focus on an aspect of contemporary or historical design. Major holdings include drawings, prints, textiles, furniture, metalwork, ceramics, glass, woodwork, and wall coverings. *2 E. 91st St., tel. 212/860–6868. Admission charged. Closed Mon.*

The **Museum of the City of New York** makes the history of the Big Apple—from its seafaring beginnings to yesterday's headlines—come to life with period rooms, dioramas, a video, and clever displays of memorabilia. *5th Ave. at 103rd St., tel. 212/534–1672. Admission charged. Closed Mon.–Tues.*

Greenwich Village   With its winding streets, town houses, and leafy squares, Greenwich Village is the closest thing to a small town in Manhattan. The Village, as New Yorkers invariably call it, is ideal for strolling, window-shopping, and café-hopping.

The preferred haunt of generations of writers, artists, musicians, and bohemians, the Village is known for the scores of famous Americans who lived and worked here and the cultural movements they defined. Perhaps those most synonymous with Greenwich Village are the countercultural artists of this century, including the abstract expressionist painters and beat writers of the late 1940s and early 1950s and the folk musicians and poets of the 1960s.

All kinds of history are encountered in a walk through the Village. Edna St. Vincent Millay and John Barrymore each lived at 75½ **Bedford Street**—at 9½ feet wide, New York's narrowest house. Theodore Dreiser wrote *An American Tragedy* at 16 St. Luke's Place, and Howdy Doody was designed in the basement of 12 Gay Street. Two houses on MacDougal Street (Nos. 127

and 129) were once owned by Aaron Burr, who held much of the land that is now Greenwich Village.

The best place to begin a walking tour is the gleaming white **Washington Arch** in **Washington Square,** at the foot of 5th Avenue. Designed by Stanford White, the arch was built in 1892 to commemorate the 100th anniversary of George Washington's presidential inauguration. Most of the buildings bordering the square belong to **New York University.** The surrounding area, around the intersection of Bleecker and MacDougal streets, attracts a young crowd to its offbeat shops, bars, jazz clubs, Off-Broadway theaters, cabarets, coffeehouses, pizza stands, fast-food stands, cafés, and unpretentious restaurants.

To the northwest, at **Sheridan Square,** is Christopher Street, the heart of New York's gay community and the location of many intriguing boutiques. West of 7th Avenue, the Village turns into a picture-book town of twisting, tree-lined streets, quaint houses, and tiny restaurants.

The gritty **East Village,** east of 4th (Lexington) Avenue, has over the centuries housed Jewish, Ukrainian, and Puerto Rican immigrants, beatniks, hippies, punk rockers, artists of various stripes, and, most recently, affluent young professionals. Soak up the eclectic atmosphere along St. Marks Place, with its seedy cafés and offbeat shops.

SoHo, Little Italy, and Chinatown   The 1970s influx of artists to **SoHo**—the area south of Houston (pronounced "How-ston") Street, bounded by Broadway, Canal Street, and 6th Avenue—transformed it seemingly overnight from a no-man's-land to a vibrant cultural and commercial center. Today, SoHo offers a range of galleries, the world's greatest concentration of cast-iron buildings, high-style shopping, and plenty of intriguing places in which to eat and drink.

West Broadway (parallel to and four blocks west of Broadway) is SoHo's main drag, with many shops and galleries. On Saturday, the big day for gallery-hopping, the sidewalks turn into a strolling fashion show of today's wildest styles. Two fine examples of **cast-iron architecture** can be found on Greene Street, at Nos. 72–76 and 28–30.

Walk one block east to Grand and Mulberry streets to enter **Little Italy,** an ever-shrinking enclave of the Italian way of life. **Mulberry Street,** lined with tenement buildings, has long been the heart of Little Italy; at this point it's virtually the entire body. Between Broome and Canal streets, Mulberry consists entirely of restaurants, cafés, bakeries, imported-food shops, and souvenir stores. Each September, the Feast of San Gennaro turns the streets of Little Italy into a bright and turbulent Italian kitchen.

In recent years, **Chinatown** has expanded beyond its traditional borders into Little Italy to the north and the formerly Jewish Lower East Side to the east. **Canal Street** abounds with crowded markets bursting with mounds of fresh seafood and strangely shaped vegetables in extraterrestrial shades of green. Food shops proudly display almond cookies and roast ducks.

Mott Street is the principal business street of the neighborhood. Narrow and twisting; crammed with souvenir shops and restaurants in funky, pagoda-style buildings; crowded with pedestrians at all hours of the day or night—Mott Street looks the way you'd expect Chinatown to look. Within a few dense blocks, hundreds of restaurants serve every imaginable type of Chinese cuisine, from simple fast-food noodles or dumplings to sumptuous Hunan, Szechuan, Cantonese, Mandarin, and Shanghai feasts.

Lower Manhattan   **Lower Manhattan** is a compact area dense with attractions and contradictions: narrow streets and immense skyscrapers, Colonial-era houses and the Brave New World complex of Battery Park City, the no-nonsense intensity of Wall Street and the theme-park aura of the South Street Seaport.

Start your exploration outside the **Staten Island Ferry Terminal,** at the southernmost tip of Manhattan. To the west lies **Battery Park,** a verdant landfill loaded with monuments and sculpture, and the point of embarkation for visits to the Statue of Liberty and Ellis Island. Buy your ticket for either at **Castle Clinton,** inside the park, and be prepared to wait.

The popularity of the **Statue of Liberty** (tel. 212/363–3200) surged following its 100th-birthday restoration in 1986. Once on Liberty Island, you may have to wait three hours to take the elevator 10 stories to the top of the pedestal. The strong of heart and limb can climb another 12 stories to the crown.

Ellis Island (tel. 212/883–1986), which opened in 1990 after a $140-million restoration, was once a federal immigration facility. Between 1892 and 1954, 17 million men, women, and children—the ancestors of more than 40% of the Americans living today—were processed here.

The **World Trade Center,** a 16-acre complex, contains New York's two tallest buildings (1,350 feet high). Elevators to the observation deck on the 107th floor of 2 World Trade Center glide a quarter of a mile into the sky in only 58 seconds. The rock and soil excavated for the center begat **Battery Park City,** 100 new acres of Manhattan on the Hudson River. It includes office buildings, high-rise apartment houses, old-looking town houses, a modest selection of shops, and the **World Financial Center,** a mammoth granite-and-glass complex designed by Cesar Pelli.

Wall Street's principal facility is the **New York Stock Exchange** (tel. 212/656–5167; closed weekends), whose august Corinthian main entrance is around the corner on Broad Street. A self-guided tour, slide shows, video displays, and guides may help you interpret the chaos that seems to reign on the trading floor.

At Broad and Pearl streets is **Fraunces Tavern,** a combination restaurant, bar, and museum occupying a Colonial tavern built in 1719 and restored in 1907. Best remembered as the site of George Washington's farewell address to his officers celebrating the British evacuation of New York in 1783, it contains two fully furnished period rooms and other displays on 18th- and 19th-century American history. *Tel. 212/425–1778. Admission charged. Closed Sun.*

Back on Wall Street, a regal **statue of George Washington** stands at the spot where he was sworn in as the first U.S. president in 1789. The Federal Hall of that day was demolished when the capital moved to Philadelphia. The current **Federal Hall National Memorial** (26 Wall St., tel. 212/264–8711; closed weekends, major holidays), built in 1842, is a stately period structure that contains exhibits on New York and Wall Street.

Jet-black **Trinity Church** (Broadway and Wall St.) was New York's first Anglican parish (1646). The present structure (1846) ranked as the city's tallest building for most of the last half of the 19th century.

South Street Seaport is an 11-block historic district on the East River that encompasses a museum, shopping centers, historic ships, cruise boats, a multimedia presentation, art galleries, and innumerable places to eat and drink. You can view the historic ships from Pier 16, which is the departure point for the 90-minute **Seaport Line** (tel. 212/233–4800) harbor cruise.

Nearby is the **Brooklyn Bridge,** New York's oldest and best-known span. When it was built in 1883, it was the world's longest suspension bridge and, like so many others in turn, the tallest structure in the city. Walking across the Brooklyn Bridge is a peak New York experience. The distance is just over a mile, and thousands of commuters make the trip on foot whenever the weather allows.

Parks and Gardens

Central Park was designed by landscape architects Frederick Law Olmsted and Calvert Vaux for 843 acres of land acquired by the city in 1856. Bounded by 59th and 110th streets, 5th Avenue, and Central Park West, the park contains grassy meadows, wooded groves, and formal gardens; paths for jogging, strolling, horseback riding, and biking; playing fields; a small zoo; an ice-skating rink; a carousel; an outdoor theater; and numerous fountains and sculptures. **AAA Bikes in Central Park** (tel. 212/861–4137), beside the Loeb Boathouse parallel to 72nd Street, rents bikes.

The Bronx's **Bronx Park,** located along the Bronx River parkway and bisected by Fordham Road, contains the **Bronx Zoo** (*see* What to See and Do with Children, *below*) as well as the **New York Botanical Garden** (tel. 212/220–8700), a 250-acre botanical treasury around the dramatic gorge of the Bronx River, with a forest, a conservatory (currently closed for renovation), a museum, and 16 specialty outdoor gardens.

New York for Free—or Almost

Most museums have free hours one night a week. Free concerts, recitals, and dance presentations are given in churches, college auditoriums, and public buildings all over town. During the summer, free outdoor concerts are held in Central Park and at the **Guggenheim Bandshell** at Lincoln Center. The best sources of information are the *Village Voice* and *New York* magazine. Also, art galleries all over town are free to the public; check local newspapers and magazines for locations and current exhibitions.

What to See and Do with Children

The **Bronx Zoo** (now officially known as The International Wildlife Conservation Park; Fordham Rd. and Bronx River Pkwy., the Bronx, tel. 717/367–1010) is the largest zoo in the United States, with more than 4,000 animals on 265 acres of woods, ponds, streams, and parkland. **New York's Aquarium for Wildlife Conservation** (W. 8th St. and Surf Ave., Coney Island,

Brooklyn, tel. 718/265–3474), just off the Coney Island Board-walk, has over 20,000 creatures on display and performing in periodic exhibitions.

Shopping

You can buy almost anything you might want or need at almost any time of the day or night somewhere in New York City, but in general, major department stores and other shops are open every day and keep late hours on Thursday. Many of the upper-crust shops along upper 5th Avenue and the Madison Mile close on Sunday. Stores in such nightlife areas as SoHo and Columbus Avenue are usually open in the evenings. The bargain shops along Orchard Street on the Lower East Side are closed on Saturday, mobbed on Sunday.

Shopping Districts **Fifth Avenue** from 49th to 58th Street and **57th Street** between 3rd and 6th avenues contain many of the most famous—and expensive—stores in the world. The area extending from **Herald Square** (6th Ave. and 34th St.) along 34th Street and up 5th Avenue to 40th Street includes several major department stores and a host of lower-price clothing stores. **Madison Mile,** the 20-block span along Madison Avenue between 59th and 79th streets, consists of mainly low-rise brownstones housing the exclusive boutiques of American and overseas designers. **SoHo's** galleries, clothing boutiques, and avant-garde house-wares shops are concentrated on West Broadway. **Columbus Avenue,** between 66th and 86th streets, features far-out European and down-home preppie fashions, some antiques and vintage stores, and outlets for adult toys. The **Lower East Side** is the place for clothing bargains.

Department Stores **Bergdorf Goodman** (754 5th Ave. at 57th St., tel. 212/753–7300) is a chic and very New York place to shop for women's designer clothes; the men's department is underrated. Glitzy **Bloomingdale's** (59th St. and Lexington Ave., tel. 212/355–5900) is the quintessence of New York style—busy, noisy, crowded, and thoroughly up-to-date. **Lord & Taylor** (424 5th Ave. at 38th St., tel. 212/391–3344) is refined, well-stocked, and never overwhelming. **Macy's** (34th St. and Broadway, tel. 212/695–4400), the country's largest store, has huge housewares and gourmet-foods departments, as well as high fashion. **Saks Fifth Avenue** (611 5th Ave. at 50th St., tel. 212/753–4000) has an outstanding selection of women's and men's designer outfits.

Specialty Stores **America Hurrah** (766 Madison Ave., between 65th and 66th
Antiques Sts., 3rd floor, tel. 212/535–1930) is one of the country's premier dealers in Americana. At **Manhattan Art & Antiques Center** (1050 2nd Ave., between 55th and 56th Sts., tel. 212/355–4400), more than 100 dealers stock three floors with antiques from around the world.

Books A browser's paradise, **Gotham Book Mart** (41 W. 47th St., tel. 212/719–4448) emphasizes literature and the performing arts in books and magazines. Eight miles of shelves house more than 2 million volumes (including a rare-book collection) at the **Strand** (828 Broadway at 12th St., tel. 212/473–1452), North America's largest used-book store.

Cameras, Smart shoppers throng **47th Street Photo's** no-frills stores (67
Electronics W. 47th St., 115 W. 45th St., and 116 Nassau St., tel. 212/398–1410) for great deals with a minimum of service.

Food
: From jams, cheeses, spices, and smoked fish to a superb selection of kitchen wares, **Zabar's** (2245 Broadway at 80th St., tel. 212/787–2000) has long been a favorite with New York foodies.

Jewelry
: Every store is a jewelry shop in the **Diamond District** (47th St. between 5th and 6th Aves.); be ready to haggle. **Fortunoff** (681 5th Ave. at 54th St., tel. 212/758–6660) is a flashy discount jeweler with a wide selection of gemstones and styles. At venerable **Tiffany & Co.** (727 5th Ave. at 57th St., tel. 212/755–8000), prices can be out-of-sight, but there's always a selection of inexpensive gift items.

Music
: **Bleecker Bob's Golden Oldies** (118 W. 3rd St., tel. 212/475–9677) is a Greenwich Village spot with all the good old rock. The two **HMV**'s (2081 Broadway at 72nd St., tel. 212/721–5900; 1280 Lexington Ave. at 86th St., tel. 212/348–0800), state-of-the-art music superstores, stock hundreds of thousands of disks, tapes, and videos. **J&R Music World** (23 Park Row, tel. 212/732–8600) offers a wide selection and good prices. **Tower Records** (692 Broadway at 4th St., tel. 212/505–1500; 1965 Broadway at 67th St., tel. 212/496–2500) has a huge selection of music and videos at competitive prices.

Spectator Sports

Baseball
: **New York Mets** (Shea Stadium, Roosevelt Ave. off Grand Central Pkwy., Flushing, Queens, tel. 718/507–8499 or 718/307–6387; Apr.–Oct.). **New York Yankees** (Yankee Stadium, 161st St. and Jerome Ave., Bronx, tel. 212/293–6000; Apr.–Oct.).

Basketball
: **New York Knicks** (Madison Square Garden, 4 Penn Plaza, tel. 212/465–6741; late Oct.–mid-Apr.).

Football
: The **New York Giants** and the **New York Jets** both play at the Meadowlands Sports Complex (Rte. 3, East Rutherford, NJ, tel. 201/935–8222 or 201/935–3900; Sept.–Dec.).

Hockey
: **New York Rangers** (Madison Square Garden, tel. 212/465–6741; Oct.–Apr.).

Tennis
: The annual **U.S. Open,** in late August and early September, is one of the four grand-slam events of tennis. It is held at the **USTA National Tennis Center** in Flushing Meadows–Corona Park, Queens (tel. 718/271–5100).

Dining

Name any country, name any city or province in any country, and New York will probably have a selection of restaurants specializing in its cuisine. Enclaves of ethnic cuisines include Little India, on 6th Street between 1st and 2nd avenues, as well as Little Italy and Chinatown (*see* Exploring New York City, *above*). New York restaurants are expensive, yet savvy diners learn how to keep costs within reason—by going for lunch instead of dinner, for example, or by limiting drink orders. Be sure to make a reservation for any restaurant on a weekend, especially on Saturday night. For price ranges, see Chart 1 (A) in Chapter 1.

Very Expensive
: **Café des Artistes.** This romantic and extremely popular Lincoln Center–area institution is decorated with murals of nudes cavorting in a sylvan glade. Specialties from the country French menu include *saucisson de Lyon* (garlic sausage baked in pas-

try) and pot au feu. *1 W. 67th St. at Central Park West, tel. 212/
877–3500. Reservations required. Jacket required at dinner.
AE, DC, MC, V.*

★ **Four Seasons.** Menus and decor shift with the seasons at this
class act. The rosewood Grill Room is where movers and shak-
ers rendezvous for power lunches of high-priced, impeccably
served, and imaginative dishes that blend Oriental touches
with traditional American and French cuisine. *Seagram Building, 99 E. 52nd St., tel. 212/754–9494. Reservations required.
Jacket required. AE, DC, MC, V. No lunch Sat.; closed Sun.*

Gotham Bar and Grill. A place with a name like Gotham had
better be huge, crowded, the quintessence of sophistication—
and this is. The postmodern decor features tall columns and
high ceilings decked with parachute shades. The menu is eclectic and surprising. *12 E. 12th St., tel. 212/620–4020. Reservations advised. AE, DC, MC, V. No lunch weekends.*

★ **Le Bernardin.** On the ground floor of the midtown Equitable
building, this top-notch restaurant offers an all-seafood menu
teeming with rare treasures. For starters, try oysters with
truffle cream or black bass tartare with caviar, and go on to lobster daube or any of the fresh, artfully arranged fillets. *155 W.
51st St., tel. 212/489–1515. Reservations required. Jacket and
tie required. AE, DC, MC, V. Closed Sun.*

★ **Bouley.** In this artfully restored TriBeCa structure dramatic
arched ceilings, handsome furniture, sedate lighting, and im-
pressionistic landscapes set the tone. Chef/owner David
Bouley's cooking is exciting without being trendy—sea scallops with sea urchins, braised salmon in bandol wine, frogs'
legs in watercress consommé and Canadian chanterelles, and
his famous hot chocolate soufflé that melts when you put your
fork into it. Bouley's popularity has led to long waits for reserved tables and delays between courses, so reserve early.
The fixed-price ($65), five-plus-course meal is a bargain.
There's a very fine wine list, too. *165 Duane St. (near Hudson
St.), tel. 212/608–3852. Reservations required. Jacket and tie
required. AE, DC, MC, V. Closed Sat. lunch and Sun.*

Expensive **Alcala.** Relax in the large, exposed-brick room over a wide variety of seafood, fish, chicken, and beef dishes from Spain. Appetizers, such as fried calamari and cream of cauliflower soup,
far surpass the entrées. *349 Amsterdam Ave. (near 76th St.),
tel. 212/769–9600. Reservations advised. AE, DC, MC, V.*

★ **Il Cortile.** This classy, intimate establishment is one of the
brightest spots in the sea of restaurants for which Little Italy is
famous. An efficient, personable staff is happy to assist you in
choosing from among such dishes as the simple *scaloppine di
vitello al cognac* (tender slices of veal smothered in mushrooms
and a cognac gravy) or any of the fresh seafood dishes. *125 Mulberry St. (near Hester St.), tel. 212/226–6060. Reservations advised. AE, DC, MC, V.*

Smith & Wollensky. Plank floors, bentwood chairs, and sporting prints make this midtown steak house look like it's been
here forever. In addition to big blackened sirloins and filet mignon with pepper sauce, there are huge lobsters, veal chops,
and terrific onion rings. *201 E. 49th St., tel. 212/753–1530. Reservations advised. Jacket advised. AE, DC, MC, V.*

Moderate **Bangkok Cuisine.** New York's oldest Thai restaurant is set in an
Orientalized storefront just north of the Theater District.
Some of the spicy specialties include *tod mun pla* (deep-fried
fish patties in a sweet sauce), *pad thai* (an exciting shrimp-noo-

dle dish), and whole fish. *885 8th Ave. at 53rd St., tel. 212/581–6370. Reservations advised. AE, MC, V. No lunch Sun.*

Dawat. Classic Indian food, following the recipes of actress-author Madhur Jaffrey, carries out the promise of the sophisticated, softly lit dining room. Try the tandoori mixed grill, baked in a clay oven; the *keema matar* (ground lamb with peas and ginger); or the *kheer* (yogurt with shredded cucumber). *210 E. 58th St. (near 3rd Ave.), tel. 212/355–7555. Reservations advised. AE, DC, MC, V.*

Odeon. This converted art deco cafeteria in the TriBeCa (Triangle Below Canal [Street]) neighborhood, south of SoHo and north of the Financial District, is a lively place where everyone can feel at home. The menu mingles French brasserie-style dishes with purely American fare. *145 West Broadway at Thomas St., tel. 212/233–0507. Reservations advised. AE, DC, MC, V. No lunch Sat.*

Omen. Old brick, hardwood floors, timber ceilings, and Oriental lanterns give this former store in SoHo the relaxing ambience of a Japanese country inn. *Omen* is a dark, hot broth served with half-cooked exotic vegetables, sesame seeds, and noodles; other favorites include a boned-chicken dish called *sansho*, scallops and blanched spinach, and avocado with shrimp in miso sauce. *113 Thompson St. (between Spring and Prince Sts.), tel. 212/925–8923. Reservations advised. AE, DC. Closed Mon.*

Pig Heaven. This popular Upper East Side restaurant is gimmicky to the max, with pigs everywhere, including on an imaginative menu dominated by pork dishes, but the food is fun and good. Try Cantonese-style suckling pig or minced pork sautéed with corn, peppers, and pine nuts. *1540 2nd Ave. at 80th St., tel. 212/744–4333. Reservations advised on weekends. AE, DC, MC, V.*

★ **Rosa Mexicano.** Young professionals come to this crowded midtown hangout for chunky guacamole prepared at your table and margaritas blended with pomegranate. Grilled versions of shell steak, chicken, and snapper; pork *carnitas;* and skinned breast of duck are other noncombustible house specialties. *1063 1st Ave. at 58th St., tel. 212/753–7407. Reservations advised. AE, DC, MC, V. No lunch.*

★ **Union Square Café.** A young, monied crowd frequents this site, with light-wood floors and cream-colored walls splashed with Chagallesque murals. Executive chef Michael Romano uses nouvelle touches in such entrées as rabbit with garlic-seared artichokes in a white wine sauce, but the portions are generous and the desserts sumptuous. *21 E. 16th St., tel. 212/243–4020. Reservations advised. AE, DC, MC, V. Closed Sun.*

★ **Vince & Eddie's.** Low, beamed ceilings, sturdy oak furniture, and rough whitewashed walls lend Vince & Eddie's a country-inn flavor. A lively, preppie crowd packs this Lincoln Center-area favorite for such dishes as calves' liver with apples and onion rings and red snapper with walnuts. *70 W. 68th St., tel. 212/721–0068. Reservations required. AE, DC, MC, V.*

Inexpensive **Benito's II.** A window display of figurines and a photographic mural of the Italian coast welcome you into this one-room dining spot in the heart of Little Italy. Affable waiters arrange for eclectic appetizers of hot and cold antipasto or, for the adventurous, an entrée of octopus *polipo*, prepared in a spicy tomato sauce with plenty of garlic. *163 Mulberry St., tel. 212/226–9012. Reservations advised. No credit cards.*

Katz's Delicatessen. At this kosher deli in the heart of the Lower East Side, the noise level can be a bit much, but so are the portions of knishes, pastrami, corned beef, and brisket. *205 E. Houston St. (near Orchard St.), tel. 212/254–2246. No reservations. AE.*

★ **Mandarin Court.** Though the command of English here leaves something to be desired and the pace can be chaotic, this wildly popular *dim sum* parlor warrants the trip to Chinatown. The food—a parade of small dishes of various traditional Chinese foods, such as steamed or fried dumplings—is cheap and very fresh, and everybody sits at communal tables. *61 Mott St. (near Canal St.), tel. 212/608–3838. AE, DC, MC, V.*

Wong Kee Restaurant. Behind the columned, brushed-metal facade, diners enjoy the renowned barbecued pork, the spiced-beef *chow fun* (wide rice noodles), or maybe the sweet-and-pungent chicken (a refinement of sweet-and-sour). Wong Kee's hallmark is the reliability of its low-priced, high-quality Cantonese fare, made with fresh ingredients and served in ample portions. *113 Mott St. (north of Canal St.), tel. 212/226–9018. No reservations. BYOB. No credit cards.*

Lodging

Once you've accepted that your New York hotel room is going to cost you a lot of money, you'll have plenty of choices. The hotels usually compensate for small room size and lack of parking or landscaping with fastidious service, sprucely maintained properties, and restaurants that hold their own in a city of very knowledgeable diners.

Hundreds of B&B rooms are available in Manhattan and the outer boroughs, principally Brooklyn, and almost always cost well below $100 a night; some singles are available for under $50. Reservations may be made through **Bed and Breakfast Network of New York** (134 W. 32nd St., Suite 602, 10001, tel. 212/645–8134), **City Lights Bed and Breakfast** (Box 20355, Cherokee Station, 10028, tel. 212/737–7049), or **New World Bed and Breakfast** (150 5th Ave., Suite 711, 10011, tel. 212/675–5600 or 800/443–3800). For price ranges, see Chart 2 (A) in Chapter 1.

Very Expensive **The Carlyle.** This beautifully appointed, traditional hotel in one of the city's best residential areas has the subdued mood of an English manor house. The Café Carlyle, Bemelman's Bar, and the formal Carlyle Restaurant are all eminently worth patronizing even if you're not staying here. *35 E. 76th St. at Madison Ave., 10021, tel. 212/744–1600. 185 rooms. Facilities: restaurant, café, bar, lounge, fitness center, VCRs, stereos, fax machines, kitchenettes and pantries in larger units, meeting rooms. AE, DC, MC, V.*

The Mark. The former Madison Avenue Hotel has been completely redone by its owner, Rafael Hotels. Such extras as high-quality TVs and VCRs in all rooms, deep tubs, and kitchenettes in some rooms (stocked with beverages and basic condiments) make The Mark a serious contender among New York's elite hotels. *25 E. 77th St., 10021, tel. 212/744–4300 or 800/843–6275. 185 rooms. Facilities: restaurant, café, lounge, meeting rooms, VIP suites with terraces. AE, DC, MC, V.*

★ **The Pierre.** Since it opened, at the height of the Depression, The Pierre has symbolized dignified elegance. Guest rooms, most of them recently refurbished, are traditionally decorated in soft florals with quilted bedspreads. *5th Ave. at 61st St., 10021, tel. 212/838–8000 or 800/332–3442. 204 rooms. Facilities: restaurant, bar, tearoom, meeting rooms. AE, DC, MC, V.*

The Plaza. This New York landmark has been updated, with new color schemes in burgundy or teal blue and floral-patterned quilted spreads on the large beds. Guest rooms are among the most spacious of the city's first-class hotels. Public spaces such as the Palm Court continue to evoke the palmy fin de siècle atmosphere of the great European hotels. *5th Ave. at 59th St., 10019, tel. 212/759–3000 or 800/228–3000. 807 rooms. Facilities: 2 restaurants, café, 2 bars, art gallery, handicapped-accessible rooms, meeting rooms, large concierge staff. AE, DC, MC, V.*

The Waldorf-Astoria. Along with The Plaza, this art deco masterpiece personifies New York at its most lavish and powerful. Hilton, its owner, has spent a fortune refurbishing the original murals and mosaics, elaborate plaster ornamentation, and fine old-wood walls of both public areas and guest rooms. *301 Park Ave., 10022, tel. 212/355–3000. 1,692 rooms. Facilities: 3 restaurants, coffee shop, tearoom, lounge, ballroom, fitness center, meeting rooms. AE, DC, MC, V.*

Expensive **The Algonquin.** While this landmark property's English-drawing-room atmosphere and burnished-wood lobby are being kept intact, its working parts (the plumbing, for instance) are being improved under new Westin Hotels management. Bathrooms and sleeping quarters retain Victorian-style fixtures and furnishings, but now there are larger, firmer beds, modern TVs, and Caswell-Massey toiletries. *59 W. 44th St., 10036, tel. 212/840–6800 or 800/548–0345. 165 rooms. Facilities: restaurant, 2 lounges, meeting rooms, free parking on weekends, business center. AE, DC, MC, V.*

Hotel Elysée. This relatively small hotel, on a prime block between Madison and Park avenues, has a rather offbeat atmosphere with a lived-in, 1950s feel. *60 E. 54th St., 10022, tel. 212/753–1066. 110 rooms. Facilities: restaurant, lounge, art gallery, concierge. AE, DC, MC, V.*

★ **Manhattan East Suite Hotels.** Here's a group of good-value properties for the traveler who likes to combine full hotel service with independent pied-à-terre living. The four best are the Beekman Tower (3 Mitchell Pl.), near the United Nations; the Dumont Plaza (150 E. 34th St.), on a direct bus line to the Javits Center; the Surrey Hotel (20 E. 76th St.), near Madison Avenue art galleries and designer boutiques; and the Southgate Tower (371 7th Ave.), near Madison Square Garden and Penn Station. *Sales office: 500 W. 37th St., 10018, tel. 212/465–3700 or 800/637–8483. AE, DC, MC, V.*

The Royalton. With its witty *art moderne* design, The Royalton has a plush but slightly spooky atmosphere: The halls are narrow and dark, as are some of the strangely shaped rooms. The furnishings, however, are comfy. *44 W. 44th St., 10036, tel. 212/869–4400 or 800/635–9013. 205 rooms. Facilities: restaurant with bar, meeting rooms, game and library areas, fitness center, VCRs, stereos. AE, DC, MC, V.*

Moderate **Hotel Edison.** A popular budget stop for American and foreign tour groups, this offbeat old hotel has gotten a face-lift. Guest rooms are brighter and fresher than the dark corridors seem to suggest. *228 W. 47th St., 10036, tel. 212/840–5000. 1,000* *rooms. Facilities: restaurant, coffee shop, bar. AE, DC, MC, V.*

★ **The Roger Smith Winthrop.** This hotel, in the process of a gradual redecoration, has clean, well-decorated, and spacious guest rooms with pantries. *501 Lexington Ave. at 47th St., 10017, tel. 212/755–1400. 200 rooms. Facilities: restaurant, meeting room. AE, DC, MC, V.*

Inexpensive   **Chatwal Inns.** The six Chatwal properties, most in the Broadway-midtown area, provide clean, attractive rooms at reasonable prices. *Aberdeen (17 W. 32nd St.), Best Western Woodward (210 W. 55th St.), Chatwal Inn (132 W. 45th St.), Chatwal Inn on Park (429 Park Ave. S), President Hotel (234 W. 48th St.), and Quality Inn (157 W. 47th St.); central reservations, 234 W. 48th St., 10036, tel. 800/826–4667 or 800/621–4667 in Canada. Facilities: restaurants, small meeting rooms, lounges, depending on the property. AE, DC, MC, V.*

International House. This large nonprofit residence for graduate students from abroad, in a 10-story graystone building near Columbia University, has simply furnished guest rooms and suites available for travelers year-round, as well as single student rooms from mid-May to late August. *500 Riverside Dr. at 123rd St., tel. 212/316–8436. 11 suites, 5 guest rooms, 10–100 student rooms with shared baths. Facilities: cafeteria, lounges, laundry, sports, cultural programs. MC, V.*

New York International American Youth Hostel. In 1990 AYH opened this ambitious facility on the Upper West Side, with dorm accommodations at rock-bottom prices. Guests can rent sheets and use kitchens and dining rooms. *891 Amsterdam Ave., 10025, tel. 212/932–2300. 30 4- to 12-bed dorm rooms with hall baths. Facilities: dining area, patio, kitchen, self-service laundry, travel desk, conference rooms for nonprofit groups. MC, V.*

Motels   **Holiday Inn Crowne Plaza** (1605 Broadway, 10019, tel. 212/977–4000 or 800/465–4329), 770 rooms, 3 restaurants, coffee shop, lounge, health club, concierge level, pool; expensive. **Sheraton Park Avenue** (45 Park Ave., 10016, tel. 212/685–7676 or 800/325–3535), 149 rooms, restaurant, lounge; expensive. **Ramada Inn** (48th St. and 8th Ave., 10019, tel. 212/581–7000), 366 rooms, restaurant, lounge, pool, meeting room; moderate. **Sheraton Center Hotel and Towers** (811 7th Ave., 10019, tel. 212/581–1000 or 800/325–3535), 1,748 rooms, 2 restaurants, lounge; moderate. **Sheraton City Squire** (790 7th Ave., 10019, tel. 212/581–3300 or 800/325–3535), 720 rooms, restaurant, lounge, health club, pool; moderate. **Best Western Milford Plaza** (270 W. 45th St., 10036, tel. 212/869–3600 or 800/528–1234), 1,300 rooms, 2 restaurants, 2 lounges; inexpensive. **Howard Johnson Plaza Hotel** (851 8th Ave., 10019, tel. 212/581–4100 or 800/654–2000), 300 rooms, restaurant, lounge; inexpensive. All listed motels provide parking for a fee.

The Arts and Nightlife

Full listings of entertainment and cultural events appear in the weekly *New York* magazine; they include capsule summaries of plays and concerts, performance times, and ticket prices. The Arts & Leisure section of the Sunday *New York Times* lists and describes events but provides no service information. The Theater Directory in the daily *Times* advertises ticket information for Broadway and Off-Broadway shows. Listings of events also appear weekly in *The New Yorker, Village Voice,* and *New York Newsday*'s Friday edition.

The Arts
Theater New York boasts nearly 40 Broadway theaters, three dozen Off-Broadway theaters, and 200 Off-Off-Broadway houses. Broadway theaters are located in the Theater District, most of which lies between Broadway and 8th Avenue, from 43rd to 52nd streets. Off- and Off-Off-Broadway theaters are scattered all over town, including in Greenwich Village, on the Upper West Side, and along Theater Row, a strip of 42nd Street between 9th and 10th avenues.

At Duffy Square, on 47th Street between Broadway and 7th Avenue, and on the Mezzanine at 2 World Trade Center, **TKTS** booths sell half-price (plus $2-per-ticket service charge) day-of-performance tickets to Broadway and Off-Broadway shows. Booths open at 11 AM; lines can be long.

Music Much of New York's serious-music scene clusters around the magnificent concert halls and theaters of **Lincoln Center** (Broadway and 65th St., tel. 212/875-5400). Its **Avery Fisher Hall** (tel. 212/875-5030) is home of the New York Philharmonic Orchestra, the American Philharmonic, the Mostly Mozart festival, and visiting orchestras and soloists. **Carnegie Hall** (154 W. 57th St., tel. 212/247-7800) has epitomized a musician's ascent to the big time for over a century.

Opera The **Metropolitan Opera House** (tel. 212/362-6000), at Lincoln Center, is a sublime setting for mostly classic operas performed by world-class stars. The **New York City Opera** (tel. 212/870-5570), at Lincoln Center's **State Theater,** is a first-class company with lower ticket prices and an innovative and unpredictable schedule.

Dance The **American Ballet Theatre** (tel. 212/362-6000) is the resident dance company of the Metropolitan Opera House in Lincoln Center. The center's **New York State Theater** is home to the **New York City Ballet** (tel. 212/870-5570), which reached world-class prominence under the direction of the late George Balanchine. **City Center** (131 W. 55th St., tel. 212/581-7907) hosts innovative dance companies, such as the **Harlem Dance Center,** the **Paul Taylor Company,** and the **Joffrey Ballet.** The **Joyce Theater** (8th Ave. and 19th St., tel. 212/242-0800) houses the avant-garde **Feld Ballet.**

Film Check local newspapers for movie listings. *New York* magazine and *The New Yorker* publish programs and capsule reviews. The vast majority of Manhattan theaters are first-run houses. Among the art-film and revival houses are **The Film Forum 2** (209 W. Houston St., tel. 212/727-8110) in SoHo and **Theatre 80 St. Marks** (80 St. Marks Pl., tel. 212/254-7400) in the East Village. The **Museum of Modern Art** (*see* Exploring New York City, *above*) also offers several film series every year.

Nightlife
Cabaret **The Ballroom** (253 W. 28th St., tel. 212/244-3005) is a Chelsea *tapas* (Spanish appetizers) bar with top-name cabaret acts and outrageous revues.

Comedy Club **The Original Improvisation** (358 W. 44th St., tel. 212/765-8268), New York's original comedy showcase, is where all the big-name yucksters (Rodney Dangerfield, Richard Pryor, Robert Klein) earned their first giggles.

Discos and The **Palladium** (126 E. 14th St., tel. 212/473-7171) is New
Dance Clubs York's largest club. **Roseland** (239 W. 52nd St., tel. 212/247-0200) is the place for "touch dancing" the way they used to do it.

Jazz Clubs **The Blue Note** (131 W. 3rd St., tel. 212/475-8592) is a new incarnation of a legendary jazz club. **Michael's Pub** (211 E. 55th St., tel. 212/758-2272) has mainstream jazz, top vocalists, jazz-based revues—and Woody Allen's Dixieland band most Mondays. The **Village Gate** (160 Bleecker St., tel. 212/475-5120) presents different jazz-related acts and shows in three places simultaneously. The **Village Vanguard** (178 7th Ave. S, tel. 212/255-4037) is a basement joint that has ridden the crest of every new wave in jazz for over 50 years.

Pop, Rock, Blues, The *Village Voice* carries the best listings of who's playing
and Country where on the pop and rock scenes. **The Bitter End** (147 Bleecker St., tel. 212/673-7030) has been giving a break to folk, rock, jazz, comedy, and country acts for over 25 years. **The Bottom Line** (15 W. 4th St., off Mercer St., tel. 212/228-6300) features folk and rock headliners. **Eagle Tavern** (355 W. 14th St., tel. 212/924-0275) presents traditional Irish music, with bluegrass and comedy thrown in for variety. **The Lone Star Roadhouse** (240 W. 52nd St., tel. 212/245-2950) offers big names in country swing and big city blues.

For Singles **Ear Inn** (326 Spring St., near Greenwich St., tel. 212/226-
(Under 30) 9060) boasts an archetypal jukebox and regular poetry readings. The **Hard Rock Café** (221 W. 57th St., tel. 212/489-6565) is a shrine to rock 'n' roll. **Lucy's Restaurant** (503 Columbus Ave., tel. 212/787-3009) is a popular Upper West Side hangout. **South Street Seaport** (Water and Fulton Sts., tel. 212/732-7678) has a plethora of bars that attract an Ivy League–type crowd.

For Singles **Jim McMullen's** (1341 3rd Ave., tel. 212/861-4700) is a young,
(Over 30) upscale, Upper East Side watering hole with a large, busy bar decked with bouquets of fresh flowers. **Pete's Tavern** (129 E. 18th St., tel. 212/473-7676), a crowded, friendly saloon, is famous as the place where O. Henry wrote "The Gift of the Magi." The **White Horse Tavern** (567 Hudson St. and 11th St., tel. 212/243-9260) was one of the watering holes patronized by Dylan Thomas.

Gay Bars **Crazy Nanny** (21 7th Ave. S, tel. 212/366-6312), a women's bar, is small, but that doesn't discourage the diehard jukebox dancers. At **Eagle's Nest** (142 11th Ave., tel. 212/691-8451), a favorite cruise bar, the hormones are always running, attracting a balanced mix of men, including pool players and dancing fools (there's a DJ on board). **Uncle Charlie's Downtown** (56 Greenwich Ave., tel. 212/255-8787) is an extremely popular Village gay bar, visited by stylish young men and distinguished-looking professionals.

Excursions to the Other Boroughs

Brooklyn Brooklyn Heights—named for its enviable hilltop position—
Heights was New York's first suburb, linked to the city first by ferry and later by the Brooklyn Bridge. Some 600 buildings more than a century old remain intact today, making the Heights a kind of picture book of 19th-century American architecture. The mansard-roofed Federal-style residence at **24 Middagh Street** is the oldest home in the neighborhood; from a door in the

wall on Willow Street around the corner you can see the cottage garden and carriage house in the rear.

The **Plymouth Church of the Pilgrims** (Orange St. between Henry and Hicks Sts.) was the vortex of abolitionist sentiment in the years before the Civil War, thanks to the oratory of the eminent theologian Henry Ward Beecher. The church was a major stop on the Underground Railroad, which smuggled slaves to freedom. Around the corner at **22 Willow Street** is the house where Beecher lived. **Willow Street,** between Clark and Pierrepont streets, is one of the Heights' prettiest and most architecturally varied blocks, with houses in the Queen Anne and Federal styles. Pierrepont ends at the **Brooklyn Heights Promenade,** a quiet sliver of park lined with benches facing the Manhattan skyline.

Getting There Walk across the Brooklyn Bridge from lower Manhattan near City Hall and return on the No. 2 or 3 subway from the Clark Street station, a few blocks southwest of the walkway terminus.

Queens **Astoria** in Queens is one of New York's most vital ethnic neighborhoods; once German, then Italian, it is now heavily Greek and is filled with shops and restaurants reflecting the community. It is also the site of the **American Museum of the Moving Image** (35th Ave. at 36th St., tel. 718/784–0077; admission charged; closed Mon.), where a theater features clips from the works of leading Hollywood cinematographers; galleries offer exhibits on the techniques of filmmaking, including hands-on displays; and the collection of movie memorabilia contains costumes worn by Rudolph Valentino and Bette Davis.

Getting There Take the No. 7 train from Manhattan (Grand Central) to Queensboro Plaza, then change for the N train and get off at Broadway.

The Bronx The only New York borough attached to the mainland, the Bronx was first settled by Dutch, French, English, and Swedish country squires, who established manorial holdings there while fighting off the Native Americans. Little remains from the Colonial era, but the area dramatically illustrates another aspect of Bronx history: the influx of immigrant groups—first the Irish, then Germans, Italians, and Jews—from the 1840s on. Later waves included blacks and Hispanics, and today there are new infusions of Albanian and Cambodian immigrants.

Poe Park contains the **Edgar Allan Poe Cottage** (E. Kingsbridge Rd. and Grand Concourse, tel. 212/881–8900), where Poe and his wife, Virginia, lived between 1846 and 1849. On Fordham Road is the 85-acre campus of **Fordham University,** begun as a Jesuit college in 1841. In **Bronx Park** are the **New York Botanical Garden** (*see* Parks and Gardens, *above*) and the **Bronx Zoo** (*see* What to See and Do with Children, *above*), two world-class attractions.

Long Island

At 1,682 sq mi, Long Island is not only the largest island on America's East Coast but the most varied. From west to east, Long Island shades from suburban sprawl to the farmland of the North Fork and the world-famous resort villages of the Hamptons. It has arguably the nation's finest stretch of white-sand beach, as well as the notoriously congested Long Island Expressway (LIE).

Tourist Information

Long Island: Convention and Visitors Bureau (Nassau Veterans Memorial Coliseum, 1255 Hempstead Turnpike, Uniondale 11553, tel. 516/794–4222 or 800/441–4601). **Visitor centers:** at Eisenhower Park (parking field 6A, East Meadow), on the Southern State Parkway (between Exits 13 and 14, Valley Stream) and the LIE (Dix Hills–Deer Park), and at the Cross Sound Ferry Terminal (New London, CT).

Getting There

By Plane   In addition to **John F. Kennedy International** and **LaGuardia** airports in Queens (*see* New York City, Arriving and Departing, *above*), Long Island is served by **Long Island MacArthur Airport** in Ronkonkoma (tel. 516/467–6161 for airline information).

By Car   The **Midtown Tunnel** (I–495) and the **Triborough Bridge** (I–278) connect Long Island with Manhattan. The **Throgs Neck Bridge** (I–295) provides access from the Bronx and New England.

By Train   The **Long Island Railroad** (tel. 516/822–5477) has frequent service from Penn Station in Manhattan to all major towns on Long Island.

By Bus   **Hampton Jitney** (tel. 212/936–0440) links Manhattan with towns on the southeastern end of Long Island.

Exploring Long Island

The best way to get a feel for Long Island and explore its museums, stately mansions, nature preserves, and coastal villages is to avoid the traffic-choked LIE and take the more leisurely roads that parallel the coasts. On the North Shore, your best bet is Rte. 25A; on the South Shore, Rte. 27 (Sunrise Highway).

The stretch of wealthy suburbs just outside New York City on the North Shore is known as the Gold Coast. **Roslyn Harbor** is home to Long Island's largest art museum, the **Nassau County Museum of Art,** set amid 145 acres of formal gardens, outdoor art, and rolling fields, and housed in the former country home of Henry Clay Frick. The 10 galleries are hung with changing exhibits. *Rte. 25A, tel. 516/484–9337. Admission charged. Closed Mon.*

Farther east, in the town of **Oyster Bay,** is the **Planting Fields Arboretum** (Planting Fields Rd., tel. 516/922–9200; admission charged), 150 acres of immaculately landscaped grounds surrounding a Renaissance-style mansion. Nearby is **Sagamore Hill** (Cove Neck Rd., 1 mi north of Rte. 25A, tel. 516/922–4447;

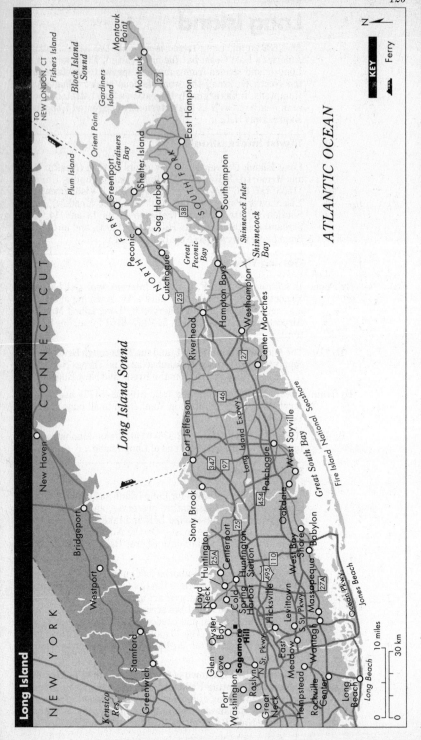

Long Island

N

NEW YORK

CONNECTICUT

Long Island Sound

ATLANTIC OCEAN

Block Island Sound

Montauk Point

Fishers Island

Gardiners Island

TO NEW LONDON, CT

Plum Island

Orient Point

Greenport

Gardiners Bay

Shelter Island

Montauk

Sag Harbor

Peconic

Cutchogue

NORTH FORK

SOUTH FORK

East Hampton

Southampton

Great Peconic Bay

Shinnecock Inlet

Shinnecock Bay

New Haven

Bridgeport

Westport

Stamford

Greenwich

Kensico Res.

Riverhead

Hampton Bays

Westhampton

Center Moriches

Port Jefferson

Long Island Expwy

Stony Brook

Patchogue

West Sayville

Oakdale

Great South Bay

Fire Island National Seashore

Fire Island

Huntington

Lloyd Neck

Centerport

Cold Spring Harbor

Huntington Station

Hicksville

Levittown

West Bay Shore

Babylon

Oyster Bay

Glen Cove

Sagamore Hill

Roslyn

East Meadow

Wantagh

Massapequa

Port Washington

Great Neck

Hempstead

Rockville Centre

Long Beach

Ocean Beach

Jones Beach

Ocean Pkwy

N St Pkwy

S St Pkwy

10 miles

30 km

admission charged), the Victorian summer White House of President Theodore Roosevelt.

The North Fork, the upper part of Long Island's eastern "tail," is beautiful farm country, with a thriving wine-growing business concentrated in **Cutchogue** and **Peconic. Hargrave Vineyard** (Rte. 48, Cutchogue, tel. 516/734–5158), the pioneer winery in the region, offers tours and tastings.

The Hamptons, on the South Fork, are a string of seaside villages that the East Coast upper crust "discovered" in the late 19th century and transformed into elegant summer resorts. At the pinnacle of fashion and fame is **East Hampton,** which, despite the hordes of celebrities and tourists who descend each summer, retains the grace and dignity of its Colonial heritage. Main Street has the town's classic white Presbyterian Church (built in 1860) and stately old homes and inns, and the side streets are lined with Shingle-Style mansions.

Sag Harbor, on the north shore of the South Fork, looks much as it did in the 1870s, when it was an important whaling center. The **Whaling Museum** displays logbooks, scrimshaw, and harpoons. *Garden and Main Sts., tel. 516/725–0770. Admission charged. Closed Oct.–Memorial Day.*

Beautiful and historic **Shelter Island,** in Gardiners Bay, nestled between the North and South forks, was among the first parts of Long Island to be settled by the British and is now primarily a summer resort and boating center. You can use the island as a scenic stepping-stone between one fork and the other, taking the ferries that leave from **Greenport** on the North Fork (tel. 516/749–0139) and **North Haven** on the South Fork (tel. 516/749–1200).

At Long Island's eastern tip, **Montauk** has the double allure of extremity and the sea. Though the village is rather touristy, the beaches are unsurpassed. **Hither Hills State Park** (Rte. 27, tel. 516/668–2461) preserves miles of rolling moors and forests of pitch pine and scrub oak. From the 110-foot **Montauk Lighthouse** (Rte. 27, tel. 516/668–2544) you can see all the way to Rhode Island.

What to See and Do with Children

Lewin Farms (Rte. 48, Wading River, tel. 516/929–4327) is the island's largest pick-your-own farm, with apples, berries, and vegetables. **Long Island Game Farm** (Chapman Blvd., Manorville, tel. 516/878–6644; closed mid-Oct.–mid-Apr.) has baby animals for children to bottle-feed, a wild-tiger show, and train rides.

Shopping

Long Island is known for its shopping malls, the largest of which is the **Roosevelt Field Mall** (tel. 516/742–8000) in Garden City, with 150 stores and more on the way. Branches of many New York City department stores are located in Garden City (on Franklin Ave.). **Manhasset's "Miracle Mile,"** along Rte. 25A, has department stores and designer boutiques. If you're looking for bargains, visit the **Flea Market** at Roosevelt Raceway (Old Country Rd., Westbury, tel. 516/222–1530) every Wednesday and Sunday.

Sports and Outdoor Activities

Boating   **Captree Boatmen's Association** (Captree State Park, Box 5372, Babylon 11707, tel. 516/669–6464) has a fleet of 34 open and charter-fishing boats with courteous crews. **Oyster Bay Sailing School** (Box 447, West End Ave., Oyster Bay 11771, tel. 516/624–7900) offers classes and three- to five-day vacation packages from April through October.

Spectator Sports

Hockey   **New York Islanders** (Nassau Coliseum, Hempstead Turnpike, Uniondale, tel. 516/794–4100; Oct.–Apr.).

Horse Racing   **Belmont Park** (Hempstead Turnpike, Elmont, tel. 718/641–4700; May–July, late Aug.–Oct.) is home to the third jewel in horse racing's triple crown, the Belmont Stakes, held in early June.

Beaches

Jones Beach State Park (Wantagh Pkwy., Wantagh, tel. 516/785–1600), a wide, sandy stretch of ocean beach, is the most crowded but also the biggest and most fully equipped of Long Island beaches, with a restaurant, concession stands, changing rooms, a boardwalk, a theater, and sports facilities. Due east, **Robert Moses State Park** (Robert Moses Causeway, Babylon, tel. 516/660–0049), on Fire Island, is a far less crowded, beautiful, sandy ocean beach.

Dining and Lodging

Long Island restaurants run the gamut from fast-food chains, pizzerias, and family-style eateries to ethnic restaurants and elegant country inns. Not surprisingly, the island draws on the bounty of the surrounding waters, especially on the east end, where commercial fishing remains a vital industry.

Recent years have brought all of the major motel chains to Long Island, as well as a resurgence in hotel construction. Resort hotels and country inns are concentrated in the Hamptons. For those who prefer the bed-and-breakfast route, most local chambers of commerce, particularly on the east end, have information on B&Bs in their towns. For price ranges, see Charts 1 (A) and 2 (A) in Chapter 1.

Amagansett   **Napeague.** The decor is nautical to match the fresh seafood, in-
Dining   cluding mako shark caught off Long Island. Rounding off the seafood specialties—bouillabaisse, broiled swordfish, lobster *fra diavolo*—are Continental meat dishes, such as beef Wellington. *Montauk Hwy., tel. 516/267–3332. Reservations advised. AE. Closed early Nov.–late Apr. Moderate.*

Lodging   **Sea Crest.** These efficiency apartments are located on 500 feet
★   of oceanfront, putting them several notches above ordinary motel fare. You have your choice of poolside or more expensive oceanside rooms. *Box 7053, 11930, tel. 516/267–3159 or 800/732–3297. 74 rooms. Facilities: heated pool, tennis, barbecue grills. MC, V. Very Expensive.*

East Hampton   **The Palm at the Huntting Inn.** A powerful crowd of high-profile
Dining   Upper East Siders come here on weekends to see and be seen,

as much as to treat themselves to the lavish portions of steak and lobster for which the place is famous. *94 Main St., tel. 516/ 324–0410. Reservations for parties of 4 or more only. AE, DC, MC, V. No lunch. Very Expensive.*

Hobson's Choice. Unlike its namesake, you *do* have many choices—from tacos to duck—at this popular, informal eatery. The two rooms and bar in a 100-year-old building have an English-pub look. All desserts are made on the premises. *47 Montauk Hwy., tel. 516/324–9793. AE, MC, V. Moderate.*

Lodging
★
Maidstone Arms. This historic inn, built in the 1830s, is the coziest and most comfortable in town. It also has one of the best locations—right across from a pond and a pristine park, surrounded by East Hampton's oldest streets and most beautiful homes. *207 Main St., 11937, tel. 516/324–5006. 16 rooms, 3 cottages. Facilities: restaurant, bar. AE, MC, V. Expensive.*

Garden City
Lodging
★
Garden City Hotel. This all-new hotel is more luxurious, more sophisticated, and even more expensive than the original. It is a world-class hotel, the most opulent on Long Island and the rival of the finest Manhattan has to offer. *45 7th St., 11530, tel. 516/747–3000 or 800/547–0400. 275 rooms. Facilities: 2 restaurants, bar, lounge, nightclub, health club, indoor pool, beauty salon, shopping arcade. AE, D, DC, MC, V. Expensive.*

Greenport
Dining
Claudio's. Two large dining rooms, decorated with artifacts from the J-boats that raced in the America's Cup during the 1930s, face the harbor through large picture windows. Local seafood is the specialty. The new clam bar offers alfresco dining at umbrella-shaded tables on a wharf overlooking Peconic Bay. *Foot of Main St., tel. 516/477–0627. MC, V. Closed mid-Jan.–mid-Apr. Moderate.*

Jericho
Dining
Milleridge Inn. Basic, old-fashioned American food, including prime rib, is served in a Colonial mansion, complete with fireplaces and antiques. *Hicksville Rd., tel. 516/931–2201. Reservations advised. AE, D, DC, MC, V. Closed Christmas. Inexpensive.*

Montauk
Dining
Gosman's. This huge, classy fish restaurant, jam-packed in the summer, offers a spectacular location—at the entrance to Montauk Harbor—and the freshest possible fish, served indoors or out. You may have a long wait in peak season. *West Lake Dr., tel. 516/668–5330. No reservations. No jogging shorts. MC, V. Closed mid-Oct.–Mar. Moderate.*

Sag Harbor
Lodging
Baron's Cove Inn. This renovated motel sits next to the water near the boats of an adjacent marina. The air-conditioned rooms have kitchenettes, and some have private patios or balconies with water views. *West Water St., 11963, tel. 516/725–2100. 66 rooms. Facilities: pool, tennis, fishing, meeting rooms. AE, D, MC, V. Expensive.*

Motels
Best Western Hotel & Conference Center (80 Clinton St., Hempstead 11550, tel. 516/486–4100 or 800/343–7950), 182 rooms, restaurant, lounge, exercise room, pool; expensive. **Holiday Inn of Riverhead** (Box 883, Riverhead 11901, tel. 516/369–2200), 100 rooms, restaurant, bar, pool; expensive. **Ramada Inn** (8030 Jericho Turnpike, Woodbury 11797, tel. 516/921–8500), 102 rooms, pool, meeting rooms; moderate.

Spa

★ **Gurney's Inn Resort and Spa.** Long popular for its fabulous location, on a bluff overlooking 1,000 feet of private ocean beach, Gurney's has become even more famous in recent years for its European-style health and beauty spa. The large, luxurious rooms all have ocean views. *Old Montauk Hwy., Montauk 11954, tel. 516/668–2345. 125 rooms. Facilities: restaurant, bar, health club, indoor saltwater pool, golf and tennis privileges, extensive spa facilities, barber, beauty shop, recreation room, meeting rooms. AE, D, DC, MC, V. Very Expensive.*

Campgrounds

Hither Hills State Park (*see* Exploring Long Island, *above*) has both tent and RV sites.

The Arts and Nightlife

Check the Friday edition of *Newsday*, the Long Island newspaper, which has a weekend supplement containing an abundance of information about Long Island arts and entertainment, as well as the magazine *Long Island Monthly*.

The Arts **Jones Beach Marine Theatre** (Jones Beach, Wantagh, tel. 516/221–1000) hosts major outdoor concerts by contemporary pop artists during summer months. **Nassau Coliseum** (Hempstead Turnpike, Uniondale, tel. 516/794–9300) has major rock and pop concerts throughout the year. **Westbury Music Fair** (Brush Hollow Rd., Westbury, tel. 516/334–0800) features live concerts, shows, and theater.

Nightlife Long Island is a hot place for singles and young couples. Clubs feature the loudest in music and the fanciest in video displays, and there are big, glitzy discos. **Oak Beach Inn** (Ocean Pkwy., Oak Beach, tel. 516/587–0097) has sing-along upstairs, top-40 downstairs, deli food, and live bands on weekends. **The Savoy** in the Huntington Hilton (598 Broad Hollow Rd., Melville, tel. 516/845–1000) is one of the hottest clubs on the island from happy hour on. **Sonny's** (3603 Merrick Rd., Seaford, tel. 516/826–0973) features live jazz nightly.

The Hudson Valley

The landscape along the Hudson River for the 140 mi from Westchester County to Albany, the state capital, is among the loveliest in America. Indeed, this natural beauty—dramatic palisades, pine forests, cool mountain lakes and streams—inspired an entire art movement, the Hudson River School, in the 19th century. Also a rich agricultural region, the valley has scores of orchards, vineyards, and farm markets along country roads. Proximity to Manhattan makes this a viable destination for day trips, but the numerous country inns, B&Bs, and resorts make more leisurely journeys especially attractive.

Tourist Information

Albany County: Convention & Visitors Bureau (52 S. Pearl St., Albany 12207, tel. 518/434–1217 or 800/258–3582). **Columbia County:** Chamber of Commerce (527 Warren St., Hudson

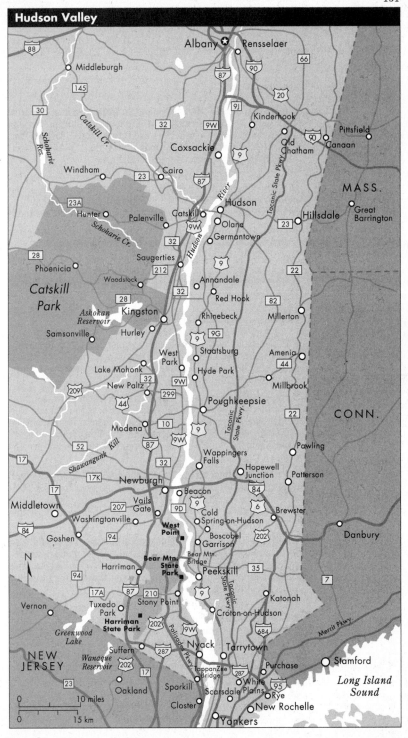

Hudson Valley

12534, tel. 518/828–4417). **Dutchess County:** Tourism Promotion Agency (46 Albany Post Rd., Box 2025, Hyde Park 12538, tel. 914/229–0033 or 800/445–3131). **Hudson River Valley:** Association (42 Catherine St., Poughkeepsie 12601, tel. 800/232–4782).

Getting There

By Plane   **LaGuardia, John F. Kennedy,** and **Newark** airports (*see* New York City, *above*) are manageable distances from the Hudson Valley. In the area itself, **Stewart International Airport** (tel. 914/564–2100) in Newburgh and **Albany County Airport** (tel. 518/869–9611) are served by major airlines.

By Car   From New York City, pick up the New York State Thruway (I–87), which parallels the west bank of the Hudson River, or the more scenic Taconic Parkway, which parallels the east bank. I–84 provides access to the region from southern New England.

By Train   **Amtrak** provides service to Hudson, Rhinecliff, Rensselaer (Albany), and points west and north of Poughkeepsie.

By Bus   **Adirondack and Pine Hill Trailways** (tel. 914/339–4230 or 800/225–6815) has daily service between New York's Port Authority Bus Terminal and New Paltz, Kingston, Albany, and other Hudson Valley towns.

Exploring the Hudson Valley

U.S. 9 hugs the east bank of the Hudson, passing through many picturesque towns, including Tarrytown, Hyde Park, Rhinebeck, and Hudson. Rte. 9W hugs the west bank from Newburgh to Catskill.

Sunnyside (W. Sunnyside La. off U.S. 9, Tarrytown, tel. 914/591–8763; admission charged), just south of the Tappan Zee Bridge, was the romantic estate of Washington Irving, author of *The Legend of Sleepy Hollow* and *Rip Van Winkle*. The 17 rooms include Irving's library and many of his original furnishings.

Harriman and **Bear Mountain state parks** (off Palisades Pkwy., tel. 914/786–2701) are the most famous parks of the vast Palisades Interstate system. Together they offer 54,000 acres and plenty of outdoor activity year-round, including boating, swimming, hiking, fishing, and cross-country skiing.

West Point (U.S. 9W, West Point, tel. 914/938–2638 or 914/938–7049), America's oldest and most distinguished military academy, is situated on bluffs overlooking the Hudson River. The museum at Olmstead Hall houses one of the world's foremost military collections.

Across the river in Garrison stands **Boscobel** (Rte. 9D, tel. 914/265–3638; admission charged), a fully restored early 19th-century mansion surrounded by beautiful gardens that afford a breathtaking view of the Hudson River. Nearby **Cold Spring-on-Hudson** is a small 19th-century village with quiet streets for strolling and shops full of antiques and crafts.

Farther up the river at **Hyde Park** are the **Franklin Delano Roosevelt National Historic Site** and nearby **Val-Kill,** the cottage where Eleanor Roosevelt lived from 1945 to 1962. The large Roosevelt family home contains original furnishings and a museum displaying manuscripts and personal documents. At Val-Kill, set on 172 wooded acres, the tour includes the film biography *First Lady of the World*. Two miles north of here, the elaborately decorated 54-room **Vanderbilt Mansion,** a former home of Frederick and Louise Vanderbilt, offers panoramic views of the Hudson. *All 3 sites: U.S. 9, tel. 914/229–9115. Admission charged. Val-Kill: Closed Jan.–Mar.; weekdays Nov.–Dec., Mar.–Apr. Others: Closed Tues.–Wed. Nov.– Mar., major holidays.*

A short distance away is the country's most respected cooking school, **The Culinary Institute of America** (U.S. 9, Hyde Park, tel. 914/452–9600). Founded in 1946, the institute has 1,900 students enrolled in two 21-month culinary arts or baking and pastry arts programs. Facilities include 36 kitchens and bakeshops, plus eight instructional dining rooms, of which four are student-staffed restaurants open to the public by reservation (*see* Dining and Lodging, *below*).

The **Mohonk Mountain House** (tel. 914/255–1000; admission charged for day use of facilities; *see also* Dining and Lodging, *below*) in **Lake Mohonk,** west of New Paltz over the Walkill River, is a resort high above the Hudson River valley on several thousand unspoiled acres of the Shawangunk Mountains. The mountains are ideal for hiking, bird-watching, golf, ice-skating, horseback riding, and cross-country skiing.

Woodstock became a rock-music legend after the 1969 concert (actually held 50 mi away, in Bethel). Today the town is an ideal place for walking, crafts shopping, and people-watching.

Frederic Church, the leading artist of the Hudson River School, built **Olana,** his 37-room Moorish-style castle, on a hilltop with panoramic vistas of the valley. *Rte. 9G, Hudson, tel. 518/828–0135. Admission charged. Closed Nov.–Apr.; Mon.*

In **Albany,** the **Albany Urban Cultural Park Visitors Center** (25 Quackenbush Sq., corner of Broadway and Clinton Ave., tel. 518/434–5132) has two permanent hands-on exhibits depicting Albany's past and present and offers guided and self-guided walking and driving tours. The **Henry Hudson Planetarium** here offers star shows and a free orientation to Albany.

Albany's **Empire State Plaza** (tel. 518/474–2418) is a half-mile concourse with modern art and sculpture and a blend of government, business, and cultural buildings. The plaza includes the **Corning Tower,** with a free observation deck on the 42nd floor. Also on site is the **New York State Museum** (tel. 518/474–5877), where life-size exhibits depict the state's natural and cultural history. A new exhibit includes a reproduction of an Iroquois village with a full-size longhouse. Free guided tours of the adjacent **State Capitol** (tel. 518/474–2418), including the Executive and Legislative Chambers, are conducted daily on the hour, except holidays.

What to See and Do with Children

Troy's **Junior Museum** (282 5th Ave., tel. 518/235–2120; closed Mon.–Tues.) offers everything from constellation shows in a Sky Dome Theater to reproductions of log cabins. "Team Earth" is a new environmental exhibit featuring live animals.

Sports and Outdoor Activities

Fishing The Hudson River estuary contains a remarkable variety of fish, most notably American shad, black bass, smallmouth and largemouth bass, and sturgeon. For information on licenses (required in fresh waters) and restrictions, as well as fishing hot spots and charts, contact the **New York State Department of Environmental Conservation** (21 S. Putt Corners Rd., New Paltz 12561, tel. 914/255–5453; 50 Wolf Rd., Albany 12233, tel. 518/457–3521; or Stony Kill Farm, Rte. 9D, Wappingers Falls 12590, tel. 914/831–8780).

Golf **Beekman Country Club** (11 Country Club Rd., Hopewell Junction, tel. 914/226–7700) has 27 holes; **Dinsmore Golf Course** (Rte. 9, Staatsburg, tel. 914/889–4751) and **James Baird State Park Golf Course** (Pleasant Valley, tel. 914/452–1489) have 18.

Ski Areas

Cross-country **Bear Mountain State Park** (Bear Mountain 10911, tel. 914/786–2701) has 10 mi of trails. **Clermont State Historic Site** (1 Clermont Ave., Germantown 12526, tel. 518/537–4240) has 6 mi of trails. **Mills-Norrie State Park** (Old Post Rd., Staatsburg 12580, tel. 914/889–4646 or 914/889–4111) has 6 mi of trails. **Olana State Historic Site** (RD-2, Hudson 12534, tel. 518/828–0135) has 7 mi of trails. **Rockefeller State Park** (Rte. 117, North Tarrytown 10591, tel. 914/631–1470) has 14 mi of trails.

Downhill **Catamount** (Rte. 23, Hillsdale 12529, tel. 518/325–3200) has a 1,000-foot vertical drop, 6 lifts, and 23 trails.

Dining and Lodging

For price ranges, see Charts 1 (B) and 2 (B) in Chapter 1.

Albany **Ogden's.** On the ground floor of a 1903 brick-and-limestone
Dining building, Ogden's has two-story arched windows built into 30-
★ foot-high ceilings. The menu focuses on Continental cuisine, including grilled Norwegian salmon, veal dishes, and pasta. *42 Howard St., tel. 518/463–6605. Reservations advised. AE, DC, MC, V. No lunch Sat.; closed Sun. Expensive.*

Lodging **Mansion Hill Inn.** Albany's only downtown B&B is in an urban setting around the corner from the Executive Mansion. Two of the three Civil War–era buildings have been completely renovated; the rooms are spacious, with cherry furniture and floral prints, and some have full kitchens and decks. *115 Philip St., 12202, tel. 518/465–2038 or 518/434–2334. 12 rooms. Facilities: restaurant. AE, D, DC, MC, V. Expensive.*

Bear Mountain **Bear Mountain Inn.** For more than 50 years, this chalet-style
Lodging resort has been known for both its bucolic location (in Bear Mountain State Park on the shores of Hessian Lake) and its warm hospitality. There are rooms in the main inn and units in five lodges across the lake. *Rte. 9W, 10911, tel. 914/786–2731. 60 rooms. Facilities: restaurant, lounge, outdoor pool, ice-skating, picnic grounds, hiking trails. AE, D, MC, V. Moderate.*

The Inn at Shaker Mill. This converted 1823 mill has a setting (woods, streams, and a waterfall outside your window), an interior (expert workmanship and Shaker antiques), and a host (Ingram Paperny—fascinating and friendly) that add up to an exceptional stop on your journey. *Cherry La., off Rte. 22, Canaan 12029, tel. 518/794–9345; fax 518/794–9344. 20 rooms. Facilities: restaurant, swimming pond, sauna. MC, V. Moderate.*

Cold Spring
Dining
★
Plumbush Inn. This opulent Victorian-style inn offers dining by candlelight in a setting of rose-patterned wallpaper, dark oak paneling, and paintings by local artists. Fixed-price and à la carte menus feature fresh seafood, veal, and Swiss specialties. *Rte. 9D, tel. 914/265–3904. Reservations advised. Jacket required at dinner. AE, MC, V. Closed Mon.–Tues. Expensive.*

Lodging
Olde Post Inn. This restored 1820 inn offers bed and breakfast in an Old World setting with such modern amenities as air-conditioning. Its stone tavern features jazz entertainment on weekends. *43 Main St., 10516, tel. 914/265–2510. 5 rooms share 2 baths. Facilities: tavern, patio, garden. No credit cards. Moderate.*

Hyde Park
Dining
Culinary Institute of America. The institute (*see* Exploring the Hudson Valley, *above*) has four public restaurants. **The Escoffier** (expensive) features classical haute cuisine. **American Bounty** (moderate–expensive) offers American regional fare. **Caterina de Medici** (moderate–expensive) focuses on regional Italian cooking, both traditional and modern. The informal **St. Andrew's Cafe** (moderate) specializes in meals prepared according to sound nutritional guidelines. *U.S. 9, tel. 914/471–6608 weekdays 9–5. Reservations advised. Jacket required in some rooms. AE, D, DC, MC, V. Closed school holidays and 1st 3 wks of July.*

Kingston
Dining
★
Skytop Steak and Seafood House. Panoramic views of the Hudson Valley are part of the attraction at this hilltop spot near the New York State Thruway. The menu features meats grilled over a charcoal pit and fresh lobster and seafood. *Rte. 28, tel. 914/338–6161. AE, DC, MC, V. No lunch except Sun. Moderate.*

New Paltz
Dining and Lodging
★
Mohonk Mountain House. On a lake amid 7,500 acres in the heart of the Shawangunk Mountains is this great resort with a stately Victorian feel. Room rates include three hearty American-style meals in the large, busy dining rooms and afternoon tea. Theme programs include mystery weekends (originated here in 1976), swing-dance weekends, and hikers' holidays. *Lake Mohonk, 12561, tel. 914/255–4500. 276 rooms. Facilities: 3 dining rooms, fitness center, 6 tennis courts, beach, basketball court, croquet, lawn bowling, shuffleboard, softball, volleyball, horseback riding, carriage rides, 85 mi of hiking trails, nature preserve, cross-country skiing, ice-skating. AE, DC, MC, V. Expensive.*

Rhinebeck
Dining and Lodging
★
Beekman Arms. This inn in the village center comprises 10 buildings, including smallish Colonial-style rooms in the original 1766 building and Victorian-style rooms in a mid-19th-century house a block away. All rooms have private baths and telephones; 22 have fireplaces. The inn's restaurant, the **Beekman 1766 Tavern,** serves American regional fare and incorporates the old taproom. *4 Mill St. (U.S. 9), 12572, tel. 914/876–7077 (restaurant: tel. 914/871–1766). 59 rooms. Reservations advised. AE, DC, MC, V. Moderate.*

West Point **Hotel Thayer.** On the grounds of the academy, this stately brick
Lodging hotel steeped in history and tradition has been welcoming military and civilian guests for more than 60 years. Many guest
rooms have views of the river and the West Point grounds. *U.S.
9W, 10996, tel. 914/446–4731 or 800/247–5047. 197 rooms. Facilities: restaurant, lounge. AE, D, DC, MC, V. Expensive.*

Woodstock **The Artist's Grill.** This charming restaurant 2½ mi from town is
Dining housed in a restored 150-year-old farmhouse. The menu emphasizes French country cuisine and fresh seafood. *Rte. 212, tel.
914/679–5977. Reservations advised. AE, DC, MC, V. No
lunch; closed Mon.–Wed. Oct.–May. Moderate.*

Motels **Days Inn** (16 Wolf Rd., Albany 12205, tel. 518/459–3600 or 800/
325–2525), 167 rooms, health club, pool, Continental breakfast;
moderate. **Holiday Inn Crowne Plaza** (66 Hale Ave., White
Plains 10601, tel. 914/682–0050 or 800/227–6963), 401 rooms,
restaurant, lounge, exercise room, indoor pool, whirlpool, sauna, free parking, airport and train shuttle, gift shop; moderate.
Howard Johnson Lodge (Rte. 9W, 416 Southern Blvd., Albany
12209, tel. 518/462–6555), 177 rooms, restaurant, lounge, exercise room, pool, sauna, indoor tennis courts, playground, laundry; inexpensive. **The Roosevelt Inn** (38 Albany Post Rd., Hyde
Park 12538, tel. 914/229–2443), 25 rooms, coffee shop (breakfast only), tennis, golf, cross-country skiing; inexpensive.

The Arts and Nightlife

The **Nelson A. Rockefeller Performing Arts Center** (Madison
Ave. and S. Swan St., Albany, tel. 518/473–1061) features drama, dance, and musical events. Lively bars and clubs are found
in some of the larger towns, including Nyack, New Paltz, and
Albany.

The Catskills

The Catskill Mountains have a beauty and variety dispropor-
tionate to their modest size. Just a two- or three-hour drive
from New York City, the area offers streams for fly-fishing,
paths for hiking, cliffs for rock-climbing, hills for skiing, and
back roads for leisurely driving. Once known as the "borscht
belt" for the resort complexes that catered to families from the
city, the region now tends to attract wilderness lovers and
craftspeople.

Tourist Information

Catskill: Association for Tourism Services (CATS; Box 449,
Catskill 12414, tel. 518/943–3223 or 800/542–2414). **Delaware
County:** Chamber of Commerce (97E Main St., Delhi 13753, tel.
800/642–4443). **Greene County:** Promotion Department (Box
527, Catskill 12414, tel. 518/943–3223 or 800/542–2414). **Sullivan County:** Office of Public Information (100 North St., Box
5012, Monticello 12701, tel. 914/794–3000, ext. 5010, or 800/
882–2287).

Getting There

By Plane **Albany County Airport** (*see* The Hudson Valley, *above*) is an
hour's drive from the heart of the Catskills. **Oneonta Municipal**

Airport (tel. 607/431–1076) is in the northwest corner of the region.

By Car The northern Catskills can be reached off I–87 from Catskill (Rte. 23) and Kingston (Rte. 28). The resort region lies on both sides of Rte. 17 north from I–87 at Harriman or from I–84 at Middletown.

By Bus **Adirondack Trailways** (tel. 800/858–8555) offers regular service to several Catskills communities, including Kingston, New Paltz, Phoenicia, Hunter, and Fleischmanns, from New York City and Albany. **Shortline** (tel. 800/631–8405) connects a half-dozen Sullivan County communities, including Bloomingburg, Monticello, and Wurtsboro, with New York City.

Exploring the Catskills

In the northeastern section of the Catskills is the actual village of **Catskill,** which has its share of museums and quaint buildings. Here the **Catskill Game Farm** is home to 2,000 birds and animals, including a large collection of rare hooved species, and has a petting zoo and a playground. *400 Game Farm Rd., tel. 518/678–9595. Admission charged. Closed Nov.–mid-Apr.*

In the area known as the High Peaks, Rte. 214 from **Phoenicia** north to the ski resort town of **Hunter** winds through **Stoney Clove,** a spectacular mountain cleft that has inspired countless tales of the supernatural. Another scenic route out of Phoenicia is across the Esopus River and south up lovely **Woodland Valley** to the well-marked trail to **Slide Mountain,** the highest peak in the Catskills.

Delaware County, newly discovered by big-city vacationers and second-home buyers, has gentler terrain than the High Peaks region. Fishermen prize the east and west branches of the Delaware River, and the county's more than 500 farms offer honey, eggs, cider, and maple syrup at numerous roadside stands. **Roxbury,** on Rte. 30, has a picture-perfect Main Street that Norman Rockwell would have loved.

What to See and Do with Children

Delaware & Ulster Rail Ride (Rte. 28, Arkville, tel. 607/652–2821) runs a three-hour scenic route between Arkville and Fleischmanns. In Catskill, try **Peelings Reptile Land** (Rte. 32, tel. 518/678–3557), where kids get to see snakes and lizards up close, or the **Catskill Game Farm** (*see* Exploring the Catskills, *above*).

Shopping

Shopping is a major diversion in the Catskills, with a scattering of auctions, flea markets, crafts fairs, antiques shops, and galleries. The Lower Catskills have a number of factory outlets and shopping villages. **Apollo Plaza** (E. Broadway, Monticello, tel. 914/794–2010) is an enclosed mall with 35 outlet stores selling housewares, men's and women's apparel and jewelry, toys, gifts, and more at discounts of up to 70%.

Sports and Outdoor Activities

Canoeing The 79-mi **Upper Delaware Scenic and Recreational River** is one of the finest streams for paddling in the region. For a list of trip planners and rental firms, contact the **Sullivan County Office of Public Information** (*see* Tourist Information, *above*).

Fishing Trout are abundant in Catskill streams; smallmouth bass, walleye, and pickerel can be found in many lakes and in six reservoirs. For the "Catskill Fishing" brochure and map, write to **CATS** (*see* Tourist Information, *above*).

Golf The region has 43 golf courses, many of which are located at the big resorts. For the "Golf Catskills" brochure, write to **CATS** (*see* Tourist Information, *above*).

Hiking The New York State Department of Environmental Conservation (50 Wolf Rd., Albany 12233) puts out a brochure on the 200 mi of marked hiking trails through the **Catskill Forest Preserve.**

Tubing **Town Tinker** (Bridge St., Phoenicia, tel. 914/688–5553) rents tubes for beginner and advanced routes along the Esopus Creek between Shandanken and Mount Pleasant.

Spectator Sports

Horse Racing **Monticello Raceway** (Rtes. 17 and 17B, Monticello, tel. 914/794–4100), offers year-round harness racing.

Ski Areas

Cross-country **Belleayre Mountain** (*see* Downhill, *below*) has 5 mi of trails. **Hyer Meadows** in Tannersville (Box 198, Rte 23A, 12485, tel. 518/589–5361) has 16 mi.

Downhill Downhill ski areas in the Catskills have snowmaking capabilities, because the snow cover has been unreliable in recent years. **Belleayre Mountain** (Box 313, Highmount 12441, tel. 914/254–5600), with 33 runs, eight lifts, and a 1,340-foot vertical drop, is the only state-run ski facility in the Catskills. **Hunter Mountain** (Box 295, Hunter 12442, tel. 518/263–4223) has 47 runs, 15 lifts, and a 1,600-foot drop. **Ski Windham** (C.D. Lane Rd., Windham 12496, tel. 518/734–4300) has 33 runs, seven lifts, and a 1,600-foot drop.

Dining and Lodging

While the region offers some outstanding food, the most inspiring aspect of its restaurants is often their setting. The Catskills are best known for mammoth resort hotels, but there are plenty of B&Bs and country inns that provide a personal touch, as well as ski-center condos and cabins in the woods. For price ranges, see Charts 1 (B) and 2 (B) in Chapter 1.

Big Indian **Rudi's Big Indian.** Established in the 1960s as a vegetarian
Dining sandwich shop and antiques store, Rudi's has evolved into a so-
★ phisticated spot for dining on pasta, couscous, grilled light meats, fresh local vegetables, and home-baked bread and pastries. *Rte. 28, tel. 914/254–4005. AE, DC, MC, V. Moderate.*

Elka Park
Dining and Lodging
★

Redcoat's Return. The ambience of an English country inn is offered in beautiful Platte Clove. Dinner, served in a room with a view of surrounding mountains or in the cozy library, might include Yorkshire pudding or steak-and-kidney pie. *Dale La., 12427, tel. 518/589–6379. 14 rooms (9 share baths). Facilities: breakfast, restaurant. Reservations advised. AE, DC, MC, V. Closed Nov., Apr.–Memorial Day. Moderate.*

Ellenville
Dining and Lodging
★

Nevele Hotel. This legendary Catskills superresort is set in five buildings on a woodsy, mountainous site with lakes and landscaping. The lobby is decorated in extravagant 1950s style with big bulky chairs, faux columns, and brass, but the rooms are strictly contemporary. The restaurant has a changing international menu to cater to convention guests, and big-name entertainers often perform here. *Nevele Rd., 12428, tel. 914/647–6000 or 800/647–6000. 400 rooms. Facilities: restaurant, nightly entertainment, indoor and outdoor pools, golf course, 15 tennis courts, fitness center, ice rink, horseback riding, skiing, sledding, private lake, boating, fishing. AE, DC, MC, V. Expensive.*

Glenford
Dining

La Grillade. This charming French country restaurant spent 21 prosperous years in Manhattan before moving to the Catskills. Now Manhattanites have to drive up here for the duck confit, leg of lamb, seafood, and French pastries. *Maverick Rd., Rte. 28, tel. 914/657–8630. AE, MC, V. Closed Tues. Moderate.*

Hunter
Dining and Lodging
★

Scribner Hollow Lodge. There are 22 fireplaces in this ultramodern lodge, plus such theme rooms as Future World (sunken bath, waterfall, environmentally controlled bed chamber) and Hunting Lodge (Remington prints, sporty decor). The underground "grotto pool" has a cocktail bar and live entertainment on weekends. The restaurant overlooks the mountains; rates are MAP. *Rte. 23A, 12442, tel. 518/263–4211. 38 rooms. Facilities: restaurant, pool, whirlpool, sauna. AE, D, MC, V. Expensive.*

Kiamesha Lake
Dining and Lodging
★

Concord Resort Hotel. One of the most enduring Catskill resorts, the Concord offers big-name entertainment, extensive sporting facilities, and nearby skiing. The American Plan hotel annually serves more than 2.5 million strictly kosher meals in dining rooms that can seat more than 3,000 people at a time. *Kiamesha Lake 12751, tel. 914/794–4000 or 800/431–3850. 1,200 rooms. Facilities: 6 dining rooms, 3 nightclubs, health clubs, fitness center, 2 pools, 3 golf courses, 40 indoor and outdoor tennis courts, horseback-riding trails, indoor-outdoor skating rink, volleyball, basketball, shuffleboard, toboggan run. AE, D, DC, MC, V. Expensive.*

Shandaken
Dining and Lodging
★

Auberge des 4 Saisons. At this French-style inn, some rooms are in a chalet, others in a former hunting lodge where baths are shared. The rooms are simple and wood-paneled with white and dark-red accents, and some have balconies. The lodge has a fireplace, and a patio outside for drinks. The restaurant serves French bistro cuisine, with specialties from different provinces featured on weekends. *Rte. 42, 12480, tel. 914/688–2223. 36 rooms (10 share baths). Reservations advised. AE, DC, MC, V. Restaurant closed weekdays Nov.–Memorial Day, except Christmas holidays. Moderate.*

Tannersville
Dining and Lodging

Deer Mountain Inn. This circa-1900 mansion on a 15-acre wooded enclave is lushly packed with mountain ambience:

moose heads, boar heads, bearskin rugs, paintings of European mountain villages, and heavy overstuffed furniture. The
dining room, bracketed by two huge stone fireplaces, offers
American fare—trout, veal, and seafood—with a European accent. *Rte. 25, 12485, tel. 518/589–6268. 7 rooms. MC, V. Expensive.*

Windham **La Griglia.** Elegant country dining here features northern Ital-
Dining ian cuisine. A house specialty is the *penne pepperata* (pasta
★ with sautéed sun-dried tomatoes, sweet red pepper, basil, and
a whisper of light cream). The wine list may be the best in upstate New York. *Rte. 296, tel. 518/734–4499. Reservations advised. AE, D, DC, MC, V. Expensive.*

Dining and **Thompson House.** Guests are remembered by their first names
Lodging at this resort run by five generations of the same family for over
★ a century. Guest rooms, furnished with four-poster beds and
antiques, are located in the 1860s-era main house, the Victorian Spruce Cottage, and newer buildings. The restaurant serves
Continental and American food from a changing menu. *Rte.
296, 12496, tel. 518/734–4510. 110 rooms. Facilities: restaurant, heated pool, tennis, putting greens, recreation room.
MC, V. Closed Nov.–Apr. except ski season. Moderate.*

Wurtsboro **The Repast.** This is an elegant eatery in a country sort of way.
Dining Such entrées as salmon Dijon and *poulet portofino* (sautéed
★ breast of chicken with a banana-liqueur sauce), seafood, and
big lamb chops are served with Caesar salad and homemade
desserts. *Sullivan St., tel. 914/888–4448. Reservations advised. D, MC, V. No dinner Mon.–Thurs. Moderate.*

Motels **Red Carpet Motor Inn** (Rtes. 10 and 23, Stamford 12167, tel.
607/652–7394), 36 rooms, restaurant, lounge, pool, tennis
court; moderate. **Wolfe's Pioneer Motel** (Rte. 97, Narrowsburg
12764, tel. 914/252–3385), 16 rooms, picnic area; inexpensive.

The Arts and Nightlife

Several well-established regional organizations offer a full
menu of performing and decorative arts year-round; in summer
the cultural calendar is especially busy. The wide array of performances embraces music, theater, and dance, as well as film
and literary series and changing art exhibits. Hunter has some
lively night spots during ski season and summers. The large resorts, such as the Concord and the Nevele (*see* Dining and
Lodging, *above*), offer dancing and big-name acts.

Saratoga Springs
and the North Country

Saratoga Springs, about 30 mi north of Albany, is one of American high society's oldest summer playgrounds. The five-week
Thoroughbred-racing season, starting the last week in July, is
the high point of the year. Northwest of Saratoga, and in stark
contrast, are the rugged mountains, immense forests, and
abundant lakes and streams of the Adirondack Park, the largest park expanse in the United States outside Alaska. The
North Country—anchored by the resort towns of Lake Placid
and Lake George—hums with summer hikers and fall leaf-

peepers, returning to life when the winter-sports enthusiasts descend.

Tourist Information

Greater Saratoga: Chamber of Commerce (494 Broadway, Saratoga Springs 12866, tel. 518/584–3255). **Lake Placid:** Visitors Bureau (Olympic Center, 12946, tel. 518/523–2445 or 800/447–5224). **Saranac Lake:** Chamber of Commerce (30 Main St., 12983, tel. 518/891–1990).

Getting There

By Plane The principal gateways are New York City (207 mi south of Lake George) and Montreal (177 mi north of Lake George). Other airports serving the region are in Albany, Syracuse, and Burlington, Vermont.

By Car The primary route through the region is the Northway (I–87), which links Albany and Montreal.

By Train Amtrak's *Adirondack* operates daily between New York and Montreal, with North Country stops in Saratoga Springs, Glens Falls, Fort Ticonderoga, Westport, and Plattsburgh.

By Bus **Adirondack Pinehill Trailways** (tel. 800/225–6815) provides bus service to Saratoga Springs, Lake Placid, Lake George, Chestertown, Watertown, Bolton Landing (summer only), and many other towns throughout the region.

Exploring Saratoga Springs and the North Country

Saratoga Springs has been frequented for its medicinal springs since the late 18th century. In the late 19th century, it emerged as one of North America's principal resorts, both for the spa waters and for its gambling casino. It also became a horseracing center in the 1890s, and August still brings crowds for the race meet and yearling sale.

Across from the **Saratoga Race Course** (*see* Spectator Sports, *below*), site of the renowned horse races (and listed on the National Register of Historic Places), is the **National Museum of Racing.** Its centerpiece is the Hall of Fame, which has video clips of races featuring the horses and jockeys enshrined here. *Union Ave., tel. 518/584–0400. Admission charged.*

Also on Union Avenue is **Yaddo,** a highly regarded retreat for artists and writers. The 400-acre grounds and rose garden are open to the public.

The **National Museum of Dance** features rotating exhibits on the history and development of the art form, as well as the Hall of Fame, honoring dance luminaries. New studios allow visitors to watch or participate in a dance class. *Rte. 9S, tel. 518/ 584–2225. Admission charged. Closed Labor Day–Memorial Day; Mon.*

Housed in **Canfield Casino**—the only building in downtown's Congress Park, off Broadway—is the **Historical Society of Saratoga Springs,** with a museum devoted to Saratoga's colorful history as a gambling center, a contemporary art gallery, and a museum store. *Tel. 518/584–6920. Admission charged. Closed Mon.–Tues. Nov.–Mar.*

In the Adirondack Mountain range, the 6-million-acre **Adirondack Park** encompasses 1,000 mi of rivers and more than 2,500 lakes and ponds. The southern sections are more developed, while the High Peaks region in the north-central sector offers the greatest variety of wilderness activities. *Visitor Interpretive Centers: Paul Smiths, tel. 518/327–3000; Newcomb, tel. 518/582–2000.*

Lake George, 40 mi north of Saratoga, is a tourist town catering to families, with amusement parks, souvenir shops, and miniature golf. Cruises from the town dock are extremely popular from May through October; contact **Lake George Shoreline Cruises** (tel. 518/668–4644) and the **Lake George Steamboat Company** (tel. 518/668–5777). If you have an interest in the French and Indian War, you will want to visit **Ft. William Henry** (tel. 518/668–5471), reconstructed on the original 1755 site at the foot of Lake George.

Just south of town is **Great Escape Fun Park,** the North Country's largest amusement park. *U.S. 9, tel. 518/798–1084. Admission charged. Closed Sept.–May.*

Blue Mountain Lake is home of the **Adirondack Museum,** which covers the entire cultural and historical spectrum of the region with exhibits of boats, Adirondack furniture, and sporting paraphernalia, among other things. *Rtes. 28 and 30, tel. 518/352–7311. Admission charged. Closed mid-Oct.–Memorial Day.*

Lake Placid, the hub of the northern Adirondacks, has a Main Street lined with shops and motels, two lakes in its backyard, and the **winter Olympics facilities** all around it. The Olympic Ice Arena and speed-skating oval are right in the center of town, the ski jump is 2 mi out, Whiteface Mountain (scene of the downhill competitions) is a 10-minute drive away on Rte. 86, and the bobsled run at Mt. Van Hoevenberg on Rte. 73 is 15 minutes away. All sites are open to the public.

During the summer, you can ascend 4,867-foot **Whiteface Mountain** either by chair lift or by car on Veterans Memorial Highway. A short walk to the summit provides a superb view: Lake Placid in one direction, Lake Champlain in another, and the High Peaks to the south. Go on a clear day if possible.

Self-guided tours can be made of the **John Brown Farm,** home and burial place of the famed abolitionist, who operated the farm for runaway slaves. *Off Rte. 73 past the Olympic ski jumps, tel. 518/523–3900. Admission free. Closed late Oct.–early May.*

The serenity and mountain air of **Saranac Lake** (elevation: 1,600 ft) made it a famous health resort for the tubercular in the late 19th century. Ten miles west of Lake Placid, it is today the jumping-off point for canoe trips (*see* Sports and Outdoor Activities, *below*). Much of the lake is part of the **St. Regis Canoe Area,** which is off-limits to powerboats.

Cranberry Lake is the largest body of water in the relatively unexplored northwestern corner of the park. Several long and gentle hiking trails wind through the area around the lake, and the quick and easy hike to a lookout from Bear Mountain provides a sweeping view of the lake and the unspoiled countryside beyond.

There is much more to the region called the **Thousand Islands** than the island-studded area of the St. Lawrence River. The name usually refers to an area defined by the Adirondacks to the east, the St. Lawrence to the north, and Lake Ontario to the west. Most of the region is flat or rolling farmland, but the economy is heavily dependent on the St. Lawrence Seaway. The scenic **Seaway Trail,** a combination of Rtes. 37, 12, and 12E, follows the river and the Lake Ontario shore. In **Massena,** huge cargo vessels pass through the **Eisenhower Lock;** call ahead (tel. 315/769–2422) to find out what time a ship is scheduled to pass through.

What to See and Do with Children

The area has several amusement parks, the largest of which is **Great Escape Fun Park** (*see* Exploring Saratoga Springs and the North Country, *above*). Those not big on hiking can sample the beauty of the Adirondack region at **Ausable Chasm,** on U.S. 9 just north of Keeseville; **High Falls Gorge,** off Rte. 86 near Wilmington; and **Natural Stone Bridge and Caves** (tel. 518/494–2283), at Exit 26 of I–87 near Pottersville.

Shopping

The region's maple syrup and sharp Cheddar cheese make good gifts. The **Adirondack North Country Craft Center** (93 Saranac Ave., Lake Placid 12946, tel. 518/523–2062) offers a guide to shops, dealers, and craftspeople in the North Country. **Blue Mountain Lake** and **Lake Placid** are good bets for crafts hunting. Look for baskets and pottery with pinecones, unique to the area; you'll also find an array of jewelry, leatherwork, and quilting. **All Seasons Outfitters** (168 Lake Flower Ave., Saranac Lake, tel. 518/891–6159) sells and rents gear for canoeing, skiing, snowshoeing, and hiking.

Sports and Outdoor Activities

McDonald's Adirondack Challenges (Box 855, Saranac Lake 12983, tel. 518/891–1176) leads tours and provides guides for individuals or groups in canoeing, snowshoeing, cross-country skiing, hiking, and orienteering.

Biking   Roadside signs mark several bike routes, most quite hilly, that wind through the North Country. For a map of routes in the Saranac Lake area, contact the **Saranac Lake Chamber of Commerce** (*see* Tourist Information, *above*).

Canoeing   The 170-mi **Raquette River** and the **St. Regis Canoe Area,** east of Saranac Lake, are among the best and most popular canoe routes in the North Country.

Fishing   Brook and lake trout are taken year-round on the lakes and streams of the North Country. Licenses can be obtained at town or county clerk offices, sporting-goods stores, and outfitters.

Golf   Among the more challenging courses are those at the **Whiteface Resort** (Whiteface Inn Rd., Lake Placid, tel. 518/523–2551; 18 holes), the **Sagamore** (110 Sagamore Rd., Bolton Landing, tel. 518/644–9400; 18 holes), the **Saranac Inn Golf Club** (Upper Saranac Lake, tel. 518/891–1402; 18 holes), and the **Westport Country Club** (Lake Champlain, tel. 518/962–4470; 18 holes).

Hiking   The most popular area for hiking is the High Peaks region, accessible from the Lake Placid area in the north, Keene and Keene Valley in the east, and Newcomb in the south. For more information, contact **ADK Lodges** (Box 867, Lake Placid 12946, tel. 518/523–3441) or the **Adirondack Mountain Club** (RR3, Box 3055, Lake George 12845, tel. 518/668–4447).

Rafting   **Hudson River Rafting Co.**—with offices in North Creek (tel. 518/251–3215), Lake Luzerne (tel. 518/696–2964), and Watertown (tel. 315/782–7881)—offers day trips on the Hudson, the Sacandaga, and the Black River from April to September.

Spectator Sports

For information on Lake Placid summer and winter athletic competitions, contact the **Olympic Regional Development Authority** (tel. 518/523–1655 or 800/462–6236). Events include concerts, distance and free-style aerial ski jumping, and figure-skating shows.

Horse Racing   The five-week Thoroughbred-racing session starts the last week of July at **Saratoga Race Course** (Union Ave., Saratoga Springs, tel. 518/584–6200). **Saratoga Harness** (Nelson Ave., Saratoga Springs, tel. 518/584–2110) is open throughout the year, except for periods in April and December.

Ski Areas

Cross-country   **Mt. Van Hoevenberg** on Rte. 73 has 50 km of groomed tracks, which connect with the **Jackrabbit Trail,** a 23-mi network of ski trails through the High Peaks region connecting Lake Placid, Saranac Lake, and Keene. For information and conditions, contact **Adirondack Ski Touring Council** (Box 843, Lake Placid 12946, tel. 518/523–1365).

Downhill   **Whiteface Mountain Ski Center** (Wilmington 12997, 8 mi east of Lake Placid, tel. 518/946–2223) has 65 runs, 10 lifts, a 3,216-foot vertical drop, and snowmaking.

Dining and Lodging

Saratoga is indisputably the North Country's culinary champion in quality and variety, with Lake Placid a distant second. Elsewhere expect large portions, home cooking, and rustic atmosphere. Lodging runs the gamut from roadside motels to resorts. For information on B&Bs, contact the **Bed and Breakfast Association of Saratoga, Lake George, and Gore Mountain Region** (Box 99, Lake Luzerne 12846, tel. 518/696–9912) or **American Country Collection of Bed & Breakfast Accommodations** (4 Greenwood La., Delmar 12054, tel. 518/439–7001 or, for reservations only, 800/800–5908, ext. 21). For price ranges, see Charts 1 (B) and 2 (B) in Chapter 1.

Bolton Landing   **The Sagamore.** Each of the three dining rooms at this island re-
Dining   sort has its own atmosphere and cuisine, ranging from the for-
★   mal, slightly nouvelle touches of the Trillium to the hearty burgers and steaks of the Club Grill. *Tel. 518/644–9400. Reservations required. Jacket required Apr.–Oct. AE, D, DC, MC, V. No lunch at Trillium. Expensive.*

Chestertown
Dining and
Lodging
★

Balsam House Inn and Restaurant. This elegantly restored inn, on a bluff overlooking Friends Lake, dates to 1860. A spiral staircase, lots of wicker, and charming bedrooms all help to evoke the past. The candle-lit dining room is a regional favorite for French cuisine. *Atateka Dr., Box 365, 12817, tel. 518/494–2828; fax 518/494–4431. 20 rooms. Reservations advised. AE, DC, MC, V. Expensive.*

Lake Placid
Dining

Artist's Cafe. This popular spot has an enclosed lakeside deck and a cozy dining room and bar. Seafood, steaks, hearty soups, and imaginative sandwich combinations headline the menu. The paintings, by local artists, are for sale. *Main St., tel. 518/523–9493. AE, DC, MC, V. Inexpensive.*

Dining and
Lodging
★

Lake Placid Manor. One of the private "great camps" built before the turn of the century, this small, personal hotel stands as a prime example of Adirondack rustic architecture. Sophisticated meals with a Continental flair are served in a dining room with a panoramic view of Lake Placid and Whiteface Mountain. *Whiteface Inn Rd., 12946, tel. 518/523–2573. 31 rooms. Facilities: restaurant, lounge, beach, rental boats. AE, MC, V. Closed Apr., Nov. Expensive.*

Saranac Lake
Dining

Red Fox. Locals heartily endorse this restaurant's consistently good American food and generous libations. Each of the four intimate rooms has a fireplace, wood paneling, and subdued lighting. *Rte. 3, Tupper Lake Rd., tel. 518/891–2127. MC, V. Moderate.*

Dining and
Lodging

The Point. Onetime home of William Avery Rockefeller, this elegantly rustic inn is the Adirondacks' most exclusive retreat. It is operated in the manner of a sophisticated private home with no commercial overtones, and guests are required to dress for dinner. *HCR 1, Box 65, 12983, tel. 518/891–5674 or 800/255–3530. 11 rooms. Facilities: restaurant, lounge, open bar, game room, swimming, sailing, cross-country skiing. AE. Expensive.*

Saratoga Springs
Dining
★

Eartha's Kitchen. This small bistro is a local favorite, especially for the mesquite-grilled seafood dishes from the ever-changing, eclectic menu. The cinnamon-bread pudding with brandy-cream sauce is a house specialty. *60 Court St., tel. 518/583–0602. Reservations required. AE, DC, MC, V. No lunch. Moderate.*

Lodging

Sheraton Saratoga Springs. Adjacent to the City (Civic) Center, this elegantly furnished brick-and-mahogany hotel, inside an office-building exterior, was totally renovated in 1992. *534 Broadway, 12866, tel. 518/584–4000. 235 rooms, 5 suites. Facilities: restaurant, indoor pool, gift shop, newsstand, valet service. AE, D, DC, MC, V. Moderate.*

Warrensburg
Lodging

Donegal Manor. Antiques and Irish hospitality greet you in this homey B&B. Documentation is still in the works, but it is believed James Fenimore Cooper was a guest here while researching *The Last of the Mohicans. 117 Main St., 12885, tel. 518/623–3549. 4 rooms. MC, V. Moderate.*

Motels

Howard Johnson Resort (90 Saranac Ave., Lake Placid 12946, tel. 518/523–9555 or 800/858–4656), 92 rooms, restaurant, indoor pool, whirlpool, laundry; expensive. **Blue Spruce Motel** (Main St., Box 604, Old Forge 13420, tel. 315/369–3817), 13 rooms; moderate. **Days Inn of Lake George** (Rte. 9, Box 3202, Lake George 12845, tel. 518/793–3196 or 800/325–2525), 91 rooms, restaurant, indoor pool, valet service, baby-sitting; moderate. **Travelodge of Lake George** (Rte. 9, Lake George 12845, tel. 518/668–5421 or 800/234–0586), 90 rooms, restaurant, outdoor pool, lawn games, arcade; moderate. **Empress Motel** (Rtes. 4, 29, and 32; 177 Broadway, Schuylerville 12871, tel. 518/695–3231), 12 rooms; inexpensive.

Campgrounds

Adirondak Loj Wilderness Campground (Box 867, Lake Placid 12946, tel. 518/523–3441) provides information about camping throughout the High Peaks region and operates a campground around Heart Lake with 34 tent sites and 13 lean-tos, water, no gas or electric, picnic table, seasonal showers, and toilets. **KOA Lake Placid–Whiteface Mountain** (HCR 2, Box 38, Fox Farm Rd., Wilmington 12997, tel. 518/946–7878) has 90 tent sites and 144 RV sites, water and electric, hot showers, toilets, and laundry.

The Arts

The **Adirondack Lakes Center for the Arts** in Blue Mountain Lake (tel. 518/352–7715) features concerts, dramatic presentations, films, and demonstrations of arts and crafts throughout the summer. The **Saratoga Performing Arts Center** (tel. 518/587–3330) hosts the New York City Opera, the New York City Ballet, the Philadelphia Orchestra, and Newport Jazz Festival-Sartoga, as well as big-name pop stars from June to September.

Elsewhere in the State

Leatherstocking Country and the Finger Lakes

Getting There The Leatherstocking region is 200–300 mi from New York City via the New York State Thruway and Rte. 28 from Kingston. I–90 runs east–west through both Leatherstocking Country and the Finger Lakes, connecting Albany with Buffalo. I–88 runs northeast–southwest, leading to Binghamton.

What to See and Do The early Yankees in their leather leggings gave the region its nickname; it is quintessential rural America, with gently rolling countryside, community chicken barbecues, and tree-shaded small towns. **Cooperstown** is home to the **National Baseball Hall of Fame,** where displays, paintings, and audiovisual presentations honor the heroes, recall great moments, and trace the history of the game. *Main St., tel. 607/547–9988. Admission charged. Closed Thanksgiving, Christmas, New Year's Day*.

Binghamton has the **Roberson Museum and Science Center** (30 Front St., tel. 607/772–0660), a complex of museums, ballet studios, a planetarium, and a theater; and the wooded **Ross Park Zoo** (60 Morgan Rd. and 185 Park Ave., tel. 607/724–5461), where animals (including tigers and a timberwolf pack) live in their natural habitat. You can relive the old days of canal transport, including a ride in a horse-drawn canal boat, at **Erie Canal Village** (Rte. 49W, Rome, tel. 315/336–6000, ext. 250), a reconstructed ca. 1840 village.

The 11 **Finger Lakes,** from Conesus Lake south of Rochester to Otisco Lake near Syracuse, offer waterfalls, gorges, and diverse terrain. The region is studded with vineyards, and local wineries—the **Taylor Wine Co.** (Country Rd. 88, south of Hammondsport, tel. 607/569–6111) is the area's largest—are open for tours and tastings, most from May to October, some year-round.

Rochester is the headquarters of the **Eastman Kodak Company.** The **George Eastman House,** onetime home of the company founder and photographic innovator, now houses the **International Museum of Photography,** the world's largest museum devoted to photographic art and technology. *900 East Ave., tel. 716/271–3361. Admission charged. Closed Mon.*

Rochester was also home to **Susan B. Anthony,** whose **house** (17 Madison St., tel. 716/235–6124) is furnished in the style of the mid-1800s. It was here that the 19th-century women's-rights advocate wrote *The History of Woman Suffrage.*

In **Corning,** the **Corning Museum of Glass** contains a world-class collection of glass, as well as a time-line exhibit describing 3,500 years of glass-making, a library covering everything ever written about glass, and a tour of the Steuben glass factory. *Off Rte. 17, tel. 607/974–8229. Admission charged.*

Ithaca, at the tip of Cayuga Lake, is the home of **Cornell University** and the starting point for the **Cayuga Wine Trail.** The town is more spectacular than most in the Finger Lakes because of the deep gorges and more than 100 waterfalls that lace it.

About 5 mi west of the north end of Cayuga Lake is **Seneca Falls,** where, on July 18, 1848, 300 people attended America's first women's-rights convention, held at the **Wesleyan Methodist Chapel** (126 Falls St.).

For more information, contact the **Cooperstown Chamber of Commerce** (31 Chestnut St., 13326, tel. 607/547–9983); **Leatherstocking Country, NY** (327 N. Main St., Herkimer 13350, tel. 315/866–1500 or 800/233–8778); and the **Finger Lakes Association** (309 Lake St., Penn Yan 14527, tel. 315/536–7488 or 800/548–4386).

Buffalo, Chautauqua, and Niagara Falls

Getting There Access from the east, west, and south is primarily via I–90, the New York State Thruway.

What to See and Do **Buffalo** is a city of Victorian elegance, with many churches and strongly ethnic neighborhoods. The **Albright-Knox Art Gallery** (1285 Elmwood Ave., tel. 716/882–8700) has a superb collection of contemporary art.

The 50-mi drive from **Silver Creek** to **Ripley,** along the shores of Lake Erie, is known as the **Chautauqua Wine Trail,** sprinkled with five wineries and numerous farm stands and antiques shops.

Niagara Falls, the most accessible and famous waterfall in the world, is actually three cataracts: the American and Bridal Veil Falls, in New York, and the Horseshoe Falls, in Ontario, Canada. More than 750,000 gallons of water flow each second in the summer. For a good orientation to the falls, stop at the Niagara Visitor's Center in the **Niagara Reservation State Park** (Prospect Park, Niagara Falls 14303–0132, tel. 716/278–1770), the oldest state park in the nation. **Goat Island** provides the closest view of the American falls; cross to the Canadian side for the best view of Horseshoe Falls. The famous *Maid of the Mist* boat ride lets you view the falls from the water.

Dining   For price ranges, see Chart 1 (B) in Chapter 1.

The Red Coach Inn. With a spectacular view of the upper rapids, this 1923 inn has an old-England atmosphere, plus wood-burning fireplaces and an outdoor patio for summer dining. Specialties include prime rib, Boston scrod, and seafood-sausage mornay. *2 Buffalo Ave., Niagara Falls, tel. 716/282–1459. Reservations advised. AE, D, DC, MC, V. Moderate.*

Top of the Falls. If you like the feeling of being on top of the falls, stop in here for the usual luncheon fare. *Goat Island, tel. 716/285–3316. AE, D, DC, MC, V. No dinner; closed Nov.–Apr. Moderate.*

Lodging   For price ranges, see Chart 2 (B) in Chapter 1.

Days Inn Falls View. A longtime landmark, this bustling property has recently undergone a much-needed renovation. The top floors with a view of the upper rapids are best. *201 Rainbow Blvd., Niagara Falls 14303, tel. 716/285–9321. 200 rooms. Facilities: dining room, cocktail lounge. AE, D, MC, V. Expensive.*

Coachman Motel. Just three blocks from the Convention Center and the falls, this motel represents one of the area's best values. *523 3rd St., Niagara Falls 14301, tel. 716/285–2295. 18 rooms. AE, D, DC, MC, V. Closed Jan.–Apr. Inexpensive.*

For more information, contact the **Greater Buffalo Convention and Visitors Bureau** (107 Delaware Ave., Buffalo 14202, tel. 716/852–0511), the **Chautauqua County Vacationland Association** (4 N. Erie St., Mayville 14757, tel. 716/753–4304 or 800/242–4569), and the **Niagara Falls Official Information Center** (4th and Niagara Sts., 14301, tel. 716/284–2000 or 800/338–7890).

RHODE ISLAND

By Nigel Fisher

Capital	Providence
Population	1,003,464
Motto	Hope
State Bird	Rhode Island Red
State Flower	Violet

Visitor Information

Rhode Island Department of Economic Development, Tourism Division (7 Jackson Walkway, Providence 02903, tel. 401/277–2601 or 800/556–2484). **Greater Providence:** Convention and Visitors Bureau (30 Exchange Terr., 02903, tel. 401/274–1636 or 800/233–1636). **Newport County:** Convention and Visitors Bureau (23 America's Cup Ave., Newport 02840, tel. 401/849–8048 or 800/326–6030). **South County:** Tourism Council (Box 651, Narragansett 02882, tel. 401/789–4422 or 800/548–4662).

Scenic Drives

With 400 mi of shoreline, coastal scenes are Rhode Island's forte. The western coastline from Watch Hill to Narragansett Pier along **Rtes. 1 and 1A** (with a detour down to Jerusalem and Galilee) takes you past state parks, forest areas, vast stretches of sandy beaches, and the marshes of Point Judith Pond. And nothing compares with the grand mansions along **Newport's Ocean Drive.**

National and State Parks

State Parks Rhode Island has no national parks, but it does have 37 state parks and recreational grounds, most of which are along the south coast between Westerly and Jamestown. **Burlingame State Park, Charlestown Breachway, Fishermen's Memorial State Park, George Washington Camping Area,** and the **Ninegret Conservation Area** allow camping. For information about the state parks, contact the Department of Economic Development (*see* Visitor Information, *above*).

Around Rhode Island

Coastal Rhode Island is undervisited compared with other parts of New England, though not for lack of appeal: Some of its white-sand beaches rival Cape Cod's best, and a diversity of coastal environments makes for enjoyable drives (*see* Scenic Drives, *above*). Newport, with its grandiose mansions, is lively on both land and water. Providence, the state capital and an Ivy League college town, is rejuvenating its historic heritage.

Getting There

By Plane The **Theodore Francis Green State Airport** (tel. 401/737–4000), 3 mi northeast of Warwick and 5 mi south of Providence, is served by major U.S. airlines and regional carriers. **Corporate**

Air Newport (tel. 401/848–5550) flies charters to **Newport State Airport** (tel. 401/846–2200), 3 mi northeast of the city.

By Car   I–95 cuts diagonally across the state and is the fastest route to Providence from Boston, coastal Connecticut, and New York City. I–195 links Providence with New Bedford and Cape Cod. U.S. 1 follows the coast east from Connecticut before turning north to Providence.

By Train   **Amtrak** stops at Westerly, Kingston, and Providence's Union Station (100 Gaspee St.).

By Bus   **Greyhound** (tel. 401/454–0790) and **Bonanza Bus Lines** (tel. 401/751–8800) link northeast cities with the **Providence Bus Terminal** (Cemetery St., off I–95 Exit 25). **Rhode Island Public Transit Authority** (tel. 401/781–9400, 401/847–0209, or 800/662–5088 in RI) provides local transportation in Providence and some service to other parts of the state.

By Ferry   **Interstate Navigation Co.** (tel. 401/783–4613) operates car ferries from Providence's India Street Pier to Newport and Block Island and from Point Judith's Galilee State Pier to Block Island. Reservations are required for cars, and service is irregular in the off-season.

Exploring Rhode Island

The South Coast   **Watch Hill** is a pretty Victorian-era resort town, with miles of beautiful beaches, a number of Native American settlements, and an active fishing port. On Bay Street is a **statue of Ninigret,** a 17th-century chief of the Rhode Island branch of the Niantic tribe. Nearby is the **Flying Horse Carousel,** built in about 1867, and the oldest merry-go-round in America. *Bay St., no phone. Admission charged. Closed Labor Day–June 15.*

Ocean House (2 Bluff Ave., tel. 401/348–8161) is one of several Victorian-era hotels in this part of Watch Hill. A walk to the end of Bay Street and a left into Fort Road will take you in the direction of the path (at the end of Fort Road) to **Napatree Point,** one of the best long beach walks in the state.

Charlestown is a resort filled with summer cottages and much history of the Narragansett Indians, native to the area. Its **Indian Church** is the last of three Christian Indian churches built in Rhode Island. The **Indian Burial Ground,** resting place of the Narragansett tribe, is on Narrow Lane, south of town off Rte. 2/112.

U.S. 1 brings you to **South Kingstown,** an area made up of many small Colonial villages, full of crafts shops and galleries. It is also home to the **University of Rhode Island** and rowdy **Matunuck Beach.**

In the village of **Wakefield** is the old Washington County Jail, built in 1792, which now houses the **Pettaquamscutt Historical Society.** Here you can see jail cells and rooms from the Colonial period, a Colonial garden, and changing exhibits. *1348 Kingstown Rd., tel. 401/783–1328. Admission free. Closed Mon., Wed., Fri., Sun.; Nov.–Apr.*

The section of **Narragansett** known as **Narragansett Pier** was a posh resort in the late 19th century. At Sprague Park is the **Narragansett Indian Monument.** The 23-foot monument is made from a single piece of wood, the trunk of a giant Douglas fir.

South on Ocean Road are beaches and, at land's end, the **Point Judith Lighthouse** (tel. 401/789–0444), open during daylight hours. North, in **Galilee,** one of the busiest fishing ports on the East Coast, is a ferry terminal for Block Island. The village has several excellent seafood restaurants.

Drive north through the village of **Wickford** to the intersection of Rte. 1A and U.S. 1; take U.S. 1 north and turn right onto Richard Smith Drive for **Smith's Castle,** built in 1678 and the site of many orations by Roger Williams, Rhode Island's most famous historical figure. *Tel. 401/294–3521. Admission charged. Closed Mon.–Wed., holidays; Nov.–Apr.*

Newport Bounded on three sides by water, **Newport** is one of the great sailing cities of the world. It is also host to world-class jazz, blues, and classical music festivals, as well as international tennis tournaments.

Newport's first age of prosperity was in the late 1700s, and many homes and shops built in that era still stand in the Colonial section of the city. In the 19th century, Newport became a summer playground for America's wealthiest families.

A walk around **Colonial Newport**—the northwestern section of the city, clustered around the harbor—begins at the 1748 **Hunter House,** at 54 Washington Street. The carved pineapple over the doorway is a symbol of hospitality. *Tel. 401/847–1000. Admission charged. Closed weekdays Apr. and Oct.*

Thames (pronounced "Thaymz") Street is the main street of Colonial Newport. Continue south on Thames to Washington Square. **The Brick Market,** built in 1760, was designed by Peter Harrison, who was also responsible for the city's Touro Synagogue and the Redwood Library. The market houses shops.

Facing the market on Washington Square is the **Old Colony House.** Built in 1739, it was the headquarters of the Colonial and state governments, and from its balcony the Declaration of Independence was read to Newporters. *Tel. 401/846–2980. Tours Mon.–Sat. in summer.*

Newport's oldest house, the **Wanton-Lyman-Hazard House,** displays a "two-room" plan typical of the time. As well as a Colonial garden, it offers demonstrations of 18th-century cooking. *17 Broadway, tel. 401/846–0813. Admission charged. Closed Sun.–Mon.; Oct.–May.*

On Marlborough Street is the **White Horse Tavern** (tel. 401/849–3600). In operation since 1687, the White Horse claims to be the oldest tavern in America, and its cozy yet elegant tables epitomize Newport's Colonial charm.

On the same corner stands the **Friends Meeting House,** built in 1699 and the oldest Quaker meeting house in America. *29 Farewell St., tel. 401/846–0813. Donation requested. Closed Sun.–Wed. mid-Aug.–mid-June.*

South, across Washington Square, on Touro Street, is the site of the oldest surviving synagogue in the country. **Touro Synagogue** (85 Touro St., tel. 401/847–4794), dedicated in 1763, is very simple on the outside but elaborate within.

Newport

Coasters Harbor
Coasters Harbor Island

MIANTONOMI MEMORIAL PARK

TO NEWPORT STATE AIRPORT

138 Newport Bay Bridge

Admiral
Kalbfus Rd.
Broadway
Garfield St.
Van Zandt Ave.
Washington St.
Warner St.
Kay St.

Rose Island

Old Colony House
Common Burial Ground
Friendship
Friends Meeting House
Brick Market
Wynton-Lyman-Hazard House
Hunter House
Rosecliff
Goat Island
Washington Sq.
Touro St.
Catherine St.
Easton's Pond

Narragansett Bay

Touro Synagogue
Church St.
Newport Historical Society
Trinity Church
Old Beach Rd.
Easton Beach
Redwood Library
Memorial Blvd.
Cliff Walk (Begins)

Kingscote
International Tennis Hall of Fame and Tennis Museum

FT. ADAMS STATE PARK
Newport Harbor
KING PARK AND BEACH
The Elms
Museum of Yachting
Brenton Cove
Wellington Ave.
Thames St.
Spring St.
Bellevue Ave.
Ochre Pt.

Castle Hill Cove
Holdan Ave.
Webster
St.
Hammersmith Farm
Fort Adams Rd.
Ridge Rd.
Harrison
Moorland Rd.
Wickham Rd.
Chateau-sur-Mer
Victoria Ave.
The Breakers

Castle Ave.
Brenton Rd.
Hazard Rd.
Lily Pond
Rosecliff
Winans Ave.
Harrison Ave.
Ocean Ave.
Almy Pond
Beechwood
The Ocean Drive
Bellevue Ave.
Marble House
Pirate's Cove
Ocean Ave.
Gooseberry Island
Cliff Walk (Ends)
Belcourt Castle
BRENTON POINT STATE PARK

Rhode Island Sound

N

ATLANTIC OCEAN

0   1 mile
0   1 km

At 82 Touro Street is the headquarters of the **Newport Historical Society,** departure point for walking tours. Its museum features a large collection of Newport memorabilia, furniture, and maritime items. *Tel. 401/846–0813. Admission free. Closed Sat.–Mon.*

South of Washington Square, at the corner of Spring and Church streets, is **Trinity Church** (tel. 401/846–0660), built in 1724. The three-tier wineglass pulpit inside is the only one of its kind in America.

East along Church Street is the 1748 **Redwood Library,** the oldest library in continuous use in the United States. Although the building is made of wood, the original exterior paint was mixed with sand to make it resemble stone. The library houses a collection of paintings by early American artists . *50 Bellevue Ave., tel. 401/847–0292. Admission free. Closed Sun.*

South on Bellevue are the **Newport Art Museum and Art Association** (76 Bellevue Ave., tel. 401/847–0179), with exhibits of Rhode Island art past and present, and the **International Tennis Hall of Fame** and **Tennis Museum** (194 Bellevue Ave., tel. 401/849–3990), housed in a magnificent Stanford White building, the Newport Casino.

Six Newport mansions are maintained by the **Preservation Society of Newport County** (tel. 401/847–1000). A combination ticket gives you a discount on individual admission prices. Each mansion provides a guided tour that lasts about an hour.

Kingscote (closed Nov.–Mar.; weekdays Apr., Oct.), on Bowery Street, was built in 1840 for a plantation owner from Savannah, Georgia. It is furnished with antique furniture, glass, and Oriental art and has a number of Tiffany windows.

South on Bellevue Avenue is **The Elms** (closed weekdays Nov.–Mar.), one of Newport's most graceful mansions. Classical in design, it was built for a coal baron at the turn of the century. A broad lawn, fountains, and formal gardens surround it.

Chateau-sur-Mer (closed weekdays Nov.–Mar.), the first of Bellevue Avenue's stone mansions, is modest compared with the opulence that came later. Built in 1852 and enlarged by Richard Morris Hunt for a China-trade tycoon, the mansion houses a toy collection; in December it is decorated on a Victorian Christmas theme.

On Ochre Point Avenue is **The Breakers** (closed Nov.–Mar.), built in 1893 for Cornelius Vanderbilt II and his small family. The 70-room showplace took more than 2,500 workmen two years to complete and required 40 servants to keep it running.

Return to Bellevue Avenue for **Rosecliff** (closed Nov.–Mar.), built in 1902. Modeled after the Grand Trianon at Versailles, this 40-room mansion includes a heart-shaped staircase designed by Stanford White. Rosecliff has appeared in several movies, including *The Great Gatsby*.

At **Beechwood,** built for the Astors, actors in period costume play the parts of family members including Mrs. Astor, the belle of New York and Newport society; servants; and household guests. *580 Bellevue Ave., tel. 401/846–3772. Admission charged. Closed weekdays Jan.–Apr.*

The last of the Preservation Society's Bellevue Avenue properties is **Marble House** (closed weekdays Nov.–Mar.). With its extravagant gold ballroom, this palace in marble was the gift of William Vanderbilt to his wife, Alva, in 1892.

Belcourt Castle, just down the road, was designed by Richard Morris Hunt, based on Louis XIII's hunting lodge. The castle contains an enormous collection of European and Oriental treasures. *Tel. 401/846–0669 or 401/849–1566. Admission charged. Closed Jan. 26–Mar. 31.*

Take Ocean Drive to **Hammersmith Farm,** the childhood summer home of Jacqueline Bouvier and the site of her wedding to John F. Kennedy. It is also the only working farm in Newport. The gardens were designed by Frederick Law Olmsted. *Near Ft. Adams, tel. 401/846–7346. Admission charged. Closed mid-Nov.–Mar., but with special openings during Christmastime.*

Out at **Ft. Adams State Park** is a Revolutionary War–era fort named after John Quincy Adams, whose grounds now host the annual Newport jazz and folk festivals, as well as the **Museum of Yachting,** with four galleries of pictures: Mansions and Yachts, Small Craft, America's Cup, and the Hall of Fame for Single-handed Sailors. *Ocean Dr., tel. 401/847–1018. Admission charged. Closed Mon.; Nov.–mid-May.*

Block Island   Newport (along with Galilee) is another jumping-off point for **Block Island,** 13 mi off the coast. Despite its popularity, the 11-sq-mi island's beauty and privacy are intact. Its freshwater ponds are a haven for migrating birds; its harbors are a sanctuary for yachtsmen; and its narrow roads and walking trails are ideal for relaxed exploring. The **Block Island Chamber of Commerce** (Drawer D, 02807, tel. 401/466–2982) can help with reservations at hotels and guesthouses. Aside from the ferry service (*see* Getting There, *above*), **New England Airlines** (tel. 401/596–2460 or 800/243–2460) offers air service to the island from Westerly State Airport.

Providence   Thirty miles north of Newport is the state's capital, **Providence,** founded by Roger Williams in 1635 as a refuge for free-thinkers and religious dissenters. Brown University, the Rhode Island School of Design (RISD), and the Trinity Square Repertory Company are major forces in New England's intellectual and cultural life. Historic walking-tour maps of the city are available at the tourist office (*see* Visitor Information, *above*).

Four Brown brothers had a major part in Providence's development in the 18th century. John Brown traded slaves, opened trade with China, and aided the American Revolution. Joseph Brown's architectural designs changed the face of the city. Moses Brown founded the Quaker School that bears his name. Nicholas Brown rescued the failing Rhode Island College—known today as Brown University.

The **Providence Athenaeum,** established in 1753, is one of the oldest lending libraries in the world. The library has a collection of Rhode Island art and artifacts, as well as an original set of the folio *Birds of America* prints by John J. Audubon. *251 Benefit St., tel. 401/421–6970. Admission free. Closed Sun.*

Down the street is the **Rhode Island School of Design Museum of Art.** This small but comprehensive museum exhibits textiles,

Japanese prints, Paul Revere silver, 18th-century porcelain, French Impressionist paintings, and a mummy from c. 300 BC. *224 Benefit St., tel. 401/331–3511. Admission charged (free Sat.). Closed Mon.*

Also on **Benefit Street**—known as the "Mile of History"—is a long row of small early Federal and 19th-century candy-colored houses crammed shoulder-to-shoulder on a steep hill overlooking downtown Providence. The **Ambrose Burnside mansion** (314 Benefit St.), a redbrick Victorian house with a turret, was built in 1850 for the Civil War general and later Rhode Island governor.

Along South Water Street is **Market House** (Market Sq., S. Main St.), designed by Joseph Brown. Tea was burned here in March 1775, and the upper floors were used as a barracks during the Revolutionary War. North on South Water Street and west onto Westminster Mall is the **Arcade** (65 Weybosset St., tel. 401/456–5403; closed Sun.), built in 1828 and America's first indoor shopping mall. Now a National Historic Landmark, the three-story Greek Revival Arcade still houses shops.

On Smith Street is the **State House,** built in 1900. Its dome— the first unsupported marble dome in America—is the world's second-largest after St. Peter's Basilica in Rome. On display is the original parchment charter granted by King Charles to the colony of Rhode Island in 1663. *82 Smith St., tel. 401/277–2357. Admission charged. Closed weekends.*

South along Benefit Street is the **First Unitarian Church of Providence** (1 Benevolent St., tel. 401/421–7970), built in 1816. The bell tower houses the largest bell ever cast in Paul Revere's foundry, a 2,500-pounder.

On Power Street is the **John Brown House,** designed by Joseph Brown for his brother in 1786. This three-story Georgian mansion is replete with elaborate woodwork and furniture, silver, pewter, glass, linens, Chinese porcelain from the late 18th and early 19th centuries, and an antique-doll collection. *52 Power St., tel. 401/331–8575. Admission charged. Closed Mon.; Jan.–Feb. by appointment.*

What to See and Do with Children

Norman Bird Sanctuary (583 3rd Beach Rd., Middletown, tel. 401/846–2577) is a 450-acre sanctuary with nature trails, guided tours, and a small natural-history museum. In Newport, **The Children's Theatre** (tel. 401/848–0266) stages several major productions each year.

Shopping

Newport is a city for shoppers, though not for bargain hunters. Its specialties include antiques, traditional clothing, and marine supplies. Art and antiques shops, and boutiques with traditional clothing line Thames Street. Spring and Franklin streets and the Brick Market area between Thames and America's Cup Avenue have some 50 shops with crafts, clothing, antiques, and toys. Bowen's and Bannister's wharves feature shops with a nautical theme.

Sports and Outdoor Activities

Biking In Newport, **Ten Speed Spokes** (18 Elm St., tel. 401/847–5609) has bikes and **Newport Rent-a-Ped** (2 Washington St., tel. 401/846–7788) has mopeds. For information on trails in Providence, call the **Department of Public Parks** (tel. 401/785–9450).

Boating In Newport, **Old Port Marine Services** (Sayer's Wharf, tel. 401/847–9109) offers harbor tours, yacht charters, and rides on a harbor ferry. **Sight Sailing of Newport** (Bowen's Wharf, tel. 401/849–3333) organizes two-hour sailing tours of Newport Harbor in a six-passenger sailboat with a U.S. Coast Guard–licensed captain.

Beaches

The southern coast of Rhode Island boasts mile after mile of beautiful, mostly sandy ocean beaches with clear, clean water. The best are at **Westerly, Charleston, South Kingstown,** and **Narragansett.** Newport has several beaches: **Easton's Beach** (Memorial Blvd.), also known as First Beach, is popular for its miniature golf and children's carousel. **Ft. Adams State Park** (Ocean Dr.) has a small beach with a picnic area, lifeguards, and beautiful views of Newport Harbor. **King Park** (Wellington Ave.), popular with scuba divers, also has lifeguards.

Dining and Lodging

Traditional Rhode Island fare includes johnnycake, a sort of corn cake cooked on a griddle, and quahogs (pronounced "KO-hawgs"), the local clams, served steamed, stuffed, fried, in chowder, or in a pie. Particularly popular are "shore dinners," which include clam chowder, steamers, clam cakes, baked sausage, corn on the cob, lobster, watermelon, and Indian pudding (a steamed pudding made with cornmeal and molasses).

While the big chain hotels are represented in Rhode Island, many visitors prefer to stay in smaller inns and B&Bs (**Bed and Breakfast of Rhode Island, Inc.,** Box 3291, Newport 02840, tel. 401/849–1298). Entering Newport from the direction of Providence, you will find dozens of motels where room rates are considerably lower than those in downtown. Along the south shore there are many small motels along Rte. 1, especially on the outskirts of Westerly, and on the Post Road in North Kingston.

Low-season prices are reduced by as much as 50% from high-season rates. For price ranges, see Charts 1 (A) and 2 (A) in Chapter 1.

Newport **The Black Pearl.** Known to yachtsmen throughout the world,
Dining this waterfront restaurant has a tavern for casual fare and
★ drinks and a more formal (and more expensive) dining room for such appetizers as black and blue tuna with red-pepper sauce, and oysters warmed with truffles and cream. Entrées may include swordfish with Dutch-pepper butter or duck breast with green-peppercorn sauce. *Bannister's Wharf, tel. 401/846–5264. Reservations required. Jacket required. AE, DC, MC, V. Expensive.*

Brick Alley Pub. Low ceilings, small tables, plants, and American memorabilia give this place a friendly atmosphere. An extensive menu includes fresh fish, chowder, steaks, and homeymade pasta. *140 Thames St., tel. 401/849–6334. AE, DC, MC, V. Moderate.*

Salas'. Movie posters, red-and-white plastic tablecloths, and lines of waiting customers create a lively, good-natured waterfront dining spot. Pastas, lobster, clams, and corn on the cob are the principal fare. Spaghetti and macaroni are served by the quarter, half, and full pound. *341 Thames St., tel. 401/846–8772. Reservations advised. AE, V. Moderate.*

Lodging **The Marriott.** This harborfront hotel has a courtyard-type atrium lobby with marble floors and a gazebo. Guest rooms, bordering the atrium or overlooking the skyline or the water, are decorated in mauve and seafoam, with either a king-size bed or two double beds. Prices vary greatly according to season and whether the room overlooks the harbor or the parking lot. *25 America's Cup Ave., 02840, tel. 401/849–1000. 310 rooms, 7 suites. Facilities: restaurant, disco, indoor pool, health club. AE, DC, MC, V. Expensive–Very Expensive.*

The Inn at Castle Hill. Perched on an oceanside cliff 3 mi from Newport, this rambling inn was built as a summer home in 1874, and much of the original furniture remains. Some smaller unrefurbished rooms are much less expensive than those that have recently been renovated. The inn's Sunday brunches are famous—be sure to make reservations. *Ocean Dr., 02840, tel. 401/849–3800. 10 rooms (3 share baths). Facilities: Continental breakfast, restaurant (closed Nov.–Mar.), 3 private beaches. AE, MC, V. Closed Dec. 24–25. Expensive–Very Expensive.*

The Francis Malbone House. This stately 1760 house on Thames Street is beautifully restored and furnished with period reproductions. The large corner guest rooms face either the garden or the street and harbor beyond. Breakfast is served in the country kitchen. *392 Thames St., 02840, tel. 401/846–0392. 9 rooms, 1 suite. Facilities: Continental breakfast, working fireplaces in 6 rooms. AE, MC, V. Moderate–Expensive.*

Providence **Al Forno.** This restaurant cemented Providence's reputation as
Dining a culinary center in New England. The entrées, such as oven-
★ roasted chicken cakes with applesauce, as well as sinful desserts like strawberry-and-rhubarb tart, are all made with fresh local ingredients. *577 S. Main St., tel. 401/273–9760. AE, MC, V. Closed Sun.–Mon. Expensive.*

In-Prov. At this tapas place with smallish portions and a wildly varied menu, highlights include pizza with *chorizo* (Portuguese sausage), grilled peppers and wild mushrooms; and Chinese duck in ginger, soy, and saki sauce with pancakes and red-currant sauce. *Fleet Center, 50 Kennedy Plaza, tel. 401/351–8770. Reservations advised. Dress: neat but casual. AE, MC, V. No lunch Sat.; closed Sun. Moderate–Expensive.*

Angelo's Civita Farnese. On Federal Hill, in the heart of Little Italy, this family-run place has vinyl booths and fresh and simply prepared pasta. The portions are large, the volume loud. *141 Atwells Ave., tel. 401/621–8171. No credit cards. Closed Sun. Inexpensive.*

Lodging **Omni Biltmore Hotel.** The Biltmore, completed in 1922, has a
★ sleek art deco exterior, Old World charm, and an external glass elevator that offers attractive views of Providence at night. The attentiveness of the staff, the downtown location, and a recent face-lift make this an appealing perch from which to explore the city. *Kennedy Plaza, 11 Dorrance St., 02903, tel. 401/*

421–0700. 253 rooms, 18 suites. Facilities: restaurant, health club nearby, weekend packages. AE, DC, MC, V. Expensive.

C. C. Ledbetter's. The somber green exterior of this Benefit Street home belies its vibrant interior—the place is filled with two English springer spaniels, lively art, books, photographs, handmade quilts, and a warm, homey blend of contemporary furnishings and antiques. Book early for Brown University's parents' and graduation weekends. *326 Benefit St., 02903, tel. 401/351–4699. 5 rooms (4 share 2 baths). Facilities: free parking. No credit cards. Moderate.*

Holiday Inn. This high-rise motel is close to Exit 21 on I–95, near the Providence Civic Center. There is a comfortable piano bar off the lobby. *21 Atwells Ave., 02903, tel. 401/831–3900. 274 rooms. Facilities: restaurant, indoor pool, exercise room. AE, DC, MC, V. Moderate.*

Motels
Newport

Comfort Inn (936 W. Main Rd., 02840, tel. 401/846–7600), 136 rooms, restaurant, pool; expensive. **Best Western** (151 Admiral Kalbfus Rd., 02840, tel. 401/849–9880), 122 rooms, restaurant, pool; moderate.

Providence

Marriott (Charles and Orm Sts., 02904, tel. 401/272–2400), 345 rooms, restaurant, health club, 2 pools; expensive. **Days Hotel on the Harbor** (220 India St., 02903, tel. 401/272–5577), 136 rooms, restaurant, exercise room; moderate.

South Shore

Best Western (7075 Post Rd., 02852, tel. 401/884–8000), 51 rooms, restaurant, outdoor pool; moderate. **Wickford Motor Inn** (7650 Post Rd., 02852, tel. 401/884–2230), 18 rooms, some with refrigerators; inexpensive.

Nightlife

The tourist offices (*see* Visitor Information, *above*) have listings of concerts, shows, and special events, as do the Newport and Providence newspapers.

In Newport: **The Ark** (348 Thames St., tel. 401/849–3808) features jazz on Sunday. **Clark Cooke House** (Bannister's Wharf, tel. 401/849–2900) offers two discos, one upstairs overlooking the harbor. **Club Thames** (337 America's Cup Ave., tel. 401/849–9840) plays high-energy dance music and videos.

In Providence: **Oliver's** (83 Benevolent St., tel. 401/272–8795), a hangout for Brown University types, has a pool table and good pub food. **American Cafe** (1 Throop Alley, tel. 401/861–1996) offers live rock weeknights and a DJ on weekends. **The Living Room** (212 Promenade St., tel. 401/521–2520) showcases local and national bands.

VERMONT

By Mary Frakes

Capital	Montpelier
Population	563,000
Motto	Freedom and Unity
State Bird	Hermit thrush
State Flower	Red clover

Visitor Information

Vermont Department of Travel and Tourism (134 State St., Montpelier 05602, tel. 802/828–3236). **Vermont Chamber of Commerce** (Box 37, Montpelier 05602, tel. 802/223–3443).

Scenic Drives

Rte. 100, up the spiny backbone of the state, passes through a sampling of the faces of Vermont: small towns oriented to nearby ski areas, the eastern edge of Green Mountain National Forest, Mad River Valley, Stowe, and on to Canada.

National and State Parks

National Park The 300,000-acre **Green Mountain National Forest** (Rutland 05701; or Green Mountain Club, Rte. 100, Box 650, Waterbury Center 05677, tel. 802/244–7037) runs through the center of the state, from Bristol south to the Massachusetts border.

State Parks The 40 parks owned and maintained by the **Department of Forests, Parks and Recreation** (Waterbury 05676, tel. 802/244–8711) offer nature and hiking trails, campsites, swimming, boating facilities, and fishing. Especially popular are the **Champlain Islands** sites: **Burton Island, Kill Kare** (*see* Northwestern Vermont, *below*), and **Sand Bar.**

Southern Vermont

Southern Vermont is the cradle of the state's tradition of independence and rebellion. Many of the towns with village greens and white-spired churches were founded in the early 18th century as frontier outposts and later became trading centers. In the western region, the Green Mountain Boys fought off both the British and claims by land-hungry New Yorkers. The influx of new residents in the past 20 years means that the quaintness often comes with a patina of sophistication or funk; shoppers can find not only antiques but New Age crystals, Vermont-made salsa, and the highest-tech ski gear.

Tourist Information

Bennington: Area Chamber of Commerce (Veterans Memorial Dr., 05201, tel. 802/447–3311). **Brattleboro:** Chamber of Commerce (180 Main St., 05301, tel. 802/254–4565). **Manchester:** and the Mountains Chamber of Commerce (Adams Park Green, Box 928, 05255, tel. 802/362–2100). **Rutland:** Region Chamber of Commerce, Convention and Visitors' Division (Box 67,

05702, tel. 802/773–2747). **Woodstock:** Area Chamber of Commerce (4 Central St., 05091, tel. 802/457–3555).

Getting There

By Car I–91 runs north–south along the eastern edge of Vermont. U.S. 7 goes north–south through western Vermont, and Rte. 9 runs east–west across the state through Bennington and Brattleboro.

By Train **Amtrak** stops at Brattleboro and Bellows Falls.

By Bus The local **Greyhound** subsidiary, **Vermont Transit** (tel. 802/864–6811 or 800/451–3292), links Bennington, Brattleboro, and smaller towns with nearby states and the rest of the country. **Bonanza Bus Lines** (tel. 802/442–4808) goes from Danbury, Connecticut, to Bennington.

Exploring Southern Vermont

It was at **Bennington** that Ethan Allen formed the Green Mountain Boys, who helped capture Ft. Ticonderoga in 1775. The **Bennington Battle Monument** (15 Monument Ave., tel. 802/447–0550), a 306-foot-tall stone obelisk, commemorates General John Stark's defeat of the British in their attempt to capture Bennington's stockpile of supplies. Piled higgledy-piggledy in cases at the **Bennington Museum** (W. Main St. [Rte. 9], tel. 802/447–1571) is a rich collection of Early American artifacts, including decorative arts, glassware, and the folk art of Grandma Moses.

Manchester has been a popular summer retreat since the mid-19th century (Mary Todd Lincoln visited here). Its tree-shaded marble sidewalks and stately old houses reflect the luxurious resort lifestyle of a century ago, while upscale factory-outlet stores appeal to the ski crowd. **Hildene** (Rte. 7A, 2 mi north of intersection with Rtes. 11 and 30, tel. 802/362–1788), the 412-acre summer home of Abraham Lincoln's son Robert, features Georgian Revival symmetry and formal gardens.

The **Southern Vermont Art Center** (West Rd., tel. 802/362–1405) offers a permanent painting collection and rotating exhibits. Its 375-acre Manchester site is dotted with contemporary sculpture, and concerts, dramatic performances, and films are presented here. The **American Museum of Fly Fishing** (Rte. 7A, tel. 802/362–3300) displays the tackle of such noted anglers as General George Patton, Daniel Webster, and Winslow Homer. The steep 5.2-mi drive to the top of **Mt. Equinox** (Rte. 7A, tel. 802/362–1114) brings you to the Saddle, where the views are outstanding.

In **Rutland's** **Vermont Marble Exhibit** (off Rte. 3, tel. 802/459–3311), northwest of town, visitors can watch the transformation of the rough stone into slabs, blocks, and gift items. The **Chaffee Art Gallery** (16 Main St., tel. 802/775–0356) houses the work of 250 Vermont artists.

On the eastern side of the state on U.S. 4, **Woodstock** is the quintessential quiet New England town. Exquisitely preserved Federal houses surround the tree-lined village green. The **Vermont Institute of Natural Science's Raptor Center** (Church Hill Rd., tel. 802/457–2779) features nature trails and 26 species of birds of prey. A half-mile north of town, the recon-

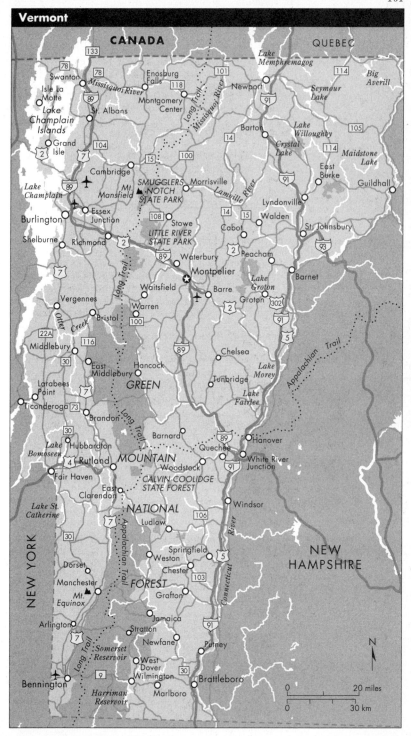

Vermont

CANADA

QUEBEC

133

78

Swanton

78 Missisquoi River

Enosburg Falls

101

114

Big Averill

Lake Memphremagog

Isle La Motte

89

118

Newport

91

Seymour Lake

Lake Champlain Islands

St. Albans

Montgomery Center

Long Trail

Missisquoi River

Barton

Lake Willoughby

105

2 Grand Isle

104

14

Crystal Lake

114

Maidstone Lake

7

15

100

East Burke

Cambridge

SMUGGLERS NOTCH STATE PARK

Morrisville

Lamoille River

Guildhall

Lake Champlain

89

Mt. Mansfield

Lyndonville

91

Essex Junction

108

14

15

Walden

St. Johnsbury

Burlington

Stowe

LITTLE RIVER STATE PARK

Cabot

2

93

Shelburne

Richmond

2

Waterbury

Peacham

89

Montpelier

Barnet

Vergennes

Waitsfield

Barre

Lake Groton

Otter Creek

Warren

2

Groton

302

22A

100

Bristol

91

5

Middlebury

116

89

Chelsea

Appalachian Trail

30

East Middlebury

Hancock

GREEN

Tunbridge

Lake Morey

Larabees Point

7

Lake Fairlee

Ticonderoga

73

Long Trail

Barnard

89

Hanover

Brandon

30

Lake Bomoseen

Hubbardton

MOUNTAIN

Quechee

White River Junction

4 Rutland

Woodstock

91

Fair Haven

East Clarendon

CALVIN COOLIDGE STATE FOREST

Lake St. Catherine

NATIONAL

106

Windsor

30

7

Ludlow

NEW YORK

Appalachian Trail

Springfield

5

Connecticut River

NEW HAMPSHIRE

Dorset

Weston

Chester

Manchester

FOREST

103

Grafton

Mt. Equinox

Jamaica

91

Arlington

7

Stratton

Newfane

Putney

Long Trail

Somerset Reservoir

West Dover

30

Bennington

9

Wilmington

Brattleboro

Harriman Reservoir

Marlboro

N

0   20 miles

0   30 km

structed farmhouse, school, general store, and workshop at the **Billings Farm and Museum** (Rte. 12, tel. 802/457–2355) demonstrate the daily activities and skills of early Vermonters.

The mile-long **Quechee Gorge,** carved by a glacier and the Ottauquechee River, is visible from U.S. 4, but you can also scramble down one of the several descents. In the town of **Quechee,** at **Simon Pearce** (Main St., tel. 802/295–2711), you can watch potters and glassblowers at work.

What to See and Do with Children

The **New England Maple Museum** (U.S. 7, Pittsford, tel. 802/ 483–9414), near Rutland, gives historical perspectives on the process of making maple syrup, back to its Native American origins.

Shopping

Antiques and traditional and contemporary crafts are everywhere. Particularly good are **U.S. 7** north of Manchester to Danby and the **Antiques Center at Hartland** (U.S. 5, tel. 802/ 436–2441). The **Bennington Potters Yard** (324 County St., tel. 802/447–7531) has a huge selection of Bennington Pottery factory seconds. **Manchester,** with its designer names and factory outlets, has become to Vermont what Freeport is to Maine.

Sports and Outdoor Activities

Biking **Vermont Bicycle Touring** (Box 711, Bristol 05443, tel. 802/453–4811) and **Bike Vermont** (Box 207, Woodstock 05091, tel. 802/ 457–3553) operate guided tours.

Canoeing The **Connecticut River** and the **Battenkill** offer easygoing canoe outings. Rentals are available from **Battenkill Canoe** (Arlington, tel. 802/375–9559).

Fishing The **Battenkill River** is famous for trout. The **Orvis Co.** (Rte. 7A, Manchester, tel. 802/362–3900) runs an annual fly-fishing school. The necessary fishing license is easily available through tackle shops, or call the **Department of Fish and Wildlife** (tel. 802/244–7331).

Golf In Manchester, **Equinox** (tel. 802/362–3223) and **Haystack Country Club** (tel. 802/464–8301) are public 18-hole courses.

Hiking and Backpacking The southern half of the **Long Trail** is part of the **Appalachian Trail** and runs from just east of Rutland to the state's southern boundary. The **Green Mountain Club** (*see* National and State Parks, *above*) maintains the trail and staffs huts along it in summer, as well as mapping hiking elsewhere in Vermont.

Ski Areas

For up-to-date snow conditions in the state, call 802/229–0531. All downhill ski areas listed have snowmaking equipment.

Cross-country **Bolton Valley** (Box 300, Bolton 05477, tel. 802/434–2131), 62 mi of trails. **Mt. Snow** (400 Mountain Rd., Mt. Snow 05356, tel. 802/ 464–3333), 62 mi of trails. **Stratton** (Stratton Mountain 05155, tel. 802/297–2200 or 800/843–6867), 20 mi of trails. **Woodstock Ski Touring Center** (Woodstock 05091, tel. 802/457–2114), 47 mi of trails.

Downhill **Bromley** (Box 1130, Manchester Center 05255, tel. 802/824–5522), 35 runs, 10 lifts, 1,334-foot vertical drop. **Killington** (400 Killington Rd., Killington 05751, tel. 802/773–1330), 107 runs, 19 lifts, 3,175-foot drop. **Mt. Snow** (*see* Cross-country, *above*), 84 trails, 18 lifts, 1,700-foot drop. **Stratton** (*see* Cross-country, *above*), 92 slopes, gondola, 11 lifts, 2,000-foot drop.

Dining and Lodging

The **Vermont Travel Information Service** (tel. 802/276–3120) offers centralized lodging referrals. For price ranges, see Charts 1 (B) and 2 (B) in Chapter 1.

Bennington **Main Street Cafe.** A few minutes from downtown, this small
Dining storefront café draws locals with its northern Italian cuisine and a casual-chic atmosphere. *Rte. 67A, North Bennington, tel. 802/442–3210. Reservations advised. AE, DC, MC, V. Closed Thanksgiving, Christmas. Expensive.*
The Brasserie. The fare is hearty and creative, the decor as clean-lined as the Bennington Pottery sold in the same complex. *324 County St., tel. 802/447–7922. MC, V. Closed Tues. Moderate.*

Lodging **South Shire Inn.** Canopy beds in lushly carpeted rooms, ornate plaster molding on the ceilings, and the dark mahogany fireplace in the library add up to turn-of-the-century grandeur in a quiet residential neighborhood. *124 Elm St., 05201, tel. 802/447–3839. 9 rooms, 7 with fireplace. Facilities: full breakfast. No smoking indoors. AE, MC, V. Moderate–Expensive.*

Dining and Lodging **Four Chimneys.** This palatial estate provides Old World formality in enormous guest rooms. The dining room's heavy silverware and candlelight set the tone for such classic French dishes as steak flambéed in cognac with green peppercorns. *21 West Rd., 05201, tel. 802/447–3500. 7 rooms. Facilities: restaurant (reservations advised; jacket and tie advised), outdoor pool, sauna. AE, DC, MC, V. Closed Mon., Jan. 2–Feb. 14. Expensive.*

Manchester **Chantecleer.** The Swiss-inspired menu may mix air-dried
Dining Swiss beef with such French classics as frogs' legs in garlic butter. The converted dairy barn has a huge fieldstone fireplace and is divided into intimate dining rooms. *U.S. 7, 5 mi north of Manchester in East Dorset, tel. 802/362–1616. Reservations required. DC, MC, V. No lunch; closed Mon.–Tues. Expensive.*
Garden Cafe. This sunny room has a terrific view of the spacious Southern Vermont Art Center grounds, an outdoor terrace, and such dishes as sautéed trout with almonds. *West Rd., tel. 802/362–4220. No credit cards. Closed mid-Oct.–Memorial Day. Moderate.*
The Quality Restaurant. The model for Norman Rockwell's *War News* painting, this family-owned spot features sturdy New England standbys, such as hot open-faced roast beef or turkey sandwiches with gravy. *Main St., tel. 802/362–9839. AE, MC, V. Moderate.*

Lodging **1811 House.** Staying here feels like staying at an elegant En-
★ glish country house filled with antiques. The pub-style bar is decorated with horse brasses and equestrian paintings. *Rte. 7A, 05254, tel. 802/362–1811. 14 rooms. Facilities: full breakfast, lounge. No smoking. AE, MC, V. Expensive.*
Barnstead Innstead. This 1830s barn was transformed in 1968

into a handful of rooms that combine exposed beams and barn-board walls with modern plumbing and cheerful wallpaper. *Rte. 30, 05255, tel. 802/362–1619. 12 rooms. Facilities: cable TV, outdoor pool. MC, V. Moderate.*

Dining and Lodging **The Equinox.** This white-columned resort was a landmark on Vermont's tourism scene even before Abraham Lincoln's family began summering here. The rooms, renovated in 1985, are furnished in Vermont pine. The front porch is perfect for watching the passing parade. The health center offers a medically supervised spa program. *Manchester Village 05254, tel. 802/362–4700 or 800/362–4747. 119 rooms, 18 suites, 9 3-bedroom town houses. Facilities: restaurant, tavern, tennis courts, golf course, 2 pools. AE, D, DC, MC, V. Very Expensive.*

Reluctant Panther. Spacious rooms with goose-down duvets and Pierre Deux linens are the standard here; many rooms have fireplaces. The dining room features a huge fieldstone fireplace, a small solarium area, and an ambitious menu of Vermont regional dishes and seafood. *West Rd., Box 678, 05254, tel. 802/362–2568. 14 rooms. Facilities: restaurant (reservations required; closed Wed.), lounge. AE, MC, V. Expensive.*

Rutland **Back Home Cafe.** Wooden booths, black-and-white linoleum
Dining tile, and exposed brick lend atmosphere at this second-story
★ café where dinner might be baked stuffed fillet of sole with spinach, mushrooms, feta cheese, and tarragon sauce. *21 Center St., tel. 802/775–2104. MC, V. Moderate.*

Lodging **Comfort Inn.** Rooms at this chain hotel are a cut above the standard, with an upholstered wing chair and blond-wood furnishings. *170 S. Main St., 05701, tel. 802/775–2200. 103 rooms. Facilities: restaurant, fitness center, pool, tennis courts. AE, D, DC, MC, V. Expensive.*

The Inn at Rutland. In this renovated Victorian mansion, an ornate oak staircase leads to rooms with such turn-of-the-century touches as botanical prints, elaborate ceiling moldings, and frosted glass. *70 N. Main St., 05701, tel. 802/773–0575. 12 rooms. Facilities: Continental breakfast. AE, D, MC, V. Moderate.*

Woodstock **The Prince and the Pauper.** This romantically candlelit Colonial
Dining setting serves a prix-fixe menu of nouvelle French with a Ver-
★ mont accent. *24 Elm St., tel. 802/457–1818. Reservations advised. D, MC, V. No lunch; closed Sun.–Mon. late fall and early spring. Expensive.*

Bentley's. Antique silk-fringed lampshades, long lace curtains, and a life-size carving of a kneeling, winged knight lend a tongue-in-cheek Victorian air to burgers, chili, homemade soups, and entrées like duck in raspberry puree, almonds, and Chambord. *3 Elm St., tel. 802/457–3232. AE, MC, V. Moderate.*

Dining and Lodging **Kedron Valley Inn.** One of the state's oldest hotels, built in the
★ 1840s, has rooms decorated with family quilts and antiques. The motel units in back feature exposed log walls. The dining room offers classical French technique and Vermont ingredients. *Rte. 106, 05071, tel. 802/457–1473. 28 rooms. Facilities: full breakfast, restaurant, swimming/skating pond, lounge. D, MC, V. Closed Apr. Expensive.*

Woodstock Inn and Resort. This massive facility presides over the village green like a dowager duchess. The rooms' modern ash furnishings are enlivened by patchwork quilts and original

Vermont landscape paintings. The menu in the dining room is nouvelle New England. *U.S. 4, 05091, tel. 802/457–1100 or 800/ 448–7900. 146 rooms. Facilities: dining room (jacket required at dinner), pool, tennis, golf course, sports center, cross-country and downhill skiing. AE, MC, V. Expensive.*

Village Inn at Woodstock. The rooms in this renovated Victorian mansion are decorated simply with country antiques, chenille bedspreads, and dried flowers. *U.S. 4, 05091, tel. 802/457– 1255. 8 rooms (2 share bath). Facilities: restaurant, lounge. MC, V. Closed early Nov., Thanksgiving. Moderate.*

Motels

Aspen Motel (Box 548, Manchester 05255, tel. 802/362–2450), 24 rooms, cable TV, outdoor pool; moderate. **Pond Ridge Motel** (U.S. 4, Woodstock 05091, tel. 802/457–1667), 21 rooms, some with refrigerator and stove; moderate. **Harwood Hill Motel** (Rte. 7A, Bennington 05201, tel. 802/442–6278), 16 rooms; inexpensive.

Campgrounds

The campsites in the **Green Mountain National Forest** (*see* National and State Parks, *above*) operate on a first-come, first-served basis. The state park system runs nearly 40 campgrounds with more than 2,000 campsites; contact the forests department (*see* National and State Parks, *above*). The official state map lists private campgrounds.

The Arts and Nightlife

Like most things in Vermont, the arts and nightlife tend to be low-key. The summer **Marlboro Music Festival** (Marlboro Music Center, tel. 802/257–4333) and the fall **New England Bach Festival** (Brattleboro Music Center, tel. 802/257–4523) are among the best classical music festivals in the country. Most nightlife is concentrated at and around the ski resorts.

Northwestern Vermont

More mountainous than the southern part of the state, northern Vermont is also less populated and contains the closest thing Vermont has to a seacoast—Lake Champlain—as well as the state capital. Its recorded history dates from 1609, when Samuel de Champlain explored the lake now named for him.

Tourist Information

Central Vermont: Chamber of Commerce (Box 336, Barre 05641, tel. 802/229–5711). **Lake Champlain:** Regional Chamber of Commerce (209 Battery St., Box 453, Burlington 05402, tel. 802/863–3489). **Smugglers' Notch:** Area Chamber of Commerce (Box 3264, Jeffersonville 05464, tel. 802/644–2239). **Stowe:** Area Association (Main St., Box 1320, Stowe 05672, tel. 802/ 253–7321).

Getting There

By Plane **Burlington Airport** (South Burlington, tel. 802/863–2874) is 4½ mi east of town off Rte. 2 and is served by major airlines. **E. F. Knapp Airport** (tel. 802/223–2060), served by regional airlines, lies between Barre and Montpelier.

By Car I–89 runs from White River Junction to Vermont's northwest corner at the Canadian border.

By Train **Amtrak** stops at Montpelier, Waterbury, Essex Junction, and St. Albans.

By Bus **Vermont Transit** (tel. 802/864–6811 or 800/451–3292) connects Burlington, Stowe, Montpelier, Barre, St. Johnsbury, and Newport.

Exploring Northwestern Vermont

On the western edge of the region, **Middlebury** is Robert Frost country; Vermont's former poet laureate spent 23 summers at a farm near here. East of Middlebury on Rte. 125 is the **Robert Frost Wayside Trail,** which winds through quiet woodland with Frost quotations posted along the way.

The 100-acre **Shelburne Museum'**s 35 buildings contain one of the largest Americana collections in the country. Exhibits include 18th- and 19th-century houses and furniture, fine and folk art, farm tools, carriages and sleighs, and an old sidewheel steamship. *U.S. 7, 5 mi south of Burlington, tel. 802/985–3346. Admission charged.*

At the 1,000-acre **Shelburne Farms,** visitors can see a working dairy farm, attend nature lectures, or stroll the grounds along a stretch of Lake Champlain's waterfront. *Off U.S. 7, 3 mi south of Burlington, tel. 802/985–8686. Admission charged.*

Burlington is enlivened by the 10,000 students at the **University of Vermont. Church Street Marketplace,** with its down-to-earth shops, chic boutiques, and an appealing menagerie of sidewalk cafés, food and crafts vendors, and street performers, is an animated downtown focal point. The *Spirit of Ethan Allen* (Perkins Pier, tel. 802/862–9685), a replica of the paddle wheelers that once plied Lake Champlain, offers daily narrated cruises in summer.

A scenic summer alternative to I–89 east toward Stowe takes you through **Smugglers' Notch** (Rte. 15 to Jeffersonville, then south on narrow, twisting Rte. 108), the bouldered pass over Mt. Mansfield said to have given shelter to 18th-century outlaws. There are roadside picnic tables and a spectacular waterfall view.

Stowe is best known as a venerable ski center, but in summer you can take the 4½-mi toll road to the top of Vermont's highest peak, **Mt. Mansfield** (entrance on Mountain Rd., 7 mi from Rte. 100, tel. 802/253–3000). At the road's end is a short and very scenic walk. Another way to ascend Mt. Mansfield is in the gondola that shuttles from the base of the ski area up 4,393 feet to the section known as "the Chin," where there are scenic views and a restaurant.

In the state capital of **Montpelier,** the interior of the **Vermont State House** (State St., tel. 802/828–2228) is decorated with quotes about Vermont. The **Vermont Museum** (109 State St., tel. 802/828–3391), on the ground floor of the Vermont Historical Society offices, can tell you why New England bridges are covered and what a "niddy-noddy" is.

What to See and Do with Children

The University of Vermont's **Morgan Horse Farm** (Rte. 23, 2.5 mi from Middlebury, tel. 802/388–2011) offers tours of the stables and paddocks. Just south of Stowe is the Mecca, Nirvana, and Valhalla of ice-cream lovers, **Ben and Jerry's Ice Cream Factory** (Rte. 100, 1 mi north of I–89, tel. 802/244–5641), which gives tours.

Shopping

The **Vermont State Craft Center at Frog Hollow** (Mill St., Middlebury, tel. 802/388–3177; Church St., Burlington, tel. 802/863–6458; Rte. 7A, Manchester, tel. 802/362–3321) is a juried display of the work of more than 250 Vermont artisans. Burlington's **Church Street Marketplace** is a pedestrian thoroughfare lined with boutiques.

Sports and Outdoor Activities

Biking   In addition to the numerous back roads along the Champlain Valley, Stowe has a recreational path, and Burlington has a 9-mi path along its waterfront. Several operators offer guided tours throughout the state (*see* Southern Vermont, *above*).

Fishing   Lake Champlain contains salmon, lake trout, bass, pike, and more. Marina services are offered by **Malletts Bay Marina** (228 Lakeshore Dr., Colchester, tel. 802/862–4077) and **Point Bay Marina** (Thompson's Point, Charlotte, tel. 802/425–2431).

Golf   Public courses include **Ralph Myhre's** 18 holes (Rte. 30, Middlebury, tel. 802/388–3711) and 9 holes at **Montpelier Country Club** (U.S. 2, just south of U.S. 302, Montpelier, tel. 802/223–7457).

Hiking and   Aside from the Long Trail (*see* Southern Vermont, *above*), day
Backpacking   hikes in northern Vermont include the **Little River** area in Mt. Mansfield State Forest near Stowe and **Stowe Pinnacle.**

Tennis   Stowe's **Grand Prix Tournament** is in early August (Stowe Area Association, tel. 802/253–7321). Most resorts' courts are open only to guests. Tennis schools are offered at **Smugglers' Notch Tennis Camp** (Smugglers' Notch 05464, tel. 802/644–8851) and **Sugarbush Tennis School** (Sugarbush Sports Center, R.R.1, Box 350, Warren 05674, tel. 802/583–2381).

Beaches and Water Sports

The center for water activities in Vermont is Lake Champlain. Marinas, rentals, and charters are available in or near Vergennes and Burlington. In Burlington, **North Beach Park** (North Ave., tel. 802/864–0123) offers swimming at a long, sandy beach; **McKibben Sailing Vacations** (tel. 802/864–7733) has charter sailboats; **Burlington Rent All** (tel. 802/862–5793) rents rowboats and motorboats; and **Burlington Community Boathouse** (Burlington Harbor at College St., tel. 802/865–3377) rents sailboats and sailboards. **North Hero State Park** (tel. 802/372–8727) has a children's play area nearby. **Kill Kare State Park** (off Rte. 36, south of St. Albans, tel. 802/524–6021) has sailboard rentals and the ferry to Burton Island.

Ski Areas

For statewide snow conditions, tel. 802/229–0531. All downhill areas listed have snowmaking.

Cross-country **Burke Mountain** (Box 247, East Burke 05832, tel. 802/626–3305 or 800/541–5480) has 37 mi of trails and a ski school. Alpine resorts (*see* Downhill, *below*) that also have cross-country trails include **Jay Peak**, 25 mi; **Smugglers' Notch**, 23 mi; **Stowe**, 18 mi of groomed trails, 12 mi of back-country trails; and **Sugarbush**, 15 mi.

Downhill **Jay Peak** (Rte. 242, Jay 05859, tel. 802/988–2611 or 800/451–4449), 43 trails, six lifts, 2,153-foot vertical drop. **Mad River Glen** (Rte. 17, Waitsfield 05673, tel. 802/496–3551), 33 runs, three lifts, 2,000-foot drop. **Smugglers' Notch** (Smugglers' Notch 05464, tel. 802/644–8851 or 800/451–8752), 56 runs, five lifts, 2,610-foot drop. **Stowe** (5781 Mountain Rd., Stowe 05672, tel. 802/253–3000), 45 trails, nine lifts, 2,360-foot drop. **Sugarbush** (R.R. 1, Box 350, Warren 05674, tel. 802/583–2381), 107 trails, 16 lifts, 2,600- and 2,400-foot drops.

Dining and Lodging

For price ranges, see Charts 1 (B) and 2 (B) in Chapter 1.

Burlington **The Daily Planet.** At one of Burlington's hippest restaurants, a
Dining jukebox plays Aretha Franklin or Big Band sounds, the food is Mediterranean with Oriental flourishes, and a solarium lightens the turn-of-the-century bar. *15 Center St., tel. 802/862–9647. Reservations advised. AE, DC, MC, V. Moderate.*

★ **Déjà Vu.** The atmosphere here blends high-gothic booths made from ornately carved church pews with brass accents and romantic candlelight. The cuisine runs to fancily prepared game with a Continental touch. *185 Pearl St., tel. 802/864–7917. AE, DC, MC, V. Moderate.*

★ **Five Spice Cafe.** In this tiny, funky spot, the chef plays with a variety of Asian cuisines to create an extensive selection of vegetarian dishes as well as a weekend dim sum brunch. *175 Church St., tel. 802/864–4045. AE, DC, MC, V. Inexpensive.*

Lodging **Queen City Inn.** The rooms in the restored Victorian house have baskets of potpourri and magnificent architectural detailing. The motel rooms next door, while simple, also admit lodgers to Continental breakfast in the sunny sitting room. *428 Shelburne Rd., South Burlington 05403, tel. 802/864–4220. 25 rooms. AE, MC, V. Moderate–Expensive.*

Dining and Lodging **Sheraton-Burlington.** As the biggest hotel in the city and the closest to the airport, the Sheraton-Burlington is popular for large conferences. Upholstered wing chairs and dust ruffles in the mauve and burgundy rooms give a New England touch. *870 Williston Rd., 05403, tel. 802/862–6576. 309 rooms. Facilities: health club, pool, cable TV, handicapped-accessible rooms. AE, D, DC, MC, V. Expensive.*

Middlebury **Woody's.** In addition to cool jazz, diner-deco light fixtures, and
Dining abstract paintings, Woody's offers a view of Otter Creek just
★ below. The menu has nightly specials, and usually there's a

Vermont lamb dish. *5 Bakery La., tel. 802/388–4182. Reservations advised. DC, MC, V. Expensive.*

Rosie's. This family place serves simple, straightforward food at reasonable prices. *U.S. 7 (1 mi south of Middlebury), tel. 802/388–7052. MC, V. Inexpensive.*

Dining and Lodging   **Middlebury Inn.** White fluted columns and a black marble fireplace in the lobby speak of this 1827 inn's heritage. Rooms in the main building mix formal and country antiques; the 20 motel rooms have quilt hangings and floor-to-ceiling windows. The blue-and-white Colonial dining room offers an all-you-can-eat buffet. *Court House Sq., 05753–0798, tel. 802/388–4961 or 800/842–4666. 75 rooms. Facilities: restaurant, lounge. AE, MC, V. Expensive.*

Montpelier   **Tubb's.** The staff are all students at the New England Culinary
Dining   Institute. A well-prepared, inventive menu changes daily but stays along the lines of swordfish with spinach and cherry tomatoes. The atmosphere is more formal than that of its sister operation down the block, the Elm Street Cafe. *24 Elm St., tel. 802/229–9202. Reservations advised. MC, V. Closed Sun. Expensive.*

Horn of the Moon. The bowls of honey on the tables and the bulletin board of political notices hint at Vermont's prominent progressive contingent. This vegetarian restaurant's cuisine includes a little Mexican, a little Thai, a lot of flavor, and not too much tofu. *8 Langdon St., tel. 802/223–2895. No credit cards. No dinner Sun.–Mon. Moderate.*

Lodging   **The Inn at Montpelier.** This spacious early 1800s house was
★   renovated in 1988 and features architectural detailing, antique four-posters, stately tapestry-upholstered wing chairs, and classical guitar on the stereo. *147 Main St., 05602, tel. 802/223–2727. 19 rooms. Facilities: Continental breakfast. AE, MC, V. Expensive.*

Stowe   **Stubb's.** The chef updates traditional New England dishes, as
Dining   in calves' liver with a sauce of balsamic vinegar and shallots. Marbleized walls and pink-over-burgundy linens give a sophisticated note to the rustic beams and the fireplaces at either end of the two rooms. *Mountain Rd., tel. 802/253–7110. Reservations advised. AE, DC, MC, V. Moderate–Expensive.*

★   **Villa Tragara.** A farmhouse interior has been converted into a number of intimate dining nooks where romance reigns. Specialties include four-cheese ravioli with a tomato-cream sauce. *Rte. 100, 10 minutes south of Stowe, tel. 802/244–5288. Reservations advised. AE, MC, V. Moderate–Expensive.*

Lodging   **The Gables.** This farmhouse is a warren of charming rooms furnished with antiques. The tiny, plant-filled sunroom is perfect for lazy mornings, and the full breakfasts are generous. *Mountain Rd., 05672, tel. 802/253–7730 or 800/422–5371. 17 rooms. Facilities: pool, hot tub, handicapped-accessible room. AE, MC, V. Closed late Apr.–May. Expensive.*

★   **The Inn at the Brass Lantern.** Home-baked cookies in the afternoon, a freshly filled basket of logs by the fireplace, and stenciled hearts along the wainscoting all speak of the care taken in renovating this 18th-century farmhouse. *Rte. 100, 1 mi north of Stowe, 05672, tel. 802/253–2229. 9 rooms, some with fireplace. Facilities: full breakfast. AE, MC, V. Moderate.*

Dining and Lodging   **10 Acres Lodge.** Rooms in the main inn are smaller than those in the newer building high on the hill but all are carefully decorated. Contemporary pottery complements antique horse brasses over the living-room fireplace. *Luce Hill Rd., Box 3220, 05672, tel. 802/253–7638 or 800/327–7357. 18 rooms, 2 cottages. Facilities: full breakfast, restaurant, lounge, pool. AE, MC, V. Expensive.*

Motels

Econo Lodge (101 Northfield St., Montpelier 05602, tel. 802/223–5258), 54 rooms, restaurant; moderate. **Greystone Motel** (U.S. 7, South Middlebury 05753, tel. 802/388–4935), 10 rooms; moderate.

Spa

For price range, see Chart 2 (A) in Chapter 1.

Topnotch at Stowe. The lobby of this resort, one of the state's poshest, features floor-to-ceiling windows, a freestanding circular stone fireplace, and cathedral ceilings. Rooms have thick rust carpet and a barn-board wall or an Italian print. *Mountain Rd., Stowe 05672, tel. 802/253–8585 or 800/451–8686. 92 rooms, 8 suites. Facilities: restaurant, lounge, 2 pools, 12 tennis courts, golf course. AE, DC, MC, V. Very Expensive.*

Campgrounds

Camping on the Champlain Islands state parks can be arranged through the state forests department (*see* National and State Parks, *above*).

The Arts and Nightlife

The Arts Burlington has the **Vermont Mozart Festival** (tel. 802/862–7352) and the **Champlain Shakespeare Festival** (tel. 802/656–0090) in summer. Stowe has a summer **performing arts festival** (tel. 802/253–7321).

Nightlife Burlington's nightlife caters to its college-age population, with pubs and a few dance spots. The **Vermont Pub and Brewery** (College and St. Paul Sts., Burlington, tel. 802/865–0500) is the only pub in Vermont that makes its own beers. **Comedy Zone** (Radisson Hotel, 60 Battery St., Burlington, tel. 802/658–6500) provides the laughs in town on weekends.

Elsewhere in the State

The Northeast Kingdom

Getting There Drive up I–91 on the eastern side of the state.

What to See The greatest pleasure is driving through pastoral scenery and
and Do discovering charming small towns such as Peacham, Barton, and Craftsbury Common. The chief city is **St. Johnsbury,** where the **Fairbanks Museum and Planetarium** (Main and Prospect Sts., tel. 802/748–2372) offers collections of plants and animals, Vermontiana, and a 50-seat planetarium. The **St. Johnsbury Athenaeum** (30 Main St., tel. 802/748–8291), an architectural gem with dark paneling, polished Victorian woodwork, and ornate circular staircases that rise to the gallery, contains pho-

tographer Albert Bierstadt's *Domes of Yosemite*. **St. Johnsbury Chamber of Commerce** (30 Western Ave., 05819, tel. 802/748–3678) has information on the region.

3 The Middle Atlantic States

The Middle Atlantic States

Detroit

0 _____ 100 miles
0 _____ 150 km

N

Lake Erie

Cleveland

Erie

90

Cory

Warre

Meadville

ALLEGHEN
NATIONA
FOREST

Franklin

Oil City

79

322

Clarion

80

Butler

Kittaning

422

Indiar

22

Aliquippa

76

Mill Run

Pittsburgh

Steubenville

Greensburg

70

OHIO

Ohio River

Columbus

Washington

40

Wheeling

Waynesburg

Uniontown

Paden City

Morgantown

48

Parkersburg

50

Clarksburg

Monongahela River

Fairmont

Grafton

Ravenswood

Weston

Buckhannon

Ripley

33

Elkins

77

33

WEST VIRGINIA

Ohio River

19

Harrisonburg

Milton

St.
Albans

Charleston

Huntington

South
Charleston

Richwood

250

Staunton

White
Sulphur
Springs

Waynesbor

Oak Hill

64

Logan

Beckley

Lexington

Lynchburg

KENTUCKY

Mullens

Welch

Princeton

Roanoke

81

Bedford

29

Deel

Blacksburg

Bluefield

Radford

Norton

Wytheville

Lynchburg

South
Bosto

Middlesboro

Marion

58

Danville

TENNESSEE

Galax

77

Martinsville

NORTH CAROLINA

Introduction

*By Conrad
Paulus*

In the closing decades of the 18th century, all the action in the New World was here, in the five original colonies. While the Revolutionary War still raged, Delaware passed its own constitution and became the first state; Washington's audacious crossing of the Delaware River made possible the colonists' victory in the Battle of Trenton; Virginia saw the war's final battles and surrender; Philadelphia saw the Constitution hammered out; and Maryland ceded land for the District of Columbia. Today, the people of these states remember the past, proudly tending their historic monuments and welcoming visitors.

The Middle Atlantic countryside of rolling farmland and woods, ancient, soft-edged mountains, broad rivers, and green valleys is a livable land in a manageable climate—a land much walked through and fought over. Besides the Revolution, the region suffered many of the battles of the Civil War and today commemorates their sites. On its eastern edge (part of the densely populated urban corridor that runs from Boston to Richmond), you'll find the cities and most of the history. The international, multiracial mix produces every possible cuisine, and you can buy anything on Earth in the upscale boutiques, department stores, and antiques shops.

Beyond the smog on the New Jersey Turnpike are long beaches, casino-filled Atlantic City, and Victorian Cape May to the east; horse country, ski resorts, and Philadelphia to the west. The Eastern Shore's Delaware and Maryland beaches are sedate or swinging; Virginia Beach is both. And the seafood anywhere near the Chesapeake Bay is superb. Baltimore combines historic buildings with new restaurants and shops; Annapolis and Oxford are ports for boaters gunkholing around the Chesapeake. Washington, D.C., seat of government, is a wonderful showplace for visitors, with myriad treasure houses among the cherry trees. Alexandria's historic district and Georgetown's splendid town houses recall the capital's early years. In Williamsburg you'll hear echoes of the Revolution and sample 18th-century life.

West of the Tidewater, the towns are smaller and farther apart. Continuing on a circuit past Richmond, with its glorious capitol, you'll come to Charlottesville, Mr. Jefferson's hometown; farther west rise the Blue Ridge Mountains and West Virginia's Appalachians, sprinkled with palatial 19th-century resorts. At the stunning confluence of the Shenandoah and Potomac rivers sits Harpers Ferry, where John Brown met his fate; and back in Pennsylvania are Gettysburg and the Amish country. These are the habitats of the country auction, the wonderful local restaurant, and the farmhouse bed-and-breakfast—the secret places off the beaten track that you'll love to discover for yourself.

Tour Groups

Tours in the Middle Atlantic states highlight the region's natural and historic riches. Besides the operators listed in Chapter 1, the following firms offer tours of the region:

Gadabout Tours (700 E. Tahquitz Way, Palm Springs, CA 92262, tel. 619/325–5556 or 800/952–5068) offers 11-day "West

Virginia Country Roads" and 10-day "Blossom-Time in Washington, D.C." tours. **Globus** (5301 S. Federal Circle, Littleton, CO 80123, tel. 303/797–2800 or 800/221–0090) has a "Historic East" tour that includes Washington, D.C., Monticello, Williamsburg, Gettysburg, Valley Forge, and Philadelphia; Globus's budget-minded affiliate, **Cosmos Tourama** (same address), has a similar tour. **Maupintour** (Box 807, Lawrence, KS 66044, tel. 913/843–1211 or 800/255–4266) arranges a week-long visit to the Baltimore area and eight- and 10-day "Colonial Cities" tours. **Talmage Tours** (1223 Walnut St., Philadelphia, PA 19107, tel. 215/923–7100) offers four-day drives in Virginia and a paddle-wheeler cruise down the Ohio River through West Virginia and Pennsylvania. **Tauck Tours** (11 Wilton Rd., Box 5027, Westport, CT 06881, tel. 203/226–6911 or 800/468–2825) takes an eight-day drive through Williamsburg, Washington, D.C., Gettysburg, Monticello, and Philadelphia.

When to Go

In the cool early **spring,** Washington's pink cherry blossoms bloom for a few spectacular days. The many equestrian events in Maryland and Virginia also herald the season. **Summer** is swampy in Washington, Baltimore, and Philadelphia, with temperatures in the 80s, yet thousands flock to all three for monuments and baseball. Ocean bathers head to the Jersey Shore, Rehoboth, Ocean City, and Virginia Beach. The dazzling **autumn** foliage in Virginia's Shenandoah Valley draws hordes and also signals the opening of the orchestra, theater, and ballet seasons in the cities, most notably Philadelphia. In **winter,** when temperatures average in the 40s, workaday Washington grinds to a halt after just a sprinkling of snow, but Pennsylvania, Virginia, and West Virginia offer downhill and cross-country skiing, weather permitting.

Festivals and Seasonal Events

Jan. 1: The Mummers Parade in Philadelphia, Pennsylvania, ushers in the year with some 30,000 sequined and feathered marchers between Broad Street and City Hall. *Tel. 215/636–1666.*

Early Apr.: The National Cherry Blossom Festival takes place in Washington, D.C., with a parade, a marathon, and a Japanese lantern-lighting ceremony. *Tel. 202/737–2599.*

Mid-Apr.: The Azalea Festival in Norfolk, Virginia, features a parade, an air show, concerts, a ball, and the coronation of a queen from a NATO nation. *Tel. 804/622–2312.*

Early May: Virginia Gold Cup steeplechase horse races, held near Middleburg, have been among the most prominent social and sporting events in Virginia since the 1920s. *Tel. 703/253–5001.*

Late May: The Preakness, held in Baltimore, is the second event of horse racing's Triple Crown, after the Kentucky Derby and before the Belmont Stakes. *Tel. 410/837–4636.*

Early June: The Blue and Grey Reunion in Philippi, West Virginia, is four days of music, food, crafts, and a costumed reenactment of the Civil War's first land battle. *Tel. 304/457–3700.*

Late June, early July: The Festival of American Folklife, held on the Mall in Washington, celebrates music, arts, crafts, and foods of regional cultures. *Tel. 202/357–2700.*

Early July: The Philadelphia Freedom Festival features parades, hot-air balloon races, ceremonies at Independence Hall, a restaurant festival, and July 4 fireworks. *Tel. 215/686–1776.*

Late July, early Aug.: The Virginia Highlands Festival in Abingdon offers crafts and farm animals on exhibit, antiques for sale, and country musicians in concert. *Tel. 703/628–8141.*

Mid-Sept.: The Miss America Pageant in Atlantic City, New Jersey, headlines concerts by top stars during three days of judging that culminate in a tearful coronation ceremony. *Tel. 609/345–7571.*

Early, mid-Oct.: United States Sailboat and Powerboat Shows, the world's largest events of their kind, take place in Annapolis, Maryland. *Tel. 410/268–8828.*

Nov., Dec.: Yuletide at Winterthur is a Christmas-theme tour of the treasure-filled rooms at this vast museum near Wilmington, Delaware. *Tel. 302/888–4600 or 800/448–3883.*

Early Dec.–Jan. 1: The National Christmas Tree Lighting/Pageant of Peace in Washington, D.C., begins on the second Thursday in December, when the president lights the tree, followed by nightly choral performances at the Ellipse. *Tel. 202/619–7222.*

Getting Around the Middle Atlantic States

By Plane American, Continental, Delta, Northwest, TWA, United, and USAir, among others, serve **Philadelphia International Airport** (tel. 215/492–3181), **Greater Pittsburgh International Airport** (tel. 412/778–2601), **Baltimore-Washington International Airport** (tel. 410/849–7111), **Washington National Airport** (tel. 703/685–8003), and **Washington Dulles International Airport** (tel. 703/685–8000).

By Car I–95, the major East Coast artery, runs through all of these states except West Virginia. The New Jersey Turnpike, a toll road, fills in for I–95 in the Garden State. The 470-mi Pennsylvania Turnpike, also a toll road, runs from the Ohio border to Valley Forge, just outside Philadelphia. I–64 runs east–west, intersecting I–95 at Richmond, Virginia. At Staunton, Virginia, I–64 intersects I–81, which runs north–south through the Shenandoah Valley, toward West Virginia and Tennessee.

By Train Amtrak (tel. 800/872–7245) serves the region both north–south and east–west, with major lines along the coast and inland lines through Pennsylvania, Virginia, and West Virginia. **NJ Transit** (tel. 201/762–5100 or 215/569–3752), **Southeastern Pennsylvania Transportation Authority** (SEPTA; tel. 215/580–7800), and **Maryland Area Rail Commuter** (MARC; tel. 800/325–7245) provide service within states.

By Bus Greyhound (tel. 215/931–4000 or 800/231–2222) serves all these states. NJ Transit (tel. 201/762–5100 or 215/569–3752) provides bus service to many areas of the Garden State.

DELAWARE

By Marcia
Andrews

Updated by
Carolyn Price

Capital	Dover
Population	680,000
Motto	Liberty and Independence
State Bird	Blue hen
State Flower	Peach blossom

Visitor Information

Delaware Tourism Office (99 Kings Hwy., Box 1401, Dover 19903, tel. 302/739–4271 or 800/441–8846. **Information centers:** I–95, between Rtes. 896 and 273 (tel. 302/737–4059), and at Delaware Memorial Bridge (tel. 302/571–6340).

Scenic Drives

From Wilmington's west edge, a **30-mi loop** follows winding Rte. 100 past well-screened estates, a state park, and the meandering Brandywine Creek; a section of U.S. 1W in Pennsylvania past several historical attractions; and, back in Delaware, Rte. 52 (locally called "Château Country") to antiques-shop-lined villages, horse farms, and Winterthur, a major du Pont estate turned museum. A drive south along **Rte. 9** from New Castle to Dover slides past tidal marshes and across creeks on one-lane bridges; side roads veer into bird sanctuaries or out to points of land with a view of Delaware Bay.

National and State Parks

National Parks **Bombay Hook National Wildlife Refuge** (Rte. 9, east of Smyrna; RD 1, Box 147, Smyrna 19977, tel. 302/653–6872) is over 15,000 acres of ponds and fields filled with resident and migrating waterfowl between April and November. **Prime Hook National Wildlife Refuge** (County Rd. 236, just off Rte. 16; RD 3, Box 195, Milton 19968, tel. 302/684–8419) is a smaller, well-developed preserve with boat ramps, canoe trails, and a boardwalk trail through marshes.

State Parks A dozen parks run by the **Delaware Division of Parks and Recreation** (89 Kings Hwy., Richardson and Robbins Bldg., Box 1401, Dover 19903, tel. 302/793–4405 or 302/793–4702) are set up for hiking, fishing, and picnicking. The chief inland parks, with freshwater ponds, add boat rentals, beaches, and modern showers to basic amenities. Parks are open year-round, but weekends only between Labor Day and Memorial Day.

Cape Henlopen (42 Henlopen Dr., Lewes 19958, tel. 302/645–8983; Seaside Nature Center, tel. 302/654–6852), east of Lewes, has more than 150 campsites in pinelands. **Delaware Seashore** (850 Inlet, Rehoboth Beach 19971, tel. 302/227–2800; marina, tel. 302/227–3071) has both ocean surf and calm bay waters, and rustic and hookup campsites. **Lums Pond State Park** (Rtes. 301 and 71, south of Newark; 1068 Howell School Rd., Bear 19701, tel. 302/368–6989) has campsites. **Trap Pond** (off Rte. 24, east of Laurel; RD #2, Box 331, Laurel 19956, tel.

302/875–5153) includes part of the Great Cypress Swamp and has rustic sites under a canopy of loblolly pines.

Wilmington

Surrounded by big, pressure-cooker cities, Wilmington is one of the quieter, less-stressed stops on the eastern corridor. It began as an early (1638) Swedish settlement and was quickly taken over successively by the Dutch and the English. More recently, it was "all chemists and chickens," a reference to employees at DuPont company headquarters and nearby poultry ranches. Now the city's pro-business policies have enticed corporations whose towers of granite and glass reflect (literally) the Colonial stonework next door. The multinationals imported employees, and at some recent but unmarked instant, the city became home to more newcomers than natives. Still, Colonial roots, artifacts, and style are highly prized in Wilmington.

Two nearby towns—Newark, home of the University of Delaware, and New Castle, the state's beautifully restored Colonial capital—are linked to Wilmington by a few miles of neighborhoods and strip malls and are important to the city's cultural, commercial, and social mix.

Tourist Information

Greater Wilmington: Convention and Visitors Bureau (1300 Market St., Suite 504, 19801, tel. 302/652–4088 or 800/422–1181).

Arriving and Departing

By Plane **Philadelphia International Airport** (tel. 215/492–3000) is about 30 mi north of downtown Wilmington and is served by all major U.S. and international airlines. Taxi fare is about $25 to Wilmington. Door-to-door shuttle buses—**Airport Shuttle Service** (tel. 302/655–8878) or **Delaware Express Shuttle** (tel. 302/454–7634 or 800/648–5466)—cost $19 or $20 and require reservations (24-hour advance notice is recommended).

By Car Located between Baltimore and Philadelphia, Wilmington is bisected by I–95 north–south and linked to small-town Pennsylvania by U.S. 202 and Rtes. 52 and 41.

Train Station **Wilmington Train Station** (Martin Luther King Blvd. and French St., tel. 800/872–7245) has **Amtrak** service, as well as **SEPTA** (tel. 215/580–7800) commuter service to Philadelphia.

Bus Station **Greyhound** (101 N. French St., tel. 302/655–6111).

Getting Around Wilmington

Downtown is compact enough to stroll, but visits to New Castle, Newark, or the museums and parks ringing Wilmington require a car. Downtown parking is mid-priced in garages and hopeless on the streets in the jam-packed office district. Buses are geared to commuters, not explorers.

Exploring Wilmington

Remnants of three centuries of prosperity survive in Wilmington's architectural stew. **Eden Hall Lodge** (206 W. 10th St.), an 1889 Norman Gothic, has a dark stone facade and cupolas with mismatched tops that look like a melted-together chess set. More buildings in the heavily decorated styles of the late 1800s line streets radiating from **Baynard Boulevard,** from 18th Street to Concord Pike. Some vivid 1920s Victorians edge spottily renovated blocks along nearby **Washington Street.** Farther up the Brandywine Creek the Colonial Revival style was favored for large houses built around **Rockford Park** during World War I. Mid-19th-century millworkers' row houses, once Quaker plain, are constantly renovated as stylish town houses along **Ivy Street.**

Just to the east is the **Delaware Art Museum** (2301 Kentmere Pkwy., tel. 302/571–9590), which houses a major collection of post-1840 American painting and illustration, as well as the foremost assemblage of English pre-Raphaelite paintings and decorative arts in the United States.

A tour of city center starts on the four-block Market Street Mall. The **Grand Opera House** (818 Market St. Mall, tel. 302/658–7897) is a working theater. Built by the Masonic Order in 1871 and restored in 1971, the four-story Grand's facade is cast iron painted white in French Second Empire style, to mimic the old Paris Opera.

Across the Mall, the **Old Town Hall Museum** is a two-story Georgian-style building with meeting rooms, changing exhibits, and a jail to tour. The hall and museum shop were restored as headquarters for the Historical Society of Delaware, which has its hands full of 18th- and early 19th-century buildings. *512 Market St. Mall, tel. 302/655–7161. Admission charged. Closed Sun.–Mon.; Jan.–Feb.*

Five blocks north is the **Hercules Building** (1313 Market St.), built in the 1980s with ziggurat walls and a 20-foot-diameter clock. The core of the building is a 14-story atrium, with ground-level shops and a jungle of plants. Indoor and outdoor pools mirror sculptures and large marble globes rolling on columns of water.

Across Brandywine Creek, cherished Colonial remnants, such as the row of ca. 1770 houses at 18th and Market streets, stand amid drab commercial buildings in what was once Brandywine Village.

About 10 blocks east of the Mall (not an easy walk), a monument to the 1638 landing of a Swedish expedition marks the first permanent settlement in the Delaware Valley. At the **Kalmar Nyckel Shipyard/Museum** (823 E. 7th St., tel. 302/429–7447; admission charged), volunteers are building a replica of that first Swedish vessel. Nearby stand **Old Swedes Church and Hendrickson House Museum** (606 Church St., tel. 302/652–5629). The church, built in 1698, with its hipped roof and high wooden pulpit unchanged, is still regularly used for religious services. The farmhouse, built in 1690 by Swedish settlers, is furnished with period pieces.

In the Vicinity   **New Castle,** 5 mi south of Wilmington on Rte. 9, is a barely commercialized gem rich in lovingly restored Colonial houses, cob-

Wilmington

TO NEMOURS

TO ROCKWOOD

Rockford Park

Delaware Art Museum

Kentmere Pkwy.

TO WINTERTHUR

TO HAGLEY MUSEUM

Ivy Rd.

17th St.

Delaware Ave.

Broom St.

Baynard Blvd.

Concord Ave.

Monroe St.

Washington St.

PUBLIC GOLF COURSE

Pennsylvania Ave.

Greenhill Ave.

Brandywine Park

Park Dr. S.

18th St.

Market St.

30th St.

Brandywine Zoo

Dupont Rd.

Cleveland Ave.

Lincoln St.

10th St. 9th St.

8th St. 7th St.

6th St. 5th St.

4th St. 3rd St.

2nd St.

Hercules Building.

Washington St.

Walnut St.

26th St.

Eden Hall Lodge

Lancaster Ave.

Union St.

Broom St.

Oak St.

Grand Opera House

Old Town Hall Museum

Market Street Mall

Spruce St.

Church St.

Brandywine Creek

Dupont Rd.

TO NEWARK

Maryland Ave.

Old Swedes Church

R.R. Station

Kalmar Nyckel Shipyard/Museum

Christina River

Christina Ave.

TO NEW CASTLE

0   750 yards

0   750 meters

N

KEY

— Rail Lines

---

blestone streets, and historic sites along the Delaware River. **William Penn's first landing** in North America is noted in Battery Park. Two blocks west of the waterfront, the **New Castle Court House** (211 Delaware St., tel. 302/323–4453), Delaware's Colonial capitol, is a pristine museum of state history in three stolid brick wings. Its white cupola and spire were the compass point for the arc of the state's boundary with Pennsylvania.

Also in New Castle, the **George Read II House** was built in 1797 in Federal style by a signer of both the Declaration of Independence and the Constitution. Twelve rooms of the big brick house are open, including three furnished in period style. *42 The Strand, tel. 302/322–8411. Admission charged. Closed weekdays Jan.–Feb.*

On the northwest edges of Wilmington, along Rte. 52, former du Pont family properties have become impressive museums of the Brandywine Valley's industrial history. At the **Hagley Museum** (298 Buck Rd., tel. 302/658–2400; admission charged), the Du Pont company's beginnings in 1802 as an explosives manufacturer are recalled by gunpowder mills, a 19th-century machine shop, and the family home and gardens, all set on 230 acres.

Winterthur Museum and Gardens focuses on Henry Francis du Pont's passion for collecting furniture and decorative arts made or used in America from 1640 to 1860. The nine-story, 196-room hillside stucco mansion and newly added museum wing shelter a world-class collection in period settings. The naturalistic gardens showcase native and exotic plants. *Rte. 52, Winterthur,* *tel. 302/888–4600 or 800/448–3883. Admission charged. Topical tours by reservation only.*

Nemours Mansion and Gardens shows another du Pont family's preference for fine automobiles, European antiques, Louis XVI–style architecture, and formal French gardens. *Rockland Rd., tel. 302/651–6912 (reservations required). Admission charged. Closed Dec.–Apr.*

Odessa is a tiny, mostly residential village set on the banks of the Appoquinimink River, about 23 mi south of Wilmington off Rte. 13. Originally a grain-shipping port, it stopped growing in the mid-19th century when disease attacked its peach crops and the railroad passed it by. What you'll find today is an immaculate, quiet community of 303 people that is a bit of living history—until a few years ago, muskrat still topped the menu at the town's one-and-only restaurant. A newly installed branch of the **Winterthur Museum** (tel. 302/378–4069; admission charged) includes four 18th- and 19th-century houses and the **Brick Hotel Gallery,** which houses rotating exhibits of American furniture and decorative arts.

Parks and Gardens

In the center of town, in **Brandywine Park,** shady paths pass Colonial stone walls and a tiny brick church that was built in 1740 and used for British wounded during the Revolutionary War. Lush Brandywine Creek and a millrace attract fishermen and splashing children.

Rockwood Museum (610 Shipley Rd., tel. 302/761–4340; admission charged) displays a collection of unusual specimen plants on 6 acres of cultivated grounds and 62 acres of woodlands.

What to See and Do with Children

Wilmington's **Brandywine Zoo** (North Park Dr., tel. 302/571–7747; admission charged Apr.–Oct.; exotic-animal house closed Nov.–Mar.) tucks outdoor exhibits into cliffs along Brandywine Creek. The **Delaware Children's Theatre** (1014 Delaware Ave., Wilmington, tel. 302/655–1014) is headquartered in a well-preserved early 1900s stucco town house.

Shopping

Delaware's lack of a sales tax may lure out-of-staters for big-ticket items (cars), but outlet malls in Maryland and Pennsylvania are the magnets for many Delaware shoppers. The anchor stores at Newark's **Christiana Mall** (Rte. 7 at I–95 Exit 42, tel. 302/731–9815), which has 130 stores, are Macy's and Wanamaker's. Among the 87 stores at Wilmington's **Concord Mall** (4737 Concord Pike, tel. 302/478–9271), Strawbridge & Clothier and Boscov's are the department-store biggies.

Dining

During the '80s boom, Wilmington's kitchens multiplied as new companies' globe-circling employees pushed for diversity. The best-established restaurants are Italian and Asian. It's safest to reserve on weekends, and jackets are preferred in the expensive places. For price ranges, see Chart 1 (B) in Chapter 1.

Expensive **Green Room.** The place is unique. French cuisine, complete with elaborate sauces, is served in a dramatic, wood-paneled setting of 19th-century opulence with a 20th-century touch: original Andrew Wyeth paintings on the walls. *Hotel du Pont, 11th and Market Sts., tel. 302/594–3154. Reservations required. Jacket advised. AE, D, DC, MC, V.*

★ **Positano.** The intimate room caters to small groups with discerning tastes in Italian cuisine—from fresh fish to intricate desserts. *The Devon, 2401 Pennsylvania Ave., tel. 302/656–6788. Reservations advised. AE, D, DC, MC, V.*

Moderate **Ming Gardens.** Classic Chinese dishes, such as beef with orange
★ flavor, are tender, well seasoned, and accompanied by crisp vegetables. The room is spacious, with pastel walls, art deco chandeliers, and lacquered furniture. *618 N. Union St., tel. 302/429–9292. AE, D, DC, MC, V.*

Mirage. In a colorful, contemporary space divided by arches into private dining pavilions, young servers (this is a university town) deliver such regional American specialties as poached salmon with vegetable broth and blue poppy seeds or sautéed veal with artichoke hearts, tomatoes, and leeks. The only fine-dining option in Newark, Mirage lures Wilmington visitors south with a low-priced menu—the most expensive entrée is under $20. *100 Elkton Rd., Newark, tel. 302/453–1711. AE, D, MC, V.*

Ristorante Carruci. Don't let the stylish black-and-white room or the piano and live opera distract you from such updated Italian dishes as flaky mahimahi topped with pine nuts, basil, and little clams. *Wawaset Plaza, 504 Greenhill Ave., tel. 302/654–2333. Reservations advised. Jacket advised. AE, MC, V.*

Inexpensive **Cellar Gourmet.** Day-trippers, itinerant cyclists, and families packed in station wagons come here for a bite to eat on the spot or a picnic to take along to New Castle's promenade bordering the Delaware River. This environmentally conscious restaurant serves sandwiches, soups, and vegetarian and low-cholesterol dishes on recyclable paper plates. Freshly baked sweets and ice-cream treats give travelers a welcome relief after a long, hot summer day of Colonial history and architectural appreciation. *208 Delaware St., New Castle, tel. 302/323–0999. No credit cards.*

Coyote Cafe and Restaurant. The room is colorful and quirky, with the signature animal in various forms. A few vegetarian and Caribbean dishes keep the updated Mexican menu interesting. *1801 Lancaster Ave., tel. 302/652–1377. AE, MC, V.*

Di Nardo's. This crowded, casual tavern—more plastic than rustic, with Formica tables and unpadded chairs—specializes in seafood. The catch of the day is always fresh, and the spicy (or ask for plain, steamed) hard-shell crabs are famous. *405 N. Lincoln St., tel. 302/656–3685. AE, D, DC, MC, V.*

★ **India Palace.** The authentic Indian food served here includes spicy curry dishes and clay-oven specialties (tandoori). The neighborhood isn't fancy, but bits of traditional art (paintings of the Taj Mahal and smoky-eyed women) and the service are sparkling. *101 Maryland Ave. (Rte. 4), tel. 302/655–8772. No credit cards.*

Lodging

Most Wilmington-area hotels are designed for business travelers, with less emphasis on resort amenities and more on efficiency and value. For variety, there are restored Colonial inns (not modern adaptations) and a few B&Bs. Two reservation services—**Bed & Breakfast of Delaware, Inc.** (3650 Silverside Rd., Box 177, Wilmington 19810, tel. 302/479–9500) and **Guesthouses, Inc.** (Box 2137, West Chester, PA 19380, tel. 800/950–9130)—help locate moderately priced lodgings. For price ranges, see Chart 2 (B) in Chapter 1.

Expensive **Christiana Hilton Inn.** This modern high rise southwest of Wilmington is convenient to I–95. The rooms are furnished traditionally, but the restaurant, Ashley's, is notable. *100 Continental Dr., Newark 19713, tel. 302/454–1500. 266 rooms. Facilities: 2 restaurants, bar, outdoor pool, free shuttle to downtown Wilmington. AE, D, DC, MC, V.*

★ **Guest Quarters Suite Hotel Wilmington.** This former store, tucked into a nondescript downtown block, has dramatic contemporary architecture, suites with rich traditional furnishings, and a popular lounge. *707 King St., 19801, tel. 302/656–9300 or 800/543–9106; fax 302/656–2459. 49 suites. Facilities: restaurant, bar. AE, DC, MC, V.*

Hotel du Pont. A 1993 renovation of this posh and popular downtown hotel created large rooms with living areas set off by mahogany dividers. The furnishings are 18th-century reproductions. *11th and Market Sts., 19801, tel. 302/594–3100 or 800/441–9019. 10 suites, 206 rooms. Facilities: 2 restaurants, bar, spa. AE, D, DC, MC, V.*

★ **Janvier-Black House Bed & Breakfast.** This Federal-style merchant's house on the Delaware River is beautifully restored and vividly furnished in Victoriana. It's in the historic district on a cobblestone street, overlooking formal gardens. *17 The Strand, New Castle 19720, tel. 302/328–1339. 2 rooms, 1 suite. MC, V.*

Moderate **The David Finney Inn.** The restored 17th-century inn on New Castle's town square, amid boutiques and historic sites, is furnished with antiques. *216 Delaware St., New Castle 19720, tel. 302/322–6367 or 800/334–6640. 13 rooms, 4 suites. Facilities: restaurant, bar. AE, DC, MC, V.*

Radisson Hotel Wilmington. This refurbished hotel in northwest Wilmington has quiet, amply sized traditional rooms. *4727 Concord Mall, Rte. 202, 19803, tel. 302/478–6000 or 800/441–7378. 154 rooms. Facilities: restaurant, lounge, outdoor pool. AE, D, DC, MC, V.*

Sheraton Suites Wilmington. The hotel has good views of Wilmington from the top floors of its sleek high rise in the middle of town. Suites are adequate and colorful. *422 Delaware Ave., 19801, tel. 302/654–8300 or 800/228–9290; fax 302/654–6036. 230 suites. Facilities: restaurant, lounge, indoor pool, sauna, exercise room. AE, DC, MC, V.*

William Penn Guest House. Irma and Dick Burwell have run this wonderful and affordable B&B in the heart of New Castle since 1956. Floorboards in their handsomely restored Colonial are hewn from soft Delaware pine; an 18th-century chandelier lights the formal dining room; and a claw-foot tub in one bathroom provides perfect therapy for bone-weary cyclists. A Continental breakfast is included in the room rate. *208 Delaware St., New Castle 19720, tel. 302/328–7736. 4 rooms. No credit cards.*

Inexpensive **Fairfield Inn.** Close to the University of Delaware and about 9 mi west of Wilmington, this Marriott-owned inn is Spartan but convenient. *65 Geoffrey Dr., Newark 19713, tel. 302/292–1500. 135 rooms. AE, D, DC, MC, V.*

Red Roof Inn. This three-story, gallery-style motel just off I–95 has simple, well-maintained rooms with standard Formica and floral fabrics. *415 Stanton-Christiana Rd., Newark 19713, tel. 302/292–2870 or 800/843–7663. 119 rooms. AE, D, DC, MC, V.*

Rodeway Inn. Nonsmoking rooms (rare in Delaware) and proximity to historic New Castle are two advantages of this traditional motor inn. *111 S. DuPont Hwy., New Castle 19702, tel. 302/328–6246 or 800/321–6246; fax 302/328–9493. 40 rooms. AE, D, DC, MC, V.*

The Atlantic Coast

As you drive Rtes. 9 and 1 south between farm fields and stands of 10-foot-high grasses, it's hard to believe the broad Delaware River and Bay are out there. Then, as you slide by a low spot in the marsh grass, the disembodied deck house of a boat comes into view, evidence of the small, mostly recreational fishing marinas along the shore. The water view opens up at Lewes and Cape Henlopen State Park; then sand dunes and wide, white Atlantic beaches mark the resort towns. The small inland towns house historic sites and dining and lodging alternatives.

Tourist Information

Bethany-Fenwick: Chamber of Commerce and Information Center (Rte. 1, N. Fenwick Island; Box 1450, Bethany Beach 19930, tel. 302/539–2100 or 800/962–7873). **Lewes:** Chamber of Commerce and Visitors Bureau (Savannah Rd. and Kings Hwy., Box 1, 19958, tel. 302/645–8073). **Milton:** Chamber of Commerce (101 Federal St., 19968, tel. 302/684–1101). **Rehoboth Beach–Dewey Beach:** Chamber of Commerce (501 Rehoboth Ave., Box 216, Rehoboth Beach 19971, tel. 302/227–2233 or 800/441–1329).

Delaware Today magazine (Box 4440, Wilmington 19807, tel. 302/656–1809 or 800/285–0400) publishes a monthly report on planned events and region-wide restaurant listings.

Getting There

By Car From the north, exit I–95 to U.S. 13S at Wilmington. Take U.S. 113 at Dover and Rte. 1 at Milford. From the south, the scenic route to Delaware's northern shores crosses Chesapeake Bay at Annapolis and continues east via U.S. 301/50; follows U.S. 50 to Rte. 404 at Wye Mills, Maryland; then crosses Delaware on Rtes. 404/18 to Rte. 1 at Lewes.

By Bus **Greyhound** links Rehoboth Beach with Wilmington, New Castle, and Dover.

By Ferry **Cape May–Lewes Ferry** (tel. 302/645–6346 or 302/645–6313 for recorded information) is a 70-minute ride from Cape May, New Jersey, to Lewes, Delaware.

Exploring the Atlantic Coast

It's wise to check current beach-pollution conditions with local tourism offices. Public access to the Atlantic surf and 23 mi of sand is ample, though crowds pour in from Washington, D.C., and points west on holidays. The Broadkill River, Rehoboth Bay, Indian River Bay, and Little Assawoman Bay offer sheltered waters.

Just west of the beaches are some of the state's historic villages and scenic bay-side parks (*see* National and State Parks, *above*). In **Milton,** once a major shipbuilding center at the head of the Broadkill River, the whole downtown area is a historic district of 18th- and 19th-century architecture, including old cypress-shingle houses. **Lewes,** a 1631 Dutch settlement at the mouth of Delaware Bay, cherishes its seafaring past with a marine museum and draws visitors with good restaurants, shops, and lodging that's away from the hectic beach resorts.

Coastal towns include **Rehoboth Beach,** the largest, with a busy boardwalk for noshing/strolling/shopping expeditions, and adjacent **Dewey Beach. Bethany Beach, South Bethany,** and **Fenwick Island** (founded as a church camp and known for its fishing), south of the Indian River Inlet, are the quiet resorts, especially compared with Ocean City, Maryland, to the south.

Sports and Outdoor Activities

Biking   **Fenwick Islander Bicycle Shoppe** (Rte. 1, Fenwick Island, tel. 302/537–2021) is a source for rentals and sales. Rehoboth has several bicycle concessions and uncrowded neighborhoods to ride in but restricts biking on the boardwalk to 5–10 AM in summer. **Bob's Bike Rentals** (1st St. and Maryland Ave., Rehoboth Beach) has bikes and roller skates.

Fishing   Charter boats, for either deep-sea or bay (trout, bluefish) fishing, book day or half-day trips, including all the gear. Book through your hotel, or try **Angler's Fishing Center** (tel. 302/645–5775 or 302/654–8212), or **Fisherman's Wharf** (tel. 302/645–8862 or 302/645–8541), both in Lewes.

Water Sports   Marinas on Rehoboth Bay and Delaware Bay (at Lewes) rent sailboards, sailboats, and motorboats. Sailboats, catamarans, and sailboards are for rent at **Fenwick Island State Park,** among others.

Dining and Lodging

Resort mavens from Washington, D.C., and Baltimore have sparked a growing variety of hotels and restaurants in the region. Seeking culinary thrills as far north as Milford, these weekenders support good chefs in off-beach towns. The resort strips, from Rehoboth Beach to Fenwick Island, are chockablock with two- and three-story balconied hotels and occasional high rises striving for ocean views. A few inns and B&Bs at Lewes and Milford are the quiet alternative. For price ranges, see Charts 1 (B) and 2 (B) in Chapter 1.

Bethany Beach   **Rusty Rudder.** In this barnlike space with nautical decor over-
Dining   looking Rehoboth Bay, the specialties are down-home service and local seafood, such as crab imperial. *Dickinson St., on the bay, tel. 302/227–3888. AE, D, DC, MC, V. Moderate.*

Lewes   **Kupchick's.** This is the best that Lewes has to offer. Expect
Dining   American cuisine with some Continental specialties at both the
★   grill and the formal Victorian dining room. Certified Angus beef, rack of lamb, and supernal seafood characterize the menu

here. Budget-minded guests enjoy the year-round 25% discount before 6 PM. *3 E. Bay Ave., tel. 302/645-0420. Reservations advised on weekends. AE, D, DC, MC, V.*

Rose & Crown. A dark, paneled, old-English pub, with British and American cooking, may stretch the imagination, but it works here—especially on fresh seafood and good steaks. A large selection of imported ale and beer is the main draw. *108 2nd St., tel. 302/654-2373. AE, DC, MC, V. Expensive.*

Lodging
★
The New Devon Inn. Each room's antique furnishings and linens are unique and have a story, often documented by a local historian. The lobby and the parlor/breakfast room are treasuries of Early Americana. *2nd and Market Sts., Box 516, 19958, tel. 302/645-6466. 24 rooms, 2 suites. MC, V. Expensive.*

Milford
Dining and Lodging
★
Banking House Inn. The country-French cooking in this restored Victorian bank building means less sauce and a lighter approach. Upstairs from the vivid Victoriana of the restaurant, the guest rooms—some with fireplaces—are traditionally decorated. *112 N.W. Front St., 19963, tel. 302/422-5708. 5 rooms. Facilities: restaurant. MC, V. Moderate.*

Lodging
Traveler's Inn Motel. Rooms in this two-story, balconied motel are plain, with two double beds and minimal furnishings (a hanging rack, no closet). *1036 N. Walnut St., 19963, tel. 302/422-8089. 38 rooms. AE, MC, V. Inexpensive.*

Millsboro
Dining
The Marina Restaurant at Pot-Nets. The food is ordinary (crab cakes, steaks) and quality is uneven, but the view of the marina, a playground, and Indian River Bay are worth it. *Pot-Nets (campground/development) off Long Neck Rd., Long Neck (east of Millsboro), tel. 302/945-0300. AE, MC, V. Inexpensive.*

Rehoboth Beach
Dining
★
La La Land. The converted cottage is decorated in movie memorabilia, and the menu is fun, too: an inventive mix of southwest American, Native American, and Asian influences. Try the sautéed Norwegian salmon wrapped in rice paper. *23 Wilmington Ave., tel. 302/227-3887. Reservations required. AE, DC, MC, V. Expensive.*

Club Potpourri Restaurant. The room is clubby, with easy chairs at the bar, lots of plants, and a skylight. Creatively sauced dishes with fresh fish and hand-cut meats set the chef apart. *316 Rehoboth Ave., tel. 302/227-4227. AE, DC, MC, V. Moderate.*

Sydney's Side Street Restaurant and Blues Place. The dining tables are on an enclosed porch; after dinner, the band plays near the bar, inside. Contemporary California-style cooking issues from the kitchen. California shrimp-and-scallop stir-fry with spinach, pine nuts, and ginger over rice is a specialty. The innovative "grazing menu" is great for light eaters or those who like to sample several choices. *25 Christian St., tel. 302/227-1339. Reservations advised. AE, D, DC, MC, V. Moderate.*

Grotto Pizza. For years, come Labor Day weekend baby boomers who summered at the Delaware resorts have had to be weaned from this pizza they knew as mother's milk. It isn't a pretty sight. Grotto's has several beach locations. *36 Rehoboth Ave., tel. 302/227-3451; The Boardwalk, tel. 302/227-3601; Rte. 1, Dewey, tel. 302/227-3407. No reservations. No credit cards. Inexpensive.*

Pierre's Pantry. Pierre's does a fast takeout business but has a few tables inside. The attractions are breakfasts, kosher items, and fresh seafood salads, plus some vegetarian entrées. *28 Wilmington Ave. (entrance on 1st St.), tel. 302/227–7537. No credit cards. Inexpensive.*

Dining and Lodging **The Corner Cupboard Inn.** This big old house has homey bedrooms and a popular restaurant that offers traditional Eastern Shore cooking, featuring seafood and poultry. *50 Park Ave., 19971, tel. 302/227–8553. 38 rooms. Facilities: restaurant (closed Labor Day–Memorial Day). Moderate.*

Lodging **Atlantic Sands Hotel.** This is one of the area's few mid-rise buildings (five floors), with a rare beachfront pool. Most of the pink-and-green tropical-pattern rooms have balconies and ocean views. *Boardwalk and Baltimore Ave., 19971, tel. 302/227–2511 or 800/422–0600. 114 units. Facilities: hot tub, free parking. AE, D, MC, V. Expensive.*

Best Western Gold Leaf. The rooms at this hotel, a half block from the beach and across the street from the bay, are traditionally furnished and pleasant. Fourth-floor rooms have water views. *1400 Hwy. 1, 19971, tel. 302/226–1100 or 800/422–8566. 75 rooms. Facilities: outdoor pool. AE, D, MC, V. Expensive.*

Brighton Suites. Each suite includes a traditionally furnished king-size bedroom and a living room with refrigerator and wet bar. *34 Wilmington Ave., 19971, tel. 302/227–5780 or 800/227–5788. 66 suites. Facilities: indoor pool, free parking. AE, D, DC, MC, V. Expensive.*

Atlantic Budget Inn. Rooms at this two-story brick inn are crowded, with double or king-size beds and side tables in motel-moderne style (hanging racks, no closets). *4353 Hwy. 1, 19971, tel. 302/227–0401. 74 rooms. AE, DC, MC, V. Inexpensive.*

Elsewhere in the State

Dover

Getting There North and south approaches to Dover are on U.S. 13; Rte. 10 links it with Goldsboro, Maryland.

What to See and Do An oasis of Colonial preservation in a bustling government center, the heart of the tree-shaded state capital is the **capitol complex** historic area, on a square laid out in 1722 to William Penn's 1683 plan. The **Margaret O'Neill Visitor Center** (Federal St., 19903, tel. 302/739–4266) and the **Kent County Tourism Corporation** (tel. 800/233–5368) have information. Southeast of town is the **Dover Air Force Base** (tel. 302/677–3379 for tours) and its C-5 Galaxies (the largest aircraft in the world), visible from U.S. 13.

MARYLAND

By Francis X. Rocca

Capital	Annapolis
Population	4,781,468
Motto	Manly Deeds, Womanly Words
State Bird	Oriole
State Flower	Black-eyed Susan

Visitor Information

The **Maryland Office of Tourism Development** (217 E. Redwood St., Baltimore 21202, tel. 410/333–6611 or 800/543–1036) provides free publications and runs seven information centers.

Scenic Drives

On **U.S. 50,** over the William Preston Lane, Jr., Memorial Bridge, cars soar across the Chesapeake Bay and then swoop down over sailboats docked in the narrows between Kent Island and the Eastern Shore. **U.S. 40** passes through the Cumberland Narrows, a break in the Alleghenies through which westward-bound settlers passed in the 18th century.

National and State Parks

National Parks **Assateague Island National Seashore** (Rte. 611, 7206 National Seashore La., Berlin 21811, tel. 410/641–1441 or 410/641–3030) is a 37-mi-long Atlantic barrier island that extends south into Virginia. Swimming, biking, hiking, fishing, picnicking, and camping are permitted, and there are boat ramps.

State Parks There are 18, including **Point Lookout** (Box 48, Scotland 20687, tel. 301/872–5688), with a dramatic prospect of the bay from the southernmost tip of the Western Shore. **Patapsco State Park** (8020 Baltimore National Pike, Ellicott City 21043, tel. 410/461–5005) offers horseback riding. The Office of Tourism Development (*see* Visitor Information, *above*) has information about each of the parks.

Baltimore

Before 1980, it was a joke to speak of Baltimore as a tourist destination. Then Inner Harbor, a decaying downtown neighborhood refurbished in the 1970s, became a showcase of expensive hotels, shops, office buildings, and museums. Ever since, it has been drawing visitors to the city where Babe Ruth was born, where Edgar Allan Poe died, and where stalwart citizens under fire inspired the composition of the national anthem.

Tourist Information

Baltimore: Area Convention and Visitors Association (100 Light St., 12th Floor, 21202, tel. 410/659–7300). Area Visitors Center (300 W. Pratt St., 21201, tel. 410/837–4636 or 800/282–6632). Office of Promotion (200 W. Lombard St., 21201, tel.

410/752–8632). International Visitors Center (World Trade Center, Suite 1353, 21202, tel. 410/837–7150).

Arriving and Departing

By Plane **Baltimore Washington International Airport** (tel. 410/859–7111), 10 mi south of town, is a destination for most major domestic and foreign carriers. Taxi fare to downtown is roughly $17. **Amtrak** and **Maryland Area Rail Commuter** (MARC; tel. 800/325–7245) trains run between the airport station (10 minutes from the terminal via free shuttle bus) and Penn Station, about 20 minutes away. **Shuttle Express** (tel. 410/859–0800) has motor coach service to downtown hotels.

By Car Baltimore is located on I–95, the major east-coast artery.

Train Station **Penn Station** (Charles St. at Mt. Royal Ave., tel. 410/291–4260).

Bus Station **Greyhound** (210 W. Fayette St., tel. 410/744–9311).

Getting Around Baltimore

Most attractions are a walk or a short trolley ride (tel. 410/752–2105) from Inner Harbor. Beyond that a car is useful; the metro line is limited, and bus riding can mean lots of transfers (**Mass Transit Administration**, tel. 410/539–5000).

Exploring Baltimore

The city fans out northward from Inner Harbor, with newer attractions like the National Aquarium and Orioles Park concentrated at the center and more historic neighborhoods and sites out toward the edges. Running along the center, the major northbound artery is Charles Street; cross streets are "East" or "West" relative to it.

Charles Street Head north on Charles Street from Baltimore Street toward the impossible-to-miss Washington Monument. Restaurants and art galleries lend an urbane tone to this neighborhood, a mix of 19th-century brownstones and modern office buildings. A block west of Charles is the **Basilica of the Assumption** (Mulberry St. at Cathedral St.), the oldest cathedral in the United States, built in 1821.

At the **Walters Art Gallery,** international art from antiquity through the 19th century is housed in an Italiante palace. *N. Charles and Centre Sts., tel. 410/547–9000. Admission charged.*

The **Washington Monument,** built in 1829, is a 178-foot marble column topped by a 16-foot statue of the first president. A 228-step spiral staircase within leads to a unique view of the city.

Surrounding the monument is **Mt. Vernon Square,** flanked by four block-long parks. Note the bronze sculptures in the parks and the elegant brownstones along East Mt. Vernon Place. The **Peabody Library** (17 E. Mt. Vernon Pl., tel. 410/659–8179) has a handsome reading room with a skylight in its five-story-high ceiling. At the nearby **Maryland Historical Society** (201 W. Monument St., tel. 410/685–3750), the eclectic display of state memorabilia includes the original manuscript of "The Star Spangled Banner."

Baltimore

192

Broadway

N

1500 yards

1500 meters

KEY

Rail Lines

Madison Square

Eden St.

Chase St.

Eager St.

Harford Ave.

Johnson Square

Biddle Street

Greenmount Ave.

State Penitentiary

45

83

TO BALTIMORE MUSEUM OF ART, JOHNS HOPKINS UNIVERSITY

Guilford St.

Calvert St.

Chase St.

Saint Paul St.

Eager St.

Cathedral St.

Read St.

Howard St.

Biddle St.

Madison St.

Monument St.

Washington Monument

Washington Pl.

Mt. Vernon Place

Walters Art Gallery

Centre St.

Maryland Historical Society

Greyhound Bus Terminal

Peabody Library

Basilica of the Assumption

Park Ave.

Mulberry St.

Eutaw St.

Howard St.

Charles St.

Liberty St.

Saint Paul Pl.

Sun Papers Building

Davis St.

Peale Museum

Pleasant St.

Holliday St.

Gay S

Gay St.

The Fallsway

Low St.

Gay St.

Orleans St.

Ensor St.

Front St.

Hillen St.

Train Station

Madison St.

Monument St.

Old Town Mall

McElderry St.

147

40

Aisquith St.

Main Post Office

Fayette St.

Fairmont St.

Church Home Hospital

0

0

The **Baltimore Museum of Art** (Charles and 31st Sts., tel. 410/396–7101), 1½ mi north, displays works by Rodin, Matisse, Picasso, Cézanne, Renoir, and Gauguin. The 140-acre campus of **Johns Hopkins University** is next door to the museum.

Inner Harbor and Environs

Harborplace comprises two glass-enclosed shopping malls with more than 100 specialty shops and gourmet markets. Other waterfront attractions are nearby. At the **Maryland Science Center** (601 Light St., tel. 410/685–5225), the biggest draw is an IMAX movie theater with a five-story-high screen. There is also a planetarium. In 1797 the **USF** *Constellation* (tel. 410/539–1797), now docked at Pier 1, became the first commissioned ship of the United States Navy. The **World Trade Center** (401 Pratt St., tel. 410/837–4515) is the world's tallest pentagonal building (32 stories); its 27th-floor observation deck offers a terrific view of the city. The World War II submarine USS *Torsk* and the lightship *Chesapeake* make up the **Baltimore Maritime Museum** (Pier 3, Pratt St., tel. 410/396–3854).

The **National Aquarium** is home to 500 species of marine life, birds, reptiles, and plants. A rooftop "rain forest" is inhabited by parrots, iguanas, and red-bellied piranhas. Three 10-foot beluga whales live next door in a million-gallon pool. *Pier 3, tel. 410/576–3810. Admission charged.*

East of Inner Harbor is the **Star-Spangled Banner House** (Pratt and Albemarle Sts., tel. 410/837–1793), where the flag that inspired the national anthem was woven. Around Lombard Street courtyard between Front and Albemarle streets are the four institutions of **Museum Row** (Baltimore City Life Museums, tel. 410/396–3523). Highlights are a row house where actors perform short plays set in 1840 and the elegant town house of a signer of the Declaration of Independence. At East Fayette and Front streets is the **Old Shot Tower,** a 234-foot-high brick tower used to make ammunition a century ago (closed due to subway construction; may reopen in 1994).

North of Inner Harbor on Holliday Street are the golden-domed **Baltimore City Hall,** built in 1875 and completely supported by ironwork, and the **Peale Museum** (tel. 410/396–1149), the oldest museum in the United States (1814), showing paintings by Charles Willson Peale and his family.

Other Attractions

A 10-minute trolley ride from Inner Harbor is **Fells Point,** once a thriving shipbuilding center and now a neighborhood of cobblestone streets and historic redbrick houses, many of them shops, galleries, restaurants, and taverns. At Broadway and Thames (pronounced "thaymz") Street is an operating tugboat pier.

West of Inner Harbor are the **H. L. Mencken House** (1524 Hollins St., tel. 410/396–7997), from which "the Sage of Baltimore" ruled American letters from the 1920s to the 1940s; the **Poe House** (203 N. Amity St., tel. 410/396–7932), where Edgar Allan Poe wrote his first horror story; and the **Westminster Church Churchyard** (W. Fayette and Greene Sts.), where Poe is buried.

The 50,000-seat **Oriole Park at Camden Yards** (Camden and Howard Sts., tel. 410/685–9800) opened in 1992, sporting a 700-square-foot video scoreboard, several restaurants, and a cocktail lounge. Its brick facade and asymmetric playing field evoke the big-league parks of the early 1900s. Built on the site of a former railroad depot, it is served by MARC trains from Washington, Light Rail System (LRS) trains from the Baltimore suburbs, and the local Metro. Two blocks west is **Babe Ruth's Birthplace** (216 Emory St., tel. 410/727–1539), where the baseball legend was born in 1895.

Locomotives and railroad cars are on display at the **B&O Railroad Museum** (Pratt and Poppleton Sts., tel. 410/752–2490), on the site of the country's first railroad station.

At the end of the peninsula bounding the Patapsco River's northwest branch is **Ft. McHenry,** a star-shaped brick building famous for its role in the national anthem. "The Star-Spangled Banner" that Francis Scott Key saw "by the dawn's early light" on September 14, 1814, was the one flying above the fort. *Fort Ave., from Light St. via Key Hwy., tel. 410/962–4299. Admission charged. Boat rides from Inner Harbor, Memorial Day–Labor Day.*

Parks and Gardens

Sherwood Gardens (Stratford Rd. and Greenway, 3 mi from Inner Harbor, east of St. Paul St., tel. 410/366–2572) is worth a special trip in late April and early May to see thousands of peaking tulips and azaleas. South of Inner Harbor is **Federal Hill Park** (Battery St. and Key Hwy.), with an excellent view of the downtown skyline and a jogging track in adjacent **Rash Field.**

What to See and Do with Children

Baltimore's Child (tel. 410/367–5883) is published monthly during the school year and given away at public libraries.

The Cloisters (10440 Falls Rd., 7 mi from Inner Harbor, tel. 410/823–2550) is a fanciful mock-Tudor/Gothic Revival "castle" on 50 leafy acres, where youngsters can step in and out of a supersize storybook or a child-size indoor "village."

Shopping

The city's most diverse and colorful shopping areas are the malls of **Harborplace** and the shops of **Fells Point** (*see* Exploring Baltimore, *above*). There are more than three dozen first-rate shops on **Antique Row** (700 and 800 blocks, N. Howard St.; 200 block, W. Read St.). At **Kelmscott Bookshop** (32 W. 25th St., tel. 410/235–6810), you can browse among an enormous stock of rare books in the coziness of a converted town house. Baltimore has a number of indoor food markets; at least 100 years old are **Belair Market** (Gay and Fayette Sts.), **Broadway Market** (Broadway and Fleet Sts.), **Cross Street Market** (Light and Cross Sts.), **Hollins Market** (Hollins and Arlington Sts.), **Lexington Market** (Lexington and Eutaw Sts.), and **Northeast Market** (Monument and Chester Sts.).

Spectator Sports

Baseball **Orioles** (Oriole Park at Camden Yards, Camden and Howard Sts., tel. 410/685–9800; Apr.–Sept.).

Dining

Seafood, especially Chesapeake Bay blue crab (steamed in the shell, fried in a crab cake, or baked with a white cream and wine sauce), is the specialty, but every major cuisine is available, including the ethnic offerings of the Greek and Italian neighborhoods. For price ranges, see Chart 1 (B) in Chapter 1.

Expensive   **The Brass Elephant.** The rooms of this grand 19th-century house are variously decorated, one with "moss" painted over pink walls. Sautéed veal Valdostano (veal sautéed in butter, shallots, and mushrooms with a cream–white wine sauce) and hot antipasto stand out on the northern Italian menu. *924 N. Charles St., tel. 410/547–8480. Reservations required. Jacket and tie advised. AE, MC, V.*

Da Mimmo. Big favorites here are shrimp with garlic baked in cognac and *stracciatelle* (egg-drop soup). This is the best of the Little Italy eateries, and therefore often crowded and noisy. *217 S. High St., tel. 410/727–6876. Reservations required. Jacket and tie advised. AE, DC, MC, V.*

★ **Tio Pepe.** Paella à la Valenciana (chicken, sausage, shrimp, clams, mussels, and saffron rice) is served often in these candlelit cellar dining rooms, as is the lesser-known Basque red snapper (with clams, mussels, asparagus, and boiled egg). *10 E. Franklin St., tel. 410/539–4675. Reservations required. Jacket and tie required at dinner. AE, DC, MC, V.*

Moderate   **Acropolis.** Try the lamb Giouvetsi (braised in olive oil and baked
★ with orzo in a sauce of tomatoes, green peppers, and onions) or any seafood dish at this relaxing family eatery. *4718 Eastern Ave., tel. 410/675–3384. Reservations required. AE, D, DC, MC, V. Closed Mon.*

Bertha's. Mussels are the specialty here, served steamed (with a choice of eight butter-based sauces) or as a Turkish appetizer (stuffed with sweet-and-spicy rice). The decor is nautical. *734 S. Broadway, tel. 410/327–5795. MC, V.*

8 East. This cozy and discreet restaurant serves such dishes as scallops sautéed with sun-dried tomatoes and chicken marsala (sautéed with shallots and mushrooms). *Tremont Hotel, 8 E. Pleasant St., tel. 410/576–1199. Reservations advised. Jacket and tie advised. AE, DC, MC, V.*

Haussner's. The 100-item menu features everything from sauerbraten and pigs' knuckles to crab imperial. On the walls are 600 paintings, among them originals by Rembrandt, Van Dyck, and Gainsborough. *3244 Eastern Ave., tel. 410/327–8365. No reservations at dinner. Dress: neat but casual. AE, D, DC, MC, V. Closed Sun.–Mon.*

Midtown Yacht Club. A jukebox, dartboards, and video games keep things hopping until 2 AM. The spicy Cajun menu, available until midnight, includes jambalaya (rice with clams and mussels) and seafood gumbo (a crab-and-shrimp stew). *15 E. Centre St., tel. 410/837–1300. AE, MC, V.*

Pierpoint. When Chesapeake meets Mediterranean, results include Brussels sprout coleslaw, smoked Silver Queen corn chowder, Eastern Shore rabbit sausage, and smoked crab cakes. With modern Italian art on the walls and jazz in the background, the setting is almost as eclectic as the menu. *1822 Aliceanna St., tel. 410/675–2080. Reservations advised. Dress: neat but casual. AE, DC, MC, V.*

Inexpensive **Donna's.** A good bet for both fresh-baked morning scones and after-theater espresso (open till 1 AM on Fri. and Sat.), this Italian coffee bar also serves a variety of pastas, salads, and innovative sandwiches from mid-day on. *1 Mt. Vernon Sq. (2 W. Madison St. at Charles St.), tel. 410/385-0180. Reservations accepted for groups. AE, MC, V.*

The Buttery. At this beloved institution on Mt. Vernon Square, sit at the counter or in a booth and order pancakes or a triple-decker sandwich. Coffee is always fresh, as is (notably in such a place) the seasonal fruit. *1 E. Centre St., tel. 410/837-2494. No reservations. No credit cards.*

Lodging

Staying around Inner Harbor means ready access to the major attractions. Away from the water, as far north as Mt. Vernon, are reminders of an older Baltimore and some relative bargains in accommodations. For price ranges, see Chart 2 (A) in Chapter 1.

Very Expensive **Harbor Court.** Since 1986 this redbrick tower with an ersatz
★ English-country-house interior (à la Ralph Lauren) has been Baltimore's most prestigious transient address. The priciest rooms have a harbor view. *550 Light St., 21202, tel. 410/234-0550 or 800/824-0076, fax 410/659-5925. 195 rooms, 8 suites. Facilities: 2 restaurants, bar, indoor pool, sauna, workout room. AE, D, DC, MC, V.*

Expensive **Latham Hotel.** The dark-wood-paneled lobby of the former Peabody Court hotel suggests a men's club, but the guest rooms are largely in pastels, with horticultural prints on the wall. Park views are the most sought after. *612 Cathedral St., 21201, tel. 410/727-7101 or 800/528-4261, fax 410/789-3312. 104 rooms, 10 suites. Facilities: 2 restaurants. AE, DC, MC, V.*

Sheraton Inner Harbor. Guest rooms are among the smallest in town, but all were renovated in 1993 and feature coffee makers. The Sheraton's is the only Orthodox-Union-certified kosher hotel kitchen in town. *300 S. Charles St., 21201, tel. 410/962-8300 or 800/325-3535, fax 410/962-8211. 339 rooms, 20 suites. Facilities: restaurant, bar, indoor pool, sauna, workout room. AE, D, DC, MC, V.*

Society Hill Hotel. The VIP suite, where the mayor's guests stay, is off-limits to paying customers, but the regular Victorian rooms are just fine. Wine and fruit are served afternoons in the parlor. *58 W. Biddle St., 21201, tel. 410/837-3630, fax 410/837-4654. 15 rooms. Facilities: restaurant, bar, Continental breakfast. AE, DC, MC, V.*

Tremont Hotel. This small hostelry on a quiet downtown block has a locally unsurpassed level of service: The concierge will arrange free local transportation, and the staff will do guests' personal shopping. All suites have kitchens and were renovated in 1992. *8 E. Pleasant St., 21202, tel. 410/576-1200 or 800/638-6266, fax 410/685-4216. 60 suites. Facilities: restaurant, bar. AE, DC, MC, V.*

★ **Tremont Plaza.** A plain gray 37-story tower has suites decorated in gentle earth tones. All units have kitchens, and those numbered 06 have the best views. *222 St. Paul Pl., 21202, tel. 410/727-2222 or 800/638-6266, fax 410/685-4215. 230 suites. Facilities: restaurant, deli, bar, outdoor pool, sauna, workout room. AE, DC, MC, V.*

Motels **Days Inn Inner Harbor** (100 Hopkins Pl., 21201, tel. or fax 410/
576–1000 or 800/325–2525), 250 rooms, 8 suites, restaurant,
pool, bar; moderate. **Courtyard by Marriott Hunt Valley** (221 International Circle, Hunt Valley 21030, tel. 410/584–7070 or 800/
321–2211, fax 410/584–8151), 146 rooms, 12 suites, restaurant,
pool, exercise room; inexpensive. **Hampton Inn Hunt Valley**
(11200 York Rd., Hunt Valley 21031, tel. 410/527–1500 or 800/
426–7866, fax 410/771–0819), 126 rooms; inexpensive.

The Arts and Nightlife

Events listings appear in the Friday *Baltimore Sun*, the
Thursday *Evening Sun*, the monthly *Baltimore* magazine, and
the *City Paper*, a free weekly distributed in shops and at
street-corner machines.

The Arts **Center Stage** (700 N. Calvert St., tel. 410/332–0033) is the state
theater of Maryland. Other venues: **Friedberg Hall** (Peabody
Conservatory, E. Mt. Vernon Pl. and Charles St., tel. 410/659–
8124), **Lyric Opera House** (Mt. Royal Ave. and Cathedral St.,
tel. 410/685–5086), **Meyerhoff Symphony Hall** (1212 Cathedral
St., tel. 410/783–8000), and **Morris A. Mechanic Theater** (Baltimore and Charles Sts., tel. 410/625–1400).

Nightlife The rooftop **Skyline Café** (Belvedere Hotel, N. Charles and
Chase Sts., tel. 410/539–1355) and the harborside **Explorer's
Club** (Harbor Court Hotel, tel. 410/234–0550) offer jazz and re-
markable views. **8x10** (8 E. Cross St., tel. 410/625–2000) is the
spot for blues and rock. Move to the latest dance mixes at the
Baja Beach Club (55 Market Pl., tel. 410/727–0468). Laughter
is the sound heard at the **Comedy Factory Outlet** (Lombard and
Light Sts., tel. 410/523–3837), while the talk is all sports at
Balls (200 W. Pratt St., tel. 410/659–5844) and the **Orioles
Sports Bar** (Sheraton Inner Harbor hotel, tel. 410/962–8300).

Maryland's Chesapeake

Maryland encompasses the top half of the Chesapeake Bay,
where the attractions are, naturally, quite water-oriented: Annapolis is a world yachting capital, the Eastern Shore is a major
duck-hunting ground, and Ocean City is a bustling Atlantic resort. Yet bayside towns are also rich in history, with many well-
preserved 18th-century buildings.

Tourist Information

Calvert County: Department of Economic Development (Coun-
ty Courthouse, Prince Frederick 20678, tel. 410/535–4583).
Dorchester County: Tourism (Box 26, Cambridge 21613, tel.
410/228–1000). **Queen Anne's County:** Visitors Service (102 E.
Main St., Suite 103A, Stevensville 21666, tel. 410/758–2300).
St. Mary's County: Department of Economic and Community
Development (Box 653, Leonardtown 20650, tel. 301/475–4626
or 800/327–9023). **Wicomico County:** Visitors Bureau (500 Glen
Ave., Salisbury 21801, tel. 410/548–4914). **Worcester County:**
Tourism (Box 208, Snow Hill 21863, tel. 410/632–3617). **Annapolis:** Conference and Visitors Bureau (1 Annapolis St., 21401,
tel. 410/280–0445). **Ocean City:** Convention and Visitors' Bureau (4001 Coastal Hwy., 21842, tel. 410/289–2800 or 800/626–

2326). **St. Michael's:** Talbot County Chamber of Commerce (805 Goldsborough St., Easton 21601, tel. 410/822–4606).

Getting There

By Car **To Annapolis:** From Baltimore, follow Rte. 3/97 to U.S. 50 (Rowe Blvd. exit). **To the Western Shore:** From Annapolis, take Rte. 2S, which becomes Rte. 4 in Calvert County. **To the Eastern Shore:** From Baltimore or Annapolis, cross the Bay Bridge (there is a toll) northeast of Annapolis and stay on U.S. 50.

By Bus **Baltimore Mass Transit** (tel. 410/539–5000) provides service—express on weekdays, local on weekends—between Annapolis and Baltimore. **Carolina Coach** (tel. 410/727–5014) links Annapolis to Ocean City and intermediate points on the Eastern Shore.

Exploring Maryland's Chesapeake

Annapolis Start on the waterfront. Sailboats dock right at the edge of **Market Square,** where there is a visitor information booth.

On the riverside campus of the **United States Naval Academy** (known to West Pointers as the "country club on the Severn"), the most prominent structure is the bronze-domed **U.S. Naval Chapel,** burial place of the Revolutionary War hero John Paul ("I have not yet begun to fight!") Jones. Outdoors, full-dress parades of midshipmen are a stirring sight. *Tel. 410/263–6933 or 410/267–3363. Admission free.*

The **Hammond-Harwood House** (19 Maryland Ave., tel. 410/269–1714), the **Chase-Lloyd House** (22 Maryland Ave., tel. 410/263–2723), and the **William Paca House** (186 Prince George St., tel. 410/263–5553) are all outstanding specimens of redbrick Colonial architecture. **St. John's College** (College Ave., tel. 410/263–2371) is the third-oldest college in the country and the home of a 600-year-old tree.

The **Maryland State House** (tel. 410/974–3400) is the oldest state capitol in continuous legislative use and the only one that has housed the U.S. Congress. Charles Willson Peale's painting *Washington at the Battle of Yorktown* hangs inside.

The Western Shore Calvert County offers plenty of striking bayside scenery, including the imposing **Calvert Cliffs** (some 100 feet high) and several miles of beaches. The forest primeval is open for inspection from an elevated boardwalk at the **Battle Creek Cypress Swamp Sanctuary** (Rte. 2/4 to Rte. 506, tel. 410/535–5327), which boasts the northernmost naturally occurring stand of the ancient bald cypress tree in the United States. To see the cliffs and beaches, stop at **Calvert Cliffs State Park** (Rte. 2/4, Lusby, tel. 301/856–8987). For a glimpse of the Eastern Shore on a clear day, try the observation deck at the **Calvert Cliffs Nuclear Power Plant** (tel. 410/586–4676) next door.

Down at the tip of the peninsula is **Solomons,** a still-tranquil but increasingly fashionable sailing town. At its **Calvert Marine Museum** (Rte. 2/4 at Solomons Island Rd., tel. 410/326–2042), boats from various epochs and a 19th-century screw-pile lighthouse are on display.

Across the Patuxent in St. Mary's County is **Historic St. Mary's City** (Rte. 5, tel. 301/862–0990), where the first colonists dispatched by Lord Baltimore, according to a grant of Charles I, settled in 1634. Until 1694 this was the capital of Maryland. Reconstructions of 17th-century buildings and of the ship that the settlers came on are to be seen at this less spectacular but more peaceful version of Virginia's Colonial Williamsburg. Plantation buffs may want to visit the partially restored **Sotterley** (Rte. 235, tel. 301/373–2280) to the north.

The Eastern Shore The William Preston Lane, Jr., Memorial Bridge links Annapolis to the Eastern Shore, passing along the way through **Kent Island,** the bay's largest island. This is the site of the first English settlement in Maryland—agents of Virginia's governor set up a trading post here in 1631. Rte. 50 continues south past historic towns near the bay and then leads east to the Atlantic.

In the town of **Wye Mills** (Rte. 662) is the state tree, the 400-year-old, 95-foot-tall **Wye Oak;** and a reconstructed, working 17th-century gristmill. The affluent town of **Easton** has a 17th-century Quaker meeting house and an 18th-century courthouse.

On the Miles River is **St. Michaels** (on Rte. 33), once a shipbuilding center and now a fashionable yachting destination. On display at its **Chesapeake Bay Maritime Museum** is everything from a Native American dugout canoe to a modern sailboat still under construction. Exhibitions of stuffed waterfowl, decoys, and guns are extensive. *Navy Point, tel. 410/745–2916. Admission charged. Closed weekdays Jan.–Mar.*

The **Oxford-Bellevue Ferry** has been running since 1683, and today it takes cars and pedestrians across the Tred Avon River from a spot 7 mi south of St. Michaels to the 17th-century town of **Oxford.** Few of the surviving buildings in Oxford date to before the mid-1800s, but the bigger (and less charming) town of **Cambridge** 15 mi to the southeast has several from the 1700s.

Southwest of Cambridge is the **Blackwater National Wildlife Refuge** (Rte. 335, tel. 410/228–2677), 11,000 acres of marshland inhabited by Canada geese, ospreys, and bald eagles. Visitors can take it in on foot, by bicycle, or from an observation tower.

On the Atlantic side of the peninsula is **Ocean City,** with 10 mi of white sand beach and a flashy 27-block boardwalk. Coastal Highway, with blocks of high-rise condos, runs down the center of town. More than 300,000 vacationers flock here every summer.

What to See and Do with Children

Vintage aircraft are parked outside the **Naval Air Test and Evaluation Museum** (Rte. 235 and Shangri-la Dr., Lexington Park [Western Shore], tel. 301/863–7418). Indoors, failed contraptions on display include the improbable Goodyear Inflatoplane. **Trimper's Amusement Park** (Boardwalk and S. 1st St., Ocean City, tel. 410/289–8617), with a huge roller coaster and other rides, celebrated its centennial in 1990.

Sports and Outdoor Activities

Biking **Viewtrail 100** is a 100-mi circuit in Worcester County, between Berlin and Pocomoke City. In **Ocean City,** the right-hand lanes of Coastal Highway are for buses and bikes. Many boardwalk shops rent bikes.

Fishing The principal catches are black drum, channel bass, flounder, bluefish, white perch, weakfish, croaker, trout, and large-mouth bass. One-week licenses are sold at many sporting goods stores, one-year licenses from the **Department of Natural Resources** (Box 1869, Annapolis 21404, tel. 410/974–3211). **Anglers** (435 Revel Hwy., Annapolis, tel. 410/757–3442) sells and rents equipment. **Bunky's Charter Boats** (Solomons Island Rd., Solomons, tel. 410/326–3241) and **Scheibels** (Wynne Rd., Ridge, south of Lexington Park, tel. 301/872–5185) will arrange bay charters. **The Fishing Center** (Shantytown Rd., West Ocean City, tel. 410/213–1121) runs private charters and daily deep-sea trips, and **Bahia Marina** (22nd St. and the bay, Ocean City, tel. 410/289–7438) arranges deep-sea charters.

Golf **Eisenhower Golf Course** (Generals Hwy., northwest of Annapolis, tel. 410/222–7922) and the **Bay Club** (Rte. 818, west of Ocean City, tel. 410/641–4081) have 18 holes. **Ocean City Golf and Yacht Club** (Rte. 611, tel. 410/641–1779) has 36.

Beaches and Water Sports

Sandy Point State Park (Rte. 50, 12 mi east of Annapolis) is a good spot for fishing, swimming, or launching boats. Otherwise, Western Shore beaches are for strolling and looking. There are no Chesapeake Bay beaches of any consequence on the Eastern Shore. On the Atlantic, south of Ocean City, is the northern portion of **Assateague Island National Seashore** (*see* National and State Parks, *above*).

Northeast Wind Yachts (222 Severn Ave., Annapolis, tel. 410/267–6333) charters sailboats, with or without crews. **Annapolis Sailing School** (601 6th St., tel. 410/267–7205 or 800/638–9192) offers outfitting and instruction. **Zanhiser's Sailing Center** (C St. at Back Creek, Solomons, tel. 410/326–2166) arranges yacht charters. **Town Dock Marina** (305 Mulberry St., St. Michaels, tel. 410/745–2400) and **Sailing, Etc.** (5305 Coastal Hwy., Ocean City, tel. 410/723–1144) rent sailboats.

Dining and Lodging

Restaurants in Annapolis and the less expensive Western Shore, though reliable for seafood, do not warrant a special trip. Across the bay are innovative kitchens and classic crab houses.

Lodging reservations are necessary as much as a year in advance of the Annapolis sailboat and powerboat shows in October, Naval Academy commencement in May, and Easton's Waterfowl Festival in November.

For price ranges, see Charts 1 (B) and 2 (B) in Chapter 1.

Annapolis **The Corinthian.** Cheerful waiters lend this oil lamp–lit dining
Dining room its sporty air. The distinctive crab cakes have an angel-hair-pasta binder, and the New York strip is three-week-aged. *Loews Annapolis Hotel, 126 West St., tel. 410/263–7777. Reservations advised. Jacket and tie advised. AE, DC, MC, V. Expensive.*

★ **Little Campus Inn.** This cozy local favorite has a dark-paneled main dining room and a lively tavern. Menu highlights include Greek mariner's salad (with crabmeat and shrimp) and soft-shell crab. *63 Maryland Ave., tel. 410/263–9250. Reservations advised. AE, MC, V. Closed Sun. Moderate.*

Lodging **Annapolis Marriott Waterfront.** Amenities such as bathroom phones typify the rooms, which face the water, the historic district, or—from private balconies—the bustle of City Dock. *80 Compromise St., 21401, tel. 410/268–7555, 800/336–0072, or 800/228–9290, fax 410/269–5864. 150 rooms. Facilities: restaurant, 2 bars. AE, D, DC, MC, V. Expensive.*

★ **Governor Calvert House.** This expanded 18th-century town house, one of four neighboring properties owned by Historic Inns of Annapolis, has Victorian as well as Colonial rooms. *58 State Circle, 21401, tel. 410/263–2641 or 800/847–8882, fax 410/268–3813. 55 rooms. AE, DC, MC, V. Expensive.*

Calvert County **Solomons Crabhouse.** Inside this converted firehouse, diners
Dining smash hard-shell crabs with wood mallets to the tune of country-and-western music over the stereo. *H&W Shopping Center, Rte. 2/4, Solomons, tel. 410/326–2800. Reservations advised. AE, MC, V. No lunch weekdays. Moderate.*

Lodging **Back Creek Inn.** Rooms in this 19th-century wood-frame house feature brass beds with colorful quilts and views of the water, a garden, or a quiet street. *Calvert and A Sts., Solomons 20688, tel. 410/326–2022. 4 rooms (3 share bath), 2 suites, cottage. Facilities: whirlpool. No credit cards. Closed mid-Dec.–mid-Feb. Expensive.*

St. Mary's County **Evans Seafood.** Ask for a water view, then order lobster stuffed
Dining with crab imperial, or the spicy, secret-recipe hard-shell crab. *Rte. 249, Piney Point, tel. 301/994–2299. Reservations advised for 10 or more. No credit cards. No lunch weekdays. Moderate.*

Lodging **Potomac View Farm.** This 19th-century wood-frame farmhouse is furnished with simple oak furniture, quilts, and a life-size wooden cow in the living room. A mile away is an affiliated marina. Full breakfast is included. *Rte. 249, Tall Timbers 20690, tel. 301/994–0418, fax 301/994–2613. 7 rooms, 1 suite, 1 cottage. Facilities (at the marina): restaurant, bar, outdoor pool, beach. AE, MC, V. Moderate.*

Ocean City **The Hobbit.** Murals and carved lamps portray J. R. R. Tolkien
Dining characters in this dining room with a two-angled view of Assawoman Bay. Veal with pistachios and sautéed catch of the day are menu highlights. *101 81st St., tel. 410/524–8100. Reservations advised. Dress: neat but casual. MC, V. Expensive.*
Lombardi's. Cozy wood booths, and tables and walls decorated with photos, provide the setting for outstanding thin-crust pizza. Cheese steaks and cold-cut sandwiches are the alternatives. *9203 Coastal Hwy., tel. 410/524–1961. No reservations. MC, V. Closed Wed. Inexpensive.*

Lodging **Carousel Hotel and Resort.** Once a weekend playground for
★ Washington politicians, it is now a well-equipped family recreational facility. The indoor ice rink is an unusual beachfront attraction. *118th St. and Coastal Hwy., 21842, tel. 410/524–1000 or 800/641–0011, 410/524–1286. 265 rooms. Facilities: restaurant, delicatessen, 3 bars, indoor pool, saunas, exercise room, 3 lighted tennis courts, skating rink. AE, D, DC, MC, V. Expensive.*

St. Michaels **208 Talbot.** An antiques-filled late-19th-century house is the
Dining setting for regional cuisine. Maryland's own rockfish is sautéed
★ with wild mushrooms in an oyster cream. Fresh Bay oysters

are served with a champagne cream sauce, prosciutto, and pistachio nuts. *208 N. Talbot St., tel. 410/745–3838. Reservations advised. MC, V. Expensive.*

Crab Claw. The bang-them-yourself steamed blue crabs are first-rate at this harborside eatery. The spicy deep-fried hard crab is worthwhile too, as is the vegetable crab soup. *Navy Point, tel. 410/745–2900. Reservations advised. No credit cards. Closed Dec.–Feb. Moderate.*

Dining and Lodging ★ **Inn at Perry Cabin.** This early 19th-century farmhouse has been made to resemble an English country house, with antiques and Laura Ashley in the bedrooms, a cozy library, spectacular gardens, and a formal dining room. Menu standouts are crab-and-lobster cake with black truffles, and rabbit with grilled squash and smoked bacon. *308 Watkins La., 21663, tel. 410/745–2200 or 800/722–2949, fax 410/745–3348. 27 rooms, 14 suites. Facilities: restaurant, bar, indoor pool. AE, DC, MC, V. Expensive.*

Motels **Dunes Motel** (27th St. and Baltimore Ave., Ocean City 21842, tel. 410/289–4414), 103 rooms, café, outdoor pool, wading pool; closed Dec.–mid-Feb.; moderate. **Holiday Inn Conference Center and Marina** (155 Holiday Dr., Box 1099, Solomons 20688, tel. 410/326–6311 or 800/465–4329, fax 410/326–1069), 325 rooms, restaurant, 2 bars, outdoor pool, 2 tennis courts, Nautilus equipment, sauna; moderate. **St. Michaels Motor Inn** (Rte. 33 and Peaneck Rd., St. Michaels 21663, tel. 410/745–3333, fax 410/745–2906), 93 rooms, 1 suite, 2 pools; moderate.

The Arts and Nightlife

The Arts During the summer, the **U.S. Naval Academy Band** performs at Annapolis's City Dock on Tuesday evenings, and the **Starlight Series** takes place on Sunday evenings. **Ocean City** (tel. 410/289–2800 or 800/626–2326) sponsors free boardwalk concerts. When the **Colonial Players** (108 East St., Annapolis, tel. 410/268–7373) go on vacation, **Annapolis Summer Garden Theater** (Compromise and Main Sts., tel. 410/268–0809) takes over.

Nightlife Ocean City has plenty of places for dancing to rock, live or recorded; there is even an under-21 club, **Night Light** (Boardwalk at Worcester St., tel. 410/289–6313), for those too young to drink. Bars in Annapolis, Solomons, and St. Michaels are favored by more subdued, and in many cases middle-aged, crowds.

Elsewhere in the State

Western Maryland

Getting There From Baltimore, I–70 runs westward through Frederick and up to the state's narrowest point, pinched between West Virginia and Pennsylvania. U.S. 40 passes through into the "Panhandle."

What to See and Do In **Frederick,** the Visitor Center (19 E. Church St., 21701, tel. 301/663–8703) has information on several Civil War sites. These include the **Barbara Fritchie House** (154 W. Patrick St., tel. 301/698–0630), where, according to legend and poetry, an old woman defied Stonewall Jackson by waving the Stars and Stripes.

Near Sharpsburg is **Antietam National Battlefield** (Rte. 65, tel. 301/432–5124), where Union troops repelled Lee's invasion in 1862. **Hagerstown,** also in Washington County (Tourism Office, 1826 Dual Hwy., 21740, tel. 301/791–3130), was a frontier town founded by Germans in the early 18th century; several buildings from that period have been preserved.

The mountain scenery grows rugged in aptly named **Allegany County** (Office of Tourism, Canal St., Cumberland 21502, tel. 301/777–5905), where the Cumberland Gap provides an opening for U.S. 40, formerly the "National Road" taken by westward-bound settlers in the early years of the Republic. Here and in neighboring **Garrett County** (Promotion Council, 200 S. 3rd St., Oakland 21550, tel. 301/334–1948) there are plenty of opportunities for outdoor recreation, including skiing.

NEW JERSEY

By Alexandra Roll Kenney

Updated by Rathe Miller

Capital	Trenton
Population	7,721,000
Motto	Liberty and Prosperity
State Bird	Eastern goldfinch
State Flower	Purple violet

Visitor Information

New Jersey Department of Commerce, Energy, and Economic Development (Division of Travel and Tourism, 20 W. State St., CN-826, Trenton 08625–0826, tel. 609/292–2470 or 800/537–7397; fax 609/633–7418). There are eight **welcome centers** around the state, one in Trenton.

Scenic Drives

The **Garden State Parkway** rolls north–south through landscaped suburbs, farmland, and pine woods from the New York state border to Cape May. For Hudson River views, take the **Palisades Interstate Parkway** north from the George Washington Bridge to the state line, or **River Road** from Weehawken north to Fort Lee. Both **Rte. 23** northwest from Newfoundland through High Point State Park and **Rte. 15** northwest from I–80 offer lakes, rural estates, and higher-elevation vistas.

National and State Parks

National Parks   Sandy Hook Unit of Gateway National Recreation Area (*see* The Jersey Shore, *below*). On the Delaware River boundary between New Jersey and Pennsylvania is the **Delaware Water Gap National Recreation Area** (visitor center, Kittatinny Point, off I–80; mailing address, Bushkill, PA 18324; tel. 908/496–4458; *see also* Pennsylvania). The 38,000-acre **Edwin B. Forsythe National Wildlife Refuge, Brigantine Division** (Box 72, Great Creek Rd., Oceanville 08231, tel. 609/652–1665) has an 8-mi wildlife drive and nature trails especially popular during spring and fall bird migrations.

State Parks   New Jersey has the third-largest state-park system in the nation, with 36 parks, 11 forests, four recreation areas, 41 natural areas, 23 historic sites, and four marinas. The **Department of Environmental Protection and Energy** (New Jersey Division of Parks and Forestry, CN-404, Trenton 08625, tel. 609/292–2797) provides information and publications. The 108,000-acre **Wharton State Forest** (R.D. 9, Hammonton 08037, tel. 609/561–3262) contains the **Batsto State Historic Site** (Rte. 542), a restored early 19th-century iron- and glass-making community.

The Jersey Shore

The Jersey Shore is 127 mi of public beachfront, stretching like a pointing index finger along the Atlantic Ocean from the Sandy Hook Peninsula in the north to Cape May at the southern tip. The beach sand changes from Sandy Hook's gray, coarse grit, full of ground silicates washed down over centuries from the Hudson River's Lower New York Bay and New York Harbor, to the finely powdered white sand of Wildwood, to the smoothly polished yellow pebbles off Cape May.

The shore offers saltwater fishing from pier, bridge, dock, or boat (licenses are not required) and other water sports, birdwatching, and bicycling or strolling on the ubiquitous woodplank or concrete boardwalks. In Atlantic City are the famed gambling casinos; in Cape May, Victorian bed-and-breakfasts.

Tourist Information

Monmouth County: Department of Public Information/Tourism (27 E. Main St., Freehold 07728, tel. 908/431–7476, or 800/523–2587; fax 908/294–5930). **Ocean County:** Tourism Advisory Council (CN 2191, Administration Bldg., Toms River 08753, tel. 908/929–2138 or 800/365–6933). Southern Ocean County Chamber of Commerce (265 W. 9th St., Long Beach Island 08008, tel. 609/494–7211 or 800/292–6372; fax 609/494–5807). **Atlantic City:** Convention & Visitors Bureau (2314 Pacific Ave., 08401, tel. 609/348–7100 or 800/262–7395; fax 609/345–3685). **Cape May:** Convention & Visitors Bureau (Box 403, 08204, tel. 800/528–7328). County Chamber of Commerce (Court House, Box 74, 08210, tel. 609/465–7181). **Wildwood:** Department of Tourism (Box 609, 08260, tel. 609/522–1408; fax 609/729–2234).

Getting There

By Plane **Philadelphia International** (*see* Pennsylvania), **Newark International** (tel. 201/961–6000), and the **New York City airports** (*see* New York) are closest to Atlantic City and Shore points. The southern Shore has its own airport, **Atlantic City International** (tel. 609/645–7895), with scheduled service to metropolitan airports.

By Car The main road serving the Jersey Shore is the Garden State Parkway, a north–south toll road that ends in Cape May. From New York City, I–80 and the New Jersey Turnpike (toll) connect with the Garden State. From Philadelphia and southern New Jersey suburbs, take the Atlantic City Expressway (toll). From the south, take the Delaware Memorial Bridge and continue north on the New Jersey Turnpike. At the northern end of the Shore, Rte. 36, turning off to Rte. 71 and then Rte. 35 swing scenically down along the coast toward Seaside Heights. Toms River, Barnegat, and Tuckerton are linked by U.S. 9.

By Train **Amtrak** (Kirkman Blvd. at Missouri Ave.) serves Atlantic City. **New Jersey Transit** (tel. 800/772–2222) operates local commuter service to Atlantic City and the shore towns of Monmouth and Ocean counties from New York City.

By Bus **New Jersey Transit** (*see* By Train, *above*) offers bus service to most Jersey Shore towns. **Academy Bus Line** (tel. 212/964–6600) and **Asbury Park–Transit Lines** (tel. 908/291–1300) also run buses between New York City and Shore points. **Greyhound** serves Atlantic City (tel. 609/344–7550 or 609/345–6617). Ask Atlantic City casino hotels about direct service to their properties.

By Ferry The **Cape May–Lewes Ferry** (tel. 609/886–2718 or 302/645–6313 in DE) is a year-round, 70-minute car-ferry link (800 passengers, 100 cars per ferry) across Delaware Bay between Cape May and Lewes, Delaware. The cost is $4.50 one-way per foot passenger; $18 per car and driver plus $4.50 per additional passenger.

Exploring the Jersey Shore

The **New Jersey Coastal Heritage Trail** (tel. 609/785–0676), which opened in spring 1993 and is run by the National Park Service, connects historic sites along the coast. A series of five mapped routes marking various types of sites is under construction. The first, featuring maritime history, is now open; the others are scheduled to follow within two years.

At the Shore's north end, the **Sandy Hook Unit of the Gateway National Recreation Area** (Box 530, Ft. Hancock 07732, tel. 908/872–0115) is east of Atlantic Highlands on Rte. 36. Here on this peninsula of barrier beach you can glimpse the distant Manhattan skyline; splash in the usually gentle, shallow surf; and explore sleepy **Ft. Hancock,** built in 1895.

One of America's first resorts, founded with strict moral codes in the late 18th century, **Long Branch** lured seven U.S. presidents for Shore visits. Presidents Grant, Garfield, Arthur, McKinley, Hayes, Harrison, and Wilson worshiped in the former Church of the Presidents, now the **Long Branch Historical Museum,** which has a collection of books, photos, and memorabilia from the area's past. *1260 Ocean Ave., tel. 908/229–0600 or 908/222–9879. Admission free. Open by appointment only.*

A century ago **Asbury Park** was the Shore's toniest resort, but efforts to revive that glory have so far been disappointing. Nowadays it is known for its place in rock history: The metal gate at 702 Cookman Avenue led to the second-floor **Upstage Club,** where the young Bruce Springsteen performed in the 1960s. Asbury Park still has a boardwalk, with rides and amusements, plus a minimall (tel. 908/988–8585) with antiques vendors and auctions.

Ocean Grove has 19th-century Victorian-ornate hotels and inns, relatively quiet beaches, a boardwalk, and sidewalk cafés. The imposing **Ocean Grove Great Auditorium** (Auditorium Sq., tel. 908/775–0035 or 800/388–4768) presents summer concerts. In **Belmar,** at the **Municipal Marina** (Rte. 35, tel. 908/681–2266) on the Shark River, you can board party and charter boats that head for the ocean daily in search of blackfish, blues, fluke, tuna, and shark. **Point Pleasant Beach** has **Jenkinson's Beach and Boardwalk Amusement Center** (tel. 908/892–3274) for rainy-day diversion. **Bay Head** tries to maintain itr dnd-of-the-commuter-line exclusivity.

In **Toms River,** once a pirate and privateering port, the **Ocean County Historical Society** (26 Hadley Ave., tel. 908/341–1880) has a museum with artifacts and exhibits on the dirigibles that flew from **Lakehurst Naval Air Warfare Center** (Rte. 547,

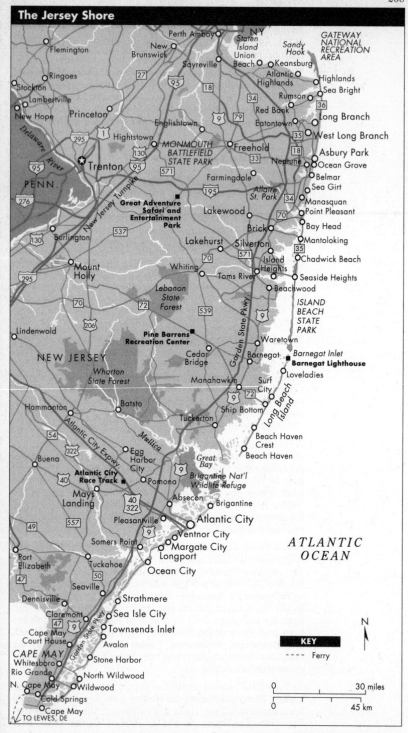

The Jersey Shore

Lakehurst, tel. 908/323–2527)—site of the 1937 *Hindenburg* airship tragedy.

On Barnegat Peninsula, **Seaside Park,** Ocean County's "party city," has two major amusement piers. South of this is narrow **Island Beach State Park** (tel. 908/793–0506), 10 mi of ocean and bay beaches with almost no evidence of human habitation.

Return inland through Toms River, then head south on U.S. 9 and east on Rte. 72 over Barnegat Bay to **Long Beach Island. Barnegat Lighthouse** (tel. 609/494–2016; admission charged), known locally as "Old Barney" and completed in 1858, is to the north. To the south is **Beach Haven,** the island's commercial center, with Victorian houses ranged around the town square and the small museum of the **Long Beach Historical Society** (Engleside and Beach Aves., tel. 609/492–0700), which conducts walking tours of the historic district.

Back on the mainland, the Garden State Parkway leads to **Atlantic City.** It was originally popular for seaside holidays in fabulous stone hotels and for promenades on the **boardwalk,** the nation's first elevated wood walkway (1870), where saltwater taffy is still sold. Today some 33 million people flood the town annually to gamble, dropping about $8 million daily in the **casinos.** (Be alert outside at night—the city has a high crime rate.) The dozen casino hotels are outrageous, from the prow-shaped **Showboat** and adjacent glitzy **Taj Mahal** on the oceanside boardwalk to the pair of quieter, marina casinos on the bay.

Some of Atlantic City's famous ocean **amusement piers** can still be seen: Howard's Pier (Kentucky Ave. and the boardwalk) dates from 1882; the Moorish Revival Central Pier began as Applegate Pier in 1884; the Steel Pier, most famous of them all, is closed for renovation; Garden Pier is the only one owned by the city. The annual mid-September **Miss America Pageant** takes place in **Convention Hall** (tel. 609/345–7571).

South on Rte. 52 is **Ocean City,** across Great Egg Harbor. Begun as a Methodist retreat (Billy Graham got his start here as a radio preacher in the 1940s), Ocean City is one of only two dry (that is, no alcohol sold) towns on the Shore. Its **boardwalk** and **boardwalk parades** are family-oriented, and summer evening concerts are traditional at the **Music Pier** (Moorlyn Terr.).

Savor a quiet walk on **Strathmere** beach before heading on to the five little boroughs of **Wildwood.** The 2-mi **Wildwood boardwalk** boasts the single greatest concentration of outdoor **amusement rides** on the Shore.

For a change of pace and scene, travel to the southern tip of the Shore and the re-created world of Victorian **Cape May.** Believed to be the state's oldest ocean resort, it was named for the Dutch captain who sighted it in 1620. Cape May today hosts myriad mostly-for-grownups bed-and-breakfasts, most in elaborately gingerbreaded Victorian houses. (Many B&Bs and restaurants are closed January through March.) Early October **Victorian Week** combines madcap frivolity with serious lectures on period history and restoration (make reservations well in advance); the July 4 celebration is vintage Americana.

What to See and Do with Children

The entire Jersey Shore is a children's playground, with its
sandy beaches, usually gentle and shallow surf, and casual
boardwalk snack bars. Towns with **amusement parks** or **rides**
with child-appeal include Asbury Park, Seaside Heights, and
Long Beach Island. **Lucy the Elephant** (Atlantic and Decatur
Aves., Margate, tel. 609/823–6473 or 609/822–6519), an ele-
phant-shaped building seven stories high, appeals to kids of all
ages.

Six Flags Great Adventure is a huge theme park comprising an
amusement park with a multitude of rides, as well as a drive-
through Safari Park. *Rte. 537, via Garden State Pkwy. to I–95
Exit 16, Jackson, tel. 908/928–1821. Admission: $23 adults,
$15 children. Closed mid-Sept.–May.*

Shopping

The **Englishtown Auction** (tel. 908/446–9644), a giant flea market held in Englishtown on weekends March–January, covers
50 acres. Arrive at sunrise for the best buys.

Sports and Outdoor Activities

Biking   Boardwalks are grand for biking if you don't mind dodging
weekend walkers and joggers. The road around Cape May
Point takes you past the Cape May Lighthouse and Cape May
Point State Park.

Canoeing   Try the many freshwater creeks, streams, and tributaries in
the 1.1-million-acre **Pinelands Pine Barrens National Reserve**
around Chatsworth (tel. 609/894–9342).

Fishing   Monmouth County has more charter and party boats than any
other area along the Shore; its largest marina is the **Brielle Marine Basin** (tel. 908/528–6200) in Brielle. In Ocean County, numerous party and charter boats sail from Point Pleasant and
Long Beach Island. State marinas are in **Leonardo** (tel. 908/
291–1333), **Forked River** (tel. 609/893–5045), and **Atlantic City**
(tel. 609/441–8482).

Spectator Sports

Horse Racing   Before Atlantic City started sponsoring attention-getting boxing matches, horse racing was the Shore's most popular spectator sport. **Monmouth Park** (Oceanport Ave., Oceanport, tel.
908/222–5100) is the area's best-known track, with Thoroughbred races June through September. The **Atlantic City Race
Course** (junction of Black Horse Pike and U.S. 40, McKee City,
tel. 609/641–2190) has Thoroughbred racing June through September. **Freehold Raceway** (junction of U.S. 9 and Rte. 33,
Freehold, tel. 908/462–3800) offers harness racing mid-August
through May.

Beaches and Water Sports

From Memorial Day to Labor Day the **Water Information Hotline** (tel. 609/777–3373) supplies information about the Shore's
water quality and beach conditions. **Island Beach State Park**
(*see* Exploring the Jersey Shore, *above*) is the most scenic natu-

ral beach on the Jersey Shore. Shore beaches usually charge a
fee from Memorial Day or mid-June to Labor Day for everyone
12 and older. Windsurfing is especially good in the calm waters
of the open bays. Sailing, rowing, or powerboating is superb on
sheltered Barnegat Bay in Ocean County.

Dining and Lodging

Though the restaurant fare ranges from cheap snacks to pricey
haute cuisine, seafood is the Jersey Shore's biggest deal, with
local catches featured on most menus. Ocean City and Ocean
Grove do not allow the sale of liquor. For price ranges, see
Chart 1 (A) in Chapter 1.

Lodgings should be booked far in advance in summer.
Beachfront rooms are more expensive. Rooms in Atlantic City
casino hotels are the most popular, the most costly, and the
most difficult to reserve, especially on weekends from mid-
June to Labor Day. Chambers of commerce (*see* Tourist Information, *above*) can provide assistance. **Bed & Breakfast of New
Jersey** (103 Godwyn Ave., Suite 132, Midland Park 07432, tel.
201/444–7409 or 800/992–2632) handles inns and private homes
statewide. For price ranges, see Chart 2 (A) in Chapter 1.

Atlantic City
Dining
★

Le Palais. Favorites such as the shellfish/vegetable mélange
Olga, rack of lamb with rosemary and pine nuts, and individual
dessert soufflés (order these at the start of the meal) are elegantly served in this lavish mirrored and art-hung dining
room. *Merv Griffin's Resorts Casino Hotel, North Carolina
Ave. and boardwalk, tel. 609/344–6000 or 800/438–7424. Reservations advised. Jacket requested. AE, D, DC, MC, V. Closed
Mon.–Tues., holidays. Very Expensive.*

The Meadows. Though French haute cuisine is featured, one
can dine casually in this rustic, wood-paneled setting overlooking the bay. Specialties include rack of lamb, duckling with
cherry sauce, and crab-stuffed lobster. *Harrah's Casino Hotel,
1725 Brigantine Blvd., tel. 609/441–5000, 800/242–7724, or after 4 PM 609/441–5050. AE, D, DC, MC, V. No lunch; closed
Mon.–Tues. Very Expensive.*

★ **Dock's Oyster House.** Owned and operated by the Dougherty
family since 1897, the city's oldest restaurant features seafood,
naturally, in a large, bustling setting. *2405 Atlantic Ave., tel.
609/345–0092. Reservations advised. AE, MC, V. Closed Jan.
Expensive.*

Knife and Fork Inn. Established in 1912 in its Tudor-accented
Flemish building and owned by the same family since 1927, this
local institution serves straightforward seafood and steaks. *Albany and Atlantic Aves., tel. 609/344–1133. Jacket required.
AE, DC, MC, V. Closed Mon. Expensive.*

Cousin's Country House. The extensive menu includes duckling
with fruit sauce. There's piano-bar entertainment Thursday
through Sunday in an elegant atmosphere. *3373 Bargaintown
Rd., Bargaintown, tel. 609/927–5777. AE, DC, MC, V. No
lunch Sat. Moderate.*

Renault Winery Gourmet Restaurant. Atop the country's oldest
winery, this popular candlelit spot features fixed-price meals
with wine. *Bremen Ave., Egg Harbor City, tel. 609/965–2111.
Reservations advised. AE, DC, MC, V. No lunch Mon.–Sat.;
brunch Sun. Moderate.*

★ **Angelo's Fairmount Tavern.** The locals flock here for lots of good
Italian fare served up by the Mancuso family, the owners since

1935. *2300 Fairmount Ave., tel. 609/344–2439. No credit cards. No lunch weekends. Inexpensive.*

White House Sub Shop. It claims to have sold more than 16 million overstuffed sandwiches (known as subs) since 1946. Photo walls proclaim its celebrity fans. *2301 Arctic Ave., tel. 609/345–1564 or 609/345–8599. No reservations. No credit cards. Inexpensive.*

Lodging ★ **TropWorld Casino and Entertainment Resort.** TropWorld's two white towers house guests in cool, modern rooms, while the vast casino floor and public areas keep them entertained. *Brighton at Boardwalk, 08401, tel. 609/340–4000 or 800/257–6227; fax 609/343–5211. 1,019 rooms. Facilities: 7 restaurants, 2 lounges, comedy club, 1,700-seat showroom, theme park (admission charged), fun house, saloon, 2 tennis courts, 2 pools, exercise room, whirlpool, sauna. AE, D, MC, V. Very Expensive.*

Trump Castle Casino Resort. The 26-story Castle on the Bay adjoins the largest state-owned marina. The seafood restaurant offers one of the nicest views of Atlantic City. *Huron Ave. and Brigantine Blvd., 08401, tel. 609/441–2000 or 800/365–8786; fax 609/345–2021. 725 rooms, including 162 suites. Facilities: 10 restaurants, 3 lounges, boat docking, 6 tennis courts, health club, pool, exercise room, whirlpool, sauna. AE, D, DC, MC, V. Very Expensive.*

★ **Flagship Resorts.** A pleasant, modern salmon-colored condo hotel, located across from the boardwalk facing Brigantine and the Absecon Inlet, it's quietly away from the casino action. *60 N. Main Ave., 08401, tel. 609/343–7447; fax 609/344–2702. 440 kitchen-equipped suites. Facilities: restaurant, bar, health club, pool, whirlpool, sauna. AE, D, DC, MC, V. Expensive.*

Holiday Inn Diplomat. Completed in 1989, the Diplomat is a noncasino hotel located opposite the TropWorld. Its contemporary rooms are pleasant and functional; some have ocean views. *Chelsea Ave. at Boardwalk, 08401, tel. 609/348–2200 or 800/548–3030; fax 609/345–5110. 212 rooms, 8 two-bedroom suites. Facilities: restaurant, bar, pool. AE, D, DC, MC, V. Moderate.*

Quality Inn Boardwalk. Another smaller alternative, this one's near Merv Griffin's casino. It has a 17-story guest-room wing plus a lower building with a restaurant. *S. Carolina and Pacific Aves., 08401, tel. 609/345–7070 or 800/356–6044; fax 609/345–0633. 199 rooms, 4 suites. Facilities: restaurant, bar. AE, D, DC, MC, V. Moderate.*

Cape May *Dining* **Mad Batter.** You can choose dishes from the eclectic menu in the skylighted Victorian dining room or outdoors on the porch or garden terrace. *19 Jackson St., tel. 609/884–5970. MC, V. Closed Jan.–Feb.; weekdays Mar.–mid-May and mid-Oct.–Dec. Expensive.*

Lodging **The Mainstay.** This 1870 gambling and men's club, restored as a B&B, captures the feel of another era with 14-foot ceilings, oversize guest rooms with lace curtains and William Morris wallpapers, harmoniously arranged antiques, and lavish plantings. *635 Columbia Ave., 08204, tel. 609/884–8690. 12 rooms. Facilities: dining room (breakfast and tea), game room. No credit cards. Closed mid-Dec.–mid-Mar. Expensive.*

The Queen Victoria. In the center of the historic district, the inn's three green-trimmed restored Victorian houses are blessed with a genteel air. Beautiful handmade quilts cover the beds in rooms furnished with antiques, such as marble-top tables and dressers. *102 Ocean St., 08204, tel. 609/884-8702. 23 rooms, 6 suites. Facilities: 2 dining rooms (breakfast and tea), bicycles, free beach tags, parking. MC, V. Expensive.*

Captain Mey's Inn. Two blocks from the beach and in the historic district, this 1890 inn beckons with wraparound veranda, fireplaced sitting room, Dutch antiques, and original Tiffany stained-glass windows. *202 Ocean St., 08204, tel. 609/884-7793. 9 rooms (3 share bath). Facilities: full breakfast, afternoon tea, free beach tags, parking. MC, V. Closed weekdays Jan.-mid-Mar. Moderate-Expensive.*

The Manor House. On a quiet tree-lined street two blocks from the beach, this guest house mixes antiques, art, and dashes of whimsy, including a barber's chair and a player piano. *612 Hughs St., 08204, tel. 609/884-4710. 6 rooms, 1 suite. Facilities: fireplace, free beach tags, parking. MC, V. Closed Jan. Moderate.*

Ocean City
Lodging

The Flanders Hotel. One of the last grand hotels on the Jersey Shore sits on the boardwalk. Spanish Colonial-style on the outside, it has old woods, antiques, and a polished, elegant '20s look inside. *Boardwalk at 11th St., 08226, tel. 609/399-1000 or 800/345-0211; fax 609/399-0194. 214 rooms (some share baths). Facilities: restaurant, pool, sauna, lawn games, parking. AE, DC, MC, V. Moderate.*

Red Bank
Lodging
★

Oyster Point. The sleek, new five-story hotel overlooks the Navesink River, an easy walk from the marina and town. Some rooms have patios or balconies. *146 Bodman Pl., 07701, tel. 908/530-8200 or 800/345-3484; fax 908/747-1875. 58 rooms. Facilities: restaurant, bar, exercise room. AE, DC, MC, V. Expensive.*

Spring Lake
Lodging

The Breakers. Toward the northern end of the Shore, one of the few remaining Victorian oceanfront hotels has been modernized and has rooms with contemporary furnishings. *1507 Ocean Ave., 07762, tel. 908/449-7700; fax 908/449-0161. 64 rooms. Facilities: restaurant, bar, pool. AE, DC, MC, V. Moderate.*

Toms River
Dining
★

Old Time Tavern. This is a good bet for complete meals at bargain prices. Italian dishes, steak, seafood, and sandwiches are the lures. *N. Main St., tel. 908/349-8778. AE, DC, MC, V. Inexpensive.*

Motels

Ascot Motel (Iowa and Pacific Aves., Box 1824, 08404, tel. 609/344-5163 or 800/225-1476), 80 rooms, pool; moderate. **Best Western Bayside Resort at Golf & Tennis World** (8029 Black Horse Pike, West Atlantic City 08232, tel. 609/641-3546 or 800/999-9466; fax 609/641-4329), 110 rooms, restaurant, 6 tennis courts, exercise room, whirlpool, pool, casino shuttle; moderate. **Midtown-Bala Motor Inn** (Indiana and Pacific Aves., 08401, tel. 609/348-3031 or 800/624-0986; fax 609/347-6043), 300 rooms, restaurant, bar, 2 pools, free valet parking; moderate. **Sandpiper** (Boulevard at 10th St., Ship Bottom 08008, tel. 609/494-6909), 20 rooms, refrigerators; closed Nov.-Apr.; inexpensive.

The Arts and Nightlife

Garden State Arts Center (Garden State Pkwy.; Exit 116, Holmdel, tel. 908/442-9200, June-mid-Sept.) has a summer roster of performing-arts groups, star acts, and ethnic festivals. Nightlife is fierce at the **Atlantic City casino hotels,** between the gambling action and the nationally famous nightclub acts; call the casino box offices for show reservations.

Elsewhere in the State

The Northwest Corner

Getting There Rtes. 23 and 15 northwest from I–80 provide easy access to this region from Manhattan.

What to See and Do This less-crowded region of small lakes and low mountains—including the state's highest elevation (1,803 feet) at **High Point State Park** (tel. 201/875–4800), 7 mi northwest of Sussex—entices outdoorsy types in warm weather and skiers in winter.

The most popular ski areas, clustered around the nondescript town of **McAfee,** are fully blanketed with artificial snowmaking equipment, have both day and evening skiing, are family-oriented, and provide a good mix of all-ability ski terrain. **Vernon Valley/Great Gorge** (Rte. 94, McAfee 07428, tel. 201/827–3900; 14 chair lifts, 53 trails) is the largest and liveliest complex, with slopes on two sides of the mountain. In the summer, this one becomes **Action Park** (tel. 201/827–2000; admission charged; closed Sept.–Apr.), with about 75 action rides (motorbikes, race cars) and an abundance of water rides. **Hidden Valley** (Rte. 515, Vernon 07462, tel. 201/764–4200; 3 chair lifts, 14 trails) is a lively alternative. **Craigmeur Ski Area** (Rte. 513, Newfoundland 07435, tel. 201/697–4500), small and friendly, is best for rank beginners or families with younger children.

Central New Jersey

Getting There U.S. 202 connecting with U.S. 206 links Morristown and Princeton. The junction of I–78 and I–287 is about equidistant from these two anchor points.

What to See and Do This is chic horse country, with estates and meadows edged with wood fencing, especially around **Bedminster,** where many locals ride in hunts. **Far Hills** is the home of the U.S. Golf Association and its museum, **Golf House** (Liberty Corner Rd., tel. 908/234–2300).

South of residential **Morristown** is the **Morristown National Historical Park** (Washington Pl., tel. 201/539–2085), which commemorates the 1779–80 winter that George Washington and his Continental army spent here. The park includes the elegant Ford Mansion, once Washington's quarters, and soldiers' log huts. The pretty university town of **Princeton** is where Washington and his troops defeated the British army by surprise attack in the 1777 Battle of Princeton, marked by the **Princeton Battle Monument** (Monument Dr., off Stockton St.; admission free). Though Princeton was the new nation's capital for a few months in 1783, Washington stayed at nearby **Rockingham** (east off U.S. 206, Rocky Hill, tel. 609/921–8835), where he wrote his "Farewell Orders to the Armies." (**Chamber of Commerce of the Princeton Area,** Box 431, Princeton 08542, tel. 609/921–7676 or 609/520–1776.)

The state governor's mansion, **Drumthwacket,** is in Princeton, but the state capital offices are in nearby **Trenton,** a small Delaware River city undergoing a quiet rebirth from its days as a leading Colonial pottery and manufacturing center. (**Mercer County Chamber of Commerce,** 214 W. State St., Trenton 08608, tel. 609/393-4143.)

Newark and Jersey City

Getting There I-78 passes through Jersey City and Newark; U.S. 1, 9, and 22 go through Newark.

What to See and Do Jersey City and neighboring Hoboken offer superb views of the broad Hudson River and the Manhattan skyline. **Newark,** the state's largest city, is undergoing major rebuilding. The **Newark Museum** (49 Washington St., tel. 201/596-6550; admission free) has outstanding fine arts, science, and industry collections. (**Metro Newark Chamber of Commerce,** 1 Newark Center, 07102, tel. 201/242-6237; fax 201/824-6587.)

Jersey City is the site of **Liberty State Park** (Exit 14B, New Jersey Turnpike, tel. 201/915-3400), where boats leave for the **Statue of Liberty** and the century-old, restored **Ellis Island Immigration Museum** (for both, tel. 212/363-3200), less than 2,000 feet offshore. Within the park is the new **Liberty Science Center** (tel. 201/451-0006), with the world's largest Omnimax theater (a domed screen 88 feet across and 6 stories high); an anchored replica of Henry Hudson's ship, the *Half Moon,* and the **New Netherland Museum** (tel. 201/433-5900); and the restored, open-sided **Central Railroad of New Jersey Terminal,** once a major transportation hub and now an exhibition and festival venue. (**Hudson County Division of Cultural and Heritage Affairs,** 114 Clifton Pl., Jersey City 07304, tel. 201/915-1212 or 800/542-7894.)

PENNSYLVANIA

By Alan Hines

Updated by
Carolyn Price
and Mark Porter

Capital	Harrisburg
Population	11,881,643
Motto	Virtue, Liberty, and Independence
State Bird	Ruffed grouse
State Flower	Mountain laurel

Visitor Information

Pennsylvania Department of Commerce, Office of Travel Marketing (453 Forum Bldg., Harrisburg 17120, tel. 717/787–5453; 800/847–4872 for free publications). **Welcome centers:** on major highways around the state.

Scenic Drives

In Bucks County, **River Road** wends 40 mi along the Delaware River, offering views of 18th- and 19th-century stone farmhouses, tucked-away villages, and fall foliage along wooded hills. In the Poconos, **Rte. 209,** from Stroudsburg to Milford, passes untouched forests and natural waterfalls.

National and State Parks

National Park The 500,000-acre **Allegheny National Forest** (Box 847, Warren 16365, tel. 814/723–5150; visitor center, tel. 814/726–1291 May–Sept.), in the northwestern part of the state, has hiking and cross-country ski trails, three rivers suitable for canoeing, and outstanding stream fishing.

State Parks Pennsylvania's 114 state parks include more than 7,000 campsites. The **Bureau of State Parks** (Box 1467, Harrisburg 17120, tel. 800/847–4872) provides information on the parks and campsite reservations. **Hickory Run State Park** (RD 1, Box 81, White Haven 18661, tel. 717/443–9991) and **Promised Land State Park** (RR 1, Box 96, Greentown 18426, tel. 717/676–3428) in the Poconos offer fishing, hiking, and camping; ski resorts are nearby. The 18,719-acre **Ohiopyle State Park** (Box 105, Ohiopyle 15470, tel. 412/329–8591) has hiking, camping, swimming, and skiing, both downhill and cross-country. **Presque Isle State Park** (Rte. 832, Erie 16505, tel. 814/871–4251), a 3,202-acre sandy peninsula that extends 7 mi into Lake Erie, is popular for fishing, swimming, boating, and camping.

Philadelphia

Almost a century after English Quaker William Penn founded Philadelphia in 1682, the city became the birthplace of the nation and the home of its first government. Today, for visitors and natives alike, Philadelphia is synonymous with Independence Hall, the Liberty Bell, cheesesteaks and hoagies, ethnic neighborhoods, theaters, buoyant classical music—and city streets teeming with life. With close to 1.6 million people, Penn's "City of Brotherly Love" is the fifth-largest city in the country yet maintains the feel of a friendly small town.

Tourist Information

Philadelphia: Convention and Visitors Bureau (1515 Market St., Suite 2020, 19102, tel. 215/636–3300 or 800/537–7676). Visitors Center (16th St. and John F. Kennedy Blvd., tel. 215/636–1666 or 800/537–7676). **Greater Philadelphia:** Chamber of Commerce (1234 Market St., Suite 1800, 19107, tel. 215/545–1234).

Arriving and Departing

By Plane **Philadelphia International Airport** (tel. 215/492–3181), 8 mi southwest of downtown, has scheduled flights by most major domestic and foreign carriers. A **SEPTA** (*see* Getting Around Philadelphia, *below*) rail line connects the airport with center-city stations; the trip takes 25 minutes and costs $4.75. Airport shuttle services, such as **Airport-Limelight Limousine** (tel. 215/342–5557) and **Philadelphia Airport Shuttle, Inc.** (tel. 215/969–1818), charge about $8 per person. Taxis are plentiful; they cost about $20 plus tip.

By Car The main north–south highway through Philadelphia is I–95; to reach center city, take the Vine Street exit off I–95S or the Broad Street exit off I–95N. From the west, the Schuylkill Expressway (I–76) has several exits to center city. From the east, the New Jersey Turnpike and I–295 provide access to either U.S. 30/I–676, which enters the city via the Benjamin Franklin Bridge, or New Jersey Rte. 42 and the Walt Whitman Bridge.

Train Station **Amtrak** serves **30th Street Station** (30th and Market Sts., tel. 215/824–1600).

Bus Station **Greyhound** (10th and Filbert Sts., tel. 215/931–4000). **NJ Transit** (30th Street Station, tel. 215/569–3752).

Getting Around Philadelphia

The traditional heart of the city is Broad and Market streets, where City Hall now stands. Market Street divides the city north and south. North–south streets are numbered, starting with Front (1st) Street, at the Delaware River, and increasing to the west. Most historical and cultural attractions are easy walks from the midtown area, which is comparatively safe during the day. After dark, ask hotel personnel about the safety of places you're interested in visiting, but in general, cabs are safer than walking.

By Car These narrow streets were designed for Colonial traffic, and driving can be difficult. On-street parking is often forbidden during rush hours (parking facilities at 41 N. 6th St.; 15th St. and Kennedy Blvd.; 10th and Locust Sts.; 1500 Arch St.). During rush hours avoid the major arteries leading into and out of the city, particularly I–95, U.S. 1, and the Schuylkill Expressway.

By Public **SEPTA** (tel. 215/580–7800; fare $1.50, transfers 40¢; exact
Transportation change required) operates an extensive network of buses, trolleys, subways, and commuter trains. Certain lines run 24 hours a day. SEPTA's **Day Pass,** good for a day's unlimited riding, can be purchased at the Visitors Center (*see* Tourist Information, *above*) for $4.

By Taxi Cabs are plentiful during the day—especially along Broad Street and near hotels and train stations. At night and outside center city, taxis are scarce and you may have to call for service. The main companies are **Quaker City Cab** (tel. 215/728–8000), **United Cab** (tel. 215/238–9500), and **Yellow Cab** (tel. 215/922–8400).

Orientation Tours

Gray Line Tours (tel. 215/569–3666) offers a 5½-hour tour of historic and cultural areas. To combine lunch or dinner with a sightseeing cruise on the Delaware River, climb aboard the *Spirit of Philadelphia* (tel. 215/923–1419).

Walking Tours **Audio Walk and Tour** (Norman Rockwell Museum, 6th and Sansom Sts., tel. 215/925–1234) offers a city historic tour with cassette player and map. **Centipede Tours** (tel. 215/735–3123; May–Oct.) offers guided candlelight strolls through Old Philadelphia.

Carriage Tours **Philadelphia Carriage Co.** (tel. 215/922–6840), **'76 Carriage Co.** (tel. 215/923–8516), and **Society Hill Carriage Co.** (tel. 215/627–6128) offer narrated tours of the historic area in antique horse-drawn carriages with costumed drivers.

Water Taxi **Philadelphia Water Taxi, Inc.** (tel. 215/351–4170) stops at various waterfront entertainment spots, eating holes, and attractions, including Penn's Landing.

Exploring Philadelphia

Historic District Most sites in "the most historic square mile in America" are part of **Independence National Historical Park** (tel. 215/597–8974). Except as noted, all have free admission and are open daily.

Across from the **Visitors Center** (3rd and Chestnut Sts.) are the **First Bank of the United States,** the country's oldest bank building, and **Carpenter's Hall** (Carpenter's Ct.; closed Mon.), where the First Continental Congress convened in September 1774.

Philosophical Hall (104 S. 5th St., tel. 215/627–0706)—just off **Independence Square,** where, on July 8, 1776, the Declaration of Independence was first read in public—is the headquarters of the American Philosophical Society. Founded by Benjamin Franklin in 1743 to promote "useful knowledge," it is the oldest learned society in America. Its library, **Library Hall** (105 S. 5th St., tel. 215/440–3400; closed weekends), contains a copy of the Declaration handwritten by Thomas Jefferson.

Also on Independence Square is **Independence Hall** (Chestnut St. between 5th and 6th Sts., tel. 215/597–8974), which was opened in 1732 as the State House for the colony of Pennsylvania. It was here that the Second Continental Congress convened on May 10, 1775; that the Declaration of Independence was adopted a year later; that the Articles of Confederation were signed in 1778; and that the Constitution was formally signed by its framers on September 17, 1787. The west wing is **Congress Hall,** formerly the Philadelphia County Courthouse, and the meeting place of the U.S. Congress from 1790 to 1800. The first floor was the House of Representatives; President John Adams was inaugurated here in 1797. In the second-floor Senate chamber, George Washington was inaugurated for his second term in 1793. Tours of Independence Hall are given year-round; from early May to Labor Day, expect a wait.

Philadelphia

Delaware River

Delaware Ave.

Delaware Ave.

Spring Garden St.

Front St.

Front St.

Willow St.

Penn's Landing

Head House Square

Elfreth's Alley

Arch St.

2nd St.

Betsy Ross House

Christ Church

Independence National Historical Park

Visitors Center

Chestnut St.

First Bank of the United States

Bishop White House

3rd St.

4th St.

U.S. Mint

Library Hall

Todd House

Carpenter's Hall

Spruce St.

Pine St.

5th St.

Race St.

Liberty Bell

Independence Square

Independence Mall

Philosophical Hall

Washington Square

6th St.

Callowhill St.

Franklin Square

Independence Hall

8th St.

9th St.

Lombard St.

South St.

7th St.

Filbert St.

Locust St.

Ridge Ave.

10th St.

Pennsylvania Convention Center

Sansom St.

Quince St.

KEY

Subway

Market East Station

Reading Terminal Market

11th St.

Vine St.

Race St.

Philadelphia Savings Fund Society Building

12th St.

Buttonwood St.

Masonic Temple

John Wanamaker Store

13th St.

Juniper St.

Broad St.

Broad St.

Callowhill St.

Pennsylvania Academy of the Fine Arts

City Hall

Locust St.

15th St.

Academy of Music

16th St.

Cathedral of SS. Peter and Paul

17th St.

Suburban Station

Pine St.

Lombard St.

Free Library of Philadelphia

18th St.

Academy of Natural Sciences

19th St.

Ludlow St.

Chestnut St.

Sansom St.

Rittenhouse Square

Spruce St.

19th St.

Logan Circle

Benjamin Franklin Parkway

Hamilton St.

Rodin Museum

Franklin Institute

John F. Kennedy Blvd.

Market St.

20th St.

Brandywine St.

Spring Garden St.

N

Cherry St.

Arch St.

21st St.

Walnut St.

Locust St.

22nd St.

Philadelphia Museum of Art

TO GERMANTOWN

23rd St.

24th St.

25th St.

440 yards

400 meters

30th St. Station

Schuylkill River

One block up the mall in front of Independence Square is the **Liberty Bell.** To keep it from falling into British hands during the Revolution, the bell was spirited 60 mi north by horse and wagon to Allentown. You can touch the 2,080-pound bell and read its biblical inscription: "Proclaim liberty throughout all the land unto all the inhabitants thereof."

Christ Church (2nd St. north of Market St., tel. 215/922–1695) is where noted Colonials, including 15 signers of the Declaration, worshiped. East of Market Street is **Elfreth's Alley,** one of the oldest continually occupied residential streets in America, dating back to 1702; **No. 126** (tel. 215/574–0560; closed weekdays Jan.–mid-Feb.) has been restored as a Colonial craftsman's home. The **Betsy Ross House** (239 Arch St., tel. 215/627–5343; closed Mon.) is where the seamstress supposedly sewed the first American flag.

The **United States Mint** (5th and Arch Sts., tel. 215/597–7350), built in 1969, is the largest mint in the world and stands two blocks from the first U.S. mint, which opened in 1792. Tours and exhibits on coin-making are available.

The Waterfront and Society Hill The spot where William Penn stepped ashore in 1682 is today a 37-acre park known as **Penn's Landing;** docked here are the restored USS *Olympia,* Commodore George Dewey's flagship in the Spanish-American War, and the USS *Becuna,* a World War II submarine that is especially appealing to kids. In warm weather, the Great Plaza is the scene of concerts, festivals, and other events. *Spruce St., tel. 215/922–1898. Admission charged.*

Docked a block north is the *Gazela of Philadelphia.* Built in 1883, it is the last of a Portuguese fleet of cod-fishing ships and the oldest wooden square-rigger still sailing. *Between Walnut and Spruce Sts., tel. 215/923–9030. Closed Oct.–May, weekdays June–Sept.*

The **Bishop White House** (309 Walnut St.), built in 1786 as the home of the rector of Christ Church, has been restored to Colonial elegance. Nearby is the simply furnished **Todd House** (4th and Walnut Sts., tel. 215/597–8974). The Visitors Center offers a free tour that includes both houses. Built in 1775, it has been restored to its appearance in the 1790s, when its best-known resident, Dolley Payne Todd (later Mrs. James Madison), lived here.

Head House Square (2nd and Pine Sts.) was once an open-air Colonial marketplace. Today, on summer weekends, it is the site of crafts fairs, festivals, and other activities.

City Hall and Environs **City Hall,** topped by a bronze statue of William Penn, is not only the geographic center of Penn's original city but also the governmental center. Inside are the mayor's ornate reception room, the City Council Chambers, and the Pennsylvania Supreme Court. *Broad and Market Sts., tel. 215/567–4476. Closed weekends.*

Philadelphia is the mother city of American Masonry, and the **Masonic Temple** is home to the Grand Lodge of Free and Accepted Masons of Pennsylvania. The temple's collection includes handwritten letters from George Washington and Benjamin Franklin's printing of the first book on Freemasonry published in America. *1 N. Broad St., tel. 215/988–1917. Admission free. Closed Sat. July–Aug.*

The city's classiest park, **Rittenhouse Square** (between 18th and 19th Sts. at Walnut St.) frequently hosts arts festivals. The **Academy of Music** (Broad and Locust Sts., tel. 215/893–1900 or 215/893–1930 for tickets), modeled on Milan's La Scala opera house, is home to the Philadelphia Orchestra and the Opera Company of Philadelphia. The **John Wanamaker Store** (13th and Market Sts., tel. 215/422–2000) has a nine-story grand court with a 30,000-pipe organ. A block away is the **Philadelphia Savings Fund Society Building** (12th and Market Sts., tel. 215/629–7000), one of the city's first skyscrapers.

The sprawling **Reading Terminal Market** (12th and Filbert Sts., tel. 215/922–2317; closed Sun.) has 79 stores and stalls, with the city's widest variety of eating places and fresh foods to cook. Next door, the new **Pennsylvania Convention Center** (1101 Market St., tel. 215/574–2070) is second in size only to New York City's Jacob Javits Center. It's *mammoth*. The main exhibit hall opened its doors in June 1993. By January 1994, you'll be able to view all 1.3 million square feet of it.

Museum District The **Benjamin Franklin Parkway** angles across the grid of city streets from City Hall to Fairmount Park. Lined with distinguished museums, hotels, and apartment buildings, this 250-foot-wide boulevard inspired by the Champs-Elysées was built in the 1920s. Off the parkway you'll find the **Free Library of Philadelphia** (19th St., tel. 215/686–5322), with more than 2 million volumes; the **Academy of Natural Sciences** (19th St., tel. 215/299–1020), America's first museum of natural history; the **Rodin Museum** (22nd St., tel. 215/787–5431), which has the largest collection of Auguste Rodin's works outside France; and the **Franklin Institute** (20th St., tel. 215/448–1200), a science museum with an abundance of hands-on exhibits.

Atop Faire Mount, the plateau at the end of the parkway, stands the **Philadelphia Museum of Art.** Modeled on ancient Greek temples but on a grander scale, it houses more than 500,000 works in its 200 galleries. Climb the steps and, before entering, turn to savor the view down the parkway. *26th St. and Benjamin Franklin Pkwy., tel. 215/763–8100; 215/787–5488 for recording. Admission charged (free Sun. 10–1). Closed Mon., holidays.*

Behind the museum is **Fairmount Park** (accesses from East River Dr., West River Dr., and Belmont Ave.). At 4,500 acres it is among the largest city parks in the world, following both banks of the Schuylkill River through woodlands, meadows, rolling hills, and a forested gorge. Within the park's bounds are tennis courts, ball fields, playgrounds, trails, an exercise course, several celebrated cultural institutions (such as the **Ellen Phillips Samuel Memorial Sculpture Garden**), and some fine Early American country houses (**Laurel Hill, Strawberry Mansion,** and others). An excellent map of the park is available at most park sites for 25¢. Don't miss **Boathouse Row,** on the banks of the Schuylkill, 11 architecturally varied 19th-century buildings that are home to 13 rowing clubs. In the northwest section of the park is the **Wissahickon,** a 5½-mi gorge carved out by Wissahickon Creek. Of the Philadelphia that William Penn encountered, this trail-laced area of cliffs, towering trees, and wildlife has changed the least.

The Pennsylvania Academy of the Fine Arts is the oldest art institution in the United States. Its collection ranges from Winslow Homer and Benjamin West to Andrew Wyeth and Red Grooms. *Broad and Cherry Sts., tel. 215/972–7600. Admission charged (free Sat. 10–1).*

The Italian Renaissance–style **Cathedral of Saints Peter and Paul** (18th and Race Sts., tel. 215/561–1313), built between 1846 and 1864, is the basilica of the Roman Catholic archdiocese of Philadelphia.

Germantown In 1683, Francis Pastorius led 13 Mennonite families out of Germany to seek religious freedom in the New World; they settled 6 mi northwest of Philadelphia in what is now Germantown, and many became Quakers. **Cliveden** (6401 Germantown Ave., tel. 215/848–1777), an elaborate country house built in 1763, was occupied by the British during the Revolution. On October 7, 1777, Washington's attempt to dislodge them resulted in his defeat in the Battle of Germantown. During the yellow-fever plague of 1793–94, George Washington lived in the **Deshler-Morris House** (5442 Germantown Ave., tel. 215/596–1748) to avoid the unhealthy air of sea-level Philadelphia.

Parks and Gardens

Fairmount Park (*see* Exploring Philadelphia, *above*) is the city's largest, encompassing varied terrains as well as many cultural sites. The University of Pennsylvania's **Morris Arboretum** (Hillcrest Ave. between Germantown and Stenton Ave., Chestnut Hill, tel. 215/247–5777), an example of Victorian garden design, is 166 acres of romantically landscaped seclusion. America's first zoo, the **Philadelphia Zoological Gardens** (34th St. and Girard Ave., tel. 215/243–1100) displays 1,600 animals on 42 acres.

Philadelphia for Free

Get a copy of the *Calendar of Events* at the Visitors Center (*see* Tourist Information, *above*) for listings of Philadelphia's myriad free events and attractions. Several museums schedule a period when admission is free to all.

What to See and Do with Children

The **Please Touch Museum** (210 N. 21st St., tel. 215/963–0667), designed for children age seven and younger, encourages hands-on participation. The **Annenberg Center Theater for Children** (37th and Walnut Sts., tel. 215/898–6791) schedules productions in November, February, and April. **Sesame Place and Twiddlebug Land** (100 Sesame Rd., Langhorne, tel. 215/ 757–1100), a 30-minute drive north of the city, is an amusement park based on the popular public-television show. A wide assortment of attractions—such as slides, sandboxes, a nature maze and a 10,000-square-foot wave pool—makes this Anheuser-Busch theme park suitable for children aged 3 to 15.

Shopping

Pennsylvania's 6% sales tax does not apply to clothing, medicine, or food bought in stores.

Shopping Districts **Walnut Street,** between Broad Street and Rittenhouse Square, and the intersecting streets just north and south are filled with upscale boutiques and galleries. **Jewelers' Row,** centered on Sansom Street between 7th and 8th streets, is one of the world's oldest and largest markets of precious stones. Pine Street from 9th to 12th streets is **Antiques Row.** Along **South Street** are more than 180 unusual stores selling everything from New Age books and health food to avant-garde art. For local color, visit the outdoor stalls and indoor stores of the **Italian Market,** on 9th Street between Christian and Washington streets.

Department Stores **John Wanamaker** (tel. 215/422–2200) occupies the entire block bounded by 13th, Juniper, Market, and Chestnut streets. **Strawbridge and Clothier** (tel. 215/629–6000), at 8th and Market streets, was founded in 1868.

Specialty Stores **Architectural Antiques Exchange** (715 N. 2nd St., tel. 215/922–3669) handles everything from embellishments from Victorian saloons and apothecary shops to stained and beveled glass. **Bauman Rare Books** (1215 Locust St., tel. 215/546–6466) has volumes from the 19th century and earlier on law, science, English literature, and travel. **Wine Reserve** (205 S. 18th St., tel. 215/560–4529) deals exclusively in fine wines and cognacs. **J. E. Caldwell** (Juniper and Chestnut Sts., tel. 215/864–8829), a local landmark for jewelry since 1839, is adorned with antique hand-blown crystal chandeliers by Baccarat. For fine furniture, stop in at **Thomas Moser Cabinetmakers** (210 W. Washington Sq., tel. 215/922–6440). Gorgeous renderings of pencil-post beds, clocks, lecterns, and more in solid, premium-grade cherry-wood reveal elegant, uncompromised craftsmanship and uncommon restraint in design. Beside her White Dog Cafe (*see* Dining, *below*) in West Philadelphia, restaurateur Judith Wicks runs a wonderful crafts store, **The Black Cat** (3424 Sansom St., tel. 215/386–6664), with nine colorful rooms of American and imported fabrics, jewelry, notions, and furniture.

Spectator Sports

Baseball **Philadelphia Phillies** (Veterans Stadium, Broad St. and Pattison Ave., tel. 215/463–1000; Apr.–Oct.).

Basketball **Philadelphia 76ers** (Spectrum, Broad St. and Pattison Ave., tel. 215/336–3600; Oct.–Apr.).

Football **Philadelphia Eagles** (Veterans Stadium, tel. 215/463–5500; Aug.–Dec.).

Hockey **Philadelphia Flyers** (Spectrum, tel. 215/336–3600; Oct.–Apr.).

Dining

Dining experiences in Philadelphia can range from street-corner pretzel vendors and cheese-steak shops to world-class cuisine. For price ranges, see Chart 1 (A) in Chapter 1.

Very Expensive **The Fountain.** Nestled in the lavish yet dignified lobby of the
★ Four Seasons, the Fountain offers predominantly local and American entrées, such as roast Pennsylvania pheasant with bacon-flavored cabbage. *1 Logan Sq., tel. 215/963–1500. Reservations required. AE, DC, MC, V.*

★ **Le Bec-Fin.** The most prestigious restaurant in Philadelphia is fit for a king: apricot silk walls, crystal chandeliers, and gilt-framed mirrors. The cuisine is haute French. *1523 Walnut St.,* *tel. 215/567–1000. Reservations required. Jacket and tie advised. AE, DC, MC, V. Closed Sun.*

Old Original Bookbinder's. This favorite haunt of celebrities, politicians, and athletes, full of dark paneling and Tiffany-style glass, tends to be a bit overpriced and touristy. The seafood is good but not great. *125 Walnut St., tel. 215/925–7027. Reservations advised. AE, D, DC, MC, V.*

Expensive **Meiji-En.** This huge waterfront property on the Delaware River, with indoor wishing ponds, paper lanterns, Oriental screens, and rock gardens, proves that "chain" isn't necessarily a dirty word in restaurants. Fine Japanese cuisine is featured at dinner: salmon-wrapped scallops, tempura, broiled eel, shabu-shabu. A knockout Sunday brunch includes sushi, omelets, lox and bagels, sesame noodles, and other confusingly eclectic but savory delectables. *Pier 19, N. Delaware Ave., tel. 215/592–7100. Reservations advised. AE, DC, MC, V.*

★ **Osteria Romana.** This fine Italian restaurant, with stucco walls and white tile floors in the style of a Roman *ristorante*, features such entrées as suckling pig. Homemade gelato is the star dessert. *935 Ellsworth St., tel. 215/271–9191. Reservations advised. AE, DC, MC, V. Closed Mon.*

★ **Susanna Foo.** In an un-Chinese atmosphere, with Tchaikovsky playing in the background, Chef Foo presents an imaginative Chinese menu that includes steamed bass with scallion-and-ginger sauce. *1512 Walnut St., tel. 215/545–2666. Reservations required. AE, MC, V. Closed Sun.*

Moderate **Sansom Street Oyster House.** This Philadelphia favorite serves
★ first-rate raw shellfish and grilled and blackened dishes. It's unpretentiously paneled in dark wood, with uncovered tables. *1516 Sansom St., tel. 215/567–7683. Reservations only for parties of 5 or more. AE, D, DC, MC, V. Closed Sun.*

Victor Cafe. Waiters at this family-owned restaurant are opera singers. The northern Italian cuisine is fair, but people come for the music and the atmosphere. *1303 Dickinson St., tel. 215/468–3040. Reservations required weekends. AE, DC, MC, V. Closed Mon.*

★ **White Dog Cafe.** The place teems with pleasure: ready University of Pennsylvania students huddling in the bar over "Leg Lifter Lager," tweedy academics engaging in provocative breakfast chats over flapjacks, sybarites lost in the wonders of a celestial crème brûlée (7,000 were sold in 1992). Attracting them all is the fine homemade fare using organic ingredients, a great children's menu, a wide price range, and monthly theme meals. *3420 Sansom St., tel. 215/386–9224. AE, DC, MC, V.*

Inexpensive **Joe's Peking Duck House.** Known for Peking duck and barbe-
★ cued pork, Joe's is the best Chinese restaurant in Chinatown. *925 Race St., tel. 215/922–3277. Reservations advised. No credit cards.*

★ **Melrose Diner.** This classic Philadelphia diner serves nothing elaborate but offers top-quality ingredients at diner prices—and is open 24 hours. *1501 Snyder Ave., tel. 215/467–6644. No credit cards.*

Triangle Tavern. This South Philly neighborhood Italian bar-restaurant offers good food and local color. *10th and Reed Sts., tel. 215/467–8683. No credit cards.*

Lodging

Philadelphia's hotels run the gamut from commonplace to world-class. Most B&Bs operate under the auspices of booking agencies, such as **Bed and Breakfast, Center City** (1804 Pine St., 19103, tel. 215/735–1137), or **Bed and Breakfast of Philadelphia** (Box 252, Gradyville 19039, tel. 215/358–4747 or 800/733–4747). For price ranges, see Chart 2 (A) in Chapter 1.

Very Expensive **The Barclay.** The elegant lobby leads to a registration area sparkling with crystal chandeliers. Some rooms in this carefully renovated 1929-vintage hotel have four-poster beds, and furniture is antique in style throughout. *Rittenhouse Sq. E, 19103, tel. 215/545–0300 or 800/421–6662. 235 rooms. Facilities: restaurant, lounge, concierge. AE, D, DC, MC, V.*

★ **Four Seasons.** Built in 1983, this eight-story hotel is Philadelphia's most expensive. Rooms are furnished in the Federal style, with romantic views overlooking Logan Circle. *1 Logan Sq., 19103, tel. 215/963–1500. 371 rooms. Facilities: restaurant, café, exercise room, indoor pool, concierge, nonsmoking floors. AE, DC, MC, V.*

Latham. At this small, elegant hotel with a European accent and an emphasis on personal service, guest rooms have marble-top bureaus and French writing desks. *17th St. at Walnut St., 19103, tel. 215/563–7474 or 800/528–4261. 139 rooms. Facilities: restaurant, lounge. AE, DC, MC, V.*

Expensive **Adam's Mark.** Guest rooms are small here with an English-
★ country motif, request one on an upper floor facing south toward Fairmount Park and the downtown skyline. The hotel's big attraction is the nighttime activity at Quincy's, its turn-of-the-century nightclub. *City Ave. and Monument Rd., 19131, tel. 215/581–5000 or 800/444–2326. 449 rooms, 66 suites. Facilities: 3 restaurants, lounge, sports bar, exercise room, 2 pools. AE, D, DC, MC, V.*

Holiday Inn Center City. This is an above-average Holiday Inn with an excellent location. All rooms in the 25-floor hotel have a mauve color scheme and contemporary decor. *1800 Market St., 19103, tel. 215/561–7500. 445 rooms. Facilities: restaurant, lounge, exercise room, outdoor pool, nonsmoking floors. AE, D, DC, MC, V.*

Moderate **Quality Inn Historic Downtown Suites.** The out-of-the-way 1890
★ building was once the Bentwood Rocker Factory. Guest rooms have a rustic, homey atmosphere. *1010 Race St., 19107, tel. 215/922–1730 or 800/221–2222. 92 suites. Facilities: lounge, health club. AE, D, DC, MC, V.*

Society Hill Hotel. Rooms in this 1832 former longshoreman's house are furnished with antiques. Continental breakfast is brought to your room with fresh-squeezed juice and hand-dipped chocolates. *301 Chestnut St., 19106, tel. 215/925–1394. 10 rooms, 2 suites. Facilities: restaurant, outdoor café, piano bar. AE, DC, MC, V.*

Thomas Bond House. Spend the night in the heart of the Olde City the way Philadelphians did 220 years ago. Built in 1769, this four-story house has rooms that feature marble fireplaces and four-poster Thomasville beds. *129 S. 2nd St., 19106, tel. 215/923–8523. 10 rooms, 2 suites. AE, DC, MC, V.*

Inexpensive **Chamounix Mansion.** This youth hostel is located on a wooded bluff overlooking the Schuylkill River (and, unfortunately, the Schuylkill Expressway). The 1802 estate is loaded with character; the drawbacks are dorm-style living and shared baths. *Chamounix Dr., 19131, tel. 215/878–3676. 6 rooms with 48 beds. No credit cards. Closed mid-Dec.–mid-Jan.*

International House. At this residence for students and professors on the University of Pennsylvania campus, a limited number of rooms are available for overnight guests from the end of May to the end of August. *3701 Chestnut St., 19104, tel. 215/ 387–5125. 379 rooms. Facilities: cafeteria, bar. College affiliation preferred. MC, V.*

The Arts and Nightlife

Philadelphia magazine (on newsstands), *Calendar of Events* and *Philadelphia Spotlite* (free at the Visitors Center), and the *Inquirer* and the *Daily News* (the city's daily papers) list arts and entertainment events. The **Donnelley Directory Philadelphia Events Hotline** (tel. 215/337–7777, ext. 2540) is an automatic 24-hour service.

The Arts
Theater Performances by touring companies and pre-Broadway productions can be seen at the **Shubert Theater** (250 S. Broad St., tel. 215/732–5446), the **Forrest Theater** (1114 Walnut St., tel. 215/923–1515), and the **Walnut Street Theater** (9th and Walnut Sts., tel. 215/574–3550). The **Philadelphia Drama Guild** performs at the Annenberg Center (3680 Walnut St., tel. 215/898–6791). **Freedom Theater** (1346 N. Broad St., tel. 215/765–2793) is the oldest and most active black theater in Philadelphia.

Concerts The **Philadelphia Orchestra** performs at the Academy of Music (Broad and Locust Sts., tel. 215/893–1900) in winter and at the Mann Music Center (W. Fairmount Park, tel. 215/878–7707) in summer. The **Philly Pops** (tel. 215/735–7506), conducted by Peter Nero, performs at the Academy of Music.

Opera The **Opera Company of Philadelphia** (tel. 215/981–1450) performs at the Academy of Music. **Pennsylvania Opera Theater** (1315 Walnut St., tel. 215/440–9797) is known for innovative stagings of lesser-known operas.

Dance The classical **Pennsylvania Ballet** (tel. 215/551–7014) dances at the Academy of Music. **Philadelphia Dance Company** (tel. 215/ 387–8200) performs modern dance in spring and fall.

Nightlife Call radio station WRTI's "Jazz Line" (tel. 215/787–5277) for an up-to-the-minute listing of music in town.

Bars, Lounges, and Cabarets **Chestnut Cabaret** (3801 Chestnut St., tel. 215/382–1201) is a concert hall/dance club that attracts a crowd mostly in their twenties and early thirties. **Top of the Centre Square** (15th and Market Sts., tel. 215/563–9494) has a bar with the best view in town—from 41 stories up. **Trocadero** (1003 Arch St., tel. 215/ 922–0194), a rock-and-roll club, occupies a former burlesque house where W. C. Fields and Mae West performed. **Woody's** (202 S. 13th St., tel. 215/545–1893) is the city's most popular gay bar.

Comedy **Comedy Works** (126 Chestnut St., tel. 215/922–5997) features top young comedians from both coasts.

Miscellaneous By day, **Painted Bride Art Center** (230 Vine St., tel. 215/925–9914) is an art gallery. By night, it's a club featuring performance art, readings, dance, and theater.

Excursion to Bucks County

Getting There From Philadelphia, follow I–95N to the Yardley exit, then go
north on Rte. 32 toward New Hope. The trip takes one hour.

What to See Bucks County is known for antiques, covered bridges, and
and Do country inns. **New Hope** is a hodgepodge of art galleries, old
stone houses, and shops along crooked little streets. William
Penn's reconstructed Georgian-style mansion, **Pennsbury
Manor** (U.S. 13 off Tyburn Rd., Morrisville, tel. 215/946–
0400), and **Washington Crossing Historic Park** (Rtes. 532 and
32, tel. 215/493–4076), where George Washington and his
troops crossed the river on Christmas Night 1776, are nearby.
Contact the **Bucks County Tourist Commission** (Box 912, Dept.
95, Doylestown 18901, tel. 215/345–4552) or the **New Hope Information Center** (1 W. Mechanic St., at Main St., 18938, tel.
215/862–5880) for more information.

Excursion to Valley Forge

Getting There Take the Schuylkill Expressway (I–76) west from Philadelphia
to Exit 25. Take Rte. 363 to North Gulph Road and follow signs
to Valley Forge National Historical Park, 18 mi from the city.

What to See The monuments, huts, and headquarters on the 3,500 acres of
and Do rolling hills of the **Valley Forge National Historical Park** (Rtes.
23 and 363, Valley Forge, tel. 215/783–1077) preserve the moment in American history when George Washington's Continental Army endured the bitter winter of 1777–78. Nearby
attractions include **Mill Grove** (Audubon and Paulings Rds.,
Audubon, tel. 215/666–5593), the home of naturalist John
James Audubon; the studio/residence of painter and
woodcarver **Wharton Esherick** (Horseshoe Trail, Paoli, tel.
215/644–5822); and **The Court and The Plaza** (Rte. 202 and N.
Gulph Rd., King of Prussia, tel. 215/265–5727), one of the nation's largest shopping complexes. For more information, contact the **Valley Forge Convention and Visitors Bureau** (Box 311,
Norristown 19404, tel. 215/278–3558 or 800/441–3549).

Excursion to the Brandywine Valley

Getting There Take U.S. 1S from Philadelphia about 25 mi to the valley.

What to See The Brandywine River valley has inspired generations of
and Do Wyeths and du Ponts—the Wyeths to capture its peaceful harmony on canvas, the du Ponts to recontour the landscape with
grand gardens, mansions, and mills. The **Brandywine River
Museum** (U.S. 1 and Rte. 100, Chadds Ford, tel. 215/388–
7601), in a preserved 19th-century gristmill, celebrates the
Brandywine School of artists. **Longwood Gardens** (U.S. 1,
Kennett Sq., tel. 215/388–6741), Pierre-Samuel du Pont's 350
acres of ultimate estate gardens, has established an international reputation. **Brandywine Battlefield State Park** (U.S. 1,
Chadds Ford, tel. 215/459–3342) is the site of one of the more
dramatic turns in the American Revolution. The region is dotted with antiques shops and cozy inns. **The Tourist Information
Center for the Brandywine Valley** (Box 910, Dept. VG U.S. 1,
Kennett Sq., 19348, tel. 215/388–2900 or 800/228–9933) has information.

Pennsylvania Dutch Country

First of all, the Pennsylvania Dutch aren't Dutch; the name comes from *Deutsch* (German). In the 18th century, this rolling farmland 65 mi west of Philadelphia became home to the Amish, the Mennonites, and other German and Swiss immigrants escaping religious persecution. Today their descendants continue to turn their backs on the modern world—and in doing so, attract the world's attention. In summer, busloads of tourists jam Rte. 30, the main thoroughfare. But there is still charm on the back roads, where you will discover Amish farms, hand-painted signs advertising quilts, fields worked with mules, and horse-drawn buggies.

Tourist Information

Pennsylvania Dutch Convention & Visitors Bureau (501 Greenfield Rd., Lancaster 17601, tel. 717/299–8901). **Mennonite Information Center** (2209 Millstream Rd., Lancaster 17602, tel. 717/299–0954).

Getting There

By Car   From Philadelphia (65 mi away), take the Schuylkill Expressway (I–76) west to the Pennsylvania Turnpike, leaving the pike at Exit 20, 21, or 22.

By Train   **Amtrak** has service from Philadelphia to Lancaster.

By Bus   **Greyhound** (tel. 215/931–4000) has three runs daily from Philadelphia to Lancaster.

Exploring Pennsylvania Dutch Country

In **Lancaster,** several furnished farmhouses offer simulated, up-close looks at how the Amish live, including **The Amish Homestead** (2034 Lincoln Hwy. E, tel. 717/392–0832) and **The Amish Farm and House** (2395 Lincoln Hwy. E, tel. 717/394–6185). Abe, of **Abe's Buggy Rides** (Rte. 340, Bird-in-Hand, no phone), chats about the Amish during a 2-mi spin down country roads in an Amish family carriage.

The **Historic Lancaster Walking Tour** (tel. 717/392–1776), a two-hour stroll through the heart of this charming old Colonial city, is conducted by guides who impart lively anecdotes about local architecture and history. **Central Market** (Penn Sq., tel. 717/291–4740) is one of the oldest covered markets in the country; this is where the locals shop for fresh produce, meats, and baked goods. The Old City Hall, reborn as the **Heritage Center Museum** (King and Queen St., tel. 717/299–6440), shows the work of Lancaster County artisans and craftspeople.

Wheatland (1120 Marietta Ave. [Rte. 23], 1½ mi west of Lancaster, tel. 717/392–8721), a restored 1828 Federal mansion, was the home of the only president from Pennsylvania, James Buchanan.

In **Strasburg,** the **Strasburg Railroad** (Rte. 741, tel. 717/687–7522) is a scenic 9-mi excursion in a wooden coach pulled by a steam locomotive. The **Railroad Museum of Pennsylvania** (Rte. 741, tel. 717/687–8628) features colossal engines, railcars, and memorabilia documenting railroading in the state.

In **Ephrata,** the 18th-century Protestants of the **Ephrata Cloister** (Rte. 272, tel. 717/733–6600) led an ascetic life, living examples of William Penn's "Holy Experiment." Guides now give tours of the restored medieval-style German buildings.

Lititz, west of Ephrata, was founded by Moravians who settled in Pennsylvania to do missionary work among the Native Americans. It's a lovely town with a tree-shaded main street of 18th-century cottages and shops. Pick up a Historical Foundation walking-tour brochure at the General Sutter Inn (14 E. Main St.).

Shopping

Antiques   Antiques malls are located on Rte. 272 between Adamstown and Denver, 2 mi east of Pennsylvania Turnpike Exit 21; **Barr's Auctions** (tel. 215/267–2861), **Renninger's Antique and Collector's Market** (tel. 215/267–2177), and **Stoudt's Black Angus** (tel. 215/484–4385) all feature indoor and outdoor sales.

Crafts   Places to see fine local crafts include the **Weathervane Shop** at the Landis Valley Museum (2451 Kissel Hill Rd., Lancaster, tel. 717/569–9312), **The Tin Bin** (Landis Valley Rd. and Rte. 501, Neffsville, tel. 717/569–6210), and the 28-shop **Kitchen Kettle Village** (Rte. 340, Intercourse, tel. 717/768–8261).

Farmers Markets   In addition to Lancaster's **Central Market** (*see* Exploring Pennsylvania Dutch Country, *above*), the **Green Dragon Farmers Market and Auction** (R.D. 4 just off Rte. 272, Ephrata, tel. 717/738–1117) is an old, traditional agricultural market with a country-carnival atmosphere.

Sports and Outdoor Activities

Hot-air Ballooning   **Great Adventure Balloon Club** (tel. 717/397–3623) offers a bird's-eye view of Pennsylvania Dutch Country.

Dining and Lodging

Like the German cuisine that influenced it, Pennsylvania Dutch cooking is hearty. To sample such regional fare as ham, buttered noodles, chowchow, and shoofly pie, eat at one of the bustling restaurants where diners sit with perhaps a dozen others and the food is passed around family style. A number of farm families open their homes to visitors and allow them to observe and even participate in day-to-day farm life. Most of these are heavily booked in summer. For information, contact the Convention & Visitors Bureau (*see* Tourist Information, *above*). For price ranges, see Charts 1 (B) and 2 (B) in Chapter 1.

Bird-in-Hand   **Bird-in-Hand Family Restaurant.** This family-owned spot spe-
Dining   cializes in hearty Pennsylvania Dutch home cooking. *Rte. 340, just west of N. Ronks Rd., tel. 717/768–8266. No credit cards. Closed Sun. Inexpensive.*

Churchtown   **Churchtown Inn.** This restored 1735 fieldstone mansion over-
Lodging   looking an Amish farm has cozy bedrooms with pencil-post can-
★   opy, brass, and high-back Victorian beds. A five-course

breakfast is served in the glass-enclosed garden room. *Rte. 23 between Morgantown and New Holland, 5 mi from PA Turnpike Exit 22 (Box 135, R.D. 3, Narvon 17555), tel. 215/445–7794. 8 rooms (2 share bath), 1 suite. MC, V. Moderate–Expensive.*

Ephrata
Dining

The Restaurant at Doneckers. Classic and country-French cuisine is served downstairs amid Colonial antiques and upstairs in a country garden. *333 N. State St., tel. 717/738–2421. Reservations advised. AE, DC, MC, V. Closed Wed. Moderate–Expensive.*

Lodging

Smithton Country Inn. At this B&B in a former stagecoach inn, guest rooms have handmade antiques, fireplaces, and canopy beds. Full breakfast is included in the rates. *900 W. Main St., 17522, tel. 717/733–6094. 8 rooms, 1 4-room suite. AE, MC, V. Moderate–Expensive.*

Lancaster
Dining
★

The Log Cabin. Steak, lamb chops, and seafood are prepared on a charcoal grill in this expanded log cabin, which was a speakeasy during Prohibition. The atmosphere is elegant. *11 Lehoy Forest Dr., Leola (5 mi north of Lancaster), tel. 717/626–1181. Reservations advised. Jacket advised. AE, DC, MC, V. Closed Sun. Expensive.*

Lodging

Best Western Eden Resort Inn. Spacious contemporary rooms and attractive grounds contribute to a pleasant stay here. The suites have kitchens and fireplaces. *222 Eden Rd. (U.S. 30 and Rte. 272), 17601, tel. 717/569–6444. 274 rooms, 40 suites. Facilities: 3 restaurants, disco, nightclub, indoor pool, whirlpool. AE, D, DC, MC, V. Expensive.*

Lititz
Lodging
★

Swiss Woods. This comfortable, friendly, European-style B&B on 30 acres looks like a Swiss chalet and offers contemporary country decor. *500 Blantz Rd., 17543, tel. 717/627–3358 or 800/594–8018; fax 717/627–3483. 6 rooms, 1 suite. Facilities: dining room (closed Apr.–Oct.). No smoking. D, MC, V. Moderate–Expensive.*

Mount Joy
Dining
★

Groff's Farm. Hearty Mennonite farm fare, such as chicken, farm relishes, and cracker pudding, is served in a restored 1756 farmhouse decorated with country fabrics and fresh flowers. *650 Pinkerton Rd., tel. 717/653–2048. Reservations required for dinner, advised for lunch. AE, DC, MC, V. Closed Sun.–Mon. Expensive.*

Lodging

Cameron Estate Inn. Rooms in this sprawling Federal redbrick mansion on 15 wooded acres have Oriental rugs, antique and reproduction furniture, and canopy beds; seven have working fireplaces. *1895 Donegal Springs Rd., 17552, tel. 717/653–1773. 18 rooms (2 share bath). Facilities: Continental breakfast, restaurant. AE, DC, MC, V. Moderate–Expensive.*

Strasburg
Dining

Washington House Restaurant. The restaurant at the Historic Strasburg Inn offers American cuisine by candlelight in three Colonial-style dining rooms. *Rte. 896, tel. 717/687–7691. AE, D, DC, MC, V. Moderate.*

Lodging
★

Limestone Inn. This 1786 B&B is furnished with Colonial and primitive antiques and reproductions. A multicourse breakfast is served. The proprietors are happy to set you up for dinner at a local Amish home; reserve ahead. *33 E. Main St., 17579, tel. 717/687–8392. 6 rooms. AE. Moderate–Expensive.*

Campgrounds The Convention & Visitors Bureau (*see* Tourist Information, *above*) has a list of area campgrounds. Two of the best are **Mill Bridge Village and Campresort** (½ mi south of U.S. 30 on Ronk's Rd.; Box 86, Strausberg 17579, tel. 717/687–8181), attached to a restored 18th-century village, and **Spring Gulch Resort Campground** (Rte. 897; 475 Lynch Rd., New Holland 17557, New Holland, tel. 717/354–3100).

The Arts and Nightlife

Dutch Apple Dinner Theater (510 Centerville Rd., at U.S. 30, Lancaster, tel. 717/898–1900) offers a buffet plus Broadway musicals and comedies. Plays and concerts, as well as performances by the **Lancaster Symphony Orchestra** and the **Lancaster Opera,** are presented at the **Fulton Opera House** (12 N. Prince St., Lancaster, tel. 717/394–7133), a restored 19th-century Victorian theater and National Historic Landmark.

Excursion to Reading

Getting There From Exit 22 off the Pennsylvania Turnpike, take I–276N to U.S. 422W into downtown Reading—it's about an hour from Lancaster.

What to See and Do Reading, a 19th-century industrial city, today promotes itself as the "Outlet Capital of the World." If you're in the mood for a diversion after a shopping spree, **Skyline Drive** is a meandering road with miles of unspoiled vistas and an expansive view of the city. The **Daniel Boone Homestead** (tel. 215/582–4900) is a renovation of the frontiersman's home. For information contact **Berks County Visitors Information** (VF Factory Outlet Complex, Park Rd. and Hill Ave., Box 6677, Wyomissing 19610, tel. 215/375–4085).

Excursion to Hershey

Getting There Take I–76 to Exit 20 and follow signs—it's about 45 minutes from Lancaster.

What to See and Do The streets have names like Cocoa Avenue, and the streetlights look like Hershey's Kisses. A family-oriented amusement park called **Hersheypark** (U.S. 422, tel. 717/534–3900) offers Pennsylvania Dutch, German, and English theme areas. At **Chocolate World** (Park Blvd., tel. 717/534–4900), you can take an eight-minute ride through the process of chocolate-making. Contact the **Hershey Information Center** (Hershey 17033, tel. 717/534–3005).

Excursion to Gettysburg

Getting There From Lancaster, take U.S. 30E to Gettysburg (about 1½ hours).

What to See and Do The battle of Gettysburg, in July 1863, was the turning point of the Civil War. At the **Gettysburg National Military Park** (Visitor Center, 95 Taneytown Rd., tel. 717/334–1124), you can follow the course of the fighting along roads through the battleground and on an enormous electronic map. The **Gettysburg Travel Council** (35 Carlisle St., 17325, tel. 717/334–6274) provides information on the region.

Pittsburgh

At the point where the Monongahela and Allegheny rivers meet to form the Ohio River is a natural fortress first named Ft. Pitt and later Pittsburgh. Prosperity in coal, iron, and steel made the city a giant in the industrial age—and earned it the nickname "Smoky City." Today the smoke has cleared and Pittsburgh—recently rated one of the "nation's most livable cities"—has been recast into an artful blend of turn-of-the-century architectural masterpieces and modern skyscrapers.

Tourist Information

Greater Pittsburgh: Convention and Visitors Bureau (4 Gateway Center, 15222, tel. 412/281–7711). **Visitor Information Centers:** Downtown (Gateway Center, tel. 412/281–9222), Oakland (Forbes Ave., tel. 412/624–4660), Mount Washington (Grandview Ave., tel. 412/381–5134). **Visitors Hotline** (tel. 412/456–2719).

Arriving and Departing

By Plane **Greater Pittsburgh International Airport** (tel. 412/778–2601), served by most major airlines, is 14 mi west of downtown, to which cab fare is about $27. **Airlines Transportation Co.** (tel. 412/471–8900) provides motorcoach service to the major downtown hotels for $10 one-way and $17 round-trip.

By Car From the north or south, take I–79 to I–279, which leads into downtown. From the east or west, take the Pennsylvania Turnpike (I–76), then I–376 to the Grant Street exit.

Train Station **Amtrak** (Liberty and Grant Sts., tel. 412/471–6170).

Bus Station **Greyhound** (11th St. and Liberty Ave., tel. 412/391–2300).

Getting Around Pittsburgh

Port Authority Transit operates daily bus and trolley service (tel. 412/231–5707). The downtown subway, known as the **"T"** (fare 75¢ after 7 PM), is free during the day between Gateway Center, Wood Street, Steel Plaza, and Penn Station. Two cable cars—the *Duquesne Incline,* from West Carson Street west on the Ohio River to the restaurant area of Grandview Avenue, and the *Monongahela Incline,* from Station Square on the Monongahela to Grandview Avenue—carry passengers from river level to the hilly south side of the city.

Exploring Pittsburgh

Downtown, a triangle framed by the three rivers, contains **Point State Park** (*see* Parks and Gardens, *below*) and major hotels, restaurants, and theaters. **PPG Place** (Stanwix St. and 4th Ave.), with its spires and towers that evoke a medieval castle, exemplifies the Pittsburgh renaissance, as do the beautifully restored or maintained commercial and public buildings from the early boom days. Chief among these are **Two Mellon Bank Center** (5th Ave. and Grant St.), Daniel Burnam's Union Station, now **The Pennsylvanian** (Grant St. and Liberty Ave.), the **Oliver Building** (6th Ave. and Smithfield St.), and H.H. Richardson's great **Allegheny County Courthouse and Jail** (5th

Pittsburgh

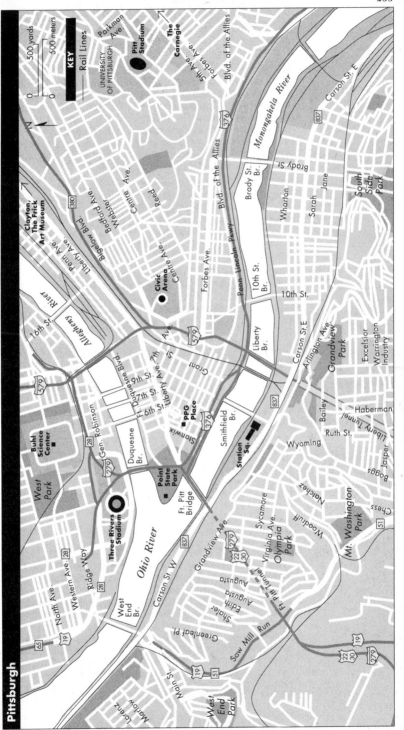

Ave. and Grant St.). **Station Square** (tel. 412/471–5808), on the Monongahela across the Smithfield Bridge, is a restored turn-of-the-century rail station with boutiques, restaurants (*see* Dining, *below*), and nightclubs.

East of downtown, **Oakland** is the headquarters of many of the city's cultural, educational, and medical landmarks. **The Carnegie** is an opulent cultural center with the **Museum of Art,** the **Museum of Natural History,** the **Music Hall,** and the **Carnegie Library** all under one Beaux Arts roof. Don't miss the 19th-century French and American paintings; the Hall of Architecture, which re-creates in plaster some of the world's architectural masterpieces; the dinosaur collection; and the extravagant Music Hall lobby. *4400 Forbes Ave., tel. 412/622–3131; tours, tel. 412/622–3289.*

The Frick Art & Historical Center (7200 Penn Ave., tel. 412/ 371–0606 or 412/371–0600) consists of **Clayton,** the turn-of-the-century home of Henry Clay Frick that preserves the original furnishings and art, a carriage museum, and **The Frick Art Museum,** which possesses a small, choice collection of Old Master works.

The huge **Three Rivers Stadium** commands the north side of the Allegheny River. In the neighborhood is The Carnegie's **Buhl Science Center** (Allegheny Center, tel. 412/237–3300), an indoor amusement park with hands-on science adventures.

In the Vicinity Northeast of Pittsburgh, the **Laurel Highlands** region has Revolutionary War–era forts and battlefields, restored inns and taverns, lush mountain scenery, and **Fallingwater** (Rte. 381, Mill Run, tel. 412/329–8501), the acclaimed stone, concrete, and glass house that Frank Lloyd Wright built over a waterfall. The Highlands are also noted for whitewater rafting, hiking, and other recreational pleasures. Contact **Laurel Highlands, Inc.** (Ligonier Town Hall, 120 E. Main St., Ligonier 15658, tel. 412/238–5661).

Parks and Gardens

In the 36-acre **Point State Park** is the **Ft. Pitt Blockhouse** and **Ft. Pitt Museum** (tel. 412/281–9284). **Schenley Park** has a lake, trails, golf, and cross-country skiing. **Phipps Conservatory** (Schenley Park, tel. 412/622–6915) is Henry Phipps's Victorian gardens—outdoors and under glass.

Shopping

Pittsburgh's best downtown department stores are **Saks Fifth Avenue** (513 Smithfield St.), **Horne's** (200 Stanwink St.), and **Kaufmann's** (5th Ave. and Smithfield St.). Nearby are the shopping complexes **Fifth Avenue Place, 1 Oxford Centre** on Grant Street, and **PPG Place.** In the **Strip District** (betweeen Liberty and Penn Aves. and 7th and 10th Sts.) are streets lined with farmers' market stalls, imported foods, and dry-goods merchants. Antiques shops and art galleries are along Carson Street East on the South Side. In **The Shops at Station Square** (*see* Exploring Pittsburgh, *above*) are 70 shops and restaurants.

Spectator Sports

Baseball **Pittsburgh Pirates** (Three Rivers Stadium, 400 Stadium Cir., tel. 412/321–2827 or 800/321–2827; Apr.–Oct.).

Football **Pittsburgh Steelers** (Three Rivers Stadium, tel. 412/323–1200; Nov.–Apr.).

Hockey **Pittsburgh Penguins** (Civic Arena, Center Ave. and Auditorium Pl., tel. 412/642–7367; Oct.–Apr.).

Dining

For price ranges, see Chart 1 (B) in Chapter 1.

Expensive **Common Plea.** This restaurant courts many of the city's lawyers and judges in its two dining rooms—one subdued in dark wood, the other flashy with glass and mirrors. Recommended are the fresh seafood and the veal dishes, including veal Romano (tender veal sautéed in an egg-and-Romano-cheese batter). *310 Ross St., tel. 412/281–5140. Reservations advised. Jacket and tie advised. AE, DC, MC, V.*

★ **The Grand Concourse/Gandy Dancer Saloon.** Set in a dazzling restored Beaux Arts railroad terminal, the restaurant features seafood, homemade pastas, and gracious service. In the Saloon, the emphasis is on raw-bar platters and lighter dishes. *1 Station Sq., Carson and Smithfield Sts., tel. 412/261–1717. Reservations advised. AE, D, DC, MC, V.*

★ **LeMont Restaurant.** The emphasis is on Italian and French cuisine, served in quietly classic contemporary surroundings with a spectacular view of the downtown triangle. *1114 Grandview Ave., tel. 412/431–3100. Reservations essential. Jacket required. AE, D, DC, MC, V. No lunch.*

Moderate **The Georgetowne Inn.** Wraparound windows offer a majestic view from the Colonial-style dining rooms. The quality of the American food is exceptional; the low-key atmosphere makes this a good place to take the family. *1230 Grandview Ave., tel. 412/481–4424. AE, DC, MC, V. No lunch Sun.*

Inexpensive **Gallagher's Pub.** In this relaxed neighborhood hangout, salads, burgers, hoagies, and Irish stew are on the menu. *2 S. Market Sq., tel. 412/261–5554. AE, DC, MC, V. Closed Sun.*

★ **Richest Restaurant.** Long, narrow, and evocative of the decade it opened, this kosher-style deli established in 1936 serves up classic deli fare in the heart of the cultural district. *140 6th St., tel. 412/471–7799. AE, D, DC, MC, V. Closed Sun.*

Lodging

Choice hotels are limited in downtown Pittsburgh—and most are pricey. Nationally affiliated hotels are located in Oakland and in outlying suburban areas. For price ranges, see Chart 2 (B) in Chapter 1.

Expensive **Vista International.** The dramatically designed lobby leads to a 21-story tower where the rooms have contemporary decor. *1000 Penn Ave., 15222, tel. 412/281–3700 or 800/445–8667. 584 rooms, 36 suites. Facilities: restaurant, lounge, fitness center, pool. AE, D, DC, MC, V.*

★ **Westin William Penn.** Pittsburgh's grand hotel, anything but stuffy, has a sumptuous lobby with coffered ceiling, intricate plasterwork, and crystal chandeliers. It is always filled with peo-

ple relaxing over drinks or designer coffee from the resident
espresso bar. The guest rooms are light-filled and large enough
for a couch and wing chair. *530 William Penn Pl., Mellon Sq.,
15230, tel. 412/281–7100. 595 rooms, 47 suites. Facilities: 2 restaurants, lounge, spa, beauty salon. AE, D, DC, MC, V.*

Moderate   **Holiday Inn—At University Center.** At this modern, 10-story
hotel adjacent to the University of Pittsburgh, guest rooms are
furnished in contemporary style. *100 Lytton Ave., 15213, tel.
412/682–6200. 253 rooms. Facilities: restaurant, lounge, pool,
sauna. AE, D, DC, MC, V.*

★   **The Priory.** This European-style hotel is furnished with antiques and reproductions. A hearty Continental breakfast is
served. *614 Pressley St., 15212, tel. 412/231–3338. 24 rooms.
AE, D, DC, MC, V.*

Inexpensive   **Clubhouse Inn Pittsburgh.** At this garden-style hotel 5 mi from
★   the airport, guest rooms overlook a courtyard. The breakfast
buffet is complimentary. *5311 Campbells Run Rd., 15205, tel.
412/788–8400. 126 rooms, 26 suites. Facilities: pool, free airport transportation. AE, D, DC, MC, V.*

Howard Johnson Hotel University Center. This modern nine-story hotel in the heart of Oakland provides easy access to the university and the museum district. *3401 Blvd. of the Allies,
15213, tel. 412/683–6100 or 800/245–4444. 119 rooms. Facilities: restaurant, lounge, pool. AE, D, DC, MC, V.*

The Arts and Nightlife

The Arts   The **Pittsburgh Symphony Orchestra** appears at the Heinz Hall
for the Performing Arts (tel. 412/392–4800). The **Pittsburgh
Opera** (tel. 412/281–0912) and the **Pittsburgh Ballet** (tel. 412/
281–0360) are at the Benedum Center for the Performing Arts
(tel. 412/456–6666). **The Pittsburgh Playhouse Theatre Center**
(tel. 412/621–4445) presents theater, dance, and films.

Nightlife   Station Square (Carson at Smithfield St.) has **Chauncy's** (tel.
412/232–0601) for dining and dancing, the **FunnyBone Comedy
Club** (tel. 412/281–3130), and **Pittsburgh Sports Garden** (tel.
412/281–1511), a sports-theme entertainment center.

Elsewhere in the State

The Poconos

Getting There   I–80W leads to Delaware Water Gap, I–84W to Milford. From
the south, U.S. 611N skirts the Delaware River and takes you
into Stroudsburg. Stroudsburg is 98 mi from Philadelphia, 135
mi from Harrisburg, and 318 mi from Pittsburgh by road.

What to See   The Poconos, in the northeast corner of the state, encompass
and Do   2,400 sq mi of mountainous wilderness bordering the Delaware
River, with lakes, streams, waterfalls, resorts, and enchanting
country inns. A back-roads drive will turn up quaint villages
such as **Jim Thorpe** (Rte. 209), a late-Victorian mountain-re-
sort town that has first-rate antiques shops and galleries. Winter brings downhill and cross-country skiing, skating, and
snowmobiling; summer offers golf, boating, horseback riding,
and hiking. **Pocono Mountain Vacation Bureau** (Box CIB,
Stroudsburg 18360, tel. 717/424–6050 or 800/762–6667) provides information.

VIRGINIA

By Francis X.
Rocca

Capital   Richmond
Population   6,015,100
Motto   Thus Always to Tyrants
State Bird   Cardinal
State Flower   Dogwood

Visitor Information

Virginia Division of Tourism (1021 E. Cary St., Richmond 23219, tel. 804/786–2051 or 800/932–5827). **Welcome centers:** in Bracey (on I–85), Bristol (I–81), Clearbrook (I–81), Covington (I–64), Fredericksburg (I–95), Lambsburg (I–77), Manassas (I–66), New Church (U.S. 13), Rocky Gap (I–77), and Skippers (I–95).

Scenic Drives

Skyline Drive, the **Blue Ridge Parkway,** and **Goshen Pass** offer spectacular mountain scenery (*see* Western Virginia, *below*). A 25-mi drive north along **Rte. 20** from Charlottesville to Orange takes you through gently rolling green countryside, past horse farms and vineyards. For a stirring panorama of the famous buildings and monuments of Washington, D.C., drive north from Alexandria on the **George Washington Memorial Parkway.** Between Virginia Beach and the Eastern Shore stretches the 17½-mi **Chesapeake Bay Bridge-Tunnel,** where you are surrounded by sea without leaving your car; there is an observation pier and a restaurant along the way.

National and State Parks

National Parks   **Shenandoah National Park** (Rte. 4, Box 348, Luray 22835, tel. 703/999–2266)—195,000 acres with a vertical change in elevation of 3,500 feet—offers hiking, horseback riding, and fishing. Also in western Virginia are the 1.5-million-acre **George Washington National Forest** (Harrison Plaza, Box 233, Harrisonburg 22801, tel. 703/433–2491) and the 700,000-acre **Jefferson National Forest** (210 Franklin Rd. SW, Roanoke 24001, tel. 703/982–6270), which offer camping, boating, hiking, fishing, swimming, hunting, and horseback riding; and **Mt. Rogers National Recreation Area** (Rte. 1, Box 303, Marion 24354, tel. 703/783–5196), with 116,000 acres, including the state's highest point—5,729 feet above sea level.

State Parks   The **Division of Conservation and Recreation** (203 Governor St., Richmond 23219, tel. 804/786–1712) has information on Virginia's 35 state parks, which range in size from 500 to 4,500 acres. **Douthat State Park** (Rte. 1, Box 212, Millboro 24460, no phone) and **Seashore State Park** (2500 Shore Dr., Virginia Beach 23451, no phone) are the most popular.

Western Virginia

Residents of Charlottesville, in the Piedmont region of rolling plains, call it "Mr. Jefferson's Country." They speak of "The Sage of Monticello" as if he were still writing, building, and governing. Yet aware as it is of its past, Charlottesville is anything but backward. Home to the state university, and a fashionable retreat for tycoons and movie stars, it is one of America's most sophisticated small cities, often called the Santa Fe of the East.

In and along the Shenandoah Valley are small towns that were once frontier outposts; well-traveled driving routes with turnouts overlooking breathtaking scenery; many opportunities for outdoor recreation, on water and solid ground; and accommodations and restaurants to suit all tastes.

Tourist Information

Bath County: Chamber of Commerce (Rte. 220, Box 718, Hot Springs 24445, tel. 703/839–5409). **Roanoke Valley:** Convention and Visitors Bureau (114 Market St., Box 1710, Roanoke 24008, tel. 703/342–6025). **Shenandoah Valley:** Tourist Information Center (Box 1040, New Market 22844, tel. 703/740–3132). **Charlottesville:** Thomas Jefferson Visitors Bureau and Center (Rte. 20, Box 161, 22902, tel. 804/977–1783). **Lexington:** Visitor Center (102 E. Washington St., 24450, tel. 703/463–3777). **Winchester:** Chamber of Commerce (1360 S. Pleasant Valley Rd., 22601, tel. 703/662–4135 or 800/662–1360).

Getting There

By Plane **Charlottesville-Albemarle Airport** (tel. 804/973–8341) is 8 mi north of town on Rte. 29. **Roanoke Regional Airport** (tel. 703/362–1999) is 6 mi north of town on Rte. 581.

By Car Charlottesville is where U.S. 29 (north–south) meets I–64. I–81 and U.S. 11 run north–south the length of the Shenandoah Valley and continue south into Tennessee. I–66 meets I–81 and U.S. 11 at the northern end of the valley; I–64 connects the same highways with Charlottesville. Rte. 39 into Bath County connects with I–81 just north of Lexington.

By Train **Amtrak** has service to Charlottesville's Union Station (810 W. Main St., tel. 804/296–4559), to Clifton Forge (for The Homestead resort in Bath County), and to Staunton.

By Bus **Greyhound** serves Charlottesville (310 W. Main St., tel. 804/295–5131), Lexington (tel. 804/254–5937), Roanoke (26 Salem Ave., tel. 703/342–6761), and Staunton (1211 Richmond Rd., tel. 703/886–2424).

Exploring Western Virginia

Charlottesville Jefferson built his beloved **Monticello** on a "little mountain" over a period of 40 years, 1769–1809. In the details and the overall conception, Monticello was a revolutionary structure, a neoclassical repudiation of the Colonial style with all its political connotations. Throughout the house are Jefferson's inventions, including a seven-day clock and a two-pen contraption for copying letters as he wrote them. It is impossible to see it all in one visit. *Rte. 53, tel. 804/295–8181 or 804/295–2657. Admission charged.*

Next door is a more modest presidential residence, James Monroe's **Ash Lawn.** The cozy rooms evoke the fifth president—our first to spring from the middle class. Outside, peacocks roam the grounds of this working plantation. *James Monroe Pkwy. (southwest of Rte. 53), tel. 804/293–9539. Admission charged.*

The nearby **Historic Michie Tavern** is an 18th-century building moved here in the 1920s from a neighboring location. The period rooms are a bit too tidy but otherwise convincing. *Rte. 53, tel. 804/977–1234. Admission charged.*

There is little to see in downtown Charlottesville besides a pedestrian shopping mall that takes up six brick-paved blocks of Main Street. At the west end of town is the **University of Virginia** (tel. 804/924–7969), founded and designed by Thomas Jefferson and still widely acclaimed as "the proudest achievement in American architecture." Pavilions flank the lawn as it flows down from the Rotunda, a half-scale replica of the Pantheon in Rome. Behind the pavilions, gardens and landscaping are laced with serpentine walls.

The Shenandoah Valley At the top of the valley, and almost at the northernmost tip of the state, is **Winchester.** Because of its strategic location, the town has drawn more than its share of military action over the years. A young Colonel George Washington spent over a year here during the French and Indian War; the log cabin he worked out of is now **George Washington's Office Museum** (Braddock and Cork Sts., tel. 703/662–4412). Up the street is **Stonewall Jackson's Headquarters** (415 N. Braddock St., tel. 703/667–3242), where the Confederate general planned the First Battle of Winchester (there were eventually three). The town is the site of happier activity, including parades and a beauty pageant, during the **Shenandoah Apple Blossom Festival** every May (tel. 703/665–0765). September is apple time at pick-your-own orchards throughout the surrounding countryside.

Belle Grove, just south of Middletown, is a grand 1790s house designed with the help of Thomas Jefferson. It served as headquarters for the victorious Union general Philip Sheridan during the Battle of Cedar Creek (1864) and is today a working farm. *U.S. 11, tel. 703/869–2028. Admission charged.*

Shenandoah National Park (*see* National and State Parks, *above*), encompassing some 60 peaks, runs more than 80 mi along the Blue Ridge, south from Front Royal to Waynesboro. Mountain meadows open up to gorgeous views of the range. Hiking, camping, fishing, and horseback riding are all available. For information on seasonal activities, pick up the free *Shenandoah Overlook* upon entering the park.

Skyline Drive winds 105 mi over the mountains of the park, affording panoramas of the valley to the west and the rolling country of the Piedmont to the east. On holidays and weekends in spring and fall, crowds slow down traffic to much less than the maximum of 35 mph. Many lodges, campsites, and eating places, and sometimes stretches of the drive itself, are closed from November through April.

Luray Caverns, the largest caves in the state, are just west of Skyline Drive. Water seepage over millions of years has created striking rock and mineral formations. Tours begin every 20 minutes. *Rte. 211, Luray, tel. 703/743–6551. Admission charged.*

At **New Market,** the site of a costly Confederate victory late in the Civil War, the **New Market Battlefield Historical Park** has exhibits on the battle and the war. *I–81 Exit 67, tel. 703/740–3102. Admission charged.*

In **Staunton** (pronounced *"Stan-*ton"), the **Woodrow Wilson House** (24 N. Coalter St., tel. 703/885–0897) has been restored to its appearance in 1856, when the 28th U.S. president was born here. Just outside town is the **Museum of American Frontier Culture** (230 Frontier Dr., tel. 703/332–7850), an outdoor living museum that re-creates early American agrarian life on four genuine 18th-century farmsteads, right down to the animals and crops.

The 470-mi **Blue Ridge Parkway,** a continuation of Skyline Drive, runs south through the **George Washington National Forest** (*see* National and State Parks, *above*) to Great Smoky Mountains National Park in North Carolina and Tennessee. Less pristine than the drive, the parkway offers better, higher views—and free admission. **Peaks of Otter Recreation Area,** just off the parkway northeast of Roanoke, offers a 360-degree panorama.

In **Lexington,** the sixth-oldest college in the country, **Washington and Lee University,** is named for the first U.S. president (an early benefactor) and the Confederate commander Robert E. Lee, who served as college president after the Civil War. Among the campus's white-columned redbrick buildings is the **Lee Memorial Chapel and Museum** (tel. 703/463–8768; admission free), where a saintly statue of the recumbent general behind the altar marks his tomb.

Next door are the imposing neo-Gothic buildings of the all-male **Virginia Military Institute,** established in 1839. Here the **George C. Marshall Museum** (tel. 703/463–7103; admission free) preserves the memory of the general, secretary of state, and Nobel Peace Prize winner. On display at the **Institute Museum** (tel. 703/464–7232; admission free) is Stonewall Jackson's horse, stuffed and mounted. Jackson's private life can be glimpsed nearby at the **Stonewall Jackson House** (8 E. Washington St., tel. 703/463–2552; admission charged).

Between Lexington and **Bath County** (the site of thermal springs once used for medical treatments and still a popular resort area) runs **Goshen Pass,** a stunning 3-mi stretch of Rte. 39 that follows the Maury River as it winds its way through the Alleghenies. The countryside is lush with rhododendrons in May.

Natural Bridge, south of Lexington, is a 215-foot-high, 90-foot-long arch gradually carved out of limestone by the creek below it. It really *is* a bridge, supporting U.S. 11. *I–81 Exit 49 or 50, tel. 703/291–2121. Admission charged.*

Roanoke is a quiet and cheerful railroad hub. A restored downtown warehouse called **Center in the Square** (Market Sq., tel. 703/342–5700) houses a theater, a local historical museum, an art gallery, and a science museum with a planetarium. A stroll away is the **Virginia Museum of Transportation** (303 Norfolk

Ave., tel. 703/342–5670; admission charged), where dozens of original train cars and engines are on display.

A restored plantation southeast of Roanoke, **Booker T. Washington National Monument,** is the birthplace of the great black educator and a living museum of life under slavery. *Rte. 122, tel. 703/721–2094. Admission charged.*

About two hours east of Roanoke, and less than two hours south of Charlottesville, is the village of **Appomattox Court House,** restored to its appearance on April 9, 1865, when Lee surrendered to Grant in the parlor of the McLean house here. A slide show supplements a self-guided tour, and costumed interpreters answer questions in summer. *Rte. 24, tel. 804/352–8987. Admission charged.*

What to See and Do with Children

At Charlottesville's **Virginia Discovery Museum** (400 Ackley La., tel. 804/293–5528), children can step inside a giant kaleidoscope or an authentic log cabin; plays and concerts are also performed here. The **Science Museum of Western Virginia** in Roanoke (Market Sq., tel. 703/342–5726) offers interactive exhibits, including computer games, that entertain youngsters while informing them on such topics as energy resources and natural history.

Shopping

Lewis Glaser Quill Pens (107 W. Main St., Charlottesville, tel. 804/293–8531) sells feather pens and pewter inkwells of the kind it has made for the U.S. Supreme Court and the British royal family. **Paula Lewis** (4th and Jefferson Sts., Charlottesville, tel. 804/295–6244) specializes in quilts by the Amish and Mennonite communities of Pennsylvania and Ohio.

Sports and Outdoor Activities

Canoeing **Front Royal Canoe** (Rte. 340, tel. 703/635–5440) and **Downriver Canoe** (Rte. 613, tel. 703/635–5526) are both near Front Royal. **Shenandoah River Outfitters** (Rte. 3, tel. 703/743–4159) is near Luray.

Fishing To take advantage of the abundance of trout in some 50 streams of **Shenandoah National Park,** get a five-day Virginia fishing license, available in season (early Apr.–mid-Oct.) at concession stands along Skyline Drive.

Golf **Caverns Country Club Resort** (Rte. 211, Luray, tel. 703/743–6551). **Greene Hills Golf Club** (Rte. 619, Stanardsville, tel. 804/985–7328). **The Homestead** (Rte. 220, Hot Springs, tel. 703/839–5500 or 800/336–5771). **Wintergreen** (Rte. 664, Nellysford, tel. 804/325–2200 or 800/325–2200).

Hiking The stretch of the **Appalachian Trail** running through Shenandoah National Park takes hikers along the Blue Ridge skyline, offering stunning views of the Piedmont and the Shenandoah Valley in the distance; white-tailed deer often appear at arm's length. The main pathway's proximity to Skyline Drive and frequent parking lots make hike lengths flexible. For deep wilderness, 500 mi of marked side trails lead into the backcountry.

Skiing **The Homestead** (*see* Golf, *above*) has cross-country, downhill, and night skiing. **Massanutten Village Ski Resort** (Rte. 33, McGaheysville, tel. 703/289–9441) offers rentals and snowmaking. **Wintergreen** (*see* Golf, *above*) maintains 17 slopes and trails.

Tennis **Caverns Country Club Resort, The Homestead,** and **Wintergreen** (*see* Golf, *above*) also offer tennis.

Spectator Sports

The **University of Virginia** (tel. 804/924–8821) is nationally or regionally ranked in several varsity sports. The *Cavalier Daily* has listings.

Equestrian Events The **Virginia Horse Center** (Lexington, tel. 703/463–2194) stages show jumping, hunter trials, and multibreed shows year-round.

Dining and Lodging

B&B reservations in the region can be made through **Bed & Breakfasts of the Historic Shenandoah Valley** (402 N. Main St., Woodstock 22664, tel. 703/459–4828), **Blue Ridge Bed & Breakfast** (Box 3895, Berryville 22611, tel. 703/955–1246), **Guesthouse Bed & Breakfast** (Box 5737, Charlottesville 22905, tel. 804/979–7264), and **Virginia's Inns of the Shenandoah Valley** (Box 1387, Staunton 24401, tel. 703/332–3972).

For price ranges, see Charts 1 (B) and 2 (B) in Chapter 1.

Bath County **The Homestead.** Famous for its mineral waters since 1766, this
Dining and Lodging is today one of the country's most luxurious resorts. The spacious guest rooms have Victorian decor. The 15,000-acre property includes 100 mi of riding trails, four ski slopes, and 4 mi of streams stocked with rainbow trout. In the formal dining room a dance band plays every night. *Rte. 220, Hot Springs 24445, tel. 703/839–5500 or 800/336–5771; fax 703/839–7670. 592 rooms. Facilities: 7 restaurants, indoor pool, 2 outdoor pools, 3 golf courses, 19 tennis courts, bowling alley, spa, horseback riding, skiing, fishing. AE, MC, V. Expensive.*
Inn at Gristmill Square. These five buildings (gristmill, miller's house, country store, blacksmith's house, and hardware store) are a state historic landmark; a walk-in wine cellar is set among the gears of the original waterwheel. Entrées may include such dishes as breast of chicken stuffed with wild rice, sausage, apple, and pecans. The guest rooms are done in a rustic Colonial Virginia motif. *Rte. 645, Box 359, Warm Springs 24484, tel. 703/839–2231. 11 rooms, 2 suites, 2 apartments. Facilities: restaurant (reservations advised), 3 tennis courts, outdoor pool, sauna. MC, V. Expensive.*

Blue Ridge **Doe Run Lodge.** The location, on the crest of the Blue Ridge,
Parkway means grand vistas of the Piedmont and proximity to golf, ski-
Lodging ing, and hunting. Each rustic condominium unit or villa has a fireplace and floor-to-ceiling windows. *Mile Post 189, Rte. 2, Box 338, Hillsville 24343, tel. 703/398–2212; fax 703/398–2833. 39 apartments, 2 villas. Facilities: restaurant, 3 tennis courts, outdoor pool, sauna, stocked fishing pond. MC, V. Expensive.*
Wintergreen. From December through February, guests at this 11,000-acre resort may ski and golf on the same day; and there are plenty of sports options all year long. Accommoda-

tions range from studio apartments to six-bedroom houses, all wood buildings that blend in with the leafy surroundings. *Rte. 664, Box 706, Wintergreen 22958, tel. 804/325–2200 or 800/325–2200; fax 804/325–6760. 330 units. Facilities: 6 restaurants, bar, indoor pool, 5 outdoor pools, 25 tennis courts, lake, 2 golf courses, 17 ski slopes and trails, 25 mi of hiking trails, exercise room, sauna. AE, MC, V. Expensive.*

Rocky Knob Cabins. These log cabins, hidden away in the woods a short hike from spectacular Rock Castle Gorge, have kitchens but no bathtubs or phones. *Mile Post 174, Box 5, Meadows of Dan 24120, tel. 703/593–3503. 7 cabins. DC, MC, V. Closed Labor Day–Memorial Day. Inexpensive.*

Charlottesville
Dining

C&O Restaurant. A boarded-up storefront hung with an illuminated Pepsi sign conceals a stark-white formal dining room. Appetizers include *terrine de campagne* (pâté of veal, venison, and pork). Among the entrées is coquilles St. Jacques. The informal bistro downstairs serves light meals. *515 E. Water St., tel. 804/971–7044. Reservations required upstairs; no reservations downstairs. Jacket and tie required upstairs. MC, V. Closed Sun. Expensive.*

Eastern Standard. Specialties served in the casual but subdued upstairs dining room include rainbow trout stuffed with shiitake mushrooms, wild rice, and fontina cheese; and loin of lamb with mint pesto. The lively downstairs bistro serves pastas and light fare. *Downtown Mall, tel. 804/295–8668. Reservations advised. MC, V. No lunch; upstairs closed Sun.–Wed. Moderate.*

Crozet Pizza. There are up to 30 toppings to choose from, including snow peas and asparagus spears in season. The hardwood booths are always full, and takeout must be ordered hours in advance. *Rte. 240, Crozet, west of Charlottesville, tel. 804/823–2132. Reservations advised. No credit cards. Closed Sun.–Mon. Inexpensive.*

Dining and Lodging

Boar's Head Inn. At this resort built around a restored early 19th-century gristmill set on two small lakes, the simple but elegant guest rooms are furnished chiefly with Victorian antiques. Some suites have fireplaces. *U.S. 250W, Box 5307, 22905, tel. 804/296–2181 or 800/476–1988; fax 804/977–1306. 173 rooms, 11 suites. Facilities: 3 restaurants, 3 pools, 17 tennis courts, 3 squash courts, biking, fishing, hot-air ballooning. AE, D, DC, MC, V. Expensive.*

Silver Thatch Inn. The interior of this 18th-century farmhouse is decorated in Colonial Americana, each guest room unique. In the restaurant, provisioned by three organic farms, the fish is always fresh and the rabbits and chickens are locally raised. The wine cellar wins national awards. *3001 Hollymead Dr., 22901, tel. 804/978–4686; fax 804/973–6156. 7 rooms. Facilities: restaurant, outdoor pool, 2 tennis courts. MC, V. Expensive.*

English Inn. This large-scale B&B has a Tudor-style lobby, but the guest rooms are in decor; modern suites have sitting rooms and reproduction antiques. *2000 Morton Dr., 22901, tel. 804/971–9900; fax 804/977–8008. 67 rooms, 21 suites. Facilities: Continental breakfast, indoor pool, sauna, exercise equipment. AE, DC, MC, V. Moderate.*

Lexington
Dining and Lodging

Maple Hall. In this mid-19th-century plantation house set on 56 acres, guest rooms are furnished with period antiques and modern amenities. The main dining room has a large fireplace.

Notable entrées include beef fillet with a green-peppercorn sauce. *Rte. 11, 11 N. Main St., 24450, tel. 703/463–2044; fax 703/463–7262. 21 rooms. Facilities: restaurant (reservations advised; no lunch), hiking trails, fishing pond, outdoor pool, tennis court. MC, V. Expensive.*

Roanoke
Dining

La Maison du Gourmet. The 12 dining rooms in this 1927 Georgian Colonial–style house range from grand to cozy. Filet mignon is flambéed tableside and served as steak Diane. Veal, chicken, and lamb are among the alternatives. *5732 Airport Rd., tel. 703/366–2444. Reservations advised. AE, D, DC, MC, V. No lunch weekends. Expensive.*

Texas Tavern. The sign says "We serve a thousand, ten at a time." The tavern is often packed, especially at night, so you may have to wait for one of the 10 stools; but the tough-looking guys behind the counter will fill your order quickly. Chili is the specialty. *114 Church Ave., tel. 703/342–4825. No reservations. No liquor. No credit cards. Inexpensive.*

Staunton
Dining

Rowe's Family Restaurant. This bright dining room filled with booths has been operated by the same family since 1947. Specialties include Virginia ham, steak, chicken, and homemade pies (try the mincemeat). *I–81 Exit 222, tel. 703/886–1833. D, MC, V. Moderate.*

Lodging

Frederick House. Three restored town houses dating from 1810 make up this inn in the center of the historic district. Guest rooms are decorated with antiques. *18 E. Frederick St., 24401, tel. 703/885–4220. 14 rooms. Facilities: full breakfast. No smoking. AE, D, DC, MC, V. Moderate.*

Dining and Lodging

Belle Grae Inn. The classic Continental entrées include grilled lamb chops with mint sauce and grilled medallions of beef with béarnaise sauce. The dining rooms in this restored Victorian house are appointed with brass wall sconces and Oriental rugs. Guest rooms feature rocking chairs and canopy or brass beds. *515 W. Frederick St., 24401, tel. 703/886–5151; fax 703/886–6641. 16 rooms. Facilities: full breakfast, restaurant (reservations advised; closed Mon.–Tues.). AE, DC, MC, V. Expensive.*

Motels

Holiday Inn Civic Center (501 Orange Ave., Roanoke 24016, tel. 703/342–8961 or 800/465–4329; fax: 703/342–8961 ext. 121), 153 rooms, restaurant, bar, outdoor pool, parking; moderate. **Roseloe Motel** (Rte. 2, Box 590, Hot Springs 24445, tel. 703/839–5373), 14 rooms, parking; inexpensive.

Campgrounds

In **Shenandoah National Park,** the **Big Meadows Campground** (tel. 800/365–2267) accepts reservations. Other campsites in the park are available on a first-come, first-served basis; for information, contact the park.

The Arts and Nightlife

The Arts
Charlottesville

For details on performances at the University of Virginia, check the *Cavalier Daily*. **McGuffey Art Center** (201 2nd St. NW, tel. 804/295–7973), which houses the studios of painters and sculptors, also hosts concerts and plays.

Shenandoah Valley

Garth Newel Music Center (Hot Springs, tel. 703/839–5018) hosts chamber-music concerts on summer weekends. **Lime Kiln Arts Theater** (Lexington, tel. 703/463–3074) is an outdoor rock-wall pit—the ruins of a lime kiln—where plays and concerts (folk and classical) are performed throughout the summer. **Roanoke Ballet Theatre** (tel. 703/345–6099) performs in spring and fall. **Roanoke Valley Chamber Music Society** (tel. 703/774–2899) hosts visiting performers from October to May.

Nightlife In Charlottesville, the large and comfortable **Miller's** (109 W. Main St., Downtown Mall, tel. 804/971–8511) hosts folk and jazz musicians. In Roanoke, **Billy's Ritz** (102 Salem Ave., tel. 703/342–3937) has pop music and a young professional crowd. At **The Homestead** in Hot Springs (*see* Dining and Lodging, *above*), there's ballroom dancing to live music nightly.

Northern Virginia

The affluent and cosmopolitan residents of this region look more to neighboring Washington, D.C., than to the rest of the Commonwealth for direction. Yet they take pride in being Virginians and in protecting the historic treasures they hold in trust for the rest of the nation. Here is found some of America's most precious acreage, including Mount Vernon and the Civil War battlefield of Manassas (Bull Run). The real estate is valuable in a less exalted sense, too: Tysons Corner in Fairfax County is said to have more commercial office space than Miami, Florida. The gracious Old South lives on, however, in the fox hunting and steeplechases of Loudoun County. On the nearby Northern Neck, visitors can combine historic sightseeing with fishing and water sports.

Tourist Information

Fairfax County: Tourism and Convention Bureau (8300 Boone Blvd., Suite 450, Vienna 22182, tel. 703/790–3329). **Loudoun County:** Visitor Center (108D South St. SE, Leesburg 22075, tel. 703/777–0519). **Northern Neck:** Travel Council (Box 312, Reedville 22539, tel. 800/453–6167). **Alexandria:** Convention and Visitor's Bureau (221 King St., 22314, tel. 703/838–4200). **Fredericksburg:** Visitor Center (706 Caroline St., 22401, tel. 703/373–1776).

Getting There

By Plane Two major airports serve both northern Virginia and the Washington, D.C., area. The busy and often crowded **Washington National Airport** (tel. 703/685–8000) in Arlington has scheduled daily flights by all major U.S. carriers. **Dulles International Airport** (tel. 703/661–2700) in Loudoun County, 26 mi west of Washington, is a modern facility served by the major U.S. airlines and many international carriers.

By Car I–95 runs north–south along the eastern side of the region. I–66 runs east–west. Fredericksburg is 50 mi south of Washington, D.C., on I–95. Rte. 3 runs the length of the Northern Neck.

By Train **Amtrak** stops in Alexandria (110 Callahan Dr., tel. 703/836–4339) and Fredericksburg (Caroline St. and Lafayette Blvd., tel. 703/786–0160).

By Bus **Greyhound** serves Fairfax (4103 Rust St., tel. 703/273–7770), Fredericksburg (1400 Jefferson Davis Hwy., tel. 703/373–2103), and Springfield (6583 Backlick Rd., tel. 703/451–5800).

Exploring Northern Virginia

George Washington's **Mount Vernon** is the most visited house museum in the country. The elegant, porticoed farmhouse, built from Washington's own plans starting in 1754, has been restored to its appearance during the years (1759–75, 1783–89, and 1797–99) the first president lived here. And here, in the land they loved, Washington and his wife, Martha, are buried. *Rte. 235, tel. 703/780–2000. Admission charged.*

Washington's nephew Lawrence Lewis lived at nearby **Woodlawn** (U.S. 1, tel. 703/780–4000; admission charged), designed by the architect of the Capitol and begun in 1800. The formal gardens include a large collection of rare old-fashioned roses. Also on the grounds is the small **Pope-Leighey House,** designed by Frank Lloyd Wright and built in 1940.

South of Mount Vernon is the relatively unvisited but meticulously restored **Gunston Hall** (Rte. 242, tel. 703/550–9220; admission charged), the plantation home of George Mason, one of the framers of the Constitution.

North of Mount Vernon, on the Potomac, is **Alexandria,** a suburb of Washington, D.C., with an identity based on 2½ centuries of history. The Old Town is a neighborhood of 18th- and 19th-century town houses, most of them redbrick. Its major sights can be seen on foot within 20 blocks or so. Parking is usually scarce, but the Convention and Visitor's Bureau provides a three-day pass.

The bureau—the best place to start a tour—is located in the town's oldest structure, **Ramsay House** (221 King St., tel. 703/838–4200), built in 1724 in Dumfries (25 mi south) and moved here in 1749. Like it, the **Old Presbyterian Meeting House** (321 S. Fairfax St., tel. 703/549–6670) and the grand **Carlyle House** (121 N. Fairfax St., tel. 703/549–2997) are 18th-century reminders of the town's Scottish heritage.

George Washington frequented the **Stabler-Leadbeater Apothecary Shop** (105–107 S. Fairfax St., tel. 703/836–3713; admission charged), **Gadsby's Tavern** (134 N. Royal St., tel. 703/838–4242; admission charged), and **Christ Church** (Washington and Cameron Sts., tel. 703/549–1450). Another member of Christ Church was Robert E. Lee; the **Lee boyhood home** (607 Oronoco St., tel. 703/548–8454; admission charged) is practically around the corner.

The homes of less famous residents help to fill out a picture of 18th- and 19th-century life. The block of Prince Street between Fairfax and Lee, lined by imposing three-story houses, is called **Gentry Row,** and the cobblestone block of humbler residences between Lee and Union is **Captain's Row.**

Alexandria's cultural heritage is honored at the **Lyceum** (201 S. Washington St., tel. 703/838–4994), with displays of decorative arts and exhibits on local history. Work by local artists is shown at the **Atheneum** (201 Prince St., tel. 703/548–0035). At the **Torpedo Factory Art Center** (105 N. Union St., tel. 703/838–4565), a renovated waterfront building where torpedos were made during both world wars, 180 artists and craftspeople make and sell their wares.

Possibly too far to walk to, but impossible to miss, is the 333-foot-high **George Washington National Masonic Memorial.** Rel-

Northern Virginia

Harper's Ferry
Morven Park
Leesburg
MARYLAND
TO BALTIMORE
Potomac River
15
7
270
29
95
1
Oatlands
Loudoun County
George Washington Memorial Parkway
Reston
DISTRICT OF COLUMBIA
95 495
50
Dulles International Airport
Tyson's Corner
Vienna
Arlington
Washington
TO MIDDLEBURG
50
Falls Church
Arlington National Cemetery
Manassas National Battlefield Park
66
Fairfax
Annandale
Alexandria
400
28
Capital
The Pentagon
Torpedo Factory Art Center
Manassas
95
Beltway
1
Pope-Leighey House
Woodlawn
235
Mount Vernon
301
234
Fort Belvoir
242
Gunston Hall
Woodbridge
N
Quantico U.S. Marine Corps Reservation
Potomac River
301
17
1
301
95
218
3
Fredericksburg
Fredericksburg and Spotsylvania National Military Park
Westmoreland State Park
208
2
17
Fort A.P. Hill
Rappahannock River
George Washington's Birthplace
Robert E.Lee's Birthplace
TO RICHMOND

0   10 miles
0   15 km

ics of the first president and exhibits on the Masonic Order are on display inside, and the top offers a spectacular view of Alexandria and nearby Washington. *Shooter's Hill, tel. 703/683–2007. Admission free.*

For information on **Arlington National Cemetery** and the **Pentagon,** *see* Washington, D.C.

Fredericksburg, about an hour south, rivals Alexandria and Mount Vernon for associations with the Washington family. The future first president lived across the Rappahannock River at Ferry Farm from age 6 to 16. His sister Betty and her husband lived at **Kenmore** (1201 Washington Ave., tel. 703/373–3381; admission charged), a house whose plain facade belies a lavish interior. The home of his brother Charles Washington later became the **Rising Sun Tavern** (1306 Caroline St., tel. 703/371–1494; admission charged), a watering hole for such revolutionaries as Patrick Henry and Thomas Jefferson. The **Home of Mary Washington** (Charles and Lewis Sts., tel. 703/373–1569; admission charged) is a modest house George bought for his mother during her last years.

The future fifth president also lived in Fredericksburg, and the **James Monroe Museum and Memorial Library** (908 Charles St., tel. 703/899–4559; admission charged) is set in the tiny one-story building where he practiced law from 1787 to 1789.

At the **Hugh Mercer Apothecary Shop** (Caroline and Amelia Sts., tel. 703/373–3362; admission charged), the guide's explicit descriptions of amputations, cataract operations, and tooth extractions can make latterday visitors wince.

Four Civil War battlefields—Fredericksburg, Chancellorsville, the Wilderness, and the Spotsylvania Courthouse—make up the **Fredericksburg and Spotsylvania National Military Park.** All the sites are within 17 mi of Fredericksburg, where a **visitor center** has an introductory slide show and exhibits. *1013 Lafayette Blvd. (U.S. 1), tel. 703/373–6122. Admission free.*

Rte. 3 east of Fredericksburg takes you into the **Northern Neck,** a strip of land bounded by the Potomac and the Rappahannock rivers. At the top of the Neck is Westmoreland County, which produced both the "father of our country" and the greatest tragic hero of the Civil War.

George Washington's Birthplace National Monument, in Wakefield, preserves the memory of the first president with a working farm and a reproduction of the original early 18th-century plantation house (which burned down Christmas day, 1779). Washington's family members are buried on the property. *Rte. 204, tel. 804/224–1732. Admission charged.*

Stratford Hall, birthplace of Robert E. Lee, is an elegant original, built in the shape of an *H* in the 1730s, with brick and timber produced on the site. Farmers still cultivate 1,600 of the original acres, and their yield, a variety of cereals, is for sale. Lunch is served in a log cabin from April through October. *Rte. 214, tel. 804/493–8038. Admission charged.*

At the far end of the Neck, in **Irvington,** is a jewel of Tidewater architecture: **Christ Church** (jct. of Rtes. 646 and 709, tel. 804/438–6855), a redbrick sanctuary of cruciform design, built in 1732.

A 26-mi drive west of Washington is the monumentally important **Manassas National Battlefield,** or Bull Run, where the
Confederacy won two major victories and Stonewall Jackson
won his nickname. *Rte. 234 off I–66, tel. 703/361–1339. Admission charged.*

Farther west is horse country. In **Loudoun County's** fashionable towns of **Leesburg** and **Middleburg,** the residents (many of
them Yankee transplants) keep up the local traditions of fox
hunts and steeplechases. The county visitor center in Leesburg
(*see* Tourist Information, *above*) can suggest scenic drives.

Oatlands (U.S. 15, 6 mi south of Leesburg, tel. 703/777–3174;
admission charged) is a restored Greek Revival plantation
house whose manicured fields host public and private equestrian events spring through fall. The Greek Revival mansion at
Morven Park (Rte. 7, 1 mi north of Leesburg, tel. 703/777–
2414; admission charged), a White House look-alike, contains
two museums: one of horse-drawn carriages, the other of
hounds and hunting. And here in the midst of Thoroughbred
country is the **American Workhorse Museum** (Rte. 662,
Paeonian Springs, tel. 703/338–6290; admission free), a tribute
to an unsung hero of this nation's economic history.

What to See and Do with Children

Wolf Trap Farm Park (*see* The Arts and Nightlife, *below*) hosts
mime, puppet, and animal shows, as well as concerts, plays,
and storytelling, mid-June–Labor Day. Events are often free.
Emus, monkeys, a zebra, giant tortoises, and domestic farm
animals inhabit **Reston Animal Park** (Rtes. 7 and 606, Hunter
Mill Rd., Lake Fairfax, tel. 703/759–3636 or 703/759–3637).

Shopping

Tysons Corner Center (1961 Chain Bridge Rd., jct. Rtes. 7 and
123) houses 240 retailers, including **Bloomingdale's** and
Nordstrom. Next door, **The Galleria at Tysons II** (2001 Interna-
tional Dr.) has 125 more, including **Saks Fifth Avenue** and
Neiman Marcus. The first area branch of **Tiffany & Co.** (8045
Leesburg Pike) is a few minutes away.

The old towns of Alexandria and Fredericksburg are dense
with **antiques** shops, many quite expensive, that are particularly strong in the Federal and Victorian periods. The town visitor
centers (*see* Tourist Information, *above*) have maps and lists of
the stores.

Sports and Outdoor Activities

Biking The 19-mi **Mount Vernon Bicycle Trail** (tel. 703/285–2598) runs
along the Potomac and through Alexandria. The 4.7-mi **Burke
Lake Park Bicycle Trail** (tel. 703/323–6600) in Fairfax County
circles the lake. The Arlington Parks and Recreation Bureau
(tel. 703/358–3317) offers a free map of the **county Bikeway System.**

Golf **Algonkian Park** (600 Potomac View Rd., Sterling, tel. 703/450–
4655), **Burke Lake Park** (Fairfax Station, tel. 703/323–1641),
and **Shannon Green Resort** (Rte. 3, Fredericksburg, tel. 703/
786–8385) have public courses. **The Tides Inn** (tel. 804/438–

5501; *see* Dining and Lodging, *below*) offers 18- and 9-hole courses.

Water Sports The Northern Neck gives sailors, water-skiers, and windsurfers access to two rivers and the Chesapeake Bay. For information, contact the **Northern Neck Travel Council** (*see* Tourist Information, *above*).

Dining and Lodging

Old Town Alexandria's restaurants are many and varied, but they are also pricey and, on weekend nights, crowded. Arlington's Little Saigon, on and around Wilson Boulevard, has many excellent and affordable Vietnamese restaurants.

Lodging prices are high, but so are the standards of comfort and luxury. B&Bs tend to be more elegant here because many serve as romantic weekend hideaways for regular customers from Washington. For listings, try **Bed & Breakfast Ltd.** (Box 12011, Washington, DC 20005, tel. 202/328–3510). **Princely Bed & Breakfast** (819 Prince St., Alexandria 22314, tel. 703/683–2159) lists accommodations in historic Old Town homes.

For price ranges, see Charts 1 (A) and 2 (A) in Chapter 1.

Alexandria **Le Gaulois.** At this quiet country bistro whose white walls are
Dining hung with scenes of southern France, the specialties include *pot-au-feu gaulois*, a beef-and-chicken stew with whole vegetables; and cassoulet, a rich bean casserole with sausage and beef. *1106 King St., tel. 703/739–9494. Reservations advised. Dress: neat but casual. AE, DC, MC, V. Moderate.*
Scotland Yard. The kilted owner holds forth in the narrow, wood-paneled dining room while in the kitchen his children prepare such Caledonian favorites as venison game pie. Original recipes include lobster Drambuie and flaming whiskey steak. *728 King St., tel. 703/683–1742. Reservations advised. Dress: neat but casual. AE, MC, V. No lunch; closed Mon. Moderate.*
★ **Taverna Cretekou.** Surrounded by whitewashed stucco walls and brightly colored macramé tapestries, or outside in the canopied garden, diners enjoy such dishes as lamb *Exohikon* (baked in a pastry shell) and swordfish kabob. All the wines are Greek. *818 King St., tel. 703/548–8688. Reservations advised. AE, DC, MC, V. Closed Mon. Moderate.*
Hard Times Café. Recorded country-and-western music and framed photographs of Depression-era Oklahoma set the tone at this casual, always crowded hangout. Three kinds of chili are served—Texas (spicy), Cincinnati (mild), and vegetarian. *1404 King St., tel. 703/683–5340. No reservations. AE, MC, V. Inexpensive.*

Lodging **Holiday Inn Old Town.** The mahogany-paneled lobby and the hunting prints in the guest rooms suggest a men's club. Marble bathtubs, modem-ready phones, and extraordinary service (for example, exercise bikes are brought to your room upon request) make this an exceptional member of the chain. *480 King St., 22314, tel. 703/549–6080; fax 703/684–6508. 227 rooms. Facilities: restaurant, lounge, indoor pool, sauna. AE, D, DC, MC, V. Expensive.*
★ **Morrison House.** Butlers unpack for guests in rooms furnished with four-posters, and tea is served every afternoon at this convincing Federal-style house (built in 1985). Most extraordinary of all, the employees never accept tips. *116 S. Alfred St., 22314,*

tel. 703/838–8000; fax 703/684–6283. 43 rooms, 2 suites. Facilities: restaurant. AE, DC, MC, V. Expensive.

Arlington
Dining

Cafe Dalat. The specialties at this restaurant, a favorite among the neighborhood's large Vietnamese population, include the "Fairy Combination" (crisp noodles with chicken, scallops, shrimp, and mixed vegetables) and beef wrapped in grape leaves. *3143 Wilson Blvd., tel. 703/276–0935. MC, V. Inexpensive.*

Lodging

Marriott Crystal Gateway. Black marble, blond wood, and lots of greenery distinguish this hostelry for big-budget business travelers and tourists who want to be pampered. *1700 Jefferson Davis Hwy., 22202, tel. 703/920–3230; fax 703/979–6332. 626 rooms, 71 suites. Facilities: 3 restaurants, lounge, nightclub, indoor and outdoor pools, whirlpool, sauna, exercise rooms. AE, D, DC, MC, V. Expensive.*

Ritz-Carlton Pentagon City. This soundproofed enclave of luxury five minutes from the airport boasts Persian carpets in the lobby and silk wallpaper in the reproduction Federal bedrooms. *1250 S. Hayes St., 22202, tel. 703/415–5000; fax 703/415–5060. 304 rooms, 41 suites. Facilities: restaurant, bar, indoor pool, exercise room, sauna. AE, D, DC, MC, V. Expensive.*

Best Western Arlington. The rooms are in unexceptional modern decor. The attraction here is convenience: easy access to I-395 and a free shuttle to the airport. *2480 S. Glebe Rd., 22206, tel. 703/979–4400 or 800/426–6886; fax 703/685–0051. 325 rooms. Facilities: restaurant, outdoor pool, exercise room, laundry and valet service. AE, D, DC, MC, V. Moderate.*

Fairfax
Lodging

The Bailiwick Inn. Guest rooms in this 18th-century house opposite the County Courthouse are furnished with period reproductions; four have fireplaces, two have whirlpools. *4023 Chain Bridge Rd., 22030, tel. 703/691–2266; fax 703/934–2112. 13 rooms, 1 suite. Facilities: full breakfast. AE, MC, V. Expensive.*

Fredericksburg
Dining

Le Lafayette. The cuisine served in this pre-Revolutionary Georgian house could be called "Virginia French." The menu may offer grilled breast of duck in red-currant sauce over braised red cabbage or poached salmon fillet in saffron broth with mussels, leeks, and tomatoes. *623 Caroline St., tel. 703/373–6895. Reservations advised. Dress: neat but casual. AE, D, DC, MC, V. Moderate.*

Ristorante Renato. At this unlikely candlelit Italian restaurant in the midst of a Colonial town, the specialties include "Romeo and Juliet" (veal and chicken topped with mozzarella in white-wine sauce) and shrimp scampi Napoli with lemon-butter sauce. *Williams and Prince Edward Sts., tel. 703/371–8228. Reservations advised weekends. AE, MC, V. Moderate.*

Lodging

The Richard Johnston Inn. This three-story row house across from the visitor center has parking in the rear under magnolia trees. Guest rooms are furnished with Empire-style and Chippendale antiques; the suites open onto a patio. *711 Caroline St., 22401, tel. 703/899–7606. 7 rooms, 2 suites. Facilities: Continental breakfast. AE, DC, MC, V. Moderate.*

Best Western Johnny Appleseed. This generic, two-story, family-oriented hotel is five minutes from the battlefields. The most pleasant views are of the pool. *543 Warrenton Rd. (U.S. 17 and I-95), 22405, tel. 703/373–0000; fax 703/373–5676. 87 rooms.*

Facilities: restaurant, outdoor pool, playground, nature trail. AE, D, DC, MC, V. Inexpensive.

Great Falls **L'Auberge Chez François.** White stucco, dark exposed beams,
Dining and a garden just outside create a country-inn ambience 20
minutes from Tysons Corner. The Alsatian cuisine includes
salmon soufflé with salmon-and-scallop mousse and white-wine
or lobster sauce. *332 Springvale Rd. (Rte. 674), tel. 703/759–
3800. Reservations required 2 wks in advance. Jacket required.
AE, DC, MC, V. No lunch; closed Mon. Expensive.*

Northern Neck **The Tides Inn** At this 20-acre Colonial resort on a Rappahan-
Lodging nock tributary, almost all the rooms have water views. For an
even closer look, guests can take a dinner cruise on one of the
inn's two yachts. *Rte. 200, Box 480, Irvington 22480, tel. 804/
438–5000 or 800/843–3746; fax 804/438–5222. 92 rooms, 18
suites. Facilities: 4 restaurants, lounge, marina, 2 golf
courses, outdoor pool, 4 tennis courts, sailboats, canoes,
paddleboats, summer children's programs, privileges at nearby fitness center. AE, D, DC, MC, V. Very Expensive.*

Tysons Corner **Clyde's.** Quality is high, service attentive, and the tone always
Dining lively in these art deco dining rooms. The long, eclectic menu
includes fresh fish, often in such preparations as trout Parmesan. *8332 Leesburg Pike, tel. 703/734–1901. Reservations advised. AE, D, DC, MC, V. Moderate.*

Motel **Hampton Inn** (2310 Plank Rd., Fredericksburg 22401, tel. 703/
371–0330 or 800/426–7866; fax 703/371–1753), 165 rooms, 1
suite, outdoor pool; inexpensive.

The Arts and Nightlife

The Arts **Fairfax County Council of the Arts** (tel. 703/642–0862) acts as a
clearinghouse for information about performances and exhi-
bitions throughout northern Virginia. **Wolf Trap Farm Park**
(I–495, Exit 10B to Rte. 7W, Vienna, tel. 703/255–1860 or 703/
938–2404), one of the major performing-arts venues in the
greater Washington area, presents top musical and dance performers in a grand outdoor pavilion during the warmer months
and in 18th-century farm buildings during other seasons.

Nightlife **Whitey's** (2761 Washington Blvd., Arlington, tel. 703/525–
9825) often features live bluegrass. **Murphy's Grand Irish Pub**
(713 King St., Alexandria, tel. 703/548–1717) hosts Irish and
folk performers. **Two Nineteen** (219 King St., Alexandria, tel.
703/549–1141) has jazz upstairs and a sports bar in the basement. **Clyde's** (8332 Leesburg Pike, Tysons Corner, tel. 703/
734–1901) attracts unattached professionals.

Richmond and Tidewater

Strictly speaking, Tidewater Virginia is the region east of the
fall line of the rivers that flow into the Chesapeake Bay; but
"Tidewater" has also come to stand for the genteel Old South.
Richmond, on the fall line of the James, straddles Tidewater
and the Piedmont region of rolling plains; so, too, it bridges
Virginia past and present, with remnants of the Confederacy
preserved amid the cultural and commercial bustle of a modern
state capital. An hour southeast are two former capitals: Colonial Williamsburg, restored to its 18th-century splendor; and
Jamestown, the very first, long deserted and all the more stir-

ring. With Yorktown, where the Colonies won their independence, these pre-Revolutionary towns form the Historic Triangle.

Tourist Information

Metro Richmond: Visitor Center (1710 Robin Hood Rd. [Exit 78 off I–95 and I–64], 23220, tel. 804/358–5511). **Petersburg:** Visitors Center (425 Cockade Alley, 23803, tel. 804/733–2400). **Williamsburg:** Area Tourism and Conference Bureau (Drawer GB, 23187, tel. 804/253–0192 or 800/368–6511). Colonial Williamsburg (Box C, 23187, tel. 800/447–8679). **Yorktown:** Colonial National Historical Park (Box 210, 23690, tel. 804/898–3400).

Getting There

By Plane **Richmond International Airport** (tel. 804/226–3000) is served by six airlines. **Newport News–Williamsburg International Airport** (tel. 804/877–0924) in Newport News and **Norfolk International Airport** (tel. 804/ 857–3351) also serve the region.

By Car Richmond is at the intersection of I–95 and I–64; U.S. 1 runs north–south by the city. Petersburg is 20 mi south of Richmond on I–95. Williamsburg is west of I–64 and 51 mi southeast of Richmond; the Colonial Parkway joins it with Jamestown and Yorktown.

By Train **Amtrak** serves Richmond (7519 Staples Mill Rd., tel. 804/264–9194) and Williamsburg (468 N. Boundary St.).

By Bus **Greyhound** serves Richmond (2910 N. Boulevard, tel. 804/254–5910) and Williamsburg (468 N. Boundary St., tel. 804/229–1460).

Exploring Richmond and Tidewater

Richmond Most of **Richmond's** historic attractions lie north of the James River, which bisects the city in a sweeping curve. West of downtown are such gracious residential neighborhoods as Monument Avenue, with its statues of Civil War heroes. Streets fan out southwesterly from Park Avenue to form the gaslit **Fan District,** a hip neighborhood of restored turn-of-the-century town houses.

The heart of old Richmond is the **Court End** district, which contains seven National Historic Landmarks, three museums, and 11 more buildings on the National Register of Historic Places—all within eight blocks. At any museum you will receive a self-guided walking tour with the purchase of a discount block ticket, good for any admission fees. The museums include the **John Marshall House** (9th and Marshall Sts., tel. 804/648–7998), home of the early U.S. chief justice; and the **Museum and White House of the Confederacy** (1201 E. Clay St., tel. 804/649–1861), the official residence of President Jefferson Davis, with a newer building next door housing such relics as Robert E. Lee's sword.

The **Virginia State Capitol,** designed by Thomas Jefferson in 1785, contains a wealth of sculpture, including busts of the eight Virginia-born U.S. presidents and a life-size statue of George Washington. It was here that Lee accepted command of

Richmond

James River

Jefferson Ave.

Richmond National Battlefield Park
St. John's Episcopal Church

25th St.
24th St.
23rd. St.
22nd St.
21st St.

20th St.
19th St.
18th St.
17th St.

Mayo's Bridge

White House of the Confederacy

15th St.

14th St.

12th St. Governor St.
11th St.
10th St.
9th St.

Begin Canal Walk

Brown's Island

Court End District

Virginia State Capitol

Manchester Bridge

John Marshall House

8th St.
7th St.
6th St.
5th St.
4th St.

Grace St.
Franklin St.
Main St.

Robert E. Lee Bridge

Broad St.

3rd St.
2nd St.
1st St.
Foushee St.

Cary St.

Canal St.

Jackson St.
Leigh St.
Clay St.
Marshall St.

Adams St.
Jefferson St.
Madison St.
Monroe St.

Brook St.

Henry St.

Belvidere St.

440 yards
400 meters

Belvidere St.

Gilmer St.
Goshen St.

Laurel St.
Cherry St.
Linden St.

Harrison St.

Hancock St.
Harrison St.

Beech St.
Morris St.

Randolph St.

Kinney St.
Bowe St.
Lombardy St.

Harvie St.

Plum St.
Lombardy St.

Vine St.

Lombardy St.

Idlewood St.

Allen Ave.

Allen Ave.

Granby St.

Allen Ave.

Grayland St.
Rosewood St.

Hermitage Rd.

Science Museum of Virginia

Broad St.
Grace St.
Monument Ave.

Park Ave.
Stuart Ave.
Hanover Ave.
Grove Ave.

Meadow St.
Rowland St.
Shields Ave.
Addison St.

Parkwood St.

Cary St.

Agecroft Hall

Stafford St.
Davis St.
Robinson St.

Floyd St.
Main St.

Mulberry St.

Museum of Fine Arts

The Boulevard

Colonial St.

the Confederate forces. *Capitol Sq., tel. 804/786–4344. Admission free.*

Canal Walk, beginning at 12th and Main streets, follows the locks of the James River–Kanawha Canal proposed by George Washington. Plaques along the way note points of historic interest. The walk (under 1 mi) continues over a footbridge to **Brown's Island,** the site of sculptures and outdoor concerts.

In the Church Hill Historic District, east of downtown, is **St. John's Episcopal Church.** It was here, on March 23, 1775, that Patrick Henry demanded of the Second Virginia Convention: "Give me liberty or give me death!" *25th and Broad Sts., tel. 804/648–5015. Admission charged.*

The visitor center for **Richmond National Battlefield Park** provides a movie and a slide show about the three campaigns fought here, as well as maps for a self-guided tour. *3215 E. Broad St., tel. 804/226–1981. Admission free.*

Heading west again, one finds the **Science Museum of Virginia** housed in a massive, domed former train station. The planetarium doubles as a movie theater with a huge curved screen. *2500 W. Broad St., tel. 804/367–1013. Admission charged.*

Aptly situated at the base of the artsy Fan District is the **Virginia Museum of Fine Arts,** whose collection includes paintings by Goya, Renoir, Monet, and van Gogh, as well as African masks, Roman statuary, Oriental icons, and five Fabergé eggs. *Boulevard and Grove Ave., tel. 804/367–0844. Admission charged.*

Just west of the Fan District stands **Agecroft Hall,** a 15th-century English house reassembled here in 1925, surrounded by formal gardens, and extensively furnished with Tudor and early Stuart art and furniture. *4305 Sulgrave Rd., tel. 804/353–4241. Admission charged.*

Petersburg   Twenty miles south of Richmond on I–95 lies Petersburg, the town that was the so-called last ditch of the Confederacy: Its fall in 1865 led to the fall of Richmond and the surrender at Appomattox. At **Petersburg National Battlefield** you can tread the ground where 60,000 soldiers died. The 1,500-acre park, laced with miles of earthworks, includes two forts. *Rte 36, tel. 804/732–3531. Admission charged.*

In Old Towne Petersburg the Civil War is examined from a local perspective at the **Siege Museum** (15 W. Bank St., tel. 804/733–2402). Outstanding relics of antebellum Petersburg include the eccentric **Trapezium House** (244 N. Market St., tel. 804/733–2404), built with no right angles; and the **Centre Hill Mansion** (Centre Hill Ct., tel. 804/733–2401), remodeled in Victorian style at the turn of this century. The pre-Revolutionary **Old Blanford Church** (319 S. Crater Rd., tel. 804/733–2396) is today a Confederate shrine, surrounded by the graves of 30,000 southern dead. The Memorial Day tradition is said to have begun in this cemetery.

The James River   Southeast of Richmond on Rte. 5, along the north bank of the
Plantations   James River, lie four historic plantations. **Shirley,** the oldest in Virginia, has belonged to the same family, the Carters, for 10 generations. Robert E. Lee's mother was born here. The 1723 house is filled with family silver, ancestral portraits, and rare

books. The hall staircase rises three stories with no visible supports. *Rte. 608, tel. 804/829–5121. Admission charged.*

Virginians say that the first Thanksgiving was celebrated not in Massachusetts but right here, at **Berkeley,** on December 4, 1619. Benjamin Harrison, a signer of the Declaration of Independence, and William Henry Harrison, the short-lived ninth president, were born here. The 1726 Georgian brick house has been restored and furnished with period antiques, and the boxwood gardens are well tended. There is a restaurant and outdoor tables for picnickers. *Rte. 5E, tel. 804/829–6018. Admission charged.*

Westover was home to the flamboyant Colonel William Byrd II, member of the Colonial legislature and author of one of the region's first travel books (as well as a notorious secret diary). The 1735 house, celebrated for its moldings and carvings, is open only during April Garden Week, but the grounds and gardens can be visited all year. *Rte. 5, tel. 804/829–2882. Admission charged.*

At 300 feet, **Sherwood Forest** may be the longest frame house in the country. Built in 1720, it was the retirement home of John Tyler, the 10th U.S. president, and remains in his family. The house, furnished with heirloom antiques, and the five outbuildings are open daily. *Rte. 5, tel. 804/829–5377. Admission charged.*

The Historic Triangle **Colonial Williamsburg** is a marvel: an improbably sanitary but otherwise convincing re-creation of the city that was the capital of Virginia in the years 1699–1780. The restoration project, financed by John D. Rockefeller, Jr., began in 1926; the work of the archaeologists and historians of the Colonial Williamsburg Foundation continues to this day. (To obtain an extensive packet of information, *see* Tourist Information, *above.*)

On Colonial Williamsburg's 173 acres, 88 original 18th- and early 19th-century structures, such as the **Courthouse,** have been meticulously restored; another 50, including the **Capitol** and the **Governor's Palace,** were reconstructed on their original sites. In all, 225 period rooms have been furnished from the foundation's collection of more than 100,000 pieces of furniture, pottery, china, glass, silver, pewter, textiles, tools, and carpeting. Period authenticity also governs the landscaping of the 90 acres of gardens and public greens.

All year long, hundreds of costumed interpreters, wearing bonnets or three-cornered hats, rove and ride through the cobblestone streets. Dozens of costumed craftspeople, such as the bootmaker and the gunsmith, demonstrate and explain their trades inside their workshops; their wares are for sale nearby. Three taverns serve fare approximating that of 200 years ago.

One million people visit Colonial Williamsburg annually. The restored area must be toured on foot, as all vehicles are banned between 8 AM and 6 PM. Free shuttle buses run (available to ticketholders only) continually to and from the visitor center and around the edge of the restored area. Vans for the disabled are permitted by prior arrangement, and all structures have ramps. *I–64 Exit 56, tel. 804/229–1000. Admission charged.*

Jamestown Island, site of the first permanent English settlement in North America (1607) and the capital of Virginia until 1699, is now uninhabited. Foundation walls show the layout of the settlement, and push-button audio stations narrate the local history. The only standing structure is the ruin of a 1639 church tower. A 5-mi nature drive ringing the island is posted with historical markers. *Colonial Pkwy., tel. 804/229–1733. Admission charged.*

Adjacent to the island is **Jamestown Settlement,** a living-history museum with a reconstructed fort manned by "colonists," and an "Indian Village" inhabited by buckskin-clad interpreters. At the pier are reproductions of the *Godspeed*, the *Discovery*, and the *Susan Constant*, the ships that brought the settlers. *Rte. 31 off Colonial Pkwy., tel. 804/229–1607. Admission charged.*

At **Yorktown Battlefield** in 1781, American and French forces surrounded British troops and forced an end to the American War of Independence. Today the museum here displays George Washington's original field tent; dioramas, illuminated maps, and a short movie tell the story. After a look from the observation deck, you can rent the taped audio tour and explore the battlefield by car or join a ranger-led free walking tour. *Colonial Pkwy., tel. 804/898–3400. Admission free.*

The **Yorktown Victory Center** next door features a Continental army encampment, with tents, a covered wagon, and interpreters—costumed as soldiers or female auxiliaries—who speak to visitors in the regional dialects of the time. Also on site are a small working tobacco farm and a museum focusing on the experience of ordinary people during the Revolution. *Rte. 238 off Colonial Pkwy., tel. 804/887–1776. Admission charged.*

Unlike Jamestown, **Yorktown** remains a living community, albeit a small one. Rte. 238 leads into **Main Street,** with an array of preserved 18th-century buildings on a bluff overlooking the York River. **Moore House,** where the terms of surrender were negotiated, and the elegant **Nelson House,** the residence of a Virginia governor and a signer of the Declaration of Independence, are open for tours in summer (tel. 804/898–3400). On adjacent Church Street, **Grace Church,** built in 1697, remains an active Episcopal congregation; its walls are made of marl (a mixture of clay, sand, and limestone containing fragments of seashells).

What to See and Do with Children

The 100-plus rides at **King's Dominion** (I–95, Doswell exit, tel. 804/876–5000; closed Nov.–Mar.), north of Richmond, include simulated white-water rafting, a stand-up roller coaster, and a monorail through a game preserve. East of Williamsburg is **Busch Gardens, the Old Country** (U.S. 60, tel. 804/253–3350; closed Nov.–Mar.). Rides include an especially fast and steep roller coaster, and nine re-creations of European hamlets offer the cuisine and entertainment of different countries.

Shopping

Fresh produce is for sale at Richmond's **Farmers Market** (17th and Main Sts.); art galleries, boutiques, and antiques shops are nearby. The **Colonial Williamsburg Crafts Houses** (Merchants Sq., tel. 804/220–7747) sell approved reproductions of the antiques on display in the houses.

Sports and Outdoor Activities

Open to the public in Richmond—for free or at a nominal charge—are more than 150 tennis courts, 11 swimming pools, a golf driving range, and about 7 mi of fitness trails. The **Department of Recreation and Parks** (tel. 804/780–6091) has listings.

Biking In Colonial Williamsburg, ticket holders can rent bicycles at the **lodge** on South England Street; others can try **Bikesmith** (York St., tel. 804/229–9858).

Golf **The Crossings** (jct. of I–95 and I–295, Glen Allen, tel. 804/266–2254), north of Richmond, has an 18-hole course open to the public. **Colonial Williamsburg** (tel. 804/220–7696) operates three courses. **Kingsmill Resort** (tel. 804/253–3906), east of Williamsburg near Busch Gardens, has two courses.

Rafting **Richmond Raft** (tel. 804/222–7238) offers guided white-water rafting through the heart of the city (class 3 and 4 rapids), float trips upriver, and overnight trips from April through October.

Tennis **Colonial Williamsburg** (tel. 804/220–7794) has eight tennis courts; **Kingsmill** (tel. 804/253–3945) has 15 courts open to the public; additional public courts in Williamsburg are at **Kiwanis Park** on Long Hill Road and **Quarterpath Park** on Pocahontas Street.

Dining and Lodging

The established upmarket dining rooms of Richmond are dependable, but keep an eye out for intriguing new bistros, often short-lived, in the Fan District. In Williamsburg, remember that dining rooms within walking distance of the restored area are often crowded, and reservations are advised.

Richmond's hotel rates are fair for its size, but standards of service lag behind those of many smaller communities. Williamsburg has a greater range of lodging choices for the money, but vacancies are scarce in summer.

For price ranges, see Charts 1 (B) and 2 (B) in Chapter 1.

Richmond **La Petite France.** The emerald green walls are hung with En-
Dining glish landscapes and portraits. Tuxedoed waiters serve lobster
★ baked in puff pastry with whiskey sauce and Dover sole amandine, among other specialties. *2108 Maywill St., tel. 804/ 353–8729. Reservations advised. Jacket and tie advised. AE, DC, MC, V. Closed Sun.–Mon. Expensive.*

Mr. Patrick Henry's. Antiques and fireplaces create the Colonial ambience in the main room; there's also a basement pub and a garden café. Menu favorites include unusual crab cakes (crabmeat and spices in a puff pastry) and crisp roast duck with plum sauce. *2300 E. Broad St., tel. 804/644–1322. Reservations advised. AE, DC, MC, V. No dinner Sun. Expensive.*

Joe's Inn. The specialty at this Fan District hangout is Greek spaghetti, with feta and provolone baked on top; all the sandwiches are oversize. Regulars make newcomers feel right at home. *205 N. Shields Ave., tel. 804/355–2282. AE, MC, V. Inexpensive.*

Lodging **Jefferson Grand Heritage Hotel.** This 1895 National Historic
★ Landmark has a grand lobby, with a tall staircase straight out of *Gone with the Wind.* The rather small guest rooms have reproduction 19th-century furnishings. *Franklin and Adams*

Sts., 23220, tel. 804/788–8000 or 800/424–8014; fax 804/225–
0334. 274 rooms, 26 suites. Facilities: 2 restaurants, bar, spa
privileges. AE, DC, MC, V. Expensive.

Omni Richmond. Guest rooms in this luxury hotel have a contemporary look, but the marble lobby, with its green velvet
chairs, equestrian statues, and Romanesque vases, calls to
mind a Venetian foyer. 100 S. 12th St., 23219, tel. 804/344–7000;
fax 804/648–6704. 364 rooms. Facilities: 3 restaurants, bar, indoor and outdoor pools, saunas. AE, D, DC, MC, V. Expensive.

Radisson Hotel. Triangular rooms at the point of this wedge-
shape hotel have views of the skyline and the river. The three-
story atrium lobby features a waterfall. 555 E. Canal St.,
23219, tel. 804/788–0900; fax 804/788–7087. 300 rooms. Facilities: restaurant, bar, indoor pool, health club, saunas. AE, D,
DC, MC, V. Expensive.

Massad House Hotel. This modest Tudor-style hotel is five
blocks from the capitol in the business district, a quiet area after 6 PM. Guest rooms are small with stucco walls and are well
maintained. 11 N. 4th St., 23219, tel. 804/648–2893. 64 rooms.
Facilities: restaurant. MC, V. Inexpensive.

Williamsburg **Regency Room.** Crystal chandeliers, Oriental silkscreen
Dining prints, and full silver service set the tone. Rack of lamb is
★ carved at the table; other specialties are lobster bisque and rich
ice-cream desserts. Williamsburg Inn, 136 E. Francis St., tel.
804/229–1000. Reservations advised. Jacket and tie required at
dinner and Sun. brunch. AE, MC, V. Expensive.

The Cascades. Bare polished-wood tables are piled with all-
American fare: baked crab imperial, Cheddar-cheese soup,
sugar-cured ham, fried chicken, pecan pie. The daily Hunt
Breakfast buffet includes fried chicken and oysters in season.
Visitor Center area, tel. 804/229–1000. Reservations advised.
AE, MC, V. Moderate.

Le Yaca. The country-French dining room is done in soft pastels with hardwood floors, candlelight, and a central open fireplace where leg of lamb roasts nightly on a spit. 1915
Pocahontas Trail, tel. 804/220–3616. Reservations advised.
AE, DC, MC, V. Closed Sun., early Jan. Moderate.

The Trellis. Hardwood floors, ceramic tiles, and green plants
evoke Napa Valley. The menu may include grilled swordfish
with crisp fried leeks and sautéed onions, and for dessert,
Death by Chocolate: seven layers of chocolate topped with
cream sauce. Merchants Sq., tel. 804/229–8610. Reservations
advised. AE, MC, V. Moderate.

Lodging **Quality Suites.** At this quiet all-suite hotel, built in 1987 on 11
wooded acres, the decor is heavily mauve California contemporary. 152 Kingsgate Pkwy., 23185, tel. 804/229–6800 or 800/
333–0924; fax 804/220–3486. 169 suites. Facilities: indoor pool,
whirlpool. AE, D, DC, MC, V. Expensive.

Williamsburg Hospitality House. This four-story redbrick
building, constructed in 1973, faces the College of William and
Mary. Guest rooms are furnished with Chippendale reproductions; some look onto a cobblestone courtyard with a fountain.
415 Richmond Rd., 23185, tel. 804/229–4020 or 800/932–9192;
fax 804/220–1560. 309 rooms. Facilities: restaurant, bar, outdoor pool. AE, D, DC, MC, V. Expensive.

★ **Williamsburg Inn.** This is the local grand hotel, built in 1932
and decorated in English Regency style. The surrounding Colonial houses, equipped with modern kitchens and baths, are

also part of the inn. *136 E. Francis St., 23185, tel. 804/229–1000 or 800/447–8679; fax 804/220–7096. 235 rooms. Facilities: restaurant, bar, outdoor pool, tennis, golf, health club. AE, MC, V. Expensive.*

Heritage Inn. Room furnishings include beds with two-poster headboards and an armoire concealing a TV. Some rooms open directly onto the parking lot, but this is an unusually quiet, leafy site, and the pool is set in a garden. *1324 Richmond Rd., 23185, tel. 804/229–6220 or 800/782–3800; fax 804/229–2774. 54 rooms. AE, DC, MC, V. Moderate.*

War Hill Inn. Built in 1970 on a 32-acre operating cattle farm, the inn was designed to resemble an 18th-century brick-and-wood structure and has been furnished with appropriate antiques and reproductions. *4560 Long Hill Rd., 23188, tel. 804/565–0248. 5 rooms, cottage. AE, MC, V. Moderate.*

Yorktown Dining
Nick's Seafood Pavilion. In this simply decorated riverside dining room, the fare may include seafood shish kebab (lobster, shrimp, scallops, tomatoes, peppers, mushrooms, and onion, served with rice pilaf and topped with brown butter) or a buttery lobster pilaf, with baklava for dessert. *Water St., tel. 804/887–5269. No reservations. AE, DC, MC, V. Moderate.*

Motels
The Woodlands (Information Center Dr., Williamsburg 23187, tel. 804/229–1000 or 800/447–8679; fax 804/221–8942), 315 rooms, restaurant, 3 pools, miniature golf, putting green, tennis court, playground; expensive. **Days Inn North** (1600 Robin Hood Rd., Richmond 23220, tel. 804/353–1287; fax 804/355–2659), 87 rooms, restaurant, bar, outdoor pool; moderate. **Duke of York Motel** (508 Water St., Yorktown 23690, tel. 804/898–3232), 57 rooms, restaurant, outdoor pool; moderate. **Governor Spotswood Motel** (1508 Richmond Rd., Williamsburg 23185, tel. 804/229–6444 or 800/368–1244), 78 rooms, outdoor pool, playground; inexpensive.

The Arts and Nightlife

The Arts
Barksdale Theatre (Hanover Tavern, Richmond, tel. 804/537–5333), founded in 1953, was the first dinner theater in the country. **Swift Mill Creek Playhouse** (Richmond, tel. 804/748–4411), another dinner theater, is housed in a 17th-century gristmill. **TheatreVirginia** (Richmond, tel. 804/367–0831), an Equity theater maintained by the Virginia Museum of Fine Arts, has a strong repertory. The **Richmond Symphony** (tel. 804/788–1212) often features internationally known soloists. **Concert Ballet of Virginia** (Richmond, tel. 804/780–1279) performs modern and experimental works. The **Richmond Ballet** (614 N. Lombardy St., tel. 804/359–0906) is the city's classical-ballet company.

Nightlife
Bogart's (203 N. Lombardy St., Richmond, tel. 804/353–9280) is a cozy jazz club. **The Flood Zone** (18th and Main Sts., Richmond, tel. 804/643–6006) is a rock-and-roll dance club in a converted recording studio. **J.B.'s Lounge** at the Fort Magruder Inn near Williamsburg (tel. 804/220–2250) features Top 40, country, or rock most nights.

Elsewhere in the State

Hampton Roads, Virginia Beach, and the Eastern Shore

Getting There **Norfolk International** and **Newport News–Williamsburg International airports** (*see* Richmond and Tidewater, *above*) are served by USAir. I–64 connects Richmond with Hampton Roads. U.S. 58 and Rte. 44 connect I–64 with Virginia Beach; U.S. 13 runs between Virginia Beach and the Eastern Shore via the Chesapeake Bay Bridge-Tunnel. **Greyhound** serves Virginia Beach (1017 Laskin Rd., tel. 804/422–2998) and various locations along U.S. 13 on the Eastern Shore.

What to See and Do The cities of Newport News and Hampton on the north and Norfolk on the south flank the enormous port of **Hampton Roads,** where the James empties into the Chesapeake. In **Newport News,** the **Mariner's Museum** (I–64 Exit 258A, tel. 804/595–0368) displays tiny hand-carved models of ancient vessels and full-size specimens of more recent ones, including a gondola and a Japanese submarine. The very latest in transportation can be viewed in **Hampton** at the **Virginia Air and Space Museum** (600 Settlers Landing Rd., tel. 804/727–0800), which opened in 1992; the exhibits include a lunar rock and an Apollo capsule. At Hampton's **Ft. Monroe** (Rte. 258, tel. 804/727–3391), the **Casemate Museum** tells the Civil War history of the moat-enclosed Union stronghold—object of the battle between the *Monitor* and the *Merrimac*, and President Jefferson Davis's prison after the Confederacy's defeat.

Norfolk is best known for the **U.S. Naval Base** (Hampton Blvd., tel. 804/444–7955), home to more than 125 ships of the Atlantic and Mediterranean fleets, including the nuclear-powered USS *Theodore Roosevelt*—the world's second-largest warship. The sights are gentler at the **Norfolk Botanical Gardens** (I–64, airport exit, tel. 804/441–5830), 175 acres supporting an abundance of azaleas, camellias, and roses—plus a lone palm tree. The arts are preserved at the **Hermitage Foundation Museum** (7637 North Shore Rd., tel. 804/423–2052), a reconstructed Tudor mansion that houses a large collection of Oriental art; and at the **Chrysler Museum** (Olney Rd. and Mowbray Arch, tel. 804/622–1211), whose collection ranges from Gainsborough to Roy Lichtenstein. Of historical interest are the elegant **Moses Myers House** (323 Freemason St., tel. 804/627–2727), built in 1792 by Norfolk's first Jewish resident; and the **Douglas MacArthur Memorial** (Bank St. and City Hall Ave., tel. 804/441–2965), burial place and museum of the controversial war hero.

The heart of **Virginia Beach,** 6 mi of crowded public beach and a raucous 40-block boardwalk, has been a popular summer gathering place for many years. One advantage of the commercialism is easy access to sailing, surfing, and scuba rentals. Almost 2 mi inland, at the southern end of Virginia Beach, is one of the state's most visited museums, the **Virginia Marine Science Museum** (717 General Booth Blvd., tel. 804/425–3474), where visitors can use computers to predict the weather, bird-watch in a salt marsh, and take a simulated journey to the bottom of the sea. Inland from the bay shore, and a throwback to much quieter times, is the 1680 **Adam Thoroughgood House** (1636 Parish

Rd., tel. 804/627–2737), said to be the oldest non-Spanish brick house in the country.

On the Eastern Shore, U.S. 13 takes you past historic 17th- to 19th-century towns, such as **Eastville**, with its 250-year-old courthouse. **Onancock** has a working general store established in 1842 and a wharf from which to catch that east-coast rarity: a sunset over the water (that is, the bay).

Assateague Island is a 37-mi-long wildlife refuge and recreational area that extends north into Maryland (*see* Maryland). Smaller and closer to shore is neighboring **Chincoteague Island,** where, despite invasive tourism and overdevelopment, at least one tradition survives from a simpler time: Every July the wild ponies from Assateague are driven across the channel and placed at auction here; the unsold swim back home. All year long, the fine beaches and natural beauty next door justify a visit to Chincoteague. On nearby **Wallops Island** is NASA's **Wallops Flight Facility** (Rte. 175, tel. 804/824–2298), where a museum tells the story of the space program on the site of early rocket launchings.

For further information on the region, contact **Virginia Beach Visitors Center** (2100 Parks Ave., 23451, tel. 804/437–4888 or 800/822–3224), **Chincoteague Chamber of Commerce** (Box 258, 23336, tel. 804/336–6161), or **Eastern Shore of Virginia Chamber of Commerce** (Box R, Melfa 23410, tel. 804/787–2460).

Lodging **Norfolk Waterside Marriott.** Next door to the convention center and connected by a walkway to the Waterside mall, this hotel opened in late 1991. *235 E. Main St., 23510, tel. 804/627–4200 or 800/228–9290; fax 804/628–6452. 405 rooms. Facilities: 2 restaurants, lounge, health club, indoor pool. AE, D, DC, MC, V. Expensive.*

Omni International. Built in 1976 and renovated in 1993, this hotel offers views of the harbor from about half its rooms. *777 Waterside Dr., 23510, tel. 804/622–6664 or 800/843–6664, fax 804/625–4930. 442 rooms. Facilities: restaurant, lounge, health club, outdoor pool. AE, D, DC, MC, V. Expensive.*

WASHINGTON, D.C.

By John F. Kelly

Population   606,900
Official Bird   Wood thrush
Official Flower   American Beauty rose

Introduction

Washington, the District of Columbia, was founded in 1791 as the world's first planned national capital. It's a city of unforgettable memorials, a place where the striking image of the Washington Monument is never far from sight and the stirring memories of a young democratic republic are never far from mind.

The capital's attractions are more than just governmental, though; visitors will find world-class theaters, music, parks and gardens, and the many museums of the Smithsonian Institution. Washington is a showcase city and, like America itself, opens its arms to everyone.

Tourist Information

Washington, D.C., Convention and Visitors Association information center (1455 Pennsylvania Ave., NW, 20005 tel. 202/789–7000; events recording: tel. 202/737–8866). **Dial-A-Park** (tel. 202/619–7275) is a recording of events at National Park Service attractions.

Arriving and Departing

By Plane   **National Airport** (tel. 703/685–8000) in Virginia, 4 mi south of downtown Washington, has scheduled flights by most major domestic carriers. It is often cramped and crowded, but it's a convenient 20-minute subway ride from the center of Washington ($1.25, depending on the time of day). Cab fare downtown should average $9, including tip.

Many transcontinental and international flights arrive at **Dulles International Airport** (tel. 703/685–8000), a modern facility 26 mi west of Washington in Virginia. **Baltimore-Washington International (BWI) Airport** (tel. 410/859–7111) is in Maryland, about 25 mi northeast of Washington.

Bus service is provided to National and Dulles airports by **Washington Flyer** (tel. 703/685–1400) and to BWI by **The Airport Connection** (tel. 301/441–2345).

By Car   I–95 approaches Washington from the north and south, encircling the city in Maryland and Virginia as the Beltway. I–66 leads west through Virginia; I–270, northwest into Maryland.

Train Station   **Union Station** (50 Massachusetts Ave., NE, tel. 202/484–7540).

Bus Station   **Greyhound** (1005 1st St., NE, tel. 301/565–2662).

Getting Around Washington, D.C.

Washington's best-known sights are a short walk—or a short Metro ride—from one another.

By Car   A car can be a drawback in Washington. Traffic is horrendous, especially at rush hours (6:30–9:30 AM and 3:30–7 PM). Parking is also an adventure: Free spots are hard to find, private lots expensive. There is free, three-hour parking around the Mall on Jefferson Drive and Madison Drive, though these spots always seem to be filled. You can park free—in some spots all day—in parking areas south of the Lincoln Memorial on Ohio Drive and West Basin Drive in West Potomac Park.

By Public   The **Washington Metropolitan Area Transit Authority** (tel. 202/
Transportation   637–7000; TDD 202/638–3780) provides Metrorail and Metrobus service in the District and in the Maryland and Virginia suburbs. The base fare is $1; the actual price you pay depends on the time of day and the distance traveled (all bus rides within the District are $1). Children under five ride free when accompanied by a paying passenger. A $5 **Metro Tourist Pass** entitles you to one day of unlimited subway travel any weekend or holiday (except July 4).

By Taxi   Taxis in the District are not metered but operate on a curious zone system. Two major companies are **Capitol Cab** (tel. 202/
546–2400) and **Diamond Cab** (tel. 202/387–6200). Maryland and Virginia taxis are metered but cannot take passengers between points within Washington.

Orientation Tours

Buses from **Tourmobile** (tel. 202/554–7950 or 202/554–5100) and **Old Town Trolley Tours** (tel. 301/985–3021) ply routes around the city's major attractions, allowing passengers to get on and off as often as they like. **Gray Line Tours** (tel. 301/386–8300) offers a four-hour motorcoach tour of Washington, Embassy Row, and Arlington National Cemetery; four-hour tours of Mount Vernon and Alexandria; and a combination of both.

Walking Tour   Not a specific walking route but a group of sites within historic neighborhoods, the **Black History National Recreation Trail** (brochure available from National Park Service, 1100 Ohio Dr., SW, 20242, tel. 202/619–7222) illustrates aspects of African-American history in Washington, from slavery days to the New Deal.

Exploring Washington, D.C.

The Mall is the logical first stop for visitors to Washington. Ringing it are the major museums and galleries of the Smithsonian Institution. At the east end is the U.S. Capitol, to the west are the city's major monuments, and just a stone's throw away is the White House. Start your visit here to see Washington the capital, then venture farther afield to see Washington the city.

The Mall   The first museum built by the Smithsonian was architect James Renwick's Norman-style **Castle.** Today it's home to the **Smithsonian Information Center;** an orientation film inside provides an overview of the various Smithsonian offerings, and television monitors announce the day's special events. *1000 Jefferson*

Dr., SW. For all Smithsonian museums: tel. 202/357–2700, TDD 202/357–1729. Admission free.

Walking counterclockwise around the Mall, you'll come to the Smithsonian's **Arts and Industries Building** (900 Jefferson Dr., SW), a treasure trove of Victoriana, then the striking **Hirshhorn Museum and Sculpture Garden** (7th St. and Independence Ave., SW), featuring modern art.

Across the street is the most visited museum in the world: the **National Air and Space Museum** (Jefferson Dr. at 6th St., SW). Twenty-three galleries tell the story of aviation, from man's earliest attempts at flight to travels beyond our solar system. Breathtaking IMAX films are shown on the five-story screen of the museum's Langley Theater (admission charged), while images of celestial bodies are projected on a domed ceiling in the Albert Einstein Planetarium.

On the north side of the Mall are the two buildings of the **National Gallery of Art:** architect John Russell Pope's domed West Building and I. M. Pei's angular East Building. Modern works are generally shown in the East Building, while the West Building's more than 100 galleries provide a survey of Western art from the 13th to the 20th century. *Madison Dr. and 4th St., NW, tel. 202/737–4215, TDD 202/842–6176. Admission free.*

The **National Museum of Natural History** (Madison Dr. between 9th and 12th Sts., NW) is filled with bones, fossils, stuffed animals, and other natural delights, including the popular Dinosaur Hall, the Hope Diamond, and a sea-life display featuring a living coral reef.

The three floors of the **National Museum of American History** (Madison Ave. between 12th and 14th Sts., NW) trace the social, political, and technological history of the United States. Here you'll find a 280-ton steam locomotive, a collection of first ladies' inaugural gowns, and the Bunkers' living room furniture from the TV series "All in the Family."

Across the Mall are three more Smithsonian museums: the **Freer Gallery of Art** (12th St. and Jefferson Dr., SW), a repository of Oriental art that's also known for James McNeill Whistler's stunning *Peacock Room;* the **Arthur M. Sackler Gallery** (1050 Independence Ave., SW), whose collection includes works from China, the Indian subcontinent, Persia, Thailand, and Indonesia; and the **National Museum of African Art** (950 Independence Ave., SW), dedicated to the collection, exhibition, and study of the traditional arts of sub-Saharan Africa.

The Monuments   Washington is a city of monuments. Those dedicated to the most famous Americans are west of the Mall on ground reclaimed from the marshy flats of the Potomac.

The tallest of them all is the **Washington Monument,** toward the Mall's western end. Construction of the 555-foot obelisk was started in 1848, interrupted by the Civil War (the reason for the color change about a third of the way up), and finally completed in 1884. An elevator takes those who wait out the sometimes long lines to the top of the monument, where the view is unequaled. *Constitution Ave. at 15th St., NW, tel. 202/426–6840. Admission free.*

On the south bank of the **Tidal Basin** is the **Jefferson Memorial,** honoring America's third president. One of the best views of

Washington, D.C.

Washington Nat'l Cathedral

National Zoological Park

California St.

T St.

16th St.

15th St.

14th St.

Massachusetts Ave.

S St.

S St.

Florida Ave.

Decatur Pl.

R St.

Sheridan Circle

R St.

Phillips Collection

Q St.

New Hampshire Ave.

Corcoran St.

Q St.

R St.

Church St.

Church St.

DUPONT CIRCLE

Massachusetts Ave.

Dupont Circle

P St.

O St.

30th St.

29th St.

28th St.

27th St.

R St.

P St.

O St.

Rock Creek

N St.

22nd St.

21st St.

20th St.

19th St.

18th St.

Connecticut Ave.

N St.

17th St.

O St.

Rhode Island Ave.

Scott Circle

16th St.

15th St.

Thomas Circle

GEORGE-TOWN

M St.

M St.

New Hampshire Ave.

M St.

19th St.

18th St.

M St.

L St.

L St.

L St.

26th St.

25th St.

Washington Circle

K St.

K St.

FARRAGUT NORTH

Hay-Adams Hotel

St. John's Episcopal Church

McPHERSON SQUARE

FOGGY BOTTOM

I St.

I St.

Pennsylvania Ave.

FARRAGUT WEST

Decatur House

H St.

Lafayette Park

National Museum Women in the

24th St.

23rd St.

22nd St.

Virginia Ave.

G St.

F St.

Renwick Gallery

Blair House

New Yo

14th St.

Old Executive Office Building

The White House

Treasury

Willa

Octagon House

Corcoran Gallery of Art

Hotel Washington

Natio Aqua

E St.

Memorial Continental Hall (D.A.R. Museum)

D St.

The Ellipse

17th St.

FEDE TRIAN

C St.

Constitution Ave.

Vietnam Veterans Memorial

National Museum of American History

Me

Washington Monument

Arlington National Cemetery

Lincoln Memorial

Reflecting Pool

SMITH

Memorial Bridge

U.S. Holocaust Memorial Museum

Independence Ave.

Kutz Bridge

Ohio Dr.

West

Potomac River

Potomac

W. Basin Dr.

Tidal Basin

Columbia Island

Park

Outlet Bridge

Jefferson Memorial

N

395

the White House can be seen from the top steps of the memorial, John Russell Pope's reinterpretation of the Pantheon in Rome. *Tel. 202/426–6821. Admission free.*

Cherry trees ring the approach to the **Lincoln Memorial,** at the west end of the Mall. Henry Bacon's monument is considered by many to be the most moving spot in the city, a mood enhanced by Daniel Chester French's somber statue of the seated president gazing out over the **Reflecting Pool.** Visit this memorial at night for best effect. *Tel. 202/426–6895. Admission free.*

In Constitution Gardens, the **Vietnam Veterans Memorial**—a black granite *V* designed by Maya Ling and a sculptural group by Frederick Hart—is another landmark that encourages introspection. The names of more than 58,000 Americans are etched on the face of the wall in the order of their deaths. *23rd St. and Constitution Ave., NW, tel. 202/634–1568. Admission free.*

The President's Neighborhood The president's schedule is usually too busy to allow sightseeing, even in his immediate neighborhood. If he did have the time, he'd find an area of town that includes some of Washington's most interesting buildings and museums.

Overlooking **Lafayette Park** is the **White House,** the most famous residence in Washington. The house was designed by Irishman James Hoban, who based it on the Georgian design of Leinster Hall near Dublin and of other Irish country houses. To get a glimpse of some of the public rooms—including the East Room and the State Dining Room—join the (usually long) line that forms along the east fence of the White House. Between Memorial Day and Labor Day you'll need tickets to tour the mansion—go early (by 8 AM to be safe; one ticket per person), and get them at the blue-and-green ticket booth on the **Ellipse,** just south of the White House. *1600 Pennsylvania Ave., NW, tel. 202/456–7041 (recorded information) or 202/619–7222. Admission free. Closed Sun.–Mon.*

Just across Lafayette Square is the golden-domed **St. John's Episcopal Church** (16th and H Sts., NW, tel. 202/347–8766), the so-called Church of the Presidents. Across 16th Street stands the **Hay-Adams Hotel** (*see* Lodging, *below*), one of the most opulent hostelries in the city and a favorite with Washington insiders and visiting celebrities.

The first floor of the redbrick, Federal-style **Decatur House** (748 Jackson Pl., NW, tel. 202/842–0920; admission charged) is decorated as it was when naval hero Stephen Decatur lived there in 1819. The green canopy at 1651 Pennsylvania Avenue marks the entrance to **Blair House,** the residence used by visiting heads of state. (When dignitaries are visiting the president, you'll often see their country's flag flying from the lampposts on Pennsylvania Avenue.) Across the street is the **Old Executive Office Building,** a French Empire–style structure in which the vice president has his office.

Facing the avenue is the Smithsonian's **Renwick Gallery** (Pennsylvania Ave. and 17th St., NW), devoted to American decorative arts.

A few blocks away is the **Corcoran Gallery of Art.** One of the few large museums in Washington outside the Smithsonian family, the Corcoran has a collection that ranges from works by early

American artists to late 19th- and early 20th-century paintings from Europe. A highlight is the entire 18th-century Grand Salon of the Hôtel d'Orsay in Paris. *17th St. and New York Ave., NW, tel. 202/638–1439. Admission charged. Closed Tues.*

Despite its name, the 1801 **Octagon House** has six sides. The Treaty of Ghent, ending the War of 1812, was signed in an upstairs study. Exhibits relating to architecture, decorative arts, and Washington history are mounted here today. *1799 New York Ave., NW, tel. 202/638–3105, TDD 202/638–1538. Admission charged. Closed Mon.*

On 17th Street is **Memorial Continental Hall,** headquarters of the Daughters of the American Revolution. The 50,000-item collection of the **D.A.R. Museum** includes fine examples of Colonial and Federal silver, china, porcelain, stoneware, earthenware, and glass. *1776 D St., NW, tel. 202/879–3240. Admission free. Closed Sat.*

Across the Ellipse is the venerable **Hotel Washington** (515 15th St., tel. 202/638–5900). The view from the rooftop Sky Top Lounge (open May–Oct.) is one of the best in the city. Across 14th Street is the huge, Greek Revival **Treasury Building,** home to the Department of the Treasury.

Capitol Hill   Pierre L'Enfant, the French designer of Washington, called Capitol Hill (then known as Jenkins Hill) "a pedestal waiting for a monument." That monument is the **U.S. Capitol,** the gleaming white-domed building in which elected officials toil. George Washington laid the cornerstone on September 18, 1793, and in November 1800 Congress moved down from Philadelphia. The Capitol building has grown over the years and today contains some of the city's most beautiful art, from Constantino Brumidi's *Apotheosis of Washington,* the fresco at the center of the dome, to the splendid Statuary Hall. There are also live attractions: senators and representatives speechifying in their respective chambers. *East end of the Mall, tel. 202/224–3121 or 202/225–6827. Admission free.*

East of the Capitol are the three buildings of the **Library of Congress,** whose 90 million reference items are available to readers 18 and older. The green-domed **Jefferson Building** (1st St. and Independence Ave., SE, tel. 202/707–8000), with its grand, octagonal Main Reading Room and mahogany reader's tables, is the centerpiece of the system.

Behind the Jefferson Building stands the **Folger Shakespeare Library.** Inside are a reproduction of an inn-yard theater and a gallery, designed in the manner of an Elizabethan Great Hall, that hosts rotating exhibits from the library's collection of works by and about the Bard. *201 E. Capitol St., SE, tel. 202/544–4600. Admission free. Closed Sun.*

After being shunted around several locations, including a spell in a tavern, the **Supreme Court** got its own building in 1935. The impressive, colonnaded white-marble temple was designed by Cass Gilbert. *1st and E. Capitol Sts., NE, tel. 202/479–3000. Admission free. Closed weekends.*

Union Station (50 Massachusetts Ave., NE) is now a shopping center as well as a train station. The Beaux Arts building's wonderful main waiting room is a perfect setting for the inaugural ball that's held here every four years.

Old Downtown and Federal Triangle

Before the glass office blocks around 16th and K streets, NW, became the business center of town, Washington's mercantile hub was farther east. The open-air markets are gone, but some of the 19th-century character of Washington's east end remains. More recent is Federal Triangle, a humongous complex built in the 1930s to accommodate the expanding federal bureaucracy.

The massive redbrick **Pension Building,** built in the 1880s to house workers who processed the pension claims of veterans and their survivors, is home to the **National Building Museum** (F St. between 4th and 5th Sts., NW, tel. 202/272–2448; admission free), devoted to architecture and the building arts.

Judiciary Square is Washington's legal core, with local and district court buildings arrayed around it. At the center is the **National Law Enforcement Officers Memorial,** a 3-foot-high wall bearing the names of more than 15,000 American police officers killed in the line of duty since 1794. Not far away is Washington's compact **Chinatown,** bordered by G, E, 5th, and 8th streets, NW.

Two more Smithsonian museums—the **National Portrait Gallery,** with its paintings and photographs of presidents and other notable Americans, and the **National Museum of American Art,** whose collection ranges from Colonial times to the present—are in the Greek Revival Old Patent Office Building (8th and G Sts., NW).

A few blocks away is **Ford's Theatre** (511 10th St., NW, tel. 202/426–6924; admission free), where Abraham Lincoln was assassinated by John Wilkes Booth on April 14, 1865. A museum in the basement displays items connected with Lincoln's life and untimely death.

The Beaux Arts **Willard Hotel,** on the corner of 14th Street and Pennsylvania Avenue, is one of the most luxurious in Washington. The **Commerce Department Building** forms the base of **Federal Triangle.** Inside Commerce is the **National Aquarium,** the country's oldest public aquarium, featuring tropical and freshwater fish, moray eels, frogs, turtles, piranhas, even sharks. *14th St. and Pennsylvania Ave., NW, tel. 202/482–2825. Admission charged.*

The tour of the hulking **J. Edgar Hoover Federal Bureau of Investigation Building** outlines the work of the FBI and ends with a live-ammo firearms demonstration. In high tourist season there may be up to an hour's wait to get inside. *10th St. and Pennsylvania Ave., NW (tour entrance on E St., NW), tel. 202/324–3447. Tours weekdays.*

The Declaration of Independence, the Constitution, and the Bill of Rights are on display in the Rotunda of the **National Archives.** *Constitution Ave. between 7th and 9th Sts., NW, tel. 202/501–5000. Admission free.*

Across 7th Street is the **Navy Memorial,** a statue of a lone sailor staring out over the largest map in the world. In summer the memorial's concert stage is the site of military-band performances (tel. 202/737–2300).

Georgetown

Georgetown, a former tobacco port, is Washington's poshest neighborhood, home to some of its wealthiest and best-known citizens. It's also the nucleus of Washington's nightlife scene, with dozens of bars and restaurants dotting Wisconsin Avenue and M Street, Georgetown's crossroads.

Starting in Georgetown and running parallel to the Potomac is the **Chesapeake & Ohio Canal,** a 19th-century waterway that once carried lumber, coal, iron, and flour into northwest Maryland. Joggers tread its scenic towpath, and in summer mule-drawn barges ply its placid waters (tickets available at the Foundry Mall, 1055 Thomas Jefferson St., NW, tel. 202/472–4376).

Georgetown Park (3222 M St., NW), home to such high-ticket stores as F.A.O. Schwarz, Williams-Sonoma, and Polo/Ralph Lauren, is a multilevel shopping extravaganza that answers the question "If the Victorians had invented shopping malls, what would they look like?"

At the western edge of Georgetown is **Georgetown University,** the oldest Jesuit school in the country. When seen from the Potomac or from Washington's high ground, the Gothic spires of the university's older buildings give it an almost medieval look.

To the north is **Dumbarton Oaks,** an estate comprising two museums—one of Byzantine works, the other of pre-Columbian art—and 10 acres of stunning formal gardens designed by landscape architect Beatrix Farrand. *Art collections: 1703 32nd St., NW, tel. 202/338–8278. Admission charged. Closed Mon. Gardens: 31st and R Sts., NW. Admission charged Apr.–Oct.*

Arlington, Virginia   Though these attractions are across the Potomac, they're a part of any visit to the nation's capital. (For more suburban Virginia sites—including Mount Vernon and Old Town Alexandria—*see* Virginia.)

At **Arlington National Cemetery,** visitors can trace America's history through the aftermath of its battles. Dominating the cemetery is the Greek Revival **Arlington House,** onetime home of Robert E. Lee, which offers a breathtaking view across the Potomac to the Lincoln Memorial and the Mall. On a hillside below are the **Kennedy graves.** John F. Kennedy is buried under an eternal flame; nearby, marked by a simple white cross, is the grave of his brother Robert. Also in the cemetery is the **Tomb of the Unknowns.** *West end of Memorial Bridge, tel. 703/692–0931. Admission free.*

Just north of the cemetery is the **United States Marine Corps War Memorial,** honoring Marines who have given their lives since the Corps was formed in 1775. The memorial statue, sculpted by Felix W. de Weldon, is based on Joe Rosenthal's Pulitzer Prize–winning photograph of six soldiers raising a flag atop Mt. Suribachi on Iwo Jima on February 19, 1945. (A word of caution: It is dangerous to visit the memorial after dark.)

The **Pentagon,** headquarters of the Department of Defense, is an exercise in immensity: 23,000 military and civilian employees work here; it is as wide as three Washington Monuments laid end to end; inside are 17½ mi of corridors, 7,754 windows, and 691 drinking fountains. Visitors can take a 75-minute tour. *Off I-395, tel. 703/695–1776. Tours weekdays every half-hour 9:30–3:30. Closed on federal holidays.*

Other Attractions   The **Bureau of Engraving and Printing** is the birthplace of all paper currency in the United States. Despite the fact that there are no free samples, the 20-minute self-guided tour—

which takes visitors past presses that turn out some $22.5 million a day—is one of the city's most popular. *14th and C Sts., SW, tel. 202/847–3019. Admission free. Closed weekends.*

Alongside the city's many museums celebrating the best of humanity's accomplishments is one that illustrates what humans at their worst are capable of. The **United States Holocaust Memorial Museum,** which opened in April 1993, tells in almost cinematic fashion the story of the 11 million Jews, Gypsies, Jehovah's Witnesses, homosexuals, political prisoners, and others killed by the Nazis between 1933 and 1945. *100 Raoul Wallenberg Pl., SW (14th St. and Independence Ave., SW), tel. 202/653–9220. Admission free.*

The **Phillips Collection** was the first permanent museum of modern art in the country. Holdings include works by Braque, Cézanne, Klee, Matisse, Renoir, and John Henry Twachtman. *1600–1612 21st St., NW, tel. 202/387–2151. Admission charged.*

The **National Geographic Society's Explorers Hall** is the magazine come to life. Interactive exhibits encourage visitors to learn about the world. The centerpiece is a hand-painted globe, 11 feet in diameter, that floats and spins on a cushion of air, showing off different features of the planet. *17th and M Sts., NW, tel. 202/857–7588. Admission free.*

The 160-acre **National Zoological Park,** part of the Smithsonian Institution, is one of the foremost zoos in the world. Innovative compounds show animals in naturalistic settings, and the ambitious Amazonia re-creates the complete ecosystem of a South American rain forest. *3001 Connecticut Ave., NW, tel. 202/673–4717. Admission free.*

The **Frederick Douglass National Historic Site** is at Cedar Hill, the Washington home of the noted abolitionist. The house displays mementos from Douglass's life and has a wonderful view of the Federal City, across the Anacostia River. *1411 W St., SE, tel. 202/426–5961. Admission free.*

The **National Museum of Women in the Arts** displays the works of prominent female artists from the Renaissance to the present, including Georgia O'Keeffe, Mary Cassatt, Elisabeth Vigée-Lebrun, and Judy Chicago. *1250 New York Ave., NW, tel. 202/783–5000. Admission charged.*

The **Washington Navy Yard** is the Navy's oldest shore establishment. A former shipyard and ordnance facility, the yard today is home to the **Navy Museum** and the **Marine Corps Museum,** which outline the history of those two services from their inception to the present. *9th and M Sts., SE, tel. 202/433–4882. Admission free.*

It took 83 years to complete the Gothic-style **Washington National Cathedral,** the sixth-largest cathedral in the world. Besides flying buttresses, naves, transepts, and barrel vaults that were built stone by stone, it is adorned with fanciful gargoyles created by skilled stone carvers. *Wisconsin and Massachusetts Aves., NW, tel. 202/537–6200. Admission free.*

Parks and Gardens

The 444-acre **National Arboretum** blooms with all manner of plants, including clematis, peonies, rhododendrons, and azaleas. Also popular are the National Bonsai Collection, National Herb Garden, and an odd and striking hilltop construction of old marble columns from the U.S. Capitol. *3501 New York Ave., NE, tel. 202/475–4815. Admission free.*

Rock Creek Park (tel. 202/426–6829) is a cool tongue of green jutting down into the center of Washington. Its 1,800 acres include picnic sites and biking, hiking, and equestrian trails that wend through groves of dogwood, beech, oak, and cedar.

The **United States Botanic Garden,** just below the Capitol, is a peaceful, plant-filled conservatory that includes a cactus house, a fern house, and a subtropical house filled with orchids. *1st St. and Maryland Ave., SW, tel. 202/225–8333. Admission free.*

Shopping

Shopping Districts **Georgetown** (centered on Wisconsin Ave. and M St., NW) is probably Washington's densest shopping area, with specialty shops selling everything from antiques to designer fashions. **Adams-Morgan** (around 18th St. and Columbia Rd., NW) is a bit funkier, with lots of used book and clothing stores and a bohemian atmosphere.

The Shops at National Place (13th and F Sts., NW, tel. 202/783–9090) is a glittering, three-story collection of stores, including Banana Republic, Victoria's Secret, and The Sharper Image. **Union Station** (50 Massachusetts Ave., NE, tel. 202/371–9441) has trendy clothing boutiques like Cignal and Martinaro and neat special-interest shops like the Nature Company (decorative natural objects) and Political America (campaign buttons and memorabilia). **Mazza Gallerie** (5300 Wisconsin Ave., NW, tel. 202/966–6114) is an upmarket mall straddling the Maryland border that's anchored by the ritzy Neiman Marcus.

Department Stores Washington's two main department stores are downtown, by the Metro Center subway stop. Both **Hecht's** (12th and G Sts., NW, tel. 202/628–6661) and **Woodward & Lothrop** (11th and F Sts., NW, tel. 202/347–5300) are bright and spacious, with a wide selection of items, sensibly grouped.

Specialty Stores Every museum in Washington has a gift shop; in each, the range of items reflects the museum's collection and extends far beyond the mere souvenir. The largest is probably in the **National Museum of American History** (*see* Exploring Washington, *above*).

Spectator Sports

Basketball **Bullets** (Capital Centre, 1 Harry S. Truman Dr., Landover, MD, tel. 202/432–7328; Sept.–Apr.).

Football All regular **Redskins** home games at RFK Stadium (E. Capitol and 22nd Sts., SE, tel. 202/546–2222; Aug.–Dec.) are sold out to season-ticket holders. If you're willing to pay dearly, you can get tickets from brokers who advertise in *The Washington Post* classifieds.

Hockey **Capitals** (Capital Centre, tel. 202/432–7328; Oct.–Apr.).

Dining

Washington's restaurants aren't exactly innovators, but neither are they blind to fashion. That means trends started elsewhere—nouvelle cuisine, New American, southwestern—quickly show up in the capital. Good ethnic meals can be found in Adams-Morgan (lots of Ethiopian), Georgetown (Afghani to Indonesian), and Chinatown. For price ranges, see Chart 1 (A) in Chapter 1.

Very Expensive

★ **Jean-Louis at the Watergate Hotel.** This small restaurant is a showcase for the cooking of Jean-Louis Palladin. The contemporary French fare is based on regional American ingredients—crawfish from Louisiana, wild mushrooms from Oregon, game from Texas—combined in innovative ways. *2650 Virginia Ave., NW, tel. 202/298–4488. Reservations required. Jacket and tie required. AE, DC, MC, V. No lunch; closed Sun. and last 2 weeks in Aug.*

Le Lion d'Or. The superior entrées at this French restaurant include lobster soufflé, ravioli with foie gras, and crepes with oysters and caviar. Don't forget to place an order for a dessert soufflé—it will leave you breathless. *1150 Connecticut Ave., NW, tel. 202/296–7972. Reservations advised. Jacket and tie required. AE, DC, MC, V. No lunch Sat.; closed Sun.*

Expensive

★ **i Ricchi.** At this airy Tuscan restaurant, the spring/summer menu includes such offerings as rolled pork and rabbit roasted in wine and fresh herbs, while the fall/winter list brings grilled lamb chops and sautéed beef fillet. *1220 19th St., NW, tel. 202/835–0459. Reservations advised. Jacket and tie advised. AE, DC, MC, V. No lunch Sat.; closed Sun.*

Occidental Grill. Part of the stately Willard Hotel complex, this popular restaurant offers innovative dishes, attentive service, and lots of photos of politicians and other power brokers past and present. The menu changes frequently, but you can count on grilled poultry, fish, and steak, as well as salads and sandwiches. *1475 Pennsylvania Ave., NW, tel. 202/783–1475. Reservations advised. AE, DC, MC, V.*

Sam and Harry's. Here is the quintessential steak house. The surroundings are understated and genteel and the bar is a popular downtown gathering place. The main attractions are the porterhouse steak and the prime rib. *1200 19th St., NW, tel. 202/296–4333. Reservations advised. Jacket and tie advised. AE, DC, MC, V. No lunch Sat.; closed Sun.*

Moderate

★ **Bacchus.** Appetizers are especially well executed at this Lebanese restaurant offering impeccable versions of *hummus* and *baba ghannouj*, as well as more exotic concoctions of ground beef, eggplant, and yogurt. *1827 Jefferson St., NW, tel. 202/785–0734. Reservations advised. Dress: neat but casual. AE, MC, V. No lunch Sat.; closed Sun.*

Notte Luna. Diners at this Italian restaurant sit in a dramatic black-and-fuchsia neon dining room while chefs work in an open kitchen around a wood-burning pizza oven. The ordinary here often has an unexpected twist; you can order your pizza topped with gravlax or lamb sausage, your pasta with grilled salmon. *809 15th St., NW, tel. 202/408–9500. Reservations advised. Dress: neat but casual. AE, DC, MC, V. No lunch weekends.*

Old Glory. Always teeming with visiting Texans, Georgetown students, and closet Elvis fans, Old Glory sticks to barbecue basics: sandwiches and platters of pulled and sliced pork, beef brisket, and smoked and pulled chicken, ribs, and sausage. The open pit will also roast vegetables, but they're an unusual choice here. *3139 M St., NW, tel. 202/337–3406. Reservations for large groups only. AE, DC, MC, V.*

Sushi-Ko. At Washington's first sushi bar, the menu includes—in addition to the à la carte items and fresh sushi and sashimi—seafood and vegetable tempuras, fish teriyaki, and *udonsuki* (noodles with seafood and vegetables). *2309 Wisconsin Ave., NW, tel. 202/333–4187. Reservations advised. Dress: neat but casual. AE, MC, V. No lunch weekends; closed Mon.*

Inexpensive **American Café.** Healthy food—but not health food—served here includes roast beef on humongous croissants, fresh fish, seafood pie, and barbecued ribs. Weekend brunches offer such temptations as strawberry-banana-nut waffles and stuffed French toast. *1211 Wisconsin Ave., NW, tel. 202/547–8500. Reservations for large groups only. AE, DC, MC, V.*

Café Atlantico. This lively spot in Adams-Morgan serves Caribbean specialties in a casual atmosphere. Appetizers include conch, cod, and yucca fritters, as well as shrimp and potato croquettes, all beautifully fried. Pork loin, jerk chicken, and lamb curry are among the main courses. *1819 Columbia Rd., NW, tel. 202/575–2233. No reservations. AE, MC, V. No lunch.*

Madurai. The extensive menu and well-prepared dishes at this all-vegetarian Indian establishment make up for its lackluster decor. Cost-conscious diners can take advantage of the Sunday all-you-can-eat buffet (noon to 4 and 5 to 10 PM), which offers curries, basmati rice, and Indian breads. *3318 M St., NW, tel. 202/333–0997. AE, MC, V.*

★ **Meskerem.** Among Adams-Morgan's many Ethiopian restaurants, Meskerem is distinctive for a balcony where you can eat Ethiopian-style: seated on the floor on leather cushions, with large woven baskets for tables. For a truly authentic experience, order the *injera* (spongy bread) made with *teff*, a grain grown only in Ethiopia and Idaho that imparts a distinctive sourness. *2434 18th St., NW, tel. 202/462–4100. Reservations advised. Dress: neat but casual. AE, DC, MC, V. No lunch Mon.–Thurs.*

Lodging

Many Washington hotels, particularly those downtown, offer special reduced rates and package deals on weekends, and some are available midweek; be sure to ask about them at the hotel of your choice. To find reasonably priced accommodations in small guest houses and private homes, contact **Bed 'n' Breakfast Ltd. of Washington, D.C.** (Box 12011, 20005, tel. 202/328–3510) or **Bed and Breakfast League, Ltd.** (3639 Van Ness St., NW, 20008, tel. 202/363–7767). For price ranges, see Chart 2 (A) in Chapter 1.

Very Expensive ★ **Four Seasons Hotel.** This contemporary hotel, conveniently situated between Georgetown and Foggy Bottom, is a gathering place for Washington's elite. Guest rooms have traditional furniture upholstered in light colors. The quieter rooms face the courtyard; others have a view of the C&O Canal. *2800 Pennsylvania Ave., NW, 20007, tel. 202/342–0444. 167 rooms, 30 suites. Facilities: 2 restaurants, bar, nightclub, health club, pool. AE, DC, MC, V.*

★ **Hay-Adams Hotel.** Italian Renaissance in design, this hotel looks like a mansion in disguise. Seventeenth-century Medici tapestries adorn two lobby walls, while guest rooms are the most brightly colored in the city, decorated in 20 different English country-house schemes. *1 Lafayette Sq., 20006, tel. 202/ 638–6600 or 800/424–5054. 120 rooms, 23 suites. Facilities: 3 restaurants, bar. AE, DC, MC, V.*

The Ritz-Carlton. Exclusive and intimate, this Dupont Circle hotel has an English-hunt club theme, reflected in an extensive collection of 18th- and 19th-century English art heavy on horses and dogs. *2100 Massachusetts Ave., NW, 20008, tel. 202/ 293–2100. 215 rooms, 17 suites. Facilities: restaurant, access to health club. AE, DC, MC, V.*

Expensive **Latham Hotel.** A Colonial-style hotel in the city's liveliest
★ neighborhood, the redbrick Marbury is popular with Europeans, sports figures, and devotees of Georgetown. Some rooms are underground; others have views of the C&O Canal or busy M Street. *3000 M St., NW, 20007, tel. 202/726–5000 or 800/368–5922. 134 rooms, 9 suites. Facilities: room service 7 AM–10:30 PM, 2 restaurants, 2 bars, outdoor pool. AE, DC, MC, V.*

Phoenix Park Hotel. Just steps from Union Station and four blocks from the Capitol, this high-rise hotel has a wood-paneled and brass Irish men's-club theme and is the home of The Dubliner (*see* The Arts and Nightlife, *below*), one of Washington's best bars. Guest rooms are bright, traditionally furnished, and quiet. *520 N. Capitol St., NW, 20001, tel. 202/638–6900 or 800/824–5419. 82 rooms, 6 suites. Facilities: 2 restaurants. AE, DC, MC, V.*

★ **The Washington Hilton and Towers.** One of the city's busiest convention hotels, this high rise also attracts travelers who like to be where the action is. The light-filled but compact guest rooms are furnished in hotel *moderne* and have marble bathrooms. *1919 Connecticut Ave., NW, 20009, tel. 202/483–3000. 1,062 rooms, 88 suites. Facilities: 3 restaurants, 2 bars, 3 tennis courts, outdoor pool. AE, DC, MC, V.*

Moderate **Channel Inn.** This informal establishment, on an inlet of the Potomac a few blocks from the new Waterfront Metro station, offers views of bobbing boats and tranquil parkland across the water. Air traffic can be noisy during the daytime. *650 Water St., SW, 20024, tel. 202/554–2400 or 800/368–5668. 98 rooms, 2 suites. Facilities: restaurant, bar, coffee shop, outdoor pool. AE, DC, MC, V.*

Hotel Anthony. A good value, this small hotel has a courteous staff, offers the basics in the midst of the K and L streets business district, and is close to the White House. Some rooms have a full kitchen, some a wet bar; king, queen, or extra-long double beds are available. *1823 L St., NW, 20036, tel. 202/223–4320 or 800/424–2970. 99 rooms. Facilities: room service 7 AM–10 PM, 2 restaurants. AE, DC, MC, V.*

★ **Hotel Tabard Inn.** Three Victorian town houses near Dupont Circle were linked in the 1920s to form an inn that is still welcoming guests today. Furnishings are broken-in Victorian and American Empire antiques, and a Victorian-inspired carpet cushions the labyrinthine hallways. *1739 N St., NW, 20036, tel. 202/785–1277. 40 rooms (17 share baths). Facilities: restaurant. MC, V.*

Inexpensive **Washington International Hostel.** Guests sleep in four- to 14-person dormitories (some "couple" rooms are available, but reservations are required). Guests must bring their own linens or rent them from the hostel. The maximum stay is six days in summer, when reservations are highly recommended; off-season reservations are necessary only for groups. *1009 11th St., NW, 20001, tel. 202/737–2333. 250 beds. MC, V.*

The Arts and Nightlife

Area arts and entertainment events are listed in the Weekend section in Friday's *Washington Post*, the free *City Paper*, *Washingtonian* magazine (on newsstands), and *Where: Washington* (free in hotels).

The Arts **TicketPlace** (L St. between 15th and 16th Sts., NW, tel. 202/842–5387; closed Sun.) sells half-price, day-of-performance tickets for selected shows. **TicketMaster** (tel. 202/432–7328 or 800/551–7328) takes phone charges for events around the city. All manner of cultural events, from ballet to classical music, are offered at the **John F. Kennedy Center for the Performing Arts** (New Hampshire Ave. and Rock Creek Pkwy., NW, tel. 202/467–4600 or 800/444–1324).

Theater **Arena Stage** (6th St. and Maine Ave., SW, tel. 202/488–3300) has three theaters and is the city's most respected resident company. The historic **Ford's Theatre** (511 10th St., NW, tel. 202/347–4833) is host mainly to musicals. The **National Theatre** (1321 E St., NW, tel. 202/628–6161) presents pre- and post-Broadway shows. Now in a new home, the **Shakespeare Theatre** (450 7th St., NW, tel. 202/393–2700) presents classics by the Bard. Many scrappy smaller companies—including Source, Studio, and Woolly Mammoth—are clustered near 14th and P streets, NW.

Music The **National Symphony Orchestra** (tel. 202/416–8100) performs at the Kennedy Center from September through June and during the summer at Wolf Trap Farm Park (tel. 703/938–2404) in Virginia.

The **Armed Forces Concert Series** offers free military-band performances from June through August, Sunday through Friday evenings, on the West Terrace of the Capitol and at the Sylvan Theater on the Washington Monument grounds. *Air Force, tel. 202/767–5658; Army, tel. 703/696–3718; Marines, tel. 202/433–4011; Navy, tel. 202/433–2525.*

Opera The **Washington Opera** (tel. 202/416–7800 or 800/876–7372) presents seven operas each season in the Kennedy Center's Opera House and Eisenhower Theater.

Dance **Dance Place** (3225 8th St., NE, tel. 202/269–1600) hosts a wide assortment of modern and ethnic dance. The **Washington Ballet** (tel. 202/362–3606) performs mainly at the Kennedy Center.

Nightlife **Georgetown, Adams-Morgan, Dupont Circle,** and **Capitol Hill** are the main nightlife centers in Washington.

Bars **The Brickskeller** (1523 22nd St., NW, tel. 202/293–1885) sells more than 500 brands of beer—from Central American lagers to U.S. microbrewed ales. **The Dubliner** (Phoenix Park Hotel, 520 N. Capitol St., NW, tel. 202/737–3773) features snug, paneled rooms; thick, tasty Guinness; and nightly live Irish entertainment.

Cabaret Two troupes offering political song and satire perform regularly in Georgetown clubs: the **Capitol Steps** (tel. 202/298–8222 or 703/683–8330) and **Gross National Product** (tel. 202/783–7212).

The **Marquee Lounge** (Omni-Shoreham Hotel, 2500 Calvert St., NW, tel. 202/745–1023) is home to funny lady Joan Cushing and occasional song and dance acts.

Jazz   **Blues Alley** (rear 1073 Wisconsin Ave., NW, tel. 202/337–4141) books some of the biggest names in jazz. **One Step Down** (2517 Pennsylvania Ave., NW, tel. 202/331–8863) is an intimate, smoky space that's a favorite with hardcore devotees.

Rock and Reggae   **The Bayou** (3135 K St., NW, tel. 202/333–2897) in Georgetown features live rock. **Kilimanjaro** (1724 California St., NW, tel. 202/328–3838) specializes in "international" music from the Caribbean and Africa. The **9:30 Club** (930 F St., NW, tel. 202/393–0930) books an eclectic mix of local, national, and international artists, playing what used to be known as "new wave" music.

Excursions from Washington

Washington is within an easy drive of such cities as Annapolis, Baltimore, and Frederick in Maryland, and such Virginia attractions as Mount Vernon and Fredericksburg. For details, *see* Maryland and Virginia, *above*.

WEST VIRGINIA

*By Dale
Leatherman*

Capital	Charleston
Population	1,801,000
Motto	Mountaineers Are Always Free
State Bird	Cardinal
State Flower	Rhododendron maximum

Visitor Information

West Virginia Division of Tourism and Parks (Bldg. 6, Room B564, Charleston 25305, tel. 800/225–5982).

Scenic Drives

In the eastern part of the state, the **Highland Scenic Highway** (Rte. 150 between Cranberry Glades and U.S. 219/Rte. 55 north of Edray) and the **Highland Trace** (Rte. 55 between the Virginia border and Elkins) wind through the Potomac Highlands, the state's high-mountain region. In the south, the historic **Midland Trail** (U.S. 60) runs east–west for 120 mi between White Sulphur Springs and Charleston, tracing the 200-year-old path through the Appalachians first used by buffalo and Native Americans.

National and State Parks

National Parks The **Monongahela National Forest** (200 Sycamore St., Elkins 26241, tel. 304/636–1800) and **George Washington National Forest** (Lee Ranger District, Rte. 1, Box 31A, Edinburg 22824, tel. 703/984–4101) encompass 900,000 and 100,000 acres, respectively, near the Virginia border.

State Parks West Virginia is unique in that eight of its 35 state parks have fine lodges with restaurants and resort amenities, such as downhill skiing or golf courses. Most have cabins and campsites with full hookups. **Cacapon Resort State Park** (Berkeley Springs 25411, tel. 304/258–1022) is noted for its Robert Trent Jones golf course; amenities include 30 cottages and a 49-room lodge with restaurant. At **Canaan Valley Resort State Park** (Rte. 1, Box 330, Davis 26260, tel. 304/866–4121), the 250-room lodge, restaurant, and lounge are bustling year-round; the park has an alpine-skiing area, an 18-hole golf course, and a new indoor pool and fitness center. **Pipestem Resort State Park** (Pipestem 25979, tel. 304/466–1800), southeast of Beckley, has two lodges (143 rooms) with restaurants, 25 deluxe cottages, and 82 campsites, as well as golf, indoor and outdoor pools, an aerial tramway, and cross-country skiing.

Eastern West Virginia

It's easy to slip into West Virginia from the east, through the time tunnel of Harpers Ferry, Charles Town, and Shepherdstown, where buildings predate the Revolutionary War and bear the scars of the Civil War. To the west, the scene changes to one of rugged splendor in a swath of mountainland blessed with Canadian weather patterns—and the ski industry to prove it. In the spring, the focus shifts to white-water rafting on some of the nation's most exciting rivers.

Tourist Information

Potomac Highlands: Convention and Visitors Bureau (Executive Office Plaza, Suite 113, Elkins 26241, tel. 304/636–8400 or 800/347–1453). **Southern West Virginia:** Convention and Visitors Bureau (Box 1799, Beckley 25802, tel. 800/847–4898).

Getting There

By Plane   The region is served by Beckley's **Raleigh County Memorial Airport** (tel. 304/255–0476), Bluefield/Princeton's **Mercer County Airport** (tel. 304/327–5308 or 800/428–4332), Charleston's **Yeager Airport** (tel. 304/344–8033 or 800/241–6522), **Elkins/Randolph County Airport** (tel. 304/636–2726), and Lewisburg's **Greenbrier Valley Airport** (tel. 304/645–3961).

By Car   Three interstates traverse the region: I–64, between White Sulphur Springs and Beckley; I–77, Princeton to Charleston; and I–81, in the Eastern Panhandle. U.S. 340 enters Harpers Ferry from the east. From the west, U.S. 50, I–79, and I–64 provide the best access.

By Train   **Amtrak** has stations in Harpers Ferry, Martinsburg, Charleston, and White Sulphur Springs.

By Bus   **Greyhound** has terminals in major towns.

Exploring Eastern West Virginia

Old and new mingle here in surprising harmony. In the Eastern Panhandle you can explore pre–Revolutionary era buildings, shop for the latest in fashions, and relax in a Roman bath, all in the same day. To the west and south, the mountain roads are scenic but sometimes narrow and limited to 40 mph. Do your driving in the daytime—for safety's sake, and to enjoy the many overlooks and small towns reminiscent of the 1950s.

On the state's eastern tip is **Harpers Ferry National Historic Park** (tel. 304/535–6223; admission free), where the Shenandoah and Potomac rivers join. Hand-carved stone steps lead to the overlook where Thomas Jefferson proclaimed the view "worth a trip across the Atlantic." The town grew around a U.S. armory built in 1740, and many buildings have been preserved.

Lining the cobblestoned streets are shops and museums, where park employees in period costume demonstrate Colonial skills. The **John Brown Wax Museum** depicts the abolitionist's raid on the town. *Tel. 304/535–6342. Admission charged. Closed weekdays Feb.–Mar.*

In commerce-minded **Martinsburg** (*see* Shopping, *below*), two **pre–Civil War roundhouses** at the foot of Martin Street attract railroad buffs, though they're in poor condition. Downtown, pre–Civil War structures of Federal and Greek Revival style can be seen on John, Race, and North Spring streets.

From Martinsburg, Rte. 9 leads to **Berkeley Springs,** the nation's first spa, and George Washington's favorite. **Berkeley**

Springs State Park (tel. 304/258–5860; bathhouse closed Fri. Dec.–Feb.) offers heated Roman baths and massages.

Driving south, U.S. 50 and Rte. 93 take you over the mountains to **Davis** and the **Canaan Valley,** home of the **Canaan Valley** and **Timberline ski areas** (*see* Ski Areas, *below*). The high-tundralike **Dolly Sods Wilderness Area** of the Monongahela National Forest (*see* National and State Parks, *above*) is used for hiking, cross-country skiing, and nature studies.

A southwesterly route leads through the **Potomac Highlands,** an area with boundless opportunities for outdoor recreation, to the **National Radio Astronomy Observatory** in Green Bank, where huge radio telescopes listen for life in outer space. The process is explained during a bus tour and slide presentation. *Rte. 28/92 Tel. 304/456–2011. Admission free. Closed weekdays Memorial Day–mid-June and Labor Day–Oct., Mon.–Tues. mid-June–Labor Day; Nov.–Memorial Day.*

Nearby is **Cass Scenic Railroad State Park,** where visitors ride up Cheat Mountain in open railcars drawn by steam locomotives that pulled lumber cars in the early 1900s. *Rte. 66, Cass, tel. 304/456–4300. Admission: $11 adults, $5 children. Closed Nov.–May.*

Near Cass, the **Greenbrier River Trail State Park** (Star Rte., Caldwell, tel. 304/799–4087, 304/572–3771, or 800/336–7009), centered on a 76-mi former railroad bed, is now devoted to hikers (*see* Sports and Outdoor Activities, *below*), bikers, and cross-country skiers.

The towns of **Snowshoe** and **Slatyfork** mark the location of several downhill ski areas and miles of cross-country trails (*see* Ski Areas, *below*). **White Sulphur Springs** is the site of **The Greenbrier** (*see* Dining and Lodging, Spas, *below*), an elegant four-seasons resort visited by U.S. presidents and heads of state from around the world. The area's restorative springs have been an attraction for more than 200 years.

The **Lewisburg National Historic District** (tel. 304/645–1000) encompasses 236 acres and more than 60 18th-century buildings, many of native limestone or brick. At night, gas lamps flicker on quaint storefronts and signs, and no overhead power lines spoil the image of a bygone era.

To the south is **Winterplace ski resort** (*see* Ski Areas, *below*) and **Pipestem Resort State Park** (*see* National and State Parks, *above*). North is a land of raging waters that have played a major role in West Virginia tourism since the 1970s. Major whitewater rafting areas (*see* Sports and Outdoor Activities, *below*) include the **New River Gorge National River** (tel. 304/465–0508) and the **Gauley River National Recreation Area** (tel. 304/574–0704).

What to See and Do with Children

With its wide range of outdoor sports, this area is one big natural amusement park for children. Rafting, on all rivers except the Gauley, is suitable for youngsters, as are the **Cass Scenic Railroad** and the **National Radio Astronomy Observatory** (*see* Exploring Eastern West Virginia, *above*).

Shopping

Fairs and festivals are plentiful, and perfect places to shop for mountain handicrafts; check with local tourist offices for schedules. **Martinsburg** has several outlet centers, including the **Blue Ridge Outlet Mall** (Stephen and Queen Sts., tel. 304/263–7467 or 800/445–3993), which houses 50 major stores.

Sports and Outdoor Activities

Biking   Rentals, instruction, and tours are available from **Blackwater Bikes** (Davis, tel. 304/259–5286) and the **Elk River Touring Center** (Slatyfork, tel. 304/572–3771).

Canoeing   The **Greenbrier River** is one of the country's best paddling rivers. Area outfitters can put you on this and other waterways; for a list of operators, contact the Division of Tourism and Parks (*see* Visitor Information, *above*).

Fishing   Trout are abundant in faster streams and rivers, while bass, crappie, and walleye lurk in the lakes. Licenses are available at sporting and convenience stores. Most rafting companies also organize fishing trips.

Golf   **Cacapon** and **Canaan Valley Resort state parks** (*see* State Parks, *above*) offer 18 holes each; **The Greenbrier** in White Sulphur Springs (*see* Dining and Lodging, Spas, *below*), 54 holes; **Pipestem Resort State Park** (*see* National and State Parks, *above*), 27 holes; **The Woods in** Hedgesville (tel. 304/754–7977 or 800/248–2222), 18 holes.

Hiking and Backpacking   State and national parks have extensive trail systems. The **Appalachian Trail** (Harpers Ferry 25425, tel. 304/535–6331), the **Big Blue Trail** (Potomac Appalachian Trail Club, 1718 N St., NW, Washington, DC 20036, tel. 703/242–0965), and the **Greenbrier River Trail** (Slatyfork 26291, tel. 304/572–3771) run through this region.

Horseback Riding   Trail riding is available in most state parks.

Rafting   The **New, Gauley,** and **Cheat** are West Virginia's most heavily traveled rivers, followed by the **Tygart** and **Shenandoah**. First-timers can tackle all but the Gauley. For information on nearly 50 outfitters that run white-water excursions, contact the Division of Tourism and Parks (*see* Visitor Information, *above*).

Ski Areas

Cross-country   **Elk River Touring Center** (*see* Sports and Outdoor Activities, Biking, *above*) and the **White Grass Ski Touring Center** (Rte. 1, Davis, tel. 304/866–4114) offer rentals, instruction, and tours.

Downhill   Call 800/225–5982 for snow conditions at these ski areas: **Canaan Valley State Park** (Davis, 21 trails, 3 chair lifts, vertical drop 850 ft, 1¼-mi run), **Silver Creek** (Snowshoe, 14 trails, 4 chair lifts, vertical drop 663 ft, 4,700-ft run), **Snowshoe** (Snowshoe, 30 trails, 8 chair lifts, vertical drop 1,500 ft, 1½-mi run), **Timberline** (Davis, 15 trails, 2 chair lifts, vertical drop 1,000 ft, 2-mi run), and **Winterplace** (Flat Top, 20 trails, 3 chair lifts, vertical drop 603 ft, 1¼-mi run).

Dining and Lodging

Real West Virginia cooking is hearty, simple, and usually homemade from local ingredients—buckwheat cakes for breakfast, beef stew for lunch, brook trout or game for dinner—but more urbane fare is usually available. As for accommodations, you can find the "Ritz" in West Virginia, or motels where "the light's always left on for you," but local B&Bs afford access to the state's greatest treasure: its people (tel. 800/225–5982 for B&B listings and booklet). For price ranges, see Charts 1 (B) and 2 (B) in Chapter 1.

Berkeley Springs **The Country Inn.** This restaurant's atmosphere suits its
Dining name—lots of natural wood and old prints. The best menu choices are steaks or Oriental chicken. *207 S. Washington St., tel. 304/258–2210. AE, DC, MC, V. Moderate.*

Lodging **Cacapon Resort State Park.** Locally crafted heavy oak pieces
★ furnish the main lodge's rooms and woodsy dining room, which overlook the golf course or Cacapon ridge. Rustic cabins are tucked in the surrounding woods. *Off U.S. 522, Rte. 1, Box 304, 25411, tel. 304/258–1022; fax 304/258–5323. 49 lodge rooms, 30 cabins. Facilities: restaurant, tennis courts, lake, golf course. AE, MC, V. Inexpensive (winter)–Moderate (summer).*

Davis **Blackwater Falls State Park.** The stone-pillared dining room,
Dining furnished in handmade red oak, perches on the rim of the Blackwater Canyon. Diners' favorites are the breakfast bar, charbroiled chicken breast, and prime rib. *Rte. 32 to Blackwater Falls State Park Rd., tel. 304/259–5216. AE, MC, V. Moderate.*

Lodging **Canaan Valley Resort State Park.** The rooms here are motel-style but spacious and newly refurbished, and the resort's wooded setting is superb. *Rte. 1, Box 330, 26260, tel. 304/866–4121 or 800/225–5982; fax 304/866–4172. 250 rooms. Facilities: restaurant, lounge, indoor pool, golf course, downhill ski area. AE, D, DC, MC, V. Inexpensive–Moderate.*

Shepherdstown **Bavarian Inn and Lodge.** In four alpine chalets overlooking the
Dining and Lodging Potomac River, the rooms are luxurious, with canopy beds,
★ fireplaces, and whirlpool tubs. The dining areas are decorated with antiques and fine china. The German and American cuisine includes wild pheasant, venison, and boar. *Rte. 1, Box 30, 25443, tel. 304/876–2551; fax 304/876–9355. 42 units. Facilities: restaurant (Moderate), pool, tennis courts, bike rentals. AE, DC, MC, V. Very Expensive.*

Snowshoe/Slatyfork **Red Fox Restaurant.** This restaurant offers an extensive menu
Dining and exceptional service. The chefs use local meats, fish, herbs,
★ and cheeses for such specialties as wild game pâtés or roast highland quail cooked with apples, country ham, sausages, and applejack brandy. *Snowshoe Mountain Resort, off U.S. 219, tel. 304/572–1111. AE, MC, V. No lunch Dec.–Mar.; closed Apr.–May, Nov., Mon.–Tues. June–Oct. Expensive–Very Expensive.*

Lodging **Snowshoe/Silver Creek Mountain Resort.** Accommodations vary from motel-style rooms to luxury condos. Snowshoe has an assortment of natural-wood structures in the forest fringing the ski slopes, and Silver Creek has lodgings in a high rise. *Off U.S. 219, Box 10, Snowshoe 26209, tel. 304/572–5252. 1,250 houses and condos, 301 lodge rooms. Facilities: 11 restaurants,*

8 pubs, 2 indoor pools, exercise room, 2 downhill ski areas, golf course, tennis courts. AE, MC, V. Inexpensive–Expensive.

Motel **Sheraton Inn–Martinsburg** (301 Foxcroft Ave., Martinsburg 25401, tel. 304/267–5500), 120 rooms, restaurant, coffee shop, lounge, indoor and outdoor pools and tennis courts, health club, parking; moderate.

Spas For price ranges, see Chart 2 (A) in Chapter 1.

★ **The Greenbrier.** One of the best hotels in the country, this 6,500-acre spa is done in grand turn-of-the-century style. Massive white columns rise six stories against a white facade, while inside, nine lobbies offer vast, chandeliered common areas. Every guest room is different, decorated in Dorothy Draper pastel prints. Restaurant menus feature such dishes as farm-raised striped bass and rack of lamb. *Off I–64, White Sulphur Springs 24986, tel. 304/536–1110 or 800/624–6070; fax 304/536–7854. 700 units. Facilities: 4 dining rooms, lounge, health club, tennis, indoor/outdoor pool, 3 golf courses, horseback riding. AE, DC, MC, V. Very Expensive.*

★ **Coolfont Resort.** Accommodations are in modern chalets, rustic cabins, or lodge rooms. Special programs for losing weight, reducing stress, and stopping smoking are offered. The soup/salad/bread bar is exceptional, as are the daily buffet and the fresh brook trout. *Rte. 1, Box 710, Berkeley Springs 25411, tel. 304/258–4500 or 800/888–8768; fax 304/258–5499. 82 units. Facilities: restaurant (Moderate), lounge, indoor pool, lake, health club, tennis. AE, D, DC, MC, V. Moderate–Very Expensive.*

Campgrounds State park camping facilities (*see* State Parks, *above*) and more than 100 commercial campgrounds are listed in a camping booklet (tel. 800/225–5982).

The Arts

West Virginians celebrate everything from potatoes and apple butter to the coming of spring with festivals and fairs (tel. 800/225–5982). Staged at Grandview State Park's **Theatre West Virginia** (tel. 304/256–6800 or 800/666–9142) are the state's premier outdoor theatrical productions: *Honey in the Rock*, a Civil War story, and *Hatfields and McCoys*, depicting the famous feud.

Western West Virginia

The Charleston/Huntington area is a center of commerce and culture quite different from the mountain wilderness to the east and farmland to the north. Skilled craftspeople, such as those who supplied the Kennedy White House with glassware, make their homes in the mid–Ohio River valley. The Northern Panhandle suffers from steel-industry troubles, but its fine old mansions and Victorian architecture are reminders of better times. Wheeling's Oglebay Park is a cultural and environmental jewel.

Tourist Information

Charleston: Convention and Visitors Bureau (200 Civic Center Dr., 25301, tel. 304/344–5075 or 800/733–5469). **Wheeling:** Convention and Visitors Bureau (1233 Main St., Suite 1000, 26003, tel. 800/828–3097). **Northern West Virginia:** Convention and Visitors Bureau (709 Beechurst Ave., Morgantown 26505, tel. 800/458–7373).

Getting There

By Plane The region is served by Charleston's **Yeager Airport** (*see* Eastern West Virginia, *above*), Huntington's **Tri-State Airport** (tel. 304/453–6169), Parkersburg's **Wood County Airport** (tel. 304/464–5113), Clarksburg/Fairmont's **Benedum Airport** (tel. 304/842–3400), and the **Morgantown Municipal Airport/Hart Field** (tel. 304/291–7461).

By Car Major routes into the region are I–64, Charleston to Huntington; Clarksburg to I–77 north–south, Parkersburg to Charleston; I–79 north–south, Clarksburg to Charleston; and I–70, crossing the Northern Panhandle at Wheeling.

By Train **Amtrak** provides service from White Sulphur Springs through Charleston to Huntington.

By Bus **Greyhound** has terminals in major towns.

Exploring Western West Virginia

Apart from the Mountain Lakes region, this area is heavily influenced by the Ohio River. Charleston and Huntington set an urban tone with museums, shopping malls, and cultural and entertainment centers, but the hustle is balanced by lazy days on the river. Moving north through valley farmland, you can watch glassblowers and other craftspeople at work. The boom and bust of the 1890s is reflected throughout the area in grand mansions and nicely preserved Victorian architecture.

In **Charleston,** the Italian Renaissance **Capitol** merits a visit for its massive gilt dome and its two-ton chandelier of Czechoslovakian crystal. *1900 Washington St. E, tel. 304/558–3809. Admission free. Closed Sun. Labor Day–Memorial Day.*

Within the Capitol complex is the **Cultural Center** (Greenbrier and Washington Sts., tel. 304/558–0162; admission free), with its marble **Great Hall** and the **State Museum,** which traces West Virginian history.

Overlooking the Capitol are the **Sunrise Museums,** two historic mansions that house art galleries, a children's museum, and a planetarium. Outside are gardens and wooded trails. *746 Myrtle Rd., tel. 304/344–8035. Admission charged. Closed Mon.*

Downtown are a large civic center and the pleasant **Town Center** shopping area. Eight styles of 19th-century architecture are represented in the **East End Historic District,** bordered by Bradford, Quarrier, and Michigan streets and Kanawha Boulevard.

It takes an hour by I–64 to reach metropolitan Huntington, but it's more fun to take all day by way of the Kanawha and Ohio rivers on the 1,200-passenger *West Virginia Belle* (tel. 800/327–1381 or 800/543–0227 in WV; operates Apr.–Oct.), one of several paddle wheelers offering sightseeing and dinner cruises.

The streets of **Huntington,** a river and rail town, are lined with stately turn-of-the-century houses, particularly in the **9th**

Charleston, West Virginia

Street West Historic District. There the streets are brick, the houses Victorian frame bordered with wrought-iron fences. The **Huntington Museum of Art** (2033 McCay Rd., tel. 304/529–2701; admission charged; closed Mon.), the state's largest museum, covers 52 acres and houses a Junior Art Museum, a celestial observatory, an auditorium, and an amphitheater.

Near Huntington, at **Milton,** is the **Blenko Glass Visitor Center and Factory Outlet,** one of more than a dozen hand-blown-glass factories between Huntington and Parkersburg, to the north. *Exit 28 off I–64 to U.S. 60, tel. 304/743–9081. Admission free. No glassblowing weekends, some holidays.*

Another thriving Ohio River town, **Parkersburg** has many restored turn-of-the-century houses, but its main attraction is **Blennerhassett Island Historic Park and Mansion.** In 1800 Harman Blennerhassett's magnificent island estate was the talk of the Northwest Territory, but he was later arrested with Aaron Burr for treason. Besides the Palladian-style mansion, you can visit a crafts village and take horse-drawn-wagon tours of the island, which is reached aboard a sternwheeler. *Blennerhassett Museum, 2nd and Juliana Sts., tel. 304/428–3000. Admission charged. Closed Mon.–Tues. Memorial Day–Labor Day, weekdays May and Sept.–Oct.*

In the heart of the state is the Mountain Lakes region, dotted with prime fishing areas (*see* Sports and Outdoor Activities, *below*) and a number of Civil War landmarks, such as **Carnifex Ferry Battlefield State Park.** The battle here dashed the South's hopes of controlling the Kanawha Valley. The **Patteson**

House, which marked the line between Union and Confederate forces, has been restored as a museum and displays artifacts and a film on the battle. *Rte. 2, Summersville, tel. 304/872-3773. Admission free. Closed Labor Day–Memorial Day.*

North of Clarksburg is **Morgantown,** home of **West Virginia University,** where the world's first fully automated transportation system carries students between campuses. There's all the bustle of a college town here, plus 1,700-acre **Cheat Lake,** which is served by three marinas (Blosser's, tel. 304/594-2541; Edgewater, tel. 304/594-2630; Sunset Harbor, tel. 304/594-1100).

In the Northern Panhandle, **Wheeling** was once the gateway to the West. Parks, museums, riverboat rides, and a wealth of restored Victorian houses (Victorian House Tours, tel. 304/233-2003) are reminders of the old days. **Oglebay Park** (tel. 304/243-4000) is a 1,500-acre municipal park/resort with a hotel (*see* Dining and Lodging, *below*), a 65-acre zoo, a planetarium, a museum, a swimming pool, and a small ski area (3 lifts, snowmaking).

What to See and Do with Children

Riverboating, fishing, and canoeing are prime attractions in this region. Charleston's **Sunrise Museums** and Wheeling's **Oglebay Park** (*see* Exploring Western West Virginia, *above*) are geared for children.

Shopping

Antiques and native crafts, particularly hand-blown glass, are abundant in this region. Venues vary from roadside shops to outdoor fairs to sprawling glass-factory outlets (*see* Exploring Western West Virginia, *above*).

Sports and Outdoor Activities

Canoeing The area's many lakes (contact the Army Corps of Engineers, tel. 304/529-5258) are ideal for canoeing.

Fishing Native trout are abundant in the faster streams and rivers, while bass, crappie, and walleye lurk in the lakes. Licenses are available at sporting and convenience stores. Rafting companies organize fishing trips. **Sutton Lake** (Sutton, tel. 304/765-2705) and **Stonewall Jackson Lake** (Weston, tel. 304/452-8830) are prime areas.

Golf **Coonskin Golf Course** (Coonskin Dr., Charleston, tel. 304/341-8013), 18 holes. **Oglebay Park's Crispin and Speidel courses** (Wheeling, tel. 304/243-4000 or 800/624-6988), 36 holes. **Twin Falls Resort State Park Golf Course** (Mullens, tel. 304/294-4000 or 800/225-5982), 18 holes. **Worthington Golf Club** (3414 Roseland Ave., Parkersburg, tel. 304/428-4297), 18 holes.

Hiking and Backpacking The **Allegheny Trail** (633 West Virginia Ave., Morgantown 26505, tel. 304/296-5158) and the **Kanawha Trace** (733 7th Ave., Huntington 25701, tel. 304/523-3408) pass through state and national forests and wilderness areas with rocky overlooks and thickets of rhododendron and mountain laurel.

Horseback Riding Trail riding is available in most state parks.

Rafting The white waters of the **Cheat** and **Tygart** rivers flow through this region. More than 50 outfitters (tel. 800/225–5982) guide trips.

Dining and Lodging

For price ranges, see Charts 1 (B) and 2 (B) in Chapter 1.

Charleston **Chilton House.** In a charming Victorian house with seven ga-
Dining bles, this restaurant overlooks the Coal River. Menu highlights
★ include oysters Rockefeller, orange roughy with sesame sauce,
and steak Diane flambé. *2 6th Ave., St. Albans, tel. 304/722–
2918. Reservations advised. AE, D, MC, V. Closed Sun. Moderate.*

Wheeling **Oglebay Park.** Connected to the rustic lodge, which has a huge,
Lodging stone-floored lobby and a stone fireplace, are motel-style
rooms and once-detached chalets. Nearby cabins sleeping 12 to
20 are rustic outside and ultramodern inside. (*See* Exploring
Western West Virginia *and* Sports and Outdoor Activities,
above.) *Rte. 88N, 26003, tel. 800/624–6988; fax 304/243–4070.
204 lodge rooms, 16 suites, 34 deluxe cabins. Facilities: dining
room, golf, tennis, swimming, horseback riding, zoo, lake,
museum, glass center, festivals. AE, D, DC, MC, V. Moderate.*

Dining and Lodging **Stratford Springs.** This historic inn, composed of two turn-of-
★ the-century houses, is secluded on 30 wooded acres. The rooms
are Colonial style, with cherrywood or Amish furniture.
Among the restaurants, which cater mainly to nonguests, the
formal Stratford Room (jacket and tie required) serves such
dishes as stuffed strip steak or baby coho salmon. *355 Oglebay
Dr., 26003, tel. 304/233–5100; fax 304/232–6447. 3 rooms, 3
suites. Facilities: 4 restaurants, heated pool, athletic center,
spa. AE, MC, V. Moderate–Expensive.*

Motel **Charleston Marriott** (200 Lee St. E, Charleston 25301, tel. 304/
345–6500, fax 304/353–3722), 354 rooms, restaurant, lounge,
indoor pool, health club, tennis; inexpensive.

Campgrounds The state tourism department (*see* Visitor Information, *above*)
has listings of commercial campgrounds as well as facilities in
more than a dozen state parks.

The Arts

Wheeling's **Capitol Music Hall** (1015 Main St., tel. 800/624–
5456), home of WWVA radio's "Jamboree USA," has live performances by country-music greats and two big-name jambo-
rees in July and August.

4 The Southeast

The Southeast

ATLANTIC OCEAN

KENTUCKY

TENNESSEE

VIRGINIA

NORTH CAROLINA

SOUTH CAROLINA

GEORGIA

ALABAMA

MISSISSIPPI

Nashville

Knoxville

GREAT SMOKY MTS. NAT'L PARK

Asheville

Florence

Decatur

Huntsville

Gadsden

Dalton

Rome

Anniston

Birmingham

Bessemer

Tuscaloosa

Eutaw

Selma

Montgomery

Auburn

Phenix City

Eufaula

Enterprise

Montevallo

Dothan

Alabama River

Columbus

La Grange

Atlanta

Decatur

Griffin

Macon

Warner Robins

Milledgeville

Athens

Gainesville

Anderson

Greenville

Spartanburg

Shelby

Hickory

Winston-Salem

Greensboro

High Point

Durham

Chapel Hill

Raleigh

Goldsboro

Warsaw

New Bern

Elizabeth City

Manteo

Cape Hatteras Nat'l Seashore

Cape Lookout Nat'l Seashore

Wilmington

Lumberton

Fayetteville

Bennettsville

Florence

Conway

Myrtle Beach

Georgetown

Charleston

Beaufort

Hilton Head Island

Savannah

Brunswick

Waycross

Jessup

Hazlehurst

Vidalia

Statesboro

Waynesboro

Augusta

Aiken

Batesburg

Orangeburg

Lake Moultrie

Walterboro

Columbia

Rock Hill

Charlotte

Concord

Moultrie

Albany

Ochlockonee River

Savannah River

Congaree River

Black River

Hartwell

Knoxville

Nashville

KEY
—— Amtrak Lines

Gulf of Mexico

FLORIDA

BAHAMAS

Gulf Islands Nat'l. Seashore

St. Simons Island
Cumberland Island Nat'l. Seashore

Jacksonville
St. Augustine
Daytona Beach
Ocala
Gainesville
Valdosta
Thomasville
Tallahassee
Panama City
Ft. Walton Beach
Pensacola
Mobile

OKEFENOKEE NAT'L WILDLIFE REFUGE

Orlando
Walt Disney World
Lakeland
Tampa
Clearwater
St. Petersburg
Bradenton
Sarasota
Ft. Myers
Naples

Merritt Island
Cocoa
Melbourne
Kissimmee
Vero Beach
Ft. Pierce
Lake Kissimmee
Lake Okeechobee
Belle Glade
Palm Beach
West Palm Beach
Ft. Lauderdale
Hollywood
Hialeah
Miami
Coral Gables

EVERGLADES NAT'L. PARK

Florida Keys
Key West

Great Abaco
Grand Bahama
Nassau
New Providence
Andros Island

Fla. Tpk.

150 miles
225 km

Introduction

By Conrad Paulus

From pine to palm, lapped by the Atlantic Ocean and the Gulf of Mexico, stretch North and South Carolina, Georgia, Florida, and Alabama. While the world tends to think of southerners as dreaming life away on the veranda, julep in hand, among the magnolias and Spanish moss, still biting the black hand that feeds them, times have changed. Not too long ago nostalgia for times gone by and the Confederacy's lost cause shaped the region's point of view, but nowadays it is clearly dealing in the present, planning for tomorrow, and busily exploiting its plantation past in novels and as movie sets and B&Bs. Surprisingly, perhaps, the Southeast is also the most racially integrated part of the country, and one of the liveliest.

With the exception of Florida, all these states have both mountains (with resorts and sports) and the sea (with beaches and boating); Florida's watery edges are never more than 50 mi away. It's a good thing, too, because the region's temperatures and humidity are fierce, although air-conditioning has transformed the summers.

Post–Civil War poverty prevented much of the tearing down and rebuilding common in the rest of the East and forced people to make do with that outmoded old Chippendale and Sheraton furniture they had hoped to replace with the new machine-made Victorian marvels. Today dozens of Greek Revival mansions containing their original furnishings are open to visitors. The shabby white-columned houses have been restored, and travelers can often sleep in those tall mahogany and walnut beds.

Some of the cities are charmingly old-fashioned; in Savannah and Charleston, Edenton and Mobile, you can wander through houses on shady squares with brick courtyards and gardens of astonishing fecundity. There are modern cities, too—the dynamic Raleigh–Durham–Chapel Hill college triangle; the booming crossroads that is Atlanta; Birmingham, the former steel town that became a medical center; and Miami, now infused with Cuban culture—not to mention Disney World, already in the 21st century.

Food in the Southeast today bears little resemblance to the familiar greasy fare of yore. Having absorbed every cuisine that has come its way, the region is prepared to serve you fancy nouvelle, down-home soul, and spicy Cajun and Caribbean, along with the deep-fried classics. That adaptability is characteristic of a people who really do want to please: This is the basis of southern hospitality. Southerners are an easygoing bunch—talkative, courteous, and witty, with a talent for laughter and enjoying life.

Tour Groups

From the heights of the Blue Ridge Mountains to the Florida marshes, the South offers unparalleled scenic beauty, and the small towns and bustling cities across the region reveal the diverse lifestyles of southern America. Tours of this region are equally varied.

Domenico Tours (751 Broadway, Bayonne, NJ 07002, tel. 201/823–8687 or 800/554–8687) offers a 10-day tour of Florida's

highlights, a six-day "Orlando Delight" tour, and an eight-day tour of the southeastern states, including Florida. **Gadabout Tours** (700 E. Tahquitz Way, Palm Springs, CA 92262, tel. 619/325–5556 or 800/952–5068) takes a nine-day tour of Florida that includes a cruise to the Bahamas. It also offers a 15-day tour of the "Sentimental South," from New Orleans to Savannah and Charleston, and a three-week tour of "Mansions and Magnolias" during the magnificent southern springtime. **Globus** (5301 S. Federal Circle, Littleton, CO 80123, tel. 303/797–2800 or 800/221–0090) offers a week-long "Old South" excursion, including Charleston and Hilton Head Island in South Carolina; Savannah, Georgia; and Jacksonville, Florida. Or swing through "the Best of Florida" on a 10-day tour that includes St. Augustine, Miami, Key West, and Orlando and Disney World. For similar Florida tours at bargain prices, check out Globus's budget-minded affiliate, **Cosmos Tourama** (same address). **Maupintour** (Box 807, Lawrence KS 66044, tel. 913/843–1211 or 800/255–4266) offers eight-day tours of the Carolinas and Georgia. **Talmage Tours** (1223 Walnut St., Philadelphia, PA 19107, tel. 215/923–7100) has a six-day tour to Myrtle Beach and Charleston, South Carolina, and a five-day tour highlighting the sights of Key West, Florida. **Tauck Tours** (11 Wilton Rd., Box 5027, Westport, CT 06881, tel. 203/226–6911 or 800/468–2825) heads north from Jacksonville, Florida, for an eight-day tour that includes Savannah, Georgia, and Hilton Head and Charleston, South Carolina. Week-long and 10-day tours of Florida resorts and attractions are also available.

When to Go

The best times to visit the South are **spring** and **fall**, when temperatures are in the 70s and 80s. That's when golf and tennis buffs converge on the region en masse. Spring also brings the magnficent azaleas, magnolias, and other flora of the region to life, and visitors come to ooh and aah their way through the gardens and historic homes that traditionally open to the public at this time of year. Fall, when colors reach their peak in the mountains of Alabama, Georgia, and the Carolinas, draws thousands of leaf worshipers. Autumn is a popular season for senior citizens to visit the region, taking advantage of smaller crowds and lower rates in beach and resort areas. **Winter** can be quite pleasant in the Southeast, especially in the more temperate, lower coastal regions of Georgia and Florida. In the higher elevations of western North Carolina and Georgia, temperatures often drop to freezing between mid-November and mid-March, producing ideal conditions for area ski resorts. **Summer** tends to be hot and muggy, with temperatures often soaring into the 90s, especially in Florida and at the lower elevations of Alabama, Georgia, and the Carolinas. That's when "flatlanders" flock to the mountains to cool off.

Festivals and Seasonal Events

Festivals are a way of life in the Southeast. Even the smallest communities have planned celebrations around offbeat and often obscure themes, such as chitlins, hollering contests, and the woolly worm.

Mid-Jan.: Art Deco Weekend spotlights Miami Beach's historic district with a street fair, a gala, and live entertainment. *Tel. 305/672-2014.*

Late Jan.: Bamboleo Festival in Tampa, Florida, combines the old Gasparilla and Pirate Fest with a parade and other street festivities celebrating the city's Spanish heritage. *Tel. 813/223-1111.*

Mid-Feb.: Mardi Gras in Mobile, Alabama, is an uproarious, pre-Lenten celebration similar to its more famous cousin in New Orleans. *Tel. 205/434-7304 or 800/252-3862.*

Mid-Mar.: The Aiken (SC) Triple Crown, featuring Thoroughbred trials, harness races, and steeplechases, draws thousands of equestrian enthusiasts. *Tel. 803/641-1111.*

Mar. 17: St. Patrick's Day Celebration in Savannah, Georgia, is one of the country's largest honoring Ireland's patron saint. *Tel. 800/444-2427.*

Early Apr.: Master's Golf Tournament in Augusta, Georgia, attracts top golf pros to this tournament of tournaments. *Tel. 706/823-6600 or 800/726-0243.*

Mid-May–early June: Spoleto USA, a festival featuring world-renowned performers and artists in Charleston, South Carolina, gets global attention. *Tel. 803/853-8000.*

Late May–early June: The Sun Fun Festival in Myrtle Beach, South Carolina, features sand sculpting, beauty queens, and other activities. *Tel. 803/626-7444.*

Early–mid-June: June Jam is a 10-day Alabama festival that climaxes with an outdoor concert hosted by the music group Alabama in their hometown of Fort Payne. *Tel. 205/845-9300.*

Mid-July: Annual Highland Games and Gathering of the Scottish Clans, held in the high meadows of Grandfather Mountain in North Carolina, is one of the largest Scottish celebrations in the world. *Tel. 704/733-2013.*

Mid-July: The Hemingway Days Festival features look-alike contests and play and short-story competitions in Key West, Florida. *Tel. 305/294-4440.*

Late July–early Aug.: Folkmoot USA: North Carolina International Folk Festival, held in Haywood County and surrounding areas over a two-week period, features dancers and singers from around the globe. *Tel. 704/452-2997.*

Early–mid-Aug.: The Georgia Mountain Fair is a 12-day celebration in Hiwassee that features authentic mountain crafts, music, dancing, and exhibits. *Tel. 706/878-2181.*

Mid-Oct.: Alabama's National Shrimp Festival, held in Gulf Shores, features seafood, arts and crafts, music, sky divers, and hot-air balloons. *Tel. 205/968-7511.*

Late Nov.–Dec.: Christmas at Biltmore brings festive decorations, musical concerts, and candlelit tours to this North Carolina estate for six weeks. *Tel. 800/543-2961.*

Mid-Dec.: Salem Christmas is celebrated in the restored Moravian village section of Winston-Salem, North Carolina. *Tel. 919/721-7331.*

Mid-Dec.: The Grand Illumination in St. Augustine, Florida, features torchlit processions, caroling, and other activities. *Tel. 904/829-5681.*

Getting Around

By Plane The region is served by most major domestic airlines, including American, Continental, Delta, Northwest, TWA, United, USAir, and several foreign carriers. Some of the busiest airports in the nation and the world are located in the Southeast, including Atlanta's **Hartsfield International Airport** (tel. 404/530-6830), **Miami International Airport** (tel. 305/876-7000), and **Orlando International Airport** (tel. 407/825-2001). Other major airports in the region are **Birmingham (AL) Airport** (tel. 205/595-0533), **Charleston (SC) International Airport** (tel. 803/767-1100), and **Charlotte-Douglas (NC) International Airport** (tel. 704/359-4000).

By Car More than a dozen interstate highways, including I-10, I-16, I-20, I-26, I-40, I-59, I-65, I-75, I-77, I-85, and I-95, crisscross the Southeast, linking major cities and providing easy access to other parts of the country. In some cases, interstates and federal highways, such as U.S. 1 along the Florida Keys, link the region's many islands to the mainland. In other cases, ferries (*see* By Boat, *below*) are the only means of transport. Scenic highways include South Carolina's Foothills Parkway and the Blue Ridge Parkway, the latter traversing the Virginia and North Carolina mountains. Interstate and federal highways are usually well maintained; some secondary roads are narrow, a few unpaved, and in mountain sections often very curvy.

By Train **Amtrak** (tel. 800/872-7245) provides service to major southern cities, including Charlotte, North Carolina; Charleston and Columbia, South Carolina; Atlanta and Savannah, Georgia; Miami and Orlando, Florida; and Birmingham and Mobile, Alabama.

By Bus The major intercity carrier is **Greyhound** (tel. 404/522-6300 in Atlanta, 205/252-7171 in Birmingham, 803/722-7722 in Charleston, 704/527-9393 in Charlotte, 305/374-7222 in Miami, 407/843-7720 in Orlando, or 800/231-2222).

By Boat Traveling by boat along the Southeast's extensive waterways and rivers is a quite popular (and, in some cases, essential) mode of transportation. The **Intracoastal Waterway,** which extends from New England around Florida to the Gulf of Mexico, is filled with north-south traffic, and many of the region's major rivers are navigable. Ferries connect major islands and the mainlands of Alabama, the Carolinas, Georgia, and Florida. For more information on waterways and ferry schedules, contact the highway departments of individual states.

ALABAMA

Updated by Dick
Pivetz and Sylvia
Higginbotham

Capital	Montgomery
Population	4,135,000
Motto	We Dare Defend Our Rights
State Bird	Yellowhammer
State Flower	Camellia

Visitor Information

Alabama Bureau of Tourism and Travel (401 Adams Ave., Box 4309, Montgomery 36103, tel. 205/242–4169 or 800/252–2262). **Welcome centers:** I–59, at Valley Head and at Cuba; I–65, at Elkmont; I–10, at Robertsdale and at Grand Bay; I–20, at Heflin; I–85, at Valley; U.S. 231, at Slocomb.

Scenic Drives

Lookout Mountain Parkway is a 100-mi scenic stretch in northeast Alabama, encompassing Rtes. 117, 89, and 176; markers indicate routes for side trips to Little River Canyon, De Soto Falls, and Yellow Creek Falls. Maps are available at the welcome center off I–59 near the Georgia state line (tel. 205/635–6522). In and around Mobile, the well-marked **Azalea Trail** twines for 37 mi; the blooms are at their best in March and April. **Rte. 163S** from Mobile joins Rte. 193 south of Mon Louis, affording views of Mobile Bay and the Gulf of Mexico.

State Parks

Alabama's 22 state parks include several with resorts providing lodging and recreational activities. **De Soto State Park Resort** (Rte. 1, Box 210, Fort Payne 35967, tel. 205/845–5380), nearly 5,000 acres along the Little River Canyon, features a spectacular 100-foot waterfall. **Gulf State Park Resort** (HC 79, Box 9, Gulf Shores 36543, tel. 205/948–4853 or 800/544–4853) is a 6,000-acre park on the Gulf. **Joe Wheeler State Park Resort** (Drawer K, Rogersville 35652, tel. 205/247–5461 or 800/544–5639), on the Tennessee River, offers a marina and golf. **Lake Guntersville State Park Lodge** (Star Rte. 63, Box 232, Guntersville 35976, tel. 205/571–5440 or 800/548–4553) is popular with fishermen. Contact **Alabama State Parks** (64 N. University St., Montgomery 36130, tel. 800/252–7275) for reservations or information on Alabama's state parks.

The Highlands and Plantation Country

This region encompasses the hilly Highlands around Birmingham, the state's largest city, and the antebellum history of the state capital, Montgomery, 90 mi south of Birmingham.

Tourist
Information
Birmingham: Convention & Visitors Bureau (2200 9th Ave. N, 35203–1100, tel. 205/252–9825 or 800/962–6453). **Montgomery:**

Area Chamber of Commerce (41 Commerce St., 36104, tel. 205/834–5200). Visitors Center (401 Madison Ave., 36104, tel. 205/262–0013).

Getting There

By Plane Major domestic airlines serve **Birmingham Airport** (tel. 205/595–0533) and Montgomery's **Dannelly Field** (tel. 205/281–5040).

By Car I–59 runs northeast from Birmingham into Georgia and Tennessee and southwest into Mississippi. I–20 runs east–west through the city. I–65 is the north–south route connecting Birmingham with Montgomery. I–85 leads southwest from Atlanta to Montgomery.

By Train **Amtrak** serves Birmingham, Montgomery, and other cities and towns in the area. *The Gulf Breeze* links Montgomery and Birmingham with Mobile, and connects with *The Crescent*, which stops at Birmingham on its New Orleans–New York run.

By Bus **Greyhound** (tel. 205/252–7171 in Birmingham, 205/264–4518 in Montgomery) serves major towns in the region.

Exploring the Highlands and Plantation Country

Birmingham blossomed with the rise of coal mines and the iron industry in the 19th century. Today its largest employer is the University of Alabama at Birmingham, home to one of the country's largest medical centers. The city has restored many of its 19th-century buildings and is a hospitable and beautiful metropolis. The **Lightning Route Trolley** (tel. 205/262–7321; closed Sun.) can take you to several points of interest in the downtown area.

The **Alabama Sports Hall of Fame Museum** (corner of 22nd St. N and Civic Center Blvd., tel. 205/323–6665), in the Civic Center, displays memorabilia of such Alabama athletic heroes as coach Bear Bryant, Jesse Owens, Willie Mays, and Hank Aaron. The Kelly Ingram Park area, southwest of the center, includes the **16th Street Baptist Church** (16th St. and 8th Ave. N, tel. 205/251–9402), a civil rights landmark. Here numerous protests were staged during the 1960s. Here, too, four children lost their lives when a bomb exploded in 1963; a plaque is erected to their memory. Across the street is the new **Birmingham Civil Rights Institute** (6th Ave. and 16th St. N, tel. 205/323–2276), new in 1992, which uses exhibits, multimedia presentations, music, and storytelling to document the civil rights movement from the 1920s to the present.

Heading back east via 1st Avenue North, look for signs for **Sloss Furnace.** The massive ironworks plant used ore dug from the hills around Birmingham between 1882 and 1971. Retired blast-furnace workers give guided tours through this National Historic Landmark. *1st Ave. N and 32nd St., tel. 205/324–1911. Admission free. Closed Mon.*

South on U.S. 31 is the **Discovery 2000 Red Mountain Museum** (1421 22nd St. S, tel. 205/933–4104; closed Mon.), which displays samples of the rocks, fossils, and minerals found in the area. The only solar telescope in North America open to the public is located here; don't miss the chance to view the sun's surface. South of the museum, sitting atop Red Mountain, is

Vulcan (Valley Ave. at U.S. 31S, tel. 205/328–6198; admission charged), the world's tallest cast-iron statue. From the enclosed observation deck at the base, you'll have a wonderful panoramic view of the city.

Forty miles from the city (head southeast on U.S. 280 to Childersburg, then east on Rte. 76) is **De Soto Caverns,** a network of vast onyx caves used as a Native American burial ground 2,000 years ago. Rediscovered by Spanish explorer Hernando de Soto in 1540, the caverns later served as a Confederate gunpowder mining center and a Prohibition speakeasy. Tours of the stalagmite and stalactite formations culminate in a sound, water, and laser-light show in the 12-story-high Great Onyx Cathedral. *Tel. 205/378–7252 or 800/933–2283. Admission charged.*

Southwest of Childersburg, near Mountain Creek off U.S. 31, is **Confederate Memorial Park,** with a museum containing Civil War memorabilia and a cemetery where more than 300 Confederate veterans and their wives are buried. *Children Rd., Marbury, tel. 205/755–1990. Admission free.*

Montgomery, 90 mi south of Birmingham via I–65, is a city steeped in antebellum history. Today many of its old houses have been restored, and the city has become known as a cultural capital of the South. The **Visitors Center** (*see* Tourist Information, *above*) shows a brief slide presentation on the city; you can park your car here and visit many attractions on foot.

The handsome **State Capitol** (Bainbridge St. at Dexter Ave., tel. 205/242–3184) reopened in 1993, following extensive restorations. Built in 1852, it served as the first capitol for the Confederate States of America. One block west is the **Dexter Avenue King Memorial Baptist Church** (tel. 205/263–3970), where Dr. Martin Luther King, Jr., began his career as a minister in 1955; a mural in the basement depicts people and events associated with the civil rights movement. At the corner of Washington Avenue and Union Street stands the **First White House of the Confederacy** (tel. 205/242–1861). Built in 1840, it contains many possessions that belonged to Jefferson Davis, the Confederate president, as well as Civil War artifacts.

At 400 Washington Avenue, in front of the Southern Poverty Law Center, is the **Civil Rights Memorial** (tel. 205/264–0286). Created by Maya Lin, designer of the Vietnam Veterans' Memorial in Washington, D.C., it features a plaza and a pool from which water flows over a 40-foot black granite wall. Inscribed on the wall is Dr. Martin Luther King's "I have a dream . . . " speech, along with the names of many who gave their lives to the civil rights movement.

What to See and Do with Children

The **Birmingham Zoo** (2630 Cahaba Rd., tel. 205/879–0408) is famous for its breeding of Siberian tigers and golden spider monkeys. At **Discovery 2000** (1320 22nd Ave. S, tel. 205/939–1176), children can pretend to be policemen, firemen, and ambulance drivers or put together the bones of a skeleton.

Shopping

Birmingham's **Riverchase Galleria** (tel. 205/985–3039), at the intersection of I–459 and U.S. 31S, is one of the largest shopping malls in the Southeast, with at least 200 stores. In **Boaz**, about 75 mi northwest of Birmingham, there are more than 140 outlet stores.

Dining and Lodging

Throughout Alabama, especially north of Mobile, Old South dishes—fried chicken, barbecue, roast beef, country-fried steak—prevail, though in recent years a number of upscale restaurants have opened in Birmingham and Montgomery. In Birmingham, hotels and motels offer weekend specials but are often crowded during football season; the same holds true in Montgomery when the state legislature is in session. For price ranges, see Charts 1 (B) and 2 (B) in Chapter 1.

Birmingham
Dining
★

Highlands: A Bar and Grill. Grand gourmet feasts prepared by owner-chef Frank Stitt are served in a sophisticated setting, accented with fine paintings and brass. Delicacies include fillet of sole with wine sauce; quail with raspberry sauce; and tomatoes stuffed with chunks of lobster, crab, shrimp, and corn. *2011 11th Ave. S, tel. 205/939–1400. Reservations for dinner only. AE, DC, MC, V. Closed Sun. Expensive.*

John's. This large family restaurant gets raves for fresh seafood dishes—trout amandine, whole red snapper, lightly fried jumbo shrimp—served with John's famous cole slaw and corn sticks. *112 21st St. N, tel. 205/322–6014. Reservations for 5 or more only. AE, D, DC, MC. V. Closed Sun. Moderate.*

Michael's Sirloin Room. This popular steak house and sports bar is decorated with photographs of local sports greats. The specialty is a hefty 2-inch-thick cut of charbroiled prime steer butt. *431 20th St. S, tel. 205/322–0419. Reservations for 5 or more only. AE, DC, MC, V. Closed Sun. Moderate.*

Lodging
★

Tutwiler. This National Historic Landmark was built in 1913 as luxury apartments and converted into a hotel in 1987. The elegant lobby has marble floors, chandeliers, antiques, and lots of flowers; guest rooms are furnished with antique reproductions. *Park Pl. at 21st St. N, 35203, tel. 205/322–2100 or 800/228–0808. 96 rooms, 53 suites. Facilities: restaurant, pub, use of nearby YMCA. AE, D, DC, MC, V. Expensive.*

Wynfrey Hotel. This deluxe hotel rises 15 stories above the Riverchase Galleria. The lobby is elegant, with Italian marble floor, Chippendale furniture, Oriental rug, enormous floral arrangement, and brass escalator. Rooms are furnished in English and French traditional styles. *1000 Riverchase Galleria (U.S. 31S), 35244, tel. 205/987–1600 or 800/522–5282. 329 rooms, 19 suites. Facilities: restaurant, café, lounge, health club, pool, whirlpool. AE, DC, MC, V. Expensive.*

Mountain Brook Inn. This eight-story glass-walled hotel at the foot of Red Mountain features a marble-floor lobby and bilevel suites with spiral staircases and Oriental decor. *2800 U.S. 280, 35223, tel. 205/870–3100 or 800/523–7771. 161 rooms, 8 suites. Facilities: restaurant, lounge, pool. AE, D, DC, MC, V. Moderate.*

Montgomery
Dining
★

Sahara Restaurant. At Montgomery's finest restaurant, Joe and Mike Deep carry on a family tradition of friendly service. The snapper, grouper, and scampi are broiled to taste, and the choice steaks are grilled over coals. *511 E. Edgemont Ave., tel. 205/262–1215. Reservations advised. AE, DC, MC, V. Closed Sun. Expensive.*

Jubilee Seafood Company. In a small café setting you'll find some of the finest and freshest seafood in town. Try the crabmeat omelet, steamed Florida clams in season, and Cajun-style oysters. *1057 Woodley Rd., Cloverdale Plaza, tel. 205/262–6224. No reservations. AE, MC, V. Closed Sun. Moderate.*

Chris' Hot Dog Stand. A Montgomery tradition for more than 50 years, this small eatery is always busy at lunchtime. Mr. Chris's famous sauce combines chile peppers, onions, and a variety of herbs that give his hot dogs a one-of-a-kind flavor. *315 Dexter Ave., tel. 205/265–6850. No reservations. No credit cards. Closed Sun. Inexpensive.*

Lodging

Madison Hotel. Elvis Presley slept here, but you're more likely to run into legislators and businessmen than rock stars at this downtown hotel. The six-story atrium lobby is filled with lush greenery, fountains, and exotic caged birds. Rooms were recently renovated. *120 Madison Ave., 36104, tel. 205/264–2231. 184 rooms, 6 suites. Facilities: 2 restaurants, 2 lounges, pool. AE, DC, MC. Expensive.*

Red Bluff Cottage. In this delightful cottage in the heart of downtown, guests can eat breakfast in the dining room or on a veranda overlooking the Alabama River. Rooms have ceiling fans and are furnished with antiques. There's a living room with fireplace and a music room/library where guests frequently congregate. *551 Clay St., 36104, tel. 205/263–1727. 4 rooms. No credit cards. Expensive.*

Riverfront Inn. Housed in a converted turn-of-the-century railway depot near the Civic Center, the hotel retains many original details. Every guest room has a brass bed; second-floor rooms have cathedral ceilings and original brick and beams. *200 Coosa St., 36104, tel. 205/834–4300. 124 rooms, 6 suites. Facilities: restaurant, lounge, coffee shop, pool. AE, DC, MC, V. Expensive.*

Motels

Hampton Inn (1401 East Blvd., Montgomery 36117, tel. 205/277–2400 or 800/426–7866), 103 rooms, 2 suites, pool; inexpensive. **Motel Birmingham** (7905 Crestwood Blvd., Birmingham 35210, tel. 205/956–4440 or 800/338–9275), 242 rooms, restaurant, pool; inexpensive.

The Arts

In Montgomery, at the world-class **Alabama Shakespeare Festival** (Eastern By-Pass exit off I–85, tel. 205/271–5353; closed Sept.–Oct.), Shakespearean plays, modern drama, and musicals are performed on two stages.

Mobile and the Gulf Coast

In Mobile, a busy port and one of the oldest cities in Alabama,
antebellum buildings survive as a bridge to the treasured past,
and azaleas bloom in profusion each spring. The country's first
Mardi Gras was created here, and today the predominantly
Catholic city still glories in its pre-Lenten parades and merry-
making. South of Mobile, across the bay, the area around Gulf
Shores encompasses 50 mi of white sandy beaches, including
those on Pleasure and Dauphin islands. The eastern shore of
Mobile Bay has the laid-back atmosphere of the past, with live
oaks laced with Spanish moss and sprawling clapboard houses
with wide porches overlooking the bay.

Tourist Information

Alabama Gulf Coast Area: Convention and Visitors Bureau
(Hwy. 59, 3150 Gulf Shores Pkwy., Drawer 457, Gulf Shores
36542, tel. 205/968–7511). **Mobile:** Chamber of Commerce (Box
2187, 451 Government St., 36652, tel. 205/433–6951). **Orange
Beach:** Chamber of Commerce (Hwy. 182, Drawer 399, 36561,
tel. 205/981–8000).

Getting There

By Plane **Mobile Municipal Airport** (tel. 205/633–0313) is served by most
major domestic carriers, as is Florida's **Pensacola Regional Airport** (tel. 904/433–7800), 40 mi east of Gulf Shores.

By Car I–10 leads west from Florida to Mobile and continues into Mississippi. I–65 leads south from Birmingham and Montgomery
and ends at Mobile. Gulf Shores is connected with Mobile via
I–10 and Rte. 59; Rtes. 180 and 182 are the main beach routes.

By Train Amtrak's *Gulf Breeze* travels between Birmingham, Montgomery, and Mobile, with stops at Greenville, Evergreen, and
Atmore.

By Bus **Greyhound** has stations in Mobile (201 Government St., tel.
205/432–1861) and Pensacola, Florida (505 W. Burgess Rd.,
tel. 904/476–4800).

Exploring Mobile and the Gulf Coast

Ft. Condé was the name the French gave in 1711 to what would
become **Mobile.** The city's French origins survive in its Creole
cuisine. **Ft. Condé,** too, survives, thanks to a $2.2 million resto-
ration. One hundred fifty years after it was destroyed, remains
of the fort were discovered during construction of the I–10 interchange. A reconstructed portion houses the city's **visitor
center,** as well as a museum and several re-created rooms. Costumed guides conduct tours. *150 S. Royal St., tel. 205/434–
7304 or 800/252–3862. Admission free.*

At the visitor center you can also get information on the major
annual events hosted by Mobile, the biggest of which is **Mardi
Gras,** featuring balls, parties, and parades. The **Azalea Trail
Festival** is held in March or April, depending upon when blooms
peak. The **Historic Mobile Homes Tour** in March opens 36 town
houses, cottages, and antebellum plantation homes to the public.

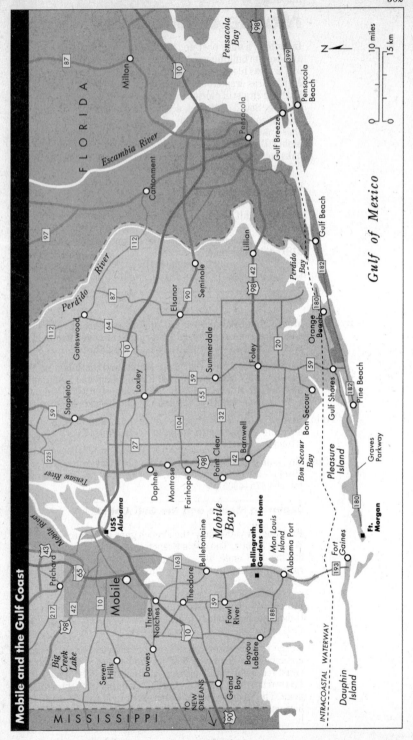

Mobile and the Gulf Coast

MISSISSIPPI

FLORIDA

Gulf of Mexico

Mobile Bay

Pensacola Bay

Perdido Bay

Bon Secour Bay

Escambia River

Perdido River

Tensaw River

Mobile River

Big Creek Lake

Pleasure Island

Dauphin Island

INTRACOASTAL WATERWAY

Graves Parkway

Milton

Pensacola

Pensacola Beach

Gulf Breeze

Cantonment

Lillian

Gulf Beach

Seminole

Elsanor

Gateswood

Stapleton

Loxley

Summerdale

Foley

Orange Beach

Gulf Shores

Pine Beach

Daphne

Montrose

Fairhope

Point Clear

Barnwell

Bon Secour

Bellefontaine

USS Alabama

Bellingrath Gardens and Home

Mon Louis Island

Alabama Port

Fort Gaines

Ft. Morgan

Mobile

Prichard

Theodore

Three Notches

Fowl River

Dawes

Seven Hills

Bayou LaBatre

Grand Bay

TO NEW ORLEANS

N

10 miles

15 km

One block north of the fort via Government Street is **Oakleigh** (350 Oakleigh Pl., tel. 205/432–1281; admission charged). The high-ceilinged, half-timbered mansion, built between 1833 and 1838, showcases fine period furniture, portraits, silver, jewelry, kitchen implements, toys, and more. Tickets may be purchased next door, at the **Cox-Deasy House,** an 1850s cottage furnished with simple 19th-century pieces.

The battleship USS *Alabama* is anchored in Mobile Bay, east of the city. A tour gives a fascinating glimpse into the operation of the World War II vessel, which had a crew of 2,500. Anchored next to it is the USS *Drum*, a World War II submarine. Other exhibits in the 100-acre **Battleship Park** include the B–52 bomber *Calamity Jane* and a P–51 Mustang fighter plane. *Battleship Pkwy., tel. 205/433–2703. Admission and parking fee charged.*

Southwest of here via I–10 and Bellingrath Road lies **Bellingrath Gardens and Home,** site of one of the world's most magnificent azalea gardens. Here, amid a 905-acre semitropical landscape, are 65 acres of gardens that bloom in all seasons: 200 species of azaleas in spring, 2,500 rosebushes in summer, 60,000 chrysanthemum plants in autumn, and fields of poinsettias in winter. The onetime home of Coca-Cola bottling pioneer Walter D. Bellingrath, who started the gardens with his wife in 1917, offers one of the finest collections of antiques in the Southeast. *Tel. 205/973–2217. Admission charged.*

From here you may continue south on Rte. 193 toward the Gulf or return to Mobile and take I–10 and Rte. 59S to **Gulf Shores,** a family-oriented beach area with hotels, restaurants, and attractions. There's ample free parking along the white-as-snow beach, though the traffic is bumper-to-bumper at peak times. At the western tip of **Pleasure Island,** 20 mi west of Gulf Shores at the end of Rte. 180, is **Ft. Morgan** (Mobile Point, tel. 205/540–7125; admission charged), built in the early 1800s to guard the entrance to Mobile Bay. In 1864, Confederate torpedoes sank the ironclad *Tecumseh*, on which Admiral David Farragut commanded, "Damn the torpedoes! Full speed ahead!"

Sports and Outdoor Activities

Biking
Gulf State Park Resort (tel. 205/948–7275 or 800/252–7275) in Gulf Shores has bike trails through pine forests; rentals are available.

Canoeing
Sunshine Canoe Rentals (tel. 205/344–8664) runs canoe trips at Escatawpa River, 15 mi west of Mobile. The river has no rapids and makes for leisurely travel past lots of white sandbars.

Fishing
Freshwater and saltwater fishing here are excellent. In Gulf Shores, **Gulf State Park** (*see* State Parks, *above*) has fishing from an 825-foot pier and rents flat-bottom boats for lake fishing. Deep-sea fishing from charter boats is very popular; Gulf Shores has the ***Moreno Queen*** (tel. 205/981–8499), and nearby **Orange Beach** has 90 charter boats to choose from. You can obtain a fishing license from most local bait shops. For more information, contact the **Department of Conservation and Natural Resources** (tel. 205/242–3829).

Water Sports
In Orange Beach, **Fun Marina** (tel. 205/981–8587) rents Jet Skis, pontoon boats, and 16-foot bay-fishing boats. In Gulf

Shores, **Island Recreation Services** (tel. 205/948–7334) rents boogie boards, body boards, surf boats, and sailboats.

Dining and Lodging

In Mobile and throughout the Gulf area, the specialty is fresh seafood, often prepared Creole style, with peppery spices, crabmeat dressing, and sometimes a tomato-based sauce. For price ranges, see Charts 1 (B) and 2 (B) in Chapter 1.

Gulf Shores **Original Oyster House.** Dining at this plant-filled restaurant
Dining overlooking the bayou has become a local tradition. Oysters on
★ the half-shell, plucked fresh from nearby Perdido Bay, are the specialty of the house. The Cajun-style gumbo—a concoction of crab claws, shrimp, amberjack, grouper, redfish, okra and other vegetables, and Cajun spices—has won 20 culinary awards. *Bayou Village Shopping Center, Rte. 59, tel. 205/948–2445. No reservations. AE, DC, MC, V. Moderate–Expensive.*

Lodging **Gulf Shores Plantation.** This 320-acre family resort, 8 mi east of Ft. Morgan on the Gulf, offers condominiums with fully equipped kitchens in high rises overlooking the beach. Abundant recreational activities are available. *Rte. 180W, Box 1058, 36542, tel. 205/540–2291 or 800/554–0344. 518 units. Facilities: 2 restaurants, lounge, indoor and outdoor pools, tennis courts, access to golf course, other sports facilities, gift shop. Moderate–Expensive.*

Mobile **La Louisiana.** At this antiques-filled old house on the outskirts
Dining of town the seafood is fresh and prepared with a touch of
★ French Creole. *2400 Airport Blvd., tel. 205/476–8130. Reservations advised. Jacket and tie advised. AE, MC, V. No lunch; closed Sun. Expensive.*

Wintzell's Oyster House. Local celebrities and anyone else wanting to see and be seen gather at the raw bar of this 50-year-old favorite. The seafood is fresh from the Gulf, served fried or broiled, and perfectly complemented by good draft beer. *605 Dauphin St., tel. 205/433–1004. No reservations. AE, DC, MC, V. Closed Sun. Inexpensive–Moderate.*

Lodging **Radisson Admiral Semmes Hotel.** The hotel is popular with local politicians and partygoers, the latter for its excellent location directly on the Mardi Gras parade route. Rooms are furnished in Queen Anne and Chippendale styles. *251 Government St., Box 1209, 36633, tel. 205/432–8000. 147 rooms, 22 suites. Facilities: restaurant, lounge, pool, whirlpool. AE, DC, MC, V. Expensive.*

The Malaga Inn. A delightful, romantic getaway, The Malaga has a lobby furnished with 19th-century antiques and opening onto a tropically landscaped central courtyard with a fountain. The rooms are large, airy, and furnished with massive antiques. *359 Church St., 36602, tel. 205/438–4701. 40 rooms. Facilities: restaurant, lounge, outdoor pool. AE, DC, MC, V. Inexpensive–Moderate.*

Orange Beach **Dempsey's Restaurant.** The tropical setting at this lakeside din-
Dining ing room is enhanced by a 20-foot waterfall. Cajun seafood specialties are arranged temptingly at the all-you-can-eat dinner buffet, which includes such dishes as stuffed jumbo shrimp. Blues is played nightly, and there's a small dance floor. *Rte. 182, tel. 205/981–6800. No reservations. AE, D, MC, V. Moderate.*

★ **Hazel's Family Restaurant.** This plain family-style restaurant serves a good, hearty breakfast (the biscuits are famous), soup-and-salad lunches, and adequate buffet dinners featuring such seafood dishes as flounder Florentine and crab-stuffed broiled snapper. *Gulf View Square Shopping Center, Rte. 182, tel. 205/981–4628. No reservations. AE, MC, V. Inexpensive.*

Lodging
★ **The Original Romar House.** This unassuming beach cottage is filled with surprises—from the Caribbean-style upstairs sitting area to the Purple Parrot Bar to the luxurious art deco-style guest rooms. *23500 Perdido Beach Blvd. (Rte. 182), 36561, tel. 205/981–6156 or 800/487–6627. 6 rooms. Facilities: Continental breakfast, hot tub, tandem bicycle. MC, V. Expensive.*

Perdido Beach Hilton. The eight- and nine-story towers of this Mediterranean-style hotel are stucco and red tile; the lobby is tiled in terra-cotta and decorated with mosaics by Venetian artists. Luxurious rooms have beach views and balconies. *Rte. 182E, Box 400, 36561, tel. 205/981–9811 or 800/634–8001. 329 rooms, 16 suites. Facilities: restaurant, café, heated indoor/outdoor pool, pool bar, exercise room overlooking beach, whirlpool, sauna, 4 lighted tennis courts. AE, DC, MC, V. Expensive.*

Point Clear
Dining and Lodging
★ **Marriott's Grand Hotel.** Set within 550 acres of beautifully landscaped grounds on Mobile Bay, the "Grand" has been a cherished tradition since 1847. Extensively refurbished by Marriott, it is one of the South's premier resorts. Spacious rooms and cottages are traditionally furnished. Food is elegantly prepared and served in the restaurants, including the award-winning Magnolia's Room. *U.S. Scenic 98, 36564, tel. 205/928–9201 or 800/544–9933. 282 rooms, 24 suites. Facilities: 3 restaurants, lounge, coffee shop, pool, 10 tennis courts, 36 holes golf, horseback riding, bicycle riding, marina with rental boats, sailing, charter fishing, children's day camp. AE, DC, MC, V. Expensive.*

Elsewhere in the State

U.S. Space and Rocket Center

Getting There Huntsville is 100 mi north of Birmingham via I–65 and U.S. 72E.

What to See and Do Home to the **U.S. Space Camp,** the center offers a bus tour of the NASA labs and shuttle test sites; a 33-minute OMNIMAX film, *Speed*, which traces modes of travel from bicycles to rocketships; hands-on exhibits in the museum; and an outdoor park filled with spacecraft. *1 Tranquillity Base, Huntsville, tel. 205/837–3400. Admission: $11.95 adults, $7.95 children.*

FLORIDA

By Donna Singer

Capital	Tallahassee
Population	13,642,540
Motto	In God We Trust
State Bird	Mockingbird
State Flower	Orange blossom

Visitor Information

Florida Division of Tourism (126 Van Buren St., Tallahassee 32301, tel. 904/487–1462 or 904/487–1463). **Information centers:** on U.S. 301 at Hilliard, U.S. 231 near Graceville, I–75 near Jennings, I–10 at Pensacola, and I–95 near Yulee, and in the lobby of the capitol building in Tallahassee.

Scenic Drives

In **Everglades National Park,** the 38-mi drive from the Main Visitor Center to Flamingo reveals a patchwork of ecosystems, including mangrove and cypress forests, sawgrass marshes, and a variety of wildlife. Although traffic jams abound during the winter tourist season, the **Overseas Highway** (U.S. 1) from Key Largo to Key West offers spectacular vistas of the Atlantic, Florida Bay, the Gulf of Mexico, and the myriad islands of the keys.

Rte. 789 along the Gulf Coast south from Holmes Beach in Bradenton to Lido Beach in Sarasota, and from Casey Key south of Osprey to Nokomis Beach, passes over several picturesque barrier islands. Along the Atlantic coast, the **Buccaneer Trail** (Rte. A1A) from Mayport to the old seaport town of Fernandina Beach passes through marshlands and along pristine beaches. **U.S. 98** winds east from historic Pensacola through the lush coastal landscape of the Panhandle.

National and State Parks

National Parks **Everglades and Biscayne national parks** (*see* Elsewhere in the State, *below*). In southwest Florida, **Big Cypress National Preserve** (20 mi east of Ochopee on U.S. 41; HCR 61, Box 110, Ochopee 33943, tel. 813/695–2000 or 813/262–1066), noted for the bald and dwarf cypress that line its marshlands, is a sanctuary for alligators, bald eagles, and the endangered Florida panther.

Florida boasts three national forests. The 556,500-acre **Apalachicola National Forest** (Rte. 65; Edward Ball Wakulla Spring State Park, Wakulla Spring Rd., Wakulla 32305, tel. 904/653–9419) is popular for canoeing and hiking, and has a recreational facility designed for the disabled. **Ocala National Forest** (Rte. 40 east of Ocala; Forest Visitor Center, 10863 E. Hwy. 40, Silver Springs 34488, tel. 904/625–7470) has lakes, springs, hiking trails, campgrounds, and historic sites. **Osceola National Forest** (north of Lake City on I–10; Osceola Ranger District, Box 70, Olustee 32072, tel. 904/752–2577) is dotted with cypress swamps and offers good fishing and hunting. In addition, the state has five national monuments, two national seashores, and eight national wildlife refuges.

State Parks The state administers hundreds of parks, nature preserves, and historic sites. Among these are **Blackwater River State Park** (40 mi northeast of Pensacola on I–10; Rte. 1, Box 57C, Holt 32564, tel. 904/623–2363), popular with canoeists; **Delnor-Wiggins Pass State Recreation Area** (North Naples; 1100 Gulfshore Dr. N, Naples 33963, tel. 813/597–6196), with miles of beaches, picnic areas, and fishing spots; **Florida Caverns State Park** (Rte. 167, two hours north of Panama City; 3345 Caverns Rd., Mariana 32446, tel. 904/482–9598), comprising 1,783 acres of caves and nature trails; **Ft. Clinch State Park** (*see* Elsewhere in the State, *below*); and **St. Andrews State Recreation Area** (east end of Panama City Beach in the Panhandle; 4415 Thomas Dr., Panama City Beach 32408, tel. 904/233–5140), encompassing 1,038 acres of beaches, pinewoods, and marshes for swimming, pier fishing, and dune hiking. For more information contact the **Florida Department of Natural Resources** (Marjory Stoneman Douglas Bldg., MS 525, 3900 Commonwealth Blvd., Tallahassee 32399–3000, tel. 904/488–9872).

Miami

With more than half of its nearly 2 million people Hispanic in origin, it's no wonder Miami is called the capital of Latin America. Indeed, Miami is a city of superlatives. This growing metropolis boasts one of the largest airports and *the* largest cruise ship port in the world. More than 100 companies base their international operations in the city, and big-league sports are big news here. Undergirding all this energy and prosperity is a flourishing drug culture that fuels get-rich-quick lifestyles. Although Hurricane Andrew devastated south Miami in 1992, the storm did little damage to the areas that tourists visit most.

Tourist Information

Greater Miami: Convention and Visitors Bureau (701 Brickell Ave., Suite 2700, 33132, tel. 305/539–3063 or 800/283–2707). **Miami Beach:** Chamber of Commerce (1920 Meridian Ave., 33130, tel. 305/672–1270). **South Dade County:** Visitors Information Center (160 U.S. 1, Florida City, 33034, tel. 305/245–9180 or 800/852–8675).

Arriving and Departing

By Plane **Miami International Airport** (tel. 305/876–7000) has scheduled service by most major domestic and Latin American airlines and many transatlantic carriers. It is 6 mi west of downtown via Rte. 836. Rental cars are available at the airport. Cab fare downtown is about $15; the flat fare to and from the Port of Miami, where cruise ships dock, is $14 plus tip. **SuperShuttle** (tel. 305/871–2000) vans go from the airport to area hotels. Bus service (fare $1.25, exact change required; 25¢ transfer) is available across the lower-level lanes in the center of the airport.

By Car I–95, which runs north–south along Florida's east coast, flows into the heart of Miami. From the northwest, I–75 leads to the city. Rte. 836 (also called East–West Expressway or Dolphin Expressway), connecting the airport to downtown (toll eastbound only, 25¢), continues across I–395 and the MacArthur Causeway to lower Miami Beach and the Art Deco District. Rte. 112 (Airport Expressway) connects the airport with midtown (toll eastbound only, 25¢) and continues across I–195 and the Julia Tuttle Causeway to mid–Miami Beach.

Train Station Amtrak (8303 N.W. 37th Ave., tel. 305/835–1200).

Bus Station Greyhound (700 Biscayne Blvd., tel. 305/374–6160).

Getting Around Miami

Greater Miami resembles Los Angeles in its urban sprawl and traffic congestion. You'll need a car to get from one area of the city to another. Metromover, a light-rail mass-transit system, circles the heart of the city on twin elevated loops; use it to tour the downtown area. The Deco District in Miami Beach and the heart of Coconut Grove are best explored on foot.

By Car Miami is laid out in quadrants: northwest, northeast, southwest, southeast. These meet at Miami Avenue, which separates east from west, and Flagler Street, which separates north from south. Avenues and courts run north–south; streets, terraces, and ways run east–west. Roads run diagonally, northwest–southeast. In Miami Beach, avenues run north–south; streets, east–west. Streets in Coral Gables have names, not numbers.

By Public Transportation The **Metro-Dade Transit Agency** (tel. 305/638–6700) runs the Metrorail, Metromover, and Metrobus. **Metrorail** (fare $1.25) runs from downtown Miami north to Hialeah and south along U.S. 1 to Dadeland. **Metromover** (fare 25¢), a separate system, has two loops that circle downtown Miami, linking major hotels, office buildings, and shopping areas. **Metrobus** (fare $1.25) stops are marked by blue-and-green signs with a bus logo and route information. Frequency of service varies widely.

By Taxi Be on your guard when traveling by cab in Miami. Some drivers are rude and unhelpful and may take advantage of visitors unfamiliar with their destinations. The fare is $1.10 for the first ⅓ mi, 20¢ for each additional ⅓ mi, plus 20¢ per ⅔ minute of waiting time and a $1 surcharge on airport departures. Major cab companies include **Central Taxicab Service** (tel. 305/534–0694), **Diamond Cab Company** (tel. 305/545–7575), **Magic City Cab Company** (tel. 305/757–5523), **Metro Taxicab Company** (tel. 305/888–8888), and **Yellow Cab Company** (tel. 305/444–4444).

Orientation Tours

Bus Tour **Old Town Trolley of Miami** (tel. 305/374–8687) runs 90-minute narrated city tours leaving Bayside Marketplace every half hour between 10 and 4.

Boat Tours *Island Queen* and *Good Times Too* (tel. 305/379–5119) offer 90-minute water tours of Miami from Bayside Marketplace.

Walking Tours The **Miami Design Preservation League** (tel. 305/672–2014) runs a 90-minute tour of Miami Beach's Art Deco District 10:30 AM Saturday and 5 PM Wednesday, leaving from the Leslie Hotel (1244 Ocean Dr., Miami Beach). Metro-Dade Community College history professor **Paul George** (tel. 305/858–6021) offers walking tours through downtown and other historic districts.

Exploring Miami

Downtown Begin your tour of downtown Miami at the 3.3-acre **Metro-Dade Cultural Center** (101 W. Flagler St.), a Mediterranean expression of architect Philip Johnson's postmodern style. An elevated plaza provides a serene haven from the city's pulsations. Within the complex are several arts venues, including the **Center for the Fine Arts** (tel. 305/375–1700). In the tradition of the European *Kunsthalle* (exhibition gallery), this art museum has no permanent collection but offers temporary exhibitions, such as 1994's scheduled "Portrait Drawings from the Portrait Gallery of London." Also in the Cultural Center are the **Historical Museum of Southern Florida** (tel. 305/375–1492), with artifacts from prehistory to the present, such as Tequesta and Seminole Indian ceramics and a 1920 streetcar; and the **Main Public Library** (tel. 305/375–2665), with more than 3 million holdings and art exhibits in its auditorium and second-floor lobby.

East of here, between Biscayne Boulevard and Biscayne Bay, is **Bayside Park.** Japanese sculptor Isamu Noguchi redesigned the park just before his death in 1989; it now includes a memorial to the *Challenger* astronauts, an amphitheater, and a fountain honoring the late Florida congressman Claude Pepper and his wife.

Bayside Marketplace (tel. 305/577–3344), between Bayfront Park and the entrance to the Port of Miami, is a waterside entertainment and shopping center. Its 235,000 square feet of retail space include 150 specialty shops, outdoor cafés, and an international food court. The center adjoins the **Miamarina,** where you can see luxurious yachts moored and ride in an authentic Venetian gondola (tel. 305/579–6955). Pier 5 extends to a fisherman's wharf, offering fresh seafood and fishing charters.

Northeast of here on Biscayne Boulevard is the **Freedom Tower** (600 Biscayne Blvd.), where the Cuban Refugee Center processed more than 500,000 immigrating Cubans in the 1960s. Built in 1925 and renovated as office space in 1990, this imposing Spanish Baroque–style structure was inspired by the Giralda, an 800-year-old bell tower in Seville, Spain.

South of downtown proper, several architecturally interesting condominiums rise between Brickell Avenue and Biscayne Bay. Israeli artist Yacov Agram painted the rainbow-hued exterior of **Villa Regina** (1581 Brickell Ave.). The 20-story **Atlantis** (2025 Brickell Ave.), where a palm tree grows in a hole in the building between the 12th and 16th floors, formed a backdrop for the opening credits of the television series "Miami Vice."

Miami Beach Made up of 17 islands in Biscayne Bay, Miami Beach is officially a separate city from Miami. In recent years this "American Riviera" has revived its fortunes by renewing its mile-square Art Deco District, now on the National Register of Historic Places. Decorative streamlined moderne facades dating from the Depression were repainted in lively pastels as residents reveled in their architectural heritage. Today the district is Florida's preeminent place for people-watching.

Miami

ATLANTIC OCEAN

Virginia Key

Causeway

Rickenbacker

Biscayne

CRANDON PARK

KEY BISCAYNE

BILL BAGGS
CAPE FLORIDA
STATE RECREATION
AREA

0   3 km

0   3 miles

Bric.

Grove Isle

S.W. 22nd St.

Bay Shore Dr.

S. Dixie Hwy.

COCONUT GROVE

Waterway

Miracle Mile

953

Coral Gables

CORAL GABLES

University of Miami

972

S.W. 57th Ave.

Coral Way

Bird Rd.

976

Sunset Dr.

Old Cutler Rd.

MATHESON HAMMOCK PARK

Red   Rd.

S.W. 72nd St.

1

Snapper Creek Canal

Ludlam Rd.

986

Start at Ocean Drive and 6th Street, where the **Art Deco District** begins. Proceed north past pastel-hued deco hotels (outlined in brilliant neon at night) on your left and the palm-fringed beach on your right. The neighborhood's two main commercial streets are **Collins Avenue**, one block west of Ocean Drive, and, one block farther west, **Washington Avenue**. The latter is a colorful mix of Jewish, Cuban, Haitian, and more familiar American culture, containing delicatessens, produce markets, shops selling religious artifacts, and many of the best restaurants in the metropolis. West of Washington Avenue, the **Lincoln Road Mall**, a pedestrian shopping street that declined in popularity in the 1960s, has begun to enjoy a comeback thanks to artists and vendors attracted to low-rent sidewalk shops.

At 17th Street and Washington Avenue is the **Miami Beach Convention Center** (tel. 305/673–7311), where the Jackie Gleason television show once originated. North of here, the **Bass Museum of Art** (2121 Park Ave., tel. 305/673–7530) has a diverse collection of European works. Return to Collins Avenue and drive north: The triumphal archway that looms ahead is a work of illusionary art by Richard Haas that depicts the **Fontainebleau Hilton Resort and Spa** (4441 Collins Ave., tel. 305/538–2000), which actually sits behind it. The hotel is the largest in south Florida, with more than 1,200 rooms.

Little Havana More than 30 years ago, the tidal wave of Cubans fleeing the Castro regime flooded an older neighborhood just west of downtown with refugees. The area became known as Little Havana, although today more than half a million Cubans live throughout Greater Miami. On the southwest corner of Flagler Street and Teddy Roosevelt Avenue is the **Plaza de la Cubanidad** (S.W. 17th Ave.), where redbrick sidewalks surround a fountain and monument inscribed with words from José Martí, a leader in Cuba's struggle for independence from Spain: *Las palmas son novias que esperan* ("The palm trees are girlfriends who will wait").

South of here is **Calle Ocho** (S.W. 8th St.), the main street of Little Havana. Visit **Versailles** (3555 S.W. 8th St., tel. 305/445–7614), a Cuban restaurant whose menu and decor will immerse you in Cuban-American popular culture. At Calle Ocho and Memorial Boulevard (S.W. 13th Ave.) stands the **Brigade 2506 Memorial**, which commemorates the victims of the unsuccessful 1961 Bay of Pigs invasion of Cuba by an exile force. The **Cuban Museum of Art and Culture** (1300 S.W. 12th Ave., tel. 305/858–8006; closed Mon.–Tues.), created by Cuban exiles to preserve and interpret their heritage, now includes exhibits from the entire Hispanic art community.

Coral Gables, South Miami, Coconut Grove Developed during the 1920s by visionary George Merrick, Coral Gables has remained remarkably true to his dream of a planned community, with broad boulevards, Spanish Mediterranean architecture, and a busy commercial downtown. South Miami was a pioneer farming community that grew into a suburb while still managing to retain a small-town charm. Coconut Grove is the oldest section of Miami, begun during the 1870s and annexed to the city in 1925. Its earliest settlers included New England intellectuals, bohemians, Bahamians, and, later, artists, writers, and scientists who established winter homes. The Grove still reflects the pioneers' eclectic origins, with posh estates next to rustic cottages and starkly modern dwellings.

Coral Way runs east–west through **Coral Gables,** becoming **Miracle Mile** at Douglas Road (S.W. 37th Ave.). This is the heart of downtown Coral Gables, with more than 150 shops and a concentration of fine restaurants. Along Coral Way west of LeJeune Road (S.W. 42nd Ave.), the **Granada Golf Course** (2001 Granada Blvd., tel. 305/460–5367) is one of two public courses amid Coral Gables' largest historic district. **Coral Gables Merrick House** (907 Coral Way, tel. 305/460–5361), George Merrick's boyhood home, has been restored to its 1920s appearance and contains family furnishings and artifacts.

South on Granada Boulevard is the **DeSoto Plaza and Fountain,** a classical column on a pedestal with water flowing from the mouths of four sculpted faces. Northeast one block is the stunning **Venetian Pool** (2701 DeSoto Blvd., tel. 305/460–5356; admission charged), a municipal swimming pool created from a rock quarry. South of here is the 260-acre main campus of the **University of Miami,** with about 13,000 students—the largest private university in the Southeast. Its **Lowe Art Museum** (1301 Stanford Dr., tel. 305/284–3536) has a permanent collection of 8,000 works.

Fine old homes and mature trees line **Sunset Drive,** the city-designated "historic and scenic road" to and through downtown **South Miami.** Go south on Red Road to reach the grounds of the **Parrot Jungle,** one of Miami's oldest and most popular attractions. Many of the 1,000 parrots, macaws, cockatoos, and other exotic birds fly free, but they'll come to you for seeds, sold in old-fashioned gumball machines. You can watch a trained-bird show, stroll among exotic plants and trees, and see a cactus garden. *11000 S.W. 57th Ave., tel. 305/666–7834. Admission: $10.50 adults, $7 children.*

Just south of here is the 83-acre **Fairchild Tropical Garden** (10901 Old Cutler Rd., tel. 305/667–1651), the largest tropical botanical garden in the continental United States. North of the garden, Old Cutler Road traverses Dade County's oldest and most scenic park, **Matheson Hammock Park** (9610 Old Cutler Rd., tel. 305/666–6979), dating from the days of the Civilian Conservation Corps in the 1930s. The most popular feature is a bathing beach, where the tide flushes a saltwater "atoll" pool through four gates.

In **Coconut Grove,** northwest of South Miami, the **Plymouth Congregational Church** (3400 Devon Rd., tel. 305/444–6521), a handsome coral-rock structure, dates from 1917. Main Highway brings you to the historic **Village of Coconut Grove,** a trendy commercial district with redbrick sidewalks and more than 300 restaurants, stores, and art galleries. Parking is often a problem, so be prepared to walk several blocks to the heart of the district.

The apricot-hued, Spanish Rococo–style **Coconut Grove Playhouse** (3500 Main Hwy., tel. 305/442–4000), dating from 1926, presents traditional plays, musical revues, and experimental productions. Across the street is **The Barnacle** (3485 Main Hwy., tel. 305/448–9445; closed Tues.–Wed.), a 19th-century pioneer residence that is now a state historic site. The house has a broad, sloping roof and deeply recessed verandas to channel sea breezes inside; many furnishings are original. In the village center is **Cocowalk,** a multilevel open mall of

Mediterranean-style brick courtyards and terraces overflowing with restaurants, bars, and shops.

East of here is **Dinner Key Marina,** Greater Miami's largest marina, and the 105,000-square-foot **Coconut Grove Convention Center** (2700 S. Bayshore Dr., tel. 305/579–3310), site of antiques, boat, and home-furnishings shows. Nearby, decorated with nautical-motif art deco trim, is **Miami City Hall** (3500 Pan American Dr., tel. 305/250–5400), built in 1934 as terminal for the Pan American Airways seaplane base at Dinner Key.

North on South Bayshore Drive is **Our Lady of Charity Shrine** (3609 S. Miami Ave., tel. 305/854–2405), a 90-foot-high conical shrine built to overlook the bay so that worshipers face Cuba. Half a mile west is the **Miami Museum of Science and Space Transit Planetarium** (3280 S. Miami Ave., tel. 305/854–4247), with hands-on sound, gravity, and electricity exhibits and laser-light planetarium shows. Across the street is the **Vizcaya Museum and Gardens** (3251 S. Miami Ave., tel. 305/579–2813), a showplace of antiquities. The Italian Renaissance–style villa was built in the early 20th century as the winter residence of Chicago industrialist James Deering. Continue north to **Simpson Park** (55 S.W. 17th Rd., tel. 305/856–6801), a fragment of the dense jungle that once covered the entire 5 mi from downtown Miami to Coconut Grove.

Virginia Key and Key Biscayne   The waters of Government Cut and the Port of Miami separate densely populated Miami Beach from Greater Miami's playground islands, Virginia Key and Key Biscayne. Parks and stretches of dense mangrove swamp occupy much of both keys. To reach the keys, take the **Rickenbacker Causeway** across Biscayne Bay at Brickell Avenue and S.W. 26th Road, about 2 mi south of downtown Miami. Across the high bridge is the 6,536-seat **Miami Marine Stadium** (3601 Rickenbacker Causeway, tel. 305/361–6732), site of summer pop concerts, and the **Miami Seaquarium** (4400 Rickenbacker Causeway, tel. 305/361–5705), featuring sea lion, dolphin, and killer-whale performances and a 235,000-gallon tropical-reef aquarium.

Key Biscayne's commercial center is a mix of posh shops and stores catering to neighborhood needs. At the key's south end is the **Bill Baggs Cape Florida State Recreation Area** (1200 Crandon Blvd., tel. 305/361–5811), with 1¼ mi of pine- and palm-topped white-sand beach.

The keys took a hit from Hurricane Andrew, and hotels suffered damage, as did the well-known public golf course. If you are planning a visit to Virginia Key and Key Biscayne, contact Greater Miami Convention and Visitors Bureau (*see* Tourist Information, *above*) for an update on conditions.

Other Attractions   Southwest of Dade County's urban core is the 290-acre **Metro Zoo** (12400 Coral Reef Dr., tel. 305/251–0400), a favorite destination for area residents. Unfortunately, the zoo took a beating from Hurricane Andrew and, although reopened, was still undergoing major repairs at press time.

Next door is the **Gold Coast Railroad Museum** (12450 Coral Reef Dr., tel. 305/253–0063), whose collection includes a 1949 Silver Crescent dome car and the *Ferdinand Magellan*, the only Pullman car ever constructed specifically for U.S. presidents.

Shopping

Shopping is everywhere in Florida except the Everglades. Malls, an international free zone, and specialty shopping districts are the attractions in Miami. Many local shopping areas have an ethnic flavor. Store hours vary.

Shopping Districts More than 500 garment manufacturers sell their clothing in more than 30 factory outlets and discount fashion stores in the **Fashion District,** east of I–95 along 5th Avenue from 25th to 29th streets. Most stores in the district are open Monday through Saturday 9–5 and accept credit cards. The **Miami Free Zone** (2305 N.W. 107th Ave., tel. 305/591–4300) is an international wholesale trade center supervised by the U.S. Customs Service, where you can buy goods duty-free for export or pay duty on goods released for domestic use. At **Cauley Square** (22400 Old Dixie Hwy., Goulds, tel. 305/258–3543)—a complex of clapboard, coral-rock, and stucco buildings that housed railroad workers at the turn of the century—shops sell antiques, crafts, and clothing. To get there, turn right off U.S. 1 at S.W. 224th Street.

Sports and Outdoor Activities

Diving Summer diving conditions in greater Miami have been compared with those in the Caribbean. Winter diving can bring rough, cold waters. Fowey, Triumph, Long, and Emerald reefs are shallow 10- to 15-foot dives good for snorkelers and beginning divers. **Divers Paradise** (4000 Crandon Blvd., Key Biscayne, tel. 305/361–3483) offers dive charters, rentals, and instruction. In Miami, **Omega Diving International** (13885 S.W. 70th Ave., tel. 305/238–3039 or 800/255–1966) offers private instruction, equipment consultation, and specialty courses, including instructor training and underwater photography, and **Bubbles Dive Center** (2671 S.W. 27th Ave., tel. 305/856–0565) is an all-purpose dive shop. All shops are PADI-affiliated.

Golf Dade County has more than 30 private and public courses (tel. 305/579–2968 for county information, 305/575–5256 for Miami information, and 305/673–7730 for Miami Beach information).

Sailing **Dinner Key** and the **Coconut Grove** waterfront remain the center of sailing in Greater Miami, although moorings and rentals are found elsewhere on the bay and up the Miami River. **Easy Sailing** (Dinner Key Marina, 3400 Pan American Dr., tel. 305/858–4001 or 800/780–4001) offers instruction and a fleet (19 to 127 feet) for rent by the hour or by the day.

Tennis Greater Miami has 11 tennis centers open to the public. **Biltmore Tennis Center** (1150 Anastasia Ave., Coral Gables, tel. 305/460–5360) has 10 hard courts. **Flamingo Tennis Center** (1000 12th St., Miami Beach, tel. 305/673–7761) has 19 clay courts. **International Tennis Center** (7300 Crandon Blvd., Key Biscayne, tel. 305/361–8633) has 17 Laykold Cushion Plus hard courts, six of them lighted; reservations are necessary for night play.

Water Sports **Beach Sports International** (2401 Collins Ave., Miami Beach, tel. 305/538–0752) rents Windsurfers and other water-sports equipment and runs a parasailing service.

Spectator Sports

Baseball **Florida Marlins** (Joe Robbie Stadium, 2269 N.W. 199th St., Miami, tel. 305/620–2578 or 305/779–7070; Apr.–Oct.).

Basketball **Miami Heat** (Miami Arena, 721 NW 1st Ave., Miami, tel. 305/577–4328; Nov.–Apr.).

Football **Miami Dolphins** (Joe Robbie Stadium, tel. 305/620–2578; Aug.–Dec.).

Jai Alai In this, the fastest game on Earth, *pelotas*, the hard balls thrown from hand-held cowled baskets called *cestas*, travel at speeds above 170 mph. **Miami Jai Alai** (3500 N.W. 37th Ave., Miami, tel. 305/633–6400), the oldest fronton in America, presents games November–April and mid-May–late September.

Beaches

Millions visit Dade County's beaches annually. The broadest is along **Miami Beach,** where a boardwalk runs from 21st to 46th streets; within this stretch, various groups tend to congregate in specific areas. From 1st to 14th streets, senior citizens often gather early in the day. A younger crowd, including families, appears later. The beaches opposite the Art Deco District, between 6th Street and 21st Street, attract a mix of locals and European and Asian tourists. Here topless bathing, although officially illegal, is tolerated. University of Miami students like the stretch of beach along Millionaires' Row, around 46th Street, where the big hotels have outdoor concession stands on the beach. High-school groups gather at 1st, 10th, 14th, and 85th streets for volleyball and football. Quieter beaches can be found at 35th, 53rd, or 64th streets. Miami Beach's municipal beaches are open daily with lifeguards. **Bal Harbour** and **Surfside,** beach communities just north of Miami Beach, have no lifeguards. Beaches are free in all three, with metered parking nearby.

North of Bal Harbour via Collins Avenue, **Haulover Beach Park** (10800 Collins Ave., tel. 305/947–3525) is a less crowded Atlantic Ocean public beach. In Key Biscayne, **Crandon Park** (4000 Crandon Blvd., tel. 305/361–5421) is an Atlantic Ocean beach popular with young couples and families. Also in Key Biscayne is the **Bill Baggs Cape Florida State Recreation Area** (*see* Exploring Virginia Key and Key Biscayne, *above*).

Dining

Miami is gaining a world reputation for its fusion of tropical ingredients with the nouvelle-inspired remake of classical French cooking. Gourmet centers of the city are downtown Coral Gables and the Deco District of Miami Beach, with pockets of fine dining also in ethnic neighborhoods, such as Little Havana, and in popular nightlife districts, such as Coconut Grove and Bayside downtown. For price ranges, see Chart 1 (A) in Chapter 1.

Very Expensive **A Mano.** This highly acclaimed exemplar of Miami's nouvelle-
★ tropical cuisine features chef Norman Van Aken's imaginative use of fresh Florida seafoods. Decor in this striking restaurant in the Deco District's Betsy Ross Hotel features terra-cotta floor tiles and an orange, black, and aqua color scheme. *1440*

Ocean Dr., Miami Beach, tel. 305/531–6266. Reservations advised. AE, DC, MC, V. No lunch; closed Mon.

★ **Casa Rolandi.** Popular among the fashionable, this elegant restaurant features high ceilings and Italian art. The cuisine is a combination of northern Italian and Swiss, with Latin influences. *1930 Ponce de Leon Blvd., Coral Gables, tel. 305/444–2187. Reservations required. Jacket advised. AE, DC, MC, V. No lunch weekends; closed Thanksgiving, Christmas, New Year's Day.*

Grand Cafe. This upscale spot features a bilevel room with pink tablecloths and floral bouquets. International cuisine here means everything from Maine lobster to squid-ink linguine. *2669 S. Bay Shore Dr., Coconut Grove, tel. 305/858–9600. Reservations advised. Jacket advised. AE, DC, MC, V.*

The Pavillon Grill. The English-club ambience at this downtown restaurant is heightened by mahogany and marble accents and leather furniture. The attentive staff serves regional American fare, such as grilled medallions of venison with roasted figs and cassis sauce. *Inter-Continental Hotel, 100 Chopin Plaza, tel. 305/577–1000. Reservations advised. Jacket required. AE, DC, MC, V. No lunch (except Sun. brunch).*

Expensive **Café Chauveron.** Unrepentantly traditional French cuisine, such as broiled pheasant with truffle and goose-liver pâté, is served to a loyal clientele in this classically formal dining room overlooking Indian Creek. *9561 E. Bay Harbor Dr., Bay Harbor Islands, tel. 305/866–8779. Reservations advised. Jacket required. AE, DC, MC, V. Closed June–Sept.*

★ **Chef Allen's.** In an art-deco setting of glass and neon, diners' gazes are drawn to the kitchen, visible through a large picture window, where chef Allen Susser creates new American masterpieces. Dishes such as honey-chilled roasted duck with stir-fried wild rice and green-apple chutney are *almost* too pretty to eat. *19088 N.E. 29th Ave., North Miami Beach, tel. 305/935–2900. AE, MC, V.*

★ **Mark's Place.** At this popular restaurant, owner-chef Mark Militello excels with regional fare prepared in an oak-burning oven from Genoa. The menu changes nightly to take advantage of fresh local produce. *2286 N.E. 123rd St., North Miami, tel. 305/893–6888. Reservations advised. AE, DC, MC, V.*

★ **Yuca.** This high-styled Cuban eatery, decorated with striking modern art prints and blond wood, attracts chic young Cubans and other fashionable types. Chef Douglas Rodriguez prepares dazzling nouvelle tropical dishes. *177 Giralda Ave., Coral Gables, tel. 305/444–4448. Reservations required. AE, DC, MC, V. No lunch weekends.*

Moderate **Acapulco.** Enjoy authentic Mexican cuisine while surrounded by Mexican-tile tabletops and adobe walls adorned with festive sombreros and serapes. The restaurant is on the fringe of Little Havana, between the airport and downtown. *727 N.W. Unity Blvd. (N.W. 27th Ave.), tel. 305/642–6961. Reservations advised weekends. AE, DC, MC, V.*

Café des Arts. French provincial cuisine is served in an art-deco setting amid tropical plants, antiques, and an art gallery with changing exhibits. Outdoor seating in the heart of the Deco District is a plus. *918 Ocean Dr., Miami Beach, tel. 305/534–6267. Reservations advised. AE, MC, V. No lunch.*

Las Tapas. *Tapas*—little dishes of various Spanish foods—come in appetizer-size portions to give you a variety of tastes during a single meal. Full-size meals are also served at this

Bayside Marketplace restaurant, typically packed at all hours. *401 Biscayne Blvd., tel. 305/372–2737. No reservations except large parties. AE, DC, MC, V.*

Los Ranchos. There's nothing nouvelle at this Nicaraguan restaurant west of town, where Argentine-style beef (lean, grass-fed tenderloin) is lovingly served to a loyal following. *125 S.W. 107th Ave., tel. 305/221–9367. Reservations advised. AE, DC, MC, V.*

★ **Unicorn Village Restaurant & Marketplace.** This outstanding natural-foods restaurant, serving such dishes as spinach lasagna and vegetable spring rolls, has the added advantage of a Riviera-like setting on a waterway off Biscayne Bay. If your meal inspires you, the 16,000-square-foot market next door is an incomparable source of natural foods. *3565 N.E. 207th St., Aventura, tel. 305/933–8829. No reservations. MC, V.*

Inexpensive **Chez Moy International.** This bustling restaurant with friendly staff is *the* choice in Little Haiti. Caribbean cuisine includes boiled spiced pork, conch with garlic and hot pepper, sugary fruit drinks, and sweet-potato pie for dessert. *1 N.W. 54th St., tel. 305/757–3056. No credit cards.*

★ **Hy Vong.** This tiny restaurant seating 36 is popular with locals, who come for such Vietnamese dishes as barbecued pork with sesame seeds and fish sauce. Expect a wait if you come after 7 PM. *3458 S.W. 8th St., Little Havana, tel. 305/446–3674. Reservations for 5 or more only. No credit cards. No lunch; closed Mon., 2 weeks in Aug.*

The News Cafe. This hip spot on Ocean Drive (open 24 hours) is always packed with people-watchers and those who enjoy such eclectic dishes as huge fresh-fruit bowls, burgers, bagels, pâtés, and chocolate fondue. *800 Ocean Dr., Miami Beach, tel. 305/538–6397. No reservations. AE, DC, MC, V.*

Shorty's Bar-B-Q. Miami's choice for barbecue and all the trimmings since the 1950s, Shorty's serves meals family style at long picnic tables. *9200 S. Dixie Hwy., Kendall, tel. 305/665–5732. No reservations. MC, V.*

Lodging

Few urban areas can match Greater Miami's diversity of lodging options. The area has hundreds of hotels and motels in all price categories, from $10 a night for a hostel bed to $2,000 for a luxurious presidential suite. For B&B accommodations, contact **Bed & Breakfast Company, Tropical Florida** (Box 262, Miami 33243, tel. 305/661–3270). Lodgings are concentrated in Miami Beach and downtown Miami, around the airport, and in Coral Gables, Coconut Grove, and Key Biscayne. Winter is peak season; summer is also busy but rates are lower. For price ranges (which reflect high-season rates), see Chart 2 (A) in Chapter 1.

Very Expensive **The Colonnade Hotel.** The twin 13-story towers of this $65 million swank hotel, office, and shopping complex dominate downtown Coral Gables. Oversize rooms feature sitting areas, built-in armoires, and traditional mahogany furnishings. *180 Aragon Ave., Coral Gables 33134, tel. 305/441–2600 or 800/533–1337; fax 305/445–3929. 140 rooms, 17 suites. Facilities: 2 restaurants, outdoor pool, 2 saunas, exercise equipment. AE, DC, MC, V.*

Fontainebleau Hilton Resort and Spa. The Miami area's foremost convention hotel boasts an opulent lobby with massive chandeliers and a sweeping staircase. Room decor varies; you can request a room with a '50s look or one with contemporary furnishings. Upper-floor rooms in the Chateau Building have the best views. *4441 Collins Ave., Miami Beach 33140, tel. 305/538–2000; fax 305/531–9274. 1146 rooms, 60 suites. Facilities: 12 restaurants, nightclub, ocean beach with 30 cabanas, 2 outdoor pools, water-sports equipment, 7 tennis courts, health club. AE, DC, MC, V.*

★ **Grand Bay Hotel.** This modern high rise overlooking Biscayne Bay features rooms with traditional furnishings and original art. The stepped profile, like a Mayan pyramid, gives each room facing the bay a private terrace. *2669 S. Bayshore Dr., Coconut Grove 33133, tel. 305/858–9600; fax 305/859–2026. 150 rooms, 49 suites. Facilities: restaurant, lounge, health club, outdoor pool, poolside bar, afternoon tea in lobby. AE, DC, MC, V.*

Sonesta Beach Hotel & Tennis Club. Public areas display museum-quality modern art by notable painters and sculptors. Some of the rooms are in villas with full kitchens and screened-in pools. *350 Ocean Dr., Key Biscayne 33149, tel. 305/361–2021 or 800/766–3782; fax 305/361–3096. 267 rooms, 12 suites, 11 villas. Facilities: restaurant, lounge, snack bar, deli, health club, outdoor pool and whirlpool, 10 tennis courts, water sports, gift shop. AE, DC, MC, V.*

★ **Turnberry Isle Resort.** Guests can choose from the new Mediterranean-style annex, the European-style Marina Hotel, the Yacht Club, or the Country Club Hotel beside the golf course at this 300-acre resort and condominium complex in North Dade. Oversize rooms feature light woods and earth tones. *1999 W. Country Club Dr., Aventura 33180, tel. 305/932–6200 or 800/327–7028; fax 305/933–6560. 300 rooms, 40 suites. Facilities: 5 restaurants; lounge; beachfront club; 4 outdoor pools; 24 tennis courts; 2 golf courses; marina; full-service spa with physician, nutritionist, beauty treatments, and exercise equipment; water sports; other sports facilities. AE, DC, MC, V.*

Expensive **Alexander Hotel.** Every room here is a large suite with two baths, ocean or bay views, and antique or reproduction furnishings. The hotel is renowned for service. *5225 Collins Ave., Miami Beach 33140, tel. 305/865–6500; fax 305/864–8525. 212 suites. Facilities: restaurant, coffee shop, 2 outdoor pools, ocean beach with cabanas, water-sports equipment rentals. AE, DC, MC, V.*

Grove Isle. This luxurious mid-rise urban resort sits on a 26-acre island adjoining equally posh condominium apartment towers and a private club. The oversize rooms have patios, bay views, ceiling fans, and tropical decor. *4 Grove Isle Dr., Coconut Grove 33133, tel. 305/858–8300; fax 305/858–5908. 40 rooms, 9 suites. Facilities: restaurant, outdoor pool and whirlpool, 12 tennis courts, running track, marina. AE, DC, MC, V.*

Hyatt Regency Miami. This centrally located, 24-story convention hotel adjoins the James L. Knight International Center. The best rooms are on the upper floors, facing east toward Biscayne Bay. *400 S.E. 2nd Ave., Miami 33131, tel. 305/358–1234; fax 305/858–0529. 590 rooms, 25 suites. Facilities: 2 restaurants, lounge, outdoor pool, access to health club. AE, DC, MC, V.*

Moderate **Essex House.** Long one of the finest hotels in the Deco District, the Essex has undergone an outstanding restoration. Soundproofed rooms are typically deco-small but supplied with designer linens and feather-and-down pillows. *1001 Collins Ave., Miami Beach 33139, tel. 305/534-2700 or 800/553-7739; fax 305/532-3827. 51 rooms, 9 suites. Facilities: breakfast room. AE, MC, V.*

★ **Hotel Place St. Michel.** The finest small hotel in metropolitan Miami, this ivy-clad Mediterranean-style building has Art Nouveau chandeliers suspended from vaulted lobby ceilings, mosaic-tile floors, and an excellent French restaurant. Rooms contain English, French, and Scottish antiques. *162 Alcazar Ave., Coral Gables 33134, tel. 305/444-1666 or 800/247-8526; fax 305/529-0074. AE, DC, MC, V.*

Park Central. Across the street from a glorious stretch of beach, this seven-story deco hotel is a favorite of visiting fashion models and other trendsetters. An Italian theme prevails, from the Barocco Beach restaurant to the espresso bar. The stylish guest rooms have mahogany furnishings. *640 Ocean Dr., Miami Beach 33139, tel. 305/538-1611; fax 305/534-7520. 85 rooms. Facilities: restaurant, bar. AE, DC, MC, V.*

Inexpensive **Bay Harbor Inn.** Here's down-home hospitality in the county's most affluent area. The older building is furnished in antiques; the newer faces Indian Creek and has mid-century modern decor a cut above comfortable motel style. *9660 E. Bay Harbor Dr., Bay Harbor Islands 33154, tel. 305/868-4141; fax ext. 602. 24 rooms, 12 suites. Facilities: Continental breakfast, champagne tea, 2 restaurants, lounge, outdoor pool. AE, DC, MC, V.*

Clay Hotel and International Youth Hostel. Pauper digs on a princely street, accommodations here are in dorms (separate for men and women) or in single or double rooms, some with private bath. *1438 Washington Ave., Miami Beach 33139, tel. 305/534-2988. 50 rooms, 180 dorm beds. Facilities: kitchen, laundry room. No credit cards.*

★ **Miami River Inn.** This hidden treasure is a 10-minute slow walk to the heart of downtown. The turn-of-the-century inn consists of five clapboard buildings on a grassy, palm-studded compound. Rooms are filled with antiques. *118 S.W. S. River Dr., Miami 33130, tel. 305/325-0045; fax 305/325-9227. 40 rooms. Facilities: Continental breakfast, outdoor pool. AE, D, DC, MC, V.*

Spa **Doral Saturnia International Spa Resort.** Formal Italian
★ gardens contain the spa pool and a waterfall under which guests can enjoy natural hydromassage from the falling water. The spa combines European pampering techniques with state-of-the-art American fitness programs. *8755 N.W. 36th St., Miami 33178, tel. 305/593-6030 or 800/331-7768; fax 305/591-9268. 48 suites. Facilities: restaurant, 4 exercise studios, 2 outdoor pools, indoor pool, fitness equipment, beauty salon. AE, DC, MC, V. Very Expensive.*

The Arts and Nightlife

The best sources for events are the widely distributed free weeklies *Miami Today* and *New Times; The Miami Herald* publishes a Friday "Weekend" section. If you read Spanish, rely on *El Nuevo Herald* (a Spanish version of *The Miami Herald*). Sunday's *Herald* is best for updates on museums and galleries.

The Arts The **Coconut Grove Playhouse** (3500 Main Hwy., tel. 305/442–
Theater 4000) stages Broadway-bound plays and musical revues, as well
as experimental productions. **Jackie Gleason Theater of the
Performing Arts** (1700 Washington Ave., Miami Beach, tel. 305/
673–7300) is home of the Broadway Series (tel. 305/673–8300)
and other stage events. **Teatro Avante** (Box 453005, 33245, tel.
305/858–4155) produces Spanish-language theater, including a
Hispanic-theater festival held each May.

Music **New World Symphony** (541 Lincoln Rd., Miami Beach, tel. 305/
673–3331), conducted by Michael Tilson Thomas, is a national
orchestral academy for young musicians. **Concert Association
of Florida** (555 Hank Meyer Blvd. [17th St.], Miami Beach
33139, tel. 305/532–3491) is the South's largest presenter of
classical artists.

Opera **Greater Miami Opera** (1200 Coral Way, Miami, tel. 305/854–
7890) presents two complete casts in five operas a year.

Ballet **Miami City Ballet** (905 Lincoln Rd., Miami Beach, tel. 305/532–
7713) is an acclaimed troupe under the direction of Edward
Villella.

Nightlife The liveliest scenes are in SoBe (Miami Beach's Deco District)
and Coconut Grove, but clubs can be found in the suburbs,
downtown, in Little Havana, and in Little Haiti.

Bars with Music **Tobacco Road** (626 S. Miami Ave., Miami, tel. 305/374–1198) is
one of Miami's oldest bars, with excellent blues on weekends.
Mac's Club Deuce (222 14th St., Miami Beach, tel. 305/673–
9537) is a funky—some might say weird—SoBe spot where top
international models come to shoot pool. **Cactus Cantina** (630
6th St., Miami Beach, tel. 305/532–5095), another SoBe hangout, features open blues jams and Latin jazz jams.

Dance Club The **Baja Beach Club** (in Cocowalk, 3015 Grand Ave., tel. 305/
445–0278) is the place to be in Coconut Grove; it's three clubs on
two levels, with balconies overlooking the downtown strut.

Nightclubs Some of the city's nightclubs offer a nostalgic look at the Miami
of yore. **Les Violins Supper Club** (1751 Biscayne Blvd., Miami,
tel. 305/371–8668) offers Las Vegas–style revues, a live dance
band, and full dinners. **Club Tropigala at La Ronde** (Fontainebleau Hilton, 4441 Collins Ave., Miami Beach, tel. 305/672–
7469)—whose seven-level round room is decorated with orchids, banana leaves, and philodendrons to resemble a tropical
jungle—features resplendent revues and live dance music.

Disney World
and the Orlando Area

Cosmopolitan Orlando is a growing international business center and tourist mecca, largely due to the presence of Walt Disney World. Many other attractions, interesting shopping areas,
and a varied nightlife make the area an exciting, if sometimes
frenetic and crowded, vacation destination. Away from the
tourist areas, hundreds of spring-fed lakes surrounded by
graceful oak trees recall Orlando's slower-paced past. About an
hour's drive from the city, on the Atlantic coast, are the Cocoa
Beach area and the Kennedy Space Center, Spaceport USA.

Tourist Information

Kissimmee/St. Cloud: Convention and Visitor's Bureau (1925 E. Irlo Bronson Memorial Hwy., Kissimmee 32742, tel. 407/ 363–5800, 407/847–5000, or 800/327–9159). **Orlando/Orange County:** Convention and Visitor's Bureau (8445 International Dr., Orlando 32819, tel. 407/363–5800).

Getting There

By Plane **Orlando International Airport** (6086 McCoy Rd., off the Bee Line Expressway, tel. 407/825–2000) is served by major U.S. airlines, as well as many foreign airlines. **Delta Dream Vacations** (tel. 800/872–7786) offers travel packages to Disney World.

By Car From Jacksonville, take I–95S, then I–4 from Port Orange. From Tampa/St. Petersburg, take I–4E. From Miami, take I–95N and connect with the northbound Florida Turnpike at White City. From Atlanta, take I–75S and connect with the Florida Turnpike.

By Train **Amtrak** stops at Sanford, Winter Park, Orlando, and Kissimmee.

By Bus **Greyhound** (tel. 407/843–7720) provides service from major Florida cities and from outside the state.

Exploring Walt Disney World and the Orlando Area

Walt Disney World The focal point of an Orlando vacation is **Walt Disney World** (Box 10040, Lake Buena Vista 32830, tel. 407/824–4321), a collection of theme parks and attractions connected by extensive bus, monorail, motor-launch, and ferry systems (free if you stay at a Disney hotel/resort). Admission is not cheap: A one-day ticket to *either* the Magic Kingdom, the Epcot Center, or Disney–MGM is $33 for adults and $26 for children 3–9. Your best bet, even if you plan to stay only two or three days, may be to purchase a Four-Day Super Pass or a Five-Day Super Duper Pass; both admit you to all three parks, allow you to visit more than one on any given day, and include unlimited use of Disney transport.

The Magic Kingdom Sprawling before you when you enter the Magic Kingdom is **Main Street U.S.A.**—a shop-filled boulevard with Victorian-style stores, and dining spots. Stop at **City Hall** (on your left as you enter Town Square) for information or to snap a picture with the Disney characters who frequent the spot. Other Main Street attractions include a cinema that runs vintage Disney cartoons and the Penny Arcade, a historical version of today's electronic game rooms. Walk two blocks along Main Street and you'll enter Central Plaza, with **Cinderella Castle** rising directly in front of you. This is the hub of the Kingdom; all the "lands" radiate out from it.

A great way to get an overview of the Kingdom is to hop aboard the WDW Railroad and take a 14-minute, 1½-mi ride around the perimeter of the park. You can board at the Victorian-style station by Town Square. Other stations are in Frontierland and at Mickey's Starland on the border between Tomorrowland and Fantasyland.

Orlando Area

Altamonte Springs

Apopka

North Orange Blossom Tr.

436

I-4

17 92

Bear Lake

Maitland

Maitland Lake

436

Lake Apopka

Lockhart

Park Ave.

Aloma Ave.

441

Lake Fairview

Fairbanks Ave.

Winter Park

Pine Hills

50

Orlando Arena

Colonial Dr.

50

Florida's Tnpk.

East - West Expwy.

Windermere   Lake Down

Apopka-Vineland Rd.

Orange Ave.

Orlando

Lake Butler

Turkey Lake Rd.

441 17-92

Lake Tibet

Universal Studios Florida

Sand Lake Rd.

482

528

EXIT 29

Fun 'N Wheels

528

Orlando International Airport

Lake Sheen

International Dr.

527

Magic Kingdom

Big Sand Lake

Bee Line Expwy.

Sea World

South Orange Blossom Tr.

Florida's Tnpk.

Walt Disney World

Walt Disney World Village

Gatorland Zoo

Epcot Center

Disney–MGM Studios

192

I-4

192

17 92

Kissimmee

27

TO CYPRESS GARDENS

0   750 yards

0   750 meters

N

The Magic Kingdom is divided into seven lands (of which Main Street U.S.A. is the first). Stories are told of tourists who spend an entire day in one land, thinking they have seen all the park; don't let that happen to you. The following are the highlights.

Adventureland is a mishmash of tropical and swashbuckling attractions that are among the most crowded in the Kingdom. Visit as late in the afternoon as possible or, better yet, in the evening. **Swiss Family Robinson Treehouse** (popular; all ages) is a good way to get some exercise and a panoramic view of the park. Visitors walk up the many-staired tree in single file, a trip that can take up to a half hour. **Jungle Cruise** (very popular; all ages) takes visitors along the Nile, across an Amazon jungle, and so on. The tour guide's narration is corny but nevertheless brings laughs. **Pirates of the Caribbean** (very popular; all ages) is a journey through a world of pirate strongholds and treasure-filled dungeons. The Audio-Animatronics pirates are first-rate.

Liberty Square is a journey back to Colonial America. The **Hall of Presidents** presents an electronic view of the history of the United States, while the **Mike Fink Keel Boats** and **Liberty Square Riverboat** cruise the Rivers of America. The star attraction here is Disney's special-effects extravaganza, the **Haunted Mansion**. Scary, but not terrifying, this ride on a "doom buggie" takes you past a plethora of dust, cobwebs, tombstones, and creepy characters.

Frontierland's big draw is **Big Thunder Mountain Railroad** (very popular; all ages), a scream-inducing roller coaster. Children must be at least 4'2". Try to go in the evening when the mountain is lit up and lines are relatively short. **Splash Mountain** (very popular; all ages), an elaborate water flume ride, is the newest attraction at the Magic Kingdom. Based on Disney's 1946 film "Song of the South," the ride includes characters from the movie as well as some of the songs. The eight-person hollowed-out log takes you on a half-mile journey that passes through Br'er Rabbit's habitat. The final plunge is down Chickapin Hill at speeds reaching up to 40 mph.

Fantasyland is, as the map says, "where storybook dreams come true." Fanciful gingerbread houses, gleaming gold turrets, and streams sparkling with shiny pennies dot the landscape, and its rides—such as **Dumbo, Peter Pan,** and the **Mad Tea Party**—are based on Disney's animated movies. Kids of all ages love the antique **Cinderella's Golden Carousel,** which encapsulates the entire Disney experience in its 90 prancing horses. Small children adore **It's A Small World,** a boat ride accompanied by its now-famous theme song of international brotherhood. Lines can be long for **20,000 Leagues Under the Sea,** a ride exploring the underwater life in an 11.5-million-gallon pool.

Mickey's Starland, the newest of Disney's lands, was built in 1988 to celebrate Mickey Mouse's 60th birthday. Here, in Duckburg, visitors can view Mickey's cartoons and films, visit Mickey's house, and have photos taken with Mickey in his Hollywood Theater dressing room. This is a good opportunity for weary parents to rest their feet while children explore a maze, pet young farm animals, or run around the playground.

Tomorrowland's top attraction is **Space Mountain** (very popular; children must be at least 3 years old, and children under 7 must be accompanied by an adult), a space-age roller coaster. It may never reach speeds above 20 mph, but the experience in the dark, with everyone screaming, is thrilling, even for hardcore roller-coaster fans. To see the interior without taking the ride, hop aboard the WEDway PeopleMover. Also here is the CircleVision 360 **"American Journeys,"** which places you squarely in the middle of a circle of images—it will make you gasp.

Epcot Center Visitors familiar with the Magic Kingdom find something entirely different at Epcot Center. For one thing, Epcot is twice as large. For another, Epcot's attractions all have an educational dimension.

Future World features the **Spaceship Earth** geosphere—the giant, golfball-shaped Epcot icon whose ride explores the development of human communications—as well as seven corporate-sponsored pavilions covering energy, the "Wonders of Life," Technology, motion, the seas, the land, and imagination. With the exception of the Wonders of Life, the creatively educational exhibits include a self-contained ride and an occasional post-ride showcase.

World Showcase offers an adventure very different from what you will experience in either Epcot's world of the future or the Magic Kingdom's world of fairy tales. In 11 pavilions, an ideal image—a Disney version—of life in various countries is presented through native food, entertainment, and wares. Most of the nations have done an imaginative and painstaking job of recreating scale models of their best-known monuments, such as the Eiffel Tower, a Mayan temple, and a majestic Japanese pagoda. During the day these structures are impressive enough, but at night, when the darkness inhibits one's ability to judge their size, you get the sense that you are seeing the real thing. It's a wonderful illusion, indeed.

Unlike Future World and the Magic Kingdom, the Showcase doesn't offer amusement-park-type rides (except in Mexico and Norway). Instead, it features breathtaking films, ethnic art, cultural entertainment, Audio-Animatronics presentations, and dozens of fine shops and restaurants featuring national specialties. The most enjoyable diversions in World Showcase are not inside the national pavilions but in front of them: Throughout the day, each pavilion offers some sort of live street show, featuring comedy, song, or dance routines and demonstrations of folk arts and crafts. Don't be shy about trying to improve your foreign-language skills!

Disney–MGM The **Backstage Studio Tour** and the **Animation Tour** are for
Studios Theme those who want a close-up, behind-the-scenes look at a real stu-
Park dio. The backstage tour takes up to two hours, but half of it is on a tram that will take you through costuming, into a shop where scenery is made, down a back-lot "residential" street, into Catastrophe Canyon for a look at special effects, and for a quick glance at more back-lot props before the walking part of the guided tour begins. The walking portion—which includes following Roger Rabbit's pink paw prints through the Looney Bin—takes in a water-effects tank, special-effects workshops, soundstages, postproduction work, and a theater previewing new movies. The Animation Tour takes visitors step-by-step

through the process by looking over the artists' shoulders from a raised, glass-enclosed walkway. **Star Tours** is one of Disney's more recent simulator thrill rides. Created under the direction of George Lucas, the five 40-seat theaters become spaceships, and you are off to the moon of Endor. Be forewarned: Lines are long, and the ride is rough.

Other Attractions Other Disney World attractions are the aquatic parks, **Typhoon Lagoon** (tel. 407/560–4142; admission: $18.50 adults, $14.75 children) and **River Country** (Ft. Wilderness Resort, tel. 407/824–2760; admission: $12 adults, $9.50 children), and the nature sanctuary **Discovery Island** (tel. 407/824–2875; admission: $8 adults, $4.50 children).

The Orlando Area **Universal Studios Florida** is the largest working film studio outside Hollywood. Visitors view live shows, participate in movie-themed attractions, and tour back-lot sets. The tour showcases the special-effects magic of creative consultant Steven Spielberg and the animation wizardry of Hanna-Barbera. *Exit 30B off I–4, tel. 407/363–8000. Admission: $34 adults, $27 children.*

Performing dolphins and killer whales and a moving sidewalk through a shark tank capture your attention at **Sea World.** The park also has penguins, tropical fish, otter habitats, walrus-training exhibits, botanical gardens, and other educational diversions. *7007 Sea World Dr., Orlando, tel. 407/351–3600 or 800/327–2424. Admission: $31.95 adults, $27.95 children.*

Beautiful **Cypress Gardens** offers walks through exotic gardens, bird and alligator shows, and the famous waterskiing-maidens show. *Off Rte. 540, east of Winter Haven, tel. 813/324–2111 or 800/282–2123. Admission: $19.95 adults, $13.95 children.*

In the **Cocoa Beach** area, 47 mi east of Orlando via Rte. 50 or the Bee Line Expressway, is the **Kennedy Space Center, Spaceport USA.** Here the wonders of space travel unfold through a superb film presentation and bus tours of spacecraft hangars and launch sites. *Tel. 407/452–2121 or 800/432–2153. Admission charged. Closed Christmas.*

What to See and Do with Children

In addition to the Disney parks (*see* Exploring Walt Disney World, *above*), the Orlando area offers children the delights of **Gatorland Zoo** (U.S. 17/92 near Kissimmee, tel. 407/855–5496 or 800/393–5297), with alligators, crocodiles, and other Florida wildlife; and **Fun'N Wheels** (6739 Sand Lake Rd. at International Dr., tel. 407/351–5651), with go-carts, bumper cars and boats, and other rides.

Shopping

Unique native goods are available at the various country pavilions in the **World Showcase** at **Epcot Center. Altamonte Mall** (Rte. 436 in Altamonte Springs, tel. 407/830–4400), the largest mall in central Florida, offers 165 specialty shops and five major department stores. The festive **Mercado Mediterranean Village** (8445 International Dr., tel. 407/345–9337) has specialty shops, an International Food Pavilion, and free entertainment. **Flea World** (U.S. 17/92 between Orlando and Sanford, tel. 407/

321–1792) has more than 1,500 booths selling everything from citrus products to auto parts.

Sports and Outdoor Activities

Fishing The area's plentiful freshwater lakes and rivers provide a year-round fisherman's paradise, with seasons for perch, catfish, and largemouth black bass. Contact the Orlando visitors bureau (*see* Tourist Information, *above*) for information. Fishing camps on **Lake Tohopekaliga,** a favorite destination for anglers, include **Red's Fish Camp** (4715 Kissimmee Park Rd., St. Cloud, tel. 407/892–8795) and **Richardson's Fish Camp** (1550 Scotty's Rd., Kissimmee, tel. 407/846–6540). Along the Atlantic coast, fishermen can troll for tuna, blue and white marlin, and sailfish; surf-cast for pompano and flounder; or deep-sea fish for grouper and red snapper. Deep-sea charters at Port Canaveral include **Cape Marina** (800 Scallop Dr., tel. 407/783–8410).

Golf Golf facilities open to the public include **Orange Lake Country Club** (8505 W. U.S. 192, Kissimmee, tel. 407/239–0000), **Poinciana Golf & Racquet Club** (500 Cypress Pkwy., 18 mi southeast of Kissimmee, tel. 407/933–5300), and **Timacuan Golf and Country Club** (550 Timacuan Blvd., Lake Mary, tel. 407/321–0010). There are three championship courses within **Walt Disney World.**

Horseback Riding **Ft. Wilderness Campground** (in Walt Disney World, tel. 407/824–2803) and **Poinciana Riding Stables** (3705 Poinciana Blvd., Kissimmee, tel. 407/847–4343) offer trail rides.

Tennis **Orlando Tennis Center** (649 W. Livingston St., tel. 407/246–2162) has 16 lighted courts. Many of the hotels and resorts within **Walt Disney World** also have courts.

Spectator Sports

Basketball **Orlando Magic** (Orlando Arena, off I–4 at Amelia, tel. 407/839–3900; Nov.–Apr.).

Dog Racing **Seminole Greyhound Park** (2000 Seminola Blvd., Casselberry, tel. 407/699–4510; May–Oct.) and **Sanford-Orlando Kennel Club** (301 Dog Track Rd., Longwood, tel. 407/831–1600; Nov.–May) have dog racing Monday through Saturday nights.

Beaches and Water Sports

A plethora of water sports are available in the Orlando area. Marinas at resorts in **Walt Disney World** rent all types of boats, from canoes and catamarans to pedal boats. **Orange Lake Water Sports** (8505 W. Irlo Bronson Memorial Hwy., tel. 407/239–4444) offers waterskiing and Jet Skiing. Just north of the Kennedy Space Center, the **Canaveral National Seashore** (Box 2583, Titusville 32780, tel. 904/428–3384) has 25 mi of unspoiled, uncrowded beaches with facilities for swimming and boating.

Dining and Lodging

Dining is an adventure in the Orlando area, where international cuisines, fresh fish and seafood, and such exotic local dishes as grilled alligator tail tempt the hungry. Besides hotels in Walt Disney World, you'll find accommodations in Orlando;

Kissimmee, just east of Disney World; and Lake Wales, south of Disney World near Cypress Gardens. Lodging options include luxury hotels and resorts, family resorts, and motel chains. For price ranges, see Charts 1 (B) and 2 (A) in Chapter 1.

Cocoa Beach **Mango Tree Restaurant.** Candles, fresh flowers, paintings by
Dining local artists, and a garden aviary enhance the dining experience here. Broiled grouper topped with scallops, shrimp, and hollandaise is a menu favorite. *Cottage Row, 118 N. Atlantic Ave., tel. 407/799–0513. Reservations advised. AE, MC, V. Expensive.*

Lodging **Pelican Landing Resort on the Ocean.** This family-oriented beachfront motel offers ocean views, a microwave in each room, picnic tables, and boardwalks to the beach. *1201 S. Atlantic Ave., 32931, tel. 407/783–7197. 11 rooms. MC, V. Inexpensive.*

Kissimmee **The Spaghetti House.** This rather kitschy two-story restaurant
Dining lets you design your own Italian meal. Start with your favorite entrée (there are 31), then pick a sauce (primavera, bolognese, pesto) to go over your choice of pasta (available in spinach, whole wheat, and cholesterol-free versions). *4951 Sunward Dr., tel. 407/351–3407. AE, D, DC, MC, V. Moderate.*

Lodging **Casa Rosa Inn.** This no-frills, Spanish-style motel offers clean, serviceable accommodations close to major Orlando attractions. *4600 W. Irlo Bronson Memorial Hwy. (U.S. 192), 32746, tel. 407/396–2020 or 800/432–0665; fax 407/396–6249. 54 rooms. Facilities: pool. AE, MC, V. Inexpensive.*

Lake Wales **Chalet Suzanne.** This family-owned, Swiss-style country inn
Dining and Lodging and restaurant nestled amid orange groves offers an intriguing
★ mix of furnishings, reflecting its piecemeal expansion since the 1930s. The houses and cabins have balconies, thatched roofs, and old-fashioned tubs and basins. Dining is a memorable experience, with such specialties as shad roe, broiled grapefruit, and crepes Suzanne. *U.S. 27S, Drawer AC, 33859, tel. 813/676–6011; fax 813/676–1814. 30 rooms. Facilities: restaurant (reservations advised; jacket required; closed Mon. June–Aug.). AE, DC, MC, V. Expensive.*

Orlando **Chatham's Place.** The office exterior belies what's inside—a
Dining small, unpretentious restaurant that is one of Orlando's finest.
★ Enjoy such tantalizing entrées as black grouper with pecan butter and grilled duck breast. *7575 Dr. Phillips Blvd., tel. 407/345–2992. Reservations advised. MC, V. No lunch. Moderate–Expensive.*
Florida Bay Grill. Tasty, well-prepared, and fairly priced seafood is served in an atmosphere reminiscent of a Key West yacht club, with a turquoise-and-gray color scheme and cement floors. Try the grilled shrimp and mixed greens special. *8560 International Dr., tel. 407/352–6655. AE, D, DC, MC, V. Moderate.*
Hard Rock Cafe Orlando. At Universal Studios, this guitar-shaped eatery offers all-American burgers, fries, and shakes amid a rock music atmosphere conveyed by lots of memorabilia. *5401 S. Kirkman Rd., tel. 407/363–7655. AE, MC, V. Inexpensive.*

Lodging **Peabody Orlando.** The bland facade gives no hint of this 27-story
★ hotel's beautifully decorated interior, with marble floors, fountains, and modern art. Many rooms have views of Walt Disney World. *9801 International Dr., 32819, tel. 407/352–4000 or*

800/732–2639; fax 407/351–9177. 891 rooms. Facilities: 3 restaurants, health club, pool, tennis courts. AE, DC, MC, V. Expensive–Very Expensive.

Best Western–Grosvenor Resort. This British-colonial-style hotel, with comfortable rooms, plentiful recreational facilities, and spacious public areas, is one of the best deals in the area. Rooms are average size but include refrigerator/bars and VCRs. *1850 Hotel Plaza Blvd., Lake Buena Vista 32830, tel. 407/828–4444 or 800/624–4109; fax 407/808–8120. 630 rooms. Facilities: 3 restaurants; 2 pools; 2 tennis courts; racquetball, volleyball, and basketball courts; children's playground; game room. AE, DC, MC, V. Expensive.*

Walt Disney World Dining The **World Showcase** in **Epcot Center** offers some of the best dining in the Orlando area, with country specialties that will appeal to every taste. Phone reservations are open only to those staying at a Disney hotel (tel. 407/824–4000); otherwise, reservations, which are strongly advised, must be made in person at one of Epcot's WorldKey computer terminals. Reserve early in the day, before beginning your sightseeing.

L'Originale Alfredo di Roma Ristorante, in Italy of course, has pasta and such classic dishes as veal piccata, served by singing waiters (Expensive). For a hearty portion of fish-and-chips with a Guinness stout, visit Britain's **Rose and Crown** pub on the shores of the lagoon (Moderate). For more exotic fare, try Moroccan couscous at **Restaurant Marrakesh** (Moderate).

Lodging Although hotels and resorts on Disney property cost more than comparable facilities elsewhere, there are many perks to staying at one of them. For example, Disney guests get preference for golf tee-off times and restaurant reservations, and transportation to all parks is free. Book all Disney hotels—including the following—through the **Walt Disney World Central Reservations Office** (Box 10100, Suite 300, Lake Buena Vista 32830, tel. 407/934–7639; fax 407/354–1866).

★ **Grand Floridian Beach Resort.** With its brick chimneys, gabled roof, sweeping verandas, and stained-glass domes, this resort exudes Victorian charm yet has all the conveniences of a modern hotel. Water sports are a focal point at the marina. *900 rooms, 12 suites. Facilities: 6 restaurants, health club, pool, shops, child care. AE, MC, V. Very Expensive.*
The Caribbean Beach Resort. Set on a 42-acre tropical lake, this resort has several villages named after Caribbean islands, each with its own pool and beach. Facilities include a 500-seat food court, a 200-seat lounge, and an island in the lagoon with bike paths, trails, and play areas. *2,112 units. Facilities in each village: cafeteria-style food pavilion, pool, watercraft rentals, nature trails. AE, MC, V. Moderate.*

Motels U.S. 192 is crammed with motels that offer the basics at affordable prices, in a location near Disney World. Rates range from inexpensive to moderate, and most places have a pool, with few other extras. Among these are **Best Western, Comfort Inn,** and **Econo Lodge** (*see* Appendix, Toll-Free Numbers).

Campgrounds **Ft. Wilderness Campground Resort** (Walt Disney World Central Reservations Office, *see* Lodging, *above*) is 730 acres of forests, streams, and small lakes within Disney World. You can rent a trailer or bring your own to campsites with electrical outlets, outdoor grills, running water, and waste disposal. Tent sites with water and electricity but no sewage are also available.

The Arts and Nightlife

The Arts **Carr Performing Arts Centre** (401 Livingston St., Orlando, tel. 407/849–2020) hosts dance, music, and theater performances. **Orange County Convention and Civic Center** (International Dr., Orlando, tel. 407/345–9800) presents big-name performers.

Nightlife Walt Disney World offers a variety of nightly entertainment, including the laser show **"IllumiNations"** at Epcot Center and the **Polynesian Revue** at the Polynesian Village Resort (tel. 407/934–7639). **Pleasure Island** (tel. 407/934–7781) is an entertainment complex offering theme nightclubs, a comedy club, movie theaters, and a teenage dance center. In Orlando, **Church Street Station** (129 W. Church St., tel. 407/422–2434) is a popular entertainment complex in an authentic 19th-century setting. **Medieval Times** (4510 W. Irlo Bronson Memorial Hwy. [U.S. 192], Kissimmee, tel. 407/239–0214, 800/239–8300, or 800/432–0768 in FL) is one of many exciting area dinner shows.

The Florida Keys

The string of 31 islands—or keys—placed like a comma between the Atlantic Ocean and the Gulf of Mexico at the southern tip of Florida presents a paradox to the visitor. On the one hand, the Keys are natural wonders of lush vegetation, tropical birds, and wildlife, washed by waters teeming with more than 600 kinds of fish, where swimming, fishing, and boating are a way of life. But the Keys are also a highly commercialized tourist attraction that has brought a clutter of unsightly billboards, motels, and shopping malls to the Overseas Highway linking the islands to the mainland. Although the 110-mi drive from Key Largo to Key West is often clogged with traffic, it is still a mesmerizing journey into expanses of blue water and blue sky, especially where the road is the only thing separating the ocean from the Gulf.

Tourist Information

Florida Keys & Key West: Visitors Bureau (Box 1147, Key West 33041, tel. 305/296–3811 or 800/352–5397). **Greater Key West:** Chamber of Commerce (402 Wall St., 33040, tel. 305/294–2587 or 800/527–8539). **Key Largo:** Chamber of Commerce (MM106, BS, 105950 Overseas Hwy., 33037, tel. 305/451–1414 or 800/822–1088).

Getting There

By Plane Flights from Miami (**American Eagle** and **USAir**), Fort Lauderdale (**Delta ComAir**), Orlando (**USAir** and **Delta ComAir**), and Tampa (**USAir** and **Delta ComAir**) arrive at **Key West International Airport** (S. Roosevelt Blvd., tel. 305/296–5439).

By Car From Miami, take U.S. 1S to Florida City; just south of here U.S. 1 also becomes the Overseas Highway. To avoid Miami traffic, take the Homestead Extension of the Florida Turnpike (toll road) south until it links with U.S. 1.

By Bus **Greyhound** (tel. 305/374–7222) buses make eight scheduled stops between Miami and Key West, but you can flag down a bus anywhere along the route.

By Boat You can travel to Key West via the Intracoastal Waterway through Florida Bay or along the Atlantic coast. Marinas abound in the Keys, but be sure to make docking reservations in advance. For more information, contact the **Florida Marine Patrol** (MM49, OS, 2835 Overseas Hwy., Marathon, tel. 305/ 289–2320).

Exploring the Florida Keys

The Keys are divided into the Upper Keys (from Key Largo to Long Key Channel), the Middle Keys (from Long Key Channel to Seven Mile Bridge), and the Lower Keys (from Seven Mile Bridge to Key West). Pause to explore the flora and fauna of the backcountry and the fragile reefs and aquatic life of the surrounding waters as you weave your way south to historically rich Key West. Addresses are listed by island or mile marker (MM) number. Residents use the abbreviation BS for the Bay Side of the Overseas Hwy. (U.S. 1) and OS for the Atlantic Ocean side of the highway.

The Upper Keys are dominated by **Key Largo,** with its wildlife refuges and nature parks. To view the elusive crocodile, drive through **Crocodile Lakes National Wildlife Refuge** (no tel.) on Card Sound Road in North Key Largo. **Key Largo Undersea Park** (51 Shoreland Dr., tel. 305/451–2353) includes an underwater museum that you have to snorkel or dive to; for groups of at least six there is an air-conditioned grotto theater with a multimedia slide show on the history of man and his relation to the sea. Through high-tech communications, audiences can interact with the divers in the 30-foot-deep lagoon where guides lead scuba and snorkel tours.

Continuing south on the Overseas Highway, stop at **Indian Fill Key** (MM78) to visit three unusual state parks accessible only by water (all charge admission). Take a glass-bottom dive and snorkel boat to **San Pedro Underwater Archaeological Preserve** (MM79.5, OS, Islamorada, tel. 305/664–2211), which features the 1733 wreck of a Spanish treasure ship. State-operated boat tours leave from the dock on Indian Fill Key (MM78.5) to take you to **Indian Key State Historical Site,** commemorating the 1840 Indian massacre of a pioneer settlement, and **Lignumvitae Key State Botanical Site** (closed Tues.–Wed.), with a virgin hardwood forest and ca. 1919 house and gardens. For information and reservations, contact **Long Key Recreation Area** (Box 776, Long Key, tel. 305/664–4815).

The bridge over **Long Key Channel** (one of 42 bridges on the drive) leads to the fishing and retirement community of **Conch Key,** gateway to the Middle Keys. At the **Dolphin Research Center** (MM59, BS, Marathon Shores, tel. 305/289–0002; closed Mon.–Tues.) on **Grassy Key,** you can swim with dolphins. At **Marathon** (MM53–47), explore **The Museum of Natural History of the Florida Keys** (MM50, BS, 5550 Overseas Hwy., tel. 305/ 743–9100) and the nearby exotic-plant arboretum and archaeological sites.

After crossing **Seven Mile Bridge,** the world's longest segmented bridge, you'll enter the Lower Keys. The delicate Key deer can be viewed at **National Key Deer Refuge** (off Watson Blvd., no tel.) on **Big Pine Key** (MM 32–30).

The journey ends at **Key West,** famous for its semitropical climate, laid-back lifestyle, colorful heritage, and 19th-century architecture. The town's rich ethnic past comes alive in the **Bahama Village** area (Thomas and Petronia Sts.), with the peach, yellow, and pink homes of early Bahamian settlers, and at the **San Carlos Institute** (516 Duval St., tel. 305/294–3887), the Cuban-American heritage center. History buffs head for **Ft. Zachary Taylor State Historic Site** (Southard St., tel. 305/292–6713), an important fort during the Civil and Spanish-American wars, and the **Lighthouse Museum** (938 Whitehead St., tel. 305/294–0012), with its 92-foot lighthouse and 1847 keeper's cottage. Nature lovers will want to visit the **Audubon Nature and Gardens** (205 Whitehead St., tel. 305/294–2116), with its tropical gardens and large collection of Audubon engravings. For literary types there is the **Hemingway House** (907 Whitehead St., tel. 305/294–1575), a museum dedicated to the life and work of the author who wrote the majority of his works here.

What to See and Do with Children

Two outstanding attractions are **Key Largo Undersea Park** (*see* Exploring the Florida Keys, *above*) and **Theater of the Sea** (MM84.5, OS, Islamorada, tel. 305/664–2431), with dolphin and sea-lion shows, a touch tank, and a "living reef" aquarium.

Shopping

The Keys are a thriving artists' community, so art is in good supply here. **The Rain Barrel** (MM86.7, BS, 86700 Overseas Hwy., Islamorada, tel. 305/852–3084) is a 3-acre crafts village with eight resident artists. **Key West**'s unique specialty shops, such as **Fast Buck Freddie's** (500 Duval St., tel. 305/294–2007), selling banana-leaf-shaped furniture, have gained an international reputation.

Sports and Outdoor Activities

Biking   A **bike path** parallels the Overseas Highway from Key Largo to Plantation Key (MM106–86). Trails crisscross the Marathon area; most popular is the 2-mi section of the **old Seven Mile Bridge** leading to Pigeon Key. Cycling is one of the best ways to explore Key West. For rentals, contact **Key Largo Bikes** (MM99.4, 99275 Overseas Hwy., tel. 305/451–1910), **KCB Bike Shop** (MM53, 11518 Overseas Hwy., Marathon, tel. 305/289–1670), or **Keys Moped & Scooter** (523 Truman Ave., Key West, tel. 305/294–0399).

Diving   The Keys are a diver's paradise, with miles of living coral reefs populated with 650 species of rainbow-hued tropical fish, as well as four centuries of shipwrecks, to explore. Outstanding diving areas include **John Pennekamp Coral Reef State Park** (MM102.5, OS, Key Largo, tel. 305/451–1202) and **Looe Key Reef,** 5 mi off Ramrod Key (MM27.5). Dive shops include **Florida Keys Dive Center** (MM90.5, OS, 90500 Overseas Hwy., Tavernier, tel. 305/852–4599 or 800/433–8946) and **Looe Key Dive Center** (MM27.5, OS, Ramrod Key, tel. 305/872–2215 or 800/942–5397).

Fishing and Boating   Deep-sea fishing on the ocean or gulf and flat-water fishing in the backcountry shallows are popular. Check with local chambers of commerce for information on charter- and party-boat

operators. Numerous marinas rent all types of boats and water-sports equipment. Particularly popular are the various
glass-bottom-boat tours to the coral reefs.

Golf **Key Colony Beach Par 3** (MM53.5, 8th St., Key Colony Beach
near Marathon, tel. 305/289–1533; 9 holes) and **Key West Resort
Golf Course** (6450 E. Junior College Rd., Key West, tel. 305/
294–5232; 18 holes) are open to the public.

Beaches

Since the natural shorelines of the Keys are a combination of
marshes, rocky outcroppings, and grassy wetlands, most
beaches for sunbathing and swimming are man-made from imported sand. **Bahia Honda State Recreation Area** (MM36.5, OS,
Bahia Honda Key, tel. 305/872–2353) offers a sandy beach, plus
a nature trail, campground, marina, and dive shop. Of the several Key West beaches, **Smathers Beach** (S. Roosevelt Blvd.)
has 2 mi of sandy beach and good windsurfing, and **Higgs Memorial Beach** (White St.) is popular for sunbathing.

Dining and Lodging

The Keys have gained a reputation for fine cuisine. Many dishes
have a Caribbean accent, mixing papaya, kiwi, and other tropical fruits, vegetables, and spices with local fish and citrus. Local specialties include conch chowder, Florida lobster, and Key
lime pie. Accommodations, from historic hotels and guest
houses to large resorts and run-of-the-mill motels, are more expensive here than elsewhere in southern Florida. For price
ranges, see Charts 1 (B) and 2 (A) in Chapter 1.

Islamorada **Cheeca Lodge.** This 27-acre resort preserves its beautiful sur-
Lodging roundings with a science camp for children and an extensive re-
★ cycling program. Guest rooms and suites feature periwinkle
blue/strawberry, and green/hot orange color schemes; all have
furniture of tightly woven wicker, cane, and bamboo. Each
suite has a full kitchen and a screened balcony; fourth-floor
rooms in the main lodge open onto bay- or ocean-view terraces.
*MM82, Upper Matecumbe Key, Box 527, Islamorada 33036,
tel. 305/664–4651 or 800/327–2888; fax 305/664–2893. 139
rooms, 64 suites. Facilities: 2 restaurants, lounge, 9-hole golf
course, 6 tennis courts, 3 pools, fishing pier, water-sports rentals. AE, D, DC, MC, V. Very Expensive.*

Key Largo **Crack'd Conch.** This unpretentious restaurant with a screened
Dining outdoor porch tempts hungry diners with conch chowder,
★ conch fritters, fried alligator, and 89 kinds of beer. *MM105,
OS, 105045 Overseas Hwy., tel. 305/451–0732. No reservations.
AE, D, MC, V. Closed Wed.; also Tues. Easter–Memorial
Day, Sept.–Christmas. Moderate.*
★ **Mrs. Mac's Kitchen.** Popular with locals, this open-air restau-
rant offers nightly dinner specials and a tasty bowl of chili any-
time in an informal room where beer cans, bottles, and license
plates from around the world festoon the walls. *MM99.4, OS,
tel. 305/451–3722. No reservations. No credit cards. Closed
Sun. Inexpensive.*

Lodging **Largo Lodge.** A tropical garden surrounds the guest houses at
★ this vintage-1950s resort, where every room is decorated dif-
ferently. *MM101.5, BS, 101740 Overseas Hwy., 33037, tel. 305/
451–0424 or 800/468–4378. 6 apartments with kitchen, 1 effi-*

ciency. Facilities: boat ramp and 3 slips. AE, MC, V. Moderate.

Sunset Cove Motel. In addition to standard motel rooms with carpeted or tile floors and hand-painted murals, Sunset Cove offers a dorm-style group house with kitchen for up to 15 people. Senior citizens and members of conservation groups get special discounts. *MM99.5, BS, Overseas Hwy., Box 99, 33037, tel. 305/451–0705. 10 rooms, 1 house. Facilities: boat ramp, fishing pier, free water-sports equipment. MC, V. Moderate.*

Key West
Dining
★

Louie's Backyard. Abstract art and old Key West paintings adorn the interior of this local institution, while outside you dine under the mahoe tree and feel the cool breeze off the sea. The ambience, however, takes second place to chef Doug Shook's expertise. The loosely Spanish-Caribbean menu changes twice yearly but might include such house specials as loin of venison with port, wild mushrooms, and goat-cheese strudel, or pan-cooked grouper with Thai peanut sauce. Top off the meal with Louie's lime tart or an irresistible chocolate brownie brûlée. *700 Waddell Ave., tel. 305/294–1061. Reservations advised. AE, DC, MC, V. Expensive.*

★ **Pier House Restaurant.** Steamships from Havana once docked at this pier jutting out into the Gulf of Mexico. Now it's an elegant place in which to dine, indoors or out, and to watch boats gliding by in the harbor. At night the restaurant shines lights into the water, attracting schools of brightly colored parrot fish. The menu emphasizes tropical fruits, spices, and fish and includes grilled sea scallops with black-bean cake and *pico de gallo* (tomato, shallots, cilantro, chopped chayote); lobster ravioli with a creamy pesto sauce and salmon caviar; and fresh catch prepared with tomatillo vinaigrette and saffron aïoli. *1 Duval St., tel. 305/296–4600, ext. 555. Reservations advised. AE, DC, MC, V. Expensive.*

Half Shell Raw Bar. Eat indoors or at outdoor picnic tables overlooking the deep-sea fishing fleet. Originally a fish market, this popular spot offers such daily specials as seafood linguine marinara. *Land's End Marina, tel. 305/294–7496. No reservations. No credit cards. Inexpensive–Moderate.*

El Siboney. Specializing in such traditional Cuban dishes as roast pork with black beans and rice, this family-style restaurant has a relaxed, friendly atmosphere. *900 Catherine St., tel. 305/296–4184. No reservations. No credit cards. Closed major holidays, 2 wks in June. Inexpensive.*

Lodging
★

The Marquesa Hotel. Key West architect Thomas Pope supervised the restoration of this four-story 1884 home and added onto it in a compatible style. The lobby resembles a Victorian parlor, with antique furniture, Audubon prints, fresh flowers, and wonderful photos of early Key West. Rooms have Queen Anne and eclectic antique and reproduction furnishings and dotted Swiss curtains. There are marble vanities in some baths, marble floors in others. Continental breakfast is served poolside ($6 extra). *600 Fleming St., 33040, tel. 305/292–1919 or 800/869–4631; fax 305/294–2121. 15 rooms. Facilities: heated pool, room service, 24-hr staff, in-room safe, free off-street parking. AE, MC, V. Very Expensive.*

The Curry Mansion Inn. Wicker furniture and pastel colors characterize this modern guest house, which blends beautifully with the adjoining turn-of-the-century Curry Mansion (open for self-guided tours). *511 Caroline St., 33040, tel. 305/294–5349; fax 305/294–4093. 15 rooms. Facilities: Continental* *breakfast, happy hour, pool, privileges at Pier House Beach Club. AE, DC, MC, V. Expensive–Very Expensive.*

★ **La Concha Holiday Inn.** This seven-story art deco hotel in the heart of downtown is Key West's tallest building and dates from 1926. The lobby's polished floor of pink, mauve, and green marble and a conversation pit with comfortable chairs are among the details beloved by La Concha's guests. Large rooms are furnished with 1920s-era antiques, lace curtains, and big closets. The restorers kept the old building's original louvered room doors, light globes, and floral trim on the archways. *430 Duval St., 33040, tel. 305/296–2991 or 800/745–2191; fax 305/ 294–3283. 158 rooms, 2 suites. Facilities: pool and sun deck, whirlpool, fitness room, restaurant, 3 bars, bicycle and motor scooter rentals. AE, D, DC, MC, V. Expensive–Very Expensive.*

Pier House. Easily accessible to Key West attractions, yet offering the tranquillity of a tropical-island escape within its grounds, this hotel complex has a beach club, a fitness center, and an elegant restaurant (*see* Dining, *above*). The Caribbean Spa section has rooms and suites with hardwood floors and two-poster plantation-style beds. *1 Duval St., 33040, tel. 305/296– 4600 or 800/327–8340; fax 305/296–7569. 109 rooms, 33 suites. Facilities: 5 restaurants, pool, 5 bars. AE, DC, MC, V. Expensive–Very Expensive.*

Marathon **Ship's Pub and Galley.** The 40-item salad bar with all-you-can-
Dining eat steamed shrimp and the mile-high shoofly mud pie are just two reasons to dine here. Photos of the Keys' railroad days adorn the walls. *MM61, OS, tel. 305/743–7000, ext. 3627. AE, DC, MC, V. Moderate.*

Lodging **Sombrero Resort & Lighthouse Marina.** This complex of one- to three-story buildings offers rooms with marina or pool views. Most suites have kitchens. *MM50, OS, 19 Sombrero Blvd., 33050, tel. 305/743–2250 or 800/433–8660; fax 305/743–2998. 99 suites, 25 villa efficiencies. Facilities: restaurant, commissary, bar, pool, 54-slip marina with electric cable and phone hookups, boat ramp. AE, DC, MC, V. Expensive.*

Plantation Key **Marker 88.** Savor the gorgeous Keys sunset as you sample such
Dining imaginative specialties as banana-blueberry bisque, sautéed
★ conch, or alligator steak in this bayside restaurant. *MM88, BS, Overseas Hwy., tel. 305/852–9315. Reservations advised. AE, DC, MC, V. No lunch; closed Mon. Moderate.*

The Arts and Nightlife

Key West is the Keys hub for artistic performances and nightlife. The most popular entertainment is the nightly gathering of street vendors, performers, and visitors on **Mallory Square Dock** to celebrate the sunset. The **Tennessee Williams Fine Arts Center** (Florida Keys Community College, 5901 W. Junior College Rd., Key West, tel. 305/296–9081, ext. 326) offers dance, music, plays, and star performers. Among the many discos and clubs are two landmarks noted for their connection with Ernest Hemingway: **Capt. Tony's Saloon** (428 Greene St., tel. 305/294–1838) and **Sloppy Joe's** (201 Duval St., tel. 305/294– 5717).

Southwest Florida

Swimming, sunbathing, sailing, and shelling draw increasing numbers of visitors to the 200-mi coastal stretch between the Tampa Bay area and the Everglades. Venturing inland from the miles of sun-splashed beaches along the Gulf of Mexico, many visitors discover the culturally rich and ethnically diverse towns, interesting historical sites, and stellar attractions, such as Busch Gardens. Often this something-for-everyone mix is available at more affordable prices than elsewhere in Florida. The region is most accessible if divided into three areas: Tampa Bay (including Tampa, St. Petersburg, Clearwater, and Tarpon Springs), Sarasota (including Bradenton and Venice), and the Fort Myers/Naples area.

Getting There

By Plane Most major U.S. airlines serve at least one of the region's airports. **Tampa International** (tel. 813/870–8700), 6 mi from downtown, is also served by international airlines. **Sarasota-Bradenton Airport** (tel. 813/359–5200) is just north of Sarasota off U.S. 41. **Southwest Florida Regional Airport** (tel. 813/768–1000) is about 12 mi south of Fort Myers and 25 mi north of Naples.

By Car From the Georgia–Florida border, it's a three-hour drive via I–75S to Tampa, four hours to Sarasota, five to Fort Myers, and six to Naples. U.S. 41 (the Tamiami Trail) also traverses the region, but because it passes through many towns' business districts, traffic can be heavy. Naples is linked to Fort Lauderdale, on the eastern side of the state, via Alligator Alley (Rte. 84).

By Train **Amtrak** connects most of the country with Tampa (601 N. Nebraska Ave., tel. 813/221–7600).

By Bus **Greyhound** provides statewide service, including stops at Tampa (tel. 813/229–2112), St. Petersburg (tel. 813/898–1496), Sarasota (tel. 813/955–5735), and Fort Myers (tel. 813/334–1011). For local bus service, contact **Hillsborough Area Regional Transit** (tel. 813/254–4278) for the Tampa area, **Sarasota County Area Transit** (tel. 813/951–5850) for Sarasota, and **Lee County Transit System** (tel. 813/939–1303) for the Fort Myers area.

The Tampa Bay Area

Tourist Information **Greater Tampa:** Chamber of Commerce (Box 420, 33602, tel. 813/228–7777). **St. Petersburg:** Chamber of Commerce (100 2nd Ave. N, 33701, tel. 813/821–4069). **Tampa/Hillsborough:** Convention and Visitors Association (111 Madison St., Suite 1010, Tampa 33602, tel. 800/826–8358).

Exploring the Tampa Bay Area **Tampa** is the commercial center of southwest Florida, with a bustling international port and the largest shrimp fleet in the state. It's also home to historic ethnic neighborhoods, such as Ybor City, where early Cuban immigrants established a cigar-making industry.

In Tampa, reserve a day for a journey through the Dark Continent at **Busch Gardens** (3000 Busch Blvd., tel. 813/987–5082; admission: $27.95), a 300-acre African theme park with rides, live shows, and a fascinating monorail "safari." East of downtown is the **Seminole Indian Village** (5221 Orient Rd., Exit 5 off I-4, tel. 813/620–3077), where alligator wrestling and demonstrations of traditional Seminole crafts are presented.

Ybor City is Tampa's Cuban melting pot and thrived on cigar-making at the turn of the century. To get there, take I-4W to Exit 1 (22nd St.) and go south five blocks to 7th Avenue. Here you're in the heart of Ybor City, where the smell of cigars mingles with old-world architecture. Take a stroll past the ornately tiled Columbia Restaurant and the stores lining the street. **Ybor Square** (1901 13th St.) is a restored cigar factory that is now a mall with boutiques, offices, and restaurants.

On the Gulf about 25 mi north of Tampa is colorful **Tarpon Springs.** Famous for its sponge divers, the town reflects the heritage of its predominantly Greek population. A drive north from Tampa on U.S. 19, the area's major north–south artery, offers opportunities to view the endangered manatees, or sea cows, in springs and rivers. At **Weeki Wachee Spring** (45 mi north of Tampa on U.S. 19, Weeki Wachee, tel. 904/596–2062; admission: $14.95 adults, $10.95 children), "mermaids" present shows in an underwater theater.

About 15 mi farther north is **Homosassa Springs State Wildlife Park** (U.S. 19 to Rte. 490–A, tel. 904/628–2311; admission charged), where you can watch manatees up close, visit reptile and alligator shows, cruise the Homosassa River, and view sea life in a floating observatory.

Heading south from Tampa, cross Old Tampa Bay on I-275 to get to the heart of neighboring **St. Petersburg.** Set on a peninsula bordered on three sides by bays and the Gulf of Mexico, the city offers beautiful beaches. **Great Explorations!** (1120 4th St. S, tel. 813/821–8885; admission charged) is a hands-on museum divided into theme rooms such as the Body Shop, which explores health; the Think Tank, which features mind-stretching puzzles and games; and the Touch Tunnel, a 90-foot-long, pitch-black maze you crawl through.

South from St. Petersburg on U.S. 19 to I-275 takes you toward Sarasota via the **Sunshine Skyway** suspension bridge, with breathtaking views of Tampa Bay.

What to See and Do with Children
Adventure Island has water slides and man-made waves. *4545 Bougainvillea Ave., Tampa, tel. 813/987–5660. Admission: $13.95. Closed Dec.–Feb.*

Shopping
Seven blocks of fine shops and restaurants line Tampa's Swan Avenue in **Old Hyde Park Village** (tel. 813/251–3500). In Pinellas Park is **Wagonwheel** (7801 Park Blvd., tel. 813/544–5319), a weekend flea market with about 2,000 vendors. For unique gifts, shop for natural sponges on Dodecanese Boulevard in **Tarpon Springs** or for Cuban cigars in **Ybor City** on Tampa's east side.

Dining
The ethnic diversity of the region makes for some adventurous dining, from honey-soaked Greek baklava to Cuban saffron-rice casserole. For price ranges, see Chart 1 (B) in Chapter 1.

★ **Bern's Steak House.** This renowned steak house boasts an extensive wine list, organically grown vegetables from the owner's farm, and scrumptious desserts served in upstairs rooms equipped with TV and radio. *1208 S. Howard Ave., Tampa, tel.*

813/251–2421. Reservations advised. AE, DC, MC, V. No lunch. Expensive.

Columbia. An institution in Ybor City, this light and spacious Spanish restaurant serves excellent paella, with some flamenco dancing on the side. *2117 E. 7th Ave., Tampa, tel. 813/248–4961. AE, DC, MC, V. Moderate.*

Louis Pappas' Riverside Restaurant. This waterfront landmark is always crowded with diners savoring the fine Greek fare, including the Greek salad made with feta cheese, onions, and olive oil. *10 W. Dodecanese Blvd., Tarpon Springs, tel. 813/937–5101. Reservations advised. AE, DC, MC, V. Moderate.*

Lodging A generous mix of roadside motels, historic hotels, and sprawling resorts can be found here. For price ranges, see Chart 2 (A) in Chapter 1.

★ **Don CeSar Beach Resort.** Soak up the ambience of this palatial pink rococo resort along the Gulf, frequented by writer F. Scott Fitzgerald in the 1920s and '30s. *3400 Gulf Blvd., St. Petersburg Beach 33706, tel. 813/360–1881; fax 813/367–7597. 277 rooms. Facilities: 2 restaurants, lounge, pool, beach, saunas, tennis court. AE, DC, MC, V. Very Expensive.*

Holiday Inn Busch Gardens. This family-oriented motor lodge is just 1 mi west of Busch Gardens (transport provided). Rooms are bright and spacious; some look out on a central courtyard with garden and pool. *2701 E. Fowler Ave., Tampa 33612, tel. 813/971–4710; fax 813/977–0155. 399 rooms. Facilities: restaurant, lounge, exercise room, pool, sauna. AE, DC, MC, V. Moderate.*

The Arts and Nightlife Professional theater, dance, and music events are presented at **Tampa Bay Performing Arts Center** (1010 W.C. MacInnes Pl., Tampa, tel. 813/221–1045 or 800/955–1045) and **Ruth Eckerd Hall** (1111 McMullen Booth Rd., Clearwater, tel. 813/791–7400). The area's numerous discos and clubs include the **Comedy Works** (3447 W. Kennedy Blvd., Tampa, tel. 813/875–9129).

The Sarasota Area

Tourist Information Sarasota: Convention and Visitors Bureau (655 N. Tamiami Trail, 34236, tel. 813/957–1877 or 800/522–9799).

Exploring the Sarasota Area Known for its plentiful, clean beaches and profusion of golf courses, the Sarasota area, south of Tampa Bay via U.S. 41 or U.S. 301, is also a growing cultural center and winter home of the Ringling Brothers Barnum & Bailey Circus. At **DeSoto National Memorial** (75th St. NW, Bradenton, tel. 813/792–0458), costumed guides recount Spanish conquistador Hernando de Soto's 16th-century landing and expedition. Near Bradenton is **Gamble Plantation State Historical Site** (3708 Patten Ave., Ellenton, tel. 813/723–4536), the only surviving pre–Civil War plantation house in south Florida.

U.S. 41S brings you to **Sarasota** and the **Ringling Museums** (U.S. 41, tel. 813/355–5101), which include the Venetian-style mansion of circus magnate John Ringling, his art museum with its world-renowned collection of Rubens paintings, and a circus museum. Farther south on U.S. 41 are the **Marie Selby Botanical Gardens** (800 S. Palm Ave., tel. 813/366–5730), acclaimed for their orchid displays. For a good beach escape, head for the barrier islands of **Siesta Key** (*see* Beaches and Water Sports, *below*), **Longboat Key,** and **Lido Key.** Lido Key is reached via Rte.

789W; this same road leads north from Lido to Longboat Key. To reach Siesta Key, in southern Sarasota, take Rte. 41 south to Siesta Drive or Stickney Point Rd., which lead west to the island. In south Sarasota County, you can walk into a prehistoric Indian shell midden (an ancient refuse heap containing layers of archaeological relics) or try your hand at sizing oranges at the 19th-century citrus packing house at **Historic Spanish Point** (U.S. 41, Osprey, tel. 813/966–5214).

What to See and Do with Children Along with the **Ringling Circus Museum** (*see* Exploring the Sarasota Area, *above*), children enjoy the bird and reptile shows at **Sarasota Jungle Gardens** (3701 Bayshore Rd., tel. 813/355–5305).

Shopping Art lovers can browse through the **art galleries** on Main Street and Palm Avenue in downtown Sarasota. A British telephone booth or an Australian boomerang is available for a price at the unique shops of Harding Circle on fashionable **St. Armand's Key**, west of downtown Sarasota across the Ringling Causeway.

Dining The area boasts fine raw bars and seafood restaurants, many Continental restaurants, and several family-style places run by members of the large Amish community here. For price ranges, see Chart 1 (B) in Chapter 1.

★ **Cafe L'Europe.** One of the best restaurants along the Gulf Coast, the café specializes in fresh seafood and veal dishes graciously served in a plant- and art-filled room. *431 St. Armand's Circle, Sarasota, tel. 813/388–4415. Reservations advised. AE, DC, MC, V. Expensive.*
Crab Trap. Try the wild pig or seafood dishes at this rustic spot near Bradenton. *U.S. 19 at Terra Ceia Bridge, Palmetto, tel. 813/722–6255. No reservations. D, MC, V. Moderate.*
Ophelia's on the Bay. Sample mussel soup, eggplant crepes, chicken pot pie, seafood linguine, or cioppino, among other things, at this waterfront restaurant. *9105 Midnight Pass Rd., Siesta Key, tel. 813/349–2212. Reservations advised. AE, D, DC, MC, V. Moderate.*

Lodging Tamiami Trail (U.S. 41), which traverses the region, is lined with inexpensive motels, while the islands have more expensive resort complexes and high-rise hotels. For price ranges, see Chart 2 (A) in Chapter 1.

Hyatt Sarasota. This contemporary hotel is ideally located, near city center and the major art and entertainment venues. Some rooms overlook Sarasota Bay. *1000 Blvd. of the Arts, Sarasota 34236, tel. 813/366–9000; fax 813/952–1987. 297 rooms. Facilities: restaurant, lounge, health club, sauna, pool, dock. AE, DC, MC, V. Expensive.*
Holiday Inn Riverfront. Suites overlook a courtyard at this Spanish-style motor lodge near the Manatee River. Rooms, with burgundy carpeting and mahogany furnishings, tend to be a bit dark. *100 Riverfront Dr. W, Bradenton 34205, tel. 813/747–3727; fax 813/746–4289. 77 rooms, 76 suites. Facilities: restaurant, lounge, pool, whirlpool. AE, DC, MC, V. Moderate.*

The Arts and Nightlife Sarasota is fast becoming one of Florida's cultural meccas. Broadway plays, concerts, dance, ice skating, and other shows are held at the **Van Wezel Performing Arts Hall** (777 N. Tamiami Trail, Sarasota, tel. 813/953–3366). Other major venues in the city are the **Florida West Coast Symphony Center** (709 N. Tamiami Trail, tel. 813/953–4252), the **Sarasota Opera** and the **Sarasota Ballet** (Opera House, 61 N. Pineapple Ave., tel. 813/953–7030), and the **Asolo Center for the Performing Arts** (5555 N. Tamiami Trail, tel. 813/351–8000).

The Fort Myers/Naples Area

Tourist Information
Lee County: Visitor and Convention Bureau (2180 W. 1st St., Fort Myers 33902, tel. 813/338–3500 or 800/533–4753). **Naples Area:** Chamber of Commerce (3620 N. Tamiami Trail, 33940, tel. 813/262–6141). **Sanibel-Captiva:** Chamber of Commerce (Causeway Rd., Sanibel 33957, tel. 813/472–1080).

Exploring the Fort Myers/Naples Area
The bustle of commercially oriented Fort Myers gives way to the relaxed atmosphere of the Gulf communities in growing Lee County. Beach lovers head for the resort islands of Estero (popular with young singles) Captiva, and Sanibel, with its superb shelling and fine fishing. Most of the beautiful residences here are sheltered from view by tall Australian pines, but the beaches and tranquil Gulf waters are readily accessible. The sophisticated city of Naples has excellent beaches and golf courses and an upscale shopping district.

In **Fort Myers, McGregor Boulevard** is framed by hundreds of towering royal palms. Here you'll find **Thomas Edison's Winter Home,** a 14-acre estate that includes his laboratory and a museum with his inventions, and the adjoining **Mangoes,** automaker Henry Ford's home. *2350 McGregor Blvd., tel. 813/334–3614. Admission charged. Closed major holidays.*

In the **Naples** area, return to Florida's unspoiled past at the **Corkscrew Swamp Sanctuary** (Rte. 846, east of I–75, tel. 813/657–3771), an 11,000-acre tract set aside by the National Audubon Society to protect 500-year-old trees and endangered birds. Along Naples Bay, fishing shacks have been transformed into shops and artists' studios at **Old Marine Market Place at Tin City** (1200 5th Ave. S).

What to See and Do with Children
Babcock Wilderness Adventures (Rte. 31, east of Fort Myers, tel. 813/656–6104, reservations required) offers swamp-buggy excursions through swamp and woodland areas to view wildlife. **Frannie's Teddy Bear Museum** (2511 Pine Ridge Rd., Naples, tel. 813/598–2711) displays more than 1,500 bears.

Shopping
For an eye-popping display of shells, coral, and jewelry, visit **The Shell Factory** (2787 N. Tamiami Trail, North Fort Myers, tel. 813/995–2141). For trendy boutiques selling resort wear, designer fashions, jewelry, and upscale gifts, try the **Royal Palm Square** area in **Fort Myers** (Colonial Blvd., between McGregor Blvd. and U.S. 41) and 3rd Street South and 5th Avenue South in **Naples.**

Dining
Stone-crab claw, available October through May, is a favorite dish here. It's hard to find restaurants on Sanibel and Captiva islands that aren't expensive; for budget options, you'll have better luck in Fort Myers and Naples. For price ranges, see Chart 1 (B) in Chapter 1.

★ **The Chef's Garden.** This elegant, award-winning restaurant offers Continental, traditional, and California cuisine, featuring such daily specials as Scottish smoked salmon with avocado and caviar or roast rack of lamb. *1300 3rd St. S, Naples, tel. 813/*

262–5500. Reservations advised. Jacket required. AE, D, DC, MC, V. Expensive.

Snug Harbor. This harborfront restaurant offers good seafood in a casual, rustic atmosphere. *645 San Carlos Blvd., Fort Myers Beach, tel. 813/463–8077. No reservations. AE, MC, V. Moderate.*

Woody's Bar-B-Q. This no-frills barbecue pit serves plentiful portions of mouth-watering chicken, ribs, and beef at low prices. *13101 N. Cleveland Ave. (U.S. 41), Fort Myers, tel. 813/997–1424. AE, MC, V. Inexpensive.*

Lodging In the Fort Myers/Naples area, take your choice of budget motels, all-inclusive resorts, historic hotels, or waterfront inns. Lodgings on the islands and those with waterfront views are most expensive. For price ranges, see Chart 2 (A) in Chapter 1.

★ **South Seas Plantation Resort and Yacht Harbor.** This quiet, elegant 330-acre property has nine different types of accommodations, among them harborside villas, Gulf cottages, and private homes. Numerous activities here include waterskiing, tennis, golf, and shelling. Exotic vegetation covers the landscaped grounds, which invite strolling. *South Seas Plantation Rd., Captiva 33924, tel. 813/472–5111 or 800/237–1260; fax 813/472–7541. 600 rooms. Facilities: 4 restaurants, 2 lounges, pool, fishing, golf, tennis, sailing school, children's programs. AE, DC, MC, V. Very Expensive.*

Sheraton Harbor Place. On the Caloosahatchee River in downtown Fort Myers, this modern high rise has bright rooms with peach accents and lots of windows. *2500 Edwards Dr., Fort Myers 33901, tel. 813/337–0300; fax 813/337–1530. 437 rooms. Facilities: exercise room, pool, tennis court, dock. AE, DC, MC, V. Expensive.*

Sandpiper Gulf Resort. This family-oriented motel just steps from the beach features large rooms with kitchens and private patios or balconies. *5550 Estero Blvd., Fort Myers Beach 33931, tel. 813/463–5721. 63 rooms. Facilities: 2 pools, whirlpool. MC, V. Moderate.*

The Arts and Nightlife Plays, concerts, and art exhibits are offered at the **Naples Philharmonic Center for the Arts** (5833 Pelican Bay Blvd., tel. 813/597–1111). The **Naples Dinner Theatre** is famous for its professional productions and hearty buffet (Immokalle Rd., tel. 813/597–6031).

Sports and Outdoor Activities

Biking **Sanibel Island** offers the best biking in the region, with extensive paths along the waterways and through wildlife refuges. Rent bikes at **Tarpon Bay Marina** (900 Tarpon Bay Rd., Sanibel, tel. 813/472–8900).

Boating and Sailing Sailing is popular on the calm bays and Gulf waters. Sailing schools include **O'Leary's Sarasota Sailing School** (U.S. 41, tel. 813/953–7505) and **Fort Myers Yacht Charters** (Port Sanibel Yacht Club, South Fort Myers, tel. 813/466–1800). For powerboat rentals contact **Boat House of Sanibel** (Sanibel Marina, tel. 813/472–2531) or **Brookside Marina** (2023 Davis Blvd., Naples, tel. 813/263–7250).

Canoeing Canoeists can explore many waterways here, including at **Myakka River State Park** (Rte. 72, 15 mi south of Sarasota, tel. 813/361–6511) and **J. N. "Ding" Darling National Wildlife Ref-**

uge (Sanibel, tel. 813/472–1100; rentals at **Tarpon Bay Marina,** *see* Biking, *above*). **Canoe Outpost** offers canoe and camping trips on the **Little Manatee River** (18001 U.S. 301S, Wimauma, tel. 813/634–2228) and the **Peace River** (Rte. 7, Arcadia, tel. 813/494–1215).

Fishing The Tampa Bay area and Fort Myers are major fishing centers. Speckled trout and kingfish are often caught in the Tampa Bay inlets. Deep-sea fishing enthusiasts can charter boats or join a party boat to catch tarpon, marlin, grouper, redfish, shark, and other species. Charter outfitters include **Florida Deep Sea Fishing** (4737 Gulf Blvd., St. Petersburg, tel. 813/360–2082) and **Gulf Star Marina** (708 Fisherman's Wharf, Fort Myers Beach, tel. 813/765–1500).

Golf Championship and other courses abound here. Those open to the public include **Babe Zaharias Golf Course** (11412 Forest Hills Dr., Tampa, tel. 813/932–4401), **Eastwood Golf Club** (4600 Bruce Herd La., Fort Myers, tel. 813/275–4898), **Lely Flamingo Island Golf Club** (8004 Lely Resort Blvd., Naples, tel. 813/793–2223), and **Longboat Key Club** (301 Gulf of Mexico Dr., Longboat Key, tel. 813/383–8821).

Spectator Sports

Baseball For information on the 17 major-league teams that hold their spring training and exhibition games in southwest Florida, call the **Florida Sports Foundation** (tel. 904/488–0990).

Dog Racing **Derby Lane** (10490 Gandy Blvd., St. Petersburg, tel. 813/576–1361; Jan.–June). **Naples–Fort Myers Greyhound Track** (10601 Bonita Beach Rd., Bonita Springs, tel. 813/992–2411; year-round). **Sarasota Kennel Club** (5400 Bradenton Rd., Sarasota, tel. 813/355–7744; Dec.–June). **Tampa Greyhound Track** (8300 N. Nebraska Ave., Tampa, tel. 813/932–4313; July–Dec.).

Football **Tampa Bay Buccaneers** (Tampa Stadium, 4201 N. Dale Mabry Hwy., tel. 813/461–2700 or 800/282–0683; Aug.–Dec.).

Horse Racing **Tampa Bay Downs** (Race Track Rd., Oldsmar, tel. 813/855–4401; Dec.–mid-Apr.) holds Thoroughbred races.

Beaches and Water Sports

The waters of the Gulf of Mexico tend to be cloudy, so snorkeling and diving are best done on the Atlantic side. The southwest beaches attract people who enjoy sunbathing on quiet stretches of sand, shelling, and watching spectacular sunsets.

In the Bradenton area, the popular **Manatee County Beach** on **Anna Maria Island** offers picnic facilities, showers, lifeguards, and rest rooms. **Fort Myers Beach** on **Estero Island,** 18 mi from downtown Fort Myers, attracts families and young singles; hotels, restaurants, and condominiums run its length. The island's shores slope gradually into the usually tranquil and warm Gulf waters. Along Gulf Shore Boulevard in Naples, **Lowdermilk Park** has 1,000 feet of beach, picnic tables, showers, rest rooms, and a pavilion with vending machines.

In the St. Petersburg area, the 900-acre **Ft. DeSoto Park** encompasses five islands. Its miles of beaches include fishing piers, picnic sites, and a waterskiing-and-boating area. **Lighthouse Park** at the southern end of Sanibel Island attracts a mix of singles, families, and shellers. Beautiful **Siesta Beach** on Siesta Key near Sarasota features a concession stand, picnic areas, nature trails, and facilities for soccer, softball, volleyball, and tennis. South of here, **Caspersen Beach,** on Beach Drive in south Venice, is one of the country's largest parks. Beachcombers find lots of shells and sharks' teeth here.

The Gold and Treasure Coasts

The Gold Coast exudes wealth and opulence, but it's also steeped in natural beauty. Famous for years as spring-break heaven for the college crowd, Fort Lauderdale now attracts families by offering a variety of recreational, sports, cultural, and historical activities. Farther north is the international high-society resort of Palm Beach, with its elegant mansions and world-class shopping. Inland about 50 mi is the 448,000-acre Lake Okeechobee, noted for catfish, bass, and perch fishing. Heading north from West Palm Beach to Sebastian Inlet, the Treasure Coast offers barrier islands, beaches, and sea-turtle havens to the east, and citrus groves and cattle ranches to the west.

Tourist Information

Greater Fort Lauderdale: Convention & Visitors Bureau (200 E. Las Olas Blvd., Suite 1500, 33301, tel. 305/765–4466). **Palm Beach County:** Convention & Visitors Bureau (1555 Palm Beach Lakes Blvd., Suite 204, West Palm Beach 33401, tel. 407/471–3995). Chamber of Commerce of the Palm Beaches (401 N. Flagler Dr., West Palm Beach 33401, tel. 407/833–3711).

Getting There

By Plane Major foreign and domestic carriers serve the **Fort Lauderdale–Hollywood International Airport** (4 mi south of downtown Fort Lauderdale off U.S. 1, tel. 305/357–6100) and **Palm Beach International Airport** (Congress Ave. and Belvedere Rd., West Palm Beach, tel. 407/471–7400).

By Car Two major north–south routes, I–95 and U.S. 1, connect the region with Miami to the south and Jacksonville to the north. Alligator Alley (Rte. 84) runs east–west from Fort Lauderdale to Naples.

By Train Amtrak provides daily service along the northeast coast to Fort Lauderdale, Hollywood, and Deerfield Beach in Broward County, and to West Palm Beach.

By Bus **Greyhound** stops in Fort Lauderdale (tel. 305/764–6551), and **Broward County Mass Transit** (tel. 305/357–8400) serves the surrounding county. **CoTran** buses (tel. 407/233–1111 in Palm Beach, 407/272–6350 in Boca Raton–Delray Beach) ply the greater Palm Beach area.

Exploring the Gold and Treasure Coasts

Fort Lauderdale and Palm Beach dazzle the visitor with their fabulous homes and pricey shops, shimmering beaches, plenti-

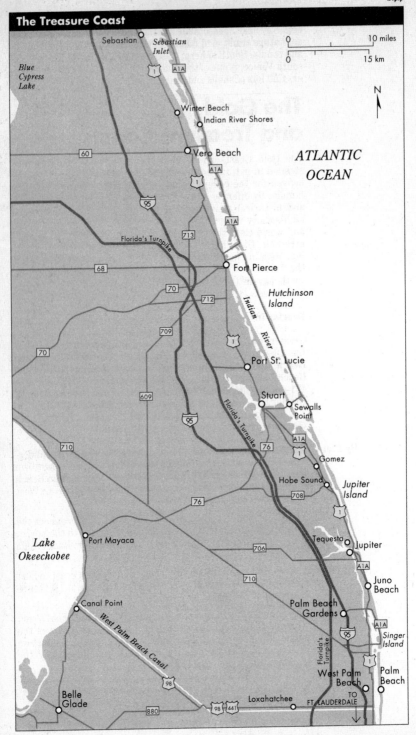

The Treasure Coast

Blue Cypress Lake

Sebastian

Sebastian Inlet

Winter Beach

Indian River Shores

Vero Beach

ATLANTIC OCEAN

Florida's Turnpike

Fort Pierce

Hutchinson Island

Indian River

Port St. Lucie

Stuart

Sewalls Point

Gomez

Hobe Sound

Jupiter Island

Port Mayaca

Lake Okeechobee

Tequesta

Jupiter

Juno Beach

Canal Point

West Palm Beach Canal

Palm Beach Gardens

Florida's Turnpike

Singer Island

Belle Glade

Loxahatchee

TO FT. LAUDERDALE

West Palm Beach

Palm Beach

0   10 miles

0   15 km

N

ful sports activities, first-class museums, and cultural events. North of Fort Lauderdale are the Treasure Coast's 70 soothing miles of sand, sea, and nature refuges.

Fort Lauderdale's picturesque **Las Olas Boulevard** takes you through **The Isles,** where expensive homes line canals dotted with yachts. After this the boulevard becomes an upscale shopping street, with Spanish-colonial buildings housing boutiques and galleries. West of here, the **Museum of Art** (1 E. Las Olas Blvd., tel. 305/525–5500; closed Mon.) has an extensive early 20th-century American art collection. Farther west, the 2-mi, palm-lined **Riverwalk** (along New River, off Broward Blvd.) features historic, scenic, and cultural attractions, all part of a $670 million redesign of downtown. Don't miss a drive through the **Henry E. Kinney Tunnel** (on U.S. 1), the only tunnel in Florida, and a jaunt along the **"Strip"** (Rte. A1A), with the beach on one side and an unbroken string of motels, shops, and restaurants on the other. For an interesting side trip, head south a few miles to the **Seminole Native Village** (4150 N. Rte. 7, tel. 305/961–3220) to observe Native American lifestyles and arts.

As you travel north from Fort Lauderdale along U.S. 1, pause to admire the 1920s Spanish-style architecture in affluent **Boca Raton.** A turn onto Rte. A1A brings you to the posh island community of **Palm Beach.** Rub shoulders with the rich and famous as you stroll along the 12-mi-long island's **Worth Avenue,** one of the world's premier shopping streets. To recapture the glitter and flamboyance of Florida's boom years, when railroad magnate Henry M. Flagler first established Palm Beach as a playground for the wealthy, visit his ornate hotel, **The Breakers,** a legendary bastion of wealth and privilege (*see* Dining and Lodging, *below*). Nearby is his palatial mansion, **Whitehall** (Cocoanut Row at Whitehall Way, tel. 407/655–2833; closed Sun.–Mon.), now a museum, with original furnishings and an art collection.

After driving past the secluded mansions along County Road and around the northern tip of the island, cross Lake Worth to **West Palm Beach,** on the mainland. Its **Norton Gallery of Art** (1451 S. Olive St., tel. 407/832–5194; closed Sun.–Mon.) has a fine collection of French Impressionists. Southwest of the city, at **Lion Country Safari** (Southern Blvd./Rte. 80, tel. 407/793–1084; admission: $11.95 adults, $9.95 children), you can drive through a cageless zoo where 1,000 animals, including lions and elephants, roam free.

It's an abrupt shift from the man-made world of Palm Beach into primitive Florida at **Arthur R. Marshall Loxahatchee National Wildlife Refuge,** a wilderness of marshes, wetlands, and bountiful wildlife. Stroll the nature trails, fish for bass and panfish, or paddle your own canoe through the waterways. *South of West Palm Beach, west of Boynton Beach; headquarters at U.S. 441 between Rtes. 804 and 806, tel. 407/932–3684 or 407/ 734–8303. Admission charged.*

Explore the upper Treasure Coast at a leisurely pace by taking U.S. 1 and Rte. A1A north from West Palm Beach along the Indian River, which separates the barrier islands from the mainland. Of major interest from April to August are the sea turtles that nest on the beaches; check with local chambers of commerce for information on turtle watches, or learn about the turtles at **Loggerhead Park Marine Life Center of Juno Beach** (1111 Ocean Dr., tel. 407/627–8280; closed Sun.–Mon.).

Drive atop the sand dunes at **Jupiter** and pause to photograph the impressive 105-foot-tall **Jupiter Lighthouse**. At **Jupiter Island's Blowing Rocks Preserve** (tel. 407/575–2297), water sprays burst through holes in the shore's limestone facade at high tide. The preserve is home to large bird communities and a wealth of plants native to beachfront dune, marsh, and hammock. North of here is **Stuart,** where revival of the downtown is transforming this onetime fishing village of fewer than 15,000 into a magnet for people who want to live and work in a small-town atmosphere. The affluent community of **Vero Beach** has elegant houses, many dating from the 1920s. Continuing north, you will arrive at **Sebastian Inlet,** popular with fishermen and driftwood collectors. I–95 brings you back to Fort Lauderdale.

What to See and Do with Children

The Palm Beach area is not geared to family-oriented activities, but Fort Lauderdale and surrounding Broward County offer several child-pleasing attractions. The insect zoo is one of the hands-on exhibits at the **Museum of Discovery and Science** (401 S.W. 2nd St., tel. 305/467–6637) along Fort Lauderdale's Riverwalk. **Ocean World** (1701 S.E. 17th St., Fort Lauderdale, tel. 305/525–6611) offers close-up views of sea turtles, sharks, alligators, and river otters, as well as a chance to pet and feed a dolphin.

Shopping

Both Palm Beach and Fort Lauderdale have shopping districts that cater to a high-society clientele. In Fort Lauderdale, expensive boutiques are clustered along tree-lined **Las Olas Boulevard.** In Palm Beach, more than 250 specialty shops and pricey boutiques, with such famous names as **Gucci** (256 Worth Ave., tel. 407/655–6955) and **Cartier** (214 Worth Ave., tel. 407/655–5913), beckon to well-heeled shoppers along **Worth Avenue.** A few miles west of Fort Lauderdale proper is **Sawgrass Mills Mall** (intersection of Flamingo Rd. and Sunrise Blvd., tel. 305/846–2350), reputedly the largest discount mall in America.

Sports and Outdoor Activities

Biking The beautiful **Palm Beach Bicycle Trail** runs for 10 mi along the shoreline of Lake Worth; for rentals, try **Palm Beach Bicycle Trail Shop** (223 Sunrise Ave., tel. 407/659–4583).

Diving A popular place to dive is the 23-mi-long, 2-mi-wide **Fort Lauderdale Reef,** one of 80 dive sites in Broward County. Palm Beach County offers excellent drift-diving and anchor-diving off the Atlantic coast. Contact **Pro Dive** (Bahia Mar Resort & Yachting Center, Rte. A1A, Fort Lauderdale, tel. 305/761–3413 or 800/772–3483) or **Force E** (11911 U.S. 1, North Palm Beach, tel. 407/624–7136).

Fishing Anglers can deep-sea or freshwater fish year-round. Pompano, amberjack, and snapper are caught off the numerous piers and bridges, while Lake Okeechobee yields bass and perch. Sailfish are a popular catch on deep-sea charters, offered by such companies as **Bahia Mar Resort & Yachting Center** (*see* Diving, *above*) and **B-Love Fleet** (314 E. Ocean Ave., Lantana, tel. 407/588–7612).

Golf Among the 50-plus golf courses in greater Fort Lauderdale are **Colony West Country Club** (6800 N.W. 88th St., Tamarac, tel. 305/726–8430). Palm Beach County boasts 145 private, public, and semiprivate courses; those open to visitors include **Emerald Dunes Golf Club** (2100 Emerald Dunes Dr., West Palm Beach, tel. 407/684–4653) and **Royal Palm Beach Country Club** (900 Royal Palm Beach Blvd., Royal Palm Beach, tel. 407/798–6430).

Spectator Sports

Baseball The Gold and Treasure Coasts host spring training for several major-league teams: **New York Yankees** (Fort Lauderdale Stadium, 5301 N.W. 12th Ave., tel. 305/776–1921); **Atlanta Braves** and **Montreal Expos** (West Palm Beach Municipal Stadium, 1610 Palm Beach Lakes Blvd., tel. 407/683–6012); **Los Angeles Dodgers** (Holman Stadium, Vero Beach, tel. 407/569–4900); and **New York Mets** (St. Lucie County Sport Complex, 525 N.W. Peacock Blvd., Port St. Lucie, tel. 407/871–2115).

Dog Racing Greyhounds race at **Palm Beach Kennel Club** (1111 N. Congress Ave., Palm Beach, tel. 407/683–2222; year-round) and **Hollywood Greyhound Track** (831 N. Federal Hwy., Hallandale, tel. 305/454–9400; Jan.–Apr.).

Horse Racing **Gulfstream Park Race Track** (901 S. Federal Hwy., tel. 305/454–7000; Jan.–mid-Mar.). **Pompano Harness Track** (1800 S.W. 3rd St., Pompano Beach, tel. 305/972–2000; schedule varies, call ahead).

Polo This sport of the wealthy has three major organizations in Palm Beach County, including the **Palm Beach Polo and Country Club** (13420 South Shore Blvd., West Palm Beach, tel. 407/793–1440), which has games on Sunday, January–April.

Beaches

Crystal-clear, warm waters are the main draw of the miles of beaches along the Atlantic coast. Each coastal town has a public beach area; many, like **Pompano Beach,** have fishing piers. The area is popular with snorkelers and divers.

The "**Strip,**" along Rte. A1A between Las Olas Boulevard and Sunrise Boulevard in Fort Lauderdale, is the most crowded beach in the region; shops, restaurants, and hotels line the road. South of here, in Dania, the **John U. Lloyd Beach State Recreation Area** (6503 N. Ocean Dr.) offers a fine beach; picnicking, fishing, and canoeing facilities; and 251 acres of mangroves to explore. **Bathtub Beach** on Hutchinson Island, north of Jupiter, has placid waters and a gentle sea slope, making it ideal for children.

Dining and Lodging

The Gold and Treasure Coasts have a mix of American, European, and Caribbean cuisines, all featuring local fish and seafood. Accommodations are expensive in the Palm Beach area, but many inexpensive motels line U.S. 1 and the major exits of I–95 throughout the region. B&B accommodations are popular in Palm Beach County; contact **Open House Bed & Breakfast** (Box 3025, Palm Beach 33480, tel. 407/842–5190). For price ranges, see Charts 1 (B) and 2 (A) in Chapter 1.

Boca Raton
Dining
★

La Vieille Maison. Closets transformed into private dining nooks are part of the charm of this 1920s home turned elegant French restaurant serving such dishes as pompano fillets with a pecan-chardonnay sauce. *770 E. Palmetto Park Rd., tel. 407/ 391–6701. Reservations advised. Jacket advised. AE, D, DC, MC, V. Expensive.*

Tom's Place. It's worth the wait in line to relish the mouth-watering ribs or chicken in homemade barbecue sauce and the sweet-potato pie in this casual, family-run eatery. *7251 N. Federal Hwy., tel. 407/997–0920. No reservations. MC, V. Closed Sept. Inexpensive.*

Fort Lauderdale
Dining

Down Under. Under a bridge approach by the Intracoastal Waterway, this Aussie-run restaurant specializes in Florida blue-crab cakes, Florida lobster, and stone crab. *3000 E. Oakland Park Blvd., tel. 305/563–4123. Reservations advised. AE, D, DC, MC, V. Expensive.*

Shirttail Charlie's. After dining on crab balls or coconut shrimp with piña colada sauce on the outdoor deck or in the upstairs dining room of this 1920s-style restaurant, enjoy a free cruise on the New River (Sun.–Thurs. after dinner only). *400 S.W. 3rd Ave., tel. 305/463–3474. Reservations advised upstairs. AE, D, MC, V. Moderate.*

Lodging
★

Riverside Hotel. Amid the upscale shops on Las Olas Boulevard, this hotel boasts an attentive staff, murals by a well-known artist in some rooms and on the facade, and rooms with refrigerators and antique oak furnishings. *620 E. Las Olas Blvd., 33301, tel. 305/467–0671 or 800/325–3280; fax 305/462– 2471. 116 rooms, 5 suites. Facilities: 2 restaurants, pool, poolside bar, volleyball court, dock. AE, DC, MC, V. Expensive.*

Hutchinson Island
Dining and Lodging
★

Indian River Plantation. This luxury resort on 192 island acres evokes a Victorian seaside ambience with its latticework trim, tin roofs, and cool verandas. Feast on steak Diane or fresh snapper at The Inlet, an intimate, elegant restaurant, or experience the Sunday champagne brunch at Scalawags. *555 N.E. Ocean Blvd., 34996, tel. 407/225–3700 or 800/444–3389; fax 407/225– 0003. 200 rooms, 54 1- and 2-bedroom oceanfront apartments with kitchens. Facilities: 5 restaurants, 3 pools, 13 tennis courts, 7 lighted golf courses, outdoor spa, marina, watersports rentals, beach club. AE, DC, MC, V. Very Expensive.*

Lake Worth
Dining

John G's. Although short on decor, this beachfront breakfast and lunch place is long on crowd-pleasing dishes, such as stuffed sandwiches, eggs prepared every conceivable way, and such seafood creations as Greek shrimp on linguine with feta cheese. *Off Rte. A1A, Lake Worth public beach, tel. 407/585– 9860. No reservations. No credit cards. No dinner. Inexpensive.*

Palm Beach
Dining

Ta-boo. Open 24 hours, this re-creation of a 1940s bistro offers such fare as gourmet pizzas and grilled chicken with arugula in three settings: a courtyard, a parlor with fireplace, and a gazebo. *221 Worth Ave., tel. 407/835–3500. Reservations advised. Jacket advised. AE, MC, V. Moderate.*

Lodging

Sea Lord Hotel. This comfortable, off-the-beaten-track motel in a garden setting offers rooms that overlook the pool, the ocean, or Lake Worth. *2315 Ocean Blvd., 33480, tel. and fax 407/582–1461. 40 rooms. Facilities: restaurant, beach, pool. No credit cards. Moderate–Expensive.*

Dining and Lodging
★

The Breakers. Formality blends with a tropical-resort ambience at this historic oceanfront hotel that resembles an Italian Renaissance palace, with cool pink, green, floral, and white interiors and original 1920s furniture. Dine on rack of lamb Dijonnaise in the tapestry-filled Florentine Dining Room or the skylighted Circle Dining Room. *1 S. County Rd., 33480, tel. 407/655–6611 or 800/833–3141; fax 407/659–8403. 484 rooms, 42 suites. Facilities: 4 restaurants, lounge, health club, saunas, beach, heated pool, 20 tennis courts, 2 golf courses, shopping arcade, other recreational activities. AE, DC, MC, V. Very Expensive.*

Spas

Fort Lauderdale

Bonaventure Resort and Spa. Part of a hotel and convention center complex, the resort's spacious rooms have tropical decor and balconies overlooking a lake or a golf course. The spa dining room is decorated in soft colors, with bamboo screens and mirrors. Menus follow the nutritional guidelines of the American Heart Association and the American Cancer Society. *250 Racquet Club Rd., 33326, tel. 305/389–3300, 800/327–8090, or 800/432–3063 in FL. 493 rooms. Facilities: restaurant, indoor and outdoor pools, 23 tennis courts, 2 golf courses, boating, other sports facilities, exercise equipment, individualized fitness programs, massage, beauty treatments. AE, D, DC, MC, V. Very Expensive.*

Palm-Aire Spa Resort. This 700-acre resort has both a luxurious resort hotel and a spa complex that promotes physical fitness and stress reduction. Large guest rooms have separate dressing rooms, king-size beds, and private terraces. *2601 Palm-Aire Dr. N, Pompano Beach 33069, tel. 305/972–3300 or 800/272–5624. 192 rooms. Facilities: 2 restaurants, 2 pools, 37 tennis courts, 5 golf courses, other recreational facilities, exercise equipment, massage, beauty treatments. AE, DC, MC, V. Very Expensive.*

Palm Beach

Hippocrates Health Institute. Personalized programs here are highly structured and emphasize holistic health and lifestyle management. Guests stay in a spacious hacienda or at private cottages in the 20-acre wooded estate. *1443 Palmdale Ct., West Palm Beach 33411, tel. 407/471–8876, 407/471–8868, or 800/882–2125. 15 rooms. Facilities: outdoor pool, supervised exercise programs, massage. AE, MC, V. Very Expensive.*

Spa at PGA National Resort. At this sybaritic getaway where golf and tennis pros exercise during tournaments, the spa facilities include the signature mineral pools with salts from around the world. Choose from large guest rooms with tropical decor or cottage units with two bedrooms and a kitchen. *400 Ave. of the Champions, Palm Beach Gardens 33818, tel. 407/627–2000 or 800/633–9150. 336 rooms, 85 cottages. Facilities: 3 restaurants, 2 pools, 5 golf courses, 19 tennis courts, 26-acre sailing lake, other sports facilities, exercise equipment and personalized programs, massage, beauty treatments. AE, DC, MC, V. Very Expensive.*

The Arts and Nightlife

Fort Lauderdale and the Palm Beach area offer a full roster of performing arts events. Major venues include **Broward Center for the Performing Arts** (201 S.W. 5th Ave., Fort Lauderdale, tel. 305/522–5334) and **Raymond F. Kravis Center for the Performing Arts** (701 Okeechobee Blvd., West Palm Beach, tel. 407/832–7469). Vero Beach is the Treasure Coast's cultural center, with its resident Equity troupe at the **Riverside Theatre** (3250 Riverside Park Dr., tel. 407/231–6990) and its **Center for the Arts** (3001 Riverside Park Dr., tel. 407/231–0707). The **Jupiter Theatre** (formerly the Burt Reynolds Jupiter Theater, 1001 E. Indiantown Rd., Jupiter, tel. 407/747–5566) is known for the Broadway and film stars who regularly perform in its productions. Fort Lauderdale has the liveliest nightlife, with comedy clubs, discos, and clubs featuring music for all ages and tastes; popular clubs include **Confetti** (2660 E. Commercial Blvd., tel. 305/776–4081), the in spot for the 35- to 50-year-old crowd, and **Musician Exchange** (729 W. Sunrise Blvd., tel. 305/764–1912), featuring an eclectic mix of blues, jazz, and rock-and-roll.

Elsewhere in the State

Everglades and Biscayne National Parks

Getting There Miami International Airport (*see* Miami, *above*) is about 35 mi from Homestead–Florida City, gateways to the national parks. Traveling south by car, take U.S. 1, the Homestead Extension of the Florida Turnpike, or Krome Avenue (Rte. 997) to the gateway towns.

What to See Everglades National Park (Box 279, Homestead 33030; Main
and Do Visitor Center, Rte. 9336, 11 mi west of Homestead, tel. 305/242–7700), the country's largest remaining subtropical wilderness, contains more than 1.4 million acres—half land, half water—that can be explored by boat, by bike, on foot, and partly by car. This slow-moving "river of grass" is a maze of sawgrass marshes, mangrove swamps, salt prairies, and pinelands that shelter a variety of plants and animals.

Biscayne National Park (Park Headquarters, N. Canal Dr.; Box 1639 Homestead 33090, tel. 305/247–7275) covers about 274 sq mi, mostly underwater, and has several ecosystems. Shallow Biscayne Bay is home to the manatee; the upper Florida Keys harbor moray eels and brilliantly colored parrot fish in a 150-mi-long coral reef; bald eagles and other large birds inhabit the mainland mangrove forests. A glass-bottom-boat tour, canoeing, snorkeling, and scuba diving are popular ways to experience the park.

The Panhandle: Northwest Florida

Getting There Pensacola Regional Airport (tel. 904/435–1746) serves the region. I–10 and U.S. 90 are the main east–west highways across the top of the state, while U.S. 231, 331, and 29 and Rte. 85 traverse the Panhandle north–south.

What to See The Panhandle has been dubbed the Emerald Coast for its pro-
and Do fusion of pine forests, magnolias, live oaks dripping with Spanish moss, lush bayous and swamps, and white-sand beaches

lapped by blue-green waters. Historical and archaeological sites vie for attention with beautiful beaches, golf, hunting, hiking, water sports, and outstanding fishing.

Stroll through the historic districts of **Pensacola** and absorb some of the city's colorful Spanish, French, British, and Civil War past. East on coastal U.S. 98 is **Fort Walton Beach,** a family vacation playground famous for its beaches and spectacular sand dunes. Here you can tour **Eglin Air Force Base** (U.S. 98, tel. 904/678–2323), the largest military base in the Western Hemisphere. Also here is the **Indian Temple Mound Museum** (139 Miracle Strip Pkwy. [U.S. 98], tel. 904/243–6521), which details the lives of the peoples who lived in the region during the past 10,000 years.

Farther along this coastal route is the bustling fishing village of **Destin,** popular with anglers, sun worshipers, and gourmets. For simple relaxation, head for the snow-white beaches, plentiful waterways, and amusement parks of **Panama City Beach,** a prime vacation area and the new in spot for students on spring break. The **Pensacola Convention & Visitors Information Center** (1401 E. Gregory St., 32501, tel. 904/434–1234 or 800/874–1234) provides information on the region.

Northeast Florida

Getting There   **Jacksonville International Airport** (tel. 904/741–4902) serves the region. I–10 is the major east–west artery through the north, and I–4 from Tampa enters the region near Daytona Beach. The primary north–south routes are I–95 along the east coast and I–75, south from Valdosta, Georgia.

What to See and Do   Variety is the key word for northeast Florida, where you can see live-oak-framed roads and plantations that recall the Old South along the **St. Johns River;** Thoroughbred horse farms in **Ocala;** impressive savannas in **Gainesville;** the Civil War heritage of the state capital at **Tallahassee;** and the cosmopolitan city of **Jacksonville.** The beaches range from rocky shorelines to the glistening sand beaches of Jacksonville and the famous hard-packed, driveable beach at **Daytona.** The annual **Daytona 500** auto race is held at **Daytona International Speedway** (U.S. 92, tel. 904/254–2700), and Jacksonville hosts collegiate football's **Gator Bowl** (tel. 904/396–1800).

St. Augustine, the oldest city in the United States, is a popular tourist destination (**Visitor Information Center,** 10 Castillo Dr., 32084, tel. 904/825–1000). Explore the 300-year-old Spanish fortress of **Castillo de San Marcos National Monument** (1 Castillo Dr., tel. 904/829–6506), guarding Matanzas Bay. Stroll down **St. George Street** through the restored Spanish-colonial village **San Agustin Antiguo** and glimpse life in the 1700s. Drink from the spring reputed to be the fountain of youth discovered by Ponce de Leon in 1513 at **Fountain of Youth Archaeological Park** (155 Magnolia Ave., tel. 904/829–3168).

Silver Springs (Rte. 40, 1 mi east of Ocala, tel. 904/236–2121; admission: $20 adults, $15 children), the world's largest formation of clear artesian springs, offers glass-bottom-boat tours and a jungle cruise. **Amelia Island** (**Amelia Island–Fernandina Beach Chamber of Commerce,** 102 Centre St., Fernandina Beach, 32034, tel. 904/261–3248), just north of Jacksonville, contains the historic town of **Fernandina Beach,** with its 19th-century mansions, and **Ft. Clinch State Park** (tel. 904/261–4212; admission charged), with its brick fort, nature trails, swimming, and living history reenactments.

For more information on the region, contact the **Jacksonville and Its Beaches Convention & Visitors Bureau** (6 E. Bay St., Suite 200, 32202, tel. 904/353–9736) or the **Tallahassee Area Convention and Visitor Bureau** (200 E. College Ave., 32302, tel. 904/681–9200 or 800/628–2866).

GEORGIA

By Mitzi
Gammon

Capital	Atlanta
Population	6,478,216
Motto	Wisdom, Justice, and Moderation
State Bird	Brown thrasher
State Flower	Cherokee rose

Visitor Information

Georgia Department of Industry, Trade and Tourism (Box 1776, Atlanta 30301, tel. 404/656–3545). **Information centers** in Atlanta, Savannah, and 23 other areas around the state.

Scenic Drives

Along the coast, Jekyll Island's **North Riverview Drive** offers scenery ranging from historic homes in Jeckyll Island Club Historic District to vast expanses of marshland. **Rte. 157N** from Cloudland Canyon State Park to the Tennessee border at Lookout Mountain affords views of northwest Georgia's Cumberland Mountains. **U.S. 76E** from Dalton to the Chattooga River traverses the North Georgia Mountains and takes in the most beautiful sections of the Chattahoochee National Forest.

National and State Parks

National Parks **Andersonville National Historic Site** (Rte. 1, Box 800, Andersonville 31711, tel. 912/924–0343) is where 13,000 Union soldiers died in a Confederate prison camp between 1864 and 1865. **Chattahoochee River National Recreation Area** (1978 Island Ford Pkwy., Dunwoody 30350, tel. 404/399–8070) offers river swimming, hiking trails, and picnic areas. **Cumberland Island National Seashore** (*see* The Golden Isles, *below*). **Kennesaw Mountain National Battlefield** (900 Kennesaw Mountain Rd., Kennesaw 30144, tel. 404/427–4686), a 2,900-acre park outside Atlanta, commemorates one of the Civil War's most decisive battles and offers 17 mi of hiking and biking trails. **Martin Luther King, Jr., National Historic District** (*see* Atlanta, *below*). **Okefenokee Swamp National Wildlife Refuge** (*see* Elsewhere in the State, *below*).

State Parks **Cloudland Canyon State Park** (Rte. 2, Box 150, Rising Fawn 30738, tel. 706/657–4050), on the west side of Lookout Mountain in the state's northwest corner, offers dramatic scenery and waterfalls. **Stephen C. Foster State Park** (*see* Elsewhere in the State, *below*). **Stone Mountain Park** (*see* Atlanta, *below*). **Vogel State Park** (7485 Vogel State Park Rd., Blairsville 30512, tel. 706/745–2628), a 221-acre park surrounded by the Chattahoochee National Forest, includes a 17-acre lake with swimming and fishing.

Atlanta

Atlanta is a city in transition—for the better. It continues to evolve from its beginnings as a railroad depot into one of the country's major metropolitan centers and a hub for aviation, commerce, and industry as it prepares to host the 1996 Olympic Games. Newly erected glass-and-stone office towers stretching along Peachtree Street stand as evidence of the city's progress. But for all its modernity, the city's winning character is still defined by the genteel charm of southern hospitality and by its picture-perfect residential neighborhoods.

Tourist Information

Atlanta: Chamber of Commerce (235 International Blvd., 30303, tel. 404/586–8403). Convention and Visitors Bureau information centers (Peachtree Center Mall, 233 Peachtree St. NE, Suite 2000, 30303, tel. 404/521–6600 or 404/222–6688; Underground Atlanta, 65 Upper Alabama St. and Lenox Square Mall, 3393 Peachtree Rd. NE).

Arriving and Departing

By Plane **Hartsfield International Airport** (tel. 404/762–1186) has scheduled flights by most major domestic and foreign carriers. Traffic to downtown Atlanta, about 13 mi north of the airport via I–75N and I–85N, can be congested during rush hour. Cab fare is about $15 for one person, $8 each for two people, and $6 each for three. Cabs are found near the baggage-claim area. The **Metropolitan Atlanta Rapid Transit Authority** (MARTA, tel. 404/848–4711; fare $1.25) rapid-rail subway train service is one of the quickest and easiest ways to reach the downtown, midtown, and Buckhead districts.

By Car Atlanta is commonly referred to as the "Crossroads of the South," for good reason. Between South Carolina and Alabama, I–85 runs northeast–southwest through Atlanta and I–20 runs east–west; I–75 runs north–south from Tennessee to Florida. I–285 makes a 65-mi loop around the metropolitan area.

Train Station **Amtrak** serves **Brookwood Station** (1688 Peachtree St., tel. 404/881–3060).

Bus Station **Greyhound** (81 International Blvd., tel. 404/522–6300).

Getting Around Atlanta

Atlanta is a spread-out city, but it does contain a number of walkable neighborhoods and districts boasting interesting architecture and attractions. Wheels are a necessity if you hope to go beyond the downtown district.

By Car Major public parking lots downtown are at **CNN Center** (entrance off Techwood Dr.), the **Georgia World Congress Center** (off International Blvd.), **Macy's** (entrance off Carnegie Way), **Peachtree Center,** and **Underground Atlanta.** In the Buckhead and midtown areas, more on-street parking and lots are available. Rush hours are typically 6:30–9 AM and 4–6 PM on weekdays; traffic at these times is especially congested along the

Buckhead strip of Peachtree Street between Roswell and Lenox roads.

By Public Transportation MARTA (tel. 404/848–4711) operates buses and a modern rapid-rail subway system. Fare for each is $1.25; exact change or a token is required. The rapid-rail trains operate from 5 AM to 1 AM; bus schedules depend upon the route.

By Taxi You can hail a cab fairly easily in the downtown or Buckhead districts, either on the street or at hotels. **Executive Limousine** (tel. 404/223–2000), **North Atlanta Cab** (tel. 404/451–4524), and **Yellow Cabs** (tel. 404/521–0200) offer 24-hour service.

Orientation Tours

Van and Bus Tours **Atlanta Tours** (tel. 404/872–5238) picks you up at area hotels for customized sightseeing or shopping tours. **Burton's Tours** (1029 Edgewood Ave. SE, tel. 404/525–3415) specializes in guided tours of landmarks in black history.

Walking Tours The **Atlanta Preservation Center** (156 7th St. NE, Suite 3, tel. 404/876–2040) offers seven guided tours of historic and other city sights from April through November; a tour of the Fox Theatre is offered year-round.

Exploring Atlanta

Beginning downtown, you can move north past an eclectic mix of Renaissance Revival towers and contemporary glass-and-steel skyscrapers; through midtown's genteel, garden-filled neighborhoods punctuated by parks and museums; into the glamour of Buckhead, lined with mansions and shopping centers bursting with designer-name boutiques and upscale department stores.

Downtown Atlanta had its inauspicious beginning as a 19th-century cow crossing and later a railway depot; a few sites from the earliest days are preserved downtown. The three-level entertainment and shopping center called **Underground Atlanta** (Peachtree and Alabama Sts., tel. 404/523–2311) encompasses some of the original city center's storefronts and streets. **Atlanta Heritage Row** (55 Upper Alabama St., tel. 404/584–7879), within the complex, offers a multimedia presentation about the city. Around the corner is **The World of Coca-Cola Pavilion** (55 Martin Luther King Jr. Dr., tel. 404/676–5151), with three floors of memorabilia from the soft-drink company. To avoid the lines that frequently form outside the pavilion, take your tour early in the day.

Four blocks from here, at the corner of Marietta Street and Techwood Drive, is the **CNN Center** (100 International Blvd., tel. 404/827–1500; admission charged), headquarters of media mogul Ted Turner's Cable News Network. Guided tours of the behind-the-scenes workings, including newscasters in action, are given daily.

Woodruff Park, at the corner of Peachtree Street and Park Place, is named for Robert W. Woodruff, the late Coca-Cola magnate. In warm weather, the park is a favorite alfresco lunch spot. Thrusting into the sky a block north of the park are the striking angles of the **Georgia-Pacific Building**'s red-marble tower. Built on the site of Loew's Grand Theatre, where *Gone with the Wind* premiered in 1939, the corporate flagship

---

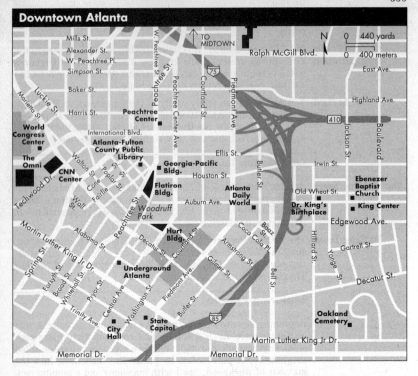

Downtown Atlanta

building houses the downtown branch of the **High Museum of Art** (133 Peachtree St., tel. 404/577–6940; *see also* Midtown, *below*), a small gallery that features a variety of temporary exhibits. Close by is the **Atlanta History Center's Information Center** (140 Peachtree St., tel. 404/814–4150), where you can see exhibits on Atlanta's history and pick up maps and information about the area.

Walking tours of **Auburn Avenue,** east of downtown, are offered at the **National Park Service Rangers Station** (526 Auburn Ave., tel. 404/331–5190). The route enters the **Martin Luther King, Jr., National Historic District,** where the civil-rights leader was born. Information on the district's history is available at the **African American Panoramic Experience** (135 Auburn Ave., tel. 404/521–2654).

The Queen Anne Victorian structure that was **Dr. King's birthplace** (501 Auburn Ave., tel. 404/331–5190) is open for tours. Three generations of the King family preached at the **Ebenezer Baptist Church** (407 Auburn Ave., tel. 404/688–7263). Adjacent to it is the **King Center** (449 Auburn Ave., tel. 404/524–1956; admission free), established by King's widow, Coretta Scott King. Inside the center are a museum, a library, and a gift shop; in front is King's tomb, where an eternal flame burns.

The **Georgia State Capitol** (206 Washington St., tel. 404/656–2844; closed weekends), several blocks southwest, houses government offices and a museum. Its dome is gilded with gold leaf from ore mined in northern Georgia. North on **Peachtree Street,** the city's main thoroughfare, is **Peachtree Center** (tel.

404/659–1111), a climate-controlled complex filled with shops and chain restaurants. In the center's Marquis Two Tower is the **Atlanta International Museum of Art and Design** (285 Peachtree Center Ave., tel. 404/688–2467; closed Mon.), specializing in international crafts exhibitions.

Midtown The heart of Atlanta's hippie scene during the 1970s, this former wasteland of neglected apartment buildings and empty lots north of downtown is today crowded with new high rises. Midtown is considered the city's arts district for its museums and theaters, but the recent influx of corporations has also made this a lively business center.

The Moorish/Egyptian–style **Fox Theatre** (660 Peachtree St., tel. 404/881–2100), the city's oldest movie palace, hosts a summer film series, as well as theatrical performances; tours are offered year-round (*see* Orientation Tours, *above*). North of here is the **High Museum of Art** (1280 Peachtree St., tel. 404/898–9540), a glossy, white-enamel showplace designed by architect Richard Meir and housing a major collection of contemporary, decorative, and African folk arts. Farther north is **Rhodes Hall** (1516 Peachtree St., tel. 404/881–9980), headquarters for the **Georgia Trust for Historic Preservation.** The renovated stone mansion houses a permanent exhibit on Atlanta architecture.

Buckhead Buckhead, 5 mi north of midtown on Peachtree Street, is to Atlanta what Beverly Hills is to Los Angeles. This residential and shopping area is home to fine dining, designer boutiques, and multimillion-dollar homes. To see the manicured lawns and mansions of Atlanta's elite, take a scenic drive along Tuxedo, Blackland, and Habersham roads.

Tours of the white-columned **Georgia Governor's Mansion** (391 W. Paces Ferry Rd., tel. 404/261–1776; closed Fri.–Mon.), decorated with an impressive collection of Federal-period antiques, give an insider's look at the lifestyles of this area's elite residents. Off West Paces Ferry Road is the **Atlanta History Center** (3101 Andrews Dr., tel. 404/814–4000), a 32-acre site that includes the Italianate-style Swan House, an 1840s frame farmhouse, and McElreath Hall, where historical artifacts are displayed and lectures given.

Parks and Gardens

In midtown between 10th and 14th streets is **Piedmont Park,** the city's premier urban green space, containing a children's playground, tennis courts, a swimming pool, and paved paths for biking, running, and roller skating. You can rent bikes and skates across the street at **Skate Escape** (1086 Piedmont Ave., tel. 404/892–1292).

Adjoining the park is the 60-acre **Atlanta Botanical Garden,** with landscaped gardens and the climate-controlled Fuqua Conservatory, containing tropical, desert, and Mediterranean plants. *1345 Piedmont Ave., tel. 404/876–5859. Admission charged. Closed Mon., major holidays.*

Fernbank Science Center (*see* What to See and Do with Children, *below*) has a botanical garden and walking trails through forest. **Stone Mountain Park** (U.S. 78, tel. 404/498–5690; admission charged), northeast of the city, features the world's largest sculpture memorial to Confederate war heroes Jeffer-

son Davis, Robert E. Lee, and Stonewall Jackson. The 3,200-
acre park also contains an antebellum plantation and historical
museums and offers such recreational activities as nightly laser
shows in summer.

Atlanta for Free

Performance stages in Piedmont Park are the scene of free concerts in summer and early fall. The **Atlanta Symphony Orchestra** (*see* The Arts and Nightlife, *below*) performs free Sunday
evening concerts in summer. *Creative Loafing* (tel. 404/688–
5623) is a weekly publication listing free events around the city.

What to See and Do with Children

The *Atlanta Journal-Constitution*'s Saturday weekend guide
has a "Kids" listing that highlights special happenings. **Fernbank Science Center** (156 Heaton Park Dr., tel. 404/378–4311)
features an authentic Apollo spacecraft, a planetarium, a botanical garden, and a 65-acre forest with 2 mi of paved walking
trails. The **Center for Puppetry Arts Museum** (1404 Spring St.,
tel. 404/873–3391) displays puppets from around the world and
stages original productions. **SciTrek** (395 Piedmont Ave., tel.
404/522–5500), in Midtown, is a physical-science museum with
hands-on exhibits and a special area for two- to seven-year-
olds. **Zoo Atlanta** (800 Cherokee Ave., tel. 404/624–5600) is in
Grant Park, south of the downtown area.

Six Flags over Georgia (I–20W at Six Flags Dr., tel. 404/948–
9290) is a major theme park offering dozens of rides, musical
revues, and concerts by top-name artists.

Shopping

Shopping Districts   Atlanta's shopping centers are generally open Monday through
Saturday 10–6 and Sunday noon–5; many stay open until 9 or
9:30 several weeknights and most weekends. The primary
downtown shopping area is **Underground Atlanta** (tel. 404/523–
2311), where specialty boutiques, chain stores, and merchandise kiosks mix with restaurants and nightclubs. North of
downtown, **Lenox Square** (3393 Peachtree St. NE, tel. 404/233–
6767) attracts shoppers from throughout the Southeast; among
its climate-controlled levels are more than 200 shops ranging
from designer boutiques to chain stores. Across the street is
Phipps Plaza (tel. 404/261–7910), another prestigious shopping
address, with numerous exclusive shops including Gucci and
Tiffany & Co. **Peachtree Center** (*see* Exploring Atlanta, Downtown, *above*) has a number of shops.

Specialty Stores   Shops selling antique pine pieces, collectibles, and unique
Antiques   crafts line **Bennett Street** in Buckhead. European furnishings
and fine art are offered in the more than 20 shops lining the cobblestone courtyard of Buckhead's **2300 Peachtree Road** (tel.
404/355–5799) complex. The **Miami Circle** area, also in
Buckhead off Piedmont Road, is another mecca for lovers of antiques, with such stores as **The Gables Antiques** (711 Miami Circle, tel. 404/231–0734) and **Williams Antiques** (631 Miami
Circle, tel. 404/264–1142).

Spectator Sports

Baseball **Atlanta Braves** (Atlanta-Fulton County Stadium, 521 Capital Ave., tel. 404/577–9100; Apr.–Oct.).

Basketball **Atlanta Hawks** (Omni, 100 Techwood Dr. NW, tel. 404/827–3865; Nov.–Apr.).

Football **Atlanta Falcons** (1 Georgia Dome, tel. 404/223–8000; Aug.–Dec.).

Dining

Italian and French food are as easy to find in Atlanta as offerings of the Deep South—the city prides itself on a wide selection of international restaurants. For price ranges, see Chart 1 (A) in Chapter 1.

Very Expensive **Abruzzi.** Some of the city's finest Italian cuisine is served at this elegant, understated restaurant. Traditional pasta, veal, and fresh seafood dishes shine; service is attentive. *2355 Peachtree Rd., tel. 404/261–8186. Reservations advised. Jacket advised. AE, DC, MC, V. No lunch weekends; closed Sun.*

City Grill. The grand setting of this downtown restaurant in the historic Hurt Building includes high ceilings, bucolic murals, and romantic table lamps. The menu features free-range chicken, lamb, and vegetable specialties. *50 Hurt Plaza, tel. 404/524–2489. Reservations advised. Jacket required. AE, D, DC, MC, V. No lunch weekends.*

★ **The Dining Room, in the Ritz-Carlton, Buckhead.** Chef Guenther Seegar has earned international acclaim for his imaginative haute cuisine, which incorporates such regional ingredients as Vidalia onions. The menu changes daily. *3434 Peachtree Rd., tel. 404/237–2700. Reservations required. Jacket advised. AE, D, DC, MC, V. No lunch; closed Sun.*

Expensive **Bone's.** Steaks, chops, and seafood are served in a New York–style atmosphere favored by the city's power brokers. Hash browns and baked potatoes rolled in salt are justly famous. *3130 Piedmont Rd., tel. 404/237–2663. Reservations advised. Jacket and tie advised. AE, DC, MC, V. No lunch weekends.*

Ciboulette. French-bistro food and atmosphere have Atlantans lining up for the variety of salmon specialties, the duck confit, the artichoke terrine. *1529 Piedmont Ave., tel. 404/874–7600. No reservations. Jacket advised. AE, DC, MC, V. No lunch.*

Pricci. The stamp of acclaimed designer Patrick Kuleto is apparent in the chic decor of this recently opened hot spot. Deceptively simple Italian fare is accompanied by Pricci's own breads. *500 Pharr Rd., tel. 404/237–2941. Reservations advised. AE, D, DC, MC, V. No lunch Sun.*

Moderate **Buckhead Diner.** This ritzy establishment with shimmering
★ metallic exterior serves modern American cuisine ranging from chips smothered in blue cheese to upscale sandwiches, pasta dishes, and gourmet pizzas. *3073 Piedmont Rd., tel. 404/262–3336. No reservations. AE, D, DC, MC, V.*

Indigo. Creative seafood—fried, baked in parchment, broiled, or sautéed—is served in this funky neighborhood bistro. Expect a wait. *1397 N. Highland Ave., tel. 404/876–0676. No reservations. AE, MC, V. No lunch.*

Inexpensive **Rocky's Brick Oven Pizzeria.** Sicilian and Neapolitan pizzas are
★ the house specialty at this bustling bistro in Buckhead. Gener-

ous salads and pasta dishes are also popular with a regular crowd of professionals, families, and students. *1770 Peachtree St., tel. 404/876–1111. No reservations. AE, MC, V.*

The Varsity. No-frills American fare is this sprawling landmark diner's specialty. Chili dogs, onion rings, and glorified hamburgers are favorites. *61 North Ave., tel. 404/881–1706. No reservations. No credit cards.*

Lodging

The city's booming convention business means hotel and motel options in all price ranges. The downtown and Buckhead areas have the greatest concentration of lodging places. For price ranges, see Chart 2 (A) in Chapter 1.

Very Expensive **Marriott Marquis.** The lobby of this popular convention hotel seems to stretch forever to the skylighted roof 50 stories above. Traditionally furnished guest rooms open onto this central atrium. *265 Peachtree Center Ave., 30303, tel. 404/521–0000; fax 404/586–6299. 1,671 rooms, 71 suites. Facilities: 5 restaurants, 4 bars and lounges, health club, indoor and outdoor pools. AE, D, DC, MC, V.*

★ **Ritz-Carlton, Buckhead.** An elegant lobby featuring fine art, overstuffed couches, and a fireplace invites lingering over afternoon tea before returning to rooms containing luxury linens, marble baths, and reproduction furnishings. *3434 Peachtree Rd., 30326, tel. 404/237–2700; fax 404/239–0078. 524 rooms, 29 suites. Facilities: 2 restaurants, lounge, health center, indoor pool. AE, D, DC, MC, V.*

Swissôtel. An international clientele frequents this European-style luxury hotel, featuring a chic contemporary glass-and-white-enamel exterior and sophisticated Biedermeier-style interiors. *3391 Peachtree Rd., 30326, tel. 404/365–0065 or 800/253–1397; fax 404/365–8787. 362 rooms, 15 suites. Facilities: 2 restaurants, 2 lounges, health club, indoor pool. AE, D, DC, MC, V.*

Expensive **JW Marriott.** Next door to Lenox Square, this 25-story hotel's subdued style focuses on intimacy and comfort. Irregularly shaped rooms have oversize baths with separate shower stall and tub. *3300 Lenox Rd., 30326, tel. 404/262–3344; fax 404/262–8689. 371 rooms, 30 suites. Facilities: restaurant, 2 lounges, health club, indoor pool. AE, D, DC, MC, V.*

Moderate **Ansley Inn.** This Tudor mansion in an exclusive midtown neigh-
★ borhood boasts deluxe public areas decorated with Chinese porcelains and reproduction furnishings. Guest rooms are spacious. *253 15th St., 30309, tel. 404/872–9000; fax 404/892–2318. 11 rooms, 1 suite. Facilities: free access to athletic club. AE, D, DC, MC, V.*

Embassy Suites. This Buckhead high rise is just blocks from two of the city's top shopping centers, Phipps Plaza and Lenox Square. Suites range from basic bedroom/sitting room combinations to luxurious rooms with wet bars; a few standard rooms are available. *3285 Peachtree Rd., 30326, tel. 404/261–7733; fax 404/261–6857. 313 suites, 15 rooms. Facilities: restaurant, lounge, fitness room, indoor and outdoor pools. AE, D, DC, MC, V.*

Motels **Days Hotel Atlanta** (3377 Peachtree Rd., 30326, tel. 404/264–1111 or 800/325–2525; fax 404/231–3497), 300 rooms, restaurant, outdoor pool, exercise rooms; moderate.

The Arts and Nightlife

Arts and nightlife events are listed in *Atlanta* magazine, *Atlanta Main Events*, and *Presenting the Season*, available at newsstands, and in *Where: Atlanta, Guest Informant*, and *KNOW ATLANTA*, available at visitor information centers and in hotels. Ticket brokers include **TicketMaster** (tel. 404/249–6400), the city's largest, and **Tic-X-Press** (tel. 404/231–5888).

The Arts   Most touring Broadway productions make their way to Atlanta's **Fox Theatre** (*see* Exploring Atlanta, Midtown, *above*), **Center Stage** (1374 W. Peachtree St., tel. 404/873–2500), **Variety Playhouse** (1099 Euclid Ave., tel. 404/524–7354), or **Civic Center** (395 Piedmont Ave., tel. 404/523–6275). The **Alliance Theater Company** (1280 Peachtree St., tel. 404/892–2414) is one of the city's leading theatrical groups. Woodruff Arts Center's **Symphony Hall** (1280 Peachtree St., tel. 404/892–2414) is the home of the acclaimed **Atlanta Symphony Orchestra**. The **Atlanta Ballet Company** (tel. 404/873–5811) performs at various venues.

Nightlife   **Underground Atlanta** (*see* Shopping, *above*) and the **Buckhead, Virginia Highlands,** and **Little Five Points** neighborhoods are Atlanta's nightlife centers. Virginia Highlands' **Atkins Park Bar & Grill** (794 N. Highland Ave., tel. 404/876–7249), one of the city's oldest neighborhood bars, attracts a 30-something crowd. The open-air deck at Buckhead's **Three Dollar Cafe** (3002 Peachtree Rd., tel. 404/266–8667), equipped with TVs and a volleyball net, caters to a younger crowd. **Blind Willie's** (828 N. Highland Ave., tel. 404/873–2583) offers New Orleans–and Chicago-style blues. Ditto **Blue's Harbor** (2293 Peachtree St., tel. 404/605–0661). For contemporary rock, try the **Cotton Club** (1021 Peachtree St., tel. 404/874–9524) and **The Point** (420 Moreland Ave., tel. 404/659–3522).

Savannah

Four hours southeast of Atlanta, and a world away from the bustling, modern metropolis, lies Savannah, wrapped in a mantle of old-world grace. Established in 1733, the city preserves its heritage in a 2½-sq-mi historic district, the nation's largest urban landmark. Here 1,000 structures have been restored, and families still live in the 18th-century mansions and town houses. Known as the "City of Festivals," Savannah rarely lets a weekend pass without some sort of celebration, from a St. Patrick's Day celebration that rivals New York's and the spring azalea and dogwood festivals to the house tours and concerts at Christmas.

Tourist Information

Savannah: Convention and Visitors Bureau (222 W. Oglethorpe Ave., 31401, tel. 912/944–0456). Visitors Center (301 Martin Luther King Jr. Blvd., 31499, tel. 912/944–0455).

Arriving and Departing

By Plane   **Savannah International Airport,** served by major airlines, is 10 mi west of town on I–16. There is no bus service into town, but

McCall's Limousine Service (tel. 912/966–5364 or 800/673–9365) runs a van shuttle between the airport and the city for $12 a person.

By Car I–95, running north–south along the coast, and I–16, leading east from Macon, intersect west of Savannah; I–16 dead-ends downtown. The Coastal Highway (U.S. 17) runs north–south through town and U.S. 80 runs east–west.

Train Station The **Amtrak** station (2611 Seaboard Coastline Dr., tel. 912/234–2611) is 4 mi southwest of downtown.

Bus Station **Greyhound** (610 W. Oglethorpe Ave., tel. 912/233–7723).

Getting Around Savannah

Savannah's historic district, though large, should be seen on foot to better observe the intricate architectural details. It's laid out in a grid pattern, and a number of strategically placed benches allow for frequent rests. If you bring a car, park it in one of the numerous metered and off-street pay lots here.

Exploring Savannah

A good way to start a tour is by picking up information at the **Savannah Visitors Center** (*see* Tourist Information, *above*), in the old Central Georgia railway station. Nearby is the restored **City Market**, a four-block area of shops, art galleries, restaurants, and jazz clubs.

Two blocks from City Market, narrow cobblestone streets wind from Bay Street down to Factors Walk and, below it, to River Street and the revitalized **River Front** district. A multimillion-dollar face-lift in 1977 transformed this once-musty warehouse district into a nine-block marketplace with boutiques, restaurants, and taverns. Also here is the **Ships of the Sea Museum** (503 E. River St., tel. 912/232–1511), with memorabilia ranging from models of Columbus's ships and nuclear submarines to a fine collection of Royal Doulton nautical figurines.

Within easy walking distance of the River Front is the **Isaiah Davenport House** (324 E. State St., tel. 912/236–8097), one of the city's finest examples of Georgian architecture, furnished with Chippendale, Hepplewhite, and Sheraton antiques. Within the graceful **Telfair Mansion** (121 Barnard St., tel. 912/232–1177), designed by William Jay, is the South's oldest public art museum, displaying American, French, and German Impressionist paintings from the 18th and 19th centuries along with classical sculptures. The **Juliette Gordon Low Girl Scout National Center** (142 Bull St., tel. 912/233–4501), in a Regency mansion that was the city's first registered National Historic Landmark, displays memorabilia and original family furnishings of the founder of the Girl Scouts of the U.S.A., who was born here.

East of here on McDonough Street is **Colonial Park Cemetery**, the burial ground for some of the city's earliest and most notable residents, such as Button Gwinnett, a signer of the Declaration of Independence. Two blocks away is the French Gothic–style **Cathedral of St. John the Baptist** (222 E. Harris St., tel. 912/233–4709), a late-19th-century structure containing Aus-

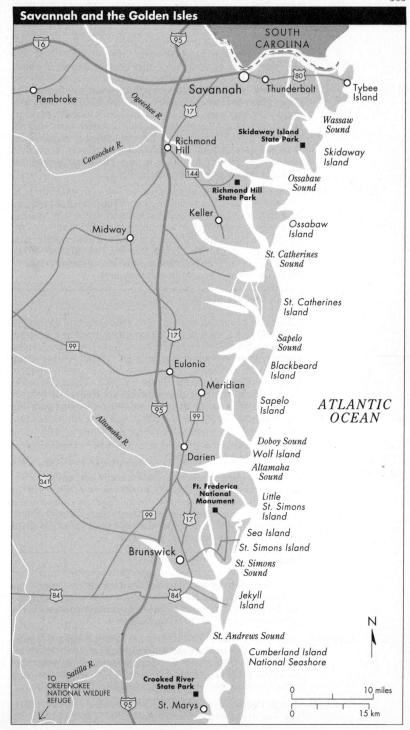

Savannah and the Golden Isles

trian stained-glass windows, an Italian marble altar, and German Stations of the Cross.

Across the street and through Lafayette Square is the 1849 **Andrew Low House** (329 Abercorn St., tel. 912/233–6854), the childhood home of Juliette Gordon Low's husband, William. Some of the city's most impressive ironwork decorates the exterior; inside is a fine collection of 19th-century antiques. The **Green-Meldrim House** (1 W. Macon St., tel. 912/233–3845), several blocks west, was built in 1850 for Low's business partner, cotton merchant Charles Green. Now a parish house for St. John's Episcopal Church, it has been meticulously restored and is furnished with 16th- and 17th-century antiques that reflect the original owner's luxurious tastes. The house is open for viewing; call ahead to make sure it's open.

In the Vicinity From Savannah, a 30-minute drive east on Victory Drive (U.S. 80/Tybee Rd.) leads across a bridge to **Tybee Island.** About 5 mi long and 2 mi wide, Tybee offers expansive white-sand beaches for shelling, crabbing, and swimming, as well as covered picnic facilities, a marina, and a wide variety of seafood restaurants, motels, and shops. The **Tybee Museum** (tel. 912/786–4077), which faces the **Tybee Lighthouse,** the state's oldest and tallest, traces the island's history from Indian days.

Parks and Gardens

Integral to Savannah's design is its park system of 24 squares large and small, each with a historic monument or a graceful fountain, that dot the historic district. Near City Market is the earliest, **Johnson Square;** food carts are typically parked along its edges, so you can grab a snack while resting on a bench. Near the Green-Meldrim House on West Macon Street is **Forsyth Park,** where outdoor concerts are frequently held; at the center of its shady 20 acres, including a jogging path and the Fragrant Garden for the Blind, is a graceful white fountain.

Shopping

Savannah's many specialty shops sell such merchandise as English antiques and Low Country handmade quilts. Stores in the historic district are housed in ground floors of mansions and town houses or in renovated warehouses along the waterfront. The **River Front** and **City Market** areas have a variety of shops (*see* Exploring Savannah, *above*).

Dining

Savannah offers an abundance of restaurants serving regional seafood; barbecue is also popular. If you want something fancier, the city has a number of fine Continental restaurants. For price ranges, see Chart 1 (B) in Chapter 1.

Expensive
★ **Elizabeth on 37th.** The restaurant has earned a regional reputation for the fine seafood and delicate sauces of owner-chef Elizabeth Terry. The cuisine is complemented by the renovated mansion's authentic Savannah decor. *105 E. 37th St., tel. 912/ 236–5547. Reservations required. AE, MC, V. Closed Sun.*

Moderate **Johnny Harris.** What started as a small roadside stand in 1924 is now one of the city's culinary mainstays. The menu includes steaks, fried chicken, seafood, and barbecued meats spiced with the restaurant's famous sauce. *1651 E. Victory Dr., tel. 912/354–7810. AE, DC, MC, V. Closed Sun.*

Inexpensive **Mrs. Wilkes Boarding House.** Come to this unassuming basement restaurant for homey cooking served family-style. Patrons line up at breakfast and lunch for such quintessential southern dishes as biscuits, grits, collard greens, mashed potatoes, and fried chicken. *107 W. Jones St., tel. 912/232–5997. No credit cards. No dinner; closed weekends.*

★ **Seashell House.** Forget the unprepossessing decor and dig into the combination platters of fresh steamed crab, shrimp, and oysters. Also on the menu is Low Country Boil, a regional dish of shrimp, sausages, and vegetables. *3111 Skidaway Rd., tel. 912/352–8116. AE, MC, V.*

Lodging

For price ranges, see Chart 2 (B) in Chapter 1.

Expensive **Ballastone Inn.** At this handsome stucco inn, centrally located on the city's major thoroughfare, 18th- and 19th-century antiques decorate the double parlor. The old-world decor continues in the guest rooms, each with its own color scheme and some with working fireplaces. *14 E. Oglethorpe Ave., 31401, tel. 912/236–1484 or 800/822–4553; fax 912/236–4626. 17 rooms. AE, MC, V.*

DeSoto Hilton. This popular convention hotel has comfortable guest rooms and an expansive lobby with discreet seating areas and fresh flowers. Suites have kitchens, and the corner king rooms provide good city views. *15 E. Liberty St., 31401, tel. 912/232–9000 or 800/426–8483; fax 912/232–6018. 254 rooms, 9 suites. Facilities: restaurant, lounge, outdoor pool, golf and tennis privileges at area clubs. AE, DC, MC, V.*

★ **The Gastonian.** The city's most deluxe accommodations are found at this inn two blocks from Forsyth Park. The two adjacent Regency Italianate mansions have been beautifully restored and maintained by live-in owners. Full breakfasts and tea are served in lushly appointed rooms filled with period antiques. *220 E. Gaston St., 31401, tel. 912/232–2869; fax 912/234–0006. 13 rooms, 2 suites. Facilities: gas fireplaces in rooms, sun deck with hot tub. AE, MC, V.*

Moderate **Magnolia Place Inn.** Striking two-story verandas overlooking lushly landscaped Forsyth Park wrap around this well-proportioned and ideally located Victorian house. Guest rooms are comfortable. *503 Whitaker St., 31401, tel. 912/236–7674 or 800/238–7674. 7 rooms, 6 suites. Facilities: garden hot tub. AE, MC, V. Closed Jan.–mid-Feb.*

Inexpensive **Days Inn.** This older property's best asset is its location, near the City Market and a block off River Street. Be prepared for typical motel-style modular furnishings and Spartan decor. *201 W. Bay St., 31401, tel. 912/236–4440 or 800/325–2525; fax 912/232–2527. 235 rooms. Facilities: restaurant, pool. AE, DC, MC, V.*

Nightlife

Savannah's nightlife is a reflection of the city's laid-back, easy-going personality. Some clubs feature live reggae, hard rock, and other contemporary music, but most stay with traditional

blues, jazz, and piano bar vocalists. **Congress Street Station**
(121 W. Congress St., tel. 912/236–7309) is the city's liveliest
music hall, featuring name performers in a variety of musical
styles. **Hard-Hearted Hannah's** (in the DeSoto Hilton, 15 E.
Liberty St., tel. 912/232–9000) is a rambunctious blues and
rock club. **City Slickers** (9 W. Bay St., tel. 912/233–6999), despite its name, is the place for country music.

The Golden Isles

An hour south of Savannah lie the Golden Isles, a chain of barrier islands stretching along Georgia's coast to the Florida state
line. The three most developed—Jekyll Island, Sea Island, and
St. Simons Island—are the only ones accessible by car; they
are connected to the mainland near Brunswick by a network of
causeways. A ferry from St. Marys connects Cumberland Island National Seashore with the mainland, and a launch transports visitors from St. Simons to Little St. Simons, a private
vacation retreat. Spring, when temperatures are mild, is the
ideal time for a visit; the superb beaches attract large crowds in
summer.

Tourist Information

Cumberland Island: National Seashore (National Park Service,
Box 806, St. Mary's 31558, tel. 912/882–4335). **Jekyll Island:**
Convention and Visitors Bureau (901 Jekyll Island Causeway,
31520, tel. 912/635–3636). **Little St. Simons Island** (*see* Dining
and Lodging, *below*). **St. Simons Island:** Chamber of Commerce
(Neptune Park, 31522, tel. 912/638–9014). **Sea Island:** (The
Cloister, 31561, tel. 912/638–3611 or 800/732–4752).

Getting There

By Plane **Glynco Jetport,** on the mainland 6 mi outside Brunswick, is
served by **Atlantic Southeast Airlines** (tel. 800/282–3424) and
USAir. International airports are an hour's drive north in Savannah and an hour's drive south in Jacksonville, Florida. Jekyll and St. Simons islands maintain small airstrips for private
planes.

By Car From Brunswick, take the Jekyll Island Causeway ($1 toll) to
Jekyll Island or the Torras Causeway (35¢) to St. Simons. From
St. Simons you can reach Sea Island via the Sea Island Causeway. Only residents and park service personnel are allowed to
drive cars on Cumberland Island.

By Boat To reach Cumberland Island, you must reserve passage on the
Cumberland Queen ferry, which leaves from St. Marys for the
45-minute journey. For a schedule or reservations, contact the
Cumberland Island National Seashore (*see* Tourist Information, *above*).

By Bus **Greyhound** connects Brunswick (tel. 912/265–2800) and St.
Marys with surrounding towns and cities, including Savannah
and Jacksonville, Florida.

Exploring the Golden Isles

St. Simons Island   St. Simons, north of Jekyll and Cumberland islands, offers the contrasting beauties of white-sand beaches and salt marshes. As large as Manhattan, with more than 14,000 residents, it's the Golden Isles' most complete and commercial resort destination: Visitors here are well served with numerous hotels, rental cottages, and condominiums, as well as four golf-course developments.

At the island's south end, the village area is dotted with T-shirt and souvenir shops, boutiques, restaurants, and a public pier for fishing and crabbing. Adjacent to the village and overlooking the ocean is **Neptune Park,** with a playground, a miniature golf course, and picnic tables shaded by a canopy of live oaks. Also in the park is the **St. Simons Lighthouse,** built in 1872; climb to the top for a panoramic view of the beachfront, or visit the **Museum of Coastal History** (101 12th St., tel. 912/638–4666) in the former lightkeeper's cottage.

At the other end of the island is **Ft. Frederica National Monument,** which contains the foundation ruins of a fort and buildings inhabited by English soldiers and civilians in the mid-18th century. Tours begin at the **National Park Service Visitors Center** (Frederica Rd., tel. 912/638–3639). On your way to and from the fort you will pass the Gothic-style **Christ Episcopal Church** (Frederica Rd., tel. 912/638–8683). The quaint, gingerbread-trimmed structure was rebuilt in 1886 after serving as a cattle slaughterhouse for Union troops during the Civil War.

Little St. Simons Island   Accessible by private boat from St. Simons, Little St. Simons is a Robinson Crusoe–style getaway just 6 mi long and less than 3 mi wide. Owned and operated by one family since the early 1900s, the island's "retreat" (*see* Dining and Lodging, *below*) accommodates just 24 guests in rugged comfort. There's a 7 mi stretch of beach for swimming and water sports; other activities include horseback riding, nature walks, fishing, and shrimping and crabbing expeditions.

Sea Island   Across a marshy expanse from St. Simons is Sea Island, whose main attraction is **The Cloister,** a Spanish Mediterranean–style resort built in 1928 (*see* Dining and Lodging, *below*). This luxurious, low-key property encompasses a beach club with health spa, formal and casual restaurants, and such recreational activities as tennis, golf, horseback riding, sailing, and biking. The resort's roster of celebrity guests includes President George Bush and Barbara Bush, who honeymooned here and returned in 1991 to celebrate their wedding anniversary. Outside the resort, beautiful mansions line Sea Island Drive.

Jekyll Island   Now a state-run park, Jekyll Island was once the favored retreat of Vanderbilts, Rockefellers, Morgans, Pulitzers, and other American aristocrats. Many of these millionaires' elegant mansions (which they called cottages) are part of the **Jekyll Island Club Historic District** (Exit 6 off I–95, tel. 912/635–2236; admission charged) and are open for tours. The lengthy system of bike paths crisscrossing the island and a golf course are year-round recreational pursuits here. Quiet beaches and an 11-acre water park, **Summer Waves** (210 Riverview Dr., tel. 912/635–2074), rank as top summer attractions.

Cumberland Island National Seashore Cumberland Island National Seashore, the largest and most remote of the Golden Isles, offers 18 mi of sandy beaches. You can tour the unspoiled terrain and the ruins of Thomas Carnegie's **Dungeness** estate on your own, or join history and nature walks led by park-service rangers (*see* Tourist Information, *above*). *Note:* You must bring whatever food, beverages, sunscreen, and insect repellent you may need with you; the island has no shops or markets.

Sports and Outdoor Activities

Biking The flat terrain along the islands' coastlines is ideal for biking. Sea Island, Jekyll Island, and St. Simons have paved bike paths. You can rent bikes from **The Cloister** on Sea Island (tel. 912/638–3611) or, on St. Simons, from **Barry's Beach Service** (1300 Ocean Blvd., tel. 912/638–8053) and **Benjy's Bike Shop** (238 Retreat Pl., tel. 912/638–6766).

Fishing The Intracoastal Waterway and the Atlantic Ocean are teeming with trout, barracuda, snapper, amberjack, and other fish. On St. Simons, **Island Charters** (tel. 912/261–0630 or 912/638–8799) and **Golden Isles Charter Co.** (tel. 912/638–5678) organize river and deep-sea fishing expeditions, and **Taylor Fish Camp** (tel. 912/638–7690) offers guided fishing trips through the marshes.

Golf St. Simons Island has four courses: **Hampton Club** (100 Tabbystone Dr., tel. 912/634–0255), **The Island Club** (100 Kings Way, tel. 912/638–5131), **Sea Island Golf Club** (100 Retreat Ave., tel. 912/638–5110), and **Sea Palms** (5445 Frederica Rd., tel. 912/638–3351). Jekyll Island has the **Oceanside 9 Hole Course** (Beachview Dr., tel. 912/635–2170), constructed by the original millionaire residents, and the **Indian Mound Oleander & Pine Lake Course** (tel. 912/635–2368).

Beaches and Water Sports

Wide expanses of clean sand beaches skirt all the islands. Choose the one where you'll spread your beach towel according to how you want to spend your afternoon. St. Simons's **East Beach** attracts large groups and families and offers sailboat rentals. The beaches rimming **Jekyll Island** are usually not too busy during the week but become more crowded on weekends. The dunes and beaches of **Cumberland Island National Seashore** offer peaceful isolation.

Dining and Lodging

For price ranges, see Charts 1 (B) and 2 (A) in Chapter 1.

Cumberland Island *Dining and Lodging* **Greyfield Inn.** This turn-of-the-century house, the island's only lodging, stands by itself in the primitive landscape; its wide colonnaded porches beckon invitingly. The inn is furnished like a private residence. Spacious rooms are filled with seashell collections, and burnished hardwood floors are warmed by antique rugs. Rates include all meals, which are delightful: hearty breakfasts, box lunches packed and left in the old-fashioned kitchen, and festive dinners. *Box 900, Fernandina Beach, FL 32035, tel. 904/261–6408. 5 rooms share 2 baths (and outdoor shower house); 1 suite. MC, V. Expensive.*

Jekyll Island
Dining and Lodging

Jekyll Island Club Hotel. This renovated 1887 hotel is a turreted Victorian, complete with wraparound veranda and croquet lawn. Guest rooms are spacious and decorated to reflect the hotel's 19th-century origins. The Grand Dining Room serves gourmet cuisine; meal-plan rates are available. *371 Riverview Dr., 31527, tel. 912/635–2600 or 800/528–1234; fax 912/635–2818. 118 rooms, 16 suites. Facilities: 2 restaurants, outdoor pool. AE, D, DC, MC, V. Expensive–Very Expensive.*

Little St. Simons Island
Dining and Lodging

Little St. Simons Island Retreat. Guests stay in spacious, airy rooms with private baths in one of four buildings: a two-bedroom cottage with screened porch and deck; the 1917 Hunting Lodge, with two antique-filled guest rooms; or one of two houses with four guest rooms each. The buildings have screened porches and wrap-around decks. Meals, which are included in the rate, are served family-style in the main dining room and include platters heaped with fresh fish, home-baked breads, and pies. *Box 1078, 31522, tel. 912/638–7472; fax 912/634–1811. 11 rooms. Facilities: horseback riding, canoeing, fishing, guided nature walks, pool. AE, MC, V. Closed Dec.–Feb. Minimum 2-night reservations. Group booking only June–Sept. Very Expensive.*

St. Simons Island
Dining

Emmeline & Hessie. This informal eatery, the island's only waterfront restaurant, offers spectacular views of the marina and marshes. Specialties are seafood dishes, steaks, and lobster. *Golden Isles Marina, tel. 912/638–9084. AE, MC, V. Inexpensive–Moderate.*

The Crab Trap. Count on a crowd in high season at this spot popular for fresh seafood with side orders of hush puppies, cole slaw, corn on the cob, and batter-dipped fries. *1209 Ocean Blvd., tel. 912/638–3552. No credit cards. Inexpensive.*

Lodging

King and Prince Hotel and Villa. This beachfront hotel-and-condominium complex recently underwent a multimillion-dollar renovation that updated its spacious guest rooms and two- and three-bedroom villas. *201 Arnold Rd., 31522, tel. 912/638–3631 or 800/342–0212; fax 912/634–1720. 125 rooms, 45 villas. Facilities: restaurant, lounge, indoor and outdoor pools, tennis courts, access to golf course. AE, DC, MC, V. Moderate–Expensive.*

Days Inn of America. Opened in 1989, this chain motel offers sizable, clean rooms with microwaves and minifridges. *1701 Frederica Rd., 31522, tel. 912/634–0660; fax 912/638–7115. 101 rooms. Facilities: Continental breakfast, pool. AE, MC, V. Inexpensive–Moderate.*

Sea Island
Dining and Lodging
★

The Cloister. At this classic resort, contemporary oceanside villas, condominiums, and rental homes have grown up around a 1920s Spanish Mediterranean–style hotel with large guest rooms. Formal dining, casual grill lunches, and seafood and breakfast buffets are included in the full American Plan. A new spa facility adjacent to the resort's Beach Club features a fully equipped workout room, daily aerobics classes, facials, massages, and other beauty treatments. *Sea Island 31561, tel. 912/638–3611 or 800/732–4752; fax 912/638–5159. 264 rooms, 450 cottages, 44 condominiums. Facilities: 4 restaurants, 2 pools, tennis, golf, horseback riding, spa. No credit cards. Very Expensive.*

Campgrounds

Cumberland Island National Seashore (*see* Tourist Information, *above*) maintains two tent campgrounds, one with rest rooms and showers, the other with cold-water spigots only.

Elsewhere in the State

Okefenokee Swamp National Wildlife Refuge

Getting There The refuge is near the Georgia-Florida border, 40 minutes northwest of Jacksonville, Florida, and 40 minutes southwest of the Golden Isles. From Atlanta, take I–75S to U.S. 82 into Waycross. From the Golden Isles, take U.S. 84W to U.S. 301S.

What to See and Do The **Okefenokee Swamp National Wildlife Refuge** (tel. 912/496–7836)—a vast peat bog once part of the ocean floor and now 100 feet above sea level—covers more than 700 sq mi. Its thick vegetation is inhabited by at least 54 reptile species (including alligators), 41 mammal species, and 225 types of birds. The **Okefenokee Swamp Park** (8 mi south of Waycross, tel. 912/283–0583; admission charged) is a major gateway to the refuge. Boardwalks lead to an observation tower; guided boat tours are offered. There's an eastern entrance at the **Suwanee Canal** near Folkston (tel. 912/496–7156; admission charged), an 11-mi waterway built over a century ago, and a western entrance at **Stephen C. Foster State Park** (Rte. 1, Fargo, tel. 912/637–5274; admission free), an 80-acre park with boat rides through a swamp, nature trails, and a large forest of cypress and black gum.

Paradise Garden

Getting There Paradise Garden is a couple of blocks off U.S. 27 just north of Summerville, about midway between Atlanta and Chattanooga. From Atlanta, take I–75N to Exit 128, then Rte. 140W to U.S. 27N to Summerville.

What to See and Do Best-known among Georgia's folk artists is the Rev. Howard Finster. His **Paradise Garden** (tel. 706/857–2926) is a complex of buildings, sculptures, and artwork. There's a church and a chapel, as well as a two-story-tall sculpture created from old bicycles, and a shop where Finster's artwork is for sale. On the way you can stop at the **Adairsville Inn** (100 S. Main St., Adairsville, tel. 706/773–2774), which serves excellent lunches (except Sat. and Mon.) and dinners (Fri. and Sat. only).

Clayton

Getting There From Atlanta, take I–85N to Rte. 365, then U.S. 441 to Clayton, in the north Georgia mountains.

What to See and Do **Main Street Gallery** (Box 641, Clayton 30525, tel. 706/782–2440) features local mountain artists as well as regional carvers and painters. A few miles north on U.S. 441 is the **Dillard House** (U.S. 441, Dillard, tel. 706/746–5348), a restaurant famous throughout the mountains for fried chicken, ham and vegetables prepared country style and served family style.

NORTH CAROLINA

By Carol Timblin

Capital	Raleigh
Population	6,689,726
Motto	To Be Rather Than to Seem
State Bird	Cardinal
State Flower	Dogwood

Visitor Information

North Carolina Division of Travel and Tourism (430 N. Salisbury St., Raleigh 27611, tel. 919/733–4171 or 800/847–4862). **Welcome centers:** I–77S near Charlotte, I–77N near Dobson, I–85S near Kings Mountain, I–85N near Norlina, I–95S near Rowland, I–95N near Roanoke Rapids, I–26 near Columbus, and I–40W near Waynesville.

Scenic Drives

The **Blue Ridge Parkway** (*see also* Virginia) in the western part of the state extends from the Virginia state line to the Great Smoky Mountains National Park entrance near Cherokee—more than 250 mi of mountain views, nature exhibits, historic sites, parks, and hiking trails. **U.S. 440** from Cherokee to Gatlinburg, Tennessee, cuts through the middle of the national park for about 35 mi, climbing to a crest of 6,642 feet at Clingmans Dome, a short distance from Newfound Gap. Portions of **U.S. 64** travel through the Hickory Nut Gorge between Lake Lure and Chimney Rock and the Cullasaga Gorge between Lake Toxaway and Franklin, affording spectacular views of mountain peaks and cascading waterfalls. **Rte. 12,** connecting the Outer Banks, offers great views of the ocean and a landscape dotted with lighthouses and weathered beach cottages.

National and State Parks

The state tourism division's travel guide (*see* Visitor Information, *above*) includes a complete listing of state and national parks and recreation areas, as well as educational state forests.

National Parks **Cape Hatteras National Seashore** (Rte. 1, Box 675, Manteo 27954, tel. 919/473–2111) stretches 75 mi from Nags Head to Ocracoke and encompasses 30,318 acres of marshland and sandy beaches—a natural habitat for hundreds of species of birds, wild animals, and aquatic life.

Cape Lookout National Seashore (3601 Bridgett St., Suite 4, Morehead City 28557, tel. 919/728–2250) extends 55 mi from Portsmouth Island to Cape Lookout and includes 28,400 acres of uninhabited land and marsh, accessible only by boat or ferry. Portsmouth, a deserted village that was inhabited from 1753 until 1984, is being restored, and wild ponies roam the Shackleford Banks.

Great Smoky Mountains National Park (Gatlinburg, TN 37738, tel. 615/436–5615), with 8.5 million visitors a year, is the most visited national park in the country. Its 514,757 acres straddle the North Carolina-Tennessee border and offer camping, hiking, fishing, historic sites, and nature lore (*see also* Tennessee). To enter the park from North Carolina, take U.S. 441N from Cherokee.

State Parks On the Intracoastal Waterway south of Wilmington, 1,773-acre **Carolina Beach State Park** (Box 475, Carolina Beach 28428, tel. 919/458–7710, marina tel. 910/458–7770) offers camping, fishing, swimming, boating, picnicking, and hiking. **Ft. Macon** (Box 127, Atlantic Beach 28512, tel. 919/726–3775) centers on the fort built in 1834 to guard Beaufort Inlet. **Hanging Rock State Park** (Box 186, Danbury 27016, tel. 910/593–8480) offers rock climbing and rappelling, hiking, camping, picnicking, and swimming. **Jockey's Ridge State Park** (Box 592, Nags Head 27959, tel. 919/441–7132) offers hang-gliding instruction and flights from a 140-foot sand dune, the tallest in the East. **Kerr Reservoir State Recreation Area** (Rte. 3, Box 800, Henderson 27536, tel. 919/438–7791) encompasses 106,860 acres and includes eight designated recreation sites around a huge manmade lake. **Merchant's Millpond** (Rte. 1, Box 141–A, Gatesville 27938, tel. 919/357–1191) can be explored by canoe. **Mt. Mitchell** (Rte. 5, Box 700, Burnsville 28714, tel. 704/675–4611) offers camping on the highest mountain in the East (6,684 feet).

The Piedmont

The Piedmont is the heartland of North Carolina, a vast area of rolling hills that extends from where the coastal plain begins, east of the Triangle area (Raleigh, Durham, and Chapel Hill), to the foothills of the Blue Ridge Mountains, west of Charlotte and the Triad area (Greensboro, Winston-Salem, and High Point). Scattered along the major arteries of the region, including interstates 40, 77, and 85, are the state's largest towns, cities, and industries—banks, tobacco, textiles, and furniture. Here also are large rivers, man-made lakes, and woodlands; historic villages dating to the mid-1700s; crafts, antiques, and outlet shops; world-renowned colleges and universities; and one of the largest concentrations of golf courses in the world.

Tourist Information

Charlotte: Visitor Information Center (122 E. Stonewall St., 28202, tel. 704/371–8700 or 800/231–4636). **Durham:** Convention & Visitors Bureau (101 E. Morgan St., 27701, tel. 919/688–2855 or 800/772–2855). **Raleigh:** Capital Area Visitor Center (301 N. Blount St., 27611, tel. 919/733–3456). Convention and Visitors Bureau (225 Hillsborough St., Suite 400, 27602, tel. 919/834–5900 or 800/849–8499). **Winston-Salem:** Convention & Visitors Bureau (Box 1408, 27102, tel. 910/725–2361 or 800/331–7018).

Getting There

By Plane Major carriers serve **Charlotte-Douglas International Airport** (Charlotte, tel. 704/359–4000), **Raleigh-Durham International Airport** (Raleigh, tel. 919/840–2123), and **Piedmont Triad International Airport** (Greensboro, tel. 910/665–5666). Taxi and limousine services are available at all airports.

By Car I–40 and U.S. 74 run east–west through the Piedmont; I–77 runs north from Charlotte; I–85 runs from Charlotte northeast through Greensboro and the Raleigh area.

By Train **Amtrak** serves Charlotte, Greensboro, and Raleigh. *The Carolinian* connects the three cities daily.

By Bus **Greyhound** provides service to Charlotte (tel. 704/527–9393), Raleigh (tel. 919/828–2567), Durham (tel. 919/687–4800), Chapel Hill (tel. 919/942–3356), and Winston-Salem (tel. 910/723–3663).

Exploring the Piedmont

A reasonable starting point is **Charlotte,** the region's largest city. Its premier attraction is **Discovery Place,** an award-winning hands-on science museum. Here you can enjoy a touch tank, aquariums, an indoor rain forest, an OMNIMAX theater, and a planetarium, plus special exhibits. *301 N. Tryon St., tel. 704/372–6261 or 800/935–9553. Admission charged.*

East of here, the **Hezekiah Alexander Homesite** (3500 Shamrock Dr., tel. 704/568–1774), built in 1774, is the city's oldest dwelling. Named for the settler who built it, the site includes a log kitchen; costumed docents give guided tours.

South of here via Eastway Drive, the **Mint Museum of Art** (2730 Randolph Rd., tel. 704/337–2000), built in 1837 as a U.S. mint, has served as a home for art since 1936. In recent years it has hosted internationally acclaimed exhibits.

It's a three-hour drive north on I–85 to **Durham,** a city once known for its tobacco production but today better known for **Duke University,** with its outstanding medical school. **Duke University Chapel** (tel. 919/684–2572), an ornate Gothic-style cathedral, serves as the focal point of the campus. It is open for tours and free organ concerts.

From Durham, drive for 30 minutes on I–40E to **Raleigh,** the state capital. You can walk to most of the government buildings and historical attractions downtown. The **State Capitol** (tel. 919/733–4994), built in 1840 and restored in 1976, commands the highest point in Capitol Square. Its appearance contrasts with the more contemporary Legislative Building, one block north, where sessions are currently held. Half a block north is the **North Carolina Museum of Natural Sciences** (102 N. Salisbury St., tel. 919/733–7451), a favorite destination for children, who love its resident snakes and animal exhibits. Two more blocks north, the **North Carolina Museum of History** (109 E. Jones St., tel. 919/733–3894) has period costumes, guns, and other exhibits that chronicle the state's history. The nearby **Executive Mansion** (200 N. Blount St., tel. 919/733–3871), a turn-of-the-century Queen Anne–style structure in brick with gingerbread trim, is the governor's home.

Several miles from the state government complex, the **North Carolina Museum of Art** (2110 Blue Ridge Blvd., tel. 919/833–1935) exhibits art ranging from ancient Egyptian to contemporary. The Museum Cafe is a favorite place for lunch, afternoon tea, or dinner on Friday night.

West of Raleigh on I–40 is **Winston-Salem.** In **Old Salem,** a restored 18th-century village, docents and craftsmen re-create the life and times of the Moravians, a Protestant sect that settled in the area in 1743. Also in the village is the **Museum of Early Southern Decorative Arts,** featuring period furnishings. Tour tickets are required to get into the buildings, but you may wander the streets free of charge. *600 S. Main St., tel. 910/721–7300. Admission: $10 adults, $5 children. Closed major holidays.*

What to See and Do with Children

Enjoy thrilling rides at **Paramount's Carowinds** (15423 Carowinds Blvd., tel. 704/588–2600 or 800/822–4428), an 83-acre theme amusement park straddling the North Carolina–South Carolina border near Charlotte. In Chapel Hill, 15 minutes south of Durham on U.S. 15/502, children can stargaze at the University of Carolina's **Morehead Planetarium** (tel. 919/962–1236). In Durham, the **North Carolina Museum of Life and Science** (433 Murray Ave., tel. 919/220–5429) exhibits life-size dinosaur models.

Shopping

The Piedmont is a mecca for lovers of **antiques and crafts;** towns such as Waxhaw, Pineville, and Matthews are devoted almost entirely to antiques. For directions and information, call Charlotte's visitor center (*see* Tourist Information, *above*). One of the country's largest antiques centers is **Metrolina Expo** (7100 Statesville Rd., tel. 704/596–4643), near Charlotte.

The Seagrove area, between Greensboro and Pinehurst, offers nearly 40 shops that produce and sell handmade **pottery.** Burlington, between Greensboro and Durham, is a hub for **outlet stores.** Charlotte and Raleigh are major retail centers; the latter is home to the **North Carolina State Flea Market** (tel. 919/832–0361) and one of the largest **farmers' markets** in the Southeast.

Sports and Outdoor Activities

Golf The Sandhills area, in the southern part of the Piedmont, has more than three dozen courses, including Pinehurst's famous No. 2. For details, contact the **Pinehurst Area Convention & Visitors Bureau** (Box 2270, Southern Pines 28388, tel. 910/692–3330 or 800/346–5362).

Spectator Sports

Basketball **Charlotte Hornets** (Charlotte Coliseum, Tyvola Rd., off Billy Graham Pkwy., tel. 704/522–6500 or 800/543–3041; Nov.–Apr.).

The Raleigh–Durham area is a college-basketball fan's dream, with **Duke University** (tel. 919/681–2583), **North Carolina State** (tel. 919/515–2104), **North Carolina Central University** (tel. 919/560–6574), and **University of North Carolina—Chapel Hill** (tel. 919/962–2211) offering games from November through March.

NASCAR Racing The Coca-Cola 600, All Pro Auto Parts 300, and Mello Yello 500 races draw huge crowds to the **Charlotte Motor Speedway** (tel. 704/455–3200) off I–85 near Concord.

Dining and Lodging

The Piedmont has a growing number of upscale restaurants and ethnic eateries, as well as restaurants that specialize in the more traditional barbecue, fresh seafood, fried chicken, and country ham. Lodging is available at economy motels, upscale convention hotels, bed-and-breakfasts, and resorts. Breakfast may be included in the room rate, and children often stay free in their parents' room. Many city hotels offer weekend packages with discounted rates and extra amenities. For price ranges, see Charts 1 (B) and 2 (B) in Chapter 1.

Chapel Hill
Dining

Catherine's on Providence. Great home cooking, including casseroles and bakery goods made on the spot, is the selling feature of this Myers Park eatery. Try the Sunday brunch. *829 Providence Rd., tel. 919/372–8199. AE, MC, V. Closed Mon. Inexpensive.*

Dining and Lodging
★

Fearrington House. Set on an old farm, this elegant French-style country inn is a member of Relais & Châteaux. Rooms are decorated with chintz and antiques, and the cuisine is a deft blend of regional and French. *Fearrington Village Center, Pittsboro 27312, tel. 919/542–2121, 800/334–5475, or 800/277–0130; fax 919/542–4202. 19 rooms. Facilities: 2 restaurants, pool, bicycles, shops. MC, V. Expensive.*

Charlotte
Dining
★

Bravo Ristorante and Lounge. The in place for special celebrations (also great for Sunday brunches), this hotel restaurant is known not only for its authentic Italian cuisine but also for its singing waitstaff. *Adams Mark Hotel, 555 S. McDowell St., tel. 704/372–5440. Reservations advised. Jacket advised. AE, D, MC, V. Expensive.*

The Lamplighter. A converted home in the Dilworth neighborhood includes a cozy lounge with a fireplace. A favorite menu item is the trio entrée of beef, veal, and lamb or seafood. *1065 E. Morehead St., tel. 704/372–5343. Reservations advised. Jacket advised. AE, DC, MC, V. Expensive.*

PizZarrelli Trattoria. Wood-burning brick ovens are the key to delicious pizzas at this popular Italian restaurant. The owner is a former opera star who often sings for his patrons. *9101 Pineville-Matthews Rd., Pineville, tel. 704/543–0647. No credit cards. Inexpensive–Moderate.*

Dining and Lodging

The Dunhill. Built in 1929, the hotel features reproduction 18th-century furnishings. The restaurant, Monticello's, gets rave reviews for beautifully presented California cuisine. *237 N. Tyron St., 28202, tel. 704/332–4141 or 800/354–4141; fax 704/376–4117. 59 rooms, 1 penthouse with whirlpool. Facilities: Continental breakfast, restaurant, piano bar. AE, D, DC, MC, V. Expensive.*

Hyatt Charlotte at Southpark. Rooms ring a four-story atrium lobby at this modern hotel, popular with business travelers. The restaurant features northern Italian cuisine. *5501 Carnegie Blvd., 28209–3462, tel. 704/554–1234; fax 704/554–8319. 259 rooms, 3 suites. Facilities: restaurant, lounge, pool, health club. AE, MC, V. Expensive.*

The Morehead Inn. Though it caters to corporate clients, this Dilworth inn, built in the '20s as a private residence and restored in the '80s, has all the comforts of a luxurious home. Guests are served a complimentary Continental breakfast. *1122 E. Morehead St., 28204, tel. 704/376–3357 or 800/322–*

3945; fax 704/335–1110. 11 rooms. Facilities: meeting rooms. AE, MC, V. Expensive.

Durham
Dining

Bullock's Bar-B-Cue. Patrons of this casual eatery queue up as early as four in the afternoon for the best Brunswick stew, barbecue, southern fried chicken, and hush puppies for miles around. *3330 Wortham St., tel. 919/383–3211. No reservations. No credit cards. Closed Sun. Moderate.*

Lodging
★

Washington Duke Hotel & Golf Club. This luxurious inn on the campus of Duke University overlooks the Robert Trent Jones golf course. Duke family memorabilia are displayed in the public rooms; the bar is called the Bull Durham. *3001 Cameron Blvd., 27706, tel. 919/490–0999 or 800/443–3853; fax 919/688–0105. 171 rooms. Facilities: restaurant, lounge, outdoor pool, jogging trails, golf course. AE, DC, MC, V. Expensive.*

Raleigh
Dining
★

The Angus Barn, Ltd. Housed in a huge rustic barn, this Raleigh fixture is known for its steaks, baby-back ribs, prime rib, homemade desserts, and 35-page wine list. *U.S. 70W at Airport Rd., tel. 919/781–2444. Reservations advised (no reservations Sat.). AE, DC, MC, V. Moderate–Expensive.*

42nd St. Oyster Bar. This favorite gathering place for businesspeople and politicians serves fresh seafood daily. *West and Jones Sts., tel. 919/831–2811. AE, DC, MC, V. Moderate–Expensive.*

Lodging
★

The Oakwood Inn. This 1871 B&B in the Oakwood Historic District downtown is furnished with Victorian period pieces. *411 N. Bloodworth St., 27604, tel. 919/832–9712. 6 rooms. AE, D, MC, V. Expensive.*

Radisson Plaza Hotel Raleigh. This downtown hotel, with an expansive atrium and Colonial-style brick inside and out, is connected to the civic center via a walk-through shopping plaza. *420 Fayetteville St. Mall, 27601, tel. 919/834–9900; fax 919/833–1217. 350 rooms, 12 suites. Facilities: 2 restaurants, takeout deli, indoor pool, whirlpool. AE, D, DC, MC, V. Moderate–Expensive.*

Velvet Cloak Inn. This elegant brick hotel with delicate wrought-iron decorations is a favorite spot for wedding receptions and political gatherings. Recently redecorated rooms have traditional, European-style decor. Curtis, the suavely attired bellman, has been greeting guests for years, and afternoon tea is a tradition. *1505 Hillsborough St., 27605, tel. 919/828–0333, 800/334–4372, or 800/662–8829 in NC; fax 919/828–2656. 172 rooms, 4 suites. Facilities: restaurant, lounge, indoor pool and tropical garden. AE, DC, MC, V. Moderate–Expensive.*

Winston-Salem
Dining

Old Salem Tavern Dining Room. Moravian dishes, such as chicken pie and rack of lamb, are served by waiters in Moravian costume. In summer you can dine outside under the arbor. *736 S. Main St., tel. 910/748–8585. AE, MC, V. Moderate.*

Lodging

Brookstown Inn. Sleep under a handmade quilt before the fireplace, relax in the whirlpools that come in some rooms, and enjoy wine and cheese in the lobby or the complimentary Continental breakfast at this B&B, built in 1837 as a textile mill. *200 Brookstown Ave., 27102, tel. 910/725–1120 or 800/845–4262; fax 919/773–0147. 71 rooms. AE, DC, MC, V. Expensive.*

The Arts and Nightlife

The Arts   In Winston-Salem, the **North Carolina School for the Arts** (tel. 910/721–1945) stages events and performances. Charlotte offers monthly **Gallery Crawls** (tel. 704/371–8700 or 800/231–4636; Sept.–May) and the new **North Carolina Blumenthal Center for the Performing Arts** (tel. 704/333–4686), which hosts operas, concerts, plays, and other cultural events. The **North Carolina Symphony Orchestra** (tel. 919/831–6060) is based in Raleigh.

The Coast

A chain of barrier islands flanks the entire North Carolina coast. The Outer Banks stretch some 130 mi from the Virginia state line south to Cape Lookout; the southern coast, to the South Carolina line, includes the Cape Fear River region and Wilmington, the state's primary port. To these shores English settlers came more than 400 years ago to establish a colony on Roanoke Island, then mysteriously disappeared. Called the "Graveyard of the Atlantic" for the hundreds of ships that met their demise here, the Outer Banks proved a safe hiding place for notorious marauding pirates in the 1700s. For many years the region remained isolated, home only to a few fishermen and their families, but now, linked by bridges and ferries, the islands are a popular vacation spot. The Historic Albemarle Region, nearby, comprises charming towns full of early architecture. Hundreds of films have been shot in Wilmington, which boasts a restored historic district and waterfront. On the surrounding coast visitors can tour old plantation houses and azalea gardens, study sea life, and bask in the sun at nearby beaches.

Tourist Information

Cape Fear Coast: Convention and Visitors Bureau (24 N. 3rd St., Wilmington 28401, tel. 910/341–4030 or 800/222–4757). **Carteret County:** Tourism Development Bureau (Box 1406, Morehead City 29557, tel. 919/726–8148 or 800/786–6962). **Craven County:** Convention and Visitors Bureau (Box 1413, New Bern 28503, tel. 919/637–9400 or 800/437–5767). **Dare County:** Tourist Bureau (Box 399, Manteo 27954, tel. 919/473–2138 or 800/446–6262). **Northeastern Historic Places, Historic Albemarle Tour, Inc.** (Box 759, Edenton 27932, tel. 919/482–7325). **North Carolina Coast Host** (Box 5044, Station 1, Wilmington 28403, tel. 910/395–4012). **Outer Banks:** Chamber of Commerce (Box 1757, Kill Devil Hills 27948, tel. 919/441–8144). **Ocracoke:** Visitor Center (Cedar Island, tel. 919/928–4531).

Getting There

By Plane   The closest airports are **Raleigh–Durham International** (*see* The Piedmont, *above*), **New Hanover International Airport** in Wilmington (tel. 919/341–4333), and Virginia's **Norfolk International** (tel. 804/857–3200). From Norfolk, **Southeast Airlines** (tel. 919/473–3222 or 800/927–3296) provides commuter service to **Dare County Regional Airport** (Airport Rd., tel. 919/473–2600) at the north end of Roanoke Island.

By Car Roads link the mainland to the Outer Banks at their northern end: U.S. 158 enters from the north near Kill Devil Hills, and U.S. 64/264 enters Manteo, on Roanoke Island, from the west. These connect with Rte. 12, the main route in the region, running south from Corolla to Ocracoke Island. Toll ferries connect Ocracoke (tel. 919/928-3841) with Cedar Island (tel. 919/225-3551), to the south, and with Swan Quarter (tel. 919/926-1111) on the mainland; a free ferry travels from Hatteras Island to Ocracoke Island. From I-95 near Raleigh, U.S. 70 leads to Cedar Island via New Bern and Morehead City, and I-40 serves Wilmington.

By Bus **Greyhound** serves Elizabeth City (tel. 919/335-5183), on the Albemarle Sound; Wilmington (tel. 910/762-6625); and Norfolk, Virginia (tel. 804/625-7500).

By Boat Marinas are scattered all along the Intracoastal Waterway, including **Pirates Cove Yacht Club** (tel. 919/473-3906) and the **Park Service Docks** (tel. 919/473-2111) in Ocracoke. Elizabeth City is a popular stopover. The Wilmington area has public marinas at Carolina Beach State Park (tel. 910/458-7770) and Wrightsville Beach (910/256-6666). A river taxi runs (mid-June–Labor Day) across the Cape Fear River in Wilmington. For more information, call the Outer Banks Chamber of Commerce (*see* Tourist Information, *above*).

Exploring the Coast

Start your tour of the Outer Banks at Nags Head and Kill Devil Hills, where the Cape Hatteras National Seashore begins (*see* National and State Parks, *above*). You can drive from Nags Head to Ocracoke in a day, but be sure to allow plenty of time in summer, when ferries are crowded. During major storms and hurricanes, follow the evacuation signs to safety.

At **Kill Devil Hills,** the site of man's first flight, stands the **Wright Brothers National Memorial,** a tribute to Wilbur and Orville's feat of December 17, 1903. A replica of *The Flyer* is housed in the visitor center. *U.S. 158 Bypass, tel. 919/441-7430. Admission charged. Closed major holidays.*

Roanoke Island, accessible from U.S. 158 Bypass via U.S. 64/264, is the site of several attractions. ***The Lost Colony*** outdoor drama (tel. 919/473-3414 or 800/488-5012; admission charged; closed Sept.–mid-June) reenacts the story of the first colonists, who settled on Roanoke Island in 1584 and then disappeared. **The Elizabethan Gardens** (U.S. 64, Manteo, tel. 919/473-3234; admission charged; closed weekends Dec.–Jan.) are a lush memorial to the first colonists. **Ft. Raleigh National Historic Site** (tel. 919/473-5772; admission free) is a reconstruction of what is thought to be the original fort. The *Elizabeth II* **State Historic Site** (tel. 919/473-1144; admission charged), a recreation of a 16th-century vessel, is moored in Manteo Harbor.

Take a day trip to visit **Elizabeth City,** on the Albemarle Sound, and its **Museum of the Albemarle** (1116 U.S. 17S, tel. 919/335-1453; admission free; closed Mon.). Then continue west to **Edenton,** the state capital from 1722 to 1743. In 1774, to protest English taxation, 51 local women staged the Edenton Tea Party. Be sure to see the Jacobean-style **Cupola House and Gardens,** built in about 1725; the 1767 **Chowan County Courthouse;** and **St. Paul's Church.**

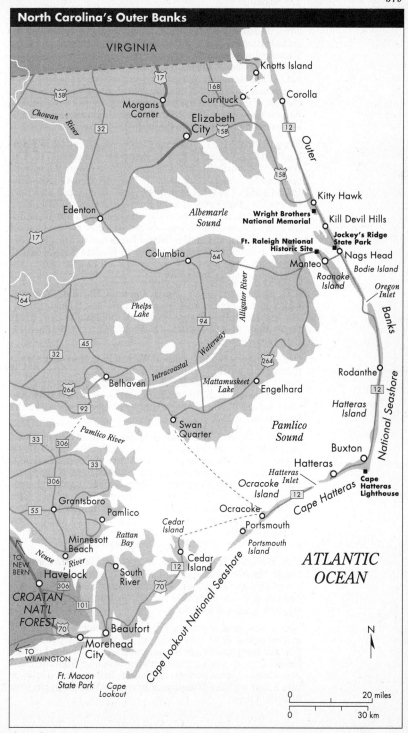

North Carolina's Outer Banks

hea

Back on the Outer Banks, traveling south on Rte. 12, you'll cross the **Bonner Bridge,** which arches for 3 mi over Oregon Inlet to **Hatteras Island,** where the blue marlin reigns. The **Cape Hatteras Lighthouse** (tel. 919/995–4474), at 208 feet, is the tallest lighthouse in America. The visitor center has a small museum. At the south end of the island you can board the free ferry for the half-hour trip to **Ocracoke Island,** which was cut off from the rest of the world for so long that natives speak with a quasi-Elizabethan accent. The 1823 **Ocracoke Lighthouse** is the oldest operating lighthouse in the state.

From Ocracoke Island, take the Cedar Island ferry to the mainland and Rte. 12 and U.S. 70 to **Beaufort,** settled in 1710. The **Beaufort Historic Site** in the center of town comprises several restored buildings dating from 1767 to 1859, including the Carteret County Courthouse and the Apothecary Shop and Doctor's Office. Don't miss the Old Burying Grounds (1731). Here Otway Burns, a privateer in the War of 1812, is buried under his ship's cannon; a nine-year-old girl who died at sea is buried in a keg of rum; and an English soldier is buried upright in his grave, saluting the king. Tours on an English double-decker bus depart from here. *138 Turner St., tel. 919/728–5225. Admission charged. Closed Sun.*

Also in Beaufort is the **North Carolina Maritime Museum,** which documents the state's seafaring and coastal history. Every August, at the Strange Seafood Exhibition, you get to eat the exhibits at a $15 buffet. *315 Front St., tel. 919/728–7317. Admission free.*

U.S. 70 crosses the Intracoastal Waterway to **Morehead City,** a fishing and boating center across Bogue Sound from Bogue Banks, where Atlantic Beach and Emerald Isle are popular family beaches. U.S. 70 continues northwest to **New Bern,** the state capital during English rule and immediately after the Revolution.

The reconstructed **Tryon Palace at New Bern,** an elegant Georgian building, was the Colonial capitol and the home of Royal Governor William Tryon in the 1770s. An audiovisual orientation is given, costumed interpreters conduct tours of the house and gardens, and (in summer) actors deliver monologues describing a day in the life of the governor. The stately **John Wright Stanly House** (ca. 1783), **Dixon-Stevenson House** (ca. 1826), and **New Bern Academy** (ca. 1809) are a part of the Tryon Palace Complex. *610 Pollock St., tel. 919/638–1560. Admission: $12 adults, $6 students. Closed major holidays.*

U.S. 17S leads to **Wilmington,** where the USS *North Carolina* **Battleship Memorial** (tel. 910/251–5797; admission charged), the city's major attraction, is permanently docked off U.S. 421. You can take the river taxi from Riverfront Park (in summer only) for a self-guided tour.

Spend some time exploring Wilmington's restored waterfront and historic district, where you can see 18th-century churches, the 1770 **Burgwin-Wright House,** and the 1852 **Zebulon Latimer House.** Pick up a self-guided walking-tour map from the Cape Fear Coast visitors bureau (*see* Tourist Information, *above*) or take a tour with the **Wilmington Adventure Tour Company** (tel. 910/763–1785).

The **Cape Fear Museum** traces the natural, cultural, and social history of Cape Fear River country. *814 Market St., tel. 910/ 341-7413. Donations suggested. Closed Sun.-Mon. and holidays.*

U.S. 421 leads south to the **Ft. Fisher State Historic Site** (Kure Beach, tel. 910/458-5538; admission free; closed Mon. Nov.-Mar.), the largest (and a very important) Confederate earthwork fortification of the Civil War. There's a reconstructed battery and a display of war relics and artifacts from sunken Confederate blockade runners. Nearby is one of the free **North Carolina Aquariums** (tel. 910/458-8258), where there are picnic tables.

On the west side of the Cape Fear River, south of Wilmington on Rte. 133, a passenger ferry links Southport and **Bald Head Island** (tel. 910/457-5003; $15 round-trip adults, $8 children). On the island you can take a historic tour and see the 109-foot Old Baldy lighthouse, dating from 1817; have a picnic or lunch at one of the restaurants; play golf; or go fishing and swimming.

What to See and Do with Children

Children may enjoy flying a kite from the tallest sand dune in the East (about 140 feet), in **Jockey's Ridge State Park** (*see* National and State Parks, *above*). Three **North Carolina Aquariums** are open free of charge: on Roanoke Island (tel. 919/473-3493); at Pine Knoll Shores on Bogue Banks (tel. 919/247-4003); and at Ft. Fisher (*see* Exploring the Coast, *above*).

Shopping

You can find **nautical items** at antiques shops and **hand-carved wooden ducks and birds** at local crafts shops in Duck, a few miles north of Nags Head, and in Wanchese, at the south end of Roanoke Island. **Kitty Hawk Kites** in Nags Head (tel. 919/441-4124 or 800/334-4777) offers every type of kite and windsock known to humanity. New Bern and Wilmington are centers for **antiques;** in Wilmington, many shops are at Chandler's Wharf, the Cotton Exchange, and Water Street Market on the waterfront.

Sports and Outdoor Activities

Boating You can travel hundreds of miles over the sounds and inlets of this vast region along the Intracoastal Waterway. For marina and docking information, contact the Elizabeth City Chamber of Commerce (tel. 919/335-4365) or the Brunswick County Chamber of Commerce (tel. 910/754-6644).

Fishing The region teems with bass, billfish, flounder, mullet, spot, trout, and other fish. Fishing is permitted from piers all along the coast and from certain bridges and causeways. Charter boats for deep-sea fishing are available at the **Oregon Inlet Fishing Center** (tel. 919/441-6301), **Gould's Charter Boats** (tel. 919/726-3821) in Morehead City, **Tropico Charters** (tel. 910/ 791-8324 or 800/876-7426) in Wilmington, and elsewhere. Licenses are available at local tackle shops or from the state's **Divison of Boating and Inland Fishing** (tel. 919/733-3633).

Golf Among the public and semiprivate courses in the Greater Wilmington area is the breathtaking **Bald Head Island Golf Course** (tel. 910/457-7310), designed by George Cobb. Ocean Isle, near the South Carolina line, also has a number of outstanding courses. Contact the Cape Fear visitors bureau (*see* Tourist Information, *above*) or the Brunswick County Chamber of Commerce (*see* Boating, *above*).

Hang Gliding At **Jockey's Ridge State Park** (*see* National and State Parks, *above*), where national champions gather for the Hang Gliding Spectacular every May, you can try your hand at the daring sport. Instruction and gear are available from **Kitty Hawk Kites** (U.S. 158 at Milepost 13, Nags Head, tel. 919/441–4124).

Scuba Diving With over 600 known shipwrecks off the coast of the Outer Banks, diving opportunities are legion. Dive shops include **Hatteras Divers** (tel. 919/986–2557), **Nags Head Pro Dive Shop** (tel. 919/441–7594), and **Entropy Charters** (tel. 910/350–0039) in Wilmington.

Surfing and The region offers ideal conditions for these sports. **Kitty Hawk**
Windsurfing **Kites** (*see* Hang Gliding, *above*) provides gear and instruction. Rentals are also available at shops in Wilmington, Wrightsville Beach, and Carolina Beach.

Beaches

Within the area's 300-plus mi of oceanfront, the **Cape Hatteras National Seashore** has lifeguard stations at Coquino Beach, Salvo, Cape Hatteras, Frisco, and Ocracoke. Visitors also flock to **Atlantic Beach** and **Emerald Isle** on Bogue Banks near Morehead City, to **Wrightsville, Carolina, and Kure beaches** near Wilmington, and to **Ocean Isle** farther south.

Dining and Lodging

Fresh seafood is in abundant supply, prepared almost any way. Hearty southern cooking, with chicken, ham, and fresh vegetables, is also popular. Cottages, condominiums, motels, resorts, B&Bs, and country inns abound all along the coast. Most places offer lower rates from September through May. Condos and beach cottages may be rented through local realtors by the week or month. For price ranges, see Charts 1 (B) and 2 (B) in Chapter 1.

Beaufort **The Beaufort House Restaurant.** Fresh seafood (including such
Dining specials as seafood supreme and shrimp-and-crabmeat au gra-
★ tin), steaks, and homemade desserts are the main agenda at this contemporary dockside eatery. *Boardwalk, tel. 919/728–7541. MC, V. Closed Jan.–Feb. Moderate.*

Lodging **Langdon House.** Sleep with history surrounded by antiques, at
★ this B&B built in 1733. Sumptuous southern breakfasts are created by host Jimm Prest. *135 Craven St., 28516, tel. 919/728–5499. 4 rooms. No credit cards. Expensive.*

Duck **Sanderling Inn Resort.** For special pampering, come to this re-
Dining and Lodging mote beachside resort. Though the inn was built in 1985 and of-
★ fers modern amenities, its stately, mellow look makes it appear older. The restaurant, housed in an old lifesaving station, offers such delicacies as crab cakes, roast Carolina duckling with black-cherry sauce, and fricassee of shrimp. *1461 Duck Rd., Box 319Y, 27949, tel. and fax 919/261–4111. 60 rooms, 28 efficiencies. Facilities: restaurant, lounge, pool, tennis courts, health club, golf privileges, bicycles. D, MC, V. Expensive.*

Kill Devil Hills
Dining

Etheridge Seafood Restaurant. The fish comes straight from the boat to the kitchen at this family-owned restaurant decorated with fishing gear. *U.S. 158 Bypass at Milepost 9.5, tel. 919/441–2645. No reservations. MC, V. Closed Nov.–Feb. Moderate.*

Lodging

The Figurehead Bed and Breakfast Inn. Fly a kite, ride a bike, or relax in a beach chair at this weathered beach house on the Albermarle Sound, minutes from the ocean and several restaurants. *417 Helga St., 27948, tel. 919/441–6929 or 800/221–6929. 3 rooms. MC, V. Expensive.*

Manteo
Dining

The Weeping Radish Brewery and Restaurant. This Bavarian-style restaurant serves Hoplen beer, brewed on the premises, and German cuisine. Tours of the brewery are given upon request. *U.S. 64, tel. 919/473–1157. Reservations advised. MC, V. Moderate.*

Lodging

Tranquil House Inn. This 19th-century-style waterfront B&B is only a few steps from shops and restaurants, and bikes are provided for adventures beyond. Guests gather about the library fireplace. *Queen Elizabeth Ave., Box 2045, 27954, tel. 919/473–1404 or 800/458–7069. 28 rooms. AE, D, DC, MC, V. Expensive.*

Morehead City
Dining
★

Sanitary Fish Market and Restaurant. In business for over a half century, this basic, pine-paneled institution built out over the edge of Bogue Sound continues to please with heaping platters of fresh seafood—served fried, steamed, or broiled, with hush puppies, cole slaw, and french fries. *501 Evans St., tel. 919/247–3111. MC, V. Closed Dec.–Jan. Moderate.*

Nags Head
Dining
★

Lance's Seafood Bar & Market. You can contemplate the fishing and hunting memorabilia while you dine on steamed or raw seafood. Shells are disposed of through the hole in the table. *U.S. 158 Bypass, Milepost 14, tel. 919/441–7501. MC, V. Moderate.*

Lodging

First Colony Inn. Enjoy the view of the nearby ocean from the veranda of this historic B&B, which was built in 1932. Rooms have four-poster or canopy beds, armoires, and English antiques. *6720 Virginia Dare Trail, 27959, tel. 919/441–2343 or 800/368–9390; fax 919/441–9234. 26 rooms, 4 suites. Facilities: pool, afternoon tea. AE, D, MC, V. Moderate–Expensive.*

New Bern
Dining
★

The Harvey Mansion Restaurant and Lounge. Swiss owner-chef Beat Zuttel excels in regional and international award-winning dishes. Original art decorates the walls of her restaurants, in a 1797 house near the confluence of the Trent and Neuse rivers. *221 Tryon Palace Dr., tel. 919/638–3205. Reservations advised. MC, V. Closed Sun. Moderate–Expensive.*

Lodging
★

Harmony House Inn. At this historic B&B, convenient to all the attractions, you can sleep in spacious rooms, furnished with a mixture of antiques and reproductions, where Yankee soldiers stayed during the Civil War. The inn serves a hot breakfast buffet. *215 Pollock St., 28560, tel. 919/636–3810 or 800/392–6231. 9 rooms. AE, MC, V. Expensive.*

Ocracoke
Dining and Lodging

The Island Inn and Dining Room. This well-worn turn-of-the-century inn has third-floor rooms with cathedral ceilings and lovely views. The dining room is known for oyster omelets, crab cakes, and hush puppies. *Rte. 12, Box 9, 27960, tel. 919/928–4351 (inn) or 919/928–7821 (dining room). 35 rooms. Facilities: outdoor pool. MC, V. Inexpensive–Moderate.*

Southport
Dining and Lodging

Bald Head Island. A self-contained, carless community complete with grocery store, restaurant, and golf course, reached by ferry from Southport, the island evokes images of Cape Cod with its modern, bleached-wood villas and shingled cottages. Guests travel the island on foot, bicycles, or in golf carts. *Bald Head Island 28461, tel. 919/457–5000 or 800/234–1666; fax 919/ 457–9232. 100 units. Facilities: restaurant, pool, canoes, bicycles, golf, sailing, tennis, fishing, nature walks. AE, MC, V. Expensive.*

Wilmington
Dining
★

The Pilot House. Resembling an elegant southern porch overlooking the Cape Fear River, with nautical prints, lanterns, and linen tablecloths, this Chandler's Wharf restaurant is known for its seafood, pastas, and vegetables, as well as for Sunday brunches. You can dine indoors or on a riverside deck. *2 Ann St., tel. 910/343–0200. Reservations advised. AE, D, MC, V. Inexpensive–Moderate.*

Lodging

Blockade Runner Resort Hotel. This two-story, 1960s-vintage oceanside complex is widely known for both its food and its service. Guest rooms, which open off the exterior balcony, overlook either the inlet or the ocean. The Ocean Terrace Restaurant serves an especially popular Saturday seafood buffet and Sunday brunch. *275 Waynick Blvd., Wrightsville Beach 28480, tel. 910/256–2251 or 800/541–1161; fax 910/256–2251. 150 rooms. Facilities: restaurant (reservations advised), pool, health spa, meeting rooms, sailing center, bike rentals, golf privileges. AE, D, DC, MC, V. Expensive.*

★ **Inn at St. Thomas Court.** In the heart of the historic district, this trio of former commercial buildings (including a convent) has been transformed into luxurious studios and suites decorated in turn-of-the-century style. The owners offer private sailing lessons. *101 S. 2nd St., 28401, tel. 910/343–1800 or 800/ 525–0909; fax 910/251–1149. AE, D, DC, MC, V. Expensive.*

Campgrounds

Camping is permitted in designated areas of the **Cape Hatteras National Seashore** from mid-April through mid-October and at **Carolina Beach State Park** near Wilmington (*see* National and State Parks, *above*). Private campgrounds are scattered all along the coast. For more information, contact the state's division of tourism (*see* Visitor Information, *above*).

The Arts and Nightlife

In Wilmington, plays and concerts take place in **Thalian Hall Center for the Performing Arts** (tel. 910/343–3664 or 800/523–2820), built in 1855–58 and recently restored. A favorite haunt on the waterfront is the **Ice House** (tel. 910/371–2890), an indoor-outdoor bar featuring live rhythm and blues.

On Roanoke Island, visitors can take in **"Pastime with Goode Companie,"** a five-course Renaissance dinner show at the Elizabethan Inn in Manteo. *Tel. 919/473–2101 or 800/346–2466. Admission: $25 adults, $14 children. Closed Nov.–mid-June and Sat.–Mon. mid-June–Aug.*

Elsewhere in the State

Biltmore Estate

Getting There You can get to Asheville via I–40E or W. I–26 begins in Asheville and heads south, connecting with I–240, which circles the city. U.S. 23/19A runs through the city.

What to See and Do I–40E to U.S. 25 leads to the astonishing **Biltmore Estate,** built as the home of George Vanderbilt in the 1890s. The 255-room French Renaissance–style château, designed by Richard Morris Hunt, is now a museum filled with priceless antiques and art treasures. The grounds, landscaped by Frederick Law Olmsted, include 17 acres of elaborate gardens and a state-of-the-art winery that occupies the former dairy. *Exit 50 off I–40E, tel. 704/543–2961 or 800/543–2961. Admission: $21.95 adults, $16.50 children. Live music at sunset Fri.–Sat. late May–Aug.; Christmas candlelight tours late Nov.–early Jan.*

High Country

Getting There The High Country—the Boone–Blowing Rock–Banner Elk area—is reached off I–40 via U.S. 321 at Hickory, Rte. 181 at Morganton, and U.S. 221 at Marion. U.S. 421 is a major east-west artery. The Blue Ridge Parkway bisects the region, traveling over mountain crests in the High Country.

What to See and Do This once-remote region in the Blue Ridge Mountains now offers a wealth of sports and family activities. **Blowing Rock** refers to both a quiet mountain village and the nearby 4,000-foot rock for which it was named. Visitors to this looming outcrop enjoy views from its observation tower (tel. 704/295–7111) and its gardens of mountain laurel and other native plants.

North of here on U.S. 321 is **Tweetsie Railroad,** a theme park built around a historic narrow-gauge train. Besides train rides, the park offers gold panning, saloon shows, and a petting zoo. *Tel. 704/264–9061 or 800/526–5740. Admission: $12.95 adults, $10.95 children. Closed Nov.–Apr.*

About 10 mi south via the Blue Ridge Parkway, **Grandfather's Mountain** soars 6,000 feet and affords sweeping views of the High Country from its Swinging Bridge. The **Natural History Museum** here features exhibits on native flora and fauna, and the **Environmental Habitat** is home to bald eagles, deer, cougars, and black bears. *Tel. 704/733–4337 or 800/468–7325. Admission charged. Closed weekdays Dec.–Feb.*

The High Country offers five alpine ski areas, plus many cross-country trails. Downhill skiing is available at **Appalachian Ski Mountain** at Blowing Rock (tel. 704/295–7828); **Hound Ears Club** (tel. 704/963–4321) and **Ski Hawksnest** (tel. 704/963–6561) at Foscoe; **Ski Beech** at Beech Mountain (tel. 704/387–2011); and **Sugar Mountain** at Banner Elk (tel. 704/898–4521).

SOUTH CAROLINA

By Carol Timblin

Capital	Columbia
Population	3,560,000
Motto	While I Breathe, I Hope
	Prepared in Mind and Resources
State Bird	Carolina wren
State Flower	Yellow jessamine

Visitor Information

South Carolina Division of Tourism (1205 Pendleton St., Box 71, Columbia 29202, tel. 803/734–0235). **Welcome centers:** U.S. 17, near Little River; I–95, near Dillon, Santee and Lake Marion, and Hardeeville; I–77, near Fort Mill; I–85, near Blacksburg and Fair Play; I–26, near Landrum; I–20, at North Augusta; and U.S. 301, near Allendale.

Scenic Drives

The **Cherokee Foothills Scenic Hwy.** (Rte. 11), passing small towns, peach orchards, and historical sites, traverses 130 mi of Blue Ridge foothills in the northwest corner of the state. The **Ashley River Road** (Rte. 61), which parallels the river for about 11 mi north of Charleston, leads to South Carolina's most famous plantations and gardens.

National and State Parks

National Parks
At **Cowpens National Battlefield** (Rte. 11, Box 308, Chesnee 29323, tel. 803/461–2828), the American patriots soundly defeated the British in 1781; exhibits in the visitor center explain the battle. **Kings Mountain National Military Park** (I–85 near Blacksburg, Box 40, King's Mountain, NC 28086, tel. 803/936–7922), where the ragtag patriot forces whipped the redcoats in 1780, offers exhibits and dioramas depicting the famous battle. A paved self-guided trail leads through the battlefield. For white-water enthusiasts, the **Chattooga National Wild and Scenic River** (U.S. Forestry Service, 1835 Assembly St., Columbia 29201, tel. 803/765–5222) forms the border between South Carolina and Georgia for 40 mi, dropping more than 493 feet on its journey from the Blue Ridge Mountains in North Carolina.

State Parks
Several of South Carolina's 48 state parks operate like resort communities, with everything from deluxe accommodations to golf. **Hickory Knob State Resort Park** (Rte. 1, Box 199-B, McCormick 29835, tel. 803/391–2450), on Strom Thurmond Lake, offers fishing, golf, and skeet shooting. **Devil's Fork State Park** (161 Holcombe Circle, Salem 29676, tel. 803/944–2639), which opened in 1991, has luxurious accommodations overlooking beautiful Lake Jocassee. **Calhoun Falls State Park** (Rte. 81, Calhoun Falls 29628, tel. 803/447–8267), which opened last year, features a full-service marina, a campground, nature trails, and a picnic area.

The state's coastal parks—known for broad beaches, camping facilities, and nature preserves—draw the most visitors. They include **Huntington Beach State Park** (Murrells Inlet 29576, tel. 803/237–4440), **Myrtle Beach State Park** (U.S. 17, Myrtle Beach 29577, tel. 803/238–5325), and **Hunting Island State Park** (St. Helena Island 29920, tel. 803/838–2011). For more information, contact the **South Carolina Division of State Parks** (1205 Pendleton St., Columbia 29201, tel. 803/734–0156).

Charleston

Charleston has withstood three centuries of epidemics, earthquakes, fires, and hurricanes to become one of the South's best-preserved and most beloved cities. Residents have rescued and restored block after block of old downtown homes and commercial buildings, as well as more than 180 historic churches. Each spring the city celebrates its heritage with symphony galas in stately drawing rooms, plantation oyster roasts, candlelight tours of historic homes and churches, and the renowned Spoleto Festival USA, a massive celebration of the arts staged in streets and performance halls throughout the city.

Tourist Information

Charleston: Trident Convention and Visitors Bureau (Box 975, 29402, tel. 803/853–8000).

Arriving and Departing

By Plane **Charleston International Airport** (tel. 803/767–1100) is served by several major domestic carriers. Taxis to downtown cost $14. Hotels also provide shuttle service from the airport. It's a 12-mi drive along I–26 east to downtown Charleston.

By Car I–26 traverses the state from northwest to southeast and terminates at Charleston. U.S. 17, a north–south coastal route, passes through the city.

By Boat Boaters arriving at Charleston Harbor via the Intracoastal Waterway may dock at **City Marina** (Lockwood Blvd., tel. 803/724–7357) or at the Isle of Palms' **Wild Dunes Yacht Harbor** (tel. 803/886–5100). Marinas sell detailed maps.

Train Station **Amtrak** (4565 Gaynor Ave., N. Charleston, tel. 803/744–8263).

Bus Station **Greyhound** (3610 Dorchester Rd., N. Charleston, tel. 803/722–7721).

Getting Around Charleston

You can park your car and walk in the city's historic district, but you'll need a car to see attractions in outlying areas. South Carolina Electric and Gas Company provides bus service within the city and to North Charleston, and operates the trolley-style Downtown Area Shuttle buses, called **DASH** (tel. 803/724–7420). Fare on the latter is 75¢, or $1 for a one-day pass. Taxi companies include **Yellow Cab** (tel. 803/577–6565). Another option that's very popular here is a horse-drawn carriage tour. Guides are generally very knowledgeable and often provide unusual snippets of history and humor. Tours conducted by the **Old South Carriage Company,** whose guides wear Confederate uniforms, depart from the corner of Anson and North

Market streets; **Carolina Carriage Company** tours leave from Market Square.

Exploring Charleston

You can get a quick orientation to the city by viewing *Forever Charleston,* a 24-minute multimedia presentation (admission charged) shown at the **Visitor Reception and Transportation Center** (375 Meeting St., tel. 803/853–8000). Across from the center (where there's free two-hour parking) is the **Charleston Museum,** founded in 1773 and the oldest city museum in the country. Now housed in a $6 million contemporary complex, the collection includes Charleston silver, fashions, toys, and snuff-boxes, as well as exhibits on natural history, archaeology, and ornithology. *360 Meeting St., tel. 803/722–2996. Admission charged.*

Also part of the museum are three historic homes. The **Joseph Manigault House** (350 Meeting St.), just down the street, was designed in 1803 and is noted for its carved-wood mantels and elaborate plasterwork. Furnishings are British, French, and American antiques, including rare tricolor Wedgwood pieces. The **Aiken-Rhett Mansion** (48 Elizabeth St.), a few blocks north, was the headquarters of Confederate general P. G. T. Beauregard during the Civil War. Its ornate interior is furnished in a variety of 19th-century styles. Many blocks south, the **Heyward-Washington House** (87 Church St.) was the residence of President George Washington during his 1791 visit. The mansion is notable for fine period furnishings by local craftsmen and includes Charleston's only restored 18th-century kitchen open to visitors. You can purchase a combined ticket for admission to the museum and all three houses.

The heart of Charleston is the **Old City Market,** between Meeting and East Bay streets, with restaurants, shops, and open-air produce stands. Here you can buy vegetables, fruits, benne (sesame) seed wafers, sweetgrass baskets (*see* Shopping, *below*), and other local craft items.

South of the market, **Dock Street Theatre** (135 Church St., tel. 803/723–5648) combines the reconstructed early Georgian playhouse that originally stood on the site and the 1809 Old Planter's Hotel. At the corner of Meeting and Broad streets is **St. Michael's Episcopal Church** (tel. 803/723–0603), modeled on London's St. Martin's-in-the-Fields. Completed in 1761, this beautiful structure is Charleston's oldest surviving church.

Ft. Sumter National Monument, a man-made island in Charleston Harbor, is where the first shot of the Civil War was fired, on April 12, 1861. National Park Service rangers conduct free tours of the restored structure, which includes a historical museum with displays and dioramas. To get here, take a boat from Patriots Point (*see* What to See and Do with Children, *below*) or the Municipal Marina on Lockwood Boulevard. *Tel. 803/722–1691. Charge for boat ride.*

Plantations, Parks, and Gardens

Charleston is famous for its public parks, magnificent plantations, and secret gardens that lie hidden behind the walls of private homes. **White Point Gardens,** on the point of the narrow Battery peninsula bounded by the Ashley and Cooper rivers, is

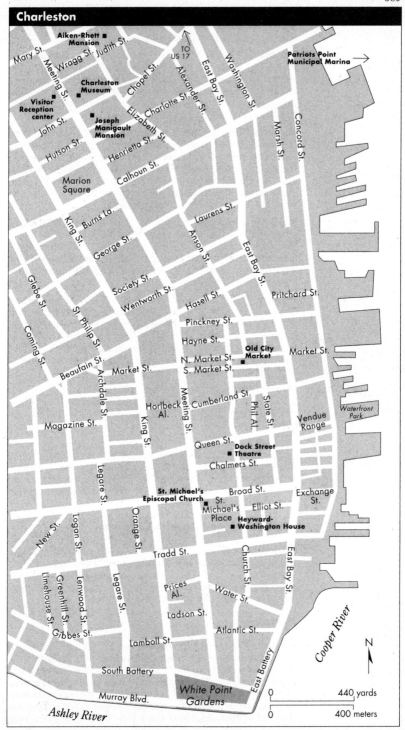

Charleston

Aiken-Rhett Mansion

Mary St.
Meeting St.
Wragg St.
Judith St.

TO
US 17

Patriots Point
Municipal Marina

Chapel St.
Charlotte St.
Alexander St.
East Bay St.
Washington St.

Charleston
Museum

Visitor
Reception
center

John St.

Elizabeth St.

Joseph
Manigault
Mansion

Hutson St.

Henrietta St.

Calhoun St.

Concord St.

Marsh St.

Marion
Square

Burns La.

King St.

George St.

Laurens St.

Anson St.

East Bay St.

Glebe St.

St. Philip St.

Society St.

Wentworth St.

Hasell St.

Pritchard St.

Coming St.

Pinckney St.

Hayne St.

Beaufain St.

Archdale St.

Market St.

N. Market St.
S. Market St.

Old City
Market

Market St.

Horlbeck
Al.

Cumberland St.

Phil Al.

State St.

Magazine St.

King St.

Meeting St.

Queen St.

Dock Street
Theatre

Vendue
Range

Waterfront
Park

Legare St.

Chalmers St.

St. Michael's
Episcopal Church

Broad St.

St.
Michael's
Place

Elliot St.

Exchange
St.

New St.

Logan St.

Orange St.

Heyward-
Washington House

Tradd St.

Church St.

East Bay St.

Limehouse St.
Greenhill St.
Lenwood St.

Legare St.

Prices
Al.

Water St.

Gibbes St.

Ladson St.

Atlantic St.

Cooper River

Lamboll St.

South Battery

East Battery

N

White Point
Gardens

Murray Blvd.

Ashley River

0   440 yards

0   400 meters

the most popular gathering spot in the city. The new **Waterfront Park**, on the Cooper River, features a fishing pier, fountains, and landscaped gardens.

Drayton Hall (tel. 803/766–0188), built between 1738 and 1742, is 8 mi west of downtown via Ashley River Road (Rte. 61). Considered the nation's finest example of Georgian Palladian architecture, the plantation house is unfurnished to better highlight the original plaster moldings, opulent hand-carved woodwork, and other ornamental details.

Magnolia Plantation and Gardens (tel. 803/571–1266) is 3 mi farther on Rte. 61. Begun in 1686, the gardens boast one of the largest collections of azaleas and camellias in North America. Nature lovers may canoe through the 125-acre Waterfowl Refuge, see the 30-acre Audubon Swamp Garden along boardwalks and bridges, explore 500 acres of wildlife trails, and enjoy the petting zoo and minihorse ranch.

Middleton Place (tel. 803/556–6020 or 800/782–3608), 4 mi north of Magnolia Plantation on Rte. 61, is the site of the nation's oldest landscape gardens, dating from 1741. Much of the mansion was destroyed during the Civil War, but a restored wing houses impressive collections of silver, furniture, paintings, and historical documents.

If **Boone Hall Plantation** (tel. 803/884–4371), 8 mi north of Charleston on U.S. 17, looks familiar to you, it may be because of the plantation's avenue of oaks—said to have been the inspiration for the painting that MGM filmed to represent Tara in *Gone with the Wind*. Visitors may explore the gardens, the first floor of the mansion, and the original slave quarters. Lunch is served in the old cotton gin.

Charles Towne Landing State Park (1500 Old Town Rd., tel. 803/556–4450) is built on the site of a 1670 settlement. It includes a reconstructed village and fortifications, a replica of a 17th-century sailing vessel, gardens with bike trails and walking paths, and an animal park.

I–26N leads to **Cypress Gardens** (U.S. 52, tel. 803/553–0515), a swamp garden created from what was once the freshwater reserve of a vast rice plantation. You can explore the inky waters by boat or walk along paths lined with moss-draped cypress trees and flowering bushes.

What to See and Do with Children

Patriots Point (U.S. 17, tel. 803/884–2727 or 800/327–5723) in Mount Pleasant is the world's largest naval and maritime museum. Berthed here are the aircraft carrier *Yorktown*, the nuclear ship *Savannah*, the World War II submarine *Clamagore*, the cutter *Ingham*, and the destroyer *Laffey*.

Shopping

The three-block **Old City Market** (*see* Exploring Charleston, *above*) yields colorful produce and varied gifts, including the beautiful sweetgrass baskets unique to this area. The craft was originally imported by slaves from Africa and is now practiced by only a handful of their descendants. The baskets come in all sizes and range in price from $10 to more than $100. (They are also sold at open-air stands along U.S. 17 north of town, near

Mount Pleasant.) Elegant antiques shops line King Street,
among them **Geo. C. Birlant & Co.** (191 King St., tel. 803/722–
3842), with 18th- and 19th-century English selections. **Livingston Antiques,** offering period furniture, clocks, and other
items, has two locations (163 King St., tel. 803/723–9697; 2137
Savannah Hwy., tel. 803/556–6261). **Historic Charleston Reproductions** (105 Broad St., tel. 803/723–8292) has superb reproductions. Among the town's chic art galleries are the **Birds I
View Gallery** (119–A Church St., tel. 803/723–1276), with bird
paintings and prints by noted artists, and the **Virginia Fouche
Bolton Art Gallery** (127 Meeting St., tel. 803/577–9351), selling
paintings and limited-edition lithographs of Charleston scenes.

Beaches

South Carolina's climate allows swimming from April through
October. There are public beaches at **Beachwalker Park,** on
Kiawah Island; **Folly Beach County Park** and **Folly Beach** on
Folly Island; the **Isle of Palms;** and **Sullivan's Island.** Resorts
with private beaches include **Fairfield Ocean Ridge** on Edisto
Island; **Kiawah Island Resort** (*see* Lodging, *below*); **Seabrook Is-
land;** and **Wild Dunes Resort** on the Isle of Palms. For more in-
formation, contact Charleston's visitors bureau (*see* Tourist
Information, *above*).

Dining

Best known for its Low Country specialties—she-crab soup,
sautéed shrimp, grits, and variations on pecan pie—Charleston is also a hotbed of a new American cuisine that blends
down-home cooking with haute cuisine. For price ranges, see
Chart 1 (B) in Chapter 1.

Expensive **Restaurant Million.** French nouvelle cuisine is served on Li-
moges china in a building dating from 1788. The rack of lamb is
outstanding. *2 Unity Alley, tel. 803/577–7472. Reservations
required. Jacket and tie required. AE, DC, MC, V. Closed Sun.*

★ **Robert's of Charleston Dinner Restaurant.** To a background of
light-operetta tunes sung by Chef Robert Dickson, diners enjoy a fixed-price ($70) six-course meal that may include lobster
pâté, sliced duck breast, beef, or seafood. The price includes
wine and gratuity. *Planters Inn, Market and Meeting Sts., tel.
803/577–7565 or 800/729–0094. Reservations required. Jacket
and tie required. AE, MC, V. No lunch; closed Sun. and usually Mon. Weekdays, 1 seating at 8 PM; Sat., seatings at 6 and 8.*

Moderate **Barbadoes Room.** Seafood dishes, such as sautéed jumbo
shrimp and scallops with creamy mushroom sauce, are served
in this large, airy, plant-filled space overlooking a garden. The
generous southern-style breakfast and brunch are popular.
*Mills House Hotel, 115 Meeting St., tel. 803/577–2400. Reser-
vations required for Sun. and holiday brunch, advised for dinner. Jacket and tie advised. AE, D, DC, MC, V.*

★ **Gaulart and Maliclet French Cafe.** This chic, upbeat café serves
ethnic and bistro French food. The menu of soups, salads, and
sandwiches is enlivened by such evening specials as coq au vin
and paella. *98 Broad St., tel. 803/577–9797. AE, DC, MC, V.*

Inexpensive **Magnolias—Uptown/DownSouth.** Housed in an 1823 warehouse
★ and decorated with a magnolia theme, the restaurant is prized
for its Low Country fare, which includes grilled dolphin-fish fil-

let topped with creamed crabmeat and fresh herbs. *185 E. Bay St., tel. 803/577–7771. Reservations advised. AE, MC, V.*

Mike Calder's Deli & Pub. Soups, salads, sandwiches, daily specials, and 12 different draft beers are offered in an antique setting, once a pharmacy in the historic district. *288 King St., tel. 803/577–0123. No reservations. D, MC, V.*

Shem Creek Bar & Grill. This pleasant dockside spot is popular for its oyster bar and light fare, as well as a wide variety of seafood entrées. A menu highlight is the pot of steamed lobsters, clams, oysters, and sausages with melted lemon butter or hot cocktail sauce. *508 Mill St., Mount Pleasant, tel. 803/884–8102. No reservations. AE, D, MC, V.*

Lodging

Hotels and inns on the peninsula are generally more expensive than those in outlying areas of the city. Rates tend to increase during festivals, when reservations are essential. During Visitors' Appreciation Days (mid-Nov.–mid-Feb.), rates drop by as much as 50%. World-class resorts are located nearby, including Kiawah Island and Seabrook Island Resorts. For price ranges, see Chart 2 (A) in Chapter 1.

Very Expensive ★ **The John Rutledge House Inn.** The 1763 main house, built by a signer of the U.S. Constitution, and two carriage houses (each with four rooms) opened in 1989 as a luxury B&B inn. Rooms feature high ceilings, plaster molding, and wood floors, and are decorated with antiques and four-poster beds. Complimentary wine and tea are served in the ballroom. *116 Broad St., 29401, tel. 803/723–7999 or 800/476–9741; fax 803/720–2615. 19 rooms. Facilities: Continental breakfast. AE, MC, V.*

Kiawah Island Resort. This plush resort on 10,000 wooded acres offers accommodations in rooms, suites, or villas. All are decorated with light colors and have balconies with ocean or forest views. *21 mi from Charleston via U.S. 17S; Box 12357, Charleston 29422, tel. 803/768–2121 or 800/654–2924; fax 803/768–6099. 150 rooms, 48 suites, 300 villas. Facilities: 3 restaurants, lounge, championship golf course, tennis courts, beaches, water sports. AE, DC, MC, V.*

Expensive **Brasington House.** The innkeepers love spoiling their guests with wine and cheese in the afternoon, evening chocolates and liqueurs, and family-style breakfasts in the dining room. This elegant B&B in the Ansonborough neighborhood is within walking distance of the visitors center and Old City Market. *328 E. Bay St., 29401, tel. 803/722–1274 or 800/722–1274. 4 rooms. No smoking. MC, V.*

Hawthorn Suites at the Market. This deluxe hotel features a restored entrance portico from an 1874 bank, a refurbished 1866 firehouse, and three lush gardens. The spacious suites, decorated with 18th-century reproductions and canopy beds, include full kitchens or wet bars. *181 Church St., 29401, tel. 803/577–2644 or 800/527–1133; fax 803/577–2697. 17 rooms, 164 suites. Facilities: full breakfast, afternoon refreshments, fitness center, pool, valet parking. AE, D, DC, MC, V.*

Mills House Hotel. This luxurious property in the historic district is a reconstruction of a 19th-century hotel that once stood on the site. Antique furnishings and period decor lend charm to rooms and public areas. The Barbadoes Room (*see* Dining, *above*) serves some of the city's best seafood. *115 Meeting St., 29401, tel. 803/577–2400 or 800/465–4329; fax 803/722–2112.*

215 rooms. Facilities: restaurant, 2 lounges, pool. AE, D, DC, MC, V.

★ **Omni Hotel at Charleston Place.** Rooms are furnished with period reproductions at this graceful low rise in the historic district near upscale boutiques and specialty shops. Louis's Charleston Grill, with its mahogany-paneled walls and wrought-iron chandeliers, is an elegant backdrop for such dishes as pan-seared scallops with corn sauce and buttermilk tart with raspberries. *130 Market St., 29401, tel. 803/722–4900; fax 803/722–0728. 394 rooms, 46 suites. Facilities: 2 restaurants, 2 lounges, fitness center, indoor pool, sauna, concierge floor with complimentary food and drink service. AE, D, DC, MC, V.*

Moderate **Comfort Inn Riverview.** Only blocks from the historic district is this seven-story inn, whose yellow-brick exterior is in keeping with the historic character of the area. Inside, furnishings are contemporary, with a teal-and-mauve color scheme. *144 Bee St., 29401, tel. 803/577–2224; fax 803/577–9001. 123 rooms. Facilities: Continental breakfast, pool. AE, D, DC, MC, V.*

Inexpensive **Hampton Inn–Historic District.** Opened in 1992, this downtown property features hardwood floors in the lobby, extra-large guest rooms furnished in period reproductions, a courtyard garden, and a pool. *345 Meeting St., 29403, tel. 803/723–4000 or 800/426–7866; fax 803/722–3725. 171 rooms. Facilities: Continental breakfast, pool. AE, D, DC, MC, V.*

Motels

Days Inn–Historic District (155 Meeting St., 29401, tel. 803/722–8411 or 800/325–2525; fax 803/723–5361), 124 rooms, restaurant, pool; moderate. **Heart of Charleston Quality Inn** (125 Calhoun St., 29401, tel. 803/722–3391 or 800/845–2504; fax 803/577–0361), 126 rooms, restaurant, lounge, pool; moderate.

The Arts and Nightlife

The Arts **Spoleto Festival USA** (Box 157, 29402, tel. 803/722–2764), a world-class annual celebration founded by maestro Gian Carlo Menotti in 1977, showcases opera, dance, theater, symphonic and chamber music performances, jazz, and the visual arts from late May through early June. The **Southeastern Wildlife Exposition** (tel. 803/723–1757 or 803/723–1748), held each February, features art by renowned wildlife artists.

Nightlife Top Charleston-area music clubs include **Windjammer** (tel. 803/886–8596), on the Isle of Palms, an oceanfront spot featuring live rock music; and **Henry's Restaurant** (tel. 803/723–4363) for live jazz on weekends. You can find authentic Irish music at **Tommy Condon's Irish Pub & Restaurant** (tel. 803/577–3818). Other options are watching films from around the world at **Stage One Cinema** (tel. 803/722–1900) or dining and dancing on the luxury yacht *Spirit of Charleston* (tel. 803/722–2628).

The Coast

The South Carolina coast is a land of extremes. The Grand Strand, from the state's northeast border to historic George-town, is one of the East Coast's family-vacation megacenters and the state's top tourist area. It offers 60 mi of beaches, championship golf courses, campgrounds, seafood restaurants, giant shopping malls, factory outlets, and amusements. The Low Country comprises the area between Georgetown and the state's southeast boundary, including Beaufort, as well as the barrier islands of Hilton Head, Edisto, and Fripp. Beaufort is a gracious antebellum town with a compact historic district of lavish 18th- and 19th-century homes. Hilton Head's exclusive resorts and genteel good life make it one of the coast's most popular vacation getaways.

Tourist Information

Beaufort: Chamber of Commerce (Box 910, 1006 Bay St., 29901–0910, tel. 803/524–3163). **Georgetown:** Chamber of Commerce and Information Center (U.S. 17, Box 1776, 29442, tel. 803/546–8436 or 800/777–7705). **Hilton Head Island:** Chamber of Commerce (Box 5647, 29938, tel. 803/785–3673). **Myrtle Beach:** Chamber of Commerce and Information Center (1301 N. Kings Hwy., Box 2115, 29578–2115, tel. 803/626–7444 or 800/356–3016, ext. 136).

Getting There

By Plane The **Myrtle Beach Jetport** (tel. 803/448–1589) is served by USAir, American, and Delta's Atlantic Southeast Airlines (tel. 803/626–2338 or 800/282–3424). **Hilton Head Island Airport** is served by American Eagle and **USAir Express** (tel. 803/681–8244). The **Savannah airport** (*see* Georgia) is about an hour's drive from Hilton Head.

By Car Major interstates connect with U.S. 17, the principal north–south coastal route.

By Train **Amtrak** does not make stops in this area, although several of its stops are within driving distance: Florence is about 70 mi northwest of the Grand Strand; Yemassee, about 22 mi northwest of Beaufort; and Savannah, about 40 mi southwest of Hilton Head.

By Bus **Greyhound** serves Myrtle Beach (tel. 803/448–2471), Beaufort (tel. 803/524–4646), and Savannah (tel. 912/232–2135).

By Boat The South Carolina coast is accessible by boat via the Intra-coastal Waterway. At Myrtle Beach, you may dock at **Hague Marina** (tel. 803/293–2141). Hilton Head has several marinas, including **Shelter Cove Marina** (tel. 803/842–7001), **Harbour Town Marina** (tel. 803/671–2704), and **Schilling Boathouse** (tel. 803/689–5873).

Exploring the Coast

With its high-rise beachfront hotels, nightlife, and amusement parks, **Myrtle Beach** is the hub of the Grand Strand. Downtown has a festive look, with its T-shirt shops, ice-cream and fudge parlors, and various amusements, including the **Myrtle Beach**

Pavilion and Amusement Park (9th Ave. N and Ocean Blvd., tel. 803/448–6456), **Ripleys Believe It or Not Museum** (901 N. Ocean Blvd., tel. 803/448–2331), and the **Myrtle Beach National Wax Museum** (1000 N. Ocean Blvd., tel. 803/448–9921). Attractions are open daily from mid-March through early October, but the schedule varies the rest of the year; all charge admission.

From Myrtle Beach, U.S. 17S leads to **Murrells Inlet,** a picturesque fishing village where you'll find fishing charters as well as some of the most popular seafood restaurants on the Strand. **Brookgreen Gardens** (tel. 803/237–4218; admission charged), a few miles farther south, are set on four former Colonial rice plantations. Begun in 1931, the gardens include more than 2,000 plant species, as well as more than 500 sculptures, including works by Frederic Remington and Daniel Chester French. Several miles farther on U.S. 17S is **Pawleys Island.** Four mi long and ½ mi wide, it's characterized by weathered old summer cottages nestled in the groves of oleander and oak. The famed Pawleys Island hammocks have been made by hand here since 1880.

On the shores of Winyah Bay at the end of the Grand Strand is **Georgetown.** Founded in 1729, it soon became the center of America's Colonial rice empire. Today tourists enjoy its quaint waterfront and historic homes and churches. The **Rice Museum** (Front and Screven Sts., tel. 803/546–7423; admission charged) traces the history of rice cultivation through maps, tools, and dioramas. It is housed in the former market-meeting building, a graceful structure topped by an 1842 clock and tower.

Twelve miles south of Georgetown on U.S. 17 is **Hopsewee Plantation,** noted for its moss-draped live oaks, magnolias, tree-size camellia shrubs, and manor house. *Tel. 803/546–7891. Admission charged. Closed Nov.–Feb., except by appointment, and Sat.–Mon. Mar.–Oct.*

About 18 mi east of U.S. 17 on U.S. 21 (about 70 mi southeast of Charleston) is the waterfront town of **Beaufort.** Established in 1710, it achieved prosperity at the end of the 18th century, when Sea Island cotton became a major cash crop. A few lavish houses built by wealthy landowners and merchants have been converted into bed-and-breakfast inns or house museums; others are open for tours part of the year. The **Beaufort Museum** (713 Craven St., tel. 803/525–7471; closed Sun.), built in 1795 and remodeled in 1852, offers exhibits on prehistoric relics, Native American pottery, the Revolutionary and Civil wars, and decorative arts.

Hilton Head Island, a 42-sq-mi semitropical barrier island, was settled by cotton planters in the 1700s and developed as a resort destination in the 1960s and 1970s. Oak and pine woods, lagoons, and a temperate climate provide an incomparable environment for tennis, water sports, and world-class golf. Choice stretches of the island are occupied by resorts, many of which have shops, restaurants, marinas, and recreational facilities that are open to the public.

Hilton Head is also blessed with vast nature preserves, including the **Sea Pines Forest Preserve,** a 605-acre wilderness tract within the resort of the same name (tel. 803/671–7170; admission charged for nonguests). The preserve's most interesting site is the 3,400-year-old Native American shell ring. Also inside the bounds of Sea Pines are the **Stoney-Baynard Ruins,** the

site of a plantation dating from 1793 that is now being excavated.

What to See and Do with Children

Called the "Miniature Golf Capital of the World," Myrtle Beach
has courses on such themes as dinosaurs, tropical islands,
ghosts, and pirates, as well as **Hawaiian Rumble** (3210 Rte.
17S, tel. 803/272–7812), with a volcano that really shakes. **Myrtle Waves Water Park** (U.S. 17 Bypass and 10th Ave. N, Myrtle
Beach, tel. 803/448–1026) is one of many area water parks.

Shopping

The Grand Strand is a great place to find bargains. **Waccamaw
Pottery and Outlet Park** (U.S. 501 at the Waterway, Myrtle
Beach, tel. 803/236–0797) is one of the nation's largest outlet
centers. In North Myrtle Beach, shoppers head for the **Barefoot Landing** shopping center (tel. 803/272–4946). **The Hammock Shops at Pawleys Island** (tel. 803/237–8448) sell the
famous handmade hammocks. Hilton Head specialty shops include **Harbour Town Antiques** (tel. 803/671–5999), **Red Piano
Art Gallery** (tel. 803/785–2318), and, for shell and sand-dollar
jewelry, **The Bird's Nest** (tel. 803/785–3737).

Sports and Outdoor Activities

Biking Pedaling is popular along the firmly packed beaches and pathways of Hilton Head Island. Rentals are available at most hotels and resorts, and at such shops as **Harbour Town Bicycles**
(tel. 803/785–3546) and **South Beach Cycles** (tel. 803/671–7300).

Fishing Because offshore waters along the South Carolina coast are
warmed by the Gulf Stream, fishing is usually good from early
spring through December. The Grand Strand has several piers
and jetties, and fishing and sightseeing excursions depart from
Murrells Inlet, North Myrtle Beach, Little River, and the Intracoastal Waterway at Rte. 544. Fishing tournaments, are
very popular. On Hilton Head, you can fish, pick oysters, dig
for clams, or cast for shrimp. Licenses (required for fresh- and
saltwater fishing from a private boat) can be purchased at local
tackle shops.

Golf The Grand Strand has nearly 80 public courses, many of championship quality. **Golf Holiday** (tel. 803/448–5942 or 800/845–
4653) offers package plans throughout the year. Some of Hilton
Head's 22 courses are ranked among the world's top 100; several are open to the public, including **Palmetto Dunes** (tel. 803/
785–1138 or 803/785–1140), **Sea Pines** (tel. 803/671–2446 or 803/
671–2436), and **Port Royal and Shipyard plantations** (tel. 803/
689–5600). Sea Pines' **Harbour Town Golf Links** (tel. 803/842–
1892 or 800/845–6131) hosts the annual MCI Heritage Golf
Classic.

Horseback Riding On Hilton Head, trails wind through woods and nature preserves; horses can be rented at Sea Pines' **Lawton Stables** (tel.
803/671–2586).

Tennis There are more than 150 courts throughout the Strand, including free municipal courts in Myrtle Beach, North Myrtle
Beach, and Surfside Beach. Hilton Head offers more than 300

courts; four resorts on the island—**Sea Pines, Shipyard Plantation, Palmetto Dunes,** and **Port Royal**—are rated among the top 50 tennis destinations in the United States. Each April, top women professionals participate in the Family Circle Magazine Cup Tennis Tournament at Sea Pines Racquet Club.

Water Sports In Myrtle Beach, surfboards, Hobie Cats, Jet Skis, Windsurfers, and sailboats are for rent at **Downwind Sails** (Ocean Blvd. at 29th Ave. S, tel. 803/448–7245). On Hilton Head you can take windsurfing lessons and rent equipment from **Windsurfing Hilton Head,** located at Sea Pines Resort's South Beach Marina (tel. 803/671–2643) or Shelter Cove Plaza (tel. 803/686–6996).

Beaches

Almost all Grand Strand beaches are open to the public. The widest expanses are in North Myrtle Beach. The ocean side of Hilton Head Island features wide stretches of gently sloping white sand, extending the island's 12-mi length. Although resort beaches on Hilton Head are reserved for guests and residents, there are about 35 public beach entrances from Folly Field to South Forest Beach near Sea Pines.

Dining and Lodging

Freshwater and ocean fish and shellfish reign supreme throughout the region, from family-style restaurants—where they're served with hush puppies and cole slaw—to elegant resorts and upscale restaurants featuring haute cuisine. You can have your choice of hotels, cottages, villas, and high-rise condominiums. Attractive package plans are available between Labor Day and spring break. For price ranges, see Charts 1 (B) and 2 (A) in Chapter 1.

Beaufort **Rhett House Inn.** If this lovely 1820 Greek Revival house in the
Dining and Lodging center of town were on a plantation, you would think you'd been transported to Tara. Completely refurbished by the owners, the house is filled with antiques and original art. Continental breakfast and Low Country high tea in the afternoon are included in the tariff; dinner by reservation is extra. *1009 Craven St., 29902, tel. 803/524–9030; fax 803/524–1310. 9 rooms, 1 suite. MC, V. Expensive.*

Georgetown **1790 House.** Built in the center of town after the Revolution,
Lodging when Georgetown's rice culture was at its peak, this restored white Georgian house with a wraparound porch contains Colonial antique and reproduction furnishings. Guests are treated to gourmet breakfasts, evening refreshments, and the use of bicycles. *630 Highmarket St., 29440, tel. 803/546–4821. 6 rooms. AE, MC, V. Moderate–Expensive.*

Hilton Head Island **Harbourmaster's.** With sweeping views of the harbor, this spa-
Dining cious, multilevel restaurant offers such dishes as chateaubriand and New Zealand rack of lamb with brandy demiglaze. After dining, guests linger in Neptune's Lounge. *Shelter Cove Marina off U.S. 278, tel. 803/785–3030. Reservations required. Jacket required at dinner. AE, DC, MC, V. Closed Sun., Jan. Expensive.*
The Crazy Crab. This casual restaurant serves the freshest seafood on the island, prepared any way you like it. The steamed seafood pot and Crazy Crab boil are locally famous. *Harbour*

Town Yacht Basin, tel. 803/363–2722. No reservations. AE, DC, MC, V. No lunch. Inexpensive.

Lodging
★
The Westin Resort, Hilton Head Island. Among the island's most luxurious properties, this sprawling, horseshoe-shaped hotel enjoys a lushly landscaped oceanside setting. The expansive guest rooms have a pleasing mix of reproduction and contemporary furnishings. The Barony restaurant offers Low Country and Continental cuisine in an upscale French atmosphere. *Port Royal Plantation, 135 S. Port Royal Dr., 29928, tel. 803/681–4000; fax 803/681–1087. 415 rooms, 38 suites. Facilities: 3 restaurants, 2 lounges, health club, pool, beach, water sports. AE, D, DC, MC, V. Very Expensive.*

Marriott's Grande Ocean Resort. Though built as a time-share property in Sea Pines Plantation, this beautiful new condo development offers a limited number of rentals. The luxuriously furnished two-bedroom, two-bath villas come with kitchens and Jacuzzis. *51 S. Forest Beach Dr., 29928, tel. 803/785–2000 or 800/473–6674; fax 803/842–3413. Facilities: golf, tennis, pools. AE, MC, V. Expensive.*

Palmetto Dunes Resort. This huge complex includes the Hyatt Regency Hilton Head, the island's largest resort hotel. It recently completed a $32 million renovation, and rooms have been lavishly redecorated. The complex also includes the Hilton Resort, formerly the Mariner's Inn. Spacious oceanfront rooms here have kitchenettes and are colorfully decorated. *Hyatt: Box 6167, 29938, tel. 803/785–1234; fax 803/842–4695. 505 rooms. Hilton: Box 6165, 29938, tel. 803/842–8000; fax 803/842–4988. 324 rooms, 28 suites. Facilities: restaurants, lounges, health clubs, pools, golf courses, tennis courts. AE, D, DC, MC, V. Expensive.*

Murrells Inlet
Dining
Planter's Back Porch. Sip cool drinks in the spring house of a turn-of-the-century farmhouse, then enjoy seafood in a garden setting reminiscent of a 19th-century southern plantation. *U.S. 17 and Wachesaw Rd., tel. 803/651–5263 or 803/651–5544. AE, MC, V. Closed Dec.–mid-Feb. Moderate.*

Myrtle Beach
Dining
★
Sea Captain's House. This picturesque restaurant with nautical decor and a fireplace has sweeping ocean views. Home-baked breads and desserts accompany Low Country fare. *3002 N. Ocean Blvd., tel. 803/448–8082. AE, MC, V. Closed mid-Dec.–mid-Feb. Moderate.*

Lodging
Radisson Resort Hotel. Set amid 145 acres of oceanside woodlands, this 20-story glass-sheathed tower is part of the Kingston Plantation complex of shops, restaurants, hotels, and condominiums. Guest rooms have bleached-wood furnishings and attractive art; some have kitchenettes. *9800 Lake Dr., 29577, tel. 803/449–0006; fax 803/497–1017. 513 suites. Facilities: 2 restaurants, lounge, privileges at sports/fitness complex. AE, D, DC, MC, V. Very Expensive.*

Holiday Inn Oceanfront. This inn in the heart of town has a spacious, plant-filled recreation center that includes a pool and an exercise room. The large rooms are decorated in cool sea tones. *415 S. Ocean Blvd., 29577, tel. 803/448–4481; fax 803/448–0086. 310 rooms. Facilities: restaurant, 2 lounges, oceanfront pool with bar, indoor pool, sauna, game room, gift shop. AE, D, DC, MC, V. Expensive.*

North Myrtle Beach
Dining

Marina Raw Bar. This casual eatery overlooking Vereen's Marina is famous for its fresh oysters, clams, and other seafood, served broiled, grilled, or fried. *1203 U.S. 17N, tel. 803/249–3972. AE, MC, V. Moderate.*

Pawleys Island
Dining

Poogan's Porch. This sister restaurant to the Charleston spot of the same name specializes in such unusual Low Country fare as fried Carolina alligator in buttermilk batter, tossed with lettuce, cabbage, and jalapeño-honey dressing. *The Hammock Shops, U.S. 17S, tel. 803/237–4848. Reservations advised. AE, MC, V. Closed Sun. Moderate.*

Lodging

Litchfield by the Sea Resort and Country Club. Contemporary gray-blue wood units are built on stilts within the 4,500-acre grounds, which include three golf clubs. The beach is a short walk away. *U.S. 17, 2 mi north of Pawleys Island, 29585, tel. 803/237–3000 or 800/845–1897; fax 803/237–4282. 97 suites. Facilities: restaurant, lounge, 2 pools, racquetball court, tennis courts, golf. AE, MC, V. Moderate–Expensive.*

The Arts and Nightlife

The Arts

Area festivals include the **Canadian/American Days Festival** in March, the **Sun Fun Festival** in early July, and the **Atalaya Arts Festival** in fall. At **Art in the Park,** held in Myrtle Beach's Chapin Park three times each summer, you can buy handmade crafts and original artwork by local artists. Hilton Head's **Community Playhouse** (Arrow Rd., tel. 803/785–4878) presents up to 10 musicals or dramas each year and offers a theater program for youth. During the warmer months, there are free outdoor concerts at **Harbour Town** and **Shelter Cove.**

Nightlife

Country-western shows are popular along the Grand Strand, which is fast emerging as the eastern focus of country-music culture. Music lovers have six shows to choose from: the 2,250-seat **Alabama Theater** (U.S. 17N, N. Myrtle Beach, tel. 803/272–1111), opened in summer 1993; **Carolina Opry** (82nd Ave. N, Myrtle Beach, tel. 803/238–8888 or 800/843–6779); **Dixie Jubilee** (U.S. 17 Bus., N. Myrtle Beach, tel. 803/249–4444 or 800/843–6779); Dolly Parton's **Dixie Stampede** (8500 N. Kings Hwy., Myrtle Beach, tel. 803/497–9700); **Myrtle Beach Opry** (1901 N. Kings Hwy., Myrtle Beach, tel. 803/448–6779); and **Southern Country Nights** (U.S. 17 Bus., Surfside Beach, tel. 803/238–8888 or 800/843–6779). Shagging (the state dance) is popular at **Studebaker's** (U.S. 17 at 21st Ave. N, Myrtle Beach, tel. 803/626–3855 or 803/448–9747) and **Duck's** (229 Main St., N. Myrtle Beach, tel. 803/249–3858). Hilton Head's hotels and resorts feature a variety of musical entertainment.

Elsewhere in the State

Columbia

Getting There

I–20 leads northeast from Georgia to Columbia. I–77 runs south to Columbia, where it terminates. I–26 runs north-south through town.

What to See and Do

Columbia, in the middle of the state, was founded in 1786 as the capital city. The Italian Renaissance–style **State Capitol,** completed in 1855, contains marble and mahogany accents and a replica of Houdon's statue of George Washington. *Main and*

Gervais Sts., tel. 803/734–2430. Admission free. Guided tours every half hour. Closed weekends.

The South Carolina State Museum (301 Gervais St., tel. 803/737–4921; admission charged), set in a refurbished textile mill, interprets state history through exhibits on archaeology, fine arts, and scientific and technological accomplishments.

At **Riverbanks Zoological Park,** 2 mi from the capitol area via I–26, more than 450 species of birds and animals (some endangered) are cared for in their natural habitats. The park also offers a cage-free aviary, a reptile house, an aquarium, and facilities for breeding rare and fragile species. A new botanical garden is under construction at the zoo. *Junction of I–126 and Greystone Blvd., tel. 803/779–8717. Admission charged. Closed Christmas.*

The **Greater Columbia Convention and Visitors Bureau** (1012 Gervais St., 29202, tel. 803/254–0479) Visitor Center has brochures, maps, and advice for travelers.

5 The Mississippi Valley

The Mississippi Valley

Kansas City

St. Louis

KANSAS

MISSOURI

ILLINOIS

24

Padu

Ma

Pa

Eureka Springs

62

Calico Rock

Fayetteville

71

ARKANSAS

White River

Jonesboro

Blytheville

7

OKLAHOMA

40

Arkansas River

7

65

67

49

55

51

Jacks

Ft. Smith

10

Mt. Ida

Little Rock

North Little Rock

West Memphis

Memphis

Selme

78

Holly Springs

Ca

45

Benton

40

61

55

Oxford

Hot Springs

70

79

Helena

Tupelo

30

Pine Bluff

Clarksdale

Hope

79

65

Saline

Mississippi River

Cleveland

6

Texarkana

71

82

Camden

El Dorado

Greenwood

82

Columbus

Magnolia

Greenville

55

Yazoo City

Bossier City

Minden

Bastrop

61

MISSISSIPPI

Ruston

Monroe

Vicksburg

Meridian

Shreveport

20

Jackson

20

Mansfield

165

59

Natchitoches

Winnfield

Port Gibson

49

Laurel

TEXAS

Toledo Bend Lake

Many

Cloutierville

84

Natchez

Pearl River

Hattiesbu

Alexandria

Red R.

61

McComb

LOUISIANA

171

Baton Rouge

55

Bogalusa

Biloxi

Opelousas

49

Hammond

12

10

P

Sulphur

Eunice

Lafayette

Breaux Bridge

Lake Pontchartrain

Gulfport

O

Sp

Lake Charles

10

St. Martinville

New Iberia

Franklin

10

Grand Chenier

Avery Island

Morgan City

90

Houma

New Orleans

Gulf of Mexico

Mississippi Delta

INDIANA

Cincinnati
Newport
Covington

OHIO

WEST VIRGINIA

Wabash River

Louisville

Ohio River

Ashland
Morehead

Frankfort

71 75 27

64 23

Bardstown
Pleasant Hill
Danville
Berea
London
Hazard
Cumberland

Lexington

64

15

Henderson
Owensboro
Madisonville
Elizabethtown

KENTUCKY

Ohio River

65 68

127

Cumberland River

24

Hopkinsville
Bowling Green

68

Middlesboro

75

23

VIRGINIA

field

ah

Clarksville

70

27

Nashville

40

Murfreesboro

TENNESSEE

24

13

40

Columbia

65

Lawrenceburg

Fayetteville

Oak Ridge

Athens

Cleveland

Maryville

Knoxville

Clingmans Dome

Morristown

Kingsport

81

Johnson City
Greeneville

Gatlinburg

NORTH CAROLINA

GREAT SMOKY MTS. N.P.

Chattanooga

inth

SOUTH CAROLINA
Columbia

Birmingham

Atlanta

GEORGIA

ALABAMA

Montgomery

Savannah

rg

Mobile

ascagoula

cean

rings

Pensacola

FLORIDA

KEY
Amtrak Lines

N

0   150 miles
0   225 km

Introduction

Stand on a shore of the Mississippi River and you're swept with large emotions: Here are the waters that have sweetened the delta and fed the imagination of the South. The five states that constitute the Mississippi Valley all sweat history; each has Civil War battlefields and citizens with long, long memories. You can find the New South here, of course, but the Old South—of Cotton Is King, of Christ Is Coming, of aristocracy and its flip side, poverty—is never far away.

The soil is rich: No sight in the world affects a southerner like the fields of cotton ready for harvest. The region isn't only farmland, though; Tennessee, Kentucky, and Arkansas are blessed with some of the most beautiful mountain scenery in America. The metropolises, from Louisville to Shreveport to Jackson, have their big-city grandeur and decay. Outside them you'll see the regal old plantation houses, but you'll also pass along godforsaken stretches of state road with tumbledown shanties that can look more desolate than any city slum.

Yet the folk culture that sprouted among the poor people of these states took root and spread its branches far out into the world. Nashville calls itself the capital of country music; Memphis will always mean blues; New Orleans is the cradle of jazz. And all three cities—all three musics—had a hand in delivering rock and roll. Graceland, the Memphis mansion where Elvis lived and died in tacky majesty, stands now as an unofficial monument to the best American art and the worst American taste.

The region gave us soul music, too—and soul food. A visitor can find ambrosial ribs in the barbecue palaces of Memphis or at hole-in-the-wall luncheonettes on Arkansas roadsides. Those lucky enough to have tasted fried chicken or fried catfish down here have been known to lose their taste for chicken and catfish anywhere else. Forget low-fat. Forget nouvelle. The scent of collard greens stewing in pork fat, of sweet potatoes glistening with sugar and butter, emanates from some deep place as central to the culture as the one that produced the Mississippi blues of Muddy Waters and the long, hypnotic periods of Faulkner.

Farther downriver, the spirit changes. The sauces become more complex; the music turns airier, and so does the mood. The fundamentalism of the Bible Belt loosens into a good-time Catholicism whose motto is *Laissez les bons temps rouler*—let the good times roll. Cajun festivals, for everything from gumbo to petroleum, are just about constant—any excuse for a party. The biggest excuse, of course, is Mardi Gras, the day before Lent, which is celebrated all through south Louisiana. By the time the Mississippi gets this close to the Gulf, its width is monumental, but the water is warm, unhurried. And so is New Orleans. It's as though the river chose this city as the place to deposit all the richness it has picked up on its long journey. You come here to slow down, relax, enjoy the good life, and dedicate your days to pleasure.

Tour Groups

If you're ready for a visit to Cajun country, the Ozarks, a cruise along the Mississippi, or an excursion through country-western capitals, the tours below offer just what you want.

Domenico Tours (751 Broadway, Bayonne, NJ 07002, tel. 201/823–8687 or 800/554–8687) visits Nashville and the Smoky Mountains in seven days, including Opryland and Gatlinburg. **Gadabout Tours** (700 E. Tahquitz Way, Palm Springs, CA 92262, tel. 619/325–5556 or 800/952–5068) travels Tennessee and Kentucky in depth for 12 days, as well as the Ozarks in 16 days. **Globus** (5301 S. Federal Circle, Littleton, CO 80123, tel. 303/797–2800 or 800/221–0090) offers eight days of "Country-Western U.S.A.," including the Smokies, Memphis, Nashville, and Opryland, as well as various tours of the New Orleans region. **Cosmos Tourama** (same address) offers budget country-western tours. **Maupintour** (Box 807, Lawrence, KS 66044, tel. 913/843–1211 or 800/255–4266) takes an eight-day steamboat ride down the Mississippi to New Orleans, as well as an eight-day tour of New Orleans and the Cajun country of Louisiana. **Talmage Tours** (1223 Walnut St., Philadelphia, PA 19107, tel. 215/923–7100) has a seven-day "Grand Ole Opry" tour of Tennessee and a five-day tour of New Orleans. **Tauck Tours** (Box 5027, Westport, CT 06881, tel. 203/226–6911 or 800/468–2825) views the Ozarks in eight days, including Memphis, Hot Springs, Arkansas, Lake of the Ozarks, St. Louis, and cruises on the Mississippi; it also offers a nine-day tour of New Orleans and Cajun country.

When to Go

The best times to visit the Mississippi Valley states are April and October, when temperatures and humidity are comfortable: in Louisiana and Mississippi, the mid-70s; in the mountains of Arkansas, Kentucky, and Tennessee, the 60s, cooling off to the mid-40s at night. In **spring** everything is in glorious bloom, while in the **fall** the trees, especially in the mountains, are bright with turning leaves. You can tour magnificent historic mansions in spring and fall.

If you dislike crowds, avoid New Orleans during Mardi Gras (February or March, depending on the date of Easter) and Louisville during the Kentucky Derby (the first Saturday in May). Visits during these times require flight and hotel reservations long in advance; hotel prices also jump.

Festivals and Seasonal Events

Jan.–Feb.: The **Dixie National Rodeo/Western Festival/Livestock Show** in Jackson, Mississippi, offers rodeos and other events. *Tel. 601/960–1891 or 800/354–7695.*

Feb. 5–15: Mardi Gras in New Orleans, Louisiana, is two weeks of madness—street festivals, parades with fantastic floats, marching bands, and eye-popping costumes. *Tel. 504/566–5031.*

Mar.–Apr.: In Mississippi, **spring pilgrimages** to elegant antebellum mansions are held throughout the state, with Natchez (tel. 800/647–2290) claiming grande-dame status, followed by Columbus and Vicksburg.

Apr.–May: The **Memphis in May International Festival** celebrates music on Beale Street, along with other events. *Tel. 901/543-5300.*

Apr.–Aug.: Wonders: The Memphis International Cultural Series presents a major collection of art and artifacts from Napoleonic France. *Tel. 901/576-1290 or 800/755-8777.*

Late Apr.: The **Annual Arkansas Folk Festival** in Mountain View salutes the folk culture of the Ozarks with music, dance, crafts, a parade, and a rodeo. *Tel. 501/269-3851.*

Late Apr.–early May: The **New Orleans Jazz & Heritage Festival** draws thousands of musicians, fans, and artisans for a 10-day all-out jam session. *Tel. 504/522-4786.*

May 1: In Louisville, the **Kentucky Derby,** one of horse racing's premier events, is preceded by a 10-day festival with parades, riverboat races, and many a mint julep. *Tel. 502/636-4400.*

Memorial Day Weekend: The **Annual Riverfest** in Little Rock, Arkansas, celebrates the visual and performing arts with music, dance, theater, food, and fireworks. *Tel. 501/682-1088.*

Mid-June: The **International Country Music Fan Fair** in Nashville, Tennessee, lets country music fans mix with their favorite stars in a week-long celebration featuring live shows, exhibits, autograph sessions, and special concerts. *Tel. 615/889-7503.*

Late Aug.: Louisville's **Kentucky State Fair** draws some half-million people with rooster-crowing contests, top-name concerts, a horse show, and an amusement park. *Tel. 502/367-5000.*

Getting Around the Mississippi Valley

By Plane **New Orleans International Airport** (tel. 504/464-0831), **Cincinnati/Northern Kentucky International Airport** (tel. 606/283-3151), and **Standiford Field** (Louisville, tel. 502/367-4636) are served by American, ComAir, Continental, Northwest, TWA, United, and USAir.

By Car I-30 goes north–south through Arkansas. I-40 goes east–west through central Arkansas and central Tennessee. I-24 cuts diagonally across eastern Kentucky. I-64 runs east–west through Louisville. I-65 is a north–south route through Tennessee and central Kentucky. I-75 runs north–south through eastern Kentucky and Tennessee. I-55 runs from south Louisiana north through Mississippi and Arkansas. I-10 runs east–west through southern Mississippi and New Orleans. I-20 is the major east–west road through northern Louisiana and Mississippi. There are bridges over the Mississippi River in New Orleans, Destrehan, Donaldsonville, and Baton Rouge, Louisiana, and in Vicksburg, in Natchez, and near Greenville, Mississippi. The river is bridged in Arkansas at Lake Village and Helena; in Tennessee at Memphis and east of Dyerburg; and in Kentucky at Hickman, Columbus, and Cairo.

By Train **Amtrak** (tel. 800/872-7245) serves all states of the Mississippi Valley.

By Bus **Greyhound** (Jackson, MS, tel. 601/352-4096; Little Rock, AR, tel. 501/372-1861; Louisville, KY, tel. 502/585-3331; Memphis, TN, tel. 901/523-7676; Nashville, TN, tel. 615/255-3556; New

Orleans, LA, tel. 504/525–9371; or 800/231–2222) provides service to cities and towns throughout the region.

By Boat In Louisiana, ferries operate across the Mississippi River in New Orleans, Lutcher, Carville, and St. Francisville. In Tennessee, there are ferries across the Cumberland River near Nashville, Cumberland City, and at Dixon Springs; and across the Tennessee River at Dayton, Clifton, Saltillo, and near Decatur.

The **Delta Queen Steamboat Company** (Robin St. Wharf, New Orleans, LA 70130, tel. 800/543–1949), the nation's only overnight riverboat, offers paddle-wheeler cruises on the Mississippi, Ohio, Tennessee, and Cumberland rivers, as far east as Chattanooga and as far north as Minneapolis.

ARKANSAS

By Delta Willis

Updated by
Brenda Blagg

Capital	Little Rock
Population	2.4 million
Motto	The People Rule
State Bird	Mockingbird
State Flower	Apple blossom

Visitor Information

Arkansas Department of Parks and Tourism (1 Capitol Mall, Little Rock 72201, tel. 501/682–7777 or 800/872–1259).

Scenic Drives

Arkansas has 18 million acres of forests, and the Ozark Mountains rival New England for beautiful fall colors. The 70-mi stretch of Rte. 7 from **Harrison to Russellville** is one of the best foliage trails in the nation. **Rte. 7** to Hot Springs and Arkadelphia passes through the Ouachita National Forest. The **Talimena Scenic Drive** runs west on Rte. 88 for 55 mi from Mena, Arkansas, to Talihina, Oklahoma, and spans the Ouachita Mountains, the highest range between the Appalachians and the Rockies. The **Great River Road** (Rte. 1 from Helena to Lake Village) runs along the levees that border the Arkansas and Mississippi rivers. The elevated, graveled road is especially good for bird-watching, with egrets and herons year-round.

National and State Parks

National Parks   The **Buffalo National River** (Box 1173, Harrison 72602, tel. 501/741–5443), in the northwestern part of the state, became the first national river in 1972. You can canoe, camp, hike, and fish along the 132-mi-long river's limestone bluffs year-round and go white-water rafting in early spring. Yellville and Marshall are gateway towns to the park. The 65,000-acre **Felsenthal National Wildlife Refuge** (Box 1157, Crossett 71635, tel. 501/364–3167) is a mosaic of wetlands, with bayous, lakes, and two rivers, the Saline and the Ouachita.

The **Ouachita National Forest** (USFS Box 1270, Hot Springs 71902, tel. 501/321–5202) extends from Pinnacle Mountain State Park, west of Little Rock, into Oklahoma, and includes 350 mi of walking trails. The **Ozark National Forest** (Box 1008, Russellville 72801, tel. 501/968–2354) offers camping facilities, a view from the highest point in the state (Magazine Mountain, 2,753 feet), and caverns to explore near Blanchard Springs.

State Parks   Arkansas has 47 state parks. Check the *Camper's Guide* and the annual "Arkansas State Parks" brochure, both available from the state tourism office (*see* Visitor Information, *above*), for locations, lodge prices, camping fees, RV sites, and hook-up fees. For information on fishing in Arkansas parks, contact the **Arkansas Game & Fish Commission** (tel. 501/223–6300).

Bull Shoals State Park (Rte. 178, Bull Shoals 72619, tel. 501/431–5521) is in the Ozark Mountains below Bull Shoals Dam on the White River. **Crater of Diamonds State Park** (Rte. 1, Box 364, Murfreesboro 71958, tel. 501/285–3113) is the only diamond deposit in the United States open to the public. **DeGray Lake Resort State Park** (Rte. 7, Bismark 71929–8194, tel. 501/865–4501) borders the northern shore of the 13,800-acre Lake DeGray. **Ozark Mountain State Park** (Box 500, Mountain View 72560, tel. 501/269–3851 or 800/264–3655), a unique park dedicated to preserving and perpetuating the Ozark Mountain way of life, offers traditional crafts demonstrations, music, and dancing, plus a gift shop, a lodge, and a restaurant in season. **Petit Jean State Park** (Morrilton 72455, tel. 501/727–5441) is 3,471 acres on Petit Jean Mountain in the Ozarks, with waterfalls and hiking trails, a lodge, and cabins. **Toltec Mounds Archeological State Park** (1 Toltec Mounds Rd., Scott 72142–9502, tel. 501/961–9442) is the site of the state's highest Indian burial mounds, which have yielded evidence of a sophisticated ceremonial and government settlement.

Little Rock

Like the state of Arkansas itself, Little Rock combines the sophisticated and the homespun. Though the skyline is dominated by shiny office towers and glittering hotels, residents continue to extend small-town hospitality.

With its sister city of North Little Rock, the capital is located along the banks of the Arkansas River, which brought Northern European and Spanish explorers here in the 16th and 17th centuries. ("La Petite Roche," the small outcrop that served as a landmark for early river travelers, is now part of Riverfront Park, in the downtown area.) The capital moved here in 1821 from Arkansas Post, the first settlement west of the Mississippi.

Little Rock is not only the governmental and financial center of the state but also its geographical center, with diverse terrain almost equally divided between forested highlands north and west of the city, and fertile agricultural lowlands to the south and east. The city is a major convention hub, with good restaurants and an exceptional Arts Center. Nevertheless, most visitors come to Arkansas to enjoy outdoor sports and the beautiful wild scenery, which begins within a few minutes' drive of the restored Victorian district downtown.

Tourist Information

Little Rock: (Box 3232, 72203, tel. 501/376–4781 or 800/844–4781).

Arriving and Departing

By Plane Most major airlines fly into **Little Rock Regional Airport** (tel. 501/372–3439), 5 mi east of downtown off I–440. There are no scheduled flights between Arkansas cities. For charters from Little Rock, call **USAir Express** (tel. 800/428–4322). Some fishing lodges have private airstrips. Major Little Rock hotels provide airport shuttles. The cab fare from the airport to downtown is about $8. Call **Black & White Cabs** (tel. 501/374–0333) or **Capitol Cabs** (tel. 501/568–0462).

By Car I–40 and I–30 lead to the city, as do U.S. 65 and U.S. 67. All major car-rental agencies have offices near the airport.

Train Station Amtrak (1400 W. Markham St.).

Getting Around

By Car Little Rock traffic is civilized, there are plenty of parking facilities, and taxis are readily available.

By Bus **Central Arkansas Transit** (tel. 501/375–1163) serves the Little Rock area.

Exploring Little Rock

Driving in the city is easy, but you can see a great deal by walking in the downtown area.

The **Quapaw Quarter** is a restored 19th-century neighborhood that includes homes, churches, and some of the city's oldest buildings. Free self-guided walking tours are offered by the quarter's headquarters, an 1881 Italianate structure called the **Villa Marre.** Originally built by saloonkeeper Angelo Marre, it now serves as a house-museum. The facade is featured in the TV series "Designing Women." *1321 Scott St., tel. 501/374–9979. Admission charged. Closed Sat.*

On a hilltop west of the downtown area, the **State Capitol,** built between 1899 and 1916 as a ¾-scale model of the U.S. Capitol, features a rotunda and massive staircases made of "Batesville marble," a local ivory-colored limestone. *Woodlawn and Capitol, tel. 501/682–5080. Admission free.*

The **Arkansas Territorial Restoration,** a group of 14 buildings from the early 1800s, includes a log cabin moved here from nearby Scott. Also here are an exhibit center and an excellent collection of Arkansas crafts for sale. *Scott and 3rd Sts., tel. 501/324–9351. Admission charged.*

A fine example of Greek Revival architecture, the **Old State House** was built between 1833 and 1842 and served as the state capitol until 1911. It was also the site of President Bill Clinton's election-night celebration. It now contains a state museum, two restored legislative chambers and a governor's office from the 19th century, and a giftshop featuring Arkansas-related books. *300 W. Markham St., tel. 501/324–9685. Donations accepted. Closed major holidays.*

The **Arkansas Museum of Science and History** has exhibits on geology and ornithology. The building, part of an arsenal built in 1838, was the birthplace of General Douglas MacArthur. *MacArthur Park, tel. 501/324–9231. Admission charged.*

Adjacent to the museum, the **Arkansas Arts Center** houses six art galleries, a museum school, a children's theater, a gift shop, a restaurant, and various performing-arts organizations (*see* The Arts and Nightlife, *below*). The **Decorative Arts Museum,** set in an 1841 mansion near the Arts Center, features arts and crafts, including elaborate and colorful quilts. *7th and Rock Sts., tel. 501/372–4000, ext. 358. Donation suggested.*

Parks and Gardens

Burns Park (tel. 501/758–2400), on 1,575 acres in North Little Rock, has hiking and jogging trails, a golf course, indoor and outdoor tennis and racquetball courts, and a crossbow range. The **Old Mill** (Lakeshore Dr. and Fairway, North Little Rock, tel. 501/758–2400) is an authentic re-creation of a stone grist-mill in a beautiful setting—it appeared in the opening scene of *Gone with the Wind*.

Pinnacle Mountain State Park (Hwy. 10, tel. 501/868–5806), 15 mi west of Little Rock, comprises more than 1,800 acres, five trails, a picnic area, and the mountain for which it is named. Staff naturalists offer interpretive programs.

Riverfront Park edges both sides of the Arkansas River. Along the southern bank, at Little Rock's La Harpe Boulevard behind the Statehouse Convention Center, is an amphitheater for bands, a history pavilion containing an open-air display of pictures and text on the early role of the city, and playgrounds, all with a view of passing river traffic. Docked on the north bank is the *Spirit* (tel. 501/376–4150), a paddle wheeler offering cruises from North Little Rock.

War Memorial Park (W. Markham St. and Fair Park Ave., tel. 501/663–9817) features football and baseball stadiums, a public golf course, and an amusement park.

What to See and Do with Children

The **Little Rock Zoo** (1 Jonesboro Dr., tel. 501/663–4733) is near the **amusement park** in War Memorial Park (*see* Parks and Gardens, *above*).

Granny's Attic, a hands-on exhibit at the Old State House Museum (*see* Exploring Little Rock, *above*), lets children learn about life during the Victorian era, play with toys, and try on period clothing.

Shopping

Little Rock has major department stores at **Park Plaza Mall** (University Ave. and Markham St.) and **University Mall** (500 S. University Ave.). More interesting are shops selling traditional crafts, from quilts to wood carvings to jams and antiques, the best of which are at the **Arkansas Territorial Restoration** and the **State Capitol** gift shop (*see* Exploring Little Rock, *above*). The Arkansas Industrial Development Commission (1 Capitol Mall, tel. 501/682–1121) publishes a catalog of state products.

Dining

Eating out in Little Rock is relatively inexpensive, and portions tend to be large. Outside the city, some counties are dry. For price ranges, see Chart 1 (B) in Chapter 1.

Expensive   **Alouette's.** This first-class French restaurant features such entrées as fresh duck in vinegar sauce with prunes. Dinner for two can be nearly $100. The wine list is excellent. *11401 Rodney Parham Rd., tel. 501/225–4152. Reservations advised weekends. AE, DC, MC, V. Closed Sun.*

★ **Ashley's.** In The Capital Hotel downtown is this romantic restaurant with fresh flowers and elegant china and silver. Lunch can be busy, with local celebrities and executives. Especially recommended is the appetizer of goat cheese in pastry with spinach and red peppers. Fresh fish is a specialty. *111 W. Markham St., tel. 501/374-7474. Reservations advised. AE, DC, MC, V.*

★ **Coy's.** Excellent steaks and seafood are featured at this popular restaurant where dinner is served by candlelight. *11400 Rodney Parham Rd., tel. 501/224-2000. Reservations advised weekends. AE, D, DC, MC, V. No dinner Sun.*

Moderate **André's.** At its two locations, one of Little Rock's best restaurants offers authentic French accents and service with a flourish. Soups and fish, including soft-shell crab and baked halibut, are excellent. *1121 Rodney Parham Rd., tel. 501/224-7880 (closed Mon.); 605 N. Beechwood St., tel. 501/666-9191. Reservations advised. AE, DC, MC, V.*

Blue Mesa Grill. This lively place with spicy dishes from the Southwest serves strong margaritas, grilled seafood, and wild game, including quail. Decorated with abstract prints and Sante Fe crafts, the restaurant also has a bar with a dance floor of black and white tiles. *1719 Merrill Dr., tel. 501/221-7777. No reservations except for large groups. AE, DC, MC, V.*

Cajun's Wharf. Set in an old warehouse near the Arkansas River, this seafood restaurant has a popular singles bar. Try the warm bread with honey butter, and shrimp or Cajun dishes. *2400 Cantrell Rd., tel. 501/375-5351. Reservations advised. AE, MC, V. Closed Sun.*

★ **Juanita's.** This downtown hot spot is famous for its spinach enchiladas; the best live bands in town appear at the bar next door. *1300 S. Main St., tel. 501/372-1228. No reservations. AE, DC, MC, V.*

Inexpensive **Franke's Cafeteria.** With three locations, family-owned Franke's has for decades been *the* practical place for eating lunch. Help yourself to simple, good food. *400 Broadway, tel. 501/372-1919, and 300 S. University Ave., tel. 501/663-4461, in Little Rock; 3929 McCain Blvd., North Little Rock, tel. 501/758-8144. No reservations. No credit cards.*

Lodging

For price ranges, see Chart 2 (B) in Chapter 1.

Expensive **Arkansas Excelsior.** A large, downtown high rise atop the Statehouse Convention Center, this glittering hotel has several suites with whirlpools. *Markham and Louisiana Sts., 72201, tel. 501/375-5000 or 800/527-1745; fax 501/375-7320. 411 rooms and suites. Facilities: restaurant, bars, convention facilities, concierge floor, parking. AE, DC, MC, V.*

The Capital Hotel. Exquisitely decorated in antebellum style, the Capital has an atrium lobby topped by a stained-glass dome and a grand balcony where you expect to see Rhett Butler carrying Miss Scarlett off to one of the suites with four-poster beds. Ashley's on the ground floor is one of the city's best restaurants (*see* Dining, *above*). *111 W. Markham St., 72201, tel. 501/374-7474 or 800/766-7666; fax 501/370-7091. 123 rooms. Facilities: restaurant, lounge. AE, DC, MC, V.*

★ **Carriage House Bed & Breakfast.** This private house has only two guest rooms and a shared sitting room but offers peace and quiet. Breakfast is included in the rates, and afternoon tea is served in the courtyard. Each bedroom has a private bath and is decorated with antiques. *1700 Louisiana St., 72201, tel. 501/ 374–7032. 2 rooms. No credit cards.*

Moderate **Camelot.** Located downtown near the Arkansas River, this partially renovated high-rise hotel was built in 1972 and has seen better days. *W. Markham St. and Broadway, 72201, tel. 501/ 372–4371 or 800/937–2789; fax 501/372–0518. 303 rooms. Facilities: 2 restaurants, bar, heated pool, meeting rooms, parking, airport shuttle. AE, D, MC, V.*

Guesthouse Inn. This hotel on University Avenue near the Medical Center offers quiet suites with kitchenettes. A breakfast of coffee and donuts is included. *301 S. University Ave., 72205, tel. 501/664–6800; fax 501/663–7043. 71 rooms. Facilities: shuttle service to the airport and downtown. AE, DC, MC.*

Radisson Legacy Hotel. Spacious and tastefully decorated rooms are offered by the Radisson chain. *625 W. Capitol Ave., 72201, tel. and fax 501/374–0100. 116 rooms with living areas, 9 suites, 3 penthouse suites. Facilities: restaurant, bar, pool. AE, DC, MC, V.*

Motels **Days Inn West** (10524 W. Markham St., 72205, tel. 501/225–7366 or 800/325–2525; fax 501/224–4238), 150 rooms, restaurant, pool, meeting rooms; inexpensive. **Hampton Inn I–30** (6100 Mitchell Dr., 72209, tel. 501/562–6667; fax 501/568–6832), 122 rooms, pool; inexpensive.

The Arts and Nightlife

The Arts The free newspaper *Spectrum* and the Friday issue of the *Arkansas Democrat–Gazette* list events. For a "What's Happening" report, call 501/372–3399.

Little Rock is also home to the **Arkansas Arts Center** (9th and Commerce Sts., tel. 501/372–4000); the **Arkansas Repertory Theatre** (601 Main St., tel. 501/378–0445); the **Arkansas Opera** (20919 Denning Rd., tel. 501/821–7275), **Ballet Arkansas** (various locations, tel. 501/664–9509), the **Arkansas Symphony Orchestra** (various locations, tel. 501/376–4781), and **Wildwood Park for the Performing Arts** (20919 Denning Rd., tel. 501/821–7275).

Broadway Theatre Series (1501 N. University Ave., tel. 501/ 661–1500), the **Community Theatre of Little Rock** (13401 Chenal Pkwy., tel. 501/663–9494), **Maurry's Dinner Theater** (6323 Asher Ave., tel. 501/562–3131), **Robinson Center** (7 State House Plaza, tel. 501/376–4781), and the **University of Arkansas Little Rock Fine Arts Galleries and Theater** (2801 S. University Ave., tel. 501/569–3183) offer a variety of performing-arts productions.

Nightlife There is good music and dancing in Little Rock, especially at restaurants like **Juanita's, Cajun's Wharf,** and the **Blue Mesa Grill** (*see* Dining, *above*). Jazz pianist Art Porter is a regular at the **Atrium Bar** in the Excelsior hotel (*see* Lodging, *above*).

Northwest Arkansas

Whether your penchant is for forested mountains and deep blue lakes, breathtaking vistas or comfortable camaraderie, Northwest Arkansas has it. The region is booming, as it did in the 1800s when Eureka Springs' much-acclaimed curative waters began drawing travelers to the Ozarks. The Victorian village that developed around those vaunted springs is still a treasure trove of arts-and-crafts shops and other attractions; from mid-October to mid-November, you can watch crafts artisans at work during the annual crafts festival. Driving here is a treat in itself: The ride offers spectacular Ozark vistas, colorful fall foliage, historic Civil War battlefields at Pea Ridge and Prairie Grove, and beautiful lakes and rivers fringed with excellent fishing lodges.

Getting There

Though travel by car is the easiest way to get around, commercial flights to some destinations are available, and charter planes and buses can be booked from Little Rock. There is no passenger train service, except for short runs in the Ozarks.

By Plane   **USAir Express** runs charters.

By Car   To reach Fayetteville, Springdale, and Rogers from Little Rock, take I–40W to Rte. 71, currently being expanded to four lanes. From Rogers, Hwy. 62 will take you eastward to Eureka Springs.

By Bus   **All Around Arkansas Tour** (tel. 501/376–8033 or 800/648–8199) runs charters.

Eureka Springs

Tourist Information   **Eureka Springs Chamber of Commerce** (Box 551, 72632, tel. 501/253–7333).

Exploring Eureka Springs   A Victorian village in the Ozark Mountains near the Missouri border, **Eureka Springs** has beautifully restored hotels and gingerbread-trimmed houses, which can be viewed by trolley car. **Thorncrown Chapel** (U.S. 62W, tel. 501/253–7401), designed by architect Fay Jones, is a magnificent glass structure in the forest. The historic downtown area has several art and crafts galleries on Spring Street, and the **Hammond Museum of Bells** (2 Pine St., tel. 501/253–7411). In October, the four-day **War Eagle craft festival** features everything from sunbonnets to antiques (War Eagle Mills Farm, tel. 501/789–5398). From late June to mid-July, opera is performed at **Inspiration Point** (U.S. 62W, tel. 501/253–8595). Breakfast, lunch, and dinner are served aboard the steam-powered **Eureka Springs & North Arkansas Railway** (tel. 501/253–9623), which makes short trips through the Ozarks daily.

Dining and Lodging   There are more than 40 restaurants in the area; the exceptional **War Eagle Mill Farm** (Rte. 98, tel. 501/789–5343) is worth the drive. **Dairy Hollow House** (515 Spring St., 72632, tel. 501/253–7444) is a small country inn as authentic as the owner's name: Crescent Dragonwagon (author of *The Dairy Hollow House Cookbook*). Reservations are required for both the restaurant and the inn, which has fireplaces, antiques, and locally made quilts.

There are more than 150 lodging facilities here, including several historic hotels. Convenient to shopping and slightly funky is the **Basin Park Hotel** (12 Spring St., 72632, tel. 501/253–7837 or 800/643–4972; fax 501/253–9551). The **Crescent Hotel** (75 Prospect St., 72632, tel. 501/253–9766 or 800/342–9766), on the mountaintop overlooking the city, is a National Historic Landmark. The **Bed and Breakfasts Association, Cabins and Cottages of Eureka Springs** (6 King's Hwy., 72632, tel. 800/653–6067) has information on a wide range of lodgings.

Fishing Lodges **Gaston's White River Resort.** This lodge attracts anglers from all over the nation; many fly their private planes onto the Gaston airstrip. Some cottages have fireplaces. *Rte. 1, Box 176NW, Lakeview 72642, tel. 501/431–5202. 73 cottages. Facilities: restaurant, gift and tackle shop, fishing guides. MC, V. Expensive.*

Spider Creek Resort. These cabins and houses are on the White River northwest of Eureka Springs. *Rte. 2, Box 418, Eureka Springs 72632, tel. 501/253–9241. 9 cabins, 2 houses. Facilities: tackle shop. DC, MC, V. Moderate.*

Sportsman's Resort. Guided fishing trips on the White River are available through this resort, offering accommodations in air-conditioned cottages with cooking facilities. *Box 96, Flippin 72634, tel. 501/453–2424 or 800/626–3474. 20 cottages. Facilities: pool, hot tub. D, MC, V. Inexpensive.*

Numerous other facilities on the White River serve fishing enthusiasts. A sampling includes **Charlie's Riverfront Cabins** (tel. 501/253–9125) and **Riverview Resort** (tel. 501/253–8367). **Fletcher's Devil's Dive Resort** (tel. 417/271–3396) in Eagle Rock, Missouri, 10 mi north of Eureka, has fishing on White River and Table Rock Lake.

Fayetteville

Tourist Information **Fayetteville:** Chamber of Commerce (Box 4216, 72702, tel. 501/521–1710 or 800/766–4626).

Exploring Fayetteville The **Arkansas Air Museum** (tel. 501/521–4947), housed in a historic wooden hangar at Drake Field, is a showcase of aviation history, airplane engines, and antique aircraft. **Headquarters House** (118 E. Dickson St., tel. 501/521–2970), built in 1853 by Judge Jonas Tebbets, served as both Union and Confederate army headquarters at different times during the Civil War. President and Mrs. Clinton's first home and offices are at the **University of Arkansas Law School,** which is also where you can root for the Arkansas Razorbacks and other spectator sports year-round. **Prairie Grove Battlefield Park** (tel. 501/846–2480), west of Fayetteville on Hwy. 62, preserves the site of the Civil War battle that saved Missouri from the Union. **Walton Arts Center** (tel. 501/443–9216), the region's largest performing- and visual-arts facility, opened for its premier season in 1992.

Springfest, held each April on colorful Dickson Street, ushers in the warm weather. June's **Music Festival of Arkansas** (tel. 501/521–4166) offers audiences the chance to hear internationally renowned artists and aspiring performers in classical, chamber, and light pops concerts. In October, **Autumnfest** celebrates fall-foliage season with the Harvest Ball, parades, and three days of special events.

Springdale

Tourist Information
Springdale: Chamber of Commerce (Box 166, 72765, tel. 501/751–4694 or 800/972–7261).

Exploring Springdale
Shiloh Historic District and Museum (118 W. Johnson St., tel. 501/750–8165) documents the history of local industry. Tontitown, just west on Hwy. 412, is a community settled in 1897 by Italian immigrants. The Arts Center of the Ozarks (tel. 501/751–5441) provides year-round theater, music, and dance performances. The Arkansas and Missouri Railroad (tel. 501/751–5763) offers journeys back to the golden age of rail travel via restored turn-of-the-century railcars.

Rodeo of the Ozarks (tel. 501/751–4694 or 800/972–7261), held every July 1–4, is nationally renowned. Albert E. Brumley Sundown to Sunup Gospel Sing, held the first week in August, draws music fans to hear southern gospel quartets. War Eagle Arts and Crafts weekends bring visitors to the region the first weekend in May and the third weekend in October. The latter is the annual War Eagle Fair, the granddaddy of regional crafts fairs; approximately 20 other crafts fairs are held throughout Northwest Arkansas that same weekend (a list is available from the Springdale Chamber of Commerce).

Western Arkansas

The spectacular terrain of western Arkansas includes beautiful lakes and forested hills rich with the history of the frontier. Fort Smith, on the state's western border, celebrates that frontier heritage, preserving a hangin' judge's courtroom and gallows and such unusual sites as the only bordello on the National Register of Historic Places. The Ouachita (pronounced "*Wauch*-it-taw") Mountains cradle Hot Springs, perhaps the best-known vacation destination in Arkansas. Nestled amid the five "diamond lakes," so named for their crystal-clear water and this diamond-bearing and quartz-rich region, the Spa City features naturally thermal waters, historic Bath House Row, and Oaklawn Park—a Thoroughbred horse-racing track. Hot Springs was the haunt of one former president (Harry Truman) and the boyhood home of our current one. Nearby Crater of Diamonds State Park is the only place in North America where you can dig for diamonds and keep any you find. Drive farther south to find Hope, President Clinton's birthplace, and Old Washington Historic State Park, site of Arkansas's Confederate capitol. James Black, a local blacksmith, forged the famous Bowie knife here. The Ozark Highlands Trail, one of Arkansas's 242 hiking trails, begins just west of Little Rock and extends into Oklahoma; it's 168 mi long, with many short spurs.

Getting There
Preferred travel is by car. There is no passenger train service, although charter flights, buses, and limousines are available from Little Rock to Hot Springs.

By Plane
USAir Express runs charters.

By Car
To reach Hot Springs from Little Rock, take I–30 to U.S. 70 for 53 mi. Hot Springs can also be approached via scenic Rte. 7.

By Bus
All Around Arkansas Tours (tel. 501/376–8033 or 800/648–8199) runs charters.

Hot Springs and the Ozarks

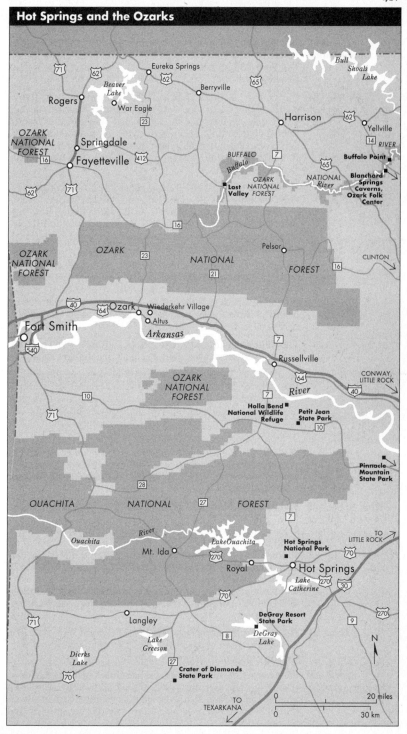

Rogers

Eureka Springs

Berryville

Bull Shoals Lake

Beaver Lake

War Eagle

OZARK NATIONAL FOREST

Springdale

Fayetteville

Harrison

Yellville

RIVER

Buffalo Point

BUFFALO

Buffalo

Blanchard Springs Caverns, Ozark Folk Center

Lost Valley

OZARK NATIONAL FOREST

NATIONAL River

OZARK NATIONAL FOREST

OZARK

NATIONAL

FOREST

Pelsor

CLINTON

Ozark

Wiederkehr Village

Altus

Fort Smith

Arkansas

Russellville

CONWAY, LITTLE ROCK

OZARK NATIONAL FOREST

River

Holla Bend National Wildlife Refuge

Petit Jean State Park

Pinnacle Mountain State Park

OUACHITA

NATIONAL

FOREST

Ouachita

River

Mt. Ida

Lake Ouachita

Hot Springs National Park

LITTLE ROCK

TO

Royal

Hot Springs

Lake Catherine

Langley

DeGray Resort State Park

DeGray Lake

Dierks Lake

Lake Greeson

Crater of Diamonds State Park

TO TEXARKANA

N

0   20 miles

0   30 km

Hot Springs

Tourist Information	**Hot Springs:** Convention and Visitors Bureau (134 Convention Blvd., Hot Springs 71902, tel. 501/321–2277 or 800/772–2489). The **Fordyce Bathhouse** (tel. 501/623–1433) features a Visitor Center downtown.

Exploring Hot Springs

During the '20s this was a gambling town famous for its therapeutic bathhouses, which drew from the 47 thermal springs that explorer Hernando de Soto called Valley of the Vapors. Pure spring water has been bottled here for more than a century. Several spa hotels have been renovated; along Bath House Row is the **Arlington,** once the haunt of former President Harry Truman.

In addition to the facilities at the major hotels (*see* Lodging, *below*), you can enjoy a mineral bath and massage without checking into a hotel. The **Buckstaff Baths** (Bath House Row, tel. 501/623–2308), a National Historic Landmark built in 1912, offers baths and massages for about $12 each (closed during lunch hours and on Sunday).

There is Thoroughbred horse racing at **Oaklawn Park** (tel. 501/623–4411 or 800/722–3652) from early January to late April. The downtown has many new art galleries (tel. 501/321–2277 or 800/772–2489 for gallery walks), and the city is surrounded by beautiful lakes. Local geologic formations have produced fantastic quartz crystals, sold at roadside stands and in shops.

The *Belle of Hot Springs* (Rte. 7S, tel. 501/525–4438) is a 400-passenger riverboat that features lunch and dinner cruises.

At **Mountain Valley Spring Water** (13 mi north of the city, on Rte. 7N, tel. 501/624–1635) visitors can sample the water and view the hot springs through a glass dome. Mountain Valley's headquarters (150 Central Ave., downtown Hot Springs, tel. 501/623–6671) is a restored turn-of-the-century building with exhibits.

On U.S. 270W past Lake Ouachita is the town of **Mount Ida** (Chamber of Commerce, Box 6, 71957, tel. 501/867–3541), with several crystal shops and the **Stanley Gem and Mineral Museum** (501/623–5836).

What to See and Do with Children

Mid-America Museum (off U.S. 270W at 400 Mid-America Blvd., tel. 501/767–3461) is a hands-on museum of energy and science. **Alligator Farm** (847 Whittington Ave., tel. 501/623–6172) has alligators large and small, plus a small zoo, including white-tail deer and mountain lions; children can feed the animals. **Castleberry Riding Stable** (Rte. 7N to Walnut Valley Rd., tel. 501/624–7291) offers hayrides, riding lessons, and overnight camping trips by horseback. **National Park Aquarium** (209 Central Ave., tel. 501/624–3474) has a large exhibit of fish and reptiles.

Shopping

Hot Springs Factory Outlet Mall (4382 Central Ave., tel. 501/525–0888), south of downtown, has discount name-brand merchandise in more than two dozen stores.

Sports and Outdoor Activities

For a map of the **hiking** trails, contact **Ouachita National Forest** (Box 1270, Hot Springs 71902, tel. 501/321–5202). The lakes around Hot Springs feature good bass **fishing,** with an annual tournament. (*See* Lodging, *below,* for fishing guides and boats.)

Dining   For price ranges, see Chart 1 (B) in Chapter 1.

Expensive   **Hamilton House.** Lace tablecloths, soft piano music, and candlelight set the tone in this romantic '20s villa on Lake Hamilton, where fresh seafood, aged beef, and rack of lamb are served. The wine list is extensive. Arrive by car or by boat. *Rte. 7S, tel. 501/525–2727 or 501/525–1717. Reservations advised. AE, D, MC, V.*

Moderate   **Cajun Boilers.** Red-checkered tablecloths and a tin roof belie the exceptional crayfish, lobster, shrimp, and crabs, which come as hot and spicey as you can take it. Try the "Rajun Cajun" seafood platter. *Albert Pike, tel. 501/767–5695. No reservations. AE, DC, MC, V. Closed Sun.*

Sawmill Depot. In this brick and wood-paneled old train station, downtown lunch fare includes robust sandwiches and dinners run to steak, seafood, and salad bar. *100 Broadway Terr., tel. 501/623–3082. No reservations Feb.–Apr. weekends. AE, D, DC, MC, V. Closed Sun.*

The Venetian Room. This elegant setting, complete with chandeliers and candlelight, in the famous Arlington hotel is best for elaborate buffet brunches with live piano music on Sunday. The cuisine is Continental. *Central and Fountain Sts., tel. 501/623–7771. Reservations advised. AE, D, MC, V.*

Inexpensive   **Cookin' With Jazz.** This small, friendly place features gumbo dishes and po'boy sandwiches. *3907 Central Ave., tel. 501/525–5629. No reservations. AE, MC, V. BYOB. Closed Mon.*

Lodging   For price ranges, see Chart 2 (B) in Chapter 1.

Expensive   **Lake Hamilton Resort and Conference Center.** On a peninsula on Lake Hamilton, this luxurious all-suite resort built in 1984 is contemporary in design, with generous use of wood and stone. All rooms have balconies and lake views. *U.S. 270W, Box 2070, 71914, tel. 501/767–5511 or 800/426–3184. 114 suites. Facilities: restaurant, lounge, indoor pool, tennis court, boat rentals. AE, D, DC, MC, V.*

Mountain Harbor Resort. Rustic cabins on Lake Ouachita and luxury condominiums with fireplaces are part of this new complex near the town of Mount Ida, which also includes studios and motel units. *22 mi west of Hot Springs on U.S. 270, Box 807, Mount Ida 71957, tel. 501/867–2191 or 800/832–2276. 76 units. Facilities: restaurant, tennis, 2 pools, marina, airport shuttle. AE, MC, V.*

Moderate   **The Arlington.** This beautifully renovated spa hotel is decorated with opulent clusters of art-deco chandeliers and acres of chintz. Half- and full-day beauty programs are available, so you can glow alongside all the silver and brass. *Central and Fountain Sts., 71901, tel. 501/623–7771 or 800/626–9768; fax 501/623–6191. 486 rooms. Facilities: 3 restaurants, 2 pools, mountainside hot tub, bathhouse, tennis courts, conference facilities, shopping arcade, golf, hiking trails. AE, D, MC, V.*

The Majestic Resort Spa. This renovated hotel features thermal mineral baths and wonderful massages administered by veteran hands. A weekend package for two is $150. *Park and Central Ave., 71901, tel. 501/623–5511 or 800/643–1504. 250 rooms. Facilities: pool, conference facilities, shops. AE, MC, V.*

Inexpensive   **Edgewater Resort.** These clean, air-conditioned cottages with knotty-pine interiors and kitchenettes are set on the shore of Lake Hamilton. *200 Edgewater Dr., 71913, tel. 501/767–3311 or*

800/234–3687. 9 cottages. Facilities: boat dock and ramp. MC, V.

Campgrounds   There are several public campsites on lakes Ouachita, Catherine, and DeGray. For a recreation directory, contact **Ouachita National Forest** (*see* Sports and Outdoor Activities, *above*). **Hot Springs National Park** (800 McClendon Rd., Hot Springs 71901, tel. 501/624–5912) has campsites with electricity, showers, pool, laundry, and RV hookups.

Fort Smith

Tourist   **Fort Smith:** Chamber of Commerce (Box 1668, 72902, tel. 501/
Information   783–6118).

Exploring Fort   Fort Smith is where east met west in frontier days. The site of
Smith   the original **fort** (3rd and Rogers Aves., tel. 501/783–3961) is
preserved as a National Historic Site commemorating events relating to the federal government's policy on Native Americans during the 1800s. Also preserved here is the historic courtroom from which Judge Isaac C. Parker dispensed frontier justice. The court, the famous "Hell on the Border" jail, and the old gallows have been restored. Nearby is the **Old Fort Museum** (320 Rogers Ave., tel. 501/783–7841) and **Miss Laura's Social Club** (North B St. and Clayton Expressway), the only former bordello on the National Register of Historic Places.

Hope

Tourist   **Hope-Hempstead County:** Chamber of Commerce (108 W. 3rd
Information   St., tel. 501/777–3640).

Exploring Hope   Hope's latest claim to fame is as the birthplace of President Bill Clinton. The city is also long renowned for champion watermelons. Melons weighing 150 to 200 pounds are common here, celebrated each August with the **Hope Watermelon Festival.** The city itself offers a taste of small-town life in Arkansas. Nearby is **Old Washington Historic State Park** (Box 98, Carrol St., Hope 71862, tel. 501/983–2684), an important resting stop on the rugged Southwest Trail and the Confederate capital of Arkansas following the capture of Little Rock. Within a short drive of Hope is the **Crater of Diamonds State Park** (Hwy. 301, tel. 501/285–3113) near Murfreesboro. The park features the only public diamond mine in the world, and you can keep what you find.

Elsewhere in the State

Helena

Getting There   Helena is on the banks of the Mississippi River and can be reached by Rte. 49. The St. Francis National Park extends north to Marianna, and the White River Wildlife Refuge is west toward Arkansas Post.

What to See   **The Delta Cultural Visitors' Center,** housed in a 1912 train de-
and Do   pot, opened in late 1990 as the first phase of an $8.5 million project delving into local heritage. The museum documents area roots of Delta blues (B. B. King and other great blues musicians played at Helena's infamous Hole in the Wall club during the '40s), the river life described by Mark Twain, and pioneer

days when local farmers were defeated by floodwaters. Also here are an excellent gift shop and an information desk that serves as a visitor center for the area. *Missouri and Natchez Sts., tel. 501/338–8919. Admission free.*

In October the **King Biscuit Blues Festival** (tel. 501/338–9144) attracts musicians from all over the nation. The town also has the **Edwardian Inn** (317 Biscoe St., tel. 501/338–8247), a restored 1904 Victorian mansion with 12 bedrooms. For further information, contact the **Phillips County Chamber of Commerce** (Box 447, Helena 72342–0447, tel. 501/338–8327).

Texarkana

Getting There Texarkana is on the Arkansas border with Texas and can be reached via I-30.

What to See and Do The **Perot Theater** (221 Main St., tel. 903/792–4992) hosts symphony orchestras, pop and country concerts, and ballet. The theater is named after Texarkana native H. Ross Perot, who financed the restoration of the 1924 structure. The **Texarkana Historical Museum** (219 State Line Ave., tel. 903/793–4831) has artifacts of the Caddo Indians and turn-of-the-century furniture and farm implements. The **Ace of Clubs House** (420 Pine St., tel. 903/793–7108) is a rare 1885 Victorian built from the winnings of a poker game. Each room is furnished in a different period.

There is a **Bluegrass Festival** in Fagan Park on both Memorial Day and Labor Day weekends. For further information, contact the **Texarkana Chamber of Commerce** (Box 1468, 75501, tel. 903/792–7191).

KENTUCKY

By John
Filiatreau

Capital	Frankfort
Population	3,660,257
Motto	United We Stand, Divided We Fall
State Bird	Cardinal
State Flower	Goldenrod

Visitor Information

Kentucky Department of Travel Development (2200 Capital Plaza Tower, Frankfort 40601, tel. 502/564–4930 or 800/225–8747). **Welcome centers:** I–75S at Florence, I–65N at Franklin, I–64W at Grayson, I–24E at Paducah, I–75N at Williamsburg, and U.S. 68 at Maysville.

Scenic Drives

A loop drive of the rugged **Red River Gorge** in the eastern Kentucky mountains starts near Natural Bridge State Park on **Rte. 77** near Slade. **Forest Development Road 918** is a 9-mi National Scenic Byway in the Daniel Boone National Forest near Morehead. The 35-mi stretch of **Little Shepherd Trail** (U.S. 119) between Harlan and Whitesburg is breathtaking in fall. **Old Frankfort Pike** between Lexington and Frankfort passes through classic Bluegrass countryside.

National and State Parks

National Parks **Daniel Boone National Forest** (U.S. 27, Whitley City; 100 Vaught Rd., Winchester 40391; tel. 606/745–3100) offers spectacular mountain scenery, especially in the Red River Gorge Geological Area, known for its natural arches, native plants, and 300-foot cliffs. **Land Between the Lakes** (100 Van Morgan Dr., Golden Pond 42211, tel. 502/924–5602) is an uninhabited 40-mi-long peninsula between Kentucky and Barkley lakes, run as a demonstration project in environmental education and resource management. **Mammoth Cave National Park** (entrances on Rte. 70, 10 mi west of Cave City, and on Rte. 255, 8 mi northwest of Park City; Mammoth Cave 42259, tel. 502/758–2328) is a 350-mi-long complex of twisting underground passages full of colorful mineral formations.

State Parks Kentucky's 34 state parks reflect a nice balance between letting nature take its course and providing for visitors' amusement. Many are ideal for hiking or simply taking in the beauty of the countryside, but most also offer facilities for picnicking, camping, water sports, and horseback riding. Sixteen have rustic but comfortable lodges and/or cottages; 28 have tent and trailer sites (Apr.–Oct.); 13 have year-round campgrounds. For information contact **Kentucky Department of Parks** (Capital Plaza Tower, Frankfort 40601, tel. 800/255–7275).

Central Kentucky

Louisville

Louisville (locally pronounced "LOO-uh-vul") was founded in 1778 by a Revolutionary War hero, Gen. George Rogers Clark, and named for King Louis XVI in gratitude for France's help during the war. The city's charter was signed in 1780 by Thomas Jefferson, then governor of Virginia, of which Kentucky was the westernmost district. Louisville's culture and history are owed largely to its location, inside a bend in the mighty Ohio River, smack in the center of the eastern half of the nation. During the first half of the 19th century the city was a bustling river port. With the advent of the railroads, it became a hub of train traffic. Waves of European immigrants settled into colorful neighborhoods that retain much of their character today. Louisville attracts crowds of visitors every May for the nation's premier horse race: the Kentucky Derby.

Tourist Information

Louisville: Area Chamber of Commerce (1 Riverfront Plaza, 40202, tel. 502/566–5000). Convention & Visitors Bureau (400 S. 1st St., 40202, tel. 502/584–2121, 800/626–2646, or 800/633–3384 in KY). **Preservation Alliance of Louisville and Jefferson County** (716 W. Main St., Louisville 40202, tel. 502/583–8622).

Arriving and Departing

By Plane **Standiford Field** (tel. 502/367–4636) is 15 minutes south of downtown on I–65. It has a modern, spacious, comfortable terminal and is served by most major carriers. Cab fare from the airport to downtown Louisville runs about $13.

By Car Louisville is well served by interstates. I–64 runs east–west, I–71 northeast, and I–65 north–south. I–264, also known as the Henry Watterson Expressway, rings the city. These converge downtown in a ramp-ridden area known as Spaghetti Junction; confusion here can result in a quick trip to Indiana.

Bus Station **Greyhound** (720 W. Muhammad Ali Blvd., tel. 502/585–3331).

Getting Around Louisville

The downtown area is defined north–south by Broadway and the Ohio, east–west by Preston and 18th streets. **Transit Authority of River City** (1000 W. Broadway, tel. 502/585–1234) operates local buses (fare: 60¢ at peak times, 35¢ other times), as well as a free trolley along 4th Avenue between Broadway and the river. A car is needed for explorations beyond downtown.

Exploring Louisville

Downtown The heart of Louisville is thick with historic sites and is best explored on foot. **West Main Street** has more examples of 19th-century cast-iron architecture than anyplace else in the country except New York City's SoHo. The **Hart Block** (728 W. Main St.), a five-story building designed in 1884, at the height of Louisville's Victorian era, has a facade that is a jigsaw puzzle of cast-iron pieces bolted together. Other historic attractions include the tiny **St. Charles Hotel** (634 W. Main St.), constructed before 1832, and the Roman Catholic **Cathedral of the Assump-**

tion (443 S. 5th St.), a Gothic Revival structure built between 1849 and 1852. The **Jefferson County Courthouse** (531 W. Jefferson St.), a Greek Revival landmark, was designed by Gideon Shyrock in 1835 with the intent of luring the state government to Louisville.

More contemporary sights include the grand, eclectic **Humana Building** (500 W. Main St.), designed by Michael Graves and finished in 1985. The **American Life and Accident Building** (3 Riverfront Plaza), designed by Mies van der Rohe and completed in 1973, is known as the "rusty building" for its covering of oxidized Cor-ten steel. Just off the riverfront Belvedere, the 1988 **Louisville Falls Fountain** spews water in the form of a 375-foot-tall fleur-de-lis, the city's symbol.

The nearby **Kentucky Center for the Arts** (*see* The Arts and Nightlife, *below*), on Riverfront Plaza, is home to a distinguished collection of 20th-century sculpture by such artists as Alexander Calder, Tony Smith, and Jean Dubuffet. The **Museum of History and Science/IMAX Theatre** (727 W. Main St., tel. 502/561–6103; admission charged), a 19th-century warehouse full of science arcades and demonstrations, includes an Egyptian mummy's tomb, a Foucault pendulum, and lots of hands-on exhibits.

While near the river, check out the ***Belle of Louisville*** (tel. 502/625–2355), usually moored at the City Wharf at 4th and River streets with its calliope wailing. The gingerbread-trim steamboat, built in 1914, is the oldest Mississippi-style sternwheeler still afloat. Should you grow foot-weary, you can hire an elegant horse-drawn carriage from **Derby City Horse Carriage** (tel. 502/895–7268) or **Louisville Horse Trams** (tel. 502/581–0100).

Other Attractions **Butchertown,** east of downtown, was settled in the 1830s, largely by Germans who worked in nearby meat-packing plants and lived in "shotgun" and "camelback" houses built in the shadow of the (still-in-business, often redolent) **Bourbon Stock Yards.** To the west is **Portland,** a community of French settlers that sprang up in 1814 where goods came ashore to be portaged past the Falls of the Ohio. Today barges carry 4.3 million tons of cargo per month through the **McAlpine Locks and Dam** (27th St.).

The **Cherokee Triangle,** a few miles southeast of downtown, is a classic Victorian village of grand homes on broad tree-lined streets, built between 1870 and 1910. A few miles out Bardstown Road from the Triangle is **Farmington** (tel. 502/452–9920; admission charged), a Federal-style mansion built in 1810 after a design by Thomas Jefferson, whose special touches include two octagonal rooms and an adventurously steep hidden staircase.

Old Louisville, just south of downtown, is the most elegant of Louisville's neighborhoods. Its architectural styles include Victorian Gothic, Richardsonian Romanesque, Queen Anne, Italianate, Châteauesque, and Beaux Arts; leaded- and stained-glass windows, turrets, and gargoyles are much in evidence. On the area's southern edge is the **University of Louisville** campus, where you'll find the **J. B. Speed Art Museum** (2035 S. 3rd St., tel. 502/636–2893; closed Mon.), with masterworks by Rembrandt, Rubens, Picasso, Henry Moore, and many others, as well as frequent contemporary exhibits.

Just south of the university is **Churchill Downs** (700 Central Ave., tel. 502/636-4400; admission charged; Apr.-June, Oct.-Nov.), world-famous as the home of the Kentucky Derby. Since the track's opening in 1875, scores of heroic three-year-old Thoroughbreds have thundered past its famous Twin Spires into legend. During the normal racing seasons, check out **"Dawn at the Downs"** (tel. 502/636-3351), a program in which fans may visit the track shortly after daybreak on Saturday, when the horses are out for exercise and the infield grass and flower beds are dew-bejeweled. It's magical. The **Kentucky Derby Museum** (tel. 502/637-1111; separate admission charged) documents the careers of the champions. If you plan a trip to Louisville during the annual Kentucky Derby Festival—the two weeks leading up to and including Derby Day (the first Saturday in May)—be prepared to pay more for everything from lodging to transportation.

Just east of Louisville is pastoral **Locust Grove** (tel. 502/897-9845; admission charged), once the home of Louisville's founder. Three presidents—James Monroe, Andrew Jackson, and Zachary Taylor—slept here.

In the Vicinity In the bourbon-whiskey country near Louisville is **Bernheim Forest** (on Rte. 245 just off I-65, about 25 mi south of the city, tel. 502/543-2451). This 10,000-acre preserve features 1,800 species of plants, a nature center, a museum, picnic areas, hiking trails, and lakes; in spring it has the state's best show of rhododendrons and azaleas. A few miles southeast on scenic Rte. 245 is Clermont, site of the **Jim Beam American Outpost Museum** (tel. 502/543-9877), which has a collection of the famous Jim Beam bourbon decanters and a film about making bourbon.

Farther southeast on Rte. 245 is **Bardstown,** the bucolic, historic city best known as the site of **My Old Kentucky Home** (tel. 502/348-3502; closed Mon. Jan.-Feb.). This Georgian Colonial mansion was visited by Stephen Foster in 1852, shortly before he wrote the famous song that makes tears well up in the eyes of all Kentuckians when it's sung on Kentucky Derby Day. **Old Bardstown Village and Civil War Museum** (near 1st St. and Broadway, tel. 502/348-5204 or 502/348-6501) has war displays and a fine 52-minute multimedia presentation about Kentucky's history and culture. Both Bardstown sites charge admission.

Southeast of Bardstown on Rte. 52, near Loretto, is **Maker's Mark Distillery** (tel. 502/865-2881; closed weekends Jan.-Feb.), a National Historic Landmark and a working distillery that you can tour for free. Southwest of Bardstown is the **Abraham Lincoln Birthplace National Historic Site** (3 mi south of Hodgenville on U.S. 31E/Rte. 61, tel. 502/358-9474), where Lincoln was born on February 12, 1809. About 110 acres of the original Thomas Lincoln farm are included in the 116-acre park.

Parks and Gardens

In 1891, Louisville's Board of Parks hired Frederick Law Olmsted, designer of New York's Central Park, to design a system of public lands to be "free to all forever." Among the results were **Shawnee Park** in the west, a plain of river bottomland; **Cherokee Park** in the east, where Beargrass Creek wanders among woods and meadows; and **Iroquois Park** in the south, a tall, rugged escarpment offering vistas of the city. Sometimes overlooked by visitors and natives alike is little **Tyler Park** on Baxter Avenue, an Olmsted-designed jewel that serves as an envelope of solitude in the midst of city bustle.

What to See and Do with Children

The Louisville Zoo (1100 Trevilian Way, tel. 502/459–2181) exhibits more than 1,300 animals in naturalistic environments. In summer, **Kentucky Kingdom Amusement Park** (Kentucky Fair and Exposition Center, tel. 502/366–2231) has rides and games, including three roller coasters, a water park, and a playground for young children. **Stage One: The Louisville Children's Theatre** (425 W. Market St., tel. 502/584–7777 or 800/283–7777) offers professional productions on weekends from October to May.

Shopping

The Galleria (4th Ave. between Liberty St. and Muhammad Ali Blvd.), a glass-enclosed mall with 80 stores and 11 fast-food restaurants, is a city melting pot and the best place to shop downtown. **Bardstown Road,** southeast of downtown, is a 2-mi strip for strolling and browsing in antiques shops, bookstores, and boutiques. The **Jefferson Mall** (tel. 502/968–4101), 10 mi south of downtown on Outer Loop, is a huge enclosed mall, with more than 100 stores. The **Biggs** "hyperstore" (12975 Shelbyville Rd., Middletown, tel. 502/244–4760) is what its name suggests—big. It has everything from pastries to chainsaws, at bargain prices. **Lazarus** (tel. 502/966–1809), in the Jefferson Mall, is the city's leading department store. The **Kentucky Art & Craft Gallery** (609 W. Main St., tel. 502/589–0102) sells top-quality crafts. **Baer Fabrics** (515 E. Market St., tel. 502/583–5521) has been working on a world-renowned collection of buttons since 1905. **Joe Ley Antiques** (615 E. Market St., tel. 502/583–4014) has an outstanding 2-acre litter of hardware, fixtures, and doodads.

Spectator Sports

Horse Racing The Kentucky Derby at **Churchill Downs** (*see* Exploring Louisville, Other Attractions, *above*) is a *very* tough ticket—unless you're willing to join tens of thousands of seatless young revelers in the infield, where you're unlikely even to get a glimpse of a horse.

Dining

Louisville has eating options to suit any taste or pocketbook. Dining alternatives range from sophisticated gourmet restaurants with adventurous menus and tuxedoed waiters to no-frills family-style eateries where a server might put a thumb through your sandwich. In general, a casual atmosphere prevails; you won't often encounter dress codes. For price ranges, see Chart 1 (B) in Chapter 1.

Expensive **Cafe Metro.** An ever-changing, ever-unusual menu offers such entrées as grilled salmon with a sauce of capers, cucumbers, and dill. The ambience is street-smart and suggestive of Paris.

1700 Bardstown Rd., tel. 502/458–4830. AE, MC, V. Closed Sun.

Equus. The decor is dark and elegant, with fresh flowers, crisp napery, and paintings of horses. The food is classic in style, prepared with flair. A house specialty is shrimp Jenkins: poached with brown sugar, garlic, lemon juice, fresh rosemary, and Tabasco, then splashed with Kentucky bourbon. *122 Sears Ave., tel. 502/897–9721. AE, DC, MC, V.*

★ **Lilly's.** One of Louisville's most daring restaurants has a menu that changes frequently and always features dishes made with fresh, homegrown ingredients, such as pork tenderloin topped with a fig-and-port *beurre rouge.* The glittery, vaguely art deco–style dining room, in green, black, and purple, is as bold as the cuisine. *1147 Bardstown Rd., tel. 502/451–0447. Reservations advised. AE, MC, V.*

★ **Vincenzo's.** Deep leather chairs, 17th-century paintings, and crisp tablecloths complement just-so service. For the main course, consider *vitello alla Sinatra* (spinach-stuffed veal scaloppine with wine sauce). *Humana Bldg., 150 S. 5th St., tel. 502/580–1350. Reservations advised. AE, D, DC, MC, V. Closed weekends.*

Moderate **Asian Pearl.** The walls sport full-color portraits of Oriental meals. A standout from the menu is Uncle Lin's chicken (lightly battered chunks sautéed with fresh zucchini and Chinese vegetables, with hot-and-spicy sauce). *2060 S. Hurstbourne Pkwy., tel. 502/495–6800. Reservations advised Fri. and Sat. and for large groups. AE, MC, V.*

★ **Cafe Mimosa.** This dark, quiet nook offers American and French fare but specializes in Vietnamese dishes. A good starter is *goi cuon* (delicate rice-paper cylinders surrounding shrimp, chicken, vermicelli, and vegetables, with sweet peanut sauce for dipping). *1216 Bardstown Rd., tel. 502/458–2233. AE, MC, V. Closed Mon.*

Jade Palace. The decor is suburban-shopping-center Mandarin, and service is variable, but the Friday–Sunday *dim sum* (a lavish buffet of Chinese appetizers and finger foods) is justly famous, and the dinner menu has just about everything your heart desires. If you're feeling adventurous, try *kwai may far chi* (sautéed squid with mushrooms, snow peas, onions, and Chinese vegetables with a 10-flavor hot sauce). *1109 Herr La., tel. 502/425–9878. AE, MC, V.*

La Paloma. Tile floors, strings of garlic and chile peppers, wood beams, and plenty of light deck this pleasant dining room. The menu offers creative variations on Mediterranean themes, such as Tuscan chicken (half a bird rubbed with olive oil and served with a shallot-port sauce). *3612 Brownsboro Rd., tel. 502/895–5493. MC, V.*

★ **Mark's Feed Store.** The atmosphere is decidedly no-frills, with concrete floors, rough-hewn wooden walls, and rolls of paper towels on the tables. What attracts the hordes of sauce-slathered diners are generous servings of tender, hickory-smoked, western Kentucky–style barbecue—slow-cooked, never refrigerated or reheated, and "pulled" rather than sliced. If you have the capacity, try Mark's homemade buttermilk pie for dessert. *11422 Shelbyville Rd., tel. 502/244–0140. AE, MC, V.*

Inexpensive **Check's Cafe.** In this Germantown eatery the fare, like the atmosphere and the service, is decidedly down-home. Among menu favorites are chili, fish, and bratwurst sandwiches. *1101 E. Burnett Ave., tel. 502/637–9515. No credit cards.*

Jessie's Family Restaurant. There's nothing fancy about Jessie's Formica tables and vinyl-covered booths. There's nothing fancy about the good food either: Plate-lunch favorites include panfried pork chops and pepper steak with rice. *9609 Dixie Hwy., tel. 502/937–6332. No credit cards.*

The Rudyard Kipling. This diner in a renovated 19th-century house in Old Louisville has music and poetry most nights and becomes a dinner theater (separate admission; reservations advised) on Thursday, Friday, and Saturday. Try crêpes Delbert (ham, black beans, and mushrooms in a sauce of cheese, mustard, and Chablis). *420 W. Oak St., tel. 502/636–1311. AE, DC, MC, V. Closed Sun.*

Lodging

Like any port city, Louisville has a long tradition of hospitality to visitors. You can choose from lovingly restored, pricey downtown hotels, to Roaring Twenties elegance, or opt for a budget room in a place that promises to leave the light on for you. B&B accommodations can be found through **Kentucky Homes B&B** (1431 St. James Ct., Louisville 40208, tel. 502/635–7341). For price ranges, see Chart 2 (B) in Chapter 1.

Expensive **The Brown.** This 16-story historic hotel (built in 1923) has been fully restored, with old-English-style furnishings, artwork, atmosphere, and service. *4th St. and Broadway, 40202, tel. 502/583–1234 or 800/866–7666; fax 502/587–7006. 294 rooms. Facilities: restaurant, bar, exercise equipment. AE, D, DC, MC, V.*

Hyatt Regency Louisville. Hyatt's familiar plant-bestrewn atrium and glass-and-brass lobby are the focus of this 18-story hotel. The rooms have been redone on a back-to-nature theme, with redwood and soft pastels. *320 W. Jefferson St., 40202, tel. 502/587–3434; fax 502/581–0133. 388 rooms. Facilities: restaurant, bar, indoor pool, spa, tennis, supervised children's activities, concierge. AE, D, DC, MC, V.*

★ **The Seelbach.** The refurbished guest rooms in this 11-story landmark (built in 1905), part of the Doubletree chain, have four-poster beds, armoires, and marble baths with gold fixtures. *500 4th Ave., 40202, tel. 502/585–3200 or 800/626–2032; fax 502/585–3200, ext. 292. 322 rooms. Facilities: restaurant, bar, concierge. AE, D, DC, MC, V.*

Moderate **Courtyard by Marriott.** This four-story motor hotel has large, light rooms around a spacious, trademark central courtyard. Warm pastels, light woods, and greenery soothe travelers. *9608 Blairwood Rd., 40222, tel. 502/429–0006; fax 502/429–5926. 151 rooms. Facilities: restaurant, bar, pool, valet service, exercise equipment. AE, D, DC, MC, V.*

The Executive Inn. The English Tudor style of this six-story hotel near the airport is carried through from the public areas to the rooms, which may look snug or gloomy, according to your taste. Some have private patios or balconies. *978 Phillips La. (off I–64), 40209, tel. 502/367–6161, 800/626–2706, or 800/222–8284 in KY; fax 502/367–6161. 465 rooms. Facilities: restaurant, bar, indoor and outdoor pools, exercise room. AE, D, DC, MC, V.*

★ **Galt House East.** Overlooking the river, this downtown hotel has an elaborately landscaped, modern 18-story atrium, but the room furnishings are of the grandpa's-overstuffed-chair variety, emphasizing old-timey comfort. *141 N. 4th Ave., 40202,* *tel. 502/589-3300 or 800/843-4258; fax 502/585-4266. 600 rooms. Facilities: restaurant, bar, pool. AE, D, DC, MC, V.*

Old Louisville Inn Bed & Breakfast. The guest rooms in this 1901 brick house have elaborately carved mahogany woodwork and are furnished with antiques. The atmosphere and service have a pleasant time-machine quality. *1359 S. 3rd St., 40208, tel. 502/635-1574; fax 502/637-5892. 11 rooms. MC, V.*

Inexpensive **Breckinridge Inn.** This two-story motor hotel is clean, plain, and comfortable. The predominant style is art deco in the recently refurbished guest rooms. *2800 Breckinridge La. (at I-264), 40220, tel. 502/456-5050; fax 502/451-1577. 123 rooms. Facilities: restaurant, bar, indoor pool, sauna, valet service, tennis. AE, D, DC, MC, V.*

★ **Days Inn Downtown.** This conveniently located eight-story motor hotel has clean, spacious rooms decorated with muted colors in Early American style. *101 E. Jefferson St., 40202, tel. 502/585-2200; fax 502/585-2200, ext. 123. 177 rooms. Facilities: restaurant, bar, indoor pool, whirlpool, valet service. AE, D, DC, MC, V.*

Wilson Inn. Far from downtown and painted a horrid salmon color outside, this five-story motor hotel has a pleasant, tree-filled lobby. Milder pastels and earth tones predominate in the plain, contemporary rooms. *9802 Bunsen Pkwy. (I-64 at Hurstbourne La.), 40299, tel. 502/499-0000 or 800/333-9457; fax 502/499-0000, ext. 152. 44 rooms, 32 suites. Facilities: valet service. AE, D, DC, MC, V.*

The Arts and Nightlife

For news of arts and entertainment events, look for the Chamber of Commerce's *Louisville* magazine on newsstands and for the Friday and Saturday editions of *The Courier-Journal* newspaper.

The Arts **Actors Theatre of Louisville** (316 W. Main St., tel. 502/585-1210) is a Tony Award–winning repertory theater in a ca. 1837 bank building designated a National Historic Landmark. **The Broadway Series** (611 W. Main St., tel. 502/584-7469) hosts touring productions of Broadway's best. **Shakespeare in the Park** (Central Park at S. 4th St., tel. 502/634-8237) transforms Louisville into the Bard's town on summer weekends.

The three stages at the **Kentucky Center for the Arts** (5 Riverfront Plaza, tel. 502/562-0100 or 800/283-7777) are alive with entertainment ranging from Broadway to Bach, bagpipes to bluegrass. The **Louisville Orchestra** (609 W. Main St., tel. 502/584-7777 or 800/283-7777) has received international attention for its recordings of contemporary works.

Nightlife The **Funny Farm Comedy Niteclub** (1250 Bardstown Rd. in the Mid-City Mall, tel. 502/459-0022) and the **Legends Comedy Club** (9700 Bluegrass Pkwy. in the Hurstbourne Hotel & Conference Center, tel. 502/459-0022) present circuit comics of the stand-up variety. **LaBo's** (Lebanon Junction, about 30 minutes south of Louisville on I-65, tel. 502/833-4707 or 502/833-9307) is a down-home venue for country music and dancing. **Uncle Pleasant's** (2126 S. Preston Hwy., tel. 502/634-4804) presents local and touring bands whose music ranges from practically blues to almost-country to rock to purt'near punk.

Lexington and the Bluegrass

Lexington, the world capital of racehorse breeding and burley tobacco (a thin-bodied, air-curved variety), was named by patriotic hunters who camped here in 1775, shortly after hearing news of the first battle of the Revolutionary War, at Lexington, Massachusetts. A log structure built by a member of that historic hunting party is preserved to this day, on the campus of Transylvania University. The Bluegrass is a lush region of rolling hills, meandering streams, and manicured horse farms.

Tourist Information

Frankfort/Franklin County: Tourist and Convention Commission (100 Capital Ave., Frankfort 40601, tel. 502/875–8687). **Lexington:** Greater Lexington Convention & Visitors Bureau (Suite 363, 430 W. Vine St., 40507, tel. 606/233–1221 or 800/845–3959). **Richmond:** Tourism Commission (Box 250, City Hall, 40476, tel. 606/623–1000).

Getting There

By Plane   **Lexington Bluegrass Airport** (4000 Versailles Rd., tel. 606/254–9336), 4 mi west of downtown Lexington, is served by Delta, USAir, and regional lines.

By Car   The Lexington area and the Bluegrass are well served by I–64 east–west, I–75 north–south, and the state parkway system, a toll network that bisects the state east–west.

Exploring Lexington and the Bluegrass

Lexington   Downtown, take a hike—or a tour in a horse-drawn carriage from **Lexington Livery Co.** (tel. 606/259–0000; $25 for a 30-minute tour). In the **Gratz Park Historic District,** near 2nd Street and Broadway, are two fine houses from 1814: the lavish, privately owned **Gratz House** (231 N. Mill St.), built by a rich hemp manufacturer, and the **John Hunt Morgan House** (201 N. Mill St., tel. 606/253–0362), the former home of a swashbuckling Confederate general and his namesake great-grandson, who won a Nobel Prize in 1933 for proving the existence of the gene. Check out the statue of General Morgan on the lawn of the **Fayette County Courthouse** (215 W. Main St.). When it was unveiled in 1911, it caused quite a stir because it portrays the Rebel raider astride a stallion though his best-known mount was a mare, Black Bess.

The Greek Revival campus of **Transylvania University** (300 N. Broadway, tel. 606/233–8120), the first college west of the Alleghenies (established in 1780), has left its mark on two U.S. vice presidents, 50 senators, 34 ambassadors, and 36 Kentucky governors. The 1832 **Mary Todd Lincoln House** (578 W. Main St., tel. 606/233–9999) belonged to the parents of Abraham Lincoln's wife and displays Lincoln and Todd family memorabilia. U.S. Senator Henry Clay, "The Great Compromiser," was a green 20-year-old lawyer when he came to Lexington in 1797 and opened his **law office** (176–178 N. Mill St.).

Two attractions at the **University of Kentucky** (Euclid Ave. and
S. Limestone St.) are the **Anthropology Museum** (201 Lafferty
Hall, tel. 606/257–7112), with exhibits on evolution and Kentucky culture; and the **Art Museum** (121 Singletary Center for
the Arts, tel. 606/257–5716), which has an interesting permanent collection and frequent special exhibits.

A Lexington curiosity is the huge **Castle** (just west of the city
on Versailles Rd.), with eight turrets and 70-foot-tall corner
towers. It was started by a Fayette County developer in 1969 as
his private residence but never finished. The **Headley-Whitney
Museum** (Old Frankfort Pike, tel. 502/255–6653; admission
charged) is an eclectic, personal three-building collection of Oriental porcelains, masks, paintings, shells, and jeweled bibe-
lots.

The Bluegrass Kentucky's Bluegrass area boasts more than 400 horse farms,
some with Thoroughbred barns as elegant as French villas.
Among the famous breeding farms is **Calumet** (just west of the
city on Versailles Rd./U.S. 60), which has produced a record
eight Kentucky Derby winners. The antebellum mansion at
Manchester farm (nearby on Van Meter Rd.) is said to have
been the inspiration for Tara in *Gone with the Wind*. **Spend-
thrift** (Ironworks Pike, tel. 606/299–5271) is one of the few
farms that routinely welcomes visitors. Famous horses from
the **C. V. Whitney** farm on Paris Pike have included Regret, the
first filly to win the Kentucky Derby, and the appropriately
named Upset, the only horse ever to finish in front of the legendary Man o'War. **Normandy** (a bit farther out on Paris Pike) has
a famous L-shape barn built in 1927, with a clock tower and roof
ornaments in animal shapes. You'll note that the plank fencing
these farms use to separate their paddocks is sometimes
painted white, sometimes black. Some farm operators claim
that the traditional white provides better visibility for the
horses and is more attractive. Others note that black requires
less frequent repainting—a serious economic factor for farms
that must maintain miles of such fences, which cost about
$18,000 per mile to install (painting's extra).

Southward on scenic U.S. 25 is **Ft. Boonesborough State Park**
(tel. 606/527–3131 or 800/255–7275; admission charged), a reconstruction of one of Daniel Boone's early forts, with a museum and demonstrations of pioneer crafts. In **Richmond,** visit
White Hall State Historic Site (tel. 606/623–9178; admission
charged), the home of the abolitionist Cassius Marcellus Clay, a
cousin of Henry and an ambassador to Russia. The elegant
mansion combines two houses and two styles, Georgian and
Italianate.

In **Berea,** where the Bluegrass meets the mountains, you'll find
charming, tuition-free **Berea College** (tel. 606/986–9341),
founded in 1855, whose 1,500 students—most of them from Ap-
palachia—work for their education. On the campus is the **Appalachian Museum** (Jackson St., tel. 606/986–9341, ext. 6078),
which charts regional history through arts and crafts.

The **Shaker Village of Pleasant Hill** (Hwy. 68, tel. 606/734–
5411; admission charged), 25 mi southwest of Lexington, features 27 restored buildings of frame, brick, or stone, erected
between 1805 and 1859 by members of a religious sect noted for
industry, architecture, and furniture making. In nearby
Harrodsburg, the first permanent settlement in Kentucky, **Old**

Ft. Harrod State Park (tel. 606/734–3314; admission charged) has a full-scale reproduction of the old fort, built on its original 1774 site.

About 15 mi south of Lexington, the beautiful, deep-blue-green **Kentucky River** flows gently but relentlessly through the Bluegrass. The combination of rolling river and rugged rock faces makes for dramatic landscapes. Take Jacks Creek Pike from Lexington through one of the most enchanting parts of Kentucky to **Raven Run Nature Sanctuary** (tel. 606/255–0835), a place of rugged, forested hills and untouched wildlife along the Kentucky River.

In lovely **Danville,** 30 mi southwest of Lexington, you can visit the **McDowell House and Apothecary Shop** (125 S. 2nd St., tel. 606/236–2804; admission charged), the residence and shop of Dr. Ephraim McDowell (a noted surgeon of the early 19th century), refurnished with period pieces. West of Danville on U.S. 150 and north on U.S. 68 is **Perryville Battlefield** (tel. 606/332–8631), the site of Kentucky's most important (and bloodiest) Civil War battle, where 4,241 Union soldiers and 1,822 Confederates were killed or wounded.

Frankfort, between Louisville and Lexington on I–64, was chosen as the state capital in 1792 as a compromise between those cities' rival claims and has been caught in the middle ever since. The **State Capitol** (tel. 502/564–3449), overlooking the Kentucky River at the south end of Capitol Avenue, is notable for its Ionic columns, high central dome, and lantern cupola; guided tours are given. Outside the capitol is the famous **Floral Clock,** a working outdoor timepiece whose face—made of thousands of plants—is swept by a 530-pound minute hand and a 420-pound hour hand.

In Frankfort Cemetery, on East Main Street, you can visit **Daniel Boone's Grave** (he died in Missouri, but his remains were returned to Kentucky in 1845). The restored, Georgian-style **Old Governor's Mansion** (420 High St., tel. 502/564–3000), built in 1798, served as the residence of 33 governors until a new mansion was built in 1914. The later **Governor's Mansion** (tel. 502/564–3449; free tours) is styled after the Petit Trianon, Marie Antoinette's villa at Versailles (France, not Kentucky).

What to See and Do with Children

Kentucky Horse Park (4089 Iron Works Pike, off I–75, Lexington, tel. 606/233–4303) is not just a Thoroughbred showcase; it offers films, a breeds show, and farm tours, as well as a museum and art gallery and campgrounds. The interactive exhibits at the **Lexington Children's Museum** (401 W. Main St., tel. 606/258–3253) include an archaeology dig. **Lexington Children's Theatre** (tel. 606/254–4546) offers performances for young audiences.

Shopping

In Lexington, **Fayette Mall** (3473 Nicholasville Rd., tel. 606/272–3493) has more than 80 stores and a dozen places to eat. For something out of the ordinary, try **Dudley Square** (380 S. Mill St.), in a restored 1881 school building; its shops feature antiques, prints, quilts, and the like. **Victorian Square** (401 W. Main St.) is an entire downtown block of renovated Victorian buildings that now contain tony retail and dining establish-ments. At nearby **Festival Market** (325 W. Main St., tel. 606/254–9888) you can dine in an open-air café or take a spin on an old-time carousel. Lexington also has a plethora of **antiques shops;** the Convention & Visitors Bureau (*see* Tourist Informa-tion, *above*) maintains a list.

Spectator Sports

Horse Racing **Keeneland Race Course** (4201 Versailles Rd., Lexington, tel. 606/254–3412 or 800/456–3412; Apr., Oct.).

Sports and Outdoor Activities

Kentucky's lakes and streams are great for **fishing** for more than 200 species. You're seldom more than a 30-minute drive away from a public **golf** course. The state parks and national forests are full of **hiking** trails. **Hunting** is available on public lands, including the Primitive/Pioneer Weapons Area in Daniel Boone National Forest (*see* National and State Parks, *above*), the first preserve of its kind in the nation. Eastern Kentucky has several rivers with mild to moderate **white-water rafting.** For information, contact the parks department (*see* National and State Parks, *above*), the tourism offices (*see* Tourist Infor-mation, *above*), or the state **Department of Fish and Wildlife Resources** (1 Game Farm Rd., Frankfort 40601, tel. 502/564–4336).

Dining and Lodging

While Lexington offers varied dining options, including Conti-nental and ethnic cuisines, most restaurants outside the city are decidedly down-home. Menus tend to feature country-fried steak, country ham, and fried chicken. Many of the best places to dine are so out of the way and unimpressive-looking that you probably won't discover them on your own. Don't be bashful about asking the locals for guidance. For price ranges, see Chart 1 (B) in Chapter 1.

Most of the best places to lay one's weary head are restored his-toric properties, often modestly priced, that are short on amenities but long on charm. State park lodges and cottages are bargain-priced, rustic but comfortable. In many rural are-as, you'll have to settle for bare-bones accommodations. In Lexington, **Dial-A-Accommodations** (430 W. Vine St., tel. 606/233–7299) can help with reservations. For price ranges, see Chart 2 (B) in Chapter 1.

Berea
Dining and Lodging
★
Boone Tavern. This grand old Colonial-style hotel (1909) is op-erated by Berea College and outfitted with furniture hand-made by students. The restaurant is famous for its spoon bread, chicken flakes in bird's nest, and Jefferson Davis pie. *Box 2345, Main and Prospect Sts., 40403, tel. 606/986–9358 or 606/986–9359. 57 rooms. Facilities: restaurant (jacket required evenings, Sun.), drugstore. AE, D, DC, MC, V. Moderate.*

Harrodsburg
Dining and Lodging
Beaumont Inn. Guest rooms at this exemplar of southern hospi-tality are scattered among four timeworn (but polished) build-ings furnished with antiques. The restaurant specializes in corn pudding and cured Kentucky country ham. *638 Beaumont Dr., 40330, tel. 606/734–3381. 33 rooms. Facilities: restaurant,*

pool, tennis. Closed mid-Dec.–mid-Mar. AE, D, DC, MC, V. Moderate.

Inn at Pleasant Hill. Rooms in 27 restored buildings (ca. 1800)—some with four floors and no elevators—are furnished with Shaker reproductions and hand-woven rugs and curtains. The restaurant, Trustees' House at Pleasant Hill, serves hearty family-style meals and specializes in a tangy Shaker lemon pie that people have been known to drive 100 mi for. *3500 Lexington Rd., 40330, tel. 606/734–5411. 80 rooms. Facilities: restaurant (reservations required), riverboat cruises. No credit cards. Closed Dec. 24–25. Moderate.*

Lexington
Dining
★ **Fleur-de-lys.** This French flower has the ambience of a New York City bistro, with mirrored walls and wide windows offering views of downtown. The cuisine is more country French than haute and may include roast breast of duckling with sauce of sun-dried cherries. *120 S. Upper St., tel. 606/252–7946. Reservations advised. AE, MC, V. Closed Sun.–Mon. Expensive.*

★ **Le Café Français.** Murals of fox-hunting scenes lend a Bluegrass atmosphere to this chic, cozy, markedly French restaurant in a building long occupied by a well-loved, now-defunct eatery called The Stirrup Cup. Menu favorites include escargots in a champagne-garlic sauce and rack of lamb bathed in Dijon mustard and topped with a honey-thyme sauce. *735 E. Main St., tel. 606/266–6646. Reservations advised weekends. AE, MC, V. Expensive.*

A la Lucie. This chef-owned eatery has a cosmopolitan feel, with a tin roof, terrazzo floors, hot colors, green plants, and eclectic art. French, German, and American dishes appear on the menu, but the specialty is whatever fresh seafood is at its seasonal best. *150 N. Limestone St., tel. 606/252–5277. AE, DC, MC, V. Closed Sun. Moderate.*

★ **Alfalfa Restaurant.** In this small, homey, woody, old-fashioned restaurant, the fare is home-cooked international, organically grown vegetarian, and ethnic dishes. The menu, written on a chalkboard, may include ham-and-apple quiche; the house salad is lavish. *557 S. Limestone St., tel. 606/253–0014. No credit cards. Closed Mon. Moderate.*

Dudley's Restaurant. Chic but unpretentious, this restaurant in a 100-year-old schoolhouse has a courtyard shaded by huge tulip poplar trees. A favorite on the Continental menu is pasta with chicken, sun-dried tomatoes, and vegetables. *380 S. Mill St., tel. 606/252–1010. Reservations advised at dinner. AE, MC, V. Moderate.*

A. P. Suggins Bar & Grill. This casual dining spot in Chevy Chase has a menu as long as your leg: Choose from beef, chicken, fish, Kentucky favorites, burgers, salads, soups, and Mexican food. *345 Romany Rd., tel. 606/268–0709. AE, MC, V. Inexpensive.*

★ **Joe Bologna's.** This longtime college hangout occupies a church built in 1890; the original stained-glass windows are still in place. You can feast on small or large servings of an assortment of pastas, as well as pizza. *120 W. Maxwell St., tel. 606/252–4933. MC, V. Inexpensive.*

Lodging **Gratz Park Inn.** In an elegantly refurbished three-story medical building dating from 1887, the guest rooms are furnished with antiques. *120 2nd St., 40507, tel. 606/231–6666 or 800/227–4362; fax 606/233–7593. 44 rooms, 8 suites. Facilities: restaurant, bar, concierge. AE, D, DC, MC, V. Expensive.*

★ **Marriott's Griffin Gate Resort.** This gleaming, seven-story, contemporary resort hotel caters to a youngish crowd that likes physical activities and physical comforts. The rooms have private patios or balconies. *1800 Newtown Pike, 40511, tel. 606/ 231–5100; fax 606/231–5100, ext. 7580. 409 rooms. Facilities: restaurant, bar, health club, indoor pool, tennis, valet service. AE, D, DC, MC, V. Expensive.*

Campbell House Inn. Striving for a bed-and-breakfast ambience, this three-story motel has modern but homey rooms, with traditional furnishings. *1375 Harrodsburg Rd., 40504, tel. 606/ 255–4281, 800/354–9235, or 800/432–9254 in KY; fax 606/254– 4368. 370 rooms. Facilities: restaurant, bar, pool, valet service, tennis. AE, D, DC, MC, V. Moderate.*

Courtyard by Marriott. The trademark of this three-story motel is a sunny, gardenlike central courtyard. The green, brown, and mauve rooms are modern, with light woodwork and oversize desks. *775 Newtown Ct., 40511, tel. 606/253–4646; fax 606/ 253–9118. 146 rooms. Facilities: restaurant, bar, indoor pool, whirlpool, valet service, exercise equipment. AE, D, DC, MC, V. Moderate.*

Wilson Inn. This newly built five-story motor hotel resembles its Louisville counterpart: well away from downtown, contemporary in style, with a tree-filled lobby, and colored a horrid salmon outside and pleasant pastels and earth tones inside. *2400 Buena Vista Dr., 40505, tel. 606/293–6113 or 800/333– 9457; fax 606/293–6113, ext. 157. 110 rooms. Facilities: Continental breakfast. AE, D, DC, MC, V. Inexpensive.*

The Arts and Nightlife

The Arts Lexington's performing-arts scene is vigorous. For information on performances contact the **Actors' Guild** (tel. 606/233– 0663), **Lexington Ballet** (tel. 606/233–3925), **Lexington Philharmonic** (tel. 606/233–4226), and **Opera of Central Kentucky** (tel. 606/245–2373). Concerts, plays, and lectures are also presented at **Transylvania University** and the **University of Kentucky.**

Nightlife After-dark offerings in Lexington are pretty sparse and pretty tame. You might check out **The Brewery,** a friendly country-western bar, and **Breeding's,** where the music is mainstream pop-rock (both at 509 W. Main St., tel. 606/255–2822); **Comedy on Broadway** (144 N. Broadway, tel. 606/259–0013), where stand-up comics crack wise; and **The Wrocklage** (361 W. Shore St., tel. 606/231–7655), the place for alternative, punkish rock.

LOUISIANA

By Honey Naylor

Capital   Baton Rouge
Population   4,419,723
Motto   Union, Justice, and Confidence
State Bird   Pelican
State Flower   Magnolia

Visitor Information

Louisiana Office of Tourism (Box 94291, Baton Rouge 70804–9291, tel. 800/334–8626).

Scenic Drives

Rtes. 56 and 57 form a circular drive south of Houma, where shrimp boats dock along the bayous from May to December. Another circular drive is the **Creole Nature Trail** (Rte. 27) out of Lake Charles. **Rte. 82** runs through the coastal marshes and wildlife refuges along the Gulf of Mexico. The **Longleaf Trail Scenic Byway** south of Natchitoches is a 17-mi highway through the Kisatchie National Forest, linking Rtes. 117 and 119.

National and State Parks

National Parks   The **Jean Lafitte National Historical Park and Preserve** (U.S. Custom House, 423 Canal St., New Orleans 70130, tel. 504/589–3882) preserves coastal wetlands south of New Orleans and offers nature trails and canoeing through exotic swampland. The 100,000-acre **Kisatchie Ranger District** of the **Kisatchie National Forest** (Box 2128, Natchitoches 71457, tel. 318/473–7160) has hiking and equestrian trails through hardwood and pine forests.

State Parks   A prehistoric Native American site dating from ca. 1800 BC to 500 BC, the 400-acre **Poverty Point State Commemorative Area** (Rte. 577, HC-60, Box 208A, Epps 71237, tel. 318/926–5492) is one of the country's most important excavations, with ancient Native American mounds, hiking trails, and an interpretive center. The 600-acre **Louisiana State Arboretum** (Rte. 3, Box 494, Ville Platte 70586, tel. 318/363–6289), lush with trees and plants native to the state, has 2½ mi of nature trails. Fishing, boating, camping, and cabins are available in the 6,500-acre **Chicot State Park** (Rte. 3, Box 494, Ville Platte 70586, tel. 318/363–2403) and at **Bayou Segnette** near New Orleans (7777 Westbank Expressway, Westwego 70094, tel. 504/436–1107), **Lake Bistineau State Park** (Box 589, Doyline 71023, tel. 318/745–3503), **Lake Fausse Point State Park** (Rte. 5, Box 5648, St. Martinville 70582, tel. 318/229–4764), **North Toledo Bend State Park** (Box 56, Zwolle 71486, tel. 318/645–4715), and **Sam Houston Jones State Park** (Rte. 4, Box 294, Lake Charles 70601, tel. 318/855–2665).

New Orleans

Strategically located on the Mississippi River, New Orleans is Louisiana's largest and most important city. From its beginnings in 1718 the city has played a vital role in the nation's history. To wrest control of the port city from the French in 1803, President Thomas Jefferson paid Napoleon $15 million and got the entire Louisiana Territory in the bargain.

"The Big Easy" is the home of the splashiest festival in all of North America: Mardi Gras, which is held each February or March. New Orleans is a fun-loving city with an insouciant spirit reminiscent of the Caribbean. As Jelly Roll Morton said, New Orleans is "the place where the birth of jazz originated." And local chefs gave the world the exotic Creole cuisine. The French Quarter, with its honky-tonk Bourbon Street, is one of the nation's favorite partying places.

Tourist Information

New Orleans: Tourist Commission (1520 Sugar Bowl Dr., 70112, tel. 504/566–5031). Welcome Center (529 St. Ann St., in the French Quarter).

Arriving and Departing

By Plane **New Orleans International Airport** (aka Moisant Field, tel. 504/464–0831), 15 mi west of New Orleans, is served by most major domestic and some foreign carriers. Cab fare for the 20- to 30-minute trip downtown is $21 for one or two passengers, $8 for each additional passenger. The 24-hour **Airport Shuttle** (tel. 504/522–3500) drops passengers off at all hotels. Buses operated by **Louisiana Transit** (tel. 504/737–9611) run between the airport and the Central Business District; the fare is $1.10 (exact coin change).

By Car I–10 is the major east–west artery through the city; I–55, which runs north–south, connects with I–10 west of town. I–59 heads for the northeast. U.S. 61 and 90 also run through the city.

Train and Bus **Union Passenger Terminal** (1001 Loyola Ave., tel. 504/528–
Station 1610).

Getting Around New Orleans

The French Quarter is best savored on leisurely strolls; the Central Business District (CBD) is also easily walkable.

By Car Driving in New Orleans can be maddening. French Quarter streets are often clogged with traffic, street signs are indecipherable, and tow trucks operate with lightning speed. Leave your car in a secured garage until it's needed for excursions.

By Public The **Regional Transit Authority,** or RTA (tel. 504/569–2700,
Transportation TDD 504/569–2838), operates the bus and streetcar system, staffs a 24-hour information line, and puts out a route map that is available free at the tourist welcome center.

Bus and **St. Charles Streetcar** fare is $1 (exact change); the **Easy Rider/CBD Shuttle,** which runs between the Superdome and the Convention Center, costs 50¢. **The Riverfront Streetcar**

($1.25 exact change) links attractions along the Mississippi. The **Vieux Carré shuttle** runs through the French Quarter to the foot of Canal Street. VisiTour passes good on all RTA buses and streetcars cost $4 (one-day) and $8 (three-day).

By Taxi Cabs cruise the French Quarter and the CBD, but not beyond. Reliable companies with 24-hour service are **United Cabs** (tel. 504/522–9771) and **Yellow-Checker Cabs** (tel. 504/943–2411). The fare is $1.70 at the flag drop, 20¢ for each additional ⅕ mi.

By Ferry A ferry (Crescent City Connection, tel. 504/364–8100; free outgoing, $1 returning) crosses the Mississippi from the Canal Street Wharf to Algiers, leaving the pier every 25 minutes.

Orientation Tours

Walking Tours **Friends of the Cabildo** (tel. 504/5233–3939) offers tours of the French Quarter. Rangers of the **Jean Lafitte National Historical Park and Preserve** (tel. 504/589–2636) conduct free tours of the Quarter and the Garden District. **Heritage Tours** (tel. 504/949–9805) offers literary tours of the Quarter. **Save Our Cemeteries** (tel. 504/588–9357) conducts tours of aboveground cemeteries. Free maps for self-guided walking tours are available at the New Orleans Welcome Center (*see* Tourist Information, *above*).

Bus and Van Tours Two- to three-hour city tours, as well as full- and half-day tours to plantation country, are available from **Gray Line** (tel. 504/587–0861), **New Orleans Tours** (tel. 504/592–0560, 504/592–1991, or 800/543–6332), and **Tours by Isabelle** (tel. 504/367–3963). Gray Line and New Orleans Tours also offer two-hour nightclub tours. **Le 'Ob's Tours** (tel. 504/288–3478) runs a daily black-heritage city tour.

Cruises Riverboat sightseeing and dinner/jazz cruises are offered by the **New Orleans Steamboat Company** (tel. 504/586–8777) and **New Orleans Paddle Wheels** (tel. 594/524–0814). Bayou tours are offered by **Honey Island Swamp Tours** (tel. 504/641–1769) and **Cypress Swamp Tours** (tel. 504/581–4501).

Exploring New Orleans

After touring the French Quarter and the adjacent CBD, you can head upriver (west) to the Garden District and Uptown. Mid-City, between the Quarter and Lake Pontchartrain, is home to lush City Park and the Fair Grounds Race Track. North of town, Lake Pontchartrain, popular for boating and fishing, is lined with marinas, picnic grounds, and seafood restaurants.

The French Quarter and the CBD The French Quarter (also called the Vieux Carré) is the original colony founded in 1718 by French Creoles. A carefully preserved historic district as well as a residential district, the Quarter is also home to some famous French Creole restaurants and many a jazz club. An eclectic crowd ambles in and out of small two- and three-story frame, old-brick, and pastel-painted stucco buildings, most of which date from the mid-19th century. Baskets of splashy subtropical plants dangle from the eaves of buildings with filigreed galleries, dollops of gingerbread, and dormer windows. Secluded courtyards are awash in greenery and brilliant blossoms.

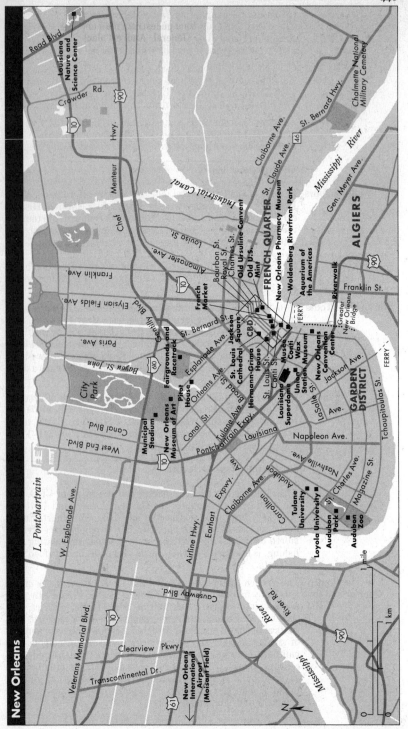

440

New Orleans

L. Pontchartrain

Read Blvd.

Louisiana Nature and Science Center

Crowder Rd.

Menteur Hwy.

Chef

Industrial Canal

Claiborne Ave.

St. Claude Ave.

Mississippi River

St. Bernard Hwy.

Chalmette National Military Cemetery

FRENCH QUARTER

ALGIERS

Gen. Meyer Ave.

Almonaster Ave.

Louisa St.

New Orleans Pharmacy Museum
Woldenberg Riverfront Park
Aquarium of the Americas
Riverwalk

Franklin Ave.

Franklin Ave.

Elysian Fields Ave.

Bourbon St.
Royal St.
Chartres St.
Old Ursuline Convent
Old U.S. Mint

French Market

Franklin St.

Gentilly Blvd

Paris Ave.

St. Bernard St.

CBD

FERRY

Greater New Orleans Bridge

Bayou St. John

Esplanade Ave.

St. Louis
St. Louis Jackson
Square
Cathedral

Musee
Conti
Wax
Museum

New Orleans
Convention
Center

City Park

Fairgrounds and Racetrack

Pitot House

Orleans Ave.

Broad

Hermann-Grima
House

Jackson Ave.

GARDEN
DISTRICT

FERRY

Tchoupitoulas St.

Canal Blvd.

New Orleans Museum of Art

Canal St.

Tulane Ave.

Louisiana
Superdome

Union
Station

LaSalle St.

Ave.

West End Blvd.

Municipal Stadium

Pontchartrain Expwy.

Louisiana

Napoleon Ave.

Nashville Ave.

Charles Ave.

Claiborne Ave.

Carrollton

Audubon

Magazine St.

Earhart
Expwy.

Airline Hwy.

Tulane
University

Loyola University

Audubon
Park

Audubon
Zoo

Causeway Blvd.

W. Esplanade Ave.

Veterans Memorial Blvd.

Clearview Pkwy

Transcontinental Dr.

New Orleans
International
Airport
(Moisant Field)

River Rd.

Mississippi

1 mile

1 km

N

The heart of the Quarter is **Jackson Square,** a pretty green park surrounded by a flagstone pedestrian mall and centered by an equestrian statue of General Andrew Jackson. Originally known to the Creoles as Place d'Armes, the square was renamed in the mid-19th century for the man who defeated the British in the Battle of New Orleans. The mall is alive with sidewalk artists, food vendors, Dixieland bands, tap dancers, and clowns.

St. Louis Cathedral, soaring above the square, is a quiet reminder of the city's spiritual life. The present church dates from 1794 and was restored in 1849. Tours are conducted daily except during services.

The church is flanked by two 18th-century buildings of the **Louisiana State Museum.** As you face the church, the **Cabildo** is on the left, the **Presbytère** on the right. Transfer papers for the Louisiana Purchase of 1803 were signed on the second floor of the Cabildo. It now holds historic documents and artifacts of the region, including a death mask of Napoleon. Damaged by fire in 1988, the structure is expected to reopen by early 1994. The Presbytère, originally built as a home for priests of the church, today houses changing exhibits. *For both: tel. 504/568–6968. Admission charged. Closed Mon. and major holidays.*

Alongside the church are **Pirate's Alley** and **Père Antoine's Alley,** two ancient flagstone passageways redolent of bygone days. You can see what life was like for upscale 19th-century Creole apartment dwellers in the **1850s House,** also part of the state museum, which contains period furnishings, antique dolls, and a quaint kitchen. *525 St. Ann St., tel. 504/568–6968. Admission charged. Closed Mon. and major holidays.*

The **Pontalba Buildings** that line Jackson Square on St. Ann and St. Peter streets are among the oldest apartment houses in the country. Built between 1849 and 1851, they boast some of the city's loveliest ironwork galleries.

The promenade of **Washington Artillery Park,** across Decatur Street, affords a splendid perspective on the square and Old Man River. Nearby is the **French Market**—a complex of shops, offices, and eating places in a row of renovated buildings that once housed markets during Spanish and French rule. Here **Café du Monde** provides a 24-hour haven for café au lait and beignets (square doughnuts).

Downriver from the square, the **Old U.S. Mint** houses exhibits on jazz and Mardi Gras. This was the first branch of the U.S. Mint, in operation from 1838 until 1861. It's now part of the Louisiana State Museum. *400 Esplanade Ave., tel. 504/568–6968. Admission charged. Closed Mon. and major holidays.*

The **Old Ursuline Convent** (1114 Chartres St.), erected in 1749 by order of Louis XV, is the only building remaining from the original colony. The Sisters of Ursula, who arrived in New Orleans in 1727, occupied the building from 1749 to 1824. It is now an archival and research center for the archdiocese and is not open to the public.

The **Gallier House** was built in about 1857 by famed architect James Gallier, Jr., as his family home. This is one of the best-researched house-museums in the city and a fine example of how well-heeled Creoles lived. *1118-32 Royal St., tel. 504/523–6722. Admission charged. Closed Sun. and major holidays.*

The tattered cottage at 941 Bourbon Street—dating from 1772 and typical of houses built by the earliest settlers—is **Lafitte's Blacksmith Shop,** a popular neighborhood bar. According to legend, the cottage was once a front for pirate Jean Lafitte's smuggling and slave trade. The **LaBranche House** (740 Royal St.), dating from about 1840, wraps around the corner of Royal and St. Peter streets. Its filigreed double galleries are the most photographed in the city.

The **New Orleans Pharmacy Museum** is a musty old place where the nation's first licensed pharmacist lived and worked. It's full of ancient and mysterious medicinal things. *514 Chartres St., tel. 504/524–9077. Admission charged. Closed Mon.*

At the **Hermann-Grima House,** guides take you through the Georgian-style town house, built in 1831, and its picturesque outbuildings. On Thursdays in winter you can get a taste of Creole cuisine during cooking demonstrations. *820 St. Louis St., tel. 504/525–5661. Admission charged. Closed Sun. and major holidays.*

Not to be missed are the tableaux in the **Musée Conti Wax Museum,** which wax lifelike on such Louisiana legends as Andrew Jackson, Jean Lafitte, and Marie Laveau, the 19th-century voodoo queen. *917 Conti St., tel. 504/525–2605. Admission charged. Closed Mardi Gras and Christmas.*

Canal Street, the upriver border of the Quarter, is a main thoroughfare of the CBD, as well as the dividing line between Uptown and Downtown. Nerve center of the nation's second-largest port, the CBD has the city's newest high-tech convention hotels, along with ritzy shopping malls, fast-food chains, stores, foreign agencies, and the mammoth Superdome.

At the foot of Canal Street, hard by the Mississippi River, is the **Aquarium of the Americas,** which offers close encounters with aquatic creatures in 60 displays in four major environments. The 16-acre Woldenberg Riverfront Park around the aquarium affords an excellent view of the river. *Tel. 504/565–3033. Admission charged. Closed Christmas.*

The ferry landing is across from the aquarium, and adjacent to it is **Riverwalk.** This busy area comprises Spanish Plaza, a broad, open expanse of mosaic tile with a magnificent fountain; the Riverwalk shopping mall; and docks for various sightseeing riverboats.

The Garden District and Uptown Nestled between St. Charles, Louisiana, and Jackson avenues and Magazine Street, the Garden District is aptly named. Shunned by the French Creoles when they arrived in the early 19th century, American settlers built palatial estates upriver and surrounded them with lavish lawns. Many of the elegant Garden District houses were built during New Orleans's Golden Age, from 1830 until the Civil War. Some of these private homes are open to the public during Spring Fiesta tours.

"Uptown" is the area just upriver of the Garden District. **Tulane** and **Loyola** universities stand side by side on St. Charles Avenue, across from **Audubon Park** (*see* Parks and Gardens, *below*).

Mid-City Located in **City Park** (*see* Parks and Gardens, *below*), the **New Orleans Museum of Art** displays Italian paintings from the 13th to the 18th century, 20th-century European and American paintings and sculptures, Chinese jades, and the Imperial Treasures by Peter Carl Fabergé. *Lelong Ave., tel. 504/488–2631. Admission charged (free to LA residents on Thurs.). Closed Mon. and major holidays.*

Across Bayou St. John from City Park, the **Pitot House** is a West Indies–style house built in the late 18th century. It is furnished with Louisiana and other American 19th-century antiques. *1440 Moss St., tel. 504/482–0312. Admission charged. Closed Sun.–Tues. and major holidays.*

Parks and Gardens

City Park (City Park Ave., tel. 504/482–4888), in Mid-City, is a 1,500-acre urban oasis shaded by majestic live oak trees. Its offerings include golf courses and tennis courts; lagoons for boating, canoeing, and fishing; botanical gardens; and a children's amusement park with puppet shows and storytelling, a carousel, and pony rides.

Smaller but no less lush, the 400-acre **Audubon Park** (6500–6800 blocks of St. Charles Ave.) features a 2-mi jogging trail with exercise stations, a riding stable, a swimming pool, tennis courts, a golf course, and a zoo.

The **Audubon Zoo** covers 58 acres of the park. Wooden walkways afford an up-close look at more than 1,100 animals in natural-habitat settings, including a Louisiana swamp and an African savanna. There's also a petting zoo and elephant and camel rides. *6500 Magazine St., tel. 504/861–2537. Admission charged. Closed major holidays.*

New Orleans for Free—or Almost

Ferry rides (*see* Getting Around New Orleans, *above*) are inexpensive and scenic. **Street musicians** perform daily in Jackson Square and Woldenberg Riverfront Park and on Bourbon, Royal, and Chartres streets. **Free concerts** are given regularly in Dutch Alley and the French Market. The **New Orleans Museum of Art** is free to Louisiana residents each Thursday (*see* Exploring New Orleans, *above*). **Free walking tours** of the French Quarter and the Garden District are conducted by the Park Service (*see* Orientation Tours, *above*). **Mardi Gras,** featuring fabulous floats and eye-popping costumes, is called The Greatest Free Show on Earth.

What to See and Do with Children

The **Aquarium of the Americas** and the **Musée Conti Wax Museum** (*see* Exploring New Orleans, *above*), **City Park** and the **Audubon Zoo** (*see* Parks and Gardens, *above*), as well as the city's many **festivals and parades,** are always a hit with kids. The **Louisiana Children's Museum** (428 Julia St., tel. 504/523–1357) features hands-on activities that are both educational and fun. **Le Petit Théâtre du Vieux Carré** (*see* The Arts and Nightlife, *below*) presents children's shows. **Louisiana Nature and Science Center** (11000 Lake Forest Blvd., tel. 504/246–9381) has a planetarium and nature trails through forests and wetlands.

Shopping

Louisiana's **Tax-Free Shopping** program grants shoppers from overseas a sales-tax rebate. Retailers who display the tax-free sign issue vouchers for the 9% sales tax, which can be redeemed on departure. Present the vouchers with your passport and international plane ticket at the tax-rebate office at New Orleans International Airport, and receive up to $500 in cash back. If the amount redeemable exceeds $500, a check for the difference will be mailed to your home address.

Store hours are generally 10 to 5:30 or 6 Monday through Saturday, noon to 5 on Sunday. Many stores in the French Quarter and in malls stay open till 9 PM. Sales are advertised in the daily *Times-Picayune*.

Shopping Districts Most of the **French Quarter's** ritzy antiques stores, musty bazaars, art galleries, and boutiques are housed in quaint 19th-century structures. The sleek indoor malls of the **CBD** include **Riverwalk** (1 Poydras St.), with more than 200 specialty shops and restaurants; **Canal Place** (1 Canal Pl.), with more than 40 tony shops, a food court, and cinemas; and **New Orleans Centre** (600 Poydras St.), connected by a walkway to the Superdome and a hotel. The **Warehouse District** neighborhood of the CBD, especially Julia Street, below St. Charles Ave. is a major center for art galleries. Upriver from the CBD, **Magazine Street** has 6 mi of antiques stores and boutiques, many of them in once-grand Victorian houses, and **Uptown Square** and **Riverbend** have specialty shops and restaurants cradled in small Creole cottages.

Department Stores **Maison Blanche** (901 Canal St., CBD) is the local department store, with branches in suburban shopping centers. **Woolworth's** (737 Canal St., CBD) has budget shopping.

Specialty Stores
Antiques **Royal Street** in the Quarter is lined with elegant antiques stores; **Magazine Street** has everything from Depression glass to Persian rugs. The Royal Street Guild and the Magazine Street Merchants' Association publish pamphlets that are available free at the New Orleans Welcome Center (*see* Visitor Information, *above*).

Flea Market Locals as well as tourists turn out for the **French Market Flea Market** daily from 7 to 7.

Food **Bayou to Go** (New Orleans International Airport, Concourse C, tel. 504/468–8040) has packaged Louisiana food products. **Old Town Praline Shop** (627 Royal St., tel. 504/525–1413) has the best pralines in town.

Jazz Records For hard-to-find vintage stuff, go to **Record Ron's** (1129 Decatur St. and 407 Decatur St., tel. 504/524–9444).

Masks Handmade Mardi Gras masks are available at **Hidden Images** (523 Dumaine St., tel. 504/524–8730) and **Rumors** (513 Royal St., tel. 504/525–0292).

Spectator Sports

Football **New Orleans Saints** (Superdome, 1 Sugar Bowl Dr., tel. 504/522–2600; Sept.–Dec.). The annual **Sugar Bowl Classic** (tel. 504/525–8573) is played in the Dome on New Year's Day.

Horse Racing There is Thoroughbred racing April to November at **The Fair Grounds** (1751 Gentilly Blvd., tel. 504/943–2200).

Dining

New Orleans is renowned for Creole and Cajun cuisine. The essence of Creole is in sauces, herbs, and the prominent use of seafood. Cajun cooking, with lots of herbs and spices, tends to be red-hot. For price ranges, see Chart 1 (A) in Chapter 1.

Very Expensive **Antoine's.** Established in 1840, Antoine's is the oldest restaurant in the United States under continuous family ownership. An elegant place, it originated oysters Rockefeller, pompano *en papillote*, and puffed-up soufflé potatoes. There is a moderately priced luncheon menu. *713 St. Louis St., French Quarter, tel. 504/581–4422. Reservations advised weekends. Jacket required for dinner. AE, DC, MC, V.*

★ **Commander's Palace.** Housed in a renovated Victorian mansion, this elegant restaurant offers the best sampling of old Creole cooking prepared with a combination of American and French touches. Entrées include veal chop Tchoupitoulas (hickory grilled with Creole seasoning—peppercorn, honey, and roasted peppers) and trout with roasted pecans. *1403 Washington Ave., Garden District, tel. 504/899–8221. Reservations required. Jacket required. AE, DC, MC, V.*

★ **Grill Room.** At this top-rated spot, New American cuisine with strong Continental overtones is served in an opulent setting highlighted by original artworks. As the name suggests, there is a grill, over which much good fish is prepared. *Windsor Court Hotel, 300 Gravier St., CBD, tel. 504/522–1992. Reservations advised. AE, DC, MC, V.*

Expensive **Arnaud's.** Beveled glass, ceiling fans, and tile floors create an
★ aura of traditional southern dining. The lively Sunday jazz brunch is a classic New Orleans experience. Pompano *en croûte* and veal Wohl (medallions of veal in a port wine sauce with crawfish tails) are good entrées; there is little on the menu that isn't excellent. *813 Bienville St., French Quarter, tel. 504/523–5433. Reservations required. Jacket required. AE, DC, MC, V.*

K-Paul's Louisiana Kitchen. National celebrity chef Paul Prudhomme's restaurant is a shrine to New Orleans Cajun cooking. Strangers often must share tables, and a no-reservations policy makes for long lines outside, but the food is great. *416 Chartres St., French Quarter, tel. 504/524–7394. No reservations. AE. Closed weekends.*

Moderate **Chez Hélène.** Stuffed bell peppers, fried chicken, Creole gumbo, and smothered okra are just some of the fine recipes of chef Austin Leslie. The soul and Cajun specialties are marked by spices and fresh herbs. The corn bread is a joy. *1540 N. Robertson St., Mid-City, tel. 504/945–0444. AE, MC, V.*

★ **Galatoire's.** Operated by the fourth generation, Galatoire's is a tradition in New Orleans. Every imaginable Creole dish is served in a large, brightly lit room with mirrors on all sides. Avoid the long lines by arriving after 1:30 PM. *209 Bourbon St., French Quarter, tel. 504/525–2021. No reservations. Jacket and tie required after 5 PM and all day Sun. MC, V. Closed Mon.*

Gautreau's. This small café converted from an old pharmacy is one of the most popular restaurants in the Uptown area. The food is straightforward but imaginative and comfortably Creole. Lunches are very light and include many good soups and salads with the entrées. The dinner menu consists entirely of specials. *1728 Soniat St., Uptown, tel. 504/899–7397. Reservations advised. MC, V. No lunch; no dinner Sun.*

The Palace Cafe. A split-level restaurant with the ambience of a Parisian café, The Palace has a spiral staircase, a tile floor, wood paneling, and splashy murals. Specialties are seafood, game, and rotisseried chicken basted in garlic oil. Wait till you see the menu of chocolate desserts. *605 Canal St., CBD, tel. 504/523–1661. Reservations advised. Dress: casual but neat. DC, MC, V.*

Inexpensive
★ **Camellia Grill.** This classy lunch counter with linen napkins and a maître d' serves the best omelets in town all day long, as well as great hamburgers, pecan pie, cheesecake, and banana-cream pie. Expect long lines on weekends for breakfast. *626 S. Carrollton Ave., Uptown, tel. 504/866–9573. No reservations. No credit cards.*

Napoleon House. This ancient bar with peeling sepia walls and Napoleonic memorabilia has a limited menu, but the *muffuletta* (an Italian sandwich of meats, cheeses, and olive salad served on an oversize round roll) is one of the best in town. The taped classical music and mellow ambience make this a popular spot for chilling out. *500 Chartres St., French Quarter, tel. 504/524–9752. AE, MC, V.*

The Praline Connection. Down-home cooking in the southern-Creole style is the forte of this laid-back restaurant. The fried or stewed chicken, smothered pork chops, barbecued ribs, and collard greens are definitively done. In 1993, a branch opened at 901 South Peters Street in the Warehouse District. *542 Frenchmen St., Faubourg Marigny, tel. 504/943–3934. No reservations. AE, MC, V.*

Lodging

When planning a stay in New Orleans, try to reserve well in advance, especially during Mardi Gras or other seasonal events. Frequently, hotels offer special packages at reduced rates, but never during Mardi Gras, when rates are much higher. For price ranges, see Chart 2 (A) in Chapter 1.

Very Expensive
Fairmont Hotel. The Fairmont, in the CBD, is one of the oldest grand hotels in America. Its lobby is decked in red and gold Victorian splendor. Special touches in every room include four down pillows and electric shoe buffers. *University Pl., 70140, tel. 504/529–7111 or 800/527–4727; fax 504/529–4775. 685 rooms, 50 suites. Facilities: 4 restaurants with bars, heated outdoor pool, fitness center, 2 lighted tennis courts, beauty salon, gift shop, newsstand, valet parking. AE, D, DC, MC, V.*

★ **Windsor Court Hotel.** Consistently rated one of the top luxury hotels in the country, this CBD gem features canopy and four-poster beds, wet bars, and high tea served daily in the plush lobby lounge. *300 Gravier St., 70130, tel. 504/523–6000 or 800/262–2662; fax 504/596–4513. 58 rooms, 266 suites. Facilities: 2 restaurants, lounge, entertainment, Olympic-size outdoor pool, health club, whirlpool, steam bath, sauna, valet. AE, DC, MC, V.*

Expensive
Royal Orleans Hotel (Omni). An elegant white marble hotel in the French Quarter, the Royal O is reminiscent of a bygone era. Rooms, though not exceptionally large, are well appointed with marble baths (telephone in each) and marble-top dressers and

tables. *621 St. Louis St., 70140, tel. 504/529–5333; fax 504/529–7089. 350 rooms, 16 suites. Facilities: 2 restaurants, 3 lounges, rooftop heated pool, exercise room, gift shop, beauty salon and barbershop, valet service, parking. AE, D, DC, MC, V.*

Moderate **Holiday Inn Château Le Moyne.** The atmosphere and decor of this French Quarter inn are mostly Old World, with eight suites in restored Creole cottages that retain the original cedar ceilings and exposed beams. *301 Dauphine St., 70112, tel. 504/581–1303; fax 504/523–5709. 160 rooms, 11 suites. Facilities: restaurant, lounge, outdoor heated pool, valet parking. AE, D, DC, MC, V.*

The Josephine Guest House. European antiques fill the rooms of this restored Italianate mansion in the Garden District, built in 1870. The bathrooms are impressive in both size and decor. A complimentary Continental breakfast, served on Wedgwood china on a silver tray, can be brought to your room. *1450 Josephine St., 70130, tel. 504/524–6361. 6 rooms. AE, DC, MC, V.*

★ **Le Richelieu.** This small, friendly hotel in the French Quarter offers many amenities usually found in luxury high rises. Some rooms have mirrored walls, walk-in closets, and refrigerators; all have hair dryers. Luxury suites are available. *1234 Chartres St., 70116, tel. 504/529–2492 or 800/535–9653; fax 504/524–8179. 69 rooms, 17 suites. Facilities: restaurant, lounge, outdoor pool, valet, free parking. AE, D, DC, MC, V.*

★ **The Pontchartrain Hotel.** Maintaining the grand tradition is the hallmark of this quiet, elegant European-style hotel that has reigned in the Garden District for more than 60 years. In 1991, a $3 million renovation created larger baths and better lighting. Accommodations range from lavish sun-filled suites to small pension rooms with shower baths. *2031 St. Charles Ave., 70140, tel. 504/524–0581 or 800/777–6193; fax 504/529–1165. 60 rooms, 42 suites. Facilities: 2 restaurants, piano bar, 24-hr concierge, limousine, valet service, parking. AE, D, DC, MC, V.*

Inexpensive **French Quarter Maisonnettes.** All the units (some with two or three rooms) are functionally furnished and open directly onto a flagstone courtyard. Private baths and TVs (but no phones) are included. Well-trained pets are welcomed. *1130 Chartres St., 70116, tel. 504/524–9918. 1 room, 7 suites. No credit cards. Closed July.*

★ **St. Charles Guest House.** Room sizes in this simple, family-run guest house in the Garden District vary from large to small "backpacker" rooms with shared baths and no air-conditioning. *1748 Prytania St., 70130, tel. 504/523–6556. 26 rooms (4 share bath). Facilities: Continental breakfast, pool, lounge. AE, MC, V.*

The Arts and Nightlife

The Friday edition of the *Times-Picayune* and the weekly *Gambit* carry comprehensive calendars of events in the arts and entertainment. *New Orleans* magazine (on newsstands), *Gambit* (a free weekly newspaper), and *This Week in New Orleans* and *Where: New Orleans* (both available free in hotels) all carry calendars of events. Credit-card purchases of tickets for events at the Saenger Performing Arts Center and UNO Lakefront Arena can be made through **TicketMaster** (tel. 504/888–8181).

The Arts
Theater
The avant-garde and the satirical are among the offerings at **Contemporary Arts Center** (900 Camp St., tel. 504/523–1216). **Le Petit Théâtre du Vieux Carré** (616 St. Peter St., tel. 504/522–2081) presents more traditional fare, as well as children's theater. Touring Broadway shows and top-name talent appear at the **Saenger Performing Arts Center** (143 N. Rampart St., tel. 504/524–2490). Nationally known artists perform at **Kiefer UNO Lakefront Arena** (6801 Franklin Ave., tel. 504/286–7222).

Concerts
Free jazz concerts are held on weekends in **Dutch Alley** (French Market at St. Philip St., tel. 504/522–2621).

Nightlife
New Orleans is a 24-hour town, meaning that there are no legal closing times and it ain't over till it's over. Bourbon Street in the French Quarter is lined with clubs; many local hangouts are Uptown.

Jazz
Aboard the **Creole Queen** (Poydras St. Wharf, CBD, tel. 504/529–4567) you'll cruise with jazz and a buffet. Live traditional jazz is also on land at the **Palm Court Jazz Cafe** (1204 Decatur St., French Quarter, tel. 504/525–0200), **Pete Fountain's** (2 Poydras St., CBD, tel. 504/523–4374), and **Preservation Hall** (726 St. Peter St., French Quarter, tel. 504/523–8939).

R&B, Cajun, Rock, New Wave
An institution, **Tipitina's** (501 Napoleon Ave., Uptown, tel. 504/897–3943) is a laid-back place with a mixed bag of music. **Jimmy's Music Club** (8200 Willow St., Uptown, tel. 504/861–8200) is popular with the college crowd. Blues and reggae are at funky **Benny's Bar** (938 Valence St., Uptown, tel. 504/895–9405). Two-step to a Cajun band at the **Maple Leaf Bar** (8316 Oak St., Uptown, tel. 504/866–9359) and **Michaul's** (701 Magazine St., CBD, tel. 504/522–5517).

Bars
Pat O'Brien's (718 St. Peter St., French Quarter, tel. 504/525–4823) has three lively bars. **Lafitte's Blacksmith Shop** (941 Bourbon St., French Quarter, tel. 504/523–0066) and the **Napoleon House** (500 Chartres St., French Quarter, tel. 504/524–9752) are longtime favorite hangouts.

Casinos
Various schemes for land-based and floating casinos are under debate in Louisiana, but at press time none were in operation.

Excursion to Plantation Country

Getting There
By car, take I–10W or U.S. 61 from New Orleans and follow the signs to the various plantations. Plantation Country maps are available at the New Orleans Welcome Center (*see* Tourist Information, *above*). Many local tour operators include visits to plantations in their itineraries (*see* Orientation Tours, *above*).

What to See and Do
Plantation Country lies upriver from New Orleans. You can see what went with the wind, and hear tales of Yankee invaders and ghosts, in some of the fine restored antebellum plantations sprinkled around the Great River Road between New Orleans and Baton Rouge, the state capital. The drive is marred by industrial plants, but elegant mansions such as **Rosedown, Nottoway,** and **Houmas House** make the trip worthwhile.

Cajun Country

Tourist Information

Southwest Louisiana: Convention & Visitors Bureau (1211 N. Lakeshore Dr., Lake Charles 70601, tel. 318/436–9588). **Lafayette:** Convention & Visitors Commission (1400 NW Evangeline Thruway, Box 52066, tel. 318/232–3808, 800/346–1958 outside LA, or 800/543–5340 in Canada).

Getting There

By Plane **Lafayette Regional Airport** (tel. 318/232–2808) is served by American Eagle, Atlantic Southeast (Delta), Continental, and Northwest Airlink. **Lake Charles Regional Airport** (tel. 318/477–6051) is served by American Eagle and Continental.

By Car The fastest route from New Orleans through Cajun Country is I–10W. U.S. 90 is a slower but more scenic drive. If you've time, take the back roads for exploring this area. Ferries across the Mississippi cost $1 per car; most bridges are free.

By Train **Amtrak** serves Franklin, Schriever, Lafayette, New Iberia, and Thibodaux.

By Bus **Greyhound Southeast Lines** (tel. 504/343–4891) has frequent daily service to Lafayette, Lake Charles, and environs.

Exploring Cajun Country

Cajun Country, or Acadiana, comprises 22 parishes (counties) of South Louisiana to the west of New Orleans. This is the cradle of the Cajun craze that swept the nation in the 1980s.

Cajuns are descendants of 17th-century French settlers who established a colony they called l'Acadie ("Cajun" is a corruption of "Acadian") in the present-day Canadian provinces of Nova Scotia and New Brunswick. After the British expelled the Acadians in the mid-18th century (their exile is described in Longfellow's epic poem *Evangeline*), they eventually found a home in South Louisiana. There they have been since 1762, sharing their unique cuisine and culture with the nation and imbuing the region with a distinctive flavor summed up in the Cajun phrase *Laissez les bons temps rouler!* (Let the good times roll!).

U.S. 90 dips down south of New Orleans into Terrebonne Parish, a major center for shrimp and oyster fisheries. (The blessing of the shrimp fleets in Chauvin and Dulac is a colorful April event.) A slew of swamp tours are based here, including **Annie Miller's Terrebonne Swamp & Marsh Tours** (tel. 504/879–3934). **Hammond's Cajun Air Tours** (tel. 504/876–0584) takes passengers up for a gull's-eye view of the alligators and other critters that inhabit the coastal wetlands.

Morgan City, on the Atchafalaya River, struck it rich when the first producing offshore oil well was completed on November 14, 1947, and the Kerr-McGee Rig No. 16 ushered in the "black gold rush." In 1917, the original *Tarzan of the Apes* was filmed in Morgan City; at the town **Information Center** (725 Myrtle St., tel. 504/384–3343) a video of the film can be seen.

West of Morgan City, Rte. 182 branches off U.S. 90 and ambles northwest toward Lafayette. For much of the way the road travels along **Bayou Teche,** the largest of the state's many bayous. (*Teche* is an Indian word meaning "snake." According to an ancient legend, the death throes of a giant snake carved the bayou.) The road runs by rice paddies and canebrakes, and on the bayous you can see Cajun *pirogues* (canoelike boats) and cypress cabins built on stilts.

Traveling along Rte. 182, you'll come to **Franklin,** an official Main Street U.S.A. town (the title is bestowed by the National Trust for Historic Preservation). The street, lined with old-fashioned street lamps, rolls out beneath an arcade of live oaks. Six antebellum homes are open for tours in and around town. Franklin is nestled along a bend in Bayou Teche, and there is a splendid view of it from Parc sur le Teche.

Northwest of Franklin, **New Iberia**—the "Queen City of the Teche"—was founded in 1779 by Spanish settlers who named it for their homeland. **Shadows-on-the-Teche** (317 E. Main St., tel. 318/369-6446; admission charged), one of the south's best-known plantation homes, was built in 1834 for sugar planter David Weeks. The big pink house is virtually enveloped in moss-draped live oak trees.

Red-hot Tabasco sauce was created in Louisiana in the 19th century; on **Avery Island** at **McIlhenny's Tabasco Company** (Rte. 329, tel. 318/369-6243), southwest of New Iberia, you can tour the factory where it's still being manufactured by descendants of its creator. Here also are the 200-acre **Jungle Garden,** lush with tropical plants, and **Bird City,** a sanctuary with flurries of snow-white egrets.

Avery Island is actually a salt dome, capped by lush vegetation. So, too, is Jefferson Island, also called **Live Oak Gardens** (284 Rip Van Winkle Rd., off Rte. 14, tel. 318/365-3332). The 19th-century American actor Joseph Jefferson, who toured the country portraying Rip Van Winkle, built a winter home here. His three-story house is surrounded by lovely formal and informal gardens; admission includes a boat ride on Lake Peigneur.

Rte. 31 is a pretty country road that hugs the banks of the Teche between New Iberia and St. Martinville to the north. The little town of **St. Martinville** is awash with legends. Now a sleepy village, it was known in the 18th century as "Petit Paris," a refuge for aristocrats fleeing the French Revolution. It was also a major debarkation point for the exiled Acadians. Longfellow's poem was based on the true story of two young lovers who were separated for years during the Acadian exile. The **Evangeline Oak** (Evangeline Blvd. at Bayou Teche) is said to have been the place where the ill-starred lovers met again—albeit briefly. On the town square is **St. Martin de Tours,** mother church of the Acadians, and the **Petit Paris Museum,** where there is a Mardi Gras collection. Be sure to visit the small cemetery behind the church, where a bronze statue depicts the real-life Evangeline.

The nearby hamlet of **Breaux Bridge** calls itself the Crawfish Capital of the World. The **Crawfish Festival,** held each May, draws upwards of 100,000 people. The town's other claim to fame is the Cajun food and music spot **Mulate's** (*see* Dining and Lodging, *below*).

Fifteen minutes west of Breaux Bridge, **Lafayette** proudly proclaims itself the Capital of French Louisiana. In this part of the state, some 40% of the residents speak Cajun, an antique, 17th-century French dialect. As most Cajuns also speak standard French as well as English, this is a superb place to test your language skills. **Cajun Mardi Gras** rivals its sister celebration in New Orleans. Centrally located, Lafayette is a good base for exploring the region. **Vermilionville** (1600 Surrey St., tel. 318/233–4077 or 800/992–2968, admission charged), a 22-acre living-history museum, depicts early life in the region through architecture, food, and daily programs featuring music and dance. In restored and replica buildings, French-speaking craftspeople demonstrate Acadian craft making and engage visitors in conversation. The **Lafayette Natural History Museum** (637 Girard Park Dr., tel. 318/268–5544; admission charged), within luxuriant Girard Park, offers workshops, movies, concerts, light shows, and a planetarium. It's also the venue for the annual September **Louisiana Native Crafts Festival.** The **Acadiana Park Nature Station** (E. Alexandre St., tel. 318/235–6181; admission free) is a three-story cypress-pole structure with an interpretive center, discovery boxes for children, a nature trail, and guided tours (fee).

Eunice, a tiny speck of a town, is home of the **"Rendez-Vous des Cajuns"** (*see* The Arts and Nightlife, *below*) and of the **Eunice Museum** (220 S. C.C. Duson Dr., tel. 318/457–6540; admission charged). In a former railroad depot, the museum contains displays on Cajun culture, including its music and Mardi Gras. The area around Eunice is the major stomping grounds for the annual **Courir du Mardi Gras,** which features a band of masked and costumed horseback riders on a mad dash through the countryside. It happens annually the Sunday before Fat Tuesday (Mardi Gras).

North of Lafayette, **Grand Coteau** is a religious and educational center, and the entire peaceful little village is on the National Register of Historic Places. Of particular note here is the **Church of St. Charles Borromeo,** a simple wooden structure with an ornate high-baroque interior. Nearby **Chretien Point Plantation** (about 4 mi from Sunset on the Bristol/Bosco Rd., tel. 318/662–5876; admission charged), a splendid antebellum mansion, is a bed-and-breakfast. The staircase in *Tara,* Scarlett O'Hara's home in *Gone with the Wind,* was modeled on the one in this house.

A short drive up I–49 is **Opelousas,** the third-oldest town in the state. Founded by the French in 1720, the town was named for the Appalousa Indians, who lived in the area centuries before the French and Spanish arrived. For a brief period during the Civil War, Opelousas served as the state capital. At the intersection of I–49 and U.S. 190, the **Acadiana Tourist Commission** (tel. 318/948–6263) houses memorabilia of Jim Bowie, the Alamo hero who spent his boyhood here. The **Opelousas Museum and Interpretive Center** (329 N. Main St., tel. 318/948–2589; admission free) traces the history of this region.

Tucked away in the far southwestern corner of the state, **Lake Charles** is a straight shot (71 mi) from Lafayette on I–10. Called Charlie's Lake in the 1760s, the city has more than 50 mi of rivers, lakes, canals, and bayous. The **Imperial Calcasieu Museum** (204 W. Sallier St., tel. 318/439–3797) has an extensive collection on Lake Charles and Imperial Calcasieu Parish, including an old-fashioned pharmacy, an Audubon collection, a Gay Nineties barbershop, and a fine-arts gallery.

The **Creole Nature Trail** (*see* Scenic Drives, *above*) begins on Rte. 27 in Sulphur and continues on Rte. 82. Beautiful in the spring, this drive goes to the **Sabine Wildlife Refuge,** where a paved trail meanders into the wilds. There is an interpretive center and a tower at the end of the trail, which gives you an excellent view of the wilderness. (Take along some insect repellent!)

You can make a detour off the Creole Nature Trail and continue east on Rte. 82 (Hug-the-Coast Highway), which whips along the windswept coastal marshes through **Grand Chenier** to the **Rockefeller Wildlife Refuge.** At this 84,000-acre preserve thousands of ducks, geese, 'gators, wading birds, otters, and others while away the winter months.

Shopping

For Cajun food-to-go, try the **Cajun Country Store** (211 Evangeline Thruway, Lafayette, tel. 318/233–7977) and **B. F. Trappey's & Sons** (900 E. Main St., New Iberia, tel. 318/365–8281).

Antiques-seeking is a favorite pastime here. In Lafayette you can root around **Ruins & Relics** (802 Jefferson and Taft Sts., tel. 318/233–9163) and **Travel Treasures Antique Mall** (Hwy. 93 and W. Congress St., tel. 318/981–9414).

Sports and Outdoor Activities

Biking These flatlands and lush parks make for easy riding. Bikes can be rented at **Pack & Paddle** (601 E. Pinhook Rd., Lafayette, tel. 318/232–5854).

Canoeing Paddling is almost a breeze on the easygoing Whisky Chitto Creek. Canoes can be rented at **Arrowhead Canoe Rentals** (9 mi west of Oberlin on Rte. 26, tel. 318/639–2086 or 800/637–2086).

Fishing Trips to fish, sightsee, bird-watch, or hunt can be arranged at **Cajun Fishing Tours** (1925 E. Main St., New Iberia, tel. 318/364–7141). **Sportsman's Paradise** (tel. 504/594–2414) is a charter fishing facility 20 mi south of Houma. **Salt, Inc. Charter Fishing Service** (tel. 504/594–6626 or 504/594–7581), on Rte. 56 south of Houma at Coco Marina, offers fishing trips in the bays and barrier islands of lower Terrebonne Parish, as well as into the Gulf of Mexico. **Hackberry Rod & Gun** (tel. 318/762–3391) in Cameron is a charter saltwater-fishing service in the far southwest corner of the state.

Golf **City Park Golf Course** (Mudd Ave. and 8th St., Lafayette, tel. 318/268–5557), **Pine Shadows Golf Center** (750 Goodman Rd., Lake Charles, tel. 318/433–8681), and **Vieux Chêne Golf Course** (Youngsville Hwy., Broussard, tel. 318/837–1159) all provide 18 holes.

Hiking/Nature Trails The Old Stagecoach Road in Lake Charles's **Sam Houston Jones State Park** is a favorite for hikers who want to explore the park and the various tributaries of the Calcasieu River; the **Louisiana State Arboretum** in Ville Platte is a 600-acre facility with 4 mi of nature trails (for both, *see* National and State Parks, *above*). There are 7 mi of hiking trails in the **Port Hudson State**

Commemorative Area near Baton Rouge (756 W. Plains-Port Hudson Rd. [Hwy. 61], Zachary, tel. 504/654–3775). Near Natchitoches, backpackers and hikers explore the 8,700-acre **Kisatchie Hills Wilderness,** with its Backbone Trail, part of the Kisatchie National Forest (*see* National and State Parks, *above*).

Horseback Riding Trail rides, pony rides, and even hayrides are offered at **Broken Arrow Stables** (3505 Broken Arrow Rd., off Rte. 3013, New Iberia, tel. 318/369–7669).

Hunting Approximately 1.7 million publicly owned or managed Louisiana acres are open to hunting. For information on permits, limits, and seasons, contact the **Louisiana Department of Wildlife & Fisheries** (Box 15570, Baton Rouge 70895, tel. 504/342–5868).

Spectator Sports

NBA exhibition and collegiate basketball, professional soccer exhibition games, wrestling, and other sports events take place at the **Cajundome** (444 Cajundome Blvd., Lafayette, tel. 318/265–2100).

Thoroughbred racing can be seen April through Labor Day at **Evangeline Downs** (I–10 at I–49, Lafayette, tel. 318/896–7266).

Dining and Lodging

With the state's wealth of waterways, it is no surprise that Louisiana tables are laden with seafood in every imaginable and innovative variety. In South Louisiana, sea creatures are prepared with a Cajun flair. Sleeping accommodations run from homey bed-and-breakfasts to chain motels to luxury hotels to elegant antebellum mansions open for overnighters. For price ranges, see Charts 1 (B) and 2 (B) in Chapter 1.

Breaux Bridge **Mulate's.** This renowned roadhouse with tables covered in
Dining checkered plastic features Cajun seafood and dancing to live
★ Cajun music noon and night. *325 Mills Ave., tel. 800/42–CAJUN or 800/634–9880 in LA. Closed Christmas Day. AE, MC, V. Moderate.*

Carencro **Prudhomme's Cajun Café.** In a suburb of Lafayette, celebrity
Dining chef Paul Prudhomme's sister Enola has a country-kitchen café
★ with outstanding Cajun fare. *4676 N.E. Evangeline Thruway, tel. 318/896–7964. AE, MC, V. Closed Mon. Inexpensive–Moderate.*

Lafayette **Prejean's.** Housed in a cypress cottage, this local favorite has a
Dining cozy oyster bar, red-checked cloths, and live music nightly.
★ Huge platters of traditional and new Cajun seafood are the specialties. *3480 U.S. 167N, next to Evangeline Downs, tel. 318/896–3247. AE, DC, MC, V. Closed Thanksgiving and Christmas. Moderate.*

Lodging **Holiday Inn Central-Holidome.** Built around an atrium that's banked with greenery, this modern motel has rooms done in contemporary decor and 17 acres within which you can find almost everything you'd ever need for a long life. *Box 91807, 70509, tel. 318/233–6815 or 800/942–4868; fax 318/225–1954. 250 rooms. Facilities: restaurant, cocktail lounge, heated indoor pool with whirlpool, sauna, 2 lighted tennis courts, 24-hr* *jogging track, game rooms, playgrounds, picnic area, airport shuttle. AE, D, DC, MC, V. Moderate–Very Expensive.*

★ **Hotel Acadiana.** Near Bayou Vermilion, this is a plush hotel whose rooms have thick carpeting, marble-top dressers, and wet bars. Even-numbered rooms face the pool. *1801 W. Pinhook Rd., 70508, tel. 318/233–8120, 800/826–8386, or 800/874–4664 in LA; fax 318/234–9667. 304 rooms. Facilities: restaurant, cocktail lounge, free parking, facilities for handicapped, outdoor pool. AE, D, DC, MC, V. Inexpensive–Moderate.*

Lake Charles **Café Margaux.** Candlelight, French waiters, and a 9,000-bottle
Dining mahogany wine cellar provide the setting for specialties that
★ include rack of lamb *en croûte* and fillet of flounder with lump crabmeat and brown *meunière* sauce. *765 Bayou Pines, tel. 318/433–2902. Reservations advised. Jacket and tie advised. AE, MC, V. Closed Sun., Christmas. Moderate–Expensive.*

Lodging **Holiday Inn, Lake Charles.** Perched between the lake and the interstate, this hotel has traditional furnishings in rooms done in soothing earth tones. There are rooms for nonsmokers and for the disabled. *505 N. Lakeshore Dr., 70601, tel. 318/433–7121, 800/367–1814, or 800/433–8809 in LA; fax 318/436–8459. 269 rooms. Facilities: restaurant, coffee shop, gift shop, laundry, outdoor pool, free parking, free airport shuttle. AE, D, DC, MC, V. Moderate.*

Chateau Charles Hotel & Conference Center. Set on 25 wooded acres, the hotel includes two-bedroom suites with wet bars, microwaves, and minirefrigerators, as well as rooms for nonsmokers and easy access for the disabled. *Box 1269, 70602, tel. 318/882–6130 or 800/935–6130; fax 318/882–6601. 212 rooms, 4 suites. Facilities: restaurant, lounge, laundry. AE, D, DC, MC, V. Inexpensive–Moderate.*

Napoleonville **Madewood.** Expect gracious southern hospitality in this an-
Lodging tiques-filled Greek Revival plantation mansion, which is both
★ elegant and cozy. There are rooms in the main mansion and suites in a restored outbuilding; rates include breakfast and a candlelight dinner. *4250 Rte. 308, 70390, tel. 800/749–7151 or 800/375–7151 in LA. 5 rooms, 3 suites. AE, D, MC, V. Closed major holidays. Expensive.*

Opelousas **The Palace Café.** This down-home coffee shop on the town
Dining square, operated by the same family for 65 years, serves steaks, fried chicken, sandwiches, burgers, and seafood. Locals flock here for the homemade baklava. *167 W. Landry St., tel. 318/942–2142. MC, V. Closed major holidays. Inexpensive.*

St. Martinville **La Place d'Evangeline.** Rooms are spacious at this bed-and-
Dining and Lodging breakfast on the banks of the Bayou Teche. The restaurant
★ serves hearty portions of seafood and Cajun dishes; the homemade bread is superb. *220 Evangeline Blvd., 70582, tel. 318/394–4010. 5 rooms. AE, MC, V. Closed Christmas. Moderate.*

The Arts and Nightlife

The Arts Major concert attractions are booked into Lafayette's
Concerts **Cajundome** (444 Cajundome Blvd., tel. 318/265–2100) and **Heymann Performing Arts & Convention Center** (1373 S. College Rd., tel. 318/268–5540), and into the **Lake Charles Civic Center** (900 Lakeshore Dr., Lake Charles, tel. 318/491–1256).

Theater The **Lake Charles Little Theater** (813 Enterprise Blvd., Lake Charles, tel. 318/433–7988) puts on plays and musicals. The **Théâtre 'Cadien** (Lafayette, tel. 318/893–5655 or 318/262–5810) performs plays in French at various venues. **Lafayette Community Theater** (529 Jefferson St., tel. 318/235–1532) offers contemporary plays with a Cajun flair.

Nightlife **Mulate's** in Breaux Bridge and **Prejean's** in Lafayette (*see* Din-
Cajun Music ing and Lodging, *above*), and **Randol's** (2320 Kaliste Saloom Rd., Lafayette, tel. 318/981–7080) regularly feature Cajun music and dancing. **Belizaire's** (2307 N. Parkerson Ave., Crowley, tel. 318/788–2501) is a great place for Cajun food and dancing. **Slim's Y-Ki-Ki** (Rte. 167, Washington Rd., Opelousas, tel. 318/942–9980), a black Cajun club, is one of the best Cajun dancing places in the state. **Fred's Lounge** (420 6th St., Mamou, tel. 318/468–5411) is a bar with live Saturday-morning radio broadcasts (8 AM to 1 PM) and plenty of dancing. **"Rendez-Vous des Cajuns"** (Liberty Theatre, Park Ave. at 2nd St., Eunice, tel. 318/457–6575) is a live Saturday-night radio show, mostly in French, that's been described as a combination of the "Grand Ole Opry," the "Louisiana Hayride," and the "Prairie Home Companion."

Elsewhere in the State

Natchitoches and North Central Louisiana

Getting There I–49 cuts diagonally from southeast to northwest, connecting Lafayette with Shreveport. Rte. 1 runs diagonally from the northwest corner all the way to Grand Isle on the Gulf of Mexico.

What to See and Nestled in the piney hills of north-central Louisiana,
Do **Natchitoches** (pronounced "Nak-a-tish") is the oldest permanent European settlement of the Louisiana Purchase, four years older than New Orleans. The town has a quaint 33-block historic district with brick-paved streets and buildings garbed in lacy ironwork. In the center of the downtown area is pretty Cane River Lake, edged with weeping willows and rolling green lawns. If it all looks familiar to you, it's because Natchitoches appeared in the film version of *Steel Magnolias.* You can take trolley tours of town and cruises on the water. Popular attractions include the **Christmas Festival of Lights,** which draws about 150,000 people annually, and the **October Pilgrimage,** when several historic houses are open for tours.

Rte. 494 follows the lake southward from town, bordered by arching trees and dotted with handsome plantation houses. Famed primitive artist Clementine Hunter lived and worked at **Melrose Plantation** (Rte. 493, Melrose, tel. 318/379–0055; admission charged), where nine quaint buildings can be toured. Twenty miles south of Natchitoches, the **Bayou Folk Museum** (Rte. 495, Cloutierville, tel. 318/379–2233; admission charged) was home in the 19th century to Kate Chopin, author of *The Awakening.*

To the west of Natchitoches, 15 mi south of Many, lies **Hodges Gardens** (U.S. 171, tel. 318/586–3523; admission charged), 4,700 acres of rolling pine forests with streams, waterfalls, and formal, multilevel botanical gardens, where flowers and shrubs bloom year-round. Just to the west is the huge **Toledo Bend**

Lake, a camping, boating, and bass-fishing delight that lies along the Texas border.

The **Natchitoches Parish Tourist Commission** (781 Front St., Box 411, 71458, tel. 318/352–8072) has information on the entire area, including walking and driving tour maps.

Shreveport and North Louisiana

Getting There
Shreveport Regional Airport is served by American, Continental, Delta, Northwest, and USAir. I–20 and U.S. 80 run east–west through the northern part of the state; Rte. 1 cuts diagonally from the northwest corner to the Gulf of Mexico; I–49 connects Shreveport with South Louisiana. Other north–south routes are U.S. 171, 71, 165, and 167.

What to See and Do
While South Louisiana dances to Cajun tunes and dines on Creole and Cajun fare, most of North Louisiana has more in common with Mississippi, Georgia, and other southern states, and Shreveport's ties are largely to neighboring Texas. North of Alexandria, the flat marshlands and gray earth give way to stands of pine trees and bluffs of rich red clay. It is not for naught that Louisiana is known as Sportsman's Paradise. The north as well as the south of the state is laced with rivers and lakes, with ample places for camping, fishing, and hunting.

Shreveport and Bossier City, separated by the Red River, comprise the largest metropolitan area in North Louisiana. A cultural center, **Shreveport** has a symphony orchestra, resident opera and ballet companies, and excellent community-theater productions. The prestigious **Norton Art Gallery** (4747 Creswell Ave., tel. 318/865–4201; admission free) has superb exhibits of art of the American West, including a permanent collection of works by Frederic Remington and Charles M. Russell. The **Louisiana State Exhibit** (Fairgrounds, tel. 318/632–2020; admission free) has extensive displays and dioramas depicting the state's history, including a large collection of Native American artifacts from Poverty Point and other important excavations in Louisiana. The **American Rose Center** (Jefferson-Paige Rd., tel. 318/938–5402; admission charged), headquarters of the American Rose Society, is a 118-acre pinewoods park with over 15,000 rosebushes in more than 60 individual gardens. The place is lit up like a Christmas tree during the "Christmas in Roseland" light show, which runs from the day after Thanksgiving through New Year's Eve.

South of Shreveport, the **Mansfield Battle Park** (Rte. 2, 4 mi south of Mansfield, tel. 318/872–1474; admission charged) is the site of the last major Confederate victory of the War Between the States. More than 30,000 men were involved in the bitter battle. The site contains monuments and an interpretive center with audiovisual displays.

The **Shreveport-Bossier Convention & Tourist Bureau** (629 Spring St, Shreveport 71166; 405 Clyde Fant Pkwy., Shreveport 71101; Pierre Bossier Mall, Airline Dr., Bossier City 71111; tel. 318/222–9391 or 800/551–8682 outside LA) has free maps and information on the region.

MISSISSIPPI

By Janet Clark

Updated by Sylvia Higginbotham

Capital	Jackson
Population	2.5 million
Motto	By Virtue and Arms
State Bird	Mockingbird
State Flower	Magnolia

Visitor Information

Mississippi Division of Tourism Development (Box 22825, Jackson 39205, tel. 601/359–3291 or 800/647–2290).

Scenic Drives

The **Natchez Trace Parkway** cuts a 313-mi swath across Mississippi from northeast of Tupelo to Natchez, passing through Jackson at the center of the state. **U.S. 90** runs along the Mississippi Sound from Alabama to Louisiana, offering views of Gulf Coast beaches, ancient live oaks, and historic homes. Along the Mississippi River, **U.S. 61**—synonymous with authentic Mississippi blues—runs through flat Delta cotton land to the hills of Vicksburg, then through Natchez to Louisiana.

National and State Parks

National Parks   **Gulf Islands National Seashore** (3500 Park Rd., Ocean Springs 39564, tel. 601/875–9057) includes Ship, Horn, and Petit Bois islands and offers nature trails and expeditions into the marsh. Vicksburg's **National Military Park** (*see* Elsewhere in the State, *below*).

State Parks   **Grand Gulf Military Monument** (*see* The Natchez Trace, *below*). **J. P. Coleman State Park** (13 mi north of Iuka off U.S. 25; Rte. 5, Box 503, Iuka 38852, tel. 601/423–6515) includes scenic Pickwick Lake, which has cabins, camping, hiking, and swimming. **Tishomingo State Park** (15 mi south of Iuka and 3 mi north of Dennis off U.S. 25; Rte. 1, Box 310, Dennis 38838, tel. 601/438–6914), which vies with J. P. Coleman for the title of most spectacular Mississippi park, lies in the Appalachian foothills, making its terrain unique in Mississippi. Bring your own provisions to enjoy hiking and water sports.

The Natchez Trace

The Natchez Trace Parkway is a long, thin park running from Nashville to Natchez, crossing early paths worn by Choctaw and Chickasaw Indians, flatboatmen, outlaws, itinerant preachers, postriders, soldiers, and settlers. Meticulously manicured by the National Park Service, it is unmarred by billboards, and commercial vehicles are forbidden to use it.

Tourist Information

Natchez-Adams County: Chamber of Commerce (300 N. Commerce St., Natchez 39120, tel. 601/446–6345 or 800/647–6724).

Natchez Trace Parkway: Visitor Center (Rte. 1, NT–143, Tupelo 38801, tel. 601/680–4025). **Jackson:** Convention and Visitors Bureau (Box 1450, 39205, tel. 601/960–1891 or 800/354–7695). Visitor Information Center (at entrance to Mississippi Agriculture and Forestry Museum, 1150 Lakeland Dr., tel. 601/354–6113).

Getting There

By Plane Jackson's **International Airport** (tel. 601/939–5631), east of the city off I–20, 10 minutes from downtown, is served by Delta, American, and Northwest Airlines.

By Train **Amtrak** stops in Jackson on its way south from Memphis to New Orleans.

By Car The Trace is interrupted at Jackson, connected by I–55 and I–20, which run through the city. Natchez, the beginning of the Natchez Trace Parkway (but the end of this tour), is also served by U.S. 61.

Exploring the Natchez Trace

The Mississippi segment of the Natchez Trace begins near Tupelo, in the northeast corner of the state in a hilly area of dense forests and sparkling streams. Enjoy some of this natural beauty at **J. P. Coleman State Park** or **Tishomingo State Park** (*see* National and State Parks, *above*).

Tupelo At the Trace's milepost 266 is the **Natchez Trace Parkway Visitor Center** (*see* Tourist Information, *above*), offering exhibits and the *Official Map and Guide*, with detailed, mile-by-mile information from Nashville to Natchez.

Tupelo (named after the gum tree), the largest city in north Mississippi, sits in scenic hill country. Site of the 1864 Civil War battle of the same name, it is now famous as the site of **Elvis Presley's birthplace**, a tiny, two-room shotgun house where the singer was born on January 8, 1935. The surrounding **Elvis Presley Park** includes a gift shop and the **Elvis Presley Memorial Chapel.** *Off Old Hwy. 78, at 306 Elvis Presley Dr., tel. 601/841–1245. Admission charged.*

The three-hour trip from Tupelo to Jackson can easily take an entire day if you stop to read the brown wooden markers describing historic sites, explore nature trails, and admire the neat fields, trees, and wildflower meadows along the way. At **Ridgeland,** the **Mississippi Crafts Center** displays and sells high-quality crafts in a dogtrot log cabin created by members of the Craftsman's Guild of Mississippi. Rest rooms and picnic tables are available. *Trace milepost 102.4, tel. 601/856–7546. Admission free.*

Jackson **Jackson,** the state capital, has an interesting downtown, with many small museums and most of the city's notable architecture. **The Agriculture and Forestry Museum** includes 10 old Mississippi farm buildings, as well as a working farm and a 1920s crossroads town. The General Store sells snacks and souvenirs; just outside the gates, a shop sells Mississippi crafts and a down-home restaurant serves blue-plate lunches (veggies, crisp fried catfish). *1150 Lakeland Dr., tel. 601/354–6113. Admission charged.*

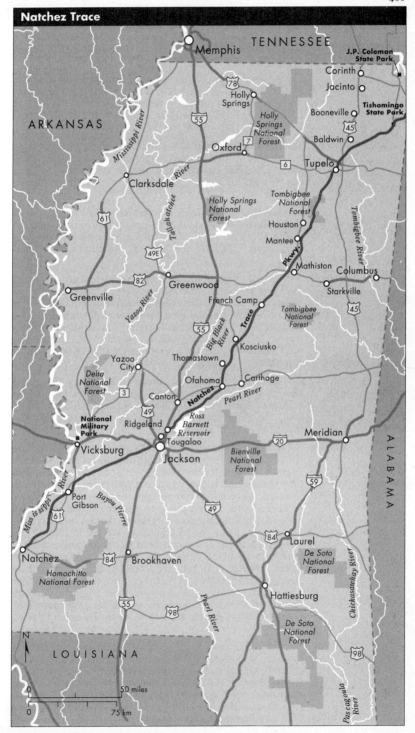

Natchez Trace

The **Mississippi Museum of Art** has changing exhibits and a permanent collection of regional paintings. Its high-tech, hands-on Impressions Gallery (free) combines art and education. *201 E. Pascagoula St., tel. 601/960–1515. Admission charged. Closed Mon.*

The **Governor's Mansion** has been the official home of the state's first family since its completion in 1841. General Sherman presumably lived here during his occupation of Jackson in 1863. It is beautifully furnished with antiques. *300 E. Capitol St., tel. 601/359–3175. Admission free.*

The **New Capitol** (1903) sits in Beaux Arts splendor, its dome surmounted by a gold-plated copper eagle with a 15-foot wingspan. Elaborate architectural details inside the building include a Tiffany window. *High St., tel. 601/359–3114. Admission free.*

The **Manship House** (1857) is a careful restoration of a small Gothic Revival home, built by the mayor who surrendered the city to Sherman. *420 E. Fortification St. (enter parking area from Congress St.), tel. 601/961–4724. Admission free. Closed Mon.*

To the south, **Port Gibson** is the earliest town to grow up along the Trace that is still in existence. Along **Church Street** many houses and churches have recently been restored; here, too, is the much-photographed **First Presbyterian Church** (1859), its spire topped by a 12-foot hand pointing heavenward. Information on the town's historic sites is available from the **Port Gibson Chamber of Commerce** (south end of Church St., tel. 601/437–4351).

Just north of Port Gibson is **Grand Gulf Military Monument** (Rte. 2, off U.S. 61, tel. 601/437–5911), site of a town left in ruins by federal gunners. Children especially love the steep trail, the observation tower, the old waterwheel, and the bloodstained uniforms on display.

Natchez   Because **Natchez** had little military significance, it survived the Civil War almost untouched (though its economy was wrecked). Today it is famous for the opulent plantation homes and stylish town houses built between 1819 and 1860, when cotton plantations and the bustling river port poured riches into the city. A number of these houses are open year-round, but others are open only during Natchez Pilgrimage weeks, when crowds flock to see them. The pilgrimages—started in 1932 by the women of Natchez as a way to raise money for preservation—are held twice a year: three weeks in October and four weeks in March and April. Tickets are available at **Pilgrimage Tour Headquarters** (Canal St. at State St. [Box 347, 39120], tel. 601/446–6631 or 800/647–6742), where all tours originate. **Carriage tours** of downtown Natchez begin at Natchez Pilgrimage Tour Headquarters (Canal St. at State St.) or the Eola Hotel (110 N. Pearl St.).

Rosalie (100 Orleans St., tel. 601/445–4555), built in 1823, established the ideal form of the southern mansion, with its white columns, hipped roof, and red bricks. Furnishings purchased for the house in 1858 include a famous Belter parlor set. A trip down south is not complete without a visit to the grand and gracious **Stanton Hall** (400 High St., tel. 601/442–6282), one of the most photographed houses in the country. Built around 1857 for cotton broker Frederick Stanton, the palatial former residence is now run as a house-museum by the Pilgrimage Garden Club. **Longwood** (140 Lower Woodville Rd., tel. 601/442–5193) is the largest octagonal house in the United States. Construction began in 1860, but the outbreak of the Civil War prevented its completion; unfinished and mysterious, it is the only Natchez mansion guaranteed to interest children. All of these houses charge admission.

What to See and Do with Children

Jackson's **Zoological Park** (2918 W. Capitol St., tel. 601/960–1575 or 601/960–1576) features animals in natural settings, including many endangered species. Also of interest to children are **Longwood** mansion in Natchez and **Grand Gulf Military Monument** outside Port Gibson (*see* Exploring the Natchez Trace, *above*).

Shopping

The Everyday Gourmet (2905 Old Canton Rd., Jackson, tel. 601/362–0723) stocks state products, including pecan pie, bread, and biscuit mixes; muscadine jelly; jams and chutneys; cookbooks; and fine ceramic tableware.

Dining and Lodging

For price ranges, see Charts 1 (B) and 2 (B) in Chapter 1.

Jackson   **400 East Capitol.** Jackson's most elegant restaurant occupies a
Dining   historic building that has been carefully restored on the outside and beautifully adapted within. Signature dishes are regional: farm-raised rabbit, quail salad, angel-hair pasta with shrimp. *400 E. Capitol St., tel. 601/355–9671. Reservations advised. Jacket and tie advised. AE, DC, MC, V. Expensive.*

Nick's. Large and elegant, this restaurant serves nouvelle versions of regional dishes. Lunch specialties are grilled catfish and pork medallions; for dinner, try eggplant stuffed with deviled crab or blackfish. *1501 Lakeland Dr., tel. 601/981–8017. No reservations Fri.–Sat. Jacket and tie required. AE, MC, V. Expensive.*

The Palette. In a light-filled gallery in the Mississippi Arts Center is one of the state's finest lunch spots. It offers such creations as Mississippi catfish sautéed in pecan butter or fresh vegetable lasagna. *201 E. Pascagoula St., tel. 601/960–2003. MC, V. No dinner; closed Mon. Moderate.*

The Mayflower. A perfect 1930s period piece with black-and-white tile floors, straight-back booths, and Formica-topped counter, this café specializes in Greek salads, fresh fish sautéed in lemon butter, and people-watching until all hours. *123 W. Capitol St., tel. 601/355–4122. No reservations. MC, V. Inexpensive–Moderate.*

The People's Cafe. Crammed with artsy memorabilia, this tiny café packs in Jackson's downtown crowd with its amazing lunch buffet, featuring fresh local vegetables and homemade breads, soups, and desserts. *232 W. Capitol St., tel. 601/353–7100. No reservations. MC, V. No dinner. Inexpensive.*

Lodging   **Edison Walthall Hotel.** The cornerstone and huge brass mailbox are almost all that remain of the original 1920s Walthall Hotel, but the marble floors and paneled library/writing room almost fool you into thinking this is a restoration. The rooms have standard hotel decor, with some wicker furniture. *225 E. Capitol St., 39201, tel. 601/948–6161 or 800/932–6161. 208 rooms. Facilities: bar, pool, whirlpool. AE, DC, MC, V. Expensive.*

Millsaps-Buie House. This 1888 Queen Anne Victorian, restored as a B&B in 1987, is listed on the National Register of Historic Places. The guest rooms are individually decorated with antiques, and the staff is attentive. *628 N. State St., 39202, tel. 601/352–0221. 11 rooms. AE, DC, MC, V. Expensive.*

Ramada Renaissance Hotel. This high-rise convention hotel in the north end of town is sleekly contemporary, but the rooms are decorated in traditional style. *1001 County Line Rd., 39211, tel. 601/957–2800 or 800/228–9898. 300 rooms. Facilities: restaurant, bar, airport van. AE, DC, MC, V. Expensive.*

Natchez
Dining

City Banc Cafe and Grill. Outstanding preparation of varied menu items served elegantly in an old bank building–cum–restaurant. Continental cuisine, with a taste of the American South. *409 Franklin St., tel. 601/445–4946. Reservations advised. AE, MC, V. Expensive.*

Cock of the Walk. The famous original of a regional franchise, this shanty overlooking the Mississippi River specializes in fried catfish fillets, fried dill pickles, hush puppies, mustard greens, and coleslaw. *200 N. Broadway, on the Bluff, tel. 601/446–8920. AE, MC, V. Inexpensive–Moderate.*

The Parlor. This parlor is a comfortable mishmash of mismatched tables and chairs, magazine racks, jazz posters, and an enclosed patio with picnic tables and umbrellas. Mexican food is a specialty; so is grilled catfish with vegetables and seafood pasta. *116 S. Canal St., tel. 601/446–8511. Reservations advised. AE, MC, V. Closed Sun. Inexpensive.*

Lodging

Dunleith. At stately, colonnaded Dunleith, a wing for overnight guests offers guest rooms with antiques, fireplaces, and wonderful views of the landscaped grounds. Guests receive a complimentary tour of the house. *84 Homochitto St., 39120, tel. 601/446–8500 or 800/647–6742. 12 rooms. AE, MC, V. Expensive.*

Monmouth. This plantation mansion (ca. 1818) was owned by Mississippi governor John A. Quitman from 1826 until his death in 1858. Guest rooms—in the main house, in servants' quarters, and in garden cottages—are furnished with tester beds and antiques. *John A. Quitman Pkwy., 39120, tel. 601/442–5852 or 800/828–4531. 17 rooms, 2 suites. AE, MC, V. Expensive.*

Eola Hotel. This beautifully restored 1920s hotel has a formal lobby and small guest rooms with antique-reproduction furniture. The Eola is listed as a Historic Hotel of America by the National Trust for Historic Preservation. *110 N. Pearl St., 39120, tel. 601/445–6000 or 800/888–9140. 122 rooms. Facilities: restaurant, lounge. AE, DC, MC, V. Expensive.*

Ramada Hilltop Motel. The typical motel decor is forgotten if your room overlooks the Mississippi River. *130 John R. Junkin Dr., 39120, tel. 601/446–6311 or 800/272–6232. Facilities: restaurant, lounge, pool. AE, DC, MC, V. Moderate.*

Tupelo
Dining

Harvey's. It's a local favorite serving consistently good chow. Specialties are prime rib and pasta. *424 S. Gloster St., tel. 601/842–6763. AE, MC, V. Closed Sun.*

Jefferson Place. This austere 19th-century house is lively inside, with red-checked tablecloths and bric-a-brac. Popular with the college crowd, it features short orders and steaks. *823 Jefferson St., tel. 601/844–8696. AE, MC, V. Closed Sun. Moderate.*

Papa Vanelli's Pizzaria. Family pictures and scenes of Greece decorate the walls of this comfortably nondescript restaurant. Specialties (all homemade) include pizza with 10 toppings, lasagna, moussaka, and Greek salad. *1302 N. Gloster St., tel. 601/ 844–4410. AE, D, MC, V. Inexpensive.*

Lodging **Ramada Inn.** This modern three-story hotel caters to business travelers and conventions as well as families. Breakfast and lunch buffets are served. *854 N. Gloster St., 38801, tel. 601/ 844–4111. 230 rooms, 10 suites. Facilities: dining room, lounge with dancing, pool, laundry. AE, DC, MC, V. Moderate.*

Best Western Trace Inn. This old, rustic inn on 15 acres near the Natchez Trace offers neat rooms and friendly service. *3400 W. Main St., 38801, tel. 601/842–5555. 165 rooms. Facilities: restaurant, pool, playground, lounge with dancing, courtesy car. AE, MC, V. Inexpensive.*

Nightlife

Jackson For live entertainment on weekends, try **Hal and Mal's** (200 S. Commerce St., tel. 601/948–0888); **The Dock** (Main Harbor Marina at Ross Barnett Reservoir, tel. 601/856–7765); and the new **Rodeos** (6107 Ridgewood Rd., tel. 601/957–1400), where patrons willingly line up outside to line-dance inside.

Natchez After dark, head for Under-the-Hill, a busy strip of restaurants, gift shops, and bars on the river. Gambling is offered at the permanently docked riverboat casino, the ***Lady Luck*** (tel. 601/445–0605), and good times are had at the **Saloon** (tel. 601/ 446–8023).

Oxford and Holly Springs

Holly Springs and Oxford, in north Mississippi, are sophisticated versions of the Mississippi small town. Courthouse towns incorporated in 1837, they offer visitors historic architecture, arts and crafts, literary associations, a warm welcome, and those unhurried pleasures of southern life that remain constant from generation to generation: entertaining conversation, good food, and nostalgic walks at twilight. Oxford and Lafayette County were immortalized as "Jefferson" and "Yoknapatawpha County" in the novels of Oxford native William Faulkner.

Tourist Information

Holly Springs: Chamber of Commerce (150 S. Memphis St., 38365, tel. 601/252–2943). **Oxford:** Chamber of Commerce (Box 965, 38655, tel. 601/234–4651).

Getting There

By Car Oxford is accessible from I–55; it is 23 mi east of Batesville on Rte. 6. Holly Springs, near the Tennessee state line, is reached via U.S. 78 and Rtes. 4, 7, and 311.

By Train **Amtrak** stops in Batesville.

By Bus   **Greyhound** has stations in Oxford (925 Van Buren Ave., tel. 601/234–1424) and in Holly Springs (490 Craft St., tel. 601/252–1353).

Exploring Oxford and Holly Springs

Oxford   **Courthouse Square** is a National Historic Landmark. At its center is the white sandstone **Lafayette** (pronounced "Luh-*fay*-it") **County Courthouse**, rebuilt in 1873 after Union troops burned it; the courtroom on the second floor is original. There's an information center at the nearby City Hall.

University Avenue, from South Lamar Boulevard to the university, is one of the state's most beautiful sights when the trees flame orange and gold in the fall, or when the dogwoods blossom in spring. **The University of Mississippi**, the state's beloved "Ole Miss," opened in 1848. Its tree-shaded campus centers on **The Grove**, surrounded by historic buildings. Facing it is the antebellum **Barnard Observatory** (tel. 601/232–5993; admission free), newly and beautifully restored, which houses **The Center for the Study of Southern Culture**, with exhibits on southern music, folklore, and literature and the world's largest blues archive (40,000 records). The **Mississippi Room** (tel. 601/232–7408; admission free; closed Sun.) in the John Davis Williams Library contains a permanent exhibit on Faulkner, including the Nobel Prize for literature he won in 1949, as well as first editions of works by other Mississippi authors.

Rowan Oak (ca. 1844) was William Faulkner's home from 1930 until his death in 1962. The two-story, white-frame house with square columns is now a National Historic Landmark owned by the university. The writer's typewriter, desk, and other personal items still evoke his presence. *Old Taylor Rd., tel. 601/234–4651. Admission free. Closed Thurs.–Fri.*

Faulkner's funeral was held at Rowan Oak, and he was buried in the family plot in **St. Peter's Cemetery** (Jefferson and N. 16th Sts.). Another Faulkner pilgrimage site is **College Hill Presbyterian Church** (8 mi northwest of Oxford on College Hill Rd.), where he and Estelle Oldham Franklin were married on June 20, 1929.

Holly Springs   **Holly Springs**, 29 mi north of Oxford on Rte. 7, contains more than 300 structures listed on the National Register of Historic Places. These include the 1858 **Montrose** (307 E. Salem Ave., tel. 601/252–2943; admission charged), open by appointment only, and the privately owned Salem Avenue mansions **Oakleigh, Cedarhurst,** and **Airliewood.**

What to See and Do with Children

In Oxford, **The Union,** the University of Mississippi's student center, has pool rooms, a video arcade, and a bookstore.

Dining and Lodging

For price ranges, see Charts 1 (B) and 2 (B) in Chapter 1.

Holly Springs   **Phillips Grocery.** Constructed in 1882 as a saloon for railroad
Dining   workers, it's decorated today with antiques and crafts and serves big, old-fashioned hamburgers. *541–A Van Dorn, tel.*

601/252–4671. No reservations. No credit cards. Closed Sun. Inexpensive.

Oxford **Downtown Grill.** The Grill could be a club in Oxford, England,
Dining but the light and airy balcony overlooking the square is pure Oxford, Mississippi. Specialties include Jesse's Famous Seafood Gumbo and breaded veal with fresh zucchini, yellow squash, onion, and shrimp. *1115 Jackson Ave., tel. 601/234–2659. Reservations advised. AE, MC, V. Moderate.*
Smitty's. Home-style cooking here features red-eye gravy and grits, biscuits with blackberry preserves, fried catfish, chicken and dumplings, corn bread, and black-eyed peas. The atmosphere is down-home. *S. Lamar Blvd., tel. 601/234–9111. No credit cards. Inexpensive.*

Lodging **Holiday Inn.** These functional rooms have no surprises. The restaurant, however, does a surprisingly good breakfast. *400 N. Lamar Blvd., 38655, tel. 601/234–3031. 100 rooms. Facilities: restaurant, pool, lounge. AE, DC, MC, V. Inexpensive.*
Oliver-Britt House. In a restored house built about 1900, this conveniently located B&B run in a helter-skelter fashion has pleasant rooms. Lunch (Tues.–Fri.) and Sunday brunch are served. *512 Van Buren Ave., 38655, tel. 601/234–8043. 5 rooms. Facilities: dining room. AE, MC, V. Moderate.*

The Arts

The annual **Faulkner and Yoknapatawpha Conference** is a week-long summer event that includes lectures by Faulkner scholars and field trips in "Yoknapatawpha County." For information, write to the Center for the Study of Southern Culture (Univ. of Mississippi, Oxford 38677).

Nightlife

In Oxford, **The Gin** (E. Harrison St. and S. 14th St., tel. 601/234–0024) offers live dance music; **The Hoka** (304 S. 14th St., tel. 601/234–3057) is a warehouse turned movie theater and restaurant; and **Syd's** (1118 Van Buren Ave., tel. 601/236–3194) serves food, drinks, rock and roll, and the blues.

Elsewhere in the State

The Delta

Getting There U.S. 61 runs from Memphis through the Delta to Vicksburg, Natchez, and Baton Rouge, Louisiana.

What to See Between Memphis and Vicksburg is the **Delta,** a vast agricul-
and Do tural plain created by the Mississippi River and an intimate set of personal relationships. Drive through it, with side trips down Rte. 1 or Rte. 8 for views of the Mississippi, timing it right for lunch in Clarksdale or Boyle and dinner at **Doe's** (tel. 601/334–3315) in Greenville. Greenville has produced an extraordinary number of writers, including William Alexander Percy, Ellen Douglas, Hodding Carter, and Shelby Foote. The **Mississippi Welcome Center** (4210 Washington St., Vicksburg 39180, tel. 601/638–4269) and the **Washington County Welcome Center** (U.S. 82 at Reed Rd., Box 6022, Greenville 38701, tel. 601/332–2378) provide information on the region.

Ocean Springs

Getting There   U.S. 90 runs through the heart of Ocean Springs.

What to See and Do   On the Mississippi Gulf Coast, this oak-shaded town originated in 1699 as a French fort. It is now known as the former home of artist Walter Anderson (1903–65). He revealed his ecstatic communion with nature in thousands of drawings and watercolors, most of them kept secret until his death. The **Walter Anderson Museum of Art** (510 Washington Ave., tel. 601/872-3164) displays his work, including his cottage studio with intricately painted walls.

Ocean Springs is also the headquarters of the **Gulf Islands National Seashore** (3500 Park Rd., tel. 601/875-9057). On the mainland there are nature trails and ranger programs. Out in the Gulf, pristine Ship, Horn, and Petit Bois islands, for which the park is named, have beaches as white and soft as sugar—some of the country's best. Excursion boats to Ship, rimmed by about 7 mi of this remarkable sand, leave from Biloxi in summer and from Gulfport May through October, and charter operators regularly take wilderness lovers to Horn and Petit Bois, both designated wilderness areas, where camping is permitted. The **Ocean Springs Chamber of Commerce** (Box 187, 39564, tel. 601/875-4424) has information on this area.

Vicksburg

Getting There   I-20 runs east–west and U.S. 61 north–south through Vicksburg.

What to See and Do   During the War Between the States, the Confederacy and the Union vied for control of this strategic location on the Mississippi Delta across the river from Louisiana. After a 47-day siege, the city surrendered to Ulysses S. Grant on July 4, 1863, giving the Union control of the river and sounding the death knell for the Confederacy. Vicksburg's **National Military Park** is second only to Gettysburg in interest and beauty. Battle positions are marked, and monuments line the 16-mi drive through the park. *Visitor Center, Clay St. (U.S. 80), 1 mi from I-20 Exit 4B, tel. 601/636-0583. Admission charged. Closed Christmas.*

TENNESSEE

By Judy Ringel

Updated by John Branston

Capital	Nashville
Population	4,877,185
Motto	Agriculture and Commerce
State Bird	Mockingbird
State Flower	Iris

Visitor Information

Tennessee Department of Tourism (Box 23170, Nashville 37202, tel. 615/741–2158).

Scenic Drives

U.S. 421 from Bristol to Trade passes through the Cherokee National Forest and crosses the Appalachian Trail. **Rte. 73** south from Townsend leads through a high valley ringed by mountains to the pioneer village of Cades Cove. **Rte. 25** from Gallatin to Springfield travels through an area of Thoroughbred farms and antebellum houses. Between Monteagle and Chattanooga, **I–24** is one of the country's most scenic stretches of mountains, valleys, and lakes.

National and State Parks

National Parks **Great Smoky Mountains National Park** (Gatlinburg 37738, tel. 615/436–5615) encompasses towering peaks and lush valleys, with excellent camping and fishing sites and more than 900 mi of horse and hiking trails.

State Parks The **Tennessee Department of Conservation, Division of State Parks** (701 Broadway, Nashville 37203, tel. 615/742–6667 or 800/421–6683) provides information on Tennessee's 50-plus state parks. The 16,000-acre **Fall Creek Falls State Resort Park** (Rte. 3, Pikeville 37367, tel. 615/881–5241) has the highest waterfall east of the Rockies. **Reelfoot Lake State Resort Park** (Rte. 1, Box 296, Tiptonville 38079, tel. 901/253–7756) in northwest Tennessee is a favorite wintering ground for the American bald eagle. **Roan Mountain State Resort Park** (Rte. 1, Box 236, Roan Mountain 37687, tel. 615/772–3303) in northeast Tennessee boasts a 600-acre natural rhododendron garden that blooms in late June.

Memphis

On the bluffs overlooking the Mississippi River, Memphis is Tennessee's largest city and the commercial and cultural center of the western part of the state. It is a blend of southern tradition and modern efficiency, where aging cotton warehouses stand in the shadow of sleek new office buildings and old-fashioned paddle wheelers steam upriver past a gleaming stainless-steel sports arena. Memphis is perhaps best known for its music and for the two extraordinary men who introduced it to the world: W. C. Handy, the "Father of the Blues," and Elvis Presley, the "King of Rock and Roll."

Tourist Information

Memphis: Convention and Visitors Bureau (47 Union Ave., 38103, tel. 901/543–5300). Visitors Information Center (340 Beale St., 38103, tel. 901/543–5333).

Arriving and Departing

By Plane **Memphis International Airport** (tel. 901/922–8000), 9 mi south of downtown, is served by most major airlines and is a hub for **Northwest Airlines.** Driving time to downtown is about 15 minutes on I–240. Cab fare runs about $16. **Huntleigh Transportation Services** (tel. 901/922–8238) operates a shuttle to downtown hotels for $8.

By Car Memphis is reached via the north–south I–55 or the east–west I–40. I–240 loops around the city.

Train Station **Amtrak** (545 S. Main St., tel. 901/526–0052).

Bus Station **Greyhound** (203 Union Ave., tel. 901/523–7676).

By Boat Memphis is one stop on the paddle-wheeler cruises of the **Delta Queen Steamboat Co.** (Robin Street Wharf, New Orleans, LA 70130, tel. 800/543–1949). The *Delta Queen* (a National Historic Landmark) and the *Mississippi Queen* (an authentic reproduction) travel between St. Louis and New Orleans.

Getting Around Memphis

Memphis's streets are well marked, and there's plenty of parking, so the city is easily explored by car. Downtown, the **Memphis Area Transit Authority** (tel. 901/274–6282) operates a trolley (fare: $1) that runs along Main Street and shuttle buses (fare: 40¢) that loop around downtown.

Exploring Memphis

Downtown Memphis begins at the Mississippi River, which is celebrated in a 52-acre theme park (tel. 901/576–7212; admission charged) on **Mud Island.** A footbridge and monorail at 125 Front Street get you to the island, where a five-block-long **River Walk** replicates the Mississippi's every twist, turn, and sandbar from Cairo, Illinois, to New Orleans. Also in the park are the **Mississippi River Museum**, the famed World War II B–17 bomber *Memphis Belle,* an amphitheater, shops, and a swimming pool.

Back in the city, opposite the north end of Mud Island, stands the 32-story, 22,000-seat stainless-steel **Pyramid Arena** (1 Auction Ave., tel. 901/521–9675), opened in 1991. Tours are available. For a look at Memphis's oldest dwelling, walk 20 minutes southeast to the **Magevney House** (198 Adams Ave., tel. 901/526–4464; admission free; closed Mon.), built in the 1830s by a pioneer schoolteacher.

Heading south on 2nd Street, you'll come to the beautifully restored **Peabody Hotel** (*see* Lodging, *below*) at the corner of Union Avenue. Farther south is **Beale Street,** where W. C. Handy played the blues in the early decades of the 20th century, and where clubs and restaurants are thriving once again (*see* The Arts and Nightlife, *below*). The **W. C. Handy Memphis Home and Museum** (329 Beale St., tel. 901/527–2583; admission charged) displays photos and other memorabilia.

Memphis

South of Beale, the motel where Dr. Martin Luther King, Jr., was assassinated in 1968 has been transformed into the **National Civil Rights Museum,** which documents the movement through interpretive exhibits and audiovisual displays. *450 Mulberry St., tel. 901/521–9699. Admission charged (free Mon. 3–5 PM). Closed Tues.*

Other Attractions In Overton Park, the popular 70-acre **Memphis Zoo and Aquarium** (2000 Galloway Ave., tel. 901/726–4775) has a new 9-acre Cat Country, opening in spring 1993. Also in the park, the **Memphis Brooks Museum of Art** (2080 Poplar Ave., tel. 901/722–3500; admission charged [free Fri.]; closed Mon.), which won a national architectural award for its 1990 renovation and addition, houses a collection of fine and decorative arts from the 13th century to the present.

Graceland, the Colonial-style mansion once owned by Elvis Presley, is 12 mi southeast of downtown. A guided tour of the home and burial site reveals the spoils of stardom, from his gold-covered piano to his glittering stage costumes. *3717 Elvis Presley Blvd., tel. 901/332–3322 or 800/238–2000 (reservations advised, especially in summer). Admission charged. Closed Tues. Nov.–Feb.*

Sun Studio, the birthplace of rock-and-roll, is where Elvis Presley, Jerry Lee Lewis, B. B. King, and Roy Orbison launched their careers. Tours are given daily. *706 Union Ave. (7 blocks east of downtown), tel. 901/521–0664. Admission charged.*

Parks and Gardens

Overton Park, a few miles east of downtown on Poplar Avenue, offers picnic areas, sports fields, hiking and biking trails, a nine-hole golf course, and a cluster of major cultural attractions. In East Memphis, the 88-acre **Memphis Botanic Garden** (750 Cherry Rd., tel. 901/685–1566) is planted with scores of different species, from camellias to cacti.

What to See and Do with Children

At **The Children's Museum of Memphis** (2525 Central Ave., tel. 901/458–2678), youngsters can touch, climb, and explore their way through a child-size city. A few blocks east is the **Memphis Pink Palace Museum and Planetarium** (3050 Central Ave., tel. 901/320–6320), which features a mix of natural- and cultural-history exhibits, plus planetarium laser shows. **Chucalissa Indian Village** (1987 Indian Village Dr., tel. 901/785–3160) is a reconstruction of a Native American village that existed on the banks of the Mississippi from AD 1000 to 1500. Skilled Choctaw craftsfolk fashion jewelry, weapons, and pottery outside the C. H. Nash Museum, which houses historic versions of the same goods.

Shopping

Oak Court Mall (530 Oak Court Dr., tel. 901/682–8928), in the busy Poplar/Perkins area of East Memphis, has nearly 70 specialty shops and two department stores. In Germantown, **Saddle Creek Shopping Center** (Poplar Ave. at W. Farmington Dr., tel. 901/761–2571) features upscale specialty stores. Off-price shopping is available at **Belz Factory Outlet Mall** (3536 Canada Rd., Exit 20 off I–40, Lakeland, tel. 901/386–3180).

Spectator Sports

Tennis   The **International Indoor Tennis Tournament** (tel. 901/765–4400) is played in February at the Racquet Club in East Memphis.

Dining

While Memphis restaurants offer a pleasing array of American and international cuisines, the local passion remains barbecue; the city has 70-odd barbecue restaurants. For price ranges, see Chart 1 (B) in Chapter 1.

Expensive   **Chez Philippe.** Chef José Gutierrez serves imaginative and so-
★   phisticated cuisine in the city's most ornate surroundings. Nightly creations may include lamb with goat cheese and garlic or halibut with fried leeks and sun-dried cherry sauce. *The Peabody, 149 Union Ave., tel. 901/529–4188. Reservations advised. Jacket and tie advised. AE, DC, MC, V. No lunch; closed Sun.*
   Justine's. Set in a gracefully restored Victorian mansion, Justine's offers New Orleans–style Continental cuisine with an emphasis on seafood. *919 Coward Pl., tel. 901/527–3815. Reservations advised. Jacket and tie advised. AE, DC, MC, V. No lunch; closed Sun.–Mon.*
   La Tourelle. This turn-of-the-century bungalow in Overton

Square has the romantic ambience of a French country inn. Four-course fixed-price meals supplement the à la carte menu. *2146 Monroe Ave., tel. 901/726–5771. Reservations advised. Jacket and tie advised. MC, V. Closed Mon.*

Moderate **Cafe Max.** The atmosphere is lively and loud at this two-story bistro in East Memphis, where menu selections emphasize pasta, seafood, and grilled meats. *6161 Poplar Ave., tel. 901/767–3633. AE, D, MC, V. No lunch (except Sun. brunch).*

Captain Bilbo's River Restaurant. This converted riverfront warehouse seats 300 and packs 'em in for such seafood dishes as fried shrimp and stuffed flounder. There's live music in the lounge every night. *263 Wagner Pl., tel. 901/526–1966. AE, DC, MC, V. No lunch.*

★ **Marena's.** At this charming midtown restaurant, the menu changes monthly to highlight foods from different Mediterranean countries, such as Spain, Greece, Israel, and Turkey. *11545 Overton Park, tel. 901/278–9774. Reservations required. AE, DC, MC, V. BYOB. No lunch.*

★ **Paulette's.** Paulette's has retained its vitality for years, serving crepes, salads, grilled items, and killer desserts in the Old World atmosphere of a European inn. *2110 Madison Ave., tel. 901/726–5128. AE, D, DC, MC, V.*

Inexpensive **Cafe Olé.** This popular midtown hangout offers "healthy" Mexican cuisine (no animal fats are used), including spinach enchiladas and chili rellenos. *959 S. Cooper St., tel. 901/274–1504. AE, D, DC, MC, V.*

★ **Cafe Roux.** Chef Michael Cahhal operates two lively cafés that offer spicy Cajun and Creole specialties. Their crawfish étouffée may be the best this side of New Orleans. *E. Memphis, 7209 Winchester Rd., tel. 901/755–7689; downtown, 94 S. Front St., tel. 901/525–7689. AE, D, MC, V.*

Charlie Vergos' Rendezvous. Tourists and locals alike flock to this downtown basement restaurant to savor Vergos's "dry" barbecued pork ribs and other barbecue specialties. *52 S. 2nd St., tel. 901/523–2746. AE, DC, MC, V. No lunch Tues.–Thurs.; closed Sun.–Mon.*

★ **Corky's.** There's always a line at this no-frills East Memphis barbecue restaurant. Once you taste the ribs (or sandwiches, or beef or pork platters), you'll understand why. *5259 Poplar Ave., tel. 901/685–9744. AE, D, DC, MC, V.*

Lodging

Memphis hotels are especially busy during the month-long Memphis in May International Festival and in mid-August, during Elvis Tribute Week; book well ahead at these times. For B&Bs, contact the **Bed & Breakfast in Memphis Reservation Service** (Box 41621, Memphis 38174, tel. 901/726–5920). For price ranges, see Chart 2 (B) in Chapter 1.

Expensive **Adam's Mark Hotel.** Set in the flourishing eastern suburbs near I–240, this 27-story glass tower offers sweeping vistas of the sprawling metropolis and its outskirts. *939 Ridge Lake Blvd., 38120, tel. 901/684–6664 or 800/843–6664. 380 rooms. Facilities: restaurant, coffee shop, lounge with live entertainment, health club, pool. AE, DC, MC, V.*

The French Quarter Suites Hotel. This pleasant Overton Square hotel is reminiscent of a New Orleans–style inn. All suites have oversize whirlpool tubs, and some have balconies.

2144 Madison Ave., 38104, tel. 901/728–4000. 105 suites. Facilities: restaurant, bar, health club, pool. AE, D, DC, MC, V.

★ **Peabody Hotel.** Even if you're not staying here, it's worth a stop to see this 12-story downtown landmark, built in 1925 and impeccably restored in 1981. The lobby preserves its original stained-glass skylights and the travertine marble fountain that is home to the hotel's resident ducks. The rooms are decorated in a variety of period styles. *149 Union Ave., 38103, tel. 901/529–4000 or 800/732–2639. 454 rooms. Facilities: 3 restaurants, lounge, bar, health club, indoor pool. AE, DC, MC, V.*

Moderate **Country Suites by Carlson.** This three-story hotel in East Memphis provides many of the comforts of home, including kitchenettes. The decor is vaguely Mesoamerican, with teal carpeting and Aztec-pattern draperies. *4300 American Way, 38118, tel. 901/366–9333 or 800/456–4000. 121 suites. Facilities: health club, pool, whirlpool. AE, D, DC, MC, V.*

★ **Holiday Inn–Memphis East/Germantown.** Close to I–240 and the bustling Poplar/Ridgeway office complex, this sleek 10-story hotel has modern gray-and-mauve rooms with large windows. *5795 Poplar Ave., 38119, tel. 901/682–7881 or 800/833–4483. 246 rooms. Facilities: restaurant, lounge, health club, pool. AE, D, DC, MC, V.*

Radisson Hotel Memphis. Across the street from the Peabody, this downtown hotel has its own lobby fountain, complete with a waterfall. Glass-walled elevators whisk guests to rooms around a 10-story atrium. *185 Union Ave., 38103, tel. 901/528–1800. 283 rooms. Facilities: restaurant, lounge, pool, whirlpool, sauna. AE, D, DC, MC, V.*

Inexpensive **Econo Lodge–Graceland.** In the Executive section of this two-story inn, rooms are extra large, with a work table, good lighting, and comfortable overstuffed chairs. All rooms have private patios. *3280 Elvis Presley Blvd., 38116, tel. 901/345–1425. 128 rooms. Facilities: restaurant, pool, wading pool, playground. AE, D, DC, MC, V.*

La Quinta Motor Inn–Medical Center. Convenient to midtown and the medical center, this two-story inn offers spacious, well-maintained rooms. *42 S. Camilla St., 38104, tel. 901/526–1050 or 800/531–5900. 130 rooms. Facilities: outdoor pool. AE, D, DC, MC, V.*

Quality Inn Airport. This completely renovated three-story motor inn not far from Graceland has modern rooms that are light, sunny, and well-maintained. *2949 Airways Blvd., 38116, tel. 901/345–1250 or 800/221–2222. 145 rooms. Facilities: restaurant, lounge with dancing and wide-screen TV, pool. AE, D, DC, MC, V.*

The Arts and Nightlife

Call the Memphis events hotline (tel. 901/681–1111) for information about performances in the city.

The Arts The **Orpheum Theatre** (203 S. Main St., tel. 901/525–7800) hosts touring Broadway shows, as well as performances by **Opera Memphis** (tel. 901/678–2706) and **Memphis Concert Ballet** (tel. 901/763–0139). The **Memphis Symphony Orchestra** (3100 Walnut Grove Rd., No. 402, tel. 901/324–3627; Oct.–May) performs at the **Vincent DeFrank Music Hall** downtown.

Nightlife

To hear the blues as they were meant to be played, head for the clubs on Beale Street. Among the most popular are **B. B. King's Blues Club** (147 Beale St., tel. 901/527–5464), where B.B. himself occasionally performs, and **Blues Hall/Rum Boogie** (182 Beale St., tel. 901/528–0150).

Nashville

Hailed as the Country Music Capital and birthplace of the "Nashville Sound," Tennessee's fast-growing capital city is also a leading center of higher education, appropriately known as the Athens of the South. The city has spawned such dissimilar institutions as the "Grand Ole Opry" and Vanderbilt University, and has prospered from them both, becoming one of the mid-South's most vibrant cities in the process.

Tourist Information

Nashville: Area Chamber of Commerce (161 4th Ave. N, 37219, tel. 615/259–4755). Visitor Information Center (I–65 and James Robertson Pkwy., Exit 85, tel. 615/259–4747).

Arriving and Departing

By Plane **Nashville Metropolitan Airport** (tel. 615/275–1675), about 10 mi east of downtown, is served by major airlines and is a hub for **American Airlines.** To reach downtown by car, take I–40W. Cab fare runs about $16. **Downtown Express Shuttle** (tel. 615/275–1180) has service to downtown hotels for $8.

By Car I–65 leads into Nashville from the north and south; I–24, from the northwest and southeast; I–40, from the east and west.

Bus Station **Greyhound** (200 8th Ave. S, tel. 615/255–3556).

By Boat The **Delta Queen Steamboat Co.** (*see* Memphis, Arriving and Departing, *above*) offers cruises on the Mississippi, Ohio, and Cumberland rivers between St. Louis and Nashville.

Getting Around Nashville

The central city is bisected by the Cumberland River; numbered avenues are west of and parallel to it, and numbered streets east of and parallel to it. **Metropolitan Transit Authority (MTA)** buses (tel. 615/242–4433; fare: $1.15, exact change) serve the county.

Exploring Nashville

Downtown Downtown attractions can be covered rather easily on foot. Overlooking the river is **Ft. Nashborough** (170 1st Ave. N, tel. 615/255–8192; admission free), a replica of the crude log fort built in 1779 by Nashville's first settlers. A left onto Church Street takes you into the **Historic 2nd Avenue Business District**—known as The District—where 19th century buildings have been handsomely restored to house offices, restaurants, boutiques, and residences.

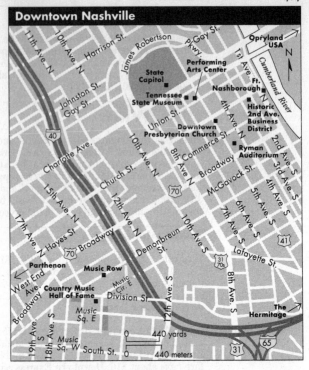

Downtown Nashville

At the corner of 5th Avenue is the **Downtown Presbyterian Church** (5th Ave. and Church St., tel. 615/254–7584) an Egyptian Revival tabernacle (ca. 1851) designed by noted Philadelphia architect William Strickland. Two blocks south is the **Ryman Auditorium and Museum** (116 5th Ave. N, tel. 615/254–1445; admission charged), the home of the "Grand Ole Opry" from 1943 to 1974—a shrine for die-hard fans.

Go north on 5th Avenue for the James K. Polk Office Building, home of the **Tennessee State Museum** (505 Deaderick St., tel. 615/741–2692; admission free; closed Mon.), where more than 6,000 artifacts trace the history of life in Tennessee. To the west along Charlotte Avenue is the Greek Revival **State Capitol** (tel. 615/741–0830; admission free), also designed by Strickland, who is interred there along with the 11th U.S. president, James K. Polk, and his wife.

Other Attractions   **Music Row** (Demonbreun St. exit off I–40) is the heart of Nashville's recording industry and the center of numerous country music attractions. A ticket to the **Country Music Hall of Fame and Museum** (4 Music Sq. E, tel. 615/256–1639; admission charged) includes admission to the legendary **RCA Studio B**, a few blocks away, where Elvis, Dolly Parton, and other greats once recorded.

Opryland USA, an attraction-filled musical theme park, offers 22 rides and more than a dozen live music shows. *2802 Opryland Dr. (via Briley Pkwy.), tel. 615/889–6600. Admission: $24.84 adults, $14.02 children. Closed Nov.–late Mar.; weekends late Mar.–May, Sept.–Oct.*

Since 1974, Opryland has also been the home of the **"Grand Ole Opry."** Each weekend top stars perform at the nation's oldest continuous radio show, which is broadcast from the world's largest broadcast studio (it seats 4,424). *2804 Opryland Dr., 37214, tel. 615/889–3060 (advance-ticket purchase advised). Admission: $14.07–$16.24 evenings; $11.91–$14.07 matinees.*

Twelve miles east of downtown (Exit 221 off I–40) is **The Hermitage,** built by the seventh U.S. president, Andrew Jackson, for his wife, Rachel. Their life and times are reflected with great care in the mansion, visitor center, and grounds. Both Jackson and his wife are entombed here. *4580 Rachel's La., Hermitage, tel. 615/889–2941. Admission charged.*

Two miles west of downtown in Centennial Park—built for the 1897 Tennessee Centennial Exposition—stands the **Parthenon,** an exact copy of the Athenian original and now used as an art gallery. *Athena Parthenos* is a 42-foot copy of a statue in the original Parthenon and the tallest indoor statue in the Western Hemisphere. *West End and 25th Aves., tel. 615/862–8431. Admission charged. Closed Mon.*

Park and Gardens

The 14,200-acre **J. Percy Priest Lake** (11 mi east of downtown off I–40, tel. 615/889–1975) is surrounded by parks where you can swim, fish, camp, hunt, hike, bike, picnic, paddle, or ride horseback. Thirty acres of gardens at the **Tennessee Botanical Gardens and Fine Arts Center at Cheekwood** (1200 Forrest Park Dr., tel. 615/356–8000; admission charged) showcase annuals, perennials, and area wildflowers.

What to See and Do with Children

Children's Discovery House (503 Maple St., Murfreesboro, tel. 615/890–2300) is a youngster's dream, with bubble blowers on the front lawn, colored chalk by the sidewalks, a play hospital, and more. At the **Cumberland Museum and Science Center** (800 Ridley Blvd., tel. 615/862–5160), children are invited to touch, smell, climb, and explore. The 50-acre **Nashville Zoo** (1710 Ridge Rd. Circle, Joelton, tel. 615/370–3333), opened in 1991, features an African savannah and a reptile house.

Shopping

Downtown, the trilevel **Church Street Centre** (7th Ave. and Church St., tel. 615/256–6644) features the **Castner-Knott** department store. The huge **Bellevue Center** mall in southwest Nashville (Bellevue exit from I–40W, tel. 615/646–8690) has 120 stores. Antiques lovers may want to browse through the shops along **8th Avenue South.** For the latest look in country-and-western wear, two-step over to **Music Row.**

Dining

If you expect Nashville dining to be all corn bread, turnip greens, and grits, you're in for a surprise. Here you will find some of Tennessee's most sophisticated restaurants. For price ranges, see Chart 1 (B) in Chapter 1.

Expensive **Arthur's.** At this romantic Continental restaurant in the renovated Union Station, the decor is lush (lace curtains, velvet upholstery) and the six-course meals are dazzling. *1001 Broadway, tel. 615/255–1494. Reservations advised. AE, DC, MC, V. No lunch (except Sun. brunch).*

★ **Mario's Ristorante Italiano.** Country-music stars, visiting celebrities, and local society come here to see and be seen—and to savor the memorable pastas created by Chef Sandro Bozzatto. *2005 Broadway, tel. 615/327–3232. Reservations required. Jacket required. AE, D, DC, MC, V. No lunch; closed Sun.*

The Merchants. This expensively built three-level restaurant has an outdoor patio. Specialties include deep-fried alligator bits, fresh seafoods, grilled meats, and Key lime pie. *401 Broadway, tel. 615/254–1892. Reservations advised. AE, DC, MC, V. No lunch weekends.*

Moderate **F. Scott's.** This popular café and wine bar has one of the largest
★ wine selections in town. Specialties include grilled chicken on black beans with roasted-pepper sauce, mango salsa, and smoked-tomato relish. *2220 Bandywood Dr., tel. 615/269–5861. AE, DC, MC, V.*

Mere Bulles, The Wine Bar and Restaurant. This intimate downtown restaurant offers river-view dining, a Continental menu, and an extensive wine list. *152 2nd Ave. N, tel. 615/256–1946. Reservations advised. Dress: casual but neat. AE, D, MC, V.*

106 Club. A black baby-grand piano and a shiny black enamel bar set the tone in this intimate art deco dining room in suburban Belle Meade. The cuisine is a mix of California nouvelle and international favorites. *106 Harding Pl., tel. 615/356–1300. Reservations advised. Jacket and tie advised. AE, D, DC, MC, V. No lunch.*

Inexpensive **Elliston Place Soda Shop.** The burgers are tasty, the sodas are frothy, and the service is friendly at this old-fashioned soda shop, where the 1950s atmosphere has been lovingly preserved. The chocolate shake is Nashville's best. *2111 Elliston Pl., tel. 615/327–1090. No credit cards. Closed Sun.*

Gerst Haus. German food prevails at this informal restaurant a mile east of downtown. Live German music on weekends adds to the oompah atmosphere. *228 Woodland St., tel. 615/256–9760. No credit cards.*

Hermitage House Smorgasbord. No need to be shy about helping yourself to the bountiful spread of salads, meats, vegetables, and desserts offered here. Don't miss the apple fritters. *4144 Lebanon Rd., Hermitage, tel. 615/883–9525. Reservations advised. No credit cards.*

★ **Loveless Cafe.** The draw here is true down-home southern cooking: feather-light homemade biscuits and preserves, country ham and red-eye gravy, and fried chicken. *8400 Hwy. 100, tel. 615/646–9700. Reservations advised. No credit cards. Closed Mon.*

Lodging

For information on B&Bs in the area, contact **Bed & Breakfast Hospitality—Tennessee** (Box 110227, Nashville 37222, tel. 615/331–5244 or 800/458–2421). For price ranges, see Chart 2 (B) in Chapter 1.

Expensive **Holiday Inn–Briley Parkway.** This hotel offers the Holidome Indoor Recreation Center, with pool, sauna, whirlpool, game room, and more. The guest rooms are spacious and well lighted. *2200 Elm Hill Pike at Briley Pkwy., 37210, tel. 615/883–9770. 381 rooms, 4 suites. Facilities: restaurant, lounge, pool, fitness center. AE, DC, MC, V.*

★ **Opryland Hotel.** This massive hotel adjacent to Opryland boasts a 2-acre glass-walled conservatory filled with 10,000 tropical plants, and a skylighted cascades area with indoor streams and a half-acre lake. *2800 Opryland Dr., 37214, tel. 615/889–1000. 1,741 rooms, 150 suites. Facilities: 5 restaurants, coffee shop, 6 lounges, pool, tennis. AE, D, DC, MC, V.*

Stouffer Nashville Hotel. This ultracontemporary high rise adjoins the Nashville Convention Center and the Church Street Centre Mall. The spacious rooms have period reproduction furnishings. *611 Commerce St., 37203, tel. 615/255–8400. 649 rooms, 24 suites. Facilities: restaurant, coffee shop, lounge, deli, health club/spa, pool. AE, D, DC, MC, V.*

Moderate **Courtyard by Marriott–Airport.** This handsome low-rise motor
★ inn offers some amenities you'd expect in higher-priced hotels: spacious rooms, king-size beds, and oversize work desks. *2508 Elm Hill Pike, 37214, tel. 615/883–9500 or 800/321–2211. 133 rooms, 12 suites. Facilities: restaurant, lounge, exercise room, pool, sauna, whirlpool. AE, D, DC, MC, V.*

Hampton Inn Vanderbilt. The rooms are colorful and spacious at this contemporary inn near Vanderbilt University. There's a hospitality suite for social or business use. *1919 West End Ave., 37203, tel. 615/329–1144 or 800/426–7866. 171 rooms. Facilities: Continental breakfast, exercise room, pool. AE, D, DC, MC, V.*

Ramada Inn Across from Opryland. This contemporary-style, low-rise motor inn is closer to the theme park than any other hotel except the Opryland. *2401 Music Valley Dr., 37214, tel. 615/889–0800 or 800/272–6232. 307 rooms, 7 suites. Facilities: restaurant, lounge, indoor pool, whirlpool. AE, D, DC, MC, V.*

Inexpensive **Comfort Inn Hermitage.** Near The Hermitage, this inn offers comfortable accommodations, some with water beds or whirlpool baths. *5768 Old Hickory Blvd., 37076, tel. 615/889–5060. 106 rooms. Facilities: Continental breakfast, pool. AE, D, DC, MC, V.*

La Quinta Motor Inn. Guest rooms are spacious and well lighted, with a large working area and an oversize bed. *2001 Metrocenter Blvd., 37227–0001, tel. 615/259–2130 or 800/531–5900. 121 rooms. Facilities: pool. AE, DC, MC, V.*

★ **Wilson Inn.** Three miles from Opryland, this five-story hotel is new, clean, and convenient. Many rooms have kitchens. *600 Ermac Dr., 37210 (Elm Hill Pike exit from Briley Pkwy.), tel. 615/889–4466 or 800/333–9457. 110 rooms. Facilities: Continental breakfast, pool. AE, D, DC, MC, V.*

The Arts and Nightlife

The Arts The **Tennessee Performing Arts Center** (505 Deaderick St., tel. 615/741–7975) holds performances by the **Nashville Ballet** (tel. 615/244–7233), **Nashville Opera** (tel. 615/292–5710), **Nashville Symphony Orchestra** (tel. 615/329–3033), and **Tennessee Repertory Theatre** (tel. 615/244–4878). The center's **Andrew Jackson**

Hall also hosts touring Broadway shows. Call **Ticketmaster** (tel. 615/737–4844) for tickets and information.

Nightlife For country music try **Boots Randolph's** (209 Printers Alley, tel. 615/256–5500), a sophisticated dinner club where Boots ("Mr. Yakkety Sax") himself performs once or twice nightly, or the **Stock Yard Bull Pen Lounge** (901 2nd Ave. N, tel. 615/255–6464), a restaurant-lounge with live entertainment and dancing. Jazz clubs include **The Merchants** and **Mere Bulls** (for both, *see* Dining, *above*), both downtown. **Exit/In** (2208 Elliston Pl., tel. 615/321–4400) and **Grapevine Cafe** (2206 Elliston Pl., tel. 615/327–3222), both near Vanderbilt University, focus on rock and blues.

East Tennessee

From the misty heights of the Great Smoky Mountains to the rippling waters of the Holston, French Broad, Nolichucky, and Tennessee rivers, East Tennessee offers a cornucopia of scenic grandeur and recreational opportunities. While mountain folkways often persist in smaller communities, cities like Knoxville and Chattanooga are up-to-date and quite diverse.

Tourist Information

Chattanooga: Area Convention and Visitors Bureau (1001 Market St., 37402, tel. 615/756–8687 or 800/322–3344). **Knoxville:** Convention and Visitors Bureau (500 Henley St., 37902, tel. 615/523–7263).

Getting There

By Plane **Knoxville Airport** (tel. 615/970–2773), served by American Eagle, Com Air, Delta, Northwest, Trans World Express, United, and USAir, is about 12 mi from town. **Chattanooga Airport** (tel. 615/855–2200), served by American Eagle, ASA, CC Air, Comair, Delta, Northwest Airlink, and USAir, is about 8 mi from town.

By Car I–75 runs north–south from Kentucky through Knoxville, then to Chattanooga. I–81 heads southwest from the Virginia border at Bristol, ending at I–40 northeast of Knoxville. I–40 enters from North Carolina and continues west to Knoxville, Nashville, and Memphis.

By Bus **Greyhound** has stops in Chattanooga (tel. 615/267–6531) and in Knoxville (tel. 615/524–0369).

By Boat The **Delta Queen Steamship Co.** (*see* Memphis, Arriving and Departing, *above*) has an annual cruise on the Tennessee River as far as Chattanooga.

Exploring East Tennessee

Founded in 1786, **Knoxville** was the first state capital when Tennessee was admitted to the Union in 1796. Today it is home to the main campus of the **University of Tennessee,** as well as the headquarters of the **Tennessee Valley Authority (TVA),** with its vast complex of hydroelectric dams and recreational lakes.

Historic sites in Knoxville include the 1792 **Governor William Blount Mansion** (200 W. Hill Ave., tel. 615/525–2375; admis-

sion charged; closed Mon.), where the governor and his associates planned the admission of Tennessee as the 16th state in the
Union; and the **Armstrong-Lockett House** (2728 Kingston Pike,
tel. 615/637–3163; admission charged; closed Mon. and Jan.–
Feb.), an 1834 farm mansion, now a showcase of American and
English furniture and English silver. The **East Tennessee Historical Center** (800 Market St., tel. 615/544–5744), housed in
the 1874 U.S. Customs House, displays books, documents, and
artifacts relating to the history of the state.

The $10.5 million **Knoxville Museum of Art** (410 10th St., in
World's Fair Park, tel. 615/525–6101; admission charged;
closed Mon.), opened in 1992, has four exhibition galleries with
contemporary prints, drawings, and paintings. The **Knoxville
Zoological Gardens** (Rutledge Pike S, off I–40 Exit 392, tel.
615/637–5331; admission charged) is famous for breeding large
cat species and African elephants, and for its reptile complex.

Southeast of Knoxville via U.S. 441/321 is **Gatlinburg,**
Tennessee's premier mountain resort town and the northern
gateway to the **Great Smoky Mountains National Park** (*see* National and State Parks, *above*). Set in the narrow valley of the
Little Pigeon River (actually a turbulent mountain stream),
Gatlinburg offers an abundance of family attractions, including
the **Gatlinburg Sky Lift** (tel. 615/436–4307) to the top of Crockett Mountain and the **Ober Gatlinburg Tramway** (tel. 615/436–
5423) to a mountaintop amusement park, ski center, and shopping mall/crafts market.

In nearby **Pigeon Forge,** about 6 mi north on U.S. 441, you'll
find **Dollywood** (700 Dollywood La., tel. 615/428–9400; admission charged; closed early Nov.–late Apr.), Dolly Parton's popular theme park. South from Gatlinburg, scenic U.S. 441
climbs to **Newfound Gap,** a haunting viewpoint on the Tennessee–North Carolina border. From here, a 7-mi spur road leads
to **Clingmans Dome**—at 6,643 feet, the highest point in Tennessee.

Southwest of Knoxville off I–75 is **Chattanooga,** a city of Civil
War battlefields, museums of all kinds (art, antiques, history,
even knives), and a famous choo-choo (*see* Dining and Lodging,
below). Chattanooga is also a city of great scenic beauty. Dominating the skyline is 2,215-foot-high **Lookout Mountain,** 6 mi
away, which offers panoramic views and the world's steepest
Incline Railway (827 E. Brow Rd., tel. 615/821–4224; admission
charged). The newest attraction here is the $45 million **Tennessee Aquarium** (1 Broad St., tel. 615/265–0695; admission
charged). Opened in 1992, this is the world's largest freshwater
aquarium, with 350 species of fish, mammals, birds, reptiles,
and amphibians.

About 100 mi northeast of Chattanooga (take U.S. 27 to I–40E
or I–75 to I–40W) is **Oak Ridge,** where atomic energy was secretly developed during World War II. The **American Museum
of Science and Energy** (300 Tulane Ave., tel. 615/576–3200; admission free) focuses on uses of nuclear, solar, and geothermal
energy, mainly for peaceful purposes.

What to See and Do with Children

The **Gatlinburg/Pigeon Forge area** is lined with amusement
parks, offbeat museums (**Guinness World Records Museum,** tel.

615/436–9100), and other attractions for children. In Knoxville, youngsters like the hands-on displays and audiovisual exhibits at the **East Tennessee Discovery Center and Akima Planetarium** (516 Beaman St., tel. 615/637–1121). Children also enjoy the **Tennessee Aquarium** in Chattanooga and the **American Museum of Science and Energy** in Oak Ridge (*see* Exploring East Tennessee, *above*).

Shopping

The **Great Smoky Arts and Craft Community** (Glades and Buckhorn Rds. off U.S. 321, 3 mi east of Gatlinburg, tel. 615/436–3301), a collection of 60 shops and crafts studios along 8 mi of rambling country road, features wood carvings, corn-husk dolls, dulcimers, handmade quilts, and other Appalachian folk crafts.

Sports and Outdoor Activities

Fishing East Tennessee's lakes offer seasonal angling for striped bass, walleye, white bass, and muskie. Gatlinburg's streams and rivers are stocked with trout from April to November. There are boat-launch ramps (but no rentals) at **Norris Dam State Resort Park** north of Knoxville (tel. 615/426–7461) and on **Lake Chickamauga,** near Chattanooga (tel. 615/894–4955).

Golf East Tennessee courses open to the public include **Brainerd Golf Course** in Chattanooga (tel. 615/855–2692), **Whittle Springs Municipal Golf Course** in Knoxville (tel. 615/525–1022), and **Bent Creek Mountain Inn and Country Club** in Gatlinburg (tel. 615/436–3947).

Hiking A scenic portion of the **Appalachian Trail** runs along high ridges in the Great Smoky Mountains National Park (Gatlinburg, tel. 615/436–5615). The trail can be easily reached at Newfound Gap from U.S. 441.

Horseback Riding **McCarter's Riding Stables** (tel. 615/436–5354; Apr.–Oct.).

Rafting and Canoeing East Tennessee has five white-water rivers: Ocoee, Hiwassee, French Broad, Tellico, and Nolichucky. For canoe rentals and guided raft trips, contact **Cripple Creek Expeditions** (Ocoee, tel. 615/338–8441) or **Rafting in the Smokies** (Gatlinburg, tel. 615/436–5008) April through October.

Ski Areas

Ober Gatlinburg Ski Resort (tel. 615/436–5423 or, Nov.–mid-Mar., 800/251–9202) has three lifts and 10 downhill slopes.

Dining and Lodging

Expect hearty food in the mountains: barbecued ribs, thick pork chops, country ham with red-eye gravy. For reservations at hotels, motels, chalets, and condominiums in Gatlinburg, contact **Smoky Mountain Accommodations Reservation Service** (Rte. 4, Box 538, Roaring Fork Rd., Gatlinburg 37738, tel. 615/436–9700 or 800/231–2230). For B&B reservations, contact **Bed & Breakfast Hospitality Tennessee** (Box 110227, Nashville 37222, tel. 615/331–5244 or 800/458–2421). For price ranges, see Charts 1 (B) and 2 (B) in Chapter 1.

Chattanooga
Dining and Lodging

Chattanooga Choo-Choo Holiday Inn. The hotel adjoins the showcase 1905 Southern Railway Terminal, with restaurants, lounges, shops, exhibits, gardens, and an operating trolley. Guest rooms stress luxurious appointments, especially the restored Victorian-era parlor cars. *1400 Market St., 37402, tel. 615/266–5000. 360 units, including suites and 48 parlor cars. Facilities: 5 restaurants, lounge, indoor and outdoor pools, whirlpools, tennis courts. AE, DC, MC, V. Moderate.*

★ **Radisson Read House.** The Georgian-style Read House dates from the 1920s and has been impeccably restored to its original grandeur. Guest rooms in the main hotel continue the Georgian motif; rooms in the annex are more contemporary. The **Green Room** restaurant (reservations advised; jacket and tie advised) offers a Continental menu. *827 Broad St., 37402, tel. 615/266–4121. 107 rooms, 131 suites. Facilities: 2 restaurants, lounge, pool, sauna, whirlpool. AE, D, DC, MC, V. Moderate.*

Gatlinburg
Dining

Burning Bush Restaurant. Reproduction furnishings evoke a Colonial atmosphere, but the menu leans toward Continental. Specialties include broiled Tennessee quail. *1151 Parkway, tel. 615/436–4669. Reservations advised. AE, D, MC, V. Moderate.*

Smoky Mountain Trout House. Trout is prepared eight ways, or you can have prime rib, country ham, or fried chicken. This restaurant is a truly rustic, mountain cottage. *410 N. Parkway, tel. 615/436–5416. No reservations. AE, DC, MC, V. Moderate. Closed Dec.–Mar.*

Lodging
★ **Buckhorn Inn.** This country inn about 6 mi outside the city has welcomed guests to its rustic rooms and cottages for more than 40 years. The mountain views are spectacular. Hearty breakfasts and dinners are included in the rates. *2140 Tudor Mtn. Rd., 37738, tel. 615/436–4668. 6 rooms, 4 1-bedroom cottages, 2 2-bedroom guest houses. No credit cards. Expensive.*

★ **Holiday Inn Resort Complex.** Near the Convention Center and the Ober Gatlinburg aerial tramway, this hotel offers the Holidome Indoor Recreation Center, with a pool, an atrium, and other attractions. *520 Airport Rd., 37738, tel. 615/436–9201. 402 rooms and suites. Facilities: 2 restaurants, lounge, 2 indoor pools, outdoor pool, whirlpool, 2 saunas, coin laundry. AE, D, DC, MC, V. Moderate.*

Knoxville
Dining
★ **Regas Restaurant.** This cozy Knoxville classic, with fireplaces and original art, has been around for 70 years. The specialty, prime rib, is sliced to order and served with a creamy horseradish sauce. *318 Gay St., tel. 615/637–9805. Reservations advised. AE, D, DC, MC, V. No lunch Sat.; no dinner Sun. Moderate–Expensive.*

Copper Cellar/Cumberland Grill. A favorite of the college crowd and young professionals, the original downstairs Copper Cellar has an intimate atmosphere. Upstairs, the Cumberland Grill features salads and sandwiches. Both offer outstanding desserts. *1807 Cumberland Ave., tel. 615/673–3411. Reservations advised. AE, DC, MC, V. Inexpensive–Expensive.*

Lodging
★ **Hyatt Regency Knoxville.** This is a handsome, contemporary adaptation of an Aztec pyramid, atop a hill overlooking the city and nearby mountains. The nine-story atrium lobby blends modern furnishings with artworks in Mesoamerican motifs. *500 Hill Ave. SE, Box 88, 37901, tel. 615/637–1234. 360 rooms, 27 suites. Facilities: 2 restaurants, lounge, exercise room, pool, playground. AE, D, DC, MC, V. Expensive.*

Luxbury Hotel. Midway between downtown Knoxville and Oak Ridge, this affordable new hotel provides oversize rooms with spacious work areas. *420 Peters Rd. N, 37922, tel. 615/539–0058. 75 rooms, 23 suites. Facilities: Continental breakfast, pool. AE, D, DC, MC, V. Inexpensive.*

The Arts and Nightlife

In Chattanooga, the **Tivoli Theater** (399 McCaulley Ave., tel. 615/757–5050) presents concerts and traveling productions. In Gatlinburg, **Sweet Fanny Adams Theatre and Music Hall** (461 Parkway, tel. 615/436–4038) stages original musical comedies and Gay '90s revues, and hotel lounges offer DJs and live entertainment.

In Knoxville, the **Bijou Theater** (803 S. Gay St., tel. 615/522–0832) offers seasonal ballet, concerts, and plays. The "Old City" boasts a variety of restaurants, clubs, and shops. Try **Manhattan's** (101 S. Central St., tel. 615/525–4463) for music. For authentic Tex-Mex music and food there's **Amigo's** (116 S. Central St., tel. 615/546–9505). And both **Patrick Sullivan's** (100 N. Central St., tel. 615/522–4511) and **Hooray's** (106 S. Central St., tel. 615/546–6729) offer saloon-style fun and food.

6 The Midwest and Great Lakes

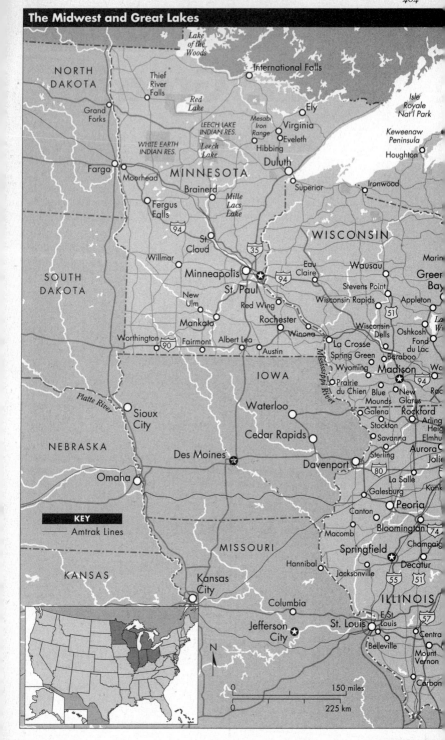

484

The Midwest and Great Lakes

Lake of the Woods

NORTH DAKOTA

Thief River Falls

Red Lake

International Falls

Ely

Virginia

Eveleth

Hibbing

Mesabi Iron Range

LEECH LAKE INDIAN RES.

Leech Lake

WHITE EARTH INDIAN RES.

Grand Forks

Fargo

Moorhead

MINNESOTA

Brainerd

Mille Lacs Lake

Duluth

Superior

Isle Royale Nat'l Park

Keweenaw Peninsula

Houghton

Ironwood

Fergus Falls

94

St Cloud

35

Willmar

SOUTH DAKOTA

Minneapolis

St Paul

WISCONSIN

Eau Claire

Wausau

Marin

Greer Bay

94

Stevens Point

Appleton

New Ulm

Red Wing

Rochester

Wisconsin Rapids

51

Oshkosh

Fond du Lac

La Wi

Mankato

Worthington

90

Fairmont

Albert Lea

Winona

Austin

La Crosse

Spring Green

Wisconsin Dells

Baraboo

Wyoming

Madison

94

Wo

IOWA

Mississippi River

Prairie du Chien

Blue Mounds

New Glares

Rac

Platte River

Sioux City

Waterloo

Cedar Rapids

Galena

Stockton

Savanna

Rockford

Arling Heig

Elmhu

NEBRASKA

Des Moines

Davenport

80

Sterling

La Salle

Aurora

Jolie

Omaha

Galesburg

Kank

KEY

Canton

Peoria

— Amtrak Lines

Macomb

Bloomington

74

MISSOURI

Springfield

Champaig

KANSAS

Hannibal

Jacksonville

Decatur

55

51

Kansas City

Columbia

St. Louis

E. St Louis

ILLINOIS

57

Jefferson City

Belleville

Centra

Mount Vernon

Carbon

N

0   150 miles

0   225 km

CANADA

Lake
Superior

Copper
Harbor

Marquette

Sault
Ste. Marie

MICHIGAN

Iron
Mountain

Escanaba

Northport

Petoskey

Beaver
Island

Mackinac
Island
Mackinaw
City

Manitoulin
Island

*Georgian
Bay*

Sudbury

Alpena

*Lake
Huron*

Toronto

*Lake
Ontario*

Sturgeon
Bay

Traverse
City

MICHIGAN

23

Manitowoc

Cadillac

Bay
City

131

Saginaw

*Lake
Michigan*

nebago

Sheboygan

43

Grand
Rapids

75

Flint

69

Port
Huron

Buffalo

NEW
YORK

kesha

Milwaukee

96

Kenosha

Waukegan

Battle
Creek

196

94

Lansing

Jackson

Kalamazoo

Ann
Arbor

Detroit

*Lake
Erie*

90

PENNSYLVANIA

Evanston

Chicago

80
90

Angola

Toledo

69

Cleveland

Port
Clinton

Sandusky

80
90

Akron

Youngstown

80

South
Bend

La
Porte

Auburn

75

Gary

65

kee

57

Huntington

Logansport

24

69

Fort
Wayne

Lima

Marion

71

Mansfield

OHIO

Canton

77

Wapakoneta

70

INDIANA

Muncie

Danville

Lafayette

Anderson

Zionsville

Dayton

70

Columbus

Zanesville

Wheeling

Crawfordsville

36

Indianapolis

Terre
Haute

Columbus

74

Marietta

Chillicothe

Cincinnati

36

WEST VIRGINIA

70

Bloomington

50

Madison

65

Vincennes

Wabash River

New
Albany

Gentryville

Corydan

Ohio R.

Louisville

KENTUCKY

54

Evansville

ale

VIRGINIA

Introduction

By Holly Hughes   The Midwest *is* America, that prototypical vision of neat farm-land, affluent suburbs, and compact, skyscrapered downtowns strung together along purposefully straight silver highways. Sauk Centre, Minnesota, was the setting for Sinclair Lewis's *Main Street;* Muncie, Indiana, was the subject of the sociological study *Middletown, USA.* It is no accident that stand-up comedians use midwestern town names—Peoria, Sheboygan, Kokomo, Kalamazoo—to mean "the heart of the country." Nevertheless, transplanted Midwesterners spend the rest of their lives longing for broad, clear horizons; thick, shady stands of beech and maple trees; hazy summer afternoons when kids sell lemonade from sidewalk stands. People seem genuinely friendlier and more down-to-earth here.

Six states—Ohio, Indiana, Michigan, Illinois, Wisconsin, and Minnesota—occupy what was originally the Northwest Territory, a vast tract of forest and meadow awarded to the United States in the 1783 Treaty of Paris. Unlike the stark Great Plains to the west, this is gently rolling landscape, punctuated by rivers, woods, and trees. It is defined by great geographical features: to the east, the Appalachian Mountains; to the north, the Great Lakes; to the south, the Ohio River; to the west, the majestic Mississippi River.

Smarting from years of being labeled as "the sticks," midwest-ern cities are always trying to prove themselves, cheerfully re-habilitating their downtowns, rooting for their major-league ball teams, building gleaming convention centers and festival malls. Ohio has no fewer than five important cities (Cleveland, Cincinnati, Columbus, Dayton, and Toledo). Minnesota's major population center comprises two cities, Minneapolis and St. Paul, which means that there are twice as many parks and mu-seums there as you'd expect. Indiana's capital, Indianapolis, is a beautifully laid-out city that's also the amateur-sports capital of the U.S.A. Michigan has Detroit, home of America's auto in-dustry, which still offers attractions despite economic prob-lems. Milwaukee, Wisconsin, poised on the western shore of Lake Michigan, is a rich melting pot of immigrant cultures, as is vibrant and powerful Chicago, Illinois, the region's one great metropolis.

But it's never more than an hour's drive from these cities to northern lake resorts, historic villages along sleepy back roads, utopian colonies, and pleasant university towns. Big swatches of forest and lakeshore are protected as parkland, and gorgeous scenic drives edge the Great Lakes and the dra-matic bluffs of the Mississippi and Ohio river valleys.

Tour Groups

From the beauty of the Upper Peninsula and the historic sites of Mackinac Island to the bustle of such cities as Grand Rapids and Chicago, tours of the Great Lakes region offer something for everyone.

Gadabout Tours (700 E. Tahquitz Way, Palm Springs, CA 92262, tel. 619/325–5556 or 800/952–5068) takes a three-week swing in May through St. Louis, Chicago, Indianapolis, and Holland, Michigan. **Globus** (5301 S. Federal Circle, Littleton, CO 80123, tel. 303/797–2800 or 800/221–0090) offers 10 days in

Michigan and the Great Lakes region, including Chicago; Agawa Canyon, Ontario; and Mackinac Island and Dearborn, Michigan. **Maupintour** (Box 807, Lawrence, KS 66044, tel. 913/843–1211 or 800/255–4266) has an eight-day Great Lakes tour that goes from Chicago to the coasts and takes in scenic features of Wisconsin, Mackinac Island, and coastal Michigan, winding up in Grand Rapids. **Talmage Tours** (1223 Walnut St., Philadelphia, PA 19107, tel. 215/923–7100) offers an eight-day trip and cruise through the Great Lakes to Mackinac Island. **Tauck Tours** (Box 5027, Westport, CT 06881, tel. 203/226–6911 or 800/468–2825) visits the scenic coastline of Lake Michigan in eight days, covering Holland, the Upper Peninsula, Mackinac Island, and Dearborn.

When to Go

Summer is the most popular time of year to visit the Midwest and the Great Lakes. Generally, the farther north you go, the fewer people you'll find. Prices in most places peak in July and August. Daily summer temperatures average in the 80s in Illinois, Indiana, and Ohio, though July and August heat waves can push them high into the 90s. In Michigan, Wisconsin, and Minnesota, summer temperatures run 10° cooler. These three states have the best **fall** foliage, though you can see good color in all six. Depending on the weather, the leaves usually begin to turn in mid-September and reach their most colorful by mid-October. In **winter** Michigan has the only significant downhill skiing in the region, but cross-country is extremely popular in Wisconsin and Minnesota. The Midwest usually gets at least one sub-zero cold snap every year. For the rest of winter, expect temperatures in the 20s and 30s, and about 10° colder in northern Michigan, Wisconsin, and Minnesota. Sudden snowstorms can make winter driving unpredictable and treacherous. **Spring** is damp and clammy, with erratic weather and temperatures ranging from the 30s to the 60s.

Festivals and Seasonal Events

Late Jan.–early Feb: The 12-day **St. Paul (MN) Winter Carnival** celebrates winter with a sleigh and cutter parade, an ice palace, car races on the ice, and ice sculptures by artists from around the world. *Tel. 612/297–6953.*

May: The month-long **Indianapolis 500 Festival** culminates in the most famous car race in the United States. *Tel. 317/636–4556 or 317/241–2500.*

May 4–14: The **Holland (MI) Tulip Festival** features flowers and Dutch traditions. *Tel. 616/396–4221.*

Late June–early July: Milwaukee holds **Summerfest,** a lakefront festival featuring rock, jazz, and popular music. *Tel. 414/273–2680 or 800/837–3378.*

July 4 and week preceding: A Taste of Chicago feeds 4 million hungry visitors to Grant Park with specialties from the city's restaurants. *Tel. 312/744–3315.*

July 15–24: The **Minneapolis Aquatennial** celebrates the lakes of Minnesota with sailing regattas, waterskiing competitions, and other water-related events. *Tel. 612/377–4621.*

July 23–24: The two-day **Chicago-to-Mackinac Boat Race** is one of the most challenging sailboat races in the country. *Tel. 312/861–7777.*

July 23–24: The **U.S. International Air Show,** Wright Patterson Air Force Base, Dayton, Ohio, is a dazzling display of flying technique. *Tel. 513/898–5901.*

July 30: The **Pro Football Hall of Fame Game** and induction ceremonies in Canton, Ohio, kick off the football season. *Tel. 216/456–8207.*

Late July: The **Cincinnati Riverfront Stadium Festival** is the largest festival in the country devoted to rhythm and blues. *Tel. 513/871–3900.*

Late July–early Aug: The **Experimental Aircraft Association Fly-in** in Oshkosh, Wisconsin, gathers close to a million people and 30,000 aircraft from around the world. *Tel. 414/426–4800.*

Early Aug.: The **Wisconsin State Fair** attracts crowds to Milwaukee for livestock and crop shows, midway attractions, and stage shows. *Tel. 414/266–7000.*

Aug. 12–22: The **Illinois State Fair** in Springfield has livestock shows, car and horse races, food, and entertainment. *Tel. 217/782–6661.*

Aug. 26–Sept. 6: The **Minnesota State Fair** attracts throngs to St. Paul. *Tel. 612/642–2200.*

Labor Day weekend: The **Detroit Montreux Jazz Festival** attracts more than 700,000 jazz fans. *Tel. 313/259–5400.*

Last Sun. in Oct.: The **Chicago Marathon** draws runners from all over the world. *Tel. 312/951–0660.*

Getting Around the Midwest and Great Lakes

By Plane The region is served by most major airlines, including American, Delta, Northwest, United, and USAir. The largest airports are Cleveland Hopkins International Airport (tel. 216/265–6000) in Ohio; Detroit Metropolitan Wayne County Airport (tel. 313/942–3550) in Michigan; General Mitchell Field, Milwaukee, Wisconsin (tel. 414/747–5300); Indianapolis International Airport (tel. 317/248–9594) in Indiana; Minneapolis St. Paul International Airport (tel. 612/726–5555) in Minnesota; and O'Hare International Airport, Chicago, Illinois (tel. 312/686–2200).

By Car I–80 and I–90 converge near Cleveland and run along the northern borders of Ohio and Indiana until they split at Chicago. I–80 then cuts across Illinois into Iowa, while I–90 curves up through Wisconsin and goes across southern Minnesota. Other major arteries are I–70, crossing the southern parts of Ohio, Indiana, and Illinois; I–94, which goes from Detroit across Michigan, hugs Lake Michigan through Indiana and Illinois, then crosses Wisconsin and Minnesota; and I–75, which stretches from Sault Ste. Marie, Michigan, to Cincinnati, Ohio. State routes and county roads provide a closer look at the countryside and small towns and are in good repair throughout the region.

By Train Amtrak (tel. 800/872–7245) is the primary passenger railroad serving the entire region. All routes go through Chicago.

Among cities with commuter train service between the central city and the suburbs are Chicago (tel. 312/836–7000), Cleveland (tel. 216/621–9500), and Indianapolis (tel. 317/267–3000).

By Bus The major intercity carrier is **Greyhound** (tel. 312/781–2900 in Chicago or 800/231–2222). **Indian Trails** (tel. 800/248–3849) operates between Chicago and many cities in Michigan. In southern Wisconsin, **Van Galder Bus Lines** (tel. 608/257–5593 or 800/747–0094) runs from Madison and Milwaukee to Chicago's O'Hare Airport and downtown Amtrak station.

By Boat From mid-May to October, passenger and automobile **ferry** service operates between Ludington, Michigan, and Manitowoc, Wisconsin (tel. 616/845–5555).

ILLINOIS

By Elizabeth Gardner

Capital	Springfield
Population	11,466,682
Motto	State Sovereignty—National Union
State Bird	Cardinal
State Flower	Native violet

Visitor Information

Illinois Bureau of Tourism (310 S. Michigan Ave., Chicago 60604, tel. 800/223–0121).

Scenic Drives

The Illinois part of the **Lake Michigan Circle Tour** follows the shoreline along Lake Shore Drive through Chicago and passes through the elegant suburbs of the North Shore: Evanston, Winnetka, Glencoe, Highland Park, and Lake Forest. The **Great River Road** follows the Mississippi River for 500 mi, the length of Illinois from East Dubuque to Cairo (pronounced "KAY-ro").

National and State Parks

National Parks **Shawnee National Forest** (901 S. Commercial St., Harrisburg 62946, tel. 618/253–7114) blankets the southern tip of Illinois with 250,000 acres of wilderness; this is where the glaciers stopped after flattening most of the rest of the state during the last Ice Age.

State Parks Illinois has more than 100 state parks, conservation areas, fish and wildlife areas, and recreation areas. For a list of parks and their facilities, write or call the **Illinois Department of Conservation** (524 S. 2nd St., Springfield 62701, tel. 217/782–7454). **Illinois Beach State Park** (Lake Front, Zion 60099, tel. 708/662–4811), on Lake Michigan near the Wisconsin border, offers sandy beaches along 6½ mi of shoreline. **Rend Lake/Wayne Fitzgerrell State Park** (R.R. 4, Box 68, Benton 62812, tel. 618/439–3832) has the state's second-largest inland lake, where you can fish, sail, and swim. **Starved Rock State Park** (Box 116, Utica 61373, tel. 815/667–4726), on the Illinois River between LaSalle and Peru, has 18 canyons formed during the melting of the glaciers.

Chicago

Because Chicago is not as large or as famous as New York, many Chicagoans suffer from "Second City" complex, afraid that out-of-towners won't appreciate their city's charms. But these are hard to miss, from the elegance of Michigan Avenue's shops to the stunning sweep of the lakefront skyline. The Loop, Chicago's central business district, is a living museum of skyscraper architecture, while many outlying neighborhoods retain the grace and homey quality of pre–World War II America. Chicago's arts community is world-class, and strong ethnic communities embrace immigrants from Croatia to Cambodia, all of whom leave their cultural stamp on the city.

Tourist Information

Chicago: Office of Tourism (806 N. Michigan Ave., Water Tower in the Park, 60611, tel. 312/280–5740 or 800/487–2446; walk-in center at Pumping Station, 163 E. Pearson St.). The Mayor's Office of Special Events/General Information and Activities (121 N. La Salle St., 60602, tel. 312/744–3315, 312/744–3370 for taped announcement).

Arriving and Departing

By Plane Every national airline, most international airlines, and a number of regional carriers fly into **O'Hare International Airport,** some 20 mi from downtown in the far northwestern corner of the city. One of the world's busiest airports, it is a hub for United and American Airlines. The **Chicago Transit Authority** station is in the underground concourse near Terminal 2. **Continental Airport Express** (tel. 312/454–7799; fare, $13) provides express coach service to major downtown and Near North hotels. Metered taxicab service is available at O'Hare; expect to pay $25 to $30 (plus tip) to Near North and downtown locations.

Several carriers, including United, American, and Southwest Airlines, use **Midway Airport** on the southwest side. There's no convenient ground transportation from here, but **Continental Airport Express** operates to the Loop and Near North (*see above*, $9).

By Car From the east, the Indiana Toll Road (I–80/90) leads to the Chicago Skyway (also a toll road), which runs into the Dan Ryan Expressway (I–90/94); take the Dan Ryan westbound just past the turnoff for I–290 to any of the downtown eastbound exits. From the south, you can take I–57 to the Dan Ryan. From the west, follow I–80 to I–55, which is the major artery from the southwest and leads into Lake Shore Drive. From the north, I–94 or I–90 eastbound merge to form the John F. Kennedy Expressway (I–90/94) about 10 mi north of downtown.

Train Station **Amtrak** serves Chicago's **Union Station** (Jackson and Canal Sts., tel. 312/558–1075).

Bus Station **Greyhound and Indian Trails, Inc.** (630 W. Harrison St., tel. 312/408–5971).

Getting Around Chicago

The best way to see Chicago is on foot, supplemented by public transportation or taxi. Streets are laid out in a grid, the center of which is the intersection of Madison Street, which runs east–west, and State Street, which runs north–south.

By Car Leave your car behind if you're seeing the Loop, the Near North Side, or Lincoln Park. You'll need a car to go to the suburbs or outlying city neighborhoods. Downtown abounds with parking lots charging from $7 to $15 a day.

By Public Transportation Chicago's extensive public transportation network includes buses and rapid-transit trains, both subway and elevated. The **Chicago Transit Authority** and the **RTA** (for both, tel. 312/836–7000; base fare, $1.50) will provide information on how to get about on city rapid-transit and bus lines, suburban bus lines, and commuter trains.

By Taxi Taxis are metered, with fares beginning at $1.20 for the first ⅛ mi and 20¢ for each additional ⅛ mi or minute of waiting time. Taxi drivers expect a 15% tip. Major companies are **American United Cab** (tel. 312/248–7600), **Checker Cab** (tel. 312/829–4222), and **Yellow Cab** (tel. 312/829–4222).

Orientation Tours

Walking Tours The **Chicago Architecture Foundation** (Glessner House, 1800 S. Prairie Ave., tel. 312/326–1393; Archicenter, 224 S. Michigan Ave., tel. 312/922–3432) gives architectural walking tours of the Loop and other historic areas.

Bus Tours **Chicago Motor Coach Co.** (tel. 312/922–8919) offers narrated tours of Chicago landmarks in double-decker buses. Tours depart from the Sears Tower (Franklin and Adams Sts.), the Art Institute (Michigan and Adams Sts.), the bridge at Michigan and Wacker Sts., and the Water Tower (Michigan and Pearson Sts.).

Water Tours **Wendella Sightseeing Boats** (lower Michigan Ave. at the Wrigley Bldg., tel. 312/337–1446) and **Mercury Skyline Cruises** (lower Wacker Dr., tel. 312/332–1353) offer guided tours of the Chicago River and Lake Michigan. **Interlude Enterprises** (Wabash Ave. and Wacker Dr., tel. 312/641–1210) offers lunch cruises with an architectural narration.

Exploring Chicago

Outside downtown and the Loop, Chicago is a city of neighborhoods whose rich ethnic diversity gives the city its special air.

The Loop Walking through Chicago's central business district (defined by the "loop" of the elevated train) is like taking a course in the history of American commercial architecture. From the Monadnock Building, the tallest structure built entirely of masonry, to the Sears Tower, the tallest building of any material, Chicago's skyscrapers have unique personalities. Keep an eye out for the sculptures by Picasso, Calder, Miró, Chagall, and other artists that adorn the plazas of many buildings.

The **Chicago Public Library Cultural Center** (78 E. Washington at Michigan Ave., tel. 312/346–3278) used to be the city's main library; it's been used primarily for exhibits, lectures, and performances since the 1970s. Two splendid Tiffany-glass domes are among its treasures. **Marshall Field & Co.** (111 N. State St., at Randolph St.) is the city's largest department store. Undergoing a massive, multiyear renovation, it has 500 departments and a Tiffany dome of its own. Field's anchors the **State Street Mall**, a patently unsuccessful 1980s attempt to rejuvenate the Loop shopping district. The loss of millions of dollars' worth of merchandise to the April 1992 floodwaters that submerged the subbasements of major Loop department stores did nothing to improve the situation.

The terra-cotta **Reliance Building** (State and Washington Sts.), designed by Daniel Burnham in 1890, has the distinctive Chicago window, which juts out from the surface of the building with two side windows to catch the Lake Michigan breezes. The Corten steel **Daley Center** (Dearborn and Washington Sts.), named for the late Mayor Richard J. Daley, is headquarters for the Cook County court system; in the plaza is a terra-cotta sculpture by Picasso.

Across Clark Street from the Daley Center is the handsome neoclassical **Chicago City Hall/Cook County Building,** designed by Holabird and Roche in 1911. Inside are spacious halls, high ceilings, and plenty of marble. If you're lucky, you may catch the City Council in session—usually a good show, with plenty of hot air. A block north is a very different civic structure: Helmut Jahn's 1985 **State of Illinois Building** (Clark and Randolph Sts.), also known as Spaceship Chicago.

A few blocks to the northwest, **333 West Wacker Drive** was designed by Kohn, Pedersen, Fox in 1983 and constructed in an unpromisingly irregular shape, dictated by the triangular parcel on which it sits. A softly curving building with forest-green marble columns, a spacious plaza, and a shimmering green-glass skin, it is particularly lovely seen at sunset from the bridge over the Chicago River at Orleans Street, when the river and surrounding buildings are mirrored in the glass.

To the south, the graceful 1973 **First National Bank** (Dearborn and Madison Sts.) was one of the first skyscrapers to slope upward from its base like the letter *A.* The adjoining plaza is a popular summer hangout at lunch. A Chagall mosaic, *The Four Seasons,* is at the northeast corner.

Farther south are two handsome examples of very early skyscrapers. The 1894 **Marquette Building** (140 S. Dearborn St.), by Holabird and Roche, features an exterior terra-cotta bas relief and interior reliefs and mosaics depicting scenes from early Chicago history. The darkly handsome **Monadnock Building** (53 W. Jackson Blvd. at Dearborn St.), with walls 6 feet thick at the base, has been beautifully restored; the north half was built by Burnham and Root in 1891, the south half by Holabird and Roche in 1893.

Across the street is the Gothic-style **Fisher Building** (343 S. Dearborn St.), designed by D. H. Burnham & Co. in 1896 and exquisitely ornamented in terra-cotta with carved cherubs and fish. The **Chicago Board of Trade** (141 W. Jackson Blvd. at La Salle St.), one of the few important Art Deco buildings in Chicago, was designed in 1930 by Holabird and Roche. At the top is a gilded statue of Ceres, the Greek goddess of grain—an apt overseer of the frenetic commodities trading that goes on within.

Farther west is the **Sears Tower** (233 S. Wacker Dr. at Jackson Blvd.), the world's tallest building. A Skidmore, Owings & Merrill design of 1974, the tower has 110 stories and is almost 1,500 feet tall. The view from the Skydeck is unbeatable, but there are long lines on weekends. The Wacker Drive lobby has a jolly mobile by Alexander Calder. Two blocks north of the Board of Trade is **The Rookery** (209 S. La Salle St.), an imposing redstone building designed in 1886 by Burnham and Root; the magnificent lobby was remodeled in 1905 by Frank Lloyd Wright.

One of Louis Sullivan's outstanding works is **Carson Pirie Scott & Co.** (Madison and State Sts.), the city's "second" department store, with spectacular ornamental ironwork around the main entrance. A block south on State Street at 17 East Monroe

Chicago

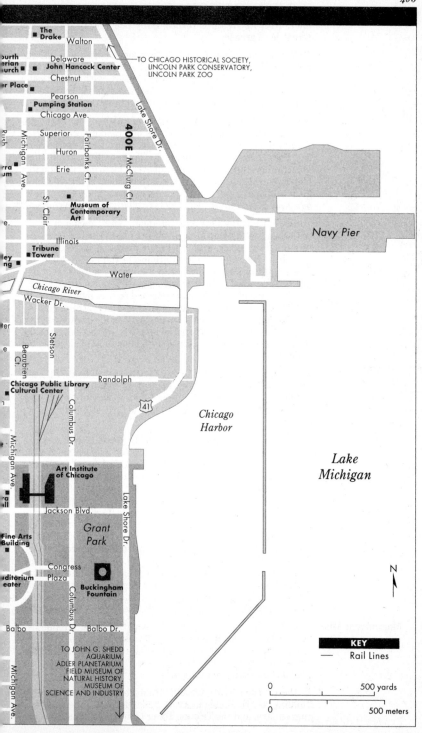

The Drake
Walton

TO CHICAGO HISTORICAL SOCIETY,
LINCOLN PARK CONSERVATORY,
LINCOLN PARK ZOO

ourth
erian
urch
Delaware
John Hancock Center
Chestnut

r Place
Pearson
Pumping Station
Chicago Ave.

Superior

Huron

Erie

400 E

Lake Shore Dr.

McClurg Ct.

Michigan Ave.

Fairbanks Ct.

St. Clair

rra
m

**Museum of
Contemporary
Art**

Illinois

ey
ng
**Tribune
Tower**

Water

Chicago River

Wacker Dr.

Navy Pier

Stetson

er

Beaubien
Ct.

Randolph

**Chicago Public Library
Cultural Center**

Columbus Dr.

41

*Chicago
Harbor*

Michigan Ave.

**Art Institute
of Chicago**

*Lake
Michigan*

Jackson Blvd.

all

*Grant
Park*

Lake Shore Dr.

**Fine Arts
Building**

Congress
Plaza

uditorium
eater

**Buckingham
Fountain**

Columbus Dr.

N

Balbo
Balbo Dr.

TO JOHN G. SHEDD
AQUARIUM,
ADLER PLANETARIUM,
FIELD MUSEUM OF
NATURAL HISTORY,
MUSEUM OF
SCIENCE AND INDUSTRY

Michigan Ave.

KEY
—— Rail Lines

0   500 yards

0   500 meters

Street is the venerable **Palmer House** hotel (*see* Lodging, *below*), with its frescoed rococo lobby one flight up from the street-level arcade.

To the east lies one of Chicago's "art zones": Michigan Avenue between Monroe Street and Congress Parkway. **Orchestra Hall** (220 S. Michigan Ave., tel. 312/435–6666), with dramatically layered balconies and steeply banked seats, is the home of the internationally acclaimed Chicago Symphony Orchestra.

Across the street is the **Art Institute of Chicago.** One of the finest museums in the world, it offers outstanding collections of Medieval and Renaissance paintings, as well as Impressionist and Post-Impressionist works; the Thorne Miniature Rooms, illustrating interior decoration in every historical style; and a meticulous reconstruction of the trading room of the old Chicago Stock Exchange, which was demolished in 1972. *S. Michigan Ave. at Adams St., tel. 312/443–3600. Admission charged.*

To the south is the **Fine Arts Building** (410 S. Michigan Ave.), with theaters showing foreign and art films. The handsome detailing on the exterior previews the marble and woodwork in the lobby. Nearby is the **Auditorium Theater** (430 S. Michigan Ave.), built in 1889 by Adler and Sullivan. The 4,000-seat hall has unobstructed sightlines and near-perfect acoustics; the interior ornamentation, including arched rows of lights along the ceiling, is breathtaking. From April to October, the mammoth **Buckingham Fountain** bubbles and gushes in **Grant Park,** two blocks directly east of the auditorium. It's worth a detour to see the profusion of nymphs, cherubs, and fish. A light show begins at dusk.

The **Harold Washington Library Center** (400 S. State St., tel. 312/747–4850), a postmodern homage to classical-style public buildings, was completed in 1991. Chicago waited 17 years for this new central library, said to be the largest building of its kind in the nation.

On a peninsula jutting into Lake Michigan at 12th Street is a cluster of museums. At the **John G. Shedd Aquarium** (1200 S. Lake Shore Dr., tel. 312/939–2426; admission charged), the dazzling new Oceanarium, with two beluga whales and several Pacific dolphins, is the big draw. But don't miss the sharks, tarpon, turtles, and myriad smaller fish and other aquatic forms in the coral-reef exhibit. The **Adler Planetarium** (1300 S. Lake Shore Dr., tel. 312/322–0300; admission charged for shows, exhibits free) is a museum with astronomy exhibits and a popular program of Sky Shows. The **Field Museum of Natural History** (Lake Shore Dr. at E. Roosevelt Rd., tel. 312/922–9410; admission charged) is one of the country's great natural-history museums. The breadth of its collections is enormous; they include Native American artifacts, endless butterflies and insects, rocks and minerals, and a Place of Wonder exhibit for children.

Magnificent Mile   The "Magnificent Mile" stretches along Michigan Avenue between the Chicago River and Oak Street, to the north. Here you'll find such high-priced shops as Gucci, Tiffany, and Bally; venerable hotels, such as The Drake and the Inter-Continental; and two fascinating art museums.

At the Chicago River are two ornate buildings: the **Wrigley Building** (410 N. Michigan Ave.), headquarters of the chewing-gum empire, and the **Tribune Tower** (435 N. Michigan Ave.), a

1930s Gothic-style skyscraper. The base of the Trib Tower incorporates pieces of other buildings, such as Westminster Abbey.

For a waterfront detour, go down the steps to Michigan Avenue's lower level at Grand Avenue and walk east about five blocks to the very end. Here's **Navy Pier** (600 E. Grand Ave.), a former shipping pier that's now being rehabbed as a European-style "pleasure garden." Even under construction it's a pleasant place for taking in a great view of the skyline. One block south and two blocks west is **North Pier** (435 E. Illinois St.), a huge old warehouse converted into a waterfront mall with boutiques, gift shops, restaurants, and miniature golf.

Follow Michigan Avenue north to Ontario Street and turn right for the **Museum of Contemporary Art** (237 E. Ontario St., tel. 312/280–5161; admission charged; closed Mon.), a fine small museum specializing in 20th-century works. Farther north on Michigan is the **Terra Museum of American Art** (666 N. Michigan Ave., tel. 312/664–3939; admission charged; closed Mon.), a small museum opened in the late 1980s with industrialist Daniel Terra's superb private collection. There are works here by almost every major American painter, including Whistler, Sargent, the Wyeths, and Mary Cassatt.

The **Water Tower,** one of the few buildings that survived the Chicago Fire of 1871, sits like a giant sandcastle at Chicago Avenue. Across the street at the **Pumping Station** is a tourist information center, where you can pick up maps and brochures and see a multimedia show about the city.

The gray-marble high rise called **Water Tower Place** (835 N. Michigan Ave.) has a host of small shops and two department stores: a branch of Marshall Field and a Lord & Taylor. In the next block is the 98-story **John Hancock Center** (875 N. Michigan Ave.), the world's third-tallest building. Across from it is the **Fourth Presbyterian Church** (126 E. Chestnut St.), a small Gothic-style jewel with a courtyard where you can find respite from the surrounding bustle. During the week, the sanctuary offers occasional organ recitals and concerts.

At the head of the Magnificent Mile is **The Drake** (140 E. Walton Pl.; *see* Lodging, *below*), one of the city's oldest and grandest hotels; take a look at the marble-and-oak lobby, complete with cherub-laden fountain, even if you're not staying here. In nice weather you may want to cross Oak Street, in front of the main entrance, and take the underground passage that leads to Oak Street Beach and the lakefront promenade. Watch for speeding bicyclists, skateboarders, and rollerbladers.

Lincoln Park "Lincoln Park" refers to an area that stretches from North Avenue (1600 N.) to Diversey Parkway (2800 N.), and from the lakefront on the east to about Racine Avenue (1200 W.) on the west. The adjoining lakefront park is also called Lincoln Park (causing visitors occasional confusion), though it stretches several miles farther north than the neighborhood.

The **Chicago Historical Society** (1601 N. Clark St., tel. 312/642–4600; admission charged) is a stately brick building with a sparkling modern glass addition on the Clark Street side. Permanent exhibits include costume collections; the much-loved diorama room, which portrays scenes from Chicago's history;

and a statue of Abraham Lincoln with a nose that gleams from having been rubbed by countless children.

Wandering north through **Lincoln Park** itself for half a mile will bring you to **Lincoln Park Zoo** (2200 N. Cannon Dr., tel. 312/294–4660; admission free), whose 35 acres are home to all the requisite zoo denizens, including koala bears and a major great-ape collection. The zoo opened in 1868, before the Chicago Fire; most of the buildings have been renovated. North of here is the **Lincoln Park Conservatory** (2400 N. Stockton Dr., tel. 312/294–4770; admission free), which has a palm house, a fernery, a cactus house, special exhibits, and large outdoor gardens. Continuing north, you'll find the **Lagoon,** where you can rent a paddleboat in summer.

At Fullerton Avenue, go west and enter the **Lincoln Park neighborhood,** where you'll pass elegant town houses and small apartment buildings from the late 1800s and early 1900s. The area declined after World War II as residents moved to the suburbs, but it was rediscovered in the 1970s, and it's not uncommon now to see million-dollar prices on some of the restored houses. The **Biograph Theater** (2433 N. Lincoln Ave., tel. 312/348–1350), where the gangster John Dillinger met his end at the hands of the FBI, is on the National Register of Historic Places and still shows first-run movies.

Other Attractions   **River North**—a former warehouse neighborhood west of Michigan Avenue, bounded roughly by Clark Street, Chicago Avenue, Sedgwick Avenue, and the Chicago River—bloomed during the mid-1980s gentrification craze and now offers a number of art galleries. The Pumping Station Information Center (Michigan Ave. at Pearson St.) carries the *Chicago Gallery News*, which lists addresses, hours, and current exhibits.

The **Museum of Science and Industry,** on the lake in Hyde Park about 7 mi south of the Loop, is a treasure trove of gadgetry, applied science, and hands-on exhibits. There's a genuine German U-boat, a coal mine, Colleen Moore's Fairy Castle (a dollhouse to end all dollhouses), actual spacecraft from early NASA missions, and a giant-screen Omnimax Theater. *5700 S. Lake Shore Dr., tel. 312/684–1414. Admission charged.*

Parks and Gardens

Most of Chicago's more than 20 mi of shoreline is parkland or beach reserved for public use. A 19-mi path stretches along the lakefront, snaking through **Lincoln Park** (*see* Exploring Chicago, *above*), **Grant Park** (just east of the Loop, with acres of rose gardens), and **Jackson Park** (just south of the Museum of Science and Industry, with a wooded island and a Japanese garden) and winding past half a dozen harbors, two golf courses, Navy Pier, Buckingham Fountain, the lakefront museums, McCormick Place, and all the city's popular beaches. Bikes are the best way to cover maximum territory; they can be rented at the concession as you enter Lincoln Park at Fullerton Avenue or from **Village Cycle Center** (1337 N. Wells St., tel. 312/751–2488). Bicycle thieves sometimes lurk in the comparatively deserted stretch south of McCormick Place; it's safe enough on weekends, but don't risk it alone during the week or at night.

There are also hundreds of parks in neighborhoods throughout the city. The **Garfield Park Conservatory** (300 N. Central Park

Blvd., tel. 312/533–1281) maintains five acres of plants and flowers under glass and holds four shows a year. The **Chicago Botanic Garden** (Lake-Cook Rd., Glencoe, tel. 708/835–8208), north of the city, covers 300 acres and has 15 separate gardens and 10 greenhouses. The **Morton Arboretum** (Rte. 53, off I–88, tel. 708/719–2465), in the western suburb of Lisle, has 1,500 acres of woody plants, woodlands, and outdoor gardens.

Chicago for Free—or Almost

The weekly *Reader* and newspapers list free events. In summer, Grant Park's **Petrillo Bandshell** offers free public concerts almost every weekend and the Grant Park Symphony performs at least one night a week. Wednesdays at 12:15, the **Chicago Cultural Center** (78 E. Washington St., tel. 312/346–3278) presents the Dame Myra Hess Memorial Concert Series, a program of recitals by rising professional classical musicians. Most **museums** have one free day a week.

What to See and Do with Children

At **Lincoln Park Zoo** (*see* Exploring Chicago, *above*), youngsters especially enjoy the Children's Zoo, the Farm-in-the-Zoo (farm animals plus a learning center with films and demonstrations), and the Kids' Corner Discovery Place, with hands-on activities. **Chicago Children's Museum** (465 E. Illinois St., tel. 312/527–1000), in the North Pier complex, has plenty of hands-on, "touch and feel" exhibits. At **Brookfield Zoo** (8400 W. 31st St., Brookfield, tel. 708/485–0263), one of the nation's best, the animals inhabit naturalistic settings that give visitors the feeling of being in the wild.

Shopping

Chicago shopping ranges from elegant department stores, small boutiques, and specialty shops to malls and bargain outlets.

Shopping Districts The **Loop** and the **Magnificent Mile** (for both, *see* Exploring Chicago, *above*) concentrate major department and upscale specialty stores. **Oak Street** between Michigan Avenue and State Street has other top-of-the-line designer shops. Three "vertical malls" combine department stores and specialty shops: **Water Tower Place** (835 N. Michigan Ave.; *see* Exploring Chicago, *above*), **The Avenue Atrium** (900 N. Michigan Ave.), and **Chicago Place** (700 N. Michigan Ave.). The **Lincoln Park neighborhood** has several worthwhile shopping strips. Clark Street between Armitage (2000 N.) and Diversey (2800 N.) avenues is home to a number of clothing boutiques and specialty stores. From Diversey north to School Street (3300 N.) are several large antiques stores, more boutiques, and some bookstores.

Department Stores **Marshall Field & Co.** (111 N. State St., at Randolph St., tel. 312/781–1000), the city's biggest department store, isn't—despite a $110 million renovation—as grand as it used to be, but you can still spend an entire day shopping here and not see the whole place. **Carson Pirie Scott & Co.** (1 S. State St., tel. 312/641–7000), Chicago's "second" department store, would be a standout anywhere else. If you like glitz, visit **Bloomingdale's**

(The Avenue Atrium, 900 N. Michigan Ave., tel. 312/440–4460) and **Nieman Marcus** (737 N. Michigan Ave., tel. 312/642–5900).

Specialty Stores   **Jazz Record Mart** (11 W. Grand Ave., tel. 312/222–1467) stocks
Music   a major collection of records, compact discs, and tapes, including many rare historic recordings and obscure imports. **Wax Trax Records** (2449 N. Lincoln Ave., tel. 312/929–0221), the place for everything in popular music, including oldies and imports, is a "must" stop if you have teenagers with you.

Outlet Stores   **Spiegel** (1105 W. 35th St., tel. 312/254–0091) and **Sears** (5555 S. Archer Ave., tel. 312/284–3200) maintain warehouse stores on the South Side. The two famous mail-order establishments offer fabulous bargains to the sharp-eyed and flexible shopper. Don't expect elegant surroundings or helpful salespeople, and do check your merchandise thoroughly before you take it home.

Spectator Sports

Baseball   **Chicago Cubs** (Wrigley Field, 1060 W. Addison St., tel. 312/404–2827; Apr.–Oct.).

Chicago White Sox (Comiskey Park, 333 W. 35th St., tel. 312/924–1000 or 312/559–1212; Apr.–Oct.).

Basketball   **Chicago Bulls** (Chicago Stadium, 1800 W. Madison St., tel. 312/943–5800; Oct.–June).

Football   **Chicago Bears** (Soldier Field, 425 E. McFetridge Dr., tel. 312/663–5100; Nov.–Apr.).

Hockey   **Chicago Blackhawks** (Chicago Stadium, tel. 312/733–5300; Oct.–Apr.).

Horse Racing   **Hawthorne Race Course** (3501 S. Laramie Ave., Cicero, tel. 708/780–3700; Oct.–Dec.) and **Arlington Park** (N. Wilke Rd. at W. Euclid Ave., Arlington Heights, tel. 708/255–4300; May–Oct.) feature flat racing. **Sportsman's Park** (3301 S. Laramie Ave., tel. 312/242–1121) has both flat racing (Feb.–May) and harness racing (June–Oct.). **Maywood Park** (North and 5th Aves., Maywood, tel. 312/626–4816) has harness racing.

Dining

Chicago has everything: from traditional aged steaks, ribs, and the ubiquitous Vienna hot dog to the loftier offerings of many excellent French and Italian restaurants to the exotic fare of Middle Eastern, Thai, and Vietnamese establishments. Most eating places listed below are in the Near North, River North, and Loop areas, within walking distance of the major hotel districts. A few are out in the city's residential neighborhoods and ethnic enclaves.

For clusters of ethnic restaurants too numerous to mention here, try Greektown (Halsted and Madison Sts.), Chinatown (Wentworth Ave. and 23rd St.), Little Italy (Taylor St. between Racine Ave. and Ashland Ave.), Argyle Street between Broadway and Sheridan Road (for Chinese and Vietnamese), Devon Avenue between 2200 W. and 3000 W. (Indian), and Clark Street from Belmont Avenue to Addison Street (Thai, Japanese, Chinese, Korean, Jamaican, Ethiopian, Mexican).

Restaurant listings appear in the monthly *Chicago* magazine and in the Friday editions of the *Chicago Tribune* and the *Sun-*

Times (Weekend section). For price ranges, see Chart 1 (A) in Chapter 1.

Very Expensive **Ambria.** In a spacious turn-of-the-century mansion, Ambria serves contemporary French food and light cuisine. Menus change seasonally; the emphasis is on using natural juices and vegetable reductions to accompany the entrées. *2300 N. Lincoln Park W, tel. 312/472–5959. Reservations required. AE, D, DC, MC, V. No lunch; closed Sun., holidays.*

★ **Charlie Trotter's.** This tastefully renovated Lincoln Park town house accommodates only 20 closely spaced tables. Owner and chef Charlie Trotter prepares extraordinary New American cuisine, with hints of Asian flavors incorporated into classic European dishes. *816 W. Armitage Ave., tel. 312/248–6228. Reservations required well in advance. Jacket required. AE, DC, MC, V. No lunch; closed Sun.–Mon.*

★ **Everest.** On the 40th floor of a postmodern skyscraper in the heart of the financial district, this restaurant serves dishes squarely in the classic French tradition but with appeal to contemporary tastes. *440 S. La Salle St., tel. 312/663–8920. Reservations required. Jacket required. AE, D, DC, MC, V. Closed Sun.–Mon., holidays.*

★ **Le Français.** Only serious eaters should make the pilgrimage to this classic haute French outpost in the northwest suburbs. Dinner takes the entire evening, and the tab can easily top $100 per person. The menu changes nightly to reflect the best ingredients available—and the whim of the chef. Try the *dégustation* menu, a bargain available weeknights. *269 S. Milwaukee Ave., Wheeling, tel. 708/541–7470. Reservations required. Jacket required. AE, D, DC, MC, V. No lunch Mon., Sat.; closed Sun.*

Spiaggia. In elegant pink-and-teal quarters overlooking the lake, Spiaggia offers the most opulent Italian dining in town, with elaborate stuffed pastas, veal chops in a vodka-cream sauce, and other richly inventive dishes. Save room for dessert. The same for less can be had next door at the more casual Cafe Spiaggia. *980 N. Michigan Ave., tel. 312/280–2750. Reservations advised. Jacket required; no denim. AE, D, DC, MC, V. No lunch Sun.*

Expensive **Avanzare.** This Italian restaurant in the Near North consistently distinguishes itself by the freshness and quality of its ingredients. The decor runs to marble, brass, and bustle. *161 E. Huron St., tel. 312/337–8056. Reservations advised. AE, D, DC, MC, V. No lunch weekends.*

Eli's the Place for Steak. Done in club style, with lots of leather and warm wood, this Chicago institution specializes in prime aged steaks prepared precisely to order. You'll also find a superb, thickly cut veal chop and, for dessert, Eli's renowned cheesecake, now sold nationally. *215 E. Chicago Ave., tel. 312/642–1393. Reservations required. Jacket required. AE, D, DC, MC, V. No lunch weekends; closed holidays.*

Morton's of Chicago. Chicago's best steakhouse offers beautiful, hefty steaks cooked to perfection. Excellent service, classy ambience, and a very good wine list add to the appeal. Vegetarians and budget watchers should look elsewhere. *1050 N. State St., tel. 312/266–4820. Reservations required. AE, D, DC, MC, V. No lunch.*

★ **Printer's Row.** Named after its recently chic loft neighborhood in the South Loop, this warm and attractive restaurant offers inventive and satisfying American cuisine. Daily specials include at least one dish low in fat and sodium. *550 S. Dearborn St., tel. 312/461–0780. Reservations advised, required on weekends. AE, D, DC, MC, V. No lunch Sat.; closed Sun.*

The Pump Room. Probably Chicago's most famous restaurant, The Pump Room offers steak and baked Alaska alongside pinenut-breaded sole with infused oils. Celebrity photos line the walls. *Omni Ambassador East, 1301 N. State Pkwy., tel. 312/266–0360. Reservations strongly advised. Jacket required. AE, D, MC, V.*

Trattoria No. 10. This former basement boiler room in the Loop has been artfully converted into an intimate grotto straight from an Italian hill town. The pastas are fresh; antipasti include sea scallops with orange-fennel relish and *rotolo di mozzarella* (homemade mozzarella rolled around layers of pesto and prosciutto). *10 N. Dearborn St., tel. 312/984–1718. Reservations advised. AE, D, DC, MC, V. No lunch weekends; closed Sun.*

Moderate–Expensive ★
Frontera Grill/Topolobampo. In the cozy, colorful grill storefront, genuine regional Mexican cooking goes way beyond burritos and chips: from charbroiled catfish (with pickled red onions and jicama salad) to garlicky skewered tenderloin (with poblano peppers, red onion, and bacon). Topolobampo, next door, shares the owners and the kitchen; it offers a more stately atmosphere and affords the chef an opportunity to experiment with more expensive ingredients. *445 N. Clark St., tel. 312/661–1434. Reservations required at Topolobampo; advised at the grill. AE, D, DC, MC, V. Closed Sun.–Mon.; no lunch Sat. at Topolobampo.*

Hatsuhana. Just east of Michigan Avenue, Hatsuhana has a long, angled sushi bar and wood tables set on purple carpeting; the white stucco walls are hung with Japanese lanterns. Besides outstanding sushi and sashimi, there are plenty of broiled and steamed dishes. *160 E. Ontario St., tel. 312/280–8287. Reservations advised. AE, DC, MC, V. No lunch Sat.; closed Sun., holidays.*

Moderate
The Bangkok. This comely and sophisticated little spot on the North Side goes well beyond the typical storefront Thai restaurant. Many of the "hot" dishes depend on subtle flavorings rather than on the one-note incendiary spicing found at lesser eateries. The two-story dining room is decorated with a profusion of Thai arts and crafts. *3542 N. Halsted St., tel. 312/327–2870. Reservations advised. AE, DC, MC, V.*

The Berghoff. This Loop institution has oak paneling, a bustling ambience, two huge dining rooms, and a splendid bar with Berghoff Beer on tap. Expect a wait of 15 minutes or so at midday. American favorites augment the menu of German classics (Wiener schnitzel, sauerbraten). *17 W. Adams St., tel. 312/427–3170. Reservations accepted for parties of 5 or more. AE, MC, V. Closed Sun.*

Cafe Ba-Ba-Reeba! Chicago's best-known purveyor of *tapas* (varied edibles, served in small portions, that originated as accompaniments to drinks in Spanish bars), this large, open restaurant and its prominent bar are usually crowded with upscale young folk. The wide selection of cold and warm tapas ranges from stuffed cannelloni to veal with mushrooms. *2024 N. Halsted St., tel. 312/935–5000. No reservations; the wait may be substantial. AE, D, DC, MC, V. No lunch Sun.–Mon.; closed holidays.*

★ Rosebud. Specializing in good, old-fashioned southern Italian cuisine, Rosebud serves a superior red sauce, and the roasted peppers, homemade sausage, and exquisitely prepared pastas are not to be missed. The wait for a table can stretch to an hour or more, despite confirmed reservations. *1500 W. Taylor St., tel. 312/942–1117. Reservations required. AE, D, DC, MC, V. No lunch weekends.*

Inexpensive **Ann Sather.** These three large, light, airy restaurants—two on the North Side, one in Hyde Park near the University of Chicago—emphasize home-style food and service. Specialties include omelets, Swedish pancakes, homemade cinnamon rolls, potato sausage, chicken croquettes, and sandwiches. *5207 N. Clark St., tel. 312/271–6677; 929 W. Belmont Ave., tel. 312/ 348–2378; 1329 E. 57th St., tel. 312/947–9323. MC, V. Closed holidays.*

Ed Debevic's. This imitation 1950s diner packs them in from morning till midnight, with gum-popping waitresses, wise-cracking signage, and blue-plate specials. The menu also includes reliable burgers, sandwiches, chili, salads, and homemade pies. *640 N. Wells St., tel. 312/664–1707. No reservations; the wait may be substantial. No credit cards.*

★ **Pizzeria Uno/Pizzeria Due.** This is where Chicago deep-dish pizza got its start. Uno has been remodeled to resemble its franchised cousins in other cities, but its pizzas retain their light crust and distinctive tang. There's usually a shorter wait for a table at Pizzeria Due (same ownership and menu, different decor and longer hours), a block away. *Uno: 29 E. Ohio St., tel. 312/321–1000. Due: 619 N. Wabash Ave., tel. 312/943–2400. No reservations, but phone-ahead orders are accepted weekdays. AE, D, DC, MC, V.*

Three Happiness. The specialty of this cavernous, kitchen-table-style Chinatown joint is its weekend dim sum brunch, served from 10 AM to 2 PM; the crowd begins to form at 9:30 on weekends. Go with a group to mix and match the little dishes of steamed and fried dumplings, rice cakes, custard squares, and other exotica. *2130 S. Wentworth Ave., tel. 312/791–1228. No reservations weekends. AE, D, DC, MC, V.*

Lodging

Chicago is the country's biggest convention town, and accommodations can be tight when major events are scheduled. Most hotels offer weekend specials when no big shows are on. Virtually every hotel chain, large or small, has at least one property in Chicago, and some have several. Hotels are concentrated in the Loop and the Near North Side. **Bed and Breakfast Chicago** (Box 14088, 60614, tel. 312/951–0085) handles more than 50 B&Bs throughout the greater Chicago area. For price ranges, see Chart 2 (A) in Chapter 1.

Very Expensive **The Drake.** The grandest of Chicago's traditional hotels was
★ built in 1920 in the style of an Italian Renaissance palace. It offers splendid lake views from two sides, and the spacious rooms are furnished with dark wood and floral upholstery for a 19th-century flavor. *140 E. Walton Pl., 60611, tel. 312/787–2200 or 800/553–7256; fax 312/951–5803. 535 rooms, 65 suites. Facilities: 3 restaurants, 2 lounges, concierge. AE, D, DC, MC, V.*

The Fairmont. This 45-story neoclassical structure of Spanish pink granite is part of the Illinois Center complex and offers fine views of the lake and Grant Park. The sizable rooms are furnished in contemporary or period styles. *200 N. Columbus Dr., 60601, tel. 312/565–8000 or 800/527–4727; fax 312/856–*

1032. 692 rooms, 72 suites. Facilities: 2 restaurants, 2 lounges, business services, valet, concierge. AE, D, DC, MC, V.

★ **The Four Seasons.** Occupying 17 floors in a major building, this luxurious hostelry offers spectacular lake and city views. Suggesting the decor of an English manor house, the smallish rooms have Italian marble, handcrafted woodwork, custom-woven rugs, and tasteful prints. *120 E. Delaware Pl., 60611, tel. 312/280–8800 or 800/332–3442; fax 312/280–9184. 344 rooms, 121 suites, 16 apartments. Facilities: restaurant, café, lounge, health club, pool, concierge. AE, D, DC, MC, V.*

Hotel Inter-Continental Chicago. This luxury property within walking distance of the Loop is a renovation of the 1929 Medinah Athletic Club. The showpiece is an Italianate Junior Olympic–size swimming pool. Guest rooms are done in beige and green, in a 1920s neoclassical style. *505 N. Michigan Ave., 60611, tel. 312/944–4100 or 800/327–0200; fax 312/944–3050. 338 rooms, 30 suites. Facilities: restaurant, bar, concierge, pool, health club. AE, D, DC, MC, V.*

Expensive **Chicago Hilton and Towers.** This huge grand hotel at the south end of the Loop was lavishly restored in the mid-1980s. The ballroom is worthy of Marie Antoinette. The guest rooms offer amenities and comfort. *720 S. Michigan Ave., 60605, tel. 312/ 922–4400 or 800/445–8667; fax 312/922–5240. 1,543 rooms. Facilities: 5 restaurants, lounge, tavern, café, pool, health club, concierge. AE, D, DC, MC, V.*

★ **Forum Hotel Chicago.** Adjoining the more plush Inter-Continental, this mid-priced high-rise business hotel is run by the same company. The 1960s-vintage building was completely renovated in 1990; both the guest rooms and the public areas are done in cool neutrals with contemporary furniture. *525 N. Michigan Ave., 60611, tel. 312/944–0055 or 800/327–0200; fax 312/944–3050. 517 rooms, 6 suites. Facilities: restaurant, access to Inter-Continental's pool and health club, concierge. AE, D, DC, MC, V.*

The Palmer House. Built over a century ago by the Chicago merchant Potter Palmer, this hotel has public areas that reflect the opulence of the era, but its modernized and recently refurbished guest rooms are more ordinary. *17 E. Monroe St., 60603, tel. 312/726–7500 or 800/445–8667; fax 312/263–2556. 1,669 rooms, 88 suites. Facilities: 6 restaurants, lounge, pool, fitness center, concierge. AE, D, DC, MC, V.*

★ **The Raphael.** On one of the nicest Near North streets, The Raphael offers the same intimacy, European-style multilingual service, and tastefully furnished and appointed rooms that other hotels provide at a higher price. *201 E. Delaware Pl., 60611, tel. 312/943–5000 or 800/821–5343; fax 312/943–9483. 172 rooms. Facilities: restaurant, lounge. AE, D, DC, MC, V.*

Moderate **Claridge Hotel.** Nestled among Victorian houses on a tree-lined
★ Near North street, this 1930s building was fully renovated in 1987. It's intimate rather than bustling, and the decor is simple but tasteful. *1244 N. Dearborn Pkwy., 60610, tel. 312/787–4980 or 800/245–1258; fax 312/266–0978. 173 rooms, 3 suites. Facilities: restaurant, bar, concierge. AE, D, DC, MC, V.*

Lenox House. Conveniently located near North Michigan Avenue, this hotel has one-room "suites," each with both a Murphy bed and a sofa bed, with wet-bar kitchens, all done in generic '80s style. *616 N. Rush St., 60611, tel. 312/337–1000 or 800/445– 3669; fax 312/337–7217. 330 suites. Facilities: restaurant, bar, concierge. AE, D, DC, MC, V.*

★ **The Richmont.** Charming rather than luxurious, comfortable rather than elegant, this small hotel east of Michigan Avenue offers an excellent value. A cold breakfast buffet is included in the tariff. *162 E. Ontario St., 60611, tel. 312/787–3580 or 800/ 621–8055; fax 312/787–1299. 193 rooms, 12 suites. Facilities: restaurant, piano bar. AE, D, DC, MC, V.*

Inexpensive **Chicago International Hostel.** Dormitory-style accommodations near Loyola University in Rogers Park cost under $20 a night, including linens. Holders of International Youth Hostel cards get a discount. *6318 N. Winthrop Ave., 60660, tel. 312/ 262–1011. 100 beds. Facilities: kitchen, laundry. No credit cards.*

Motels **Comfort Inn of Lincoln Park** (601 W. Diversey Ave., 60614, tel. 312/348–2810 or 800/221–2222; fax 312/348–1912), 74 rooms; moderate. **Best Western River North** (125 W. Ohio St., 60610, tel. 312/467–0800 or 800/727–0800; fax 312/467–1665), 149 rooms, 24 suites, restaurant, pool, health club; moderate. **Hojo Inn** (720 N. La Salle St., 60610, tel. 312/664–8100 or 800/446–4656; fax 312/664–2365), 71 rooms, 4 suites, restaurant; inexpensive. **Ohio House** (600 N. La Salle St., 60610, tel. 312/ 943–6000), 49 rooms, 1 suite, coffee shop; inexpensive.

The Arts and Nightlife

For listings of arts and entertainment events, check the monthly *Chicago* magazine (on newsstands) or the Friday editions of the *Chicago Tribune* or the *Chicago Sun-Times*. Two free weeklies, *The Reader* and *New City*, available on Fridays at stores, restaurants, and bars, are the best sources for what's happening in clubs and small theaters and for showings of noncommercial films.

The Arts Chicago is a splendid city for the arts, with more than 50 theater groups, a world-class orchestra and opera company, dozens of smaller musical ensembles, and several movie theaters that go way beyond commercial Hollywood offerings.

Theater Half-price theater tickets are available for many productions on the day of the performance at the **Hot Tix** booth (108 N. State St., tel. 312/977–1755; cash only). Among the many commercial theaters are the **Auditorium Theatre** (50 E. Congress Pkwy., tel. 312/922–2110), the **Halsted Theater Center** (2700 N. Halsted St., tel. 312/348–0110), the **Royal George Theater Center** (1641 N. Halsted St., tel. 312/988–9000), and the **Shubert Theater** (22 W. Monroe St., tel. 312/977–1700). Several small local ensembles have made the big jump into national prominence: **Steppenwolf** (1650 N. Halsted St., tel. 312/335–1650), **Remains Theater** (1800 N. Clybourn Ave., tel. 312/335–9800), and **Body Politic/Victory Gardens** (2257–61 N. Lincoln Ave., tel. 312/871–3000). The city's oldest repertory theater, the **Goodman** (200 S. Columbus Dr., tel. 312/443–3800) offers polished presentations of both contemporary works and classics.

Music The **Chicago Symphony** performs at Orchestra Hall (220 S. Michigan Ave., tel. 312/435–6666; Sept.–May) under the direction of Daniel Barenboim. In the summer, James Levine takes over the baton and the symphony moves outdoors to take part in the **Ravinia Festival** (Highland Park, tel. 312/728–4642).

Opera **Lyric Opera of Chicago** (20 N. Wacker Dr., tel. 312/332–2244; Sept.–Jan.) performs grand opera with international stars at the Civic Opera House; tickets are difficult to come by. **Chicago Opera Theatre** (2936 N. Southport Ave., tel. 312/663–0048) specializes in English-language productions of smaller works.

Dance **Ballet Chicago** (222 S. Riverside Plaza, tel. 312/993–7575) is the city's only resident classical ballet troupe. **Hubbard Street Dance Company** (tel. 312/663–0853), popular for its contemporary, jazzy vitality, usually performs in the Civic Opera House.

Film In addition to the usual commercial theaters, Chicago has several venues for the avant-garde, vintage, or merely offbeat: **Facets Multimedia** (1517 W. Fullerton Ave., tel. 312/281–4114), **Film Center of the Art Institute** (Columbus Dr. at Jackson Blvd., tel. 312/443–3737), **Fine Arts Theatre** (418 S. Michigan Ave., tel. 312/939–3700), **Music Box Theatre** (3733 N. Southport Ave., tel. 312/871–6604), and **Chicago Filmmakers** (1229 W. Belmont Ave., tel. 312/281–8788).

Nightlife Chicago comes alive at night with something for everyone, from loud and loose to sophisticated and sedate. Shows usually begin at 9 PM; cover charges generally range from $3 to $7, depending on the day of the week. Many spots have a drink minimum instead of, or in addition to, a cover charge. Most bars are open until 2 AM, and some even serve until 4 AM.

Blues Clubs In the years following World War II, Chicago-style blues grew into its own musical form. After fading in the '60s, Chicago blues is coming back, although more strongly on the trendy North Side than on the South Side, where it all began. The more famous clubs are **Blue Chicago** (937 N. State St., tel. 312/642–6261), **B.L.U.E.S.** (2519 N. Halsted St., tel. 312/528–1012), **Buddy Guy's Legends** (754 S. Wabash Ave., tel. 312/427–0333), and **Kingston Mines** (2548 N. Halsted St., tel. 312/477–4646). The **New Checkerboard Lounge** (423 E. 43rd St., tel. 312/624–3240) is in a rough neighborhood but has a long pedigree.

Comedy Clubs The granddaddy of them all is **Second City** (1616 N. Wells St., tel. 312/337–3992), which usually has two different revues playing at once. **Improvisations** (504 N. Wells St., tel. 312/782–6387) aims for spontaneity. The best stand-up comedy in town is found at **Zanies** (1548 N. Wells St., tel. 312/337–4027). **The Funny Firm** (318 W. Grand Ave., tel. 312/321–9500) has stand-up Tuesday through Saturday and improv on Sunday.

Jazz Clubs **Jazz Showcase** (636 S. Michigan Ave., tel. 312/427–4846) books nationally known groups. The **Gold Star Sardine Bar** (680 N. Lake Shore Dr., tel. 312/664–4215), a tiny spot in a splendid renovated building, books top names that attract a trendy clientele. **Pops for Champagne** (2934 N. Sheffield Ave., tel. 312/472–1000) combines small-group jazz and a popular champagne bar. **The Green Mill** (4802 N. Broadway, tel. 312/878–5552), a Chicago institution off the beaten track, books solid local acts.

Folk Clubs **No Exit** (6970 N. Glenwood Ave., tel. 312/743–3355), a coffeehouse right out of the 1960s, offers folk, jazz, and poetry readings. **Old Town School of Folk Music** (909 W. Armitage Ave., tel. 312/525–7793) mixes local talent and outstanding nationally known performers.

Rock Clubs **Avalon Niteclub** (959 W. Belmont Ave., tel. 312/472–3020) has been around for a long time, but the acts are current. **Cabaret Metro** (3730 N. Clark St., tel. 312/549–0203) presents nationally known and local artists and has a new dance floor downstairs. **The Cubby Bear** (1059 W. Addison St., tel. 312/327–1662), across from Wrigley Field, offers a variety of rock, fusion, and reggae acts. **Excalibur** (632 N. Dearborn St., tel. 312/266–1944) is a superdisco with multiple dance floors and bars. **Lounge Ax** (2438 N. Lincoln Ave., tel. 312/525–6620) offers a mix of local rock, folk, country, and reggae acts nightly. **The Wild Hare** (3530 N. Clark St., tel. 312/327–4273) is the city's premier reggae club.

For Singles Chicago's legendary "Rush Street" singles scene is actually on Division Street between Clark and State; here you'll find such bars as **Mother's** (26 W. Division St., tel. 312/642–7251) and **Butch McGuire's** (20 W. Division St., tel. 312/337–9080) jammed with young professionals. There's another cluster of bar life in the neighborhood around Halsted and Armitage streets in Lincoln Park. **North Pier** (435 E. Illinois St.) has several popular singles spots, including the **Baja Beach Club** (tel. 312/222–1992) and **Dick's Last Resort** (tel. 312/836–7870).

Gay Bars The area around Halsted Street between approximately Wellington Street and Addison Street has the city's highest concentration of gay bars.

Excursion to Oak Park

Getting There Take I–290W to Harlem Avenue and exit to the left. Turn right at the top of the ramp, head north on Harlem Avenue to Chicago Avenue, turn right, and proceed to Forest Avenue.

What to See and Do Founded in the 1850s, just west of the Chicago border, Oak Park is one of Chicago's oldest suburbs and a living museum of Prairie School residential architecture. Visit the **Frank Lloyd Wright Home and Studio** (951 Chicago Ave., corner of Forest Ave., tel. 708/848–1500; admission charged; closed major holidays), built in 1889 and, after a long period of neglect, lovingly restored by a group of citizens working with the National Trust for Historic Preservation. A few blocks away is **Ernest Hemingway's boyhood home** (600 N. Kenilworth Ave.), a gray stucco house not open to the public. The poured-concrete **Unity Temple** (875 Lake St., tel. 708/848–6225) was built for a Unitarian congregation in 1905. The **Oak Park Visitors Center** (158 N. Forest Ave., tel. 708/848–1500) can provide further information on the area.

Excursion to Baha'i House of Worship

Getting There Take Lake Shore Drive north to its end at Hollywood, then turn right onto Sheridan Road and follow it about 10 mi.

What to See and Do **Baha'i House of Worship** (100 Linden Ave., Wilmette, tel. 708/256–4400) is a sublimely lovely nine-sided building that incorporates a wealth of architectural styles and symbols from the world's religions—and symbolizes unity. The symmetry and harmony of the building are paralleled in the formal gardens that surround it.

Galena and Northwestern Illinois

The tiny town of Galena (pop. 3,900) features beautifully preserved pre–Civil War architecture, with houses in Federal, Italianate, and Gothic Revival styles; a large concentration of antiques shops; and (rare in the Midwest) hilly terrain. There's good biking, cross-country skiing, fishing, hunting, and camping in the region.

Galena's fortunes were based on the large lead deposits in the surrounding hills. Lead mining took off here in the 1820s, and Galena had a near-monopoly on shipping it down the Mississippi until the railroad came through in 1854. A depression later that decade and then the Civil War disrupted the lead trade and sent the city into an economic decline from which it never recovered. As a result, Galena today looks much as it did in the 1850s. Galena's other claim to fame is as the home of Ulysses S. Grant, commander of the Union Army in the Civil War and later the 18th president of the United States.

The region surrounding Galena is dotted with tiny towns that have been similarly bypassed by the 20th century. Among their offbeat charms are an antique-tractor museum (in Stockton) and the world's largest mallard hatchery (in Hanover). Stockton is also a time capsule of turn-of-the-century architecture, and much of Mount Carroll is registered as a National Historic District.

Tourist Information

Galena/Jo Daviess County: Convention and Visitors Bureau (101 Bouthillier St., Galena 61036, tel. 815/777–0203 or 800/ 747–9377).

Getting There

By Car   From Chicago, take I–90 86 mi to Rockford, then Rte. 20W 81 mi to Galena. From Iowa, pick up Rte. 20E at Dubuque and continue 16 mi east across the Mississippi.

Exploring Galena and Northwestern Illinois

In **Galena,** the **Ulysses S. Grant Home,** built in 1860 in the Italianate bracketed style, was presented to Grant in 1865 by Galena residents in honor of his service to the Union. The family lived there until Grant's victory in the 1868 presidential election. In 1905 Grant's children gave the house to the state; now a state historic site, the house has been meticulously restored to its 1868 appearance. *500 Bouthillier St., tel. 815/777–0248. Admission free. Closed holidays.*

The **Belvedere Mansion and Gardens** centers on an 1857 Italianate mansion built for a steamboat magnate. It has been lavishly furnished by the current owners in a fashion that some locals consider gaudy; accoutrements include the famous green drapes from the movie *Gone with the Wind* and furnishings from Liberace's estate. *1008 Park Ave., tel. 815/777–0747. Admission charged. Closed Nov.–May.*

Galena's oldest house is the 1826 **Dowling House** (220 Diagonal St., tel. 815/777–1250; admission charged). The **Historical Military Miniatures Museum** (302 S. Main St., tel. 815/777–0383; admission charged) has a collection of antique toy soldiers. The **Old General Store Museum** (223 S. Main St., tel. 815/777–9129; closed weekdays Nov.–Dec., Jan.–May) re-creates a 19th-century emporium. The shops on Main Street are also fun to browse. A **trolley tour** (220 N. Main St., tel. 815/777–1248) of the town strengthens the time-machine impression and rests hill-worn legs.

A huge swath of rolling countryside east of town, the **Galena Territory** started as a vacation-home development in the early 1980s but has taken on a life of its own as a recreation area. Hunting, fishing, and golf are popular. Watch out for deer on the back roads; they're everywhere.

Southeast of Galena, off Rte. 20 on Rte. 84, is **Hanover,** where mallard outnumber people 200 to 1. The **Whistling Wings** hatchery (113 Washington St., tel. 815/591–3512) has 200,000 of them and offers tours by appointment. Rte. 84 along the Mississippi passes through **Savanna,** which has a number of large, well-preserved 19th-century houses. East on Rte. 52, **Mount Carroll's** rolling hills and gracious 19th-century frame and masonry buildings recall a small New England town, complete with town square (rare in the Midwest). The **Campbell Center for Historic Preservation** (S. College St., tel. 815/244–1173) has workshops on architectural and fine-arts preservation.

To the north on Rte. 78 is **Stockton,** at 1,000 feet Illinois's highest town, where the business district preserves many of the lacy, cupola-topped structures beloved of the late Victorians. At **Arlo's Tractor Collection/Museum** (7871 S. Ridge Rd., tel. 815/947–2593) there are 30 restored antique tractors, all in working order.

Shopping

Galena's Main Street is lined with more than 20 antiques stores and art galleries, plus a variety of boutiques, crafts shops, and bakeries. There's more good antiquing and many artists' studios in **Stockton, Warren,** and **Elizabeth.**

Sports and Outdoor Activities

Biking   Hilly back roads around Galena offer challenging bicycling. The **Old Stagecoach Trail** runs parallel to Rte. 20, winding through Apple River and Warren. **Chestnut Mountain Resort** (*see* Dining and Lodging, *below*) rents mountain bikes, or try Dubuque, Iowa. The county tourism office (*see* Tourist Information, *above*) has maps.

Golf   **Apple Canyon Lake Golf Course** (14A400 Canyon Club Dr., Apple Canyon Lake, tel. 815/492–2182), nine holes. **Eagle Ridge Inn and Resort** in Galena Territory (*see* Dining and Lodging, *below*), one nine-hole and two 18-hole courses. **Lacoma Golf Course** (8080 Dunleith Dr., East Dubuque, tel. 815/747–3874), three nine-holes and one 18-hole course.

Hiking and   **Mississippi Palisades State Park** (4577 Rte. 84N, Savanna, tel. Backpacking   815/273–2731), about 30 mi south of Galena, offers hiking with river views. More cliffs and canyons can be found at **Apple River**

Canyon State Park (8763 E. Canyon Rd., north of Rte. 20 near Stockton, tel. 815/745–3302).

Horseback Riding Shenandoah Riding Center (Galena Territory, Rte. 20E, Galena, tel. 815/777–2373) has lessons and trails, hay and sleigh rides.

Hunting and Fishing Licenses can be purchased at marinas, bait shops, hardware stores, and other outlets, or contact the **Illinois Bureau of Tourism** (*see* Visitor Information, *above*) or the **Illinois Department of Conservation** (2612 Locust St., Sterling 61081, tel. 815/625–2968).

Ski Areas

Cross-country **Eagle Ridge Inn and Resort** (*see* Dining and Lodging, *below*) maintains more than 35 mi of groomed trails. **Lacoma Golf Course** (*see* Golf, *above*) opens its 260-acre course to skiers, but you have to break your own trails. **Mississippi Palisades State Park** and **Apple River Canyon State Park** (*see* Hiking and Backpacking, *above*) have marked trails.

Downhill It's not the Alps, or even the Catskills, but if you want downhill skiing in Illinois, try **Chestnut Mountain Resort** (*see* Dining and Lodging, *below*), with 16 runs that overlook the Mississippi.

Dining and Lodging

Galena-area restaurant fare runs to hearty steaks, burgers, and ribs. Several bakeries along Galena's Main Street offer tempting cookies and pastries. A stay in one of the area's 40-odd bed-and-breakfasts is almost de rigueur; some are right in town, others are in the Galena Territory or other rustic outlying areas. The county tourist office (*see* Visitor Information, *above*) has a complete list of B&Bs and other types of lodging; it also keeps track of vacancies. For price ranges, see Charts 1 (B) and 2 (A) in Chapter 1.

East Dubuque **Timmerman's Lodge and Supper Club.** Perched on a bluff above
Dining and Lodging the Mississippi River, this modern complex is popular with riverboat gamblers (*see* Nightlife, *below*). Most of the rooms are 1980s Holiday Inn style, but a few have antique furnishings and decor. The elegant Supper Club has spectacular views, rib-eye steaks, and candlelight. *7777 Dunleith Dr., 61025, tel. 815/747–3181 (Lodge), 815/747–3316 (Supper Club). 74 rooms, 2 suites. Facilities: restaurant, pool, sauna. AE, D, MC, V. Moderate.*

Galena **The Kingston Inn.** In an 1850s building you can sample a variety
Dining of cuisines, from French (Alsatian duckling with honey-walnut sauce) to American (roast pork whiskey Jack with horseradish). The singing waiters and waitresses are accompanied by a versatile piano player who can handle any request. *300 N. Main St., tel. 815/777–0451. Reservations advised. DC, MC, V. No lunch. Moderate–Expensive.*

Cafe d'Italia. Featured in the movie *Field of Dreams*, this cozy Italian restaurant done in 1980s wood and tile serves reliable versions of minestrone, lasagna, veal parmigiana, and other standards. *301 N. Main St., tel. 815/777–0033. AE, MC, V. No lunch; closed Mon. Nov.–Mar. Moderate.*

Baker's Oven. At this quaint bakery furnished with vintage kitchen implements and other antiques, have homemade soup, a generous sandwich, or prime rib, but save room for the delectable apple dumplings or other baked goods. *200 N. Main St., tel. 815/777–9105. MC, V. Inexpensive–Moderate.*

Dining and Lodging **Chestnut Mountain Resort.** Perched on a bank of the Mississippi, the main building has a Swiss-chalet look; the rooms are Spartan, as befits hunters and skiers. The dining room, overlooking the river, offers adequate steak-and-burger fare and a spectacular view. *8700 W. Chestnut Rd., 61036, tel. 815/777–1320 or 800/397–1320. 126 rooms. Facilities: restaurant, bar, tennis courts, indoor pool, alpine skiing. AE, D, DC, MC, V. Moderate–Expensive.*

The DeSoto House Hotel. The largest hotel in Galena has been in continuous operation for 137 years; Lincoln really did sleep here. The spacious rooms are furnished in a style reminiscent of the 1860s. An elegant curving staircase rises from the lobby to the second floor. The stately Generals' dining room serves straightforward steaks, chops, and seafood. *230 S. Main St., 61036, tel. 815/777–0090 or 800/343–6562. 55 rooms, 2 suites. Facilities: 3 restaurants. AE, D, MC, V. Moderate–Expensive.*

Farmer's Home Hotel. This restored 19th-century inn is near downtown. The rooms are furnished with original simple Victorian pieces. Breakfasts featuring organically grown ham and home-smoked salmon are a specialty. *334 Spring St., 61036, tel. 815/777–3456 or 800/373–3456; fax 815/777–3470. 7 rooms, 2 suites, 2-room cottage. Facilities: dining room, tavern, outdoor hot tub, bicycles. AE, D, DC, MC, V. Moderate–Expensive.*

Galena Territory
Dining and Lodging **Eagle Ridge Inn and Resort.** This rustic yet swanky complex is perfect for golfers (*see* Golf, *above*) and pretty good for everyone else. Guest rooms are spacious and plush, with sleeping and sitting areas done in dark woods and floral fabrics; all have views of lake or woodland. The formal restaurant offers excellent American cuisine. *Rte. 20E, Galena 61036, tel. 815/777–2444. 66 rooms; 225 condominiums, town houses, and homes. Facilities: restaurant, ice-cream parlor, indoor pool, health club, children's recreation program, alpine and cross-country skiing. AE, D, DC, MC, V. Very Expensive.*

Motels **Best Western Quiet House Suites** (Rte. 20E, Galena 61036, tel. 815/777–2577), 42 suites, pool, fitness center, some handicapped-accessible rooms; expensive. **Palace Motel** (Rte. 20W, Galena 61036, tel. 815/777–2043), 64 rooms, Continental breakfast, outdoor pool; moderate. **Grant Hills Motel** (Rte. 20E, Galena 61036, tel. 815/777–2116), 35 rooms, Continental breakfast, outdoor pool, playground, courtesy car into town; inexpensive–moderate.

Nightlife

Riverboat gambling on replicas of the Mississippi boats of the 19th century is the form of nightlife associated with normally sleepy northwestern Illinois. Check with the county tourist office (*see* Tourist Information, *above*) for boats that may be operating during your visit.

Elsewhere in the State

Springfield

Getting There I–55 runs north–south through the city. I–72 comes from Champaign and Decatur to the east. The Amtrak route from Chicago to St. Louis stops in Springfield.

What to See and Do Illinois's capital has perhaps the highest concentration anywhere of sites dedicated to Abraham Lincoln. The **Lincoln Home National Historic Site** (426 S. 7th St., tel. 217/492–4150), the **Lincoln Tomb State Historic Site** at Oak Ridge Cemetery (1500 N. Monument Ave., tel. 217/782–2717), and the **Lincoln-Herndon Law Offices** (6th and Adams Sts., tel. 217/782–4836)—all admission free—provide glimpses into his life and career before he became president. The **Old State Capitol** (Downtown Mall, tel. 217/782–4836; admission free) has been restored to the way it looked during Lincoln's legislative years. (The "new" **State Capitol Building**, at 2nd Street and Capitol Avenue, dates from the 1860s.) About 20 mi northwest of Springfield is the **Lincoln's New Salem State Historic Site** (Rte. 97 near Petersburg, tel. 217/632–4000), where Lincoln lived and studied law during his 20s.

Aside from Lincolniana, Springfield also boasts the **Dana Thomas House,** built by Frank Lloyd Wright in 1903 for a local socialite and now a state historic site. Elaborately restored in the late 1980s, it's among the most perfectly preserved examples of early Wright architecture, art glass, and furniture. *301 E. Lawrence Ave., tel. 815/782–6776. Admission free. Closed Sun.–Wed., Fri.*

The **Springfield Convention and Visitors Bureau** (109 N. 7th St., 62701, tel. 217/789–2360 or 800/545–7300) has further information on area attractions.

INDIANA

By Ann H.
Hughes and
Karen Cure

*Updated by
Bill Roberts*

Capital	Indianapolis
Population	5,544,159
Motto	Crossroads of America
State Bird	Cardinal
State Flower	Peony

Visitor Information

Indiana Department of Commerce's Division of Tourism (1 N. Capitol Ave., Indianapolis 46204, tel. 317/232–8860 or 800/289–6646).

Scenic Drives

The drive along the **Ohio River Scenic Route,** on Rtes. 56 and 156 between Madison and Aurora, takes about an hour. The 50-mi **Lincoln Heritage Trail/George Rogers Clark Trail,** on Rtes. 62 and 162 from New Albany to Gentryville, runs through the Hoosier National Forest. The 90-mi **Hoosier Heritage Trail Scenic Route,** on Rte. 66 from Newburgh through Tell City to Sulpher, begins at the Ohio River and ends up in the Hoosier National Forest. The 130-mi **U.S. Circle Tour Route** goes along U.S. 20 from the Ohio state line through the Amish country to the Indiana dunelands and Lake Michigan.

National and State Parks

National Parks **George Rogers Clark National Memorial** (401 S. 2nd St., Vincennes 47591, tel. 812/882–1776). **Lincoln Boyhood National Memorial** (Box 1816 Lincoln City 47552, tel. 812/937–4541; admission free).

State Parks Indiana's 21 state parks are operated by the Department of Natural Resources (402 W. Washington St., Indianapolis 46204, tel. 317/232–4124 or 800/622–4931) and are open daily year-round. **McCormick's Creek** (Rte. 5, Box 82, Spencer 47460, tel. 812/829–2235) highlights unique limestone formations and waterfalls along the White River, 14 mi northwest of Bloomington. At **Spring Mill** (Route 60 Box 376, Mitchell 47446, tel. 812/849–4129), a restored pioneer village with its own gristmill takes you back to the early 1800s. At **Turkey Run** (Rte. 1, Box 164, Marshall 47859, tel. 317/597–2635), Sugar Creek is a favorite with canoeists, who also enjoy the hiking trails through maple-shaded ravines.

Indianapolis

After two decades of energetic public and private investment, the 284-foot-tall monument at the center of Indianapolis that was long its most identifiable landmark is now dwarfed by jumbo sports complexes and office towers. The brick-topped street that rings the spire seems tiny compared with the wide new expressways that whoosh downtown workers to and from their jobs. The juxtaposition of old and new, though jarring, helps explain why local boosters are so proud, and why those who come on business, or to catch the annual 500-mi Memorial Day weekend auto race, leave with such pleasant memories. While new buildings make it comfortable to attend pro sports events and set a handsome scene for fine art in the city's museums, restorations of antique structures—from the nation's first Union Station and the 100-year-old State House to gracious old homes in leafy residential districts—add texture and charm.

Tourist Information

Indianapolis: City Center (210 S. Capitol Ave., 46225, tel. 317/237–5200 or 800/323–4639; hotline, tel. 317/684–2450). Convention & Visitors Association (1 Hoosier Dome, 46225, tel. 317/639–4282).

Arriving and Departing

By Plane **Indianapolis International Airport** is a USAir hub and is served by all other major and several commuter airlines. The 7-mi trip from the airport to downtown takes 10 to 15 minutes; allow 25 minutes for the trip to the north side, 35 minutes to the northeast side. By taxi or limo, the cost is $7 to downtown, $20 to the north side, $35 to the northeast side. The **AAA Airport ShuttleExpress** (tel. 317/247–7301) runs between the airport and downtown on the half-hour between 4 AM and midnight and charges $4–$7, depending upon the destination.

By Car Indianapolis is a driving city. You can get to any destination in and around Indianapolis off I–65, I–70, or I–465. Car rentals are available at major hotels and at the airport.

Train Station **Indianapolis Union Station** (350 S. Illinois St., tel. 317/263–0550) has Amtrak service.

Bus Station **Greyhound Bus Terminal** (127 N. Illinois St., tel. 317/267–8800).

Getting Around

It is easy to get around Indianapolis; the streets are numbered logically, and the center is comfortable for walking. **Metro buses** (tel. 317/632–1900 or 317/635–3344) run from 4:45 AM to 11:45 PM. Fares (75¢, $1 during rush hour) are payable upon boarding. **Metro Taxi** (tel. 317/634–1112) and **Yellow Cab** (tel. 317/847–7777) are radio-dispatched; call ahead to be sure of getting a cab, unless you're at the airport or downtown. The fare is $2.45 for the first mile and $1.50 for each additional mile.

Exploring Indianapolis

For a sense of the city's people, prowl around the downtown landmarks and marketplaces. For a sense of its culture, scout out the museums—they're scattered about town but are all worth a special trip.

Downtown **Monument Circle** is Indianapolis's centerpiece. Avenues radiate from it as in Washington, D.C. (designed by Pierre L'Enfant, of whom Indianapolis architect Alexander Ralston was a disciple). The **Indiana Soldiers' and Sailors' Monument** at the center has a panoramic observation deck (admission charged). Along the perimeter of the circle there are several other build-

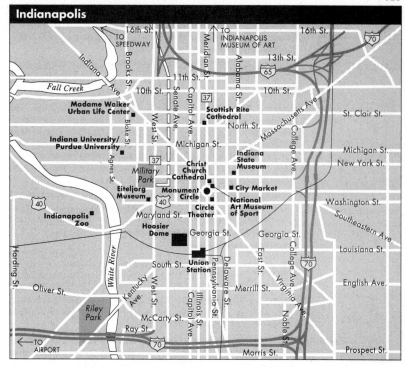

Indianapolis

ings to note. The **Circle Theatre**, a vintage movie palace opened in 1916, is now the home of the Indianapolis Symphony Orchestra (tel. 317/262–1100; admission charged; tours by appointment). **Christ Church Cathedral** (125 Monument Circle, tel. 317/636–4577; admission free; tours by appointment), built in 1857, looks straight out of the English countryside with its spire, steep gables, bell tower, and arched Tiffany-glass windows. The **National Art Museum of Sport** (111 Monument Circle, tel. 317/687–1715; admission free; closed Sun.) has a collection ranging from the 5th century BC to the present.

Assemble a meal of ethnic food at the **City Market** and savor it on the festive outside terrace where downtown office workers congregate during the lunch hour. *222 E. Market St., tel. 317/634–9266. Admission free. Closed Sun.*

The **Indiana State Museum** showcases the state's history and ecology. **Freetown Village** depicts the lifestyles of local blacks after the Emancipation. *202 N. Alabama St., tel. 317/232–1637. Admission free.*

The Gothic-Tudor-style Masonic **Scottish Rite Cathedral,** which contains a 54-bell carillon and a 7,500-pipe organ, cost $2.5 million to build in 1929. *650 N. Meridian St., tel. 317/635–2301. Admission free. Closed weekends.*

Housed in a contemporary adobe-style building that evokes images of the desert Southwest, the **Eiteljorg Museum of American Indian and Western Art** displays works by Frederic Remington and Georgia O'Keeffe, among others. *500 W. Washington St., tel. 317/636–9378. Admission charged. Closed Mon.*

The 19-story **Hoosier Dome,** its fiberglass roof supported by air pressure, is the home of the Indianapolis Colts and the **National Track & Field Hall of Fame.** *100 S. Capitol Ave., tel. 317/262–3452. Admission charged. Tours daily.*

Union Station (39 Jackson Pl., tel. 317/267–0700), restored and filled with shops and restaurants, is thronged with visitors from all over the state.

Midtown/Crosstown Ongoing revitalization efforts here aim to preserve local African-American history and culture. The **Madame Walker Urban Life Center,** in a theater where Louis Armstrong and Dinah Washington once performed, is embellished with unusual African and Egyptian motifs. "Jazz on the Avenue" concerts take place here every Friday night. *617 Indiana Ave., tel. 317/236–2099. Admission charged. Closed weekends.*

A Playscape, the world's largest water clock, and the Space Quest Planetarium make **The Children's Museum** one of the best in the country. Don't miss the turn-of-the-century carousel. *3000 N. Meridian St., tel. 317/924–5431 or 317/924–KIDS. Admission charged.*

The serene **Indianapolis Museum of Art** houses works by J.M.W. Turner, the Old Masters, and the Neo-Impressionists, as well as major Oriental and African collections. On the woodsy grounds are botanical gardens and a genteel restaurant. *1200 W. 38th St., tel. 317/923–1331. Admission charged for special exhibitions. Closed Mon.*

West Side The **Indianapolis Motor Speedway Hall of Fame Museum** displays 30 Indy-winning cars, as well as classic and antique autos. Vans bearing visitors around the famous oval depart from here. *4790 W. 16th St., tel. 317/241–2500. Admission charged. Open daily.*

Parks and Gardens

You can jog, bike, hike, golf, or do water sports at the rustic 3,800-acre **Eagle Creek Park,** on the shores of a reservoir in northwest Indianapolis. **White River State Park,** under construction, near downtown, features a ½-mi promenade along the river.

What to See and Do with Children

The **Children's Museum** and the **Speedway** (*see* Exploring Indianapolis, *above*) are essential destinations for small fry; so is the **Indianapolis Zoo** (1200 W. Washington St., tel. 317/630–2030). To give them a feel of other eras, take in the 19th-century **Benjamin Harrison Home** (1230 N. Delaware St., tel. 317/631–1898) and the antique soda fountain at **Hook's Historic Drug Store and Pharmacy Museum** at the Indiana State Fairgrounds (1202 E. 38th St., tel. 317/924–1503).

Shopping

The **Fashion Mall** (9000 Keystone Crossing, tel. 317/574–4000) is a complex of pricey specialty stores, plus **Jacobson's** (tel. 317/574–0088), a traditional department store. In **Broad Ripple Village** (62nd St. and College Ave.), you'll find one-of-a-kind secondhand bookshops, vintage-clothing stores, and antiques galleries.

Spectator Sports

Basketball **Indiana Pacers** (Market Square Arena, 300 E. Market St., tel. 317/639–2112; Oct.–Apr.).

Football **Indianapolis Colts** (Hoosier Dome, 100 S. Capitol Ave., tel. 317/262–3452 or 317/262–3389; Sept.–Jan.).

Dining

For price ranges, see Chart 1 (A) in Chapter 1.

Very Expensive **Chanteclair.** A strolling violinist and European waiters set the tone at this restaurant in the Airport Holiday Inn. Fare includes beluga caviar with sour cream and steak Diane flamed tableside. *2501 S. High School Rd., tel. 317/243–1040. Reservations required. Jacket and tie required. AE, D, DC, MC, V.*

Expensive **Chateau Normandy.** In this far northside restaurant a French Provincial–style dining room and an outdoor terrace overlooking Lake Clearwater make pleasant settings for such treats as bell-pepper ravioli with stone-crab claws and filet mignon with peppery cream sauce. *8250 Dean Rd., tel. 317/849–3970. Reservations advised. Jacket advised. AE, D, DC, MC, V.*

King Cole. The menu is in French, but the original Reynolds and Gainsborough oils on the brick-and-paneled walls make this sophisticated spot seem straight from London's Strand. Gracious service and excellent prime rib and fish continue to make this old-timer (1957) a delightful choice for elegant meals. *7 N. Meridian St., tel. 317/638–5588. Reservations advised. Jacket and tie required. AE, DC, MC, V.*

Moderate **Milano Inn.** You can smell the garlic and oregano half a block away from this 60-year-old Italian eatery in a onetime firehouse on the near-south side. The fettuccine's made from scratch and served Alfredo, primavera, or Bolognese style. *231 S. College Ave., tel. 317/264–3585. AE, DC, MC, V.*

The Teller's Cage. It's on the 35th floor of the downtown Indiana National Bank tower, so go for a table by a window. The hot-and-cold luncheon buffet challenges you to eat to capacity; evenings, the chef takes pride in his chicken Dijon, with a mustard and white-wine sauce. *1 Indiana Sq., tel. 317/266–5211. Reservations advised at dinner. Jacket and tie advised. AE, DC, MC, V.*

Inexpensive **City Taproom.** This downtown bar and grill has the atmosphere of a neighborhood tavern. Grilled swordfish with dill butter draws raves, as does the filet mignon. *28 S. Pennsylvania St., tel. 317/637–1334. AE, DC, MC, V.*

Hollyhock Hill. Prim and proper Indianapolis has been celebrating rites of passage in this country cottage on the north side for the past 60 years. Superb fried chicken, mashed potatoes, and green beans are served family style. *8110 N. College Ave., tel. 317/251–2294. Reservations advised. Jacket and tie advised. AE, MC, V.*

MCL Cafeterias. These no-frills cafeterias offer such specialties as roast beef, broiled sole, baked ham, and devil's food cake and coconut cream pie. *10 locations, including 6010 E. 10th St., tel. 317/356–1587; 8135 Pendleton Pike, tel. 317/898–5455; 3630*

S. East St., tel. 317/783–2416; 5910 Crawfordsville Rd., tel. 317/241–9497. No reservations. No credit cards.

Shapiro's Delicatessen & Cafeteria. A parking lot boasting chauffeur-driven Mercedeses and pop-up campers suggests the clientele of this nationally known 300-seat deli near the Hoosier Dome. The corned beef sandwiches, hot borscht, and chicken soup excel, and the strawberry cheesecake has been an Indianapolis institution since Shapiro's opened in 1904. *808 S. Meridian St., tel. 317/631–4041. No reservations. No credit cards.*

Lodging

For price ranges, see Chart 2 (A) in Chapter 1.

Very Expensive   **Canterbury Hotel.** This 60-year-old hostelry is now a classy European-style hotel. Massive armoires and queen-size four-poster beds make the renovated guest rooms seem cramped, but luxurious baths compensate. The Beaulieu restaurant serves chops in an elegant English-club atmosphere. *123 S. Illinois St., 46225, tel. 317/634–3000; fax 317/299–9257, ext. 7397. 99 rooms, 15 suites. Facilities: restaurant (reservations advised; jacket and tie required). AE, D, DC, MC, V.*

University Place Executive Conference Center and Hotel. This hotel on the city campus of Purdue and Indiana universities coddles its intellectual clientele with handsomely appointed rooms featuring desks, easy chairs, and 18th-century reproduction furnishings. Museum-quality original oils and watercolors add interest to the common areas. *850 W. Michigan St., 46202, tel. 317/269–9000 or 800/627–2700; fax 317/231–5168. 262 rooms, 16 suites. Facilities: 2 restaurants, bar. AE, D, DC, MC, V.*

Westin Hotel, Indianapolis. This high rise faces the Hoosier Dome on one side and the Indianapolis Zoo on the other. The executive level is especially posh, with sleeper sofas, valet stands, hair dryers, and terry-cloth robes. *50 S. Capitol Ave., 46204, tel. 317/262–8100; fax 317/231–3928. 572 rooms, 38 suites. Facilities: restaurant, bar, indoor pool. AE, D, DC, MC, V.*

Expensive   **Adam's Mark.** Tufted-leather sofas, wood paneling, and leaded glass make the common areas of this low rise feel like an English tavern. Guest rooms have writing desks big enough for both elbows and a briefcase. *2544 Executive Dr., 46241, tel. 317/248–2481 or 800/444–2326; fax 317/248–2481, ext. 7135. 407 rooms. Facilities: 2 restaurants, 2 lounges, indoor pool, health club. AE, D, DC, MC, V.*

Embassy Suites Downtown. The front desk of this contemporary property overlooks a 15-story atrium with a simulated tropical rain forest. The art-deco suites have separate living rooms with convertible sofas and minikitchens. *110 W. Washington St., 46204, tel. 317/236–1800; fax 317/236–1816. 360 suites. Facilities: restaurant, lounge, indoor pool. AE, D, DC, MC, V.*

Omni Severin Hotel. A skylighted, two-story atrium that was added in a resurrection of this railroad hotel is a perfect foil for crystal chandeliers, a marble staircase, and cast-iron balustrades in the Italian Renaissance section. Guest rooms have stark-black furnishings accented with scarlet and white accessories. *40 W. Jackson Pl., 46225, tel. 317/634–6664; fax 317/687–3619. 385 rooms, 36 suites, 11 penthouses. Facilities: restaurant, bar, indoor pool, health club. AE, DC, MC, V.*

Moderate **Courtyard Indianapolis.** This inn across from the state-offices complex has wood veneers, marble tile, and elevators with polished-brass doors. The card-accessed guest rooms have renovated baths. *501 W. Washington St., 46204, tel. 317/635–4443 or 800/666–0029; fax 317/687–0029. 233 rooms, 3 suites. Facilities: restaurant, outdoor pool, exercise room, playground. AE, D, DC, MC, V.*

Holiday Inn Union Station. Baggage carts piled high with antique steamer trunks outside this inn remind you that it occupies Union Station's old train shed. Some of the suites are in former sleeper cars named for such personalities as Jean Harlow and Rudolph Valentino and furnished with antiques and railroad memorabilia. *123 Louisiana St., 46225, tel. 317/631–2221; fax 317/236–7474. 243 rooms, 33 suites. Facilities: restaurant, lounge, indoor pool. AE, D, DC, MC, V.*

Inexpensive **Dillon Inn North.** Accessible from the beltway, and close to northwest-side office parks and a slew of restaurants ranging from gourmet to fast-food, this three-story, no-frills inn is a favorite with budget-conscious business travelers as well as families. *9090 Wesleyan Rd., 46268, tel. 317/875–7676 or 800/253–7503; fax 317/875–9051. 116 rooms. Facilities: outdoor pool. AE, D, DC, MC, V.*

Holiday Inn Southeast. Popular for business and social functions, this six-story high rise on the beltway has a lounge full of mirrors and brass and a restaurant with a country look. *5120 Victory Dr., 46203, tel. 317/783–7751; fax 317/787–1545. 140 rooms. Facilities: restaurant, lounge. AE, D, DC, MC, V.*

The Arts and Nightlife

The Arts *Indianapolis Monthly* magazine and the Sunday edition of *The Indianapolis Star* list arts and events. Tickets for plays and concerts may be obtained through **Court Side Tickets** (6100 N. Keystone Ave., tel. 317/254–9500), **Karma** (3540 W. 86th St., tel. 317/876–9603), **TicketMaster** (2 W. Washington St., tel. 317/239–1000 or 317/239–5151), or **Tickets Up Front** (1099 N. Meridian St., tel. 317/633–6400).

Music **Indianapolis Symphony Orchestra** (42 Monument Circle, tel. 317/639–4300) performs at the Circle Theatre on weekends most of the year, at Conner Prairie Pioneer Village in July and August (*see* Excursions from Indianapolis, *below*). The 88-piece **Philharmonic Orchestra of Indianapolis** (Caleb Mills Hall, Shortridge Junior High School, 3401 N. Meridian St., tel. 317/283–5242) presents classical and pops concerts throughout the year at various locations.

Opera **Indianapolis Opera Company** (250 E. 38th St., tel. 317/283–3531) stages four productions from the grand-opera repertoire and one new work each season.

Nightlife Pub crawling is best in out-of-the-way neighborhoods and on the outskirts of town. A DJ spins '50s and '60s dance tunes nightly at **Ike & Jonesy's** (17 E. Jackson Pl., tel. 317/632–4553), a.k.a. the "Fun Place Downtown." Everybody loves the drink specials and '50s menu. The **Chatterbox Tavern** (435 Massachusetts Ave., tel. 317/636–0584), in the city's art-gallery district, offers top-notch jazz. At **Durbin's Lounge** (7202 E. 21st St., tel. 317/352–1231), railroad memorabilia add interest to high-energy entertainment. Boisterous **Rick's Café Americain** at Union Station (39 Jackson Pl., tel. 317/634–6666) appeals to the under-30 set. The **Slippery Noodle Inn** (372 S. Meridian St., tel. 317/631–6974), once a stop on the Underground Railway, offers blues, poetry readings, and good food.

Excursions from Indianapolis

Zionsville Slightly more than a half hour's drive from Monument Circle is this enchanting little community (pop. 3,948) of brick streets, leafy maples, and stick-style Victorian houses. It has the only recognized hunt club in the state and one of only three Rolls-Royce dealers in the country, yet this is a community where the farmers come to gas up their trucks and chew the fat down at city hall, where school kids walk home for lunch, and where the town eccentric parks on a bench outside the hardware store.

Conner Prairie At this living-history museum just north of Indianapolis you
Pioneer Village can catch the spirit of the 1830s as you watch interpreters spinning, weaving, and learning their letters. At the Pioneer Adventure Area you can try your hand at skittles and quoits or walking on stilts. *13400 Allisonville Rd., Noblesville, tel. 317/ 776–6000. Admission charged. Closed Mon.*

Bloomington South of Indianapolis on Rte. 37 is this safe, prosperous city where you can whet your intellect as well as your appetite. It is the home of Indiana University, with one of the nation's 10 largest campuses. Nearby are five championship golf courses and Lake Monroe, the state's largest reservoir. (Bloomington/Monroe County Convention and Visitors Bureau, 2855 N. Walnut St., Bloomington 47404, tel. 812/334–8900.)

Brown County An hour south of Indianapolis on Rte. 135 is a woodsy area famous for its fall foliage, Indiana artists' colony, and state park. Brown County also offers rustic life in the hamlets of Gnaw Bone, Bean Blossom, and Story. Nashville is jammed with an amazing assortment of shops. (Brown County Convention and Visitors Bureau, Box 840, Nashville 47448, tel. 812/988–7303.)

Columbus On I-65 45 minutes south of Indianapolis, this affluent city of 30,000 boasts the headquarters of two *Fortune* 500 companies and more than 50 public and private buildings designed by world-renowned architects, such as Eero and Eliel Saarinen, I. M. Pei, and Harry Weese. Architectural walking or guided tours (by reservation) begin at the city Visitors Center (506 5th St., 47201, tel. 812/372–1954).

Southern Indiana

Southern Indiana is hardwood forests, rolling hills, majestic rivers, natural wonderlands, and picturesque towns. If you can identify with the American frontier, you'll be fascinated with this region.

Tourist Information

Southern Indiana: Convention and Visitors Bureau (540 Marriott Dr., Jeffersonville 47131, tel. 812/282–6654). **Madison Area:** Visitors Council (301 E. Main St., Madison 47250, tel. 812/265–2956). **Vincennes Area:** Chamber of Commerce (27 3rd St., Vincennes 47591, tel. 812/882–6440). **Vincennes:** Log Cabin Visitor Center (1 W. Harrison St., 47591, tel. 812/885–4339).

Getting There

By Car The major road through this region is I–64. From Indianapolis, take I–70 and U.S. 41 to Vincennes, I–65 and Rte. 7 to Madison, and I–65 to New Albany. From Louisville, Kentucky, take I–65; from Cincinnati, take I–71.

By Bus Service between Indianapolis and Vincennes is available on **Greyhound** (tel. 812/882–3426) and **I–V Coaches** (tel. 317/634–3198). **White Star** (tel. 812/265–2662) travels between Madison and Indianapolis.

Exploring Southern Indiana

In 300-year-old **Vincennes** you can visit dozens of historic sites, such as the Indiana Territory Capitol, the state's first bank and first newspaper office, a memorial to Revolutionary War general George Rogers Clark, and **Grouseland,** home of President William Henry Harrison. South on U.S. 41 to I–64 and southwest on Rte. 68 is **New Harmony** (Historic New Harmony Inc., Box 579, New Harmony 47631, tel. 812/682–4488), site of two early 19th-century communes. The present town is a delightful marriage of old and new: The Harmonists' 19th-century Workingmen's Institute and dormitories contrast sharply with architect Richard Meier's avant-garde Atheneum and Philip Johnson's Roofless Church.

Near **Gentryville,** back east on I–64 and southwest on U.S. 231, is **Lincoln State Park** (Rte. 162, Lincoln City, tel. 812/937–4710), where you can see the outdoor musical drama *Young Abe Lincoln* performed in summer. To learn more about young Abe, cross the road to the **Lincoln Boyhood National Memorial** (tel. 812/937–4757), with a museum, a working pioneer farmstead, and the grave of the president's mother, Nancy Hanks Lincoln.

The Hoosier National Forest offers spelunking in **Wyandotte Caves** (Rte. 1, Leavenworth, tel. 812/738–2782). You can see flowstone and dripstone formations in Little Wyandotte Cave or take a strenuous journey to Milroy's Temple in Big Wyandotte Cave. At **Squire Boone Caverns & Village** in Corydon (tel. 812/732–4831), a descent into labyrinthine passageways reveals waterfalls, delicate soda straws, and massive stalactites.

While in **Corydon,** Indiana's first capital, you can browse through 10,000 square feet of antiques in two downtown malls. The Federal-style **Capitol Building** (Chestnut and Capitol Sts., tel. 812/738–4890) is where the state's first constitution was drafted. The 15-mi round-trip aboard the **Scenic 1883 Railroad** (Walnut and Water Sts., tel. 812/738–8000) gives you a taste of the bucolic countryside.

New Albany is the site of the Victorian-era **Culbertson Mansion** (914 E. Main St., tel. 812/944–9600), with hand-painted ceilings, marble fireplaces, and delicate woodwork. The nearby **Falls of the Ohio State Park** (tel. 812/945–6284), accessible off Rte. 62, is great for picnics.

In **Madison,** the entire main street is listed on the National Register of Historic Places. See the gleaming white Greek Revival **Lanier Mansion** (511 W. 1st St., tel. 812/265–3526), with a cantilevered spiral staircase and a portico overlooking the Ohio River.

What to See and Do with Children

Holiday World in Santa Claus (tel. 812/937–4401 or 800/488–0890) has sledding, storytelling, and caroling when it's cold, and water rides and attractions when it's warm.

Sports and Outdoor Activities

Biking Four routes on the **Hoosier Bikeway System** run through this area. Bring your own bike.

Fishing At **Patoka Lake** (R.R. 1, Birdseye, tel. 812/685–2464) and **Markland Dam** on the Ohio River off Rte. 156, each season brings record catches of bass, carp, and catfish.

Dining and Lodging

Southern Indiana is well supplied with roadside motels and hotels, but for the ultimate lodging experience, try one of the many local bed-and-breakfasts that sprinkle this area (**Indiana Bed and Breakfast Association,** Box 48, Madison 47250). For price ranges, see Charts 1 (B) and 2 (B) in Chapter 1.

Clarksville/
Jeffersonville/
New Albany
Dining and Lodging
Lakeview Hotel and Resort. This hotel has brightened its common areas with marble and tile, and ivory-colored furnishings in the rooms are dressed up with cheery floral fabrics. The Sunday-brunch and luncheon buffets are a local institution. *505 Marriott Dr., Clarksville 47130, tel. 812/283–4411 or 800/824–7740. 325 rooms. Facilities: restaurant, lounge, indoor and outdoor pools. AE, DC, MC, V. Inexpensive.*

Madison
Dining and Lodging
Ogle Haus Inn. Whirlpool baths, dhurrie rugs, and Queen Anne–style furniture make this modified Swiss chalet east of Madison on Rte. 56 more sophisticated than you'd expect in this countrified area. Its dining room, which features both Bavarian and American cuisine, draws a clientele from a 100-mi radius. *R.R. 3, Box 177, Vevay 47043, tel. 812/427–2020, 800/826–6299, or 800/545–9360 in IN. 54 rooms. Facilities: 2 restaurants, outdoor pool. AE, DC, MC, V. Moderate.*

Lodging **Cliff House.** This historic bed-and-breakfast is furnished with antiques and canopy beds. Guests are served a Continental breakfast on Haviland china, accompanied by fine silver and crystal. *122 Fairmount Dr., 47250, tel. 812/265–5272. 9 rooms. Facilities: music room (instruments for guests' use). AE, DC, MC, V. Expensive.*

Vincennes
Dining and Lodging
Executive Inn Vincennes. Amenities include a five-story, skylighted atrium with towering palms, guest rooms with tufted headboards and marble-top tables, and gourmet dining. An unexpected plus is Las Vegas–style entertainment. *1 Executive Blvd., 47591, tel. 812/886–5000. 318 rooms. Facilities: dining room, lounge, indoor pool. AE, DC, MC, V. Moderate.*

Northern Indiana

Trekking through this part of Indiana offers variety—from the sands along Lake Michigan's shores to the horse-drawn buggies of the plain-and-simple Amish folk.

Tourist Information

Fort Wayne: Convention and Visitors Bureau (826 Ewing St., 46802, tel. 219/424–1435). **Porter County:** Convention and Visitors Bureau (528 Indian Oak Mall, Chesterton 46304, tel. 219/926–2255 or 800/283–8687). **South Bend/Mishawaka Area:** Chamber of Commerce (401 E. Colfax Ave., South Bend 46634, tel. 219/234–0079).

Getting There

By Car Major east–west roads through the region are I–80/90 and U.S. 12 and 20. Traversing the region north–south are I–65, I–69, and U.S. 31 and 41.

By Train This area is served by the **South Shore Line** (2702 W. Washington St., South Bend, tel. 219/233–3111) and **Amtrak.**

By Bus **United Limo** in Osceola (tel. 219/674–6993) provides daily service to and from Chicago. Service to and from other major Midwestern cities is available on **Greyhound** (4671 Terminal Dr., South Bend, tel. 219/287–6541).

Exploring Northern Indiana

In the **Indiana Dunes National Lakeshore** (U.S. 12, 1100 N. Mineral Springs Rd., Porter 46304, tel. 219/926–7561) arctic bearberry grows next to prickly-pear cactus, and dogwoods next to jack pines along the shores of Lake Michigan.

Hordes come to **South Bend** each year to see the **University of Notre Dame**'s Fighting Irish and the century-old murals in the landmark **Golden Dome** (tel. 219/239–7367). The university's **Snite Museum of Art** (tel. 219/239–5466) contains more than 17,000 art objects, including works by Rembrandt, Chagall, and Picasso. Downtown South Bend's **East Race Waterway** attracts tubers and rafters and is the scene of international kayak and canoe competitions.

The 75-mi ride east on U.S. 20 from South Bend to Angola takes you through Indiana's **Amish Country,** where there are festivals, flea markets, Amish restaurants, and the Amish people going about their lives. **Amish Acres** (Rte. 19, 1600 W. Market St., Nappanee, tel. 219/773–4188) is a working farm, an inn, a playhouse, and a restaurant with food prepared by Amish cooks. To the east is Auburn, where the **Auburn-Cord-Duesenberg Museum** (1600 S. Wayne St., tel. 219/925–1444; admission charged) displays more than 130 vintage cars in a historic art-deco building.

What to See and Do with Children

Off I–69 in downtown Fort Wayne is **Historic Old Fort Wayne,** where you can glimpse life as it was on the U.S. frontier during the War of 1812, complete with craftspeople in period costumes. *107 S. Clinton St., tel. 219/424–3476. Admission charged. Closed Mon.–Thurs. and Sept.–June.*

Dining and Lodging

There are enough bed-and-breakfasts in this part of Indiana to make you think the concept originated here (**Indiana Bed and Breakfast Association,** Box 48, Madison 47250). For price ranges, see Charts 1 (B) and 2 (B) in Chapter 1.

Fort Wayne
Dining and Lodging

Fort Wayne Hilton. This downtown property connects with the city's premier convention center. The oversize guest rooms have lounge chairs and Georgian-style furniture accented with mauves and blues. *1020 S. Calhoun St., 46802, tel. 219/420–1100. 250 rooms. Facilities: 2 restaurants, lounge, health spa, indoor pool, weight room. AE, D, DC, MC, V. Expensive.*

Don Hall's Guesthouse. In this local favorite, guest rooms have cherrywood Thomasville furniture, fresh carpets, and accessories in blue and rose or green and beige. *1313 W. Washington Center Rd., 46825, tel. 219/489–2524. 130 rooms. Facilities: restaurant, lounge, indoor/outdoor pool. AE, D, DC, MC, V. Moderate.*

Indiana Dunelands
Lodging

Indian Oak Inn. This contemporary cedar-and-fieldstone inn has rattan-furnished guest rooms with picture windows overlooking either lake or woods. Some suites have fireplaces. *558 Boundary Rd., Chesterton 46304, tel. 219/926–2200 or 800/552–4232. 90 rooms, 5 suites. Facilities: heated indoor pool, whirlpool, health spa. AE, D, DC, MC, V. Moderate.*

Carlton Lodge. A fieldstone fireplace and golden-oak woodwork create the ambience of a mountain lodge. Standard motel furnishings are pepped up with splashy prints in contemporary shades. *7850 Rhode Island Ave., Merrillville 46410, tel. 219/756–1600 or 800/445–6343. 112 rooms. Facilities: lounge, indoor/outdoor pool, whirlpool. AE, D, DC, MC, V. Inexpensive.*

South Bend
Dining and Lodging

South Bend Marriott Hotel. The centerpiece of this sleek glass-and-limestone property is a 32,000-square-foot atrium. Guest rooms with traditional appointments are decorated in restful shades of rose and beige. *123 N. St. Joseph St., 46601, tel. 219/234–2000; fax 219/234–2252. 300 rooms. Facilities: 2 restaurants, lounge, indoor pool, sauna/whirlpool. AE, D, DC, MC, V. Expensive.*

The Works Hotel. A Singer sewing machine factory that predates the Civil War has been converted into a trendy hotel. Green and mauve accessories complement modern oak furniture; guest rooms have kitchenettes and wet bars. *475 N. Niles Ave., 46617, tel. 219/234–1954. 56 rooms. Facilities: dining room, lounge, exercise room. AE, DC, MC, V. Moderate.*

MICHIGAN

By Don Davenport

Updated by Richard Bak

Capital	Lansing
Population	9,240,000
Motto	If You Seek a Pleasant Peninsula, Look About You
State Bird	Robin
State Flower	Apple blossom

Visitor Information

Michigan Department of Commerce Travel Bureau (Box 30226, Lansing 48909, tel. 800/543–2937). **Information centers:** I–94 at New Buffalo and Port Huron; I–69 at Coldwater; U.S. 23 at Dundee; U.S. 2 at Ironwood and Iron Mountain; U.S. 41 at Marquette and Menominee; I–75 at St. Ignace, Sault Ste. Marie, and Monroe; U.S. 27 in a rest area 1 mi north of Clare; and Rte. 108 in Mackinaw City.

Scenic Drives

Rte. BR–15 between Pentwater and Montague follows the Lake Michigan shoreline for about 25 mi. **Rte. M–23** between Tawas City and Mackinaw City follows the Lake Huron shoreline for more than 160 mi. In the Upper Peninsula, **Rte. M–28** follows the Lake Superior shoreline between Marquette and Munising.

National and State Parks

National Parks   **Isle Royale National Park** (Houghton 49940, tel. 906/482–3310), 48 mi off the Michigan coast in Lake Superior, is a wilderness park and can be reached by ferry from Houghton or Copper Harbor or by seaplane from Houghton.

Pictured Rocks National Lakeshore (Box 40, Munising 49862, tel. 906/387–2607) in the Upper Peninsula extends 40 mi along Lake Superior between Munising and Grand Marais.

Sleeping Bear Dunes National Lakeshore (9922 Front St., Box 277, Empire 49630, tel. 616/326–5134) encompasses 33 mi of Lower Michigan's Lake Michigan shore and includes the Manitou Islands. The 71,000-acre preserve has the highest sand dunes outside the Sahara.

State Parks   Michigan has 94 state parks, including 23 in the Upper Peninsula, where a number feature spectacular waterfalls. Camping is allowed in 78 parks. A motor-vehicle permit, available at each park entrance, is required for admission. The *Michigan Travel Guide*, available from the Michigan Department of Commerce Travel Bureau (*see* Visitor Information, *above*), details the state's parks and their facilities.

Brimley State Park (Rte. 2, Box 202, Brimley 49715, tel. 906/248–3422), overlooking Lake Superior's Whitefish Bay, is one of 14 parks where you may rent a tent already set up and equipped with two cots and two sleeping pads. **Porcupine Mountains State Park** (Rte. M–107, Ontonagon, tel. 906/885–5275) and **J. W. Wells State Park** (Rte. M–35, Cedar River

49813, tel. 906/863–9747) are two of 13 parks that have cabins to rent.

Detroit

Founded seven decades before the American Revolution, Detroit is a busy industrial city that produces some 26% of the nation's autos, trucks, and tractors. The riverfront harbor is one of the busiest ports on the Great Lakes. Downtown, a constant flow of traffic moves in and out of the Detroit–Windsor Tunnel, which connects Detroit with Windsor, Ontario, directly across the Detroit River.

Nearly half of Michigan's total population lives within the metropolitan area. More than 150 ethnic groups are represented, including almost 900,000 African-Americans and more than 400,000 people of Polish descent. Detroit's Bulgarian, Belgian, and Arab populations are the largest in North America. These numbers add up to a wealth of cultural diversity that's reflected in language, music, food, art, and entertainment.

Tourist Information

Detroit Visitor Information Center (2 E. Jefferson Ave., 48226, in Hart Plaza just west of the Renaissance Center, tel. 313/567–1170).

Arriving and Departing

By Plane **Detroit Metropolitan Airport** (tel. 313/942–3550) in Romulus, about 26 mi west of downtown Detroit, is served by most major airlines, with nearly 1,000 arrivals and departures daily. **Detroit City Airport** (tel. 313/267–6400), 6 mi east of downtown, is the regional hub for Southwest Airlines.

Commuter Transportation Company (tel. 313/941–3252) operates buses from the Metropolitan Airport to major downtown hotels from 6:45 AM to midnight; the fare is $14 one-way, $26 round-trip. Taxis to and from the airport take about 45 minutes; the fare is about $32.

By Car I–75 enters Detroit from the north and south, U.S. 10 from the north. Approaching from the west and northeast is I–94; from the west, I–96 and I–696. From the east, Canadian Rte. 401 becomes Rte. 3 when entering Detroit from Windsor via the Ambassador Bridge and Rte. 3B when entering via the Detroit–Windsor Tunnel.

Train Station **Amtrak Station** (16121 Michigan Ave., Dearborn, tel. 313/336–5407).

Bus Station **Greyhound** (1000 W. Lafayette St., tel. 313/963–9840 or 800/528–0447).

Getting Around Detroit

By Car Detroit is the Motor City; everyone drives. Most downtown streets are one-way; a detailed map is a necessity. The main streets into downtown are Woodward Avenue (north–south) and Jefferson Avenue (east–west). Rush hours should be avoided.

By Public Transportation	The **Department of Transportation** (tel. 313/933–1300) operates bus service throughout Detroit; the fare is $1. **Suburban Mobility Authority Regional Transportation** (tel. 313/962–5515) provides suburban bus service. The **People Mover** (tel. 313/224–2160) is an elevated, automated monorail that makes a 14-minute, 2.9-mi circuit of 13 downtown stations. Trains run about every three minutes; the fare is 50¢ (tokens are sold at each station).
By Taxi	The taxi fare is $1.10 at the flag drop, plus $1.10 per mile. Taxis can be ordered by phone or hired at stands at most major hotels. The two largest companies are **Checker Cab** (tel. 313/963–7000) and **City Cab** (tel. 313/833–7060).

Exploring Detroit

Starting from the Renaissance Center, on the banks of the river downtown, you can move outward to East Detroit, then on to the near Northwest side, the cultural heart of Detroit.

Downtown	Detroit's most prominent landmark, the big, brassy **Renaissance Center,** known as the Ren Cen, dominates the city's skyline with six office towers and the spectacular 73-story Westin Hotel, one of the tallest hotels in the world. This gleaming complex is a city within a city, with more than 90 retail stores, services, and restaurants. There's a People Mover stop right at the center.

Next to the Ren Cen is the **Old Mariner's Church** (tel. 313/259–2206), made famous in folksinger Gordon Lightfoot's song "The Wreck of the *Edmund Fitzgerald*." Adjacent to the church is the 75-acre **Civic Center,** a riverfront mecca for entertainment, festivals, and sporting activities. At the heart of the Civic Center is **Philip A. Hart Plaza,** designed by Isamu Noguchi. In warm weather, lunchtime crowds come to enjoy the open spaces, the sculpture, and the computer-controlled **Dodge Fountain.**

Two blocks north is **Cadillac Square,** site of many presidential speeches and the 1872 **Civil War Soldiers' and Sailors' Monument,** designed by Randolph Rogers, who created the bronze doors of the Capitol in Washington, D.C. Just west is the **Penobscot Building,** the state's tallest office tower. The blinking red light atop its 47 stories has been part of the Detroit skyline since 1928. Two blocks north, **Capitol Park** is the site of Michigan's first capitol. A statue of Steven T. Mason, the first governor, stands over his grave in the park.

A five-minute walk north is **Grand Circus Park,** envisioned as a full circus (circle) when Detroit was rebuilt after a disastrous fire in 1805; only half was completed. A fountain in the west park honors Thomas A. Edison.

Just to the southeast, along Monroe Street, is **Greektown,** one of Detroit's most popular entertainment districts, with markets, bars, coffeehouses, shops, boutiques, and restaurants serving authentic Greek fare with an American flair. At the center of Greektown is **Trappers Alley** (508 Monroe St.), once one of the Midwest's leading fur centers and today a shopping enclave, created by restoring, remodeling, and enclosing five century-old buildings under one roof. The complex contains some 50 shops and restaurants.

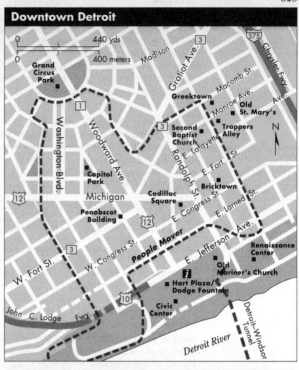

Downtown Detroit

Grand Circus Park
Madison
Gratiot Ave.
375
Greektown
Macomb St.
Monroe Ave.
Old St. Mary's
Washington Blvd.
Woodward Ave.
Second Baptist Church
Trappers Alley
Randolph St.
E. Lafayette
Capitol Park
Michigan
Cadillac Square
Bricktown
E. Fort St.
Penobscot Building
12
E. Congress St.
E. Larned St.
People Mover
3
W. Congress St.
E. Jefferson Ave.
Renaissance Center
W. Fort St.
Old Mariner's Church
Hart Plaza/ Dodge Fountain
10
Civic Center
John C. Lodge Fwy.
Chrysler Fwy.
Detroit-Windsor Tunnel
Detroit River

Greater Detroit

15
Oxford
Holly
24
53
New Baltimore
Clarkston
75
Auburn Hills
Rochester
94
Pontiac
Utica
59
Milford
59
Bloomfield Hills
Troy
Mt. Clemens
96
Cranbrook
Birmingham
1
Royal Oak
St. Clair Shores
Detroit Zoo
696
696
Roseville
Grosse Pointe Shores
Novi
Southfield
Harper Woods
Grosse Pointe
MICHIGAN
ONTARIO
Northville
Livonia
39
10
DETROIT
Lake St. Clair
96
275
University Cultural Center
Rivertown
Henry Ford Museum and Greenfield Village
Historic Ft. Wayne
SEE DOWNTOWN MAP
Ypsilanti
Dearborn
Windsor
12
Romulus
75
Lincoln Park
94
Detroit Metropolitan Wayne County Airport
24
ONTARIO CANADA
Amherstburg
Boblo Island
Detroit River

Close by, the **Second Baptist Church** (Monroe and Beaubien Sts.), organized in 1836, is Detroit's oldest black congregation. It was here that blacks gathered to celebrate the Emancipation Proclamation. **Old St. Mary's Catholic Church** (Monroe and St. Antoine Sts.), built in 1885, began as a parish of German and Irish immigrants in 1833.

Two blocks south of Greektown is **Bricktown,** a collection of dining spots and bars in a refurbished corner of downtown. Characterized by a multitude of brick facades, Bricktown is a good place for a leisurely lunch, a shopping spree, or cocktails.

East Detroit   In the 1880s the section east of the Renaissance Center, between the river and Jefferson Avenue, blossomed with lumberyards, shipyards, and railroads. Known as **Rivertown,** the area is seeing new life today—with parks, shops, restaurants, and night spots, set in rejuvenated warehouses and carriage houses. **Stroh River Place,** opened in 1988, has attracted new businesses, restaurants, and shops to a 21-acre site that stood empty for years.

Rivertown is the home of **Pewabic Pottery** (10125 E. Jefferson Ave., tel. 313/822–0954), founded in 1907, which produced the brilliantly glazed ceramic Pewabic tiles found in buildings throughout the nation. The pottery houses a ceramic museum, a contemporary gallery, a workshop, and a learning center.

Farmers and city slickers alike have gathered in the historic, open-air **Eastern Market** (2934 Russell St., tel. 313/833–1560) since 1892 to barter and bargain over fresh produce, meats, fish, and plants. Public shopping hours are Saturday 10–6; sales are in bulk only.

Near Northwest Detroit   The **University Cultural Center** is a world of art, history, and science clustered throughout some 40 city blocks 2½ mi from downtown via Woodward Avenue.

The **Children's Museum** (67 E. Kirby St., tel. 313/494–1210) has exhibits on everything from dolls and toys to birds and life in other cultures. A planetarium shows the night sky in Detroit and faraway lands. The **Detroit Historical Museum** (5401 Woodward Ave., tel. 313/833–1805) features "Collectors in Toyland," part of an ongoing exhibit of the Lawrence Scripps Wilkinson toy collection. The "Streets of Old Detroit" is a walk through the city's history from 1701.

The **Detroit Institute of Arts,** with more than 100 galleries, features 5,000 years of world-famous art treasures, including works by van Gogh, Rembrandt, and Renoir. Diego Rivera's *Detroit Industry,* four immense frescoes, is a must-see. *5200 Woodward Ave., tel. 313/833–7900. Donation suggested. Hours vary widely; call ahead.*

Home to 1.3 million books, the Cultural Center branch of the **Detroit Public Library** is the system's largest. Its Burton Historical Collection is the state's most comprehensive on Detroit, Michigan, and Great Lakes lore. *(5201 Woodward Ave., tel. 313/833–1000 or 313/833–1722 for recorded information). Closed Sun.–Mon.*

The **International Institute of Metropolitan Detroit** (111 E. Kirby St., tel. 313/871–8600) is a museum, a working social agency for the foreign-born, and a lunchtime café. Its "gallery of nations" features the arts and crafts of 43 countries. The **Mu-**

seum of **African-American History** (301 Frederick Douglass St., tel. 313/833–9800) tells the story of the black experience in America through exhibits and audiovisual presentations.

Other Attractions   Built along the river in 1843, **Historic Ft. Wayne** (6325 W. Jefferson Ave., tel. 313/297–9360) has costumed guides who tell the story of Detroit's military history. The fort is the home of the **Tuskegee Airmen Museum** and the **North American Indian Museum.**

Boblo Island, in the Detroit River between Michigan and Ontario, is a highly popular 272-acre amusement park featuring 75 rides, shows, revues, food stands, and restaurants. Ferries (90-minute ride) depart from Boblo Dock (I–75 SW to Clark Ave., Exit 47A; follow signs to dock). *4401 W. Jefferson Ave., tel. 313/843–8800. Admission (including transportation, rides, shows): $16.50 adults, $11.50 children. Closed Labor Day–late May.*

The **Detroit Zoological Park** (8450 W. 10 Mile Rd., Royal Oak, tel. 313/398–0903) features more than 1,200 animals from 300 species, displayed in natural environments without bars. Highlights include the world's largest penguinarium and a walk-through aviary with tropical birds and plants.

Dearborn's **Henry Ford Museum and Greenfield Village,** America's largest indoor-outdoor museum, details the country's evolution from a rural to an industrial society with exhibits covering communications, transportation, domestic life, agriculture, and industry. Greenfield Village preserves 80 famous historic structures, which include the bicycle shop where the Wright brothers built their first airplane, Thomas Edison's laboratory, an Illinois courthouse where Abraham Lincoln practiced law, and the Dearborn farm where Ford himself was born. A new exhibit, "The Automobile in American Life," is a lavish collection of chrome and neon that traces the country's love affair with cars. *20900 Oakwood Blvd., tel. 313/271–1620. Admission to each site: $11.50 adults, $5.75 children; combination ticket for both sites, $20 adults, $10 children. Village buildings closed Jan.–mid-Mar.*

Cranbrook, in Bloomfield Hills, is a cultural and educational center with a graduate art academy and college preparatory schools. Historic **Cranbrook House** (380 Lone Pine Rd., tel. 313/645–3149), a mansion built for newspaper publisher George Booth, features leaded-glass windows, art objects, and formal gardens with fountains and sculpture. **Cranbrook Academy of Art Museum** (500 Lone Pine Rd., tel. 313/645–3312) has major exhibitions of contemporary art and a permanent collection that includes works by Eliel and Eero Saarinen and Charles Eames. **Cranbrook Institute of Science** (550 Lone Pine Rd., tel. 313/645–3210) has intriguing hands-on physics experiments, geology displays, and dinosaur excavation exhibits.

Parks and Gardens

Belle Isle (tel. 313/267–7115), a thousand-acre island park in the Detroit River 3 mi southeast of the city center, is reached by way of East Jefferson Avenue and East Grand Boulevard. It offers woods, walking trails, outdoor sports facilities, a nine-hole golf course, and a half-mile-long beach.

Among Belle Isle's other attractions is the **Whitcomb Conservatory** (tel. 313/267–7134), with one of the largest orchid collections in the country. **Belle Isle Aquarium** (tel. 313/267–7159), the nation's oldest freshwater aquarium, exhibits more than 200 species of fish, reptiles, and amphibians. The **Belle Isle Nature Center** (tel. 313/267–7157) has changing exhibits and presentations on area nature. **Belle Isle Zoo** (tel. 313/267–7160; closed Nov.–Apr.) has an elevated walkway offering views of animals roaming in natural settings.

Also on Belle Isle, the **Dossin Great Lakes Museum** has displays about Great Lakes shipping and an ongoing exhibition, "The Storm of 1913," recalling the Great Lakes' worst-ever storm. Visitors can listen to ship-to-shore radio messages and view the river and city through a periscope. *100 Strand Dr., tel. 313/267–6440. Admission free. Closed Mon.–Tues., holidays.*

What to See and Do with Children

Many of Detroit's attractions will interest children, including the **People Mover** (*see* Getting Around Detroit, *above*); the **Children's Museum, Detroit Historical Museum,** and **Detroit Institute of Arts** (*see* Exploring Detroit, Near Northwest Detroit, *above*); **Boblo Island** amusement park, **Cranbrook Institute of Science, Detroit Zoological Park,** and **Henry Ford Museum and Greenfield Village** (*see* Exploring Detroit, Other Attractions, *above*); and **Belle Isle Aquarium, Nature Center,** and **Zoo** (*see* Parks and Gardens, *above*).

Shopping

Detroit's shops and stores are generally open Monday through Saturday from 10 to 6; many in the malls stay open until 9 PM. Some stores are open Sunday from noon to 5.

Shopping Districts The once fashionable downtown shopping district along Woodward Avenue is now largely a collection of eclectic boutiques. In the Renaissance Center is the **World of Shops,** with some 80 retail outlets. The shops of the new **Millender Center,** which can be reached by all-weather walkways from the Ren Cen or the City-County Building, include a bakery, a bank, beauty and barber shops, bookstores, and jewelers. **Trappers Alley Festival Marketplace,** in Greektown, has some 50 shops, food booths, and restaurants.

The **Eastern Market** (*see* Exploring Detroit, East Detroit, *above*) is open to the general public Saturday 10–6, and stores around it are open daily. The **New Center One Mall** (in the University Cultural Center) has weatherproof skywalks connecting its more than 50 stores, galleries, and restaurants to the Fisher Building, the General Motors Building, and the Hotel St. Regis. The **Somerset Collection,** in suburban Troy, has well-known upscale chains, such as **Neiman Marcus.**

Department Stores **Crowley's** (several locations, including in the New Center One Mall) is well-known for fashions for men, women, and children. **J. L. Hudson's** (eight metropolitan locations, including the Fairlane Town Mall in Dearborn) is a leader in fashion and home furnishings.

Spectator Sports

Baseball **Detroit Tigers** (Tiger Stadium, 2121 Trumbull Ave. at Michigan Ave., tel. 313/962–4000; Apr.–Oct.).

Basketball **Detroit Pistons** (The Palace of Auburn Hills, 2 Championship Dr., tel. 313/377–0100; Oct.–Apr.).

Football **Detroit Lions** (Pontiac Silverdome, Pontiac, 30 mi northwest of Detroit, tel. 313/335–4151; Sept.–Dec.).

Hockey **Detroit Red Wings** (Joe Louis Arena, downtown on the riverfront, tel. 313/567–6000; Oct.–Apr.).

Dining

By Jeremy Iggers The tremendous diversity of the Detroit restaurant scene may surprise first-time visitors. Each wave of immigrants to the city has made its culinary mark: You'll find soul-food restaurants in the inner city, a vibrant Mexican community on the west side, and Greek restaurants in Greektown. Detroiters often dine across the river in Windsor, Ontario, which boasts its own rich mix of ethnic restaurants (a favorable rate of exchange makes the Canadian restaurants excellent values). For price ranges, see Chart 1 (A) in Chapter 1.

Very Expensive ★ **Van Dyke Place.** The evening ritual at this restored turn-of-the-century mansion starts with dinner in main-floor dining rooms, followed by dessert and coffee in the upstairs drawing rooms. The menu offers such dishes as roast boneless quail in a potato nest. *649 Van Dyke Ave., tel. 313/821–2620. Reservations advised. Jacket and tie advised. AE, MC, V. No lunch Sat.; closed Sun.*

★ **The Whitney.** This former mansion of lumber baron David Whitney has been transformed into one of Detroit's most opulent restaurants. The imaginative, eclectic menu ranges from lobster and salmon in brioche to chicken pot pie. *4421 Woodward Ave., tel. 313/832–5700. Reservations advised. Jacket and tie advised. AE, D, MC, V. No lunch Sat.–Thurs.*

Expensive **The Caucus Club.** This venerable Detroit institution is a period piece from the era when elegant restaurants had boardroom decor, with lots of oil paintings and wood. The menu is of similar vintage: corned-beef hash, steaks, chops, Dover sole, and famous baby-back ribs. *150 W. Congress St., tel. 313/965–4970. Reservations advised. Jacket and tie advised. AE, MC, V. Closed Sun.*

MacKinnon's. The countrified decor at this charming restaurant imitates nature. The menu features experimental and often outstanding fish and game dishes, such as charcoal-grilled duck and ginger-barbecued shrimp. *126 E. Main St., Northville, tel. 313/348–1991. Reservations advised. Jacket and tie advised. AE, D, MC, V. Closed Sun.*

The Rattlesnake Club. Superchef Jimmy Schmidt's menu offers innovative treatments of pickerel, salmon, and veal, as well as the club's signature rack of lamb. The decor is contemporary in marble and rosewood, with terrific views of the Detroit River and Windsor skyline. *300 River Pl., tel. 313/567–4400. Reservations advised. Jacket and tie required in main dining room; grill, casual. AE, D, MC, V. Closed Sun.*

The Summit. This revolving restaurant on the 71st floor of the Westin Hotel has a superb view of Detroit. The menu includes charbroiled steaks and swordfish la Louisiana. *Renaissance Center, tel. 313/568–8600. Reservations advised. Jacket and tie advised. AE, D, MC, V.*

Moderate **Blue Nile.** Silverware is optional when you dine Ethiopian
★ style; richly seasoned meats and vegetables are served on communal trays covered with *injera*, a pancakelike flat bread, chunks of which are torn off to be used as scoops for the other foods. The simple but stylish casual decor features Ethiopian handicrafts. *Trappers Alley, 508 Monroe St., tel. 313/964–6699. Reservations advised. AE, DC, MC, V.*

Fishbone's Rhythm Kitchen Cafe. What could be more cosmopolitan than an authentic New Orleans–style restaurant in the heart of Greektown? Like New Orleans itself, Fishbone's is loud, brash, funky, and fun. Seasonal offerings on the spicy Creole menu include gator, gumbo, crawfish, and Gulf oysters on the half shell. The best year-round bet is the whiskey ribs. *400 Monroe St., tel. 313/965–4600. AE, D, DC, MC, V. No dinner (brunch only) Sun.*

Giovanni's Ristorante. This popular west-side family eatery sits in the dingy shadows of the Ford Rouge plant, which accounts for its comforting lack of pretension. Inside, the sounds of opera and the smell of garlic and marinara provide a perfect backdrop to such dishes as *manicotti verde pomadore* (herbed ricotta wrapped in spinach pasta and bathed in a sweet tomato sauce). *330 Oakwood Blvd., tel. 313/841–0122. Reservations suggested. AE, MC, V. No lunch Sat.; closed Sun.–Mon.*

★ **Lelli's Inn.** When Detroiters think Italian, Lelli's comes to mind. Although the decor (festoons of Christmas lights) hasn't changed in years and the waiters can be brash, the minestrone and steak Lelli are hard to beat. *7618 Woodward Ave., tel. 313/871–1590. Jacket and tie advised. AE, DC, MC, V. No dinner Mon.*

Les Auteurs. Talented chef Keith Famie pays homage to the giants of the culinary world in the decor of his trendy and popular suburban café. His ever-changing menus may offer black-bean cake studded with smoked turkey, or gourmet pizzas. *222 Sherman Dr., Washington Sq. Plaza, Royal Oak, tel. 313/544–2887. AE, MC, V. Closed Sun.*

Inexpensive **Maxie's Left Field Deli.** The decor badly needs a face-lift, but
★ the cops and robbers, judges and vagrants, who congregate at the counter of Max Silk's deli could care less. They're there for Max's sandwiches and superb homemade soups, and to shoot the breeze with the legendary octogenarian owner. *1266 Michigan Ave., tel. 313/961–7968. No credit cards. No dinner; closed Sun.*

Pegasus Taverna. Popular with the throngs who visit Greektown, the Pegasus menu includes such staples as moussaka, pastitsio, roast leg of lamb, stuffed grape leaves, and baklava. The Greektown experience isn't complete without an order of *saganaki* (flaming kasseri cheese ignited tableside) and a little retsina or ouzo to drink. *558 Monroe St., tel. 313/964–6800. Reservations advised. AE, D, DC, MC, V.*

Traffic Jam & Snug. No detail of hospitality is neglected at this charmingly funky hangout near the Wayne State campus. The wide-ranging menu includes an exotic selection of breads, cheeses, ice creams, sausages, and even hamburgers. *511 W. Canfield St., tel. 313/831–9470. No reservations. MC, V. No dinner Sun., Mon.; no lunch weekends.*

Under the Eagle. Typical of Detroit's modestly priced little Polish cafés, the cooking at the Eagle is first-rate, with generous portions of stick-to-the-ribs roast duckling and kielbasa. For the adventuresome, there's *czarnina* (duck-blood soup). *9000 Joseph Campau St., tel. 313/875–5950. No credit cards. Closed Wed.*

★ **Wah Court.** Across the river in Windsor, Ontario, is this popular no-frills Cantonese restaurant. The menu is full of such offerings as pork and duck in hot pot. Dim sum, the traditional Chinese tea snacks, are served daily, with the biggest selection on Sunday. *2037 Wyandotte Ave. W, Windsor, tel. 519/254–1388. No reservations. MC, V.*

Lodging

Accommodations in and around the Motor City range from the pricey high-rise room-with-a-view to the more moderate and closer to the ground. Downtown, near the Renaissance Center and Civic Center, you'll find Detroit's luxury mega-hotels. Accommodations in suburban Troy, with its high concentration of corporate businesses, and Dearborn, where the Ford Motor Company has its headquarters, are quickly and easily reached by freeways and expressways. Most of the hotels, motels, and inns offer reduced-price weekend packages. For price ranges, see Chart 2 (A) in Chapter 1.

Very Expensive **Hotel St. Regis.** The St. Regis has slipped a notch in service, but its convenient location (one block from the Fisher Theater and G.M. headquarters) guarantees the patronage of well known entertainers and business execs. The guest rooms are light, roomy, and tastefully decorated with simple modern furniture. The hotel is linked by skywalks to a shopping and office complex. *3071 W. Grand Blvd., 48202, tel. 313/873–3000 or 800/333–3333; fax 313/873–3000, ext. 7116. 221 rooms. Facilities: restaurant, lounge, health club, valet parking. AE, D, DC, MC, V.*

★ **Hyatt Regency Dearborn.** Opposite Ford's world headquarters, this large hotel is only five minutes from the Henry Ford Museum and Greenfield Village. Its public spaces are attractive, and many of its rooms have been renovated recently. *Fairlane Town Center, Dearborn 48126, tel. 313/593–1234; fax 313/593–3366. 771 rooms. Facilities: 2 restaurants, coffee shop, lounge, indoor pool, sauna, valet parking. AE, D, DC, MC, V.*

★ **Omni International.** One of Detroit's newest hotels, the Omni is connected by skywalk to the Renaissance Center. The rooms are bright, large, and decorated in soothing blues and whites, with luxurious furniture. *333 E. Jefferson Ave., 48226, tel. 313/222–7700; fax 313/222–6509. 253 rooms. Facilities: restaurant, lounge, indoor pool, sauna, health club, 2 tennis courts, racquetball court, concierge, valet parking, People Mover station. AE, D, DC, MC, V.*

★ **Radisson Hotel Pontchartrain.** The Pontch, as it is familiarly known, is tastefully decorated with neutral shades accented by green-and-rose fabrics. The light, airy rooms all have wonderful views of the city and the river; do not, however, accept a room at the back of the hotel—which is across the street from the fire station—unless you are a heavy sleeper. *2 Washington Blvd., 48226, tel. 313/965–0200 or 800/537–6624; fax 313/965–9464. 414 rooms. Facilities: restaurant, lounge, concierge, heated outdoor pool, health club, complimentary limo service in city. AE, DC, MC, V.*

★ **Ritz-Carlton, Dearborn.** Since opening in 1989, the Ritz has acquired a reputation for impeccable taste and service. Its mahogany-paneled walls, overstuffed settees, Chinese jardinieres, and antique art suggest a clubby, "olde English" elegance. Reinforcing that image is a traditional afternoon high tea and hors d'oeuvres served in the lobby lounge. *300 Town Center Dr., Dearborn 48126, tel. 313/441–2000; fax 313/441–2051. 308 rooms. Facilities: restaurant, grill, bar, indoor pool, sauna, fitness center. AE, D, DC, MC, V.*

★ **The Westin Hotel.** At 73 stories, this hotel is best summed up as mega-big with mega-buck prices. The rooms are neither large nor special, but each commands a waterfront view of the city and neighboring Windsor, Ontario. The lobby is sumptuously decorated in granite, marble, brass, and earth tones. *Renaissance Center, Jefferson Ave. at Randolph St., 48243, tel. 313/568–8000; fax 313/568–8666. Facilities: restaurant, lounge, indoor pool, health club, outdoor jogging track, valet parking. AE, D, DC, MC, V.*

Expensive **Dearborn Inn and Marriott Hotel.** Across from the Henry Ford Museum and Greenfield Village, this property features five replicas of historic Colonial homes, honoring such famous Americans as Patrick Henry, Edgar Allan Poe, and Walt Whitman. *20301 Oakwood Blvd., Dearborn 48124, tel. 313/271–2700; fax 313/271–7464. 222 rooms. Facilities: 2 restaurants, lounge, outdoor pool, 2 tennis courts. AE, DC, MC, V.*

Moderate– **Guest Quarters.** This suite hotel is a feast for the eyes, with an
Expensive eight-story atrium full of trees, flowers, ivy, a small fountain, and a miniwaterfall. All the decor, from carpeting to upholstery to café tablecloths, combines to create an outdoorsy ambience. A complimentary full American breakfast is served. *850 Tower Dr., Troy 48098, tel. 313/879–7500; fax 313/879–9139. 251 suites. Facilities: café, lounge, indoor pool, health club. AE, D, DC, MC, V.*

Mayflower Bed and Breakfast Hotel. The rooms have a homey atmosphere with lots of prints and pastels; some have whirlpool baths. Guests receive a complimentary full breakfast, and shopping, golf, and cross-country skiing are nearby. *827 W. Ann Arbor Trail, Plymouth 48170, tel. 313/453–1620; fax 313/453–0075. 100 rooms. Facilities: 3 restaurants, lounge. AE, D, DC, MC, V.*

Somerset Inn. This inn 25 mi north of Detroit in the heart of Troy's corporate district is a favorite with the business set. Guest rooms are rather small and standard, but the entry level is lovely, with marble floors, greenery, and several small sitting rooms tucked around the perimeter. *2601 W. Big Beaver Rd., Troy 48084, tel. 313/643–7800 or 800/228–8769; fax 313/643–2296. 250 rooms. Facilities: restaurant, bar, 2 pools, health club. AE, DC, MC, V.*

Moderate **The Drury Inn.** Decorated mostly in earth tones, the spacious rooms include brick and stucco walls and neat and clean modern furnishings, including fabric-covered tub chairs. The hotel offers a complimentary breakfast buffet. *575 W. Big Beaver Rd., Troy 48084, tel. 313/528–3330 or 800/325–8300; fax 313/528–3330, ext. 479. 154 rooms. Facilities: outdoor pool. AE, D, DC, MC, V.*

Shorecrest Motor Inn. This pleasant, no frills two-story hotel is conveniently located two blocks east of the Renaissance Center and within walking distance of downtown attractions. *1316 E.*

Jefferson Ave., 48207, tel. 313/568–3000 or 800/992–9616; fax 313/568–3002, ext. 260. 54 rooms. Facilities: restaurant. AE, DC, MC, V.

The Arts and Nightlife

The Arts *Detroit Monthly* has a comprehensive calendar of events, as does *Metro Times*, a free weekly tabloid available in downtown stores. Also check the arts sections of the *Detroit News* and *Free Press.*

Attic Theater (7339 3rd Ave., tel. 313/875–8284) presents Off-Broadway plays and works by new playwrights. **Detroit Repertory Theater** (13103 Woodrow Wilson Ave., tel. 313/868–1347) is one of the city's oldest resident professional theater companies. Touring Broadway shows and nationally known entertainers appear at the **Fisher Theater** (3011 W. Grand Blvd., tel. 313/872–1000) and the opulent **Fox Theater** (2211 Woodward Ave., tel. 313/567–6000). **Orchestra Hall** (3177 Woodward Ave., tel. 313/833–3700) is home to the **Chamber Music Society of Detroit** and the **Detroit Symphony.**

Nightlife Much of Detroit's nightlife is centered in the downtown area. In Greektown, tourists crowd the **Bouzouki Lounge** (432 E. Lafayette St., tel. 313/964–5744) to see and hear traditional Greek music, folksingers, and belly dancers. **Baker's Keyboard Lounge** (20510 Livernois Ave., tel. 313/864–1200), a dimly lit, smoke-filled jazz club, is a Detroit institution.

In Rivertown, the **Soup Kitchen Saloon** (1585 Franklin St., tel. 313/259–2643) is the home of the Detroit blues. **The Rhinoceros Restaurant** (265 Riopelle St., tel. 313/259–2208) and **Woodbridge Tavern** (289 St. Aubin, tel. 313/259–0578) are former speakeasies where downtown professionals loosen their ties and stomp their feet. Poetry readings, art exhibitions, and nononsense live acts give **Alvin's** (5756 Cass St., tel. 313/832–2355) a bohemian appeal, especially among students at nearby Wayne State University.

Elsewhere in the State

Mackinac Island

Getting There By car, take I–75N from Detroit to Mackinaw City. Island ferries depart from Mackinaw City and St. Ignace, at the north end of the Mackinac Bridge.

What to See and Do No autos are allowed on **Mackinac Island** (island, town, and straits all pronounced "MACK-i-naw"), but the quaint Victorian village begs to be explored on foot. A small park at the east end of the village, along the boardwalk, offers terrific views of the Mackinac Bridge and ships passing through the straits. Farther afield, 8 mi of paved roads circle the island; bicycles rent by the hour or day at concessions near the ferry docks on Huron Street. **Mackinac Island Carriage Tours** (Main St., tel. 906/847–3573) offer horse-drawn tours covering historic points of interest, including Ft. Mackinac, Arch Rock, Skull Cave, Surrey Hill, and the Grand Hotel.

Old Ft. Mackinac (tel. 906/847–3328), perched on a bluff above the harbor, was a British stronghold during the American Revolution and the War of 1812. Fourteen original buildings are preserved as a museum; costumed guides offer tours and reenactments. **Marquette Park,** directly below the fort along Main Street, commemorates the work of French missionary Jacques Marquette with a bark chapel patterned after those built on the island in the 1600s. The venerable **Grand Hotel** (tel. 906/847–3331), now more than a century old, charges visitors $5 just to look, but the Victorian opulence of the public rooms and the view from the world's longest porch is worth it. **Mackinac Island Chamber of Commerce** (Box 451, Mackinac Island 49757, tel. 906/847–3783) provides information on island attractions.

Keweenaw Peninsula

Getting There The Keweenaw, in the northwestern Upper Peninsula, is reached by U.S. 41.

What to See and Do Curving into Lake Superior like a crooked finger, the Keweenaw ("KEY-wa-naw") was the site of extensive copper mining from the 1840s to the 1960s. The deposits were exceptionally pure, and in its heyday the Keweenaw produced much of the world's copper. In **Hancock,** the **Arcadian Copper Mine** (tel. 906/482–7502) has a ¼-mi guided tour of workings no longer in operation. **Houghton** is home to Michigan Technical University, whose **E. A. Seaman Mineralogical Museum** (tel. 906/487–2572) has extensive displays of minerals native to the Upper Peninsula. The inland headquarters of **Isle Royale National Park** (*see* National and State Parks, *above*) are also in Houghton.

North on U.S. 41, the Victorian stone architecture in **Calumet** gives just a hint of the wealth in the copper towns during the boom days. The **Calumet Theater** (tel. 906/337–2610), built in 1910, was the stage for such stars as Lillian Russell, Sarah Bernhardt, and Douglas Fairbanks, Sr. At **Coppertown, U.S.A.** (tel. 906/337–4354), a visitor center tells the story of the mines, towns, and people of the Keweenaw. Farther north, in the old mining town of **Delaware, Delaware Copper Mine Tours** (tel. 906/289–4688) provides guided walking tours through the first level of a 145-year-old mine.

At the tip of the peninsula, **Copper Harbor,** Michigan's northernmost community, is a popular spot with campers. **Ft. Wilkins State Park** (tel. 906/289–4215) contains the restored buildings of an Army post established in 1844 and abandoned in 1870. The complex also has copper-mine shafts, hiking trails, and campgrounds. **Brockway Mountain Drive** climbs 900 feet above Copper Harbor to provide magnificent views of the peninsula and Lake Superior. **Keweenaw Tourism Council** (326 Shelden Ave., Houghton 49931, tel. 906/482–2388 or 800/338–7982) provides information on peninsula attractions.

Lake Michigan Shore

Getting There U.S. 31 edges Lake Michigan from St. Joseph to Mackinaw City.

What to See and Do The Lake Michigan shoreline, which extends from the southwest corner of the state up to the Mackinac Bridge, is one of Michigan's greatest natural resources. Its placid waters, cool breezes, and sugary beaches (including some of the largest sand dunes in the world) have attracted generations of tourists, including such regulars as Al Capone, Ernest Hemingway, and L. Frank Baum (who wrote many of his *Wizard of Oz* books over the course of several summer vacations).

Resort towns, some of which triple in population between Memorial Day and Labor Day, dot the shoreline. **St. Joseph** is a picturesque community whose turn-of-the-century downtown and two 1,000-foot-long piers make it ideal for walkers. The artists' colony of **Saugatuck** has many fine restaurants and shops, an active gay and lesbian community, and B&Bs enough to be considered the bed-and-breakfast capital of the state. **Saugatuck Dune Rides** (tel. 616/857–2253) offers freewheeling dune-buggy rides along Lake Michigan. In neighboring **Douglas**, the S.S. *Keewatin* (tel. 616/857–2151), one of the Great Lakes' last classic passenger steamboats, is permanently docked as a maritime museum.

Nearby is **Holland**, home of the famous **Tulip Time Festival** (tel. 616/396–4221), held for 10 days each May. **The De Klomp Wooden Shoe and Delftware Factory** (12755 Quincy St., tel. 616/399–1900) is the only place outside the Netherlands where earthenware is hand-painted and fired using Delft-blue glaze.

Farther north is the eastern shore's largest city, **Muskegon**. More than a Rust Belt relic, this industrial town offers the **Muskegon Winter Sports Complex** (tel. 616/744–9629), with the Midwest's only luge run. **The Frauenthal Center for the Performing Arts** (417 W. Western St., tel. 616/722–4538) is a gaudy art deco theater that is home to traveling Broadway-quality plays, silent-film showings, the West Shore Symphony Orchestra, and the Miss Michigan Pageant. Eight miles north of town is **Michigan's Adventure Amusement Park** (Russell Rd. exit off U.S. 31, tel. 616/766–3377), with more than 20 thrill rides, 10 water slides, a wave pool, shows, games, food, and the only two roller coasters in Michigan.

A two-hour drive north of Muskegon is **Traverse City**, the state's premier sports-vacation spot. Much to the chagrin of longtime residents, the area south of Grand Traverse Bay was "discovered" by sportsmen—and developers—about 25 years ago. Unfortunately, the roads have not kept pace with the boom in sailors, golfers, and skiers. The two-lane highways can resemble parking lots, particularly during the popular **National Cherry Festival** (tel. 616/947–1120), which draws an estimated 400,000 people each summer. For a pleasant diversion, follow Rte. 37 around the **Old Mission Peninsula,** filled with the cherry orchards and vineyards that, next to tourism, are the area's main industry. Spring, when crowds are low and the orchards are in bloom, is a good time to visit.

Some of the finest views of Lake Michigan are found farther north. Follow Rte. 119 between **Harbor Springs,** a resort village overlooking Little Traverse Bay, and **Cross Village,** where the **Chief Andrew J. Blackbird Museum** (tel. 616/526–7731) houses a collection of Ottawa and Ojibwa Native American artifacts. The **West Michigan Tourist Association** (136 E. Fulton St., Grand Rapids 49503, tel. 616/456–8557) provides information on lakeside attractions.

MINNESOTA

*By Don
Davenport*

*Updated by Gene
Rebeck*

Capital	St. Paul
Population	4,307,000
Motto	Star of the North
State Bird	Common loon
State Flower	Showy lady's slipper

Visitor Information

Minnesota Office of Tourism (375 Jackson St., 250 Skyway Level, St. Paul 55101, tel. 612/296–5029 or 800/657–3700). There are 11 visitor centers around the state.

Scenic Drives

U.S. 61, along the Mississippi River between Red Wing and Winona, is often compared with the Rhine Valley in beauty; between Duluth and the Canadian border, it hugs the edge of Lake Superior for 160 mi, providing spectacular views of the lake and its rocky shoreline. **Rte. 59,** between Fergus Falls and Detroit Lakes, traverses some of central Minnesota's prime lake country.

National and State Parks

National Parks **Voyageurs National Park** (*see* Elsewhere in the State, The Iron Range and Boundary Waters, *below*), in far northern Minnesota near International Falls, has 30 major lakes and is part of the watery highway that makes up the state's northern border with Canada.

State Parks Minnesota has 65 state parks, 51 of which offer camping facilities that vary from modern to primitive sites. For information, contact the **Department of Natural Resources** (DNR Information Center, 500 Lafayette Rd., Box 40, St. Paul 55155, tel. 612/296–6157).

Ft. Snelling State Park, just south of downtown St. Paul (Rte. 5 and Post Rd., St. Paul, tel. 612/725–2340), preserves the historic fort built at the junction of the Mississippi and Minnesota rivers in 1819. **Itasca State Park** (U.S. 71 and Rte. 92, Lake Itasca 56460, tel. 218/266–3654) is Minnesota's oldest state park, established in 1891 to protect the headwaters of the Mississippi River, which rises from Lake Itasca. **Tower-Soudan State Park** (Rte. 169, Soudan 55782, tel. 218/753–2245) offers hiking trails and tours of the Soudan Mine, Minnesota's oldest and largest iron mine, which operated until 1962. **Gooseberry Falls State Park** (1300 U.S. 61E, Two Harbors 55616, tel. 218/834–3855) and **Temperance River State Park** (U.S. 61E, Schroeder 55613, tel. 218/663–7476), with roaring waterfalls and scenic vistas, are typical of parks found along Lake Superior's shore.

Minneapolis and St. Paul

Drawing comparisons between Minneapolis and St. Paul is much like comparing two favorite aunts—a difficult task. St. Paul has a slightly reserved air about it; Minneapolis is brasher, noisier, and busier. Both cities have tall, gleaming glass skylines; St. Paul's is designed to blend with the city's art deco and Victorian architecture, while Minneapolis's is more eclectic. St. Paul has preserved much of its architectural heritage, while most of downtown Minneapolis is new. Both cities straddle the Mississippi River, and riverboat traffic calls at the Twin Cities from as far away as New Orleans.

There are 2.2 million people in the Greater Minneapolis/St. Paul metro region, but Minneapolis wins the population race by 90,000. The strong Scandinavian strain in the cities' ancestry has not prevented them from constructing miles-long skyway systems. Residents can drive downtown, park, walk to work, go to lunch, shop, see a show, and return to their car without once setting foot outdoors—a blessing in the blustery Minnesota winters.

Tourist Information

Minneapolis: Convention and Visitors Association (1219 Marquette Ave., Suite 300, 55403, tel. 612/348–4313). **St. Paul:** Convention and Visitors Bureau (55 E. 5th St., 55101, tel. 612/297–6985 or 800/627–6101). Visitor information booths: St. Paul Center (445 Minnesota St., tel. 612/223–5409), State Capitol (75 Constitution Ave., tel. 612/296–3962), Science Museum (30 E. 10th St., tel. 612/221–9454), Landmark Center (75 W. 5th St., tel. 612/292–3225), and City Hall/Courthouse (4th and Wabasha Sts., tel. 612/298–4012).

Arriving and Departing

By Plane **Minneapolis/St. Paul International Airport** (tel. 612/726–5555) lies between the cities on I–494, 8 mi south of downtown St. Paul and 10 mi south of downtown Minneapolis. It is served by most major domestic airlines and several foreign carriers. From the airport to either city, **Metropolitan Transit Commission** (tel. 612/827–7733) buses cost $1.10; taxis take about 30 minutes and charge $17–$20 to downtown Minneapolis and $12–$14 to St. Paul.

By Car The major north–south route through the area is I–35, which divides into I–35W bisecting Minneapolis and I–35E through St. Paul. I–94 goes east–west through both cities. A beltway circles the Twin Cities, with I–494 looping through the southern suburbs and I–694 cutting through the north.

Train Station St. Paul's **Amtrak** station (730 Transfer Rd., tel. 612/644–1127) serves both cities.

Bus Station **Greyhound** has stations in St. Paul (25 W. 7th St., tel. 612/222–0509) and in Minneapolis (29 N. 9th St., tel. 612/371–3311).

Getting Around Minneapolis and St. Paul

Both cities are laid out on a grid, with streets running north–south and east–west. However, many downtown streets parallel the Mississippi River and run on a diagonal, and not all streets cross the river. Both downtowns have extensive skywalk systems. Many St. Paul attractions can be reached on foot, but most of those in Minneapolis require wheels. Express fare on **Metropolitan Transit Commission** (tel. 612/827–7733) buses between Minneapolis and St. Paul during rush hour is $1.35. Within each city's central business district the fare is 25¢. Outside the downtown area the fare is 85¢, $1.10 during peak hours (6–9 AM and 3:30–6:30 PM). Children under six ride free.

Cabs must be ordered by phone or hired at cabstands. The fare is about $3 for the first 1¼ mi and approximately $1.20 for each additional mi. The largest taxi firms in St. Paul are **Yellow** (tel. 612/222–4433) and **City Wide** (tel. 612/292–1616); in Minneapolis, **Blue and White** (tel. 612/333–3331) and **Yellow** (tel. 612/824–4444). **Town Taxi** (tel. 612/331–8294) serves both cities and all suburbs.

Exploring Minneapolis and St. Paul

Minneapolis **Downtown** Minneapolis is easily walkable in any season. The climate-controlled skyway system connects hundreds of shops and restaurants. In general, skyways remain open during the business hours of the buildings they connect.

At the eastern edge of downtown are the Mississippi River's **Falls of St. Anthony,** discovered by Father Louis Hennepin three centuries ago. Harnessed by dams and diminished in grandeur, the historic falls are today bypassed by the **Upper St. Anthony Lock** (foot of Portland Ave.), which allows river traffic to reach industrial sections of Minneapolis. An observation deck provides views of lock operations.

Just north of the Mississippi, the **University of Minnesota,** with an enrollment of more than 50,000, has the fourth-largest campus in the country. **Dinkytown,** on the east bank, is an area of campus bars, night spots, university shops, and record and book stores. **Seven Corners,** on the west bank, features the **West Bank Theater District,** with popular after-hours hangouts, theaters, and more night spots.

The university's **James Ford Bell Museum of Natural History** (University Ave. SE at 17th Ave., tel. 612/624–7083) has dioramas of Minnesota wildlife, a wildlife-art gallery, and a "Touch and See" room where youngsters can handle the skins, bones, and skulls of a variety of animals. The **University Art Museum** (84 Church St. SE, tel. 612/624–9876) features student and faculty work and a permanent collection of American art from 1900 to 1950.

Several blocks west is downtown Minneapolis, much of it built in the past 25 years. Two of the more recent additions are the 57-story **Norwest Center** (77 S. 7th St.), designed by Cesar Pelli, and its smaller companion, **Gaviidae Common** (651 Nicollet Mall), the latest downtown shopping mecca. The mirrored, 51-story **IDS Building** (80 S. 8th St.) contains **Crystal Court,** a focal point of the skyway system, with shops, restaurants, and offices. The 42-story **Piper Jaffray Tower** (222 S. 9th St.), sheathed in aqua glass, and the 17-story **Lutheran Brotherhood Building** (625 4th Ave. SE), dressed in copper-colored glass, are sparkling additions to the skyline. At the **Foshay**

Downtown Minneapolis

Greater Minneapolis

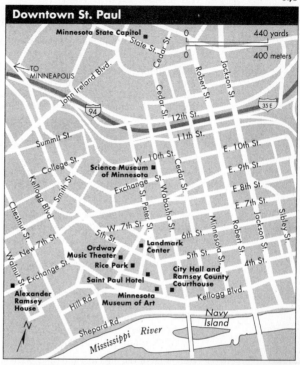

Downtown St. Paul

Minnesota State Capitol

0 — 440 yards
0 — 400 meters

State St.
Cedar St.
Jackson St.

TO MINNEAPOLIS
John Ireland Blvd.
94
35 E

Cedar St.
12th St.
11th St.
E. 10th St.
E. 9th St.
E. 8th St.
E. 7th St.

Summit St.
College St.
Smith St.
Science Museum of Minnesota
W. 10th St.
Cedar St.
Exchange St.
Wabasha St.
St. Peter St.

Chestnut St.
Walnut St.
New 7th St.
W. 7th St.
5th St.
6th St.
Minnesota St.
Robert St.
Jackson St.
Sibley St.

Exchange St.
Ordway Music Theater
Landmark Center
5th St.
4th St.

Rice Park
Saint Paul Hotel
City Hall and Ramsey County Courthouse

Alexander Ramsey House
Hill Rd.
Minnesota Museum of Art
Kellogg Blvd.

Shepard Rd.
Navy Island

Mississippi River

Greater St. Paul

Como Lake
Como Park

0 — 2 miles
0 — 3 km

Cottage Ave.
55
10
Clear Ave.

Jessamine Ave.
Maryland Ave.
31
49
Jackson St.
Mississippi St.
Westminster St.
Edgerton St.
31

Front Ave.
Children's Museum
Como Ave.
Rice St.
Rose St.

Hamline Ave.
Hubbard Ave.
Wilder Ave.
53
35 E

University Ave.
SEE DOWNTOWN MAP

Lexington Pkwy.
Victoria St.
N. Dale St.
94
Wabasha St.
Jackson St.
5
Kellogg Blvd.

TO MINNEAPOLIS
Cathedral of St. Paul
Summit Ave.
35 E
Navy Island
Lafayette Fwy.

Goodrich Ave.
Jefferson Ave.
W. 7th St.
Plato Blvd.
52

Hamline Ave.
Randolph Ave.
5
W. George St.
Hall Ave
Robert St.

Historic Ft. Snelling
Minneapolis-St. Paul International Airport
Mississippi River
W. Water St.
Smith Ave.
Minnesota Zoological Gardens
Annapolis St.
13

Tower (821 Marquette Ave., tel. 612/341–2522)—Minneapolis's first skyscraper, constructed in 1929—a 31st-floor observation deck provides spectacular views of the city April–October.

In the public library on **Nicollet Mall**—a mile-long pedestrian mall, running from 2nd Street to Grant Avenue, with an extensive system of skywalks connecting many shops—the **Minneapolis Planetarium** (tel. 612/372–6644) offers sky shows that tour the night sky and investigate the latest discoveries in space science.

Another downtown landmark, the inflated **Hubert H. Humphrey Metrodome** (900 S. 5th St., tel. 612/332–0386) is home to the Minnesota Twins baseball team and the Minnesota Vikings and University of Minnesota football teams. Behind-the-scenes tours of locker rooms, playing field, and press box are available.

A mile south of downtown, and west of I–35W, the **Minneapolis Institute of Arts** displays more than 80,000 works of art from every age and culture, including works by the French Impressionists, rare Chinese jade, and a photography collection ranging from 1863 to the present. *2400 3rd Ave. S, tel. 612/870–3131. Admission free. Closed Mon.*

Five blocks east, the **American Swedish Institute** (2600 Park Ave., tel. 612/871–4907) is set in a 33-room Romanesque château filled with decorative woodwork. The museum houses collections of art, pioneer items, Swedish glass, ceramics, and furniture relating to the area's Swedish heritage.

Just west of Loring Park and the I–94 loop, the **Walker Art Center** houses an outstanding collection of 20th-century American and European sculpture, prints, and photography. The Walker's **Minneapolis Sculpture Garden** is the largest outdoor urban sculpture garden in the nation. *725 Vineland Pl., adjoining the Guthrie Theater, tel. 612/375–7600. Admission charged. Closed Mon., holidays.*

St. Paul You can easily explore downtown St. Paul on foot, walking either on the streets or through the all-weather, climate-controlled skyway system. Keep in mind that the Mississippi makes a huge loop and runs east–west through St. Paul.

The **Minnesota Museum of Art** (305 St. Peter St., tel. 612/292–4355), in the Art Deco Jemne Building, has a permanent collection strong in Asian and 19th- and 20th-century American art, along with changing exhibits of contemporary sculpture, paintings, and photography.

Nearby, in a 20-story building of a design known as American Perpendicular, is the **City Hall and Ramsey County Courthouse** (15 W. Kellogg Blvd., tel. 612/298–4012). Here, Memorial Hall (4th St. entrance) features Swedish sculptor Carl Milles's towering *God of Peace* statue, the largest carved-onyx figure in the world, standing 36 feet high and weighing 60 tons.

Two blocks west is **Rice Park,** St. Paul's oldest urban park, dating from 1849. A favorite with downtowners, who eat lunch here in warm weather, it is an excellent place in which to stop and enjoy the flavor of the city. Facing the park on the north is the **Landmark Center** (75 W. 5th St., tel. 612/292–3225), the restored Old Federal Courts Building, constructed in 1902. The towering Romanesque Revival structure features a six-story indoor courtyard, stained-glass skylights, and a marble-tile foyer. Housed within are the offices of many of St. Paul's cultural organizations; a branch of the **Minnesota Museum of Art;** and the **Schubert Club Musical Instrument Museum** (tel. 612/ 292–3268), with an outstanding collection of keyboard instruments dating from the 1700s.

On the east side of the park is the luxurious **Saint Paul Hotel** (*see* Lodging, *below*), which hosts notables from presidents to Hollywood stars. On the south side is the block-long Italian Renaissance Revival **St. Paul Public Library.** Rice Park's most recent addition is the **Ordway Music Theater** (*see* The Arts and Nightlife, *below*), a state-of-the-art auditorium with faceted-glass walls set in a facade of brick and copper.

West of the park is the **Alexander Ramsey House,** home of the first governor of the Minnesota Territory. Built in 1872, the restored French Second Empire mansion has 15 rooms containing marble fireplaces, period furnishings, and rich collections of china and silver. *265 Exchange St., tel. 612/296–8681. Admission charged. Closed Jan.–Mar.*

North of Rice Park is the **Science Museum of Minnesota,** a favorite with both local and visiting youngsters. There are exhibits on archaeology, technology, and biology; the Physical Sciences and Technology Gallery offers many exciting hands-on exhibits. In the McKnight Omnitheater, 70-mm films are projected overhead on a massive tilted screen. *30 E. 10th St., tel. 612/221–9488. Admission charged. Closed Mon. Labor Day–Easter.*

The **Minnesota State Capitol,** to the northwest, designed by the St. Paul architect Cass Gilbert, contains more than 25 varieties of marble, sandstone, and granite. Its 223-foot-high dome is the world's largest unsupported marble dome. *University Ave. between Aurora and Cedar Sts., tel. 612/296–2881. Admission free.*

The **Cathedral of St. Paul** (239 Selby Ave., tel. 612/228–1766), a classic Renaissance-style domed church echoing St. Peter's in Rome, lies ½ mi southwest of the Capitol. Inside are beautiful stained-glass windows, statues, paintings, and other works of art and a small historical museum on the lower level.

Summit Avenue, which runs 4½ mi from the cathedral to the Mississippi River, has the nation's longest stand of intact residential Victorian architecture. F. Scott Fitzgerald lived at 599 Summit in 1918, when he wrote *This Side of Paradise.* The **James J. Hill House** (240 Summit Ave., tel. 612/297–2555), once home of the transportation pioneer and builder of the Great Northern Railroad, is a Richardsonian Romanesque mansion with carved woodwork, tiled fireplaces, and a skylit art gallery hosting changing exhibits. The **Governor's Mansion** (1006 Summit Ave., tel. 612/297–2161) is open to tours on Thursdays. **Mt. Zion Temple** (1300 Summit Ave., tel. 612/698–3881) is the home of the oldest Jewish congregation in Minnesota (1856).

Other Attractions In Minneapolis's Apple Valley suburb, the **Minnesota Zoo** houses some 1,700 animals in natural settings viewed by following six year-round trail systems. Other features are a monorail, a Zoo Lab, a seasonal children's zoo, bird and animal shows, and daily films and slide shows. *13000 Zoo Blvd., Apple Valley, tel. 612/431–9200. Admission charged.*

At the confluence of the Mississippi and Minnesota rivers is **Historic Ft. Snelling.** The northernmost outpost in the old Northwest Territories, it remained an active military post until after World War II. Seventeen buildings have been restored, and costumed guides portray 1820s fort life with demonstrations of blacksmithing, carpentry, and military ceremonies. A History Center has exhibits and short films on the fort. *Rtes. 5 and 55 near the International Airport south of St. Paul, tel. 612/725–2413. Admission charged. Fort closed Nov.–Apr.; History Center closed weekdays Nov.–Apr.*

Parks and Gardens

Minneapolis **Minnehaha Park,** on the Mississippi near the airport, contains Minnehaha Falls, made famous by Longfellow's *The Song of Hiawatha.* Above the waterfall is a statue of Hiawatha and Minnehaha. Minnehaha Parkway, which follows Minnehaha Creek, offers 15 mi of jogging, biking, and roller-skating trails running west to Lake Harriet, one of the Minneapolis chain of lakes.
Wirth Park (I–394 and Theodore Wirth Pkwy.), just west of downtown, features not only bicycling and walking paths through wooded areas but also the **Eloise Butler Wildflower Garden**—a little Eden of local forest and prairie flora. Wirth also has a moderately challenging 18-hole public golf course—a popular cross-country skiing spot in winter.

St. Paul **Como Park** (N. Lexington Ave. at Como Ave.) has picnic areas, walking trails, playgrounds, and tennis and swimming facilities. **Como Park Zoo** (tel. 612/488–5571) features large cats, land and water birds, primates, and aquatic animals. The adjacent **Como Park Conservatory** (tel. 612/489–1740), in a domed greenhouse, has sunken gardens, a fern room, biblical plantings, and seasonal flower shows.

What to See and Do with Children

At the **Children's Museum** (1217 Bandana Blvd., St. Paul, tel. 612/644–5305), youngsters can try their hand at such grown-up activities as driving a bus and playing banker or dentist in two floors of simulated settings. **The Children's Theater** (2400 3rd Ave., Minneapolis, tel. 612/874–0400) features a season of adventurous plays that appeal as much to adults as to their offspring. Among the many other Twin Cities attractions children will enjoy are **Upper St. Anthony Lock,** the **Minneapolis Planetarium,** and **Foshay Tower** (*see* Exploring Minneapolis, *above*); the **Science Museum of Minnesota** and **Minnesota State Capitol** (*see* Exploring St. Paul, *above*); the **Minnesota Zoo** and **Historic Ft. Snelling** (*see* Other Attractions, *above*); and St. Paul's **Como Park Zoo** (*see* Parks and Gardens, *above*).

Shopping

The Twin Cities offer everything from tiny specialty shops to enclosed shopping malls featuring large department stores. The skyway systems in each city connect hundreds of stores and shops.

Minneapolis Among the many shops along **Nicollet Mall** (*see* Exploring Minneapolis, *above*) are **Dayton's** (700 Nicollet Mall), the city's largest department store; and **Gaviidae Common,** the newest downtown shopping addition, with three levels of upscale shops, including branches of **Saks Fifth Avenue** and **Neiman Marcus. The Conservatory** (800 Nicollet Mall at 8th St.) has a number of fine boutiques and restaurants, accented handsomely with wood and marble. **City Center** (7th St.) features 60 shops and 19 restaurants. **Riverplace** and **St. Anthony Main,** on the east bank of the Mississippi, have large numbers of shops and specialty stores housed in historic structures. A few miles south is **Uptown,** a smaller shopping and entertainment mecca centered on **Calhoun Square** (Lake and Hennepin Aves.), which has more than 80 shops and restaurants.

St. Paul **Saint Paul Center,** in the World Trade Plaza downtown, features more than 100 specialty shops and restaurants, including **Dayton's,** the leader in fashions for men, women, and children. **Bandana Square,** in the former Great Northern Railroad repair yard in northwest St. Paul, has a variety of specialty stores. **Victoria Crossing** (857 Grand Ave.) is a collection of small shops and specialty stores that provide an anchor for the dozens of other shops that span Grand Avenue from Dale Street to Prior Avenue.

Bloomington South of Minneapolis, Bloomington is Minnesota's third-largest city (perhaps one day part of the Triplet Cities?) and home to the area's newest attraction: the **Mall of America** (Cedar Ave. and Killebrew Dr., tel. 612/851–3500). Nicknamed "the Megamall," the world's largest enclosed mall features more than 370 stores and shops, including **Macy's, Bloomingdale's, Sears,** and **Nordstrom.** Beneath its central dome is Camp Snoopy, a large amusement park.

Spectator Sports

Baseball **Minnesota Twins** (Hubert H. Humphrey Metrodome, 501 Chicago Ave. S, Minneapolis, tel. 612/375–1116; Apr.–Oct.).

Basketball **Minnesota Timberwolves** (Target Center, 600 1st Ave. N, Minneapolis, tel. 612/337–3865; Nov.–Apr.).

Football **Minnesota Vikings** (Hubert H. Humphrey Metrodome, 500 11th Ave. S, Minneapolis, tel. 612/333–8828; Aug.–Dec.).

Hockey **Minnesota North Stars** (Metropolitan Sports Center, 7901 Cedar Ave., Bloomington, tel. 612/853–9333; Oct.–Apr.).

Beaches

With 22 lakes, Minneapolis has scores of beaches. **Thomas Beach,** at the south end of Lake Calhoun, is one of the most popular. Further information is available from the Minneapolis Parks and Recreation Board (tel. 612/348–2243 or 612/348–2226).

Dining

By Karin Winegar

Despite the diverse gastronomic traditions introduced to the Twin Cities by the new immigrant population, the majority of Minnesotans of Scandinavian and German descent still demand things "toned down a bit" and are somewhat wary of any seasonings more exotic than salt and pepper. No matter what the cuisine, Minnesotans rarely dress up when they eat out. At all but the most stellar restaurants the unofficial dress code is urban-casual-but-tidy attire. For price ranges, see Chart 1 (B) in Chapter 1.

Minneapolis
Expensive

D'Amico Cucina. From the *faux-marbre* plates and peach-and-gray linens to the black marble floors and black leather chairs, this is haute urban nouvelle with a northern Italian accent. Artistic presentations from the kitchen include carpaccio of venison with juniper-berry mayonnaise. *Butler Sq., 100 N. 6th St., tel. 612/338–2401. Reservations advised. Jacket and tie advised. AE, DC, MC, V.*

Goodfellow's. The emphasis at this plush restaurant is on regional American cuisine, with such offerings as South Dakota venison, wild-rice fritters, sautéed walleye with warm new-potato salad, and cranberry-walnut compote. *Conservatory, 800 Nicollet Mall, tel. 612/332–4800. Reservations advised. Jacket advised. AE, D, MC, V. Closed Sun.*

Kincaid's Steak, Chop and Fish House. Kincaid's imposing decor of marble, brass, glass, and wood, combined with its eclectic cuisine, makes it very up-to-date. The kitchen does competent interpretations of Continental and all-American entrées, from T-bone steak to mesquite-grilled mahimahi to steamed clams and baked chicken Dijon. *8400 Normandale Lake Blvd., Bloomington, tel. 612/921–2255. Reservations advised. Jacket and tie advised. AE, D, DC, MC, V.*

Tejas. Sunlight pours down a great curved rose-marble staircase into this chic café, whose specialties include grilled shrimp enchilada with smoked-pepper cream. The southwestern theme carries over equally successfully into such desserts as dark chocolate *ancho* cake with cherimoya sauce. *Conservatory, 800 Nicollet Mall, tel. 612/375–0800. Reservations advised. AE, D, DC, MC, V. Closed Sun.*

Whitney Grille. Set in the lavish Whitney Hotel, the Grille has a flower-filled garden plaza and a hushed main dining room decorated in rich woods and muted floral fabrics. Specialties include veal medallions in Dijon-tarragon sauce and roast loin of venison served on chestnut spaghetti. *150 Portland Ave., tel. 612/339–9300. Reservations advised. Jacket required. AE, D, DC, MC, V.*

Moderate

Chez Bananas. Inflatable palm trees, vinyl bats, and windup toys on tables set the tone for Caribbean food served by Yuppies with a sense of humor in a warehouse storefront. Offerings include savory garlic-laced black beans and rice with chicken or fish. *129 N. 4th St., tel. 612/340–0032. D, DC, MC, V.*

Loring Cafe. The Loring offers a terrific view of handsome Loring Park, bohemian-chic decor, and a menu that includes manicotti with lamb and Chinese chicken salad with sesame-ginger dressing. *1624 Harmon Pl., tel. 612/332–1617. Reservations advised. AE, MC, V. No lunch weekends, no dinner Mon.*

Inexpensive

Atrium Cafe International. This informal lunch spot in a former knitting factory serves fruit and cheese, omelets, pasta, salads, stir-fry dishes, and a rotating selection of soups. *International Market Sq., Glenwood and Lyndale Aves., tel. 612/339–8000. AE, MC, V. No dinner; closed weekends.*

Black Forest Inn. This hangout of students and artists is famed for its huge selection of bottled and tap beers and for its hearty German cuisine. Owner Erich Christ is the real thing, and so are his plates of no-nonsense Wiener schnitzel with potato pancakes and applesauce. *1 E. 26th St., tel. 612/872–0812. AE, D, DC, MC, V.*

St. Paul
Moderate

Dakota Bar and Grill. The Twin Cities' best jazz club also serves an inventive menu of midwestern fare, including smoked-chicken-and-bean fritters and salmon-walleye croquettes. Like the music, the atmosphere is contemporary, cool in color and mood. Sunday brunch is served. *Bandana Sq., 1021 E. Bandana Blvd., tel. 612/642–1442. Reservations advised. AE, D, DC, MC, V. No lunch Sat.*

Khyber Pass Cafe. Set in a corner storefront in a sleepy neighborhood, this small restaurant with decor that includes antique dresses, beadwork, rugs, and photos has barely a dozen tables. The small menu of sometimes-spicy Afghani cuisine includes such dishes as chicken broiled on a skewer and served with coriander chutney. *1399 St. Clair Ave., tel. 612/698–5403. No credit cards. Closed Sun.–Mon.*

Saint Paul Grill. The Saint Paul Hotel's stylish bistro sports contemporary decor and affords a lovely view of Rice Park. The menu is American: dry-aged steaks, a variety of fish dishes, chicken potpie, and homemade roast-beef hash. *350 Market St., tel. 612/292–9292. AE, D, DC, MC, V.*

Inexpensive

Cafe Latté. This furiously successful and almost always jammed cafeteria offers an eclectic selection of soups, salads, breads, and stews. Rosemary-shrimp chowder and Japanese ginger salad are specialties, as are such desserts as towering whipped-cream fruit tortes. *850 Grand Ave., tel. 612/224–5687. AE, MC, V.*

Mickey's Diner. This quintessential streamlined 1930s diner with lots of chrome and vinyl, a lunch counter, and a few tiny booths is listed on the National Register of Historic Places. The stick-to-the-ribs fare and great breakfasts make it a local institution. *36 W. 7th St., tel. 612/222–5633. No credit cards.*

Lodging

By Karin Winegar

There is no shortage of lodging in the Twin Cities. Accommodations are available in the downtowns, along I–494 in the suburbs and industrial parks of Bloomington and Richfield (known as "the strip"), and near the Minneapolis/St. Paul International Airport. A number of hotels are attached to shopping centers as well, the better to ignore Minnesota's fierce winters and summer heat. For price ranges, see Chart 2 (A) in Chapter 1.

Minneapolis
Very Expensive

Hyatt Regency Hotel. A wide, sweeping lobby with a fountain, potted trees, and a piano bar is the focal point of this hotel, within easy walking distance of downtown. Bedrooms are decorated in contemporary jade, peach, and gray fabrics and carpeting. *1300 Nicollet Mall, 55403, tel. 612/370–1234; fax 612/370–1463. 533 rooms, 11 suites. Facilities: restaurant, coffee shop, lounge, health club, sauna, tennis and racquetball courts. AE, D, DC, MC, V.*

★ **The Whitney Hotel.** An 1880s flour mill converted into a small, elegant, genteel hotel, The Whitney provides suite accommodations; about half overlook the Mississippi. The lobby features rich woods, brass fixtures, and marble appointments. *150 Portland Ave., 55401, tel. 612/339–9300 or 800/248–1879. 54 rooms, 43 bilevel suites. Facilities: restaurant, lounge, valet parking. AE, D, DC, MC, V.*

Expensive **Marriott City Center Hotel.** At this sleek, 31-story hotel within
the City Center shopping mall, rooms have a contemporary
look in peach and jade. *30 S. 7th St., 55402, tel. 612/349–4000;
fax 612/332–7165. 499 rooms, 62 suites, and 23 bilevel suites.
Facilities: 3 restaurants, 2 lounges, valet parking, health club,
sauna. AE, D, DC, MC, V.*

Park Inn International. The desk staff is cheery enough, but
the decor in the public areas is a bit somber. Rooms in the 12-
story hotel have contemporary furniture and provide sweeping
views of downtown. *1313 Nicollet Mall, 55403, tel. 612/332–
0371; fax 612/332–0970. 320 rooms, 5 suites. Facilities: restaurant, lounge, indoor pool, sauna. AE, DC, MC, V.*

Moderate **Minneapolis Metrodome Hilton.** Located in an industrial park
near U.S. 280 and I–35W, this Hilton has sleekly contemporary
decor in brass, glass, green, and gold. *1330 Industrial Blvd.,
55413, tel. 612/331–1900; fax 612/331–6827. 254 rooms, 16
suites. Facilities: restaurant, coffee shop, lounge, indoor pool,
sauna, whirlpool, exercise room. AE, DC, MC, V.*

Omni Northstar Hotel. Guest rooms run from the seventh to the
17th floor of the Northstar Center office complex, with easy access to shops. The lobby is decorated in an Oriental style with
antique screens; rooms have contemporary American decor.
*618 2nd Ave. S, 55402, tel. 612/338–2288. 224 rooms, 2 suites.
Facilities: restaurant, lounge. AE, D, DC, MC, V.*

St. Paul **Crown Sterling Suites–St. Paul.** Built in 1980, this hotel is dec-
Expensive orated in neo–New Orleans Garden District style, with terra-
cotta, brickwork, tropical plants, and a courtyard fountain. It
is close to I–35E and within walking distance of major downtown businesses. *175 E. 10th St., 55101, tel. 612/224–5400. 210
suites. Facilities: restaurant, pool, sauna, free airport pickup.
AE, D, DC, MC, V.*

Saint Paul Hotel. Built in 1910, this stately stone hotel overlooks the center of genteel St. Paul. Renovated in 1979, the
rooms have an eclectic traditional decor, with Oriental touches.
*350 Market St., 55102, tel. 612/292–9292 or 800/292–9292. 234
rooms, 20 suites. Facilities: restaurant, bar, coffee shop,
lounge. AE, D, DC, MC, V.*

Sheraton Midway St. Paul. This contemporary four-story hotel
is in the busy district centered on Snelling and University avenues. Hallways decorated in green and gold lead into bright,
comfortable rooms (some no-smoking) with contemporary oak
woodwork. *400 Hamline Ave., 55104, tel. 612/642–1234. 185
rooms, 12 suites. Facilities: restaurant, lounge, indoor pool,
sauna, exercise room. AE, D, DC, MC, V.*

Moderate **Best Western Kelly Inn.** A popular spot for state legislators
whose home districts are far away, this hotel within walking
distance of the State Capitol has essentially remained the same
clean, efficient inn for 25 years. *161 St. Anthony St., 55103, tel.
612/227–8711; fax 612/227–1698. 125 rooms. Facilities: restaurant, lounge, pool, sauna, children's pool. AE, DC, MC, V.*

Radisson Hotel Saint Paul. This 23-story riverside tower has
rooms decorated in traditional American style, with Oriental
touches in the lobby. Most rooms have a river view. *11 E. Kellogg Blvd., 55101, tel. 612/292–1900; fax 612/224–8999. 461
rooms, 21 suites. Facilities: 2 restaurants, indoor pool. AE, D,
DC, MC, V.*

Inexpensive **Sunwood Inn Bandana Square.** In what was once a paint shop
for the Pacific Northern Railroad, this hotel is connected by

skyway to the Bandana Square shopping center. Rooms are decorated with contemporary furnishings. *1010 W. Bandana Blvd., 55108, tel. 612/647–1637. 103 rooms, 6 suites. Facilities: indoor pool, wading pool, whirlpool, sauna. AE, D, DC, MC, V.*

The Arts and Nightlife

The Arts The calendar section of the monthly *Mpls. St. Paul* magazine has extensive listings of events, as does the free monthly *Twin Cities Directory.* Events calendars are also published in the Arts sections of the *St. Paul Pioneer Press and Dispatch* and the Minneapolis-based *Star Tribune.* **Ticketmaster** (tel. 612/ 989–5151) sells tickets for sporting events, concerts, theater, attractions, and special events.

Minneapolis The West Bank theater district has the highest concentration of theaters in Minneapolis, including the **University of Minnesota Theater** (330 21st Ave. S, tel. 612/625–4001). The award-winning **Guthrie Theater** (725 Vineland Pl., tel. 612/377–2224 or 800/328–0542) has a repertory company known for its balance of classics and avant-garde productions. The **Minneapolis Chamber Symphony** (100 N. 6th St., tel. 612/339–0235) offers concerts of both classical and contemporary music during summer and winter. The acclaimed **Minnesota Orchestra** performs in Orchestra Hall (1111 Nicollet Mall, tel. 612/371–5656).

St. Paul The **Great American History Theater** (30 E. 10th St., tel. 612/ 292–4323) presents plays about Minnesota and midwestern history. The **Penumbra Theater Company** (270 Kent St., tel. 612/ 224–4601) is Minnesota's only black professional theater company. The **Ordway Music Theater** (345 Washington St., tel. 612/ 224–4222) is home to the **St. Paul Chamber Orchestra** and the **Minnesota Opera.**

Nightlife With closings at 1 AM, there's no "in the wee small hours" in the Twin Cities, but there's no lack of good places to visit. Most night spots are trendy and upscale and attract a youngish crowd. The Twin Cities also have night spots that serve a sizable, active gay and lesbian community.

Minneapolis **Acme Comedy Co.** (708 N. 1st St., tel. 612/375–1111) features top regional and national comedians. **Windows on Minnesota Lounge,** on the 50th floor of the IDS Center (Nicollet Mall and 8th St., tel. 612/349–6250), features danceable music played by a DJ and spectacular views of the Twin Cities. The best gay bar in downtown Minneapolis is the **Gay Nineties** (400 S. Hennepin Ave., tel. 612/333–7755).

St. Paul **Gallivan's** (354 Wabasha St., tel. 612/227–6688) is a downtown classic with a cozy fireplace and live entertainment. The **Heartthrob Cafe** (St. Paul Center, 30 E. 8th St., tel. 612/224–2783) has a vintage '50s atmosphere and 1990s high-tech lights and music. The **Dakota Bar and Grill** (Bandana Sq., 1021 E. Bandana Blvd., tel. 612/642–1442) is one of the best jazz bars in the Midwest and features some of the Twin Cities' finest performers. Central St. Paul's popular gay bar is **Rumours** (490 N. Robert St., tel. 612/224–0703).

Elsewhere in the State

Southeastern Minnesota

Getting There   From the Twin Cities, follow U.S. 61 southeast along the Mississippi River.

What to See and Do   This picturesque corner of the state has high, wooded bluffs that provide vast panoramas of the Mississippi River. The river towns and villages are noted for charming 19th-century architecture. **Red Wing** is famous for boots and pottery, both of which bear its name. Levee Park, Bay Point Park, and Covill Park offer views of the Mississippi, which widens into Lake Pepin here. The historic **St. James Hotel** (406 Main St., tel. 612/388–2846) has been restored to its 1875 Victorian elegance and has boutiques, shops, and an art gallery; the public spaces recall the heyday of the riverboats. The **American Museum of Wildlife Art** (3303 N. Service Dr., tel. 612/388–0755) features works by regional and national artists. Contact the **Red Wing Chamber of Commerce** (420 Levee St., Box 133, 55066, tel. 612/388–4719) for further information.

Ten miles south on U.S. 61, **Frontenac State Park** (tel. 612/345–3401) has a fur-trading post, scenic overlooks, and Native American burial grounds.

Winona is an early lumbering town settled by New Englanders and Germans. Here **Gavin Heights Scenic Wayside** (Huff St., past U.S. 14 and U.S. 61) offers picnic facilities, hiking trails, and scenic views from atop a 575-foot bluff. The **Julius C. Wilkie Steamboat Center** (foot of Main St. in Levee Park, tel. 507/454–1254), a replica of a steamboat, contains a museum with exhibits on steamboating and river life. Exhibits of the local Polish heritage found at the **Polish Cultural Institute** (102 N. Liberty Ave., tel. 507/454–3431) include family heirlooms and many religious artifacts. For more information contact the **Winona Chamber of Commerce** (67 Main St., Box 870, 55987, tel. 507/452–2272).

Away from the river, west of Winona on U.S. 14, is **Rochester,** home to the famous **Mayo Clinic** (tel. 507/284–9161), which offers tours of its facilities. **Maywood,** the former residence of Dr. Charles H. Mayo, one of the brothers who founded the clinic, has 40 rooms furnished with French, Spanish, English, and American antiques; tickets for tours are purchased at the **Olmsted County Historical Society** (3 mi southwest on Rte. 22, tel. 507/282–9447). The **Rochester Art Center** (320 E. Center St., tel. 507/282–8629) features exhibitions of major works by regional and national artists. The **Rochester Convention and Visitors Bureau** (150 S. Broadway, Suite A, 55904, tel. 507/288–4331) provides information on city attractions.

Duluth

Getting There   From the Twin Cities, head north of I–35.

What to See and Do   Set at the edge of the north-woods wilderness and the western end of Lake Superior is **Duluth,** a city of gracious old homes and one of the largest ports on the Great Lakes. **Skyline Parkway,** a 16-mi scenic boulevard above the city, offers views of Lake Superior and the harbor. Narrated boat tours of Duluth-Superior

Harbor, which has 50 mi of dock line, are offered by **Vista Fleet Excursions** (5th Ave. W and the waterfront, tel. 218/722–6218). The **Aerial Lift Bridge** (Canal Dr.), an unusual elevator bridge 386 feet long, spans the canal entrance to the harbor. Nearby, the **Depot** (506 W. Michigan St., tel. 218/727–8025), an 1892 landmark train station, houses the **Lake Superior Museum of Transportation,** with an extensive collection of locomotives and rolling stock. **Lake Superior Zoological Gardens** (72nd Ave. W and Grand Ave., tel. 218/624–1502) has a children's zoo and animals from all over the world. **The Duluth Convention and Visitors Bureau** (100 Lake Place Dr., 55802, tel. 218/722–4011 or 800/438–5884) provides information on the city.

The Iron Range and Boundary Waters

Getting There   From Duluth, take U.S. 53N.

What to See and Do   The discovery of iron ore in the north woods brought an influx of immigrants, who wove a rich and varied cultural heritage. Known as "The Range" because it encompasses the huge Mesabi and Vermilion Iron ranges, the region is ringed by deep forests and many lakes.

Eveleth, which produces taconite, a form of processed iron ore, is home to the **United States Hockey Hall of Fame** (U.S. 53 and Hattrick Ave., tel. 218/744–5167), where pictures, films, and artifacts tell the story of hockey in America. In **Virginia,** 2 mi north, rimmed with open-pit mines and reserves of iron ore, the **Mine View in the Sky observation platform,** at the south edge of town, overlooks part of the vast **Rochleau Mine** works. The **Virginia Historical Society Heritage Center** (4th St. N and 6th Ave., tel. 218/741–1136; summer only) has exhibits on iron mining and other local history.

West of Virginia on U.S. 169 is **Hibbing,** the largest town in the Mesabi Range, and the place where the Greyhound bus system began. The **Greyhound Origin Center** (Hibbing Memorial Center Bldg., 5th Ave. and 23rd St.) has displays and artifacts on the history of the company. Programs on astronomy and space exploration are offered at the **Paulucci Space Theater** (U.S. 169 and 23rd St., tel. 218/262–6720). Tours of the **Hull-Rust Mahoning Mine,** the world's largest open-pit iron-ore mine, may be arranged at the **Hibbing Area Chamber of Commerce** (211 E. Howard St., 55746, tel. 218/262–3895).

Ely, east of Virginia on U.S. 169, lies in the heart of the Superior National Forest. It is the gateway to the western portion of the **Boundary Waters Canoe Area,** a federally protected area of more than 1,000 pristine lakes surrounded by dense forests. Area outfitters rent canoes and camping equipment and provide assistance in planning canoe trips. The **Vermilion Interpretive Center** (1900 E. Camp St., tel. 218/365–3226) has exhibits on the Vermilion Iron Range, the fur trade, and Native Americans.

International Falls, at the northern terminus of U.S. 53, on the Canadian border, is known as the "icebox of the nation" because of its severe winters. The town lies at the western edge of **Voyageurs National Park** (*see* National and State Parks, *above*), where the **Rainy Lake Visitor Center** (11 mi east of International Falls on Rte. 11, tel. 218/283–9821) offers a slide show, exhibits, maps, and information, as well as guided boat tours of the lake and other points in the park. In town is the **Koochiching County Historical Museum** (214 6th Ave., tel. 218/283–4316), with exhibits on early settlement, gold mining, and Native Americans. The **International Falls Chamber of Commerce** (Box 169, 200 4th St., 56649, tel. 218/283–9400 or 800/325–5766) offers brochures and information.

OHIO

By Mary Norris
Updated by
Christopher
Johnston

Capital	Columbus
Population	10,847,115
Motto	With God, All Things Are Possible
State Bird	Cardinal
State Flower	Scarlet carnation

Visitor Information

Ohio Division of Travel and Tourism (Box 1001, Columbus 43266, tel. 800/282–5393). **Ohio Historical Society** (1982 Velma Ave., Columbus 43211, tel. 614/297–2300).

Scenic Drives

The **Lake Erie Circle Tour** consists of nearly 200 mi of state routes and U.S. highways along the Lake Erie shoreline from Toledo to Conneaut (*see* Northwest Ohio and the Lake Erie Islands, *below*). **Paint Valley,** along U.S. 50 and Rte. 41 in the Chillicothe-Bainbridge area, 45–60 mi south of Columbus (*see* Marietta, Columbus, and the Mounds, *below*), offers spectacular fall foliage, usually peaking in the third week of October.

National and State Parks

National Parks   National monuments include the **Mound City Group** (*see* Marietta, Columbus, and the Mounds, *below*) and **Perry's Victory and International Peace Memorial** in Put-in-Bay (*see* Northwest Ohio and the Lake Erie Islands, *below*). The **William Howard Taft birthplace** (2038 Auburn Ave., Cincinnati, tel. 513/684–3262) is a national historic site.

The **Cuyahoga Valley National Recreation Area** (15610 Vaughn Rd., Brecksville 44141, tel. 216/526–5256) occupies 22 mi of forested valley between Cleveland and Akron, along the Cuyahoga River.

State Parks   Of the 72 state parks, eight feature Ohio State Park Resorts (tel. 800/282–7275), which offer swimming, boating, golf, and tennis, as well as lodging, dining, and meeting facilities. For more information, contact the **Ohio Department of Natural Resources** (Division of Parks and Recreation, Fountain Sq., Bldg. C–1, Columbus 43224, tel. 614/265–7000).

Marietta, Columbus, and the Mounds

The move West began in Marietta. You can pick up a lot of history here and take it with you to Columbus, the state capital, a young, forward-looking city. South of Columbus are the prehistoric Native American mounds of the Middle Ohio Valley.

Tourist Information

Columbus: Visitors Center (10 W. Broad St., 43215, tel. 614/221–6623). **Marietta:** Tourist and Convention Bureau (316 3rd St., 45750, tel. 614/373–5178 or 800/288–2577).

Getting There

By Plane   **Port Columbus International Airport,** 10 mi east of downtown Columbus, is served by major airlines and by **Christman** (tel. 412/225–4000), **Comair** (tel. 800/354–9822), and **Skyway** (tel. 614/239–1139). A shuttle bus runs downtown. **Wood County Airport,** 6 mi south of Marietta in Parkersburg, West Virginia, is served by USAir.

By Car   Marietta is at the intersection of I–77 and Rte. 7, which meanders along the Ohio River. Columbus is at the intersection of I–70 and I–71, in the middle of the state.

By Bus   **Greyhound** serves Marietta (tel. 614/373–2237) and Columbus (tel. 614/221–5311). The **Central Ohio Transit Authority** (tel. 614/228–1776) operates buses within Columbus.

Exploring Marietta, Columbus, and the Mounds

Marietta is a picture-postcard town along the Ohio and Muskingum rivers. The **Campus Martius Museum** (601 2nd St., tel. 614/373–3750) tells the story of the town's founding. Guides on the *W. P. Snyder, Jr.,* a stern-wheeler moored in the Muskingum River (**Ohio River Museum,** 601 Front St., tel. 614/373–3717), make you nostalgic for steamboat days. *Both museums: Admission charged. Closed Mon.–Tues. Mar.–Apr. and Oct.–Nov.*

Historically, the way north from Marietta is up the Muskingum, paralleled by scenic Rte. 60 as far as Zanesville. Lock masters crank open the gates of the 11 manually operated locks and dams on the river. Another historic route, the **National Road** (U.S. 40), runs west from Zanesville. Milestones mark your progress to Columbus.

Columbus is the Hartford of Ohio (with Cleveland the New York and Cincinnati the Boston)—a center for banking and insurance as well as government. Major events include the **Ohio State Fair** (tel. 614/644–3247) in August and, of course, Columbus Day. The city's attractions include **COSI** (*see* What to See and Do with Children, *below*), Peter Eisenmann's controversial **Wexner Center for the Arts** on the Ohio State University campus (N. High St. at W. 15th Ave., tel. 614/292–3535), and the **Ohio Theatre,** a one-of-a-kind palace dating from the 1920s (*see* The Arts and Nightlife, *below*). **German Village** (tel. 614/221–8888), south of downtown, was built by immigrants in the 19th century; it or the nearby **Brewery District** makes a good lunch stop. There's a Gallery Hop the first Saturday of each month in the **Short North,** a strip of High Street north of downtown.

High Street (Rte. 23) will take you out of Columbus, through the hills that inspired those on the state seal, to **Chillicothe,** the first state capital. From there, take Rte. 104 north to the **Mound City Group National Monument.** A prehistoric burial ground comprising 23 mounds on 13 acres, this necropolis is attributed to the Hopewell Indians, who lived here from 200 BC to AD 500. *Tel. 614/774–1125. Admission charged.*

For a more remote spot, take U.S. 50 and Rte. 41 (at Bainbridge) to Rte. 73 (at Locust Grove) and visit the **Serpent Mound State Memorial.** The serpent, carpeted with grass, uncoils itself to a length of ¼ mi, on a ridge in the middle of nowhere. Its builders and meaning are shrouded in mystery. *Tel. 513/587–2796. Admission charged. Closed weekdays Apr.–May and Sept.–Oct.*

What to See and Do with Children

COSI (pronounced "co-sigh"), the Center of Science and Industry (280 E. Broad St., Columbus, tel. 614/228–2674), has colorful hands-on exhibits and traveling shows. Four generations of gorillas live at the **Columbus Zoo** (9990 Riverside Dr., tel. 614/645–3550), about 18 mi northwest of downtown off I–270.

Shopping

Columbus is world headquarters for Leslie Wexner's popular women's-clothing chain, **The Limited,** and its spinoffs **Limited Too, Express,** and **Structure** (for men). Wexner also owns **Henri Bendel, Abercrombie & Fitch,** and **Victoria's Secret,** all of which are represented in **Columbus City Center** (111 S. 3rd St., tel. 614/221–4900), a three-story atrium mall downtown. You can't miss **Lazarus** (S. High and W. Town Sts., tel. 614/463–2121), the granddaddy of Columbus department stores. Its old-fashioned water tower sticks up out of the skyline like a Tootsie Roll Pop.

Sports and Outdoor Activities

Canoeing **Little Muskingum Canoe Livery** (Rte. 1, Wingett Run, tel. 614/473–2258 or 614/473–2495), about 20 mi northeast of Marietta at Rtes. 26 and 260, runs trips through the Marietta section of the Wayne National Forest (*see* Hiking and Backpacking, *below*).

Golf Public courses near Marietta include **Lakeside Golf Course** (Rte. 60, Beverly, tel. 614/984–4265) and **Oxbow Golf & Country Club** (Rte. 85, Belpre, tel. 614/423–6771).

Hiking and Several miles of trails run through the **Wayne National Forest.**
Backpacking Information is available from the U.S. Forest Service field office (Newport Pike, Rte. 1, Reno; Box 132, Marietta 45750, tel. 614/373–9055 or 800/283–2267).

Dining and Lodging

For information about bed-and-breakfasts, try **Buckeye B&B** (Box 130, Powell 43065, tel. 614/548–4555) or **Columbus B&B** (769 S. 3rd St., Columbus 43206, tel. 614/443–3680). For price ranges, see Charts 1 (B) and 2 (B) in Chapter 1.

Columbus **Carolyn's.** The menu changes daily at this popular restaurant in
Dining a renovated German Village house, with an airy feeling and an antique bar imported from a hotel in Portsmouth, Ohio. The chef, Carolyn, experiments with regional American cuisine. *489 City Park Ave., tel. 614/221–8100. MC, V. Closed Sun. Expensive.*

★ **Rigsby's Cuisine Volatile.** The chef at this white-tiled Short North restaurant studied in San Francisco. The bread sticks are a yard long, and the New American menu is inventive. *698 N. High St. (entrance at rear), tel. 614/461–7888. Reservations advised. AE, DC, MC, V. Closed Sun. Moderate.*

Katzinger's Deli. Get your own pickle out of the barrel at this New York–style deli in German Village, famous for good rye bread. *475 S. 3rd St., tel. 614/228–3354. MC, V. Inexpensive.*

Schmidt's Sausage Haus. Homemade sausage hangs from the ceiling in this old-fashioned place, redolent of the butcher shop. *240 E. Kossuth St., tel. 614/444–6808. AE, D, MC, V. Inexpensive.*

Lodging
★ **The Great Southern Hotel.** The rooms are decorated in Victorian style in this dignified historic hotel with a rich marble-and-wood lobby. *310 S. High St., tel. 614/228–3800, 800/328–2073, or 800/228–3789 in OH. 196 rooms, 37 suites. Facilities: 2 restaurants, lounge, parking. AE, D, DC, MC, V. Expensive.*

Hyatt Regency. Adjacent to the convention center, this ultra-modern high-rise hotel caters mainly to businesspeople. (The Hyatt on Capitol Square is more for the political crowd.) *350 N. High St., 43215, tel. 614/463–1234; fax 614/463–9161. 631 rooms, 33 suites. Facilities: 2 restaurants, lounge, pool, concierge, parking. AE, D, DC, MC, V. Expensive.*

Courtyard by Marriott. This contemporary hotel is comfortable and convenient to everything. *35 W. Spring St., 43215, tel. 614/228–3200 or 800/344–2345. 165 rooms. Facilities: restaurant, lounge, pool and gym at YMCA next door for nominal charge, parking. AE, D, DC, MC, V. Moderate.*

Marietta
Dining **Adventure Galley.** Rib-eye steaks are a favorite in this high-ceilinged pub, which started out as a saloon and bowling alley in 1902. *203 2nd St., tel. 614/374–8278. MC, V. Moderate.*

Betsey Mills Dining Room. Waitresses in pinafores serve home-cooked food in a Colonial-look dining room attached to a residence for young women, near the Marietta College campus. *300 4th St., tel. 614/373–3804. V. Closed Memorial Day, July 4, Labor Day, Christmas–New Year's. Inexpensive.*

Lodging **Claire E.** This may be the only floating B&B in the Northwest Territory. Docked on the Ohio River, the room decor is Victorian. *c/o 127 Ohio St., 45750, tel. 614/374–2233, 614/374–3876, or inquire Levee House Cafe. 3 rooms share bath. MC, V. Moderate.*

Best Western Marietta. This standard motel, with a launch and docks on the east bank of the Muskingum River, caters to boaters. *279 Muskingum Dr., 45750, tel. 614/374–7211. 47 rooms, 2 suites. Facilities: Continental breakfast, pool and health club privileges at YMCA, tennis courts, golf nearby. AE, D, DC, MC, V. Inexpensive.*

Dining and Lodging
★ **Lafayette Hotel.** The theme is riverboats, and all the rooms are different in this solid brick Victorian-era hotel overlooking the Ohio River. The Gun Room restaurant is decorated with muskets. *101 Front St., 45750, tel. 614/373–5522, 800/331–9336, or 800/331–9337 in OH; fax 614/373–4684. 81 rooms, 11 suites. Facilities: restaurant, bar. AE, D, DC, MC, V. Moderate.*

Peebles
(Serpent Mound)
Lodging **The Bayberry Inn B&B.** This gray-and-white Victorian farmhouse with rocking chairs on the porch (and no TV inside) is a welcome sight—it's the only place to stay for miles. *25675 Rte.*

41 (at Rte. 32), 45660, tel. 513/587–2221. 3 rooms share bath. No credit cards. Closed Nov.–Apr. Moderate.

Motels **Buckeye Inn at OSU** (3232 Olentangy River Rd., Columbus 43202, tel. 614/261–7141 or 800/325–2525), 150 rooms, 24 suites, restaurant, lounge, pool; inexpensive. **Cross Country Inn–OSU South** (1445 Olentangy River Rd., Columbus 43212, tel. 614/291–2983), 120 rooms, pool; inexpensive. **Red Roof Inn OSU** (441 Ackerman Rd., Columbus 43202, tel. 614/267–9941), 115 rooms; inexpensive.

Campgrounds **Muskingum River Campgrounds** (Rte. 60, 2 mi south of Gaysport; 10206 South River Rd., McConnelsville 43756, tel. 614/674–6918) has tent and RV sites and a boat ramp.

The Arts and Nightlife

Columbus Monthly has complete listings of goings-on in the city.

The Arts The **Columbus Symphony Orchestra** (tel. 614/224–3291) and the **BalletMet** (tel. 614/229–4860) perform at the **Ohio Theater** (55 E. State St., tel. 614/469–1045). **The Players** perform in Columbus's **Capitol Theatre** at Vern Riffe Center (77 S. High St., tel. 614/644–8425). **Opera/Columbus** and touring Broadway shows are at the **Palace Theatre** (34 W. Broad St., tel. 614/469–1331).

Nightlife Columbus's hot spots are in the Short North. The Scottish **Mac's Cafe** (693 N. High St., tel. 614/221–6227), **700 High** (700 N. High St., tel. 614/221–7200), **Short North Tavern** (674 N. High St., tel. 614/221–2432), and **Union Station Cafe** (630 N. High St., tel. 614/228–3740) all have live music Thursday through Saturday.

Cincinnati

People who live in Cincinnati really enjoy it. It's a highly cultured, well-regulated city with a proud history, an active riverfront, and a bustling downtown. The one thing Cincinnatians complain about is the weather: Because the city is in a basin along the Ohio River, summers are hot and humid.

Tourist Information

Cincinnati: Visitors Bureau (300 W. 6th St., at Plum St., 45202, tel. 513/621–2142 or 800/344–3445).

Arriving and Departing

By Plane **Cincinnati/Northern Kentucky International Airport** is 12 mi south of downtown, off I–275, in Kentucky. It is served by major airlines and by **Comair** (tel. 800/354–9822). **Jetport Express** (tel. 606/283–3702) makes regular trips from the airport to downtown hotels ($10 one-way, $15 round-trip). Taxis downtown cost about $20.

By Car I–71, I–75, and I–74 all converge on downtown Cincinnati.

Train Station **Amtrak** serves **Union Terminal** (1301 Western Ave., tel. 513/651–3337 or 800/872–7245).

Bus Station **Greyhound** (Court St. and Gilbert Ave., tel. 513/352–6000).

Getting Around

Downtown Cincinnati is eminently walkable. Skywalks connect hotels, convention centers, stores, and garages above street level. **Queen City Metro** (tel. 513/621–4455) runs buses out of Government Square (5th St. between Walnut and Main Sts.); there is also a downtown loop bus.

Exploring Cincinnati

Fountain Square (5th and Vine Sts.) is the center of downtown Cincinnati. The city is laid out along the river, with numbered streets running east–west (2nd Street is Pete Rose Way); north–south streets have names. Vine Street divides the city into east and west.

If you have only an hour in Cincinnati, spend it at **Carew Tower** (5th and Race Sts.) looking at the gorgeous Rookwood pottery in the Arcade and at the art deco interior of the **Omni Netherland Plaza Hotel.** Its marble, rosewood, mirrors, and murals are so richly detailed that the hotel provides an architectural walking tour.

You can cross the Ohio River into Kentucky on the **Roebling Suspension Bridge,** built by John A. Roebling, who later built the Brooklyn Bridge. **Covington Landing,** a floating entertainment complex in the form of a side-wheeler and a wharf, is west of the bridge. Beyond the wharf is **BB Riverboats** (tel. 606/261–8500), running river tours year-round. **Covington** itself, east of the bridge, is a neighborhood of fine antebellum mansions, with wonderful views from Riverside Drive.

Back on the Ohio side, the narrow streets and funky houses of **Mt. Adams,** the first hill east of downtown, are reminiscent of San Francisco. The yard of the **Immaculata Church** (Pavillion and Guido Sts.) provides a sterling view of the city.

Eden Park, on the other side of Mt. Adams, is the site of the **Cincinnati Art Museum** (tel. 513/721–5204), which has an outstanding collection of Near Eastern and ancient art, and the **Krohn Conservatory** (tel. 513/352–4086), a garden center. Other bastions of culture are the **Contemporary Arts Center** (115 E. 5th St., tel. 513/721–0390) and the **Taft Museum** (316 Pike St., tel. 513/241–0343), famous for its Chinese porcelains.

You could spend a full day in the **Museum Center at Union Terminal,** which looks like a huge art-deco cabinet radio and houses both the Museum of Natural History (*see* What to See and Do with Children, *below*) and the Cincinnati Historical Society. *1301 Western Ave. (off I–75 at Ezzard Charles Dr.), tel. 513/287–7000 or 800/733–2077. Admission charged.*

Parks and Gardens

Bicentennial Commons, an outdoor recreation center at Sawyer Point, on the Ohio River, uses monuments to tell the story of Cincinnati's origins as a river town. Look for the famous flying pigs, a reminder of the city's prominence as a meat-packing center.

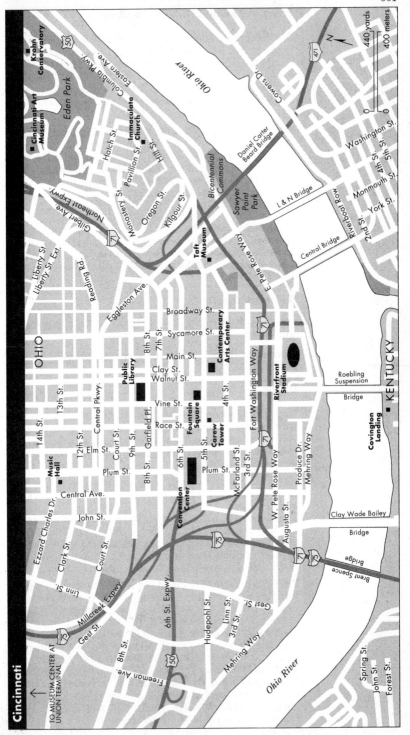

Cincinnati

TO MUSEUM CENTER AT UNION TERMINAL

OHIO

KENTUCKY

Ohio River

Eden Park

Krohn Conservatory

Cincinnati Art Museum

Immaculata Church

Columbia Pkwy.

Eastern Ave.

Hatch St.

Pavillion St.

Monastery St.

Hill St.

Oregon St.

Kilgour St.

Gilbert Ave.

Northeast Expwy.

Reading Rd.

Liberty St.

Liberty St. Ext.

Eggleston Ave.

Taft Museum

Bicentennial Commons

Sawyer Point Park

Daniel Carter Beard Bridge

L & N Bridge

Central Bridge

Cowens Dr.

Washington St.

4th St.

5th St.

Monmouth St.

York St.

2nd St.

Riverboat Row

Broadway St.

Sycamore St.

Main St.

Clay St.

Walnut St.

Vine St.

Race St.

8th St.

7th St.

Public Library

Contemporary Arts Center

Fort Washington Way

E. Pete Rose Way

Riverfront Stadium

Roebling Suspension Bridge

Covington Landing

14th St.

13th St.

Central Pkwy.

12th St.

Court St.

Elm St.

9th St.

Garfield Pl.

8th St.

6th St.

5th St.

Plum St.

Fountain Square

Carew Tower

4th St.

McFarland St.

3rd St.

W. Pete Rose Way

Produce Dr.

Mehring Way

Clay Wade Bailey Bridge

Music Hall

Central Ave.

John St.

Convention Center

Ezzard Charles Dr.

Clark St.

Court St.

Linn St.

Millcreek Expwy.

Gest St.

6th St. Expwy.

Hudepohl St.

Linn St.

Gest St.

3rd St.

Augusta St.

Brent Spence Bridge

Freeman Ave.

8th St.

Mehring Way

Ohio River

Spring St.

John St.

Forest St.

N

440 yards

400 meters

50

71

75

What to See and Do with Children

The **Museum of Natural History** in the Museum Center at Union Terminal (*see* Exploring Cincinnati, *above*) has a Children's Discovery Center, a cave with real bats (behind glass), and an Ice Age diorama that lets you go behind the glass. The **Cincinnati Zoo** (3400 Vine St., tel. 513/281–4700), famous for its white Bengal tigers, is the second-oldest zoo in the country. Follow the paw-print signs off I–75 Exit 6 or I–71 Exit 7.

Kings Island Theme Park, 24 mi north of Cincinnati in Kings Mills (I–71, Exit 25A), has seven themed areas, including a water park, the longest wooden roller coaster in the world, and a wild-animal habitat. *Tel. 513/398–5600. Admission: $21.95 adults, $11.95 children ages 3–6. Closed Jan.–Mar.*

Shopping

Shops in the **Tower Place** (4th and Race Sts.) atrium shopping mall include the city's best-loved quality women's clothing stores, **Gidding-Jenny** and **Henry Harris.** Skywalks connect Tower Place with **McAlpin's** and **Saks Fifth Avenue** (via Carew Tower).

Spectator Sports

Baseball **Cincinnati Reds** (100 Riverfront Stadium, tel. 513/421–4510; Apr.–Oct.).

Football **Cincinnati Bengals** (100 Riverfront Stadium, tel. 513/621–3550; Sept.–Dec.).

Dining

Cincinnati has more good restaurants than the most ravenous traveler could sample in any one visit, including high-rise revolving restaurants, riverboat restaurants, rathskellers, and chili parlors. For price ranges, see Chart 1 (B) in Chapter 1.

Expensive **The Celestial.** Request a table with a view at this classic spot on
★ top of Mt. Adams, serving French and American cuisine. *1071 Celestial St., tel. 513/241–4455. Reservations advised. Jacket and tie advised. AE, D, DC, MC, V. Closed Sun.*
The Maisonette. Since 1964 this has been ranked among the foremost restaurants in the United States. The food is fresh and French, the atmosphere plush and formal. *114 E. 6th St., tel. 513/721–2260. Reservations advised. Jacket required. AE, D, DC, MC, V. Closed Sun., major holidays, 1st 2 wks of July.*

Moderate **The Golden Lamb.** The oldest inn in Ohio has enough Shaker
★ furniture to qualify it as a museum. It's 33 mi north of Cincinnati, off I–71 or I–75. *27 S. Broadway, Lebanon, tel. 513/621–8373. Reservations advised. AE, DC, MC, V.*
Lenhardt's. This informal restaurant features schnitzel, Viennese and Hungarian goulash, sauerbraten, and potato pancakes. *151 W. McMillan St., tel. 513/281–3600. AE, DC, MC, V. Closed Mon., July 4, 1st 2 wks in Aug., 2 wks at Christmas.*
Montgomery Inn at the Boathouse. The barbecued ribs are famous, and you can't get any closer to the river without swimming in it. *925 Eastern Ave., tel. 513/721–7427. AE, MC, V. No lunch weekends; closed major holidays.*

Inexpensive **Rookwood Ice Cream Parlor.** Once the Tea Room at Union Terminal, this delightful green spot is decorated with vintage Rookwood pottery and serves local ice cream. *Museum Center at Union Terminal, tel. 513/721–4985. No credit cards. Closed holidays.*

Rookwood Pottery. Families consume giant hamburgers and other American fare in wood-and-brick dining rooms that contain what were once the kilns of the famous Mt. Adams pottery. *1077 Celestial St., tel. 513/721–5456. AE, DC, MC, V. Closed major holidays.*

Lodging

Downtown Cincinnati has several choice hotels. Many offer weekend packages including Reds or Bengals games. Staying in the suburbs is less expensive and forces you to learn your way around at least one neighborhood. For price ranges, see Chart 2 (B) in Chapter 1.

Expensive **Cincinnatian Hotel.** Stars are drawn to this sedate French Sec-
★ ond Empire–style hotel with an unusual contemporary interior. The young chef at The Palace has taken the town by storm with her New American cuisine. *601 Vine St., 45202, tel. 513/381–3000, 800/942–9000, or 800/332–2020 in OH; fax 513/651–0256. 147 rooms, 8 suites. Facilities: restaurant (tel. 513/381–6006; reservations strongly advised), lounge, health club, concierge, parking. AE, D, DC, MC, V.*

Hyatt Regency Cincinnati. This 22-story hotel with a four-story atrium lobby was renovated in 1989. The modern rooms are decorated in bright solid colors. Champs is an Italian chop house downstairs in this most sports-oriented of Cincinnati's downtown hotels (there's a Reds shop in the lobby). *151 W. 5th St., 45202, tel. 513/579–1234; fax 513/579–0107. 485 rooms, 22 suites. Facilities: 2 restaurants, 2 lounges, health club, pool, parking. AE, D, DC, MC, V.*

★ **Omni Netherland Plaza.** Downtown's grand art-deco hotel is in the Carew Tower (*see* Exploring Cincinnati, *above*). Reservations are recommended for dinner at Orchids, which serves American cuisine in the exquisite Palm Court. *35 W. 5th St., 45202, tel. 513/421–9100; fax 513/421–4291. 621 rooms, 12 suites. Facilities: 2 restaurants, lounge, health club, pool, concierge, parking. AE, D, DC, MC, V.*

Moderate **Amos Shinkle Town House B & B.** The master bedroom in this antebellum mansion, once home to the man who hired John A. Roebling to build a suspension bridge across the Ohio River, has a whirlpool bath and a chandelier in the bathroom. *215 Garrard St., Covington, KY 41011, tel. 606/431–2118. 7 rooms. Facilities: phones available, parking. AE, D, DC, MC, V.*

Best Western Mariemont Inn. Staying at this inn 10 mi east of downtown is like staying at Henry VIII's hunting lodge. Everything is in the Tudor style—even the cash machine! *6880 Wooster Pike (U.S. 50), Mariemont 45227, tel. 513/271–2100; fax 513/271–1057. 60 rooms. Facilities: restaurant, pub, parking. AE, D, DC, MC, V.*

Inexpensive **Caesar Creek American Youth Hostel.** Rent a sleeping bag and crash in the men's or women's dormitory, on the grounds of a state park 45 mi northeast of Cincinnati. *8823 Center Rd., Wilmington 45177, tel. 513/488–3755. 16 beds. No credit cards.*

The Arts and Nightlife

The Arts   The **Music Hall** (1241 Elm St., tel. 513/721–8222) is home to the **Cincinnati Symphony Orchestra** (tel. 513/381–3300; Sept.–Apr.), the **Cincinnati Opera** (tel. 513/241–2742; June–July), and the **Cincinnati Ballet** (tel. 513/621–5219; Oct.–May).

Nightlife   At Covington Landing, **Howl at the Moon Saloon** (tel. 606/491–7733) features dueling piano players and sing-alongs. In Mt. Adams, **Longworth's** (1108 St. Gregory St., tel. 513/579–0900) has a DJ and a garden, and the **Incline** (1071 Celestial St., tel. 513/241–4455), a sophisticated bar at The Celestial restaurant, has vocalists.

Northwest Ohio and the Lake Erie Islands

Between Toledo and Cleveland lie a stretch of the Lake Erie shore and a group of islands that constitute the Riviera and Madeira of Ohio. Families rent cottages at Catawba Point or Put-in-Bay (the port village of South Bass Island) and swim, fish, and boat, topping the week off with a trip to Cedar Point Amusement Park in Sandusky.

Tourist Information

Erie County: Visitors and Convention Bureau (231 W. Washington Row, Sandusky, 44870, tel. 419/625–2984 or 800/255–3743; covers Cedar Point, Kelleys Island, and Sandusky). **Ottawa County:** Visitors Bureau (109 Madison St., Port Clinton, 43452, tel. 419/734–4386 or 800/441–1271; covers Catawba, Lakeside, Marblehead, Port Clinton, and Put-in-Bay). **Greater Toledo:** Convention and Visitors Bureau (SeaGate Convention Center, 401 Jefferson Ave., 2nd floor, 43604, tel. 419/321–6404 or 800/243–4667). **Kelleys Island:** Chamber of Commerce (Box 783F, 43438, tel. 419/746–2360). **Put-in-Bay:** Chamber of Commerce (Box 250–BN, 43456, tel. 419/285–2832).

Getting There

By Plane   **Toledo Express Airport,** west on Rte. 2, is served by six airlines. For **Cleveland Hopkins Airport,** *see* Cleveland, *below.* **Griffing Island Airlines** (tel. 419/734–3149), out of **Port Clinton Airport** (3255 E. State Rd.), and **Griffing Flying Service** (tel. 419/626–5161), out of **Griffing-Sandusky Airport** (Rte. 6, east of Sandusky), fly to the Lake Erie islands.

By Car   The Ohio Turnpike (I–80/90) runs 5 to 10 mi below the Lake Erie shoreline. For Toledo take Exit 4 (I–75) or Exit 5 (U.S. 280); for Port Clinton, Exit 6 (Rte. 53); for Sandusky, Exit 7 (U.S. 250). Toledo is on I–75. Rte. 2 hugs the lake between Toledo and Sandusky; Rte. 269 loops out to Marblehead.

By Train   Amtrak stops in Toledo and Sandusky.

By Bus   **Greyhound** has national service from Toledo (811 Jefferson Ave., tel. 419/243–3151). **TARTA** (Toledo Area Regional Transit Authority; tel. 419/243–7433) covers Toledo and its suburbs.

By Boat   Ferries serve the Lake Erie islands from May through October. **Put-in-Bay Boat Line** (tel. 800/245–1538), from Port Clinton to Put-in-Bay, takes passengers only and offers late-night service. **Miller Boat Line** (tel. 419/285–2421), from Catawba to Lime Kiln Dock (on the opposite side of South Bass Island from Put-in-Bay) and to Middle Bass Island, takes passengers and cars (reservations required), as does **Neumann Boat Line** (tel. 419/798–5800), from Marblehead to Kelleys Island.

Exploring Northwest Ohio and the Lake Erie Islands

Though not a tourist town, **Toledo** has its attractions. Baseball fans won't want to miss the **Ohio Baseball Hall of Fame** (2901 Key St., off U.S. 24, Maumee, tel. 419/893–9481), next to Ned Skeldon Stadium, where the Mud Hens play, in the Lucas County Recreation Center. The **Toledo Museum of Art** (2445 Monroe St. at Scottwood Ave., off I–75, tel. 419/255–8000) offers a fine small collection of contemporary, abstract, and Impressionist paintings, Greek and Egyptian statues, and an important collection of glass.

Vacationland begins at **Port Clinton,** which lies at the northern base of the Marblehead Peninsula, some 30 mi east of Toledo on Rte. 2. A center for fishing excursions (*see* Sports and Outdoor Activities, *below*), the town is also the base for a ferry to South Bass Island's **Put-in-Bay** (*see* Getting There, *above*), a port village consisting of a marina, a grassy lakefront park dotted with small cannons, and a strip of shops, bars, and restaurants featuring a vintage wooden merry-go-round. Today a wild-party town, Put-in-Bay was the site of Commodore Oliver Hazard Perry's naval victory over the British in the War of 1812. From the top of **Perry's Victory and International Peace Memorial,** a single massive Doric column east of downtown, you can see all the way to Canada. A popular day excursion is to take the *Sonny S* (tel. 419/285–8774 or 419/285–4631) over to **Middle Bass Island** and sample the wares of the **Lonz Winery** (tel. 419/285–5411), which looks like a European monastery.

Back on the mainland, at the eastern tip of the peninsula is **Marblehead,** site of the oldest continuously working lighthouse on Lake Erie. From here it's a short ferry ride to **Kelleys Island,** which has two remarkable geologic features: on the north shore, glacial grooves (waves in the rock) left by the Ice Age; on the south shore, prehistoric Native American pictographs.

Sandusky, the gateway to **Cedar Point** (*see* What to See and Do with Children, *below*), makes a good touring base. It's near the highways and ferries and offers thousands of motel rooms as well as a few romantic Victorian hideaways.

What to See and Do with Children

Cedar Point Amusement Park is in the *Guinness Book of World Records* as having the most roller coasters in the world (10), among them the fastest (the Magnum XL–200) and the highest wooden one (the Mean Streak). It also has a water park (Soak City) and a mile-long sandy beach. In 1993, the park debuted Snake River Falls, the tallest, deepest, and fastest water ride in the world. *Off U.S. 250N, Sandusky, tel. 419/627–2350. Ad-*

mission: $21.95 adults, $11.95 children. Closed Oct.–May, weekdays in Sept.

Sports and Outdoor Activities

Beaches and Water Sports Lake Erie really is swimmable again, having been cleaned by zebra mussels—supposedly a pest. The best lake beach is at **East Harbor State Park,** off Rte. 163, on the Marblehead Peninsula. **Cedar Point** also offers good swimming (*see* What to See and Do with Children, *above*).

Fishing The Western Lake Erie Basin is known as the "Walleye Capital of the World." Toledo even has a **Walleye Hotline** (tel. 419/893–9740; Mar.–May). Smallmouth bass and Lake Erie perch are also plentiful. Nonresident fishing licenses are sold at bait shops, or call 419/625–8062. There's ice fishing if the lake freezes.

The breakwater in Port Clinton and the pier at Catawba Point are both good fishing spots. Per-head fishing boats leave from Fisherman's Wharf in Port Clinton (tel. 419/734–6388) and from Battery Park Marina in Sandusky (tel. 419/625–5000), among other places.

Dining and Lodging

The chambers of commerce in Put-in-Bay and on Kelleys Island (*see* Tourist Information, *above*) give advice on lodging, which should be arranged well in advance. For price ranges, see Charts 1 (B) and 2 (B) in Chapter 1.

Catawba Point
Dining **The Greenhouse.** Seafood lasagna and sunsets are among the specialties at this many-windowed restaurant full of hanging plants. *3026 N.W. Catawba Rd., tel. 419/797–4411. AE, D, DC, MC, V. Closed Jan.–Feb. Moderate.*

★ **Mon Ami.** This well-established winery and restaurant has a chalet-style dining room with 4-foot-thick stone walls and a patio surrounded by wooden casks. Pasta and fresh fish are the specialties. *3845 E. Wine Cellar Rd., off N.E. Catawba Rd. (Rte. 53), tel. 419/797–4445 or 800/777–4266. AE, MC, V. Moderate.*

Grand Rapids
Lodging **The Mill House.** This country-Victorian house on the Maumee River 40 minutes from downtown Toledo was built in 1900 as a working gristmill. Today it features three Victorian-style rooms, where guests enjoy a sumptuous three-course full breakfast and some great views of the gardens out back. *24070 Front St., 43522, tel. 419/832–6455. No credit cards. Moderate.*

Marblehead
Lodging **The Old Stone House.** The owners of this Federal-style mansion right on the lake keep curtains to a minimum so that nothing obscures the view. *133 Clemons St., 43440, tel. 419/798–5922. 13 rooms share baths, 1 suite. Facilities: parking. MC, V. Moderate.*

Port Clinton
Dining **The Garden at the Lighthouse.** Up a garden path is a Victorian house, originally built for the lighthouse keeper. Fresh fish, veal, and chicken dishes are served by candlelight. *226 E. Perry St., tel. 419/732–2151. AE, D, DC, MC, V. Closed Sun. and holidays Sept.–May. Moderate.*

Lodging **Beach Cliff Lodge.** Families who fish bunk down in this unpretentious place, close to the ferry and the state park, which has freezers and fish-cleaning services. *4189 N.W. Catawba Rd., 43452, tel. 419/797–4553. 8 rooms, 13 cottages. Facilities: pool. No credit cards. Moderate.*

Dining and Lodging **The Island House Hotel.** This 100-year-old redbrick hotel with tall windows has a dining room serving fresh fish. *102 Madison St., 43452, tel. 419/734–2166 or 800/233–7370. 37 rooms. Facilities: 2 restaurants, lounge, parking. AE, D, MC, V. Moderate.*

Put-in-Bay **The Crescent Tavern.** If you can eat only one meal in Put-in-Bay,
Dining this restaurant inside a gracious Victorian house is the place. *Delaware Ave., tel. 419/285–4211. No reservations. MC, V. Moderate.*

Frosty's. With a bar and a pool table on one side, pizza and Formica tables on the other, this noisy place caters to rowdies and families alike. *Delaware Ave., tel. 419/285–4741. No credit cards. Inexpensive.*

Lodging **Park Hotel.** This white frame hotel, dating from the 1870s, has etched glass and a gracious Victorian lobby, but it's smack in the middle of the island revelry. Bring earplugs. *Box 60, 43456, tel. 419/285–3581. 26 rooms with shared baths. MC, V. Moderate (weekend rates higher).*

Sandusky **Margaritaville.** This Mexican restaurant on the Sandusky River
Dining is mostly underground, with a garden on its roof and a minute waterfall visible from the dining room. *212 Fremont Ave., Rte. 6, tel. 419/627–8903. D, DC, MC, V. Moderate.*

Lodging **Hotel Breakers.** Built in 1905 to resemble a French château, with a five-story rotunda, stained glass, and vintage wicker furniture, this is *the* place to stay on the beach at Cedar Point, especially if you can get a turret room. *Box 5006, 44871, tel. 419/627–2106. 400 rooms. Facilities: 4 restaurants, lounge, pool, beach, shuffleboard. AE, D, MC, V. Closed Oct.–Apr. Expensive.*

Radisson Harbour Inn. This big hotel is successfully disguised as a rambling, weathered beach house. Rooms have matching spreads and draperies in patterned earth tones. *2001 Cleveland Rd. at Cedar Point Causeway, 44870, tel. 419/627–2500. 237 rooms. Facilities: restaurant, pool, exercise room, fishing, parking. AE, D, DC, MC, V. Moderate.*

Wagner's 1844 Inn. A block from downtown, this house is furnished with canopy beds and globe lamps in rooms and a common pool table, TV, and travel library. *230 E. Washington St., 44870, tel. 419/626–1726. 3 rooms. Facilities: Continental breakfast. No credit cards. Moderate.*

Toledo **Tony Packo's Cafe.** Before Max Klinger ever mentioned it on
Dining "M*A*S*H," this place was famous for its Tiffany lamps and Hungarian hot dogs. Don't miss the autographed hot-dog buns. *1902 Front St., tel. 419/691–6054. MC, V. Inexpensive.*

Lodging **Toledo Marriott Portside.** This is the only downtown hotel right on the Maumee River. Walkways connect it with office buildings and the convention center. Built in 1984, it was remodeled in 1991. *2 SeaGate/Summit St., 43604, tel. 419/241–1411 or 800/ 289–1411; fax 419/241–8161. 245 rooms, 5 suites. Facilities: 2 restaurants, lounge, fitness center, parking. AE, D, DC, MC, V. Moderate.*

Motels The great majority of area motels are in and around Sandusky, on the roads to Cedar Point. Prices reflect high-season rates (June–Aug.). **Best Western Resort Inn** (1530 Cleveland Rd.,

Sandusky 44870, tel. 419/625–9234), 105 rooms, restaurant, pool; expensive. **Comfort Inn** (11020 U.S. 250, Milan 44846, tel. 419/499–4681 or 800/228–5150), 53 rooms, pool, exercise room; moderate. **Howard Johnson's** (1932 Cleveland Rd., Sandusky 44870, tel. 419/625–1333), 68 rooms, pool; moderate.

Campgrounds **Middle Bass Island Camping and Fishing** (Apr.–Oct., Box 69, Middle Bass Island 43446, tel. 419/285–6121; Nov.–Mar., 9025 Rte. 14, Streetsboro 44241, tel. 216/626–5233) has tent and RV sites, hot showers, a beach, bike rentals, boat rentals, and charter-fishing packages.

Cleveland

A lot has changed in Cleveland in the 20 years since the fire on the river. The lake and the river have been cleaned up, new buildings have altered the skyline, and the Flats—the industrial area along the Cuyahoga River—is booming with restaurants and nightclubs.

Tourist Information

Cleveland: Visitor Information Center (lobby of Terminal Tower, downtown on Public Sq., tel. 216/621–4110 or 800/321–1001).

Arriving and Departing

By Plane **Cleveland Hopkins International Airport,** 10 mi southwest of downtown, is served by major airlines and several commuter lines. From here the **Rapid Transit Authority** rail system (tel. 216/621–9500) takes 20 minutes to Public Square and costs $1.50. A taxi takes twice as long and costs about $19.

Private planes land at **Burke Lakefront Airport,** on North Marginal Road, just east of downtown.

By Car I–90 runs east–west through downtown Cleveland. I–71 and I–77 come up from the south. Driving from the east on the Ohio Turnpike (I–80), take Exit 10 to I–71N.

Train Station **Amtrak Passenger Station** (200 Memorial Shoreway NE, tel. 216/696–5115).

Bus Station **Greyhound** (E. 15th St. and Chester Ave., tel. 216/781–1400).

Getting Around

The RTA rapid-transit system (tel. 216/621–9500), though not extensive, efficiently bridges east and west, with the Terminal Tower as the hub. RTA buses travel from Public Square on five downtown loop routes.

Exploring Cleveland

From the **Terminal Tower,** Cleveland's central landmark, cross Public Square and walk east on Superior Avenue to the **Old Arcade** (between Superior and Euclid Aves.). Built in 1890, this is still downtown's most beautiful building. Like a nave without a cathedral, it rises five stories, with brass railings, ironwork, a bridge, and a skylight. It was here in the early '80s that the renaissance of downtown Cleveland began, with a few fast-food

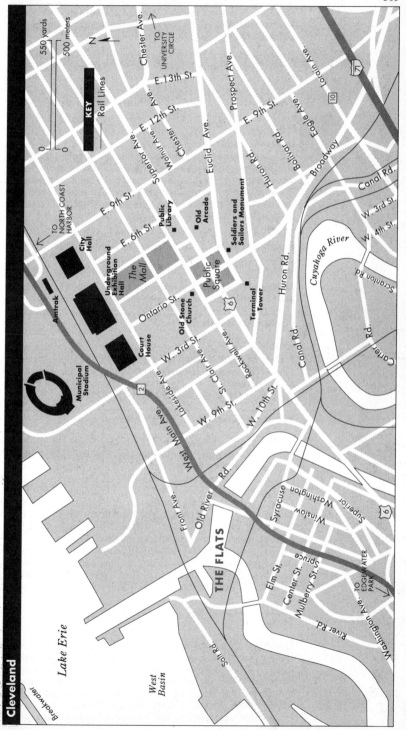

Cleveland

Lake Erie

West Basin

Breakwater

THE FLATS

Municipal Stadium

Amtrak

City Hall

Underground Exhibition Hall

The Mall

Court House

Ontario St.

Old Stone Church

Public Square

Terminal Tower

Public Library

Old Arcade

Soldiers and Sailors Monument

E. 9th St.

E. 6th St.

Superior Ave.

Walnut Ave.

E. 12th St.

Chester

Euclid Ave.

Prospect Ave.

E. 9th St.

E. 13th St.

Chester Ave.

Huron Rd.

Bolivar Rd.

Eagle Ave.

Lorain Ave.

Broadway

Canal Rd.

W. 3rd St.

W. 4th St.

Scranton Rd.

Cuyahoga River

Canal Rd.

Huron Rd.

Rockwell Ave.

St. Clair Ave.

W. 3rd St.

W. 9th St.

W. 10th St.

Lakeside Ave.

West Main Ave.

Front Ave.

Old River Rd.

Carter Rd.

Superior

Winslow

Washington

Syracuse

Elm St.

Center St.

Spruce

Mulberry St.

River Rd.

Washington Ave.

Salt Rd.

TO NORTH COAST HARBOR

TO UNIVERSITY CIRCLE

TO EDGEWATER PARK

KEY
—— Rail Lines

N

550 yards
500 meters

2

6

6

7

10

outlets and a shop called **Cleveland Reflections** (401 Euclid Ave., tel. 216/566–1566), which sells souvenirs you might actually want to buy.

To see the lake, take East 9th Street to **North Coast Harbor,** formerly the East 9th Street Pier. The steamer *William G. Mather* (tel. 216/574–6262; May–Oct.) is moored here, and on it you can learn how Cleveland became a steel town. The *Goodtime III* (tel. 216/861–5110; June–Sept.) gives sightseeing tours on the Cuyahoga River. At sunset, both the lake and the skyline glow.

University Circle, easily reached by rapid transit from downtown, boasts over 50 cultural institutions, of which the **Cleveland Museum of Art** is the centerpiece. A white marble temple set among spring-flowering trees and reflected in a lagoon, it is world-renowned for its medieval European collection, Egyptian art, and European and American paintings. *Tel. 216/421–7340. Admission free. Closed Mon.*

The **Western Reserve Historical Society** has an extensive Napoleonic collection and, in the Crawford Auto-Aviation Museum, just about every old car you might want to see. *10825 E. Boulevard, tel. 216/721–5722. Admission charged. Closed Mon.*

Severance Hall (*see* The Arts and Nightlife, *below*) has the city's most beautiful art deco interior.

Parks and Gardens

At **Edgewater Park,** just west of downtown, there is a beach with water clean enough to swim in and a startlingly close-up view of the skyline. The park also includes a fishing pier, a bait shop, a fitness course, playgrounds, and picnic facilities. The stiff wind off the lake makes for good kite flying.

What to See and Do with Children

If you can get the kids out of the **Disney Store** (tel. 216/696–8444) or **Warner Bros. Studio Store** (tel. 216/781–1550) in Tower City (*see* Shopping, *below*), they'll enjoy the **Children's Museum** (10730 Euclid Ave., tel. 216/791–5437) in University Circle or the **Cleveland Zoo** (Brookside Park, tel. 216/661–6500). Narrated tours on *Lolly the Trolley* (tel. 216/771–4484) leave from Burke Lakefront Airport. **Cedar Point Amusement Park** is an hour away, in Sandusky (*see* Northwest Ohio and the Lake Erie Islands, *above*). Another amusement park, **Geauga Lake** (tel. 216/562–7131 or 800/843–9283 in OH; May–Sept.), is off Rte. 43 in Aurora, about 20 mi southeast of Cleveland (Ohio Turnpike Exit 13 or I–271). Just down the road from it is **Sea World** (tel. 216/995–2121 recording, 216/562–8101, or 800/637–4268; June–Aug.).

Shopping

Downtown Cleveland is a pleasure for shopping: It has everything you might want, and it's rarely crowded. **The Avenue** (tel. 216/241–8550), in Tower City Center, the reborn version of the Terminal Tower, is the newest, biggest, glitziest place to shop downtown. An atrium with a marble fountain and original brass fittings, it's anchored by **Dillard's** (100 Public Sq.), a venerable department store, and has three levels of shops and a food court overlooking the Flats. **The May Company** (159 Euclid Ave.), another venerable department store, is across Ontario Street. Farther east, the **Galleria** (1301 E. 9th St., tel. 216/861–4343) is a crystal palace of a mall, with some of the same shops as The Avenue but a less formal atmosphere.

Spectator Sports

Baseball **Indians** (Cleveland Municipal Stadium, 1085 W. 3rd St., tel. 216/861–1200; Apr.–Oct.).

Basketball **Cavaliers** (The Coliseum, 2923 Streetsboro Rd., Richfield, tel. 216/659–9100; Oct.–May).

Football **Browns** (Cleveland Municipal Stadium, tel. 216/891–5000 or, for tickets, 216/696–3800; Sept.–Dec.).

Dining

Ethnic food is a specialty in Cleveland. A Polish dog is a spicy Polish sausage in a hot-dog bun—make sure you smother it with Cleveland's famous Stadium Mustard. There are restaurant rows in the Flats and in Beachwood, on the East Side. For price ranges, see Chart 1 (B) in Chapter 1.

Expensive **Jim's Steak House.** The original restaurant in the Flats (since 1930) serves traditional steaks and seafood and offers a view of the river laced with willow trees. *1800 Scranton Rd., tel. 216/241–6343. Reservations advised. AE, D, DC, MC, V. Closed Sun. (except during Browns home games), holidays.*
Sammy's. Fresh fish, a raw bar, venison, and linguine are some of the specialties of this converted warehouse with a view of bridges over the Cuyahoga. *1400 W. 10th St., tel. 216/523–5560. Reservations required. AE, D, DC, MC, V. Closed Sun., holidays.*

Moderate **Miracles.** Sandwiches are served on potato pancakes at this sleek restaurant in the Tremont area and at its Glidden House Hotel outpost in University Circle. For dessert there's homemade frozen custard. *2391 W. 11th St., tel. 216/621–6419; 1903 Ford Dr., tel. 216/231–8900. AE, MC, V. No dinner Sun.–Mon.; closed major holidays.*
Paul's Siam Cuisine. Spare furnishings and generous portions make this crowded corner establishment the best Thai restaurant in Cleveland. The mango dishes are superb. *1918 Lee Rd., tel. 216/371–9575. No reservations. No credit cards. No lunch Sat.–Thurs.*
Sweetwater's Café Sausalito. Paella is the specialty in this laidback Marin County–style bar and restaurant—a favorite for lunch at the Galleria. *1301 E. 9th St., tel. 216/696–2233. AE, DC, MC, V. Closed Thanksgiving and Christmas.*

Inexpensive **Otto Moser's.** Corned beef is king in this 100-year-old down-
★ town bar, where moose heads and photographs of old vaudevillians decorate the walls. *2044 E. 4th St., tel. 216/771–3831. No credit cards. No dinner; closed Sun., major holidays.*

Lodging

Cleveland has taken great strides in correcting the shortage of hotels downtown. The Ritz-Carlton opened in 1990, the Cleveland Marriott in 1991, and another hotel is under way in Playhouse Square. Downtown hotels offer weekend packages, whereas suburban ones have lower weekday rates. For price ranges, see Chart 2 (A) in Chapter 1.

Very Expensive **Cleveland Marriott Society Center.** Part of the newest addition to Cleveland's skyline, the Society Tower complex, this beautiful hotel faces the historic Mall and abuts Public Square. Plush accommodations are complemented by fantastic views of Lake Erie and the lights and bridges of the Flats. *127 Public Sq., 44114, tel. 216/696-9200; fax 216/696-0966. 401 rooms, 15 suites. Facilities: restaurant, 2 lounges, fitness center, concierge, parking. AE, D, MC, V.*

Radisson Suite Hotel. This downtown former apartment complex debuted in 1990 as Cleveland's first all-suite hotel. Decor is modern but warmly elegant, with decidedly private club–style furnishings. *1706 E. 12th St., 44114, tel. 216/523-8000; fax 216/861-1266. 252 suites. Facilities: restaurant, health club. AE, D, DC, MC, V.*

★ **The Ritz-Carlton.** A touch of Victorian England suits Cleveland's Tower City surprisingly well. China cabinets decorate the halls, and the rooms are furnished with antiques and easy chairs. The bar at The Grill specializes in single-malt Scotch whiskies. *1515 W. 3rd St., 44113, tel. 216/623-1300; fax 216/623-0515. 208 rooms, 21 suites. Facilities: 2 restaurants, 2 lounges, fitness center, pool, concierge, parking. AE, D, DC, MC, V.*

Stouffer Tower City Plaza Hotel. The city's original grand hotel has recently had the grandeur restored to its lobby, which features an ornate Carrara marble fountain. The rooms, done in burgundy and pale green, have period furniture and good views. *24 Public Sq., 44113, tel. 216/696-5600 or 800/678-8946; fax 216/696-3102. 492 rooms, 49 suites. Facilities: 2 restaurants, 2 bars, health club, pool, concierge, complimentary limousine (downtown). AE, D, DC, MC, V.*

Expensive **Aurora House Spa.** This rustic barn-board lodge, furnished with antiques and Victorian draperies, started out as a hair salon and grew. Mario's International has spa dining, Roman pizza, and six-course northern Italian dinners (closed Sun.). *35 E. Garfield Rd. (Rtes. 82 and 306), Aurora 44202, tel. 216/562-9171; fax 216/562-2386. 74 rooms, 1 suite, 8 cabins. Facilities: 3 restaurants, pool, jogging track, full spa, limousine, parking. AE, D, DC, MC, V. Spa closed Sun., holidays.*

Baricelli Inn. Every room is different in this turn-of-the-century brownstone mansion, now a B&B, convenient to University Circle. Contemporary European and American dinners are served in the dining room (closed Sun.). *2203 Cornell Rd., 44106, tel. 216/791-6500; fax 216/791-9131. 7 rooms. Facilities: Continental breakfast, restaurant, parking. AE, MC, V. Closed holidays.*

Clinic Center Hotel. Although it's on the grounds of the renowned Cleveland Clinic, there's nothing clinical about this luxurious international hotel. The Classics restaurant (no lunch Sat.; closed Sun.) serves French and Continental cuisine. *2065 E. 96th St. (at Carnegie Ave.), 44106, tel. 216/791-1900 or 800/321-7100; fax 216/791-7065. 292 rooms, 14 suites. Facilities: 3 restaurants, bar, access to pool and fitness center at clinic, concierge, parking. AE, D, DC, MC, V. Special rates for clinic patients.*

Sheraton Cleveland City Center Hotel. The former Bond Court Hotel has been transformed into a Sheraton geared to business travelers, with upgraded communications systems and additional phones and work space in all rooms. *777 St. Clair Ave., 44114, tel. 216/771–7600 or 800/321–1090 in OH; fax 216/771–5129. 315 rooms, 45 suites. Facilities: restaurant, health club, conference rooms, business lounge. AE, D, DC, MC, V.*

Moderate **Holiday Inn–Lakeside.** Across from Burke Lakefront Airport and convenient to the train station, this hotel, with lake views and a country-club feel, is congenial to sports fans and people who like high winds off the lake. *1111 Lakeside, 44114, tel. 216/241–5100; fax 216/241–7437. 377 rooms. Facilities: 2 restaurants, bar, pool, exercise equipment, concierge, parking. AE, DC, MC, V.*

Ramada Inn–Southeast. This seven-story suburban hotel, with a restful lobby done in blue and gray, is convenient to Sea World and Geauga Lake. *24801 Rockside Rd. (at I–271), Bedford Heights 44146, tel. 216/439–2500. 136 rooms. Facilities: restaurant, pub, pool, parking. AE, D, DC, MC, V.*

Inexpensive **Brooklyn YMCA.** Bare-bones single rooms for men are available on a first-come, first-served basis. *3881 Pearl Rd., 44109, tel. 216/749–2355. 69 rooms. Facilities: pool, gym, cafeteria, laundry, parking. No credit cards.*

Motels Motels are concentrated around the Berea–Middleburg Heights exit off I–71 (near the airport), the Rockside Road/Brecksville exit off I–77, and the Chagrin Boulevard/Beachwood exit off I–271. Closer to Aurora, rates are higher in summer. **Aurora Woodlands Best Western Inn** (800 N. Aurora Rd., Aurora 44202, tel. 216/562–9151, 146 rooms, 2 restaurants, pool, exercise room, shuttle to attractions; expensive. **Radisson Inn Beachwood** (26300 Chagrin Blvd., Beachwood 44122, tel. 216/831–5150 or 800/221–2222), 188 rooms, 6 suites, restaurant, lounge, pool, fitness center; moderate. **Budget Host Inn La Siesta Motel** (8300 Pearl Rd., Strongsville 44136, tel. 216/234–4488), 38 rooms; inexpensive. **Quality Inn Airport** (28600 Ridgehill Rd., Cleveland 16161, tel. 216/267–5100 or 800/221–2222; fax 216/267–2428), 153 rooms, restaurant, bar, 2 pools; inexpensive.

The Arts and Nightlife

The Arts **Playhouse Square Center** (1501 Euclid Ave., at E. 17th St., tel. 216/241–6000, 800/492–9696, or 800/492–6048 in OH; Sept.–May) is home to the Cleveland Ballet, Cleveland Opera, DanceCleveland, and the Great Lakes Theater Festival. The **Cleveland Play House** (8500 Euclid Ave., tel. 216/795–7000; Oct.–June) and **Karamu House** (2355 E. 89th St., tel. 216/795–7070; Oct.–June) are near University Circle. **Severance Hall** (11001 Euclid Ave., tel. 216/231–1111; Sept.–May) is home to the Cleveland Orchestra. Tickets to many events are sold through **Ticketmaster** (tel. 216/241–5555).

Nightlife Nightlife is concentrated in the Flats, where the crowd is young and into everything from darts to karaoke. At **Shorty's Delux Diner** (1540 Columbus Rd., tel. 216/521–5321) the waitresses sing '50s numbers. **Smart Bar** (1575 Merwin Ave., tel. 216/522–1575) is for people who like to get dressed up and stand in line. For a look at the Flats the way it used to be, try the **Harbor Inn** (1219 Main Ave., tel. 216/241–3232).

Elsewhere in the State

Neil Armstrong Air and Space Museum

Getting There The museum is off I–75, halfway between Cincinnati and Toledo (about an hour from either city), in Wapakoneta, Neil Armstrong's hometown.

What to See and Do Ohio is a leading producer of astronauts. The **Neil Armstrong Air and Space Museum** helps you feel what it's like to go into space. *Exit 111 off I–75, tel. 419/738–8811. Admission charged. Closed Dec.–Feb.*

Dayton

Getting There Dayton is 54 mi north of Cincinnati on I–75, just below the interchange with I–70. **Dayton International Airport** is served by several major carriers and commuter lines.

What to See and Do Aviation is central to the history of Dayton. The **Dayton/Montgomery County Convention and Visitors Bureau** (Chamber Plaza, 5th and Main Sts., 45402, tel. 513/226–8248, 800/221–8235, or 800/221–8234 in OH) publishes a helpful Visitors Guide and operates an information center at the U.S. Air Force Museum (*see below*). A self-guided tour of Dayton's Aviation Trail starts out at the **Wright Brothers Bicycle Shop** (22 S. Williams St., tel. 513/443–0793), where Wilbur and Orville Wright, native Daytonians, first hatched the idea for the airplane, and ends up at the **Wright Memorial,** near the field where the brothers practiced flying.

The **United States Air Force Museum** is an internationally popular attraction and could easily take a full day. Exhibits tell the story of flight from Icarus to Desert Storm, with 200 planes (including the only remaining B–70) in hangars and on airfields. The Space Age is also thoroughly chronicled. The IMAX theater shows flight-related films several times daily (admission charged). Also here are museum shops, a café, and picnic tables. *Wright-Patterson Air Force Base, Springfield Pike (I–75 to Rte. 4, Harshman Rd. exit), tel. 513/255–3284. Admission free.*

Pro Football Hall of Fame

Getting There The Hall of Fame is in Canton, 60 mi south of Cleveland, off I–77 (2121 George Halas Dr. NW, Canton 44708).

What to See and Do The **Pro Football Hall of Fame,** its dome shaped like a football in kickoff position, is a mecca to football fans. Two enshrinement halls are the serious purpose, but displays include a chronology of the game; mementos of the great players; and video replays showing great moments in football. A museum store, a snack bar, and vending machines are on the premises. *2121 George Halas Dr. NW (Fulton Rd. exit off I–77 and U.S. 62), tel. 216/456–8207 or 216/456–7762 (recording). Admission charged.*

The **Canton/Stark County Convention & Visitors Bureau** (229 Wells Ave. NW, Canton 44703, tel. 216/452–0243 or 800/533–4302) maintains an information center on the approach road to the Hall of Fame.

WISCONSIN

*By Don
Davenport*

Capital — Madison
Population — 4,867,000
Motto — Forward
State Bird — Robin
State Flower — Wood violet

Visitor Information

Wisconsin Tourism Development (Box 7606, Madison 53707, tel. 608/266–2161 or 800/432–8747). **Information centers:** I–90N at Rest Area 22 near Beloit; I–94E at Rest Area 25 near Hudson; I–94N at Rest Area 26 near Kenosha; I–90E at Rest Area 31 near La Crosse; Rte. 12N at Rest Area 24 near Genoa City; Prairie du Chien, at the Rte. 18 bridge; 123 West Washington Avenue, Madison; and 305 East 2nd Street, Superior.

Scenic Drives

As part of the **Great River Road,** Rte. 35 follows the Mississippi River between Prairie du Chien and Prescott, offering many scenic vistas. Rte. 107, between Merrill and Tomahawk, travels along one of the most scenic sections of the 400-mi-long **Wisconsin River Valley.** In northeastern Wisconsin, Rtes. 57 and 42 circle the **Door County Peninsula,** providing 250 mi of spectacular Lake Michigan scenery.

National and State Parks

National Parks — Apostle Islands National Lakeshore (*see* Elsewhere in the State, *below*)

State Parks — Wisconsin's state park system includes 52 parks, nine forests, and numerous trails. Camping is allowed in 36 state parks and all state forests. The **Wisconsin Department of Natural Resources** (Bureau of Parks and Recreation, Box 7921, Madison 53707, tel. 608/266–2181) offers information on the parks and their facilities.

Devils Lake State Park (S5975 Park Rd., Baraboo 53913, tel. 608/356–8301) is one of the state's most popular parks, with hiking, camping, and 500-foot-high bluffs overlooking Devils Lake. **Pattison State Park** (Rte. 2, Superior 54880, tel. 715/399–8073) offers camping, hiking, picnic facilities, and spectacular waterfalls, including the 165-foot Big Manitou Falls, Wisconsin's highest waterfall and the fourth highest east of the Rocky Mountains. **Peninsula State Park** (Rte. 42, Box 218, Fish Creek 54212, tel. 414/868–3258) covers nearly 4,000 acres on the shores of Green Bay; offering golf, hiking, bicycling, and lakeshore camping, it is one of the state's most heavily used parks. **Wyalusing State Park** (13342 County Rte. C, Bagley 53801, tel. 608/996–2261) stands at the confluence of the Wisconsin and Mississippi rivers, providing sweeping vistas of the river valleys.

Milwaukee

Set on the shores of Lake Michigan, Wisconsin's largest city is an international seaport and the state's primary commercial and manufacturing center. A small-town atmosphere prevails in Milwaukee, which is not so much a city as a large collection of neighborhoods. Modern steel-and-glass high rises occupy much of the downtown area, but the early heritage persists in the restored and well-kept 19th-century buildings that share the city skyline. First settled by Potawatomi and later by French fur traders in the late 18th century, the city boomed in the 1840s with the arrival of German brewers, and their legacy remains.

Milwaukee has also become known as a city of festivals. The **Summerfest** kicks off each summer's activities on the lakefront. Another annual highlight is the **Great Circus Parade,** a July spectacle that features scores of antique circus wagons from the famed Circus World Museum in Baraboo. August brings the **State Fair.**

Tourist Information

Greater Milwaukee: Convention & Visitors Bureau (510 W. Kilbourn Ave., 53203, tel. 414/273–3950 or 800/231–0903).

Arriving and Departing

By Plane   **General Mitchell International Airport** (5300 S. Howell Ave., tel. 414/747–5300), 6 mi from downtown via I–94E, is served by several domestic and international carriers. **Milwaukee County Transit System** (tel. 414/344–6711; fare, $1—exact change) operates buses to and from the airport. Taxis between the airport and downtown take about 20 minutes; the fare range is $13 to $15.

By Car   From the north, I–43 provides controlled access into downtown Milwaukee. I–94 provides direct access to downtown from Chicago and other points south, and from the west. I–894 bypasses the metropolitan area to the south and west and provides the best connection to I–94 west and south of the city.

Train Station   **Amtrak** (433 W. St. Paul Ave., tel. 414/933–3081).

Bus Station   **Greyhound** (606 N. 7th St., tel. 414/272–8900).

Getting Around Milwaukee

Lake Michigan is the city's eastern boundary; Wisconsin Avenue is the main east–west thoroughfare. The Milwaukee River divides the downtown area into east and west sections. The East–West Expressway (I–94/I–794) is the dividing line between north and south. Streets are numbered in ascending order from the Milwaukee River west well into the suburbs. Many downtown attractions are near the Milwaukee River and can be reached on foot. **Milwaukee County Transit System** (*see* By Plane, *above*) provides bus service. **Taxis** can be ordered by phone or at taxi stands; the fare is $2.50 for the first mile and $1.25 for each additional mile. The largest firm is **Yellow Cab** (tel. 414/271–1800).

Exploring Milwaukee

Downtown Milwaukee's central business district is a mile long and only a few blocks wide. It is divided by the Milwaukee River. On the east side, the **Iron Block Building** (N. Water St. and E. Wisconsin Ave.) is one of the few remaining ironclad buildings in the United States. Its metal facade was brought in by ship from an eastern foundry and installed during the Civil War. In the 1860s, Milwaukee exported more wheat than any other port in the world, which gave impetus to building the **Grain Exchange Room** in the Mackie Building (225 E. Michigan St.). The 10,000-square-foot trading room has three-story-high columns and painted ceiling panels that feature Wisconsin wildflowers.

The **Milwaukee Art Museum,** in the lakefront War Memorial Center designed by Eero Saarinen, houses notable collections of paintings, drawings, sculpture, photography, and decorative arts. Its permanent collection is strong in European and American art of the 19th and 20th centuries. *750 N. Lincoln Memorial Dr., tel. 414/271–9508. Admission charged. Closed Mon.*

Returning to the river, stop a moment at **Cathedral Square.** This quiet park (E. Kilbourn Ave. and Jefferson St.) was built on the site of Milwaukee's first courthouse. Across the street, **St. John's Cathedral,** dedicated in 1853, was the first church built in Wisconsin specifically as a Roman Catholic cathedral.

The banks of the Milwaukee River are busy in summer, especially at noon, when downtown workers lunch in the nearby parks and public areas, such as **Père Marquette Park,** on the river at Old World 3rd Street and West Kilbourn Avenue.

Adjacent to the park, the **Milwaukee County Historical Center** (910 N. Old World 3rd St., tel. 414/273–8288), a museum housed in a graceful former bank building, features early fire-fighting equipment, military artifacts, toys, and women's fashions. It also contains a research library with naturalization records and genealogical resources.

The river is also the departure point for cruises of Milwaukee's harbor and lakefront. **Iroquois Harbor Cruises** (Clybourn St. bridge on the west bank, tel. 414/332–4194) offers harbor cruises aboard a 149-passenger vessel. **Celebration of Milwaukee** (502 N. Harbor Dr., tel. 414/278–1113) and **Edelweiss Excursions** (1110 N. Old World 3rd St., tel. 414/272–3625) offer lunch and dinner cruises.

As you cross the river to the west side, notice that the east-side streets are not directly opposite the west-side streets and that the bridges across the river are built at an angle. This layout dates from the 1840s, when the area east of the river was called Juneautown and the region to the west was known as Kilbourntown. The rival communities had a fierce argument over which would pay for the bridges that connected them; so intense was the antagonism that citizens venturing into rival territory carried white flags. The Great Bridge War was finally settled by the state legislature in 1845, but the streets on either side of the river were never aligned.

A few blocks west of the river, the **Milwaukee Public Museum** has the fourth-largest collection of natural-history exhibits in the country, as well as outstanding fine arts and Native Ameri-

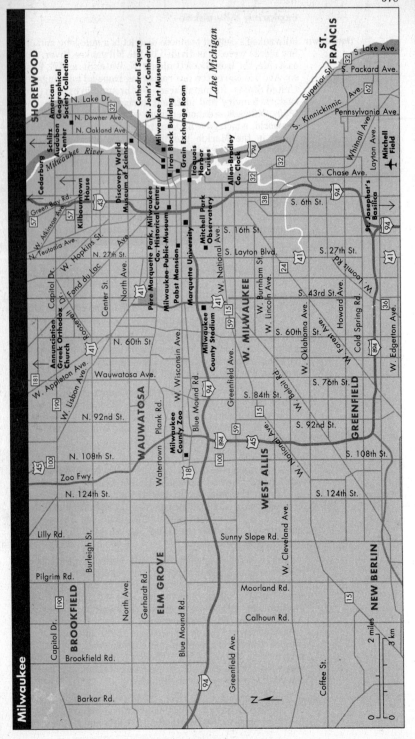

Milwaukee

American Express offers Travelers Cheques built for two.

American Express® Cheques *for Two*. The first Travelers Cheques that allow either of you to use them because both of you have signed them. And only one of you needs to be present to purchase them.

Cheques *for Two* are accepted anywhere regular American Express Travelers Cheques are, which is just about everywhere. So stop by your bank, AAA* or any American Express Travel Service Office and ask for Cheques *for Two*.

can, African, and pre-Columbian collections. Walk-through exhibits include the "Streets of Old Milwaukee," depicting the city in the 1890s; a two-story rain forest; and the "Third Planet" (complete with full-size dinosaurs), where visitors walk into the interior of the Earth to learn about its history. *800 W. Wells St., tel. 414/278–2702. Admission charged.*

Nearby, **Discovery World—Museum of Science, Economics and Technology,** in the Milwaukee Public Central Library, has a wide range of hands-on exhibits on magnets, motors, electricity, health, and computers that introduce youngsters to science, technology, and economics. It also features the "Great Electric Show" and the "Light Wave–Laser Beam Show" on weekends. *818 W. Wisconsin Ave., tel. 414/765–9966. Admission charged. Closed holidays.*

Farther west, just off Wisconsin Avenue on the central mall of the **Marquette University** campus, is **St. Joan of Arc Chapel** (601 N. 14th St., tel. 414/288–7039), a small, stone 15th-century chapel moved from its original site near Lyon, France, and reconstructed here in 1964. One of the stones was reputedly kissed by Joan before she went to her death and is said to be discernibly colder than the others. The **Haggerty Museum of Art** (12th St. and Wisconsin Ave., on the mall between Wisconsin Ave. and Clybourn St., tel. 414/288–7290) houses the university's collection of more than 6,000 works of art, including Renaissance, Baroque, and modern paintings, sculpture, prints, photography, and decorative arts; it also offers changing exhibitions.

Other Attractions Away from downtown, the **Pabst Mansion,** built in 1893 for the beer baron Captain Frederick Pabst, is one of Milwaukee's treasured landmarks. The castlelike, 37-room Flemish Renaissance–style mansion has a tan pressed-brick exterior and is decorated with carved stone and terra-cotta ornamentation outside and carved cabinets and woodwork, ornamental ironwork, marble, tile, stained glass, and carved panels inside, all imported from a 17th-century Bavarian castle. *2000 W. Wisconsin Ave., tel. 414/931–0808. Admission charged. Closed weekdays Jan.–mid-Mar.*

Milwaukee's unique **Mitchell Park Conservatory** consists of three modern 85-foot-high glass domes housing tropical, arid, and seasonal plant and flower exhibits; its displays of lilies and poinsettias are spectacular at Easter and Christmas. There are picnic facilities on the grounds. *524 S. Layton Blvd., tel. 414/ 649–9800. Admission charged.*

The **Milwaukee County Zoo** houses more than 3,000 wild animals and birds, including many endangered species, displayed in natural environments. It also offers educational programs, a seasonal children's zoo, narrated tram tours, miniature-train rides, picnic areas, and cross-country ski trails. *10001 W. Bluemound Rd., tel. 414/771–3040. Admission charged.*

North of downtown Milwaukee, the **American Geographical Society Collection,** housed in the Golda Meir Library on the University of Wisconsin–Milwaukee campus (2311 E. Hartford Ave., tel. 414/229–6282), has an exceptional assemblage of maps, old globes, atlases, and charts, plus 180,000 books and 400,000 journals. The **University of Wisconsin–Milwaukee Art Museum** (3253 N. Downer Ave., tel. 414/229–5070) displays a permanent collection of Greek and Russian icons and 20th-century European paintings and prints. The **UWM Fine Arts Gallery** (2400 E. Kenwood Blvd.) displays the works of students and faculty members; other changing exhibits are held at the **UWM Art History Gallery** (3203 N. Downer Ave.).

The **Charles Allis Art Museum** (1801 N. Prospect Ave., tel. 414/278–8295) occupies an elegant Tudor-style house built in 1911 for the first president of the Allis-Chalmers Manufacturing Co. The home has stained-glass windows by Louis Comfort Tiffany and a stunning worldwide collection of paintings and objets d'art, including works by major 19th- and 20th-century French and American painters.

The Greek Revival cream-colored brick **Kilbourntown House** (4400 W. Estabrook Dr., tel. 414/273–8288), built in 1844, is listed on the National Register of Historic Places and contains an outstanding collection of mid-19th-century furniture and decorative arts.

The **Schlitz Audubon Center,** 10 mi north of downtown, is a 186-acre wildlife area of forests, ponds, marshland, and nature trails along Lake Michigan. Popular with cross-country skiers and bird-watchers, it has an environmental research and education center. *1111 E. Brown Deer Rd., tel. 414/352–2880. Admission charged. Closed Mon., holidays.*

The **Annunciation Greek Orthodox Church** (9400 W. Congress St., tel. 414/461–9400) was Frank Lloyd Wright's last major work; the famed Wisconsin architect called it his "little jewel." Since it opened in 1961, the blue-domed, Byzantine-style church has drawn visitors from all over the world.

Just south of downtown, the **Allen-Bradley Co. Clock** (1201 S. 2nd St.) is a Milwaukee landmark and, according to the *Guinness Book of World Records,* "the largest four-faced clock in the world." Great Lakes ships often use the clock as a navigational reference point.

Built by immigrant parishioners and local craftsmen at the turn of the century, **St. Josephat's Basilica** (2336 S. 6th St., tel. 414/645–5623) is the first Polish basilica in North America and has a dome modeled after St. Peter's in Rome. The church is adorned with a remarkable collection of relics, portraits of Polish saints and leaders, stained glass, and wood carvings.

In the Vicinity About 15 mi north of Milwaukee off I–43 is **Cedarburg,** where the entire downtown district, most of it built by 19th-century pioneers of Niagara limestone, is on the National Register of Historic Places. **Cedar Creek Settlement** (N70 W6340 Bridge Rd., tel. 414/375–9390) is a collection of crafts and antiques shops in the historic Wittenberg Woolen Mill, which was built in 1864 and operated until 1969. With several levels, wooden floors, and lots of nooks and crannies, it's fun to explore. Wisconsin's last remaining **covered bridge** (off Hwy. 143) crosses Cedar Creek 3 mi north of town. The 120-foot bridge was built in 1876 and retired in 1962. Its white pine was cut and squared at a mill near Baraboo and hauled 75 mi to the bridge site. A small park beside the bridge invites picnicking.

Thirty-five mi west of Milwaukee near Eagle is the State Historical Society's living-history museum, **Old World Wisconsin,** which celebrates the state's ethnic heritage in architecture, with over 50 historic buildings on 576 acres in the **Southern Kettle Moraine State Forest.** The restored farm and village buildings gathered from across the state depict 19th- and 20th-century rural Wisconsin. All were originally built and inhabited by European immigrants; they are grouped in German, Norwegian, Danish, and Finnish farmsteads. Costumed interpreters relate the story of immigration to Wisconsin, along with each ethnic group's role in it, and perform chores necessary to rural life a century ago, such as making soap. *S103 W37890 Hwy. 67, tel. 414/594–2116. Admission charged. Closed Nov.–Apr.*

An hour north of Milwaukee off I-43 is **Kohler,** a planned, landscaped village surrounding the factories of the plumbing-fixtures manufacturer Kohler Co. The **Kohler Design Center** (101 Upper Rd., tel. 414/457–3699) houses the company's ceramic-art collection, archives, artifacts from its early factory and village, and a showroom of decorator bathrooms. A guided 2½-hour tour of the factory may be arranged by reservation (tel. 414/457–4441; must be 14 or older). Guided tours of **Waelderhaus** (Kohler Memorial Dr., tel. 414/452–4079), a reproduction of founder John M. Kohler's ancestral home in Austria, are offered daily. The **Woodlake Kohler Complex,** in nearby Sheboygan, comprises more than 25 shops, galleries, and restaurants—including **Artspace** (tel. 414/452–8602), a gallery of the John Michael Kohler Arts Center. **The American Club** (Highland Dr., 53044, tel. 414/457–8000 or 800/344–2838), built as a company-owned hotel for workers, is now a posh resort hotel on the National Register of Historic Places. The compound has two 18-hole golf courses designed by Pete Dye, a large indoor sports complex, a 500-acre wilderness preserve, and several restaurants.

Parks and Gardens

Whitnall Park (5879 S. 92nd St., in suburban Hales Corners) is one of the largest municipal parks in the nation. Its 660 acres encompass an 18-hole golf course, a variety of recreational facilities, picnic areas, and nature and cross-country skiing trails. Within the park is the internationally famous **Alfred L. Boerner Botanical Garden** (tel. 414/425–1130), with trees, shrubs, and flowers in formal and informal gardens. The park's **Wehr Nature Center** (tel. 414/425–8550) includes wildlife exhibits, woodlands and wetlands, a lake, nature trails, and wild gardens.

What to See and Do with Children

At the **Milwaukee Public Museum** (*see* Exploring Milwaukee, Downtown, *above*), the **Wizard Wing** has hands-on natural and human-history exhibits for children and families. The Milwaukee Public Central Library's **Discovery World** (*see* Exploring Milwaukee, Downtown, *above*) and the **Milwaukee County Zoo** (*see* Exploring Milwaukee, Other Attractions, *above*) both have strong appeal for the younger set. **Wm. K. Walthers, Inc.** (N. 60th St. and Florist Ave., tel. 414/527–0770), maker of model railroad equipment since 1932, has the world's largest single warehouse selection of trains, with over 300 manufacturers represented.

Shopping

Stores range from tiny ethnic and specialty shops to enclosed shopping malls featuring large department stores. Using the downtown skywalk system, it's possible to browse in hundreds of stores over several blocks without once setting foot outside. Downtown Milwaukee's major shopping street is **Wisconsin Avenue** west of the Milwaukee River. The **Grand Avenue Mall** is the major downtown retail center, spanning four city blocks. **Historic Third Ward,** a turn-of-the-century wholesale and manufacturing district on the National Register of Historic Places, is bordered by the harbor, the river, and downtown and offers many unusual shops and restaurants. **Jefferson Street,** stretching four blocks from Wisconsin to Kilbourn, offers upscale shops and stores. The **Lincoln Avenue District,** minutes from downtown off I–94, has specialty shops and ethnic restaurants in a quaint, historic Polish and German neighborhood. On Milwaukee's south side, historic **Mitchell Street** is a multicultural blend of retail shops and diverse ethnic restaurants.

Shopping centers in the metropolitan area include **Bayshore** (5900 N. Port Washington Rd.), **Brookfield Square** (95 N. Moorland Rd.), **Capital Court** (5500 W. Capitol Dr.), **Mayfair** (2500 N. Mayfair Rd.), **Northridge** (7700 W. Brown Deer Rd.), **Point Loomis** (3555 S. 27th St.), **Southgate** (3333 S. 27th St.), and **South Ridge** (5300 S. 76th St.).

Spectator Sports

Baseball **Milwaukee Brewers** (Milwaukee County Stadium, 201 S. 46th St., tel. 414/933–9000; Apr.–Oct.).

Basketball **Milwaukee Bucks** (Bradley Center, 1001 N. 4th St., tel. 414/227–0500; Oct.–Apr.).

Football **Green Bay Packers** (tel. 414/342–2717; Sept.–Dec.) play three "home" games each year at Milwaukee County Stadium.

Beaches

Lake Michigan is the place to swim, but be prepared: The midsummer water temperature is only in the 50s and 60s, and the wind adds to the chill. Among the most popular of the narrow sandy beaches are **Bradford Beach** (2400 N. Lincoln Memorial Dr.), **Doctors Beach** (1870 E. Fox Ln., Fox Point), **Grant Beach** (100 Hawthorne Ave., South Milwaukee), and **McKinley Beach** (1750 N. Lincoln Memorial Dr.). The Parks Department's Pool and Beach Hotline (tel. 414/961–6143) has information.

Dining

By Anne Schamberg

Milwaukee's culinary style was shaped to a great extent by the Germans who first settled here. Many restaurants—whether or not they are German—offer Wiener schnitzel or the meringue-based desserts called *schaumtortes*. Rye bread, sometimes crusted with coarse salt, is as common on Milwaukee tables as robins on a spring lawn. Many other ethnic groups have also donated their specialties to Milwaukee's tradition of gemütlichkeit (fellowship and good cheer).

Milwaukeeans like to relax and socialize when they eat out. Fashion isn't as important here as in faster-paced cities. Jackets and ties are customary at the most expensive restaurants, but only a few actually require them. For price ranges, see Chart 1 (A) in Chapter 1.

Very Expensive

★ **English Room.** Milwaukee's premier hotel restaurant, in the Pfister Hotel, has a dark, Victorian elegance. Chef Édouard Becker's German/American cuisine emphasizes meat dishes, though seafood is also served. Service is formal, with plenty of tableside cooking. *424 E. Wisconsin Ave., tel. 414/273–8222. Reservations advised. Jacket required. AE, D, DC, MC, V. No lunch weekends.*

★ **Grenadier's.** Knut Apitz, chef-owner, serves some of the most elegant food in Milwaukee. Imaginative dishes combine classical European style with Oriental or Indian flavors; offerings include tenderloin of veal with raspberry sauce and angel-hair pasta. The three small rooms have an air of matter-of-fact refinement; the handsome, darkly furnished piano bar also has tables. *747 N. Broadway St., tel. 414/276–0747. Reservations advised. Jacket required. AE, DC, MC, V. No lunch Sat.; closed Sun.*

Sanford. Award-winning chef Sanford D'Amato and his wife, Angie, are at the helm of one of Milwaukee's best and busiest restaurants. The innovative French–New American menu changes daily but may include such specials as seared tournedos of sea scallops. The 50-seat dining room is decorated in understated gray and black. *1547 N. Jackson St., tel. 414/ 276–9608. Reservations essential. Jacket required. AE, D, DC, MC, V. No lunch; closed Sun.*

Expensive **Boder's on the River.** Tie-back curtains, fireplaces, and lots of knickknacks give the dining rooms in this suburban restaurant a cheerful country look. The menu offers Wisconsin favorites prepared in a straightforward manner, including roast duckling and baked whitefish. *11919 N. River Rd., Mequon, tel. 414/ 242–0335. Reservations advised. AE, D, DC, MC, V. Closed Mon.*

Giovanni's. At this Old World–style Sicilian place one finds flocked wallpaper, crystal chandeliers, and large portions of rich Italian food. Veal steak Giovanni is excellent, but the pasta is disappointing. *1683 N. Van Buren St., tel. 414/291–5600. Reservations advised. MC, V. No lunch weekends.*

Harold's. Velvet-backed booths, low lighting, etched glass, and rich greenery set a romantic, if slightly generic, mood at this restaurant in the Grand Hotel. Breast of capon with pistachio nuts is representative of the ambitious but sometimes heavy-handed choices on the menu. There is also a selection of "traditional favorites," including steaks and fresh fillet of whitefish. *4747 S. Howell Ave., tel. 414/481–8000. AE, DC, MC, V. No lunch weekends.*

★ **Karl Ratzsch's Old World Restaurant.** In the authentic German atmosphere of this family-owned restaurant, such specialties as schnitzel, roast duckling, and sauerbraten are served by dirndl-skirted waitresses while a string trio schmaltzes it up. The main dining room is decorated with murals, chandeliers made from antlers, and antique beer steins. *320 E. Mason St., tel. 414/276–2720. Reservations advised. AE, D, DC, MC, V. No lunch Mon.*

Mike and Anna's. At this small, trendy restaurant in a working-class neighborhood on the south side, the changing menu features excellent nouvelle-inspired selections, such as fresh salmon with basil-and-tarragon beurre blanc. Be sure to ask for directions when making reservations. *1978 S. 8th St., tel. 414/643–0072. Reservations advised. MC, V. No lunch.*

★ **Steven Wade's Cafe.** Noted for creative, freshly prepared food, chef and co-owner Steven Wade Klindt operates this establishment in a former suburban paint-and-wallpaper store. The changing menu might include Norwegian salmon fillet poached with vanilla sauce or coconut curried lamb. *17001 W. Greenfield Ave., New Berlin, tel. 414/784–0774. Reservations required. AE, D, DC, MC, V. No lunch Sat.; closed Sun.*

Moderate **Chip and Py's.** In the northern suburbs, this stylish restaurant has light gray dual-level dining rooms, a huge fireplace, and contemporary art. The eclectic menu features chicken, beef, seafood, blackened redfish, and vegetarian entrées. Jazz is offered weekends. *1340 W. Town Square Rd., Mequon, tel. 414/241–9589. AE, D, DC, MC, V. No lunch Sun., no dinner Mon.*

Izumi's. Traditional Japanese dishes, including sushi (and tempura or noodles for those who prefer their food cooked), are the fare at this friendly, well-run restaurant. *2178 N. Prospect Ave., tel. 414/271–5278. Reservations advised. AE, MC, V. No lunch weekends.*

Jake's. There are two locations for this longtime Milwaukee favorite that earned its reputation with perfectly prepared steaks and heaps of french-fried onion rings. The best menu choices include escargot, roast duckling, and Bailey's chocolate-chip cheesecake. *6030 W. North Ave., Wauwatosa, tel. 414/771–0550; 21445 W. Capitol Dr., Brookfield, tel. 414/781–7995. Reservations advised. AE, MC, V.*

Three Brothers Bar & Restaurant. Set in an 1887 tavern is one of Milwaukee's revered ethnic restaurants, serving chicken paprikash, roast lamb, Serbian salad, and homemade desserts at old metal kitchen tables. It's about 10 minutes from downtown on the near south side. *2414 S. St. Clair St., tel. 414/481–7530. Reservations advised. No credit cards. No lunch; closed Mon.*

Inexpensive **Benjamin's Delicatessen and Restaurant.** You'll find a wide selection of such tasty specialties as matzo ball soup, corned beef sandwiches, and brisket of beef at this neighborhood deli. There are booths, tables, and a counter where the TV is usually tuned to the latest sporting event. *4156 N. Oakland Ave., Shorewood, tel. 414/332–7777. MC, V.*

Crocus Restaurant and Cocktail Lounge. Tucked away on the south side is this friendly neighborhood restaurant decorated with ethnic paintings and artifacts. Good choices among the homemade Polish dishes are braised-beef roll-ups, stuffed potato dumplings, and pierogi. *1801 S. Muskego Ave., tel. 414/643–6383. No credit cards. No lunch weekends.*

Elsa's on the Park. Across from Cathedral Square Park, this chic but casual place attracts talkative young professionals for big, juicy hamburgers and pork-chop sandwiches. The decor is a crisply stylish gray, white, and black. *833 N. Jefferson St., tel. 414/765–0615. No credit cards. No lunch weekends.*

Rudy's Mexican Restaurant. Located in Walker's Point, an area south of downtown inching toward gentrification, Rudy's serves fresh standard Mexican fare, including chile rellenos, enchiladas, and guacamole. *625 S. 5th St., tel. 414/291–0296. AE, D, DC, MC, V.*

Watts Tea Shop. This genteel spot for breakfast or lunch is located above George Watts & Sons, Milwaukee's premier store for china, crystal, and silver. Offerings include simple breakfasts, sandwiches, a juice bar, and the special custard-filled sunshine cake. *761 N. Jefferson St., tel. 414/276-6352. No shorts. AE, MC, V. Closed Sun.*

Lodging

By Anne Schamberg

Milwaukee offers a number of options for accommodations, ranging from cozy small motels to executive suites overlooking Lake Michigan and the city. Most downtown hotels are within walking distance of the theater district, the Convention Center and Arena, and plenty of shopping and restaurants. In summer, accommodations should be booked well ahead, especially for weekends. For price ranges, see Chart 2 (A) in Chapter 1.

Very Expensive **Pfister Hotel.** Many of the rooms in Milwaukee's grand old hotel, built in 1893, have been combined to make suites with enlarged bathrooms. Rooms in the Tower, built in 1975, are bright and contemporary with a Victorian accent, in keeping with the original hotel. A collection of 19th-century art hangs in the elegant Victorian lobby. *424 E. Wisconsin Ave., 53202, tel. 414/273-8222; fax 414/273-0747. 307 rooms. Facilities: 3 restaurants, nightclub, lounge, indoor pool, health club. AE, D, DC, MC, V.*

Expensive **Embassy Suites Hotel.** The sweeping atrium lobby with fountains, potted plants, and glass elevators is the focal point of this hotel in the western suburbs. The one- or two-bedroom suites are decorated in pastels and earth tones with contemporary furnishings. *1200 S. Moorland Rd., Brookfield 53005, tel. 414/782-2900; fax 414/796-9159. 203 suites. Facilities: restaurant, lounge, indoor pool, whirlpool, sauna, exercise room. AE, D, DC, MC, V.*

Hyatt Regency. This centrally located high-rise hotel has an 18-story open atrium and a revolving restaurant on top. The rooms are airy and bright, with plush contemporary furnishings. *333 W. Kilbourn Ave., 53203, tel. 414/276-1234 or 800/233-1234; fax 414/276-6338. 484 rooms. Facilities: 3 restaurants, 3 lounges. AE, D, DC, MC, V.*

Marc Plaza. Crystal chandeliers, marble-base columns, and dark woodwork in the lobby give this gracious hotel, built in 1929, a handsome appearance. Traditionally decorated rooms vary quite a bit in size. *509 W. Wisconsin Ave., 53203, tel. 414/271-7250 or 800/558-7708 outside WI; fax 414/271-1039. 500 rooms, 34 suites. Facilities: 2 restaurants, lounge, indoor pool, sauna, exercise room. AE, D, DC, MC, V.*

★ **Wyndham Milwaukee Center.** Part of the city's growing theater district, this hotel is located atop the Milwaukee Center, by the river. The opulent lobby is tiled with Italian marble; guest rooms are contemporary, large and pleasant, with mahogany furnishings. *139 E. Kilbourn Ave., 53202, tel. 414/276-8686; fax 414/276-8007. 221 rooms. Facilities: restaurant, lounge, exercise room, sauna, whirlpool, 2 steam baths, health club, jogging track. AE, DC, MC, V.*

Moderate **Grand Milwaukee Hotel.** Located across from the airport, the Grand is the largest hotel in the state. Renovated in 1992, the bright rooms are decorated in earth tones. The marble-walled lobby is illuminated with chandeliers; a swimming pool cools the central courtyard. *4747 S. Howell Ave., 53207, tel. 414/481-8000 or 800/558-3862; fax 414/481-8065. 510 rooms. Facilities: restaurant, lounge, nightclub, 2 pools, health club, 7 indoor* *tennis courts, 6 racquetball courts, movie theater. AE, DC, MC, V.*

Ramada Inn Downtown. Rough knotty-pine paneling gives the lobby of this motor hotel a casual feeling. The maroon-toned rooms are furnished in standard Ramada style. *633 W. Michigan St., 53202, tel. 414/272–8410; fax 414/272–4651. 154 rooms. Facilities: restaurant, lounge, outdoor pool, airport transportation. AE, D, DC, MC, V.*

Sheraton Mayfair. This bustling high-rise motor hotel on the west side is convenient to the County Medical Complex and the Milwaukee County Zoo. Guest rooms are bright and airy, with traditional furnishings; those near the top have fine views. *2303 N. Mayfair Rd., Wauwatosa 53226, tel. 414/257–3400; fax 414/257–0900. 150 rooms. Facilities: restaurant, lounge, indoor pool, sauna. AE, D, DC, MC, V.*

Inexpensive   **Astor Hotel.** Close to Lake Michigan, the Astor has the not-unpleasant air of a hotel past its heyday, which is documented with photographs of illustrious guests in the large lobby. Many of the rooms have been remodeled and furnished with antiques and period reproductions but retain old bathroom fixtures. *924 E. Juneau Ave., 53202, tel. 414/271–4220, 800/558–0200, or 800/242–0355 in WI; fax 414/271–6370. 96 rooms. Facilities: restaurant, lounge, garage, airport transportation. AE, D, DC, MC, V.*

Motels   **Best Western Midway Hotel-Brookfield** (1005 S. Moorland Rd., Brookfield 53005, tel. 414/786–9540 or 800/528–1234; fax 414/786–4561), 125 rooms, restaurant, lounge, indoor pool, saunas, whirlpool, recreation area; moderate. **Holiday Inn–South** (6331 S. 13th St., 53221, tel. 414/764–1500; fax 414/764–6531), 159 rooms, restaurant, lounge, indoor recreation area, heated pool, whirlpool, playground, sports court, jogging track; moderate. **Holiday Inn Express** (11111 W. North Ave., Wauwatosa 53226, tel. 414/778–0333; fax 414/778–0331), 122 rooms; inexpensive.

The Arts and Nightlife

Milwaukee Magazine (on newsstands) lists arts and entertainment events. Also check the Arts section of the Sunday *Milwaukee Journal.*

The Arts   Milwaukee's theater district is in a two-block downtown area bounded by the Milwaukee River, East Wells Street, North Water Street, and East State Street. Most tickets are sold at box offices.

The **Riverside Theater** (116 W. Wisconsin Ave., tel. 414/224–3000) and **Pabst Theater** (144 E. Wells St., tel. 414/278–3663) host touring theater companies, Broadway shows, and other entertainment. The **Milwaukee Center** (108 E. Wells St., tel. 414/224–9490) is home to the **Milwaukee Repertory Theater** and the **Milwaukee Chamber Theater.** The **Milwaukee Symphony Orchestra, Milwaukee Ballet Company, Florentine Opera Company,** and **First Stage Milwaukee** are based at the **Performing Arts Center** (929 N. Water St., tel. 414/273–7206). **Lincoln Center for the Arts** (820 E. Knapp St., tel. 414/272–2787) is home to three dance groups: the **Bauer Dance Company, Dancecircus,** and **J.U.M.P. Dance Theater.** The 1927 **Oriental Landmark Theater** (2230 N. Farwell Ave., tel. 414/276–8711) shows foreign and hard-to-find films in an exotic setting.

Nightlife The city offers a variety of nightlife, with friendly saloons (about 1,600 at last count) and a varied music scene. The **Safe House** (779 N. Front St., tel. 414/271–2007), with a James Bond spy hideout decor, is a favorite with young people and out-of-towners. **La Playa** (Pfister Hotel, 424 E. Wisconsin Ave., tel. 414/276–1200) combines a South American atmosphere with the glamour of a supper club. **Major Goolsby's** (340 W. Kilbourn Ave., tel. 414/271–3414) is regarded as one of the country's top 10 sports bars by the jocks and occasional major-league sports stars who hang out here. Jazz fans go to the **Bombay Bicycle Club** (Marc Plaza Hotel, 509 W. Wisconsin Ave., tel. 414/271–7250) or **The Estate** (2423 N. Murray Ave., tel. 414/964–9923), a cozy club offering progressive jazz four nights a week.

Elsewhere in the State

Madison and Southern Wisconsin

Getting There Take I–90W from Milwaukee to Madison.

What to See and Do **Madison,** named after President James Madison, is the state capital and home to the University of Wisconsin. The center of the city lies on an eight-block-wide isthmus between Lakes Mendota and Monona. The Roman Renaissance–style **Wisconsin State Capitol** (tours daily, tel. 608/266–0382), built between 1906 and 1917, dominates the downtown skyline. A **farmers' market** is held on Capitol Square each Saturday from May through October. The **State Historical Society Museum** (30 N. Carroll St., Capitol Sq., tel. 608/262–7700) has permanent and changing exhibits on Wisconsin history from prehistoric Native American cultures to contemporary social issues.

Capitol Square is connected to the university's campus by State Street, a mile-long, tree-lined shopping district of import shops, ethnic restaurants, and artisans' studios. The **Madison Art Center,** in the lobby of the Civic Center (211 State St., tel. 608/257–0158), has a large permanent collection and frequent temporary exhibitions.

At the foot of State Street, the **University of Wisconsin,** which opened in 1849 with 20 students, now has an enrollment of 46,000. Guided walking tours of the campus may be arranged at the visitor information center in the **Memorial Union** (800 Langdon St., tel. 608/262–2511). The university's **Elvehjem Museum of Art** (800 University Ave., tel. 608/263–2246) is one of the state's best, with a permanent collection of paintings, sculpture, and decorative arts dating from 2300 BC to the present. Away from downtown, the **University Arboretum** (1207 Seminole Hwy., tel. 608/263–7888) has more than 1,200 acres of natural plant and animal communities, such as prairie and forest landscapes, and horticultural collections of Upper Midwest specimens.

Close by, the **Henry Villas Zoo** (702 S. Randall Ave., tel. 608/266–4732) exhibits nearly 200 species of animals and has a children's zoo where youngsters can pet and feed animals. On Madison's south side, **Olbrich Park Botanical Gardens** (3330 Atwood Ave., tel. 608/246–4550) features 14 acres of outdoor rose, herb, and rock gardens and a glass-pyramid conservatory with tropical plants and flowers. The **Greater Madison Convention and Visitors Bureau** (615 E. Washington Ave., 53703, tel.

608/255–0701 or 800/373–6376) offers information on Madison attractions.

West of Madison is **Blue Mounds,** at the eastern edge of Wisconsin's lead-mining region. **Blue Mound State Park** (1 mi northwest of village, tel. 608/437–5711) offers glorious vistas from towers on the summit of one of the hills. **Cave of the Mounds** (Cave of the Mounds Rd., tel. 608/437–3038; admission charged; closed weekdays mid-Nov.–mid-Mar.) is small, but it is filled with diverse and colorful mineral formations.

Nestled in a picturesque valley nearby is **Little Norway** (3576 Hwy. JG North, tel. 608/437–8211), a restored 1856 Norwegian homestead with its original log buildings and an outstanding collection of Norwegian antiques and pioneer arts and crafts.

Another charming spot in this region is the village of **New Glarus,** founded by Swiss settlers from the canton of Glarus in 1845. It retains its Swiss character in language, food, architecture, and festivities. The **Swiss Historical Village** (612 7th Ave., tel. 608/527–2317) contains reconstructed and original buildings from early New Glarus and displays that trace Swiss immigration to America.

Frank Lloyd Wright chose the farming community of **Spring Green** on the Wisconsin River for his home, "Taliesin," and his architectural school. Wright's influence is evident in a number of buildings in the village; notice the use of geometric shapes, low flat-roofed profiles, cantilevered projections, and steeple-like spires. Tours of **Taliesin** (3 mi south of Spring Green on Hwy. 23, tel. 608/588–2511) buildings, designed and built by Wright, include his home and office for nearly 50 years, the 1903 Hillside Home School, galleries, a drafting studio, and a theater.

The extraordinary, multilevel stone **House on the Rock** stands on a chimneylike rock 450 feet above the Wyoming Valley. It was begun by artist Alex Jordan in the early 1940s and was opened to the public in 1961. The complex now includes re-creations of historic village streets, complete with shops, and extensive collections of dolls, cannons, musical machines, and paperweights.

The renowned **American Players Theater** (County Rte. C and Golf Course Rd., tel. 608/588–7401) presents Shakespeare and other classics in a beautiful, wooded outdoor amphitheater near the Wisconsin River.

On the western edge of the state, **Prairie du Chien** dates from 1673, when explorers Marquette and Joliet reached the confluence of the Wisconsin and Mississippi rivers 6 mi to the south. It became a flourishing fur market in the late 17th century, and today it is a bustling river community where the steamers *Delta Queen* and *Mississippi Queen* call in summer. The **Villa Louis Mansion** (521 Villa Louis Rd., tel. 608/326–2721) was built in 1870 by Wisconsin's first millionaire. It contains one of the finest collections of Victorian decorative arts in the country. The Astor Fur Warehouse on the grounds has exhibits on the fur trade of the upper Mississippi. Nearby is **Wyalusing State Park** (*see* National and State Parks, *above*).

Wisconsin Dells and Baraboo

Getting There Take I–90W from Milwaukee to Madison, then I–90/94 north-west to the Dells. Baraboo is off U.S. 12 to the south of I–90/94.

What to See and Do One of the state's foremost natural attractions is the **Wisconsin Dells,** nearly 15 mi of soaring, eroded rock formations created over thousands of years as the Wisconsin River cut into the soft limestone. The two small communities encompassed by the Dells—Wisconsin Dells and Lake Delton, with a combined population of less than 4,000—draw nearly 2 million visitors annually to frolic in the water parks, play miniature golf, and enjoy the rides, shows, and other man-made attractions that today nearly overshadow the scenic wonders.

You can view the river and its spectacular rock formations on the cruise boats of **Dells Boat Tours** (tel. 608/254–8555) or aboard World War II amphibious vehicles that travel both land and water at **Dells Ducks** (tel. 608/254–6080) or **Wisconsin Ducks** (tel. 608/254–8751). **Noah's Ark** (tel. 608/254–6351), **Familyland** (tel. 608/254–7766), and **Riverview Park and Waterworld** (tel. 608/254–2608) offer a thrilling variety of water slides, wave pools, inner-tube and raft rides, and a host of other diversions. The notorious Confederate spy Belle Boyd, who died here while on a speaking tour in 1910, is buried in **Spring Grove Cemetery.**

When you need a break from the nonstop action, **Mirror Lake State Park** (just south of the Dells off U.S. 12, tel. 608/254–2333) and **Rocky Arbor State Park** (2 mi north off U.S. 12, tel. 608/254–8001) offer camping, hiking, scenery, and solitude. For more information, contact the **Wisconsin Dells Visitor and Convention Bureau** (701 Superior St., Wisconsin Dells 53965, tel. 608/254–8088 or 800/223–3557).

South of Wisconsin Dells is **Baraboo,** where a fur-trading post run by a Frenchman named Baribault stood in the early 19th century. It is best known as the place where the five Ringling brothers began their circus careers in 1882 and where the Ringling Brothers Circus quartered in winter from 1884 to 1912. In the quarters now is **Circus World Museum** (426 Water St., tel. 608/356–8341; admission charged; closed mid-Sept.–Apr.), a State Historical Society site that preserves the history of the more than 100 circuses that began in Wisconsin. Along with an outstanding collection of antique circus wagons, the museum presents big-top performances featuring circus stars of today. **Baraboo Chamber of Commerce** (124 2nd St., 53913, tel. 608/356–8333) supplies information on the town.

Door County

Getting There Take I–43N from Milwaukee, Rte. 310E to Two Rivers, then Rte. 42N.

What to See and Do Jutting out from the Wisconsin mainland like the thumb on a mitten, the 70-mi-long **Door County Peninsula** is bordered by the waters of Lake Michigan and Green Bay. It was named for the Porte des Morts (Door of Death), a treacherous strait separating the peninsula from nearby offshore islands. Scores of ships have come to grief in Door County waters, and even today large Great Lakes freighters often slip through the Door to seek shelter in the lee of the islands during Lake Michigan's autumn storms. Soil conditions and climate make the peninsula ideal for cherry production, and its orchards produce as much as 20 million pounds of fruit each year. The peninsula is carpeted in blossoms when the trees bloom in late May.

A visit to the peninsula can include stops at a half-dozen charming lakeshore towns, each with its own flavor. First-time visitors often make a circle tour via Rtes. 57 and 42. The Lake Michigan side of the peninsula is somewhat less settled and the landscape rougher. The peninsula's rugged beauty attracts large numbers of artists, whose works are shown in studios, galleries, and interesting shops in all the villages.

Sturgeon Bay, the peninsula's chief community and a busy shipbuilding port, sits on a partially man-made ship canal connecting the waters of Lake Michigan and Green Bay. Here, the **Door County Maritime Museum** (2nd Ave. and Sunset Park, tel. 414/743–8139) has displays on local shipbuilding and commercial fishing, and the **Door County Historical Museum** (18 N. 4th Ave., tel. 414/743–5809) exhibits Native American relics and items from pioneer days.

Beside Rte. 57 along the peninsula's Lake Michigan side, you can see the rocky shoreline and sea caves at **Cave Point County Park** (no phone), near Valmy. Just north of **Jacksonport,** you'll cross the 45th parallel, halfway between the equator and the North Pole.

Northport, at the tip of the peninsula, is the port of departure for the daily car ferries to **Washington Island,** 6 mi offshore; passenger ferries leave from nearby **Gills Rock.** The island's 600 inhabitants celebrate their heritage with an annual Scandinavian festival in August. Narrated tram tours aboard the Washington Island **Cherry Train** (tel. 414/847–2135) or the **Viking Tour Train** (tel. 414/854–2972) leave from the ferry dock. The island has nearly 100 mi of roads and is popular with bicyclists. You may take your own bicycle on the ferry or rent one from the ferry line at Gills Rock. To really get away from it all, take the ferry from Washington Island to remote **Rock Island State Park** (tel. 414/847–2235), a wilderness area permitting only hiking and backpack camping.

Back on the mainland, on the Green Bay side of the peninsula, the villages evoke New England in atmosphere and charm and provide exceptional views of Green Bay, where sunsets can be breathtaking. **Fish Creek** is home to the **Peninsula Players Theater** (tel. 414/868–3287), called America's oldest professional resident summer theater. Here, too, is beautiful **Peninsula State Park** (tel. 414/868–3258), which offers hiking and bicycling.

No visit to Door County would be complete without sampling the region's famed fishboil, which originated more than 100 years ago. It is a simple but delicious meal that has reached legendary status in the region. A huge caldron of water is brought to a boil over a wood fire. A basket of red potatoes is then cooked in the caldron, followed by a basket of fresh local whitefish steaks. At the moment the fish is cooked to perfection, kerosene is dumped on the fire, and the flames shoot high in the air, causing the caldron to boil over, expelling most of the fish oils and fat. The steaming whitefish is then served with melted butter, potatoes, cole slaw, and another favorite, Door County cherry pie. The **Door County Chamber of Commerce** (Box 406, Sturgeon Bay 54235–0406, tel. 414/743–4456 or 800/527–3529) provides information on county attractions.

Bayfield and the Apostle Islands

Getting There Take I–94W from Milwaukee to Portage, U.S. 51N to Hurley, U.S. 2W to Ashland, and then Rte. 13N to Bayfield.

What to See and Do The commercial-fishing village of Bayfield, population 700, is the gateway to the **Apostle Islands National Lakeshore,** which comprises 21 of Lake Superior's 22 Apostle Islands and a segment of mainland near Bayfield. Named by French missionaries, who mistakenly thought the islands numbered 12, the Apostles encompass 42,000 acres spread over 600 square miles of Lake Superior. Primitive camping and hiking are allowed on most of the islands. The **Little Sand Bay Visitor Center** (13 mi north of Bayfield on Rte. 13, tel. 715/779–3459) has Lakeshore exhibits and daily guided tours of a former commercial fishing operation in summer. Sailing among the islands is a favorite pastime, as is charter boat fishing for salmon. **K–2 Charters** (tel. 715/779–3320 or 800/354–8735), **Paragon Charters** (tel. 715/779–5634), **Catchun-Sun Charter Co.** (tel. 715/779–3111), and **Superior Charters, Inc.** (tel. 715/779–5124 or 800/772–5124), all out of Bayfield, offer captained sailboat charters among the islands. For experienced sailors, **Superior Charters, Inc.** and **Sailboats, Inc.** (tel. 800/826–7010) offer bareboat sailboat charters. **Apostle Islands Cruise Service** (City Dock, Bayfield, tel. 715/779–3925) gives daily sightseeing tours of the islands, weather permitting. Camper shuttle service to many of the islands is also available. **Stockton Island,** the largest island in the National Lakeshore, has a visitor center (open daily, Memorial Day–Labor Day) with a park naturalist on duty; there are natural and cultural history exhibits. Guided tours of the **Raspberry Island Lighthouse** buildings and gardens are offered, as are guided tours of historic **Manitou Island Fish Camp,** on Manitou Island. Lakeshore headquarters (Washington Ave. and 4th St., Box 4, Bayfield 54814, tel. 715/779–3397) offers publications, exhibits, and a movie about the islands.

In **Bayfield** itself is **Booth Cooperage** (1 Washington Ave., tel. 715/779–3400)—Wisconsin's only working barrel factory and museum—where you can watch local coopers ply their trade. At **Lake Superior Big Top Chautauqua** (3 mi south of Bayfield on Rte. 13, tel. 715/373–5851), concerts, plays, lectures, and original historical musicals are performed under canvas in the spirit of old-time tent shows. **Bayfield Chamber of Commerce** (Box 138, 54814, tel. 715/779–3335 or 800/447–4094) provides information on other area attractions.

Bayfield is also the embarkation point to **Madeline Island,** where the village of **La Pointe** was established as a French trading post in the early 17th century, followed in 1793 by a permanent settlement. The island is reached via the car- and passenger-carrying **Madeline Island Ferry** (Washington Ave., tel. 715/747–2051). The **Madeline Island Historical Museum** (tel. 715/747–2415), on the site of a former fur trading post, houses exhibits on island history. Narrated island tours are given by **Madeline Island Bus Tours** (Ferry Dock, La Pointe, tel. 715/747–2051; late June–early Oct.). If you've a yen for the outdoors, consider renting a bicycle from **Madeline Island Bike Rentals** (tel. 715/747–2801) and touring the island on your own. **Big Bay State Park** (tel. 715/747–6425) has camping, a long sandy beach, picnic areas, and hiking and nature trails.

7 The Great Plains

Great Plains

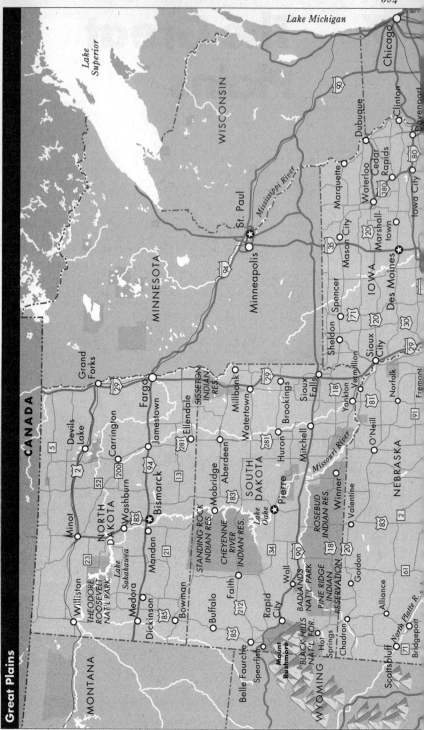

Lake Michigan

Chicago

Lake Superior

WISCONSIN

90

Dubuque

Clinton

Davenport

Marquette

Cedar Rapids

Waterloo

Iowa City

380

80

Mississippi River

St. Paul

Mason City

Marshall-town

20

Minneapolis

35

Des Moines

IOWA

94

MINNESOTA

Spencer

Sheldon

71

20

30

29

Grand Forks

Sioux City

29

Devils Lake

Fargo

SISSETON INDIAN RES.

Vermillion

18

Norfolk

CANADA

5

Jamestown

Ellendale

Millbank

29

Sioux Falls

Yankton

81

O'Neill

91

Fremont

2

Carrington

281

Watertown

Brookings

Minot

52

200

94

13

Aberdeen

281

Huron

Mitchell

Missouri River

NEBRASKA

Washburn

Bismarck

Mobridge

SOUTH DAKOTA

Pierre

Winner

Valentine

83

NORTH DAKOTA

83

Lake Sakakawea

21

STANDING ROCK INDIAN RES.

CHEYENNE RIVER INDIAN RES.

Lake Oahe

ROSEBUD INDIAN RES.

Gordon

23

Williston

Mandan

34

Faith

Wall

90

PINE RIDGE INDIAN RESERVATION

18

20

Alliance

61

THEODORE ROOSEVELT NAT'L PARK

Medora

Dickinson

Bowman

85

Buffalo

212

Rapid City

BADLANDS NAT'L PARK

Chadron

North Platte R.

MONTANA

Belle Fourche

Spearfish

BLACK HILLS NAT'L FOR.

Mount Rushmore

Hot Springs

Scottsbluff

71

Bridgeport

85

WYOMING

Introduction

By Suzanne
De Galan

The name Great Plains evokes an image of flat farmland stretching to the horizon, unbroken save for the occasional cluster of buildings marking a town or farmstead. Those who go there, however, know that the limitless terrain destroys as many preconceived images as it confirms. This seemingly uniform landscape actually encompasses the towering buttes looming over the horizons of western South Dakota and the fertile river valleys that crisscross the eastern boundaries of Missouri and Kansas. Its cultural legacy owes as much to such artists as Louis Sullivan and Grant Wood as it does to the cowboy and Indian artifacts that stud the region. And although European settlement came late here, St. Louis existed more than a decade before the Declaration of Independence was signed; Coronado had explored Kansas two centuries before that.

The area that now comprises the states of Iowa, Missouri, Oklahoma, Kansas, Nebraska, and North and South Dakota saw its greatest European settlement in the 19th century. Railroad companies lured thousands of immigrants with large, inexpensive parcels of land; towns sprang up along rail lines and pioneer trails; and Native Americans were inexorably forced into smaller and smaller territories. The sod-breaking plow and hardy winter wheat helped transform the long- and short-grass prairies of the high plains into America's bread basket. In the remaining grasslands, cattle fed where bison once reigned.

Life on the Great Plains in the 19th century was harsh and sometimes violent, but it's a life that today's residents love to re-create. Countless historical theme parks and Old West towns dot the region, along with abundant archaeological and Civil War battle sites, U.S. Army forts, pioneer trail markers, and museums of Native American and pioneer lore. Great Plains folk think nothing of journeying 100 mi to see a building covered with thousands of bushels of corn, or an arrangement of wrecked cars made to resemble the monoliths of Stonehenge. This tendency achieves its ultimate expression in Mt. Rushmore, where the 60-foot faces of four U.S. presidents have been carved into a wall of South Dakota granite.

But alongside these landmarks and oddities lies another Great Plains. To know it, you must drive its hundreds of miles of roads bisecting fields of grain; leave the highway for one of its small towns, just to walk the Main Street and see the serene and mellow old houses. Here, somewhere between myth and reality, the true spirit of this region is revealed.

Tour Groups

Gadabout Tours (700 E. Tahquitz Way, Palm Springs, CA 92262, tel. 619/325–5556) offers 10-day tours of the Missouri and Arkansas Ozarks that include stops in Kansas City, Branson, and Eureka Springs; 15-day cruises of the Mississippi River that wind past Iowa and Missouri towns en route to New Orleans; and eight-day tours of South Dakota's Badlands and Black Hills areas. **Maupintour** (Box 807, Lawrence, KS 66044, tel. 913/843–1211 or 800/255–4266) features an 11-day Mississippi River cruise that travels north past historic Missouri towns and concludes in St. Paul, Minnesota; and eight-day tours that include Badlands National Park and Mt. Rushmore National Memorial in South Dakota, and Yellowstone National Park in Wyoming.

When to Go

The traditional tourist season for most of the Great Plains is **summer,** despite the soaring temperatures and high humidity that are common throughout the region. In fact, many tourist attractions, particularly in North and South Dakota, are only open during June, July, and August. Northern states, such as the Dakotas and Nebraska, are generally cooler than southern states, with temperature averages in the 80s rather than the 90s, but you should be prepared for anything in this variable region. **Winter** weather is equally extreme, especially in Nebraska and the Dakotas, where sub-zero temperatures and snowy conditions are not uncommon. South Dakota offers excellent cross-country skiing and snowmobiling, but again, make sure hotels and restaurants are open. **Spring** and **fall** can be excellent times to visit, with temperatures moderate (anywhere from 40°F to 70°F) and crowds at a minimum. Fall in the Ozarks or such places as the eastern border of Iowa has the added attraction of colorful foliage, usually in mid- to late October.

Festivals and Seasonal Events

May: Pella (IA) Tulip Time Festival celebrates Dutch customs, arts, and crafts, and presents a staggering array of blooming flowers. *Tel. 515/628–4311.*

May: At the **Oklahoma Cattlemen's Association Range Roundup** in Guthrie, cowhands compete in saddle bronc riding, wild-cow roping, and other contests. *Tel. 405/282–3004.*

June 9–19: The **Oklahoma Mozart International Festival** features concerts, barbecues, and powwows celebrating the composer and local culture in Bartlesville. *Tel. 918/336–9900.*

Mid-June: NEBRASKAland Days is a Western hootenanny in North Platte that's highlighted by the Buffalo Bill Rodeo. *Tel. 308/532–7939.*

Mid-June: The Red Earth Native American Cultural Festival in Oklahoma City attracts hundreds of Native American dancers from the United States and Canada for competitions and performances. *Tel. 405/427–5228.*

July: Kansas City Blues & Jazz Festival features performances by nationally known blues and jazz artists on three stages. *Tel. 800/530–5266.*

July–Aug.: Dodge City (KS) Roundup Rodeo is a five-day rodeo during the city's Dodge City Days festival. *Tel. 316/225–2244.*

July 4: The VP Fair in St. Louis is a huge birthday party for America, featuring musical entertainment, air shows, fireworks, and more, held over several days on the Mississippi riverfront beneath the Gateway Arch. *Tel. 314/421–1023 or 800/ 888–3861.*

July 4: National Tom Sawyer Days in Mark Twain's hometown of Hannibal, Missouri, is a week's worth of activities, including a fence-painting contest. *Tel. 314/221–2477.*

Early July: Black Hills and Northern Plains Indian Pow-Wow and Exposition is the best-known of many powwows held annually across South Dakota. *Tel. 605/394–4115.*

Aug.: Iowa State Fair in Des Moines is a short course in farm machinery, animals, crops, and crafts; less bucolically minded visitors can enjoy carnival rides and musical entertainment. *Tel. 515/262–3111.*

Early Aug.: Days of '76 in Deadwood, South Dakota, celebrates the town's wild and woolly gold-rush days with a parade, a rodeo, and other activities. *Tel. 605/578–1876.*

Mid-Aug.: Sturgis (SD) Motorcycle Classic draws more than 200,000 bike buffs from around the country each year. *Tel. 605/347–2556.*

Mid-Aug.: Pioneer Days at Bonanzaville USA transform the pioneer village of West Fargo, North Dakota, into a living museum for two days, with costumed shopkeepers, tradespeople, and townspeople. *Tel. 701/282–2822.*

Early Sept.: United Tribes International Pow-Wow brings Native Americans from around the country to Bismarck, North Dakota, to exhibit art, hold dance competitions, and celebrate cultural ties. *Tel. 701/255–3285.*

Third weekend in Sept.: The Walnut Valley Festival in Winfield, Kansas, is four days of bluegrass and other music, including contests for the national titles in finger-pick guitar, flat-pick guitar, and mountain dulcimer. *Tel. 316/221–3250.*

Oct.: Octoberfest in Hermann, Missouri, draws thousands of people each weekend to celebrate this Missouri River town's German and wine-making heritage. *Tel. 314/486–2744.*

Early Oct.: Norsk Hostfest in Minot, North Dakota, brings in crowds from throughout the region to sample Scandinavian foods, dancing, and costumes. *Tel. 701/852–6000.*

Nov.: The American Royal Livestock, Horse Show and Rodeo is an annual celebration of Kansas City's Wild West days. *Tel. 816/221–5242 or 800/767–7700.*

Getting Around the Great Plains

By Plane Major domestic carriers serve the region, including American, Continental, Delta, Northwest, United, and USAir. The largest airports are, in Missouri, **Lambert–St. Louis International Airport** (tel. 314/426–8000) and **Kansas City International Airport** (tel. 816/243–5237); in Iowa, **Des Moines International Airport** (tel. 515/256–5050); in Oklahoma, **Will Rogers World Airport** (tel. 405/681–5311) and **Tulsa International Airport** (tel. 918/838–5000); and in South Dakota, **Sioux Falls Regional Airport** (tel. 605/336–0762).

By Car Three interstates meet at Oklahoma City: I–40, running east–west through Oklahoma; I–44, which proceeds northeast from Oklahoma City to Tulsa, Oklahoma, and through Missouri to St. Louis; and I–35, one of two major north–south arteries in the Great Plains. From Oklahoma City, I–35 proceeds north through Wichita, Kansas, Kansas City, and Des Moines. Another north–south route is I–29, which begins in Kansas City and runs along the eastern borders of Nebraska, South Dakota, and North Dakota, passing through Omaha, Sioux Falls,

Fargo, and Grand Forks. Major east–west arteries are I–94 in North Dakota, which passes through Medora, the Bismarck/ Mandan area, and Fargo; I–90 in South Dakota, running from Rapid City to Sioux Falls; I–80 through Nebraska and Iowa, which links North Platte, Lincoln, and Omaha with Des Moines and Iowa City; and I–70, which bisects Missouri and Kansas and links St. Louis with Kansas City and points west. Roads are generally in good condition throughout the region.

By Train Amtrak (tel. 800/872–7245) provides some service through the Great Plains but not necessarily to the major cities, and South Dakota and Oklahoma are not served at all.

By Bus The major intercity carrier is **Greyhound** (tel. 816/698–0080 or 800/231–2222). In addition, **Jefferson Lines** (tel. 800/735–7433) serves Lawrence and Kansas City, Kansas, and **Jackrabbit Lines** (tel. 800/444–6287) serves Wall and Rapid City in western South Dakota. Many of the Greyhound stops in this region are small towns that have no ticket booth; call to check whether you must purchase your ticket in advance.

IOWA

By Marcia Andrews

Updated by Diana Dickinson

Capital	Des Moines
Population	2,840,000
Motto	Our Liberties We Prize and Our Rights We Will Maintain
State Bird	Eastern goldfinch
State Flower	Wild rose

Visitor Information

The Division of Tourism (Iowa Dept. of Economic Development, 200 E. Grand Ave., Des Moines 50309, tel. 515/242–4705) has 18 Welcome Centers, along I–35 and I–80 and in towns throughout the state. For regional tourist information, call or write **Eastern Iowa Tourism Association** (Box 178, West Branch 52358, tel. 319/643–2848), **Central Iowa Tourism Region** (113 1st Ave. W, Newton 50208, tel. 515/792–7451), and **Western Iowa Tourism Region** (405 Reed St., Red Oak 51566, tel. 712/623–4232).

Scenic Drives

Perhaps Iowa's most beautiful scenic drive is the series of roads that takes you south along the high bluffs and verdant banks of the Mississippi River on the state's eastern border (*see* Dubuque and the **Great River Road,** *below*). In southeast Iowa, **Rte. 5** from Des Moines to Lake Rathbun, near Centerville, makes a nice detour for those heading south on I–35; to return to the interstate, take **Rte. 2W** from Centerville for about 50 mi.

National and State Parks

National Parks

Effigy Mounds National Monument (*see* Exploring Dubuque and the Great River Road, *below*) offers scenic hiking trails along prehistoric burial mounds. Iowa has four federal reservoir areas located around large man-made lakes: **Coralville Lake** (2850 Prairie du Chien Rd. NE, Iowa City 52240, tel. 319/338–3543), **Lake Rathbun** (Rte. 3, Centerville 52544, tel. 515/647–2464), **Lake Red Rock** (R.R. 3, Box 149A, Knoxville 50138–9522, tel. 515/828–7522 or 800/362–2001), and **Saylorville Lake** (5600 N.W. 78th Ave., Johnston 50131, tel. 515/276–0433 or 515/276–4656).

State Parks

Iowa's 76 state parks include 5,700 campsites, many of them with shower facilities and electrical hookups. Some well-developed parks with modern campsites, cabins, lodge rentals, and boat rentals are **Clear Lake** (tel. 515/357–4212), near Mason City; **George Wyth Memorial** (tel. 319/232–5505), near Waterloo; **Lacey-Keosauqua** (tel. 319/293–3502), near Keosauqua; and **Lake of Three Fires** (tel. 712/523–2700), near Bedford. Virgin prairie areas, part of the state park system but lacking facilities, include **Cayler Prairie,** near the Great Lakes area in northwest Iowa; **Hayden Prairie,** near the Minnesota border in the northeastern corner of the state; **Kaslow Prairie,** about 90 mi northwest of Des Moines; and **Sheeder Prairie,** about 50 mi west of Des Moines. Contact the **Department of Natural Resources** (tel. 515/281–5145) for more information.

Des Moines

Viewed from an airplane or a car topping a hill, the capital of Iowa is a cluster of office towers that seem to pop out of a green corduroy landscape. Downtown straddles the *V* of two rivers; the '80s-built skyline faces granite government buildings and a classic gold-domed capitol across four bridges. Major businesses in this relatively hassle-free city of nearly 400,000 residents include insurance, finance, government, publishing, and agribusiness. Although hardly a glittering metropolis—the city plays annual host to a horde of farmers and agriculture buffs at the Iowa State Fair—neither is Des Moines a village. The U.S. presidential race starts here with the Iowa Caucuses, and every cultural wave breaks on Des Moines's shores—eventually.

Tourist Information

Information centers are located in the **airport** lobby (tel. 515/287–4396) and in the **skywalk** above the corner of 6th and Walnut streets downtown (tel. 515/286–4960).

Arriving and Departing

By Plane **Des Moines International Airport** (tel. 515/256–5050), about 3 mi south of downtown, has scheduled service by major domestic airlines. The drive into town takes about 10 minutes in normal traffic. Cab fare, including tip, is less than $10. Hotel shuttles serve the route, and major car-rental companies are located in the airport.

By Car I–80, the major east–west thoroughfare through the state, and I–35, Iowa's main north–south route, intersect northwest of Des Moines and link with I–235, which runs across the north part of town.

Bus Station **Greyhound** and **Jefferson** share a terminal (tel. 515/243–5211) at Keosauqua Way and 12th Street.

Getting Around Des Moines

Streets in both the city and suburban Urbandale and West Des Moines are laid out in a grid and make getting around fairly easy, but a car is essential, as attractions are scattered about the city and suburbs. Downtown is compact enough to explore in comfortable shoes.

Exploring Des Moines

Downtown Start from the **Capitol Complex** (E. 9th St. and Grand Ave., tel. 515/281–5591; admission free) on the east bank of the Des Moines River. There you can see the elaborate murals in the rotunda of the Capitol building and climb into the dome, covered in 22-karat gold leaf. Nearby, the **Botanical Center** (909 E. River Dr., tel. 515/283–4148; admission charged) has flower exhibits and a three-story, dome-topped jungle. The **State Historical**

Building of Iowa (600 E. Locust St., tel. 515/281–5111; admission free), one block west of the Capitol, shakes off any dusty-old-stuff image with its postmodern design, abstract sculpture of neon and glass, and striking fountain display. The building houses the state archives, library, and museum.

Follow Locust Street west and cross over to the west side of the Des Moines River, where some of the city's most interesting historic buildings can be found. Self-guided walking tours of the **Court Avenue District,** containing a number of restored 19th-century warehouses and other commercial buildings, and the **Sherman Hill Historic District,** with impressive Victorian houses, are detailed in brochures from **Downtown Des Moines, Inc.** (Suite 100B, 601 Locust St., tel. 515/286–4981). Many of the restored buildings along Court Avenue now house shops and restaurants; the area has become a popular entertainment district.

Other Attractions   **Living History Farms,** a 600-acre open-air museum a few miles northwest of Des Moines, is well worth a half day's exploration. The farms are a trip back in time through the sights, sounds, and smells of an 18th-century Ioway camp, two working farms of 1850 and 1900, and an 1875 town. *2600 N.W. 111th St., Urbandale, tel. 515/278–2400. Admission charged. Closed Nov.–Apr.; call for special events in winter.*

Shopping

Valley Junction (tel. 515/223–3286), six square blocks 5 mi west of downtown, has a mix of antiques stores and contemporary shops selling country furnishings, collectibles, and Iowa souvenirs.

Dining

Des Moines's staple fare is Italian, followed closely by Chinese food, although lately there has been a trend toward more exotic cuisines, such as Thai, Indian, and Middle Eastern. Downtown, sample Court Avenue's lineup of pubs and Italian, Tex-Mex, and Cajun places. For price ranges, see Chart 1 (B) in Chapter 1.

Expensive   **8th Street Seafood Bar and Grill.** Lit by skylights and flanked by a busy bar, the raised dining area seats a stylish crowd. Seafood is the draw, cooked simply and well. *1261 8th St., West Des Moines, tel. 515/223–8808. AE, DC, MC, V. No lunch.*

★ **Guido's.** Located in the Savery Hotel downtown, Guido's features large chandeliers, an elevated bar, and a wall of wine bottles. The menu includes prime rib and lightened versions of Continental dishes. *400 Locust St., tel. 515/284–1272. Reservations advised. AE, MC, V. No lunch.*

Metz Continental Cuisine. This elegant restaurant in the Homestead Building downtown features an upper-level bar and an intimate dining area on the lower level. Exquisite entrées, such as *gibier à la Metz* (stuffed baked quail and grilled duck breast), and a sinful dessert cart highlight the menu. *303 Locust St., tel. 515/246–1656. Reservations advised. AE, DC, MC, V. Closed Sun.*

Moderate   **Cafe Su.** Dim sum appetizers are the specialty at this chic restaurant in the popular Valley Junction shopping area in West Des Moines. Contemporary decor compliments the traditional

Chinese cuisine. *225 5th St., tel. 515/274–5102. AE, D, DC, MC, V. Closed Sun.*

The Greenbrier. In the northern suburb of Johnston, this restaurant offers a large menu mixing elegant and basic fare with such choices as Iowa pork chops, rack of lamb, and fish. Frosted glass and dark wood accent the three dining rooms and bar. *5810 Merle Hay Rd., Johnston, tel. 515/253–0124. No reservations. MC, V. Closed Sun.*

Jesse's Embers. Just west of downtown, Jesse's is prized for grilled prime steaks. Whether it's ribs, chicken, or seafood, top ingredients make the kitchen's reputation. The room is small, plain, and crowded with neighborhood people waiting in the bar, but service is swift. *3301 Ingersoll Ave., tel. 515/255–6011. AE, MC, V.*

Johnnie's Vets Club. Beside the train tracks in West Des Moines, this restaurant has low ceilings, scruffy furnishings, and food that has suited the regulars for 47 years. It's another beef place but also serves homemade pastas and chicken dishes. *312 Lincoln Ave., tel. 515/279–9757. AE, D, DC, MC, V. Closed Sun.*

Inexpensive **Des Moines Art Center Restaurant.** For an elegant interlude with light fare, this solarium amid sculpture and a pool is unique. Lunches feature soups, salads, sandwiches, and desserts. *4700 Grand Ave., tel. 515/277–4405. MC, V. No dinner, except Thurs. by reservation; closed Sun.–Mon.*

★ **Drake Diner.** The sharp, New Age look of chrome and neon adds fun to a traditional soup, salad, and sandwich menu. Students from nearby Drake University mix with older patrons. *1111 25th St., tel. 515/277–1111. AE, MC, V.*

El Patio. Just west of downtown, this converted bungalow filled with southwestern artifacts seats diners in colorful rooms, a porch, and a covered patio. More Tex than Mex, the food is still a cut above the fare found at chain-type Mexican restaurants. *611 37th St., tel. 515/274–2303. AE, D, MC, V. No lunch; closed Mon.*

★ **New Delhi Palace.** Classic aromatic dishes range from zingy lamb vindaloo to mild tandoori chicken; a good vegetarian choice is *palak aloo*, a savory blend of spinach and potatoes. The restaurant's peach-colored walls are hung with Indian paintings, and seating is at booths and tables with armchairs *Parkwood Plaza, 86th and Douglas Sts., Urbandale, tel. 515/278–2929. AE, MC, V.*

Lodging

You'll find little in the way of historic or lavish hotels here; most establishments cater to business travelers and offer modern amenities and convenient locations. Downtown renovations or newer suburban hotels dominate, with low-cost motels clustered near interstate exits and a suburban B&B or two (**Iowa Bed and Breakfast Innkeepers' Association,** 109 S. 3rd Ave. W, Newton 50208, tel. 800/888–4667) for variety. For price ranges, see Chart 2 (B) in Chapter 1.

Expensive **Des Moines Marriott.** The downtown location on the skywalk is a plus. Rooms are plush contemporary, with unobstructed views of the city from the higher floors. The restaurant here, Quenelle's, serves rich Continental fare. *700 Grand Ave., 50309, tel. 515/245–5500; fax 515/245–5567. 415 rooms. Facilities: 2 restaurants, lounge, health club, pool. AE, D, MC, V.*

★ **Embassy Suites Hotel on the River.** Across the bridge from Court Avenue attractions, this recently opened hotel has seven balconies ringing an atrium with a waterfall. Beyond this, the hotel lacks flash, but it makes up for it with free breakfasts and lots of attentive service. *101 E. Locust St., 50309, tel. 515/244–1700 or 800/421–9871; fax 515/244–2537. 234 suites. Facilities: restaurant, 2 lounges, health club, pool, convention center. AE, MC, V.*

Holiday Inn University Park. On the west edge of town, the hotel's 10-story, plant-filled atrium and convention facilities draw business groups and local events. Rooms are big, with plush contemporary furnishings. *1800 50th St., West Des Moines 50265, tel. 515/223–1800; fax 515/223–0894. 228 rooms, 60 suites. Facilities: 2 restaurants, 2 lounges, health club, pool. AE, D, MC, V.*

Moderate **The Drake Inn.** Located next to Drake University, this attract-
★ ive, low-rise hotel has airy rooms. *1140 24th St., 50311, tel. 515/255–4000 or 800/252–7838; fax 515/255–1192. 52 rooms. Facilities: 2 meeting rooms. AE, D, MC, V.*

Holiday Inn Downtown. Just north of downtown, the hotel has fresh but ordinary rooms and a few suites with whirlpool baths. *1050 6th Ave., 50314, tel. 515/283–0151; fax 515/283–0151. 245 rooms. Facilities: restaurant, lounge, pool. AE, D, MC, V.*

Valley West Inn. Next to West Des Moines's big mall, the three-story inn has simply furnished rooms decorated in rosy fabrics and blond woods. *3535 Westown Pkwy., West Des Moines 50265, tel. 515/225–2524 or 800/833–6755; fax 515/225–9058. 136 rooms. Facilities: restaurant, lounge, meeting rooms, pool, whirlpool. AE, D, MC, V.*

Inexpensive **Airport Comfort Inn.** Two blocks from the airport, the hotel is convenient if not quiet. The three-story building has plain rooms, big beds, and morning coffee in the lobby. *5231 Fleur Dr., 50321, tel. 515/287–3434 or 800/221–2222. 57 rooms. Facilities: pool. AE, MC, V.*

★ **Heartland Inn.** On the northeast edge of Des Moines, next to an amusement complex, this three-story building is part of a new Iowa chain. Decor is rustic. *5000 N.E. 56th St., Altoona 50009, tel. 515/265–1944 or 800/334–3277. 87 rooms. Facilities: pool, spa, miniature golf in season. AE, D, MC, V.*

East-Central Iowa

This region east of Des Moines is a mix of historic towns, trim farmsteads, and forested river valleys. Cedar Rapids is the largest town in the area; Iowa City, about 25 mi south, is the home of the University of Iowa. The area is perhaps best known to tourists for the Amana Colonies, a cluster of seven villages west of Iowa City that were founded in the 19th century as a utopian religious community.

Tourist Information

Amana Colonies: Welcome Center (U.S. 151 and Rte. 220, Box 303, Amana 52203, tel. 319/622–3828 or 800/245–5465), with information and a lodging reservation service. **Cedar Rapids Area:** Convention and Visitors Bureau (119 1st Ave. SE, 52401, tel. 319/398–5009 or 800/735–5557). **Iowa City/Coralville:** Visitors Bureau (325 E. Washington St., Iowa City 52240, tel. 319/337–6592).

Getting There

By Plane The **Cedar Rapids/Iowa City Municipal Airport** (tel. 319/362–8336), 7 mi south of Cedar Rapids and just off I–380, is served by American/American Eagle, USAir, TWA, and United.

By Car I–80, the state's major east–west thoroughfare, runs from Des Moines east to Iowa City. From Iowa City, I–380N passes Lake Macbride on the way to Cedar Rapids. From Cedar Rapids, U.S. 151 meanders southwest for about 25 mi through a rural farmscape to Middle Amana, the start of the cluster of Amana Colonies.

Exploring East-Central Iowa

Start your tour at the southwestern point of the region's roughly triangular shape, at the **Amana Colonies,** encompassing the seven villages of Amana (where the **Welcome Center** is located, *see* Tourist Information, *above*), West Amana, South Amana, High Amana, East Amana, Middle Amana, and Homestead. Although the descendants of the German/Swiss immigrants who founded the community voted to end its communal way of life in 1932, much of this life is preserved here. A 25-mi circuit of the area takes in restored buildings, such as barn and kitchen museums and a schoolhouse. Craft hunters favor the shopping opportunities here, where members of the Amana community still manufacture prized woolen goods and other items.

North of the Amanas on U.S. 151 is **Cedar Rapids.** In the 19th and early 20th centuries, waves of Czechoslovakian immigrants settled in this manufacturing town; a sampling of their heritage is on view at the **Czech Village, Museum and Immigrant Home** (10–119 16th Ave. SW, tel. 319/362–8500). The city also boasts the world's largest permanent collection of paintings by renowned native son Grant Wood at its **Museum of Art** (410 3rd Ave. SE, tel. 319/366–7503).

South of here on I–380 is **Iowa City,** where the **University of Iowa's** hilly campus on the Iowa River is dominated by its **Old Capitol** (for tours, tel. 319/335–0548), which served as the seat of state government until the capital was moved to Des Moines in the mid-19th century. Today the Greek Revival building is part of the university.

West Branch, just west of Iowa City on I–80, contains the **Herbert Hoover Presidential Library and Birthplace** (Parkside Dr. and Main St., tel. 319/643–2541 or 319/643–5301). Here you can see the simple cottage where the future president was born to Quaker parents in 1874; the house contains period furnishings, many of them original.

Shopping

The commercial hub of Amana shopping is the eight-block center of Amana, just east of the welcome center. The **Woolen Mill Salesroom** (tel. 319/622–3432), **Furniture and Clock Shop** (tel. 319/622–3291), and **Millstream Brewing Co.** (tel. 319/622–3672) give visitors a look at traditional production processes. The **Old Fashioned High Amana Store** (tel. 319/622–3797), 2 mi west of

---

Eastern Iowa

the welcome center, is fragrant, creaky, and full of old-timey gifts. A block away, the **Amana Arts Guild Center** (tel. 319/622–3678) sells high-quality quilts and crafts. **Little Amana**, at I–80 and U.S. 151, is more of a quick-stop outlet for woolens, gifts, and souvenirs than a typical Amana village. The **Tanger Factory Outlet Center** (Exit 220 off I–80, Williamsburg, tel. 800/727–6885) has 55 stores selling mainly women's designer clothing at discounted prices.

Dining and Lodging

Amana kitchens are well known for both quality and quantity. Try the locally made rhubarb wine served at many establishments here. Hotels in Cedar Rapids tend to cater to business travelers, but the Amanas, like many Iowa towns, are home to a burgeoning number of B&Bs (**Iowa Bed and Breakfast Innkeepers' Association,** 109 S. 3rd Ave. W, Newton 50208, tel. 800/888–4667). Iowa City has a fair number of decent chain hotels and motels. For price ranges, see Charts 1 (B) and 2 (B) in Chapter 1.

Amana Colonies
Dining

Ox Yoke Inn. Traditional German-American food is served in an old-country-inspired setting, including walls lined with beer steins. *Main St., Amana, tel. 319/622–3441. AE, D, MC, V. Moderate.*

Bill Zuber's Restaurant. The comfortable surroundings haven't changed much since the 1950s. Neither has the menu, which is a primer on German cuisine: lots of baked or fried meat, plus salad, vegetables, and dessert, all for a reasonable price. *Main*

St., Homestead, tel. 319/622–3911. AE, D, MC, V. Inexpensive.

★ **The Brick Haus Restaurant.** Located in the middle of prime Amana shopping, the restaurant features long tables covered in checkered cloths and lots of *Wiener Schnitzel mit Spätzle* (breaded, deep-fried veal with homemade soft noodles). *Box 285, Amana, tel. 319/622–3278. AE, D, MC, V. Inexpensive.*

Lodging **Amana Holiday Inn.** For the most part this is standard Holiday Inn material, enlivened by such rustic touches as a pool and sauna in a barnlike setting. *Exit 225 off I–80, Box 187, Little Amana 52203, tel. 319/668–1175 or 800/633–9244. 156 rooms. Facilities: restaurant, lounge. AE, D, MC, V. Moderate.*

★ **Rawson's Bed & Breakfast.** Once a kitchen workers' dormitory when Homestead still practiced communal living, this unique establishment has two large, distinctive rooms, with exposed beams and brick walls, and one suite. All three feature excellent period furnishings and fabrics and lavish baths. *Box 118, Homestead 52235, tel. 319/622–6035. 2 rooms, 1 suite. D, MC, V. Moderate.*

Die Heimat Country Inn. This two-story B&B has small rooms decorated with locally made, traditional furnishings and deluxe rooms with canopy beds. *Box 160, Homestead 52236, tel. 319/622–3937. 19 rooms. D, MC. Inexpensive.*

Cedar Rapids **Collins Plaza.** In this seven-balcony hotel north of downtown, *Lodging* rooms are large, with traditional furnishings and pastel colors. *1200 Collins Rd. NE, 52402, tel. 319/393–6600 or 800/541–1067; fax 319/393–2308. 221 rooms. Facilities: 2 restaurants, lounge, pool, spa, airport shuttle. AE, D, MC, V. Expensive.*

The Roosevelt. This renovated downtown landmark, connected to the city's skywalk system, features big rooms with high ceilings and traditional furnishings. *200 1st Ave. NE, 52401, tel. 319/364–4111. 133 rooms. Facilities: restaurant, lounge, pool, health club. AE, D, MC, V. Moderate.*

Iowa City **Givanni's.** Neon lights enhance the exposed-brick walls at this *Dining* popular Italian/American/vegetarian restaurant in the downtown pedestrian mall. *109 E. College St., tel. 319/338–5967. AE, D, DC, MC, V. Moderate.*

Motel **Heartland Inn** (3315 Southgate Ct. SW, Cedar Rapids 52304, tel. 319/362–9012 or 800/334–3277), 87 rooms, pool, spa; inexpensive.

Dubuque and the Great River Road

The mighty Mississippi River forms the eastern border of Iowa, and the top third of this border, from the Minnesota line to Dubuque, combines the oldest settlements, highest bluffs, and closest river access of the entire stretch. This tour follows the Great River Road, a network of federal, state, and county roads, as it winds its way from the northwest corner of the state along this magnificent stretch of riverbank.

Tourist Information

Tourist Information Center (Port of Dubuque Welcome Center, 3rd St. and Ice Harbor, Dubuque 52001, tel. 319/556-4372).

Getting There

By Car Link up with the Great River Road from the north on U.S. 18 at Prairie du Chien, Wisconsin, or pick up the scenic route anywhere along Iowa's eastern border. For its entire length, the Great River Road is marked with a 12-spoke pilot's wheel symbol.

By Bus **Greyhound** links Dubuque to most major cities from Union Bus Station (2255 Kerper Blvd., tel. 319/583–3397).

Exploring Dubuque and the Great River Road

Spectacular views of the Mississippi start at the **Municipal Park** in Lansing and continue at the **Effigy Mounds National Monument** (tel. 319/873–3491), north of McGregor. Here hiking trails run alongside eerie prehistoric Native American burial mounds in animal shapes. One-, four-, and six-hour walks lead to clifftop views of the upper Mississippi River valley.

From **Pikes Peak State Park** (tel. 319/873–2341), 3 mi south of McGregor, the view includes the Wisconsin River as it links up with the Mississippi. The stretch of road approaching Balltown, 7 mi north of Dubuque, reveals green hills rolling down to the river.

Dubuque is full of river merchants' homes, some of them lavish Victorian houses turned B&Bs, snuggled against the limestone cliffs that back this small harbor town. Here you can get out of your car and explore **Cable Car Square** (tel. 319/583–5000) at 4th and Bluff streets, site of two dozen shops and restaurants. Ride **Fenelon Place Elevator** to the top of a 200-foot bluff for a sweeping view of the city.

The town, along with seven others on the river, has recently found popularity as a center for riverboat gambling. Don't expect high rollers here: A $200 gambling-loss limit and triple-decker boats that feature dining, sightseeing, floor shows, and video games make this a family-oriented activity (children under 21 are not allowed in gaming areas). Call **Roberts River Rides** (3rd St., Ice Harbor, tel. 319/583–1761 or 800/426–5591) for reservations on the *Casino Belle*, holding up to 3,000 passengers, or the smaller *Spirit of Dubuque*, with 377 passengers. The same company operates similar boats from Clinton and LeClaire.

What to See and Do with Children

Dyersville, 25 mi west of Dubuque on U.S. 20, found fame as a setting for the movie *Field of Dreams*. The field, about 3 mi north of town, has been preserved as a tourist attraction. Dyersville itself has several interesting museums, including the **National Farm Toy Museum** (1110 16th Ave. SE, tel. 319/875–2727).

Dining and Lodging

Ethnic and family-style restaurants line Dubuque's 4th Street at Cable Car Square. As with the rest of the state, B&Bs are proliferating here (**Iowa Bed and Breakfast Innkeepers' Association,** 109 S. 3rd Ave. W, Newton 50208, tel. 800/888–4667). For price ranges, see Charts 1 (B) and 2 (B) in Chapter 1.

Balltown   **Breitbach's Country Dining.** This funky, rambling piece of folk
Dining   architecture has a good home-style kitchen. *563 Balltown Rd.,*
★   *tel. 319/552–2220. D, MC, V. Inexpensive.*

Dubuque   **The Ryan House.** A restored Victorian house provides a lavish
Dining   period setting for updated, lightened Continental cuisine. *1375*
Locust St., tel. 319/556–2733. AE, D, MC, V. Moderate–Ex-
pensive.
Yen Ching. This café offers predictable Chinese food, with a few
spicy Hunan dishes for variety. *926 Main St., tel. 319/556–*
2574. AE, MC, V. Closed Sun. Moderate.

Lodging   **The Hancock House.** This meticulously restored Victorian
★   perched halfway up a bluff has four-poster beds, lace-covered
windows, and ornate fireplaces. The third-floor room with the
turret is a special favorite. *1105 Grove Terr., 52001, tel. 319/*
557–8989. 6 rooms. Facilities: Continental breakfast. MC, V.
Expensive.
The Redstone Inn. Coming across this establishment is like
finding a British manor on the prairie. Bedrooms are grand,
and baths are lavish, with mosaic tile and stained glass. *504*
Bluff St., 52001, tel. 319/582–1894. 15 rooms. Facilities:
lounge, breakfast. AE, D, MC, V. Moderate.
Stout House. This sturdy red-stone mansion has vivid Victorian furnishings. *1105 Locust St., 52001, tel. 319/552–1894. 6*
rooms (some share baths). AE, D, MC, V. Moderate.

Elsewhere in the State

Iowa's Great Lakes

Getting There   Take I–80W from Des Moines to U.S. 71N to Spirit Lake.

What to See   The Iowa Great Lakes lie in the northwest corner of the state.
and Do   Comprising six lakes (including West Okoboji—one of only
three blue-water lakes in the world), the region hosts a dozen
vacation resorts. Climb aboard the ***Queen II*** excursion boat
(Arnolds Park, tel. 712/332–5159) for a tour of West Okoboji.
Iowa Great Lakes Chamber of Commerce (Box 9, Arnolds Park
51331, tel. 712/332–2107).

KANSAS

By Janet Majure

Capital	Topeka
Population	2,477,574
Motto	To the Stars Through Difficulties
State Bird	Western meadowlark
State Flower	Helianthus

Visitor Information

Kansas Department of Commerce, Travel & Tourism Division (700 S.W. Harrison St., Suite 1300, Topeka 66603, tel. 913/296–2009 or 800/252–6727). **Visitor information centers:** on I–70W in Kansas City, on I–70E in Goodland, on I–35N at South Haven, and in Topeka (Capitol, 10th and Harrison Sts.).

Scenic Drives

Rte. 177S from I–70 to historic Council Grove provides lovely views—especially in late afternoon or early morning—of the undulating Flint Hills.

National and State Parks

National Parks Federal sites include **Ft. Larned National Historic Site** (*see* The Santa Fe Trail Region, *below*); **Ft. Scott National Historic Site** (Old Fort Blvd., Ft. Scott 66701, tel. 316/223–0310), built in the 1840s to keep the peace in Native American territory; and the **Cimarron National Grassland** (Box J, 242 E. Hwy. 56, Elkhart 67950, tel. 316/697–4621), less than a mile from central Elkhart, which offers a self-guided automobile tour of key Sante Fe Trail sites.

State Parks Kansas has 24 state parks, most associated with recreational lakes, run by the **Department of Wildlife and Parks** (R.R. 2, Box 54A, Pratt 67124, tel. 316/672–5911). Two of the best are **Scott State Park** (R.R. 1, Box 50, Scott City 67871, tel. 316/872–2061), containing archaeological evidence of the first white settlement in Kansas, and **Milford State Park** (8811 State Park Rd., Milford 66514, tel. 913/238–3014), with a scenic reservoir, a nature center, and an arboretum.

East-Central Kansas

Heading west from Kansas City across this land, you'll follow in the footsteps of pioneers who traveled the Oregon, Santa Fe, Smoky Hill, and Chisholm trails. Native American history, Civil War sites, and a taste of the Old West loom large along this 150-mi stretch.

Tourist Information

Abilene: Convention & Visitors Bureau (201 N.W. 2nd St., 67410, tel. 913/263–2231). **Kansas City:** Convention & Visitors Bureau (753 State Ave., Suite 101, 66101, tel. 913/321–5800). Overland Park Convention & Visitors Bureau (10975 Benson

Dr., Suite 360, 66210, tel. 913/491–0123 or 800/262–7275). **Lawrence:** Convention & Visitors Bureau (734 Vermont St., 66044, tel. 913/865–4411). **Topeka:** Convention & Visitors Bureau (120 S.E. 6th St., Suite 100, 66603, tel. 913/234–1030 or 800/235–1030).

Getting There

By Plane The biggest airport serving the area is **Kansas City International Airport** in Missouri (*see* Missouri). USAir Express serves Topeka's **Forbes Field** (tel. 913/862–6515).

By Car I–70W enters the area from Kansas City, Missouri; I–70E, from Colorado. Most attractions are just off the interstate. Note: Kansas weather is highly changeable. Listen to the radio for forecasts, as ice storms, heavy snowfalls, and high winds can making driving treacherous.

By Train Amtrak serves Lawrence, Topeka, and Kansas City.

By Bus **Greyhound** connects Kansas City, Kansas (tel. 913/371–6330), Lawrence (tel. 913/843–5622), Topeka (tel. 913/233–2301), and Abilene (at Abilene's Pride motel, tel. 913/263–2800) en route to Denver. **Jefferson Lines** (tel. 800/735–7433) serves Kansas City, Overland Park, and Lawrence.

Exploring East-Central Kansas

Along I–70 you'll encounter an array of historic sites and recreational opportunities. **Kansas City**, which straddles the border between Kansas and Missouri, was a major provisioning point for frontier travelers in the 19th century. For information on the Missouri side of Kansas City, *see* Missouri.

On the Kansas side, the **Mahaffie Farmstead & Stagecoach Stop** served the Santa Fe Trail, one of the routes established in the 19th century for trade and, later, westward expansion. Guided tours are given of the stone house, one of three buildings here that are listed on the National Register of Historic Places. *1100 Kansas City Rd., Olathe, tel. 913/782–6972. Admission charged. Closed Mon.–Tues. June–Aug., weekends Sept.–May, major holidays.*

In the Kansas City suburb of Fairway, the **Shawnee Methodist Mission** (3403 W. 53rd St., tel. 913/262–0867), a state historic site, was begun in 1839 as a school to teach English and trade skills to Native Americans. In Overland Park, another suburb, college sports history is recounted through photographs, videos, and sound tracks at the **National Collegiate Athletic Association Visitors Center** (6201 College Blvd., tel. 913/339–0000).

West about 40 mi on I–70 is **Lawrence.** The town was rebuilt after being raided and burned for its antislavery views during the Civil War by William Quantrill and a band of Confederate sympathizers; many structures dating from this time remain. Stroll Massachusetts Street through the lovely downtown area, whose turn-of-the-century buildings and retail shops retain a small-town flavor.

A few blocks away is the scenic main campus of the 26,500-student **University of Kansas.** Lining Jayhawk Boulevard are an assortment of university buildings, including the Romanesque-

style structure of native limestone that houses one of the
school's four museums: the **Dyche Museum of Natural History**
(tel. 913/864–4540), which displays fossils, mounted animals,
and rotating exhibits. Also in Lawrence is **Haskell Indian Junior College** (23rd and Barker Sts., tel. 913/749–8403), which has
provided higher education for Native Americans since 1884.

Continue west on I–70 for about 30 mi to **Topeka** and see the
outstanding Classical Revival state **Capitol** (10th and Harrison
Sts., tel. 913/296–3966), begun in 1866 and completed nearly 40
years later. Lobby murals include a striking depiction of abolitionist John Brown by Regionalist artist John Steuart Curry.
The ornate Senate chambers, featuring bronze columns and
variegated-marble accents, are magnificent. West of downtown, the **Kansas Museum of History** (6425 S.W. 6th St., tel.
913/272–8681), perversely situated in a modernist box of a
building, explains Kansas's history from the Native American
era to the present. Just outside Topeka, the **Combat Air Museum** (Hangars 602–604, Forbes Field, tel. 913/862–3303; admission charged) offers two hangars full of military aircraft dating
from World War I. **Monroe Elementary School** (1515 Monroe
St.)—where Linda Brown's attempt to attend classes led to the
historic 1954 Supreme Court ruling, in *Brown* v. *Board of Education*, that racial segregation in public schools is unconstitu-
tional—was designated a national historic site in 1992. It opens
as a museum in late 1993.

The countryside to the west is a sea of treeless hills. Extending
from Nebraska to Oklahoma, the **Flint Hills** include the last
large vestiges of tall-grass prairie that once covered much of
the Great Plains.

The small town of **Abilene,** about 85 mi west of Topeka, is famous for cattle drives and for Dwight D. Eisenhower. The **Eisenhower Center** complex includes the late president's **boyhood
home**—the 19th-century clapboard looks out of place among
the surrounding limestone buildings—as well as the **Eisenhower Museum,** the **Eisenhower Presidential Library,** and the **Place
of Meditation,** a chapel where the president, his wife, Mamie,
and their son Doud Dwight are interred. The museum displays
memorabilia of Eisenhower's life, from his youth in Abilene to
his success as a general during World War II through his popular presidency. *S. Buckeye St. at 4th St., tel. 913/263–4751. Admission charged for museum. Closed major holidays.*

Other Abilene attractions include the **Dickinson County Historical Museum** (412 S. Campbell St., tel. 913/263–2681), offering exhibits on the life of the Plains Indians, and the **Greyhound
Hall of Fame** (407 S. Buckeye St., tel. 913/263–3000), documenting the history of this illustrious canine breed.

What to See and Do with Children

Children will enjoy the dinosaur bones and live snakes at Lawrence's **Dyche Museum of Natural History** and Discovery Place
at Topeka's **Kansas Museum of History,** with hands-on exhibits
about 19th-century clothes, tools, and household items (for
both, *see* Exploring East-Central Kansas, *above*). **Gage Park** in
Topeka (635 Gage Blvd., tel. 913/295–3838) has a carousel and
is home to the **Topeka Zoo** (tel. 913/272–5821). **Golfland/
Sunsplash** (20005 W. 153rd St., Olathe, 913/764–3204), new in
1993, is a family-oriented golf and water theme park.

Sports and Outdoor Activities

Fishing Most of this region follows the Kansas River, where a series of large-scale flood-control reservoirs affords good fishing for walleye, bass, and crappie. Good sites include **Clinton State Park** (R.R. 1, Box 120E, Lawrence 66044); **Perry State Park** (R.R. 1, Box 464A, Ozawkie 66070), near Topeka; **Tuttle Creek State Park** (5020–B Tuttle Creek Blvd., Manhattan 66502); and **Milford State Park** (*see* National and State Parks, *above*). Licenses are required and can be purchased at county clerks' offices, state park offices, and some retail outlets. The **Kansas Department of Fish and Game** (tel. 316/672–5911) has further information.

Hiking and Backpacking Kansas's reservoirs (*see* Fishing, *above*) are bordered by state parks with marked nature trails. The **Konza Prairie** (5 mi off I-70 at Exit 307, McDowell Creek Rd., tel. 913/532–6620), a section of Flint Hills tall-grass prairie set aside for research and preservation, has a self-guided nature trail.

Spectator Sports

Basketball Not only did the University of Kansas hire basketball's inventor as its first coach, but the **Jayhawks** are consistently among the top-10 college basketball teams in the country. Games are memorable—if you can get a cherished ticket (tel. 913/864–3141; Nov.–Mar.).

Horse and Dog Racing The **Woodlands** (99th St. and Leavenworth Rd., Kansas City, tel. 913/299–9797) offers greyhound racing year-round, horse racing Memorial Day–Labor Day.

Dining and Lodging

Typical Kansas roadhouse fare is chicken-fried steak and fried chicken. In cities, good barbecue and Mexican food can be found. Accommodations range from business-class hotels in the Kansas City suburb of Overland Park to the basic roadside motels that predominate in the western part of the region to B&Bs (**Kansas Bed & Breakfast Association,** Rte. 1, Box 93, Wa Keeney 67672). For price ranges, see Charts 1 (B) and 2 (B) in Chapter 1.

Abilene
Dining
Kirby House. The traditional midwestern fare served here is nothing special, but the quietly elegant setting, in a restored Victorian mansion, makes up for it. *205 N.E. 3rd St., tel. 913/263–7336. Reservations advised. D, MC, V. Moderate.*

Kansas City
Dining
Tatsu's French Restaurant. At this refuge of low-key elegance in a colorless suburban shopping strip, traditional French cuisine with an Oriental accent flourishes. *4603 W. 90th St., Prairie Village, tel. 913/383–9801. Reservations advised. Jacket and tie advised. MC, V. No lunch Sat.; closed Sun. Moderate–Expensive.*

★ **Hayward's Pit Bar-B-Que.** Locals flock to this hillside restaurant for piles of succulent smoked beef, ribs, chicken, pork, and sausage. The combination plate lets you try three meats. *11051 Antioch Rd., Overland Park, tel. 913/451–8080. Reservations for large parties only. AE, MC, V. Inexpensive–Moderate.*

Lodging **Doubletree Hotel.** Adjacent to two major highways, a business park, and a scenic public jogging trail, this 18-story hotel was recently renovated to soften its former high-tech look with deeper colors and warmer fabrics. *10100 College Blvd., Overland Park 66210, tel. 913/451–6100; fax 913/451–3873. 340 rooms, 17 suites. Facilities: restaurant, lounge, health club, indoor pool, racquetball. AE, D, DC, MC, V. Expensive.*

★ **Overland Park Marriott Hotel.** This upscale hotel in a suburban business area has a lobby with marble floor and traditionally furnished rooms. The concierge level features slightly larger rooms and a lobby/lounge serving food and drinks. *10800 Metcalf Ave., Overland Park 66210, tel. 913/451–8000; fax 913/451–5914. 390 rooms, 7 suites. Facilities: 2 restaurants, lounge, health club, pool. AE, D, DC, MC, V. Expensive.*

Lawrence
Dining
★

Free State Brewing Co. Kansas's only brew pub serves such dishes as Cheddar-ale soup, bratwurst, and black-bean quesadillas to complement the selection of beers made here. Brewery tours are offered on Saturday. *636 Massachusetts St., tel. 913/843–4555. Reservations for parties of 10 or more. D, MC, V. Inexpensive–Moderate.*

Paradise Cafe. Hippies live, and they're serving consistently tasty nouveau-regional cuisine. Try the breakfast enchiladas, chicken enchiladas for lunch, and homemade pasta or seafood for dinner. Douglas County pie (a chocolate-pecan combo) is a standard. *728 Massachusetts St., tel. 913/842–5199. No reservations. D, MC, V. No dinner Sun. Inexpensive–Moderate.*

Lodging
★

Eldridge Hotel. This historic downtown hotel offers attractive suites that include a parlor and wet bar; rooms on the top (fifth) floor afford good views. The downtown location means some traffic noise but great convenience. *701 Massachusetts St., 66044, tel. 913/749–5011 or 800/527–0909; fax 913/749–4512. 48 suites. Facilities: restaurant, bar, hot tub. AE, D, DC, MC, V. Moderate.*

Topeka
Dining

Tia's Cafe. Mexican-Caribbean food is served in a spacious, bright setting. The popular chicken-and-black-bean burrito comes with sautéed squash, sweet peppers, onions, and carrots. Try "mad dog" hot sauce for serious heat. *1521 S.W. 21st St., tel. 913/232–0719. AE, D, DC, MC, V. Moderate.*

Lodging

Club House Inn. Located in western Topeka near the Kansas Museum of History, this white stucco B&B inn features spacious rooms, many overlooking a landscaped courtyard, and suites with kitchenettes. *924 S.W. Henderson St., 66615, tel. 913/273–8888 or 800/258–2466; fax 913/273–5809. 104 rooms, 17 suites. Facilities: outdoor pool, hot tub. AE, D, DC, MC, V. Moderate.*

Dining and Lodging

Heritage House. This turn-of-the-century clapboard home, once the site of the Menninger Clinic, has B&B rooms ranging from the dramatic to the cozy. Third-floor rooms have less light and more noise. The intimate restaurant serves a frequently changing Continental menu for lunch and dinner. *3535 S.W. 6th St., 66606, tel. 913/233–3800; fax 913/233–9793. 13 rooms (2 share bath). Facilities: restaurant (reservations required; jacket and tie advised). AE, D, DC, MC, V. Moderate–Expensive.*

Motels

Representatives of such chains as Motel 6, Super 8, and Econo Lodge are located along I–70 (*see* Appendix, Toll-Free Numbers). **Best Western Inn** (2210 N. Buckeye St., Abilene 67410, tel. 913/263–2050), 64 rooms, 1 suite, restaurant, lounge, indoor pool, hot tub; inexpensive.

Campgrounds **Four Seasons RV Acres** (6 mi east of Abilene off I–70, Rte. 5, Box 138, 67410, tel. 913/598–2221 or 800/658–4667). **KOA Campgrounds of Lawrence** (R.R. 3, Box 175, Lawrence 66044, tel. 913/842–3877). **KOA Campground** (Rte. 1, Grantville 66429, tel. 913/246–3419). Camping is also available in state parks at reservoirs (*see* Sports and Outdoor Activities, *above*).

The Santa Fe Trail Region

Although the Santa Fe Trail spans the entire state, the towns in western Kansas are most closely associated with its lore and history. This is the Kansas we know from film and myth: remote, flat, treeless, littered with tumbleweeds, windy, but imbued with a romance linked with such names as Wyatt Earp and Dodge City. Towns sprang up here first along the trail, then on the railroad lines that followed. Today, agriculture is the mainstay. Tourism is growing, but don't expect resorts.

Tourist Information

Dodge City: Convention & Visitors Bureau (4th and Spruce Sts., 67801, tel. 316/225–8186). **Hutchinson:** Convention & Visitors Bureau (117 N. Walnut St., 67501, tel. 316/662–3391). **Larned:** Chamber of Commerce (502 Broadway, 67550, tel. 316/285–6916).

Getting There

By Plane **Dodge City Regional Airport** (tel. 316/227–8679), about 2 mi east of downtown, is served by USAir Express.

By Car From Kansas City or Topeka, take I–70W to I–135S, then Rte. 61 to Hutchinson. Eastbound travelers enter Dodge City via U.S. 50 or U.S. 56.

By Train Amtrak serves Hutchinson and Dodge City.

By Bus **Greyhound** (tel. 316/265–7711) connects with **TNM&O Coaches** (tel. 316/227–9547) to provide service to Dodge City from Wichita. The **Hutchinson Shuttle Service** (tel. 316/662–5205) connects with other cities in central Kansas.

Exploring the Santa Fe Trail Region

Hutchinson is home to the state fairgrounds and the world's largest grain elevators, but what really makes this small town worth a visit is the **Kansas Cosmosphere & Space Center,** undergoing a $12.7 million expansion. Housing more than $100 million worth of space exhibits, the center's museum, which is doubling in size, has the largest collection outside the Smithsonian Institution. Various displays—including interactive exhibits—explain the history of space exploration and solutions to the many challenges of human flight. The center also has a planetarium and an Omnimax theater. *1100 N. Plum St., tel. 316/662–2305 or 800/397–0330. Admission charged. Closed Christmas Day.*

Head west on 4th Street (which becomes R.R. 636) for about 30 mi and keep a sharp lookout for signs to the **Quivira National Wildlife Refuge** (R.R. 3, Box 48A, Stafford 67578, tel. 316/486–

The Santa Fe Trail Region

N

30 miles

45 km

Wichita

[135]

[50] Burrton
Moundridge Halstead
McPherson [61] Arkansas River
Crawford Andale
Mount Mount Hope Cheney
Frederick Little Arkansas R. Haven Cheney Res.
Lyons Hutchinson Elmer [96] [54] Norwich
Sterling Nickerson Kingman [42]
[56] [14/96] [636] [50] Rago
Claflin Abbyville Arlington [61] Zenda
Ellinwood Sylvia Turon Nashville
[156] Quivira Nat'l Waterfowl Refuge Preston South Fork Ninnescah
Cheyenne Bottoms [484] Stafford Cunningham Sawyer [281]
Hoisington Great Bend Hudson St. John Byers Lake City Medicine Lodge
Walnut Creek Radium [19] [281] Pratt
Albert Pawnee Rock Rattlesnake River Hopewell [160]
Rush Center Santa Fe Trail Center Larned Belpre Greensburg Belvidere
[96] [183] [56] Kinsley [54] Coldwater
Fort Larned Nat'l Historic Site Arkansas River Mullinville
Alexander [156] [154] Bucklin
Bazine Burdett Hanston [50/56] [34]
Ness City Spearville [154] Kingsdown Bloom
[283] Wright Dodge City Minneola
Beeler Jetmore Pawnee River
Buckner River [154]
Kalvesta [50] Ensign Fowler

2393). More than 250 bird species have been spotted at this rest spot for migrating ducks, geese, and other birds.

Drive north through the refuge, then turn west on R.R. 484, which becomes Rte. 19, to **Larned,** where the **Santa Fe Trail Center** (2 mi west of town on Rte. 156, tel. 316/285–2054) details the history of the trail and displays artifacts from early 20th-century prairie life. About 4 mi farther west on Rte. 156 is **Ft. Larned National Historic Site** (R.R. 3, tel. 316/285–6911; admission charged), a meticulously restored prairie fort built in 1868 to protect travelers on the Santa Fe Trail and, later, railroad workers. Buffalo Soldiers (post–Civil War regiments of black soldiers) were stationed here. The site includes a museum, restored barracks, and other buildings; a video paints a distinctly unromantic picture of the fort's history and mission.

Turn south on the first road west of Ft. Larned, which intersects with U.S. 56. Follow this southwest to **Dodge City,** which capitalizes on its 19th-century reputation as the "wickedest little city in America." Founded 5 mi west of Ft. Dodge, another Santa Fe Trail outpost, in anticipation of the arrival of the Santa Fe railroad, the town thrived on the drinking and gambling of buffalo hunters and cowboys, and it is here that lawmen Bat Masterson and Wyatt Earp earned their fame.

Dodge City's **Boot Hill Museum** includes exhibits on Native American history, the Santa Fe Trail, and the town's early life; Front Street, a reconstruction of houses, saloons, and other businesses that existed before the original town burned in 1885; and a Boot Hill cemetery re-creation (the remains of those buried here were moved years ago). In summer, gunfights, medicine shows, and stagecoach rides are staged daily. *Front St., tel. 316/227–8188. Admission charged. Closed major holidays.*

Follow U.S. 50W for 9 mi to the **Santa Fe Trail tracks,** a 140-acre preserve where, more than 100 years later, ruts from wagons on the trail are still visible in the sandy prairie earth.

Sports and Outdoor Activities

Hiking At **Dillon Nature Center** in Hutchinson (3002 E. 30th St., tel. 316/663–7411), a National Recreation Trail system takes in woods, prairie, and wetlands.

Spectator Sports

Rodeo The Professional Rodeo Cowboys Association's biggest Kansas rodeo is the **Dodge City Roundup Rodeo** (tel. 316/225–2244), held for five days each summer during the Dodge City Days festival.

Dining and Lodging

Motels hold sway in this part of the state, and you'll find few fancy restaurants, though many offer fresh and flavorful food. If you're traveling in summer, make reservations early for lodging; for restaurants, reservations on weekends are advised. Note: "Red beer" on menus means beer with tomato juice. (It's good—really!) Kansas's liquor laws vary from county to county; in "dry" counties, alcohol is served only in private clubs, to which many hotels offer courtesy memberships (ask when you call to reserve). For price ranges, see Charts 1 (B) and 2 (B) in Chapter 1.

Dodge City   **El Charro.** Mexican dishes such as "enchilada delights," topped
Dining   with cheese, lettuce, tomato, and sour cream, bring in crowds. The pleasant, low-key dining room has baskets of silk flowers hanging from beamed ceilings and ornate, dark-wood chairs. *1209 W. Wyatt Earp Blvd., tel. 316/225–0371. MC, V. Closed Sun. Inexpensive–Moderate.*

★ **Saigon Market.** Fresh ingredients for Vietnamese dishes are cooked to order and colorfully presented in the restaurant half of this market, housed in a funky strip mall. The "French" coffee (a strong blend served with condensed milk over ice) could be dessert. *1202 E. Wyatt Earp Blvd., tel. 316/225–9099. No reservations. No credit cards. Closed Mon. Inexpensive–Moderate.*

Lodging   **Silver Spur Lodge & Convention Center.** You'll find clean, pleasant, undistinguished rooms at this sprawling complex just five minutes from Front Street. *1510 W. Wyatt Earp Blvd., 67801, tel. 316/227–2125. 121 rooms, 3 suites. Facilities: 2 restaurants, lounge, outdoor pool. AE, D, DC, MC, V. Inexpensive.*

Hutchinson   **Anchor Inn.** Two large, brick-walled rooms in older downtown
Dining   buildings are the setting for Mexican dishes using the restau-
★ rant's distinctive homemade flour tortillas. Portions are bounteous. *126–128 S. Main St., tel. 316/669–0311. No reservations weekend nights. No credit cards. Closed Sun. May–Sept. Inexpensive.*

Roy's Hickory Pit BBQ. This tiny restaurant seating 13 serves barbecued pork spare ribs, beef brisket, sausage, ham, and turkey. There's nothing else on the menu except beans, salad, and bread—but who needs more? *1018 W. 5th St., tel. 316/663–7421. No reservations. No credit cards. Closed Sun.–Mon. Inexpensive.*

Lodging   **Best Western Sun Dome.** This standard chain establishment is just off U.S. 50. Neutral colors and modern furnishings decorate the rooms, many of which overlook the atrium and pool area. *11 Des Moines St., South Hutchinson 67505, tel. 316/663–4444; fax 316/663–1165. 96 rooms, 1 suite. Facilities: restaurant, lounge, indoor pool, sauna, weight room. AE, D, DC, MC, V. Moderate.*

★ **Holiday Inn Holidome.** Rooms in the "minidome" section of this busy convention hotel look onto a quiet landscaped courtyard. Main-dome rooms open onto a recreation area with a putting green and a swimming pool. *1400 N. Lorraine St., 67501, tel. 316/669–9311; fax 316/669–9830. 220 rooms, 7 suites. Facilities: restaurant, lounge, indoor pool, 2 tennis courts, exercise room. AE, D, DC, MC, V. Moderate.*

Larned   **Porterhouse.** Steaks and homemade desserts are specialties in
Dining   this former Atchison Topeka & Santa Fe Railway depot. The bar is open only to members and registered guests at Townsman Inn. *320 Broadway, tel. 316/285–6939. Reservations advised. MC, V. Closed Sun. Moderate.*

Motels   Econo Lodge and Super 8 are in Dodge City (*see* Appendix, Toll-Free Numbers). **Best Western Townsman Inn** (123 E. 14th St., Larned 67550, tel. 316/285–3114), 44 rooms, pool; inexpensive. **Quality Inn City Center** (15 W. 4th St., Hutchinson 67501, tel. 316/663–1211), 100 rooms, restaurant, lounge, outdoor pool; inexpensive. **Scotsman Inn** (322 E. 4th St., Hutchinson 67501, tel. 316/669–8281), 48 rooms; inexpensive.

Campgrounds

Gunsmoke Campground (R.R. 2, W. Hwy. 50, Dodge City 67801, tel. 316/227–8247). **Melody Acres RV Park** (2201 S. Bonebrake St., Hutchinson 67501, tel. 316/665–5048). **Watersports Campground** (500 E. Cherry St., Dodge City 67801, tel. 316/225–9003 or 316/225–9325).

Nightlife

In Dodge City, the **Boot Hill Museum Repertory Co.** (*see* the Boot Hill Museum in Exploring the Santa Fe Trail Region, *above*) puts on a 19th-century Long Branch Variety Show. Also in Dodge City, the **Longhorn Saloon** (706 N. 2nd St., tel. 316/225–3546) has a 1,350-sq-ft wood dance floor for western stomping, as well as a restaurant.

Elsewhere in the State

Wichita

Getting There Wichita lies about 190 mi southwest of Kansas City on the Kansas Turnpike (I–35). Most visitors arrive by car or fly into the **Mid-Continent Airport** (tel. 316/946–4700), served by most major domestic carriers.

What to See and Do Originally a frontier town, Wichita is known today as the "Air Capital of the World"—Beech, Cessna, and Learjet are based here, and Boeing has a major installation. The city is also home to such corporate giants as Coleman, which manufactures camping equipment, and Pizza Hut.

Tourist attractions include the **Indian Center Museum** (650 N. Seneca St., tel. 316/262–5221), featuring artifacts from numerous tribes; the **Old Cowtown Museum** (1871 Sim Park Dr., tel. 316/264–0671), a re-creation of a 19th-century town; and the **Wichita Greyhound Park** (10 mi from downtown Wichita on I–135, tel. 316/755–4000 or 800/872–2894). The **Convention and Visitors Bureau** (100 S. Main St., Suite 100, 67202, tel. 316/265–2800 or 800/288–9424).

MISSOURI

By Lori Dodge Rose

Capital	Jefferson City
Population	5,117,073
Motto	Let the Welfare of the People Be the Supreme Law
State Bird	Eastern bluebird
State Flower	Hawthorn

Visitor Information

The **Missouri Division of Tourism** (Truman State Office Bldg., Box 1055, Jefferson City 65102, tel. 314/751–4133 or 800/877–1234 in MO) operates six Tourist Information Centers to serve travelers as they enter Missouri on major interstates.

Scenic Drives

Rte. 21 from St. Louis to Doniphan in extreme southern Missouri passes through national forests and rugged hill country. Scenic routes in the Ozark Mountains of southwestern Missouri include **Rte. 76, Rte. 248,** and **U.S. 65** south of Springfield.

National and State Parks

National Parks The **Ozark National Scenic Riverways** (National Park Service, Box 490, Van Buren 63965, tel. 314/323–4236), two south-central Missouri rivers that were the first to be federally protected, offer good canoeing. The **Mark Twain National Forest** (401 Fairgrounds, Rolla 65401, tel. 314/364–4621) in southern Missouri offers a wealth of outdoor opportunities.

State Parks Lake of the Ozarks State Park (*see* Exploring the Ozarks, *below*) is the largest state park in Missouri. The popular **Missouri River State Trail**, known to locals as the Katy Trail, is a walking and cycling path along the Missouri River between Sedalia and St. Charles. Other significant parks include **Elephant Rocks** (Belleview 63623, tel. 314/697–5395), **Johnson's Shut-ins** (Middle Brook 63656, tel. 314/546–2450), **Mastodon State Park** (Imperial 63052, tel. 314/464–2976), and **Onondaga Cave State Park** (Leasburg 65535, tel. 314/245–6576). For more information, contact the **Missouri Department of Natural Resources** (Box 176, Jefferson City 65102, tel. 314/751–2479 or 800/334–6946).

St. Louis

Founded as a French fur-trading settlement on the west bank of the Mississippi River in 1764, St. Louis today is best known for its soaring silver arch so impressive to travelers entering the city from the east. In its early days, the city thrived as a river port, then as a rail hub, and today it's the world headquarters for such diverse corporations as Anheuser-Busch and McDonnell Douglas. The building of the Gateway Arch more than 25 years ago did more than commemorate the city's role in westward expansion—it helped spark the rebirth of a downtown that had been abandoned in the rush for the suburbs.

Tourist Information

St. Louis: Convention and Visitors Commission (10 S. Broadway, Suite 1000, 63102, tel. 314/421–1023 or 800/888–3861) is open weekdays from 8:30 to 5. **Visitor centers** are located at the airport and downtown (308 Washington Ave., tel. 314/241–1764). The **Missouri Tourist Information Center** (tel. 314/869–7100) is just west of the Missouri–Illinois border on I–270 at the Riverview exit.

Arriving and Departing

By Plane   **Lambert–St. Louis International Airport** (tel. 314/426–8000), 10 mi northwest of downtown on I–70, has scheduled flights by most major domestic and foreign carriers. It's about 20 minutes by car from the airport to downtown St. Louis; taxis cost about $17.50. Transportation is also provided to downtown stops by the **Bi-State** bus (tel. 314/231–2345) and to hotels by **Airport Express** limousines (tel. 314/429–4950).

By Car   From I–70, I–55, and I–44, follow the exits for downtown St. Louis. From U.S. 40 (I–64) from the west, exit at Broadway.

Train Station   Amtrak (550 S. 16th St., tel. 314/331–3300).

Bus Station   Greyhound (1450 N. 13th St., tel. 314/231–4485 or 314/231–7800).

Getting Around St. Louis

Downtown sights can be explored on foot, but for the city's more far-flung attractions, you'll need a car. The Bi-State bus service's **Levee Line** (tel. 314/231–2345) offers free rides to major attractions downtown.

Exploring St. Louis

Downtown   Any visit to the Gateway City should include a trip to the top of the **Gateway Arch,** rising 630 feet above the Mississippi River. This magnificent centerpiece of the 91-acre **Jefferson National Expansion Memorial Park** was built in 1966 to commemorate the city where thousands of 19th-century pioneers stopped for provisions before traveling west. A tram takes visitors up the inside of each leg of the arch to an observation room, where you get a terrific view of the city and the mighty Mississippi. Below it is the underground visitor center and the **Museum of Westward Expansion.** *On the riverfront at Market St., tel. 314/425–4465. Admission charged. Closed major holidays.*

Just down the steps from the arch is the Mississippi riverfront and its cobblestone levee, where permanently moored riverboats house a handful of mostly fast-food restaurants. The *Huck Finn, Tom Sawyer,* and *Becky Thatcher* (tel. 314/621–4040), replicas of 19th-century steamboats, offer one-hour sightseeing trips. The new *Belle of St. Louis* riverboat (tel. 314/621–4040) provides day trips and dinner cruises. North of the arch is **Laclede's Landing,** nine square blocks of cobblestone streets and restored 19th-century warehouses now filled with shops, galleries, restaurants, and night spots.

Back on the west edge of the arch grounds is St. Louis's oldest church, **Basilica of St. Louis, the King** (209 Walnut St.), a simple

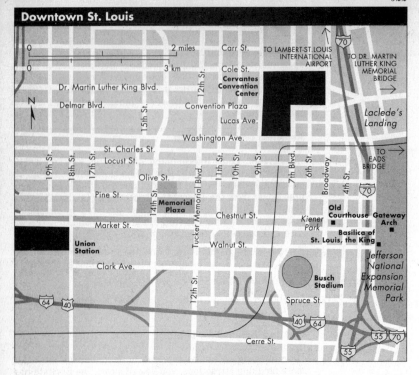

Downtown St. Louis

0   2 miles
0   3 km

Carr St.
Cole St.
Cervantes Convention Center
Convention Plaza
Lucas Ave.
Washington Ave.

TO LAMBERT-ST. LOUIS INTERNATIONAL AIRPORT
TO DR. MARTIN LUTHER KING MEMORIAL BRIDGE

Dr. Martin Luther King Blvd.
Delmar Blvd.

N

St. Charles St.
Locust St.
Olive St.
Pine St.

Laclede's Landing

TO EADS BRIDGE

19th St. 18th St. 17th St. 15th St. 14th St. 12th St. 11th St. 10th St. 9th St. 7th Blvd. 6th St. Broadway 4th St.

Memorial Plaza
Tucker Memorial Blvd.
Chestnut St.
Market St.
Union Station
Clark Ave.
Walnut St.
12th St.
Spruce St.
Cerre St.

Kiener Park
Old Courthouse
Basilica of St. Louis, the King
Gateway Arch

Busch Stadium

Jefferson National Expansion Memorial Park

64 40   40 64   55 70   55

Greek Revival structure built 150 years ago that is a favorite setting for weddings. One block west on Market Street, the **Old Courthouse** (11 N. 4th St., tel. 314/425–4465) houses displays and photographs of early St. Louis.

South of the courthouse is **Busch Stadium,** home of the St. Louis Cardinals (*see* Spectator Sports, *below*). On the northeast side of the stadium is the **St. Louis Cardinals Hall of Fame,** displaying sports memorabilia and audio and video highlights of the city's baseball history. *Tel. 314/421–3263. Admission charged. Closed weekends Jan.–Mar.*

Other Attractions St. Louis is home to the world's largest brewer, **Anheuser-Busch,** makers of Budweiser beer. Tours at the company's world headquarters in south St. Louis include the stables where some of the famous Clydesdale horses are kept. *12th and Lynch Sts., tel 314/577–2626. Admission free. Closed Sun.*

On the west edge of town is **Forest Park** (north of U.S. 40 between Kingshighway and Skinker Blvd.). On its grounds are the **St. Louis Zoo** (tel. 314/781–0900), which includes a high-tech education center, and **The St. Louis Art Museum** (tel. 314/721–0072), whose pre-Columbian and German Expressionist collections are outstanding. **St. Louis Science Center** (5050 Oakland Ave., tel. 314/289–4444) contains exhibits on ecology, space, and humanity.

A mind-boggling collection of mosaics covers the walls, ceilings, and three domes of the **Cathedral of St. Louis** (Lindell Blvd. and Newstead Ave., tel. 314/533–2824), also known as the New Cathedral.

The **Missouri Botanical Garden,** known locally as Shaw's Garden for founder Henry Shaw, is a 15-minute drive southwest of downtown. Highlights include an impressive Japanese garden and a tropical rain forest housed in a geodesic dome. *4344 Shaw Ave., tel. 314/577–5100. Admission charged.*

St. Louisans love **Ted Drewes** frozen custard (6726 Chippewa St., tel. 314/481–2652) so much they'll stand in lines that spill into the street, but don't worry—the lines move fast. You'll label yourself a tourist if you have to ask what a concrete is (it's frozen custard so thick it won't budge even when you flip the cup upside down).

What to See and Do with Children

Six Flags over Mid-America–St. Louis (I–44 and Allenton Rd., Eureka, tel. 314/938–4800), about 30 mi southwest of St. Louis, thrills visitors of all ages with roller coasters and other rides.

Shopping

For browsing in boutiques and specialty shops, try **Union Station** (18th and Market Sts.), an impressive former train station, and **Laclede's Landing** (*see* Exploring St. Louis, *above*). The **Central West End,** along Euclid Avenue east of Forest Park, is an area of hip boutiques and restaurants. The city's most sophisticated shoppers head for **Plaza Frontenac** (Clayton Rd. and Lindbergh Blvd., tel. 314/432–0604), home to upscale stores.

Spectator Sports

Baseball   The **St. Louis Cardinals** (Busch Stadium, 250 Stadium Plaza, tel. 314/421–3060; Apr.–Oct).

Dining

St. Louis's Hill neighborhood boasts an Italian restaurant on nearly every corner; other ethnic restaurants are found throughout the city. Even the abundant steak houses carry an Italian dish or two. The Central West End and Laclede's Landing have a number of restaurants, as does Clayton, the St. Louis County seat, about 7 mi west of downtown. For price ranges, see Chart 1 (B) in Chapter 1.

Expensive   **Cardwell's.** Diners can eat in the airy café, with marble-top tables and French doors, or in the more formal, elegant dining room. The frequently changing menu at this Clayton restaurant may include salmon with honey-mustard glaze; poultry mixed grill with marinated quail, squab, and duck; or maybe even wild boar. *8100 Maryland St., tel. 314/726–5055. Reservations advised. AE, MC, V. Closed Sun.*
Sidney Street Cafe. Tables for two in the atrium and a candlelit dining room lend romance to this former storefront in the Benton Park neighborhood. The eclectic cuisine includes raspberry or tequila-lime chicken. *2000 Sidney St., tel. 314/771–5777. Reservations advised. AE, DC, MC, V. Closed Sun.–Mon.*
★ **Tony's.** After more than 40 years at the north edge of downtown, this highly acclaimed restaurant has moved to the more central Equitable Building to make room for construction of the city's new domed stadium. Run by the Bommarito family

for three generations, Tony's still offers superb Italian dishes and prime steaks and remains a favorite place for celebrating special occasions. *410 Market St., tel. 314/231–7007. Reservations advised. Jacket and tie required. AE, D, DC, MC, V. No lunch; closed Sun.*

Moderate   **Blue Water Grill.** Grilled seafood with a Southwestern flair is the specialty at this small, festive restaurant near the Hill. On Monday nights diners can mix and match "Flying Saucers," an assortment of miniature entrées. *2607 Hampton Ave., tel. 314/645–0707. Reservations advised. AE, MC, V. Closed Sun.*

★ **Cunetto's House of Pasta.** There's usually a wait at this popular restaurant on the Hill, but relaxing in the cocktail lounge is part of the experience. Once seated, you'll find plenty of veal and meat dishes to choose from, as well as more than 30 different pastas. *5453 Magnolia Ave., tel. 314/781–1135. No reservations at dinner. AE, DC, MC, V. Closed Sun.*

Inexpensive   **Blueberry Hill.** This St. Louis original, in the hip University
★ City neighborhood, was into pop memorabilia long before the Hard Rock Cafe. Order a burger and a Rock & Roll beer and plunk a quarter into the famous 2,000-tune jukebox and let the good times roll. *6504 Delmar Blvd., tel. 314/727–0880. No reservations. AE, D, DC, MC, V.*

Rigazzi's. Generous, inexpensive servings of pasta keep locals coming back to this no-frills pasta house on the Hill. *4945 Daggett St., tel. 314/772–4900. Reservations advised. AE, D, DC, MC, V. Closed Sun.*

Lodging

Most of St. Louis's big hotels are downtown or in Clayton, about 7 mi west. To check out the growing number of B&Bs in town, call or write **Bed and Breakfasts of St. Louis, River Country of Missouri and Illinois** (1900 Wyoming St., St. Louis 63118, tel. 314/771–1993 or 314/965–4328). For price ranges, see Chart 2 (A) in Chapter 1.

Expensive   **Hotel Majestic.** This small European-style hotel downtown is often the choice of visiting celebrities. The 80-year-old building was renovated in 1987 and filled with reproduction antiques. *1019 Pine St., 63101, tel. 314/436–2355 or 800/451–2355; fax 314/436–2355, ext. 493. 90 rooms, 2 suites. Facilities: restaurant, lounge, valet parking. AE, D, DC, MC, V.*

Hyatt Regency St. Louis at Union Station. Most of the rooms are in a contemporary garden setting beneath the arched trusses of Union Station's original train shed. The Regency Club offers deluxe rooms and suites on the concierge club level. *1 St. Louis Union Station, 63103, tel. 314/231–1234; fax 314/436–6827. 540 rooms, 22 suites. Facilities: 2 restaurants, 2 lounges, health club, outdoor pool, valet parking. AE, D, DC, MC, V.*

The Ritz-Carlton, St. Louis. Located in Clayton, this recent addition to the luxury-hotel scene is filled with chandeliers and museum-quality oil paintings. Some rooms on the top floors have views of the downtown St. Louis skyline. *100 Carondelet Plaza, Clayton 63105, tel. 314/863–6300; fax 314/863–3525. 301 rooms, 32 suites. Facilities: 2 restaurants, 2 lounges, health club, indoor pool. AE, D, DC, MC, V.*

Moderate   **Drury Inn–Union Station.** Recent renovation managed to re-
★ tain the leaded-glass windows and marble columns of this former YMCA. There's no bellman here, but you do have

complimentary breakfasts and an excellent location, next door to Union Station. *201 S. 20th St., 63103, tel. 314/231–3900 or 800/325–8300; fax 314/231–3900. 176 rooms, 11 suites. Facilities: restaurant, indoor pool. AE, D, DC, MC, V.*

Inexpensive **Budgetel Inn West Port.** Rooms are standard size at this reliable chain hotel near West Port Plaza. Recently renovated, the hotel offers complimentary Continental breakfast. *12330 Dorsett Rd., Maryland Heights 63043, tel. 314/878–1212 or 800/428–3438; fax 314/878–3409. 145 rooms, 15 suites. AE, D, DC, MC, V.*

Motels **Fairfield Inn by Marriott** (9079 Dunn Rd., 63042, tel. 314/731–7700; fax 314/731–7700, ext. 709), 135 rooms, pool; inexpensive. **Red Roof Inn** (5823 Wilson St., tel. 314/645–0101 or 800/843–7663; fax 314/645–0101, ext. 444), 110 rooms; inexpensive.

The Arts and Nightlife

The Arts The **Fabulous Fox Theatre** (527 N. Grand Blvd., tel. 314/534–1678) hosts major shows and concerts. The **Riverport Amphitheatre** (14141 Riverport Dr., tel. 314/298–9944) stages big-name concerts. The **St. Louis Symphony Orchestra** presents programs at **Powell Symphony Hall** (718 N. Grand Blvd., tel. 314/534–1700). For tickets to major events, call **Dialtix** (tel. 314/291–7600).

Nightlife Much of St. Louis's nightlife can be found in the redeveloped areas of **Laclede's Landing,** on the riverfront, and in **Soulard,** on the south edge of downtown. For gambling, head upriver to the new **Alton Belle Riverboat Casino** (219 Piasa St., Alton, IL, tel. 618/474–7500 or 800/336–7568). To find out who's playing where, consult the *St. Louis Post-Dispatch*'s Thursday calendar section or the free weekly paper *The Riverfront Times.*

The Ozarks

From wooded mountaintops and clear, spring-fed streams to the water playgrounds of Lake of the Ozarks and Table Rock Lake, the Ozark hill region of southern Missouri offers limitless recreation and unparalleled beauty. Branson, second only to Nashville as the nation's country-music capital, attracts 4 million visitors a year to its star-studded theaters.

Tourist Information

Greater Lake of the Ozarks: Convention and Visitors Bureau (Box 98, Lake Ozark 65049, tel. 314/365–3371 or 800/325–0213). Table Rock Lake/Kimberling City Area: Chamber of Commerce (Box 495–91, Kimberling City 65686, tel. 417/739–2564). **Branson:** Branson Lakes Area Chamber of Commerce (Box 220, 65616, tel. 417/334–4136). **Springfield:** Convention and Visitors Bureau and Tourist Information Center (3315 E. Battlefield Rd., 65804–4048, tel. 417/881–5300 or 800/678–8766).

Getting There

By Car Many of the towns and attractions in this wide-ranging region can be reached from I–44, which cuts diagonally across the state from St. Louis to Springfield (about 220 mi). Branson lies

about 40 mi south of Springfield on U.S. 65. The Lake of the
Ozarks is centrally located between St. Louis and Kansas City.

Exploring the Ozarks

Central Missouri's **Lake of the Ozarks,** formed by the damming
of the Osage River in 1931, is the state's largest lake, with 1,300
mi of shoreline sprawling over 58,000 acres. In summer, crowds
of vacationing families descend on the numerous resorts, motels, and tourist attractions; better times to visit may be
spring, when the dogwoods are blooming, and fall, when the
wooded hills come alive with color.

Lake of the Ozarks State Park (U.S. 54, tel. 314/348–2694), just
south of Osage Beach, encompasses 90 mi of shoreline and offers hiking trails, other recreational activities, and tours of
Ozark Caverns, one of Missouri's 5,000 or so caves. *Tel. 314/
346–2500. Admission charged. Closed Dec.–Feb.*

You're deep in the country's "Bible Belt" when you reach
Springfield (off I–44), home to two Bible colleges and a theolog-
ical seminary and located near a number of sights and cultural
events with religious themes. For many people, though, the
first stop in Springfield has little to do with religion. The enormous **Bass Pro Shops Outdoor World** (1935 S. Campbell Ave.,
tel. 417/887–1915), dubbed the "Sportsman's Disney World,"
has cascading waterfalls, a wildlife trophy collection, and an indoor pleasure-boat showroom, not to mention clothing and
sporting gear.

The visitor center at **Wilson's Creek National Battlefield** (Rte.
ZZ, tel. 417/732–2662), southwest of Springfield, documents
the first major Civil War battle to be fought west of the Mississippi. In Mansfield, roughly 40 mi east of Springfield on U.S.
60, is the **Laura Ingalls Wilder Home** (Rte. A, tel. 417/924–
3626), recently named a National Historic Landmark, where
the much-loved children's author wrote her "Little House"
books. Museum displays include Laura's handwritten manuscripts (written with pencil on school tablets) and Pa's fiddle.
About 70 mi west of Springfield is the **Carver National Monument** (off Rte. V, tel. 417/325–4151), honoring the birthplace of
George Washington Carver, the famous black botanist and
agronomist.

About 40 mi south of Springfield on U.S. 65 is **Lake Taneycomo,**
the first of Missouri's man-made lakes. Along its riverlike
length, small resorts are concentrated in towns such as Forsyth
and Rockaway Beach. Its larger, more developed neighbor, **Table Rock State Park** (Branson, tel. 417/334–4704), has boating,
picnicking, and plenty of motels, resorts, and commercial
campgrounds. Kimberling City is the main resort town here.

Boasting some 57,000 seats in such star-studded venues as the
Roy Clark Celebrity Theatre and the Cristy Lane Theatre (*see*
The Arts and Nightlife, *below*), **Branson** is becoming a mecca
for country-music fans to rival Nashville. Most of the town's recent growth has taken place along Rte. 76, already crowded
with miniature-golf courses, bumper-car concessions, souvenir
and hillbilly-crafts shops, motels, and resorts.

A few miles west of Branson is the **Shepherd of the Hills Homestead and Outdoor Theatre,** a working pioneer homestead with
a gristmill, a sawmill, and a smith and wheelwright shop. The

Shepherd of the Hills inspirational drama is performed outdoors here. *Rte. 76, tel. 417/334–4191. Admission charged. Closed Jan.–Apr.*

What to See and Do with Children

The Ozarks region is well suited to family vacations, with boating, swimming, and many roadside attractions, such as miniature golf and water parks. **Silver Dollar City** (Rte. 76, tel. 417/338–8100), just west of Branson, features Ozark artisans demonstrating traditional crafts, along with rides and music shows. Nearby, **White Water** (Rte. 76, Branson, tel. 417/334–7488) is the place for water-soaked fun.

Shopping

Osage Village (U.S. 54, Osage Beach, tel. 314/348–2065) is a major factory-outlet mall with more than 50 stores.

Sports and Outdoor Activities

Canoeing The Ozarks have some of the finest "floating" streams in the country, such as the Current River, one of two protected as the **Ozark National Scenic Riverways** (*see* National and State Parks, *above*). For a list of outfitters, contact the Missouri Division of Tourism (*see* Visitor Information, *above*).

Fishing **Bull Shoals Lake,** Lake Taneycomo, and Table Rock Lake all offer excellent fishing, including bass, catfish, and trout. Other good spots include Lake of the Ozarks and **Truman Lake.** Contact the **Missouri Department of Conservation** (Box 180, Jefferson City 65102, tel. 314/751–4115) for information on permits, costs, and seasons.

Hiking and The partially completed **Ozark Trail** passes through national
Backpacking and state forest and parkland, as well as private property. For information and maps, contact the **Missouri Department of Natural Resources** (Box 176, Jefferson City 65102, tel. 314/751–2479 or 800/334–6946) or individual state parks (*see* National and State Parks, *above*).

Dining and Lodging

To find out about B&Bs in the area, contact the **Ozark Mountain Country Bed and Breakfast** reservation service (Box 295, Branson 65616, tel. 417/334–4720 or 800/695–1546). For price ranges, see Charts 1 (B) and 2 (B) in Chapter 1.

Branson Area **Candlestick Inn.** Fresh local trout is a specialty at this restau-
Dining rant overlooking Lake Taneycomo. The two elegant dining
★ rooms have floor-to-ceiling glass. *Rte. 76E, Branson, tel. 417/334–3633. Reservations advised. AE, D, DC, MC, V. No lunch; closed 1st 2 weeks of Jan. Moderate.*
The Outback Steak and Oyster Bar. This rustic, Australian-inspired oysters-and-steak place has a veranda overlooking its own swamp, where a fake crocodile rests on a log. Servers wear khaki and greet you with "G'day!" *1914 Rte. 76W, Branson, tel. 417/334–6306. Reservations advised. AE, D, MC, V. Moderate.*

Lodging **Holiday Inn Branson.** Although this recently renovated hotel is not on Lake Taneycomo, some rooms have views of it. Service is friendly, and the location is convenient to area attractions. *1420 Rte. 76W, Box 340, Branson 65616, tel. 417/334–5101 or 800/465–4329; fax 417/334–0789. 220 rooms, 6 suites. Facilities: restaurant, lounge, outdoor pool. AE, D, DC, MC, V. Moderate.*

Kimberling Inn Resort and Conference Center. This small resort motel on Table Rock Lake is within walking distance of the Kimberling City Shopping Village, where there are crafts shops, restaurants, and bowling. *Rte. 13, Box 159, Kimberling City 65686, tel. 417/739–4311 or 800/833–5551. 53 rooms. Facilities: 3 restaurants, lounge, 3 outdoor and indoor pools, miniature golf, tennis court, boat rentals. AE, D, DC, MC, V. Moderate.*

Lake of the Ozarks
Dining

The Blue Heron. This seasonal restaurant serving steak and seafood is popular with lake visitors, who enjoy cocktails poolside before moving to the dining room overlooking the lake. *Bus. Rte. 54 and Rte. HH, Osage Beach, tel. 314/365–4646. No reservations. AE, D, MC, V. No lunch; closed Sun.–Mon. and Dec.–Feb. Moderate.*

Shooters 21. This large, popular lakeside bar and restaurant has both casual and fine dining. Bar fare includes such favorites as spicy chicken wings, potato skins, and burgers. *Lake Rd. 54–56, Osage Beach, mile marker 21, tel. 314/348–2100. AE, D, MC, V. Inexpensive–Moderate.*

Lodging
★

Lodge of the Four Seasons. Featuring a highly rated 27-hole Robert Trent Jones golf course and fine dining in the Toledo Room, this deluxe resort offers drastically reduced winter rates. *Box 215, Lake Ozark 65049, tel. 314/365–3000 or 800/843–5253; fax 314/865–3525. 311 rooms, 23 suites. Facilities: 6 restaurants, 2 lounges, 11 indoor and outdoor pools, 17 indoor and outdoor tennis courts, lake swimming, 45 holes of golf. AE, D, DC, MC, V. Expensive.*

★

Marriott's Tan-Tar-A Resort and Golf Club. One of the top choices in the region for vacations and business meetings, the resort features numerous recreational opportunities and fine dining at its Windrose restaurant. *Rte. KK, Osage Beach 65065, tel. 314/348–3131 or 800/826–8272; fax 314/348–3206. 750 rooms, 250 suites. Facilities: 5 restaurants, 3 lounges, health club, 5 indoor and outdoor pools, 6 indoor and outdoor tennis courts, 27 holes of golf. AE, D, DC, MC, V. Expensive.*

Holiday Inn Resort and Conference Center. The hotel does not have lake access, but some slightly more expensive rooms do have a view. *Bus. Rte. 54, Box 1930, Lake Ozark 65409, tel. 314/365–2334 or 800/532–3575; fax 314/365–6887. 213 rooms, 4 suites. Facilities: restaurant, lounge, 3 indoor and outdoor pools, miniature golf, exercise room. AE, D, DC, MC, V. Moderate.*

Springfield
Dining

Hemingway's Blue Water Cafe. Located in the Bass Pro Shops Outdoor World (*see* Exploring the Ozarks, *above*), this restaurant offers seafood, steaks, pasta, and poultry in a tropical atmosphere. *1935 S. Campbell Ave., tel. 417/887–3388. AE, D, MC, V. Expensive.*

Billy's Chili and Bar Bar. Set in a 100-year-old historic-district house decorated with World War II memorabilia, Billy's is a popular lunch spot serving chili, burgers, and barbecue. *307 S. National Ave., tel. 417/865–5344. No reservations. MC, V. Inexpensive.*

Lodging **Sheraton Inn and Conference Center.** The rooms at this hotel in the south part of town were renovated in 1990. Each is equipped with a VCR, and movies can be rented in the lobby. *3333 S. Glenstone Ave., 65804, tel. 417/883–6550; fax 417/883–5720. 199 rooms, 1 suite. Facilities: restaurant, lounge, indoor and outdoor pool. AE, D, DC, MC, V. Moderate.*
University Plaza Holiday Inn. Boasting the largest conference center in Missouri, this hotel has guest rooms arranged around a nine-story atrium. *333 John Q. Hammons Pkwy., 65806, tel. 417/864–7333 or 800/465–4329; fax 417/864–7333, ext. 7177. 271 rooms, 41 suites. Facilities: 2 restaurants, 2 lounges, indoor and outdoor pool, 2 tennis courts, exercise room. AE, D, DC, MC, V. Moderate.*

Motels **EconoLodge** (2808 N. Kansas Expressway, Springfield 65803, tel. 417/869–5600), 83 rooms; inexpensive. **Red Roof Inn** (2655 N. Glenstone Ave., Springfield 65803, tel. 417/831–2100), 112 rooms; inexpensive.

Campgrounds In the Lake of the Ozarks area: **Deer Valley Park and Campground** (Sunrise Beach, tel. 314/374–5277; closed mid-Oct.–mid-Apr.); **Lake of the Ozarks State Park** (*see* Exploring the Ozarks, *above*); **Majestic Oaks Park** (Lake Ozark, tel. 314/365–1890; closed Nov.–Mar.). In the Branson area: **Blue Mountain Campground** (Branson, tel. 800/779–2114; closed Nov.–Mar.); **Port of Kimberling Marina and Campground** (Kimberling City, tel. 417/739–5377); **Silver Dollar City Campground** (Branson, tel. 417/338–8189 or 800/282–2489; closed Nov.–Mar.).

The Arts and Nightlife

Among the music shows in the Lake of the Ozarks region is the **Kin-Fokes Mountain Music Show** (Camdenton, tel. 314/346–6797). Among the music theaters in Branson: **Andy Williams Moon River Theatre** (tel. 417/334–4500), **Baldknobbers Hillbilly Jamboree Show** (tel. 417/334–4528), **Cristy Lane Theatre** (tel. 417/335–5111), **Grand Palace** (tel. 417/336–7006), the **Jim Stafford at Stars of the Ozarks** (tel. 417/335–2797), **Mel Tillis Ozark Theatre** (tel. 417/335–6635), **Mickey Gilley's Family Theatre** (tel. 417/334–3210), **Presley's Mountain Music Jubilee** (tel. 417/334–4874), **Roy Clark Celebrity Theatre** (tel. 417/334–7535), and the **Shoji Tabuchi Show** (tel. 417/334–7469). Contact the Branson Lakes Area Chamber of Commerce (*see* Tourist Information, *above*) for a complete listing.

Kansas City

Boasting more fountains (more than 200) than any city except Rome and more boulevard miles (155) than Paris, Kansas City is attractive and cosmopolitan. This spread-out metropolitan area, which straddles the Missouri–Kansas line, has a rich history as a frontier trade center and river port, where wagon trains were outfitted before heading west on the Santa Fe and Oregon trails. Through the years it has been home to the nation's second-largest stockyards, saxophone player Charlie "Bird" Parker and his Kansas City–style jazz, and some of the best barbecue in the world.

Tourist Information

Greater Kansas City: Convention and Visitors Bureau (1100 Main St., Suite 2550, tel. 816/221–5242 or 800/767–7700), in City Center Square in downtown Kansas City. Its **Visitor Information Phone** (tel. 816/691–3800) offers a weekly recording of activities. The **Missouri Information Center** (I–70 and Blue Ridge Cutoff, tel. 816/889–3330) overlooks the Truman Sports Complex.

Arriving and Departing

By Plane **Kansas City International Airport** (tel. 816/243–5237), 30 minutes northwest of downtown on I–29, is served by major domestic airlines. Taxi service is zoned; the maximum fare from the airport to downtown Kansas City is $26. **KCI Shuttle** buses (tel. 816/243–5950; fare $10–$11) will take you to major downtown hotels.

By Car From I–70 or I–35, exit at Broadway for downtown. If you're coming from the airport, I–29 from the north merges with I–35 north of the city.

Train Station **Amtrak** (2200 Main St., tel. 816/421–3622).

Bus Station **Greyhound** (12th St. and Troost Ave., tel. 816/698–0080).

Getting Around Kansas City

Attractions are located throughout the metropolitan region, making cars important for visitors. However, sightseeing trolleys (tel. 816/221–3399) travel between downtown, Crown Center, Westport, and the Country Club Plaza; the drivers are usually entertaining and well versed in local history.

Exploring Kansas City

Plaza, Midtown, Kansas City's **Country Club Plaza** (47th and Main Sts., tel. 816/
Downtown 753–0100) is known for its fine shops and restaurants, its Spanish-style architecture, and its annual display of holiday lights from Thanksgiving to January, when hundreds of thousands of gaily colored bulbs outline the Plaza's buildings. Here you'll also find many of the city's fountains and statues. Several blocks east of the Plaza is the **Nelson-Atkins Museum of Art** (4525 Oak St., tel. 816/561–4000), known principally for its outstanding Oriental art collection and its Henry Moore Sculpture Garden on the south grounds.

Before there was a Kansas City, there was a **Westport** (north of the Plaza at Broadway and Westport Rd., tel. 816/931–3400), built along the Santa Fe Trail as an outfitting center for the wagon trains heading west. Today this area is filled with renovated and new buildings housing trendy shops, restaurants, and night spots.

On the crest of a hill at the north edge of **Penn Valley Park,** north of Westport, is the **Liberty Memorial** (100 W. 26th St., tel. 816/221–1918), dedicated to those who served in World War I. From the 217-foot tower's observation deck you get a panoramic view of the city.

Just across Main Street to the east is **Crown Center** (Grand Ave. and Pershing Rd., tel. 816/274–8444), an 85-acre shopping, en-

Downtown and Midtown Kansas City

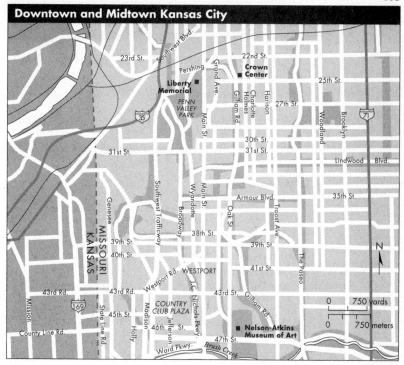

tertainment, office, and hotel complex. During the summer, free Friday night concerts are held on the terrace, and an outdoor, covered ice-skating rink is open during the winter. Kansas City–based Hallmark Cards, the largest maker of greeting cards in the world, built Crown Center and has its headquarters here. You can visit the **Hallmark Visitor's Center** (tel. 816/274–3613; closed Sun.), which features a display on the history of the greeting-card industry and a bow-making machine (you get to keep the bow).

Downtown, the **Treasures of the Steamboat *Arabia*** museum houses goods—from French perfume to buttons to coffee pots—salvaged from the *Arabia's* muddy grave 132 years after it sank in the Missouri River in 1856. *4th and Grand Sts., tel. 816/471–4030. Admission charged. Closed Mon.*

Other Attractions Just east of Kansas City is **Independence,** once the home of President Harry S Truman. His life and career are the focus at the **Harry S Truman Library and Museum** (U.S. 24 and Delaware St., tel. 816/833–1225) and the **Truman Home** (219 S. Delaware St., tel. 816/254–9929), the summer White House for Harry and Bess Truman during his administration.

Fleming Park (22807 Woods Chapel Rd., tel. 816/795–8200) in Blue Springs, south of Independence, features the 970-acre **Lake Jacomo,** as well as **Missouri Town 1855** (tel. 816/881–4431), a reproduction 1800s town created from more than 30 transplanted period houses, barns, stores, and outbuildings. Staff and volunteers dress in period clothing at this living-history museum.

Shopping

Kansas City's finest shopping is on **Country Club Plaza,** and a number of specialty shops and boutiques are concentrated in **Westport** and at **Crown Center** (for all, *see* Exploring Kansas City, *above*).

Spectator Sports

Baseball **Kansas City Royals** (Royals Stadium, Truman Sports Complex, I–70 and Blue Ridge Cutoff, tel. 816/921–8000; Apr.–Oct.).

Football **Kansas City Chiefs** (Arrowhead Stadium, Truman Sports Complex, tel. 816/924–9400; Aug.–Dec.).

Dining

Kansas City is best known for its steaks and barbecue, although locals argue over which places serve the best. Both the Plaza and Westport have a variety of good eating places, from elegant restaurants to sidewalk cafés to neighborhood joints dispensing barroom grub. For price ranges, see Chart 1 (B) in Chapter 1.

Expensive **Cafe Allegro.** Among the favorite entrées at this trendy restaurant are salmon with Chinese mustard glaze and tuna tartare. The brick interior is hung with paintings by local artists, and candles and fresh flowers grace the tables. *1815 W. 39th St., tel. 816/561–3663. Reservations advised. AE, DC, MC, V. No lunch weekends; closed Sun.*

★ **Plaza III–The Steakhouse.** This handsome, nationally known restaurant on Country Club Plaza serves excellent steaks, prime rib, and seafood; its steak soup is legendary. *4749 Pennsylvania Ave., tel. 816/753–0000. Reservations advised. AE, D, DC, MC, V.*

Savoy Grill. Locals often choose this historic, turn-of-the-century beauty when celebrating a special occasion. Maine lobster or a T-bone steak from the restaurant's own herd are good choices here. *219 W. 9th St., tel. 816/842–3890. Reservations advised. AE, D, DC, MC, V. No lunch weekends.*

Moderate **Golden Ox.** It's a little out of the way, but this steak house, featuring prime rib in a comfortable western atmosphere, is still extremely popular. *1600 Genesee St., tel. 816/842–2866. AE, D, DC, MC, V.*

★ **West Side Cafe.** This has become one of Kansas City's hottest spots—in more ways than one. The spicy tandoori chicken highlights a menu of Indian, Greek, and North African food. Seating is limited, so be ready for a wait. *723 Southwest Blvd., tel. 816/472–0010. D, MC, V. No dinner Sun.–Wed.*

Inexpensive **Arthur Bryant's.** Although there are reportedly more than 50
★ barbecue joints in Kansas City, Bryant's—low on decor but high on taste—tops the list for many Kansas Citians, who don't mind standing in line to order from the counter. *1727 Brooklyn Ave., tel. 816/231–1123. No credit cards.*

Ponak's. This large and popular restaurant is located in the flourishing Hispanic neighborhood along Southwest Boulevard. Among the menu items are soft tacos, tamales, enchiladas, and *menudo*, a Mexican soup made with tripe and hominy. *2856 Southwest Blvd., tel. 816/753–0775. No reservations weekend nights. AE, MC, V.*

Lodging

Kansas City offers a core of major hotels within walking distance of the Plaza and Westport, or in the Crown Center complex. For a listing of B&Bs, contact **Bed and Breakfast Kansas City** (Box 14781, Lenexa, KS 66285, tel. 913/888–3636). For price ranges, see Chart 2 (B) in Chapter 1.

Expensive **The Raphael.** Built in 1927 as apartments, The Raphael today
★ enjoys its status as the only intimate, European-style hotel in the city. Despite its small size, many of the rooms are large, with excellent views of the Plaza. *325 Ward Pkwy., 64112, tel. 816/756–3800 or 800/821–5343; fax 816/756–3800. 123 rooms, 72 suites. Facilities: restaurant, lounge, valet parking. AE, D, DC, MC, V.*

★ **The Ritz-Carlton.** This luxury hotel filled with crystal chandeliers, imported marble, and fine art was completely renovated in 1990. Some of the luxuriously appointed rooms have balconies and views of the Plaza. *401 Ward Pkwy., 64112, tel. 816/756–1500; fax 816/756–1635. 373 rooms, 28 suites. Facilities: 2 restaurants, 2 bars, health club, outdoor pool, valet parking. AE, D, DC, MC, V.*

The Westin Crown Center. Part of the Crown Center complex, The Westin features a bustling lobby complete with five-story waterfall and natural limestone cliff. All rooms have views; the best face Crown Center Square to the east. *1 Pershing Rd., 64108, tel. 816/474–4400; fax 816/391–4438. 725 rooms, 49 suites. Facilities: 3 restaurants, health club, outdoor pool, putting green, tennis courts. AE, D, DC, MC, V.*

Moderate **Drury Inn-Stadium.** Across from the sports complex, this chain hotel offers clean and comfortable rooms; for a few dollars more, you can have a "mini suite" with a king-size bed, a recliner, and a microwave. *3830 Blue Ridge Cutoff, 64133, tel. 816/923–3000 or 800/325–8300; fax 816/923–3000. 133 rooms, 1 suite. Facilities: outdoor pool. AE, D, DC, MC, V.*

Quarterage Hotel. Larger rooms at this intimate, brick hotel in Westport have either a queen-size bed or two doubles; smaller, less expensive rooms have one double and a balcony. *560 Westport Rd., 64111, tel. 816/931–0001 or 800/942–4233; fax 816/931–0001, ext. 157. 123 rooms. Facilities: health club, sauna. AE, D, DC, MC, V.*

Inexpensive **EconoLodge of KCI.** This inexpensive option for airport lodging offers free transportation to area restaurants. *11300 N.W. Prairie View, 64153, tel. 816/464–5082 or 800/424–4777. 58 rooms, 1 suite. AE, D, MC, V.*

The Arts and Nightlife

The Arts The **Folly Theater** (12th and Central Sts., tel. 816/842–5500) and the larger **Midland Center for the Performing Arts** (1228 Main St., tel. 816/471–8600) feature shows and concerts. The **Lyric Opera** of Kansas City and the **Kansas City Symphony** perform at the **Lyric Theatre** (11th and Central Sts., tel. 816/471–7344). Information on upcoming events can be found in the Friday and Sunday editions of *The Kansas City Star.* Call **Ticketmaster** (tel. 816/931–3330) for tickets for main events.

Nightlife Much of Kansas City's nightlife can be found in the Westport and Plaza areas. The **Grand Emporium** (3832 Main St., tel. 816/531–1504) is *the* place in town for blues. The city is justly proud of its jazz heritage, and live performances are featured at several establishments; call the **Jazz Hotline** (tel. 816/931–2888).

Elsewhere in the State

Hannibal

Getting There   Hannibal is about two hours north of St. Louis on U.S. 61.

What to See and Do   Hannibal is Mark Twain Country. The author's boyhood home is preserved at the **Mark Twain Home and Museum** (208 Hill St., tel. 314/221–9010). The **Mark Twain Cave** (Rte. 79, tel. 314/221–1656) is where Tom Sawyer and Becky Thatcher got lost in Twain's classic *The Adventures of Tom Sawyer*. **Hannibal Visitors and Convention Bureau** (320 Broadway, Box 624, 63401, tel. 314/221–2477).

Ste. Genevieve

Getting There   Ste. Genevieve is about 60 mi south of St. Louis on I–55.

What to See and Do   Numerous historic homes in this small river town, the oldest permanent settlement in Missouri, include examples of 18th-century French Creole architecture, characterized by vertical log construction. The **Great River Road Interpretive Center** (66 S. Main St., 63670, tel. 314/883–7097) houses the tourist information office.

St. Joseph

Getting There   St. Joseph is about an hour north of Kansas City on I–29.

What to See and Do   During the short experiment called the Pony Express, riders set out on the 2,000-mi trip to Sacramento, California, from what is now St. Joseph's **Pony Express Museum** (914 Penn St., tel. 816/232–8471). Nearby is the **Jesse James Home** (12th and Penn Sts., tel. 816/232–8206), where the notorious outlaw was shot and killed by a member of his own gang for the reward money. The bullet hole in the wall is still visible. **St. Joseph Area Chamber of Commerce** (3003 Frederick Blvd., 65406, tel. 816/232–4461).

NEBRASKA

Updated by
Ron Welch

Capital	Lincoln
Population	1,597,000
Motto	Equality Before the Law
State Bird	Western meadowlark
State Flower	Goldenrod

Visitor Information

The **Nebraska Department of Economic Development, Division of Travel and Tourism** (Box 94666, Lincoln 68509, tel. 800/228–4307) operates 20 rest and information areas along I–80.

Scenic Drives

Rte. 2, from Grand Island west to Crawford, is a long, lonesome road through the Sandhills that traverses 332 mi of delicate wildflowers, tranquil rivers, and placid cattle. The 130-mi drive north on **U.S. 83** from North Platte to Valentine offers a fine view of the Sandhills' native short-grass prairie. **U.S. 26** from Ogallala to Scottsbluff is a 128-mi historic segment of the Oregon Trail, passing such natural landmarks as Ash Hollow; Courthouse, Jail, and Chimney rocks; and Scotts Bluff National Monument.

National and State Parks

National Parks   **Homestead National Monument,** near Beatrice (Rte. 3, Box 47, 68310, tel. 402/223–3514), commemorates the post-1862 homestead movement and the pioneers who braved the rigors of the prairie frontier. **Nebraska National Forest,** at Halsey (Box 38, 69142, tel. 308/533–2257), is the largest man-planted forest in the country.

State Parks   The **Nebraska Game and Parks Commission** (Box 30370, Lincoln 68503, tel. 402/471–0641) manages and provides information on the seven state parks. Among them are **Ft. Robinson State Park** (*see* Exploring Northwest Nebraska, *below*); **Eugene T. Mahoney State Park** and **Platte River State Park** (*see* Exploring Southeast Nebraska, *below*); and **Indian Cave State Park,** in the state's southeast corner (2 mi north and 5 mi east of Shubert, Box 30, 68437, tel. 402/883–2575).

Southeast Nebraska

This is a land of mixed blessings, with city sophistication and country charm. Visitors can tour museums and historic buildings, shop in restored warehouses, ride riverboats, and board a vintage steam locomotive.

Tourist Information

Lincoln: Convention and Visitors Bureau (1221 N St., 68508, tel. 402/476–7511 or 800/423–8212). **Nebraska City:** Convention and Visitors Bureau (806 1st Ave., 68410, tel. 402/873–6654).

Omaha: Greater Omaha Convention and Visitors Bureau (1819 Farnam St., Suite 1200, 68183, tel. 402/444–4660 or 800/332–1819).

Getting There

By Plane   **Eppley Airfield,** about 3 mi from downtown Omaha, is served by most domestic carriers, as well as **GP Express** (tel. 402/342–3479) and **Great Lakes Airlines** (tel. 402/341–8657 or 800/554–5111). Cab fare from the airport to downtown is about $8. **Lincoln Municipal Airport,** about 3 mi from downtown Lincoln, is served by several major airlines, as well as GP Express. Cabs to downtown cost about $10. **Eppley Express** (tel. 308/234–6066 or 800/888–9793) runs an airport minibus from Lincoln Municipal Airport to Eppley Airfield ($15 fare).

By Car   I–80W from Des Moines links with Omaha (I–480 serves downtown Omaha) and Lincoln. U.S. 75S from Omaha leads to Nebraska City. From Lincoln, Rte. 2 goes to Nebraska City. To get to Beatrice, take U.S. 77S from Lincoln.

By Train   Amtrak's *Desert Wind, Pioneer,* and *California Zephyr* stop in Lincoln and Omaha.

By Bus   Omaha and Lincoln are served by **Greyhound** (tel. 402/341–1906 in Omaha, 402/474–1071 in Lincoln). Local bus service is provided in Lincoln by **StarTran** (tel. 402/476–1234) and in Omaha by **Metro Area Transit** (tel. 402/341–0800).

Exploring Southeast Nebraska

Nebraska's multistory state capitol building dominates the Lincoln skyline; the river city of Omaha is the region's center of commerce and industry. Minutes away from both downtowns are expansive prairies, state parks, and attractions that chronicle the opening of the West to settlement.

Start your tour in **Omaha,** where the **Henry Doorly Zoo** (Deer Park Blvd. and S. 10th St., tel. 402/733–8401) boasts the world's largest open-air aviary and an impressive new rain forest, the Lied Jungle. From here, it's about a 20-minute drive to **Peony Park** (8100 Cass St., tel. 402/391–6253), with the state's largest swimming pool, water slides, and carnival rides. Then head west on U.S. 6 to Father Flanagan's **Boys Town** (138th St. and W. Dodge Rd., tel. 402/498–1140), the only official village in the nation created just for children. Founded in 1917 and made famous in the 1938 movie with Spencer Tracy and Mickey Rooney, the town includes schools, churches, and farmland.

Travel south on 144th Street and east on Rte. 370, about 40 minutes in all, to **Bellevue,** home of the **Strategic Air Command Museum** (2510 Clay St., tel. 401/292–2001). Here you can stroll beneath the wings of aircraft that changed the course of history, see missiles huge and small, view rare film footage, and browse through an extensive collection of military artifacts.

In Fremont, about 50 mi northwest of Bellevue, board the historic **Fremont and Elkhorn Valley Railroad** (1835 N. Somer St., tel. 402/727–0615). The steam-powered train travels through 17 mi of lush Elkhorn Valley and offers dinner and mystery trips.

About 60 mi south of Fremont are the **Eugene T. Mahoney State Park** (near Ashland, tel. 402/944–2523) and the **Platte River State Park** (Rte. 50, then 2 mi west on Spur 13E near Louisville, tel. 402/234–2217). Both provide camping, riding, swimming, hiking, buffalo-stew cookouts, and spectacular vistas of the Platte River valley.

Take I–80W to **Lincoln,** home of the **University of Nebraska** and the state government. Scan the city's skyline from atop the **Nebraska Capitol** (1445 K St., tel. 402/471–3191), a 400-foot spire that towers over the surrounding plains. A five-minute drive north will take you to the **State Museum of Natural History** (at the university, 14th and U Sts., tel. 402/472–2642), nicknamed "Elephant Hall" for its huge collection of extinct animals that once roamed the Great Plains. A 20-minute drive west takes you to **Nine-Mile Prairie** (1 mi west of N.W. 48th St. and Fletcher Ave.), where you can park your car and get out to hike the natural prairies.

From Lincoln, you can take Rte. 2 southeast to U.S. 75, then U.S. 136 southeast to Brownville. At the Brownville State Recreation Area, the *Spirit of Brownville* riverboat (tel. 402/825–6441 or 712/625–2791) offers sightseeing, dining, and dancing cruises on the mighty Missouri River. Just south of Brownville Bridge is the **Meriwether Lewis and Missouri River History Museum** (tel. 402/825–3341), featuring a restored sidewheeler dredge once used on the river.

U.S. 75N brings you to **Nebraska City,** a tidy town rimmed with historic sites and apple orchards, including the **J. Sterling Morton Orchard** (100 Arbor Ave., tel. 402/873–9204), where you can buy apples, cider, and desserts year-round.

Hop the **Nebraska City Trolley** (tel. 402/873–3000) at stops throughout town. It links historic sites to 11 downtown factory outlets clustered around 8th and 1st Corso streets and to the **VF Factory Outlet Mall** (Rte. 2 and U.S. 75, tel. 402/873–7727), with merchandise from dishes to sweaters. The trolley also stops at **John Brown's Cave** (1924 4th Corso St., tel. 402/873–3115), a museum, a historic village, and a cave once used to hide runaway slaves.

Nearby is the **Arbor Lodge State Historical Park and Arboretum.** On the grounds are the 52-room mansion and greenhouse of J. Sterling Morton, the 19th-century politician and lover of trees who inaugurated the first Arbor Day, now observed nationwide as a day for planting trees. *2nd and Centennial Aves., tel. 402/873–7222. Admission charged. Closed late Oct.–mid-Apr.*

Shopping

Nebraska Furniture Mart (700 S. 72nd St., Omaha, tel. 402/397–6100 or 800/359–1200) is the largest furniture store west of the Mississippi. Omaha's **Old Market** (11th and Howard Sts., tel. 402/346–4445) and Lincoln's charming restored warehouse shopping district, **Historic Haymarket** (between 7th and 9th Sts., from O to R Sts., tel. 402/435–7496), feature quaint antiques stores, novelty gift shops, and some fine restaurants. Find bargains at Nebraska City's outlets (*see* Exploring Southeast Nebraska, *above*).

Sports and Outdoor Activities

Fishing The 13 Salt Valley lakes surrounding Lincoln, especially
Branched Oak (N.W. 140th St. and W. Raymond Rd.) and **Pawnee** (N.W. 98th and W. Adams Sts.), offer a variety of fish, including largemouth bass, northern pike, walleye, and channel
catfish. For more information contact the **Game and Parks
Commission** (tel. 402/471–0641).

Spectator Sports

Football The **University of Nebraska Cornhuskers** are a football powerhouse. Although tickets for games (Sept.–Nov.) are nearly impossible to get, check the Athletic Ticket Office (117 S. Stadium
St., tel. 402/472–3111).

Dining and Lodging

Dining choices in this varied region range from international
cuisine to pizza to quiche. Lodging runs from full-service hotels
to sumptuous bed-and-breakfasts (**Bed and Breakfast of Nebraska**, 230 S. Maple St., West Point 68788, tel. 402/372–5904).
For price ranges, see Charts 1 (B) and 2 (B) in Chapter 1.

Brownville **Thompson House Bed and Breakfast.** This Victorian three-sto-
Lodging ry house has a game room and parlor. Rooms are decorated
with antiques, including kerosene lamps. *Box 162, 68321, tel.
402/825–6551. 5 rooms. MC, V. Expensive.*

Lincoln **Billy's.** The elegance of a bygone era is complemented by a fas-
Dining cinating collection of political memorabilia and antiques in this
★ upscale restaurant that offers everything from steak Diane to
charbroiled chicken. *1301 H St., tel. 402/474–0084. AE, MC, V.
Moderate.*
Misty's Restaurant. Adorned with Cornhusker football paraphernalia, this is considered by locals to be the prime-rib palace
of the Plains. *6235 Havelock Ave., tel. 402/466–8424. AE, D,
MC, V. Moderate.*
Rock 'n' Roll Runza. Waitresses on roller skates serve
Runzas—a hamburger-cabbage sandwich—at this '50s-style
restaurant. *210 N. 14th St., tel. 402/474–2030. AE, MC, V. Inexpensive.*
★ **Valentino's Restaurant.** Besides pizza with original, home-
style, or deep-dish crust, the restaurant also serves Italian specials and dessert pizzas with such toppings as cherry and cream
cheese. *3457 Holdrege St., tel. 402/467–3611. MC, V. Inexpensive.*

Lodging **The Cornhusker.** The lobby of this elegant hotel has a grand
curving staircase, oak accents, and an Italian marble floor.
East- and south-wing rooms have good views of downtown Lincoln. *333 S. 13th St., 68508, tel. 402/474–7474; fax 402/474–
1847. 277 rooms, 12 suites. Facilities: restaurant, pool, exercise room, sauna. AE, D, DC, MC, V. Expensive.*
★ **The Rogers House Bed and Breakfast.** Built in 1914, this ivy-
covered brick mansion was converted into a B&B in 1984 by the
current owners. The antiques-filled rooms with oak floors include a living room with fireplace and a sun room where guests
can have breakfast. *2145 B St., 68502, tel. 402/476–6961. 8
rooms. AE, MC, V. Moderate.*

Nebraska City
Dining
★ **Teresa's Family Restaurant.** Booths line the walls of this casual, family-style place where old-fashioned food, such as homemade lemon pie and meatloaf, is offered at yesterday's prices. *812 Central Ave., tel. 402/873–9100. MC, V. Inexpensive.*

★ **Ulbrick's.** This converted gas station and café is nothing fancy, but the made-from-scratch family-style dinners of fried chicken, creamed corn and cabbage, and homemade egg noodles are exceptional. *1513 S. 11th St., tel. 402/873–5458. Reservations advised Sun. No credit cards. Inexpensive.*

Lodging **Whispering Pines.** Nestled among pines on 6½ quiet acres, this 112-year-old, two-story brick house has been completely refurbished as a B&B and filled with antiques. *Rte. 2, 68410, tel. 402/873–5850. 4 rooms. MC, V. Inexpensive.*

Omaha
Dining **Bohemian Cafe.** Gaily painted Czech plates hang on the walls of this family-style restaurant, where you can try such ethnic favorites as goulash. *1406 S. 13th St., tel. 402/342–9838. D, MC, V. Moderate.*

Johnny's Café. Since 1921 this has been *the* place to eat near the famous Omaha Stockyards. Mouth-watering steaks are the specialty, but seafood and other midwestern dishes are offered as well. *4702 S. 27th St., tel. 402/731–4774. AE, MC, V. Moderate.*

★ **Mr. C's.** Christmas lights surround you at this Italian steak house. Here the lasagna and manicotti are as good as the sirloin. *5319 N. 30th St., tel. 402/451–1998. AE, DC, MC, V. Moderate.*

Austins. Throw your peanut shells on the floor at this casual eatery where the atmosphere is western and the food pure country. Chicken-fried steak, prime rib, and barbecued ribs are the specialties. *12020 Anne St., tel. 402/896–5373. AE, MC, V. No reservations. Inexpensive.*

Garden Café. Home-style cooking with everything made from scratch is what this café in the historic Old Market is known for. Noteworthy are the potato casseroles, soups, salads, and desserts. *12th and Harvey Sts., tel. 402/422–1574. AE, DC, MC, V. Inexpensive.*

Neon Goose. The mood is lively at this casual restaurant with piano bar. Good menu choices here are the unusual quiches and the melt-in-your-mouth omelets. *1012 S. 10th St., tel. 402/341–2063. AE, D, DC, MC, V. Inexpensive.*

Lodging **The Marriott Hotel.** Built in the 1980s, this six-story hotel in suburban Omaha offers comfort but little flash. There's a gift shop here, or take advantage of nearby shopping at the upscale Regency Fashion Court area. *10220 Regency Circle, 68114, tel. 402/399–9000; fax 402/346–5722. 297 rooms, 4 suites. Facilities: 2 restaurants, pool, exercise equipment, gift shop. AE, D, DC, MC, V. Expensive.*

★ **Red Lion Hotel.** This 19-story hotel has a luxurious, chandeliered lobby and spacious rooms with mauve and mint-green color schemes. It's in the heart of downtown, close to the Old Market and Creighton University. *1616 Dodge St., 68102, tel. 402/346–7600; fax 402/346–5722. 378 rooms, 36 suites. Facilities: restaurant, pool, sauna. AE, D, DC, MC, V. Expensive.*

Motels **Oak Creek Inn** (2808 S. 72nd St., Omaha 68124, tel. 402/397–7137), 102 rooms, pool, whirlpool, sauna, spa/exercise room; moderate. **Harvester Motel** (1511 Center Park Rd., Lincoln

68512, tel. 402/423–3131), 80 rooms, pool, cocktail lounge; inexpensive.

Campgrounds **Indian Cave State Park** (*see* National and State Parks, *above*), as well as **Eugene T. Mahoney** and **Platte River state parks** (*see* Exploring Southeast Nebraska, *above*), offer excellent tent and RV camping.

Northwest Nebraska

Here the Great Plains end and the Old West begins—a rugged, beautiful land with dramatic buttes and bluffs, Ponderosa pines, craggy ridges, and canyons.

Tourist Information

Alliance: Box Butte Visitors Committee (Alliance Chamber of Commerce, Box 571, 69301, tel. 308/762–1520). **Chadron:** Chamber of Commerce (Box 646, 69337, tel. 308/432–4401). **Scottsbluff:** United Chamber of Commerce (1721 Broadway St., Scottsbluff 69361, tel. 308/632–2133).

Getting There

By Car From Omaha and Lincoln, take I–80W about 300 mi to U.S. 26, which closely follows the Oregon and Mormon trails to Scottsbluff. To bypass Scottsbluff and Gering, take I–80 to Grand Island, then scenic Rte. 2, which runs northwest of I–80 through Nebraska's Sandhills.

Exploring Northwest Nebraska

Head west on U.S. 26 to Bridgeport, then 4 mi south on Rte. 88. From the road you can see **Courthouse and Jail Rocks,** sandstone outcroppings that pioneers used as landmarks on the trail west. South of Bayard 4 mi, at the junction of U.S. 26 and Rte. 92, the **Chimney Rock National Historic Site** (tel. 402/471–4754) is an even more impressive outcropping that pioneers described as "towering to the heavens." Oregon Trail wagon ruts are still visible at the **Scotts Bluff National Monument** (3 mi west of Gering on Rte. 92, tel. 308/436–4340), an enormous bluff that rises out of the rocky plains. Once described as the "Lighthouse of the Plains," it now features a museum at its base.

About 60 mi north of Mitchell on Rte. 29, the **Agate Fossil Beds National Monument** features fossil deposits dating back 25 million years. A museum (tel. 308/436–4340) preserves and displays fossils and Native American artifacts, including personal items that belonged to Chief Red Cloud.

Continue north on Rte. 29, then east on U.S. 20 to **Ft. Robinson State Park** (tel. 308/665–2660), where activities include trail rides, historic tours, cookouts, swimming, trout fishing, hiking, and stagecoach rides.

Sports and Outdoor Activities

Hiking and Backpacking **Ft. Robinson State Park** (*see* Exploring Northwest Nebraska, *above*) and **Chadron State Park** (8 mi south of Chadron on U.S. 385, tel. 308/432–2036) offer an abundance of trails.

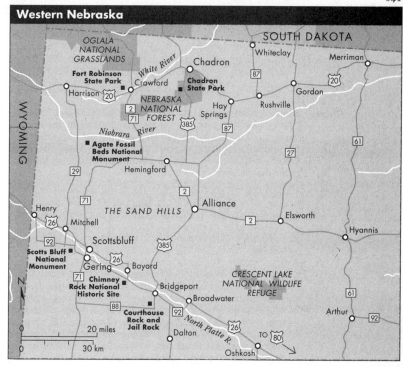

Western Nebraska

Dining and Lodging

Travelers to the region chow down at casual, out-of-the-way
restaurants, wagon-train cookouts, and ranches. Inexpensive
cattle ranches and B&Bs (**Bed and Breakfast of Nebraska,** Box
6392, Lincoln 68506, tel. 402/435–8567) provide charming alternatives to chain motels. For price ranges, see Charts 1 (B) and 2
(B) in Chapter 1.

Bayard
Dining and Lodging
★
Oregon Trail Wagon Train. Enjoy sleeping under the stars and
eating cookouts of stew, spoon bread, and vinegar pudding on
covered-wagon tours through some of Nebraska's remaining
short-grass prairieland. One- to six-day treks are available.
*Rte. 2, Box 502, 69334, tel. 308/586–1850. Reservations re-
quired. MC, V. Expensive.*

Crawford
Lodging
★
Butte Ranch Bed and Breakast. One bedroom is in a two-level
renovated barn, the others in a rustic cottage at this B&B nestled between two butte ranges east of Ft. Robinson State Park.
Bird-watching, hunting, and trail rides are popular here. *HC
76, Box 39A, 69339, tel. 308/665–2364. 4 rooms. MC, V. Inexpensive.*

Gering
Lodging
Monument Heights Bed and Breakfast. At this ranch-style
house at the base of Scotts Bluff National Monument, two bedrooms offer access to a family room with wood-burning stove.
*2665 Grandview Rd., 69341, tel. 308/635–0109. 3 rooms. Reser-
vations required. No credit cards. Inexpensive.*

Oshkosh
Dining
Thunder Valley. You can work up an appetite for ranch-style
meals of steak or hamburger by taking one of the horse or wag-

on rides offered at this working ranch. *Rte. 2, Box 16, tel. 308/772–3906. No credit cards. Expensive.*

Scottsbluff
Dining

Grampy's Pancake House. This large, family-style restaurant is divided into three dining rooms with booths and tables, where hearty breakfasts such as peanut butter or strawberry pancakes are featured. Lunch and dinner are also served here. *1802 E. 20th Pl., tel. 308/632–6906. MC, V. Inexpensive.*

Motels

Scottsbluff Inn (1901 21st Ave., Scottsbluff 69361, tel. 308/635–7646), 138 rooms, pool, sauna, weight room, restaurant/lounge; moderate. **Landmark Inn** (246 Main St., Bayard 69334, tel. 308/586–1375), 9 rooms; inexpensive. **Town Line Motel** (Box 423, Crawford 69339, tel. 308/665–1450), 24 rooms with kitchenettes; inexpensive.

Ranches

Verde Valley Guest Ranch. Bed-and-breakfast or all-inclusive packages are offered at this working cattle ranch 60 mi north of Lake McConaughy. Rooms are available in the 1915 Mission-style home or in modern cabins. Those who opt for the meal-and-activities plan can take part in riding, hunting, sailing, and swimming. *Box 228, Hyannis 69350, tel. 308/458–2220. 7 rooms, 3 cabins. Facilities: dining room, pool, recreational activities. MC, V. Moderate–Expensive.*

Meadow View Ranch Bed and Breakfast Bunkhouse. Guests stay in the converted bunkhouse of this 5,000-acre working ranch 18 mi from the South Dakota border. Accommodations include a kitchenette and living room. Complimentary breakfast is served in the ranch kitchen, and picnic lunches are packed on request. Activities include fishing, hiking in the nearby Sandhills, wagon rides, and cattle drives. *HC 91, Box 29, Gordon 69343, tel. 308/282–0679. 2 rooms. No credit cards. Closed Nov.–Apr. Moderate.*

Campgrounds

Chadron State Park (*see* Hiking and Backpacking, *above*) and **Ft. Robinson State Park** (*see* Exploring Northwest Nebraska, *above*) offer tent and RV camping.

Elsewhere in the State

Lake McConaughy and Ogallala

Getting There

From Lincoln and Omaha, take I–80W to Ogallala.

What to See and Do

Lake McConaughy State Recreation Area and the **Kingsley Dam** (9 mi north of Ogallala on Rte. 61, tel. 308/284–3542 or 308/284–6571) annually attract thousands of visitors who come to camp, fish, go boating, and enjoy the natural white-sand beaches here. In Ogallala, **Front Street** (tel. 308/284–4601) depicts an 1880s Main Street and features nightly western shows Memorial Day through Labor Day. Nearby are **Mansion on the Hill** (tel. 308/284–2237), a museum with exhibits on 19th-century cattle drives, and **Boot Hill Cemetery**, three blocks west of the mansion.

Red Cloud

Getting There

From Lincoln and Omaha, take I–80W to Grand Island, then U.S. 34S to U.S. 281, then U.S. 281S.

What to See and Do

Red Cloud was the home of Pulitzer Prize–winning author Willa Cather. The **Willa Cather Historical Center** (338 N. Webster

St., tel. 402/746–3285) is dedicated to the author, who loved the Plains—610 acres of which are preserved as the **Cather Memorial Prairie** (5 mi south of Red Cloud).

The Great Platte River Road

Getting There From Omaha and Lincoln, take I–80W.

What to See and Do Westward-bound pioneers on the Mormon and Oregon trails once hugged the shores of the Platte River, a verdant natural roadway. Today I–80 follows the same route, cutting through the state's heartland and affording glimpses of this pioneer past. **Sculpture gardens** dot the landscape along the highway for 500 mi across the Nebraska plains. At nine rest areas large stone and metal artworks constitute what some critics have called a "museum without walls."

In **Grand Island,** the **Stuhr Museum of the Prairie Pioneer** (junction of U.S. 34 and U.S. 281, tel. 308/381–5316) houses Native American artifacts and features a 60-building "Railroad Town," complete with a steam-powered train. From early March to mid-April, visitors flock to an area near Grand Island and Kearney to witness the migration of thousands of Sandhill cranes as they pause here before resuming their flight north. The **Platte River Whooping Crane Habitat Maintenance Trust** (tel. 308/384–4633) and the **Lillian Row Audubon Sanctuary** (tel. 308/236–7574) offer tours.

Ft. Kearny State Historical Park (4 mi south of I–80 on Rte. 44 and 4 mi east of L–50A, tel. 308/234–9513) has a re-created stockade and interpretive exhibits detailing the role of the outpost on the frontier.

Harold Warp's Pioneer Village (junction of U.S. 6, U.S. 34, and Rte. 10 in Minden, tel. 308/832–1181) has an extensive collection of pioneer memorabilia, horse-drawn covered-wagon rides, and crafts demonstrations. **Gothenburg**'s downtown Ehmen Park contains an original **Pony Express Station** (tel. 308/537–2680). The Wild West comes alive in **North Platte,** where Buffalo Bill Cody and his famous Wild West show began. You can tour his ranch house in the **Buffalo Bill Ranch State Historical Park** (tel. 308/535–8035), 6 mi northwest of North Platte.

Sandhills/Valentine Region

Getting There From Lincoln and Omaha, take I–80W to Grand Island. Go north on U.S. 281 to Rte. 22 and then follow it west 9 mi to Rte. 11N. At Burwell, follow Rte. 91W to U.S. 183N to U.S. 20W to Valentine.

What to See and Do **Ft. Hartsuff State Historical Park** (3 mi north of Elyria, off Rte. 11, tel. 308/346–4715) is a restored 1870s infantry post with guides in period uniforms and costumes.

For a glimpse of the Great Plains as they once were you can take a drive through hundreds of miles of mixed-grass prairie, where outdoor attractions beckon. The **Niobrara, Dismal,** and **Calumus rivers** draw canoeists from throughout the state. Outfitters include **Dryland Aquatics** (Box 33C, Sparks 69220, tel. 402/376–3117), **A&C Canoe Rentals** (HC 13, Box 36B, Sparks 69220, tel. 402/376–2839), **Brewers Canoers** (433 E. U.S. 20, Valentine 69201, tel. 402/376–2046), **Graham Canoe**

Outfitters (HC 13, Box 16A, Valentine 69201, tel. 402/376–3708), **Little Outlaw Canoe Rentals** (Box 15, Valentine 69201, tel. 402/376–1827), and **Super Tube** (310 W. U.S. 20, Valentine 69201, tel. 402/376–2956). Native wildlife is abundant at the **Valentine National Wildlife Refuge** (HC 14, Box 67, Valentine 69201, tel. 402/376–3789), south of Valentine on U.S. 83. Its 70,000 acres of prairie and wetlands shelter ducks, geese, hawks, eagles, deer, coyotes, beavers, and other species. There are trails for driving or hiking through this open country; information kiosks are located at entrances to the refuge.

Nearby, the **Ft. Niobrara National Wildlife Refuge** (HC 14, Box 67, Valentine 69201, tel. 402/376–3789), 5 mi east of Valentine on Rte. 12, has a more forested terrain and larger species, such as bison, elk, and Longhorn cattle.

NORTH DAKOTA

By Kevin
Bonham

Updated by
Ron Welch

Capital	Bismarck
Population	638,800
Motto	Liberty and Union, Now and Forever, One and Inseparable
State Bird	Western meadowlark
State Flower	Wild prairie rose

Visitor Information

North Dakota Department of Parks and Tourism (Liberty Memorial Bldg., 604 E. Blvd., Bismarck 58505, tel. 800/435–5663). **Welcome centers:** along I–94E, 1 mi west of Beach; off I–94 at the Oriska rest area, 12 mi east of Valley City; off I–29N at the Lake Agassiz Rest Area, 8 mi south of Hankinson interchange; along I–29S, 1 mi north of the Pembina interchange; one block west of the junction of U.S. 2 and U.S. 85 in Williston; at the junction of U.S. 12 and U.S. 85 in Bowman; at the 45th Street interchange off I–94W in Fargo; and on U.S. 2, 10 mi east of Grand Forks at Fisher's Landing.

Scenic Drives

The **Pembina Gorge** in northeast North Dakota is a beautiful forested valley created by glaciers and the winding Pembina River; from I–29 at the Joliette exit near the northern boundary of the state, drive west on Rte. 5, then north on Rte. 32 to Walhalla. Theodore Roosevelt National Park's **South Unit loop road** begins near park headquarters in Medora and winds 36 mi through an eerie world of lonesome pinnacles and spires, steep gorges and ravaged buttes. The 26-mi **North Unit loop road** begins at the park entrance along U.S. 85, 15 mi south of Watford City; the high ground above the Little Missouri River has dramatic overlooks, and a lower area near the visitor center features a series of slump rocks, huge sections of bluff that gradually slid intact to the valley floor.

National and State Parks

National Park   Theodore Roosevelt National Park (*see* Exploring the Badlands, *below*).

State Parks   North Dakota's state parks are open year-round. Among the most scenic are **Cross Ranch State Park,** 50 mi north of Bismarck, off Rte. 200A (HC2 Box 152, Sanger 58567, tel. 701/794–3731); **Devils Lake State Parks,** four parks on U.S. 2, Rte. 1 (Box 165, Devils Lake 58301, tel. 701/766–4015); **Ft. Abraham Lincoln State Park** (*see* Exploring the Missouri River Corridor, *below*); **Icelandic State Park,** on Rte. 5, 5 mi west of Cavalier (Rte. 1 Box 64A, Cavalier 58220, tel. 701/265–4561); and **Lake Sakakawea State Park** (Box 832, Riverdale 58565, tel. 701/487–3315), 3 mi west of Riverdale on Rte. 200. All parks listed offer camping facilities.

Missouri River Corridor

The Missouri River is both a geographic and a symbolic barrier between the two North Dakotas—the east and the west. The state capital of Bismarck, on the east bank of the river, is a busy political hub, while a short drive northwest leads to sprawling Lake Sakakawea, where urban life seems a world away.

Tourist Information

Bismarck-Mandan: Convention and Visitors Bureau (Box 2274, 523 N. 4th St., Bismarck 58702, tel. 701/222–4308). **Minot:** Convention and Visitors Bureau (1020 20th Ave. SW, 58702, tel. 701/852–6000).

Getting There

By Plane   **Bismarck Municipal Airport** (tel. 701/222–6502) is served by Northwest, Continental, United Express, and Northwest Air Link Big Sky (tel. 701/255–3845). The airport is about 5 mi from downtown; cab fare is about $5.

By Car   I–94, the state's major east–west thoroughfare, runs through the Bismarck-Mandan area. U.S. 83 runs north from Bismarck to Minot, the state's fourth-largest city.

By Train   **Amtrak** stops in Minot, Stanley, and Williston.

By Bus   **Greyhound** (tel. 701/223–6576) serves Bismarck. **Triangle Transportation** (tel. 701/223–6576) serves Minot from Bismarck.

Exploring the Missouri River Corridor

As with the rest of North Dakota, most of the attractions described here are open in the summer only (often Memorial Day–Labor Day); be sure to call ahead before you visit. The 19-story **State Capitol** building (600 East Blvd., 58505, tel. 701/224–2000) in north **Bismarck** is visible for miles across the Dakota prairie; tours of the limestone-and-marble art deco structure, built in the 1930s, are offered weekdays year-round and also on weekends Memorial Day to Labor Day. Just down the hill is the **North Dakota Heritage Center** (600 East Blvd., tel. 701/224–2666), which serves as the state museum and archives. Exhibits include Native American and pioneer artifacts and natural-history displays. The **Former Governor's Mansion** (4th St. and Ave. B, tel. 701/224–2666 or 701/255–3819) is an elegant Victorian structure containing political memorabilia and period furnishings. The *Lewis and Clark Riverboat* (tel. 701/255–4233) offers summer cruises on the Missouri River, plying the same route taken by the traders, trappers, and settlers of the last century.

The boat docks at **Ft. Abraham Lincoln State Park** (Rte. 2, Mandan, tel. 701/663–9571). You can also reach the park from Bismarck by crossing the river on I–94 to Mandan, then either traveling 4 mi south on Rte. 1806 or taking the 9-mi **Ft. Lincoln Trolley** (tel. 701/663–9018) from south Mandan. Among the reconstructed buildings at the fort, built in the 1870s to protect settlers, is the **Custer House,** a replica of the house where Gen. George Armstrong Custer lived with his wife, Libby, before his fateful expedition to Little Big Horn. Nearby is the reconstructed **On-A-Slant Indian Village,** once home to the Mandan tribe.

From Bismarck, take U.S. 83 to Washburn, then Rte. 200A west to the **Knife River Indian Villages National Historic Site.** The area preserves depressions formed by the Hidatsa and Mandan Indians' earth lodges, circular mud and timber structures. Thousands of pottery shards and other artifacts are displayed at the recently opened museum and interpretive center here. A full-size replica of an earth lodge is under construction. *3 mi north of Stanton, tel. 701/745–3309. Admission free. Closed Oct.–Apr.*

Twenty miles north is the 600-sq-mi **Lake Sakakawea,** affording countless recreational opportunities including swimming and boating. State parks and small resort communities are sprinkled along its shores. Free tours of the **Garrison Dam Power Plant** are conducted by the U.S. Army Corps of Engineers (tel. 701/654–7441). For more information on the lake, contact the Parks and Tourism department (*see* Visitor Information, *above*) or the **Mercer County Tourism Center** (Mercer County Economic Development, 801 Highway Dr., Hazen 58545, tel. 701/745–3242).

Sports and Outdoor Activities

Biking   The 246-mi **Lewis and Clark Bike Tour** follows the Missouri River along Rtes. 1804, 200, and 22, from the South Dakota border to the Montana border. Contact the Parks and Tourism department (*see* Visitor Information, *above*) for details. **Dakota Cyclery** (211 S. 3rd St., Bismarck, tel. 701/222–1218) rents bicycles and can provide information about area biking.

Canoeing   The Missouri River offers challenging stretches. For information on rentals and guides, contact the Parks and Tourism department (*see* Visitor Information, *above*).

Fishing   Walleye and northern pike are the big catches on Lake Sakakawea. The **North Dakota Game and Fish Department** (100 N. Bismarck Expressway, Bismarck 58505, tel. 701/221–6300) provides a list of area fishing guides. The *North Dakota Hunting and Fishing Guide* outlines seasons and regulations and is available through the Parks and Tourism department (*see* Visitor Information, *above*).

Hiking   The 17-mi **Roughrider Trail** along Missouri River bottomland is a treasure. For details, contact the Parks and Tourism department (*see* Visitor Information, *above*).

Dining and Lodging

For a listing of area B&Bs, contact the Parks and Tourism department (*see* Visitor Information, *above*). For price ranges, see Charts 1 (B) and 2 (B) in Chapter 1.

Bismarck   **Peacock Alley Bar and Grill.** Located in what was once the his-
Dining   toric Patterson Hotel, this restaurant enjoys local fame as the
★   former scene of countless political deals; period photographs recall those heady days. The menu features seafood specials such as Cajun firecracker shrimp and such regional dishes as pheasant in white-wine sauce. *422 E. Main St., tel. 701/255–7917. AE, D, MC, V. Moderate.*

Fiesta Villa. This family-run Mexican restaurant is suitably housed in a Spanish mission-style building, with arched doorways and high ceilings. Beef or chicken fajitas are a good choice here, and go well with the excellent margaritas. *4th and Main Sts., tel. 701/222–8075. D, DC, MC, V. Inexpensive.*

Lodging **Radisson Inn.** Rooms here are spacious and comfortable, with overstuffed chairs and soothing pastel color schemes. The hotel is located across from Bismarck's largest shopping mall, Kirkwood Plaza. *800 S. 3rd St., 58504, tel. 701/258–7700. 310 rooms, 5 suites. Facilities: restaurant, 2 lounges, pool, casino. AE, D, DC, MC, V. Moderate.*

Mandan **Captain's Table Restaurant.** As the name suggests, the decor
Dining follows a maritime theme. Menu selections hail from around the world; the specialty is a peppery South American–style steak whose recipe is a closely guarded secret. *Best Western Seven Seas Inn, I–94 Exit 31, tel. 701/663–3773. AE, D, DC, MC, V. Moderate.*

★ **Mandan Drug.** For a fun lunch (the place is open 9–6), follow a sandwich or homemade soup with an old-fashioned cherry soda or a Brown Cow—that's a root beer float with chocolate ice cream. The homemade candy is hard to resist. *316 Main St., tel. 701/663–5900. No credit cards. Inexpensive.*

Lodging **Best Western Seven Seas Inn and Convention Center.** Nautical decor fills the public areas, from scrimshaw displays to 200-year-old anchors to carpeting made to resemble ship's planking. Rooms continue the theme with maritime art. *I–94 Exit 31, Box 1316, 2611 Old Red Trail, 58554, tel. 701/663–7401. 100 rooms, 4 suites. Facilities: restaurant, pool. AE, D, DC, MC, V. Moderate.*

Minot **Sheraton-Riverside Inn.** Across from the State Fairgrounds,
Dining the hotel features guest rooms with windows that overlook a
and Lodging central seven-story atrium. The inn's Pavilion Supper Club (reservations advised; moderate) has a Mediterranean decor well suited to the menu: Appetizers include Greek pizza and meat pastries, while shrimp Byzantine and steak à la Grecque (with scallions and feta cheese) are popular main courses. *2200 Burdick Expressway E, 58702, tel. 701/852–2504 or 800/468–9968. 172 rooms. Facilities: 2 restaurants, indoor pool, exercise room. AE, D, DC, MC, V. Moderate.*

Lodging **Best Western International Inn.** Larger-than-average rooms
★ have contemporary furnishings at this modern, three-story hotel on a hill above downtown Minot. *1505 N. Broadway, 58701, tel. 701/852–3161. 262 rooms, 8 suites. Facilities: restaurant, lounge, casino, pool. AE, D, DC, MC, V. Moderate.*

Motel **Expressway Inn** (200 Expressway, Bismarck 58504, tel. 701/222–2900 or 800/456–6388), 165 rooms, pool, game room; moderate.

Campgrounds **Ft. Abraham Lincoln State Park** (*see* Exploring the Missouri River Corridor, *above*). **Lake Sakakawea State Park** (*see* National and State Parks, *above*).

The Badlands

Theodore Roosevelt, who ranched in western North Dakota in the late 1800s, once said, "I would never have been president if it had not been for my experiences in North Dakota." He was talking about the Badlands, where a national park named after him is now the heart of this wide-open country, largely unchanged since the president's time.

Tourist Information

Medora: Convention and Visitors Bureau (c/o Rough Riders, 1 Main St., Box 198, 58645, tel. 701/623–4422 in season, 701/623–4444 or 701/223–4800 off-season). **Williston:** Convention and Visitors Bureau (10 Main St., Drawer G, 58801, tel. 701/774–9041).

Getting There

By Plane Bismarck Municipal Airport (*see* Missouri River Corridor, *above*) is the nearest airport.

By Car I–94 crosses the Badlands, with an exit at Medora at the entrance to the South Unit of Theodore Roosevelt National Park. U.S. 85 links the park's North and South units.

By Bus **Greyhound** stops in Dickinson (tel. 701/225–6789) and Medora (tel. 701/623–4455).

Exploring the Badlands

Theodore Roosevelt National Park (Box 7, Medora 58645, tel. 701/623–4466) is divided into two units, which are separated by 50 mi of Badlands and the **Little Missouri Grasslands**. Scenic loops through both (*see* Scenic Drives, *above*) are marked with low speed limits to protect the bison, wild horses, mule deer, pronghorn antelope, and bighorn sheep that roam here. You can get a panoramic view of the Badlands from the park's **Painted Canyon Overlook and Visitors Center** (tel. 701/623–4466) on I–94, 7 mi east of Medora, a good place to start a tour. The center provides picnic tables from which to enjoy the sweeping vista.

If you're up for an hour-long horseback ride in the **South Unit** of the park, contact **Peaceful Valley Ranch** (tel. 701/623–4496), 7 mi north of the park entrance. They'll take you on some of the park's 80 mi of marked horse trails. The visitor center will provide you with maps if you prefer to hike.

The **North Unit,** off U.S. 85 south of Watford City, offers the same scenic driving and hiking opportunities but in a less crowded setting. This is a good place to spot the wildlife you may have missed in the South Unit.

Outside the park, historic **Medora** is a walkable small town with a number of tiny shops, museums, and other attractions. The **Château de Mores,** an elegant 26-room mansion on a bluff overlooking the town, was built in the mid-1880s by the Marquis de Mores, a French nobleman who ran a short-lived cattle and meat-packing industry from here. You can see a collection of antique dolls in the **Medora Doll House;** Native American artifacts, wildlife exhibits, and wax figures depicting frontier days

Western North Dakota

in the **Museum of the Badlands;** or the three-screen multimedia show *The Rough Rider Time Machine* in the Town Hall Theater. For information on these and other Medora attractions, contact the Medora Convention and Visitors Bureau (*see* Tourist Information, *above*).

Ft. Buford State Historic Site (tel. 701/572–9034), 22 mi southwest of Williston via Rte. 1804, is built around the 1866 fort that once imprisoned famous Native American leaders, including Sioux leader Sitting Bull and Nez Percé Chief Joseph. Two mi north of here on Rte. 58 is the **Ft. Union Trading Post** (tel. 701/572–9083). This national historic site presents reconstructed buildings from the fort built in 1829 by John Jacob Astor of the American Fur Company. Ft. Union dominated the fur trade along the Upper Missouri River for many years and played host to such notable visitors as John Jacob Audubon and Prince Maximillian of Austria.

Shopping

Specialty shops lining Medora's Main Street include **Dakota Arts and Crafts** (tel. 701/623–4805), offering a variety of craft items, gifts, and souvenirs; and **Kite Heights** (tel. 701/623–4855), specializing in (what else?) kites, along with model airplanes and other hobby kits.

Sports and Outdoor Activities

Biking The loop roads in the North and South Units of Theodore Roosevelt National Park are challenging and scenic.

Hiking and Both units of Theodore Roosevelt National Park offer spectacu-
Backpacking lar hiking and backpacking opportunities. The Little Missouri National Grasslands, which stretches between the two park units, is also a popular spot (for information, contact the Parks and Tourism department, *see* Visitor Information, *above*).

Dining and Lodging

For price ranges, see Charts 1 (B) and 2 (B) in Chapter 1.

Medora **Rough Rider Hotel Dining Room.** Housed in a two-story wood
Dining frame building, this rustic restaurant features barbecued buf-
★ falo ribs, along with prime rib and other beef specialties. *Main St., tel. 701/623–4433. MC, V. Closed Sept.–mid-May. Moderate.*
Chuckwagon Cafeteria. This large, wood-paneled cafeteria with western decor often features patio cookouts. Main courses include prime rib and ham; a large array of side dishes, soups, and salads are offered. *Main St., tel. 701/623–4444. MC, V. Closed Sept.–mid-May. Inexpensive.*
Theodore Roosevelt Foundation Pitchfork Fondue. Three times a week from Memorial Day through Labor Day weekend, the town plays host to this western cookout, featuring 12-ounce rib-eye steaks cooked over an open spit. There's no set schedule, so call the visitor center to see if it's on or just ask one of the locals. *Outside the Burning Hills Amphitheater, tel. 701/623–4444. Inexpensive.*

Williston **El Rancho Restaurant.** The Old West atmosphere here was re-
Dining cently replaced by the earthy colors and art of the Southwest,
★ but beef—especially prime rib—remains the specialty. Seafood and chicken are also on the menu. *1623 2nd Ave. W, tel. 701/572–6321. AE, D, DC, MC. V. Moderate.*

Motels **El Rancho Motor Hotel** (1623 2nd Ave. W, Williston 58801, tel. 701/572–6321), 92 rooms, restaurant, lounge, coffee shop; moderate. **Hospitality Inn** (I–94 and Rte. 22, Dickinson 58601, tel. 701/227–1853), 149 rooms, restaurant, lounge, casino, pool, Jacuzzi, sauna, gameroom; moderate. **Badlands Motel** (Box 198, Medora 58645, tel. 701/623–4422), 116 rooms, pool; closed Oct.–Apr.; inexpensive. **Medora Motel** (E. River Rd., Medora 58645, tel. 701/623–4422), 190 rooms, pool; inexpensive.

Campgrounds **Buffalo Gap** (7 mi west of Medora on I–94 Exit 4, tel. 800/437–2077 or 800/472–2100 in ND). **Cottonwood Campground** (5 mi inside Theodore Roosevelt National Park, tel. 701/623–4466). **Medora Campground** (Medora, tel. 701/623–4435).

Nightlife

The *Medora Musical* (tel. 701/623–4444), in the outdoor **Burning Hills Amphitheater,** is a stage-show tribute to western Americana featuring everything from singing to history to fireworks.

Elsewhere in the State

The Lakes Region

Getting There U.S. 2 is the principal east–west route through the region, connecting with I–29 at Grand Forks. U.S. 281 runs north–south through the region, with secondary roads leading to lakes and area attractions. Devils Lake is served by **Northwest Air Link Mesaba. Amtrak** stops in Devils Lake and Rugby.

What to See **Devils Lake,** the heart of the lakes region, is surrounded by
and Do hundreds of smaller lakes and prairie potholes. A major breeding ground for North America's migratory waterfowl, the area offers fine duck and geese hunting. Devils Lake itself has excellent jumbo perch and walleye fishing and uncrowded beaches. For more information on hunting and fishing in the area, contact the **Game and Fish Department** (100 N. Bismarck Expressway, Bismarck 58505, tel. 701/221–6300). On the Devils Lake Sioux Indian Reservation is the **Ft. Totten Historic Site** (Rte. 57, tel. 701/766–4441), the best-preserved military fort west of the Mississippi River. Built in 1867, it later served as one of the nation's largest government-run schools for Native Americans.

At Rugby, west of Devils Lake on U.S. 2, is the **geographical center of North America.** Marked by a stone monument, the landmark includes a spacious **Geographical Center Historical Museum** (tel. 701/776–6414; admission charged) containing thousands of objects, such as 19th-century farming equipment and antique cars. The **International Peace Garden** (tel. 701/263–4390; admission charged), 30 mi northwest of Belcourt on Rte. 30, is a 2,300-acre garden straddling the border between Canada and the United States and planted as a symbol of peace between the two nations. In addition to the 140,000 flowers planted annually, the garden includes an 18-foot floral clock, a Peace Tower, and a Peace Chapel. (**Devils Lake Convention and Visitors Bureau,** U.S. 2E, Box 879, Devils Lake 58301, tel. 701/662–4903.)

Dining **The Birchwood.** Cajun specialties and delicious prime rib are staples at this lakeside restaurant bordering Canada. *North of Rte. 43, Lake Metígoshe, 701/263–4283. MC, V. Moderate.*

Mr. & Mrs. J's. The "Pig-out Omelette" is the specialty; a huge salad bar complements Mexican and traditional foods. *U.S. 2E, Devils Lake, tel. 701/662–8815. MC, V. Inexpensive.*

Campground **Grahams Island State Park** (Rte. 1, Box 165, Devils Lake 58301, tel. 701/766–4015) is 15 mi southwest of Devils Lake off Rte. 19.

The Red River Valley

Getting There I–94 links Fargo with Minneapolis–St. Paul to the east and with Billings, Montana, to the west. I–29 connects Fargo with Grand Forks, 75 mi north, and with Sioux Falls, South Dakota, to the south. Fargo and Grand Forks both have airports. **Amtrak** also serves both cities. **Greyhound** provides service in Fargo (tel. 701/293–1222) and Grand Forks (tel. 701/775–4781).

What to See The **Red River of the North** forms the eastern boundary of
and Do North Dakota with Minnesota. The fertile valley formed by the river was the destination of Scandinavian and other northern European immigrants in the late 19th century and still contains

more than one-third of the state's population. The region is an enormous shopping hub, drawing bargain hunters from Minnesota, Canada, and the rest of North Dakota.

Fargo, the state's largest city, is the site of the **Roger Maris Baseball Museum** (I–29 and 13th Ave., tel. 701/282–2222), which honors baseball's all-time best single-season home-run hitter. In Wahpeton, about 50 mi south, is the **Ehnstrom Nature Center and Chahinkapa Park Zoo** (10 mi east of I–29, tel. 701/ 642–2811), containing native species such as eagles, bison, and elks. Ten mi west and 50 mi south of Fargo, at Mooreton, is the **Bagg Bonanza Farm** (tel. 701/274–8989; closed weekdays), a national historic site that re-creates the life of sprawling "bonanza" farms of the late 1800s and early 1900s. Five of 24 original buildings have been restored. **Ft. Abercrombie Historic Site** (tel. 701/553–8513 or 701/224–2666), 20 mi north of Mooreton off I–29, offers a museum and reconstructed blockhouses from this frontier fort, which was besieged by the Sioux during the 1862 Minnesota Uprising. Twenty-five mi north of here is **Bonanzaville USA** (I–94, West Fargo, tel. 701/282–2822). This pioneer village and museum uses exhibits and furnishings in 40 original and re-created buildings to show life in late-19th-century Dakota Territory.

Seventy-five miles north of Fargo on I–29 is **Grand Forks,** the state's cultural and technological center. It's home to the **North Dakota Museum of Art** (Centennial Dr., tel. 701/777–4195) and the **Center for Aerospace Sciences** (4125 University Ave., tel. 701/777–2791), both at the **University of North Dakota.** Seventy mi north of Grand Forks via I–29 is the **Pembina State Museum** (tel. 701/825–6209; closed Sept.–May). It uses exhibits and artifacts to tell the story of the early 19th-century European fur traders and the Sioux and Chippewa tribes that once inhabited this area. Farther north, in **Icelandic State Park** (*see* National and State Parks, *above*), the **Pioneer Heritage Interpretive Center** (tel. 701/265–4561) uses artifacts and exhibits to showcase the ethnic diversity of the region. For further information on the area, contact the **Fargo/Moorhead Convention and Visitors Bureau** (Box 404, Fargo 58107, tel. 800/235–7654), **Grand Forks Convention and Visitors Bureau** (200 N. 3rd St., Suite 200, 58206, tel. 800/866–4566), or **Wahpeton Convention and Visitors Bureau** (120 4th St. N, 58075, tel. 701/642–8559).

Dining **Old Broadway.** Featuring Gay '90s decor under 18-ft ceilings, with a plethora of antiques, the restaurant is located in the circa-1903 Stern's clothing store. Page after page of staple and exotic choices fill the menu. *22 N. Broadway, Fargo, tel. 701/237–6161. AE, D, DC, MC, V. Moderate.*

Sanders 1907. Tiny, elegant, and intimate, Sanders restaurant has lots of mirrors, exceptional local artwork, and exuberantly rosemaled booths. Fabulous pâté, wonderful salads and breads, such entrées as tenderloin in green-peppercorn sauce, and desserts like walnut tortes and "Chocolate Decadence" make this a delightful gastronomic experience. *312 Kittson Ave., Grand Forks, tel. 701/746–8970. AE, MC, V. Moderate.*

OKLAHOMA

By Matt Schofield

*Updated by
Barbara Palmer*

Capital	Oklahoma City
Population	3,145,585
Motto	Labor Conquers All Things
State Bird	Scissor-tailed flycatcher
State Flower	Mistletoe

Visitor Information

Oklahoma Tourism and Recreation Department (Box 60789, Oklahoma City 73146, tel. 405/521–2409 or 800/652–6552). **State Historical Society** (2100 N. Lincoln St., Oklahoma City 73105, tel. 405/521–2491).

Scenic Drives

Rte. 49 through the Wichita Mountains Wildlife Refuge (*see* Exploring Southwestern Oklahoma, *below*) and **Rte. 10** from Wyandotte through Grove to Gore (*see* Exploring Northeastern Oklahoma, *below*) are both scenic. **Rte. 1** through the northern section of the Ouachita National Forest (*see* National and State Parks, *below*), from Talihina east about 50 mi to the state border, makes a beautiful drive in autumn, when the forest foliage is most colorful.

National and State Parks

National Parks The **Ouachita National Forest** (HC64, Box 3467, Heavener 74937, tel. 918/653–4462) in southeastern Oklahoma is a scenic region of small mountain ranges.

State Parks Some of the best are **Alabaster Caverns State Park** (Rte. 1, Box 32, Freedom 73842, tel. 405/621–3381), **Beavers Bend State Park** (Box 10, Broken Bow 74728, tel. 405/494–6300), **Great Salt Plains State Park** (*see* Elsewhere in the State, *below*), **Quartz Mountain State Park** (*see* Exploring Southwestern Oklahoma, *below*), and **Red Rock Canyon State Park** (Box 502, Hinton 73047, tel. 405/542–6344).

Oklahoma City

Where else but in Oklahoma will you find oil wells pumping on the grounds of the state capitol? The state's dual themes of oil and the Wild West can be explored in Oklahoma City's museums and historic centers. Twenty mi north on I–35 is Victorian Guthrie, the state capital from territorial days until after statehood, 1889–1910. Much of the town is now included in a 1,400-acre historic district, the largest on the National Register.

Tourist Information

Oklahoma City: Convention and Visitor's Bureau (1 Santa Fe Pl., 73102, tel. 405/278–8900 or 800/225–5652). **Guthrie:** Chamber of Commerce (202 W. Harrison St., 73044, tel. 405/282–

1947 or 800/299–1889). The *Daily Oklahoman*'s Friday weekend section lists events.

Arriving and Departing

By Plane The **Will Rogers World Airport** (tel. 405/681–5311), in the southwest section of the city, is served by major domestic airlines. It's about a 20-minute drive from downtown on I–44N; cab fare is about $14. There's no bus service from the airport, but several hotels in town offer transportation.

By Car Interstates 35, 40, and 44 form a loop around the downtown area. I–235 cuts through the middle of town. Downtown exits include Lincoln Boulevard, 23rd Street, and May Avenue.

By Bus **Greyhound** (427 W. Sheridan St., tel. 405/235–6425).

Getting Around Oklahoma City

A car is a necessity here; although the downtown can be explored on foot, the rest of the city is spread out. Traffic is rarely a problem.

Exploring Oklahoma City

Oklahoma City sprawls over four counties, but the major points of interest are all within 10 mi of one another and generally northeast of the downtown area.

At the **Oklahoma State Capitol** those oil wells you see on the grounds aren't just for show: Although the earliest well dried up in 1986, the remainder actually do pump oil. The Corinthian columns of the limestone-and-granite capitol were designed to support a dome, but construction was canceled when the cost of steel soared during World War I. *N.E. 23rd St. and Lincoln Blvd., tel. 405/521–3356. Admission free.*

The **National Cowboy Hall of Fame and Western Heritage Center,** north of the capitol building off I–44, has vast collections of paintings, sculpture, and artifacts, including John Wayne's kachina collection. A sod house, a saloon, and a mine are part of a re-created frontier town. *1700 N.E. 63rd St., tel. 405/478–2250. Admission charged.*

The **Kirkpatrick Center** (2100 N.E. 52nd St., tel. 405/427–5461), about 2½ mi south via Martin Luther King Avenue, houses science and art museums, a Native American museum, the International Photography Hall of Fame, and four other institutions.

A walk through the **Crystal Bridge Tropical Conservatory,** a glass botanical tube at the I. M. Pei–designed **Myriad Gardens,** takes visitors through habitats that range from rain forest, with a 35-foot waterfall, to desert. *301 W. Reno Ave., tel. 405/297–3995. Admission charged. Closed Christmas.*

Shopping

This is a good place to buy Native American crafts and artwork. Try the **Choctaw Indian Trading Post** (1520 N. Portland St., tel. 405/947–2490) or the **Oklahoma Indian Art Gallery** (2335 S.W. 44th St., tel. 405/685–6162).

Dining

Remember, you're in beef country: Plain food and large portions of meat are standard here. The Bricktown neighborhood, a renovated section of downtown, is a favorite dining spot for locals. For price ranges, see Chart 1 (B) in Chapter 1.

Expensive **The Greystone Restaurant.** Brass accents and lots of plants enliven the decor at this large restaurant about 15 minutes north of downtown. The steaks are excellent. *1 N. Sooner Rd., Edmond, tel. 405/340–4400. Reservations advised. Jacket and tie advised. AE, D, DC, MC, V. No lunch weekends; closed Mon.*

★ **The Waterford Dining Room.** Candlelit dining lends romance to this large, elegant restaurant in the Waterford Hotel. It specializes in seafood, especially swordfish and tuna. *6300 Waterford Blvd., tel. 405/848–4782. Reservations advised. Jacket and tie required. AE, DC, MC, V.*

Moderate **The Sand Plum.** In historic downtown Guthrie, about 20 minutes north of Oklahoma City, this elegant Victorian-style restaurant serves an enormous Sunday brunch buffet, with everything from Caesar salad to eggs Benedict to cheesecake. *1st and Harrison Sts., Guthrie, tel. 405/282–7771. Reservations advised. AE, MC, V.*

Inexpensive **Bricktown Brewery.** Even the shrimp are steamed in beer in this airy brewpub, where blowups of historical photographs are displayed against exposed brick. Land Run Lager and Copperhead Ale complement a menu heavy on comfort foods: chicken pot pie, fish-and-chips, bratwurst. *1 Oklahoma Ave., tel. 405/232–2739. AE, D, DC, MC, V.*

★ **The Cattleman's Cafe.** Beef is the star attraction at this classic steak house, where diners are surrounded by western murals and paraphernalia such as cattle branding irons. *1309 S. Agnew Ave., tel. 405/236–0416. AE, D, DC, MC, V.*

The County Line. Pretty Boy Floyd was a regular when this was a Prohibition-era roadhouse. Now the Deco-style barbecue restaurant serves smoked baby-back ribs and chicken, accompanied by loaves of freshly baked bread and eucalyptus-scented hot towels. *1226 N.E. 63rd St., tel. 405/478–4955. AE, D, DC, MC, V.*

Lodging

Hotels here offer few surprises. The more expensive ones have restaurants, clubs, and lounges, but rooms generally differ little from those of more moderately priced establishments. If you don't plan to spend a lot of time at the hotel, you may be better off stopping at one of the chain motels along the highways. For price ranges, see Chart 2 (B) in Chapter 1.

Hotels **Clarion.** This 15-story glass-and-stone building in the heart of
Expensive downtown underwent major renovations in 1992–93. The rooms enfold you in mauve and deep green, with traditional-style furniture and state-of-the-art electronics. *1 N. Broadway, 73102, tel. 405/235–2780; fax 405/272–0369. 400 rooms, 22 suites. Facilities: restaurant, lounge, pool, miniature golf. AE, D, MC, V.*

The Waterford Hotel. At this nine-story redbrick, about 15 minutes from downtown, the large rooms feature mahogany armoires concealing TVs. *6300 Waterford Blvd., 73118, tel. 405/848–4782 or 800/992–2009; fax 405/843–9161. 192 rooms. Facil-*

ities: 2 restaurants, 2 lounges, athletic club, squash and tennis courts. AE, DC, MC, V.

Moderate **Harrison House Bed and Breakfast Inn.** Rooms are furnished in turn-of-the-century antiques and named for former Guthrie residents, such as Tom Mix (he tended bar down the street) and Carry Nation. Specify one of the 21 rooms in the original inn or the adjacent Freeman Block; other rooms are not nearly as charming. *124 W. Harrison St., Guthrie 73044, tel. 405/282–1000 or 800/375–1001; fax 405/282–4304. AE, D, DC, MC, V.*

Hilton Inn. Some rooms at this recently renovated contemporary hotel offer views of nearby Hefner Lake. Be sure to ask about corporate rates when you call, as the hotel frequently makes them available to noncorporate guests. *2945 N.W. Expressway, 73112, tel. 800/848–4811; fax 405/843–4829. 219 rooms, 4 suites. Facilities: restaurant, lounge. AE, D, DC, MC, V.*

Inexpensive **Quality Inn.** This modern, no-frills hotel is located in Norman, home of the University of Oklahoma. There's a tropical dome with a heated pool—especially welcome if you've just sat through a chilly football game at the nearby campus. *2600 W. Main St., Norman 73069, tel. 405/329–1624; fax 405/360–7412. 100 rooms. Facilities: restaurant, lounge, pool. AE, D, DC, MC, V.*

Motels **Motel 6** has several locations here: Airport (820 S. Meridian, 73108, tel. 405/946–6662), 129 rooms, outdoor pool; North (11900 N.E. Expressway, 73131, tel. 405/478–8666), 101 rooms, outdoor pool; South (1417 N. Moore Ave., 73160, tel. 405/799–6616), 121 rooms, outdoor pool; Midwest City (6166 Tinker Diagonal, Midwest City 73110, tel. 405/737–6676), 93 rooms, outdoor pool. All are inexpensive.

Ranches **Island Guest Ranch.** The owners of this 2,800-acre working
★ ranch 90 mi north of Oklahoma City will meet you at the airport upon request. Guests help herd cattle, ride horses, attend staged powwows, fish, hike, and tour the ranch's own ghost town. Rooms, each with private bath, are in two rustic bunkhouses; hearty meals are served in the main log lodge. Rates include all meals and activities; reservations should be made at least several weeks in advance. *Ames 73718, tel. 405/753–4574. 10 rooms. MC, V. Closed Oct.–Mar. Expensive.*

Northeastern Oklahoma

The Grand Lake O' the Cherokees is a popular vacation spot, and the region's cowboy image makes for an area thick with rodeos and western museums. The infamous Cherokee Trail of Tears—along which thousands of Cherokee traveled in the 1830s when they were forcibly resettled from their Georgia homes—ended here. Four other tribes traveled similar trails to eastern Oklahoma. Today tribal governments are vital once again and Native American art, language, and customs are actively preserved.

Tourist Information

Tahlequah: Chamber of Commerce (101 S. Muskogee Ave., 74464, tel. 918/456–3742). **Tulsa:** Visitor Information Center and Chamber of Commerce (616 S. Boston St., 74119, tel. 918/585–1201).

Getting There

By Plane   **Tulsa International Airport** (tel. 918/838–5000), about 10 mi northeast of downtown Tulsa, is served by major domestic airlines. Average cab fare to the downtown area is about $12. Major hotels have shuttle bus service.

By Car   In Tulsa, I–44 and I–244 form a downtown loop. The Keystone, Cherokee, and Broken Arrow expressways also lead downtown. From Tulsa, U.S. 75 leads north to the Bartlesville area. I–44 is the main route northeast from Tulsa and connects with many smaller, more scenic highways. A 400-mi segment of old Rte. 66 travels through Oklahoma; the 100-mi leg that connects with I–35 north of Oklahoma City and I–44 just west of Tulsa is the easiest to follow. The old gas stations and tiny groceries in such towns as Chandler and Sapulpa are part of a vanishing past.

By Bus   **Greyhound.** (317 S. Detroit St., tel. 918/584–4427) serves Tulsa.

Exploring Northeastern Oklahoma

The friendly city of **Tulsa** has a number of cultural attractions. About 3 mi from the downtown area is the **Gilcrease Museum** (1400 Gilcrease Museum Rd., tel. 918/582–3122). Its collection, dedicated to western art and Americana, includes paintings by such artists as Frederic Remington and James McNeill Whistler, as well as a wide-ranging selection of Native American art. A few miles southeast of downtown is the **Philbrook Museum of Art** (2727 S. Rockford Rd., tel. 918/749–7941). Housed in the Italianate villa of former oil baron Waite Phillips, the collection runs the gamut from Italian Renaissance to Native American art. The oil money that built Tulsa in the 1920s left a legacy of Art Deco architecture. Stop by the Chamber of Commerce (*see* Tourist Information, *above*) for a walking-tour map including more than a dozen downtown buildings.

North of Tulsa on Rte. 123 is the **Woolaroc Museum,** perhaps the top attraction in the state. It includes a drive-through wildlife preserve where bison and 40 other species roam (visitors must remain in their vehicles). The preserve surrounds a museum complex packed with western lore: gun and rifle exhibits, Native American crafts, and such western memorabilia as Theodore Roosevelt's saddle. The lodge, formerly used by oilman Frank Phillips, is filled with every animal trophy imaginable. *Box 1647, Bartlesville, tel. 918/336–0307. Admission charged. Closed Mon.*

Follow Rte. 123 north to **Bartlesville**, site of the **Frank Phillips Home** (1107 S. Cherokee St., tel. 918/336–2491), a 26-room Greek Revival mansion built in 1909. A couple of blocks northwest is the **Price Tower,** designed by Frank Lloyd Wright, which houses the **Bartlesville Museum** (6th and Dewey Sts., tel. 918/336–8708). Wright envisioned the 19-story building, completed in 1956, as a "tower in a country town." Its magnificent cantilevered exterior, adorned with copper plates and gold-tinted glass, is still a landmark on the small city's skyline. The interior still contains many of Wright's original furnishings.

Northeastern Oklahoma

Southeast of Bartlesville by way of Nowata lies the **Will Rogers Birthplace** (near Oologah, tel. 918/275–4201). The childhood home of the great humorist is a large log-and-clapboard structure containing period furnishings. Nearby, on Rte. 88 in Claremore, is the **Will Rogers Memorial** (tel. 800/324–9455), where Rogers and his family are buried. The site contains a museum and a theater that shows Rogers's movies and newsreels.

You can take I-44 and U.S. 59 to **Grove** and the **Grand Lake O' the Cherokees.** Numerous recreational options here include a ride aboard the *Cherokee Queen* riverboat (tel. 918/786–4272).

Travel south about 50 mi on Rte. 10—a scenic drive through a region of dense forest, hills, and lakes—to **Tahlequah,** home to the Cherokee Nation. The **Cherokee Heritage Center,** 3 mi south of town off U.S. 62, offers daily summer performances of the drama *The Trail of Tears;* the **Cherokee National Museum/ Adams Corner** here includes a re-creation of the 16th-century Cherokee village Tsa-La-Gi. *Willis Rd., tel. 918/456–6007. Admission charged. Closed weekends Sept.–May; Sun., June– Aug.*

The Cherokee were hardly the region's first settlers, as the **Spiro Mounds Archaeological State Park** attests. The park contains remains of 12 earthen mounds used as dwellings by the Spiro, a prehistoric people who lived here from about AD 900 to 1400. A 1½-mi trail runs alongside the mounds, and a visitor center contains artifacts. *6 mi northwest of Spiro, tel. 918/962– 2062. Admission free. Closed Mon. May–Oct.; Mon.–Tues. Nov.–Apr.*

Shopping

Native American crafts and art make the best mementos of your visit. Look for **Lyon's Indian Store** (702 S. Main St., Tulsa, tel. 918/582–6372) and **Mister Indian's** (1000 S. Main St. in nearby Sapulpa, tel. 918/224–6511). Malls in Tulsa include **Utica Square** (21st St. and Utica Ave., tel. 918/742–5531) and the **Woodland Hills Mall** (7021 S. Memorial Dr., tel. 918/250–1449).

Sports and Outdoor Activities

Fishing   There's plenty of it here, especially striped and largemouth bass, crappie, and catfish. *Tulsa World's* sports section has up-to-date fishing information, or check with the **Department of Wildlife and Conservation** (tel. 405/521–3855). Fishing licenses can be purchased in most local tackle shops.

Hiking and   Every park in the area has hiking trails (*see* National and State
Backpacking   Parks, *above*). For general information, call the **Tourism and Recreation Department** (*see* Visitor Information, *above*).

Dining and Lodging

Tulsa probably has the best dining in the state, and you'll look hard to find any restaurants that qualify as expensive. Outside the city there are always the fast-food chains; a better option may be to pack a picnic lunch. Tulsa also offers a fair number of comfortable though unexciting hotels. For price ranges, see Charts 1 (B) and 2 (B) in Chapter 1.

Bartlesville   **Hotel Phillips.** From the street, this seven-story yellow-brick
Lodging   hotel looks like a 1950s-era hospital, but you'll find lots of wood
★   and rich upholstery inside. The management specializes in details: The simplest room-service breakfast is served on Battenberg lace, and the *Wall Street Journal* is delivered to your door. *821 S. Johnstone Ave., 74003, tel. 918/337–6600 or 800/331–0706; fax 918/336–0350. 165 rooms. Facilities: restaurant, bar, fitness room. AE, D, DC, MC, V. Moderate.*

Tulsa   **Atlantic Sea Grill.** This quiet, intimate restaurant features oak
Dining   and brass fixtures, marble floors, and an aquarium. Seafood, including lobster, dominates the menu. *8321 E. 61st St., Eton Sq., tel. 918/252–7966. AE, MC, V. Moderate.*
Fifteenth Street Grill. The chef at this storefront grill learned to cook "unfussy" on an Oklahoma farm. Everything—herbs, vegetables, bread—is fresh, and the seafood is flown in daily. Wine labels from the 1920s decorate the walls. *1542 E. 15th St., 74102, tel. 918/583–0571. AE, D, DC, MC, V. Moderate.*
Jamil's. A good choice for families, this residence-turned-restaurant features smoked chicken and ribs served with complimentary tabouli and cabbage rolls in an old-fashioned, homey atmosphere. *2833 E. 51st St., tel. 918/742–9097. AE, D, DC, MC, V. No lunch. Moderate.*
★   **Nelson's Buffeteria.** This lively, old-fashioned diner features 1940s decor and the best chicken-fried steak in town. *514 S. Boston St., tel. 918/584–9969. No credit cards. No dinner; closed weekends. Inexpensive.*

Lodging   **The Doubletree Inn Downtown.** This modern high rise features contemporary decor in hues of green, rose, and mauve. A skywalk connects the hotel to the Tulsa Convention Center; free transportation is provided to a nearby shopping mall. *616*

W. 7th St., 74127, tel. 918/587–8000; fax 918/587–1642. 386 rooms, 32 suites. Facilities: 2 restaurants, bar, spa. AE, D, DC, MC, V. Expensive.

★ **The Sheraton Kensington Hotel.** Rooms are generally spacious and comfortable; those on higher floors have good views of either downtown or the river. 1902 E. 71st St., 74136, tel. 918/ 493–7000; fax 918/481–7147. 370 rooms, 13 suites. Facilities: restaurant, 2 lounges, health club. AE, D, DC, MC, V. Expensive.

Best Western Trade Winds Central Inn. Rooms at this recently renovated property have cherrywood tables and armoires. It's on the south edge of Tulsa, with easy access to the highway. 3141 E. Skelly Dr., 74105, tel. 918/749–5561; fax 918/749–6312. 142 rooms, 35 suites. Facilities: restaurant, lounge. AE, D, DC, MC, V. Moderate.

La Quinta Inn. This no-frills chain hotel is conveniently located near the airport. 35 N. Sheridan Rd., 74115, tel. 918/836–3931; fax 918/836–5428. 100 rooms, 1 suite. Facilities: pool. AE, D, DC, MC, V. Moderate.

Motels **Best Western Trade Winds East Motor Hotel** (3337 E. Skelly Dr., Tulsa 74135, tel. 918/743–7931), 279 rooms, lounge; inexpensive. **Motel 6** (1011 S. Garnett Rd., 74128, tel. 918/234–6200), 154 rooms, outdoor pool, inexpensive; and (5828 W. Skelly Dr., 74107, tel. 918/445–0223), 153 rooms, outdoor pool, inexpensive.

Ranches **The Western Hills Guest Ranch.** This state-run resort, 50 mi
★ southeast of Tulsa in Sequoyah State Park, helps satisfy your cowboy longings with chuck-wagon cookouts, stagecoach rides, and lessons in horseback riding, shooting, and calf roping. More prosaic sports like tennis and golf are also offered. Box 509, Wagoner 74477, tel. 918/772–2545 or 800/654–8240; fax 918/772–2030. 101 lodge rooms, 54 cabins. Facilities: restaurant, nature center, pool, golf, tennis, other sports facilities. AE, D, DC, MC, V. Moderate.

Campgrounds **Tenkiller State Park** (HCR 68, Box 1095, Vian 74962, tel. 918/ 489–5643) and **Greenleaf State Park** (Rte. 1, Box 119, Braggs 74423, tel. 918/487–5196), both near Gore, have cabins and campgrounds, as does **Osage Hills State Park** (Red Eagle Rte., Box 84, Pawhuska 74056, tel. 918/336–4141), near Bartlesville. **Sequoyah State Park** (Rte. 1, Box 198–3, Hulbert 74441, tel. 918/772–2046) offers camping with a swimming beach, marina, and heated pool, as well as its guest ranch (see Ranches, above).

The Arts

Tulsa has an active cultural scene. The **Tulsa Ballet Theatre** (4512 S. Peoria Ave., tel. 918/749–6006; Sept.–Apr.) is a nationally acclaimed company. The **American Indian Theater Company** (101 E. 3rd St., tel. 918/838–3875) is one of the few Native American theater companies in the country. The **Tulsa Philharmonic** (2901 S. Harvard Ave., tel. 918/747–7445; May–Sept.) holds most performances at the Performing Arts Center downtown.

Southwestern Oklahoma

This rugged, beautiful region is rich with natural and cultural attractions. Native American lore figures largely here; every town seems to have its own museum detailing some aspect of the region's history. Magnificent parks and refuges also beckon.

Tourist Information

Anadarko: Chamber of Commerce (Box 366, 73005, tel. 405/247–6651). **Lawton:** Chamber of Commerce (Box 1376, 73502, tel. 405/355–3541).

Getting There

By Plane The **Will Rogers World Airport** gives the best access to the region (*see* Oklahoma City, *above*).

By Car As with the rest of the state, you'll need a car to tour this region. Most of the area falls between I–44 and I–40 southwest of Oklahoma City; U.S. and state highways on our tour connect with these interstates.

By Bus **Greyhound** (15 N.E. 20th St., tel. 405/355–3541) serves Lawton.

Exploring Southwestern Oklahoma

Lawton makes a good base for exploring the region. The **Museum of the Great Plains** (601 Ferris Ave., tel. 405/581–3460; admission charged) features a tiny re-created town, a Spanish-sword display, and an outdoor fort.

A short drive north on I–44 brings you to the main entrance to the **Ft. Sill Military Reservation,** built in 1869 in an effort to subdue the Native Americans of the southern plains. Seven original buildings contain exhibits on the fort's history. Geronimo's Guardhouse is named for the famous prisoner who died while interned here in 1909. *Tel. 405/351–5123. Admission free. Closed major holidays.*

A few miles farther north, I–44 crosses U.S. 49, which runs along the northern border of Ft. Sill and westward to the **Wichita Mountains Wildlife Refuge,** one of the most beautiful areas in the state. Here the wildlife is thick and the scenery—pines, cliffs, and still, clear lakes—often breathtaking. The refuge is home to bison, Longhorn cattle, and other species. Hiking trails are abundant. *Rte. 1, Indiahoma, tel. 405/429–3222. Admission free. Guided tours by reservation.*

From the western end of the refuge, U.S. 54 and 62 lead southwest to Altus. From here travel north on U.S. 283/Rte. 44 to **Quartz Mountain State Park,** site of a state-run resort (*see* Dining and Lodging, *below*). The scenery alone is worth the trip— bare rock outcroppings reflected in pristine Altus Lake, and in spring, wildflowers in abundance—but you can also explore caves, visit the park's Nature Center, or take advantage of the guided tours and special programs offered throughout the year. *Lone Wolf, tel. 405/563–2238. Admission free.*

Some 100 mi east lies the largely Native American community of **Anadarko,** site of the **Southern Plains Indian Museum and Crafts Center** (715 E. Central St., tel. 405/247–6221). Just east of the museum is the **National Hall of Fame for Famous American Indians** (U.S. 62E, tel. 405/247–5555), an outdoor collection of busts depicting well-known Native Americans. Southeast of town, **Indian City USA** (Rte. 8, tel. 405/247–5661) is a re-creation of life in seven Native American villages. At the **Susan Peters Gallery** (112 N. Main St., tel. 405/247–7515 or 800/256–3724), you'll find original works and prints by such Oklahoma Native American artists as T. C. Cannon and the Kiowa Five.

Sports and Outdoor Activities

Fishing   The best bets are Altus Lake or any of the lakes at the Wichita Mountains Wildlife Refuge (*see* Exploring Southwestern Oklahoma, *above*). The *Daily Oklahoman*'s sports section has fishing reports for the lakes in the area, or contact the **Department of Wildlife and Conservation** (tel. 405/521–3855).

Hiking and   Lots of opportunities are available. Check specific parks (*see*
Backpacking   National and State Parks, *above*) or contact the state tourism department (*see* Visitor Information, *above*).

Dining and Lodging

This is not an area where either shines. Try to pack lunches when you can for picnics in parks; at night you'll probably have to content yourself with chain restaurants. Unless you plan on camping, your hotel will probably be little more than a convenient base for exploring a fascinating region. For price ranges, see Charts 1 (B) and 2 (B) in Chapter 1.

Altus   **Val's It's About Time.** This pub-style restaurant is so packed
Dining   with memorabilia—license plates, hubcaps, and an old tuba—you might miss the vintage Altus high-school band uniform hanging on the wall. Steaks, ribs, chicken-fried steak, and seafood are featured on the menu. *800 N. Main St., tel. 405/482–4580. AE, D, DC, MC, V.*

Lodging   **Flagship Inn.** Popular with business travelers, this hotel offers a number of rooms with hair driers, refrigerators, and two phones. *2804 N. Main St., 73521, tel. 405/482–9300 or 800/465–4329; fax 405/482–2245. 101 rooms, 3 suites. Facilities: indoor pool. AE, D, DC, MC, V. Inexpensive.*

Lawton   **Chi's Fong Village.** Tablecloths and better-than-average ser-
Dining   vice at fast-food prices have made this place a favorite with locals. Orange chicken, barbecued spare ribs, and Happy Family—shrimp, beef, chicken, and pork stir-fry—are standards on the buffet. *6204 N. Cache Rd., tel. 405/536–2435. AE, MC, V. Inexpensive.*
  Garfield's. This chain restaurant has such nice touches as paper tablecloths and crayons so children can doodle while awaiting their order. The menu is large, featuring everything from fajitas to prime rib. *3134 Cache Rd., tel. 405/355–0268. AE, DC, MC, V. Inexpensive.*
★ **Woody's BBQ.** Enjoy pork ribs or beef brisket in one of two rustic dining rooms featuring ceiling fans and wood trim. Side dishes include okra, fried mushrooms, and "wood chips" (fried

potatoes with melted cheese and bacon). *1107 W. Lee Blvd., tel.
405/355–4950. MC, V. Inexpensive.*

Lodging **Holiday Inn.** Executive rooms at this downtown hotel feature
king-size beds, refrigerators, and wet bars. *3134 Cache Rd.,
73505, tel. 405/353–1682 or 800/465–4329; fax 405/353–2872.
171 rooms. Facilities: restaurant, dance club, outdoor pool.
AE, D, DC, MC, V. Moderate.*
Howard Johnson Lodge and Convention Center. The public
areas of this low-rise stucco hotel just off I–44 have eclectic decor ranging from Victorian-style frosted glass to a rustic
"chandelier" of antlers. Standard rooms have a teal-and-burnt-
orange color scheme; decor in suites ranges from pastel accents
in the bridal suite to high-tech glass and chrome in the whirlpool suites. *1125 E. Gore St., 73501, tel. 405/353–0200; fax: 405/
353–6801. 142 rooms, 11 suites. Facilities: restaurant, indoor
pool, tennis courts. AE, D, DC, MC, V. Moderate.*

Lone Wolf **Quartz Mountain Resort.** One of Oklahoma's five state-run re-
Lodging sorts in state parks, this establishment offers guests the choice
★ of rooms in the main stone-and-wood lodge, cabins, or a 64-bed
dormitory. Besides numerous sports, recreational activities include an amphitheater and a nature center. *Rte. 1, 73655, tel.
405/563–2424; fax 405/563–9125. 45 lodge rooms, 16 cabins. Facilities: restaurant, pool, nature center, golf course, other
sports facilities. AE, D, DC, MC, V. Moderate.*

Motels **Hospitality Inn** (202 E. Lee St., Lawton 73501, tel. 405/355–
9765; fax 405/355–2360), 106 rooms, coffee shop next door,
laundry, outdoor pool; inexpensive. **Ramada Inn** (601 N. 2nd
St., Lawton 73507, tel. 405/355–7155; fax 405/353–6162), 98
rooms, restaurant, lounge, free passes to local YMCA, outdoor
pool; inexpensive.

Campgrounds In addition to its lodge, Quartz Mountain State Park (*see* Exploring Southwestern Oklahoma, *above*) also has camping facilities. For camping information on other state parks in the area,
contact the state tourism department (*see* Visitor Information,
above).

Elsewhere in the State

Great Salt Plains State Park/
Salt Plains National Wildlife Refuge

Getting There Take I–35N from Oklahoma City to U.S. 60 (which becomes
U.S. 64), then head west. The drive takes about two hours. Expect gravel and dirt roads as you approach the salt flats.

What to See This park attracts visitors from around the world, probably be-
and Do cause they get to keep the selenite crystals (sand and clay formations trapped inside crystalized gypsum) they dig up in the
park's salt flats. The salt flats are part of a wildlife refuge with
hiking and drive-through trails; an adjacent state park offers
camping and water sports on Great Salt Plains Lake. *Rte. 1,
Box 28, Jet 73749, tel. 405/626–4731. Admission free. Digging
Apr.–mid-Oct.*

SOUTH DAKOTA

By Doug Cunningham

Updated by Konnie Le May

Capital	Pierre
Population	696,000
Motto	Under God the People Rule
State Bird	Chinese ring-necked pheasant
State Flower	Pasqueflower

Visitor Information

South Dakota Department of Tourism (Capitol Lake Plaza, Pierre 57501, tel. 800/843–1930 or 800/952–3625). Call the **Department of Transportation** for maps of summer road construction (tel. 605/773–3571) and winter road-condition reports (tel. 605/773–3536).

Scenic Drives

The beautiful **Needles Highway** (Rte. 87) and **Iron Mountain Road** (U.S. 16A) run through Custer State Park (*see* National and State Parks, *below*). U.S. 85 follows scenic **Spearfish Canyon.**

National and State Parks

National Parks **Badlands National Park** and **Black Hills National Forest** (*see* The West, *below*). **Jewel Cave National Monument,** 50 mi southwest of Rapid City on U.S. 16 (R.R. 1, Box 60aa, Custer 57730, tel. 605/673–2288), gets its name from the calcite formations in the world's fourth-longest cave. **Wind Cave National Park,** 50 mi south of Rapid City on U.S. 16 and 385 (R.R. 1, Box 190, Hot Springs 57747, tel. 605/745–4600), is 28,000 acres of prairie and forest above the world's sixth-longest cave.

State Park **Custer State Park** (HC 83, Box 70, Custer 57730, tel. 605/255–4464 or 605/255–4000 for campground reservations) has 73,000 spectacular acres of grasslands and pine-covered hills that are home to buffalo, deer, bighorn sheep, prairie dogs, and antelope.

The West

Unlike the agricultural eastern half of the state, this is a land of prairies, pine forests, and desolate, rocky landscapes. It's also where most of the state's tourists come, to visit such places as Deadwood, the 19th-century mining town turned gambling mecca, and Mt. Rushmore, where the stern grandeur of these giant carvings remains after 50 years.

Getting There

By Plane **Rapid City Regional Airport** (tel. 605/393–9924), 10 mi southeast of downtown via Rte. 44, is served by most major domestic carriers.

By Car Unless you are traveling with a package tour, a car is essential here. Make rental reservations early; Rapid City has a large number of business travelers, and rental agencies are often booked. I–90 bisects the state slightly south of its center; it leads to Wall and to Rapid City. From Rapid City, U.S. 14 leads to towns and attractions in the northern part of the Black Hills, while U.S. 16 winds through its southern half. Rte. 44 is an alternate route between the Black Hills and the Badlands. The Black Hills have seven tunnels with limited clearance; they are marked on state maps and in the state's tourism booklet.

By Bus **Gray Line of the Black Hills** (Box 1106, Rapid City 57709, tel. 605/342–4461 or 800/456–4461) offers bus tours of the region, including trips to Mt. Rushmore, Black Hills National Forest, and Deadwood. **Jack Rabbit Lines** (tel. 800/444–6287) serves Wall and Rapid City.

The Black Hills

Tourist Information **Black Hills, Badlands and Lakes Association** (900 Jackson Blvd., Rapid City 57702, tel. 605/341–1462; fax 605/341–4614). **Rapid City:** Chamber of Commerce and Convention & Visitors Bureau (Civic Center, Box 747, 444 Mt. Rushmore Rd., 57709, tel. 605/343–1744; fax 605/348–9217).

Exploring the Black Hills As with the rest of the state, many of the region's attractions are open only in the summer; be sure to call ahead before you visit. To the locals, **Rapid City** is West River, meaning west of the Missouri. (The tamer souls, perhaps more firmly rooted to the plains, live East River.) South Dakota's second-largest city, this cross between western town and progressive community is a good base from which to explore the Black Hills. Cowboy boots are common here, and business leaders often travel by pickup truck or four-wheel-drive vehicle. Yet the city supports a convention center and a modern, acoustically advanced performance hall and boasts more than its share of bookstores downtown and a modern shopping mall on the outskirts.

The recently expanded **Sioux Indian Museum** (515 West Blvd., tel. 605/348–0557) exhibits art and crafts from the Sioux and other Native American tribes. In Box Elder, just outside Rapid City, is the **South Dakota Air & Space Museum** (Exit 66 off I–90, tel. 605/385–5188). Located at the Ellsworth Air Force Base (base tours offered in summer), it features a ⅜-size Stealth bomber model, Gen. Dwight D. Eisenhower's Mitchell B–25 bomber, and numerous other planes.

The vast **Black Hills National Forest** (R.R. 2, Box 200, Custer 57730, tel. 605/673–2251) covers 1.3 million acres on the state's western edge. Its most famous attraction is **Mt. Rushmore National Memorial,** the granite cliff where the faces of Presidents Washington, Jefferson, Lincoln, and Theodore Roosevelt are carved. Sculptor Gutzon Borglum labored at this monumental task for more than 14 years; it was finally finished by his son, Lincoln, in 1941. The memorial is spectacular in the morning light and at night, when a special lighting ceremony (nightly mid-May–mid-Sept.) dramatically illuminates the carving. *Keystone, 21 mi southwest of Rapid City on U.S. 16, tel. 605/ 574–2523. Admission free.*

Also in Keystone, the **Rushmore-Borglum Story** museum (Main St., tel. 605/666–4448; admission charged) contains newsreel

The Black Hills

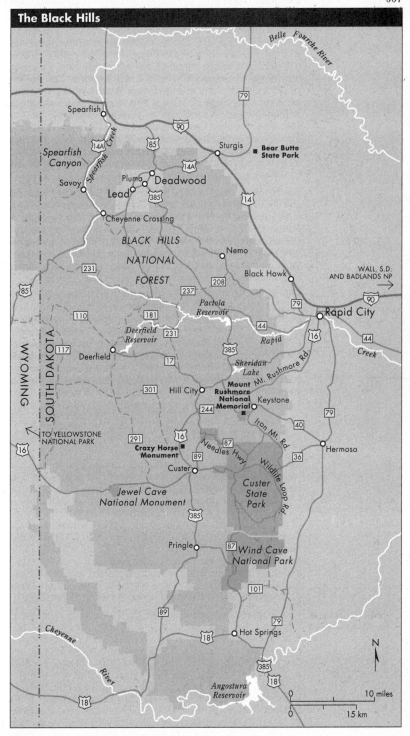

Belle Fourche River

Spearfish

79

I-90

14A

Spearfish Creek

85

Sturgis

Bear Butte
State Park

Spearfish
Canyon

14A

Savoy

Pluma

Deadwood

Lead

14

385

Cheyenne Crossing

BLACK HILLS

Nemo

NATIONAL

208

Black Hawk

WALL, S.D.
AND BADLANDS NP

231

237

79

I-90

FOREST

85

110

181

Pactola
Reservoir

44

Rapid City

Deerfield
Reservoir

231

Rapid

16

44

117

17

385

Sheridan
Lake

Creek

SOUTH DAKOTA

Deerfield

Mt. Rushmore Rd.

WYOMING

301

Hill City

Mount
Rushmore
National
Memorial

Keystone

244

40

79

TO YELLOWSTONE
NATIONAL PARK

291

16

Crazy Horse
Monument

Needles Hwy

87

Iron Mt. Rd.

Hermosa

16

89

Custer

36

Wildlife Loop Rd.

Jewel Cave
National Monument

Custer
State
Park

385

Pringle

87

Wind Cave
National Park

101

Cheyenne

89

79

Hot Springs

18

N

River

385

18

Angostura
Reservoir

0   10 miles

0   15 km

footage of the original blasting of the rockface, as well as exhibits and drawings about the project and its artist. Fifteen mi southwest of here on U.S. 385, another monumental likeness is emerging; when finished, the **Crazy Horse Memorial** (tel. 605/673–4681; admission charged) will depict the Sioux warrior who defeated General Custer at Little Bighorn. The site includes a visitor center and the **Indian Museum of North America.** Expect frequent blasting at this work-in-progress, which will be the world's largest sculpture when completed. Southeast of here is **Wind Cave National Park** (*see* National and State Parks, *above*). In Lakota tradition, it was from this cave that the first Lakota people were tricked by *Iktomi* (spider person) into stepping from their home underground and coming to live on the surface.

Lead (pronounced "Leed"), 50 mi north of Rapid City via I–90 and Alt. Rte. 14A, is a mining community born in the Black Hills gold-rush frenzy of the late 19th century. The **Homestake Mining Co.** (215 W. Main St., tel. 605/584–4673) offers tours of the aboveground operations of the country's oldest operating gold mine. Free ore samples are available. The town itself contains a number of historic houses, many once home to immigrant miners.

Sturgis, 29 mi northwest of Rapid City via I–90, is a sleepy town of about 5,600 whose population swells to between 50,000 and 125,000 the second week in August. Since 1940, the **Black Hills Motor Classic** (Sturgis Rally & Races, Box 189, Sturgis 57785, tel. 605/347–6570; fax 605/347–3245) has drawn motorcyclists and enthusiasts from around the world; many businesses turn their buildings over to sellers of leather goods, rally T-shirts, and other biker-related paraphernalia for the week.

In Spearfish, about 45 mi northwest of Rapid City via I–90, the *Black Hills Passion Play* (tel. 605/642–2646; admission charged) has since 1939 been recounting the last seven days in the life of Christ.

The 1990 Academy Award–winning *Dances with Wolves* has spawned a booming industry in the Black Hills: movie-location tours, held Memorial Day through Labor Day. **Dakota Vistas** (HC 75, Box 168, Sturgis 57785, tel. 605/347–3138) offers a Summer Camp–site tour along the Belle Fourche River. Tours of the Ft. Hays site are conducted by **Prairie Adventures** (3023 Tomahawk Dr., Rapid City 57702, tel. 605/342–4578). **Affordable Adventures** (Box 546, Rapid City 57709, tel. 605/342–7691; fax 605/341–4614) has a combination package for touring these and other sites, including some in Spearfish Canyon and Badlands National Park; the guides specialize in year-round tours of the nearby Oglala Lakota Sioux reservations of Pine Ridge.

What to See and Do with Children The fossilized remains of ancient mammoths at the **Mammoth Site** (one block north of the U.S. 18 bypass, Hot Springs, tel. 605/745–6017; admission charged) should prove fascinating to children and adults alike. The site, discovered in 1974, is believed to contain up to 100 mammoths (47 have been unearthed so far) in the sinkhole where they came to drink some 26,000 years ago. A visitor center is built over the area; excavation is in progress. **Flintstones, Bedrock City** (intersection of U.S. 16 and 385, Custer, tel. 605/673–4079) is a full-scale tribute to the enduring cartoon characters, complete with a curio shop, a train ride, a drive-in restaurant serving brontoburgers, and camping. **Bear Country U.S.A.** (8 mi south of Rapid City on U.S. 16, tel. 605/343–2290) is a drive-through wildlife park featuring black and grizzly bears, as well as wolves, coyotes, bighorn sheep, bison, moose, and most other North American wildlife. In Rapid City, **Storybook Island** (near intersection of Jackson Blvd. and Sheridan Lake Rd.) lets children romp through scenes from fairy tales and nursery rhymes, and **Dinosaur Park** (Skyline Dr.), listed on the National Register of Historic Places, features large plaster dinosaurs and a great view of the city.

Shopping Rapid City stores carry western souvenirs, crafts, and clothing. The **Red Wing Shoe Store** (519 Main St., tel. 605/343–1791) has an excellent selection of shoes and boots suitable for outdoor use and hiking. Nearly every gift shop here carries the locally famous Black Hills gold, a combination of metals that produce distinctive green and red tints; you can watch jewelry being made at the **Heirloom Black Hills Gold & Silver Co.** (603 Main St., tel. 605/341–3671). **Prairie Edge Galleries** (606 Main St., tel. 605/342–3086) displays jewelry, paintings, and crafts of the Plains Indians. **Sioux Trading Post** (913 Mt. Rushmore Rd., tel. 605/348–4822 or 800/456–3394) has a broad range of authentic Plains Indian art, crafts, music, and books and offers a catalogue for mail orders. **Everybody's Book Store** (515 6th St., tel. 605/341–3224) has a fine selection of used books, as well as new books on Native Americans and by regional authors. **Prince & Pauper Bookshop** (612 St. Joe St., tel. 605/342–7964 or 800/354–0988) has a large selection of books by regional and Native American authors.

Rushmore Mall (tel. 605/348–3378), just off I–90 outside Rapid City, contains factory-outlet stores, such as Benetton and Polo/Ralph Lauren, as well as department and western stores; among the latter is **RCC-Western Stores** (tel. 605/341–6633), which can outfit almost anyone with the requisite hat, boots, and jeans. In Piedmont, 12 mi northwest of Rapid City, **James Aplan Antiques & Art** (Exit 40 off I–90, Tilford Rd., tel. 605/347–5016) offers western art, cowboy and western items, rare books, and antiques.

Dining For price ranges, see Chart 1 (B) in Chapter 1.

Circle B Ranch. Chuck-wagon suppers include barbecued beef, biscuits, and all the trimmings. The ranch also offers western shows and wagon and trail rides. *16 mi west of Rapid City on U.S. 385, 1 mi north of junction with Rte. 44, tel. 605/348–7358. Reservations required. No credit cards. No lunch; closed Sept.–May. Moderate.*

Firehouse Brewing Co. This former firehouse serves up hearty fare, such as buffalo sausage, marinated buffalo steak, and shepherd's pie. A wide variety of beers, from light to stout, are brewed on the premises. *610 Main St., Rapid City, tel. 605/348–1915. AE, D, MC, V. Moderate.*

Fireside Inn Restaurant & Lounge. Seating in one of the two dining rooms here is around a huge slate fireplace. The large menu includes prime rib, seafood, and Italian dishes. *6.5 mi west of Rapid City on Rte. 44, tel. 605/342–3900. Reservations for 6 or more only. AE, MC, V. Moderate.*

Flying T Chuckwagon. At this converted barn, ranch-style meals of barbecued beef, potatoes, and baked beans are served on tin plates. Afterward, diners settle back to watch a western show featuring music and cowboy comedy. *6 mi south of Rapid City on U.S. 16, tel. 605/342–1905. Reservations advised. MC, V. No lunch; closed late Sept.–late May. Moderate.*

Landmark Restaurant and Lounge. This hotel restaurant is popular for its lunch buffet and for specialties that include prime rib, freshwater fish, and buffalo brochettes. *Alex Johnson Hotel, 523 6th St., Rapid City, tel. 605/342–1210. AE, D, DC, MC, V. Moderate.*

Shooters. This casual sports bar offers a typical menu of appetizers, burgers, and sandwiches. *2424 W. Main St., Rapid City, tel. 605/348–3348. AE, D, MC, V. Inexpensive–Moderate.*

World Famous Roadkill Cafe. Started by two bike-rally enthusiasts, the café promises on its Day-Glo menu to bring food "From your grill to ours!" including "The Chicken That Didn't Quite Cross the Road," "Smidgen of Pigeon," and the daily special "Guess That Mess!" The café also offers standard fare from breakfast to tuna melt and buffalo and beef burgers. *1333 Main St., Sturgis, tel. 605/347–4502. No reservations. No credit cards. Inexpensive.*

Lodging For price ranges, see Chart 2 (B) in Chapter 1.

During the summer, reservations are helpful and often required to ensure lodging; calling two or three days ahead is usually adequate. In addition to the hotels described here, several chains, including Howard Johnson's, Best Western, and Holiday Inn, have properties in and around Rapid City (*see* Appendix, Toll-Free Numbers).

Holiday Inn Rushmore Plaza. Opened in 1990, this eight-story hotel has a lobby with an atrium, glass elevators, and a 60-foot waterfall. Rooms have modern decor and mauve and gray tones. *505 N. 5th St., Rapid City 57701, tel. 605/348–4000 or 800/777–1023. 157 rooms, 48 suites. Facilities: restaurant, lounge, pool, exercise room. AE, D, DC, MC, V. Expensive.*

The Alex Johnson Hotel. Western elegance pervades this nine-story downtown hotel; the lobby features a wooden torch chandelier, leather wing chairs, and a soaring, beamed ceiling. The rooms were completely redecorated in 1992, with replicas of the original furniture that was here when the hotel opened in 1927. The hotel was officially dedicated to the Lakota Indians, so Native American patterns and artwork are dominant. *523 6th St., Rapid City 57701, tel. 605/342–1210 or 800/888–2539. 85 rooms, 35 suites. Facilities: restaurant, pub, lounge, gift shop, exercise facilities. AE, D, DC, MC, V. Moderate–Expensive.*

Campgrounds For information on state campgrounds, contact the **Department of Game, Fish and Parks** (523 E. Capitol Ave., Pierre 57501, tel. 605/773–3485). Among private facilities is **Rushmore Resort and Campground** (Box 124, Keystone 57751, tel. 605/666–4605).

Deadwood

Tourist Information **Deadwood-Lead:** Chamber of Commerce (735 Main St., Deadwood 57732, tel. 605/578–1876; fax 605/578–1033).

Exploring Deadwood Traveling through western South Dakota without stopping in Deadwood, 41 mi northwest of Rapid City, would have to qualify as sinful. Following the legalization of gambling in 1989, town planners rushed to revitalize and refurbish this once-infamous gold-mining boomtown for the projected onslaught of visitors. Streets have been repaved with cobblestones, and Main Street utility lines have been buried in order to keep all traces of the 20th century from impinging on visitors. Gaming halls and casinos now make up almost every storefront downtown; the refurbished old hotels have their own gambling rooms.

If a place with gambling can be wholesome, this is it (the maximum bet is $5), but it wasn't always so. This is the Old West town where Wild Bill Hickok was shot during a poker game and where Poker Alice Tubbs was famous for smoking big cigars. **Mt. Moriah Cemetery**, above Deadwood, is the final resting place for Hickok, Calamity Jane, and other notorious Deadwood residents. From there, one has a panoramic view of Deadwood. **The Adams Memorial Museum** (54 Sherman St., tel. 605/578–1714) has three floors of displays, including the first locomotive used in the Black Hills, photographs of the town's early days, and a gun collection.

Dining   For price ranges, see Chart 1 (B) in Chapter 1.

★ **Faro's Dining Room.** Turn-of-the-century elegance is the theme at this restaurant in the Historic Franklin Hotel. Beef is a specialty, but the homemade pasta is equally good. *700 Main St., tel. 605/578–1465. AE, D, MC, V. Moderate.*
Jake's. The fine-dining restaurant takes up the third floor of **The Midnight Star**, a renovated former clothing store owned by actor Kevin Costner and his brother. (The rest of the building contains a bar and grill and a gaming hall.) Popular dishes include steak and pork medallions. *677 Main St., tel. 605/578–3656. Reservations advised. AE, D, MC, V. Moderate.*

Lodging   For price ranges, see Chart 2 (B) in Chapter 1.

Goldiggers Hotel and Gaming Establishment. In the gaming hall downstairs, the look is more Vegas than Wild West, but the rooms upstairs have a period look, with dark wood and burgundy tones. *629 Main St., 57732, tel. 605/578–3213 or 800/456–2023. 6 rooms, 3 suites. Facilities: restaurant, lounge, gambling. AE, D, MC, V. Expensive.*
★ **Bullock Hotel.** This 1895 hotel has been meticulously restored to its ornate Victorian origins. The first floor, containing the gaming hall, has high ceilings and brass and crystal chandeliers. Guest rooms are furnished with Victorian reproductions and have large windows. *633 Main St., 57732, tel. 605/578–1745 or 800/336–1876. 26 rooms, 2 suites. Facilities: restaurant, lounge, gambling. AE, D, DC, MC, V. Moderate–Expensive.*
★ **Historic Franklin Hotel and Gambling Hall.** The front rooms have views of Main Street in this turn-of-the-century hotel in the heart of the gambling district. Wide wooden stairways to upper floors contribute to the historic feel. *700 Main St., 57732, tel. 605/578–2241 or 800/688–1876. 75 rooms. Facilities: restaurant, 2 bars, gambling. AE, D, DC, MC, V. Moderate.*

Campgrounds   For information on state campgrounds, contact the **Department of Game, Fish and Parks** (523 E. Capitol Ave., Pierre 57501, tel. 605/773–3485). Among private campgrounds around Deadwood are **Custer Crossing Campground and Store** (HCR 73, Box 1527, Deadwood 57732, tel. 605/584–1009), 15 mi south of town; **Deadwood KOA** (Box 451, Deadwood 57732, tel. 605/578–3830),

1 mi west of town; and **Wild Bill's Campground** (HCR 73, Box 1101, Deadwood 57732, tel. 605/578–2800) on U.S. 385.

The Badlands

Tourist
Information

Black Hills, Badlands and Lakes Association (*see* The Black Hills, *above*). **Wall:** Tourism Committee (Box 424, 57790, tel. 605/279–2127).

Exploring the
Badlands

Badlands National Park, 65 mi east of Rapid City, can seem like another planet. Millions of years of erosion have left these 244,000 acres with desolate gorges, buttes, and ridges colored in rust, pink, and gold. Scenic overlooks are marked. The Ben Reifel Visitor Center, 2 mi north of Interior via Rte. 377, offers information and maps. *Box 6, Interior 57750, tel. 605/433–5361. Admission charged May–Sept., free Oct.–Apr.*

South of the park, on the Pine Ridge Indian Reservation, is the **Wounded Knee Massacre monument,** where 250 Sioux men, women, and children were killed when soldiers opened fire after a brief skirmish in 1890.

If you're traveling on I–90 you'll see the ubiquitous signs every few miles ticking off the mileage to **Wall Drug** (tel. 605/279–2175), the pharmacy turned tourist mecca that enticed Depression-era travelers with offers of free ice water. The store has nearly every tourist trinket imaginable, plus a restaurant that seats more than 500, a bookstore, a chapel, a selection of knives and boots, and western art. **Wall** itself, a sleepy community on the edge of the Badlands, has several motels and restaurants.

Dining

For price ranges, see Chart 1 (B) in Chapter 1.

Cactus Family Restaurant and Lounge. This downtown Wall restaurant specializes in delicious hot cakes and pies. A giant roast-beef buffet is sometimes offered in summer. *519 Main St., Wall, tel. 605/279–2561. D, MC, V. Moderate.*

Cedar Pass Lodge Restaurant. This restaurant at a rustic hotel serves big T-bone steaks and fresh mountain trout. *Badlands National Park, Interior, tel. 605/433–5460. AE, D, DC, MC, V. Closed mid-Dec.–Mar. Inexpensive–Moderate.*

★ **The Elkton House Restaurant.** This comfortable restaurant with sun room and wood paneling has fast service and a terrific hot roast beef sandwich, served on white bread with gravy and mashed potatoes. *South Blvd., Wall, tel. 605/279–2152. D, MC, V. Inexpensive–Moderate.*

Lodging

For price ranges, see Chart 2 (B) in Chapter 1.

★ **Cedar Pass Lodge.** Located in Badlands National Park, the lodge's wood-frame cabins with knotty-pine interiors have a 1950s look. Each one- or two-bedroom cabin has a private bath. *Box 5, Interior 57750, tel. 605/433–5460. 24 cabins. Facilities: restaurant, gift shop. AE, D, DC, MC, V. Closed Oct.–Apr. Inexpensive.*

Prairie's Edge Bed and Breakfast. This small, single-story wooden farmhouse on the banks of the White River has 1940s-style furnishings. It's within hiking distance of the Badlands, and you can see spectacular sunrises and sunsets from the grounds. *Box 11, Interior 57750, tel. 605/433–5441 in season, 605/456–2836 off-season. 3 rooms. Facilities: full breakfast. No credit cards. Closed Sept.–May. Inexpensive.*

Motels **Badlands Budget Host Motel** (HC 54, Box 115, Interior 57750, tel. 605/433–5335 in season, 800/999–6116 off-season), 10 rooms, pool, playground, convenience store; closed mid-Sept.–May; inexpensive.

Campgrounds Among private campgrounds in the area is **Circle 10 Campground** (Rte. 1, Box 51½, Philip 57567, tel. 605/433–5451. For information on state campgrounds, contact the **Department of Game, Fish and Parks** (523 E. Capitol Ave., Pierre 57501, tel. 605/773–3485).

Sports and Outdoor Activities

Fishing Some of the best fishing in the state lies to the east of this area, in the large lakes along the Missouri River, but mountain streams throughout the Black Hills offer good trout fishing. Custer State Park has trout fishing in several lakes. For more information, contact the state Department of Tourism's **fishing division** (tel. 605/773–3301 or 800/445–3474).

Hiking The **Centennial Trail,** 111 mi long, runs through the Black Hills National Forest, from the Plains Indians' sacred site at Bear Butte in the north to Wind Cave National Park, passing from grasslands into the high-country hills. For more information, contact the state Department of Tourism (*see* Visitor Information, *above*).

Hunting Game, especially deer and turkey, is abundant here. A license is required; applications are available from the **Department of Game, Fish and Parks** (*see* The Badlands, Campgrounds, *above*).

Snowmobiling With about 300 mi of marked and groomed trails, the Black Hills is one of the premier spots in the country for snowmobiling. A map of the trail network is available from the Department of Tourism (*see* Visitor Information, *above*). For trail conditions, updated three times weekly, call 800/445–3474.

Ski Areas

The Black Hills' winter-sports magazine, *Romancing the Snow,* has information on cross-country and downhill skiing and is available from the Black Hills, Badlands and Lakes Association (*see* Tourist Information, *above*). For ski reports, call 800/445–3474.

Cross-country The Black Hills offer skiing on 600 mi of abandoned logging roads, railroad beds, and fire trails, as well as several trail networks including the **Big Hill,** 20 mi of trails on the rim of Spearfish Canyon. Information is available from **Ski Cross Country** (701 3rd St., Spearfish 57783, tel. 605/642–3851), a ski equipment and rental shop.

Downhill **Deer Mountain Ski Area** (Box 622, Deadwood 57732, tel. 605/584–3230) has 25 trails, a 700-foot vertical drop, and one triple chair and two poma lifts. Lessons, rentals, and cross-country trails are available. **Terry Peak Ski Area** (Box 774, Lead 57754, tel. 605/584–2165) offers a 1,052-foot vertical drop and one quad, one triple, and three double chair lifts. A rental shop, lessons, and a lodge are available.

Elsewhere in the State

Sioux Falls

Getting There Sioux Falls is located in the southeastern corner of the state, at the intersection of I–90 and I–29. **Sioux Falls Regional Airport** (tel. 605/336–0762) is served by most major domestic carriers and by Mesaba (through Northwest Airlines).

What to See and Do Sioux Falls, the state's largest city, is an ideal starting point for most attractions in the eastern part of the state. The city is a commercial hub; restaurants, hotels, and shops are numerous. The **Great Plains Zoo and Delbridge Museum of Natural History** (805 S. Kiwanis Ave., tel. 605/339–7059; admission charged) contains, besides its live-animal displays, one of the world's largest collections of mounted animals. The **Old Courthouse Museum** (200 W. 6th St., tel. 605/335–4210; admission free) is a massive Romanesque-style structure made of a native red stone called Sioux quartzite. It houses exhibits on the history of the area, including Native American artifacts. The **Pettigrew Home and Museum** (131 N. Duluth Ave., tel. 605/339–7097; admission free) was built in 1889 and was later the home of South Dakota's first full-term senator, Richard F. Pettigrew. It contains period furnishings and Native American and natural-history exhibits.

Mitchell

Getting There Mitchell is 70 mi west of Sioux Falls on I–90.

What to See and Do The city of Mitchell trumpets the "world's only" **Corn Palace** (604 N. Main St., tel. 605/996–7311 or 800/257–2676). This dubious honor goes to a fanciful structure, topped by gaily painted Moorish domes, with a facade covered with multicolored corn, grain, and grasses in various designs and murals. Inside is an exhibition hall built to showcase the state's agricultural production. The exterior designs are changed annually. Across the street is the **Enchanted World Doll Museum** (615 N. Main St., tel. 605/996–9896), with 4,000 antique and modern dolls displayed in 400 scenes. (**Mitchell Department of Tourism,** Box 776, 57301, tel. 605/996–7311 or 800/257–2676.)

DeSmet

Getting There From Sioux Falls, follow I–29N for 49 mi, then U.S. 14W for about 37 mi.

What to See and Do Fans of the *Little House* children's book series may want to visit the town where author Laura Ingalls Wilder lived for 15 years. The Ingalls family moved to DeSmet in 1879 and lived first in a shanty, then in a farmhouse, and then in a house in town that Pa Ingalls built in 1887. The first and last homes are open to the public and contain period furnishings and memorabilia. The community is also home to the annual **Laura Ingalls Wilder Pageant,** held late June–early July. (**Laura Ingalls Wilder Memorial Society,** Box 344, De Smet 57231, tel. 605/854–3383 or 605/854–3181.)

Pierre

Getting There Pierre (pronounced "Peer") is on U.S. 83, about 225 mi west of Sioux Falls.

What to See and Do The state **Capitol** (500 E. Capitol Ave., tel. 605/773–3765), a magnificent Greek Revival building completed in 1910, has a rich interior decorated with mosaic floors, stained-glass skylights, allegorical murals, and an impressive columned staircase. The state historical society has a museum and archives at the recently completed **Cultural Heritage Center** (900 Governor's Dr., tel. 605/773–3458). Exhibits focus on the history of the state with emphasis on the city of Pierre, which evolved from a French trading post in the early 1800s. The first of three phases for a "South Dakota Experience" permanent exhibit was completed in 1992. It offers a taste of the state from 1743, the year European trappers first arrived, through the beginning of the 20th century. The second phase, to be completed in the fall of 1994, focuses on the life of the Plains Indians prior to 1743. (For tourist office, *see* Visitor Information, *above*.)

8 The Southwest

The Southwest

Introduction

By Edie Jarolim   A region that seems to demand superlatives, the Southwest is the ruggedly beautiful, wide-open land out of which America's myths continue to emerge. Cowboys and Indians, Old World conquistadors and new religions, the rise and fall of fortunes in gold, copper, and oil—all feed into the vision of an untamed territory with limitless horizons.

Of course, Phoenix, Dallas, and Salt Lake City are sophisticated metropolises, and Santa Fe is coming to rival Los Angeles in wealth and number of art galleries per square foot. Las Vegas is sui generis: an unbridled, peculiarly American phenomenon. Foodies all over the country sing the praises of the delicately spiced southwestern cuisine, an outgrowth of Asian immigration into the area, now duplicated in cosmopolitan restaurants nationwide. Nor is there a region that has better Mexican food, whether you like it Tex-Mex, Sonoran, or New Mexican style. Southwestern furnishings—an eclectic blend that might include Mission chests, Navajo blankets, Mexican tinwork mirrors, strings of *ristras* (red chili peppers), and even bleached cow skulls à la Georgia O'Keeffe—have become so popular in upscale homes that they're a bit of a cliché.

But other, more ancient cultures vie here with contemporary ones. The country's largest Indian reservation, that of the Navajo nation, occupies millions of acres traversing state boundaries, and dozens of other tribes—among them Hopi, Zuni, and Apache—live in the region as well. It is their vanishing civilization and, above all, the area's natural phenomena—spectacular canyons, a vast salt lake, eerily towering rock formations, and clear, lambent light—that continue to capture the imagination of visitors and residents alike. The southwestern landscape is a glorious lesson in geologic upheaval, to be learned at such sites as Arches National Park in Utah, Carlsbad Caverns in New Mexico, and the Grand Canyon in Arizona.

Clearly anything is possible in such an unrestrained place. The heyday of the western movie may be over, but when 1990s screen heroines Thelma and Louise light out for freedom, they find it in the Southwest, still the most natural setting for outlandish deeds and grand gestures.

Tour Groups

The tours of this region reveal natural splendors from the Grand Canyon to Zion National Park and such famous cities as San Antonio, Sante Fe, and Las Vegas.

Brennan Tours (1402 3rd Ave., Suite 717, Seattle, WA 98101, tel. 206/622–9155 or 800/237–7249) offers an eight-day tour of the canyonland parks of Utah, Arizona, and Nevada, including the Grand Canyon, Monument Valley, and Bryce and Zion national parks. **Domenico Tours** (751 Broadway, Bayonne, NJ 07002, tel. 201/823–8687 or 800/554–8687) offers a 10-day excursion through Texas, beginning in Louisiana, and including a visit to the Alamo. **Gadabout Tours** (700 E. Tahquitz Way, Palm Springs, CA 92262, tel. 619/325–5556 or 800/952–5068) follows the "Blue Bonnet Trail" for a two-week tour of Texas. A number of five- to seven-day tours head to destinations in Arizona, Nevada, and Utah (Grand Canyon, Tucson, Lake Powell and Zion National Park, and Reno). Many more in-depth tours of the region are also available. **Globus** (5301 S. Federal Circle, Littleton, CO 80123, tel. 303/797–2800 or 800/221–0090) has an eight-day tour of Texas with a side trip to New Orleans and a 13-day "Parks and Canyons Spectacular" tour, which swings through six western states. Nine- and 12-day tours cover Arizona in depth, leaving from San Diego. For similar tours at bargain prices, check out Globus's budget-minded affiliate, **Cosmos Tourama** (same address). **Maupintour** (Box 807, Lawrence, KS 66044, tel. 913/843–1211 or 800/255–4266) offers four tours of Arizona or Arizona-Utah combinations, from eight days to two weeks. A 12-day tour hits the highlights of "Southwest Indian Lands." Other eight-day tours cover "Grand New Mexico" and Southwest Texas and Big Bend National Park. **Talmage Tours** (1223 Walnut St., Philadelphia, PA 19107, tel. 215/923–7100) has a five-day tour of Las Vegas and an eight-day tour of the Grand Canyon and other western national parks with a stop in Salt Lake City. **Tauck Tours** (Box 5027, Westport, CT 06881, tel. 203/226–6911 or 800/468–2825) has a number of eight-day tours. These include Texas in depth; New Mexico in depth, visiting Carlsbad Caverns, Santa Fe, and Albuquerque; "Arizona Resorts"; and "Canyonlands of Arizona and Utah."

When to Go

In the semiarid climate of most of the Southwest, **spring** is the season of choice, with cool, fresh, clear weather. In March and April, when temperatures average in the 70s, short-lived wildflowers produce carpets of extravagant color in many parts of the region, including some deserts as well as temperate areas like East Texas. **Summer** is dry and often very hot, sometimes unpleasantly so, across the Southwest; but water sports abound, and dramatic mountain chains offer another cool respite. Summer thunderstorms are typical in most areas. After spring, **fall**—September to November, in general—is the preferred time to visit, with temperatures falling back into the 70s and 80s, and gorgeous foliage to be seen in many areas. Skiers flock to slopes across the Southwest in **winter.** In general, temperatures vary greatly even within the same state and season because of the great variety of microclimates in the Southwest's mountains, deserts, plains, and forests.

Festivals and Seasonal Events

Jan. 1: The **Cotton Bowl Parade** brings floats, bands, and thousands of marchers through downtown Dallas on the same day that the Southwest Conference champion meets a highly ranked opponent at the Cotton Bowl in State Fair Park. *Tel. 214/634–7525.*

Late Jan.: The **Cowboy Poetry Gathering** in Elko, Nevada, has become famous both for the authentic characters it draws from around the Southwest and for the gentle quality of the verse these rough-hewn men and women produce. *Tel. 702/738–7508.*

Early Feb.: The **Tubac (AZ) Festival** is the state's oldest arts-and-crafts show, a nine-day extravaganza that includes exhibitions, strolling performers, and food galore. *Tel. 602/398–2704.*

Mid.-Feb.: **Washington's Birthday Celebration** in Laredo, Texas, and Nuevo Laredo, its sister city across the border, is a binational celebration of parades and fiestas honoring the first successful New World revolutionary. *Tel. 512/722–0589.*

Feb.–Mar.: Twenty thousand animals are shown at Houston's **Livestock Show & Rodeo,** a truly Texas-size event held under the curved roof of the Astrodome. Rodeos and country music abound. *Tel. 713/791–9000.*

Early Mar.: High-quality artwork is the norm at the **Heard Museum Guild Indian Fair and Market,** a juried invitational for Native American artists held in Phoenix, Arizona. *Tel. 602/252–8840.*

Late Apr.: Native Americans celebrate **American Indian Week** in Albuquerque, New Mexico, with dance, arts and crafts, and a trade show at the Indian Pueblo Cultural Center. *Tel. 505/843–7270.*

Late Apr.: Fiesta San Antonio (TX), more than a century old, commemorates the Battle of San Jacinto with a festival of music, food, sports, art shows, and the River Parade. *Tel. 512/227–5191.*

May 5: Cinco de Mayo, a fiesta celebrating Mexican history and heritage, is held in many cities and towns across the Southwest.

Late June: New Mexico's craftsmen are world-famous, and some of the best of them display and sell their work at the **New Mexico Arts & Crafts Fair** in Albuquerque. *Tel. 505/884–9043.*

Early July: The **National Basque Festival** in Elko, Nevada, celebrates the heritage of the Basque people (recruited from northern Spain for their remarkable shepherding abilities) in the American West. *Tel. 702/738–7547.*

July 8–10 and 13–17: The popular **Mormon Miracle Pageant** is a musical drama of American and Mormon history, set against the backdrop of the Temple in Manti, Utah. *Tel. 801/835–3000.*

Late July: The **Fiesta de Santiago y Santa Ana,** a colorful street party and fair, which began as a trade fair nearly 300 years ago, is the major annual event in Taos, New Mexico. *Tel. 505/758–3873 or 800/732–8267.*

July 30–Aug. 7: The **Festival of the American West,** hosted for more than 20 years by Utah State University in Logan, is famous for its fair and a multimedia pageant entitled "The West: America's Odyssey." *Tel. 801/750–1143.*

Aug. 25–29: The **Nevada State Fair,** in Reno, offers a week of rides, farm-animal competitions, livestock shows, fast food, and all the other accoutrements of a real state fair. *Tel. 702/688–5767.*

Mid-Sept.: On the first weekend after Labor Day, Zozobra, or "Old Man Gloom," is burned to open the annual **Fiestas de Santa Fe** in New Mexico. During the celebration, Santa Fe Plaza is filled with music, dancing, and food vendors. *Tel. 505/984–6760 or 800/777–2489.*

Early Oct.: The **State Fair of Texas,** the nation's largest state fair, holds its three-week annual run at Dallas' State Fair Park, declared a National Historic Landmark in 1986 for its art deco architecture. *Tel. 214/421–8716.*

Mid-Oct.: The **Albuquerque International Balloon Fiesta,** in which more than 600 colorful hot-air balloons rise in spectacular unison with the dawn, is probably New Mexico's best-known event. *Tel. 505/243–3696 or 800/284–2282.*

Early Nov.: The outdoor **Fine Folk Festival,** with 250 performers, draws some 150,000 people to Mesa, Arizona, every year. *Tel. 602/890–2613.*

Early Dec.: The ghost town of Madrid, New Mexico, is reawakened with street lights and an arts-and-crafts festival during the **Christmas Open-house Celebration.** *Tel. 505/473–0743.*

Getting Around the Southwest

By Plane America West, American, Delta, and Southwest all provide extensive service to and among the southwestern states; Continental, TWA, and United offer more limited service. The region's major airports include, in Texas, **Dallas–Fort Worth International Airport** (tel. 214/574–8888) and **Houston Intercontinental Airport** (tel. 713/230–3100); in Nevada, **Reno Cannon International Airport** (tel. 702/328–6868) and **McCarran International Airport** (tel. 702/261–5743) in Las Vegas; in New Mexico, **Albuquerque International Airport** (tel. 505/842–4366); in Phoenix, Arizona, **Sky Harbor International Airport** (tel. 602/273–3300); and in Utah, **Salt Lake International Airport** (tel. 801/575–2400).

By Car The Southwest is traversed by the country's two major east–west highways: I–80, the northern route, which passes through Salt Lake City, Utah, and Reno, Nevada; and I–40, which enters Texas at the Oklahoma border, heading to Los Angeles by way of Amarillo, Texas, Albuquerque, New Mexico, and Flagstaff, Arizona. Other east–west arteries include I–10, which links New Orleans and Los Angeles via Houston, San Antonio and El Paso, Texas, and Tucson and Phoenix, Arizona; and I–20, which connects Dallas and El Paso. The major north–south routes of the region are I–15, which heads south from Salt Lake City to Las Vegas; I–25, from Denver to El Paso by way of Albuquerque; and I–35, from Oklahoma to the Mexican border by way of Dallas and Fort Worth.

By Train Amtrak (tel. 800/872–7245) serves all the states of the region, with one major line between New Orleans and Los Angeles, and another passing through southeastern Colorado to Albuquerque and Flagstaff.

By Bus Greyhound (Dallas, TX, tel. 214/655–7000; Houston, TX, tel. 713/222–1161; Albuquerque, NM, tel. 505/243–4435; Phoenix, AZ, tel. 602/248–4040; Salt Lake City, UT, tel. 801/355–4684; Las Vegas, NV, tel. 702/382–2640; Reno, NV, tel. 702/322–4511; or 800/231–2222) provides service to towns and cities throughout the region.

ARIZONA

By Edie Jarolim

Capital	Phoenix
Population	3,000,000
Motto	God Enriches
State Bird	Cactus wren
State Flower	Saguaro cactus

Visitor Information

Arizona Office of Tourism (1100 W. Washington St., Phoenix 85007, tel. 602/542–8687).

Scenic Drives

The drive from the South Rim to the North Rim of the **Grand Canyon** passes along U.S. 89 through the Arizona Strip, a starkly beautiful, largely uninhabited part of the state. Almost all of the Grand Canyon drives are breathtaking, especially the West Rim Drive on the South Rim and the dirt-road drive to Point Sublime on the North Rim. The fall foliage is spectacular on **U.S. 89A** from Flagstaff to Sedona via Oak Creek Canyon. From Tucson, **I–10** east of Benson passes through the startling rock formations of Texas Canyon.

National and State Parks

National Parks   Canyon de Chelly (*see* Northeast Arizona, *below*). **Grand Canyon National Park** (*see* Grand Canyon National Park, *below*). **Petrified Forest National Park** (*see* Northeast Arizona, *below*). **Saguaro National Monument** (*see* Tucson and Southern Arizona, *below*). For Native American ruins in scenic settings, visit **Walnut Canyon National Monument** and **Wupatki National Monument** (*see* Elsewhere in the State, *below*, for both) in the Flagstaff area, **Tuzigoot National Monument** south of Sedona, and **Navajo National Monument** (*see* Northeast Arizona, *below*). Little-visited spots of unusual beauty include **Sunset Crater Volcano National Monument** (*see* Elsewhere in the State, *below*), west of Flagstaff, and **Chiricahua National Monument**, in the southeast part of the state.

State Parks   Arizona's state parks run a wide spectrum, from the relatively tiny 54-acre **Slide Rock** (Box 10358, Sedona 86339), near Sedona, to 13,000-acre **Lake Havasu** (1350 W. McCulloch Blvd., Lake Havasu City 86403). Boating and water-sports enthusiasts congregate at **Alamo Lake State Park** (Box 38, Wenden 85257), north of Wenden, while **Catalina** and **Picacho Peak state parks** (Box 36986, Tuscon 85704), near Tucson, are the best bets for desert activities. **Painted Rocks Park** (2015 W. Deer Valley Rd., Phoenix 85027) west of Gila Bend, is distinctive for its Native American rock carvings. All have hiking trails and, except for Slide Rock, campgrounds. For a taste of the state's lively frontier history, visit **Riordon Historical State Park** in Flagstaff, **Jerome State Historic Park** in north-central Arizona, and **Tombstone Courthouse State Historic Park** (*see* Tucson and Southern Arizona, *below*) and **Yuma Territorial Prison State**

Historic Park, both in the south. For additional information, contact the **Arizona State Parks Department** (800 W. Washington St., Suite 415, Phoenix 85007, tel. 602/542–4174).

Grand Canyon National Park

Not even the finest photographs pack a fraction of the impact of a personal experience of the Grand Canyon. This vast, eerily silent, beautiful scar on the surface of our planet is 277 mi long, 17 mi across at its widest spot, and more than 1 mi below the rim at its deepest point. Its twisted and contorted layers of rock reveal an awesome geologic profile of the Earth, including otherworldly stone monuments whose colors shift with the hours.

Tourist Information

Grand Canyon National Park (Box 129, Grand Canyon 86023, tel. 602/638–7888). South Rim: **Grand Canyon National Park Lodges** (Box 699, Grand Canyon 86023, tel. 602/638–2401); **National Park Service visitor center** (Grand Canyon Village, east of El Tovar Hotel, tel. 602/638–7888). North Rim: **Grand Canyon Lodge** (Box 400, Cedar City, UT 84720, tel. 801/586–7686). North and south rim camping: **MISTIX** (Box 85705, San Diego, CA 92138, tel. 619/452–0150 or 800/365–2267). A free newspaper, *The Guide*, containing a detailed area map, is available at both rims. Before you go, write to Grand Canyon National Park (*see above*) for a complimentary *Trip Planner*.

Getting There

By Plane **McCarran International Airport** in Las Vegas (tel. 702/739–5743) is the primary hub for flights to **Grand Canyon National Park Airport** (tel. 602/638–2446); carriers include **Air Nevada** (tel. 800/634–6377), **Grand Airways** (tel. 800/634–6616), and **Scenic Air** (tel. 800/634–6801). You can also make connections from **Sky Harbor International Airport** in Phoenix (tel. 602/273–3300) via **Arizona Pacific Airlines** (tel. 800/221–7904). The **Tusayan Grand Canyon Shuttle** (tel. 602/638–2475 or 800/472–6322) operates between Grand Canyon airport and the nearby towns of Tusayan and Grand Canyon Village. **Fred Harvey Transportation Company** (tel. 602/638–2822 or 602/638–2631) provides taxi service.

By Car In general, the best access to the Grand Canyon is from Flagstaff (*see* Elsewhere in the State, *below*), either northwest on U.S. 180 (81 mi) to Grand Canyon Village on the South Rim or, for a scenic route, north on U.S. 89 to Rte. 64W. To visit the North Rim, some 210 mi from Flagstaff, follow U.S. 89N to Bitter Springs, then take U.S. 89A to the junction of Rte. 67. From the west on I–40, the most direct route to the South Rim is via Rte. 64 to U.S. 180. Summer traffic approaching the South Rim can be quite congested around Grand Canyon Village. The more remote North Rim is closed to automobiles after the first heavy snow of the season, usually reopening around mid-May.

By Train The town closest to the Grand Canyon served by **Amtrak** is Flagstaff (tel. 602/774–8679). From Williams, you can take the historic **Grand Canyon Railway** (tel. 800/843–8724) to the South Rim.

By Bus **Greyhound** stops at Flagstaff and Williams. From both towns, **Nava-Hopi Tours** (tel. 602/774–5003 or 800/892–8687) offers bus service to the canyon's South Rim.

Exploring Grand Canyon National Park

Both the South Rim and North Rim areas of the Grand Canyon were carefully planned by the National Park Service. The down side to the park's accessibility is that large crowds converge on the South Rim every summer. Still, there are escape routes everywhere, and the most trafficked spots are popular for good reason. A walk, however brief, into the canyon itself opens up a totally new and extraordinary perspective.

South Rim **Mather Point,** at the outskirts of Grand Canyon Village, affords the first glimpse of the canyon from one of the most impressive and accessible vista points on the rim.

Scenic overlooks on the 25-mi-long **East Rim Drive** include **Yaki Point,** where the popular Kaibab Trail starts the canyon descent to the inner gorge; **Grandview Point,** which supports large stands of ponderosa and piñon pine, oak, and juniper; and **Moran Point,** a favorite spot for photographers. Three miles east of Moran Point, at the **Tusayan Ruins and Museum** (tel. 602/638–2305; admission free), partially intact rock dwellings offer evidence of early habitation in the gorge. From **Lipan Point,** the widest spot in the canyon, you get an astonishing visual profile of the area's geologic history. The highest point along the tour is **Desert View** and **The Watchtower,** site of an observatory (tel. 602/638–2736; admission charged) and a trading post with Native American art (*see* Shopping, *below*).

Back in Grand Canyon Village, the paved **Village Rim Trail** (about 1 mi round-trip) starts at **Hopi House,** one of the canyon's first curio stores (*see* Shopping, *below*). Stops along the way include the historic **El Tovar Hotel,** the jewel in the crown of the country's national park system (*see* Dining and Lodging, *below*); **Lookout Studio,** a combination lookout point, museum, and gift shop; and **Bright Angel Lodge,** with a fireplace made of regional rocks arranged in layers that match the canyon's.

On the **West Rim Drive, Trailview Overlook** affords an unobstructed view of the distant San Francisco Peaks, Arizona's highest mountains. At **Maricopa Point,** you'll see the towering headframe of an early Grand Canyon mining operation. **The Abyss** reveals a sheer canyon drop of 3,000 feet. **Pima Point** provides a bird's-eye view of the Tonto Plateau and the Tonto Trail, which winds for more than 70 mi through the canyon. **Hermits Rest,** the westernmost viewpoint, and the Boucher Trail, which descends from it (*see* Sports and Outdoor Activities, *below*), were named for Louis Boucher, a 19th-century prospector who had a roughly built home down in the canyon. The West Rim Drive is closed to auto traffic in summer; from late May through September, free shuttle buses leave daily from Grand Canyon Village for Hermits Rest.

North Rim Set in deep forest, near the 9,000-foot crest of the Kaibab Plateau in the isolated Arizona Strip, the North Rim is, for many

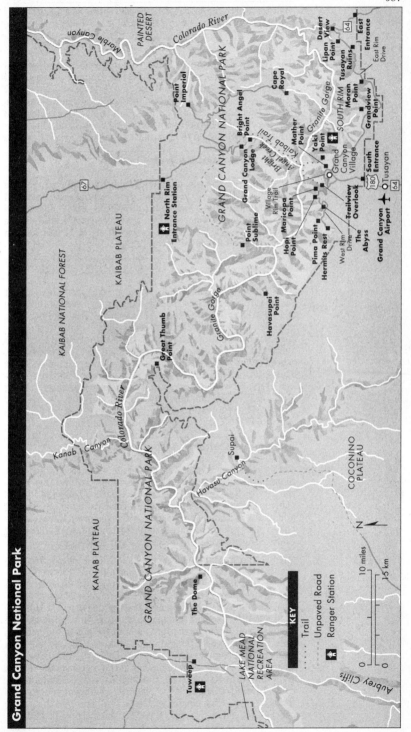

Grand Canyon National Park

KEY

······ Trail

---- Unpaved Road

Ranger Station

visitors, worth the extra miles. From central Arizona, the only route into this area is more than 200 mi of lonely road to the northwest of Flagstaff. During the winter, heavy snows close highway access to, and facilities in, the North Rim.

The trail to **Bright Angel Point,** one of the most awe-inspiring overlooks on either rim, starts on the grounds of the **Grand Canyon Lodge** (*see* Dining and Lodging, *below*), a massive stone structure built in 1928 by the Union Pacific Railroad. Two of the North Rim's most popular outlooks are **Point Imperial,** at 8,803 feet the canyon's highest viewpoint, and **Cape Royal,** the southernmost viewpoint on the North Rim.

What to See and Do with Children

Free daily programs conducted by the National Park Service may appeal especially to children. Gentle horses can be rented at the **Moqui Lodge** (Tusayan, tel. 602/638–2424). Short mule rides suitable for young children are offered on the easier trails along the North Rim; make reservations at **Grand Canyon Lodge** (tel. 801/586–7686).

Shopping

The Native American items sold at most of the lodges and at major gift shops are authentic. Among the most interesting places to browse or buy are the **Desert View Trading Post** (East Rim Dr., tel. 602/638–2360), offering a mix of Southwest souvenirs and Native American crafts; the **El Tovar Hotel Gift Shop** (near the rim in Grand Canyon Village, tel. 602/638–2631), where silver jewelry is featured; **Hopi House** (east of El Tovar Hotel, tel. 602/638–2631), with a wide variety of Native American artifacts, some of museum quality; and **Cameron Trading Post** (on U.S. 89, 1 mi north of junction with Rte. 64, tel. 602/679–2231), with jewelry, rugs, baskets, and pottery from the Navajo, Hopi, Zuni, and New Mexico Pueblo Indians.

Sports and Outdoor Activities

Hiking
Park rangers or visitor-center personnel have detailed area maps of the many canyon trails. Overnight hikes require a permit; write **Backcountry Reservations Office** (Box 129, Grand Canyon 86023). It's wise to make a reservation in advance. If you arrive without one, go to the Backcountry Reservations Office either near the entrance to Mather Campground on the South Rim or at the North Rim's ranger station.

Among the most popular and scenic hiking paths from the South Rim to the bottom of the canyon (8 mi), the well-maintained **Bright Angel Trail** has a steep (4,460-ft) ascent and should be attempted only by persons in good physical condition. The 9-mi **Hermit (Boucher) Trail,** which starts at Hermits Rest and offers some inspiring views of Hermit Gorge and the Redwall and Supai formations, is unmaintained and suitable only for experienced long-distance hikers. The steep **South Kaibab Trail** begins near Yaki Point on East Rim Drive near Grand Canyon Village and connects at the bottom of the canyon with the **North Kaibab Trail,** the only maintained trail into the canyon from the North Rim. Plan on five days if you want to hike the gorge from rim to rim. **Note:** For hikes into the gorge, carry 1-1½ gallons of water per day and drink frequently, about every 10 minutes, especially in summer. To avoid fatigue, take along high-energy snacks, such as trail mix, bananas, and fig bars.

Mule Trips Mule trips down the precipitous trails to the inner gorge are nearly as well known as the canyon itself. Inquire at the **Reservations Department** (Box 699, Grand Canyon 86023, tel. 602/638–2401) about prices and restrictions for riders, and book months in advance.

Rafting Reservations for white-water rafting trips, which last from one to several days, must often be made more than half a year ahead of time. Outfitters include **Canyoneers, Inc.** (tel. 602/526–0924), **Diamond River Adventures** (tel. 602/645–8866 or 800/343–3121), **Expeditions Inc.** (tel. 602/774–8176), and **Wilderness River Adventures** (tel. 602/645–3296 or 800/992–8022). Companies specializing in smooth-water rafting day trips include **Fred Harvey Transportation Company** (tel. 602/638–2822) and **Wilderness River Adventures** (tel. 602/645–3279 or 800/343–3121). For a complete list of river-raft companies, contact the **River Permits Office** (Grand Canyon National Park, Box 129, Grand Canyon 86023, tel. 602/638–7888).

Dining and Lodging

Restaurants throughout Grand Canyon country and northwestern Arizona cater to tourists who are moving at a good clip from one place to another; they generally offer standard American fare at reasonable prices.

It's difficult to find rooms in the South Rim area in summer. The North Rim is less crowded but has limited lodging facilities. Make reservations as soon as your itinerary is firmed up, even as much as six months in advance. If you can't find accommodations in the immediate South Rim area, try the nearby communities of Williams or Flagstaff. Camping inside the park is permitted only in designated areas. For information on park camping and reservations, contact **MISTIX** (*see* Tourist Information, *above*). Arizona Office of Tourism (*see* Visitor Information, *above*) offers a campground directory. For price ranges, see Charts 1 (B) and 2 (B) in Chapter 1.

South Rim **El Tovar Hotel.** Reminiscent of a grand European hunting
Dining and Lodging lodge, El Tovar has maintained a tradition of excellent service and luxury since 1905. The hotel's fine restaurant, set in a room of hand-hewn logs and beamed ceilings, serves Continental dishes such as veal française. *Box 699, Grand Canyon 86023, tel. 602/638–2401 (reservations) or 602/638–2631. 65 rooms, 10 suites. Facilities: restaurant, cocktail lounge, gift shop. AE, D, DC, MC, V. Expensive.*
Bright Angel Lodge. Built in 1935, this log-and-stone structure a few yards from the canyon rim offers rooms in the main lodge or in quaint cabins (some with fireplaces) scattered among the pines. The restaurant, overlooking the Abyss, is informal but memorable. *Box 699, Grand Canyon 86023, tel. 602/638–2401 (reservations) or 602/638–2631. 37 rooms (19 shared baths), 42 cabins. Facilities: restaurant, cocktail lounge, soda fountain, gift shop. AE, D, DC, MC, V. Moderate–Expensive.*

Lodging **Maswik Lodge, Yavapai Lodge, Moqui Lodge, Kachina Lodge,** and **Thunderbird Lodge.** The five other Fred Harvey Company lodges on the South Rim are all comfortable and well appointed. Moqui is on U.S. 180, just outside the park, while the others are in Grand Canyon Village. *Box 699, Grand Canyon 86023, tel. 602/638-2401 (reservations) or 602/638-2631. 1,000 rooms. Facilities: restaurants. AE, D, DC, MC, V. Moderate–Expensive.*

Camping In Grand Canyon Village, **Mather Campground** (contact MISTIX; *see* Tourist Information, *above*) has RV and tent sites, and **Trailer Village** (Box 699, Grand Canyon 86023, tel. 602/638–2401) has RV sites. Commercial and Forest Service campgrounds outside the park include **Flintstone Bedrock City** (Grand Canyon Hwy., Star Rte., Williams 86046, tel. 602/635–2600), with tent and RV sites; **Grand Canyon Camper Village** (Box 490, Grand Canyon 86023, tel. 602/638–2887) in Tusayan, with RV and tent sites; and **Ten X Campground** (Kaibab National Forest, Tusayan Ranger District, Box 3088, Grand Canyon 86023, tel. 602/638–2443), with family sites.

Bottom of the Canyon **Phantom Ranch.** Dormitory accommodations for hikers and cabins for hikers and mule riders nestle in a grove of cottonwood trees at the bottom of the canyon. The restaurant has a limited menu, with meals served family style. Arrangements—and payment—for both food and lodging should be made nine to 11 months in advance. *Box 699, Grand Canyon 86023, tel. 602/638–2401 (reservations) or 602/638–2631. 4 dorms with shared bath, 11 cabins with outside shower. Facilities: dining room. AE, D, DC, MC, V. Inexpensive.*

Dining and Lodging

Camping **Indian Gardens,** about halfway down the canyon, and **Bright Angel,** closer to the bottom, are both free campgrounds; contact the Backcountry Reservations Office (*see* Sports and Outdoor Activities, *above*).

North Rim **Grand Canyon Lodge.** The premier lodging facility on the North Rim, this historic property offers comfortable though not luxurious accommodations in an extraordinary setting. The dining room is huge. *TW Recreational Services, Cedar City, UT 84721, tel. 801/586–7686. 40 rooms, 75 cabins (4 handicapped-accessible). Facilities: dining room, cafeteria, lounge, shop, visitor center. AE, D, DC, MC, V. Moderate.*

Dining and Lodging
★

Camping Inside the park, **North Rim Campground** (contact MISTIX; *see* Tourist Information, *above*) has RV and tent sites. Forest Service facilities outside the park include **Demotte Campground** (Kaibab National Forest, North Kaibab Ranger District, Box 248, Fredonia 86022, tel. 602/643–7395), with tent and RV sites.

Northeast Arizona

Most of northeast Arizona, a vast and lonely land of shifting red dunes and soaring buttes, belongs to the Navajo and Hopi peoples. Throughout the area, excellent Native American arts and crafts may be found in shops, galleries, and trading posts. Visitors are also welcome to observe certain ancient cultural traditions, such as Hopi ceremonial dances; however, the privacy, customs, and laws of the tribes should be respected. Within the stunning landscape of Navajo National Monument and Canyon de Chelly, both on the sprawling Navajo reservation, rest the mysterious ruins of the ancient Anasazi Indian tribes, who first wandered here thousands of years ago. Just below the southeastern boundary of the Navajo reservation, straddling I–40, is Petrified Forest National Park, an intriguing geologic open book of the Earth's distant past. Above the far northwestern corner of the Navajo reservation on U.S. 80 lies Glen Canyon Dam; behind it more than 120 mi of Lake Powell's emerald waters are held in precipitous canyons of erosion-carved stone.

Tourist Information

Glen Canyon Recreation Area (Box 1507, Page 86040, tel. 602/645–2511). **Hopi Tribe Office of Public Relations** (Box 123, Kykotsmovi 86039, tel. 602/734–2441). **Navajo Tourism Department** (Box 663, Window Rock 86505, tel. 602/871–6659 or 602/871–6436). **Page/Lake Powell:** Chamber of Commerce (Box 727, Page 86040, tel. 602/645–2741).

Getting There

By Plane   No major airlines fly directly to Indian country. You'll need to make flight connections in Phoenix (*see* Phoenix, *below*) to travel on either to Flagstaff's airport (*see* Grand Canyon National Park, *above*) or to **Page Municipal Airport** (tel. 602/645–2494) near Lake Powell.

By Car   From the east or west, I–40 passes through Flagstaff, a good entry point to the region. From the north or northwest, U.S. 89 brings you to Page. From the northeast, U.S. 64 leads west from Farmington, New Mexico.

A tour of Indian country involves driving long distances among widely scattered communities, so a detailed road map is essential. Especially recommended is the map of the northeast put out by the Navajo Tourism Department (*see* Tourist Information, *above*). In this sparsely populated area, service stations are rare, so be sure to take care of necessary maintenance before your trip. Never drive into dips or low-lying road areas during a heavy rainstorm; they could be flooded.

By Train   **Amtrak** makes scheduled stops in Flagstaff (tel. 602/774–8679), a good jumping-off point for a car trip into Indian country.

By Bus   **Greyhound** goes to Phoenix (tel. 602/248–4040) and Flagstaff (tel. 602/774–4573). Travel by the **Navajo Transit System** (tel. 602/729–5449), which has fixed routes throughout the reservation, is slow.

Exploring Northeast Arizona

Some 115 mi east of Flagstaff off I–40, **Petrified Forest National Park** is strewn with fossilized tree trunks whose wood cells were replaced over the centuries by brightly hued mineral deposits. The park's 94,000 acres include portions of the **Painted Desert,** a colorful but essentially barren and waterless series of windswept plains, hills, and mesas. *Box 450, HC 30, Concho 85924, tel. 602/524–6228. Admission charged.*

Northeast of the Petrified Forest, **Window Rock** is the capital of the Navajo Nation and the business and social center for families from the surrounding rural areas. Visit the **Navajo Nation Museum** (Rte. 264, next to Navajo Nation Inn, tel. 602/871–6673; admission free; closed weekends), devoted to Navajo art, culture, and history; and the adjoining **Navajo Arts and Crafts Enterprise** (*see* Shopping, *below*), displaying local works.

Northwest of Window Rock, **Canyon de Chelly** (pronounced "deh-SHAY"), nearly 84,000 acres, is one of the Southwest's most extraordinary national monuments. Ancient 1,000-year-old pictographs made by the Anasazi people decorate some of its sheer cliff walls, and gigantic stone formations rise hundreds of feet above small streams, hogans, tilled fields, peach orchards, and grazing lands. Paved rim drives offer marvelous views; there are also horseback tours of the canyon. *Box 588, Chinle 86503, tel. 602/674-5436. Admission free.*

At the approximate center of the Navajo reservation lies the 4,000-sq-mi **Hopi reservation,** a series of stone-and-adobe villages built on high mesas. On **First Mesa** is the town of **Walpi,** built on solid rock and surrounded by steep cliffs; its 30 residents live without electricity and running water.

In **Second Mesa's** oldest and largest village, **Shungopavi,** the famous Hopi snake dances—no longer open to the public—are held in August of even-numbered years. Also on Second Mesa is the **Hopi Cultural Center,** which features shops, a pueblo-style museum, and a good restaurant and motel (*see* Dining and Lodging, *below*). *Tel. 602/734-2401; museum tel. 602/734-6650. Admission charged to museum.*

Kykotsmovi, at the eastern base of **Third Mesa,** is known for its greenery and peach orchards and is the site of the Hopi Tribal Headquarters. Atop Third Mesa, **Oraibi,** established around AD 1150, is widely believed to be the oldest continuously inhabited community in the United States.

Monument Valley, on the Utah border north of Kayenta, will look familiar if you've seen any western films. This sprawling expanse of soaring red buttes, eroded mesas, deep canyons, and naturally sculpted rock formations was originally populated by the Anasazi and has been home to generations of Navajo. Within this vast area lies the 30,000-acre **Monument Valley Navajo Tribal Park,** which offers a scenic 17-mi self-guided tour. *Visitor center, off U.S. 163, 24 mi north of Kayenta, tel. 801/727-3287. Admission charged.*

At **Navajo National Monument,** southwest of Monument Valley, off U.S. 160, two unoccupied 13th-century cliff pueblos, **Keet Seel** and **Betatakin,** stand under the overhang of soaring orange and ocher cliffs. The largest Indian ruins in Arizona, these pueblos were built by the Anasazi, whose reasons for abandoning them prior to AD 1300 are still disputed by scholars. *HC71 Box 3, Tonalea 86044, tel. 602/672-2366. Admission free.*

For information on the creation of **Glen Canyon Dam** and **Lake Powell,** 136 mi north of Flagstaff on U.S. 89, stop at **Carl Hayden Visitor Center** (Glen Canyon Dam, tel. 602/645-2511). The best way to see eerie, man-made Lake Powell as it twists through rugged canyon country is by boat (*see* Sports and Outdoor Activities, *below*); take a half-day excursion to **Rainbow Bridge National Monument,** a 290-foot red sandstone arch that straddles one of the lake's coves.

Shopping

You may find exactly what you want, at a good price, from a roadside vendor, but the following have dependable selections of Native American wares. **Cameron Trading Post** (near the junction of U.S. 89 and Rte. 64, tel. 602/679-2231) is one of the

Camping   **Cottonwood Campground** (Canyon de Chelly National Monument, near visitor center; Box 588, Chinle 86503, tel. 602/674–
5436) has individual and group sites.

Hopi Reservation-   **Tunosvongya Restaurant.** Also known as the Hopi Cultural
Second Mesa   Center Restaurant, this clean, comfortable establishment fea-
Dining   tures traditional Native American dishes, including Indian
tacos, Hopi blue-corn pancakes, fry bread, and *nok qui vi* (Hopi
lamb stew). *Rte. 264, tel. 602/734–2401. DC, MC, V. Inexpensive.*

Lodging   **Hopi Cultural Center Motel.** This pleasant pueblo-style lodging
★   high atop a Hopi mesa offers immaculate rooms with white
walls and charming Native American decor. *Rte. 264, Box 67,
86043, tel. 602/734–2401. 33 units. Facilities: restaurant, gift
shop, museum. DC, MC, V. Moderate.*

Kayenta   **Holiday Inn.** Typical of the chain except for the southwestern
Lodging   decor, this accommodation near Monument Valley has comfortable rooms. It also has one of the few swimming pools in the
western end of Indian country. *South of junction U.S. 160 and
163; Box 307, 86033, tel. 602/697–3221. 160 rooms. Facilities:
restaurant, pool, gift shop. AE, D, DC, MC, V. Expensive.*
Wetherill Inn Motel. This clean and cheerful two-story motel
without frills was named for frontier explorer John Wetherill.
*U.S. 163, Box 175, 86033, tel. 602/697–3231. 54 rooms. Facili-
ties: nearby café, gift shop. AE, D, DC, MC, V. Moderate.*

Keams Canyon   **Keams Canyon Restaurant.** At this typical rural roadside din-
Dining   ing spot, you'll find American dishes and a few Native American items, including Navajo tacos. *Keams Canyon Shopping
Center (off Rte. 264), tel. 602/738–2296. MC, V. No dinner
weekends. Inexpensive.*

Lodging   **Keams Canyon Motel.** Conveniently located near the Hopi mesas and a shopping center, this clean motel has a rustic, trading-
post setting. Rooms are basic with a hint of Native American
decor; some units have kitchenettes. *Off Rte. 264, Box 188,
86034, tel. 602/738–2297. 20 units. MC, V. Inexpensive.*

Camping   **Keams Canyon Campground** (near Keams Canyon trading post
on Rte. 264, tel. 602/738–2297) offers free camping at two sites.

Lake Powell   **Rainbow Room in Wahweap Lodge.** You can't beat the panoram-
Dining   ic views of Lake Powell from this semicircular restaurant. An
extensive menu features southwestern, standard American,
and some Continental fare; specialties include coho salmon
with a Dijon-mustard cream sauce. *U.S. 89, 5 mi north of Page,
tel. 602/645–2433 or 800/528–6154. AE, D, DC, MC, V. Moderate.*

Lodging   **Wahweap Lodge.** On a promontory above Lake Powell, the
★   lodge serves as the center for area recreational activities. Many
guest rooms, nicely furnished in oak and southwestern colors,
have lake views. *U.S. 89, 5 mi north of Page; Box 1597, Page
86040, tel. 602/645–2433 or 800/528–6154. 350 rooms. Facilities: restaurant, cocktail lounge, gift shop, rental boats,
cruises, fishing and water-skiing equipment, river-rafting excursions, houseboats. AE, D, DC, MC, V. Expensive.*

Monument Valley, **Stagecoach Restaurant.** Large windows provide splendid views
Utah   of Monument Valley; the walls are decked with memorabilia
Dining   from movies shot in the area. The standard American fare is
★   well prepared and served. *Goulding's Lodge, 2 mi west of U.S.*

163, just north of UT border, tel. 801/727–3231 or 800/874–
0902. AE, DC, MC, V. Moderate.

Lodging **Goulding's Lodge.** Featuring cozy rooms with Navajo-design
bedspreads, Native American art, and spectacular views of
Monument Valley, this comfortable motel often serves as the
headquarters for film location crews. *2 mi west of U.S. 163, just
north of UT border; Box 1, Monument Valley, UT 84536, tel.
801/727–3231 or 800/874–0902. 62 rooms. Facilities: restaurant; Native American history museum and pool (both closed
Nov. 15–Mar. 15). AE, D, DC, MC, V. Expensive.*

Camping **Mitten View Campground** (Monument Valley Navajo Tribal
Park, near visitor center, tel. 801/727–3287) is open April–
November. **Good Sam Campground** (off U.S. 163, near Gould-
ing's Trading Post, tel. 801/727–3280) operates mid-March–
October.

Navajo National   **Navajo National Monument** (*see* Exploring Northeast Arizona,
Monument   *above*) has two campgrounds with free RV and tent sites that
Camping   are open May to October.

Window Rock   **Navajo Nation Inn.** Native American government officials fre-
Dining and Lodging   quent this motel in the Navajo Nation's tribal capital. Spanish
Colonial furniture and Navajo art decorate the rooms. The in-
expensive restaurant serves American and Navajo fare, includ-
ing fry-bread, tacos, and mutton stew. *North side of Rte. 264;
Box 2340, 86515, tel. 602/871–4108 or 800/662–6189. 56 units.
Facilities: restaurant, pool. AE, DC, MC, V. Moderate.*

Metropolitan Phoenix

America's newest, fastest-growing major urban center, metropolitan Phoenix lies at the northern tip of the Sonoran Desert
in the Valley of the Sun, named for its 330-plus days of sunshine
each year. Now-chic Scottsdale began in 1901 as "30-odd tents
and a half-dozen adobe houses" put up by seekers of the healthful desert air. Glendale and Peoria on the west side and Tempe,
Mesa, and Chandler on the east constitute the nation's third-
largest Silicon Valley. Excellent golf, shopping, and dining and
some of the best luxury resorts in the country make Phoenix
desirable as a vacation spot as well as a business destination.

Tourist Information

Phoenix: Chamber of Commerce (34 W. Monroe St., 85003, tel.
602/254–5521). **Phoenix and Valley of the Sun:** Convention and
Visitors Bureau (tel. 602/254–6500; Arizona Center, 400 E.
Van Buren St., Suite 600, Phoenix 85004, Hyatt Regency Phoenix, 2nd and Adams Sts.).

Arriving and Departing

By Plane   **Sky Harbor International Airport** (tel. 602/273–3300), 3 mi east
of downtown Phoenix, is home base for **America West** and a hub
for **Southwest.** It is also served by other major airlines. Tempe
is also 3 mi from the airport; Glendale and Mesa are 15 minutes
away, and Scottsdale and Sun City 30 to 45 minutes. **Phoenix
Transit** buses (tel. 602/253–5000) connect with downtown
Phoenix or Tempe for $1. A taxi trip to downtown Phoenix costs

from $6.50 to $12. **Supershuttle** vans (tel. 602/244–9000) charge at least 25% less than taxi fares for longer trips.

By Car From the west, you'll probably come to Phoenix on I–10. I–40 enters Arizona in the northwest; U.S. 93 continues to Phoenix. From the east, I–10 brings you from El Paso into Tucson, then north to Phoenix. The northeastern route, I–40 from Albuquerque, leads to Flagstaff, where I–17 goes south to Phoenix.

Train Station Amtrak (4th Ave. and Harrison St., tel. 602/253–0121).

Bus Station Greyhound (525 E. Washington St., tel. 602/248–4040).

Getting Around Metropolitan Phoenix

If you plan to see anything beyond Phoenix's, Scottsdale's, or Tempe's pedestrian-friendly downtowns, you will need a car.

Exploring Metropolitan Phoenix

A stroll through the east end of downtown Phoenix will take you to **Heritage Square,** a city-owned block of renovated turn-of-the-century houses in a parklike setting. Nearby, **The Mercado** (Van Buren St., between 5th and 7th Sts., tel. 602/256–6322), a brightly colored, neo-Aztec fantasy of a complex, has boutiques and gift shops, many selling Latin American handicrafts. Also downtown, the **Heard Museum** (22 E. Monte Vista Rd., tel. 602/252–8840; admission charged), set in a classic Arizona adobe house, is the nation's leading museum of Native American art and culture.

Nearby **Scottsdale**'s downtown is rich in historic sites, nationally known art galleries, and lots of clever boutiques. Historic Old Scottsdale, with its rustic storefronts and wooden sidewalks, features the look of the Old West.

In the Vicinity An hour's drive south of Phoenix, **Casa Grande Ruins National Monument** provides insight into the culture of the Hohokam Indians, who began farming in this area more than 1,500 years ago. *1 mi north of Coolidge on Rte. 87, tel. 602/723–3172. Admission charged.*

What to See and Do with Children

Children can get involved with the hands-on exhibits at the **Arizona Museum for Youth** (35 N. Robson St., Mesa, tel. 602/644–2467). Attractions in Phoenix's Papago Park include the **Hall of Flame** (6101 E. Van Buren St., tel. 602/275–3473), where retired fire fighters lead tours, and the **Phoenix Zoo** (5810 E. Van Buren St., tel. 602/273–7771). **Mystery Castle** (800 E. Mineral Rd., Phoenix, tel. 602/268–1581) is chock-full of amusing oddities.

Shopping

Most of the valley's shopping is concentrated in central Phoenix and downtown Scottsdale (5th Ave.), in charming boutiques and galleries. Among the best malls are **Park Central Mall** (Central Ave. and Earll Dr., Phoenix, tel. 602/264–5575), the oldest and closest to downtown Phoenix; **Metrocenter** (I–17 and Peoria Ave., Phoenix, tel. 602/997–2641), the state's largest; **Scottsdale Fashion Square** (Scottsdale and Camelback Rds.,

Scottsdale, tel. 602/990–7800), a step upscale; and **Biltmore Fashion Park** (24th St. and Camelback Rd., Phoenix, tel. 602/955–8400), even more exclusive.

Sports and Outdoor Activities

Golf   The Valley of the Sun is the valley of year-round golf par excellence. More than 100 courses, from par-3 to PGA championship links, are available. For a detailed listing, contact the **Arizona Golf Association** (11801 N. Tatum Blvd., Phoenix 85028, tel. 602/953–5990).

Spectator Sports

Baseball   Five major-league baseball teams train in the Phoenix area (Feb.–May). Contact the **Mesa Convention and Visitor's Bureau** (120 N. Center, Mesa 85201, tel. 602/969–1307) for information.

Golf   The PGA **Phoenix Open** (tel. 602/585–4334) is held each January at the Tournament Players Club in Scottsdale.

Rodeos   **The Parada del Sol** takes place each January (8102 E. Jackrabbit Rd., Scottsdale, tel. 602/990–3179). **The Rodeo of Rodeos** (4133 N. 7th St., Phoenix, tel. 602/263–8671) is one of the Southwest's oldest and best.

Dining

Steak houses, from cowboy to fancy, abound in the area, as do excellent Mexican restaurants. Lighter, spicier, and generally more upscale fare may be found in Phoenix at the numerous restaurants serving southwestern-international cuisine. For price ranges, see Chart 1 (B) in Chapter 1.

Expensive   **Christopher's.** Here a bistro worthy of the Champs-Élysées shares an open kitchen with an elegant, monogrammed-linen-and-silver modern restaurant. Classic fish, veal, and chicken are flawlessly cooked, sauced, and presented—with delightful southwestern touches. *2398 E. Camelback Rd., tel. 602/957–3214. Reservations required. Jacket and tie advised. AE, DC, MC, V.*

Compass Room. The southwestern fare matches the spectacular views at Hyatt Regency Phoenix's rotating-crown room. Cajun croutons (crusty fried oysters in a red-pepper mayonnaise) are among the offerings. *122 N. 2nd St., tel. 602/252–1234. Reservations required. Jacket and tie advised. AE, D, DC, MC, V.*

La Bruschetta. Into this tiny space is tucked a tasty bit of Tuscany. Good choices are the light Gorgonzola-sauced pasta or delicately tender squid. *4515 N. Scottsdale Rd., tel. 602/946–7236. Reservations required. Jacket advised. AE, MC, V. Closed Sun.*

La Hacienda. Set in the chichi Scottsdale Princess Resort, this lovely tile-roof hacienda shows what happens when Sonoran food goes haute cuisine. It doesn't get much better, amigo. *7575 E. Princess Dr., 1 mi north of Bell Rd., Scottsdale, tel. 602/585–4848. Reservations required. AE, DC, MC, V.*

Marquesa. In two soft-hued, intimate rooms at the Scottsdale Princess, Catalan food is given an exciting southwestern interpretation. The stunning presentations of such dishes as pimientos stuffed with crab match the flavors. *7575 E. Princess Dr., Scottsdale, tel. 602/585–4848. Reservations required. Jacket and tie advised. AE, DC, MC, V.*

★ **Vincent's on Camelback.** One of the handful of southwestern cuisine's originators, Vincent Guerithault is among the West's master chefs *extraordinaire.* His specialties include duck tacos and lobster with smoky *chipotle* chili pasta. *3930 E. Camelback Rd., tel. 602/224–0225. Reservations advised. Dress: neat but casual. AE, DC, MC, V.*

Moderate **Greekfest.** Greek cooking meets haute cuisine in a tasteful Athens-style taverna. The feather-light spinach-pie appetizers, the sweet and succulent lamb, and fresh stuffed grape leaves make a memorable meal. *1940 E. Camelback Rd., tel. 602/265–2990. Reservations advised. AE, DC, MC, V.*

Mint Thai. At this tiny, graceful place southeast of Mesa you'll find the valley's most varied Thai menu. The *rama* beef in peanut sauce, prepared with delicacy and power, is amazing. *1111 N. Gilbert Rd., Gilbert, tel. 602/497–5366. Reservations advised on weekends. AE, MC, V.*

Rustler's Rooste. Decorated in a playful miner-cowpoke style, this droll western restaurant offers excellent steaks, juicy barbecued ribs and chicken, and homemade ice cream. *7777 S. Pointe Pkwy., tel. 602/231–9111. Reservations advised. AE, D, DC, MC, V.*

Inexpensive **Adrian's.** At this local favorite spot, set in a modest creek-rock building with wrought-iron grilles and a tiny outdoor patio, you'll find coastal Mexican dishes as well as excellent Sonoran fare. *2234 E. McDowell Rd., tel. 602/273–7957. No reservations. No credit cards.*

★ **Los Dos Molinos.** Don't come for atmosphere but for pure, hot New Mexico-style cooking: delicious rancho barbecue, multitextured *chilaquiles* (layered tortillas, cheeses, and homemade chili sauce), and other spicy delights. *Three locations: 1156 W. Main St., Mesa, tel. 602/890–1180; 260 S. Alma School Rd., Mesa, tel. 602/835–5356; 8646 S. Central Ave., Phoenix, tel. 602/243–9113. No reservations. No credit cards.*

Lodging

Famous for its world-class resorts, metropolitan Phoenix has a considerable array of lodging options, from luxury and executive hotels to no-frills roadside motels. For price ranges, see Chart 2 (B) in Chapter 1.

Expensive **The Buttes.** This is the Phoenix area's best hotel buy, joining
★ dramatic architecture, classic Southwest design, and stunning valley views. The rooms are moderate in size and comfortable. *2000 Westcourt Way, Tempe 85282, tel. 602/225–9000 or 800/843–1986. 353 rooms. Facilities: 2 restaurants, pool, health club, saunas, shops, airport shuttle. AE, D, DC, MC, V.*

Hilton Suites. A new, more luxurious version of the frequent-traveler suites concept, this property, close to downtown, is likely to become a classic. The design is modern, colorful, and bold. *10 E. Thomas Rd., Phoenix 85012, tel. 602/222–1111. 226 suites. Facilities: restaurant, bar, pool, exercise room, sauna, gift shop. AE, D, DC, MC, V.*

★ **Ritz-Carlton.** This sand-colored, neo-Federal mid-rise facing Biltmore Fashion Park mall hides a well-appointed luxury hotel that pampers the traveler. A compact, elegant health club and the daily high tea are highlights. *2401 E. Camelback Rd., Phoenix 85016, tel. 602/468–0700. 281 rooms, 14 suites. Facilities: 2 restaurants, 2 bars, pool, 2 saunas, tennis courts, concierge, gift shop, valet parking. AE, D, DC, MC, V.*

Moderate ★ **Best Western Executive Park.** One of downtown's hidden jewels, this small facility is simply but elegantly decorated. Prints by southwestern masters accent unpainted antique reproductions. *1100 N. Central Ave., Phoenix 85004, tel. 602/252–2100 or 800/426–0670. 105 rooms. Facilities: restaurant, bar, pool, health club, sauna. AE, D, DC, MC, V.*

Camelback Courtyard by Marriott. This four-story hostelry delivers compact elegance in its public areas and no-frills comfort in its rooms and suites. *2101 E. Camelback Rd., Phoenix 85016, tel. 602/955–5200 or 800/321–2211. 155 rooms, 11 suites. Facilities: restaurant, bar, exercise room, pool, spa. AE, D, DC, MC, V.*

Doubletree Suites. A mile north of the airport, this is the best of a dozen nearby choices. Suites are modest in size, with rose, blue-gray, and Navajo white furnishings. *320 N. 44th St., Phoenix 85008, tel. 602/225–0500 or 800/528–0444. 242 suites. Facilities: restaurant, bar-lounge, pool, health club, sauna, 2 tennis courts, shops, free airport shuttle. AE, D, DC, MC, V.*

Inexpensive **Ambassador Inn.** Close to the airport and shopping and recreational facilities, this cheerful hotel is set around an enclosed courtyard with a fountain. *4727 E. Thomas Rd., Phoenix 85018, tel. 602/840–7500 or 800/624–6759. 170 rooms. Facilities: restaurant, bar, pool, spa. AE, D, DC, MC, V.*

Motel 6 Scottsdale. Though amenities aren't a priority here, the best bargain in Scottsdale lodging is steps away from Scottsdale Fashion Square and Camelview Plaza, and close to the specialty shops of 5th Avenue. *6848 E. Camelback Rd., Scottsdale 85251, tel. 602/946–2280. 122 rooms. Facilities: pool, spa. AE, D, DC, MC, V.*

Resorts For price ranges, see Chart 2 (A) in Chapter 1.

Very Expensive ★ **Hyatt Regency Scottsdale at Gainey Ranch.** Modern and dramatic, this is Scottsdale's finest resort. Gondolas on a manmade lagoon and hot-air balloons are among the unusual diversions. *7500 E. Doubletree Ranch Rd., Scottsdale 85258, tel. 602/991–3388. 493 rooms. Facilities: 3 restaurants, lounge, 10 pools, 8 tennis courts, 3 golf courses, health club, concierge floor. AE, D, DC, MC, V.*

The Pointe Hilton on South Mountain. The Southwest's largest resort, it's also the most convenient—close to the airport, downtown Phoenix, and the eastern valley. Accommodations are lavishly designed and decorated. *7777 S. Pointe Pkwy., Phoenix 85044, tel. 602/438–9000 or 800/528–0428. 950 suites. Facilities: 4 restaurants, 3 pools, health center, saunas, stable, tennis, golf, hiking trails, shops, airport shuttle. AE, D, DC, MC, V.*

The Arts and Nightlife

Cultural and entertainment events are listed in the weekly *New Times* newspaper, distributed Wednesday; the Friday and Sunday Life & Leisure sections of *The Arizona Republic;* and the Marquee section of Saturday's *Phoenix Gazette.*

The Arts Downtown Phoenix's **Symphony Hall** (225 E. Adams St., tel. 602/262–7272) and **Herberger Theater Center** (222 E. Monroe St., tel. 602/252–8497) are home to many performing-arts groups. The developing "cultural district" 2 mi north, around Deck Park, offers several more.

Nightlife Nightclubs, restaurants, and upscale bars in **The Mercado** and in the **Arizona Center** in downtown Phoenix compete with lively resorts and clubs in Scottsdale and with those along Camelback Road in north-central Phoenix.

Tucson and Southern Arizona

Arizona's second-largest city, Tucson feels like a small town, albeit one enriched by its deep Hispanic and Old West roots. With its large university and myriad resorts, the city affords visitors many cultural and recreational options. It's also the gateway to southern Arizona, a relatively undiscovered treasure of mountains, deserts, canyons, and dusty little cowboy towns. Of particular interest are Bisbee and Tombstone, which give the visitor a taste of what Arizona was like in its mining and cowboy heydays.

Tourist Information

Metropolitan Tucson: Convention and Visitors Bureau (130 S. Scott Ave., Tucson, 85701, tel. 602/624–1817 or 800/638–8350). **Bisbee:** Chamber of Commerce (Drawer BA, 85603, tel. 602/432–5421). **Tombstone:** Tourist Association (Allen and 4th Sts., 85603, tel. 602/457–3939).

Getting There

By Plane **Tucson International Airport** (tel. 602/573–8000), 8½ mi south of downtown, is served by nine domestic and international airlines.

By Car From Phoenix, 111 mi northwest, or from the east, take I–10 to Tucson. From the south, take I–19. East of Tucson, U.S. 80 cuts south from I–10 to Tombstone and Bisbee.

By Train **Amtrak** (400 E. Toole Ave., tel. 602/623–4442) serves Tucson and vicinity.

By Bus **Greyhound** (2 S. 4th Ave. at E. Broadway, tel. 602/792–0972) serves the Tucson area. **Arizona Shuttle Service** (tel. 602/795–6771) runs express buses from Phoenix to Tucson.

Exploring Tucson and Southern Arizona

With weather more temperate than that of its rival city, Phoenix (it's higher in altitude, so not as hot in summer), **Tucson** of-

Tucson

fers outdoor activities year-round, as well as historical tours. The city covers more than 500 sq mi in a valley ringed by mountains, so a car is necessary. Downtown, accessible just east of I–10 off the Broadway-Congress exit, is easy to navigate on foot.

The **Presidio district** in downtown Tucson encompasses more than 130 years of the city's architectural history, including the original walled **El Presidio del Tucson**—a Spanish fortress built in 1776 when Arizona was still part of New Spain.

The city divides the **Saguaro National Monument** (tel. 602/883–6366) into two sections; the one west of town is the most heavily visited. Both are forested by the huge saguaro cactus, a native of the Sonoran Desert that is known for its towering height (often 50 ft) and arms that reach out in weird configurations.

Near Saguaro National Monument West, the **Arizona-Sonora Desert Museum** is the state's second most popular tourist attraction (after the Grand Canyon). In this desert microcosm, birds and animals busy themselves in a natural habitat ingeniously planned to allow the visitor to look on without disturbing them. *2021 N. Kinney Rd., tel. 602/883–2702. Admission charged.*

Some 10 mi north of Tucson, visitors with reservations can view the controversial, privately funded **Biosphere 2** experiment. In an exercise in recycling on a grand scale, eight people have set up housekeeping for two years in an enclosed 3-acre environment. *Off Rte. 77, Oracle, tel. 602/825–6200 or 800/828–2462. Admission charged.*

Just southwest of Tucson, the 1692 **Mission San Xavier del Bac** (off I–19, San Xavier Rd., tel. 602/294–2624) is the oldest Catholic church in the United States still serving the community for which it was built: the Tohono O'odham Indian tribe. Inside this beautiful Spanish/Moorish-style structure is a wealth of painted statues, carvings, and frescoes.

On U.S. 80, 67 mi southeast of Tucson, is **Tombstone.** Born on the site of a wildly successful silver mine, the town was headquarters of many of the West's rowdies in the late 1800s. The famous shoot-out at the OK Corral and other gunfights are replayed on Sunday on the town's main drag, **Allen Street.** As you enter Tombstone from the northwest, you'll pass **Boot Hill Graveyard,** where the victims of the OK Corral shoot-out are buried. The **Tombstone Courthouse State Historic Park** (Toughnut and 3rd Sts., tel. 602/457–3311; admission charged) offers an excellent introduction to the town's past.

Once a mining boomtown, **Bisbee,** set on a mountainside 24 mi south of Tombstone, is now an artists' colony. Arizona's largest pit mine yielded some 94 million tons of copper ore before mining activity halted in the early 1970s; at the **Lavender Pit Mine** you can still see the huge crater left by the process. The **Mining and Historical Museum** (Queens Plaza, tel. 602/432–7071; admission charged) is filled with old photos and artifacts from the town's heyday. Behind the museum is the venerable **Copper Queen Hotel** (*see* Dining and Lodging, *below*), home away from home to such guests as "Black Jack" Pershing, John Wayne, and Teddy Roosevelt.

The **Copper Queen mine tour** (1 Dart Rd., tel. 602/432–2071), led by retired miners, is an entertaining way to learn about the town's history.

What to See and Do with Children

Children will enjoy the **Arizona–Sonora Desert Museum** (*see* Exploring Tucson and Southern Arizona, *above*) and nearby **Old Tucson Studios** (201 S. Kinney Rd., in Tucson Mountain County Park, tel. 602/883–6457), a film set cum theme park where more than 250 westerns have been shot over the past 50 years.

Shopping

In Tucson, **Desert House Crafts** (2837 N. Campbell Ave., tel. 602/323–2132) and the **Kaibab Shops** next door (tel. 602/795–6905) carry a broad selection of fine southwestern crafts and clothing.

Hard-core bargain hunters usually head for **Nogales**, the Mexican border town 63 mi south of Tucson on I–19. For work by regional artists, try the **Tubac** artists' community, 45 mi south of Tucson, just off I–19 at Exit 34.

Sports and Outdoor Activities

Ballooning **Balloon America** (Box 31255, Tucson 85751, tel. 602/299–7744). **A Southern Arizona Balloon Excursion** (Box 5265, Tucson 85703, tel. 602/624–3599).

Bicycling There are many good bike paths in Tucson and the surrounding areas. **The Greater Arizona Bicycling Association** (Box 43273, Tucson 85733, tel. 602/885–8807) offers a hotline announcing group rides open to visitors.

Golf Tucson has five **municipal golf courses** (Tucson Parks and Recreation Dept., tel. 602/791–4873), as well as many excellent **resort courses,** such as those at Loews Ventana Canyon (tel. 602/299–2020), Tucson National Golf and Conference Resort (tel. 602/297–2271), Westin La Paloma (tel. 602/742–6000), and Sheraton Tucson El Conquistador (for the last, *see* Dining and Lodging, *below*). For information about other courses in the area, contact the **Arizona Golf Association** (11801 N. Tatum Blvd., Phoenix 85028, tel. 602/953–5990).

Hiking Day trips from Tucson that offer good hiking opportunities include **Tucson Mountain County Park, Mt. Lemmon,** and **Kitt Peak.** Directly south of Tucson are the Huachuca Mountains, home of **Ramsey Canyon,** a bird-watcher's paradise. The Santa Ritas, near Tucson, host another bird lovers' haven, **Madera Canyon.**

Horseback Riding Tucson stables include **Desert-High Country Stables** (6501 W. Ina Rd., tel. 602/744–3789), **Pantano Stables** (4450 S. Houghton Rd., tel. 602/298–9076), and **Pusch Ridge Stables** (11220 N. Oracle Rd., tel. 602/297–6908).

Dining and Lodging

For price ranges, see Charts 1 (B) and 2 (B) in Chapter 1.

Bisbee
Dining
★

Stenzel's. Set in a rustic wood cabin, Stenzel's serves up good ribs and grilled chicken and outstanding fettuccine Alfredo. Try the excellent Electric ale, brewed locally. *207 Tombstone Canyon, tel. 602/432–7611. No credit cards. Moderate.*

The Wine Gallery Bistro. A favorite of local yuppies, this cozy little place in one of Bisbee's venerable old buildings features tasty homemade soups at lunch. The wine list is excellent. *41 Main St., tel. 602/432–3447. No credit cards. Moderate.*

Lodging

Clawson B&B. Terrific views of town from the sun porch, a light-filled kitchen, and generous but healthy breakfasts are among the reasons to seek out this B&B on Old Bisbee's Castle Rock. *116 Clawson Ave., Box 454, 85603, tel. 602/432–5237. 3 rooms (2 share bath). MC, V. Moderate.*

★

Copper Queen Hotel. Almost 100 years old, this hotel in the heart of downtown has tiny rooms and thin walls but a lot of Victorian charm. The boom-days memorabilia throughout is fascinating. *11 Howell Ave., Drawer CQ, 85603, tel. 602/432–2216 or 800/247–5829. 43 rooms. Facilities: dining room, saloon, pool. AE, MC, V. Moderate.*

Tombstone
Dining

Longhorn Restaurant. Set up to look like an old saloon, the Longhorn is decorated with posters and artifacts from Tombstone's wilder days. Burgers, sandwiches, and the usual middle-of-the-road American food are served. *Allen and 5th Sts., tel. 602/457–3405. MC, V. Inexpensive.*

Lodging

Best Western Look-Out Lodge. This motel off U.S. 80 on the way into town has a lot of character. Rooms have western-print bedspreads, Victorian-style lamps, and views of the Dragoon Mountains and desert valley. *U.S. 80 W., Box 787, 85638, tel. 602/457–2223. 40 rooms. AE, D, DC, MC, V. Moderate.*

Buford House B&B. Built as a boarding house in 1880, this Territorial-style adobe structure has four attractively decorated theme rooms (of course, one is southwestern). Murder-mystery weekends and chuckwagon-cookout packages are offered. *113 E. Safford St., Box 38, 85638, tel. 602/457–3168 or 800/355–1880. 4 rooms (3 share bath). Facilities: hot tub, barbecue area. No credit cards. Moderate.*

Tucson
Dining
★

Janos. This historic Presidio district restaurant offers delightfully innovative southwestern cuisine, such as grilled ahi with green-chili pasta. Come here for a special, big-splurge evening. *150 N. Main Ave., tel. 602/884–9426. Reservations advised. AE, D, MC, V. Closed Sun. Nov.–mid-May; Sun.–Mon. mid-May–Oct. Expensive.*

The Tack Room. This gracious and romantic Continental restaurant has won many local awards. Arizona steak flavored with four types of mild peppercorns is a favorite. *2800 N. Sabino Canyon Rd., tel. 602/722–2800. Reservations advised. Jacket advised. AE, D, DC, MC, V. Closed 1st 2 weeks of July; Mon. mid-May–mid-Dec. Expensive.*

★

Café Terra Cotta. Everything about this restaurant says Southwest, from the decor to the food. Contemporary specialties include prawns stuffed with herbed goat cheese, and pork tenderloin with black beans. *4310 N. Campbell Ave., tel. 602/577–8100. Reservations advised. AE, D, DC, MC, V. Moderate.*

Pinnacle Peak Steakhouse. Tourists love this cowboy steak house—it's fun, it's Tucson, and the food ain't half bad either. *6541 E. Tanque Verde Rd., tel. 602/296–0911. No reservations. D, DC, MC, V. Moderate.*

★ **Café Poca Cosa.** This colorful and lively restaurant tucked into a corner of the Park Inn/Santa Rita's lobby is cheerful and thoroughly Mexican. Ingredients are fresh, and service is excellent. *88 E. Broadway, tel. 602/622–6400. Reservations advised for large parties. MC, V. No dinner Sun. Inexpensive.*

Jack's Original Bar-B-Q. If you like your Southwest cuisine messy and in big portions, this is the place. Jack's ribs are smoky, meaty, and without equal in these parts. *5250 E. 22nd St., tel. 602/750–1280. No reservations. No credit cards. Inexpensive.*

Lodging
★ **Arizona Inn.** Although this landmark 1930s-era inn is close to the university and downtown, it is secluded on 14 acres of lushly landscaped grounds. All rooms have patios and lovely period furnishings. *2200 E. Elm St., 85719, tel. 602/325–1541. 80 rooms. Facilities: restaurant, lounge, pool, 2 tennis courts, library, gift shop. AE, MC, V. Expensive.*

★ **Casa Tierra.** For a real desert experience, come to this B&B on 5 acres near Saguaro National Monument. Rooms in the beamed-ceiling adobe house are arranged around a garden courtyard. *11155 W. Calle Pima, 85743, tel. 602/578–3058. 3 rooms. Facilities: hot tub. No credit cards. Closed June–Aug. Moderate.*

Embassy Suites Tucson–Broadway. This centrally located hotel offers two-room suites (with kitchenette) opening onto a plant-filled atrium. Extras include a free cooked-to-order breakfast and complimentary happy hour. *5335 E. Broadway, 85711, tel. 602/745–2700 or 800/545–8858. 142 suites. Facilities: outdoor heated pool. AE, D, DC, MC, V. Moderate.*

★ **The Lodge on the Desert.** Although the ambience is that of an exclusive Mexican hacienda, prices at this little hotel are very reasonable. Many rooms have fireplaces. *306 N. Alvernon Way, Box 42500, 85733, tel. 602/325–3366 or 800/456–5634. 37 rooms. Facilities: restaurant, cocktail lounge, pool. AE, D, DC, MC, V. Moderate.*

Peppertrees. This establishment by the University of Arizona campus occupies two southwestern-style guesthouses in back of a restored Victorian main house well shaded by trees. Host Marjorie Martin prepares elaborate morning repasts. *724 E. University Blvd., 85719, tel. 602/622–7167. 5 rooms (4 share baths). Facilities: landscaped patio. MC, V. Moderate.*

Park Inn/Santa Rita. Conveniently located near the arts district and across from the visitor center, this hotel has ordinary rooms but a good restaurant (*see* Café Poca Cosa, *above*). *88 E. Broadway, 85701, tel. 602/622–4000 or 800/437–7275. 165 rooms. Facilities: restaurant, pool, whirlpool, sauna. AE, D, DC, MC, V. Inexpensive.*

Ranches
Tanque Verde Ranch. One of the country's oldest guest ranches covers more than 600 acres in the beautiful Rincon Mountains. The rooms are furnished in tasteful southwestern style; most have patios and fireplaces. Rates include meals. *14301 E. Speedway Blvd., 85748, tel. 602/296–6275. 65 rooms. Facilities: restaurant, indoor and outdoor pools, tennis courts, spa, exercise room, horseback riding. AE, D, MC, V. Expensive.*

★ **Westward Look Resort.** Set on 80 acres in the Santa Catalina foothills, Westward Look was refurbished in 1993. Either a city or a mountain view is available from the well-appointed rooms spread across the grounds. *245 E. Ina Rd., 85704, tel. 602/297–1151 or 800/722–2500. 244 rooms. Facilities: 2 restaurants,* *lounge, 2 pools, spas, tennis courts. AE, D, DC, MC, V. Expensive.*

White Stallion Ranch. Many scenes from the television show *High Chaparral* were shot on this family-run ranch, set on 3,000 desert mountain acres. Rates include meals. Rooms are southwestern ranch-style. The food is excellent, with great chicken and veal dishes and some Mexican specialties. *9251 W. Twin Peaks Rd., 85743, tel. 602/297–0252 or 800/782–5546. 30 rooms. Facilities: pool, tennis, volleyball, horseback riding, petting zoo. No credit cards. Closed May–Sept. Expensive.*

Resort   **Sheraton Tucson El Conquistador.** This friendly golf and tennis resort is nestled in the foothills of the Santa Catalinas. Both private casitas and the main hotel building offer appealing rooms in light woods and pastels. Biosphere 2 (*see* Exploring Tucson and Southern Arizona, *above*) is just up the road. *10000 N. Oracle Rd., 85737, tel. 602/742–7000 or 800/325–7832. 438 rooms. Facilities: 5 restaurants, golf, tennis, racquetball, horseback riding, 2 pools, fitness center, sauna, whirlpool. AE, D, DC, MC, V. Expensive.*

Spa   For price range, *see* Chart 2 (A) in Chapter 1.

Canyon Ranch. At this well-known health spa surrounded by spectacular desert scenery, guests are pampered while shaping up in the rigorous program. The food is unobtrusively healthful, and rooms are luxuriously furnished in muted southwestern tones. *8600 E. Rockcliff Rd., 85715, tel. 602/749–9000. 112 rooms, 41 suites. Facilities: restaurant, 2 pools, racket and ball courts, extensive workout equipment, spa complex, health center. D, MC, V. Very Expensive.*

Campgrounds   The public campground closest to Tucson is at **Catalina State Park** (11570 N. Oracle Rd., tel. 602/628–5798). Recreational vehicles can park in any number of facilities around town; the **Metropolitan Tucson Convention and Visitors Bureau** (*see* Tourist Information, *above*) can provide information about specific locations.

The Arts and Nightlife

The Arts   The **Tucson Symphony Orchestra** (tel. 602/882–8585) and the **Arizona Opera Company** (tel. 602/293–4336) perform in the Tucson Convention Center's Music Hall (260 S. Church St., tel. 602/791–4836). The **Arizona Theatre Company** is at Tucson's Temple of Music and Art (330 S. Scott Ave., tel. 602/622–2823) September through May.

Nightlife   In Tucson, **Cactus Moon** (5740 E. Broadway, tel. 602/748–0049), **Maverick** (4702 E. 22nd St., tel. 602/748–0456), and **Wild Wild West** (4385 W. Ina Rd., tel. 602/744–7744) are lively country-western nightclubs.

Elsewhere in the State

Sedona

Getting There   Sedona is 125 mi north of downtown Phoenix and 27 mi south of Flagstaff, at the southern end of Oak Creek Canyon on U.S. 89A.

What to See and Do Sedona is perhaps the most attractive stopover en route north from Phoenix to the Grand Canyon. Startling formations of deep-red rocks poke holes in what is almost always a clear blue sky—made to seem even bluer by the dark green of the forests. An art colony, Sedona is also a center of interest to New Age enthusiasts, who believe the area contains important vortices (energy centers).

In the town itself, shopping is the main activity; **Tlaquepaque Mall** (Rte. 179, tel. 602/282–4838) offers the largest concentration of upscale shops. The **Chapel of the Holy Cross** (Chapel Rd., tel. 602/282–4069) is worth a visit for its striking architecture and stunning vistas.

Scenic hiking spots include **Red Rock State Park** (tel. 602/282–6907), 5 mi southwest of Sedona, and **Slide Rock State Park** (*see* National and State Parks, *above*), 7 mi to the north in Oak Creek Canyon. **Jerome,** about 30 mi southwest on U.S. 89A, is a former mining boomtown perched on Cleopatra Hill; come here for outstanding views and for rows of funky boutiques. For information on the area, contact **Sedona–Oak Creek Canyon Chamber of Commerce** (North U.S. 89A and Forest Rd.; Box 478, Sedona 86339, tel. 602/282–7722 or 800/288–7336).

Dining **L'Auberge de Sedona.** One of the most romantic restaurants in Arizona, L'Auberge is done in country-French style; ask for a table overlooking the stream. The six-course prix-fixe menu ($55) might include wild game consommé with duck ravioli or filet mignon with foie gras, wild mushrooms, and truffle sauce. *L'Auberge La., tel. 602/282–1667. Reservations required. Jacket required. AE, D, DC, MC, V. Expensive.*

Heartline Café. This pretty, plant-filled café serves American food with a southwestern flavor, such as grilled salmon marinated in tequila and lime. A sampler for two allows you and your companion to try all the luscious desserts on the menu. *1610 W. U.S. 89A, tel. 602/282–0785. Reservations advised. Dress: neat but casual. AE, D, MC, V. No lunch Sun. Moderate.*

Lodging ★ **Enchantment Resort.** Set in spectacular Boynton Canyon, Enchantment has excellent sports facilities. All rooms are in pueblo-style casitas and have dazzling views of the surrounding forest and canyons; many offer fireplaces and kitchenettes, and two have private pools. *525 Boynton Canyon Rd., 86336, tel. 602/282–2900 or 800/826–4180. 162 rooms. Facilities: 2 restaurants, 4 pools, tennis courts, hiking, 6-hole golf course, fitness and health centers, lounge. AE, D, DC, MC, V. Expensive.*

★ **Sky Ranch Lodge.** An excellent value in an expensive town, the lodge has simply furnished rooms with southwestern touches, such as Mexican tiles surrounding the dressers. Some have fireplaces and others balconies offering terrific views of Sedona's red-rock canyons. *Airport Rd., Box 2579, 86336, tel. 602/282–6400. 92 rooms (20 with kitchenettes), 2 cottages. Facilities: pool, whirlpool. MC, V. Moderate.*

Flagstaff

Getting There Flagstaff is 80 mi south of the Grand Canyon, at the junction of I–40 and I–17.

What to See and Do The largest city in north-central Arizona, Flagstaff is set against a lovely backdrop of pine forests and the snowcapped San Francisco Peaks. The gateway to the Grand Canyon, the city is burgeoning with motels and fast-food places. The **downtown historic district,** near the Santa Fe railroad station, offers a glimpse of the city in its prime, as does the huge **Riordan Mansion** (1300 Riordan Ranch Rd., tel. 602/779–4395), built by two lumber-baron brothers. The **Lowell Observatory** (1400 W. Mars Hill, tel. 602/774–2096) offers educational programs on the night sky and allows visitors to peer through its 24-inch telescope on some evenings (schedules vary seasonally).

Five miles north of town on U.S. 180 is the exit for **Arizona Snowbowl** (tel. 602/779–1951), a ski lodge with fine skiing in winter; come in summer for excellent views and good hiking trails. In a lovely pine forest about 10 mi southeast of Flagstaff on I–40 is **Walnut Canyon** (Walnut Canyon Rd., tel. 602/526–3367), site of 14th-century Anasazi cliff dwellings. The 2,000-sq-mi San Francisco Volcanic Field, about 20 mi north of Flagstaff on U.S. 89, is home to **Sunset Crater Volcano National Monument** (tel. 602/556–7042) and the adjacent **Wupatki National Monument** (tel. 602/556–7040), both well worth visiting for their beauty as well as for their windows onto the area's geologic and Native American history.

The **Flagstaff Visitors Center** (101 W. Rte. 66, tel. 602/774–9541 or 800/842–7293) has information on the area.

Dining
★
Cottage Place. This elegant restaurant in a homey little 1920s cottage has a classic Continental menu with innovative touches. Try the stuffed-mushroom appetizer and the Turkish-style braised-lamb casserole. *126 W. Cottage Ave., tel. 602/774–8431. Reservations advised. AE, MC, V. No lunch; closed Mon. Moderate.*

Café Olé. This tiny, family-run Mexican restaurant downtown offers freshly made burritos, tacos, and tostadas in reasonably priced combinations. The spicy Cave Creek chili beer, with its huge peppers, will knock your socks off. *119 S. San Francisco St., tel. 602/774–8272. No credit cards. Closed weekends in winter, Sun. in summer. Inexpensive.*

Lodging
Inn at Four Ten. This quiet but convenient downtown B&B offers several spacious two-room suites in a beautifully restored 1907 building. A full breakfast is served. *410 N. Leroux St., 86001, tel. 602/774–0088 or 602/775–1424. 6 suites, 1 wheelchair-accessible room, 2 rooms share a bath. No smoking. No credit cards. Moderate.*

Little America of Flagstaff. Rooms in this popular hotel on wooded grounds are surprisingly plush, with brass chandeliers and French Provincial–style furnishings. It's one of the few places in town that offer room service. *2515 E. Butler Ave., Box 850, 86002, tel. 602/779–2741 or 800/352–4386. 248 rooms. Facilities: restaurant, 24-hr coffee shop, cocktail lounge, pool, courtesy van, garage. AE, D, DC, MC, V. Moderate.*

NEVADA

Updated by
Bobbi Zane

Capital	Carson City
Population	1,300,000
Motto	Battle Born
State Bird	Mountain bluebird
State Flower	Sagebrush

Visitor Information

Nevada Commission on Tourism (Capitol Complex, Carson City 89710, tel. 800/237–0774).

Scenic Drives

The Loneliest Road in the World is Rte. 50, in the northern part of the state from Fallon to Eureka. **Rte. 93** north from Las Vegas goes through **Great Basin National Park,** where you will see 13,061-foot **Wheeler Peak,** the highest point in the state. For a good look at the southwest desert, particularly in the spring, take **U.S. 93/95** south from Las Vegas, turning east onto Rte. 147 in Henderson, which takes you through the Lake Mead National Recreation Area to the Valley of Fire State Park (*see* Las Vegas, *below*).

National and State Parks

National Parks **Great Basin National Park** (off U.S. 93 at the Nevada–Utah border, Baker 89311, tel. 702/234–7331) is 77,092 acres of dramatic mountains, lush meadows, alpine lakes, limestone caves, and a stand of bristlecone pines (the oldest living trees in the world), with many areas for camping, hiking, and picnicking.

State Parks For information on Nevada state parks, contact the state tourism office (*see* Visitor Information, *above*). **Washoe Lake State Recreation Area** (4855 E. Lake Blvd., off U.S. 395, Carson City 89701, tel. 702/687–4319) is popular for fishing and horseback riding, with views of the majestic Sierra Nevada.

Las Vegas

Las Vegas exists for one reason: gambling. Its name, meaning "the meadows," was given to it by a Spanish scouting party who found a spring here in the 1820s. Mormons settled here briefly in 1855, but until the turn of the century, it was little more than a watering hole for the Union Pacific train that ran from Los Angeles to Salt Lake City. Las Vegas finally began to grow when lots were auctioned off in 1905. The construction of Hoover Dam in the 1930s brought a new wave of settlers seeking jobs.

The Las Vegas that we know today began shortly after World War II when mobster Benjamin "Bugsy" Siegel decided to build a gambling resort in the desert. (Gambling had been legalized in the state in 1931.) Naming it the Flamingo after his redheaded girlfriend, Virginia Hill, Bugsy built it with the money of fellow mobsters who, when the Flamingo flopped, rubbed him out. The resort eventually recovered and casino-hotels on the Las Vegas Strip caught on, and now the city is home to most of the largest hotels in the world.

Tourist Information

Las Vegas: Chamber of Commerce (711 E. Desert Inn Rd., 89101, tel. 702/737–2011). Convention & Visitors Authority (3150 Paradise Rd., 89109, tel. 702/892–0711).

Arriving and Departing

By Plane **McCarran International Airport** (tel. 702/739–5743), about a mile from the south end of the Strip, is served by major airlines. Taxi fare from the airport to Strip hotels is about $8–$10; to the downtown hotels, about $15. But the best and least expensive way to reach your hotel ($3–$4 per person) is by **Bell Trans Limousine** (tel. 702/736–4428), which you will find near the taxis.

By Car Major highways leading into Las Vegas are I–15 from Los Angeles and Salt Lake City, U.S. 95 from Reno, and U.S. 93 from Arizona.

Train Station **Amtrak** serves downtown's Union Station (1 N. Main St., tel. 702/386–6896).

Bus Station **Greyhound** (200 S. Main St., tel. 702/382–2640).

Getting Around Las Vegas

Taxis, which can easily be found in front of every hotel, are the best way to get around the city. The **Strip bus** (Las Vegas Transit, tel. 702/384–3540; fare, $1.25) links the Strip and the downtown, with stops at major hotels. If you want to drive out of town or explore the desert, you can rent a car, but be sure to gas up before you go; you won't find many stations out there.

Exploring Las Vegas

As Las Vegas is a relatively small city, it's easy to explore. But a primary caution: During the extremely hot months of June, July, and August, exploring on foot for any length of time is not recommended.

While the **downtown** is only four blocks long, this is the most brightly lighted four blocks in the world, and it is best seen at night, when it comes alive. If you recognize this stretch, it is because you have seen it in so many movies. The focal point of the downtown is Jackie Gaughan's **Jackie Gowan's Plaza Hotel and Casino** (1 N. Main St.), built on the site of the old Union Pacific train station. Walk through the casino and you will find the only train station in the world that is actually inside a casino.

Among the downtown hotel-casinos, the **Golden Nugget** (129 E. Fremont St.) has a particularly attractive lobby where you can see an enormous, 63-pound gold nugget. **Binion's Horseshoe** (128 E. Fremont St.) is an old-fashioned gambling joint that has a display of $1 million in cash. The **Four Queens Hotel** (202 E. Fremont St., tel. 702/385–4011) is the home of **Ripley's Believe**

Las Vegas

Bonanza Rd.

Squire's Park

Bonanza Rd.

Gragson Hwy.

Eastern Ave.

N. Highland Dr.

Discovery Dr.

Casino Center

Stewart Ave.

Main St.

DOWNTOWN

E. Fremont St.

Hedland Park

Rancho Dr.

Alta Dr.

Bonneville Ave.

Charleston Blvd.

Charleston Blvd.

Circle Park

Oakey Blvd.

Burnham Ave.

Eastern Ave.

Las Vegas Blvd. S.

St. Louis Ave.

Jaycee Park

Rancho Dr.

Industrial Rd.

Sahara Ave.

Sahara Ave.

Sahara Ave.

Guinness World of Records Museum

Sahara Hotel

Karen Ave.

Maryland Pkwy.

Vegas Valley Dr.

Circus Circus La.

Circus Circus

Riviera Blvd.

Las Vegas Country Club

Grand Slam Canyon

Candlelight Wedding Chapel

Riviera Hotel

Stardust Rd.

Paradise Rd.

Desert Inn Rd.

Frontier Hotel

THE STRIP

Stars' Desert Inn

Sierra Vista Dr.

Sahara Country Club

Spring Mountain Rd.

Treasure Island

Twain Ave.

Sands

Sands Ave.

The Mirage

Twain Ave.

Cambridge St.

Algonquin Dr.

Caesars Palace

Imperial Palace Hotel and Casino

Flamingo Hilton

Swenson St.

Flamingo Rd.

Flamingo Rd.

Bally's

Koval La.

Maryland Pkwy.

Las Vegas Blvd. S.

Harmon Ave.

University of Nevada, Las Vegas

Harmon Ave.

MGM Grand Hotel and Theme Park

Paradise Rd.

Tropicana

Tropicana Ave.

Tropicana Ave.

Liberace Museum

THE STRIP

Swenson St.

Eastern Ave.

Reno Ave.

Hacienda Ave.

Hacienda Ave.

Excalibur

0   1 mile

N

Luxor

0   1 km

It or Not (admission charged), where the oddities of the world are exhibited.

The Strip—a 3½-mi stretch of Las Vegas Boulevard South—begins at the Sahara Hotel (tel. 702/737–2111), at No. 2535, which has the city's largest freestanding neon sign. At No. 2780 is the Guinness World of Records Museum (tel. 702/792–3766; admission charged), which honors such record holders as the tallest man in the world and offers videos of records actually being set. Next door at No. 2880, Circus Circus (tel. 702/734–0410), the first Las Vegas hotel to cater to families with children, has a midway with carnival games, free circus acts, and a recently opened (Aug. 1993) theme park, Grand Slam Canyon (tel. 702/734–0410), modeled on the Grand Canyon. At No. 2855 is the Candlelight Wedding Chapel (tel. 702/735–4179), the busiest chapel in town.

Towers sprout from all sides at the Riviera Hotel (2901 Las Vegas Blvd. S, tel. 702/734–5110). The reclusive billionaire Howard Hughes lived in the penthouse of the Stars' Desert Inn (tel. 702/733–4444), at No. 3145, and owned the Frontier Hotel (tel. 702/794–8200), at No. 3120, as well. The Sands (tel. 702/733–5000), at No. 3355, was the home of the "Rat Pack" (Frank Sinatra, Dean Martin, and friends) in the '60s. At the $700 million palace known as The Mirage (tel. 800/639–3403), at No. 3400, a volcano erupts in a front yard landscaped with a towering waterfall, lagoons, tropical plants, and a glassed-in tigers' den. At No. 3300, adjacent to The Mirage, the new (Oct. 1993) Treasure Island resort (tel. 702/894–7111) re-creates Robert Louis Stevenson's novel—here, in an 18,000-square-foot entertainment center, pirates and sailors engage in ship-to-ship cannon battles in a half-acre lagoon.

The Imperial Palace Hotel and Casino (tel. 702/731–3311), at No. 3535, is the home of the Imperial Palace Auto Collection (admission charged): more than 300 antique and classic cars, many of them formerly owned by the famous or the infamous, such as Adolf Hitler and Al Capone. The Flamingo Hilton (tel. 702/733–3111), at No. 3555, with one of the most beautiful lighted signs in the city, was the first luxury resort on the Strip, established by Bugsy Siegel in 1946.

The curved lines and high stakes at the opulent Caesars Palace (tel. 702/731–7110), at No. 3570, attract serious gamblers. Out front at No. 3645, the enormous Bally's (tel. 702/739–4111), is a statue of a woman squirting water from her breasts. The sprawling grounds of the Tropicana (tel. 702/733–2222), at No. 3801, are especially attractively landscaped. The blue-and-pink castlelike Excalibur (tel. 702/597–7777), at No. 3850, built on a medieval/Renaissance theme, is one of the world's largest hotels. Luxor (tel. 702/795–8118), at No. 3900, is a 30-story pyramidal Egyptian-style hotel complex, which includes seven restaurants, two show rooms, and an indoor canal on which guests are transported by boat to their rooms. Two miles off the Strip is the Liberace Museum (1775 E. Tropicana Ave., tel. 702/798–5595; admission charged) in three buildings: one for the entertainer's pianos and cars, one for the costumes, and the third for general memorabilia.

In the Vicinity The awe-inspiring Hoover Dam, about 25 mi east of Las Vegas, was constructed in the 1930s to tame the destructive waters of the Colorado River and produce electricity. Tours into the 727-

foot-high, 660-foot-thick dam are offered every day but Christmas. *Rte. 93 east of Boulder City, tel. 702/293–8321. Admission charged.*

The construction of the dam created **Lake Mead** (Alan Bible Visitor Center, U.S. 93 and Lakeshore Dr., tel. 702/293–8906), the largest man-made lake in the Western Hemisphere, with more than 500 mi of shoreline. It is popular for boating, fishing, and swimming. For water tours of the lake and Hoover Dam, contact **Lake Mead Cruises** (tel. 702/293–6180).

North of Lake Mead, dramatic **Valley of Fire State Park** (Rte. 169, Overton, tel. 702/397–2088) contains distinctively colored rock formations and mysterious Pueblo petroglyphs.

Some 20 mi west of downtown, **Red Rock Canyon** descends in twisting ravines from sandstone cliffs that are becoming an internationally known mecca for rock climbers. A 12-mi loop drive begins at the canyon visitor center (Charleston Blvd., tel. 702/363–1921).

For a respite from the noise and excitement of Las Vegas and the heat of the desert, travel 35 mi northwest of the city on U.S. 95 to **Mt. Charleston,** a land of dense forests and rangy mountains that reach 10,000 feet. The hiking, camping, picnicking, and skiing in winter (Lee Canyon) are excellent.

What to See and Do with Children

Wet n' Wild (2601 Las Vegas Blvd. S, tel. 702/734–0080) is a 26-acre theme park with every water ride imaginable. **Lied Discovery Children's Museum** (833 Las Vegas Blvd. N, tel. 702/382–3445) has hands-on science exhibits. **Southern Nevada Zoological Park** (1775 N. Rancho Dr., tel. 702/648–5955) is a small but nice zoo. The **Circus Circus** midway, the Medieval Village, a shopping and dining complex, and Fantasy Faire, a kid's game room, at **Excalibur,** the **Guinness World of Records Museum,** the **Imperial Palace Auto Collection,** and **Ripley's Believe It or Not** (*see* Exploring Las Vegas, *above*) are all good bets for children as well.

Getting Married in Las Vegas

Nevada is one of the easiest—and least expensive—states in which to get married. There is no blood test or waiting period; all you have to do is get a license (about $30) at the Marriage License Bureau (200 S. 3rd St., 89155, tel. 702/455–4415) and you're ready to go. In Las Vegas, there are about 25 chapels along the Strip, not including the hotel chapels at Bally's, Circus Circus, Excalibur, Imperial Palace, and Riviera (*see* Exploring Las Vegas, *above*). Services average $35 to $50.

Casino Gambling

Most major hotels in Las Vegas (as well as in Reno and Lake Tahoe) center on large casinos. The three largest casinos in Las Vegas—and consequently in the country—are at **Excalibur,** the **Riviera Hotel,** and **Bally's** (*see below*). The games played in the casinos are slots, blackjack, baccarat, craps, roulette, keno, poker, and the Big Wheel. The major casino-hotels offer free gaming lessons, usually during the "slow" morning hours. If you don't want to bother with lessons, just head for the slot machines; thanks to the Progressive Slot Machine and to "Megabucks," both computer-controlled, wins have gone into the millions.

Like the hotels, casinos sport different themes attracting different folks. Some of the better ones are listed below.

Binion's Horseshoe Hotel and Casino (128 E. Fremont St., tel. 702/382–1600), home of the World Series of Poker, has a Wild West theme and attracts serious gambling aficionados.

Caesars Palace (3570 Las Vegas Blvd. S, tel. 702/731–7110), a sprawling ersatz temple for serious gamblers with money to burn, lays on the ancient-Rome theme, complete with toga-clad dealers and a massive chariot parked in a corner.

Circus Circus (2880 Las Vegas Blvd. S, tel. 702/734–0410) has a casino under a pink-and-white big top, where circus performers will wow you while you play the slots. Kids can watch their parents gamble away their college tuition from a midway/observation gallery surrounding the casino.

Excalibur (3850 Las Vegas Blvd. S, tel. 702/597–7777) recalls the days of King Arthur, with strolling entertainers and dealers dressed in armor as knights. There are craps tables, a race-and-sports book, and 2,630 slot machines.

Flamingo Hilton (3555 Las Vegas Blvd. S, tel. 702/731–7110) bears little resemblance to the "classy joint" created by Bugsy Siegel in the 1940s. The silly pink-flamingo theme is rampant in the huge casino, which is always mobbed. Added recently is a new sports book.

Golden Nugget Hotel and Casino (129 E. Fremont St., tel. 702/385–7111) carries a Victorian theme, replete with white marble, gold leaf, gold-plated elevators, and palm trees. The world's largest gold nugget, weighing 63 pounds, stands in the lobby.

Jackie Gowan's Plaza Hotel and Casino (1 N. Main St., tel. 702/386–2110) has the only casino in the world with its own train station; Amtrak stops here regularly.

Las Vegas Hilton (3000 W. Paradise Rd., tel. 702/732–5111) has the sports book on which betting lines are set on professional football.

Luxor (3900 Las Vegas Blvd. S, tel. 702/795–8118) re-creates ancient Egypt with reproductions of artifacts, columns, temples of Luxor and Karnak, and hieroglyphics from the Valley of the Kings, based on the real valley in Egypt.

MGM Grand Hotel and Theme Park (3805 Las Vegas Blvd. S, tel. 702/891–1111), scheduled to open in February 1994 with a Wizard of Oz theme, will be the world's largest casino, with 3,500 slot machines, baccarat, and a race-and-sports book.

Stars' Desert Inn (3145 Las Vegas Blvd. S, tel. 702/733–4444) is laid-back and elegant, appealing to an upscale clientele.

The Mirage (3400 Las Vegas Blvd. S, tel. 800/639–3403) transports you to the South Seas, with thatch-roofed gaming areas and tropical plants and flowers flanking an indoor stream and pond. High rollers—those comfortable with the $1,000 minimum bet—gamble in a separate, glassed-in area.

Tropicana (3801 Las Vegas Blvd. S, tel. 702/733–2222) is lush and tropical, with a pool and swim-up blackjack.

Shopping

Las Vegas's best shopping is on the Strip at the **Fashion Show Mall** (3200 Las Vegas Blvd. S, tel. 702/369–8382), a collection of

150 shops and department stores, including Saks Fifth Avenue and Neiman Marcus. **Forum Shops at Caesars** (3570 Las Vegas Blvd. S, tel. 702/893–4800), a complex of 70 specialty stores adjacent to Caesars Palace, dazzles shoppers with a replicated Roman Street, complete with columns, piazzas, fountains, and a cloud-filled dome ceiling. You'll find Gucci, Ann Taylor, the Museum Company, and the Warner Bros. Studio Store alongside several popular restaurants. **Boulevard Mall** (3528 S. Maryland Pkwy., tel. 702/735–8268) is a few blocks from the Strip, and **Meadows Mall** (4300 Meadows La., tel. 702/878–4849) is a few miles away. If you get hooked on gambling while in Las Vegas, **Gamblers General Store** (800 S. Main St., tel. 702/382–9903) carries all manner of paraphernalia.

Spectator Sports

Boxing Some of the major hotels, such as **Caesars Palace** and **The Mirage,** present championship bouts.

Golf The annual PGA **Las Vegas Invitational** takes place in October at the Stars' Desert Inn (tel. 702/382–6616).

Rodeo The **National Finals Rodeo** is held in December at the University of Nevada's Thomas and Mack Center (tel. 702/731–2115).

Dining

Las Vegas dining ranges from elegant gourmet at the best hotels to buffets, for which the city is known. Most hotels have buffets at breakfast ($2–$3), lunch ($3–$4), and dinner ($5–$6). The biggest buffet is at **Circus Circus,** the two best are at the **Golden Nugget** and **Bally's.** The best Sunday champagne brunch is the Sterling Buffet at **Bally's.** Foods from some 40 countries are represented in Las Vegas restaurants. For price ranges, see Chart 1 (A) in Chapter 1.

Very Expensive **Chin's.** An upscale Chinese restaurant with a bright, contemporary decor, Chin's offers such specialties as strawberry chicken and pepper-orange roughy. *Fashion Show Mall, 3200 Las Vegas Blvd. S, tel. 702/733–8899. AE, D, DC, MC, V.*

Elaine's. In the Golden Nugget downtown is this warm and intimate restaurant away from the gambling, with curtained booths, Venetian glass chandeliers, and Impressionist-style paintings. The American/Continental fare includes some unusual specials, such as gin soup (only in Las Vegas). *129 E. Fremont St., tel. 702/385–7111. Reservations advised. Jacket required. AE, D, DC, MC, V. No lunch.*

★ **Palace Court.** This flagship restaurant of Caesars Palace is a beautiful domed garden of flowers, trees, and shrubbery. The fare is classic French; chateaubriand is a specialty. *3570 Las Vegas Blvd. S, tel. 702/731–7731. Reservations advised. Jacket required. AE, D, DC, MC, V.*

Expensive **Le Montrachet.** This quiet place away from the chatter of the
★ slot machines, with elegant mohair booths and pastoral scenes on the walls, is the pride of the Las Vegas Hilton. The menu changes with the season, but the rack of lamb is always good. *3000 W. Paradise Rd., tel. 702/732–5111. Reservations advised. Jacket required. AE, D, DC, MC, V.*

Pamplemousse. The loving creation of Georges LaForges, a former Las Vegas maître d', this restaurant looks like a little French country inn. There is no menu; the waiter recites the daily specials and their method of preparation. *400 E. Sahara Ave., tel. 702/733–2066. Reservations advised. Jacket required. AE, D, DC, MC, V.*

Moderate **Alpine Village.** You can't miss this place: It looks like a Swiss chalet, inside and out. The fare is German-Swiss; the sauerbraten is something special. Below the main restaurant is a lively rathskeller with oompah music. *3003 W. Paradise Rd., tel. 702/734–6888. Reservations advised. AE, D, DC, MC, V.*

Battista's Hole in the Wall. Battista Locatelli, a former opera singer, prides himself on the quality of his mostly northern Italian food, as well as on the cleanliness of his kitchen. Decorated with wine bottles, garlic, and celebrity photos, the restaurant offers lots of specials, with all the free wine you can drink. *4041 Audrie St., tel. 702/732–1424. AE, D, DC, MC, V. No lunch.*

★ **Lombardi's.** This sidewalk café inside the Forum Shops at Caesars can be noisy, but the northern Italian fare is first-rate. Order individual pizzas, soups, salads, and luscious gelato and sorbet. *3570 Las Vegas Blvd. S, tel. 702/735–4663. Reservations advised. AE, MC, V.*

Ricardo's. This large restaurant has terrific south-of-the-border food (especially the burritos), great margaritas, and a strolling mariachi band. *2389 E. Tropicana Ave., tel. 702/798–4515. AE, D, DC, MC, V.*

The Steak House. In the center of a dark, quiet room reminiscent of 1890s San Francisco, with wood paneling and antique brass, steaks aged to perfection are cooked over an open-hearth charcoal grill. *Circus Circus, 2880 Las Vegas Blvd. S, tel. 702/794–3767. Reservations advised. AE, D, DC, MC, V. No lunch.*

★ **The Tillerman.** In a garden setting under a skylight is served seafood flown in fresh from the West Coast every day; the yellowfin tuna is especially reliable. *2245 E. Flamingo Rd., tel. 702/731–4036. No reservations. AE, D, DC, MC, V.*

Inexpensive **Baja Restaurant.** This dressed-up diner is one of the few places in Nevada where you can get spicy southwestern food: blue-corn enchiladas, chicken fajita salad, chili rellenos. *3331 E. Tropicana Ave., tel. 702/458–7300. AE, DC, MC, V.*

Lodging

Las Vegas lodging ranges from virtual palaces to simple motels. The hotels tend to be a better bet for value; for instance, the Excalibur—one of the largest resort hotels in the world—has among the lowest prices in town. The largest and most lavish hotels are on the Strip; downtown hotels are generally less expensive. For price ranges, see Chart 2 (A) in Chapter 1.

Very Expensive **Caesars Palace.** This hotel caters to an upscale clientele with
★ world-class service, superstar entertainers like Diana Ross and Julio Iglesias, and lavish restaurants. Its casino is one of the largest in town. Guest rooms are opulent, even by Las Vegas standards, and many have Roman tubs. *3570 Las Vegas Blvd. S, 89109, tel. 702/731–7110 or 800/634–6001; fax 702/731–7172. 1,301 rooms, 217 suites. Facilities: 9 restaurants, lounge, casino, showroom, health spa, 2 pools, 4 tennis courts, movie theater, shopping complex. AE, D, DC, MC, V.*

Stars' Desert Inn. Surrounded by its private golf course and offering town houses as well as televised gambling lessons, the hotel is one of the town's more restrained. The elegant rooms have a southwestern ambience. *3145 Las Vegas Blvd. S, 89109, tel. 702/733–4444 or 800/634–6906; fax 702/733–4676. 726 rooms, 95 suites. Facilities: 5 restaurants, lounge, casino, showroom, health club and spa, 10 tennis courts, golf course. AE, D, DC, MC, V.*

Expensive **Golden Nugget Hotel.** Its attractive white-and-green exterior is shaded with palm trees; the lobby is beautiful as well, with gold, white marble, and more greenery. Guest rooms reflect the same elegance. *129 E. Fremont St., 89101, tel. 702/385–7111 or 800/634–3454; fax 702/386–8362. 1,812 rooms, 106 suites. Facilities: 5 restaurants, lounge, casino, showroom, health club, pool. AE, D, DC, MC, V.*

★ **The Mirage.** At one of the most extravagant and impressive hotels in the world, the colors and lush foliage outside and in bring to mind a tropical resort. Outside the block-long hotel is a series of waterfalls, surrounded by a volcano that erupts every 15 minutes after dark. *3400 Las Vegas Blvd. S, 89109, tel. 702/791–7111 or 800/627–6667; fax 702/791–7414. 2,825 rooms, 224 suites. Facilities: 9 restaurants, lounge, casino, showroom, exercise facility, pool, 4 tennis courts. AE, D, DC, MC, V.*

Moderate **Bally's.** This is the only hotel in the city with two full-size showrooms: one for superstars and one for a long-running production show. Many of the attractive guest rooms are suites, and some have round beds under mirrored ceilings. *3645 Las Vegas Blvd. S, 89109, tel. 702/739–4111 or 800/634–3434; fax 702/794–2413. 2,832 rooms and suites. Facilities: 7 restaurants, lounge, casino, 2 showrooms, comedy club, health spa, pool, 10 tennis courts. AE, D, DC, MC, V.*

Excalibur. This pink-and-blue turreted castle with a King Arthur theme is one of the largest resort hotels in the world. With knights clad in shining armor and two moats, its appeal is mostly to families. *3850 Las Vegas Blvd. S, tel. 702/597–7777 or 800/937–7777. 4,032 rooms. Facilities: 7 restaurants, lounge, casino, showroom, pool, shops. AE, D, DC, MC, V.*

Flamingo Hilton. This neon-encrusted structure, originally called simply the Flamingo and now part of the Hilton chain, offers dramatic views of the busiest intersection of the Strip from contemporary rooms recently redecorated in bright colors and soft textures. *3555 Las Vegas Blvd. S, 89109, tel. 702/733–3111 or 800/732–2111; fax 702/733–3528. 3,334 rooms, 196 suites. Facilities: 8 restaurants, lounge, casino, showroom, health spa, 2 pools, 4 tennis courts. AE, D, DC, MC, V.*

Harrah's Las Vegas. A Las Vegas–neon Mississippi river gambling boat marks the entrance to what was formerly the largest Holiday Inn in the world. The rooms are modest by Strip standards, with lavender doors, gray walls, blue bedspreads and curtains, and dark-wood furniture. *3475 Las Vegas Blvd. S, 89109, tel. 702/369–5000 or 800/634–6765; fax 702/369–6014. 1,725 rooms. Facilities: 5 restaurants, lounge, casino, showroom, exercise room, pool. AE, D, DC, MC, V.*

Las Vegas Hilton. With 29 floors and three wings, the hotel is one of the most recognizable in town. The rooms are large, with soft colors; those on the higher floors have great views. Elvis used to perform here, and his spirit is said to roam the suite that bears his name. *3000 Paradise Rd., 89109, tel. 702/732–5111 or 800/732–7117; fax 702/794–3611. 3,174 rooms and suites. Facilities: 13 restaurants, lounge, casino, showroom,* *spa, pool, putting green, 6 tennis courts, youth hotel. AE, D, DC, MC, V.*

Luxor. This bronze-color pyramid recalls ancient Egypt with interior waterways, a replica of King Tut's tomb, and outside elevators that angle up the slope of the pyramid. *3900 Las Vegas Blvd. S, 89119, tel. 702/262–4000. 2,521 rooms, 14 suites. Facilities: 7 restaurants, lounge, casino, showroom, entertainment complex, shops. AE, D, DC, MC, V.*

MGM Grand Hotel and Theme Park. Set to open in January 1994, this movieland-theme megaresort will be the largest in the world. Three emerald green hotel towers reflect a Wizard of Oz theme; a 33-acre theme park re-creates Hollywood backlots with rides and attractions. *3805 Las Vegas Blvd. S, 89119, tel. 702/891–1111 or 800/929–1111. 5,021 rooms, 733 suites. Facilities: 8 restaurants, lounge, casino, showroom, health club, 3 pools, tennis courts, child-care center, game room. AE, D, DC, MC, V.*

Rio Suites. Opened in 1990, this red-and-blue 21-story structure offers suites furnished on a Brazilian theme. Ask for a unit high and on the east side, facing the Strip. *3700 W. Flamingo Rd. (at Valley View), 89109, tel. 702/252–7777 or 800/888–1808; fax 702/253–6090. 430 suites. Facilities: 7 restaurants, lounge, showroom, casino, health club, pool. AE, D, DC, MC, V.*

Riviera Hotel. One of the city's most famous and venerable hotels, the Riviera has one of the largest casinos in the world. Guest rooms are large, comfortable, and recently renovated. *2901 Las Vegas Blvd. S, 89109, tel. 702/734–5110 or 800/634–6753; fax 702/794–9663. 2,220 rooms. Facilities: 3 restaurants, food court, casino, 5 showrooms, health club, pool, 2 tennis courts. AE, D, DC, MC, V.*

Sands Hotel. This 1950s landmark, the first circular building in town, rises nine stories, with a cluster of low rises around a V-shaped pool. Tower rooms offer views of the Strip. John F. Kennedy, Richard Nixon, and Ronald Reagan were guests in the Presidential Suite. *3355 Las Vegas Blvd. S, 89109, tel. 702/733–5000 or 800/634–6901; fax 702/733–5632. 750 rooms. Facilities: 4 restaurants, lounge, casino, showroom, health club, 2 pools, putting green, 6 tennis courts, convention center. AE, D, DC, MC, V.*

Treasure Island Resort. This hotel is based on Robert Louis Stevenson's novel, set in the South Seas. There's lush landscaping inside and out, a re-created 18th-century pirate village, and pirate-theme rooms. *3300 Las Vegas Blvd. S, 89109, tel. 702/894–7111; fax 702/894–7446. 3,000 rooms. Facilities: 5 restaurants, lounge, casino, showroom, health club, pool, shopping arcade. AE, D, DC, MC, V.*

Tropicana. A 22-story tower rises above the most beautiful grounds in Las Vegas, complete with waterfalls and swans. Room decor evokes tropical images with bamboo and pastels. *3801 Las Vegas Blvd. S, 89109, tel. 702/739–2222 or 800/634–4000; fax 702/739–2469. 1,818 rooms, 94 suites. Facilities: 7 restaurants, lounge, casino, showroom, health club, 3 pools, 4 tennis courts, racquetball. AE, D, DC, MC, V.*

Inexpensive **Circus Circus.** Catering exclusively to families with children, the hotel has painted circus tents in the hallways and a generally chaotic atmosphere. The brightly decorated rooms (red carpets and chairs; red, pink, and blue striped wallpaper) are small but clean. *2880 Las Vegas Blvd. S, 89109, tel. 702/734–0410 or 800/634–3450; fax 702/734–5897. 2,793 rooms. Facili-*

ties: 5 restaurants, casino, 3 pools, wedding chapel, large RV park. AE, D, DC, MC, V.

Sahara Las Vegas Hotel. Like many of its neighbors, the Sahara began as a small motor hotel and built itself up by adding towers. Unlike its neighbors, it has retained a small, gardenlike ambience. The older rooms are small; tower rooms are larger and overlook the Strip. *2535 Las Vegas Blvd. S, tel. 702/737–2111 or 800/634–6666; fax 702/791–2027. 2,100 rooms. Facilities: 5 restaurants, lounge, casino, showroom, health club, 2 pools. AE, D, DC, MC, V.*

Sam's Town Hotel and Casino. This friendly hotel outside town on U.S. 95W presents an Old West theme that seems authentic because the place is so close to the desert. The comfortable rooms offer views of the desert and mountains. *5111 Boulder Hwy., 89109, tel. 702/456–7777 or 800/634–6371; fax 702/454–8014. 200 rooms. Facilities: 5 restaurants, lounge, casino, pool, bowling alley, RV park. AE, D, DC, MC, V.*

Stardust. From its first incarnation as a motor hotel to its later nine-story tower to its recent 32-story tower, the Stardust is one of the best-known hotels on the Strip. The newer tower rooms are the best. *3000 Las Vegas Blvd. S, 89109, tel. 702/732–6111 or 800/634–6757; fax 702/732–6296. 2,500 rooms. Facilities: 3 restaurants, lounge, casino, showroom, health club, pool, 2 tennis courts. AE, D, DC, MC, V.*

Jackie Gowan's Plaza Hotel and Casino. This casino-hotel was built on the original site of the Union Pacific train station and now houses an Amtrak station. Rooms are decorated in traditional style, in light mauve tones; those facing east have a great view of downtown. *1 N. Main St., 89101, tel. 702/386–2110 or 800/634–6575; fax 702/382–8281. 1,037 rooms. Facilities: 3 restaurants, lounge, casino, showroom, pool. AE, D, DC, MC, V.*

Motels **Motel 6** (195 E. Tropicana Ave., 89109, tel. 702/798–0728; fax 702/798–5657), 877 rooms, 2 pools; inexpensive. **Town Hall** (4155 Koval La., 89109, tel. 702/731–2111 or 800/634–6541; fax 702/731–1113), 360 rooms, coffee shop, pool; inexpensive. **Westward Ho** (2900 Las Vegas Blvd. S, 89109, tel. 702/731–2900 or 800/634–6803; fax 702/731–6154), 1,000 rooms; restaurant, 3 pools; inexpensive.

The Arts and Nightlife

The Arts Most arts events in Las Vegas are associated with the **University of Nevada, Las Vegas** (tel. 702/739–3011). For additional information, call the **Allied Arts Council** (tel. 702/731–5419).

Nightlife No city in America—perhaps even in the world—has more to do at night than Las Vegas.

Showrooms Hotel showrooms seat from several hundred to 2,000 (at the Las Vegas Hilton, the largest showroom). Most are luxurious and small enough to permit a close view of the star. At most hotels tickets are sold only on the day of the show or the day before; the ticket indicates your seat location. When a show is expected to sell out, hotel guests are given ticket preference.

The four main kinds of entertainment offered in showrooms are **superstar shows,** such as Frank Sinatra, Julio Iglesias, and Diana Ross; **big production shows,** such as "Jubilee!" at Bally's or the Tropicana's "Folies Bergères," which may include a major act as well as the ubiquitous revue—topless showgirls strutting their stuff in flashy costumes; **small production shows,** such as "Melinda, First Lady of Magic" at the Lady Luck; and the **lounge shows,** offered all over town, where orchestras play dance music and the only price of admission is the cost of a drink.

The major hotels' entertainment offerings are as follows (*see* Exploring Las Vegas or Lodging, *above,* for addresses and phone numbers): **Bally's,** superstars and large production show; **Caesars Palace,** superstars; **Excalibur,** large production show; **Flamingo Hilton,** large production show; **Harrah's Las Vegas,** small production show; **Imperial Palace,** small production show; **Las Vegas Hilton,** superstars; **Mirage,** two permanent shows: Siegfried & Roy and Cirque du Soleil; **Rio,** small production show; **Riviera,** large and small production shows, sometimes superstars; **Sahara,** small production show; **Stardust,** large production show; **Stars' Desert Inn,** superstars; **Tropicana,** large production show.

Comedy Clubs Bally's has **Catch a Rising Star,** the Riviera has **An Evening at the Improv,** and the Tropicana has **The Comedy Stop.**

Jazz The **Four Queens Hotel**'s Monday night jazz program, hosted by Alan Grant, is broadcast on National Public Radio.

Reno

Reno, once the gambling and divorce capital of the country, is smaller, less crowded, friendlier, and prettier than Las Vegas. Begun in 1859 as a trading station at a bridge over the Truckee River, Reno grew with the nearby silver mines, the railroad, and gambling (introduced in 1867). Its first major casinos opened in 1935.

Tourist Information

Reno-Sparks: Convention and Visitors Authority (4590 S. Virginia St., Reno 89504, tel. 702/827–7366 or 800/367–7366).

Arriving and Departing

By Plane **Reno Cannon International Airport** (tel. 702/328–6400), served by national and regional airlines, is on the east side of the city and minutes from downtown.

By Car The major highways leading to Reno are I–95 (east–west) and U.S. 95 (north–south).

Train Station **Amtrak** (135 E. Commercial Row, tel. 702/329–8638). A seasonal weekend **Fun Train** (tel. 800/783–0783, Feb.–Mar. weekends) connects Reno with California's Bay Area.

Bus Station **Greyhound** (155 Stevenson St., tel. 702/322–2970).

Getting Around Reno

Reno is such a small city that the best way to get around it is on foot or by taxi. Taxis (like rental cars) are easily hired at the airport and in front of the major hotels; the main taxi firms are **Reno-Sparks Cab Co.** (tel. 702/333–3333), **Whittlesea Checker** (tel. 702/322–2222), and **Yellow** (tel. 702/331–7171). **Reno Citifare** (tel. 702/348–7433) provides local bus service. Many large hotels have courtesy buses on call.

Exploring Reno

One advantage Reno has over Las Vegas is weather: Its summer temperatures are much more agreeable and thus much more pleasant for strolling. The city's focal point is the famous Reno arch, a sign over the lower end of Virginia Street proclaiming it "The Biggest Little City in the World."

As in Las Vegas, gambling is a favorite pastime. While not as garish as their Vegas counterparts, Reno's casinos still offer plenty of glitter and glitz. With the exception of the Reno Hilton, Peppermill, and John Ascuaga's Nugget, they are crowded into five square blocks downtown. **Reno Tahoe Gaming Academy** (135 N. Sierra St., tel. 702/329–5665) conducts behind-the-scenes tours of casinos. Some of the better casinos are listed below.

Circus Circus (500 N. Sierra St., tel. 800/648–5010), marked by a neon clown sucking a lollipop, is the best stop for families with children. Complete with clowns, games, fun-house mirrors, and circus acts, the midway overlooking the casino floor is open from 10 AM to midnight.

Comstock (200 W. 2nd St., tel. 800/648–4866) re-creates an Old West mining town.

Fitzgerald's (255 N. Virginia St., tel. 702/785–3300) celebrates the Irish with a large green casino, home of good luck and leprechauns. On the second floor you can kiss the only Blarney stones ever to leave Ireland and admire a collection of more than 50 antique slot machines.

Flamingo Hilton in Reno (255 N. Sierra St., tel. 800/648–4882) reproduces its Vegas counterpart, complete with large bright pink-feathered neon flamingos.

Harold's (250 Virginia St., tel. 702/329–0881), opened in 1935, was the first major casino in Nevada. Its advertising inspired the *"Harold's Club or Bust"* signs seen for years around the world. It has a collection of working three-reel slots from the 1950s.

Harrah's (219 Center St., tel. 800/648–3773), which debuted in 1937 as the Tango Club, was Nevada's second casino. A pair of sprawling buildings cover almost two city blocks and contain a sports casino with a new sports book and a children's arcade. There are low minimums and friendly patrons and workers.

Nevada Club (224 N. Virginia St., tel. 702/329–1721) takes you back to the 1950s. Its slots are old-fashioned one-arm bandits; line up three cherries and you might win a classic hot rod. There's a 1950s-style diner on the second floor.

Three casinos lie outside the downtown area: **Reno Hilton** (2500 E. 2nd St., tel. 800/648–5080), with 100,000 square feet, is the largest casino in Reno. **Peppermill** (2707 S. Virginia St., tel. 800/648–6992) is the gaudiest, glitziest, and noisiest. And **John Ascuaga's Nugget** (1100 Nugget Ave., Sparks, tel. 800/648–1177) is lively and fun.

Besides the hotel-casinos, Reno has a number of cultural attractions. On the University of Nevada campus, the sleekly designed **Fleischmann Planetarium** (1600 Virginia St., tel. 702/784–4811) offers films and star shows. The **Nevada Museum of Art** (160 W. Liberty St., tel. 702/329–3333), the state's largest, features changing exhibits. More than 220 antique and classic automobiles, including an Elvis Presley Cadillac, are on display at the **William F. Harrah Foundation National Automobile Museum** (Mill and Lake Sts., tel. 702/333–9300). The **Nevada Historical Society** (1650 N. Virginia St., tel. 702/688–1190) features mining exhibits and Native American artifacts.

Downtown River Walk (S. Virginia St. and the river, tel. 702/334–2077) is a festive scene year-round, with street performers, musicians, dancers, food, art displays, games, and contests. **Victorian Square** (B St. and Rock Blvd., Sparks), fringed by restored turn-of-the-century houses and Victorian-dressed casinos and storefronts, is a parklike setting with a bandstand-gazebo.

In the Vicinity Only 25 mi from Reno (U.S. 395S to Rte. 341), **Virginia City** was once the largest city in Nevada, with more than 30,000 residents and 110 saloons. The Comstock Lode, one of the largest gold and silver discoveries of the 19th century, had turned Virginia City into a boomtown. Today it's one of the liveliest and most authentic ghost towns in the West. Little has changed in more than 100 years. You can still belly up to the grand mahogany bar and hear honky-tonk piano music at the **Bucket of Blood** (tel. 702/847–0322) saloon on Main Street. The lavish interiors of **Mackay Mansion** (D St., tel. 702/847–0173), **Savage Mansion** (D St., tel. 702/847–0574), and the **Castle** (B St., no phone) offer a glimpse into the past with such adornments as Oriental rugs, Italian marble, and Brussels lace, as well as table settings made from the silver mined beneath these houses. **Virginia and Truckee Railroad** (Washington and F Sts., tel. 702/847–0380) takes visitors on historic steam-powered locomotives through the Comstock mining region. Virginia City's most famous resident was Mark Twain, who lived here from 1861 to 1864 while working as a reporter for the *Territorial Enterprise;* the **Mark Twain Museum** (109 S. C St., tel. 702/847–0525) has mementos of his life. For more information, contact the **Virginia City Chamber of Commerce** (S. C St.; Box 464, 89440, tel. 702/847–0311).

South of Virginia City is **Carson City,** the state capital. The **Nevada State Museum** (600 N. Carson St., tel. 702/885–4810; admission charged), once a U.S. mint, has exhibits on early mining days, antique gaming devices, and willow baskets woven by Washoe artists. The **Nevada State Railroad Museum** (2180 S. Carson St., tel. 702/687–6953) has an extensive historic collection of passenger and freight cars and two restored Virginia and Truckee trains. The **Carson City Chamber of Commerce** (1900 S. Carson St., tel. 702/882–1565) has information on the town's attractions.

Genoa, the oldest settlement in Nevada, is a quaint Victorian town about 20 mi south of Carson City on U.S. 395. **Mormon Station State Historic Park** (Foothill Rd. and Genoa La., tel. 702/687–4379) contains an early log cabin and Mormon artifacts. **Walley's Hot Springs Resort** (2001 Foothill Rd., tel. 702/782–8155), reputed to have the oldest bar in the state, has hot mineral pools dating from 1862.

What to See and Do with Children

Of particular interest to children in Reno are the **Fleischmann Planetarium** and the **William F. Harrah Foundation National**

Automobile Museum (*see* Exploring Reno, *above*). **Wilbur D. May Great Basin Adventure** (1502 Washington St., tel. 702/785–4064), in Rancho San Rafael Park, traces the evolution of the Great Basin through mining and other exhibits, including a dinosaur pit; also available here are a petting zoo, pony rides, and a touch-and-feel discovery room. In nearby Sparks, **Wild Island** (250 Wild Island Ct., tel. 702/331–9453) is a family theme park that includes a water park, a 36-hole minigolf course, and a state-of-the-art video arcade.

Shopping

The two best places in Reno for shopping are the **Park Lane Mall** (310 E. Plumb La., downtown, tel. 702/825–7878) and the **Meadowood Mall** (Virginia St. at McCarran Blvd., tel. 702/827–8450). **Harold's Club Antique Slots** (250 N. Virginia St., tel. 702/329–0881) sells slot machines for about $600.

Dining

Reno dining options range from plush gourmet restaurants and extensive hotel buffets to interesting little eateries scattered around the city. As in Las Vegas, the least expensive places are the hotel-casino breakfast, lunch, and dinner buffets. The best are at **John Ascuaga's Nugget** and the **Peppermill** (*see* Exploring Reno, *above*). For price ranges, see Chart 1 (B) in Chapter 1.

Expensive **Harrah's Steak House.** The hotel-casino's dark and romantic restaurant serves excellent steaks. *219 N. Center St., tel. 702/786–3232. Reservations advised. AE, D, DC, MC, V.*

Le Moulin. Located in the Peppermill casino, the intimate Le Moulin has subdued lighting and touches of neon and art deco. The fare, as you would expect, is French. Choose from among steaks, light Italian entrées such as pastas with veggies in a light cream sauce, and chicken; there's a prime rib-and-lobster early-bird special from 5 to 7. *2707 S. Virginia St., tel. 702/826–2121. Reservations advised. AE, D, DC, MC, V. No lunch.*

Moderate **Casanova.** This old-fashioned Renaissance-theme restaurant specializes in game, seafood, homemade pasta, and sinfully rich desserts. *1695 S. Virginia St., tel. 702/786–6633. Reservations advised. AE, DC, MC, V.*

La Strada. This excellent northern Italian restaurant is in the heart of the Eldorado casino. The pastas and sauces are homemade, and there are inventive pizzas as well. *345 N. Virginia St., tel. 702/786–5700. Reservations advised. AE, D, DC, MC, V. No lunch.*

Presidential Car. On the seventh floor of Harold's, this restaurant has an excellent view of the city. Decorated as a turn-of-the-century railroad car, it features prime rib, steak, and seafood. *250 N. Virginia St., tel. 702/329–0881. AE, MC, V.*

Inexpensive **Bertha Miranda's Mexican Restaurant.** Begun as a little hole-in-the-wall, it has grown into a highly successful establishment. The food is made fresh by Bertha's family. Try the salsa. *336 Mill St., tel. 702/786–9697. MC, V.*

La Trattoria. At this family-owned and -operated restaurant the food of southern Italy is served. Raviolis in red-wine sauce is a specialty. *719 S. Virginia St., tel. 702/323–1131. Reservations advised. DC, MC, V.*

Louis' Basque Corner. Basque shepherds once populated

northern Nevada, and this is the best place to sample authentic Basque food served family-style at tables for eight covered with red cloths in a wood-paneled dining room. Dishes include oxtail, shrimp, and tongue. *301 E. 4th St., tel. 702/323–7203. AE, DC, MC, V.*

Nevada Annie's. In Harold's Club, Nevada Annie's offers hearty steaks and seafood in a rustic setting. All meals are served with Annie's "pigtails"—curly fried potatoes. *250 N. Virginia St., tel. 702/329–0881. AE, MC, V.*

19th Hole. This restaurant on the Lakeridge Golf Course has a great view of the city and nearby mountains. The menu offers American and Continental food. *1200 Razorback Rd., tel. 702/825–1250. Reservations advised. D, MC, V.*

Lodging

Most of Reno's hotels are downtown. For price ranges, see Chart 2 (B) in Chapter 1.

Expensive   **Flamingo Hilton in Reno.** The former Reno Hilton was spruced up in 1989 and given a new casino. The medium-size guest rooms have a nice view of the mountains. *255 N. Sierra St., 89501, tel. 702/322–1111 or 800/445–8667. 604 rooms. Facilities: 4 restaurants, lounge, casino. AE, D, DC, MC, V.*

Harrah's. This is the most luxurious hotel in downtown Reno. Large, conservatively decorated guest rooms offer good views of the mountains. *219 N. Center St., 89501, tel. 702/788–3773 or 800/648–3773. 565 rooms. Facilities: 4 restaurants, casino, showroom, health club, pool, shopping arcade. AE, MC, V.*

Reno Hilton. This 27-story hotel near the airport, formerly Bally's, began a massive two-year, $72 million renovation in late 1993 that's changing its theme from Hollywood to the western United States. The casino and public areas now feature rivers, trees, and lush vegetation of the Northwest, mountainscapes and rock formations of the Southwest. *2500 E. 2nd St., 89595, tel. 702/789–2000 or 800/648–4882. 2,001 rooms. Facilities: 6 restaurants, lounge, casino, showroom, health club, pool, tennis courts, shopping arcade, wedding chapel. AE, D, DC, MC, V.*

Moderate   **Eldorado.** Known for its fine food and attention to detail, the Eldorado offers cushy, restful rooms overlooking the mountains. *345 N. Virginia St., 89501, tel. 702/786–5700 or 800/648–4597. 800 rooms. Facilities: 8 restaurants, lounge, casino, pool. AE, D, DC, MC, V.*

John Ascuaga's Nugget. This casino-hotel in neighboring Sparks offers some of the largest and most luxurious rooms around, as well as a resident elephant named Bertha. *1100 Nugget Ave., Sparks 89431, tel. 702/356–3300 or 800/648–1177. 983 rooms. Facilities: 7 restaurants, lounge, casino, showroom, pool, free shuttle to downtown Reno. AE, D, DC, MC, V.*

Inexpensive   **Circus Circus.** This smaller version of the giant Las Vegas hotel has the same atmosphere. The rooms are small, but some have a view of the mountains. *500 N. Sierra St., 89503, tel. 702/329–0711 or 800/648–5010. 1,625 rooms. Facilities: 3 restaurants, lounge, casino. AE, DC, MC, V.*

Comstock. The lobby and casino reflect an Old West theme. Recently renovated rooms are small, with Victorian-style decor and city or mountain views. *200 W. 2nd St., 89501, tel. 702/329–*

1880 or 800/824–8167. 310 rooms. Facilities: 3 restaurants, lounge, casino, health club, pool. MC, V.

Peppermill. The home of Reno's most colorful casino is 3 mi from downtown, but its rooms are plush and sedate. *2707 S. Virginia St., 89502, tel. 702/826–2121 or 800/684–6992. 631 rooms. Facilities: 3 restaurants, lounge, casino, health club, pool. AE, D, DC, MC, V.*

The Arts and Nightlife

The Arts Most of the arts in Reno—such as the **Nevada Festival Ballet** (tel. 702/329–2552), the **Nevada Opera Association** (tel. 702/786–4046), the **Reno Philharmonic** (tel. 702/825–5905), and the **Performing Arts Series** (tel. 702/826–0880)—center on the **University of Nevada, Reno** (tel. 702/784–1110).

Nightlife As in Las Vegas, Reno area nightlife breaks down into four categories: superstars, big production shows, small production shows, and lounge acts. Offerings at the major Reno hotels (*see* Lodging, *above,* for addresses and phone numbers): **Circus Circus,** continual circus acts; **Flamingo Hilton Reno,** large production show; **Harrah's Reno,** superstars; **John Ascuaga's Nugget,** superstars (mostly country-western); **Reno Hilton,** superstars and large production show.

Lake Tahoe

Southwest of Reno, Lake Tahoe's vast expanse of crystal-blue water surrounded by rugged peaks is a playground for natives and visitors alike. Half in Nevada and half in California, it is the largest alpine lake in North America, 22 mi long and 12 mi wide. The region offers outstanding skiing in winter; boating, fishing, and mountain sports in summer; and casino entertainment year-round.

Tourist Information

Lake Tahoe: Visitors and Convention Bureau (969 Tahoe Blvd., Incline Village 89451–9508, tel. 702/832–1606 or 800/468–2463).

Getting There

By Plane The closest major airport to Lake Tahoe is **Reno Cannon International Airport** (*see* Reno, *above*). However, three regional airlines offer limited service from several California cities to the recently reopened **Lake Tahoe Airport** (tel. 916/541–4080) near Stateline.

By Car From Reno, U.S. 395S to U.S. 50 leads to Lake Tahoe.

Exploring Lake Tahoe

A scenic drive circling Lake Tahoe (Rtes. 28 and 89) offers stunning lake, forest, and mountain vistas. You also can explore the lake aboard the *MS Dixie* (Zephyr Cove, tel. 702/588–3508). **Crystal Bay,** the northernmost community on the Nevada shore, has a small-town, outdoorsy feel, along with several casinos.

To the south, affluent **Incline Village** has lakeshore homes, inviting shopping areas, and, south of town, **Ponderosa Ranch,** where the TV series "Bonanza" was videotaped, complete with a Hollywood-style western town. *Rte. 28, tel. 702/831–0691. Admission charged. Closed Nov.–Apr.*

At the south end of the lake—just before the neon signs of **Stateline,** where five towering casinos cluster in one block just east of the Nevada–California border (*see* Dining and Lodging, *below*)—a road southeast takes you to the **Heavenly Ski Area** (tel. 702/586–7000), where the tram lifts you to unbeatable views over the water.

What to See and Do with Children

Aside from water sports on the lake, **Ponderosa Ranch** (*see* Exploring Lake Tahoe, *above*) is the chief attraction for children.

Sports and Outdoor Activities

Fishing The lake is renowned for mighty mackinaws and rainbow trout. Nonresident fishing permits are available at most sporting-goods stores. For more information, call the **Department of Fish and Game** (tel. 702/688–1500).

Golf **Edgewood at Tahoe** (Stateline, tel. 702/588–3566; 18 holes). **Glenbrook Golf Course** (Glenbrook, tel. 702/749–5201; 9 holes). **Incline Village Championship Golf Course** (955 Fairway Blvd., tel. 702/832–1144; 18 holes). **Incline Village Executive Course** (690 Wilson Way, tel. 702/832–1150; 18 holes).

Hiking More than 100 mi of hiking trails traverse the area, many through high mountain passes and along streams and meadows with sweeping views. Contact the **U.S. Forest Service** (tel. 916/573–2600) for information.

Ski Areas

Lake Tahoe offers more than 15 world-class alpine (downhill) resorts and nearly a dozen Nordic (cross-country) skiing centers—all within an hour of one another. Elevations range from 6,000 to 10,000 feet, with vertical drops up to nearly 4,000 feet. More than 150 lifts operate during the season, which usually lasts from November through May.

Cross-country **Diamond Peak** (1210 Ski Way, Incline Village 89450, tel. 702/832–1177) has 35 km of groomed high-elevation track with skating lanes.

Downhill **Diamond Peak** (*see* Cross-country, *above*) has seven lifts, 29 runs, and a 1,840-foot vertical drop. **Heavenly Ski Area** (Box 2180, Stateline 89449, tel. 916/541–1330 or 800/243–2836), straddling the Nevada–California border, has 25 lifts, 71 trails (including the longest run in Tahoe), and a 3,600-foot drop. **Mt. Rose** (22222 Mt. Rose Hwy., Reno 89511, tel. 702/849–0704) has the highest base elevation in the area, with unequaled powder skiing, five lifts, 41 runs, and a 1,440-foot drop.

Dining and Lodging

For price ranges, see Charts 1 (B) and 2 (B) in Chapter 1.

Incline Village/Reno Dining

Galena Forest Inn. Set in the heart of the mountains, the Galena appropriately serves Swiss-Austrian alpine fare. The forest terrine features venison and rabbit. *17025 Mt. Rose Hwy., tel. 702/849–2100. Reservations advised. D, MC, V. No lunch. Expensive.*

Hugo's. This restaurant in the Hyatt Regency Hotel has one of the best views of the lake. Specialties include duck, fish, and steak; there's a salad and dessert buffet. *Country Club Dr. at Lakeshore, Incline Village, tel. 702/831–1111. Reservations advised. AE, D, DC, MC, V. Moderate.*

Stateline Dining

Empress Court. Plush velvet booths and etched-glass partitions provide the setting for traditional Chinese cuisine. A specialty is the grilled-squab salad. *Caesars Tahoe, Rte. 50, tel. 702/588–3515. Reservations advised. AE, DC, MC, V. No lunch. Expensive.*

Le Posh. One of the most elegant restaurants in northern Nevada, Le Posh features American regional cuisine, such as Maine lobster. *Caesars Tahoe, Rte. 50, tel. 702/588–3515. Reservations advised. AE, D, DC, MC, V. No lunch. Expensive.*

The Sage Room Steak House. A historic landmark in Lake Tahoe, this romantic restaurant is a descendant of the Wagon Wheel Saloon and Gambling Hall, the beginning of Harvey's Resort. Sautéed prawns Mediterranean are elegantly but unpretentiously served, and excellent. *Harvey's Resort Hotel/ Casino, Rte. 50, tel. 702/588–2411. Reservations advised. AE, D, DC, MC, V. Moderate.*

The Summit. This 16th-floor restaurant affords a wonderful view. The creative menu features artfully presented salads, seafood entrées, and decadent desserts. *Harrah's Casino/ Hotel Lake Tahoe, Rte. 50, tel. 702/588–6611. Reservations advised. AE, D, DC, MC, V. Moderate.*

El Vaquero. Wrought iron, a fountain, and tiles give this restaurant an authentic Old Mexico feel. The traditional Mexican fare includes enchiladas and chimichangas. At the Taco Cart, you can make your own. *Harvey's Resort Hotel/Casino, Rte. 50, tel. 702/588–2411. AE, D, DC, MC, V. Inexpensive.*

The Forest. On the 18th floor of Harrah's, this restaurant offers buffet-style dining with an excellent view. The interior simulates a forest. *Rte. 50, tel. 702/588–6611. No reservations. AE, DC, MC, V. Inexpensive.*

Lodging

Caesars Tahoe. Once you negotiate the lobby stairs and casino areas, you find hallways with faux Corinthian columns and plush rooms in fantasyland color schemes, such as hot pink and mint green. The indoor pool has a waterfall and a swim tunnel. *Box 5800, 89449, tel. 702/588–3515 or 800/648–3353. 440 rooms, 50 suites. Facilities: 5 restaurants, lounge, casino, showroom, health club, pool, tennis courts. AE, D, DC, MC, V. Expensive.*

★ **Harrah's Casino/Hotel Lake Tahoe.** The rooms are large and comfortable, and all have two full bathrooms, complete with telephones and TVs. Most rooms also have excellent views of the lake and the mountains. *Rte. 50, Box 8, 89449, tel. 702/588– 6606 or 800/648–3773. 533 rooms, 79 suites. Facilities: 7 restaurants, casino, showroom, health club, indoor pool. AE, DC, MC, V. Expensive.*

Hyatt Regency Lake Tahoe. This elegant resort was recently renovated. Rooms are large and attractive, with warm color schemes and lake views. Amenities include a private beach, water sports, Camp Hyatt for kids, and a forest-theme casino.

Country Club Dr. at Lakeshore, Incline Village 89450, tel. 702/ 832–1234 or 800/553–3288. 460 rooms. Facilities: 3 restaurants, lounge, casino, health club, pool. AE, DC, MC, V. Expensive.

Harvey's Resort Hotel/Casino. This family-owned hotel is Lake Tahoe's largest resort. The rooms are comfortably furnished in American traditional, with soft colors. Most have a view of the lake and the mountains. *Rte. 50, Box 128, 89449, tel. 702/588–2411 or 800/648–3361. 717 rooms. Facilities: 8 restaurants, lounge, casino, health spa, tennis courts. AE, D, DC, MC, V. Moderate.*

Nightlife

Lake Tahoe nightlife centers on the top-name entertainment and production shows at the casino-hotels. **Caesars Tahoe** and **Harrah's** (*see* Lodging, *above*) both present superstars.

NEW MEXICO

By Ron Butler

Capital	Santa Fe
Population	1.5 million
Motto	It Grows as It Goes
State Bird	Roadrunner
State Flower	Yucca

Visitor Information

New Mexico Department of Tourism (Lamy Bldg., 491 Old Santa Fe Trail, Santa Fe 87503, tel. 505/827–7400 or 800/545–2040). **USDA Forest Service, Southwestern Region** (Public Affairs Office, 517 Gold Ave. SW, Albuquerque 87102, tel. 505/842–3292). **Indian Pueblo Cultural Center** (2401 12th St. NW, Albuquerque 87102, tel. 505/843–7270).

Scenic Drives

An alternative to the more direct route from Santa Fe to Taos, the old **High Road** takes you through rolling hillsides studded with orchards and tiny picturesque villages set against a rugged mountain backdrop. No visit to northern New Mexico is complete without the 90-mi trip through the **Enchanted Circle,** a breathtaking panorama of deep canyons, passes, alpine valleys, and towering mountains of the verdant Carson National Forest. **Rte. 66,** America's most nostalgic highway, includes a colorful stretch that now constitutes Albuquerque's Central Avenue. The old route between Albuquerque and Santa Fe, the **Turquoise Trail,** snakes up through a portion of Cibola National Forest and a number of ghost towns.

National and State Parks

National Parks   **Carlsbad Caverns National Park** (*see* Elsewhere in the State, *below*) is a spectacular system of caves and rock formations.

State Parks   New Mexico's 45 state parks range from the high mountain lakes and pine forests of the north to the Chihuahuan Desert lowlands in the south. Pristine and unspoiled, they offer every conceivable outdoor recreational facility. For maps and brochures, contact the **State Parks and Recreational Division** (Energy, Minerals, and Natural Resources Dept., 408 Galisteo St., Box 20003, Santa Fe 87504, tel. 505/827–7465 or 800/451–2541).

Native American Reservations

Two general classifications of Native Americans live in New Mexico: the Pueblos, who established an agricultural civilization here many centuries ago, and the descendants of the nomadic tribes who came into the area much later—the Navajos, Mescalero Apaches, and Jicarilla Apaches. The settlements of various **Pueblo** tribes are described in the Santa Fe and Albuquerque sections below.

The **Jicarilla Apaches** live on a 750,000-acre reservation in north-central New Mexico. The tribe has a well-defined tourist program promoting big-game hunting, fishing, and camping on a 20,000-acre game preserve; for details, contact the **Tourism Department, Jicarilla Apache Tribe** (Box 507, Dulce 87528, tel. 505/759–3242).

A reservation of a half-million acres of timbered mountains and green valleys in southeastern New Mexico is home to the **Mescalero Apaches.** The tribe owns and operates the most elegant luxury resort in the state, Inn of the Mountain Gods, as well as Ski Apache, 16 mi from Ruidoso. Contact the **Mescalero Apache Tribe** (Box 176, Mescalero 88340, tel. 505/671–4494) for additional information.

The **Navajo Reservation,** home to the largest Native American group in the United States, covers 16 million acres in New Mexico, Arizona, and Utah. There are a few towns on the reservation, but for the most part it is a vast area of stark pinnacles, colorful rock formations, high desert, and mountains. The tribe encourages tourism; write or call the **Navajo Tribal Tourism Office** (Box 663, Window Rock, AZ 86515, tel. 602/871–6659 or 602/871–7371).

Santa Fe

With its crisp, clear air and bright, sunny weather, New Mexico's capital couldn't be more welcoming. Perched on a 7,000-foot-high plateau at the base of the Sangre de Cristo Mountains, Santa Fe is surrounded by the remnants of a 2,000-year-old Pueblo Indian civilization and filled with evidence of the Spanish, who founded the city in 1609 (St. Augustine, Florida, is the only U.S. city that's older). The rows of chic art galleries (Santa Fe is the country's third most important art center, after New York and Los Angeles), smart restaurants, and shops selling southwestern furnishings and cowboy gear combine to make it uniquely appealing. Its population, an estimated 56,000, swells to nearly double that during the peak summer season and again in the winter when skiers arrive, lured by the challenging slopes of the Santa Fe Ski Area and those of nearby Taos Ski Valley.

Tourist Information

Santa Fe: Chamber of Commerce (510 N. Guadalupe St., De Vargas Center N, 87501, tel. 505/983–7317). Convention and Visitors Bureau (201 W. Marcy St., Box 909, 87504, tel. 505/984–6760 or 800/777–2489).

Arriving and Departing

By Plane **Albuquerque International Airport** (tel. 505/842–4366), 65 mi southwest of Santa Fe, serves both cities. Major airlines link it with the rest of the country. **Mesa Airlines** (tel. 505/473–4118) operates air-shuttle service between Albuquerque and **Santa Fe Airport.**

By Car Santa Fe is accessible from points north and south on I–25 or U.S. 84/285.

Train Station **Amtrak's** nearest station is in Lamy, 17 mi from Santa Fe, to which it is linked by an Amtrak shuttle-bus service (tel. 505/982–8829 in Santa Fe, 505/988–4511 in Lamy).

Bus Station **Greyhound** (858 St. Michaels Dr., tel. 505/471–0008).

Getting Around Santa Fe

The downtown area is easily maneuvered on foot. You'll need a car to visit attractions in the outer reaches; there's no bus service, and public transportation in town is monopolized by **Capital City Cab Company** (tel. 505/989–8888).

Exploring Santa Fe

The heart of Santa Fe is its historic **Plaza.** Laid out in 1609–10 as the center for the city's religious and military activities, it was later the terminus of the Santa Fe Trail, where freight wagons unloaded after completing their arduous journeys. Today the Plaza is lined with shops, art galleries, and restaurants. Bordering the north side is the oldest public building in the United States: the Pueblo-style **Palace of the Governors,** which houses the city's **History Museum** (tel. 505/827–6474; admission charged; closed Mon. Jan.–Feb.). Under the building's arcade, **local Native American vendors** display and sell their wares as they've been doing for centuries. Across the street, the Pueblo Revival **Museum of Fine Arts** (107 Palace Ave., tel. 505/827–4455; admission charged; closed Mon. Jan.–Feb.) emphasizes the work of regional artists, including Georgia O'Keeffe, as well as Mexican (such as Diego Rivera), southwestern, and Native American artists. At the far corner of the Plaza is Santa Fe's landmark hotel, **La Fonda** (*see* Lodging, *below*).

A block east, the magnificent French Romanesque–style **Cathedral of St. Francis** (131 Cathedral Pl., tel. 505/982–5619) houses the crypt of its builder, Jean Baptiste Lamy, Santa Fe's first archbishop, and the 17th-century statue *La Conquistadora* (Our Lady of the Conquest), carried to Santa Fe by a Spanish explorer.

Across the street, in an expanded state-of-the-art facility in the renovated former post office, is the **Museum of the Institute of American Indian Arts** (Cathedral Pl., tel. 505/988–6281; admission charged), which has the largest collection of contemporary Native American art in the United States. Its paintings, photography, and traditional crafts showcase the work of students and teachers, past and present, of the prestigious **Institute of American Indian Arts,** across town on Cerrillos Road, where it was founded as a one-room studio classroom in the early 1930s. Allan Houser, Fritz Scholder, Kevin Red Star, and Earl Biss are only a few of the top-flight Native American artists associated with the school.

A number of the city's sights trace the path of the **Old Santa Fe Trail.** The **Loretto Chapel** (212 Old Santa Fe Trail, tel. 505/984–7971; admission charged) is known for the "Miraculous Staircase"—an engineering marvel many of the faithful consider to have been built by St. Joseph—that leads to the choir loft. The adobe **San Miguel Mission** (401 Old Santa Fe Trail, tel. 505/983–3974; admission free), built in 1636 by the Tlaxcala Indians and the oldest church still in use in the United States, houses the San Jose Bell, said to have been cast in Spain in 1356, and a number of priceless statues and paintings. **Barrio De Analco** (now called East De Vargas St.), lined with historic houses, is

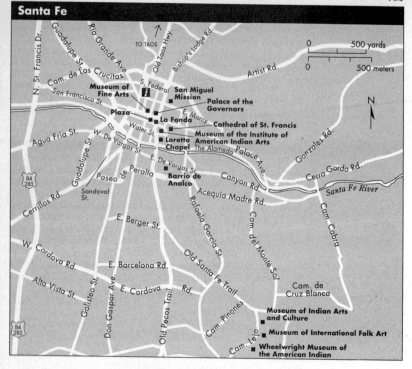

believed to be one of the oldest continuously inhabited streets
in the United States.

The fascinating **Museum of International Folk Art** (706 Camino
Lejo, tel. 505/827–6350; admission charged) is the premier museum of its kind in the world, with textiles, dolls, jewelry, ornaments, and other folk-art objects from many countries. Behind
the museum is the privately owned **Wheelwright Museum of the
American Indian** (704 Camino Lejo, tel. 505/982–4636; admission free), housed in a building shaped like a traditional Navajo
hogan and displaying works of all Native American cultures.
The **Museum of Indian Arts and Culture** (710 Camino Lejo, tel.
505/827–6344; admission charged) focuses on the history and
contemporary culture of New Mexico's Pueblo, Navajo, and
Apache tribes.

In the Vicinity   Situated on a rolling mesa at the base of the rugged Sangre de
Cristo, about 60 mi northeast of Santa Fe, **Taos** is an enchanted
town of romantic courtyards, stately elms and cottonwood
trees, narrow streets, and adobe walls. It's also a world-famous
art and literary center, and a popular ski resort in winter. The
Taos Pueblo—2 mi north of the commercial center of Taos, at
the base of the 12,282-foot-high Taos Mountain—is the home of
the Taos-Tiwa Indians, whose apartment house–style pueblo
dwelling is one of the oldest continuously inhabited communities in the United States. A farming and ranching community of
adobe houses, **Ranchos de Taos**, 4 mi south of town, has one of
the most beautiful churches in the Southwest. With its massive, buttressed adobe walls and graceful towers, the **San
Francisco de Asis Church** is a revered sanctuary to local parish-

ioners, as well as a prime example of early Mission architecture.

Just under 200 mi northwest of Santa Fe, in **Chaco Culture National Historic Park,** are the remains of 13 fully developed pueblos and about 400 smaller settlements. At this site is Pueblo Bonito, the largest prehistoric Southwest Indian dwelling ever excavated. Its magnificent kivas, a 1,200-mi network of paved roads, and a solstice marker testify that the area was the highest point in the Anasazi culture, which peaked in about AD 1150. *Star Rte. 4, Box 6500, Bloomfield 87413, tel. 505/988–6716. Admission charged.*

Forty-five minutes north of Santa Fe, **Los Alamos,** birthplace of the atomic bomb, spreads over fingerlike mesas at an altitude of 7,300 feet. While research continues at the Los Alamos National Laboratory (in such fields as lasers, nuclear energy, superconductivity, and medicine), the community now emphasizes its link to the prehistoric past, promoting the more than 7,000 archaeological sites in the area, including **Bandelier National Monument** (HCR1, Box 1, Suite 15, Los Alamos 87544, tel. 505/672–3861; admission charged).

About 25 mi southeast of Santa Fe, **Pecos National Historic Park** is the site of what was perhaps the greatest Indian pueblo. An early trading center, Pecos was the largest and easternmost pueblo reached by the Spanish conquistadors, who built two missions here, and it became a major landmark on the Santa Fe Trail. *Drawer 418, Pecos 87552, tel. 505/757–6032. Admission charged.*

Pueblos Near Santa Fe
The Native American pueblos near Santa Fe vary in their craft specialties and the recreational facilities they offer to tourists. Most have ceremonial dances on feast days that are open to the public, but policies on taking photographs, tape recording, or sketching differ from pueblo to pueblo. Permission to visit is sometimes required, and in some cases admission is charged. Call ahead for regulations.

Jemez Pueblo (Box 100, Jemez 87024, tel. 505/834–7359), in the red sandstone canyon of the Jemez River, is noted for its polychrome pottery and fine yucca-frond baskets. The beautiful **San Diego de Jemez Mission** (tel. 505/834–7419), founded in the early 1600s, is at the Jemez State Monument (Rte. 4, tel. 505/829–3530) 20 mi north.

Pojoaque Pueblo (Rte. 11, Box 71, Santa Fe 87501, tel. 505/455–2278) has a visitor center, tourist information office, and shops offering an extensive selection of northern New Mexican pottery and other traditional arts and crafts.

San Ildefonso Pueblo (Rte. 5, Box 315-A, Santa Fe 87501, tel. 505/455–2273) was the home of the most famous of all pueblo potters, Maria Martinez, whose exquisitely designed red-and-black pottery is on display throughout the Southwest. The pueblo still boasts a number of highly acclaimed potters, as well as other artists and craftspeople, many of whom open their homes to prospective buyers. San Ildefonso is one of the more active pueblos in maintaining its ceremonial dances and customs.

The picturesque **San Juan Pueblo** (Box 1099, San Juan 87566, tel. 505/852–4400) is headquarters of the Eight Northern Indian Pueblo Council. In its beautiful arts center, the pueblo's special thick-walled red-and-black pottery can be purchased. Two handsome kivas, a French Romanesque–style church, and a restaurant complete the town.

Santa Clara Pueblo (Box 580, Espanola 87532, tel. 505/753–7326) is the home of the beautiful 740-room **Puye Cliff Dwellings.** It is also famous for its shiny red-and-black engraved pottery and for its many well-known painters and sculptors; visitors who knock on the doors with signs announcing pottery will be invited inside to meet the artists.

What to See and Do with Children

The **Museum of International Folk Art** (*see* Exploring Santa Fe, *above*) is a great place to take children any day, but its **Saturdays Are for Kids** program is especially fun. **Santa Fe Adventures for Kids** (Sambusco Market Center, 500 Montezuma Ave., tel. 505/983–0111) runs a variety of exciting—and well-supervised—programs for children. **Santa Fe Children's Museum** (1050 Old Pecos Trail, tel. 505/989–8359) offers hands-on exhibits in the arts and sciences.

Shopping

Santa Fe has 125 art galleries and no one knows how many painters; the Convention and Visitors Bureau (*see* Tourist Information, *above*) has a full listing. *The Wingspread Collectors Guide to Santa Fe and Taos* (Wingspread, Box 13566-T, Albuquerque 87192) is a good bet if you are seriously interested in buying art here.

People also come to the city to buy something called Santa Fe style, characterized by clean lines and strong colors and including an eclectic blend of items from various local cultures—everything from Spanish Mission–style furniture to Mexican tinwork mirrors and Native American blankets.

Canyon Road is Santa Fe's most famous and expensive shopping district. The **downtown** offers a mix of shops, galleries, restaurants, and crafts nooks within a five-block radius of the Plaza. At the southwest perimeter of town, the **neighborhood** around the Guadalupe Church at the intersection of Guadalupe Street, Alameda, and Agua Fria Street, is great for strolling and for taking a shopping break at a sidewalk café.

The cowboy past is very much alive in the dozens of stores in town that sell anything western you can think of. **Cerrillos Road Mercantile and Trading Company** (3741 Cerrillos Rd., tel. 505/471–6329) sells peace pipes, tomahawks, Hopi masks, and muskets at some of the best prices in town. **Santa Fe Western Mercantile** (6820 Cerrillos Rd., tel. 505/471–3655) offers a seemingly inexhaustible supply of hats, boots, jeans, buckles, and belts. **Trader Jack's Flea Market** (7 mi north of Santa Fe on U.S. 84/285; tel. 505/455–7874) has a wide variety of bargains.

The Montecristi Custom Hat Works (118 Gallisteo St., tel. 505/983–9598) is where the smart set goes for custom-made straw hats that fit so perfectly they're all but guaranteed to stay on, even in an open convertible. Felt toppers with bejeweled and unusual (rattlesnake skin) hatbands are also featured.

Sports and Outdoor Activities

Horseback Riding **Camel Rock Ranch** (U.S. 285, tel. 505/986–0408). **Rocking S Ranch** (Madrid Hwy., south of Santa Fe, tel. 505/438–7333). **Santa Fe Stage Line** (Galisteo, south of Santa Fe, tel. 505/983–6565 or 800/338–6877).

Hot-air Ballooning **Balloons Over Santa Fe** (1874 Calle Quedo, Santa Fe 87505, tel. 505/982–8178).

River Rafting **New Wave Rafting Company** (107 Washington Ave., tel. 505/984–1444). **Rio Bravo River Tours** (Hwy. 58, between Taos and Espanola, tel. 800/525–4966). **Santa Fe Rafting Company and Outfitters** (80 E. San Francisco St., tel. 505/988–4914 or 800/584–6011).

Ski Areas

Santa Fe Central Reservations (tel. 505/983–8200 or 800/982–7669) provides information on skiing in the area. The **Santa Fe Ski Area** (1210 Luisa St., 87501, tel. 505/982–4429 or 505/983–9155) has a 1,650-foot vertical drop, 38 trails, and six lifts.

Cross-country **Carson National Forest** (Box 558, Taos 87571, tel. 505/758–6200) has 440 mi of trails. **Enchanted Forest Cross-Country Ski Area** (Box 521, Red River 87558, tel. 505/754–2374) near Taos has 18 mi of trails.

Downhill Taos offers four **downhill** ski resorts within a 90-mi radius: **Angel Fire Resort** (Drawer B, Angel Fire 87710, tel. 505/377–6401 or 800/633–7463), 2,180-foot drop, 55 trails, six lifts. **Red River Ski Area** (Box 900, Red River 87558, tel. 505/754–2382), 1,600-foot drop, 41 trails, six lifts. **Sipapu Lodge and Ski Area** (Rte. Box 29, Vadito 87579, tel. 505/587–2240), 865-foot drop, 18 trails, three lifts. **Taos Ski Valley** (Box 90, Taos Ski Valley 87525, tel. 505/776–2291), 2,612-foot drop, 72 trails, 11 lifts.

Spectator Sports

Horse Racing **Santa Fe Downs** (Rte. 14, tel. 505/471–3311; mid-June–Labor Day).

Dining

A delicious mixture of Pueblo Indian, Spanish Colonial, Mexican, and American-frontier cooking, Santa Fe cuisine is like none other. The city has nearly 200 restaurants to suit all tastes and budgets, from a riot of fast-food outlets on the outskirts, particularly along Cerrillos Road, to elegant spots near the Plaza. For price ranges, see Chart 1 (B) in Chapter 1.

Santa Fe **The Compound.** This restaurant shimmers with Old World elegance. The American-Continental menu includes chicken in
★ champagne, roast loin of lamb, Russian caviar, and New Zealand raspberries. *653 Canyon Rd., tel. 505/982–4353. Reservations required. Jacket and tie required. AE. No lunch; closed Sun.–Mon. Expensive.*

★ **Pink Adobe.** Easily the best-known restaurant in town, the Pink Adobe serves Continental, New Orleans Creole, and local New Mexican favorites in several cozy dining rooms in a three-century-old adobe. *406 Old Santa Fe Trail, tel. 505/983–7712. Reservations required. AE, DC, MC, V. Expensive.*

Staab House. In a delightful conservatory setting, dine on seafood and such northern New Mexican favorites as *fajitas del norte* (tortillas filled with chunks of pork, beef, or chicken). In summer you can sit out on the patio beside a bubbling fountain. *330 E. Palace Ave., tel. 505/986–0000. Reservations advised. Jacket and tie advised for dinner. AE, DC, MC, V. Expensive.*

★ **Coyote Cafe.** Formerly a Greyhound bus depot, this is now one of the trendiest spots in town, thanks to the cheerful ambience and an imaginative menu, which changes daily. Northern New Mexican offerings include a 26-ounce rib-eye steak called The Cowboy, served with barbecued black beans and onion rings. *132 W. Water St., tel. 505/983–1615. Reservations advised. Jacket and tie advised at dinner. AE, MC, V. Closed Tues. in winter. Moderate.*

El Nido. A favorite of Santa Fe Opera fans and performers, this institution has been serving in its cozy, firelit rooms for more than 50 years. The menu features seafood—including excellent broiled salmon and swordfish steak—as well as choice aged beef, prime rib, and New Mexican specialties. *Rte. 592 (22) at Bishop's Lodge Rd., 1 mi from Tesuque, tel. 505/988–4340. Reservations advised. MC, V. Closed Mon. Moderate.*

La Tertulia. Almost as well known for its splendid Spanish Colonial art collection as for its fine New Mexican cuisine and extraordinary house sangria, this lovely restaurant is set in a converted 19th-century convent. *416 Agua Fria St., tel. 505/ 988–2769. Reservations required. Closed Mon. AE, MC, V. Moderate.*

Maria Ysabel Restaurante. This little jewel of a restaurant in an old adobe is a favorite of locals. It's not on one of Santa Fe's most fashionable streets (you can get there by taking a shortcut through the Hilton's parking lot), but a string of twinkling lights outside sets a festive mood. Menu specialties include green-chili chicken enchiladas and *taquitos compuestos* (small tacos filled with guacamole, sour cream, and melted cheese, or with beef and chili verde). *409 Water St., tel. 505/986–1662. Reservations advised. MC, V. Moderate.*

Ore House on the Plaza. This restaurant is perfectly located, with a dining balcony overlooking the Plaza. Seafood and steaks are artfully prepared; margaritas come in 64 flavors. *50 Lincoln Ave., tel. 505/983–8687. Reservations advised. AE, MC, V. Moderate.*

Plaza Café. This busy-beehive restaurant has been a fixture on the Plaza since 1918. From all appearances, the decor hasn't changed much since then—a red leather banquette, black Formica tables, tile floors, and vintage Santa Fe photos, all topped by a coffered tin ceiling. Standard American fare is featured, along with such southwestern specialties as sizzling enchiladas and a nice selection of beers and wines. *54 Lincoln Ave., tel. 505/982–1664. No reservations. MC, V. Moderate.*

★ **Cafe Pasqual's.** Only a block southwest of the Plaza, this cheerful, informal place serves regional specialties. Forget the pancakes and order a *chorizo burrito* (Mexican sausages, scrambled eggs, home fries, and scallions wrapped in a flour tortilla and doused with red or green chili sauce). Expect a line outside. *121 Don Gaspar Ave., tel. 505/983–9340. Reservations advised for dinner. MC, V. Inexpensive–Moderate.*

★ **Maria's New Mexico Kitchen.** You haven't been to Santa Fe until you've eaten at this landmark, in business for over 40 years and decorated with ceramic pottery and colorful paper flowers. Mexican specialties include homemade tamales, rellenos, blue-corn tamales, and green-chili stew. *555 W. Cordova Rd., just east of St. Francis St., tel. 505/983–7929. Reservations advised. AE, D, MC, V. Inexpensive.*

The Shed. Great homemade pies and tasty New Mexican cuisine make this a favorite for lunch. Housed in a rambling adobe hacienda dating from 1692, the restaurant is decorated throughout with festive folk art. Try the red-chili enchiladas or *posole* (corn chowder). *113½ E. Palace Ave., tel. 505/982–9030. No reservations. No credit cards. No dinner; closed Sun. Inexpensive.*

Taos **Apple Tree.** Situated in a historic adobe Territorial house, this cozy and casual restaurant is a popular luncheon, early dinner, and Sunday brunch spot. A series of intimate dining rooms connected by open archways have pastel walls and wooden tables flanked with straw-seated chairs. Among the excellent entrées are mango chicken, enchiladas, shrimp quesadillas, and lamb steak (made from organically raised local lambs). Two homemade soups are prepared daily. *123 Bent St., tel. 505/758–1900. Reservations advised. AE, DC, MC, V. Expensive.*

Brett House. The former home and literary salon of Lady Dorothy Brett, friend and traveling companion of Frieda and D. H. Lawrence, offers superb views of the Sangre de Cristo Mountains and excellent southwestern and international cuisine. *Rtes. 7 and 150, tel. 505/776–8545. Reservations advised. AE, MC, V. Expensive.*

★ **La Cocina de Taos.** A typical New Mexican adobe building on the north side of the Taos Plaza houses yet another popular restaurant offering regional specialties—chili rellenos, *pollo mole poblano* (chicken with a spicy chocolate sauce), fajitas—as well as American standards. The two main dining rooms are separated by stained-glass murals. *North Plaza, tel. 505/758–2412. Reservations advised. Jacket and tie advised. AE, MC, V. Moderate.*

★ **La Cigale Cafe de Paris.** A turn-of-the-century French bistro resurrected in Taos, La Cigale features traditional bistro cooking from the four corners of France—the *bisteck* and *pommes frites* are excellent—at almost turn-of-the-century prices. There's live jazz evenings and Sunday brunch. *Pueblo Alegre Mall, tel. 505/751–0500. AE, MC, V. No lunch Sun. Inexpensive.*

Lodging

Hotel rates, which fluctuate considerably from place to place, are generally lower from November through April (excluding the Thanksgiving and Christmas holidays), and then they soar. B&Bs in Santa Fe and Taos often offer less expensive—and usually charming and characterful—accommodations (**Bed and Breakfast of New Mexico,** Box 2805, Santa Fe 87504, tel. 505/ 982–3332). For price ranges, see Chart 2 (A) in Chapter 1.

Santa Fe **Eldorado Hotel.** One of the city's most luxurious hotels, the Eldorado, in the heart of downtown, has rooms furnished in southwestern style. Many have balconies, and all offer mountain views. The Old House restaurant is outstanding. *309 W. San Francisco St., 87501, tel. 505/988–4455; fax 505/982–0713. 218 rooms. Facilities: 2 restaurants, bar, pool, nightly entertainment, shopping arcade. AE, D, DC, MC, V. Very Expensive.*

Inn of the Anasazi. Santa Fe's newest showpiece offers rooms with beamed ceilings, kiva fireplaces, and handcrafted furnishings. Amenities include concierge and twice-daily maid service, and delivery of exercise bikes to your room upon request. *113 Washington Ave., 87501, tel. 505/988–3030 or 800/688–8100; fax 505/988–3277. 51 rooms, 8 suites. Facilities: restaurant, wine cellar. AE, DC, MC, V. Very Expensive.*

La Posada de Santa Fe. This Spanish Colonial inn near the Plaza sits amid beautifully landscaped gardens and expansive green lawns. Guest rooms have fireplaces, beamed ceilings, and Native American rugs. *330 E. Palace Ave., 87501, tel. 505/986–0000 or 800/727–5276; fax 505/982–6850. 119 rooms, 33 suites. Facilities: restaurant, bar, pool, health-club privileges. AE, DC, MC, V. Expensive–Very Expensive.*

★ **Inn of the Governors.** Just two blocks from the Plaza, this is one of the nicest hotels in town. Standard rooms have a Mexican theme, with bright colors, hand-painted folk art, southwestern fabrics, and handmade furnishings. *234 Don Gaspar Ave. (at Alameda St.), 87501, tel. 505/982–4333 or 800/234–4534; fax 505/989–9149. 100 rooms. Facilities: restaurant, piano bar, pool, parking. AE, DC, MC, V. Expensive.*

★ **La Fonda.** Built in 1864 on a site established in 1610, this may be the only hotel in the world that can boast having had both Kit Carson and John F. Kennedy as guests. Each room is unique, featuring hand-decorated wooden furniture and motifs painted by local Pueblo Indian artists. *100 E. San Francisco St., 87501, tel. 505/982–5511 or 800/523–5002; fax 505/988–2952. 164 rooms, 35 suites. Facilities: restaurant, lounge, bar, pool, spa. AE, D, DC, MC, V. Expensive.*

Hotel Santa Fe. Owned by the Picuris Pueblo Indians, this 1991 hotel—the largest off-reservation Indian-owned hotel in the country—offers rooms decorated in traditional southwestern style. Its gift shop, the only tribe-owned gift shop in Santa Fe, offers prices lower than those of most nearby retail stores, and guests get an additional 25% discount. *1501 Paseo de Peralta, 87504, tel. 505/982–1200 or 800/825–9876; fax 505/984–2211. 40 rooms, 91 suites. Facilities: bar, deli. AE, D, DC, MC, V. Moderate–Expensive.*

★ **Inn of the Animal Tracks.** Three blocks east of the Plaza, this enchanting 90-year-old restored adobe has beamed ceilings, hardwood floors, handcrafted furniture, and fireplaces. Each guest room is decorated with an animal theme. A full breakfast and high tea are served. *707 Paseo de Peralta, 87504, tel. 505/988–1546. 5 rooms. AE, MC, V. Moderate–Expensive.*

Taos **Hotel La Fonda de Taos.** Built in 1937, La Fonda catered to Eu-
★ ropean and American celebrities in its heyday. Today it is well past its prime, but the locale—on the south side of Taos's Plaza—is ideal and the experience of staying there enchanting. The lobby is a showcase of framed newspaper and magazine stories, posters, photos, paintings, and Native American artifacts. In the office of owner Saki Karavas is one of Taos's most celebrated "treasures," a collection of so-called erotic paintings by D. H. Lawrence; a fee of $3 gets you in for a peek. *Taos Plaza, Box 1447, 87571, tel. 505/758–2211 or 800/833–2211. 24 rooms. MC, V. Expensive.*

★ **Taos Inn.** Only steps from the Plaza, this sprawling hotel is a prized local landmark—parts of the structure date from the 1600s—exemplifying southwestern rustic charm. Guest rooms are individually furnished, featuring hand-loomed Zapotec Indian bedspreads and furniture built by local artists. *125 Paseo del Pueblo Norte, 87571, tel. 505/758–2233 or 800/826–7466;*

fax 505/758–5776. 39 rooms. Facilities: restaurant, bar, lounge, library, wine shop. AE, DC, MC, V. Expensive.

★ **Las Palomas de Taos/The Mabel Dodge Luhan House.** This Pueblo Indian–style structure, set on spectacular grounds, was the home of heiress Mabel Dodge Luhan. The 12 guest rooms in the main house are furnished with turn-of-the-century pieces; rooms in the newer guest house have regional hand-carved furnishings. *Morada La., 87571, tel. 505/758–9456. 22 rooms (6 share baths). MC, V. Moderate.*

Sagebrush Inn. Graceful portals, romantic patios, and charming adobe architecture make this one of the prettiest hotels in town. Many of the rooms have kiva fireplaces; some have balconies looking onto the mountains. Georgia O'Keeffe once lived and painted here. *1508 Paseo del Pueblo Sur, Box 557, 87571, tel. 505/758–2254 or 800/428–3626; fax 505/758–9009. 83 rooms. Facilities: 2 restaurants, lounge, nightly entertainment, pool, spas, tennis courts. AE, DC, MC, V. Moderate.*

Koshari Inn. Nestled under centuries-old silver aspens in the foothills of Taos Canyon is this beautifully converted former motel. Rooms are spacious, with handmade furnishings; each has a private entrance. *910 E. Kit Carson Rd., Box 6612, 87571, tel. 505/758–7199. 12 units. Facilities: pool. D, MC, V. Inexpensive.*

Resorts

Santa Fe **The Bishop's Lodge.** Three miles north of downtown Santa Fe, in the rolling foothills of the Sangre de Cristo Mountains, this family-oriented resort houses guests in one- and three-story lodges with Old Southwest furnishings. The dining room is one of the area's best. *Bishop's Lodge Rd., 87504, tel. 505/983–6377; fax 505/989–8739. 56 rooms, 18 suites. Facilities: restaurant, bar, pool, whirlpool, horseback riding, hiking, skeet shooting, tennis, golf, supervised children's programs. No credit cards. Closed Jan.–Apr. Very Expensive.*

Rancho Encantado. This elegantly casual resort offers a full range of activities in the rolling, piñon-covered hills above the sprawling Rio Grande Valley. Guest rooms have fine Spanish and western antiques; some have fireplaces and/or private patios. The restaurant is a treat by itself. *U.S. 285 near Tesuque, 8 mi north of Santa Fe (Rte. 4, Box 57C), 87504, tel. 505/982–3537. 12 rooms, 10 suites, 30 2-bedroom condos. Facilities: restaurant, 2 pools, spa, tennis, horseback riding, hiking, jogging, skiing. AE, DC, MC, V. Very Expensive.*

Taos **Quail Ridge Inn and Tennis Ranch.** Five miles north of Taos Plaza, the Quail Ridge offers a touch of modern elegance against a magnificent natural backdrop. What it lacks in rustic charm it makes up for in a host of recreational amenities, from organized trail rides to hot-tub soaks. *Ski Valley Rd. (Rte. 150), Box 707, 87571, tel. 505/776–2211 or 800/624–4448; fax 505/776–2949. 115 rooms, 60 suites. Facilities: restaurant, lounge, fitness center, pool, hot tub, tennis courts, squash, volleyball. D, DC, MC, V. Expensive.*

★ **Austing Haus.** This enormous timber-frame building offers stunning views of the Taos Ski Valley from its glass-paneled front. Guest rooms are spare and functional, but the dining room is excellent. *Taos Ski Valley Rd. (Rte. 150), Box 8, 87525, tel. 505/776–2649, 505/776–2629, or 800/748–2932; fax 505/776–*

8751. 26 rooms. Facilities: restaurant, hot tub, satellite TV. MC, V. Moderate.

Campgrounds

La Bajada Welcome Center (La Bajada Hill, 13 mi southwest of Santa Fe on I–25, tel. 505/471–5242) provides information on private campgrounds. The **Santa Fe National Forest** (1220 S. St. Francis Dr., Box 1689, 87504, tel. 505/988–6940), right in the city's backyard, has public sites open from May through October. Inside the city, **Los Campos Recreational Vehicle Park** (3574 Cerrillos Rd., 87501, tel. 505/473–1949) has RV hookups and a pool. Operated by the Tesuque Pueblo Indians, **Tesuque Pueblo RV Campground** (Tesuque 87501, tel. 505/455–2661) has hookups and tent sites.

The Arts and Nightlife

Check the entertainment listings in Santa Fe's daily newspaper, the *New Mexican,* or the complimentary *Inside Santa Fe,* available at most hotels and shops, for special performances and events.

The Arts Artistically and visually the city's crowning glory, the famed **Santa Fe Opera** (Rte. 285, tel. 505/982–3855) is housed in a strikingly modern indoor-outdoor amphitheater carved into a hillside 7 mi north of the city. The **Santa Fe Symphony** (tel. 505/983–3530; Sept.–May) performs at Sweeney Center (201 W. Marcy St.). The **Orchestra of Santa Fe** (tel. 505/988–4640) plays at the Lansic Theater (211 W. San Francisco St.; Sept.–May). The **Santa Fe Chamber Music Festival** (tel. 505/983–2075) is held at the St. Francis Auditorium of the Museum of Fine Arts (The Plaza; July–Aug.).

Nightlife The lounges, hotels, and night spots of Santa Fe offer a wide variety of entertainment options. **The Cargo Club** (519 Cerrillos Rd., tel. 505/989–8790) has the hottest dance music in town. **Rodeo Nites** (2911 Cerrillos Rd., tel. 505/473–4138) attracts a country-western crowd.

Albuquerque

A large city—its population is nearing the half-million mark—Albuquerque spreads out in all directions, with no apparent ground rules. The city seems as free-spirited as the hot-air balloons that take part in its annual October Balloon Festival. Like the rest of New Mexico, Albuquerque blends its cultures—Native American, Spanish, and Anglo—well.

Albuquerque began as an important trade and transportation station on the Old Chihuahua Trail, an extension of the Santa Fe Trail that wound down into Mexico. The original four-block downtown, known as Old Town, is the city's tourist hub, with galleries and trendy Mexican and New Mexican restaurants.

Tourist Information

Albuquerque: Convention and Visitors Bureau (Springer Sq. Bldg., 121 Tijeras Ave. NE, Box 26866, 87125, tel. 505/842–9918 or 800/284–2282).

Arriving and Departing

By Plane **Albuquerque International Airport** (tel. 505/842–4366) is 5 mi
south of downtown; the trip takes 10–15 minutes. Taxis charge
about $7 (plus 35¢ for each additional rider). **Sun Tran** buses
(tel. 505/843–9200), which cost 75¢, pick up at the sunburst
signs about every 15 minutes.

By Car I–25 enters Albuquerque from points north and south; I–44,
from points east and west.

Train Station **Amtrak** serves **Albuquerque Station** (314 1st St. SW, tel. 505/
842–9650).

Bus Station **Greyhound: Transportation Center** (300 2nd St. SW, tel. 505/
243–4435).

Exploring Albuquerque

Albuquerque sprawls in all directions, so you'll need transportation to get wherever you're going. Historic and colorful Rte.
66 is Albuquerque's Central Avenue, unifying, as nothing else,
the diverse areas of the city—Old Town cradled at the bend of
the Rio Grande, the University of New Mexico to the east, and
Nob Hill, a lively strip of restaurants, boutiques, galleries, and
shops, farther east. The river and the railroad tracks, running
almost neck and neck and traversed by Central Avenue, divide
the city into quadrants: SW, NW, SE, NE.

The city began in 1706, in Old Town, and tree-shaded **Old Town
Plaza** remains the heart of Albuquerque's heritage. The **San
Felipe de Neri Church** (2005 Plaza NW, tel. 505/243–4628), enlarged and expanded several times over the years, faces the plaza, its massive adobe walls and other original sections intact.
Most of the old adobe houses surrounding the plaza have been
converted into shops, galleries, and restaurants.

The striking 1986 glass-and-sand-colored **New Mexico Museum
of Natural History** offers an active volcano, a frigid Ice Age
cave, dinosaurs, and an Evolator (short for Evolution Elevator), a six-minute high-tech ride through 35 million years of
New Mexico's geologic history. *1801 Mountain Rd. NW, tel.
505/841–8837. Admission charged.*

A short drive north of Old Town, the **Indian Pueblo Cultural
Center** holds the largest collection of Native American arts and
crafts in the Southwest, a valuable resource for the study of the
region's first inhabitants. The center is owned and operated by
the 19 Pueblo tribes of New Mexico, each of which has an alcove
devoted to its arts and crafts. Free performances of ceremonial
dances are given in summer and on special holidays. *2401 12th
St. NW, tel. 505/843–7270. Admission charged.*

For an overview of Albuquerque—and half of New Mexico, for
that matter—head for **Sandia Crest**, the 10,678-foot summit of
the Sandia Mountains. **Sandia Peak Aerial Tramway**, the
world's longest single-span tramway, makes an awesome 2.7-
mi climb from a point outside the city limits to the top of Sandia
Peak. At sunset the desert skies are a kaleidoscope of colors. *10
Tramway Loop NE, tel. 505/296–9585. Admission: $10.50
adults, $8 children. Closed weekdays 2nd and 4th weeks of
Apr.*

In the Vicinity So named because early 19th-century settlers believed they had stumbled upon the Halls of Montezuma, **Aztec Ruins National Monument,** a 3½- to four-hour drive northwest of Albuquerque, contains 500 rooms laid out in an E-shaped plan around a plaza. Archaeologists recently restored the kiva to mint condition. *Rte. 44, Box 640, Aztec 87410, tel. 505/334–6174. Admission charged.*

Coronado State Monument, a prehistoric Kuaua pueblo on a bluff overlooking the Rio Grande near Bernalillo, 20 mi north of Albuquerque, is believed to have been the headquarters of Coronado's army of 1,200, who came seeking the legendary Seven Cities of Gold in 1540. *Off I–25, Box 853, Bernalillo 87004, tel. 505/867–5589. Admission charged.*

About 180 mi southeast of Albuquerque—near the cemetery, just off Rte. 212, where Billy the Kid is buried, and the adjacent museum devoted to him—**Ft. Sumner State Monument** displays artifacts and photographs relating to the fort and the Bosque Redondo Reservation. At the latter, 9,000 Navajos were interned from 1863 to 1868, brought to the site by Kit Carson after the infamous "Long Walk" from their original homeland in Canyon de Chelly, Arizona. *Off U.S. 60 and Rte. 20, Box 356, Ft. Sumner 88119, tel. 505/355–2573. Admission charged. Closed Tues.–Wed.*

At the site of five extinct volcanoes, 8 mi west of Albuquerque, **Petroglyph National Monument** contains nearly 15,000 ancient rock drawings, inscribed on the 17-mi-long West Mesa escarpment probably between AD 1100 and 1600. *6900 Unser Blvd. NW, Albuquerque 87120, tel. 505/897–8814 or 505/873–6620. Admission free; parking charge.*

Pueblos Near Albuquerque A series of terraced adobe pueblos, dominated by the massive mission church of San Estevan del Rey, **Acoma** (Box 309, Acoma 87034, tel. 505/252–1139), also known as Sky City, sits atop a 357-foot mesa that rises abruptly from the valley floor 40 mi west of Albuquerque. Its onetime population of 6,000 has dwindled to a mere 50 who live in the village without electricity or running water. This pueblo may be visited on guided tours only.

The **Santo Domingo Pueblo** (Box 99, Santo Domingo 87052, tel. 505/465–2214), off I–25 at the Santo Domingo exit between Albuquerque and Santa Fe, operates a Tribal Cultural Center, where its outstanding *heishi* (shell) jewelry is sold. The August 4 Corn Dance is one of the most colorful and dramatic of all the Pueblo ceremonial dances.

The sun symbol appearing on the New Mexican flag was adopted from the **Zia Pueblo** (General Delivery, San Ysidro 87053, tel. 505/867–3304), at its present site since the early 1300s. Skillful Zia potters produce fine polychrome wares, and the watercolors of the tribe's painters are highly prized.

What to See and Do with Children

At the **Old Coal Mine Museum** (Madrid Star Rte., Madrid, tel. 505/473–0743), about 30 mi north of Albuquerque, children love exploring the mine tunnel, climbing aboard a 1906 steam train, and nosing through antique buildings. Sprawled over 60 acres, Albuquerque's **Rio Grande Zoological Park** (903 10th St. SW, tel. 505/843–7413) is home to more than 1,000 animals from around the world, including a rare snow leopard. The **Tinkertown Museum** (Hwy. 536, Sandia Park, tel. 505/281–5233) houses a delightful world of miniature carved-wood characters, including an animated western village and a tiny circus.

Shopping

As in most large, sprawling western cities, Albuquerque's main shopping areas are malls and shopping centers. Hours are generally weekdays 10–9, Saturday 10–6, and Sunday noon–6.

Among the major shopping centers are **Coronado Center** (Louisiana and Menaul Blvds., tel. 505/881–2700), New Mexico's largest mall; **Fashion Square** (1100 San Mateo Blvd., tel. 505/265–6931); **First Plaza Galeria** (20 1st Plaza NW, tel. 505/242–3446); and **Winrock Center** (Louisiana Blvd. exit off I–40, tel. 505/883–6132). The **Antique Specialty Mall** (4516 Central Ave. SE, tel. 505/268–8080) specializes in memorabilia from the early 1880s to the 1950s. **Ortega's de Chimayo** (324-C San Filipe Ave. NW, tel. 505/842–5624) is the Old Town showcase of the Ortega family's weaving and arts-and-crafts shop in Chimayo (on the High Rd. between Santa Fe and Taos).

Sports and Outdoor Activities

Contact the **Albuquerque Parks and Recreation Department** (Box 1293, Albuquerque 87103, tel. 505/768–3490) for information on its network of parks and recreational programs, including golf courses, paved tracks for biking and jogging, swimming pools, tennis courts, ball fields, playgrounds, and even a shooting range.

Hot-air Ballooning Reliable firms include **A&R Sky Voyages** (4600 Quartz Dr., Rio Rancho, tel. 505/891–9529), **Cameron Balloons New Mexico** (2950 San Joaquin Ave. SE, tel. 505/265–4007), **Rainbow Riders** (430 Montclaire Dr. SE, tel. 505/268–3401), and **Tours of Enchantment** (5801 Jones Pl. NW, tel. 505/831–4285).

Spectator Sports

Hot-air Ballooning The **Albuquerque International Balloon Fiesta** (8309 Washington Pl. NE, 87113, tel. 505/821–1000) attracts more than 500 registered hot-air balloons each October. An estimated 1.5 million people attend the nine-day program to watch as the balloons float over Albuquerque's backyards, setting off a serenade of barking dogs.

Dining

Many of Albuquerque's favorite dining spots specialize in northern New Mexico–style cooking, but French, Continental, Mediterranean, Italian, and standard American fare are also readily available. You can dress as casually as you like and order wine by color instead of label. Restaurants in the major business hotels tend to be a bit more formal. For price ranges, see Chart 1 (B) in Chapter 1.

Expensive **Chardonnay's.** Served in a setting reminiscent of an English
★ country house are Mediterranean saffron scallops, veal Florentine, and other Continental and French creations of Randolph Valdez, one of Albuquerque's most lauded chefs. *6815 Menaul*

Blvd., tel. 505/881–0000. Reservations advised. Jacket and tie advised. AE, D, DC, MC, V. No lunch Sat.; closed Sun.

High Noon Restaurant and Saloon. In one of Old Town's 200-year-old adobe buildings, this skylighted former woodworking shop now offers fine dining in a Territorial setting, decorated with Native American rugs and New Mexican art. Topping the menu offerings are pepper steak, steak Diane, and varying southwestern specials. *425 San Felipe Ave. NW, tel. 505/765–1455. Reservations advised. AE, D, DC, MC, V.*

Monte Vista Fire Station. Now a national historic landmark, this spacious, airy restaurant was once a working firehouse. The New American menu includes a wide variety of seafood, beef, and pasta dishes; highlights are wild-mushroom ravioli and crab cakes. *3201 Central Ave. NE, tel. 505/255–2424. Reservations advised. AE, DC, MC, V. No lunch weekends.*

Moderate ★ **Artichoke Cafe.** In a turn-of-the-century brick building just east of downtown, the café offers New American, Italian, and some French dishes and specializes in broiled salmon, veal, and lamb. Its large modern dining room, decorated with the work of local artists, spills onto a small courtyard. *424 Central Ave. SE, tel. 505/243–0200. Reservations advised Fri.–Sat. AE, MC, V. Closed Sun.*

Ciao! This tastefully decorated northern Italian restaurant, with marble floors and sculptured glass, offers spectacular views of the city lights and of the nearby Sandia Mountains. Specialties include veal *saltimbocca*, fettuccine Alfredo, and homemade pasta. *Tramway Blvd. and Indian School Rd. NE, tel. 505/293–2426. Reservations advised. Jacket and tie advised. AE, DC, MC, V. No lunch Sat.*

Maria Teresa. A restored 1840s adobe in Old Town furnished in handsome English antiques is the setting for this appealing restaurant. The menu offers aged beef, seafood, chicken, and New Mexican specialties, such as *carne adovado* (cubed, marinated pork, rolled in a flour tortilla and covered with red chilies and cheese). *618 Rio Grande Blvd. NW, tel. 505/242–3900. Reservations advised. AE, D, DC, MC, V.*

Inexpensive ★ **66 Diner.** This former transmission shop on old Rte. 66 is now a glitzy art deco establishment with black-and-white tile floors and turquoise-and-pink vinyl seats. Burgers, blue-plate specials—pot roast, chicken-fried steak, beef stew—and the separate soda fountain all add to the tone of 1950s nostalgia. *1405 Central Ave. NE, tel. 505/247–1421. AE, MC, V.*

Lodging

Albuquerque's hotels offer a comfortable mix of modern conveniences and Old West flavor, with accommodations ranging from budget motels to bed-and-breakfasts to soaring hotel towers. All are uniformly friendly and folksy, and incorporate much of the Southwest heritage in their decor and design. For price ranges, see Chart 2 (B) in Chapter 1.

Expensive **Albuquerque Marriott.** This luxury property uptown near some of the city's best shopping areas is geared to vacationers as well as executive travelers. Furnishings are contemporary, with Southwest touches. *2101 Louisiana Blvd. NE, 87110, tel. 505/881–6800; fax 505/888–2982. 410 rooms. Facilities: 2 restaurants, lounge, health club, 2 pools, free airport transfers. AE, D, DC, MC, V.*

Hyatt Regency Albuquerque. Adjacent to the Convention Center in the heart of downtown are the two soaring, desert-colored towers of this totally modern and luxurious hotel. The spacious guest rooms are finished in contemporary southwestern style with a mauve, burgundy, and tan color scheme. *330 Tijeras Ave. NW, 87102, tel. 505/842–1234; fax 505/766–6710. 395 rooms. Facilities: restaurant, 2 lounges, health club, outdoor pool. AE, D, DC, MC, V.*

Moderate– Expensive **La Posada de Albuquerque.** Opened by Conrad Hilton in 1939 (he honeymooned here with Zsa Zsa), this historic hotel in the heart of downtown oozes charm and character. Native American war-dance murals ornament the wall behind the reception desk. The large guest rooms are decorated with Southwest and Native American themes, and many have fireplaces. Despite a recent renovation, however, the hotel remains well past its prime; guests might be well advised to inspect a room before signing in. *125 2nd St. NW, 87102, tel. 505/242–9090 or 800/ 777–5732; fax 505/242–8664. 114 rooms. Facilities: 2 restaurants, bar, gift shop, free airport and Old Town transfers. AE, D, DC, MC, V.*

Moderate **Casas de Sueños.** Long a gathering spot for artists and now a
★ bed-and-breakfast on a 2-acre compound adjacent to Old Town, "Houses of Dreams" offers casitas attractively decorated with beehive fireplaces, pigskin furniture, regional paintings, and Native American rugs. *310 Rio Grande Blvd. SW, 87104, tel. 505/247–4560. 3 rooms, 9 suites. AE, MC, V.*

Radisson. This two-story motor hotel at the airport has a southwestern-Spanish flavor, with arched balconies, desert colors, a courtyard pool, and indoor and outdoor dining. The guest rooms are comfortable, if not luxurious. *1901 University Blvd. SE, 87106, tel. 505/247–0512; fax 505/843–7148. 148 rooms. Facilities: restaurant, lounge, outdoor pool, spa, free airport transfers. AE, D, DC, MC, V.*

William E. Mauger Estate. In this elegant downtown 1897 Queen Anne residence, four guest rooms are Victorian style, the other two art deco. Full breakfasts are served in guests' rooms or in the parlor. *701 Roma Ave. NW, 87102, tel. 505/242– 8755. 7 rooms. AE, DC, MC, V.*

Inexpensive **DeNaza Motor Lodge.** It's not in the best section of town, but this one- and two-story pueblo-style motel (the sign out front is shaped like a tepee) is easy on the wallet. Free Continental breakfast is served in the lobby, and minifridges are furnished upon request. Decor and furnishings are in modern Santa Fe style. *4301 Central Ave. NE, 87108, tel. 505/255–1654. 81 rooms. AE, D, MC, V.*

Campgrounds

Fifteen minutes south of Albuquerque on I–25, the **Isleta Lakes and Recreation Area** (Box 383, Isleta 87022, tel. 505/877– 0370) has complete campground facilities with tent sites and RV hookups. Within the city limits, **KOA Albuquerque Central** (12400 Skyline Rd., 87123, tel. 505/296–2729) and **Albuquerque North KOA** (1021 Hill Rd., Bernalillo 87004, tel. 505/867–5227) have tent sites and RV hookups.

The Arts and Nightlife

To find out what's on in town, check the *Albuquerque Journal* on Friday and Sunday or the *Albuquerque Tribune* on Thursday.

The Arts The **Southwest Ballet** (670 Juantabo Blvd. SW, tel. 505/294–1423) presents a wide variety of classical and contemporary performances. The **New Mexico Symphony Orchestra** (220 Gold Ave. SW, tel. 505/842–8565) is in its 60th year. The **New Mexico Repertory Theatre** (tel. 505/243–4500), the state's only resident professional theater group, stages its productions at the **KiMo Theater** (5th St. and Central Ave. NW, tel. 505/764–1700).

Nightlife **Caravan East** (7605 Central Ave. NE, tel. 505/265–7877) presents live music nightly and offers a free happy-hour buffet from 5 to 7 PM. **Midnight Rodeo** (4901 McLeod St. NE, tel. 505/888–0100), an enormous country-and-western complex, has a huge racetrack-like dance floor and several bars.

Elsewhere in the State

Carlsbad Caverns National Park

Getting There In the southeastern part of the state, the park is 320 mi from Albuquerque via I–25, U.S. 380, and U.S. 285, and 167 mi west of El Paso, Texas, via U.S. 180. **Mesa Airlines** (tel. 800/637–2247; in Carlsbad, 505/885–0245) offers air-shuttle service between Albuquerque airport and **Cavern City Air Terminal** in Carlsbad.

What to See and Do **Carlsbad Caverns National Park** (3225 National Parks Hwy., Carlsbad 88220, tel. 505/785–2232 or 505/885–2283) contains one of the largest and most spectacular cave systems in the world: 77 caves, with huge subterranean chambers, fantastic rock formations, and delicate mineral sculptures. Only two caves are open to the public. At **Carlsbad Cavern,** the descent to the 750-foot level is made by foot or elevator; either way, you can see the Big Room, large enough to hold 14 Houston Astrodomes. **New Cave** (tel. 505/785–2232; reservations required a day in advance), 25 mi from the main cavern, is much less accessible: The last few miles of the roadway are gravel, and the mouth of the cave is a half-mile climb up a 500-foot rise.

The park is the area's main lure, but the town of **Carlsbad** (Chamber of Commerce, 302 S. Canal St., 88220, tel. 505/887–6516) and such nearby attractions as **Living Desert State Park** (1504 Skyline Dr., Carlsbad 88220, tel. 505/887–5516) are also well worth visiting.

Dining For price ranges, *see* Charts 1 (B) and 2 (B) in Chapter 1.

Lucy's. A family-owned oasis of great Mexican food, Lucy's was recently remodeled in southwestern decor. Here you can enjoy such items as chapa chicken chacos (chicken tacos with guacamole) and Tucson-style chimichangas (chicken, beef, or brisket with chili, cheese, and seasonings). *701 Canal St., tel. 505/887–7714. MC, V. Moderate.*

Lodging **Best Western Stevens Motel.** An old favorite, both locally and with tour groups, this is a reliable, well-operated place. Guest rooms feature bright desert colors, mirrored vanities, and modern furnishings; some have kitchenettes and/or private patios. The hotel is owned by Carlsbad's mayor Bob Forrest, but even knowing him won't necessarily get you a table at its Silver Spur bar and lounge on Saturday night when the Chaparrals are playing. *1829 S. Canal St., 88220, tel. 505/887–2851 or 800/528–1234; fax 505/887–6338. 202 rooms. Facilities: restaurant, lounge, pool. AE, D, DC, MC, V. Moderate.*

TEXAS

By Mark Potok

Capital	Austin
Population	16,841,000
Motto	Friendship
State Bird	Mockingbird
State Flower	Bluebonnet

Visitor Information

Department of Texas Tourism (Box 5064, Austin 78763, tel. 800/888–8839).

Scenic Drives

In far southwest Texas, **Rte. 170** from Lajitas through Presidio and into the Chinati Mountains is one of the most spectacular drives in the state, plunging over mountains and through canyons along the Rio Grande (thus its name, "El Camino del Rio," or River Road). **U.S. 83** from Leakey to Uvalde is a roller coaster of a ride through the lush western edges of the central Texas Hill Country. In the northern Panhandle, **I–27** from Lubbock to Amarillo carries travelers through the buffalo grass and sheer cliffs of the Llano Estacado ("Staked Plain," so named because the lack of trees forced pioneers to tie their horses to stakes). From Center, a small town near the Louisiana border, south into the Sabine National Forest, **Rte. 87** takes you over several dramatic lakes and through one of the huge pine forests for which East Texas is famous.

National and State Parks

National Parks **Big Bend National Park** (U.S. 385 from Marathon; Superintendent, Big Bend National Park 79834, tel. 915/837–2326) is the state's premier natural attraction. This overwhelming landscape, laid bare by millions of years of erosion, includes spectacular canyons, a junglelike floodplain, the sprawling Chihuahuan Desert, and the cool woodlands of the Chisos Mountains. Spread out over 801,163 acres, Big Bend teems with animal life, from relatively rare black bears and mountain lions to coyotes, javelinas, gray foxes, beavers, deer, and jackrabbits. More than 430 bird species have been identified here, including such favorites as the roadrunner and rarities like the Colima warbler. The park is crosshatched with hundreds of miles of trails, dirt roads, and paved roads and offers wild backcountry camping (with permits). For the more timid, there are ranger-led walks, campgrounds, a trailer park, and other amenities. River outfitters offer rafting trips through remote canyons of the Rio Grande (tel. 915/424–3219 to reserve spots for longer trips).

Davy Crockett National Forest (Ratcliff Lake; 1240 E. Loop 304, Crockett, 75835, tel. 409/544–20461)—a 161,500-acre park in the "piney woods" of East Texas about 20 mi east of the historic town of Crockett on Rte. 7—offers camping, canoeing on the Neches River, a dramatic 19-mi hiking trail, and picnicking facilities and concessions around Ratcliff Lake.

Aransas National Wildlife Refuge (Rte. 2040, Tivoli, tel. 512/286–3559), on a peninsula jutting 12 mi into the Gulf of Mexico near Rockport, is the principal wintering ground of the endangered whooping crane. The best time to spot it and some 300 other species of birds is between November and March.

State Parks   **Caddo Lake State Park** (Rte. 43, tel. 903/679–3351), on the southern shore of the lake near Karnack, offers camping, cabins, fishing, swimming, and boating.

Named after the local term for "high plains," **Caprock Canyons State Park** (Rte. 1065, Quitaque, tel. 806/455–1492) in the Panhandle is marked by canyons, striking geologic formations, and an abundance of wildlife, including African aoudad sheep, mule deer, and golden eagles.

Enchanted Rock State Park (Rte. 965, Llano, tel. 915/247–3903), near Fredericksburg in the Hill Country, is so named because of the noises emitted by the underground heating and cooling of its massive, 500-foot-high dome of solid granite. The rock is the reputed site of ancient human sacrifices.

Fishing is king at **Inks Lake State Park** (Rte. 29 and Park Rd. 4, Barnet, tel. 512/793–2223), northwest of Austin at the edge of the Hill Country. Surrounding the lake's crystal-clear waters are extensive amenities, including facilities for camping, trailers, boats, and golf.

Set on the High Plains east of the Panhandle town of Canyon, **Palo Duro Canyon State Park** (Rte. 217 and Park Rd. 5, tel. 806/488–2227) is a place of rock spires and precipitous cliffs, long a favorite spot for Texan tourists. When movie director Steven Spielberg was looking for the world's most dramatic sunset for 1989's *Indiana Jones and the Last Crusade,* he found it in Palo Duro Canyon near this park. The site of the last great battle with the Comanches, the park today offers an outdoor amphitheater backed by a 600-foot cliff, where the historical drama *Texas,* written by a local playwright, is presented late June through August (Mon.–Sat.; reservations recommended, tel. 806/655–2181).

Houston and Galveston

The oil crash of the early 1980s hit once-flamboyant Houston as few other places in Texas, and the resulting strange contrast between the downtown's glass-and-steel magnificence and its boarded-up buildings may be the city's most noticeable feature. Another cause of remarkable juxtapositions is a total lack of zoning—unique among major American cities—that has yielded such results as the shacks of the poverty-stricken Fifth Ward pushing hard up against the glittering skyscrapers built during the boom years.

The nation's fourth-largest city is still an international business hub and the energy capital of the United States, a fact evidenced by the Texas-size conventions that occasionally fill its major hotels to bursting point. Its port still thrives, and its highways, while plentiful, can be nightmarish with roaring traffic. Large and varied foreign communities and a plenitude of fine ethnic restaurants and world-class cultural institutions lend Houston a distinct cosmopolitan flavor that Dallasites will claim but cannot capture. This is truly a city for city lovers.

Galveston, 50 mi to the southeast, is Houston's touristy stepchild. An island in the Gulf of Mexico, connected by causeway and bridge to the mainland, it is an odd mix of Victorian architecture and Coney Island–like beach developments. Although virtually all of its architecture dates from after 1900, when an unheralded hurricane and consequent tidal waves swept over this 32-mi-long sandbar, Galveston has managed to recapture a historic feel long lost to its northern neighbor. Once a faded has-been, the city is now enjoying a tourist-fueled renaissance evident in energetic renovation efforts. It is artsy, even precious, and well stocked with hotels and restaurants catering to visitors.

Tourist Information

Galveston Island: Convention & Visitors Bureau (2106 Seawall Blvd., in the Moody Center, tel. 409/763–4311, 800/351–4237, or 800/351–4236 in TX). Strand Visitors Center (2016 Strand, tel. 409/765–7834). **Greater Houston:** Convention & Visitors Bureau (801 Congress Ave., 77002, tel. 713/227–3100 or 800/231–7799). Information booths are located near the baggage areas at Hobby and Intercontinental airports.

Arriving and Departing

By Plane Houston's two major airports are, between them, served by about 25 airlines. (Be sure to check which airport you will be using, as many airlines serve both.) **Southwest Airlines** (tel. 713/237–1221 or 800/435–9792) offers particularly extensive, frequent, and inexpensive service among nine Texas cities. More convenient to downtown is **W. P. Hobby Airport** (tel. 713/643–4597), 9 mi to the southeast. During rush hour, the trip into the city will take about 45 minutes; taxi fare runs about $20. **Houston Intercontinental Airport** (tel. 713/230–3100), 15 mi north of downtown and closer to the Galleria area, is the city's international airport. The trip downtown during peak hours takes up to an hour and 15 minutes; cab fare will run you up to $30. **Shuttles** to several Houston locations serve both Hobby ($6; tel. 713/644–8359) and HIA ($12 adults, $5 children; tel. 713/523–8888); **city express bus service** (tel. 713/635–4000) to HIA costs $1.20. **Galveston Limousine Service** (tel. 713/223–2256 in Houston; 409/765–5288 or 409/744–0563 in Galveston) offers hourly service to island locations from both Houston airports for $15–$20.

By Car Houston is ringed by the I–610 beltway. A tighter loop, comprising several expressways, circles the downtown and provides remarkable views of the city, especially at dawn and dusk. Radiating out from these rings like spokes of a wheel are I–10, heading east to Louisiana and west to San Antonio; U.S. 59, northeast to Longview or southwest to Victoria; and I–45, southeast to Galveston (about an hour away) or north to Dallas. Traffic on all these highways can be extremely heavy during rush hours.

Train Stations In Houston, **Amtrak** (tel. 713/224–1577) trains run out of the old **Southern Pacific Station** (902 Washington Ave.).

Galveston's **Center for Transportation and Commerce** (2500 Strand, tel. 409/765–5700) serves as the terminal for the **Texas Limited** (tel. 713/864–9991), a tourist rail line that connects to Houston's **Eureka Station** (567 T. C. Jester St.). Departing Houston Friday, Saturday, and Sunday mornings and returning the same evening, the train features seven restored cars from the 1920s to the 1940s. An intermediate stop near Space Center Houston was added in 1992.

Bus Stations **Greyhound** (2121 Main St., Houston, tel. 713/222–1161). **Texas Bus Lines** (49th St. and Broadway, Galveston, tel. 409/765–7731).

Getting Around Houston and Galveston

Both Houston and Galveston almost demand cars. Attractions are spread out, and public transportation is sketchy. Houston has a city bus system (Metro, tel. 713/635–4000), but it is difficult for visitors to learn its intricacies. Similarly, Galveston offers island bus service, but of far more interest is the **Treasure Island Tour Train** (2106 Seawall Blvd., tel. 409/765–9564), which departs regularly from just outside the Convention & Visitors Bureau (*see* Tourist Information, *above*) for tours of local sights.

Exploring Houston and Galveston

Houston Houston can be neatly divided into three major areas: (1) downtown, a homage to modernism that spurred one architecture critic to declare the city "America's future" and that includes the theater district; (2) an area a couple of miles south of downtown that includes some of the Southwest's leading museums, as well as Rice University and the internationally renowned Texas Medical Center; and (3) the ritzy shopping area west of downtown that is centered on The Galleria.

Downtown You may want to start by taking in the entire urban panorama from the observation deck of I. M. Pei's **Texas Commerce Tower** (600 Travis St.; admission free; closed weekends), at 75 stories the city's tallest building and the world's highest composite tube tower. Nearby **Texas Street** is 100 feet wide, precisely the width needed to accommodate 14 Texas longhorns horn tip to horn tip in the days when cattle were driven to market along this route. Downtown's major attractions are clustered at this northwest corner, and you can get another perspective on the architecture that distinguishes the city by relaxing in **Tranquillity Park,** between Walker and Rusk streets east of Smith Street. This cool, human-scaled oasis of fountains and diagonal walkways among the skyscrapers was built to commemorate the first words of man on the moon: "Houston, Tranquillity Base here. The Eagle has landed." The plaque claiming that America has "the only system of government" capable of such a feat conveniently ignores *Sputnik* and the entire history of space exploration, but it is a true reflection of the city's bursting Texas chauvinism.

The park forms the threshold to the theater district, whose major buildings are a few steps away. The **Jesse H. Jones Hall for the Performing Arts** (615 Louisiana St.), home to the Houston Symphony Orchestra and the Society for the Performing Arts, is a huge hall that appears almost encased by a second,

Houston

colonnaded building; its teak auditorium is more attractive than the exterior. The **Alley Theatre** (615 Texas Ave.), a fortresslike but innovative low-lying structure, is the venue of the city's only resident professional theater company. The **Gus S. Wortham Theater Center** (550 Prairie Ave.), where the Houston Grand Opera and the Houston Ballet perform in two side-by-side theaters, was completed in 1987. Just behind the Wortham, **Sesquicentennial Park** was built two years later as the first phase of a beautification of the shore of Buffalo Bayou, the minor body of water bounding downtown's north end. **City Hall** (901 Bagby St.), just northwest of Tranquillity Park, is an unremarkable building whose chief interest lies in its allegorical interior murals.

On the west side of downtown, running south from Tranquillity Park, is the **Smith-Louisiana corridor,** two daunting canyons formed by towers of glass and steel, most of which were erected before oil prices plunged in 1983. A walk down these streets may be the truest measure of the city's modernism, intensified by the **outdoor sculptures** of Joan Miró, Claes Oldenburg, Louise Nevelson, and Jean Dubuffet. (Dubuffet's *Monument au Fantôme*, on Louisiana Street between Lamar and Dallas streets, is a particular delight to children.) These streets may leave you with an eerie sense of emptiness, but there is a good reason for that beyond the universal depopulation of America's urban centers: More than 70 of the major business and government buildings downtown are connected by a 6.7-mi labyrinth of **underground tunnels,** used by those in the know as a welcome escape from the humidity for which Houston is justly infamous.

A last stop downtown, particularly if you have children, might be the lobby of the **Hyatt Regency Houston** (1200 Louisiana St.). Garish and decorated with potted plants and brass aplenty, the lobby's atrium soars 30 stories, circled by balconies and topped by a revolving restaurant cocktail lounge. A ride up in the glass-enclosed cabs of the powerful elevators is dramatic, a sure winner with kids, and a trifle frightening.

The Museum District Four miles south of downtown on Main Street lies leafy **Rice University,** Texas's finest institution of higher learning; the **Texas Medical Center,** a sprawling complex best known for the famous M. D. Anderson Cancer Center; and the three world-class museums that are the city's cultural crown jewels.

The **Museum of Fine Arts'** collection is remarkable for its completeness, if exhausting in size. Housed in a complicated series of wings and galleries—many of which were designed by Ludwig Mies van der Rohe—the museum now also owns the **Bayou Bend Collection** of American decorative arts, housed across town in the River Oaks mansion neighborhood (1 Westcott St., tours by reservation only, tel. 713/529–8773). Highlights of the museum's vast offerings include the Straus collection of Renaissance and 18th-century works and the notable Samuel Kress collection of Italian and Spanish Renaissance paintings. Impressionism is also well represented in such paintings as *The Rocks,* an 1888 van Gogh that prefigures some of the artist's later, more extravagant brushstrokes. *1001 Bissonnet (north of Rice U.), between Montrose and Main Sts., tel. 713/526–1361. Admission charged (free Thurs.). Closed Mon.* `

The **Contemporary Arts Museum,** in an aluminum-sheathed trapezoid across the street, is the home of avant-garde art in Houston. It is noteworthy for the traveling exhibits that pass regularly through its spaces. *5216 Montrose St., tel. 713/526–3129. Admission free. Closed Mon.*

The Menil Collection, 10 minutes away by car on a small side street, is the city's biggest cultural surprise. Opened in 1987 in a spacious building designed by the Italian architect Renzo Piano, the museum's airy galleries contain treasures as diverse as tribal African sculpture and Andy Warhol's paintings of Campbell's soup cans. Also here are works by Léger, Picasso, Braque, and other major modern artists. Check out the wonderful Matisse cutouts, executed when the artist's eyes were failing and he could no longer paint. *1515 Sul Ross St., tel. 713/525–9400. Admission free. Closed Mon.–Tues.*

Just down the street is the moody **Rothko Chapel,** an octagonal sanctuary hung with 14 paintings by Mark Rothko. At first they appear as simple black panels; only when you come close can you see the subtle coloring. Outside the chapel, created as a site for religious meditation by all faiths, is Barnett Newman's sculpture *Broken Obelisk,* symbolizing the life and assassination of Martin Luther King, Jr. *3900 Yupon St. at Sul Ross St., tel. 713/524–9839. Admission free.*

Time Out Slicing through the center of the museum district is artsy **Montrose Street,** lined with some of the city's trendier restaurants. Though many are expensive, **Butera's** (4621 Montrose St., tel. 713/528–1500) offers reasonably priced but excellent sandwiches, salads, and pastas served buffet style.

The Galleria Area   On the west side of Houston, near the intersection of West-heimer Road and I–610, is **The Galleria,** one of the world's swankiest shopping malls. Here four major department stores and 300 other shops groan with an abundance of fashionable apparel and other pricey goods; hundreds more stores and sumptuous restaurants line the surrounding streets. Foreign shoppers are known to travel to Houston for no other reason than to spend money at The Galleria. Several deluxe hotels are also found in the area, and River Oaks, a street of multimillion-dollar mansions, is conveniently nearby.

Galveston   History is the main draw in Galveston, a city that was once the largest in Texas. Its wealthy classes built the houses that are now being restored to their former glory in a frenzy of tourist-driven rehabilitation. These homes, and some beautifully restored iron-front commercial buildings, are concentrated on the northern, bay side of the island—especially along a street known as The Strand—and on Broadway, a boulevard that runs east–west through Galveston's midsection. Also hugging the north rim of the island, from 9th to 51st streets, is the harbor, port to about 100 small fishing boats and shrimp trawlers and to the *Elissa*, the tall ship that is Galveston's pride and joy. The south, ocean side of the island is lined with beaches (*see* Beaches, *below*), hotels, parks, rental shops, and restaurants.

The Strand and   The heart of historic Galveston—and the nucleus of its new-
Broadway   found prosperity—is **The Strand,** especially the five blocks that run from 25th to 20th Street (now on the National Register of Historic Places). When Galveston was still a powerful port city—before the Houston Ship Channel was dug, diverting most boat traffic inland—this stretch of former stores, offices, and warehouses was known as the Wall Street of the South.

At its foot is the **Center for Transportation and Commerce** (which also houses the **Railroad Museum,** 2500 Strand, tel. 409/765–5700; admission charged), an art deco building that was once the Santa Fe Railroad terminal. As you stroll up the street, you'll pass dozens of trendy shops—some of them quite beautiful—and the few four- and five-story iron-front buildings that have not yet been restored, where workers are busily scurrying about to bring in still more shops, restaurants, and bars. A block away is the **Tremont House,** a onetime dry-goods warehouse converted into a hotel that conjures up visions of coaches, top hats, and Victorian elegance. Today the hotel is the best on the island. Still, it's not hard to see how new all this redevelopment is: Just at the edges of this gilded renaissance, tawdry topless bars and windowless "clubs" beckon with signs like "Lipstick Lounge" and "Exotic Dancers."

A 20-minute walk or five-minute drive to the south is Broadway, home of the "Broadway Beauties"—not employees of the above-mentioned lounges but, rather, three of the finest examples of historic restoration in Texas. The Victorian **Bishop's Palace** (1402 Broadway, tel. 409/762–2475; admission charged; closed Tues.), listed on the National Register of Historic Places, was built in 1886 for Col. Walter Gresham. The man had a fondness for fireplaces, to which the 11 rare stone and wood mantels in the limestone-and-granite castle amply attest. The building's most outstanding feature, however, is the wooden main staircase, a work of art that took 61 craftsmen seven years to carve.

Ashton Villa (2328 Broadway, tel. 409/762–3933; admission charged) is a formal Italianate villa built in 1859 of brick—appropriately so, as owner James Moreau Brown started out as a poor mason. A freethinking man, Brown had to install curtains to shield daintier guests from the naked Cupids painted on one wall. His daughter, Miss Bettie, was quite a liberated woman for her era, smoking cigars in public and raising money for the poor. Three blocks away is the 1894 **Moody Mansion** (2618 Broadway, tel. 409/762–7668; admission charged), another brick mansion, with interiors of exotic woods and gilded trim. Taped voices replicate "typical" period conversations based on historical documents.

North of Broadway, the **East End Historical District** is a trove of wooden Victorian houses built for people somewhat less wealthy. Sealy and Ball streets are particularly lovely. For a sense of how the other half lived in this slaveholding society, stop by the twin "shotgun houses" at 1722–24 Winnie Street, typical of the way poor of all colors long lived in much of Texas.

The Elissa   In 1961, a marine archaeologist and naval historian named Peter Throckmorton spotted a rotting iron hulk in the shipyards outside Athens, Greece. While it looked much like hundreds of other Greek cargo ships, Throckmorton realized the 150-foot boat was what remained of a beautiful square-rigger constructed almost a century earlier, in 1877. Through successive owners, its bark rig had been cut down to a single cargo mast, its proud sailing bow sliced off to change its telltale profile during a spell as a smuggler. Today, after almost 20 years of work, the Scottish-built *Elissa*—the oldest ship on the Lloyd's Register—has been restored to its former glory by the Galveston Historical Foundation and hundreds of volunteers. The *Elissa* spends most of the year berthed just off The Strand, but every August the crew takes it out to sail on the high seas. The ship, which in the last century carried cargoes to Galveston Harbor, may be toured above and below decks and is the centerpiece of the **Texas Seaport Museum,** which opened in late 1991. *Pier 21, tel. 409/763–1877. Admission charged.*

Parks and Gardens

Houston   A short drive south of downtown on Main Street is **Hermann Park,** 545 acres of luxuriant trees, lawns, duck-graced reflecting pools, picnic areas, and an 18-hole golf course. Sitting on the northern perimeter of the Texas Medical Center, the park is also home to the Houston Zoo and the Museum of Natural History (*see* What to See and Do with Children, *below*), the Garden Center, and the Miller Outdoor Theater. This park is the city's playground.

Memorial Park, several miles west of downtown, is 1,500 acres of mostly virgin woodland. A wonderful spot for walkers, joggers, and bikers, this serene and enormous park is where former president George Bush runs for exercise.

The small downtown **Sam Houston Park,** bounded by Bagby, McKinney, and Dallas streets, preserves a few of the city's 19th-century buildings. Tickets for daily guided tours are available at the Heritage Society (tel. 713/655–1912), on the Bagby side.

Galveston **Stewart Beach Park** (Seawall Blvd. at Broadway, tel. 409/765–5023) offers a complete bathhouse, an amusement park, bumper boats, a miniature golf course, and even bungee jumping.

Toward the western, unpopulated end of the island, **Galveston Island State Park** (13 Mile Rd., tel. 409/737–1222) is a 2,000-acre natural habitat ideal for bird-watching and walking.

What to See and Do with Children

Houston In Hermann Park, the Zoological Gardens, commonly known as the **Houston Zoo** (1513 N. MacGregor St., tel. 713/523–5888), includes a petting zoo, an aquarium, and other attractions. In the same park, a miniature train and paddleboat rides are favorites with children. The excellent **Museum of Natural History** (1 Hermann Circle Dr., tel. 713/639–4600), also on park grounds, includes the **Baker Planetarium** and **Wortham IMAX Theatre,** with a six-story-high projection screen.

Astroworld and Waterworld (8400 Kirby Dr., at I–610, tel. 713/799–1234), forming one of the country's major amusement complexes, are perennial favorites. Among the 100 rides are the "Texas Cyclone," a terrifying roller coaster, and the "Thunder River" water ride. Other attractions for children include the **Houston Fire Museum** (2403 Milam St., tel. 713/524–2526), the **Houston Police Museum** (17000 Aldine Westfield Rd., tel. 713/230–2300), and the wacky **Orange Show** (2402 Munger St., tel. 713/926–6368; closed Jan.–Feb.), an irreverent and bizarre labyrinth built over 26 years by a Houston eccentric as a tribute to the orange—a Houston must-see.

Adults as well as children may enjoy **Space Center Houston,** 25 mi south of Houston (I–45 to the Alvin exit, then 3 mi east on NASA Rd. 1, tel. 713/244–2105 or 800/972–0369). The huge new center's exhibits include a movie and a dramatic mock-up of a space shuttle. Tram tours take you through NASA's adjacent **Johnson Space Center,** where several rockets are displayed. When it's not in use, you can visit Mission Control as well.

Galveston The island's main draws for children, inevitably, are its 32 mi of beaches and the beachside rides at **Stewart Beach Park** (*see* Parks and Gardens, *above*). Other choices are the recently expanded **Lone Star Flight Museum** (at Scholes Field Municipal Airport, tel. 409/740–7722) and the collection of classic automobiles at **David Taylor Classics** (1918 Mechanic St., tel. 409/765–6590).

Shopping

Houston The city's premier shopping area is **The Galleria** (Post Oak Blvd. and Westheimer Rds.), famed for high-quality stores like Neiman Marcus, Marshall Field, and Tiffany & Co. On **Post Oak Boulevard** north to San Felipe is another stretch of luxury stores. East of The Galleria, **Westheimer Road** offers an array of galleries and artsy shops. Probably the most expensive merchandise is found at the **River Oaks Shopping Center** (Shepherd Dr. and Gray St.). Good boots and other western gear are available at **Stelzig's Western Wear** (3123 Post Oak Blvd.). Downtown, the **Parks Shops in Houston Center** (1200 McKinney St.), with 70 stores, is a recently built mall that provides a convenient entrance to the city's tunnel system (another is at the downtown Hyatt Regency), which is lined with retail shops. Tunnel maps are free at most banks.

Galveston The historic stretch of The Strand is the best place to shop in Galveston, with offerings ranging from the **Old Strand Emporium** (2112 Strand), a deli and gourmet grocery, to the superb **Simply Guatemala** (2402 Strand), selling crafts from that country. Antiques, collectibles, and peanut products are found at the **Old Peanut Butter Warehouse** (100 20th St.).

Spectator Sports

Houston Baseball **Houston Astros** (Astrodome, 8400 Kirby Dr., tel. 713/799–9500; Apr.–Oct.).

Basketball **Houston Rockets** (The Summit, 10 Greenway Plaza, tel. 713/627–2115; Oct.–Apr.).

Football **Houston Oilers** (Astrodome, tel. 713/797–1000; Aug.–Dec.).

Beaches

Galveston Galveston's ocean beaches are all open to the public. The eastern end of the island, especially around Stewart Beach Park, is rife with amenities of all kinds, including rentals of surfboards, sailboats, chairs, and umbrellas. To the west are less crowded beaches, with a quieter, more natural atmosphere.

Dining

For price ranges, see Chart 1 (B) in Chapter 1.

Houston **Anthony's.** Serving the same French food as Tony's (1801 Post Oak Blvd.) in less lavish surroundings, Anthony's is in the heart of the trendy museum district. Chef Bruce McMillian changes the menu frequently, but the veal Gragnon, prepared with shallots, artichokes, and marsala, is usually available and always superb. *4611 Montrose St., tel. 713/524–1922. Reservations advised. Jacket and tie advised. AE, DC, MC, V. No lunch weekends. Expensive.*

Cafe Annie. Don't be put off by the shopping-strip entrance— the food served up at large, isolated tables is the finest American cuisine in town. The mussel soup and the venison are favorites, but the rabbit enchiladas may be the café's most unusual offering. *1728 Post Oak Blvd., tel. 713/840–1111. Reservations required. Jacket and tie advised. AE, D, DC, MC, V. Closed Sun. Expensive.*

Athens Bar & Grill. It's not easy to find, in an industrial area near the ship channel, but you can tell it's authentic when Greek sailors stride in late at night and begin breaking plates. There's live music nightly, belly dancing on weekends. *8037 Clinton Dr., tel. 713/675–1644. Reservations required. AE, DC, MC, V. Moderate.*

Spanish Flower. A bit of a trek north of downtown, this is *the* Mexican restaurant for those in the know in Houston. It's open 24 hours a day (except on Tuesday night)—a cheerful place of ceramic tiles, potted plants, and outdoor dining. *4701 N. Main St., tel. 713/869–1706. AE, D, DC, MC, V. Moderate.*

This Is It. And so it is, if you're looking for genuine soul food. In the Fifth Ward just west of downtown, this eatery offers a buffet of oxtails, pork hocks, chitterlings, black-eyed peas, and the like. This can be a tough neighborhood, so you may want to stick to lunch. *239 W. Gray St., tel. 713/523–5319. No credit cards. Inexpensive.*

Galveston **Wentletrap.** Light woods and brick abound in this fine Continental restaurant in The Strand historic district. The veal medallions are a local favorite, the ever-changing seafood dishes trustworthy. *2301 Strand, tel. 409/765–5545. Reservations advised. AE, DC, MC, V. Closed Sun. Expensive.*

Gaido's. Founded in 1911 by the Gaidos, this restaurant is still in the same politically important Italian family and still serves some of the best seafood in town. Try their famous grilled red snapper, lump crabmeat, or oysters as you gaze out picture windows at the gulf. *39th and Seawall Blvd., tel. 409/762–9625. AE, MC, V. Moderate–Expensive.*

Benno's on the Beach. There's a Coney Island feel to this little red, white, and blue joint, cited by some as the best place in Galveston for deep-fried seafood. *1200 Seawall Blvd., tel. 409/762–4621. AE, MC, V. Inexpensive–Moderate.*

Shrimp N' Stuff. You can tell by the mix—including cops, businesspeople, and high-school students—that this place, with a brick-walled courtyard, is a great deal for fresh seafood. *3901 Ave. O, tel. 409/763–2805. AE, DC, MC, V. Inexpensive.*

Lodging

For price ranges, see Chart 2 (A) in Chapter 1.

Houston **Ritz-Carlton.** It's no surprise that Margaret Thatcher, Adnan Khashoggi, and hosts of other rich and famous types frequent the Ritz, where rooms were created at a cost of $200,000 each and where chef Todd Rogers runs a superb restaurant. With hallways perfumed by exotic flowers and rooms affording dramatic views, the Ritz is convenient to The Galleria, the museum district, and the superposh River Oaks neighborhood. *1919 Briar Oaks La., 77027, tel. 713/840–7600; fax 713/840–8036. 207 rooms, 25 suites. Facilities: 2 restaurants, bar, tearoom, rooftop pool, health club, valet parking. AE, D, DC, MC, V. Very Expensive.*

Hyatt Regency Houston. Every room opens onto a balcony overlooking the dramatic atrium, and the revolving rooftop restaurant/cocktail lounge, Spindletop, offers panoramic views of the city. Convenient to all downtown locations, this hotel is a business traveler's choice. *1200 Louisiana St., 77002, tel. 713/654–1234; fax 713/951–0934; telex 775–791. 907 rooms, 52 suites. Facilities: 4 restaurants, 2 bars, pool, nearby health club, valet parking. AE, D, DC, MC, V. Expensive.*

Allen Park Inn. This pleasant motor inn, with rooms circling an outdoor swimming pool, is convenient to downtown, fairly priced, and well maintained. *2121 Allen Pkwy., 77019, tel. 713/521–9321 or 800/231–6310; fax 713/521–9321, ext. 350. 249 rooms, 22 apartments. Facilities: restaurant, 2 bars, health club. AE, D, DC, MC, V. Moderate.*

Sara's Bed & Breakfast & Inn. A pretty example of the Queen Anne–style architecture that populates the Houston Heights neighborhood, about 4 mi northwest of downtown, this turn-of-the-century B&B has a cupola, several porches, and a family atmosphere. *941 Heights Blvd., 77008, tel. 713/868–1130 or 800/593–1130. 10 rooms (5 share baths), 1 suite. AE, DC, MC, V. Inexpensive–Moderate.*

Galveston **San Luis Hotel and Condominiums.** Balconied rooms overlooking the gulf are the norm at this spiffy if isolated high-rise resort complex, where hotel rooms are in one wing and more expensive condominiums in another. *5222 Seawall Blvd., 77551, tel. 409/744–1500, 800/445–0090, or 800/392–5937 in TX; fax 409/744–8452. 244 hotel rooms, 106 condominiums. Facilities: 2 restaurants, 2 bars, entertainment, pool, health club, tennis courts. AE, D, DC, MC, V. Very Expensive.*

Tremont House. Walking into this hotel, right off The Strand in the heart of old Galveston, is a progressive pleasure, from the Victorian elegance of its facade to the hand-carved 1888 mahogany bar of the narrow, four-story atrium that forms the lobby. But it's not until you reach your room, decorated in elegant black-and-white vertical patterns and Italian tile, with soaring ceilings and 11-foot windows, that you truly appreciate the grandeur. *2300 Mechanic's Row, 77550, tel. 409/763–0300 or 800/874–2300; fax 409/763–1539. 116 rooms. Facilities: restaurant, bar, access to health club. AE, DC, MC, V. Expensive.*

Commodore. Hard on the beach, this is a functional hotel with a large pool and gulf views from many room balconies. *3618 Seawall Blvd., 77552, tel. 409/763–2375, 800/231–9921, or 800/543–0074 in TX; fax 409/763–2379. 91 rooms. AE, D, DC, MC, V. Moderate.*

The Arts and Nightlife

The Arts Houston's performing-arts scene is a busy one, as reflected in
Houston the venues described above (*see* Exploring Houston, Downtown). Ticket information on the city's **symphony orchestra, opera, ballet,** and **Society for the Performing Arts,** which books dance, orchestras, and solo artists, may be obtained by calling 713/227–2787. Dramas are regularly presented at the **Alley Theatre** (615 Texas Ave., tel. 713/228–8421). Complete listings of events are carried in the *Houston Chronicle, Houston Post,* and *Key Magazine.*

Galveston The recently restored **Grand 1894 Opera House** (2020 Post Office St., tel. 409/765–1894), where performances of various kinds are held from time to time, is worth visiting for the architecture alone. Sarah Bernhardt and Anna Pavlova once played this storied stage, which is just 70 feet from the farthest seat. The **Strand Street Theater** (2317 Ship's Mechanic Row, tel. 409/763–4591) is another venue for occasional dramas.

Nightlife Possibly the most interesting bar in Houston is a brick-fronted
Houston hole-in-the-wall, **La Carafe** (813 Congress Ave., tel. 713/229–9399), in the oldest commercial building in Houston. A top venue for an eclectic mix of pop performers—from the Neville Brothers to fiddler Vassar Clements—is **Fitzgerald's** (2706 White Oaks Dr., tel. 713/862–7580). **Cody's** (3400 Montrose Blvd., tel. 713/522–9748) is a well-known jazz club with a decent Italian kitchen and the very best view of the downtown skyline in Houston.

San Antonio and the Hill Country

The Alamo—symbol either of Texan heroism or of Anglo arrogance—is by no means the only reason to visit San Antonio. A mélange of easily mingling ethnic groups, it is in many ways Texas's most beautiful and atmospheric city. To the northwest is the Hill Country, an anomaly in generally flat Texas, rich with pretty landscapes, early American history, and echoes of the linen-to-silk story of Lyndon Baines Johnson, the nation's 36th president.

Tourist Information

Hill Country: Tourism Association (1001 Junction Hwy., Kerrville 78028, tel. 210/895–5505). **Bandera:** Convention & Visitors Bureau (1206 Cypress St.; Box 171, 78003, tel. 210/796–3045 or 800/364–3833). **Fredericksburg:** Convention & Visitors Bureau (106 N. Adams St., 78624, tel. 210/997–6523). **Kerrville:** Convention & Visitors Bureau (1700 Sidney Baker St., 78028, tel. 210/792–3535 or 800/221–7958). **San Antonio:** Alamo Visitor Center (216 Alamo Plaza; Box 845, 78293, tel. 210/225–8587). Convention & Visitors Bureau (121 Alamo Plaza, 78205, tel. 210/270–8700 or 800/447–3372).

Getting There

By Plane More than a dozen airlines serve the **San Antonio International Airport,** about a 15-minute drive north of downtown. Inexpensive shuttle services operate 24 hours a day. **Southwest Airlines** (tel. 210/617–1221) provides regional service.

By Car Good highways serve San Antonio from most directions, including I–35 from Dallas and I–10 from Houston. I–410 rings the city, and several highways take you downtown.

By Train **Amtrak** serves San Antonio's station (1174 E. Commerce St., tel. 210/223–3226), with daily trains north to Fort Worth, Dallas, East Texas, and Chicago; east to New Orleans and beyond; and west to Los Angeles.

By Bus Buses run out of San Antonio's **Greyhound Bus Station** (500 N. St. Mary's St., tel. 210/270–5800) to all major cities as well as to most local towns.

Exploring San Antonio and the Hill Country

Much of San Antonio can be explored on foot, although some of its attractions will require transportation. For the Hill Country, a car is a must; you can cover several towns in a day, catching some of the landscapes in between as you drive.

San Antonio At the heart of San Antonio, the **Alamo** stands as a repository of Texas history, a monument to the 189 volunteers who died there in 1836 during a 13-day siege by the Mexican dictator General Santa Anna. They fought not for Texan independence, but for adherence to the liberal 1824 constitution of Mexico, of which Texas was then a part. When the Alamo was finally breached on March 6, at dreadful cost to the Mexican Army, the slaughter that followed would be remembered to history as the

San Antonio

major turning point of the Texas Revolution. Santa Anna claimed victory, but, as a liberal aide wrote privately, "One more such 'glorious victory' and we are finished." Three weeks later, at Goliad, Santa Anna ordered the massacre of 343 Texan prisoners. But he was captured and the revolution completed on April 21, when Sam Houston led his sharpshooting volunteers—crying "Remember the Alamo! Remember Goliad!"—to victory against two-to-one odds at San Jacinto. Today the Alamo is filled with guns and other paraphernalia belonging to William Travis, Davy Crockett, James Bowie, and the other martyrs. *Alamo Plaza, tel. 210/225–1391. Admission free.*

Another sight on Alamo Plaza is the 1859 **Menger Hotel.** In its moody, mahogany bar—a precise replica of the pub in London's House of Lords—Teddy Roosevelt supposedly recruited his Rough Riders, cowboys off the Chisholm Trail drank to excess and fought, and cattlemen closed deals with a handshake over three fingers of rye whiskey.

Beginning and ending at the Alamo, the **Texas Star Trail** is a 2.6-mi walking tour designated by blue disks in the sidewalks. Information on the trail, which takes you past 80 historic sites and landmarks, is available at the Alamo Visitor Center at Alamo Plaza.

Nearby, reached by dozens of stairways, is **River Walk,** the city's leading tourist attraction. Built a full story below street level, River Walk is several miles of scenic stone pathways built on both banks of the San Antonio River downtown. In some places it is peaceful and quiet, in others a mad conglomeration of restaurants, bars, hotels, and strolling mariachi bands, all of which can be seen from river taxis or charter boats—as Queen Elizabeth II did on her 1991 visit. In January, when parts of the river are drained to clear the bottom of debris, locals revel in the River Bottom Festival and Mud Parade. A pleasure at all times, River Walk should be experienced at night.

Southeast of the walk is **Hemisfair Park,** onetime site of a World's Fair and currently home to the 750-foot **Tower of the Americas** (tel. 210/299–8615), where an observation deck and a rotating restaurant offer bird's-eye views of the city. Just beyond is the **Institute of Texan Cultures** (Hemisfair Plaza, tel. 210/226–7651), a university-run, interactive museum focusing on the 26 ethnic groups who made Texas what it is today. Among the many exhibits you'll find an elaborately engraved 16th-century conquistador's helmet of the type favored by Vasquez de Coronado, the "Castroville Hearse," and a full-size, walk-through replica of a sharecropper's house.

A little farther south is the **King William Historic Area,** settled by leading German merchants in the late 19th century. The elegant Victorian mansions, set in a quiet, leafy neighborhood, are a pleasure to behold; Madison and Guenther streets are particularly pretty for a stroll or drive. A few houses, like the 1876 **Steves Homestead** (509 King William St., tel. 210/225–5924), offer daily tours. While you're in the vicinity, you might want to stop in at **Guenther House** (205 E. Guenther St., tel. 210/227–1061). Home of the adjacent Pioneer Flour Mills' founding family, it was built in 1860 and today offers tours, a small museum of mill memorabilia, a gift shop, and a cheerful restaurant serving fine German pastries and full breakfasts and lunches.

Continuing south from downtown, you can pick up the **Mission Trail,** connecting four of the Spanish stone missions built along the San Antonio River (the first of which, established in 1718, later came to be known as the Alamo). Meant to Christianize the Native Americans, these religious outposts were surrounded by *presidios* (rustic stone compounds). All are beautiful, in their way. **Mission Concepción** (807 Mission Rd.) is known for its frescoes; **San José** (6539 San Jose Dr.), "Queen of Missions," has had its outer wall, Native American dwellings, granary, and workshops restored; **Espada** (10040 Espada Rd.), the southernmost, is a favorite of serious students and includes an Arab-inspired aqueduct that was part of the missions' famous *acequia* water-management system. Pick up trail maps at the downtown information centers, as the missions are hard to find (tel. 210/229–5701; admission free).

Heading back downtown, you'll pass close by the **Lone Star Brewery** (600 Lone Star Blvd., tel. 210/270–9469)—"Home of the National Beer of Texas"—which makes for an interesting tour. The grounds also contain the old Buckhorn Bar, once San Antonio's leading saloon; a cottage used by the writer O. Henry; and the **Buckhorn Hall of Horns, Fins and Feathers** (tel. 210/270–9400), said to contain the world's largest collection of animal horns. Back in town, just west of the river, the **San Fernando Cathedral** (Commerce and Flores Sts.) is where Santa Anna raised his no-quarter flag for the Alamo defenders to tremble at. The seat of a bishopric, it was visited by Pope John Paul II in 1987. Nearby is the beautiful **Spanish Governor's Palace** (105

Plaza de Armas, tel. 210/224–0601), seat of Spanish power in Texas.

San Antonio's arts scene is marked by a strong southwestern flavor. The **San Antonio Museum of Art** (200 W. Jones Ave., tel. 210/978–8100) houses pre-Columbian, Native American, Spanish colonial, and other art. The **Southwest Craft Center** (300 Augusta St., tel. 210/224–1848) is filled with crafts but may be most remarkable for its building, once an Ursuline school for girls.

The Hill Country It's a long, pleasing drive through the Hill Country from San Antonio. Starting a slow, clockwise loop to the northwest, it's less than an hour's trip to the Kerrville area on I–10. However, you may want to catch the far prettier Rte. 16, a hilly road that leads to **Bandera** (population: 877). One of the nation's oldest Polish communities (dating from 1855) and site of an 1854 Mormon colony, Bandera is today replete with working and guest ranches. On I–10, **Boerne** (population: 4,274) is another early immigrant settlement, founded by Germans and named after a German writer. One of its fine early buildings is the **Kuhlmann-King House**, which can be toured by appointment with the local historical society (402 E. Blanco St., tel. 210/249–2030). Nearby **Cascade Caverns** (Exit 543 off I–10, tel. 210/755–8080) is a dramatic, active wet cave with a 90-foot underground waterfall and visitor facilities including RV camping and a pool.

Kerrville, a town of little obvious interest, is said to have the best climate in the nation. This has led to a proliferation of hotels, children's summer camps, guest ranches, and religious centers. **Kerrville State Park,** 500 acres along the cypress-edged Guadalupe River, is a good place to spot the white-tailed deer that abound in the area. From Kerrville, it's 24 mi to **Fredericksburg,** probably the Hill Country's prettiest town and heart of its predominantly German-American population. Its main street (duly co-signed as Hauptstrasse) is a sort of German version of a classic Western movie scene—but lined with chic stores, antiques shops, and small German eateries rather than rowdy saloons. One of Fredericksburg's famous sons was Chester W. Nimitz, commander in chief of the U.S. Pacific fleet in World War II. The restored Nimitz Steamboat Hotel now forms part of the **Admiral Nimitz Museum** (304 E. Main St., tel. 210/997–4379), which displays restored hotel rooms, exhibits on the war in the Pacific, and a "Garden of Peace" donated by the Japanese people.

Heading east, you may want to duck onto Rte. 1376 and into **Luckenbach** (population: 25)—a speck on the map made famous by the Waylon Jennings and Willie Nelson duet "Let's Go to Luckenbach, Texas"; by the late humorist Hondo Crouch, who once owned the general store; and by the chili contests that draw people from nearby states. Founded in 1850, the hamlet has since changed little, with one unpainted general store and tavern, a rural dance hall, and a blacksmith's shop. The rustic little complex is open daily except Wednesday, but you may want to stop by on Sunday afternoon, when informal groups of fiddlers, guitarists, and banjo pickers gather under the live oaks.

Anyone who has read a biography of Lyndon Johnson will want to visit **Johnson City** to see the place where the gawky, huge-eared child who would one day lead America through some of

The Hill Country

its most troubled moments grew up. While his was not a Horatio Alger story, Johnson certainly came from an unremarkable town, a dusty, poor place that was no doubt one reason for the burning ambition that marked his rise. His small white-frame boyhood home is about the nicest place in town, and it is not spectacular. A short walk takes you to Johnson Settlement, the ranch complex once owned by LBJ's family, and an 1856 dogtrot cabin similar to those the early Johnsons lived in. Free bus tours of these sites and of Johnson's birthplace, one-room school, and grave depart several times a day from the **LBJ State Historical Park** (tel. 210/644–2252), just east of Stonewall on U.S. 290. Exhibits also highlight the history of the Hill Country.

Nearby **Blanco,** the onetime county seat that also figures in the Johnson clan's long history, is ornamented by a fine bit of classic Texas: the Second Empire–style **Old Blanco County Courthouse.** About 6 mi northwest of Blanco (turn west by the laundromat on Park Road 23, left on Rte. 102, then right on Rte. 103) is the **myrrh-weeping icon of New Sarov** at Christ of the Hills Eastern Orthodox Monastery (tel. 210/833–5363). The icon, a rendition of the Mother of God, is said to have begun five months of weeping on May 7, 1985, and still weeps on occasion. The monks and nuns who inhabit the place claim thousands of miracles, including cures of deadly diseases, through the anointing with tears that is offered to all visitors.

The drive back to San Antonio on U.S. 281 is a pretty one, but if you have time, go by way of **San Marcos** on Rte. 32. This road, which skips along parts of a ridge called the **Devil's Backbone,** is a classic Hill Country drive, replete with deer sightings and appealing landscapes.

What to See and Do with Children

San Antonio In the heart of San Antonio are several attractions that will keep children occupied for hours. The **Cowboy Museum and Gallery** (209 Alamo Plaza, tel. 210/229–1257), a surprisingly zippy little museum with goodies like a Sioux necklace made of human-finger bones, and **Ripley's Believe It or Not/Plaza Theatre of Wax** (301 Alamo Plaza, tel. 210/224–9299) both face the Alamo. Nearby, in the Rivercenter mall, the **Alamo IMAX Theatre** (849 E. Commerce St., tel. 210/225–4629) shows the 45-minute *Alamo . . . the Price of Freedom* on a giant screen five times a day. The **San Antonio Zoo** (3903 N. St. Mary's St., tel. 210/734–7183) has the nation's third-largest animal collection, including koala bears, most kept in outdoor habitats. The **Buckhorn Hall of Horns, Fins and Feathers** and the **Institute of Texan Cultures** (*see* Exploring San Antonio, *above*) are other child-pleasing possibilities.

West of downtown, the $140 million **Sea World of Texas** (Ellison Dr. and Westover Hills Blvd., tel. 210/523–3000, 800/527–4757, or 800/722–2762 in TX) has five stadiums and the usual complement of killer whales, walruses, otters, and dolphins.

The Hill Country **Cascade Caverns** (*see* Exploring the Hill Country, *above*) are near Boerne. The remarkable **Natural Bridge Caverns** (follow signs from Rte. 1863 between San Antonio and New Braunfels, tel. 210/651–6101) are a mile-long series of awesome, multicolored subterranean rooms and corridors. On Rte. 306, 2 mi southwest of Sattler, you'll find **Dinosaur Flats,** with 100-million-year-old "thunder lizard" tracks.

Shopping

San Antonio With its rich ethnic heritage, the city is a wonderful place to buy Mexican imports, most inexpensive and many of high quality. Try **El Mercado,** the Mexican market building that is part of **Market Square** (514 W. Commerce St., tel. 210/299–8600). The building contains about 30 shops, including places like **Casa de Artes,** good for blankets, Mexican dresses, men's *guayabera* shirts, and strings of brightly painted papier-mâché vegetables. **La Villita** (418 Villita St., tel. 210/299–8610), a restored village a few blocks south of downtown, is now a conglomeration of crafts shops and small restaurants, some in adobe buildings dating from the 1820s. It's noteworthy for such Latin American importers as **Casa Manos Alegres** and the demonstrations of its resident glassblower. **Rivercenter** (849 E. Commerce St., tel. 210/225–0000) is a more familiar, if very ritzy, shopping mall right on the river. **Paris Hatters** (119 Broadway), run for three generations by the Cortez family, is a truly atmospheric place to buy western hats.

The Hill Country While the area is generally is no shopping mecca, **Fredericksburg**'s main street is lined with antiques shops and imaginative stores like **The Huntsman** (231 Fredericksburg St., tel. 210/997–9624), selling upscale sportswear.

Sports and Outdoor Activities

Water Sports Rafting, tubing, and canoeing are popular on the Guadalupe River between Canyon Lake north of San Antonio and New Braunfels. Try **Jerry's Rentals** (River Rd. north of New Braunfels, tel. 210/625–2036) or **Rockin' R River Rides** (tel. 210/ 629–9999) or **Gruene River Co.** (tel. 210/625–2800), both on the river in New Braunfels. Canyon Lake, one of the most scenic lakes in Texas with its surrounding steep evergreen hills, has two yacht clubs, two marinas, a water-skiing club, and excellent fishing—an 86-pound flathead catfish is just one local record.

Spectator Sports

Basketball **San Antonio Spurs** (Convention Center Arena, 200 E. Market St., tel. 210/554–7773; mid-Oct.–mid-Apr.).

Horse Racing **Bandera Downs** (Rte. 16, Bandera, tel. 210/796–7781; Fri.– Sun. Mar.–Nov.).

Dining and Lodging

The Bandera and Kerrville visitors bureaus (*see* Tourist Information, *above*) have information on guest ranches. The Hill Country is chock-full of bed-and-breakfasts, particularly in tourist towns like Fredericksburg. Ask for listings at local visitors and convention bureaus, or try the reservations services **Be My Guest** (402 W. Main St., Fredericksburg 78624, tel. 210/ 997–7227 or 210/997–8555) and **Gastehaus Schmidt** (231 W. Main St., Fredericksburg 78624, tel. 210/997–5612). For price ranges, see Charts 1 (B) and 2 (A) in Chapter 1.

San Antonio **Polo's.** Inside the elegant Fairmount hotel, Polo's is equally ele-
Dining gant and chic. A blend of southwestern nouvelle and Oriental cuisine—fare that has made the cover of *Texas Monthly*—the menu includes delights like black pasta stuffed with lobster and crab. *401 S. Alamo St., tel. 210/224–8800. Reservations advised. Jacket and tie advised. AE, DC, MC, V. Expensive.*
The Bayous. Overlooking a pleasant curve of River Walk, the restaurant has a chef who specializes in fine Creole cookery— crawfish pasta, blackened fish, oyster specialties, and the like. *517 N. Presa St., tel. 210/223–6403. AE, DC, MC, V. Moderate–Expensive.*
Rio Rio Cantina. The Tex-Mex fare served here is unusually imaginative. The restaurant sits on one of the busier—sometimes annoyingly so—stretches of River Walk. *421 E. Commerce St., tel. 210/226–8462. AE, D, DC, MC, V. Moderate.*
County Line Barbeque. Texas is famous for its barbecued ribs, smoked brisket, and related fare. In San Antonio there's only one contender. *On Rte. 1604, ½ mi west of U.S. 281, tel. 210/ 496–0011. AE, MC, V. Inexpensive–Moderate.*
Mi Tierra. At Market Square directly across from the entrance to El Mercado, this huge, cheerful, and famous restaurant boasts good Tex-Mex food, wandering mariachis, and a Mexican bakery, all 24 hours a day! *218 Produce Row, tel. 210/225– 1262. AE, DC, MC, V. Inexpensive.*

Lodging **Fairmount.** This historic luxury hotel made the *Guinness Book of World Records* when its 3.2-million-pound brick bulk was moved six blocks—and across a bridge—to its present location. It's marked by a superrefined but grandmotherly atmosphere of canopy beds, overstuffed chairs, and marble baths. *401 S. Alamo St., 78205, tel. 210/224–8800, 800/642–3363, or 800/642–3339 in TX; fax 210/224–2767. 19 rooms, 17 suites. Facilities: restaurant, bar. AE, DC, MC, V. Very Expensive.*

La Mansion del Rio. A Spanish motif marks this large hotel on a quiet portion of the River Walk. Inside and out it's replete with Mediterranean tiles, archways, and soft wood tones. Rooms are very modern. *112 College St., 78205, tel. 210/225–2581, 800/531–7208, or 800/292–7300 in TX; fax 210/226–1365. 322 rooms, 15 suites. Facilities: 2 restaurants, bar, pool. AE, D, DC, MC, V. Very Expensive.*

Menger Hotel. Since its 1859 opening, the Menger has lodged Robert E. Lee, Ulysses S. Grant, Teddy Roosevelt, Oscar Wilde, Sarah Bernhardt, even Roy Rogers and Dale Evans—all of whom must have appreciated the charming, three-story Victorian lobby, its sunny dining room, and the flowered courtyard. Rooms in the oldest part of the hotel have four-poster beds and antique-patterned wallpapers; new rooms are spacious and tastefully modern. *204 Alamo Plaza, 78205, tel. 210/223–4361 or 800/345–9285; fax 210/228–0022. 320 rooms, 23 suites. Facilities: restaurant, outdoor pool, health club, shops, bar. AE, D, DC, MC, V. Expensive.*

Emily Morgan. On the other side of Alamo Plaza, this neo-Gothic hotel is named for the so-called Yellow Rose of Texas, the beautiful mulatto slave who supposedly occupied Santa Anna's attentions at San Jacinto while sending secret messages encouraging the Texans to attack (this tale is discounted by most serious historians). *705 E. Houston St., 78205, tel. 210/225–8486 or 800/824–6674; fax 210/225–7227. 177 rooms. Facilities: 2 restaurants, bar, outdoor pool/whirlpool, exercise room, sauna. AE, D, DC, MC, V. Moderate–Expensive.*

Bullis House. The rooms in this historic mansion are spacious and well restored—and a good deal in a town where lodging is surprisingly expensive. The premises also include a modern youth hostel in a separate building next door. *621 Pierce St., 78208, tel. 210/223–9426. 7 rooms (6 share baths); hostel, 35 beds. Facilities: pool. AE, D, MC, V. Inexpensive.*

The Hill Country **Friedhelm's.** This Bavarian restaurant is known as the best in
Dining town, no small feat in a place of such intense Germanic influence. Try the Bavarian schnitzel, a breaded cutlet topped with Emmentaler cheese and jalapeño sauce. *905 W. Main St., Fredericksburg, tel. 210/997–6300. AE, D, MC, V. Closed Mon. Inexpensive–Moderate.*

Lodging **Y.O. Ranch Hilton.** This sprawling, ranch-theme hotel is named after a well-known 50,000-acre dude ranch to which regular excursions are arranged. The large rooms carry out the western theme with such decor as cattle horns. *2033 Sidney Baker St., Kerrville 78028, tel. 210/257–4440 or 800/531–2800 in TX; fax 210/896–8189. 188 rooms, 12 suites. Facilities: restaurant, bar, ballroom, pool, hot tub, tennis. AE, D, DC, MC, V. Moderate–Expensive.*

The Arts and Nightlife

The Arts At San Antonio's **Mexican Cultural Institute** (600 Hemisfair Plaza, tel. 210/227–0123), Mexican culture is depicted in film, dance, art, and other exhibits. A 1929 movie/vaudeville theater has been restored to its baroque splendor as the **Majestic Per-**

forming Arts Center (224 E. Houston St., tel. 210/226–3333), venue for touring Broadway shows and home to the San Antonio Symphony Orchestra. **Kerrville** annually hosts one of the country's largest folk festivals.

Nightlife Around the 3000 block of San Antonio's **North St. Mary's Street,** you'll find a colorful assortment of bars and restaurants in converted commercial buildings, many featuring live entertainment. **River Walk** favorites include **Durty Nellie's Pub** (Hilton Palacio del Rio, 200 S. Alamo St., tel. 210/222–1400), where sing-alongs are popular, but a more interesting choice may be **The Landing** (Hyatt Regency Hotel, 123 Losoya St., tel. 210/223–7266), where the world-class Jim Cullum's Jazz Band has attracted the attention of foreign and U.S. critics for its superb Dixieland jazz. Another great choice is the **Menger Hotel Bar** (*see* Exploring San Antonio, *above*).

Dallas and Fort Worth

These twin cities, separated by 30 mi of suburbs, may be the oddest couple of all in a state of odd couples. Dallas—one of those unfortunate places whose chief global fame emanates from a TV show—is glitzy and ritzy, a swelling, modernistic business metropolis whose inhabitants go to bed early and to church on Sunday. Fort Worth, sneered at as "Cowtown" by its neighbors, lives in the shadow of its wild history as a rip-roaring cowboy town, a place of gunfights and cattle drives—even though its cultural establishment is superior to Dallas's and it has seen a downtown rebirth in recent years. It's said that Fort Worth parents tell their children to be polite to everyone—that fellow in the faded jeans and cowboy hat could well be the president of the bank. In Dallas, no such care is necessary; people ostentatiously act the part their class has assigned them.

Tourist Information

Dallas: Convention & Visitors Bureau (1201 Elm St., Suite 2000, 75270, tel. 214/746–6677, 214/746–6679, or 800/232–5527). Information booths at the Municipal Airport, Love Field, Union Station, and the West End Market Place. **Fort Worth:** Convention & Visitors Bureau (415 Throckmorton St., 76102, tel. 817/336–8791 or 800/433–5747). Information booths at the Sid Richardson Collection of Western Art, at the Fort Worth Museum of Science and History, and in the Stockyards.

Arriving and Departing

By Plane One of the rare successful collaborations between the rival cities is the **Dallas–Fort Worth International Airport** (tel. 214/574–8888), sited 17 mi from the business districts of each town. The world's second-busiest airport, it is surprisingly easy to use, though encumbered by slow transportation between terminals. It may cost $30 or more to get to downtown Dallas by taxi, usually about $30 to downtown Fort Worth. Cheaper van service is offered by the 24-hour **Supershuttle** (tel. 817/329–2000) and **TBS** (tel. 214/361–7637); the **Airporter Bus Service** (tel. 817/334–0092) serves a downtown Fort Worth terminal and some hotels. Ritzier service comes from **Lone Star Limousine** (tel. 214/243–8880).

Love Field (Cedar Springs at Mockingbird La., Dallas, tel. 214/ 670–6080), about a $10 taxi ride from downtown Dallas, is the hub of **Southwest Airlines** (tel. 214/263–1717), offering extensive service within Texas, to many cities in the four contiguous states, and, with stops, to destinations as far away as Chicago and California.

By Car
The Metroplex, as the Greater Dallas–Fort Worth area is known, is well served by interstates. The main approaches include I–35 from Oklahoma to the north and Waco to the south; I–30 from Arkansas; I–20 from Louisiana or New Mexico; and I–45 from Houston. The twin cities are linked by I–20, the southern route, and I–30, generally the more useful road. Dallas is circled by the I–635 ring road, known as the L.B.J. Freeway, while Fort Worth is looped by I–820.

Train Stations
Amtrak serves both cities with daily trains to East Texas and Chicago, and others heading south to San Antonio. Dallas's terminal is **Union Station** (408 Houston St., tel. 214/653–1101); in Fort Worth, it's the **Santa Fe Depot** (1501 Jones St., tel. 817/ 332–2931), built in 1900.

Bus Stations
Greyhound has stations in Dallas (205 S. Lamar St., tel. 214/ 655–7082 or 214/655–7000) and Fort Worth (901 Commerce St., tel. 817/429–3089 or 817/332–4564).

Getting Around Dallas and Fort Worth

As much as anywhere in Texas, a car is necessary to see Dallas and Fort Worth, and getting around by car is relatively easy. Both cities have bus systems, but service is sketchy and sometimes just plain bad.

Exploring Dallas and Fort Worth

Dallas
Many thousands visit Dallas mainly because of the city's unhappy legacy as the site of the assassination of President John F. Kennedy, which occurred downtown. Also downtown is one of the most remarkable, and recent, flowerings of skyscraping architecture anywhere—that same skyline familiar to the world from the "Dallas" television show—and this is accompanied by the offerings of a revitalized West End, where restaurants and shops fill a former warehouse district. Nearby are several major cultural institutions, and only a little farther away, Deep Ellum is the hip-hopping center of the city's countercultural scene. A short car trip from downtown are historic areas that give a sense of the old Dallas. And to the north, where the city's conservative, wealthy establishment has long been entrenched, there's shopping galore.

Downtown
On November 22, 1963, shots that would shock the world rang out on Dealey Plaza, on the west end of downtown, as the presidential motorcade rounded the corner from Houston Street onto the Elm Street approach to the Triple Underpass. Eventually, the Warren Commission would conclude—to the continuing disbelief of a majority of Americans—that President Kennedy was killed by Lee Harvey Oswald, acting alone and firing from the sixth floor of the **Texas School Book Depository**. Today, a first-rate exhibit in the building—called **The Sixth Floor**—documents the hate-filled times, the enduring vision of Camelot, riveting details of the assassination, and a remarkably evenhanded account of the conspiracy theories that con-

Downtown Dallas

tinue to emerge. The spot from which Oswald is said to have
shot is maintained exactly as it was. At the end of the exhibit is
a moving log of brief messages written by visitors. *411 Elm St.,
tel. 214/653-6666. Admission charged.*

Just outside, on the Elm Street side of the building and to the
right, is the **grassy knoll** from which many believed a second
gunman fired. Visitors inevitably congregate directly across
the street, on **Dealey Plaza,** to look up at the so-called sniper's
perch. A short walk away, at Main and Market streets, is the
stark **cenotaph** designed like an empty house by architect Philip Johnson as a tribute to Kennedy, who was a personal friend.

Around the corner, the **West End Historic District** is an area of
brick warehouses built between 1900 and 1930 and brought
back to life in 1976. Now filled with restaurants, shops, and pedestrian activity, it is one of the city's biggest draws for visitors both day and night. It is anchored by the **West End Market
Place** (603 Munger Ave., tel. 214/954-4350), once a candy and
cracker factory and now a lively, five-story shopping and eating
center built around an atrium.

A few blocks south, facing the cenotaph, is the **Old Red Courthouse** (Main and Houston Sts.). This Romanesque building of
red sandstone went up in 1892 and is one of the city's oldest surviving structures and a familiar landmark. On adjacent Dallas
County Historical Plaza, the **John Neely Bryan Cabin** is the reconstructed 1841 log cabin and trading post that was the city's
first building.

The most remarkable thing about the center of downtown, where most of the famous Dallas skyline sprouts, is the fact that it is so new—almost all its major skyscrapers were completed in the 1980s. It was here that I. M. Pei, the New York architect who for so long has favored Texas, had his strongest influence. His **First Interstate Bank Tower** (1445 Ross Ave.), with its huge, green-glass triangular shapes, was built in 1986 and is arguably the city's finest skyscraper. See it at dusk, when the sun's reflections can be incredible. **Dallas City Hall** (1500 Marilla St.), with a facade that angles out sharply over a large plaza edged by three spiky flagpoles, is another striking Pei concoction.

One building Dallasites have developed an abiding love for is **First RepublicBank Plaza** (901 Main St.), whose 70 stepped stories are outlined in green argon lights and visible for miles. Another dramatic feature of the skyline is **Reunion Tower** (300 Reunion Blvd.), where the Hyatt Regency's lit-up restaurant and bar is known for spectacular views of the city. Set among nearby tall buildings, **Thanks-Giving Square** (Pacific Ave. and Ervay St.) is a small, triangular plaza designed by Philip Johnson on the theme of gratitude. With its spiraling chapel and quiet gardens, it is a peaceful spot, perfect for lunch or resting tired feet.

The **Arts District** is on the north edge of downtown and is anchored by the **Dallas Museum of Art** (1717 N. Harwood St., tel. 214/922–1200). The museum itself is gorgeous—a series of low, white limestone galleries built off a central barrel vault—but its art falls somewhat short of its architecture. Make a point of seeing Claes Oldenburg's *Stake Hitch*, a huge stake and rope, along with the remarkable pre-Columbian collection. The **Morton H. Meyerson Symphony Center** (2301 Flora St., tel. 214/670–3600) is a place of sweeping, dramatic curves, ever-changing vanishing points, and surprising views. This 1989 building, Pei's latest Dallas offering, is far more interesting inside than out. Just in front, *De Musica* is a solid iron sculpture reminiscent of musical notes, by the great Spanish Basque sculptor Eduardo Chillida.

Other Attractions **Deep Ellum,** a 20-minute walk east from downtown, was born as the city's first black neighborhood. Today it is the throbbing center of Dallas's avant-garde, a place of trend-setting art galleries, bars, clubs, and restaurants. The area centers on Commerce, Main, and Elm streets; its name is a phonetic rendering of "Deep Elm," pronounced with a southern drawl.

Just southeast of this area, **Fair Park** (1300 Robert B. Cullum Blvd., tel. 214/565–9931) is a 277-acre collection of artfully arranged rare Art Moderne buildings. Most of the grounds date from the 1936 Texas Centennial Exhibition, although the park has hosted the Texas State Fair since 1886. Murals and sculptures line the park's central Esplanade, and in the **Hall of State** (3939 Grand Ave., tel. 214/421–4500) more murals tell the story of Texas in heroic terms. The park also contains six major exhibit spaces: the **Museum of African-American Life and Culture** (tel. 214/565–9026); the **Age of Steam Railroad Museum** (tel. 214/428–0101), with the world's largest steam locomotives; the **Dallas Aquarium** (tel. 214/670–8441); the **Dallas Civic Garden Center** (tel. 214/428–7476), a large conservatory with a French-style formal park; the **Museum of Natural History** (3535 E.

Grand Ave., tel. 214/670–8458), a place of dinosaurs and mammoths; and **The Science Place** (tel. 214/428–7200).

In **East Dallas**, Swiss Avenue has the city's best representations of two distinct periods. On lower Swiss Avenue (2900 block), nearer downtown, the **Wilson Block Historic District** is an unaltered block of turn-of-the-century frame houses, restored as offices for nonprofit groups. The **Swiss Avenue Historic District** (particularly the 5000–5500 blocks) has a large number of setback Prairie-style and other mansions.

Just north of downtown, bustling bars and restaurants line trendy **McKinney Avenue**. A restored **trolley** (tel. 214/855–0006) runs up McKinney from outside the Dallas Museum of Art (at St. Paul and Ross Sts.). Farther north, you'll find a Dallas oddity in the **Biblical Arts Center** (7500 Park La., tel. 214/691–4661), where there's a replica of Christ's tomb at Calvary and where sound and light bring a 124-by-20-foot biblical mural to life. In this north end of town famous shopping malls like **NorthPark Center** and **The Galleria** (*see* Shopping, *below*) are located.

Fort Worth   Downtown Fort Worth is where you'll find the city's financial core, most of its historic buildings, and Sundance Square, the restored turn-of-the-century commercial neighborhood that is one of its greatest attractions. A few miles north, past a decrepit industrial area, the Stockyards and adjacent western-theme stores, restaurants, and hotels cluster around Main Street and Exchange Avenue. Just west of downtown, out Lancaster Avenue, the cultural district is home to four well-known museums, a fading coliseum complex, and several parks.

Downtown   Fort Worth's much underrated downtown gracefully manages something that few American cities do: an attractive marriage of modern glass-and-steel towers and the human-scale Victorian buildings of a century ago. The billionaire Bass brothers of Fort Worth are to be thanked for what may be the most eye-pleasing juxtaposition of scale: Rather than tear down several blocks of brick buildings to accommodate the twin towers of their giant City Center development, they created **Sundance Square** (bounded by Houston, Commerce, 2nd, and 3rd Sts.) by restoring the area as a center of tall-windowed restaurants, shops, nightclubs, and offices. It was here, on Main between 2nd and 3rd streets, that "King of the Gamblers" Luke Short, owner of the White Elephant Saloon, shot the colorful gunslinger Jim Courtright dead. The square's name recalls the Sundance Kid (Harry Longbaugh), who with Butch Cassidy (Robert Leroy Parker) hid out around 1898 in the nearby neighborhood, south and east of the present square, known as **Hell's Half-Acre.** This was a violent quarter of dank saloons, drunken cowboys, and dirty brothels. When a local prostitute was nailed to an outhouse, outraged citizens passed laws against guns and gambling—only to rescind them as soon as the local economy screeched to a halt. The **Sid Richardson Collection of Western Art** (309 Main St., tel. 817/332–6554) conjures up parts of this dark world in the idealized oils of Frederic Remington and Charles Russell.

Also in Sundance Square, **Fire Station No. 1** (203 Commerce St., tel. 817/732–1631) houses an exhibit on 150 years of city history. The 1907 building, which fronts on the street where cattle headed for the Chisholm Trail used to pass, once held the city's mascot panthers. Local firemen with a sense of humor acquired the pair after a Dallas newspaper claimed Fort Worth was so quiet that a panther could sleep downtown. Bored, they finally escaped.

The wedge-shaped **Flatiron Building** (1000 Houston St.), also downtown, is topped by gargoyles and panthers. Built in 1907 as medical offices, it was patterned on similar Renaissance Revival structures in New York and Philadelphia. Nearby, the former **Hotel Texas,** now the Radisson Plaza (815 Main St., tel. 817/870–2100), is a downtown landmark, the place where President Kennedy slept the night before he was assassinated.

The **Tarrant County Courthouse** (100 E. Weatherford St.), on the north edge of downtown, is an 1895 Beaux Arts building of native red granite. Main Street heads north from the courthouse onto the **Paddock Viaduct,** which takes traffic over the bluff where early pioneers kept watch for Comanches, then leads directly to the Stockyards, several miles north. On the way there's a grim reminder of one of the darker aspects of Texas history: the former **Ku Klux Klan Building** (1012 N. Main St.), now the Ellis Pecan Company.

The Stockyards The **Fort Worth Stockyards Historic District** recalls the prosperity brought to the city in 1902, when two major Chicago meatpackers, Armour and Swift, set up plants here to ship meat across the country in refrigerator cars—a new innovation. In the **Livestock Exchange Building** (131 E. Exchange Ave.), where cattle agents kept their offices, you'll find the **Stockyards Museum** (tel. 817/625–5087). Nearby, **Cowtown Coliseum** (121 E. Exchange Ave., tel. 817/625–1025) is the site of Saturday night rodeos. Also here are what's left of a complex of cattle, goat, and sheep pens; horse and mule barns; and, of course, **Billy Bob's Texas** (2520 Rodeo Plaza, tel. 817/624–7117), billed as "the world's largest honky-tonk." Exchange Avenue is lined with restaurants, clubs, western-wear stores, and famous spots like the **White Elephant Saloon** and the **Stockyards Hotel.** The **Tarantula Excursion Train** (2318 8th Ave., tel. 817/625–7245; fare: $8 adults, $4.50 children) offers tours from its south-of-downtown base to the Stockyards. Information on the area is available at the **Stockyards Visitors Center** (130 E. Exchange Ave., tel. 817/625–9715).

The Cultural Architect Louis Kahn's last and finest building was the **Kimbell**
District **Art Museum,** six long concrete vaults with skylights running the length of each. Mirrored light filters dreamily through these into large, airy galleries. "This light," Kahn explained, "will give a glow of silver to the room without touching the objects directly, yet give the comforting feeling of knowing the time of day." The envy of the curating world for its large acquisitions budget, the Kimbell has wonderful collections of early 20th-century European art and old masters. Two of the many extraordinary paintings are Munch's *Girls on a Jetty* and Goya's *The Matador Pedro Romero,* depicting the great bullfighter who killed 5,600 of the animals. *3333 Camp Bowie Blvd., tel. 817/332–8451. Admission free. Closed Mon.*

The city's three other major museums are all short walks from the Kimbell. The **Amon G. Carter Museum** (3501 Camp Bowie Blvd., tel. 817/738–1933; admission free; closed Mon.), designed by Philip Johnson, is a collection of American art centered on Remingtons and Russells. The **Modern Art Museum of**

Fort Worth (1309 Montgomery St., tel. 817/738–9215; admission free; closed Mon.) focuses on such painters as Picasso, Rauschenberg, and Warhol. Biology, geology, computer science, and astronomy are the order of the day at the **Fort Worth Museum of Science and History** (1501 Montgomery St., tel. 817/732–1631; admission charged).

In the same area, the **Will Rogers Center** (3301 W. Lancaster Ave.) is a fading coliseum-and-stock-pen complex named after the humorist and Fort Worth booster, who described the city as "where the West begins" (and Dallas as "where the East peters out"). City officials plan to refurbish the center shortly; for now, it's used chiefly for the annual Fat Stock Show, a livestock event.

Parks and Gardens

Dallas **Fair Park** (*see* Exploring Dallas, *above*), with its many museums and formal gardens, is one of the city's most visited parks; in October it hosts the three-week State Fair of Texas. At **White Rock Lake Park** (8300 Garland Rd., tel. 214/321–2125), a beautiful and popular 9.3-mi jogging and bicycling path circles the sailboat-dotted lake. Bikes and skates can be rented along the Garland Road side of the lake, where you'll also find **The Dallas Arboretum** (8525 Garland Rd., tel. 214/327–8263), 66 acres of gardens and lawns. Just south of downtown, **Old City Park** (1717 Gano St., tel. 214/421–5141) is an outdoor museum of historic log cabins, antebellum mansions, and a Victorian bandstand, all set against the Dallas skyline.

Fort Worth Downtown, **Water Gardens Park** (15th and Commerce Sts.) is a series of man-made waterfalls, walkways, and green areas that provide a cool respite from the surrounding pavement. At night, the Philip Johnson creation is illuminated and particularly striking. Just south of the cultural district, the **Fort Worth Botanical Gardens** (3220 Botanic Garden Dr. at University Dr., tel. 817/871–7686) lie on one edge of Trinity Park; their biggest draw is the tranquil **Japanese Garden.**

What to See and Do with Children

Midway between Dallas and Fort Worth, two major theme parks on I–30 beckon children of all ages: **Six Flags over Texas** (exit at Rte. 360S, tel. 817/640–8900), with parachute drops, the world's largest wooden roller coaster, and other rides; and **Wet 'N Wild** (exit at Rte. 360N, tel. 817/265–3013), with water rides like the 300-foot "Kamikaze." **Ripley's Believe It or Not/ Palace of Wax** (601 E. Safari Pkwy., tel. 214/263–2391) is a little closer to Dallas. Northeast of Dallas, the **Mesquite Rodeo** (1818 Rodeo Dr., Mesquite, tel. 214/285–8777) is the biggest around.

Dallas The many museums of **Fair Park** (*see* Exploring Dallas, *above*) are the premier attractions for kids. Older children are as fascinated as their parents by **The Sixth Floor** (*see* Exploring Dallas, *above*), with its interactive exhibits on the Kennedy assassination. The highlight of the **Dallas Zoo** (621 E. Clarendon St., tel. 214/946–5154) is the "Wilds of Africa" exhibit, featuring a monorail and lowland gorillas in a natural habitat. Consider a pilgrimage to the **graves of Bonnie Parker** (Crown Hill Cemetery, 9700 Webbs Chapel Rd.) **and Clyde Barrow**

(Western Heights Cemetery; follow signs on Fort Worth Ave. near Winnetka St.).

Fort Worth The **Stockyards** is surely the favorite kids' spot, followed by the **Fort Worth Museum of Science and History** and its Omni theater giant-screen presentations (for both, *see* Exploring Fort Worth, *above*).

Shopping

Dallas Ever since 1873, when Dallas ensured its future by finagling the intersection of two intercontinental rail lines (by sneaking in an amendment to the railroads' enabling law), the city has been the great southwestern mecca of American commerce. **The Galleria** (L.B.J. Fwy. and Dallas North Tollway, tel. 214/702–7100), with 190 retailers, is one of its best-known upscale malls, but **NorthPark Center** (Central Expressway and Northwest Hwy., tel. 214/363–7441), developed as the nation's first indoor mall by art collector Ray Nasher, may be the best. At the latter, well-chosen small shops and major stores like **Neiman Marcus**—a Dallas institution whose downtown store (1618 Main St., tel. 214/741–6911) is a huge draw—are set off against rotating, world-class art exhibits.

The **West End MarketPlace** (603 Munger Ave., tel. 214/954–4350) has a tourist bent (try nearby **Riscky's Barbecue,** at 1701 Market Street, for a real Texas lunch). If you're in the mood for the fresh fruit and vegetables for which the Rio Grande Valley is famous, stop by the **Dallas Farmer's Market** (1010 S. Pearl St., tel. 214/748–2082), on the southeast edge of downtown. There are some fine clothing stores on trendy **McKinney Avenue,** and nearby, the elegant **Crescent** (500 Crescent Ct., tel. 214/871–8600) offers *very* ritzy shops. Around the corner, on a street of fine restaurants and shops, the best place for Mexican masks, clothing, jewelry, rugs, and more is **Mariposa** (2817 Routh St., tel. 214/871–9103).

Fort Worth Both Fort Worth's attitude and its economy have always pointed west, and that's reflected in the shopping you'll find here. Most visitors head right to the **Stockyards,** where there are several good western-wear outlets. Check out **Fincher's** (115 E. Exchange Ave., tel. 817/624–7302), a western store since 1902 and before that a bank; you can still walk into the old vaults. A great place for boots is the nearby **M. L. Leddy's Boot and Saddlery** (2455 N. Main St., tel. 817/624–3149).

Downtown, **Sundance Square** is a perennial draw, with several small stores; better shopping, however, is generally found in the attached **Tandy Center** (200 Throckmorton St., tel. 817/390–3720), a large and modern indoor mall. For fine small items, try the **major museums' gift shops. Barber's Book Store** (215 W. 8th St., tel. 817/335–5469), specializing in Texana and rare and fine books, is the oldest bookshop in Texas.

Spectator Sports

Dallas **Texas Rangers** (Arlington Stadium, 1700 Copeland Rd., Arlington, off I–30, tel. 817/273–5100; Apr.–Oct.).
Baseball

Basketball **Dallas Mavericks** (Reunion Arena, 777 Sports St., tel. 214/939–2712; Nov.–Apr.).

Football **Dallas Cowboys** (Texas Stadium, 2401 E. Airport Fwy., Irving, tel. 214/579–5000; Aug.–Jan.).

Dining

For price ranges, see Chart 1 (A) in Chapter 1.

Dallas **French Room.** Wonderfully detailed nouvelle touches—such as veal that comes looking like a delicately wrought hummingbird—match the world-class service and exquisite Baroque style of the dining room of this famous restaurant, in the Adolphus hotel. *1321 Commerce St., tel. 214/742–8200. Reservations required. Jacket and tie required. AE, D, DC, MC, V. No lunch; closed Sun. Very Expensive.*

Jennivine. An intimate yet bustling feel reminiscent of an English pub makes this upscale Continental restaurant a local favorite. Try the excellent rack of lamb. *3605 McKinney Ave., tel. 214/528–6010. Reservations required. AE, DC, MC, V. Closed Sun. Expensive.*

Baby Routh. With the 1992 closing of the highfalutin Routh Street Café, this more casual sister became the main Dallas property of Stephen Pyles, one of the "gang of five" who helped develop Southwestern Nouvelle. Though the chef is Kevin Rathbun, another culinary wizard, Pyles keeps a hand in this stylish spot that delivers terrific value. Try the herb-roasted chicken with whipped leeks and *boniatos* (white yams), or the salmon with Key lime–papaya butter and roasted-banana couscous. *2708 Routh St., tel. 214/871–2345. Reservations advised. AE, DC, MC, V. No lunch Sat. Moderate–Expensive.*

Calle Doce. Head and shoulders above the Tex-Mex that most Americans think of as Mexican food is *cocina veracruzana*, superb cuisine from the Gulf of Mexico city of Veracruz. Come to this restaurant, frequented by power brokers and others who seek the very best, for such seafood delights as *huachinango* (red snapper smothered in sweet red peppers and onions) and *ceviche* (shellfish marinated in lime). *415 W. 12th St., tel. 214/941–4304. Reservations advised. AE, DC, MC, V. Moderate.*

Hoffbrau. They have steak, but it's the best hamburgers in town that make the western-theme Hoffbrau famous. *3205 Knox St., tel. 214/559–2680. AE, DC, MC, V. Inexpensive.*

Mia's. Film and stage celebrities mix with the unwashed masses in this crowded, upbeat Tex-Mex restaurant. You'll have to stand while you wait for seating, but it's worth it. *4322 Lemmon Ave., tel. 214/526–1020. MC, V. Closed Sun. Inexpensive.*

Fort Worth **Saint-Emilion.** Practically hidden away in a brick chalet set back from the street, one of Fort Worth's very best restaurants offers great food and wine for the money. The country-French cuisine, such as roast duck, is matched by a list of 120 French and California wines. *3617 W. 7th St., tel. 817/737–2781. Reservations advised. AE, D, DC, MC, V. Closed Sun. Expensive.*

Joe T. Garcia's. The city's best-known Tex-Mex restaurant, where margaritas are used to soak up huge portions, is adjacent to its own bakery/breakfast/lunch room. Joe T.'s is conveniently located on the way from downtown to the Stockyards. *2201 N. Commerce St., tel. 817/626–4356. No credit cards. Moderate.*

Benito's. In the hospital district just south of downtown, this popular Tex-Mex spot open until 3 AM is known for its tamales and rare seasonal Mexican beers, such as Noche Buena. *1450 W.*

Magnolia Ave., tel. 817/332–8633. AE, MC, V. Inexpensive–Moderate.

Bailey's Barbeque. Although almost no one gets to sit down in this tiny hole-in-the-wall, it's been crowded since 1931 with judges, lawyers, and other courthouse folk. *826 Taylor St., tel. 817/335–7469. No credit cards. No dinner; closed weekends. Inexpensive.*

Lodging

For price ranges, see Chart 2 (A) in Chapter 1.

Dallas **Adolphus.** Beer baron Adolphus Busch created this Beaux Arts building, Dallas's finest old hotel, in 1912, sparing nothing in the way of rich ornamentation inside and out. Widely admired by students of architecture, it was lavishly restored in 1981 at a cost of $60 million. *1321 Commerce St., 75202, tel. 214/742–8200 or 800/221–9083; fax 214/651–3588. 431 rooms, 27 suites. Facilities: 2 restaurants, 3 bars, access to health club. AE, D, DC, MC, V. Very Expensive.*

Hyatt Regency. A typical Hyatt with its soaring atrium and its glass-and-brass look, this downtown hotel is best known for the panoramic views from the restaurant atop its 50-story tower. *300 Reunion Blvd., 75207, tel. 214/651–1234; fax 214/782–8126. 943 rooms, 49 suites. Facilities: 3 restaurants, 3 bars, health club, jogging track, 2 tennis courts, sauna, whirlpool, pool. AE, D, DC, MC, V. Expensive.*

Stoneleigh. Just north of downtown, this fading brick hotel has long been favored by celebrities—including Oliver Stone while filming his movie on the Kennedy assassination. It is convenient to many restaurants and home to the Dallas Press Club. *2927 Maple Ave., 75201, tel. 214/871–7111 or 800/255–9299; fax 214/871–9379. 103 rooms, 27 suites. Facilities: restaurant, bar, pool. AE, D, DC, MC, V. Moderate–Expensive.*

La Quinta–North Central. While this is standard motor-inn fare, the location, on Central Expressway a short drive north of downtown, is excellent. *4440 N. Central Expressway, 75206, tel. 214/821–4220 or 800/531–5900; fax 214/821–7685. 101 rooms. Facilities: pool. AE, D, DC, MC, V. Inexpensive–Moderate.*

Fort Worth **Worthington.** Built in 1981 of white concrete, this 12-story, ultramodern hotel stretches along two city blocks, forming a dramatic glassed-in bridge (where lunch, brunch, and tea are served) over Houston Street. There's a spare austerity to its rooms and a square-lined look to the large lobby. *200 N. Main St., 76102, tel. 817/870–1000 or 800/443–5677; fax 817/332–5679. 509 rooms, 69 suites. Facilities: 3 restaurants, bar, 2 tennis courts, pool, gym, whirlpool, sundeck. AE, D, DC, MC, V. Very Expensive.*

Radisson Plaza. The former Hotel Texas was once a great cattlemen's hotel, attested to by the steers celebrated in its terracotta frieze. Modernized but still rich with history, the hotel lodged President Kennedy in Suite 850 the night before his death; other suites have housed such famous guests as Rudolph Valentino and Jack Dempsey. *815 N. Main St., 76102, tel. 817/870–2100; fax 817/882–1300. 516 rooms, 26 suites. Facilities: restaurant, bar, pool, health club, shops, sauna. AE, D, DC, MC, V. Expensive.*

Stockyards. A storybook place that's seen more than its share of cowboys, rustlers, gangsters, and oil barons, the hotel has

been used in many a movie, including some shots in the Bonnie
and Clyde Room, where the duo stayed in 1933. In the Booger
Red Saloon, the barstools are saddles. *109 E. Exchange Ave.,
76106, tel. 817/625–6427 or 800/423–8471; fax 817/624–2571. 46
rooms, 6 suites. Facilities: restaurant, bar. AE, D, DC, MC, V.
Moderate–Expensive.*

Miss Molly's. Once a prim little inn, then a raucous bordello,
this place above the Star Cafe just outside the Stockyards has
been reincarnated as an attractive bed-and-breakfast. *109½ W.
Exchange Ave., 76106, tel. 817/626–1522. 7 rooms with shared
baths, 1 suite. AE, DC, MC, V. Moderate.*

The Arts and Nightlife

The Arts
Dallas

The top performing-arts attraction in Dallas is whatever's at
the **Morton H. Meyerson Symphony Center** (*see* Exploring Dallas, *above*), home to the **Dallas Symphony Orchestra** (tel. 214/
692–0203). The **Dallas Theater Center** is a resident company
that performs at the **Kalita Humphreys Theater** (3636 Turtle
Creek Blvd., tel. 214/526–8210), the only theater ever designed by Frank Lloyd Wright. The **Majestic Theatre** (1925 Elm
St., tel. 214/880–0137), a beautifully restored 1920s vaudeville/
movie palace, hosts various groups, including the **Dallas Opera**
(tel. 214/443–1000). In Fair Park, the **Starplex** (1818 1st St., tel.
214/421–1111) hosts most big-name bands that come to town.
The **Dallas Black Dance Theater** (2627 Flora St., tel. 214/871–
2376) has become locally famous.

Fort Worth

The **Casa Mañana Theater** (3101 W. Lancaster Ave., tel. 817/
332–9319), a theater-in-the-round under one of Buckminster
Fuller's first geodesic domes, plays host to the city's summer-
musicals series. Other local theaters include the **Fort Worth
Theater** (3505 W. Lancaster Ave., tel. 817/738–6509) and **Stage
West** (312 Houston St., tel. 817/332–6238).

Nightlife
Dallas

Much of Dallas bar life swirls around lower and upper **Greenville Avenue,** north of downtown. On lower Greenville, **Flip's**
(1520 Greenville Ave., tel. 214/824–9944) has a pleasant outdoor terrace, while **Poor David's Pub** (1924 Greenville Ave., tel.
214/821–9891) may be the top club venue for popular music in a
town known for a good music scene. On upper Greenville, stop
at the **San Francisco Rose** (3024 Greenville Ave., tel. 214/826–
2020) for a quiet drink and a bite to eat inside or outdoors. For
country music and dancing, try **Cowboy's** (7331 Gaston Ave.,
tel. 214/321–0115). Journalists hang out at what could easily
pass for a real Chicago newspaper bar, **Louie's** (1839 N. Henderson St., tel. 214/826–0505).

A younger, more avant-garde scene is found in Deep Ellum,
where **Club Dada** (2720 Elm St., tel. 214/744–3232) is one of
several trend-setting music venues. **Adair's** (2624 Commerce
St., tel. 214/939–9900) is more of a neighborhood bar, complete
with pool tables, while **Crescent City Cafe** (2730 Commerce St.,
tel. 214/745–1900) offers Creole cuisine.

Fort Worth

The area around the Stockyards, in particular, is crammed
with saloons of distinctly western flavor. The best may be the
White Elephant Saloon (100 E. Exchange Ave., tel. 817/624—
1887), whose owner brought keno to Fort Worth. But the most
famous is **Billy Bob's Texas** (2520 Rodeo Plaza, tel. 817/624–
7117), built in an old cattle-pen building and offering big country-music names regularly. Downtown offers one extraordi-

nary spot: the **Caravan of Dreams** (312 Houston St., tel. 817/ 877–3000), a performing-arts center with a rooftop cactus garden that has to be seen to be believed. The club is a world-class musical venue, specializing in jazz and blues greats, but also pulling in top eclectic performers like Lyle Lovett. It's worth a visit just to see the famous jazz, dance, and theater murals.

Elsewhere in the State

East Texas

Getting There Between Dallas and Shreveport, Louisiana, lies East Texas, whose main east–west artery is I–20. Marshall, the heart of the region, is about a three-hour drive from Dallas or a half-hour from the Louisiana line. Daily **Amtrak** trains serve Marshall.

What to See and Do Heading into East Texas from the Dallas–Fort Worth area, you'll pass two great boundaries: a natural line, marking the start of a piney, hilly region totally unlike the Great Plains; and a man-made one, the beginning of what was the slaveholding part of the United States. In every way, East Texas—a region once dependent on cotton—feels more southern than western, a fact of which the local architecture will continually remind you. After Texas seceded from the union in 1861, **Marshall** became the seat of civil authority west of the Mississippi and the wartime capital of Missouri; five Confederate generals are buried in its cemetery. The town is full of historic homes, some of which—like the **Starr Family Home** (407 W. Travis St., tel. 903/ 935–3044)—can be toured; others are small hostelries. One of its charms is the beautiful **Stagecoach Road** (take Poplar Street, which heads east from U.S. 59, and follow markers); in places, the stages cut some 20 feet into the ground on this undisturbed section of the old main road to Shreveport. Off U.S. 59, signs lead to **Marshall Pottery** (tel. 903/938–9201), a huge working pottery.

Jefferson, a 20-minute drive north, is one of Texas's most historic towns, a charming place on Big Cypress Bayou that once served hundreds of steamboats coming up from New Orleans. When his offer to run track through the town was rebuffed, railroad baron Jay Gould is said to have angrily scrawled in the register of the Excelsior House hotel the prophetic words "The End of Jefferson." Today the superb **Excelsior House** (211 W. Austin St., tel. 903/665–2513), built in the 1850s, is a tribute to the restorer's art (reservations are required months in advance). Across the street is **Gould's Private Railroad Car** (admission charged).

Caddo Lake, hung with Spanish moss and edged with bald cypresses, is a fishing mecca straddling the Texas-Louisiana border. At various times it has been home to the beleaguered Caddo Indians, to bootleggers hiding out in its dense shore growth, to the great spiritual singer Leadbelly (reared at Swanson's Landing), to a thriving steamboat traffic from New Orleans, and to all manner of legend. **Caddo Lake State Park** (*see* National and State Parks, *above*) is on the south shore.

Dining **Black Swan.** The specialty here is southern cooking with a touch of Creole, served either inside the beautiful historic home or outdoors, on a second-floor balcony overlooking the main street. *210 W. Austin St., Jefferson, tel. 903/665–8922. MC, V. No dinner Sun.; closed Tues. Moderate.*

Lodging **Pride House.** Ornate woodwork and original stained glass distinguish this old Victorian mansion, one of Jefferson's finest B&Bs. *409 E. Broadway, Jefferson 75657, tel. 903/665–2675. 10 rooms. MC, V. Moderate.*

Caddo Cottage. This is the place for a family looking for a quiet time along one of the most beautiful parts of Caddo Lake. *Taylor Island, Uncertain 75661, tel. 903/679–3988. 1 apartment, sleeps 8. No credit cards. Inexpensive–Moderate.*

Weisman-Hirsch-Beil Home. Marshall's most beautiful bed-and-breakfast is set in a dark-paneled 1901 Eastlake Victorian house on the National Register of Historic Places. Hostess Gail Beil is also a local historian and newspaperwoman. *313 S. Washington St., Marshall 75670, tel. 903/938–5504. 2 rooms with shared bath. No credit cards. Inexpensive–Moderate.*

El Paso

Getting There At Texas's far southwest corner, El Paso is 11 hours' drive from San Antonio; about 12 from Dallas–Fort Worth six from Santa Fe, New Mexico; and five from Phoenix, Arizona. **El Paso International Airport** (Southwest is the major local carrier, tel. 800/435–9792) and **Amtrak** (Union Station, 700 San Francisco St.) serve the city.

What to See Dramatically situated a few miles between the southern end of
and Do the Rockies and the northern terminus of Mexico's Sierra Madre range, **El Paso** (established by the Spanish in 1598) was a major stopping point on the way west during the California gold rush. Outside the city, in El Paso's lower valley, are several important historic sites. **Mission Ysleta** (Old Pueblo Rd., Zaragosa exit off I–10 east of El Paso, tel. 915/859–9848), ca. 1681, is the oldest Spanish mission in the Southwest. The adjacent **Tigua Indian Reservation** (119 S. Old Pueblo Rd., tel. 915/859–3916), home of the oldest ethnic group in Texas, offers Tigua pottery, jewelry, art, and replicas of ancient Native American homes. To the south are **Soccoro Mission** (Rte. 258, tel. 915/859–7718), famed for its fine *vigas*—the carved ceiling beams that mark local architecture—and **San Elizario Presidio** (Rte. 258, tel. 915/851–2333), a fort built to protect the missions.

Across the Rio Grande is the Mexican city of **Juarez,** which offers often sensational shopping; try the **El Paso–Juarez International Trolley** (Santa Fe and Main Sts., tel. 915/544–0061). **Scenic Drive** (north on Mesa St., then right on Rim Rd.) offers panoramic views of El Paso. **Transmountain Road** (off I–10 west of downtown) takes you through "Smuggler's Gap," a dramatic cut across the Franklin Mountains. For more information, contact the **El Paso Convention & Visitors Bureau** (1 Civic Center Plaza, 79901, tel. 915/534–0600 or 800/351–6024).

Dining **Tigua Indian Reservation.** In a cheerful, feather- and pottery-bedecked dining room adjacent to the reservation gift shop, this Mexican-flavored restaurant offers delightful Tigua twists. *122 Old Pueblo Rd., tel. 915/859–3916. AE, MC, V. Closed Mon. Moderate.*

Lodging **Westin Paso del Norte.** This elegant brick downtown hotel is listed on the National Register of Historic Places. The jewel of the lobby is the dark-wood circular Dome Bar, which sits under a superb 1912 Tiffany skylight. Guest rooms are functional and large. *101 S. El Paso St., 79901, tel. 915/534–3000; fax 915/534–3024. 375 rooms. Facilities: 2 restaurants, bar, nightclub, pool, exercise room, sauna. AE, D, DC, MC, V. Expensive.*

South Padre Island

Getting There In the southeast corner of the state, near the Mexican border town of Matamoros, South Padre Island is reached by a bridge across the Intracoastal Waterway from Port Isabel, which, in turn, is accessible from Rtes. 48 and 100.

What to See and Do At the southern tip of one of the largest barrier islands in the world—113-mile-long Padre Island—the resort town and white-sand beaches of South Padre Island (population: 1,677) attract college students at spring break but delight nature-seekers, beach- and sun-lovers, and fishermen the rest of the year. To the north, the 80½-mile **Padre Island National Seashore** (9405 South Padre Island Dr., Corpus Christi 78418, tel. 512/937–2621; admission charged) is entirely natural, unchanged from the days when scavenging Karankawa Indians roamed among its sand dunes, sea oats, and beach morning glories. For further information, contact the **South Padre Island Convention & Visitors Bureau** (600 Padre Island Blvd.; Box 3500, 78597, tel. 512/761–6433 or 800/343–2368).

Austin

Getting There Located between Dallas–Fort Worth and San Antonio on I–35, Austin is accessible from Houston via U.S. 290. **Robert Mueller Municipal Airport** (tel. 512/472–3321) handles local flights.

What to See and Do **Austin,** created as capital of the new Republic of Texas in 1839, is perhaps the least Texan of cities: a liberal enclave in a generally conservative state and a heavily treed, hilly town in a land more commonly known for its monotonous flatness. Austin is famous throughout the Southwest for its thriving **music scene,** which plays itself out on scores of blues, country, rock, jazz, and other stages. It is also home to the nation's largest urban **bat colony,** found under the Congress Avenue bridge during the summer months. The **State Capitol** (11th and Congress Sts., tel. 512/463–0063) is a striking building of pink Texas granite. The **Lyndon B. Johnson Presidential Library and Museum** (2313 Red River Rd. on the University of Texas campus, tel. 512/482–5136) has a replica of the president's Oval Office and exhibits on his political life and programs. Further information is available at the **Austin Convention & Visitors Bureau** (412 E. 6th St., 78701, tel. 512/478–0098 or 800/888–8287).

UTAH

By Stacey Clark

Capital	Salt Lake City
Population	1,729,000
Motto	Industry
State Bird	California gull
State Flower	Sego lily

Visitor Information

Utah Travel Council (Council Hall, Capitol Hill, Salt Lake City 84114, tel. 801/538–1030). **Welcome centers** are situated near all major entrances to the state.

Scenic Drives

From Logan, **U.S. 89** runs north through a limestone canyon with steep, striated walls, cresting above Bear Lake on the Utah-Idaho border. In northeastern Utah, **U.S. 191** jogs north out of Vernal past geologic formations up to a billion years old before meeting **Rte. 44,** which gives an elongated view of Flaming Gorge National Recreation Area amid scents of desert sage and juniper. A colorful guide *Utah Scenic Byways and Highways,* is sold at welcome centers.

National and State Parks

National Parks Utah has five national parks, including **Bryce Canyon** and **Zion** (*see* Southwestern Utah, *below*) and **Canyonlands** and **Arches** (*see* Exploring Southeastern Utah, *below*). Once called "Land of the Sleeping Rainbow" because of its colorfully striped cliffs, **Capitol Reef National Park** (Torrey 84775, tel. 801/425–3791), reached via Rte. 24 off I–70/U.S. 50, has still-flourishing riverside orchards planted by early settlers. Petroglyphs line the canyon walls near the Fremont River.

Utah's six national monuments include the excavations at **Dinosaur National Monument** (Box 128, Jensen 84035, tel. 801/789–2115), the limestone caverns of **Timpanogos Cave** (Rte. 3, Box 200, American Fork 84003, tel. 801/756–0351), and the giant, stream-formed spans of **Natural Bridges National Monument** (Box 1, Lake Powell 84533, tel. 801/259–5174). **Glen Canyon National Recreation Area** (*see* Exploring Southeastern Utah, *below*) and **Flaming Gorge National Recreation Area** (Box 278, Manila 84046, tel. 801/784–3445) offer fishing and boating on huge reservoirs.

State Parks The **Division of State Parks** (1636 W. North Temple St., Salt Lake City 84116, tel. 801/538–7221) publishes a directory of Utah's 44 state parks. **Goblin Valley State Park** (Box 93, Green River 84525, tel. 801/564–3633), off I–70 on Rte. 24 in eastern Utah, has acres of wind-eroded sandstone "goblins" around a desert campground. **Pioneer Trail State Park** (2601 Sunnyside Ave., Salt Lake City 84108, tel. 801/584–8391), on the east bench of the Salt Lake Valley, details the trek of Mormon pioneers and re-creates an 1850s township, complete with cooking, crafts, and blacksmithing demonstrations.

Salt Lake City

On July 24, 1847, Mormon leader Brigham Young looked out over the Salt Lake Valley and announced to the ragged party behind him, "This is the right place." So began the religious settlement that would become Salt Lake City. The conservative influence of the Church of Jesus Christ of Latter-day Saints, as the Mormon church is officially known, continues to shape the city. Nevertheless, it has come a long way from its pioneer origins to its current position as a major winter-sports destination, a center for biomedical research, and the gateway to the natural wonders of southern Utah.

Tourist Information

Salt Lake City: Convention and Visitor's Bureau (180 S. West Temple St., tel. 801/521–2822).

Arriving and Departing

By Plane **Salt Lake International Airport** (tel. 801/575–2400) is 7 mi north of downtown. Major hotels provide shuttles, and **Utah Transit Authority** (tel. 801/287–4636) buses link the airport to regular city routes. Taxi fare to downtown averages $10, including tip.

By Car I–15 runs north–south through Salt Lake, I–80 east–west. I–215 circles the valley.

Train Station **Amtrak** serves the city's **Rio Grande Depot** (320 Rio Grande St., tel. 801/364–8562).

Bus Station **Greyhound** (160 W. South Temple St., tel. 801/355–4684).

Getting Around Salt Lake City

Salt Lake streets are laid out geometrically and numbered in increments of 100 in each direction, with Temple Square as their root. It is easy to get around by car; parking is inexpensive, and streets and highways are less crowded than those in comparable urban areas. **Utah Transit Authority** (tel. 801/287–4636; fare: 65¢) buses and trolleys serve the valley.

Exploring Salt Lake City

City attractions fan out from Temple Square. To the north is the Capitol Hill district, to the south are shopping and arts locations, to the east lie the ski resorts of the Wasatch Mountains, and to the west is the Great Salt Lake.

Historic **Temple Square** (North Visitors' Center, 50 W. North Temple St., tel. 801/240–2534) is the 10-acre core of sites central to Mormonism. Two visitor centers house exhibits and art with religious themes. The Mormon Tabernacle Choir performs on Thursdays and Saturdays in the squat, domed **Salt Lake Tabernacle.** While the six-spired granite **Salt Lake Temple** itself is closed to all but church members, the other buildings and monuments on the beautifully landscaped grounds are open to the public free of charge. In winter, the trees twinkle with thousands of lights for the holiday season.

Salt Lake City

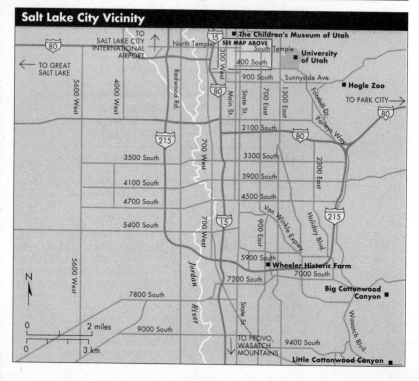

Salt Lake City Vicinity

Directly west of Temple Square are the **Museum of Church History and Art** (tel. 801/240–3310), displaying Mormon artifacts, paintings, fabric art, and sculptures; and the **Family History Library** (tel. 801/240–2331), offering free public access to the Mormons' huge collection of genealogical records.

On the corner of South Temple and State streets is the 1854 **Beehive House** (tel. 801/240–2671), the home of Brigham Young while he served as territorial governor. The **Lion House** (tel. 801/363–5466) next door received the overflow of Young's large family; it is now a social center and restaurant.

The Renaissance Revival–style **State Capitol** (tel. 801/538–3000), completed in 1915, sits on a hill at the north end of State Street. In addition to marble-walled legislative and Supreme Court chambers, the building has interesting statues and plaques tucked into niches on the main floor. Depression-era murals in the rotunda depict events from Utah's past. Scattered on the grounds are a number of historical monuments, including a bronze statue of a young soldier, honoring Vietnam veterans.

The **Pioneer Memorial Museum,** west of the capitol grounds, holds thousands of artifacts, including tools and carriages from the late 1800s and a doll and toy collection. *300 N. Main St., tel. 801/538–1050. Admission free. Closed Sun.*

The **Marmalade District**—the streets bisecting the west slope of Capitol Hill—contains many original pioneer houses. Among the well-preserved historic houses on South Temple Street east of Capitol Hill is the **Kearns Mansion,** at No. 603 (tel. 801/538–1005), the governor's residence; tours are offered.

The 26th-floor observation deck of Salt Lake's tallest structure, the **LDS Church Administration Building** (50 E. North Temple St., tel. 801/240–3789), offers the best views of the city.

In the Vicinity About 17 mi west of downtown via I–80 is the **Great Salt Lake.** Water flows into it with no outlet other than evaporation, so minerals and salts remain trapped, causing the lake to be more saline than any other body of water on Earth except the Dead Sea. There is one beach with showers, and sailboats dot the lake with color on summer days. The south and west shores and neighboring wetlands are prime nesting grounds for many species of migratory, shore, and wading birds.

Southeast of Salt Lake City, the **Wasatch Mountains** part in two scenic canyons (Rte. 190 and Rte. 210). Resorts here offer arts festivals and concerts in summer and skiing in winter (*see* Ski Areas, *below*); **Snowbird Resort,** one of the country's outstanding ski areas, has a 125-passenger tram that delivers mountaintop views year-round.

Utah's premier ski destination and only bona-fide resort town, **Park City** (*see* Ski Areas, *below*), 29 mi east of Salt Lake City on I–80, is home to the U.S. Ski Team and Ski Association. In addition to its three ski areas, it offers a historic **Main Street,** with a museum, art galleries, shops, and restaurants in restored buildings; several elegant bed-and-breakfasts; three golf courses; and a factory-outlet mall.

Parks and Gardens

Red Butte Gardens (tel. 801/581–5322), east of the University of Utah campus, has 150 acres of trees, shrubs, herbs, wildflowers, and stream-fed pools tucked into a private canyon in the Wasatch foothills. A concert series is held each summer.

What to See and Do with Children

The **Children's Museum of Utah** (840 N. 3rd West, tel. 801/328–3383) lets kids explore a 727 jet plane, a semitruck, strange light effects, and an archaeological dig. **Raging Waters** (1200 W. 1700 South, tel. 801/973–9900), Utah's largest water park, has 11 pools and 19 rip-roaring slides. **Hansen Planetarium** (15 S. State St., tel. 801/538–2098) is a dignified buff-faced building with free exhibits and a domed theater for daily star shows. **Hogle Zoo** (2600 Sunnyside Ave., tel. 801/582–1631) has 1,200 animals. Bring walking shoes and a hat; exhibits are spread out, and shade is at a premium. **Wheeler Historic Farm** (6351 S. 900 East, tel. 801/264–2212) has a well-stocked trout pond and daily "chore tours."

Shopping

Crossroads Plaza (50 S. Main St., tel. 801/531–1799) has four floors of stores, theaters, and restaurants. The neighboring **ZCMI Center** (36 S. State St., tel. 801/321–8745) features 80 stores and restaurants. **Trolley Square** (600 S. 7th East, tel. 801/521–9877) once housed electric trolleys; today it has the city's most varied shopping, as well as restaurants and movie theaters. **Mormon Handicraft** (105 N. Main St., tel. 801/355–2141) sells quilts, seasonal crafts, and clothing handmade by valley residents.

Spectator Sports

Basketball   **Utah Jazz** (Delta Center, 300 W. South Temple St., tel. 801/355–3865; Oct.–Apr.).

Ski Areas

Utah's dry powder offers exceptional downhill and cross-country skiing. Lift lines are short and tickets are reasonable at all ski areas; those listed below are about 25 mi southeast of Salt Lake City. **Guideworks** (tel. 801/363–5640) offers cross-country skiing tours and advice. For more information, call **Ski Utah** (tel. 801/534–1779; snow report, tel. 801/521–8102).

Alta (Rte. 210, tel. 801/742–3333), 39 runs, eight lifts, 2,050-foot vertical drop. **Brighton** (Rte. 190, tel. 801/943–8309 or 800/873–5512), 61 runs, five lifts, 1,745-foot drop. **Deer Valley** (Rte. 224, tel. 801/649–1000), 58 runs, 11 lifts, 2,200-foot drop. **Park City Ski Area** (Rte. 224 off I–80, tel. 801/649–8111), 83 runs, 12 lifts, gondola, 3,100-foot drop. **Park West** (Rte. 92, tel. 801/649–5400), 50 runs, seven lifts, 2,200-foot drop. **Snowbird** (Rte. 210, tel. 801/742–2222 or 800/453–3000), 45 runs, eight lifts including high-speed tram, 3,100-foot drop. **Solitude** (Rte. 190, tel. 801/534–1400), 60 runs and bowls, seven lifts, 2,030-foot drop, 11 mi of groomed cross-country track. **Sundance** (U.S. 189 off I–15, tel. 801/225–4107), 41 runs, four lifts, 2,150-foot drop.

Dining

Dining in Salt Lake offers variety and lots of food for your money. Liquor laws have some peculiarities, but mixed drinks, wine, and beer are available at most restaurants; when in doubt, call ahead. For price ranges, see Chart 1 (B) in Chapter 1.

Expensive	**LaCaille at Quail Run.** French cuisine is served in a re-created 18th-century château. Fresh flowers, candles, and roaring fires add to the ambience. *9565 Wasatch Blvd., tel. 801/942–1751. Reservations required. AE, MC, V.*

★	**Santa Fe Restaurant.** In a stream-side lodge with mountain views, southwestern concoctions are highlighted by fresh herbs and unusual sauces. *2100 Emigration Canyon Rd., tel. 801/582–5888. MC, V.*

Moderate	**Baci Trattoria.** The combination of northern and southern Ital-
★	ian food served in surroundings of marble and stained glass makes Baci a feast for the eyes and the taste buds. *134 W. Pierpont Ave., tel. 801/328–1500. AE, MC, V. Closed Sun.*
	Market Street Grill. The stylish black-and-white decor is catchy, but the food steals the show. The large menu includes creatively prepared seafood, steaks, and chicken. *48 Post Office Pl., tel. 801/322–4668. AE, MC, V.*
	Peery Pub and Cafe. Brass fixtures and wood-paneled booths promote intimate dining. The Continental menu changes seasonally with the fresh ingredients. *110 W. 300 South, tel. 801/521–8919. MC, V. Closed Sun.*

Inexpensive	**Bill and Nada's.** Satisfy cravings anytime of the day or night at this home-style café. The roast beef and lemon onions make a hearty supper, and the breakfast fare will jolt your cholesterol level. *479 S. 600 East, tel. 801/359–6984. MC, V.*

★	**Cafe Mediterranean.** This small café serves such Middle Eastern standards as falafel and tabouli, and chicken curry in pita bread. Desserts run to whole-wheat cookies and honey cheesecake. *524 E. 4th South, tel. 801/364–4914. No credit cards.*
	The Old Spaghetti Factory. This is a standard pasta purveyor, but the jumbled Victorian decor is pure fun. *Trolley Sq., 600 S. 700 East, tel. 801/521–0424. D, MC, V.*

Lodging

Salt Lake lodgings stretch from the airport east to the downtown area and south on State and Main streets. Contact the **Utah Hotel and Motel Association** (9 Exchange Pl., Suite 715, Salt Lake City 84111, tel. 801/359–0104) for further suggestions. Prices vary widely with the seasons. For price ranges, see Chart 2 (A) in Chapter 1.

Expensive–	**The Cliff Lodge at Snowbird Resort.** This angular gray struc-
Very Expensive	ture echoes the surrounding Wasatch Mountains. Large guest rooms with wide glass walls offer spectacular views winter or summer. The redwood-and-brass lobby is sumptuous. *Snowbird Resort 84092, tel. 801/521–6040 or 800/453–3000; fax 801/742–3304. 532 rooms. Facilities: 4 restaurants, 2 lounges, spa, 2 pools, valet parking. AE, D, DC, MC, V.*

Moderate–Expensive	**The Brigham Street Inn Bed and Breakfast.** The decor in each
★	room of this solid Queen Anne mansion was created by a different designer. A black-walled living room is dramatic yet invit-

ing. The breakfast room has a long common table near the marble fireplace or private tables for two with wing chairs. *1135 E. South Temple St., 84102, tel. 801/364–4461. 9 rooms. Facilities: off-street parking. AE, MC, V.*

The Inn at Temple Square. A recent renovation upgraded this 1930s redbrick hotel and added a tiled courtyard entrance with elaborate iron gates. Guest rooms are furnished with unusual touches, such as four-poster beds and lush colors. *71 W. South Temple St., 84101, tel. 801/531–1000 or 800/843–4668; fax 801/536–7272. 90 rooms. Facilities: restaurant, covered parking. No smoking. AE, D, DC, MC, V.*

Moderate **Holiday Inn.** The room decor runs to florals and stripes at this comfortable, *U*-shaped hotel. By the courtyard's wide lawn is a playground near a pretty, covered pool. *999 S. Main St., tel. 801/359–8600. 263 rooms. Facilities: restaurant, kitchenettes, lounge, pool, exercise room, sauna. AE, D, DC, MC, V.*

Little America. Private, double-tiered wings flank a central 17-story building; sunny tower rooms are decorated with gentle colors and generously upholstered furniture. The lobby and mezzanine have enormous brick fireplaces. *500 S. Main St., 84102, tel. 801/363–6781 or 800/453–9450; fax 801/322–1610. 850 rooms. Facilities: 2 restaurants, lounge, exercise room, pool, underground parking. AE, D, DC, MC, V.*

★ **Peery Hotel.** This four-story gray-brick hotel opened in 1910. Most guest rooms are furnished with eclectic antique reproductions and fanciful linens. The plush lobby lends itself to loitering. *110 W. 3rd South, 84102, tel. 801/521–4300 or 800/331–0073; fax 801/575–5014. 77 rooms. Facilities: sauna, exercise room. AE, D, DC, MC, V.*

Inexpensive **Airport Inn.** This chunky, redbrick motel near the freeway and airport offers good value. The rooms are generically furnished but reasonably quiet, considering the location. *2333 W. North Temple St., 84116, tel. 801/539–0438; fax 801/539–8852. 100 rooms. Facilities: restaurant, lounge, airport shuttle. AE, D, DC, MC, V.*

★ **Avenues Hostel.** This large white-brick hostel in a downtown residential area is brightened with flowerbeds in summer. Shared and private accommodations are available. *107 F St., 84103, tel. 801/363–8137. 20 rooms. Facilities: kitchen, laundry. No credit cards.*

★ **Skyline Inn.** On the edge of a quiet neighborhood, and near restaurants and shopping, this tan stucco motel is well maintained and friendly. *2475 E. 1700 South, 84108, tel. 801/582–5350. 24 rooms. Facilities: pool, hot tub. AE, D, DC, MC, V.*

The Arts and Nightlife

A calendar of events is available at the **Salt Lake Convention and Visitors Bureau** (*see* Tourist Information, *above*). The *Salt Lake Tribune* carries daily arts and entertainment listings.

The Arts Salt Lake's best arts bets are **Ballet West** (50 W. 2nd South, tel. 801/355–2787), **Pioneer Theater Company** (3rd South and University St., tel. 801/581–6961), **Salt Lake Acting Company** (168 W. 5th North, tel. 801/363–0525), **Utah Opera Company** (50 W. 2nd South, tel. 801/355–2787), and **Utah Symphony** (Symphony Hall, 123 W. South Temple St., tel. 801/533–6407). Concerts are presented at the **Delta Center** (300 W. South Temple St., tel. 801/325–2000).

Nightlife Many night spots are private clubs, meaning a membership is required (temporary memberships cost about $5). Weekends are wild at the **Dead Goat Saloon** (165 S. West Temple St., tel. 801/328–4628), a subterranean hangout with live music and a busy dance floor. **Port O' Call** (78 W. 400 South, tel. 801/521–0589) serves mountains of nachos and features popular local bands. The art deco–style **Zephyr Club** (301 S. West Temple St., tel. 801/355–2582) has live blues, rock, reggae, and dancing. **The Bay** (404 S. West Temple St., tel. 801/363–2623) is a smoke- and alcohol-free club with three dance floors.

Southwestern Utah

Southwestern Utah is a colorful mingling of desert, red-rock formations, and pristine forests. Heading the list of natural wonders are Zion and Bryce Canyon national parks, where clear air and high elevations create spectacular hundred-mile vistas. The picturesque towns of St. George, Cedar City, and Springdale offer historic sites and year-round warm weather.

Tourist Information

Color Country Travel Bureau (906 N. 14th West, St. George 84770, tel. 801/628–4171 or 800/233–8824).

Getting There

By Plane **St. George** and **Cedar City airports** are served by **Skywest Airlines** (tel. 800/453–9417).

By Car I–15 and U.S. 89 pass north–south through the region.

By Bus **Greyhound** stops in St. George (tel. 801/673–3457) and Cedar City (tel. 801/586–9465).

Exploring Southwestern Utah

At **Bryce Canyon National Park,** millions of years of geologic mayhem have created gigantic bowls filled with strange pinnacles and quilted drapes of stone. An 18-mi scenic drive skirts the western rim, offering views of the amphitheaters. *Rte. 12, Bryce Canyon 84717, tel. 801/834–5322. Admission charged. Some roads closed Nov.–Mar.*

Cedar City is the setting for the state's premier theatrical event: the **Utah Shakespearean Festival** (tel. 801/586–7878; June–Sept.), offering feasts, bawdy Elizabethan skits, and performances in an open-air replica of the Globe Theatre.

The Virgin River carved the towering cliffs of Zion Canyon and still flows along its floor. Spring-fed hanging gardens sprout lush greens along the walls. **Zion National Park** offers roads, tram tours, and horseback and hiking trails for exploring the beauties of the canyon and its tributaries. It can be very crowded in summer. *Rte. 9, Springdale 84767, tel. 801/772–3256. Admission charged.*

Nearby, the sleepy and picturesque towns of **Virgin, Rockville,** and **Springdale** dot the desert at the base of lofty red cliffs. To the west, in **St. George,** you can tour the historic district and **Brigham Young's Winter Home** (200 N. 100 West, tel. 801/673–2517). In **Santa Clara,** the 130-year-old **house of missionary Ja-**

cob **Hamblin** (3386 Santa Clara Dr., tel. 801/673–2161) has cotton plants and a vineyard.

Sports and Outdoor Activities

Biking **Rte. 9** through Zion, the **Bryce Canyon Scenic Loop,** and **Rte. 18** through Snow Canyon offer classic southwestern scenery. **Bicycle Utah** (tel. 801/649–5806) offers a free directory of biking routes.

Golf St. George attracts golfers year-round to seven public courses, including **Dixie Red Hills** (1000 North 700 West, tel. 801/634–5852; 9 holes) and **South Gate** (1075 Tonaquint Dr., tel. 801/628–0000; 18 holes). The **Utah Golf Association** (tel. 801/466–1132) has information.

Hiking and Backpacking Bryce and Zion national parks (*see* Exploring Southwestern Utah, *above*) have many trails of varying difficulty. Zion's paved **Gateway to the Narrows Trail** follows the Virgin River. Bryce's moderately difficult **Navajo Loop Trail** has views of towering Thor's Hammer.

Dining and Lodging

Southwestern Utah offers several dining and lodging options. **Grand Circle Reservations** (tel. 801/673–6163 or 800/233–4383) provides area-wide recommendations. For price ranges, see Charts 1 (B) and 2 (B) in Chapter 1.

Bryce Canyon *Dining and Lodging* **Bryce Lodge.** Renovated in 1991, the lobby and dining room of this rustic 1920s wood-and-sandstone lodge have high ceilings with exposed beams and massive stone fireplaces. The sturdily furnished guest rooms are geared to informal travelers. *Bryce Canyon National Park, Box 400, Cedar City 84720, tel. 801/586–7686; fax 801/586–3157. 114 rooms. Facilities: restaurant (moderate). AE, DC, MC, V. Moderate–Expensive.*
Ruby's Inn. Simply decorated guest rooms are located in a two-story annex to the rough-hewn public areas. The restaurant serves basic American fare, with creative specials. *Rte. 63, Box 1, 84717, tel. 801/834–5341 or 800/528–1234. 216 rooms. Facilities: restaurant, pool. AE, D, DC, MC, V. Moderate.*

St. George *Dining* **Pancho and Lefty's.** The Mexican cuisine served here varies from authentic tamales wrapped in corn husks to avocado-laced taco salads. The decor is spirited, and the margaritas are tart. *1050 S. Bluff St., tel. 801/628–4772. AE, MC, V. Moderate.*
The Pizza Factory. The variety of pizza toppings competes with the number of hungry patrons at this popular eatery where pasta, calzones, and sandwiches round out the menu. Dessert is scoops of chocolate-chip or oatmeal-raisin cookie dough (also available baked for traditionalists). *1 W. St. George Blvd., tel. 801/628–1234. AE, MC, V. Moderate.*

Lodging ★ **Seven Wives Inn Bed and Breakfast.** Guest rooms in two neighboring pioneer homes are named after the wives of the innkeeper's polygamous grandfather. The furnishings include quilts from the late 1800s, lace canopies, and massive wood and iron beds. *217 N. 100 West, 84770, tel. 801/628–3737. 13 rooms. Facilities: pool, off-street parking. AE, MC, V. Moderate.*

Springdale *Dining* ★ **The Bit and Spur Restaurant and Saloon.** This low-slung eatery serves innovative and healthy southwestern-style Mexican food. Works by local artists fill the pine-paneled interior, while the patio features bright flowers and scents from the herb garden. *1212 Zion Park Blvd., tel. 801/772–3498. MC, V. Closed Tues.–Wed. Nov.–Feb. Moderate.*

Flannigans. Whether you sit inside or out, Zion Canyon is the focus at this modern wood-and-glass restaurant where grilled steaks and fresh vegetables are artfully prepared. *428 Zion Park Blvd., tel. 801/772–3244. MC, V. Moderate.*

Lodging **Cliffrose Lodge and Gardens.** Acres of lawn, trees, and gardens
★ surround the low, rambling stucco wings of this hotel on the banks of the Virgin River, ¼ mi from Zion. The ample rooms are decorated in desert hues. *281 Zion Park Blvd., 84767, tel. 801/772–3234 or 800/243–8824; fax 801/772–3900. 36 rooms. Facilities: pool. AE, D, MC, V. Moderate.*

Zion Lodge and Cabins. Evenings often bring deer to the rustic front porches of duplex redwood cabins. Informal lodge rooms have views of dappled canyon walls. *Zion National Park, Box 400, Cedar City 84720, tel. 801/586–7686; fax 801/586–3157. 121 rooms and cabins. Facilities: 2 restaurants. AE, DC, MC, V. Moderate.*

Campgrounds

The region has nearly 100 national park and forest, state park, and private campgrounds from which to choose; for more information contact the **Utah Travel Council** (*see* Visitor Information, *above*). **Snow Canyon State Park** (Box 140, Santa Clara 84765, tel. 801/628–2255) and the larger **Watchman Campground** (Zion National Park, Springdale 84767, tel. 801/772–3256) have tent sites and RV hookups.

Southeastern Utah

For years southeastern Utah has captured the imagination of filmmakers, serving as the site of such western and adventure films as *Stagecoach* and *Indiana Jones and the Last Crusade.* Highlighting this canyon country, rugged Arches and Canyonlands national parks invite exploration by way of scenic drives, four-wheeling, hiking, rock-climbing, river-running, and cycling.

Tourist Information

Grand County: Travel Council (Main and Center Sts., Moab 84532, tel. 801/259–8825 or 800/635–6622).

Getting There

By Plane **Alpine Aviation** (tel. 800/748–4899) flies daily from Salt Lake City to **Canyonlands Field,** in Moab.

By Car I–70 runs east–west through the region; U.S. 191 slices north–south.

Exploring Southeastern Utah

Arches National Park, just northwest of Moab, has spectacular sandstone formations carved by wind and water from an ancient seabed. Trails and two scenic roads lead among towering pillars and arches. *Box 907, Moab 84532, tel. 801/259–8161. Admission charged.*

The landscape of nearby **Canyonlands National Park** is divided into three geologically distinct districts, each with its own visitor center. Scenic loops, trails, and four-wheel-drive roads lead to views of massive canyons or uplifts crowded with stone spires and other bizarre features. *Rte. 313, Moab 84532, tel. 801/259–7164. Admission charged.*

A sweeping view of the Canyonlands' multicolor upside-down geography is found at **Dead Horse Point State Park** (Rte. 313, tel. 801/259–6511), named for a band of wild horses once stranded on this isolated peninsula. **Glen Canyon National Recreation Area** (tel. 801/602/645–2471) surrounds **Lake Powell,** a stark mingling of water and stone that resulted from the construction of Glen Canyon Dam on the Colorado River. Renting a houseboat is the optimal way to explore the canyons and coves.

The town of **Moab,** below I–70 on Rte. 128, has become a mecca for mountain bikers. Sudden popularity hasn't harmed Moab's laid-back atmosphere, but bed-and-breakfasts, motels, museums, and bike shops have sprouted up everywhere. Just south of Moab, Utah's only commercial winery, **Arches Vineyard** (2182 S. U.S. 191, tel. 801/259–5397; closed Jan.–Feb.), gives tours and has a tasting room.

Sports and Outdoor Activities

Biking Southeastern Utah has hundreds of charted mountain-biking trails, including the **Moab Slickrock Trail,** 4 mi east of town, a 10-mi roller-coaster route marked only by dashes of paint on raw rock; and **Gemini Bridges,** where a steep ascent is followed by a ride over wavy slickrock and two giant stone spans. For rentals and advice, try **Rim Tours** (94 W. 1st North, Moab, tel. 801/259–5223 or 800/626–7335).

Hiking and Backpacking The **Moab Visitor Center** (tel. 801/259–8825) offers trail advice. Remember to bring water along on any hike in this thirsty region. The 2½-mi **Devils Garden Trail** in Arches National Park passes 10 stunning arches. **Delicate Arch** is at the end of a moderate 1½-mi march over undulating slickrock. Canyonlands National Park's **Chesler Park Trail** leads you 3 mi to a wide, grass-and-sagebrush flat ringed by huge red-and-white-banded stone needles.

Rafting The sport of river-running began here with John Wesley Powell's explorations. Outfitters offer float trips and wild white-water treks through black-granite-walled **Westwater Canyon** and the crashing rapids of **Cataract Canyon,** on the Colorado River; or through **Desolation** and **Gray** canyons on the Green River, both of which shelter Anasazi Indian ruins. **Utah Guides and Outfitters** (tel. 801/566–2662) publishes a free directory.

Dining and Lodging

Southeastern Utah is not luxurious, but clean and comfortable lodging is available throughout. Cuisine leans toward fast food and hearty meals using local produce. **Canyonlands Central Reservations** (tel. 801/259–5125 or 800/748–4386) offers suggestions. The following are all located in Moab.

Dining **Grand Old Ranch House.** This austere white ranch house is on the National Register of Historic Places. The menu includes beef and seafood, but authentic German dishes are the chef's forte. *1266 N. U.S. 191, tel. 801/259–5752. MC, V. Moderate.*
The Poplar Place. This two-story mock-adobe restaurant and watering hole has gourmet pizzas, pasta, and salads. Appetizers, dictated by the cook's whims, promise great variety. *11 E. 1st North, tel. 801/259–6018. MC, V. Inexpensive.*

Lodging **Pack Creek Ranch.** This guest ranch on a forested mountain
★ loop offers rustic log cabins and activities ranging from horseback riding—followed by a massage—to cross-country skiing and weekend entertainment. *Box 1270, 84532, tel. 801/259–5505; fax 801/259–8879. 13 cabins. Facilities: kitchens, hot tub, sauna, pool. AE, D, MC, V. Expensive.*
Sunflower Hill Bed and Breakfast. Country touches mark the decor of this stucco-and-weathered-wood dwelling built at the turn of the century. The breakfast spread might include homemade yogurt, fresh bread, or huge fruit muffins. *185 N. 3rd East, 84532, tel. 801/259–2974. 5 rooms and suites (2 share bath). MC, V. Moderate.*
The Virginian. The friendly staff is this plain two-story motel's best feature. Rooms look out on surrounding rusty cliffs. *70 E. 2nd South, 84532, tel. 801/259–5951. 20 rooms. Facilities: kitchenettes. AE, D, DC, MC, V. Inexpensive.*

Campgrounds

The **Moab Visitor Center** (*see* Sports and Outdoor Activities, *above*) has a campground directory detailing everything from overflow areas with no facilities to year-round commercial campgrounds. **Dead Horse Point State Park** (Box 609, Moab 84532; *see* Exploring Southeastern Utah, *above*) has a campground with spectacular views, a museum, a picnic area, flush toilets, and 21 campsites with hookups. **Tumbleweed RV Kampark** (3283 S. U.S. 191, Moab 84532, tel. 801/259–2988) has full hookups, laundry, showers, and cable TV.

9 The Rockies

The Rockies

NEBRASKA

Julesburg
80
Yuma
59
Cope
Last Chance
385
Burlington
76
Sterling
Greeley
Cheyenne
Meriden
Torrington
Douglas
26
Wheatland
Laramie
25
Fort Collins
Boulder
Aurora
Denver
Colorado Springs
25
Pueblo
Walsenburg
40
287
Punkin Center
70
Arkansas River
La Junta
Springfield
50
Lamar
160
350
10
Trinidad
NEW MEXICO
Casper
487
Rawlins
Continental Divide
80
Baggs
Craig
40
Colorado River
Meeker
Glenwood Springs
133
Leadville
24
COLORADO
82
Salida
285
Gunnison
50
Monte Vista
Alamosa
84
Durango
160
S. UTE INDIAN RES.
UTE MTN. INDIAN RES.
RESERVATION
Lander
287
28
Pinedale
191
Farson
181
LaBarge
30
Montpelier
30
Rock Springs
FLAMING GORGE NAT'L REC. AREA
DINOSAUR NAT'L MON.
Dinosaur
139
Fruita
Grand Junction
70
Montrose
Silverton
Sidney
Pocatello
15
Preston
86
Evanston
Salt Lake City
Great Salt Lake
UTAH
NEVADA
ARIZONA
Mountain Home
84
Gooding
Twin Falls
93
Rupert
51

N

150 miles
0
225 km
0

KEY
Amtrak Lines

Introduction

By Carolyn Price Call the Idaho Information Line, and you'll be asked to press "5" on your touch-tone phone if you would like to report a wolf sighting. Check in with the state's tourist promotion offices, and more than likely you'll be talking to a state-employed prison inmate earning $1 an hour for his or her trouble.

Wolves and outlaws haven't left the Rocky Mountain states of Idaho, Montana, Wyoming, and Colorado, and they remain part of the unpredictable charms and crimes of nature and human action that thrived in the Old West: the click of cowboy spurs and the rustling of leather chaps, the sins of Native American betrayals and broken treaties, the energy and innocence of wide-open spaces, boomtowns, and the search for gold.

But most of all, there are the mountains—a 4,000-mi-long chain that stretches from Alaska to northern New Mexico. Begun around 70 million years ago when sandstone, shale, granite, marble, and volcanic rock surged and split and gave under the plow of glacial ice, the Rockies emerged to run intermittently along what is now the Idaho–Montana boundary down to a central section sloping through western Wyoming's Yellowstone and Grand Teton national parks and into northern Colorado.

This mountain backdrop still inspires the kind of fear and wonder it did in mountain men and Native Americans. What you'll see from atop these summits is a landscape of breathtaking beauty and variety. The westernmost state, Idaho, boasts terrain encompassing everything from fruit orchards to the tallest sand dunes in the United States. Montana claims 25 million acres of public land, most of it aloft in the Northern Rockies. Its Glacier National Park is home to the ptarmigan, wolf, mountain goat, and moose. Wyoming, the ninth-largest and least populated state in the Union, is studded with thermal pools, bubbling hot springs, and, within a square-mile area in Yellowstone National Park, one-fourth of the Earth's geysers. In Colorado, the ski capital of the United States, high-country lakes, meadows frosted with blue columbine, and treeless alpine tundra assemble in one sweeping vista, while the mile-high city of Denver and the university town of Boulder attract visitors and settlers from all corners of the globe.

Tour Groups

Going West Tours (Livery Travel, 25 Neill Ave., Helena, MT 58601, tel. 406/443–1410) offers five- to seven-day bus tours through Glacier, Yellowstone, and Little Bighorn national parks. **Harmon Tours** (1529 W. Washington St., Boise, ID 83707, tel. 208/343–7915) operates one- to 32-day tours (mostly for local residents) throughout the country. **Maitland Travel Services, Inc.** (38 2nd St. E, Kalispell, MT 59901, tel. 406/755–1032) arranges custom individual tours of Glacier National Park and other destinations in the Rockies. **Off the Beaten Path** (109 E. Main St., Bozeman, MT 59715, tel. 406/586–1311) offers individually tailored tours ranging from hiking trips in the Canadian Rockies and Yellowstone to horse-pack and fly-fishing trips throughout the western Rockies. **Rocky Mountain Holiday Tours** (Box 842, Fort Collins, CO 80522, tel. 303/482–5813) organizes custom tours for individuals and groups (fly/drive) mainly to Colorado, Wyoming, South Dakota, Utah, Arizona, and New Mexico.

When to Go

Many visitors think the Rockies have only two seasons: skiing and hiking. But for those willing to risk sometimes-capricious weather, fall and spring are the Rockies' best-kept secrets. **Spring** is a good time for fishing, rafting the runoff, or birding and wildlife viewing. **Fall** may be the prettiest season of all, with golden splashes of aspen on the mountainsides, more wildlife at lower elevations, and excellent fishing during spawning. You will also pay less during these shoulder seasons, and you may have a corner of Yellowstone all to yourself. Driving in the **winter** is chancy, and, although the interstates are kept open even in fearsome weather, highway passes like the Going-to-the-Sun Highway in Glacier National Park can be blocked from late October to June. High altitude (over 7,000 feet above sea level) and latitude (the nearer you get to Canada) result in longer winters. Winter visitors should prepare for the possibility of temperatures below zero—but the climate is dry, so the cold is less cruel. Wilderness snowbanks can linger through June, so backcountry hikers generally crowd in from July through Labor Day. **Summer** temperatures rarely rise into the 90s, but the thinner atmosphere at high altitudes makes it necessary for visitors to shield themselves from ultraviolet rays.

Festivals and Seasonal Events

Early Jan.: National Western Stock Show and Rodeo in Denver is the biggest in the world, attracting all the stars of the rodeo circuit for two weeks. *Tel. 303/892–1505 or 303/295–1660 for the box office.*

3rd week in June: Telluride (CO) Bluegrass & Country Music Festival has become so popular that the organizers have had to limit the number of spectators to 10,000. *1539 Pearl St., Suite 200, Boulder, CO 80302, tel. 800/624–2422.*

Late June–mid-Aug: Colorado Shakespeare Festival, in Boulder, presents three full-scale traditional and nontraditional Shakespeare productions and one non-Shakespearean play Tuesday–Sunday nights. The actors are recruited from around the country. *Tel. 303/492–2783.*

Late June–late Aug.: Aspen Music Festival and School. Students from around the world perform with faculty, and world-class soloists and conductors are also featured. The music includes symphony orchestra, chamber, opera, and jazz. *Tel. 303/925–3254.*

July–Aug.: Grand Teton Music Festival, the most important classical music concert series in the northern Rockies, attracts musicians from the nation's finest orchestras. *Box 490, Teton Village, Jackson Hole, WY 83025, tel. 307/733–1128.*

2nd weekend in July: Green River Rendezvous, in Pinedale, Wyoming, is a two-day festival celebrating the spirit of the frontier fur trade, including parades, Native American dances, blackpowder shoots, and rodeos. *Tel. 307/367–4101.*

Last 2 weeks in July: Cheyenne (WY) Frontier Days, the rodeo "Daddy of 'em all," includes evening shows featuring the biggest names in country music, as well as parades and very popular pancake breakfasts. *Tel. 800/227–6336 or 800/543–2339 in WY.*

Late Aug.: Crow Fair in Crow Agency, Montana, is a five-day celebration of native pride, traditions, and crafts that draws tribes and visitors for parades, rodeos, powwow dancing, and horse races. *Tel. 406/638–6418.*

Nov.: Join the **Eagle Watch** to see hundreds of bald eagles gather annually in Canyon Ferry State Park, near Helena, Montana, during freshwater salmon spawning. This is one of the few places outside Alaska where you can see the eagles in such concentration. The best time to go is in November, but the eagles gather here from October to late December. *Tel. 406/442–4120.*

Getting Around

By Plane Denver's **Stapleton International Airport** (tel. 303/270–1300 or 800/247–2336) is served by most major airlines, including American, Continental, United, and USAir, with commuter airline links to smaller airports in the region. Several domestic airlines fly from Denver and Salt Lake into **Jackson Hole Airport** (tel. 307/733–4767) in Wyoming, with additional service during the ski season, including direct flights from Chicago by American Airlines. The **Boise Air Terminal** (tel. 208/382–3110) in Idaho is served by Delta, Skywest, United, and other airlines. In Montana, the **Missoula Airport** (tel. 406/543–7001) and **Glacier Park International Airport** (tel. 406/752–1028), in Kalispell, are served by major domestic airlines. **Salt Lake City Airport** (tel. 801/575–2400) also provides an access point to Wyoming and Idaho.

By Car Major interstates crisscross the region, winding their way through accessible mountain passes. The busiest, but least scenic, east–west thoroughfare is I–80, which crosses southern Wyoming, passing through Cheyenne and Laramie in the southeast corner. To reach Yellowstone National Park, you must either make the long drive north from Rock Springs or come south from I–90, which crosses southern Montana. In Colorado, I–70 runs east–west, passing through Denver and Grand Junction in the west and passing south of Rocky Mountain National Park. I–15 runs north from Salt Lake City into Idaho and connects with I–84, which heads west to Boise and on to Portland. I–90 passes through Sheridan in northeast Wyoming before crossing Montana and northern Idaho; it comes within 100 mi of Glacier National Park, which can be reached by going north from Missoula on U.S. 93 and east on U.S. 2. I–15 goes along the east side of the park; you can reach Glacier by driving west on U.S. 89. I–25 comes up from New Mexico and passes through Colorado Springs and Denver in Colorado; Cheyenne and Casper in Wyoming; and then joins I–90 in Montana. Throughout the Rockies, drivers should be extremely cautious about winter travel, when white-outs and ice are not uncommon. Because major airports are few and far between, the Rockies are a favorite of car travelers and campers, and the busy driving season is summer. Major attractions such as Glacier and Yellowstone National Park are well away from the interstates, requiring visitors to drive dozens or even hundreds of miles on scenic, two-lane highways to the entrances.

By Train **Amtrak** (tel. 800/872–7245) connects the Rockies to both coasts and all major American cities; trains run through Boise, Salt Lake City, and Denver, with other stops in between. Routes have switched back and forth between Colorado and southern Wyoming in recent years. Amtrak trains also run through northern Montana, with stops in Essex and Whitefish, along the border of Glacier National Park. Connecting motorcoach services are provided in the summer from Pocatello, Idaho, to Yellowstone National Park.

By Bus **Greyhound** (tel. 303/292–6111) has extensive service throughout Colorado and connects major cities throughout the region, including Cheyenne, Boise, Pocatello, and Missoula. Various smaller bus lines connect with Greyhound to provide service to smaller communities as well as the parks.

COLORADO

By Sandra
Widener

Capital	Denver
Population	3,294,394
Motto	Nothing Without Providence
State Bird	Lark bunting
State Flower	Columbine

Visitor Information

Colorado Tourism Board (1625 Broadway, Suite 1700, Denver 80202, tel. 303/592–5510 or 800/265–6723). **Colorado Travel-Bank** (tel. 303/320–8550; modem, tel. 303/671–7669).

Scenic Drives

Colorado has 17 designated scenic routes, which are marked by signs featuring a blue columbine. The 232-mi **San Juan Skyway** passes through historic ranching and mining towns, such as Durango, Silverton, Ouray, Telluride, and Cortez. The **Peak-to-Peak Highway** follows Rtes. 119, 72, and 7 through gold-mining towns to Rocky Mountain National Park.

National and State Parks

National Parks **Great Sand Dunes National Monument** (35 mi northeast of Alamosa off Rte. 150, Mosca 81146, tel. 719/378–2312), with shimmering mountains of sand almost 700 feet high, has a year-round campground and a nature trail. **Mesa Verde National Park** (U.S. 160, 8 mi east of Cortez, Mesa Verde Natl. Park 81330, tel. 303/529–4465) features the remarkable, well-preserved cliff dwellings of the ancient Anasazi Indians; lodging, restaurants, and camping are crowded in summer. **Rocky Mountain National Park** (Hwy. 36, Estes Park 80517, tel. 303/586–2371) offers a picturebook vision of craggy mountains, abundant wildlife, and deep-blue mountain lakes in more than 250,000 acres, with camping, hiking, lodging, and scenic drives. There is also lodging in nearby Estes Park.

State Parks The state's 40 parks offer opportunities to hunt, hike, fish, sail, and take in idyllic views. The **Colorado Division of Parks** (Dept. of Natural Resources, 1313 Sherman St., Denver 80203, tel. 303/866–3437) provides information.

Denver

Denver is a city where winter weather reports often begin with skiing conditions, and where weekends are often occupied with trips to the mountains to hike, camp, and fish after the lifts shut down for the summer. The sharp-edged new skyscrapers, clean streets, and dozens of well-used parks evoke the image of a young, forward-looking city, but much of what made Denver what it is lies in its western past. Areas like LoDo, for instance, a historic part of lower downtown, buzz with jazz clubs, restaurants, and art galleries housed in century-old buildings.

Tourist Information

Denver Metro Convention and Visitors Bureau (225 W. Colfax Ave., 80202, tel. 303/892–1112).

Arriving and Departing

By Plane The new **Denver International Airport** (tel. 303/270–1900), opened in late 1993 23 mi from downtown Denver, has flights by most major carriers. Cab fare downtown should average about $40; **RTD,** the local bus service (*see* Getting Around Denver, *below*), can also get you there. The **Airporter** (tel. 303/321–3222; reservations required) offers express-bus service from the airport to downtown hotels.

By Car I–70 (east–west) and I–25 (north–south) intersect near downtown.

Train Station **Amtrak: Union Station** (17th St. at Wynkoop St., tel. 303/534–2812).

Bus Station **Greyhound** (1055 19th St., tel. 303/292–6111).

Getting Around Denver

A free shuttle-bus service operates frequently down the length of the 16th Street Mall. For explorations beyond downtown, a car is best, although buses and taxis are available.

By Car Despite a number of one-way streets, driving in Denver is not difficult, and finding a spot in a parking lot is usually easy. Traffic on I–25 and I–70 can be congested during rush hours.

By Public Transportation The region's public bus service, **RTD** (tel. 303/299–6000 or 303/299–6700), has routes throughout Denver and to outlying towns, such as Boulder, Longmont, and Nederland. Buy bus tokens ($1) at grocery stores or with exact change on the bus.

By Taxi Cabs are available at the airport and usually at major hotels. Companies offering 24-hour service include **Yellow Cab** (tel. 303/777–7777; $1.20 minimum, $1.20 per mi) and **Metro Taxi** (tel. 303/333–3333; $1.40 minimum, $1.40 per mi).

Orientation Tours

Gray Line (tel. 303/289–2841) offers a 2½-hour city tour, a mountain parks tour, and a mountain casino tour.

Walking Tours Self-guided walking-tour brochures are available through the Convention and Visitors Bureau (*see* Tourist Information, *above*).

Exploring Denver

Denver presents its official face to the world at the **Civic Center.** The three-block park, with lawns, gardens, and a Greek amphitheater, forms a backdrop for the **State Capitol** (1475 Sherman St., tel. 303/866–2604; closed Sun.) and the **City and County Building,** which are at opposite ends. The dome of the 1894 capitol building is periodically recovered with hammered gold leaf as a reminder of the state's mining heritage. The balcony at its base affords a panoramic view of the Rockies. Just off the park are the **Colorado History Museum** (1300 Broadway, tel. 303/

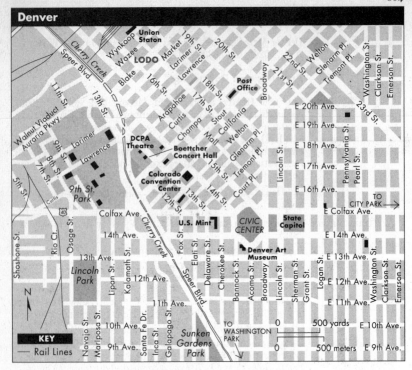

Denver

866–3682; admission charged), with Colorado and western memorabilia and dioramas, plus special exhibits; and the **Denver Art Museum** (100 W. 14th Ave. Pkwy., tel. 303/575–2793; closed Mon., major holidays), with an excellent collection of Native American art, as well as Old Masters, Impressionists, textiles, pottery, and period rooms.

Close by is the **Denver Mint** (officially known as the United States Mint), the source of all coins marked with a *D*. There are tours of this facility, where more than 5 billion coins are stamped yearly—and where the third-largest hoard of gold in the United States is on display. *W. Colfax Ave. and Cherokee St., tel. 303/844–3582. Admission free. Closed weekdays, last 2 weeks in June.*

Free shuttle buses are the only vehicles allowed on the **16th Street Mall,** which features shade trees, outdoor cafés, historic buildings, and shopping. Hop off the bus at Tremont Place and walk over a block to the **Museum of Western Art** (1727 Tremont Pl., tel. 303/296–1880), a frontier-era bordello that now celebrates artistic heroes of the western myth: Remington, Bierstadt, and Charles Russell. On the way back, peek inside the **Brown Palace** (321 17th St.; *see* Lodging, *below*), Denver's hotel empress, built in 1892 and still proud of her antique charms.

Farther down the mall is the 330-foot-tall **D&F Tower** (16th St. at Arapahoe St.), built to emulate the campanile of St. Mark's Cathedral in Venice, and **Tabor Center** (16th St. at Lawrence St.), a cheery shopping mall. South on Curtis Street is the **Den-**

ver Center for the Performing Arts (14th and Curtis Sts.), a huge complex of theaters and a symphony hall.

Across from Tabor Center behind Writer Square is historic **Larimer Square** (Larimer and 15th Sts.), Denver's most charming shopping area, which showcases some of the city's oldest retail buildings and finest specialty shops. Farther into lower downtown (**LoDo,** to the locals), north of Larimer Square between Speer Boulevard and Larimer Street, lies an equally historic, but quirkier, area featuring art galleries, nightclubs, and restaurants that range from Denver's hautest cuisine to the most down-home coffee shops.

East of downtown, the **Molly Brown House** (1340 Pennsylvania St., tel. 303/832–4092), a Victorian confection, celebrates the life and times of the scandalous unsinkable one, while the **Grant-Humphreys Mansion** (770 Pennsylvania St., tel. 303/894–2506) is a testament to the proper Denver society that looked down on Molly at the turn of the century.

Northeast of downtown in **City Park,** the popular **Denver Zoo** features a nursery for baby animals and a polar bear exhibit where visitors can watch the bears swim underwater. *E. 23rd St. between York St. and Colorado Blvd., tel. 303/331–4110. Admission charged.*

Also in City Park is the **Denver Museum of Natural History,** a rich combination of traditional collections and intriguing hands-on exhibits, plus a movie theater with a four-story screen and a planetarium. *2001 Colorado Blvd., tel. 303/322–7009. Admission charged.*

Parks and Gardens

Denver has one of the largest city park systems (tel. 303/698–4900) in the country, with over 20,000 acres in the city and nearby mountains. **City Park** features lakes, tennis, golf, museums, and the zoo (*see* Exploring Denver, *above*). Flower gardens and lakes abound in **Washington Park** (east of Downing St. between Virginia Ave. and Louisiana Ave.); this is where young Denver goes to run, rollerblade, bike, play volleyball and tennis, and hang out.

On the east side of the city are the **Denver Botanic Gardens** (1005 York St., tel. 303/331–4010; admission charged), a flowering retreat. The conservatory houses a rain forest; outside are a Japanese garden, a rock garden, and gorgeous horticulture displays at their height in summer. **Platte River Greenway** is a 20-mi biking, jogging, and rollerblading path that follows Cherry Creek and the Platte River, much of it through downtown Denver.

What to See and Do with Children

At the **Denver Children's Museum** (2121 Children's Museum Dr., tel. 303/433–7433), interactive exhibits include a working TV station and an outdoor, all-year beginners' ski hill.

Shopping

Denver is one of the top places to buy recreational equipment and clothing. Sporting goods stores have legendary ski sales around Labor Day. You can also pick up a pair of cowboy boots and other western apparel at western stores.

Shopping Districts The **Cherry Creek** shopping district, 2 mi from downtown, is Denver's best. On one side of 1st Avenue at Milwaukee Street is the **Cherry Creek Shopping Mall,** a classy granite-and-glass behemoth containing some of the nation's finest retailers. On the other side is **Cherry Creek North,** with art galleries and specialty shops. Historic **Larimer Square** (14th and Larimer Sts.) is the center of Denver specialty shopping, with antiques, housewares, and clothing boutiques. On the 16th Street Mall are **Tabor Center** and other large downtown retailers.

Specialty Stores **South Broadway** between 1st Avenue and Evans Street has **Antiques** blocks of antiques stores; prices are sometimes lower than elsewhere.

Books **The Tattered Cover** (1st Ave. at Milwaukee St., tel. 303/322–7727) has overstuffed armchairs, four stories of books (more than 175,000 titles), and a knowledgeable staff.

Sporting Goods **Gart Brothers Sports Castle** (1000 Broadway, tel. 303/861–1122) is a huge, multistory shrine to Colorado's love of the outdoors.

Western Wear **Denver Buffalo Company Trading Post** (1109 Lincoln St., tel. 303/832–0884) has top-of-the-line western clothing and high-quality souvenirs. **Miller Stockman** (16th St. Mall at California St., tel. 303/825–5339) is an old-line Denver retailer selling the genuine article.

Spectator Sports

Baseball **Colorado Rockies** (Mile High Stadium, just west of downtown across I–25, tel. 303/292–0200; Apr.–Oct.).

Basketball **Denver Nuggets** (McNichols Sports Arena, just west of downtown across I–25, tel. 303/893–3865; Oct.–Apr.).

Football **Denver Broncos** (Mile High Stadium, tel. 303/433–7466; Sept.–Dec.).

Dining

Beef, buffalo, and burritos have an honored spot in Denver's culinary history, but more sophisticated fare—from Vietnamese to casual French—is enthusiastically supported throughout the city. For dining inspiration, cruise 17th Avenue east from downtown. For price ranges, see Chart 1 (A) in Chapter 1.

Very Expensive **Cliff Young's.** Young presides over his elegant art deco restaurant with meticulous care, showering diners with attention while the kitchen prepares free-range veal. *700 E. 17th Ave., tel. 303/831–8900. Reservations advised. Jacket and tie advised. AE, D, DC, MC, V. No lunch weekends.*

Expensive **The Buckhorn Exchange.** The neighborhood has deteriorated, but this Denver landmark continues to pull in crowds eager to eat elk, buffalo, and beef on checkered tablecloths and gawk at the enormous collection of memorabilia and animal heads. *1000 Osage St., tel. 303/534–9505. Reservations advised. AE, D, DC, MC, V. No lunch weekends.*
Emil-Lene's Sirloin House. This restaurant, out in the plains at the end of a dirt road, is a locally loved throwback to the '50s,

with unrepentantly worn, ranch-style furnishings. Dinner is accompanied by iceberg-lettuce salads and relish trays, but the beef is delicious. *16000 Smith Rd., Aurora, tel. 303/366-6674. Reservations advised. AE, DC, MC, V. No lunch Sun.*

★ **European Cafe.** Housed in a converted LoDo loft that now elegantly gleams with polished brass and crystal, this restaurant serves imaginatively and beautifully presented French cuisine. Try the lamb chops with shiitake mushrooms in Madeira sauce. *1515 Market St., tel. 303/825-6555. Reservations advised. AE, D, DC, MC, V. No lunch weekends.*

★ **Strings.** This light, airy spot with its wide-open kitchen is one place in Denver to see and be seen. The food is casual-contemporary; one specialty is spaghetti with caviar and asparagus in champagne-cream sauce. *1700 Humboldt St., tel. 303/831-7310. Reservations advised. AE, D, DC, MC, V. No lunch Sun.*

Tante Louise. Set in what could be an intimate French country house 15 minutes from downtown is this restaurant with a contemporary French menu. Try the seared sea scallops with couscous and herbed vinaigrette. *4900 E. Colfax Ave., tel. 303/355-4488. Reservations advised. AE, D, DC, MC, V. No lunch (except Fri.); closed Sun.*

Moderate **Imperial Chinese Seafood Restaurant.** Denver's best Chinese food is served in a graceful dining room featuring Chinese art. Try the steamed sea bass with ginger, Hunan, or black-bean sauce. *1 Broadway, tel. 303/698-2800. Reservations only for 4 or more. AE, DC, MC, V. No lunch Sun.*

★ **Le Central.** Here you find authentic, informal, delicious French food in a French-bistro atmosphere. Favorites on the hearty menu are bouillabaisse, cassoulet, and *entrecôte au poivre.* A Sunday brunch is served. *112 E. 8th Ave., tel. 303/863-8094. No credit cards. No lunch Sat.*

Pagliacci's. This North Denver restaurant offers an old-fashioned, satisfying take on familiar Italian dishes, such as veal Parmigiana and baked manicotti. *1440 W. 33rd Ave. at Navajo St., tel. 303/458-0530. AE, DC, MC, V. No lunch.*

TransAlpin. The feel is casual, despite the white tablecloths and crystal. The menu offers food from around the globe; entrées are identified by locale, so Hungary might be next to India. Blackened-chicken tostada is a favorite. *410 E. 7th Ave., tel. 303/830-8282. MC, V. No lunch weekends.*

Inexpensive **Las Delicias.** The line that forms faithfully for dinner testifies
★ to this Mexican restaurant's popularity. On weekends, the chef makes delicious *carnitas* (tender pork simmered with green chile). *439 E. 19th St., tel. 303/839-5675. MC, V.*

T-WA Inn. This popular South Asian hole-in-the-wall serves great food, including delicate Vietnamese spring rolls and daily specials. *555 S. Federal Blvd., tel. 303/922-4584. AE, MC, V.*

Wynkoop Brewing Company. With its beer brewed on the premises, in a converted LoDo building, and its hearty pub fare, the Wynkoop has become a fast favorite of trendy Denver. Try the shepherd's pie or the bangers and mashers. *1634 18th St., tel. 303/297-2700. No reservations weekends. AE, D, DC, MC, V.*

Lodging

Denver's lodging choices range from the stately Brown Palace to the YMCA, with B&Bs and other options in between. **Bed & Breakfast Rocky Mountains** (673 Grant St., 80203, tel. 303/860-8415) handles B&Bs throughout the state. **Hostelling In-**

ternational–Rocky Mountain Council (tel. 303/442–1166) provides information about hostels in 13 Colorado locations. For price ranges, see Chart 2 (A) in Chapter 1.

Very Expensive **Brown Palace Hotel.** This grand dame of Colorado lodgings has
★ housed everyone from President Eisenhower to the Beatles. The downtown hotel's dramatic eight-story lobby is topped by a glorious stained-glass ceiling. Rooms are decorated in Victorian style. *321 17th St., 80202, tel. 303/297–3111 or 800/321–2599; fax 303/293–9204. 230 rooms, 25 suites. Facilities: 4 restaurants, 2 bars, concierge, parking. AE, D, DC, MC, V.*

Expensive **Burnsley.** Since its face-lift in the 1980s, this 16-story, Bauhaus-style tower on the southeastern edge of downtown has offered a quiet haven close to the center. The modern suites all have balconies and full kitchens. *1000 Grant St., 80203, tel. 303/ 830–1000 or 800/231–3915; fax 303/830–7676. 82 suites. Facilities: restaurant, bar, pool, parking. AE, DC, MC, V.*

Cambridge Club Hotel. This 1960s-era luxury hotel is a block from the State Capitol on a tree-lined street. Local lobbyists, politicos, and CEOs favor the bar. The suites are individually decorated, each with a firm bed and cozy reading chairs. *1560 Sherman St., 80203, tel. 303/831–1252 or 800/877–1252; fax 303/831–4724. 27 suites. Facilities: restaurant, bar. AE, D, DC, MC, V.*

Embassy Suites. In this ultramodern gray-glass skyscraper, built in 1983, suites provide more elbow room. Those on upper floors have spectacular views, while those lower down can be noisy. *1881 Curtis St., 80202, tel. 303/297–8888 or 800/733–3366; fax 303/298–1103. 336 suites. Facilities: restaurant, café, piano bar, exercise room, health club (fee), pool, whirlpool, valet parking. AE, D, DC, MC, V.*

★ **Oxford.** This fine hotel was a Denver fixture in the Victorian era; now, completely refurbished in turn-of-the-century style, it is the city's most charming small hotel. Guest rooms are exquisitely furnished in French and English antiques. *1600 17th St., 80202, tel. 303/628–5400 or 800/228–5838; fax 303/628–5413. 81 rooms. Facilities: restaurant, 2 bars, health club (fee), valet parking. AE, D, DC, MC, V.*

Moderate **Castle Marne.** This historic house with balconies, a four-story turret, and intricate stone- and woodwork is east of downtown in a shabbily genteel area near several fine restaurants. The B&B's rooms are decorated with antiques and art. *1572 Race St., 80206, tel. 303/331–0621 or 800/926–2763; fax 303/331–0623. 9 rooms. Facilities: game room, parking. AE, D, DC, MC, V.*

★ **Queen Anne Inn.** North of downtown in a reclaimed historic area, this B&B makes a romantic getaway, with fresh flowers, antiques, and turn-of-the-century charm. Full breakfast and an afternoon Colorado-wine tasting are free to guests. *2147 Tremont Pl., 80205, tel. 303/296–6666. 14 rooms. AE, D, MC, V.*

Red Lion. The hotel at the edge of town is a good bet if you plan to sidestep Denver and head immediately for the mountains. The rooms are unexceptional; service is efficient. *3203 Quebec St., 80207, tel. 303/321–3333 or 800/547–8010; fax 303/329–5233. 567 rooms. Facilities: 2 restaurants, 2 bars, exercise equipment, indoor pool, parking. AE, D, DC, MC, V.*

Inexpensive **Comfort Inn/Downtown.** The advantages to this well-worn, basic hotel are its reasonable rates and its location, right across from—and connected to—the Brown Palace in the heart of downtown. *401 17th St., 80202, tel. 303/296–0400 or 800/221–2222; fax 303/297–0774. 229 rooms. Facilities: restaurant, bar, valet parking. AE, D, DC, MC, V.*

★ **Holiday Chalet.** This turn-of-the-century house turned hotel is in the heart of Capitol Hill, immediately east of downtown. It's full of charm, with stained-glass windows and homey touches, and each room has a kitchenette stocked for breakfast. *1820 E. Colfax St., 80218, tel. 303/321–9975 or 800/626–4497; fax 303/377–6556. 10 rooms. AE, D, DC, MC, V.*

YMCA. The old standby has clean, basic rooms, some with private baths, and a great location downtown. *25 E. 16th Ave., 80202, tel. 303/861–8300. 185 rooms. Facilities: restaurant. MC, V.*

The Arts and Nightlife

Friday's *Denver Post* and *Rocky Mountain News* list entertainment events, as does *Westword*, a weekly published on Wednesday. **Ticketmaster** (tel. 303/290–8497) sells tickets to major events. The **Ticket Bus** (16th St. Mall at Curtis St., no tel.) sells tickets from 10 to 6 weekdays, and half-price tickets the day of the performance.

The Arts The modern **Denver Center for the Performing Arts** (13th and Curtis Sts., tel. 303/893–3272) complex houses most of the city's large concert halls and theaters.

Theater The **Denver Center Theater Company** (tel. 303/893–4100) offers fine repertory theater. **Robert Garner Attractions** (tel. 302/893–4100) brings Broadway-caliber plays to the city.

Music The **Colorado Symphony Orchestra** (tel. 303/893–3272) performs at Boettcher Concert Hall (13th and Curtis Sts.). The **Denver Chamber Orchestra** (tel. 303/825–4911) usually plays at historic Trinity Methodist Church (18th St. and Broadway).

Dance **Colorado Ballet** (tel. 303/298–0677) specializes in classical ballet. **Colorado Contemporary Dance** (tel. 303/892–9797) brings national dance companies to Denver. Both perform at various locations around town.

Nightlife **Downtown** and **LoDo** host most of Denver's nightlife. Downtown features more mainstream entertainment, while LoDo is home to rock clubs and small theaters. Remember that Denver's altitude makes you react sooner to alcohol.

Comedy **Comedy Works** (1226 15th St., tel. 303/595–3637) features local and nationally known stand-up comics.

Country and Western The **Grizzly Rose** (I–25 Exit 215, tel. 303/295–1330) has miles of dance floor, national bands, and country-and-western dancing lessons.

Jazz **El Chapultepec** (20th St. at Market St., tel. 303/295–9126) is a smoky, unpretentious place where visiting jazz musicians end up after hours. The **Jazz Works** (1634 18th St., tel. 303/297–0920) hosts national groups and talented locals.

Rock **Herman's Hideaway** (1578 S. Broadway, tel. 303/778–9916) is a favorite for hot local bands and national acts; some blues and reggae, too. **Rock Island** (Wazee and 15th Sts., tel. 303/572–7625) caters to the young, restless, and hip.

Excursions from Denver

Boulder   Home of the **University of Colorado,** Boulder is a quintessential college town but also home to a hard-core group of professional athletes who live to bike and run. The atmosphere is peaceful, new-age, and cultural, with the gorgeous backdrop of the mountains. One of the city's main attractions is the **Pearl Street Mall,** a see-and-be-seen pedestrian street with benches, grassy spots, great shopping, and outdoor cafés. Rich in lectures, theater, and music year-round, Boulder celebrates classical music each summer at its **Colorado Music Festival** (Chautauqua Park, tel. 303/449–1397).

Getting There   From Denver, take I–25N to the Boulder Turnpike (Hwy. 36). Denver's RTD buses make the 27-mi commute to Boulder regularly.

Central City and Blackhawk   Abandoned mines on the side of the scenic road that leads to these historic towns testifies to their silver- and gold-mining heritage. Now, however, low-stakes **gambling** has arrived, and the jingle of slot machines is a constant. The narrow, winding streets are edged with brick storefronts from the last century. The **Central City Opera House** (tel. 303/292–6700), a small Victorian jewel in the center of town, offers opera in summer.

Getting There   From I–70, take Hwy. 58 to Golden; from there, take Hwy. 6 up Clear Creek Canyon and Hwy. 119 northwest 1 mi past Blackhawk to Central City, for a total of 35 mi from Denver.

Georgetown   With its multitude of **gingerbread Victorian houses** on quiet streets, Georgetown provides a tantalizing glimpse of Colorado's heady mining past. The town, a National Historic District, has restaurants, small shops, and the **Georgetown Loop Railroad** (tel. 303/569–2403), a 3-mi narrow-gauge line that travels into the mountains and back.

Getting There   Take I–70W to the Georgetown exit, 46 mi from Denver.

Golden   **Coors** (13th and Ford Sts., tel. 303/277–2337) operates the world's largest brewery in Golden and offers a free half-hour tour that covers the basics of brewing beer and ends with a trip to the tasting rooms. Tours run daily except Sun.

Getting There   From I–70, take Hwy. 58 to Golden.

Colorado Springs and Environs

At the center of the state, 65 mi south of Denver, is Colorado's second-largest city, Colorado Springs. As well as its natural wonders, such as Pike's Peak, of "Pike's Peak or Bust" fame, the region has such man-made attractions as the Air Force Academy and the Broadmoor resort.

Tourist Information

Colorado Springs: Chamber of Commerce (2 N. Cascade Ave., 80903, tel. 719/635–1551). Visitor Center (104 S. Cascade Ave., tel. 719/635–7506 or 800/888–4748).

Getting There

By Plane **Colorado Springs Municipal Airport** (5750 E. Fountain Blvd., tel. 719/570–7755), 20 mi from the city, is served by domestic airlines.

By Car From Denver take I–25S.

By Bus **Greyhound** (120 S. Weber St., tel. 719/635–1505). **Springs Transit Management** (127 E. Kiowa St., tel. 719/475–9733) serves local routes.

Exploring Colorado Springs and Environs

The city of **Colorado Springs** has wide, tree-lined streets and Victorian houses, but its main feature is the mix of attractions around it. The **U.S. Olympic Center** (1 Olympic Plaza, tel. 719/578–4500) offers tours of the sprawling complex where hundreds of young athletes train. **The Broadmoor** (1 Lake Ave.; *see* Dining and Lodging, *below*) is a rambling ensemble of pink stucco Italian Renaissance–style hotel buildings, golf courses, gardens, an ice rink where Olympic skaters practice, and a picture-perfect lake skimmed by black swans. The **Carriage House Museum** on the grounds displays an old stagecoach, vintage cars, and carriages used at Presidential inaugurals.

Two routes—a cog railway (515 Ruxton Ave., Manitou Springs, tel. 719/685–1045) and a toll road (10 mi west on Hwy. 24, left at marked exit at Cascade)—lead up to breathtaking views atop **Pike's Peak,** the summit Zebulon Pike claimed could never be scaled by humans. The **Air Force Academy** (10 mi north on I–25, Exits 156B and 150B, tel. 719/472–1818) is notable for its forest-and-mountain setting and its Cadet Chapel, with 17 spires that rise 150 feet. The academy offers guided tours in summer. The **Garden of the Gods** (off Ridge Rd., north of U.S. 24, tel. 719/578–6939) offers picnic spots and hikes among 1,350 acres of weird, windswept red rock formations and unusual plant life.

Cripple Creek (24 mi west to Divide, then 20 mi south on Hwy. 67), until recently a creaky old mining town once known for vast deposits of gold, has gone upscale with the legalization of low-stakes gambling. The **Cripple Creek & Victor Narrow Gauge Railroad** (north end of town, tel. 719/689–2640; closed Nov.–Apr.) runs a 4-mi route past old mines and older mountains.

What to See and Do with Children

The **Cheyenne Mountain Zoo** (4250 Cheyenne Mountain Zoo Rd., tel. 719/475–9555), set on a mountainside, is a haven for endangered species—more than 100—and a home to hundreds of other animals, most in habitats closely resembling their natural ones.

Shopping

Castle Rock Factory Shops (20 mi south of Denver on I–25, tel. 303/688–4494) has more than 50 clothing and home-furnishings stores.

Central Colorado

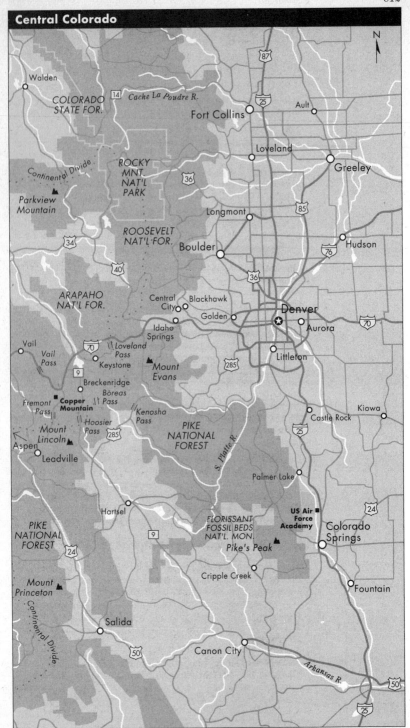

N

Walden

COLORADO STATE FOR.

14 Cache La Poudre R.

Fort Collins

87

25

Ault

Loveland

Greeley

Continental Divide

ROCKY MNT. NAT'L PARK

36

Parkview Mountain

ROOSEVELT NAT'L FOR.

Longmont

85

34

Boulder

Hudson

76

40

ARAPAHO NAT'L FOR.

Central City

Blackhawk

36

Golden

Denver

Aurora

70

Idaho Springs

Littleton

285

Vail

70

Loveland Pass

Vail Pass

9

Keystone

Mount Evans

Breckenridge

Fremont Pass

Copper Mountain

Bóreas Pass

Kenosha Pass

PIKE NATIONAL FOREST

S. Platte R.

Castle Rock

Kiowa

25

Mount Lincoln

Hoosier Pass

285

Aspen

Leadville

Palmer Lake

PIKE NATIONAL FOREST

24

Hartsel

9

FLORISSANT FOSSIL BEDS NAT'L. MON.

US Air Force Academy

Colorado Springs

24

Pike's Peak

Fountain

Mount Princeton

Cripple Creek

Continental Divide

Salida

50

Canon City

Arkansas R.

50

25

Sports and Outdoor Activities

Biking **Pike National Forest** (Ranger District Office, 601 S. Weber St., Colorado Springs, 80903, tel. 719/636–1602) has mountain-bike trails.

Fishing Lovers of trout-stream fishing flock to the **South Platte** (Rte. 67, 28 mi north of Woodland Park). **Elevenmile Reservoir** (Hwy. 24W to west edge of town of Lake George) has rainbow trout, kokanee salmon, and pike.

Golf **The Broadmoor** (1 Lake Ave., tel. 719/634–7711) has three 18-hole courses. The **Patty Jewett Golf Course** (900 E. Espanola St., tel. 719/578–6825), built in 1898, has 27 holes.

Hiking and Backpacking Colorado Springs' location provides plenty of backpacking and hiking opportunities. Check the **Visitor Center** (*see* Tourist Information, *above*) for information and maps. Some of the best trails are in **Pike National Forest** (*see* Biking, *above*).

Horseback Riding **Academy Riding Stables** (4 El Paso Blvd., tel. 719/633–5667) rents horses for guided tours through Garden of the Gods park (*see* Exploring Colorado Springs and Environs, *above*). Reservations are necessary.

Dining and Lodging

Steaks and other basic western foods, along with Mexican food, are the most popular menu options hereabouts. The Colorado Springs Visitor Center (*see* Tourist Information, *above*) offers lodging assistance. For price ranges, see Charts 1 (B) and 2 (B) in Chapter 1.

Colorado Springs
Dining **The Briarhurst Manor.** An 1878 stone mansion provides the setting for chef Sigi Krauss's offerings. Dishes such as chateaubriand are prepared with Colorado ingredients and a European touch. *404 Manitou Ave., tel. 719/685–1864. Reservations advised. AE, DC, MC, V. No lunch; closed Sun., 1st 2 wks of Jan. Expensive.*

★ **Flying W Ranch.** Chuckwagon suppers of barbecued beef, beans, biscuits, applesauce, and spice cake are served around a campfire at this working ranch. Afterward, a cowboy band gives a western show. In winter, steak-house dinners are served inside. *3330 Chuckwagon Rd., tel. 719/632–0700. Reservations required. No credit cards. Closed Sun.–Thurs. Oct.–May. Moderate.*

Dining and Lodging **The Broadmoor.** This resort is a Colorado legend. The lovely,
★ recently renovated 1918 buildings house plush, traditional rooms. The restaurants serve everything from formal French to Sunday brunch. *1 Lake Ave., 80901, tel. 719/634–7711 or 800/634–7711; fax 719/577–5700. 551 rooms. Facilities: 9 restaurants, 3 bars, health club, 16 tennis courts, 3 golf courses, 3 pools, 3 squash courts, ice skating, horseback riding, 25 shops, paddleboat and mountain-bike rentals, children's programs. D, DC, MC, V. Expensive.*

Lodging **Hearthstone Inn.** Rooms at this B&B are individually deco-
★ rated with antiques and stylish country prints. Breakfast runs to such delicacies as corn pancakes with maple syrup and fruit compote. *506 N. Cascade Ave., 80903, tel. 719/473–4413. 25 rooms (2 share bath). No smoking. AE, MC, V. Moderate–Expensive.*

Manitou Springs
Dining

Mission Bell Inn. The folks in the kitchen, who have been at it for 30 years, serve homestyle Mexican food. Among the favorites are green chili and guacamole. *178 Crystal Park Rd., tel. 719/685–9089. MC, V. No lunch; closed Mon. Inexpensive.*

Motels

Le Baron Hotel (314 W. Bijou, Colorado Springs 80905, tel. 719/471–8680 or 800/477–8610; fax 719/471–0894), 206 rooms, restaurant, lounge, pool, fitness room; moderate. **Palmer House/Best Western** (I–25, near Exit 145, 3010 North Chestnut St., Colorado Springs 80907, tel. 719/636–5201 or 800/223–9127; fax 719/636–3108), 150 rooms, restaurant, lounge, pool; moderate.

Northwestern Colorado

As you climb west from Denver, the mountains rear up, pine forests line the road, and the legendary Colorado of powder skiing, alpine scenery, and the great outdoors begins. As once-primitive mining towns have attracted skiers and scenery buffs, sophisticated dining and lodging have followed.

Tourist Information

Northwest Colorado: Visitor Information (tel. 800/327–8789). **Summit County:** Visitor's Bureau (100 Summit Blvd., Box 214, Frisco 80443, tel. 303/668–5800). **Aspen:** Information (425 Rio Grande Pl., 81611, tel. 303/925–5656). **Steamboat Springs:** Chamber of Commerce (1201 Lincoln Ave., Box 774408, 80477, tel. 303/879–0880). **Vail:** Information (100 E. Meadow Dr., 81657, tel. 303/476–1000).

Getting There

By Plane

Aspen Airport (tel. 303/920–5385) is 7 mi east of town; most flights connect from Denver. **Steamboat Springs Airport** (tel. 303/879–1204) is 3 mi northwest of town. **Vail/Beaver Creek Jet Center** (tel. 303/524–7700) is 30 mi west of Vail. All are served by regional and national airlines, but Vail has scheduled service only during ski season.

By Car

I–70 is the main route to the Summit County resorts, Vail, and Glenwood Springs. From Glenwood Springs, Hwy. 82 heads to Aspen. Hwy. 36 leads to Rocky Mountain National Park and Estes Park; Hwy. 40 heads to Steamboat Springs.

By Train

Amtrak stops in Glenwood Springs (tel. 303/945–9563), Granby, and Winter Park.

By Bus

Greyhound (tel. 303/292–6111) serves most major mountain towns.

Exploring Northwestern Colorado

Estes Park is the northern gateway to **Rocky Mountain National Park** (*see* National and State Parks, *above*), where Trail Ridge Road (closed in winter) provides a spectacular ride over one of the highest auto routes in the world. On the west side of the park is **Grand Lake,** the largest natural lake in Colorado, which has a lovely shoreline and boasts the world's highest yacht club.

The closest resort skiing from Denver is off I-70 at **Winter Park,** a family-oriented resort with a heavy slant toward intermediate skiers. It is popular with Denverites, who often travel there via the Ski Train (tel. 303/296-4754) on weekends. The mountains of **Summit County,** 70 mi from Denver off I-70, attract climbers, hikers, and skiers. The county's four ski resorts have interchangeable lift tickets. **Copper Mountain** has some terrain for most abilities, with an emphasis on intermediate skiers. The extremely well-designed ski area complements the first Club Med in North America. **Keystone Resort**'s hallmark is meticulous service in a planned village centered on a man-made lake. The resort encompasses the ski areas of **Keystone,** focused on beginning and intermediate skiers, and **A-Basin** and **North Peak,** for serious skiers. Shuttle buses serve these areas from Keystone. **Breckenridge** is an old mining town transformed into a resort with history, renovated buildings, and a sense of place, as well as fine skiing, particularly for intermediate and advanced skiers. For a change from resort atmosphere and prices, head to **Lake Dillon,** a large reservoir popular with boaters. Up U.S. 40 from I-70, **Steamboat Springs** offers the amenities of the others, plus great, uncrowded skiing for all abilities and a real western feel.

West of Summit County is **Vail,** celebrated home of the largest ski mountain in North America, with acres of skiing for every ability. Constructed from the ground up to look like a European ski village, it is huge, varied in its attractions, and pricey. It tends to be more conservative and family-oriented than Aspen (*see below*). **Beaver Creek** was created for those seeking an even more exclusive atmosphere; this is another instant Bavarian village, with more class and more expense. Its ski area is geared toward intermediate and advanced skiers.

At the turnoff for Aspen on I-70 is **Glenwood Springs,** where the main attraction, besides the scenery, is the **Glenwood Hot Springs Pool** (401 N. River St., tel. 303/945-7131), the world's largest outdoor mineral hot springs, a clean, well-run complex.

You know all about **Aspen:** the glitz, the rich, the chic-by-jowl actresses and moguls who jam this tiny town during the ski season. It's expensive—and worth it, if your passion is people-watching in an exquisitely restored mining town that happens to offer great skiing. Many prefer the other seasons, though, for the beauty of the place or the summer **Aspen Music Festival** (tel. 303/925-3254).

Within Aspen's orbit are several ski areas, each geared to a different level of ability. Skiers can get a multiday ticket to all four mountains: **Tiehack/Buttermilk,** serving primarily beginners and low-intermediate skiers; **Aspen Highlands,** for intermediate skiers, with some slopes for beginners; **Snowmass,** a perfect intermediate hill; and for experts, **Aspen Mountain,** which hosts international competitions.

What to See and Do with Children

Most ski resorts offer special programs and activities for children, especially **Winter Park** (which was the first with programs for children), **Copper Mountain, Keystone,** and **Vail.** In summer, **Breckenridge** and **Winter Park** open alpine slides.

Shopping

The town of **Silverthorne** features an outlet shopping complex
(I–70 at Silverthorne, tel. 303/468–9440) with about 50 stores.

Sports and Outdoor Activities

Biking Mountain biking is increasingly popular in the region; trails are
everywhere. Check with visitor centers.

Boating Sailing regattas are common at **Grand Lake.** Rent fishing boats
and motorboats at **Beacon Landing Marina** (Grand Co. Rd. 64,
6 mi south of Grand Lake, off Hwy. 34, tel. 303/627–3671). **Lake
Dillon Marina** (Dillon, tel. 303/468–5100) rents sail and motorboats.

Fishing **Grand Lake,** with trout lurking in its depths, and the connected
reservoirs, **Shadow Mountain Lake** and **Lake Granby,** are popular. **Dillon Reservoir** is stocked with salmon and trout. The
Lower Blue River, below Dillon Reservoir, is a Gold Medal
catch-and-release area, as is the **Upper Fryingpan River** near
Aspen.

Golf **Sheraton Steamboat Golf Club** (2200 Village Inn Ct., tel. 303/
879–2220) was designed by Robert Trent Jones, Jr. Jack
Nicklaus designed the course at the **Breckenridge Golf Club**
(200 Clubhouse Dr., tel. 303/453–9104), where reservations are
almost mandatory. The difficult **Eagle/Vail Golf Course** (0431
Eagle Dr., Avon, tel. 303/949–5267) has reduced fees in fall and
spring.

Hiking and To find out about parks and wilderness areas with great hiking
Backpacking and backpacking, contact **Holy Cross Ranger District Office**
(24747 Hwy. 24, Minturn, near Vail, tel. 303/827–5715), **Aspen
Ranger District Office** (806 W. Hallam St., tel. 303/925–3445),
and **Dillon Ranger District Office** (Blue River Pkwy.,
Silverthorne, tel. 303/468–5400).

Rafting The **Colorado River** is popular for both white-water enthusiasts
and beginners; so is the **Arkansas River,** near Buena Vista. Contact rafting firms through the **Colorado River Outfitters Association** (tel. 303/369–4632) in Denver.

Skiing For **snow conditions** at Colorado resorts, call 303/831–7669.

Cross-country **Breckenridge Nordic Ski Center** (1 mi west of Breckenridge on
Ski Hill Rd., Box 1776, Breckenridge 80424, tel. 303/453–6855)
has 30 km of trails, and **Copper Mountain/Trak Cross Country
Center** (tel. 303/968–2882) has 25 km (*see* Downhill, *below*, for
address). **Frisco Nordic Ski Center** (1 mi south of Frisco on
Hwy. 9, Box 532, Frisco 80443, tel. 303/668–0866) has 35 km of
trails.

Downhill **Aspen Highlands** (1600 Maroon Creek Rd., Aspen 81611, tel.
303/925–5300) has 552 acres of runs, 11 lifts, two pomas, and a
3,800-foot vertical drop. **Aspen Mountain** (Box 1248, Aspen
81612, tel. 303/925–1220) has 631 acres of runs, a gondola,
seven lifts, and a 3,282-foot drop. **Beaver Creek** (Box 7, Vail
81658, tel. 303/949–5750) has 1,050 acres of runs, 10 lifts, and a
3,340-foot drop. **Breckenridge** (Box 1058, Breckenridge 80424,
tel. 303/453–2918) has 1,600 acres of runs, 16 lifts, and a 3,398-
foot drop. **Copper Mountain** (Box 3533, Copper Mountain
80443, tel. 303/968–2882) has 1,200 acres of runs, 20 lifts, and a
2,760-foot drop. **Keystone** (Box 38, Keystone 80435, tel. 303/

468–2316) has 1,075 acres of runs, 15 lifts, and a 2,340-foot drop. **Snowmass** (Box 5566, Snowmass Village 80446, tel. 303/ 923–2010) has 1,500 acres of runs, 16 lifts, and a 3,600-foot drop. **Steamboat** (2305 Mt. Werner Circle, Steamboat Springs 80487, tel. 303/879–6111) has 2,500 acres of runs, a gondola, 19 lifts, and a 3,600-foot drop. **Tiehack-Buttermilk** (Box 1248, Aspen 81612, tel. 303/925–1220) has 402 acres of runs, six lifts, and a 2,030-foot drop. **Vail** (Box 7, Vail 81658, tel. 303/476–5677 or 800/525–3875) has 3,992 acres of runs, a gondola, 23 lifts, and a 3,250-foot drop. **Winter Park** (Box 36, Winter Park 80482, tel. 303/726–5514) has 1,301 acres of runs, 20 lifts, and a 3,060-foot drop.

Dining and Lodging

Dining in Colorado's resorts can be an exquisite, unforgettable experience. It can also cost you plenty. The celebrity atmosphere of towns like Aspen and Vail attracts celebrity chefs, and hot restaurants come and go as quickly as they do in New York. If you don't want to spend the money to eat with the stars, consider heading to nearby towns, where the atmosphere—and the prices—are more down-home western.

The ski resorts make getting accommodations as easy as possible. There are central numbers (Aspen, 800/262–7736; Beaver Creek, 800/622–3131; Breckenridge, 800/221–1091; Copper Mountain, 800/458–8386; Keystone, 800/222–0188; Steamboat Springs, 800/922–2722; Vail, 800/525–3875; Winter Park, 800/ 453–2525) to hook travelers up with many different kinds of accommodations. Condos are the most common and, because they have kitchens, can help cut down on food expenses. For price ranges, see Charts 1 (A) and 2 (A) in Chapter 1.

Aspen **The Restaurant at the Little Nell.** In plush, upholstered sur-
Dining roundings accented by brass railings and wide windows, Chef George Mahaffey uses local delicacies to create such dishes as roast rack of Colorado lamb with saffron couscous and pan-braised vegetables. *675 E. Durant Ave., tel. 303/920–6330. Reservations advised. AE, D, DC, MC, V. Very Expensive.*
Syzygy. Upstairs and unmarked, this restaurant is for those who like sleek modern design, track lighting, and sophisticated food that blends international flavors. *520 E. Hyman, tel. 303/ 925–3700. Reservations advised. D, MC. Expensive.*

Lodging **Hotel Jerome.** The century-old brick building has been refur-
★ bished with the charm of the original Victorian style in each room. *330 E. Main St., 81611, tel. 303/920–1000 or 800/331– 7213. 94 rooms. Facilities: 2 restaurants, 2 bars, pool, whirlpool, underground parking, shuttle bus to slopes and airport. AE, DC, MC, V. Expensive–Very Expensive.*
Snow Queen Victorian Bed and Breakfast. In the center of Aspen, in an immaculately restored Victorian house, this B&B offers telephones, coffeemakers, and televisions in most of its Victorian-wallpapered rooms. *124 E. Cooper Ave., 81611, tel. 303/925–8455. 6 rooms (2 share bath). Facilities: hot tub. AE, MC, V. Inexpensive (off season)–Expensive.*
Little Red Ski Haus. This red Victorian B&B has a large international clientele, a great location near the center of town, and is a good spot for single travelers. Breakfast is served in the worn, comfortable living room. The rooms are small and basic. *118 E. Cooper St., 81611, tel. and fax 303/925–3333. 3 rooms*

with bath, 13 with shared bath, 4 dorm rooms. Facilities: full breakfast. No smoking. AE, MC, V. Inexpensive–Moderate.

Beaver Creek
Lodging

Hyatt Regency Beaver Creek. The public rooms are a striking blend of soaring western space, huge stone fireplaces, an enormous antler chandelier, and upholstered comfort. Guest rooms are 400 sq ft, decorated in forest green and maroon. Guests leave the hotel and click on their skis. Watch for much lower rates off-season. *Box 1595, Avon 81620, tel. 303/949–1234 or 800/233–1234; fax 303/949–4164. 293 rooms. Facilities: 3 restaurants, bar, pool, 6 hot tubs, health club, ski valet. AE, D, DC, MC, V. Expensive–Very Expensive.*

Breckenridge
Lodging

Fireside Inn. This restored Victorian clapboard house in town has private rooms with carpets, brass beds, and baths, as well as shared-bath dorm rooms that sleep four. *114 N. French St., 80424, tel. and fax 303/453–6456. 4 private rooms, 5 dorm rooms. Facilities: full breakfast, hot tub. AE, MC, V. Inexpensive–Moderate.*

Glenwood Springs
Lodging

Hotel Colorado. Teddy Roosevelt and others stayed at this grande dame of Northwest Colorado to take advantage of the adjacent hot springs, and the public rooms have been returned to their former glory. The bedrooms are huge and sparsely furnished. *526 Pine St., 81601, tel. 303/945–6511 or 800/544–3998; fax 303/945–7030. 127 rooms. Facilities: 2 restaurants, bar, exercise room. AE, D, DC, MC, V. Inexpensive–Moderate.*

Grand Lake
Lodging

Grand Lake Lodge. Set majestically above Grand Lake and bordering Rocky Mountain National Park, the lodge is actually a collection of rustic cabins that accommodate two to 25 guests. Some have wood-burning stoves for heat, others share baths, but all share a comfortable, well-worn atmosphere. *Box 269, 80447, tel. 303/627–3967 in summer or 303/759–5848. 40 cabins (10 share bath). Facilities: restaurant, bar, pool, horseback riding (fee), hiking trails, mountain-bike rental. AE, D, MC, V. Closed mid-Sept.–May. Moderate.*

Keystone
Dining and Lodging
★

The Ski Tip Lodge. From the tranquil atmosphere to the public room's huge picture windows overlooking a forest, the lodge is special. So is the American regional food. Built in the 1880s, the B&B reflects the era in its period-furnished rooms. It is ½ mi from the slopes. *Box 38, 80435, tel. 303/468–4202 or 800/222–0188. 22 rooms (2 share bath). Facilities: restaurant, bar. AE, D, DC, MC, V. Moderate–Expensive.*

Lodging

Granny's Alpine Adventures. An early mining-era feeling permeates this isolated log-cabin B&B 6 mi from Keystone, where wood-burning stoves provide the heat, views of the mountains dominate the rooms, and breakfast brings great sourdough pancakes. *5435 Montezuma Rd., Montezuma 80435, tel. 303/468–9297. 3 rooms (share bath), 1 cabin. Facilities: sleigh rides and sleigh-ride dinners, horseback trail rides (fee), barbecues (fee). MC, V. Moderate.*

Silverthorne
Dining

The Old Dillon Inn. This beloved, low-key local hangout serves good Mexican food away from resort glitter and prices. *321 Blue River Pkwy, tel. 303/468–2791. No reservations. MC, V. No lunch. Inexpensive.*

Lodging

Alpine Hutte. Built to look Old World Bavarian, it offers austere but pleasant bargain lodgings and a curfew. The rooms are dormitory style, with two to eight people; lockers are underneath the beds. *471 Rainbow Dr., Box 919, 80498, tel. 303/468–*

6336. Facilities: dining room in winter, kitchen in summer; free shuttle to Summit Co. ski area. D, MC, V. Inexpensive.

Steamboat Springs
Dining

Cantina. Behind an old adobe facade, wood tables and floors provide the setting for such Mexican dishes as Santa Fe enchiladas with blue-corn tortillas. *818 Lincoln Ave., tel. 303/879–0826. No reservations. AE, D, MC, V. Inexpensive.*

Lodging

Scandinavian Lodge. The feel of far northern Europe holds sway in small, recently redone pastel rooms that have housed Olympic trainees. You can ski to the lifts; the rates include breakfast. *2883 Burgess Creek Rd., Box 774484, 80477, tel. 303/879–0517 or 800/233–8102; fax 303/879–0943. 34 rooms. Facilities: restaurant, bar, pool, sauna. No credit cards. Moderate.*

Vail
Dining
★

Sweet Basil. For a fine meal in a cheery, intimate atmosphere, this can't be beat. The menu is creative, with such offerings as lamb chops in sweet garlic sauce. *193 E. Gore Creek Dr., tel. 303/476–0125. Reservations advised. AE, MC, V. Moderate–Expensive.*

Lodging

Sonnenalp. This centrally located Bavarian-style hotel run by a German family offers small rooms with an authentically German alpine feeling. *20 Vail Rd., 81657, tel. 303/476–5656 or 800/654–8312. 191 rooms. Facilities: 5 restaurants, 2 bars, 2 pools, European health spa. DC, MC, V. Expensive–Very Expensive.*

Ranches

C Lazy U Ranch. Near Rocky Mountain National Park, this rambling, southwestern-style wooden lodge has fireplaces and Navajo rugs in its rooms and cabins. The fare ranges from old-fashioned ranch food (steak and barbecue) to lighter, health-conscious dishes, such as mountain trout stuffed with artichokes. *Box 379, Granby 80446, tel. 303/887–3344; fax 303/887–3917. 41 rooms. Facilities: dining room, 2 tennis courts, volleyball and racquetball courts, pool, sauna, horseback riding, cross-country skiing, sleigh rides, ice skating. No credit cards. Summer and holiday 1-week minimum stay. Expensive–Very Expensive.*

Home Ranch. This updated western rustic lodge in the Steamboat Springs area has some Stickley furniture in the white-walled rooms. Each log cabin has a wood-burning stove and a hot tub. *Box 822, Clark 80428, tel. 303/879–1780 or 800/223–7094; fax 303/879–1795. 8 cabins, 6 lodge rooms. Facilities: dining room, sauna, pool, horseback riding, guided hiking and fishing. AE, MC, V. Expensive–Very Expensive.*

Campgrounds

Campgrounds are everywhere in the state and national forests (*see* Sports and Outdoor Activities, *above*, for addresses and telephone numbers). Reserve camping spaces for many of the national forest campgrounds by calling 800/283–2267. **Tiger Run Resort** (3 mi north of town on Hwy. 9, Box 815, Breckenridge 80424, tel. 303/453–9690) is a resort for RVs, with tennis, pool, and game room. **Winding River Resort Village** (Box 629, Grand Lake 80447, tel. 303/627–3215) is a combination campground and low-cost dude ranch in a beautiful forest.

Southwestern Colorado

This area encompasses ski areas and red-rock deserts, cowboy hangouts and haunts of ancient cultures. The feeling is less glamorous and more down-home; you may see a cowboy in the distance riding off after a stray, or walk into a bar where ranchers discussing stock prices sit next to climbers enthusing over an ascent route.

Tourist Information

Southwest Colorado Tourism Center (Box 2102, Montrose 81402, tel. 800/933–4340). **Durango:** Chamber of Commerce (111 S. Camino Del Rio, Box 2587, 81302, tel. 800/525–8855). **Telluride:** Chamber of Commerce (666 W. Colorado Ave., Box 653, 81435 tel. 303/728–3041).

Getting There

By Plane **Durango–La Plata County Airport** (tel. 303/247–8143) is 14 mi east of Durango, and Telluride's **Montrose Regional Airport** (tel. 303/249–3203) is about 1 mi from Montrose. **Gunnison County Airport** (tel. 303/641–2304) is 23 mi south of Crested Butte.

By Car Hwy. 141 from Grand Junction to Hwy. 145 leads to Telluride; Hwy. 550 is the route from Durango to Silverton and Ouray.

By Bus The Texas, New Mexico and Oklahoma Bus Line, the local subsidiary of **Greyhound** (tel. 303/292–6111), serves Durango and such major mountain towns as Purgatory, Silverton, Ouray, Ridgeway, and Montrose.

Exploring Southwestern Colorado

Telluride is another old mining town turned ski resort, with a difference: Its relative isolation in a box canyon makes it more laid-back than many Colorado resorts, and its beauty is legendary. The resort provides terrain for skiers of all abilities. The summer brings nationally known festivals of film (tel. 303/728–4401), bluegrass (tel. 800/624–2422), and jazz (tel. 303/728–7009). South of Telluride is a complete change of scene: **Mesa Verde** (*see* National and State Parks, *above*), where the forests give way to dramatic red rock cliff dwellings.

East is **Durango,** a surprisingly large town with dramatic views of the San Juan Mountains that still cherishes its frontier traditions. A trip on the **Durango & Silverton Narrow Gauge Railroad** (479 Main Ave., tel. 303/247–2733) is worth the trouble of making reservations well in advance. The eight-hour round-trip, on tracks laid between the two towns in 1881, offers unspoiled scenery, dramatic gorge crossings, and rails dug into the mountainside. **Silverton** is a much smaller, more untouched frontier mining town.

Ouray, about 25 mi up the twisty, breathtaking Million-Dollar Highway, is a charming, sleepy western town surrounded by the magnificent red San Juan Mountains. Don't miss the **Ouray Hot Springs Pool** (tel. 303/325–4638) or, for a more rustic dip, **Orvis Hot Springs** (tel. 303/626–5324). Farther north, up Hwy. 135, is **Crested Butte,** an old Victorian mining town tucked away in another gorgeous setting that serves as base for the excellent Crested Butte ski area 2 mi away, most suited for high-intermediate and expert skiers.

Sports and Outdoor Activities

Biking The mountainous trails are challenging for experienced riders. Rent bikes in Durango and Crested Butte.

Fishing The **Dolores River,** in the San Juan National Forest (*see* Hiking and Backpacking, *below*), and the **Animas River,** near Durango, are good for trout. The **Vallecito Reservoir,** also near Durango, has pike, trout, and salmon. At **Ridgway State Park** (tel. 303/626–5822), 10 mi north of Ouray, you can catch rainbow trout.

Golf **Hillcrest Golf Course** (2300 Rim Dr., Durango, tel. 303/247–1499) offers 18 holes.

Hiking and The 469-mi **Colorado Trail,** from Durango to Denver, is a major
Backpacking route. The **San Juan National Forest District Office** (701 Camino del Rio, Room 101, Durango, tel. 303/247–4874) has information on trails in the area.

Rafting Rafting is popular on the San Miguel, Dolores, Gunnison, and Animas rivers. Arrange trips through the **Colorado River Outfitters Association** (tel. 303/369–4632).

Skiing

For snow conditions at Colorado resorts, call 303/831–7669.

Cross-country Trails abound; check with local tourist offices for details. **Purgatory Ski Touring Center** (Purgatory Ski Area, No. 1 Skier Pl., Durango 81301, tel. 303/247–9000) offers 16 km of trails; **Telluride Nordic Center** (free shuttle from alpine ski area; tel. 303/728–7570), 30 km of trails.

Downhill **Crested Butte** (off Rte. 135, Box A, 81225, tel. 303/349–2222) has 1,160 acres of runs, 13 lifts, and a 2,775-foot vertical drop. **Telluride** (Rte. 145, Box 11155, 81435, tel. 303/728–3856) has 1,050 acres of runs, 10 lifts, and a 3,155-foot drop.

Dining and Lodging

For price ranges, see Charts 1 (B) and 2 (B) in Chapter 1.

Durango **Ariano's.** Pasta made fresh daily and a sure touch with meats
Dining makes this northern Italian restaurant one of Durango's most popular. Veal scaloppine sautéed with fresh sage, garlic, and cloves is among the featured dishes. *150 E. 6th St., tel. 303/247–8146. No reservations. AE, MC, V. Moderate.*
Bar-D Chuckwagon. At this western extravaganza, beef and beans are served chuckwagon style; you carry them to long picnic tables (sheltered by canvas in bad weather) under the stars. Western entertainment accompanies the meal. *8080 County Rd. 250, tel. 303/247–5753. Reservations required. No smoking. MC, V. Closed Sept.–May. Moderate.*

Lodging **Strater Hotel.** Author Louis L'Amour made this jewel of a re-
★ stored Victorian hotel his home during frequent trips to town. The meticulously decorated accommodations match the Victorian charm of the public parlors. *699 Main Ave., 81301, tel. 303/247–4431 or 800/247–4431; fax 303/259–2208. 93 rooms. Facili-*

ties: restaurant, 2 bars, whirlpool. AE, DC, MC, V. Moderate–Expensive.

Spanish Trails. This traditional motel's lawn and playground make the clean, standard rooms, set back from the road, quieter and more appealing. *3141 Main Ave., 81301, tel. 303/247–4173. 44 rooms (10 with kitchens). Facilities: pool. MC, V. Closed Sept.–Apr. Inexpensive–Moderate.*

Ouray
Dining

The Outlaw. This Main Street fixture is dimly lit, decorated with red checked tablecloths and wagon wheels, and as western as you can get. Locals saunter in in cowboy hats, and everyone eats steak. *610 Main St., tel. 303/325–4366. MC, V. No lunch; closed Mar.–May. Moderate.*

Lodging

St. Elmo Hotel. Originally a miner's hotel, this B&B is welcoming and intimate, with Victorian antiques and charm. The Bon Ton Restaurant downstairs serves northern Italian food. *426 Main St., 81427, tel. 303/325–4951. 9 rooms. Facilities: restaurant, bar, hot tub, sauna. D, MC, V. Moderate.*

Weisbaden Hot Springs Spa and Lodgings. The rooms are clean and standard, but the attraction is the wonderful vapor caves, sauna, and hot-water pools underneath the hotel. *625 5th Ave., Box 349, 81427, tel. 303/325–4347; fax 303/325–4845. 20 rooms (5 with kitchens). Facilities: hot springs, sauna; outdoor pool with warm spring water. MC, V. Moderate.*

Silverton
Lodging

Teller House Hotel. Another miners' boardinghouse turned B&B, this one has a relaxed, young atmosphere, restored clean rooms, and breakfast at the excellent French bakery associated with the hotel. *1250 Greene St., 81433, tel. 303/387–5423. 5 rooms (3 share bath), 2 6-bed dorm rooms. Facilities: restaurant. AE, D, DC, MC, V. Inexpensive.*

Telluride
Dining
★

La Marmotte. This small, rustic restaurant is the place to go in town for a special meal. The French owners and chefs change the menu constantly, serving such dishes as duck confit or lamb with red bell pepper sauce and white beans. *150 W. San Juan Ave., tel. 303/728–6232. Reservations advised. AE, MC, V. No lunch; closed Apr.–May, mid-Oct.–mid-Nov., Tues. in summer. Expensive.*

Lodging

New Sheridan Hotel. Unprepossessing on the outside, the historic 1895 brick hotel has hung on to its heritage and now treats visitors to simple rooms and the liveliest bar in town. *231 W. Colorado Ave., Box 980, 81435, tel. 303/728–4351; fax 303/728–3807. 24 rooms (14 share baths). AE, MC, V. Inexpensive–Moderate.*

Ranches

San Juan Ranch. In the gorgeous Uncompagre Valley north of Ouray, this simple southwestern-style ranch has comfortable, unpretentious '50s decor and hearty yet health-conscious American cooking, with plenty of homegrown vegetables served family style (meals are included in the rates). *Hwy. 23, Box 2882, Ridgway 81432, tel. 303/626–5360 or 800/331–3015; fax 303/626–5457. 9 units. Facilities: dining room, children's program, horseback riding, whirlpool, sauna, free airport shuttle. 3-day minimum stay in winter, 1 week in summer. AE, MC, V. Moderate.*

Skyline Ranch. Burlap walls, pine furniture, and down comforters deck the rooms in the slab-wood buildings of this rustic western ranch. The horseback riding and fly-fishing are great. In winter, guests cross-country ski or head for downhill skiing at Telluride. The cuisine is French-American, with a menu that changes daily. *Off Hwy. 145, 8 mi south of Telluride; Box 67, Telluride 81435, tel. 303/728–3757; fax 303/728–6728. 10 lodge rooms, 6 cabins. Facilities: restaurant (Dec.–Mar.: breakfast included, lunch and dinner open to public; Apr.–Nov.: meals included, closed to public), whirlpool, sauna, free shuttle to airport and ski area. AE (winter only), MC, V. Inexpensive– Moderate.*

Campgrounds

Ranger District Offices (*see* Hiking and Backpacking, *above*) have information on campgrounds in the state and national forests. **KOA** has a campground near Durango (east on Hwy. 160, tel. 303/247–0783; closed mid-Oct.–May).

IDAHO

*Updated by
Michael McPhee*

Capital	Boise
Population	1,036,500
Motto	It Is Perpetual
State Bird	Mountain bluebird
State Flower	Syringa

Visitor Information

Idaho Travel Council (Dept. of Commerce, 700 W. State St., Boise 83720, tel. 208/334–2470 or 800/635–7820).

Scenic Drives

Idaho has 10 official scenic drives, detailed in a map available from the Idaho Travel Council (*see* Visitor Information, *above*). The **Lake Coeur d'Alene Scenic Route** follows Rtes. 3 and 97 for 70 mi along the eastern shore of one of the most beautiful lakes in the world. The **Sawtooth Scenic Byway** between Ketchum and Challis passes through spectacular mountain scenery with plenty of wildlife.

National and State Parks

National Parks Eight national forests are entirely within Idaho's borders, and seven more intrude from surrounding states, giving the state more than 21 million acres of protected land. **Challis National Forest** (Box 404, Challis 83226, tel. 208/879–2285) has some 2½ million acres and the state's highest peak. **Sawtooth National Forest** (2647 Kimberly Rd. E., Twin Falls 83301, tel. 208/737–3200) includes the **Sawtooth National Recreation Area** (Star Rte., Ketchum 83340, tel. 208/726–7672) and within that the **Sawtooth Wilderness Area** (*see* Ketchum/Sun Valley and Sawtooth, *below*). **Silent City of the Rocks National Reserve** (Box 169, Almo 83312, tel. 208/824–5519) is an eerie landscape of rock formations outside Almo in south-central Idaho.

State Parks The **Idaho Department of Parks & Recreation** (State House, Boise 83720–8000, tel. 208/327–7444) maintains 17 state parks, ranging from undeveloped, natural areas to full-scale recreational facilities. **Harriman State Park** (Rte. 20 near Yellowstone, HC 66, Box 500, Island Park 83429 tel. 208/558–7368) has a world-famous fly-fishing stream (the Henry's Fork of the Snake River) and is part of a 16,000-acre wildlife refuge. **Ponderosa State Park** (Box 17, 83638, tel. 208/634–2164) is a beautiful forested park outside McCall, popular in summer and winter.

Southern Idaho

The southern third of Idaho is a richly diverse region of mountains, desert, and farms. Roughly bisected by the Snake River, southern Idaho is predominantly agricultural in flavor, although it offers waterfalls higher than Niagara, weird volcanic formations where the lunar astronauts trained, and some of Ernest Hemingway's favorite fishing holes.

Getting There

By Plane   **Boise Air Terminal** (tel. 208/383–3110), 3 mi from downtown, is served by national and regional airlines. The **Boise Urban Stages** (tel. 208/336–1010) shuttle bus to town costs 50¢; taxis cost $7–$10.

By Car   Boise is best reached by I–84 or I–15 from the south and by I–90 from the north.

By Train   **Amtrak** (1701 Eastover Terr., in the Morrison-Knudsen building, Boise, tel. 208/336–5992).

By Bus   **Greyhound** (1212 W. Bannock St., Boise, tel. 208/343–3681) serves Boise, Twin Falls, Pocatello, and Idaho Falls.

Boise

Tourist Information   **Boise:** Convention and Visitors Bureau (Box 2106, 83701, tel. 208/344–7777 or 800/635–5240).

Exploring Boise   Founded in 1863 in the foothills of the Rockies on the Boise River as an Oregon Trail military post, Idaho's capital is now a tree-shaded, modern government, cultural, and business center. **The Boise Tour Train** (tel. 208/342–4796), a rubber-wheeled "train" pulled by a replica of an 1890 puffer-belly locomotive, offers one-hour tours starting from Julia Davis Park. At the other end of the tour is the **Idaho Historical Museum** (610 N. Julia Davis Dr., tel. 208/334–2120), with an exhibit of an Old West saloon, and the **Boise Art Museum** (670 S. Julia Davis Dr., tel. 208/345–8330), which has displays of traditional and contemporary works.

Down Warm Springs Boulevard is the **Old Idaho Penitentiary,** built in 1870 and in use until 1973. It now houses the **Idaho Transportation Museum,** the **Electricity Museum,** and the **Printing Museum.** *2445 Old Pen Rd., tel. 208/334–2844. Admission charged.*

What to See and Do with Children   **The Discovery Center of Idaho** (131 W. Myrtle St., tel. 208/343–9895) is a hands-on science learning center for children. **Birds of Prey World Center** (5666 W. Flying Hawk La., tel. 208/362–3716) is the world's largest collection of living raptors.

Dining   For price ranges, see Chart 1 (B) in Chapter 1.

Expensive   **The Gamekeeper Restaurant.** Choose between tables and booths in a room decorated with original watercolors by Idaho artists. The menu features steaks, seafood, and Caesar salads prepared at the table. *Owyhee Plaza Hotel, 1109 Main St., tel. 208/343–4611. Reservations advised. AE, D, DC, MC, V.*
Renaissance Ristorante Italiano. This elegant, intimate restaurant is in the basement of a historic quarry-stone building in Old Boise. It's very popular for its northern Italian pastas and

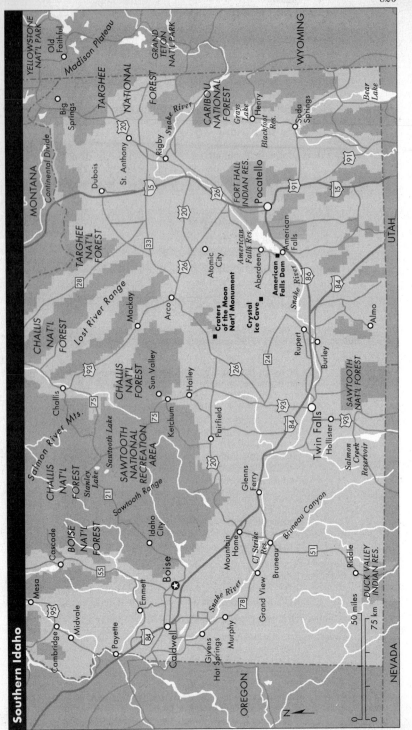

Southern Idaho

especially for its saltimbocca. *110 S. 5th St., tel. 208/344–6776. Reservations advised. AE, D, MC, V. No lunch.*

Moderate **Milford's Fish House.** In historic Old Boise, this seafood and
★ steak house has 1940s decor. The northwestern salmon is terrific. *405 S. 8th St., tel. 208/342–8382. AE, MC, V. No lunch.*
Sandpiper. Candlelight, high ceilings, oak tables, and live music on weekends make this a popular gathering place for politicians and businesspeople. Steaks and prime rib are the
specialties. *1100 W. Jefferson St., tel. 208/344–8911. Reservations advised. AE, D, DC, MC, V.*

Inexpensive **Tablerock Brewpub & Grill.** Boise's first microbrewery has a
southwestern decor, with white pine, cacti, and prints by Native American artists. The diverse menu has something for
everyone. *705 Fulton St., tel. 208/342–0944. Reservations advised for lunch. MC, V.*

Lodging For price ranges, see Chart 2 (B) in Chapter 1.

Expensive **The Idanha Hotel.** Close to business and shopping areas, this
French château–style B&B with its distinctive turrets opened
in 1901. Step back in time in the antiques-filled, turn-of-the-
century rooms. *928 Main St., 83702, tel. 208/342–3611. 40
rooms. Facilities: Continental breakfast, restaurant. AE, D,
DC, MC, V.*
★ **Owyhee Plaza Hotel.** The distinctive carved-stone ornamentation of this 1910 downtown hotel has put it on the National Register of Historic Places. Rooms are bright and spacious yet old-
fashioned; some have balconies with mountain views. *1109
Main St., 83702, tel. 208/343–4611 or 800/821–7500. 100 rooms.
Facilities: 2 restaurants, health club, pool. AE, D, DC, MC, V.*

Moderate **Red Lion Inn Downtowner.** This modern seven-story hotel on
the edge of downtown has good views, simply furnished large
rooms, and live entertainment at night. *1800 Fairview St.,
83702, tel. 208/344–7691. 182 rooms. Facilities: restaurant,
coffee shop, pool, handicapped access. AE, D, DC, MC, V.*
Sunrise Bed & Breakfast. This stone-and-wood house offers a
beautiful view of the city and nearby mountains. The large,
light rooms have lace at the windows and standard furnishings.
*2730 Sunrise Rim Rd., 83705, tel. 208/344–0805. 2 rooms share
a bath. MC, V. Closed Nov.–May.*
★ **Victoria's White House.** The imposing, pillared B&B, built in
1980, incorporates antique structural features. Each enormous, carefully decorated room has a brass bed and a sitting
area; one has a fireplace. *10325 W. Victory Rd., 83709, tel. 208/
362–0507. 2 rooms. MC, V.*

Motels **Best Western Airport Motor Inn** (2660 Airport Way, 83705, tel.
208/384–5000), 50 rooms, airport limo, handicapped access;
moderate. **Boisean Motel** (1300 S. Capitol Blvd., 83706, tel.
208/343–3645 or 800/365–3645), 136 rooms, restaurant, pool;
moderate. **Boise Super 8 Lodge** (2773 Elder St., 83705, tel. 208/
344–8871), 110 units; inexpensive.

Campgrounds Private campgrounds are located throughout the state; the
Idaho Travel Council (*see* Visitor Information, *above*) offers a
free directory. Camping is also available in nearly all of the
state and national parks; contact the state parks department
(*see* National and State Parks, *above;* tel. 800/283–2267 for reservations).

The Arts **Idaho Shakespeare Festival** holds performances in the open-air theater in Boise's Park Center (400 Park Blvd., tel. 208/336–9221; June–Sept.). The **Boise Philharmonic** performs September through May at the Morrison Center for Performing Arts (tel. 208/343–7849). The **National Old Time Fiddler's Contest** (tel. 208/549–0450), held in mid-June in Weiser, is the largest such competition in North America.

Shoshone to Craters of the Moon

Tourist Information **South Central Idaho:** Travel Committee (Box 1844, Twin Falls 83301, tel. 800/255–8946).

Exploring Shoshone to Craters of the Moon Five miles northeast of Twin Falls, in a rugged valley between towering walls of rock, the Snake River plunges 212 feet over the magnificent **Shoshone Falls.** The best viewing times are from October to April, when the river waters upstream are not being diverted for irrigation.

U.S. 26/93 heads northeast from Shoshone 60 mi to the **Craters of the Moon National Monument** (Box 29, Arco 83213, tel. 208/527–3257 or 208/527–3207), where eerie spatter cones and heaps of volcanic cinders dot charred-looking, windswept lava fields. The similarity between this area and the pockmarked surface of the moon is so striking that NASA has brought astronauts here for training.

Ketchum/Sun Valley and Sawtooth

Tourist Information **Salmon River:** Chamber of Commerce (Box 289, Riggins 83549, tel. 208/628–3778). **Stanley-Sawtooth:** Chamber of Commerce (Box 8, Stanley 83278, tel. 208/774–3411). **Sun Valley–Ketchum:** Chamber of Commerce (Box 2420, Sun Valley 83353, tel. 208/726–3423 or 800/634–3347).

Exploring Ketchum/Sun Valley and Sawtooth **Sun Valley,** America's first destination ski resort (1935) and site of the world's first chair lifts (*see* Ski Areas, *below*), is now a world-class winter and summer sport center. Nearby, in a valley surrounded by the peaks of Idaho's central Rockies, lies the town of **Ketchum.** Just outside town, beside Trail Creek, the **Ernest Hemingway Memorial** commemorates the writer's last years, which were spent in Ketchum, where he fished in Silver Creek. He is buried in the town cemetery.

One of the more scenic routes in the Rockies is the 68-mi stretch of the **Sawtooth Scenic Byway** from Ketchum, over Galena Summit, and down into the **Sawtooth Wilderness Area** to Stanley. Pick up a free cassette tape for the ride at the **Sawtooth National Recreation Area Headquarters** (tel. 208/726–7672), 8 mi north of Ketchum on Hwy. 75. Drop it off at the ranger station in Stanley, or vice versa if you're headed south.

Stop at **Galena Summit** and view the Sawtooths, as well as the landscape of the headwaters of the Salmon River. Known as the River of No Return, for the many pioneers lost trying to make it up the rugged river from Lewiston, the Salmon today is a prime lure for rafters (*see* Sports and Outdoor Activities, *below*).

At the Stanley ranger station, pick up another cassette for a similar trip down Hwy. 21 along the South Fork of the Payette River. Drop the tape off in Lowman and continue on into Boise.

Dining For price ranges, see Chart 1 (B) in Chapter 1.

Expensive **Evergreen.** The French-American menu features lamb Madeira, roast duck, and Idaho trout. Dining is in four small, friendly rooms with soft lighting, antiques, and a French-vineyards theme. *171 1st Ave., Ketchum, tel. 208/726–3888. Reservations advised. AE, MC, V. No lunch; closed May, Nov.*

Restaurant Felix. In this delightful restaurant the feel is European, with vaulted ceilings and Continental cuisine. Everything is made fresh on the premises; it's a haven for lamb connoisseurs. *Nob Hill Inn, 960 N. Main St., Ketchum, tel. 208/726–1166. Reservations advised. AE, MC, V. No lunch.*

Moderate **The Ore House.** The lobster, beef, and do-it-yourself salads make this a popular choice. *Sun Valley Mall, Sun Valley, tel. 208/622–4363. AE, MC, V. No lunch Thanksgiving–mid-Apr.; closed mid-Apr.–May, mid-Oct.–Thanksgiving.*

Warm Springs Ranch Restaurant. A mile north of town, in a cozy log cabin with roaring fireplaces and a trout pond, simple American food—steaks, chicken, barbecue, and trout—is the fare. In the snowy months, diners can step into horse-drawn sleighs for a half-hour ride across a golf course. *Warm Springs Rd., Ketchum, tel. 208/726–2609. Reservations advised in ski season. AE, DC, MC, V. No lunch.*

Inexpensive **The Kitchen.** Fresh and modern, this is the place for cereals, omelets, quiche, waffles, and salads. The teal-green kitchen opens onto a dining area with oak furniture and terra-cotta walls above white-pine paneling. *200 N. Main St., Ketchum, tel. 208/726–3856. AE, MC, V. Closed after 2 PM.*

Dining and Lodging For price ranges, see Chart 2 (A) in Chapter 1.

Sun Valley Lodge and Inn. At this Bavarian-style resort hotel at the foot of Bald Mountain's perfect slopes, the Lodge has an elegant European tone while the Inn is more sporty. Accommodations range from luxury suites to family units. The formal Lodge dining room features French cuisine. *Sun Valley Rd., Sun Valley 83353, tel. 208/622–4111 or 800/786–8259. 261 rooms. Facilities: 6 restaurants, 3 bars, lounge, 3 pools, sauna, summer children's program. AE, D, DC, MC, V. Moderate.*

Lodging For price ranges, see Chart 2 (A) in Chapter 1.

Very Expensive **Nob Hill Inn.** Brand-new, this small luxury hotel with European decor, marble, and tile is right in the center of town and has a fine dining room, Restaurant Felix (*see* Dining, *above*). *960 N. Main St., Box 800, Ketchum 83340, tel. 208/726–8010 or 800/526–8010. 24 rooms, 4 suites. Facilities: restaurant, breakfast, indoor/outdoor pool, sauna. AE, MC, V.*

Expensive **Best Western Christiania Lodge.** This two-story U-shaped gray wood motel near the center of town has rooms with contemporary decor; some have fireplaces. *651 Sun Valley Rd., Box 2196, Ketchum 83340, tel. 208/726–3351 or 800/535–3241. 38 rooms. Facilities: Continental breakfast, outdoor heated pool, hot tub. AE, D, DC, MC, V.*

Moderate **Bald Mountain Lodge.** On the National Register of Historic Places and right in the center of town, this 1929 one-story log hotel has tastefully decorated rooms, many in knotty pine. *151 S. Main St., Box 426, Ketchum 83340, tel. 208/726–9963. 10 rooms, 20 apartment units. AE, DC, MC, V.*

Sports and Outdoor Activities

Fishing Idaho is one of the best states in the union for fishing, with 39 species of game fish. The season generally runs from the Saturday before Memorial Day through November. The **Idaho Department of Fish & Game** (Box 25, 600 S. Walnut St., Boise 83707, tel. 208/334–3700) provides information and licenses.

Hiking and Backpacking For information on hiking through the wilderness, contact **Stanley-Sawtooth Chamber of Commerce** (*see* Tourist Information, *above*) or **Idaho Outfitters and Guides Association** (Box 95, Boise 83702, tel. 208/342–1919).

Hunting Idaho offers outstanding big-game hunting, with abundant elk, mule deer, waterfowl, and game birds. A hunting license and tags are required. For information on fees and licenses, contact the chamber or outfitters association listed in Hiking and Backpacking, *above*.

Rafting The king of Idaho's rafting routes is the **Middle Fork of the Salmon River,** which starts about 20 mi above Stanley, then runs northeast for about 135 mi to join the main stream. Reserve well ahead for May and June. For information about trips and guides, contact the Stanley-Sawtooth chamber (*see* Tourist Information, *above*).

Ski Areas

Cross-country The Idaho winter backcountry is ideal for Nordic skiing, with an extensive network of groomed trails. Contact **Idaho Outfitters and Guides Association** (*see* Sports and Outdoor Activities, *above*) or individual ski areas for more information.

Downhill **Bogus Basin** (2405 Bogus Basin Rd., Boise 83702, tel. 208/336–4500), 46 runs, six lifts, 1,800-foot drop. **Brundage** (Box 1062, McCall 83638, tel. 208/634–4151), 28 runs, three lifts, 1,640-foot drop. **Pebble Creek** (Box 370, Inkom 83245, tel. 208/775–4452), 24 runs, two lifts, 2,000-foot drop. **Sun Valley** (Sun Valley 83353, tel. 800/635–4150 or 800/786–8259), 66 runs, 15 lifts, 3,400-foot drop.

Ranches

For price ranges, see Chart 2 (A) in Chapter 1.

Diamond D Ranch. At the end of 28 mi of hair-raising dirt road near Stanley comes the payoff: snowcapped mountains all around, homey meals, cozy rooms with a Laura Ashley touch, and a big fireplace surrounded by overstuffed chairs. *Box 1, Clayton 83227, tel. 208/336–9772 or 313/773–5850. 20 rooms. Facilities: pool, hot tub, sauna. No credit cards. Expensive.*

Salmon River Lodge. This wilderness guest ranch offers family-style meals, hunting, fishing, horseback riding, and water trips. Cozy rooms with a rustic cedar finish can sleep four or more. On the river 70 mi from Salmon, the lodge is accessible only by the proprietors' boat. *Box 927, Salmon 83467, tel. 208/756–3033 or 800/635–4717. 8 rooms. Facilities: buffet, lounge with fireplace. AE, MC, V. Closed Dec.–Feb. Moderate.*

Northern Idaho

Northern Idaho has the greatest concentration of lakes anywhere in the country. Its clean, watery setting is home to a major population of ospreys, as well as to numerous bald eagles. Coeur d'Alene, the region's principal town, makes a good base for exploration.

Getting There

By Plane The nearest airport is **Spokane International** (tel. 509/624–1411), 20 mi from Coeur d'Alene, in eastern Washington.

By Car The major highways serving northern Idaho are I–90 east–west and U.S. 95 north–south.

By Train **Amtrak** serves Sandpoint, about 40 mi north of Coeur d'Alene.

By Bus **Greyhound** (1923½ N. 4th Ave., Coeur d'Alene, tel. 208/664–3343).

Hells Canyon and Lewis and Clark Country

Tourist Information **Lewiston:** Chamber of Commerce (2207 E. Main St., 83501, tel. 208/743–3531 or 800/473–3543). **Moscow:** Chamber of Commerce (411 S. Main St., 83843, tel. 208/882–1800). **North Central Idaho:** Travel Committee (Box 8011, Moscow 83843, tel. 208/882–3581).

Exploring Hell's Canyon Travel north from Boise up I–80 to Payette, and turn right on U.S. 95. Roughly 140 mi north is **Riggins,** headquarters for many white-water rafting and kayaking outfitters. (Note the time-zone change: Pacific time to the north, Mountain time to the south.)

About 15 mi west of Riggins is **Hell's Canyon**—at 5,500 feet, the deepest gorge in North America, even deeper than the Grand Canyon. The best way to see the canyon is by one- to six-day float or jetboat trips on the Snake River (for outfitters, contact the state tourist office or Lewiston Chamber of Commerce; reserve well ahead). Check in at **Hell's Gate State Park** (Snake River Ave., 4 mi south of Lewiston, tel. 208/743–2363) if you want to follow one of the rough roads through the rugged **Hell's Canyon National Recreation Area.**

Rte. 12, which cuts east across Idaho from Lewiston to Lolo Pass on the Montana border, follows the route on which Sacajawea, the famous female Indian guide, led Lewis and Clark through the rugged wilderness. The **Lolo Pass Visitors Center** (tel. 208/843–2261) has extensive information about the explorers; the surrounding trails are groomed for cross-country skiers in the winter.

Dining For price ranges, see Chart 1 (B) in Chapter 1.

Moderate **Jonathan's.** In this huge, elegant two-level restaurant, inverted umbrellas float above candlelit tables. The American eclectic fare includes steaks, ribs, seafood from Seattle, Mexican dishes, pastas, poultry, and salads. *301 D St., Lewiston, tel. 208/746–3438. Reservations advised. AE, DC, MC, V.*
★ **Zany Graze.** This offbeat restaurant has a carousel horse, a bathtub, and other miscellany hanging from the ceiling; jukeboxes; and an old-fashioned soda counter. It serves steaks, bar-

becued chicken, salads, pastas, and even some Mexican fare. *2006 19th Ave., Lewiston, tel. 208/746–8131. AE, D, MC, V.*

Lodging For price ranges, see Chart 2 (B) in Chapter 1.

Moderate **Carriage House Bed and Breakfast.** On a tree-shaded street of
★ historic houses, this B&B offers a 1900 French Provincial–style main house with a dining room and a gift shop, and a separate guest house with country antiques in bedrooms above a shared sitting room. *611 5th St., Lewiston 83501, tel. 208/746–4506. 2 suites. MC, V.*

Inexpensive **Sacajawea Motor Inn.** Built in 1950, this oft-remodeled motel edged with flowerbeds captures the flavor of the region. Rooms are decorated in earth tones, with sled chairs and well-lighted desks. *1824 Main St., Lewiston 83501, tel. 208/746–1393 or 800/333–1393. 90 rooms, 4 suites. Facilities: restaurant, lounge, exercise room, pool, hot tub, laundry. AE, D, DC, MC, V.*

Coeur d'Alene

Tourist Information **Coeur d'Alene:** Convention & Visitors Bureau (Box 1088, 83814, tel. 208/664–0587 or 800/544–9855). **North Idaho:** Travel Committee (Box 928, Sandpoint 83864, tel. 208/263–2161).

Exploring Coeur d'Alene **Coeur d'Alene,** the largest city in Idaho's panhandle, has become a major recreation center because of its superb location on the beautiful lake for which it is named. Surrounded by a lush green forest, the lake is home to the largest population of ospreys in the western United States. The cruiser *Mish-An-Nock* (tel. 208/765–4000) takes passengers on excursions around the lake. Along the lakefront, the luxurious **Coeur d'Alene Resort** (*see* Dining and Lodging, *below*) has the world's largest floating boardwalk, which is open to the public. For a history lesson on this city born during the gold rush of 1883, stop in at the **Museum of North Idaho** (Northwest Blvd. at the city park, tel. 208/664–3448).

What to See and Do with Children **Silverwood Theme Park** (U.S. 95, Athol, tel. 208/772–0515) is a perfectly reconstructed turn-of-the-century mining town, with rides on a narrow-gauge steam train or in a vintage biplane.

Dining For price ranges, see Chart 1 (B) in Chapter 1.

Expensive **The Cedars Floating Restaurant.** This restaurant is actually *on* the lake, which means it has wonderful views. Hawaiian broiled chicken is a specialty. *Junction of I–90 and U.S. 95, tel. 208/664–2922. AE, D, DC, MC, V. No lunch.*

Moderate **Wally's Wolf Lodge Inn.** The strictly western decor complements the steaks and seafood cooked over cherrywood on an open pit. *12025 E. Frontage St., 5 mi east of Coeur d'Alene off I–90, tel. 208/664–6655. MC, V. No lunch.*
Beachhouse. Overlooking Silver Beach Marina with docking facilities for diners, this casual waterfront restaurant features pasta and seafood on its varied menu. *2 mi east of Coeur d'Alene on I–90 at Silver Beach, tel. 208/664–6464. MC, V.*

Inexpensive **Jimmy D's.** This Continental sidewalk café is popular with locals as well as visitors. The specialties are fresh seafood and pasta, and the wine list features more than 100 selections. *320 Sherman Ave., tel. 208/664–9774. MC, V.*

Dining and Lodging
For price ranges, see Chart 2 (A) in Chapter 1.

Very Expensive
★

Coeur d'Alene Resort. On the shores of Lake Coeur d'Alene, this world-class resort offers plush guest rooms with fireplaces or lake-view lanais. The restaurant Beverly's has a beautiful view of the lake and the mountains, as well as cuisine of the Northwest and a superb wine cellar. *2nd and Front Sts., 83814, tel. 208/765–4000 or 800/688–5253. 338 rooms. Facilities: 2 restaurants, 3 lounges, exercise equipment, sauna, 2 pools, 18-hole golf course, bowling alley, private beach. AE, D, DC, MC, V.*

Lodging
For price ranges, see Chart 2 (B) in Chapter 1.

Expensive
The Blackwell House. This B&B in a charming Victorian jewel of a house is close to the lake and to shopping. Its quaint, elegant rooms have wing chairs and antique beds, and the bathtubs are big and old-fashioned. *820 Sherman Ave., 83814, tel. 208/664–0656. 8 rooms (2 share bath). MC, V.*

Moderate
Warwick Inn. Just a block from the lake's sand beach and boardwalk, this small B&B offers large guest rooms with lace curtains and quilts. *303 Military Dr., 83814, tel. 208/765–6565. 3 rooms. AE, D, MC, V.*

Motels
Bennett Bay Inn (E. 5144 I–90, 83814, tel. 208/664–6168 or 800/368–8609), 20 units (some with kitchens), pool; moderate. **Pines Resort Motel** (1422 N.W. Blvd., 83814, tel. 208/664–8244), 55 rooms, restaurant, lounge, pool; inexpensive.

The Northern Lakes

Tourist Information
Priest Lake: Chamber of Commerce (Steamboat Bay Rd. #121, Coolin 83821, tel. 208/443–3191). **Sandpoint:** Chamber of Commerce (Box 928, 83864, tel. 208/263–2161).

Exploring the Northern Lakes
Sandpoint is a resort town on the shores of **Pend Oreille,** the largest lake in northern Idaho and completely surrounded by mountains. At the southern end of the lake, 4,000-acre **Farragut State Park** (tel. 208/683–2425) offers forest walks, picnic areas, and camping.

Rte. 57 provides access to remote **Priest Lake,** with 70 mi of densely wooded shoreline, and the **Upper Priest Lake Scenic Area,** just a jump from the Canadian border. **The Grove of Ancient Cedars,** on the west side of Priest Lake, is a stand of virgin forest with trees up to 12 feet across and 150 feet high.

Dining and Lodging

Expensive
For price ranges, see Charts 1 (B) and 2 (B) in Chapter 1.

Hill's Resort. You have a choice of cabins or condos, all with kitchenettes and some with fireplaces. The restaurant features steaks and oysters, and there's dancing in the summer. *HCR 5, Box 162A, Priest Lake 83856, tel. 208/443–2551. 48 units. D, MC, V.*

Ranch
Shreffler's. There's nothing fancy about this working ranch, nestled between the Selkirk Mountains and the Cabinet Range high in Idaho's panhandle, but the owners offer real hospitality. *200 W. Center Valley Rd., Sandpoint 83864, tel. 208/263–5038. 4 rooms (shared baths). No credit cards. Inexpensive.*

Sports and Outdoor Activities

Fishing Lake Pend Oreille is famous for kamloops, Lake Priest for mackinaw, Lake Coeur d'Alene for cutthroat trout and chinook salmon. The St. Joe and Coeur d'Alene rivers are good for stream angling. (*See* Southern Idaho, Fishing, *above*, for general information.)

Hiking Extensive trail systems run through the **Selway Bitterroot Wilderness,** the **Frank Church River of No Return Wilderness,** and the **Gospel Hump Wilderness.** For information and guides, contact **Idaho Outfitters and Guides Association** (Box 95, Boise 83702, tel. 208/342–1919) or **North Central Idaho Travel Committee** (Box 8011, Moscow 83843, tel. 208/882–3581).

Rafting The **Salmon** and the **Selway** rivers are suitable for rafting. For information, contact the **Salmon River Chamber of Commerce** (*see* Ketchum/Sun Valley and Sawtooth, Tourist Information, *above*) or **Idaho Outfitters and Guides Association** (*see* Hiking, *above*).

Ski Areas

Schweitzer (Box 815, Sandpoint 83864, tel. 208/263–9555 or 800/831–8810), 47 runs, five lifts, 2,400-foot vertical drop. **Silver Mountain** (610 Bunker Ave., Kellogg 83737, tel. 208/783–1111), 44 runs, five lifts, 2,200-foot drop.

MONTANA

By Ellen Meloy

Capital	Helena
Population	799,065
Motto	Oro y Plata (gold and silver)
State Bird	Western meadowlark
State Flower	Bitterroot

Visitor Information

Travel Montana (Dept. of Commerce, 1424 9th Ave., Helena 59620, tel. 406/444–2654 or 800/541–1447).

Scenic Drives

The **Beartooth Highway,** U.S. 212 from Red Lodge to Yellowstone National Park, is a slow 68-mi route over a 10,940-foot mountain pass (open June–mid-Oct.). **I–15** and **U.S. 287 and 89,** for 187 mi between Helena and East Glacier, parallel the Rocky Mountain Front as it rises dramatically from the eastern plains. **Going-to-the-Sun Road** (*see* The Flathead and Western Montana, *below*).

National and State Parks

Millions of acres of Big Sky Country—Montana's nickname for its vast wide-open spaces—are public reserves, including national parks, monuments, and recreation areas, eight national wildlife refuges, 10 national forests, and 15 wilderness areas. Although most of Yellowstone National Park is in Wyoming, it is a logical part of a Montana itinerary.

National Parks **Glacier National Park** (*see* The Flathead and Western Montana, *below*) crowns the Continental Divide on the Montana-Canada border. **Little Bighorn Battlefield National Monument** (*see* Bighorn Country, *below*) preserves the battle site in southeastern Montana.

State Parks The **Montana Department of Fish, Wildlife and Parks** (1420 E. 6th Ave., Helena 59620, tel. 406/444–2535) manages 60 state parks, including **Bannack State Park** west of Dillon, a ghost town of homes, saloons, and a gallows. **Missouri Headwaters State Park** near Three Forks marks the site where Lewis and Clark came upon the confluence of the three rivers that form the Missouri.

The Flathead and Western Montana

Stunning peaks and lush intermontane valleys offer superb recreation and some of the Rockies' most dazzling landscapes. The northwest, or Flathead region, is a destination resort area with such attractions as Flathead Lake and Glacier National Park. In western Montana south of the Flathead, forests, lakes, and meadows mix with ranch country and small valley towns.

Tourist Information

Glacier Country: Regional Tourism Commission (945 4th Ave. E, Kalispell 59901, tel. 406/756–7128 or 800/338–5072).

Getting There

By Plane   **Glacier Park International Airport** in Kalispell and the **Missoula Airport** are served by major domestic airlines.

By Car   I–90 and U.S. 93 pass through Missoula. U.S. 93 and Rte. 35 lead off I–90 to Kalispell in the Flathead; from there, U.S. 2 leads to Glacier park. From Great Falls, take I–15 then U.S. 89 to St. Mary, at the east entrance to Glacier's Going-to-the-Sun Road (open June–Sept., depending on snowfall; off-season, leave 89 for U.S. 2 at Browning for West Glacier).

By Train   **Amtrak** (tel. 406/226–4452) stops in Essex, Whitefish, and East Glacier.

By Bus   **Intermountain Bus Co.** (tel. 406/755–4011) stops in Kalispell. **Greyhound** (tel. 406/549–2339) serves Missoula.

Exploring the Flathead and Western Montana

The Flathead   The Flathead's towns are atypical of Montana in that they are relatively close to one another. Glacier Park, Bigfork, Kalispell, and Whitefish make good touring bases; many attractions are within a day's drive.

Glacier National Park (National Park Service, West Glacier 59936, tel. 406/888–5441) preserves 1,500 spectacular acres of peaks, waterfalls, lakes, and wildlife best seen from a hiking trail (*see* Sports and Outdoor Activities, *below*) or on horseback. The 50-mi **Going-to-the-Sun Road,** the park's only through road, is a cliff-hanger and unsuitable for oversize vehicles; guided bus tours (tel. 406/226–5531) leave from either end. Most of the park, including this road, is closed to vehicles in winter.

South of Kalispell is deep, pristine **Flathead Lake,** the largest freshwater lake west of the Mississippi. An 85-mi loop drive around it takes in cherry orchards, parks, sweeping views of the Mission and Swan ranges, and the arts community of **Bigfork,** with professional repertory theater at the **Bigfork Summer Playhouse** (Electric Ave., tel. 406/837–4886).

Western Montana   **Missoula,** 60 mi south of Kalispell via I–93, is a forestry and trade center and home of the **University of Montana.** The Clark Fork, Bitterroot, and Blackfoot rivers converge here—it's not unusual to see anglers casting just down from the movie theater. The **Missoula Museum of the Arts** (335 N. Pattee St., tel. 406/728–0047) exhibits contemporary works.

North of town, Rte. 200 leads to the **Seeley-Swan Valley,** densely forested and studded with lakes. View loons and other waterfowl from turnouts along the 18-mi **Clearwater Chain-of-Lakes** scenic route (Rte. 83 from Salmon Lake to Rainy Lake).

South of Missoula on U.S. 93, the **Bitterroot Valley** stretches between the Sapphire Mountains and the Bitterroots, one of

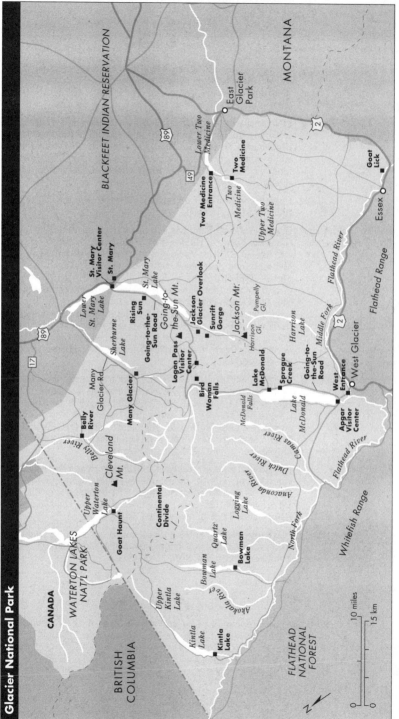

Glacier National Park

CANADA

BRITISH COLUMBIA

WATERTON LAKES NAT'L PARK

BLACKFEET INDIAN RESERVATION

MONTANA

Upper Waterton Lake

Goat Haunt

Belly River

Belly River

Cleveland Mt.

Continental Divide

Many Glacier Rd.

Many Glacier

Sherburne Lake

Lower St. Mary Lake

St. Mary Visitor Center

St. Mary

St. Mary Lake

Rising Sun

Going-to-the-Sun Road

Going-to-the-Sun Mt.

Logan Pass Visitor Center

Jackson Glacier Overlook

Sunrift Gorge

Jackson Mt.

Two Medicine

Two Medicine Entrance

Lower Two Medicine

East Glacier Park

Upper Two Medicine

Pumpelly Gl.

Harrison Gl.

Harrison Lake

Bird Woman Falls

Sprague Creek

Lake McDonald

McDonald Falls

Lake McDonald

Going-to-the-Sun Road

West Entrance

West Glacier

Apgar Visitor Center

Flathead River

Flathead River

Flathead Range

Goat Lick

Essex

Middle Fork

Upper Kintla Lake

Kintla Lake

Kintla Lake

Bowman Lake

Quartz Lake

Bowman Lake

Logging Lake

Akokala River

North Fork

Anaconda River

Dutch River

Camas River

Whitefish Range

FLATHEAD NATIONAL FOREST

N

0   10 miles
0   15 km

the northern Rockies' most rugged ranges. Jesuit missionaries founded St. Mary's Mission in 1866 at Stevensville.

Sports and Outdoor Activities

Biking Glacier's **Going-to-the-Sun Road** is a challenging ride. **Backcountry Bicycle Tours** (Box 4029, Bozeman 59772, tel. 406/586–3556) organizes five- to seven-day trips in Glacier National Park as well as the rest of the state and into Canada.

Fishing Fish for cutthroat and bull trout in the **Flathead River** or northern pike, Mackinaw, and other lake species in **Flathead Lake. Big Dipper Charters** (Kalispell, tel. 406/257–3234) offers boats and guides. In western Montana, fish the **Clark Fork, Bitterroot,** or **Blackfoot** rivers; **Rock Creek,** a blue-ribbon trout stream; or **Seeley Lake.** Local stores sell fishing licenses.

Golf **Eagle Bend Golfing Community** (Box 960, Bigfork 59911, tel. 406/837–5421), 18 holes.

Hiking and Backpacking **Glacier National Park** has 750 mi of trails at all ability levels; **Glacier Wilderness Guides** (Box 535M, West Glacier 59963, tel. 406/888–5333) leads backcountry trips. The **Great Bear, Bob Marshall,** and **Scapegoat wilderness areas** (Flathead National Forest, 1935 3rd Ave. E, Kalispell 59901, tel. 406/755–5401) constitute a million-acre refuge along the Continental Divide. The **Jewel Basin Hiking Area,** 13 mi east of Bigfork, off Rte. 83, is a short, minimal-ascent trail to high-country lakes and superb views, designed for children and inexperienced hikers. For information on backcountry hiking, contact the **U.S. Forest Service Northern Region** (200 E. Broadway, Missoula 59807, tel. 406/329–3511).

Rafting and Canoeing The three forks of the Flathead River constitute 10% of the nation's Wild and Scenic River system. Rafting outfitters include **Glacier Raft Co.** (Box 218M, West Glacier 59936, tel. 406/888–5454 or 800/332–9995). Canoes take the calmer waters of Glacier Park's **Lake McDonald.** For canoe rentals try **Glacier Park Boat Company** (Box 5262, Kalispell 59903, tel. 406/888–5727 May–Sept. or 406/752–5488 Oct.–Apr.).

In the west, most stretches of the **Clark Fork** and **Bitterroot** are runnable by raft or canoe; the **Blackfoot** is more difficult. Outfitters include **Western Rivers** (333 Knowles St., Missoula 59801, tel. 406/728–6161). North of Missoula, the **Clearwater River Canoe Trail** follows an easy 4-mi stretch.

Water Sports **Flathead Lake** supports a large sailing community, countless waterskiers and windsurfers, and cruises on the *Port Polson Princess* (Polson, tel. 800/332–7148).

Ski Areas

For ski reports call 406/444–2654 or 800/541–1447.

Cross-country Trails are found at **Glacier National Park,** in the **Flathead National Forest,** and in the **national forests** near Missoula (for information on all these sites, *see* Sports and Outdoor Activities, *above*). On Glacier's southern border, the **Izaak Walton Inn** (U.S. 2, Essex 59916, tel. 406/888–5700) has 18 mi of trails.

Downhill **Big Mountain** (Box 1400, Whitefish 59937, tel. 406/862–3511 or 800/858–5439) is Montana's largest resort, with 54 marked runs, nine lifts, and a 2,300-foot vertical drop.

Dining and Lodging

The Flathead breaks the West's traditional steak-and-burger mold by offering sophisticated dining (dress: neat but casual) and fine wines. Lodging in Glacier is seasonal (June–Labor Day); reserve well in advance here, and for the summer and ski seasons in the Flathead. For price ranges, see Charts 1 (B) and 2 (B) in Chapter 1.

Bigfork
Dining

Coyote Roadhouse. Behind a simple stucco facade lies a cozy place serving Cajun, Sicilian, and Mexican specialties. *8083 Rte. 35, tel. 406/837–4250. Reservations advised. AE, MC, V. Moderate.*

Lodging

O'Duach'ain Country Inn Bed and Breakfast. This handsome log inn sits in a quiet lodgepole pine forest near Flathead Lake and the Swan River. The main house has three guest rooms; a smaller log cabin next door has two suites. Navajo rugs adorn the walls, and two stone fireplaces keep the main house warm during cooler months. Both cabins are furnished with Old West antiques. *675 Ferndale Dr., 59911, tel. 406/837–6851. 5 rooms (3 share bath). AE, MC, V. Moderate.*

Glacier National Park
Dining and Lodging

Lodges. Glacier's grand lodges date from the early 1900s, when the Great Northern Railroad brought tourists to this remote park. The rooms in all the lodges are rustic—no TVs—but quite comfortable. **Glacier Park Lodge,** connected to East Glacier's Amtrak station by a brief walk through a garden, offers 154 rooms, golf, and a pool. **Lake McDonald Lodge,** a former hunting refuge near West Glacier, has 100 rooms in cabins, motel units, and a lodge on the lake (with boat rentals and fishing). **Many Glacier Hotel,** 12 mi west of Babb overlooking Swiftcurrent Lake, is the park's largest lodge, offering 208 rooms, boat tours, and fishing. *Glacier Park, Inc.: June–Labor Day, East Glacier 59434, tel. 406/226–5551; Labor Day–May, Greyhound Tower, Station 1210, Phoenix, AZ 85077, tel. 602/ 248–6000. Facilities: restaurants, bars, trail rides. D, MC, V. Closed Labor Day–May. Moderate–Expensive.*

Missoula
Dining

Alley Cat Grill. French, Indonesian, and seafood specials are served in a pleasant bistro atmosphere. *125½ Main St., tel. 406/ 728–3535. Reservations advised. MC, V. Moderate.*

Zimorino Brothers Red Pies Over Montana. The menu is Italian—thick-crust pizzas, lasagna, and other dishes. *424 N. Higgins Ave., tel. 406/549–7434. MC, V. Inexpensive.*

Lodging

Goldsmith's Inn. This B&B, formerly the home of University of Montana presidents, was moved to its present riverside location and restored. One room has a fireplace. The large front deck overlooks the river. *809 E. Front St., 59801, tel. 406/721– 6732. 4 rooms, 1 suite. AE, DC, MC, V. Moderate.*

Motels

Best Western Outlaw Inn (1701 Hwy. 93S, Kalispell 59901, tel. 406/755–6100 or 800/247–9707), 250 rooms, restaurant, lounge, casino, whirlpools in some rooms, 2 swimming pools; moderate. **Village Red Lion Motor Inn** (100 Madison St., Missoula 59801, tel. 406/728–3100 or 800/547–8010), 172 rooms, coffee shop, restaurant, lounge, whirlpool, outdoor pool, gift shop; moderate.

Ranch

Montana's guest ranches (for Travel Montana's listing, *see* Visitor Information, *above*) range from working ranches to deluxe cowless spreads. Those listed throughout this chapter are categorized as either Moderate (under $1,000 per week) or Expensive ($1,000–$1,900), double occupancy.

Averill's Flathead Lake Lodge. Reserve at least a year ahead for this deluxe 2,000-acre resort on the shores of Flathead Lake. The decor is rustic western. There's a big stone fireplace in each of the lodges. Rates are AP, with a one-week minimum. *Box 248, Bigfork 59911, tel. 406/837–4391. 19 rooms, 17 cottages. Facilities: dining room, sailing, waterskiing, fishing, tennis, horseback riding, hiking, cookouts. MC, V. Closed Nov.–May. Expensive.*

Hot Springs

Lost Trail Hot Springs Resort. On the Montana–Idaho border, 90 mi south of Missoula, in the Bitterroot National Forest, this resort offers rustic rooms in log cabins and a hot tub and swimming pools fed straight from the hot springs. The resort is also close to recreation areas at Lost Trail Pass. *Off U.S. 93, Box 37, Sula 59871, tel. 406/821–3574. 18 rooms in 3 lodges, 7 cabins for 2–8 people each. Facilities: restaurant, pools, nearby skiing, RV spaces. AE, MC, V. Closed Oct.–Nov., May. Inexpensive–moderate.*

Campgrounds

Glacier National Park's 17 campgrounds are available on a first-come, first-served basis; they fill by noon. Other public campgrounds are in national forests and state parks (*see* Sports and Outdoor Activities, *above*). Look for private campgrounds with RV services near towns, or check Travel Montana's directory (*see* Visitor Information, *above*).

Southwestern Montana

Montana's pioneer history began here, and the full range of the early mining frontier—from rough-and-tumble camps to the mansions of the magnates—is still evident. In the stunning high country north and west of Yellowstone National Park you'll find some of the state's best ski terrain and world-class fishing.

Tourist Information

Gold West Country: Regional Tourism Commission (1155 Main St., Deer Lodge 59722, tel. 406/846–1943). **Yellowstone Country:** Regional Tourism Commission (Box 1107, Red Lodge 59068, tel. 406/446–1005 or 800/736–5276).

Getting There

By Plane Major domestic airlines fly to Helena, Bozeman, and Butte.

By Car I–15 passes through Helena. Use I–90 for Butte and Bozeman. U.S. 191, 89, and 212 link the region with Yellowstone.

By Bus **Intermountain Bus Co.** stops in Helena (tel. 406/442–5860) and Butte (tel. 406/723–3287). **Greyhound** serves Bozeman (tel. 406/587–3110). In summer, **Karst Stages** (tel. 800/332–0504) runs between Bozeman, Livingston, and Yellowstone.

Exploring Southwestern Montana

The humble mining origins of **Helena,** Montana's capital, are visible in its earliest commercial district, **Reeder's Alley.** However, by 1888, the "Queen City of the Rockies" boasted major gold rushes and 50 resident millionaires. The mansions on the **West Side** and commercial buildings on the main street, **Last Chance Gulch,** preserve the era's grace and opulence.

Helena's vibrant arts scene includes dramatic performances and movies in the two auditoriums within the **Myrna Loy Theater** (15 N. Ewing St., tel. 406/443–0287). The **Archie Bray Foundation** (2915 Country Club Ave., tel. 406/443–3502), a nationally known center for ceramic arts, offers tours.

While the millionaires lived in Helena, the miners lived in **Butte,** a tough, wily town with a rich ethnic mix. The **Berkeley Pit,** a mile-wide open-pit copper mine, sits at the edge of the **Butte Historic District.** Near Deer Lodge, the **Grant-Kohrs Ranch National Historic Site** (316 Main St., Deer Lodge 59722, tel. 406/846–2070) preserves a 30-building 19th-century ranch, still worked by cowboys and draft horses.

Bozeman, 50 mi east of Butte on I–90, is a regional trade center, a place crazy for food, art, and the outdoors. It is also home to **Montana State University,** whose **Museum of the Rockies** (6th and Kagy Blvd., tel. 406/994–2251) offers paleontology exhibits, a hands-on dinosaur playroom, planetarium shows, and western and contemporary art exhibits.

South of town, U.S. 191 follows the Gallatin River to **West Yellowstone,** the gateway to **Yellowstone National Park** (*see* Wyoming). On the U.S. 89 approach to the park, **Livingston** sits at the head of **Paradise Valley,** bisected by the **Yellowstone River.** Another route to Yellowstone, U.S. 212, leads to **Red Lodge,** a town of distinct ethnic flavors passed down from early miners. Late summer is **rodeo season** in Livingston, Red Lodge, and Big Timber.

Sports and Outdoor Activities

Fishing Few trout streams rival the **Missouri, Beaverhead,** and **Big Hole** rivers; outfitters include **The Complete Fly Fisher** (Wise River, tel. 406/832–3175). Livingston, Ennis, and West Yellowstone are base towns for the superb fly-fishing on the **Yellowstone, Madison,** and other local rivers; **Dan Bailey's Fly Shop** (209 W. Park St., Livingston, tel. 406/222–1673 or 800/356–4052) is a Montana legend. Licenses are sold at local stores.

Golf **Big Sky Golf Course** (Rte. 64, Big Sky, tel. 406/995–4706), 18 holes.

Hiking and Backpacking Areas include the **Gates of the Mountains** near Helena (tel. 406/449–5201), the **Anaconda-Pintler Wilderness** near Anaconda (tel. 406/496–3400), and the **Lee Metcalf Wilderness** near Bozeman and **Absarokee-Beartooth Wilderness** near Livingston (tel. 406/587–6701).

Rafting and Canoeing The **Missouri River** north of Helena is easy for rafts and canoes. **Bear Trap Canyon,** on the Madison River near Ennis, and **Yankee Jim,** on the Yellowstone near Gardiner, require whitewater experience or an outfitter, such as the **Yellowstone Raft Co.** (tel. 406/848–7777).

Ski Areas

For ski reports, call 406/444–2654 or 800/541–1447.

Cross-country In winter, many national forest roads and trails become backcountry ski trails (*see* Sports and Outdoor Activities, *above*). **Lone Mountain Ranch** (Box 160069, Big Sky 59716, tel. 406/995–4644) offers 47 mi of groomed and tracked trails, food, and lodging.

Downhill Big Sky resort (*see* Dining and Lodging, *below*) has 55 runs, 10 lifts, and a 3,030-foot vertical drop.

Dining and Lodging

For price ranges, see Charts 1 (B) and 2 (B) in Chapter 1.

Big Sky **Big Sky Ski and Summer Resort.** At this resort in Gallatin Can-
Dining and yon 43 mi south of Bozeman, come back to large, bright rooms
Lodging in the ski lodge or condominiums after enjoying the extensive outdoor activities. *Box 160001, 59716, tel. 406/995–4211 or 800/ 548–4486. 204 lodge rooms, 94 condo rooms. Reservations advised. Facilities: restaurants, health club, outdoor pool, golf, horseback riding, fishing, gondola rides, skiing. AE, D, DC, MC, V. Closed mid-Apr.–early June, late Sept.–mid-Dec. Moderate–Expensive.*

Bozeman **Voss Inn.** This B&B, an 1883 Victorian house in the historic dis-
Lodging trict, is furnished with period antiques. The hosts can help with Yellowstone tour plans. *319 S. Willson Ave., 59715, tel. 406/587–0982. 3 rooms (2 share bath), carriage house for 6. No smoking. MC, V. Moderate.*

Helena **The Windbag.** Named for the hot political debates you're likely
Dining to overhear while dining on burgers, seafood, and light dishes, this saloon was a bordello until the 1970s. *19 S. Last Chance Gulch, tel. 406/443–9669. AE, MC, V. Moderate.*

Lodging **The Sanders.** Wilbur Fisk Sanders, frontier politician and vigilante, once lived in this gracious 1875 mansion, now a centrally located B&B on the National Historic Register. *328 N. Ewing St., 59601, tel. 406/442–3309. 7 rooms. AE, MC, V. Moderate.*

Livingston **Livingston Bar and Grille.** This popular local hangout serves
Dining beef, buffalo, trout, and Cajun dishes, as well as the famous, but actually difficult to find, Rocky Mountain oysters. There's a much-photographed century-old mahogany back bar. *130 N. Main St., tel. 406/222–7909. MC, V. Inexpensive.*

Motels **Bozeman Inn** (1235 N. 7th Ave., Bozeman 59715, tel. 406/587–3176 or 800/648–7515), 50 rooms, restaurant, lounge, pool, sauna, hot tub; moderate. **Jorgenson's** (1714 11th Ave., Helena 59601, tel. 406/442–1770 or 800/272–1770 in MT), 107 rooms, restaurant, lounge, indoor pool, laundry; inexpensive.

Ranch

For the price range, *see* The Flathead and Western Montana, Ranch, *above.*

Lazy K Bar. This venerable dude ranch, built in 1880, sits on 20,000 acres below the Crazy Mountains. It is a working ranch, and guests do a lot of riding, including actual cattle moving and other ranch work, if they choose. Rates are AP, with a one-week minimum stay. *Box 550, Big Timber 59011, tel. 406/537-4404. Facilities: horseback riding, fishing, square dancing, children's wrangler. No credit cards. Closed Oct.–May. Moderate.*

Hot Springs

Chico Hot Springs Lodge. Built at the turn of the century, this resort is nestled against the Absarokee Mountains 29 mi north of Yellowstone. The dining room is famous, as are the mineral hot springs. Accommodations are in condominiums or the old lodge, as well as cabins and a small motel. *Pray 59065, tel. 406/333-4933. 71 rooms. Facilities: restaurant, pools, ski trips. D, MC, V. Inexpensive–Moderate.*

Campgrounds

Public campgrounds are in national forests and state parks; private ones with RV services are near towns, or check Travel Montana's directory (*see* Visitor Information, *above*). In peak season, campgrounds near Yellowstone fill early in the day.

The Arts

The **New World Symphony** performs in Big Sky (*see* Big Sky Resort, *above*) during the **Big Sky Arts Festival** in July. Big Timber hosts August's **Montana Cowboy Poetry Gathering** (Big Timber Chamber of Commerce, tel. 406/932-5131).

Bighorn Country

Cowboy culture seems overpowering in southeastern Montana, but this is truly Indian land. A stunning country of rimrock, badlands, wide-open grasslands, and rugged mountains, it is still the home of the Northern Cheyenne and the Crow. Billings is a convenient base for touring.

Tourist Information

Custer Country: Regional Tourism Commission (Rte. 1, Box 1206A, Hardin 59034, tel. 406/665-1671).

Getting There

By Plane Major domestic airlines fly to **Logan International Airport** in Billings (tel. 406/259-7184).

By Car The main routes between Yellowstone and Broadus, in the southeast corner of the state, are I-94, I-90, and U.S. 212.

By Bus **Greyhound** (tel. 406/245-5116) and **Rimrock Stages** (tel. 406/245-5116 or 800/255-7655) serve Billings.

Exploring Bighorn Country

Booms in coal, oil, and gas made **Billings** Montana's largest town. Sprawled between steep-faced rimrocks and the Yellowstone River, it has big-city services and a stockman's heart. In summer the town puts on a nightly rodeo.

Southeast of Billings on I–94 lie the **Crow** and **Northern Cheyenne Indian reservations. Crow Fair** (tel. 406/638–2601), held in Crow Agency for five days in August, draws visitors from all over the West for parades, rodeos, dancing, and horse races.

On the Montana-Wyoming border is **Bighorn Canyon National Recreation Area** (5 Ave. B, Billings 59107, tel. 406/666–2339); **Bighorn Canyon Boat Tours** (tel. 307/548–6418) leave for trips on Bighorn Lake from Horseshoe Bend near Lovell, Wyoming.

Fifteen miles south of Hardin on I–90, **Little Bighorn Battlefield National Monument** (National Park Service, Crow Agency 59022, tel. 406/638–2621) preserves the site where, in 1876, the Cheyenne and Sioux defended their lives and homeland in a bloody battle with General George Armstrong Custer. A museum and guided tours help to unravel the history.

Sports and Outdoor Activities

Fishing Trout anglers fish the **Yellowstone River** above Columbus. Downriver, expect walleye, bass, and warmer-water fish. The **Bighorn River** below Yellowtail Dam near Pryor is trout heaven; lake species inhabit the reservoir above the dam.

Hiking and Backpacking The northern region of the arid **Pryor Mountains,** south of Billings, is on the Crow Reservation; permits for backcountry travel are issued by the Crow Tribal Council (Crow Agency 59022, tel. 406/638–2601). The southern Pryors are in Custer National Forest (2602 1st Ave. N, Billings 59103, tel. 406/657–6361).

Rafting and Canoeing Canoes, rafts, and drift boats suit the **Yellowstone River** and the **Bighorn River** below Yellowtail Dam.

Ski Area

Red Lodge Mountain (Box 750, Red Lodge 59068, tel. 406/446–2610 or 800/444–8977), an hour southwest of Billings, has 30 runs, six lifts, and a 2,016-foot vertical drop.

Dining and Lodging

For price ranges, see Charts 1 (B) and 2 (B) in Chapter 1.

Billings Dining **Golden Belle.** The Continental cuisine served here is among the city's finest. This is not your typical western ambience—crystal chandeliers hang from the ceilings, and most men wear a jacket and tie. On weekends there is live piano music. The southwestern flank steak is excellent. Also popular are the flamed desserts, usually prepared right at the tables. *1st Ave. N and Broadway, tel. 406/245–5121. Reservations advised. AE, D, MC, V. Moderate.*

Lodging **Sheraton Billings.** Centrally located downtown, this hotel is always lively, and usually filled with people in boots and Stetsons. The decor is enhanced by western art, most of it depictions of horses. *27 N. 27th St., 59101, tel. 406/252–7400 or*

800/325–3535. 297 rooms. Facilities: restaurant, health club, lounge, pool. AE, D, DC, MC, V. Moderate.

Motel **Ponderosa Inn Best Western** (2511 1st Ave. N, Billings 59101, tel. 406/259–5511), 130 rooms, restaurant, lounge, pool, sauna, fitness room; moderate.

Campgrounds

Public campgrounds are in **Custer National Forest** or **Bighorn Canyon National Recreation Area;** private ones are near towns, or check Travel Montana's listing (*see* Visitor Information, *above*).

Elsewhere in the State

Central and Eastern Montana

Getting There I–15 and U.S. 89 traverse the region north–south; U.S. 2 and I–94, east–west.

What to See and Do Montana's heartland is open grasslands and, rising abruptly from the plains, the sheer escarpment of the Rocky Mountain Front. In Great Falls, the **C. M. Russell Museum** (400 13th St. N, tel. 406/727–8787) has a formidable collection of works by the cowboy artist. Cowboy life thrives in **Miles City,** which in May hosts the **Miles City Bucking Horse Sale,** three days of horse trading, rodeo, and street dances. **Russell Country Regional Tourism Commission** (Box 1366, Great Falls 59403, tel. 406/761–5036 or 800/527–5348). **Missouri Country Regional Tourism Commission** (Box 11990, Wolf Point 59201, tel. 406/665–1671).

WYOMING

By Geoffrey
O'Gara

Capital	Cheyenne
Population	453,588
Motto	Equal Rights
State Bird	Meadowlark
State Flower	Indian paintbrush

Visitor Information

Wyoming Division of Tourism (I–25 at College Dr., Cheyenne 82002, tel. 307/777–7777; for recording/ski reports, tel. 800/ 225–5996). **Information centers** in Cheyenne, Evanston, Jackson, and Sheridan are open year-round; in Sundance, Pine Bluffs, and Chugwater, and near Laramie, they close in winter.

Scenic Drives

North of Cody and east of Yellowstone is the 60-mi **Beartooth Highway**, U.S. 212. It is a summer trip, switchbacking as it does across Beartooth Pass, at 10,947 feet the state's highest highway. Add a few miles of well-kept gravel road, and take the **Chief Joseph Scenic Highway** (Rte. 296, south from Beartooth Highway toward Cody) to see the gorge carved by the Clarks Fork of the Yellowstone River. There is more scenery than service on these roads, so gas up in Cody or at the northeastern end of the route, in Red Lodge, Montana.

National and State Parks

National Park
Devils Tower National Monument (east of Gillette, 27 mi north of I–90; Box 8, Devils Tower 82714, tel. 307/467–5283), a stone stump rising 1,280 feet above the Belle Fourche River, has been especially popular since it was featured in the film *Close Encounters of the Third Kind*.

State Parks
Wyoming's state parks are listed in brochures and on the Division of Tourism's state road map. Historic sites include **South Pass City** (125 South Pass Main, South Pass City 82520, tel. 307/ 332–3684), a history-rich gold camp near the Oregon Trail, and the **Wyoming Territorial Prison Park** (975 Snowy Range Rd., Laramie 82070, tel. 800/845–2287), where Butch Cassidy once did time. **Hot Springs State Park** in Thermopolis, on U.S. 20, features the world's largest hot spring.

Yellowstone, Grand Teton, and Jackson

When John Colter's descriptions of Yellowstone were reported in St. Louis newspapers in 1810, most readers dismissed them as tall tales. Colter had left the Lewis and Clark expedition to trap and explore in a region virtually unknown to whites, and his reports of giant elk roaming among fuming mudpots and waterfalls and geysers in a wilderness of evergreens and towering peaks were just too farfetched to be taken seriously. Sixty years and several expeditions later, however, the nation was convinced, and in 1872 Yellowstone became the country's first national park.

The Snake River emerges from Yellowstone country into the Teton Valley, where it makes its way south and west at the foot of the Grand Tetons. In the valley of Jackson Hole, just south of Grand Teton National Park and nestled between the Tetons and the Gros Ventre Mountains, the town of Jackson has been hosting visitors for over a century. The spot was first a rendezvous for fur trappers, then the gateway to the nearby parks and dude ranches, and later the center of a booming ski industry.

Tourist Information

Grand Teton National Park (National Park Service, Moose 83012, tel. 307/543–2851; visitor center, tel. 307/733–2880; recorded message, tel. 307/733–2220). **Yellowstone National Park** (National Park Service, Mammoth 82190, tel. 307/344–7381). **Jackson Hole:** Chamber of Commerce (Box E, 83001, tel. 307/733–3316). Visitors Council (Box 982, Dept. 8, 83001, tel. 800/782–0011).

Getting There

By Plane   Several airlines have daily service from Denver and Salt Lake City into **Jackson Hole Airport** (reservations, tel. 800/443–6931), 9 mi north of town and about 40 mi south of Yellowstone National Park. Major car-rental agencies serve the airport. **Yellowstone Regional Airport** (tel. 307/587–5096), at Cody, on the east side of the park, is served by commuter airlines out of Denver. *See* Montana for additional service.

By Car   To reach Yellowstone through the Teton Valley and Jackson Hole, turn north off I–80 at Rock Springs and take U.S. 191 the 177 mi to Jackson; Yellowstone is about 60 mi farther north on U.S. 191/89. You can also approach Yellowstone from the east through Cody on U.S. 14/16/20; for north and west entrances, *see* Montana. Grand Teton National Park is about 10 mi north of Jackson on U.S. 191/89.

By Bus   There is no direct bus service to Jackson. In ski season, **S.T.A.R.T.** buses (tel. 307/733–4521) operate between town and Jackson Hole Ski Resort, and the **Targhee Express** (tel. 307/733–3101 or 800/443–8146) crosses Teton Pass to the Grand Targhee Ski Resort. **TW Services** (tel. 307/344–7311) has bus tours of Yellowstone in summer and snow-coach tours in winter.

Exploring Yellowstone, Grand Teton, and Jackson

Yellowstone   Yellowstone preserves and provides access to natural treasures such as **Yellowstone Lake,** with its 110-mi shoreline and lake cruises, wildlife, waterfowl, and trout fishing; **Grand Canyon of the Yellowstone,** 24 mi long, 1,200 feet deep, in shades of red and ocher surrounded by emerald-green forest; spectacular **Mammoth Hot Springs;** and 900 mi of horse trails, 1,000 mi of hiking trails, and 370 mi of public roads. Visitor centers throughout the park offer guided hikes, evening talks, and campfire pro-

Yellowstone and Grand Teton National Parks

grams (check the park newsletter *Discover Yellowstone*). Park service literature and warnings about dealing with the wildlife—grizzly bears and bison, especially—should be taken seriously.

Roads from all five park entrances eventually join the figure-8 **Grand Loop Road,** which makes many areas of the park accessible by vehicle. If you enter from the south, start at the Old Faithful area. The best-known geyser is, of course, **Old Faithful,** the dependable crowd pleaser that erupts every hour or so. Wooden walkways lead among the other geysers, mudpots, and colorful springs and along the nearby **Firehole River.** Stay on the walkways—geysers can be dangerous. Elk and bison frequent this area. Near the west entrance is **Norris Geyser Basin;** among its hundreds of springs and geysers is the unpredictable **Steamboat Geyser,** which came back to life in 1978 and shoots water over 300 feet into the air.

Near **Canyon Village,** at the middle of the loops, is a short hike to **Inspiration, Grandview,** and **Lookout points,** where the vistas explain why Colter's accounts seemed so outlandish. The **North Rim Trail** leads to views of the cascading waters of the 308-foot **Upper** and 109-foot **Lower falls.** In the northeast corner of the park is the beautiful **Lamar Valley,** which attracts bison in the summer.

Grand Teton   Just south of Yellowstone, connected by the John D. Rockefeller Memorial Parkway (U.S. 89), is **Grand Teton National Park,** established in 1929 and expanded to its present size when the Rockefeller family donated land that it owned in Jackson Hole.

Technical climbers rope up and drag themselves to the 13,770-foot summit of **the Grand** (usually led by an experienced guide), but day hikers find many rewards, too, from a journey up **Cascade Canyon** to a ramble along a lakeshore. **Jenny, Leigh,** and **Jackson lakes** are strung out along the base of the Tetons and are popular with fishermen, canoeists, and, on Jackson Lake, windsurfers and sailors. Rafting along the **Snake River** allows views of moose or bison and a variety of smooth or fast-moving water. **Willow Flats** and **Oxbow Bend** are both excellent places to see waterfowl, and **Signal Mountain Road** affords a top-of-the-park view of the Tetons.

Jackson   The nearby national parks deserve some of the credit for the growth of Jackson, but the town has an identity and a western swing all its own. With its raised wooden sidewalks, cowboys strolling about, and old-fashioned storefronts and lettering on shop windows, Jackson may resemble a western-movie set, but it's the real thing. There are hot debates about whether and how much to control development, and most locals want to avoid what they call Aspenization. For the time being, the town remains compact and folksy, a place where genuine cowboys rub shoulders with the store-bought variety and where the antler-arched square, the whoop-it-up nightlife, and the surrounding wilderness are pretty much intact.

Jackson is walk-around size, and easy to relax in after a stint of white-water rafting, hiking, or skiing. Whether your idea of relaxing is epicurean meals, lolling in a hot tub, or dancing at the Cowboy Bar, Jackson is a good host.

What to See and Do with Children

A favorite family spot is **Granite Hot Springs,** south of Jackson off U.S. 191, 10 mi into Bridger-Teton National Forest along a gravel road. There is a shady campground by a creek, a hot-springs pool, hikes, and scenery. From December 15 through March, the **National Elk Refuge** (675 E. Broadway, Jackson, 83001, tel. 307/733–8084), just north of Jackson, offers trips on horse-drawn sleighs through the herd of over 7,000 elk in their winter preserve.

Shopping

Shopping in Jackson is centered on the town square. Western wear and outdoor clothing, some of it locally made, dominate in such stores as **Wyoming Outfitters** (12 Center St., tel. 307/733–3877), **Jackson Hole Clothiers** (north side of square, tel. 307/733–7211), and **Hideout Leather** (40 N. Center St., tel. 307/733–2422). Specialists in the latest outdoor equipment include **Teton Mountaineering** (86 E. Broadway, tel. 307/733–3595) and **Skinny Skis** (65 W. Deloney St., tel. 307/733–6094). Several galleries feature western jewelry and art, such as the **Trailside Gallery** (105 N. Center St., tel. 307/733–3186), or photography, such as **Tom Mangelsen Images of Nature Gallery** (125 N. Cache St., tel. 307/733–6179).

Participant Sports

In Jackson there are guides and services to cater to almost every interest. The **Jackson Hole Chamber of Commerce** (*see* Tourist Information, *above*) has information on various winter and summer activities and lists of outfitters. For sporting opportunities in the parks, which include skiing, horseback riding, hiking, and climbing, contact the visitor centers.

Boating Hire boats on Jackson Lake through **Pelican Bay Marina** (tel. 307/733–2811) or **Signal Mountain Marina** (tel. 307/543–2831).

Climbing Mountain climbers get a leg up from **Jackson Hole Mountain Guides** (tel. 307/733–4979) or **Exum Mountain Guides** (tel. 307/733–2297).

Fishing There are blue-ribbon trout streams all through this country, and Jackson Lake has set some records for Mackinaw trout. The necessary license for fishing in Yellowstone and Grand Teton is free at entrance gates or park offices. For fishing elsewhere, licenses can be bought at sporting-goods or general merchandise stores; or contact **Wyoming Game and Fish** (5400 Bishop Blvd., Cheyenne 82002, tel. 307/777–7735). Fly shops in Jackson include **Jack Dennis Sporting Goods** (on the square, tel. 307/733–3270) and **High Country Flies** (75 E. Broadway, tel. 307/733–7210).

Golf **Jackson Hole Golf Club** (off U.S. 89, 8 mi north of Jackson, tel. 307/733–3111) and **Teton Pines Golf Club** (3450 Clubhouse Dr., tel. 307/733–1733) both have 18 holes.

Rafting There are peaceful, scenic floats on the Upper Snake, including the beautiful Oxbow, which you can navigate yourself by canoe or kayak. Guided rafting trips are available from such outfits as **Barker-Ewing Scenic** (in Moose, tel. 307/733–1800), **Snake River Kayak & Canoe School** (Jackson, tel. 307/733–3127 or 800/

824–5375), and **Triangle X** (Moose, tel. 307/733–5500). For bouncier guided white-water trips in Snake River Canyon, try **Dave Hansen Whitewater** (Jackson, tel. 307/733–6295) or **Lewis & Clark Expeditions** (Jackson, tel. 307/733–4022 or 800/824–5375). Canoes and kayaks can be rented in Jackson from **Leisure Sports** (1075 S. U.S. 89, tel. 307/733–3040) and **Teton Aquatics** (145 W. Gill, tel. 307/733–3127).

Ski Areas

Cross-country In the winter, cross-country skiing and snowshoeing are permitted in parts of both Yellowstone and Grand Teton national parks and surrounding forests. One of the best spots is **Togwotee Pass,** within Bridger-Teton and Shoshone national forests (U.S. 26/287), where **Togwotee Mountain Lodge** (Box 91, Moran 83013, tel. 307/543–2847) offers 13½ mi of groomed tracks. **Spring Creek Ranch Resort** (*see* Dining and Lodging, *below*) has 8 mi of trails; **Jackson Hole Nordic Center** (Box 290, Teton Village 83025, tel. 307/733–2292) has 12.

Downhill **Grand Targhee Ski Resort** (Box SKI, Alta 83422, tel. 307/353–2304 or 800/443–8146), 26 runs, three lifts, 2,800-foot vertical drop. **Jackson Hole Ski Resort** (Box 290, Teton Village 83025, tel. 307/733–2292 or 800/443–6931), 58 runs, nine lifts, 4,139-foot drop (the longest of any U.S. ski area), some snowmaking. **Snow King** (Box SKI, Jackson 83001, tel. 307/733–5200 or 800/522–5464), 400 acres of slopes, two lifts, 1,571-foot drop.

Dining and Lodging

You can make reservations for a stay in Jackson or Jackson Hole Ski Resort through **Central Reservations** (tel. 800/443–6931). **Bed & Breakfast Rocky Mountains** (906 S. Pearl St., Denver 80209, tel. 303/744–8415) handles B&Bs throughout the region. For price ranges, see Charts 1 (B) and 2 (B) in Chapter 1.

Grand Teton Three of the park's lodges are operated by **Grand Teton Lodge Company** (Box 240, Moran 83013; AE, DC, MC, V).

Dining and Lodging **Jackson Lake Lodge.** This low-slung, massive brown stone edifice has huge windows overlooking Willow Flats. Guest rooms in the adjacent buildings are larger and more appealingly decorated than those in the main lodge. The Mural Room's menu sometimes features local game, such as venison or antelope. *Off U.S. 89 north of Jackson Lake Junction; Grand Teton Lodge Co., tel. 307/543–2855. 385 rooms. Facilities: 2 restaurants, pool. Closed mid-Sept.–early June. Expensive.*

★ **Jenny Lake Lodge.** The most exclusive of the resorts, set amid pines and a wildflower meadow, has cabins and rooms that are rustic yet luxurious, with sturdy pine beds covered with handmade quilts and electric blankets. The dining-room menu emphasizes Rocky Mountain cuisine, including roast prime rib of buffalo or breast of pheasant with pheasant sausage. *Jenny Lake Rd.; Grand Teton Lodge Co., tel. 307/733–4647. 30 cabins. Facilities: restaurant, lounge. Closed mid-Sept.–early June. Expensive.*

★ **Signal Mountain Lodge.** On the shore of Jackson Lake, the main building is of volcanic stone and pine shingle; inside is a cozy lounge with a fireplace, a piano, and Adirondack furniture. Guest rooms are in a separate cluster of cabinlike units. The

Aspens restaurant offers such dishes as scallops linguine and buffalo sirloin. *Teton Park Rd.; Box 50, Moran 83013, tel. 307/ 543–2831. 79 units, some with kitchenettes. Facilities: restaurant, bar, marina. AE, DC, MC, V. Closed mid-Oct.–early May. Moderate–Expensive.*

Colter Bay Village. Near the shore of Jackson Lake, the resort is made up of log cabins and less-expensive tent cabins (canvas-covered wood frames). The Chuckwagon restaurant is family-oriented, with lasagna, trout, and barbecued spare ribs. *Off U.S. 89; Grand Teton Lodge Co., tel. 307/543–2855. 209 cabins (some share baths), 72 tent cabins (communal bath). Facilities: 2 restaurants, bar, laundromat. Closed late Sept.–mid-May (tent cabins have slightly shorter season). Moderate.*

Jackson
Dining
★

The Blue Lion. In this homey, light-blue clapboard house, the fare ranges from elk Wellington to a wine-basted trout stuffed with Canadian snow crab. *160 N. Milward St., tel. 307/733–3912. AE, MC, V. Expensive.*

The Granary. Perched on a ridge and offering stunning vistas of the Tetons, the restaurant has an open-beam lodgepole-pine interior decorated with Native American art. The nouvelle western menu features such entrées as poached salmon in cucumber-dill sauce with wild rice. *Spring Creek Ranch Resort, 1800 Spirit Dance Rd., tel. 307/733–8833. Reservations required. AE, D, DC, MC, V. Expensive.*

The Bunnery. This pine-paneled whole-grain restaurant and bakery serves irresistible breakfasts, from omelets with blue cheese, mushrooms, and sautéed spinach to home-baked pastry; and sandwiches, burgers, and Mexican fare later in the day. *130 N. Cache St., Hole-in-the-Wall Mall, tel. 307/733–5474. No reservations. MC, V. Moderate.*

★ **Nani's.** The ever-changing menu at this cozy restaurant may offer braised veal shanks with saffron risotto and other regional Italian cooking. *240 N. Glenwood St., tel. 307/733–3888. DC, MC, V. Moderate.*

Lodging

The Painted Porch Bed & Breakfast. Eight miles north of town is this modern house with rooms decorated with antiques; some have Japanese soaking tubs. *Teton Village Rd., Box 7453, 83001, tel. 307/733–1981. 3 rooms. MC, V. Expensive.*

Spring Creek Ranch Resort. Isolated atop 7,000-foot East Gros Ventre Butte, just outside Jackson, the elegant group of log buildings sits amid 1,000 acres adjacent to a wildlife refuge. Guest rooms have porches with a view of the Tetons, floor-to-ceiling stone fireplaces, and Native American hangings and prints. *1800 Spirit Dance Rd., 83001, tel. 307/733–8833 or 800/ 443–6139. 117 units. Facilities: restaurant, lounge, pool, whirlpool, Nordic skiing, horseback riding. AE, D, DC, MC, V. Expensive.*

Cowboy Village Resort. Each of the pine-log cabins in this complex on a quiet side street offers bunk beds and a kitchenette, making it a popular spot for families and groups of friends who don't mind close quarters. *120 S. Flat Creek Dr., 83001, tel. 307/733–3121. 82 cabins. Facilities: 2 whirlpools. AE, D, MC, V. Moderate.*

Teton Village
Dining
★

Mangy Moose. Folks pour in here off the ski slopes with big appetites and a lot to talk about. It's noisy, but the trendy, eclectic American fare is decent. *South end of Teton Village, tel. 307/ 733–4913. AE, MC, V. Moderate.*

Dining and Lodging ★ **Alpenhof.** In the heart of the Jackson Hole Ski Resort (*see* Ski Areas, *above*), this European-style hotel is the lodge closest to the lifts. The restaurant, which serves veal, wild game, and seafood, is small, quiet, and comfortable. *Box 288, 83025, tel. 307/733–3242. 41 rooms. Facilities: restaurant, bistro, bar, pool, whirlpool, sauna. AE, D, MC, V. Expensive.*

Yellowstone The lodgings and restaurants within Yellowstone are operated by **TW Recreational Services** (Yellowstone National Park, 82190, tel. 307/344–7311 for lodging reservations; AE, D, DC, MC, V). There are numerous services, from gas stations to snack bars, throughout the park.

Dining and Lodging ★ **Lake Yellowstone Hotel.** At the north end of the lake is the park's oldest (late 1800s) and most elegant resort, with a columned, pale-yellow neoclassical facade. The spacious lobby's tall windows overlook the lake, and some rooms have brass beds and vintage fixtures. The restaurant offers such items as Thai curried shrimp or fettuccine with smoked salmon and snow peas. *Lake Village. 194 rooms, 102 cabins. Facilities: restaurant (tel. 307/242–3899; reservations required). Closed late Sept.–mid-May. Moderate–Expensive.*

★ **Old Faithful Inn.** You can loll in front of the lobby's immense stone fireplace and look up six stories at wood balconies that seem to disappear into the night sky. Guest-room decor ranges from brass beds to Victorian cherrywood to inexpensive motel-style furniture. The dining room, a huge hall centered on a fireplace of volcanic stone, serves shrimp scampi and chicken *forestière*, among other delights. *Old Faithful. 327 rooms (77 share baths). Facilities: restaurant (tel. 307/545–4999; dinner reservations required), cocktail lounge, gift shop. Closed mid-Oct.–early May. Moderate.*

Mammoth Hot Springs Hotel. Sharing its grounds with the park headquarters, this spot is a little far from some of the major attractions. The lobby has Art Deco touches; the cabins are small and ranged around "auto courts." The dining room offers regional American fare, including prime rib and chicken with Brie and raspberry sauce. The Terrace Grill, across from the lodge, is an airy room with large windows that bring in the outdoors, offering fast-food and cafeteria-style service. *Mammoth. 140 cabins, 4 with hot tubs. Facilities: 2 restaurants (dining room tel. 307/344–5314), lounge, horseback riding. Closed mid-Sept.–mid-Dec., mid-Mar.–late May. Inexpensive–Moderate.*

Old Faithful Snow Lodge. The compact, drab-looking motel tucked off to one side of the Old Faithful complex is one of only two park lodgings that stay open in winter. The rooms are nondescript motel style, but the lobby's wood-burning stove is a popular gathering spot in winter. The small restaurant serves family fare. *Old Faithful. 31 rooms (30 share baths), 34 cabins. Facilities: restaurant (no lunch early Sept.–mid-Oct.), gift shop. Closed mid-Oct.–mid-Dec., mid-Mar.–mid-May. Inexpensive.*

★ **Roosevelt Lodge.** Near the Lamar Valley in the park's northeast corner, this simple, homey log lodge is more ranch house than resort. The dining room serves barbecued ribs, Roosevelt beans, and other western fare. Accommodations are in nearby cabins. *Tower-Roosevelt. 8 cabins with bath, 78 with nearby common shower cabin. Facilities: restaurant (no reservations), lounge, gift shop. Closed early Sept.–early June. Inexpensive.*

Motels **Antler Motel** (43 W. Pearl St., Jackson 83001, tel. 307/733–2535), 107 rooms, hot tub; expensive. **Days Inn** (1280 W. Broadway, Jackson 83001, tel. 307/739–9010), 74 rooms, Continental breakfast, whirlpool, sauna; expensive. **Virginian Motel** (750 W. Broadway, Jackson 83001, tel. 307/733–2792), 159 rooms, restaurant, pool; moderate. **Motel 6** (1370 W. Broadway, Jackson 83001, tel. 307/733–1620), 155 rooms, outdoor heated pool; inexpensive.

Campgrounds

Grand Teton The **National Park Service** (P.O. Drawer 170, Moose 83012, tel. 307/733–2880) has five campgrounds within the park; none have RV hookups, but all have fire grates and rest rooms. The privately run **Colter Bay Trailer Village** (Grand Teton Lodge Co., Box 240, Moran 83013, tel. 307/543–2855) has full RV hookups.

Yellowstone Among the 11 **National Park Service** (Box 168, Yellowstone National Park 82190, tel. 307/344–7381) campsite areas in Yellowstone, **Bridge Bay** (420 sites, marina) is the largest and **Slough Creek** (29 tent-trailer sites) is the smallest. There are also 300 backcountry campsites, for which you need a permit from the park rangers.

Elsewhere in the State

Cheyenne

Getting There I–25 comes north the 100 mi from Denver. Commuter airlines fly between Denver and **Cheyenne Municipal Airport** (tel. 307/634–7071) and **Greyhound** (tel. 307/634–7744) provides bus service. **Amtrak** stops 10 mi outside the city, and a shuttle bus takes passengers into town.

What to See and Do For a whiff of corral dust, don't miss the **Frontier Days** rodeo (tel. 800/227–6336) the last week of July—a reminder that the state's capital city was once known as "Hell on Wheels." Outside the gold-domed **State Capitol** is a statue of Esther Hobart Morris, who earned Wyoming its "equality state" motto: The first woman to hold U.S. public office, she was appointed a justice of the peace in 1870. Women got the vote upon statehood, in 1890, and in 1924 Mrs. Nellie Taylor Ross became the state's and the nation's first elected female governor.

The **Frontier Days Old West Museum** (Frontier Park, 4501 N. Carey Ave., tel. 307/778–7290) displays buggies, stagecoaches, and buckboards. A favorite lodging place with travelers and state legislators is the **Hitching Post Inn** (1700 W. Lincolnway, tel. 307/638–3301 or 800/221–0125).

Cody

Getting There Cody is 52 mi east of Yellowstone on U.S. 14/16/20.

What to See and Do Most people use Cody as a way station en route to or from Yellowstone's east entrance, but the town has a museum that makes it a required stop for anyone interested in western history. The **Buffalo Bill Historical Center** (720 Sheridan Ave., tel. 307/587–4771) has a **Plains Indian Museum,** a collection of firearms, the **Buffalo Bill Museum,** and the **Whitney Gallery of**

Western Art. For information about the many fine guest ranches between Cody and Yellowstone, contact the **Wapati Valley Association** (1231 Yellowstone Hwy., tel. 307/587–3963). In town, the **Irma Hotel** (1192 Sheridan Ave., 82414, tel. 307/587–4221) has an ornate cherrywood bar and some rooms in turn-of-the-century western style. For further information, contact the **Cody Chamber of Commerce** (tel. 307/587–2297).

Sheridan

Getting There Commuter airlines fly from Denver to **Sheridan County Airport** (tel. 307/674–4222). **Powder River Transportation** (tel. 307/672–9757) buses connect with national carriers. I–90 comes into Sheridan 130 mi from Billings, Montana, and I–25 comes 140 mi north from Casper.

What to See and Do This is authentic cowboy country, with a touch of dudish sophistication. **Eaton's Ranch** (Wolf 82844, tel. 307/655–9285), on Wolf Creek near Sheridan, began hosting guests in 1904, making it the granddaddy of the area's dude ranches. The **Equestrian Center**, 12 mi south of town toward Big Horn, offers polo matches on summer weekends, as well as horse shows and steeplechase. Mosey into **King's Saddlery and Ropes** (184 N. Main St., tel. 307/672–2702 or 800/443–8919), where you can look at (and try out) hundreds of lariats, as well as hand-tooled leather saddles that sell for thousands of dollars. For information, contact the **Sheridan Chamber of Commerce** (Box 707, 82801, tel. 307/672–2485).

10 The West Coast

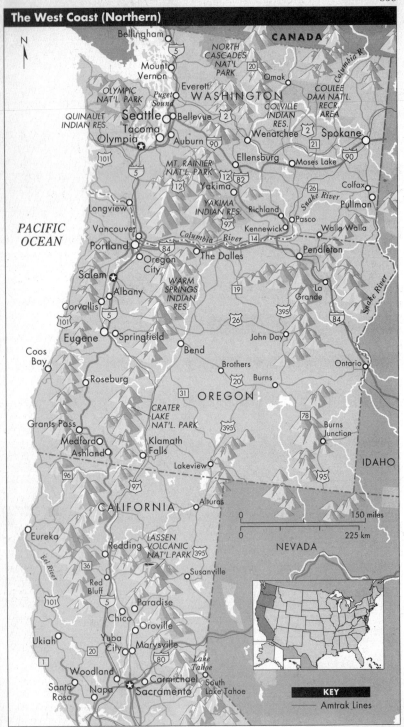

The West Coast (Northern)

The West Coast (Southern)

KEY
— Amtrak Lines

NEVADA

CALIFORNIA

PACIFIC OCEAN

ARIZONA

MEXICO

Santa Rosa
Petaluma
Novato
Woodland
Napa
Vallejo
San Francisco
Berkeley
Oakland
San Mateo
Palo Alto
San Jose
Santa Cruz
Watsonville
Monterey
Salinas
Los Banos
San Simeon
Morro Bay
San Luis Obispo
Santa Maria
Lompoc
Santa Barbara
Ventura
Oxnard
Burbank
Beverly Hills
Santa Monica
Inglewood
Long Beach
Huntington Beach
Santa Ana
Anaheim
Los Angeles
Pasadena
Riverside
San Bernardino
Twentynine Palms
Needles
San Clemente
Oceanside
Vista
Escondido
Palm Springs
San Diego
National City
Tijuana
Blythe
Brawley
El Centro
Mexicali
Yuma

Sacramento
Stockton
Modesto
Turlock
Merced
Madera
Fresno
Hanford
Visalia
Tulare
Porterville
Delano
Bakersfield
Lancaster
Barstow

Lake Tahoe
South Lake Tahoe
YOSEMITE NAT'L PARK
KINGS CANYON NAT'L PARK
SEQUOIA NAT'L PARK
DEATH VALLEY NATIONAL MONUMENT
CHANNEL ISLANDS NAT'L. PARK
JOSHUA TREE NATIONAL MONUMENT
Salton Sea

San Joaquin R.
Los Angeles Aqueduct
Colorado River

0   100 miles
0   150 km

Introduction

By Larry Peterson

Although often with an arched eyebrow, the rest of America keeps a careful watch on its West Coast, knowing that the latest thing there will almost surely be coming to a sporting-goods store, bookstore, menu, college campus, voter referendum, church, shopping mall, TV or computer screen, CD player, or theater near them. Soon.

This is the far edge of the frontier, the last stop of westward expansion. The region is shaped as much by its people's unwavering conviction that reality can be pretty much remade to their liking as by its geography. This fact characterizes and unifies cities as different as Seattle, Portland, San Francisco, Los Angeles, and San Diego. The essence of the area is also built on preconceived notions getting turned on their heads: The Spanish came in search of a mythical paradise filled with gold and found fertile land; Americans came for the land and found the gold; Lewis and Clark came looking for the Northwest Passage and found a damp, plentiful wilderness. Current notions ripe for debunking include the many clichés that the West Coast has generated about itself and the character of its citizens: The feet-on-the-ground Northwest gave us Jimi Hendrix, David Lynch, and the Simpsons. From eccentric, extravagant San Francisco came Joes DiMaggio and Montana. Southern California's hotbed of hedonism spawned Richard Nixon and Ronald Reagan.

Though more and more camouflaged by the hand of man, nature continues to offer a critical perspective on human pursuits. The ragged edges of Washington's Olympic Peninsula and the Oregon coast illustrate the power of the ocean; the mountains surrounding Seattle offer a sobering sense of scale, as does the view from Yosemite's valley floor; and tremors along the San Andreas fault tick off nanoseconds on Earth's geological clock. Every city and town along the West Coast sits amid some grand gesture of nature, and the challenge of how to preserve it is a source of both tension and creativity.

After three centuries of exploration and migration, the West Coast remains a place of myth and expectation, a land of promise. As America's proving ground for new ideas, the region continues to exert its magnetic pull on the imagination of people the world over.

Tour Groups

In the western states, where distances are long, group tours provide an attractive alternative to driving.

Domenico Tours (751 Broadway, Bayonne, NJ 07002, tel. 201/823–8687 or 800/554–8687) has seven- to 18-day tours of California, as well as shorter excursions that include such events as the Tournament of Roses. **Gadabout Tours** (700 E. Tahquitz Way, Palm Springs, CA 92262, tel. 619/325–5556) offers regional tours, including "Hearst Castle Rail Caper," "California Wine Country," and "Pacific Ports of Call" in the Northwest. **Globus/Cosmos** (150 S. Los Robles Ave., Pasadena, CA 91101, tel. 818/449–0919 or 800/556–5454) has tours encompassing the entire region, including a nine-day trip from San Francisco to Vancouver and "Focus on Calfornia" from Los Angeles to San Francisco highlighting the Monterey area, Yosemite, and Lake

Tahoe. **Gray Line of Seattle** (720 S. Forest St., Seattle, WA 98134, tel. 206/624–5813) has two- to seven-day regional tours, including a "Northwest Triangle" of Seattle, Vancouver, and Victoria. **Maupintour** (Box 807, Lawrence, KS 66044, tel. 913/843–1211 or 800/255–4266) explores the coast, with stops at San Diego, San Francisco, Portland, and Seattle.

When to Go

You can plan a West Coast vacation anytime of the year. Weather in coastal areas is generally mild year-round, with the rainy season running from October through March. Expect to encounter heavy coastal fog throughout the summer. Inland areas such as Napa Valley, the Columbia Gorge, and the High Sierras can be hot in summer, with temperatures reaching up to 90° in the high deserts and mountains; in the desert, summer temperatures can soar above 110°. The ski season in the High Sierras and Cascades runs from October through March, occasionally into April and May. Those who want to enjoy the sun-drenched delights of the desert should plan a trip between October and May; the wildflowers are at their peak in April. Whenever you visit the West Coast, expect temperatures to vary widely from night to day, sometimes by as much as 40°. Most West Coast attractions are open daily year-round, but summer is the busiest tourist season, when you can expect the most congestion and the highest prices.

Festivals and Seasonal Events

Jan. 1: Tournament of Roses in Pasadena, California, features a parade of 60 floral floats, equestrian units and marching bands, followed by the Rose Bowl football game. *Tel. 818/449–4100.*

Late Jan.–early Feb.: AT&T Pebble Beach (CA) National Pro-Am pairs 180 top professional golfers with amateurs from business, sports, and entertainment. *Tel. 408/649–1533.*

Feb.: Chinese New Year celebrations are held in San Francisco and Los Angeles, complete with dragon parades, fireworks, and sumptuous feasts. *Tel. 415/391–2000 in San Francisco or 213/617–0396 in Los Angeles.*

Mid-Feb.–late Oct.: Oregon Shakespeare Festival, held in Ashland, presents 10 classical and contemporary plays in repertory in three theaters, plus tours, concerts, and lectures. *Tel. 503/482–4331.*

Early Mar.: Mendocino (CA) Whale Festival combines whale-watching with art viewing, wine tasting, lighthouse tours, music, and merriment. *Tel. 707/961–6300.*

Apr.–May: Ramona Pageant stages the poignant love story of Ramona and Allesandro in an outdoor amphitheater near Hemet, California. *Tel. 714/658–3111.*

Memorial Day Weekend: Dixieland Jazz Jubilee brings more than 100 jazz bands to Sacramento, California, for three days of jamming. *Tel. 916/372–5277.*

Early June: Portland (OR) Rose Festival features a rose show, carnivals, celebrity entertainment, a hot-air balloon race, a national air show, visiting bands, and a world-class auto show. *Tel. 503/227–2681.*

Mid-June–early July: Oregon Bach Festival brings stellar musicians to Eugene for concerts, recitals, lectures, luncheons, and opera. *Tel. 503/687–5000.*

Mid-July–early Aug.: Seafair salutes Seattle with 50 events, including a torchlight parade and hydroplane races. *Tel. 206/728–0123.*

Late July: Pacific Northwest Arts & Crafts Fair brings the work of Northwest artists to Bellevue, Washington. *Tel. 206/454–4900.*

Early Aug.: Old Spanish Days Fiesta is Santa Barbara's biggest event, with parades, a carnival, a rodeo, and dancers in the Spanish marketplace. *Tel. 805/966–9222.*

Early Aug.: Mt. Hood Festival of Jazz brings acclaimed jazz musicians to Gresham, Oregon, for a tuneful weekend. *Tel. 503/666–3810.*

Sept.–Oct.: Renaissance Pleasure Faire draws revelers in Elizabethan-style costumes to Novato, California, for weekends of music, merriment, and theater. *Tel. 415/892–0937.*

Late Nov.: Pasadena's Doo Dah Parade satirizes the city's Rose Parade with such entries as Briefcase Brigade and Kazoo Marching Band. *Tel. 818/796–2591.*

Early Dec.: Hollywood Christmas Parade features celebrities riding festively decorated floats. *Tel. 213/469–2337.*

Getting Around the West Coast

By Plane The West Coast is served by all major domestic airlines and most international carriers. Major airports in California include **Los Angeles International Airport** (tel. 310/646–5252), plus John Wayne Orange County Airport and other regional airports at Burbank, Long Beach, and Ontario; **San Diego Lindbergh Field** (tel. 619/231–2100); and **San Francisco International Airport** (tel. 415/876–2222), plus regional airports at Oakland and San Jose. The region's other major airports are Oregon's **Portland International Airport** (tel. 503/335–1234) and Washington's **Seattle-Tacoma International Airport** (SeaTac, tel. 206/433–5217).

By Car I–5 runs north–south from the Canadian to the Mexican border, connecting Seattle, Portland, Sacramento, Los Angeles, and San Diego en route. The coastal route is designated Hwy. 101 in Oregon and Washington and Hwy. 1 in most of California, where much of it travels through coastal valleys. Major east–west routes include I–90, which bisects Washington from Spokane to Seattle; I–84, which traverses eastern Oregon and travels through the Columbia Gorge to Portland; I–80, the main highway crossing the High Sierras in California from Lake Tahoe to San Francisco; I–10, the historic route through Southern California's desert to Los Angeles; I–8, the southernmost route, hugging the Mexican border from El Centro to San Diego. I–15 is the route between Southern California and Las Vegas. The interstate highways are open all year, but you should expect temporary closures during severe winter storms. State highways crossing high mountain passes are normally closed in winter.

By Train **Amtrak** (tel. 800/872–7245) serves rail passengers in the region. Trains run daily between Seattle and Los Angeles; the trip takes 39 hours. Commuter trains serve Los Angeles from San Diego and Santa Barbara. **CalTrain** brings passengers to San Francisco from peninsula locations. **Transcontinental** trains serve Los Angeles, San Francisco/Oakland, Portland, and Seattle.

By Bus **Greyhound** (tel. 800/247–3946) provides intercity service.

By Boat **Washington State Ferries** (tel. 800/542–0810) serve 20 destinations around Puget Sound, including the San Juan Islands. Ferries can accommodate cars and recreational vehicles.

CALIFORNIA

By Aaron Shurin
and Bobbi Zane

Capital	Sacramento
Population	30,000,000
Motto	Eureka
State Bird	Valley quail
State Flower	Golden poppy

Visitor Information

California Office of Tourism (801 K St., Sacramento 95814, tel. 916/322–1397).

Scenic Drives

The land- and seascapes along the nearly 400 mi of coastline between San Francisco Bay and the Oregon border are beautiful and rugged; switchbacked **Hwy. 1,** also known as the Pacific Coast Highway, is punctuated by groves of giant redwood trees, tiny coastal towns, and secluded coves and beaches. U.S. 395 north from San Bernardino rises in elevation gradually from the Mojave Desert to the Sierra foothills and on to the east entrance to Yosemite National Park.

National and State Parks

National Parks At **Yosemite National Park** (National Park Service, Ft. Mason, Bldg. 201, San Francisco 94123, tel. 415/556–0560), glacial granite peaks and domes rise more than 3,000 feet. Yosemite Valley offers hiking, backpacking, and spectacular scenery at every turn; Yosemite Falls, at 2,425 feet, is the highest waterfall in North America. Reservations for a hotel room, cabin, or campsite must be made far in advance (Yosemite Park and Curry Co. Central Reservations, 5410 E. Home Ave., Fresno 93727, tel. 209/252–4848). Just north of San Francisco is the **Point Reyes National Seashore** (tel. 415/663–1200), whose shoreline and sand dunes attract lots of birds and migrating whales.

State Parks California's more than 200 state parks are maintained by the **Department of Parks and Recreation** (Box 942896, Sacramento 94296, tel. 916/445–6477). **Anza Borrego Desert** (tel. 619/767–5311), northeast of San Diego, has fascinating flora and rock formations. **Big Basin Redwoods** (tel. 408/338–6132), near Santa Cruz, has 18,000 acres of the big trees. **Leo Carillo State Beach** (tel. 818/706–1310), north of Malibu, has tide pools, hiking trails, and picnic areas. **Pismo Beach** (tel. 805/489–2684), near San Luis Obispo, offers a wide stretch of beach and many recreational facilities.

San Francisco

Few cities cram as much diversity into as little space as San Francisco, dramatically set on a 46.6-sq-mi tip of land between San Francisco Bay and the Pacific Ocean, with the hills of Marin and Oakland forming a backdrop in the distance. After more than a century as a port city, trafficking with countless peoples of the world, San Francisco has a tolerance for differences of custom and belief. Because of its rowdy, licentious reputation, it earned the nickname Barbary Coast, and some outsiders considered the devastating 1906 earthquake to be Heaven-sent retribution. San Franciscans didn't, and rebuilt the place in short order and in high style. The resulting blend of surviving Victorian structures and graceful post-quake, turn-of-the-century buildings created the architectural look for which the city is still renowned.

During World War II, millions of GIs passed through town, and word spread about this beautiful, sophisticated place. In the 1960s, San Francisco and the Bay Area became a hotbed of radical thought, and the Haight-Ashbury district a center of the counterculture. The 1970s saw the emergence of the city's gay community, which became a powerful political force and has made San Francisco something of a mecca for gays everywhere.

Much of the city's vitality comes from the distinct cultural, political, and ethnic identities of the neighborhoods that house its 750,000 residents. Many visitors are struck by San Francisco's overall cleanliness. This is partly a result of its weather—sea breezes don't allow smog to linger—and the fact that most of its buildings are white or light-colored, but perhaps most important, there is tremendous civic pride in the city's appearance, and maintaining its attractiveness is a high priority.

Tourist Information

San Francisco: Convention and Visitors Bureau (201 3rd St., Suite 900, 94103, tel. 415/974–6900).

Arriving and Departing

By Plane **San Francisco International Airport** (SFO, tel. 415/876–7809), 20 minutes south of the city off U.S. 101, is served by most major airlines. **Oakland Airport** (tel. 510/577–4000), across the bay but not much farther from the city, provides additional air access through several domestic airlines. The **SFO Airporter** (tel. 415/495–8404; $8 one-way, $14 round-trip) bus runs every 20 minutes between downtown and SFO. **Supershuttle** (tel. 415/871–7800; $12) will take you from SFO to anywhere within the city limits in 30–50 minutes, depending on traffic and your destination. **Taxis** between downtown and either airport take 20–30 minutes and cost about $30.

By Car I–80 comes into San Francisco from the east, crossing the Bay Bridge from Oakland. U.S. 101 runs north–south through the city and across the Golden Gate Bridge.

By Train **Amtrak** trains stop at the West Oakland depot (1707 Wood St., tel. 510/645–4607), from which buses leave for San Francisco's Transbay Terminal (*see* By Bus, *below*). Trains depart for the southern peninsula from San Francisco's **Southern Pacific** depot (4th and Townsend Sts., tel. 415/495–4560).

By Bus **Greyhound** serves San Francisco's **Transbay Terminal** (1st and Mission Sts., tel. 415/558–6789).

Getting Around San Francisco

By Car Driving in the city is a challenge. Watch out for one-way streets, curb your wheels when parking on hills, and check street signs for parking restrictions—of which there are many.

By Public Transportation Most of the light-rail and bus lines of **MUNI** (Municipal Railway System, tel. 415/673–6864) operate continuously; standard fare is $1 for adults (transfers are free), and exact change is required. Three **cable car** lines crisscross downtown; information and tokens ($3 adults) can be obtained at the main turnaround at Powell and Market streets and at major stops. **BART** (Bay Area Rapid Transit, tel. 415/788–2278) sends its sleek air-conditioned trains to the East Bay and south to Daly City; wall maps list destinations and fares. Trains run Monday–Saturday 6 AM–midnight, Sunday 9 AM–midnight.

By Taxi Rates are high—$1.70 to get in, then $1.80 per mile—and it's difficult to hail a passing cab. For a radio-dispatched taxi, try **Yellow Cab Co.** (tel. 415/626–2345).

Orientation Tours

Gray Line (350 8th St., tel. 415/558–9400) offers a variety of city tours on buses and double-deckers. The **Great Pacific Tour** (518 Octavia St., tel. 415/626–4499) takes 3½ hours; German-, French-, Spanish-, and Italian-speaking guides are available.

Walking Tours Trevor Hailey's **Castro District Tour** (tel. 415/550–8110) focuses on the history and development of the city's gay and lesbian community. The **Chinese Cultural Heritage Foundation** (tel. 415/986–1822) offers a Heritage Walk and a Culinary Walk through Chinatown.

Exploring San Francisco

Touring San Francisco is best done one neighborhood at a time, and on foot, though the hills are a challenge—dependable walking shoes are essential. You'll need a jacket for the dramatic temperature swings, especially in summer when the afternoon fog rolls in. Starting from Union Square, which is more or less in the center of things, we'll go through nearby Chinatown, and Nob Hill, then south to the Civic Center area; east through the Financial District to the Embarcadero along San Francisco Bay; then north and west through North Beach, Telegraph Hill, Fisherman's Wharf, and the Golden Gate Bridge, and on to Golden Gate Park and the Pacific Ocean.

Union Square The landmark of Union Square is the grand **Westin St. Francis Hotel** (335 Powell St., tel. 415/397–7000), San Francisco's second-oldest, on the southeast corner of Post and Powell streets. After a day exploring the stores of this major shopping district (*see* Shopping, *below*), you can relax over a traditional tea in the Westin's dramatic art deco **Compass Rose** lounge (tel. 415/774–0167).

Across Union Square is tiny **Maiden Lane,** which runs for two blocks between Stockton and Kearney streets. From 11 AM to 4 PM, the lane is closed to vehicles and becomes a chic and pricey mall. **140 Maiden Lane,** the only Frank Lloyd Wright building in San Francisco, is reminiscent of his later Guggenheim Museum in New York.

Chinatown The dragon-crowned, green-tile **Chinatown Gate** at Bush Street and Grant Avenue is the main entrance to Chinatown. The bustling, noisy, colorful stretches of Grant Avenue and Stockton Street are difficult to navigate on foot, but by car it's worse, and parking is almost impossible. Join the residents as they stroll and shop for fresh fish, vegetables, and baked goods. Nighttime here is as busy as day: Almost 100 restaurants are squeezed into these 14 blocks.

The heart of Chinatown is **Stockton Street,** where shoppers jostle one another amid the sidewalk displays. The many excellent examples of Chinese architecture here include the **Chinese Six Companies** building (843 Stockton St.), with curved roof tiles and elaborate cornices.

To learn about the area's rich immigrant history, go to the **Chinese Cultural Center,** which exhibits the work of Chinese-American artists and offers Saturday-afternoon tours of Chinatown (*see* Walking Tours, *above*). *Holiday Inn, 750 Kearney St., tel. 415/986–1822. Admission free. Closed Sun.–Mon.*

Nob Hill North of Union Square is **Nob Hill,** home to the city's elite and some of its finest hotels. The 1906 earthquake destroyed the mansions that had been built in this neighborhood by gold-rush millionaires and the later railroad barons. Although not the grandest of the bunch, the shell of railroad magnate James Flood's Italianate–style brownstone mansion (1000 California St.) managed to survive the quake, was slightly remodeled, and now houses the exclusive **Pacific Union Club. Grace Cathedral** (1051 California St.) is the seat of the Episcopal church in San Francisco. The gothic structure took 53 years to build and has bronze doors cast from Ghiberti's *Gates of Paradise* in Florence. The **Mark Hopkins Hotel** atop Nob Hill is known for the view from its **Top of the Mark** lounge (1 Nob Hill, tel. 415/392–3434).

Civic Center **City Hall** (Polk St., between Grove and McAllister Sts.), a granite-and-marble masterpiece modeled on the Capitol in Washington, faces the long **Civic Center Plaza** with a fountain, walkways, and flowerbeds. (The plaza is "home" to many transients, and caution is advised after dark.) Across Van Ness Avenue, between McAllister and Hayes streets, is the **Performing Arts Center** complex, which includes the **War Memorial Opera House** and the **Louise M. Davies Symphony Hall.** Also in the complex is the **San Francisco Museum of Modern Art** (tel. 415/863–8800; admission charged), with works by Matisse, Manet, Monet, and Picasso, as well as a museum store and a café. The **San Francisco Opera Shop** (199 Grove St., tel. 415/565–6414) carries gift items associated with the performing arts.

To the west of the Civic Center area, in a neighborhood known as the Western Addition, is the much-photographed row of six identical Victorian houses along Steiner Street, at the east end of Alamo Square.

San Francisco

PACIFIC OCEAN

Golden Gate Bridge
Ft. Point

Golden Gate
National
Recreation
Area

The Presidio

Baker Beach
Phelan Beach

Land's End
Palace of the Legion of Honor
Lincoln Park

Lake St.

Clement St.

Park Presidio Blvd.

8th Ave.

Arguello Blvd.

Gea

SEACLIFF

Point Lobos

Cliff House

43rd Ave.

34th Ave.

Geary Blvd.

25th Ave.

19th Ave.

Balboa St.

Turk Blvd.

RICHMOND

Fulton St.

M. H. de Young Memorial Museum
California Academy of Sciences
Japanese Tea Garden
Strybing Arboretum

Kennedy Dr.

Golden Gate Park

Middle Dr.

Stow Lake

Stanyan St.

Lincoln Way

Judah St.

28th St.

Funston Ave.

7th Ave.

Lawton St.

1

Clarendon Ave.

Noriega St.
Ortega St.

19th Ave.

SUNSET

Quintara St.

41st Ave.

Sunset Blvd.

14th Ave.

Dewey Blvd.

Ocean Beach

Great Highway

McCoppin Square

Taraval St.

Vicente St.

Larsen Park

Dr.

Mt. Davidson

Stern Grove

Portola

Yerba Buena Ave.

Monterey Blvd.

Miramar Ave.

San Francisco Zoo

Sloat Blvd.

STONESTOWN

Juniper Serra Blvd.

Ocean Ave.

Harding Park

San Francisco State Univ.

Holloway Ave.

Garfield St.

Plymouth Ave.

Skyline Blvd.

Lake Merced

Lake Merced Blvd.

Font Blvd.

Brotherhood Way

N

0   1 mile
0   1 km

The Financial District Bounded by the Union Square area, Telegraph Hill, Mission Street, and the Embarcadero, San Francisco's Financial District is distiguished from the rest of town by its cluster of steel-and-glass high rises and older, more decorative architectural monuments to commerce. The city's signature high rise is the 853-foot **Transamerica Pyramid** (600 Montgomery St., tel. 415/983–4100), whose 27th-floor public viewing area affords spectacular vistas. Dominating the skyline, however, is the 52-story **Bank of America** tower. High atop this granite monolith, the **Carnelian Room** (555 California St., tel. 415/433–7500) is a good spot for a sunset dinner or cocktails.

Other notable structures in this district include the **Russ Building** (235 Montgomery St.), a gothic twin to the Chicago Tribune Tower; the **Mills Building and Tower** (220 Montgomery St.), of white marble and brick; and the **Pacific Stock Exchange** (Pine and Sansome Sts.). The ceiling and entry in the **Stock Exchange Tower** (155 Sansome St.), an art deco gem, are of black marble.

The Embarcadero The tower of the romantic-looking 1896 **Ferry Building,** on the Embarcadero at the foot of Market Street, was the tallest building in town for many years. Obscured from view for the past three decades by the elevated Embarcadero Freeway, the tower was returned to prominence when the 1989 earthquake forced the roadway's dismantling. Ferries still sail from here to Sausalito (*see* Excursion to Sausalito, *below*), Larkspur, and Tiburon. The Embarcadero's waterfront promenade extends to the **San Francisco–Oakland Bay Bridge,** is great for walking and jogging, and has one of the finest views anywhere.

Across from the Ferry Building, at the end of Market Street, is the huge **Embarcadero Center,** a complex of eight buildings that include more than 100 shops, 40 restaurants, and two hotels. A three-tier pedestrian mall links the buildings. The **Hyatt Regency Hotel** (5 Embarcadero, tel. 415/788–1234) is noted for its spectacular lobby and 20-story hanging garden. In front of the hotel is **Justin Herman Plaza,** site of frequent arts-and-crafts shows and political rallies.

North Beach and Telegraph Hill **Washington Square** is the heart of North Beach, which was once considered Little Italy, though these days the elderly Italian men who come here to take in the sun share the park benches with Chinese matrons. Across from the park is the Romanesque **SS. Peter and Paul Cathedral,** with its twin-turreted terra-cotta towers.

The streets surrounding the cathedral are packed with Italian delicatessens and bakeries, coffeehouses, and, increasingly, Chinese markets. Cafés are the arteries of North Beach, and the aroma of fresh roasted coffee permeates the air.

Telegraph Hill, which rises to the east of North Beach, provides some of the best views in town. From Filbert Street, the Greenwich Stairs climb to **Coit Tower,** a monument to the city's volunteer firemen. Inside are the works of 25 muralists, most notably the great Mexican painter Diego Rivera. From the top there's a panoramic view of the bay, bridges, and islands.

The Northern Waterfront and Fisherman's Wharf **Fisherman's Wharf** and the waterfront are at the end of the Powell-Hyde cable-car line from Union Square. From the cable-car turnaround, the **National Maritime Museum** (at the foot of Polk St., tel. 415/556–8177) and Ghirardelli Square are to the west, Fisherman's Wharf and piers 39 and 41 to the east. **The Red and White Fleet** (Pier 41, tel. 415/546–2700) and the **Blue and Gold Fleet** (Pier 39, tel. 415/781–7877) offer bay cruises.

Ghirardelli Square (North Point, between Polk and Larkin Sts.) is a complex of renovated 19th-century factory buildings that once housed the famous chocolate maker; it is now filled with a variety of shops (including one that sells Ghirardelli chocolates), cafés, restaurants, and galleries. Just east of the Hyde Street Pier is **The Cannery** (2801 Leavenworth St.), a similar "adaptive re-use" of the 1894 Del Monte Fruit and Vegetable Cannery. Only a few active fishing boats of the wharf's once flourishing fleet still dock here, and restaurants and souvenir vendors are now the dominant industries.

Just south of the waterfront area, between Hyde and Leavenworth streets, is that famous stretch of **Lombard Street** known as "the crookedest street in the world." This series of sharp switchbacks was designed to compensate for the steep grade.

To the west of the waterfront area, at the edge of the **Marina** district, is the rosy, rococo **Palace of Fine Arts** (Baker St., between Bay and Marina Blvds.), with massive columns, an imposing rotunda, and a swan-filled lagoon. Built for the 1913 Pan Pacific Exposition, the city's semiofficial celebration of its rebuilding after the earthquake, the palace is a cherished San Francisco landmark. Inside is the **Exploratorium** (tel. 415/563–7337), whose imaginative, interactive exhibits have made it one of the best science museums in the world.

To reach the **Golden Gate Bridge** from here, walk along the bay or take MUNI bus No. 28 to the toll plaza. Nearly 2 mi long, the bridge looks serene and airy yet is tough enough to withstand 100 mph winds. Even when conditions are gusty and misty, as they frequently are, a walk across the bridge offers unparalleled views of the skyline, the bay, the Marin County headlands, and the Pacific Ocean.

Golden Gate Park and the Western Shore   **Golden Gate Park,** in the northwest part of town, is ideal for strolling, especially on Sunday, when it is closed to car traffic. A cluster of museums in its eastern section includes the **M. H. de Young Memorial Museum** (tel. 415/863–3330), with American art; adjoining it are the galleries of the **Asian Art Museum** (tel. 415/668–8921). The **California Academy of Sciences** (tel. 415/750–7145), a natural-history museum, is excellent. The **Steinhart Aquarium** (tel. 415/750–7145) features a cylindrical 100,000-gallon tank, the Fish Roundabout, which is home to 14,000 creatures and a coral reef. The **Strybing Arboretum** (tel. 415/661–1316) features Californian, Australian, Mediterranean, and South African plants. A long walk west brings you to Ocean Beach and the Pacific. At the north end of the beach is **Cliff House** (1066 Point Lobos Ave., tel. 415/386–3330), a restaurant where you can dine to the sound of crashing surf.

What to See and Do with Children

In **Golden Gate Park** (*see* Exploring San Francisco, *above*), the playground has a vintage carousel, and the **Steinhart Aquarium** a "Touching Tide Pool." The **Exploratorium** in the Palace of Fine Arts (*see* Exploring San Francisco, *above*) is wonderful for children. **Pier 39** (at the eastern end of North Point St. at the Embarcadero) has a carousel, roving entertainment, food stalls, and a population of noisy sea lions that have made a smelly home for themselves here, much to the chagrin of those who have to work nearby. Another good bet is the **San Francisco Zoo** (Sloat Blvd. at Great Hwy., tel. 415/753–7083), at the south end of Ocean Beach.

Shopping

Shopping is a primary activity in San Francisco, where choices include everything from the most elegant boutiques and department stores to discount outlets and vintage-clothing stores.

Shopping Districts **Union Square** is flanked by such department stores as **Macy's, Saks Fifth Avenue, I. Magnin,** and **Neiman Marcus,** with **Tiffany & Co** (252 Grant Ave.) and **Brooks Brothers** (201 Post St.) nearby.

Fisherman's Wharf is the hub of waterfront shopping and sightseeing attractions: **Pier 39, Ghirardelli Square,** and **The Cannery** (*see* Exploring San Francisco, *above*) offer shops, restaurants, a festive atmosphere, a view of the bay, and cable-car access.

Jackson Square, a preserve of beautiful Victorian town houses, also features a dozen or so of San Francisco's finest antiques dealers. The **Embarcadero Center** and **Chinatown** (*see* Exploring San Francisco, *above*) are nearby.

The area south of Market (SOMA), just below the Financial District, is packed with discount outlets in warehouses wedged between hip restaurants and art galleries. On Saturday, the factory outlets along the alleys between 3rd, 7th, Townsend, and Harrison streets open their doors to the public, offering discounts of as much as 50%. In the **660 Center Arcade** (660 3rd St.) alone, there are 16 shops.

The **Haight-Ashbury** district gets a lot of visitors wanting a look into the flower-powered past. Gentrification has changed the area, the virtual world headquarters of hippiedom in the '60s, and there are now some interesting shops, particularly on the 1500 block of Haight Street.

Specialty Stores **Paris 1925** (1954 Union St., tel. 415/567–1925) specializes in
Antiques jewelry and vintage watches. **Telegraph Hill Antiques** (580 Union St., tel. 415/982–7055) features artwork, china and porcelain, crystal, Oriental objects, and Victoriana. Also *see* **Jackson Square** in Shopping Districts, *above*.

Art **Vorpal Gallery** (393 Grove St., tel. 415/397–9200) focuses on postmodern painting and has a wide selection of graphic works.

Books **City Lights** (261 Columbus Ave., tel. 415/362–8193), a literary institution since its beginnings as a beatnik-writer gathering place, is well stocked with poetry, contemporary literature, and nature and travel books.

Clothing **Apacci Paris** (50 Grant Ave., tel. 415/982–7222) features an exclusive collection of menswear (including unique ties) from Italy, France, and Switzerland. **Eileen West** (33 Grant Ave., tel. 415/982–2275) has dresses, lingerie, linens, and more by this San Francisco designer.

Gifts **Gump's** (250 Post St., tel. 415/982–1616) sells jewelry, china, stationery, art, home accessories, and fascinating specialty-item imports.

Toys and Gadgets **Forma** (1715 Haight St., tel. 415/751–0545) has an imaginative selection of high-design housewares and home accessories, toy animals, and a variety of campy, pop-culture knickknacks.

Spectator Sports

Baseball **San Francisco Giants** (Candlestick Park, off U.S. 101, tel. 415/467–8000; Apr.–Oct.). **Oakland A's** (Oakland Coliseum, off I-880 at 66th Ave., tel. 510/638–0500; Apr.–Oct.).

Basketball **Golden State Warriors** (Oakland Coliseum, tel. 510/762–2277; Oct.–early Apr.).

Football **San Francisco 49ers** (Candlestick Park, tel. 415/468–2249; Aug.–Dec.). Games sell out far in advance.

Dining

San Francisco may have more restaurants per capita than any other American city. The Bay Area gave us "California cuisine," which uses the freshest local produce, occasional Asian flavorings, and classic French cooking techniques. This style is well represented in the city—as is every conceivable ethnic cuisine. For price ranges, see Chart 1 (A) in Chapter 1.

Very Expensive **Donatello.** Chef Patrizio Sacchetto's cooking is from the north of Italy, with admirable risotto and remarkable multicolor-striped pastas at center stage. The intimate dining rooms are exquisitely appointed and elegant. *Donatello Hotel, Post and Mason Sts., tel. 415/441–7128. Reservations advised. Jacket and tie required. AE, DC, MC, V. No lunch.*

★ **Ernie's.** This old-timer got a face-lift in 1988 and the new, young French-trained American chef, David Kinch, is preparing light versions of French classics. Even so, Ernie's is still steeped in the aura of Gay Nineties San Francisco. *847 Montgomery St., tel. 415/397–5969. Reservations advised. Jacket and tie required. AE, DC, MC, V. No lunch Sat.–Mon.; closed major holidays.*

★ **Masa's.** The artistry of the presentation is as important as the French cuisine in this understated, elegant, flower-filled dining spot. *Vintage Court Hotel, 648 Bush St., tel. 415/989–7154. Reservations advised far in advance. Jacket required. AE, DC, MC, V. No lunch; closed Sun.–Mon., 1st week in July, last week in Dec.–1st week in Jan.*

Expensive **Hayes Street Grill.** Up to 15 kinds of seafood are featured each ★ night. The fish is superbly fresh, simply grilled, and served with a choice of sauces ranging from tartar to a spicy Szechuan concoction. *320 Hayes St., tel. 415/863–5545. Reservations required, accepted no more than 1 week in advance. AE, DC, MC, V. No lunch Sat.; closed Sun., major holidays.*

★ **PosTrio.** In Wolfgang Puck's open kitchen and stunning three-level bar and dining area, the food is Californian with Mediterranean and Asian overtones, and emphasizes pastas, grilled seafood, and freshly baked breads. *545 Post St., tel. 415/776–7825. Reservations advised. AE, DC, MC, V.*

★ **Stars.** This huge dining room with a clublike ambience is the culinary temple of Jeremiah Tower, an acknowledged co-creator of California cuisine. The menu ranges from grills to ragouts to sautés, some daringly creative and some classical. *150 Redwood Alley, tel. 415/861–7827. Reservations strongly advised. AE, DC, MC, V. No lunch weekends; closed Memorial Day, Thanksgiving, Christmas.*

Moderate **Capp's Corner.** At this family-style trattoria, diners sit elbow to elbow and feast on bountiful Italian five-course dinners. *1600 Powell St., tel. 415/989–2589. Reservations advised. DC, MC, V. No lunch weekends; closed Thanksgiving, Christmas.*

★ **Fog City Diner.** The long, narrow dining room emulates a railroad dining car. The cooking is inspired by U.S. regional cuisine. *1300 Battery St., tel. 415/982–2000. Reservations weeks in advance advised. DC, MC, V. Closed Thanksgiving, Christmas.*

Hong Kong Flower Lounge. Many Sinophiles swear this spot serves the best Cantonese food in town. The seafood is spectacular, as is the dim sum, which is offered here daily. *5322 Geary Blvd., tel. 415/668–8998. Reservations advised. AE, MC, V.*

Inexpensive **Angkor Palace.** This lovely Cambodian restaurant offers such exotic fare as fish-and-coconut mousse baked in banana leaves. *1769 Lombard St., tel. 415/931–2830. Reservations advised. AE, MC, V. No lunch.*

Chevy's. At this first San Francisco branch of a popular Mexican minichain, the emphasis is on the freshest ingredients and sauces. Of note are the fajitas and the grilled quail and seafood. *4th and Howard Sts., tel. 415/543–8060. Reservations for 8 or more only. MC, V. Closed Thanksgiving, Christmas.*

Hunan. This expanded version of Henry Chung's six-star Hunanese café specializes in smoked dishes—prepared without MSG. *924 Sansome St., tel. 415/956–7727. Reservations advised. AE, DC, MC, V.*

Lodging

San Francisco has world-class hotels, renovated older buildings with European charm, Victorian homes transformed into bed-and-breakfasts, and representatives of most chains. Less expensive motel and hotel rooms can be found in the Civic Center and Lombard areas; truly budget accommodations are available at the **YMCA Central Branch** (220 Golden Gate Ave., tel. 415/885–0460). For free assistance with hotel reservations try **San Francisco Reservations** (tel. 800/677–1550). For price ranges, see Chart 2 (A) in Chapter 1.

Very Expensive **Four Seasons Clift.** Probably San Francisco's most acclaimed
★ hotel for its elegant style and service, this stately landmark has sumptuously decorated accommodations—suites in black and gray, rooms in beige and pink—in updated contemporary style. *495 Geary St. (Union Sq.), 94102, tel. 415/775–4700; fax 415/931–7417. 297 rooms, 32 suites. Facilities: restaurant, lounge. AE, DC, MC, V.*

The Sherman House. Rooms in this luxury small hotel near the Presidio, formerly a private mansion, have wood-burning fireplaces with marble mantels, four-poster beds, and Biedermeier, English Jacobean, or French Second Empire antique furniture. *2160 Green St. (Cow Hollow), 94123, tel. 415/563–3600; fax 415/563–1882. 15 rooms. AE, DC, MC, V.*

★ **Stouffer Stanford Court Hotel.** The dictionaries in each room are just one of the thoughtful touches worth noting at this world-class hotel. One of the city's finest restaurants, **Fournou's Ovens,** is located here. *905 California St. (Nob Hill), 94108, tel. 415/989–3500 or 800/227–4726; fax 415/391–0513. 402 rooms. Facilities: 2 restaurants, 2 lounges. AE, DC, MC, V.*

Expensive **Inn at the Opera.** Hearts of music and ballet lovers may quiver at the sight of this lovely small hotel where musicians and singers stay when they appear at the nearby performing-arts centers. *333 Fulton St. (Civic Ctr.), 94102, tel. 415/863–8400; fax 415/861–0821. 48 rooms. Facilities: restaurant, lounge. AE, DC, MC, V.*

★ **Petite Auberge.** The French countryside was imported to downtown San Francisco to create this charming B&B inn. Next door is the sister hotel, the White Swan, with an English-country flavor. *845 Bush St. (Union Sq.), 94108, tel. 415/928–6000; fax 415/775–5717. 26 rooms. AE, MC, V.*

Sheraton Palace. This grand hotel built in 1909 reopened in 1991 after extensive renovation. The gorgeous glass-domed Garden Court has been restored, and a Maxfield Parrish painting hangs in the famed Pied Piper lounge. The rooms have cherry-wood furnishings and a decor that is unobtrusive to the point of being unremarkable. *2 New Montgomery St. (Financial District), 94105, tel. 415/392–8600; fax 415/243–8062. 550 rooms. Facilities: 2 restaurants, 2 lounges, fitness center. AE, DC, MC, V.*

Moderate **The Cartwright.** This is a family-owned hotel with a friendly, personal touch and an ideal location. Rooms have brass or carved-wood beds and small refrigerators. *524 Sutter St. (Union Sq.), 94102, tel. 415/421–2865 or 800/227–3844; fax 415/421–2865. 114 rooms. Facilities: coffee shop. AE, DC, MC, V.*

Majestic Hotel. One of the city's first grand hotels, the Majestic has been restored and offers romantic rooms with French and English antiques and four-poster canopy beds. *1500 Sutter St. (Civic Ctr.), 94109, tel. 415/441–1100 or 800/869–8966; fax 415/673–7331. 60 rooms. Facilities: restaurant, lounge. AE, MC, V.*

★ **Marina Inn.** Cute B&B accommodations are offered here at motel prices. The rooms have an English-country feel. Continental breakfast is served in the cozy central sitting room. *3110 Octavia St. (at Lombard St.), 94123, tel. 415/928–1000; fax 415/928–5909. 40 rooms. AE, MC, V.*

Inexpensive **Adelaide Inn.** The bedspreads don't match the drapes, but the rooms are clean and cheap at this friendly small hotel popular with Europeans. *5 Isadora Duncan Ct. (off Taylor St., between Geary and Post Sts.), 94102, tel. 415/441–2474. 16 rooms (all share baths). AE, MC, V.*

★ **Grant Plaza.** This bargain-priced hotel at the entrance to Chinatown has small but clean and attractively furnished rooms. *465 Grant Ave. (Union Sq.), 94103, tel. 415/434–3883; fax 415/434–3886. 72 rooms. AE, MC, V.*

★ **San Remo Hotel.** This small European-style hotel with daily and weekly rates has tiny rooms but is tidy and pleasingly decorated with plants and antiques. It's at the far north end of North Beach, practically on the doorstep of Fisherman's Wharf. *2237 Mason St., 94133, tel. 415/776–8688; fax 415/776–2811. 62 rooms (all share baths). Facilities: restaurant. AE, DC, MC, V.*

The Arts and Nightlife

The best guide to arts and entertainment events in San Francisco is the pink "Datebook" section of the Sunday *Examiner* and *Chronicle*. The *Bay Guardian* and *S.F. Weekly*, free weeklies available throughout the city, list more neighborhood, avant-garde, and budget-priced events. **Bass** (tel. 510/762–2277 or 415/776–1999) offers charge-by-phone ticket service. Half-price, same-day tickets to many stage shows go on sale at 11 AM Tuesday–Saturday at the **TIX Bay Area** (tel. 415/433–7827) ticket booth on the Stockton Street side of Union Square.

Theater The **American Conservatory Theatre** (box office, in the Geary Theatre, 415 Geary St., tel. 415/748–2228), a repertory company, specializes in classics. The **Curran** (445 Geary St., tel. 415/474–3800) hosts touring companies.

Music The **San Francisco Symphony** plays from September to May in the Louise M. Davies Symphony Hall (201 Van Ness Ave. at Grove St., tel. 415/431–5400).

Opera Productions of the **San Francisco Opera** (War Memorial Opera House, 301 Van Ness Ave. at Grove St., tel. 415/864–3330), presented from September through December, are often sold out; standing-room tickets are usually available.

Dance The **San Francisco Ballet** (War Memorial Opera House, tel. 415/703–9400) performs classical and contemporary works February through May.

Film The Bay Area has a large number of first-run and revival movie theaters. The **San Francisco International Film Festival** (tel. 415/931–3456) takes place each spring.

Nightlife **Nob Hill** is noted for its piano bars and lounges with panoramic views, **North Beach** for its burlesque and bistros, **Union Street** for its singles scene, **South of Market** (SOMA) for its alternative clubs, and **the Castro** for gay bars.

Comedy Clubs **Cobb's Comedy Club** (2801 Leavenworth St., at Beach St., tel. 415/928–4320) features stand-up comics. **The Punch Line** (444-A Battery, tel. 415/397–7573) launched comics Jay Leno and Whoopi Goldberg.

Discos **Club DV8** (540 Howard St., tel. 415/957–1730) is a large, trendy SOMA club. **Oz** (top of the Westin St. Francis Hotel, 335 Powell St., tel. 415/397–7000) is an upscale disco.

Jazz Clubs **Kimballs** (300 Grove St., tel. 415/861–5555) is the preeminent spot for jazz, presenting such greats as Mose Allison.

Nightclubs **The Great American Music Hall** (859 O'Farrell St., tel. 415/885–0750), one of the country's great eclectic nightclubs, has top blues, folk, jazz, and rock entertainers.

Rock Clubs **Bottom of the Hill** (1233 17th St., at Texas St., tel. 415/626–4455) showcases local alternative rock and blues talent. **Slim's** (333 11th St., tel. 415/621–3330) specializes in basic rock and blues.

For Singles **The Balboa Cafe** (2199 Fillmore St., tel. 415/921–3944) is a Yuppie hangout famous for its burgers. **The Hard Rock Cafe** (1699 Van Ness Ave., tel. 415/885–1699) features an upscale rock-and-roll motif. **Perry's** (1944 Union St., tel. 415/922–9022) is a famous Union Street singles bar.

Gay and Lesbian Nightlife   San Francisco's large and active gay/lesbian community supports a multitude of bars, comedy clubs, cabarets, and discos. Check the *Bay Area Reporter* (tel. 415/861–5019) or the *San Francisco Bay Times* (tel. 415/626–8121) for the latest one-night-a-week clubs. **The Box** (Kennel Club, 628 Divisadero St., tel. 415/931–1914) has house, hip-hop, and funk sounds for a lesbian crowd. **The Elephant Walk** (Castro and 18th Sts., no tel.), one of the Castro's cozier gay bars, is among the few where the music level allows for conversation. **The End Up** (6th and Harrison Sts., tel. 415/543–7700), with a spacious dance floor and an open-air courtyard, hosts several popular gay and lesbian one-night clubs. At **The Midnight Sun** (4067 18th St., tel. 415/861–4186), giant video screens play nightly to a packed house.

· Excursions from San Francisco

Berkeley and Oakland   **Berkeley** is the home of the 178-acre **University of California at Berkeley,** a center of student protests in the 1960s. Along Telegraph Avenue south of the campus is a student-oriented business district with a dog-eared counterculture ambience. Food lovers will want to head for that cradle of California cuisine, **Chez Panisse Cafe & Restaurant** (1517 Shattuck Ave., tel. 510/548–5525; closed Sun.). In the elegantly appointed redwood-paneled dining room downstairs and the less pricey and more informal café upstairs, Alice Waters masterminds the culinary wizardry and Jean-Pierre Moulle performs as head chef, together producing such treats as roast truffled breast of guinea hen and a variety of distinctive pasta dishes.

Oakland has long been viewed as a warmer and more spacious alternative to San Francisco, and many residents commute to work across the bay from vintage houses in Oakland's hillside neighborhoods. It is also an important industrial town and the second-largest port in California. The revitalized Jack London Square, waterfront, and downtown area have attracted to the city much long-overdue attention. The **Oakland Museum** (1000 Oak St., tel. 510/834–2413; admission free) displays Californian art, history, and natural sciences through engaging exhibits and films.

Getting There   By car, take I–80 across the Bay Bridge; exit at University Avenue for Berkeley, or pick up I–580 and exit at Grand Avenue for Oakland. By BART, Berkeley is 45 minutes to an hour from the city; exit at the downtown Berkeley stop, then take the shuttle to the campus. Oakland is a half-hour BART ride from San Francisco; exit at the Lake Merritt station for the museum.

Sausalito   This hillside town on Richardson Bay, an inlet of San Francisco Bay in Marin County, feels at once like an artist's colony and something out of the Mediterranean with its usually sunny weather, resort-town ambience, yacht harbor, and superb views of the Richardson and San Francisco bays. The main street, Bridgeway, has waterfront restaurants on one side and shops, hotels, and residential neighborhoods climbing the wooded hills on the other. At the south end is an esplanade with expansive views. The **Village Fair** (777 Bridgeway), just behind the marina, is a four-story former warehouse that has been converted into a warren of clothing, crafts, and gift boutiques. Along the northern shores of Richardson Bay are some of the

400 houseboats that make up Sausalito's famous **"floating-homes community."**

Getting There By car, cross the Golden Gate Bridge and drive north a few miles to the Sausalito exit. **Golden Gate Ferry** (tel. 415/332–6600) and the **Red and White Fleet** (tel. 415/546–2896) cruise regularly from the Embarcadero and Fisherman's Wharf on breathtaking 30-minute trips to (and from) the island.

The Wine Country

California's Napa and Sonoma counties produce some of the world's finest wines. In the Napa Valley, every inch of soil is in the service of one of the 200 local wineries, and traffic on the two-lane stretch of Hwy. 29 from Napa to Calistoga slows to a crawl on weekends, when visitors jam the gift shops and restaurants. In Sonoma County, the pace is less frenetic. The wineries in both counties range from charming and rustic to palatial and high-tech, but the land that surrounds them is consistently lush.

Tourist Information

Napa Valley: Conference and Visitors Bureau (1310 Napa Town Center, 94558, tel. 707/226–7459). **St. Helena:** Chamber of Commerce (1080 Main St., Box 124, 94574, tel. 707/963–4456 or 800/767–8528). **Sonoma County:** Convention and Visitor's Bureau (10 4th St., Suite 100, Santa Rosa 94501, tel. 707/575–1191 or 800/326–7666). Russian River Wine Road (Box 46, Healdsburg 95448, tel. 707/433–6782).

Getting There

By Plane The San Francisco and Oakland airports (*see* San Francisco, *above*), served by most major carriers, are just over an hour's drive away.

By Car Although traffic on the two-lane country roads can be heavy, the best way to get around the Wine Country is by car. There are three major paths through the area: U.S. 101 north from Santa Rosa, Hwys. 12 and 121 through Sonoma County, and Hwy. 29 north from Napa. From San Francisco, cross the Golden Gate Bridge and follow U.S. 101 to Santa Rosa and points north, or take the exit east on Hwy. 37 and north on Hwy. 121 into Sonoma. Another route runs over San Francisco's Bay Bridge and along I–80 to Vallejo, where you can pick up Hwy. 29 to Napa.

By Train The **Wine Train** (tel. 707/253–2111, 800/522–4142, or 800/427–4124 in CA) serves lunch, dinner, and a weekend brunch on a restored Pullman car as it runs between Napa and St. Helena.

By Bus **Greyhound** (tel. 415/558–6789) runs buses from the Transbay Terminal at 1st and Mission streets to Napa, Sonoma, and Santa Rosa. **Sonoma County Area Transit** (tel. 707/585–7516) and **The Vine** (tel. 707/255–7631), Napa's bus service, provide local transportation.

Exploring the Wine Country

Napa Along Hwy. 29 north of the town of **Napa** toward Calistoga are some of California's most important wineries. In Yountville is **Domaine Chandon,** owned by Moët-Hennessey and Louis Vuitton. You can take a tour, or sample flutes of the luxurious sparkling wine, made by the *méthode champenoise,* for $4 a glass. *California Dr., tel. 707/944–2280. Closed Mon.–Tues., Nov.–Apr., holidays.*

Many wineries are between Yountville and St. Helena. At **Robert Mondavi** (7801 St. Helena Hwy., Oakville, tel. 707/963–9611), the 40- to 60-minute tour is encouraged before imbibing. **Christian Brothers Greystone Cellars** (2555 Main St., St. Helena, tel. 707/967–3112) is housed in an imposing 1889 stone building; tours every half hour feature displays on wine-barrel making, and a collection of corkscrews.

Calistoga, at the valley's north end, was founded as a spa and remains notable for its mineral water, hot mineral springs, mud baths, steam baths, and massages. **Dr. Wilkinson's Hot Springs** (1507 Lincoln Ave., tel. 707/942–4102) offers mineral-water showers or whirlpools and a steam room; reservations are recommended.

The **Silverado Trail** runs parallel to Hwy. 29 and, north of Napa, leads to some distinguished wineries: **Clos du Val** (5330 Silverado Trail, tel. 707/252–6711), **Stag's Leap Wine Cellar** (5766 Silverado Trail, tel. 707/944–2020), and, just off the Trail, the **Rutherford Hill Winery** (200 Rutherford Hill Rd., tel. 707/963–7194).

Sonoma East of U.S. 101 and west of the Napa Valley, Hwy. 12 goes through the hills of Sonoma County. In the town of **Sonoma** is the landmark **Buena Vista Winery** (1800 Old Winery Rd., tel. 707/938–1266), where California wine making got its start in 1857. Today the wines are produced elsewhere, but there are tours, a gourmet shop, an art gallery, a wine museum, and great picnic spots.

The wineries off U.S. 101 in Sonoma County are along winding side roads. For a historic overview, start at the imposing **Korbel Champagne Cellars** (13250 River Rd., Guerneville, tel. 707/887–2294), housed in a former railway station. **The Hop Kiln Winery** (6050 Westside Rd., Healdsburg, tel. 707/433–6491) is located in a hops drying barn that dates from the early 1900s. **Lytton Springs Winery** (650 Lytton Springs Rd., Healdsburg, tel. 707/433–7721) produces Sonoma Zinfandel, a dark, fruity wine with a high alcohol content.

What to See and Do with Children

Old Faithful Geyser of California (1299 Tubbs La., 1 mi north of Calistoga, tel. 707/942–6463) is a 60-foot tower of steam and vapor that erupts every 40 minutes or so. At the **Petrified Forest** (4100 Petrified Forest Rd., 5 mi west of Calistoga, tel. 707/942–6667) you'll see the effects of volcanic eruptions from Mt. St. Helena 6 million years ago.

Shopping

Most wineries will ship purchases, but don't expect bargains. Area supermarkets stock a wide selection of local wines at lower prices.

Sports and Outdoor Activities

Hot-air Ballooning This sport has become part of the scenery in the Wine Country. Many hotels arrange excursions, or contact **Balloons Above the Valley** (tel. 707/253–2222) or **Napa Valley Balloons** (tel. 707/253–2224 or 800/944–0228).

Dining and Lodging

For price ranges, see Charts 1 (A) and 2 (A) in Chapter 1.

Calistoga
Dining
Calistoga Inn. With the atmosphere of a village tavern, this restaurant serves nicely prepared California cuisine and excellent fish dishes. *1250 Lincoln Ave., tel. 707/942–4101. Reservations advised. MC, V. Moderate.*

Lodging
Mountain Home Ranch. This rustic ranch, built in 1913, is set on 300 wooded acres, with hiking trails, a creek, and a fishing lake. It has just one TV and no phones. *3400 Mountain Home Ranch Rd., 94515, tel. 707/942–6616; fax 707/942–8091. 6 rooms, 7 cabins. Facilities: 2 pools, tennis. MC, V. Closed Dec.–Jan. Moderate.*

Rutherford
Dining
★
Auberge du Soleil. The dining terrace of this hilltop inn, looking down across groves of olive trees to the Napa Valley vineyards, is the closest you can get to the atmosphere, charm, and cuisine of southern France without a passport. *180 Rutherford Hill Rd., tel. 707/963–1211. Reservations advised. Jacket and tie advised. AE, MC, V. Very Expensive.*

St. Helena
Lodging
Meadowood Resort. Set on 256 wooded acres is this rambling country lodge, with separate 5-suite bungalows and smaller lodges clustered on the hillside. The decor is New England seashore, and some rooms have fireplaces. *900 Meadowood La., 94574, tel. 707/963–3646 or 800/458–8080; fax 707/963–3532. 98 rooms. Facilities: 2 restaurants, 2 pools, golf, wine school. AE, DC, MC, V. Very Expensive.*

Santa Rosa
Dining
★
John Ash & Co. The chef emphasizes presentation, innovation, and freshness and uses mainly seasonal foods grown in Sonoma County. The two-level dining room overlooks vineyards. *4430 Barnes Rd., tel. 707/527–7687. Reservations advised. Jacket advised. AE, MC, V. Closed Mon. Expensive.*

Sonoma
Lodging
Thistle Dew Inn. Half a block from Sonoma Plaza, this Victorian inn features collector-quality Arts and Crafts furnishings and antique quilts. *171 W. Spain St., 95476, tel. 707/938–2909. 6 rooms. AE, MC, V. Expensive.*

Yountville
Dining
★
Mustard's Grill. Grilled fish, hot smoked meats, fresh local produce, and a good wine list are offered in a simple, unassuming dining room. *7399 St. Helena Hwy., tel. 707/944–2424. Reservations essential. MC, V. Expensive.*

Elsewhere in Northern California

The Gold Country

Getting There Sacramento Metropolitan Airport (tel. 916/929–5411) is served by most major domestic airlines. **Greyhound** serves Sacramento, Auburn, Grass Valley, and Placerville from San Francisco. The most convenient way to see the area is by car, since few towns have public transportation. I–80 intersects with Hwy. 49, the main route through the region, at Auburn; U.S. 50 intersects with Hwy. 49 at Placerville.

What to See and Do When gold was discovered at **Coloma** in 1848, people came from everywhere in the world to get some of it, and when the rush was over California was a very different place. Today, clustered along Hwy. 49 are restored villages and ghost towns, antiques shops, crafts stores, and vineyards.

At the northern end of Hwy. 49 is **Downieville,** one of the prettiest of the gold-rush towns; its quiet streets are lined with lovely old houses. Fifty miles south is **Nevada City,** with the 1865 **Nevada Theatre,** California's oldest theater in continuous use. In **Grass Valley** is the **Empire Mine** (10791 E. Empire St., tel. 916/273–8522), now a state park with exhibits on gold mining. The **Marshall Discovery State Historical Park** (tel. 916/622–3470; $5 per car admission), 8 mi north of Placerville on Hwy. 49, has a replica of **Sutter's Mill,** where it all started. At the southern end of Hwy. 49 is **Columbia State Historic Park** (tel. 209/532–4301), where you can ride a stagecoach, pan for gold, or watch a blacksmith working at his anvil.

In **Sacramento,** the state capital and largest city of the Gold Country, the **visitor center** (1104 Front St., tel. 916/442–7644) will key you in to such attractions as the **Sacramento History Museum** (101 I St., tel. 916/264–7057) and the **California State Railroad Museum** (125 I St., tel. 915/448–4466), which displays 21 restored locomotives and railroad cars.

Lake Tahoe

Getting There **Reno Cannon International Airport,** 58 mi northeast of the lake, is used by national and regional airlines (*see* Nevada). **Lake Tahoe Airport** on Hwy. 50, 3 mi south of the lakeshore, is served by American Airlines' **American Eagle.** There is an **Amtrak** station in Truckee. **South Tahoe Area Ground Express** (tel. 916/573–2080) and **Tahoe Area Regional Transit** (tel. 916/581–6365) offer local buses. The 198 mi northeast from San Francisco can be driven in under five hours. The major route is I–80 through the Sierra Nevada; U.S. 50 from Sacramento is the direct route to the south shore. Caution: Tire chains are sometimes necessary in winter.

What to See and Do Visitors to Lake Tahoe's California side, where gambling isn't legal, come to ski, hike, fish, camp, and boat in the spectacular mountains 6,000 feet above sea level in the High Sierra. Ski resorts, such as Incline Village and Squaw Valley, open at the end of November and operate as late as May, when the **U.S. Forest Service Visitors Center** (tel. 916/573–2674) opens on the south shore. Tourist information is also provided at the **Lake Tahoe Visitors Authority** (tel. 916/544–5050).

The 72-mi shoreline is best seen along a route through wooded flatlands and past beaches, climbing to vistas on the rugged west side of the lake. It should take about three hours but can be slow going in summer and on holiday weekends.

Past South Lake Tahoe, where the shore route becomes Hwy. 89, is the **Pope-Baldwin Recreation Area** (tel. 916/541–5227), where three grand century-old mansions are open to the public. The **Lake Tahoe Visitors Center** (tel. 916/573–2564) on Taylor Creek is also near the site of a onetime Washoe Indian settlement, and there are trails through meadow, marsh, and forest. **Emerald Bay** is famed for its jewellike shape and color. *The Tahoe Queen* (tel. 916/541–3364), a glass-bottom sternwheeler, cruises on the lake and visits Emerald Bay year-round from Ski Run marina, off U.S. 50 in South Lake Tahoe. Beyond Emerald Bay is **D. L. Bliss State Park** (tel. 916/525–7277), with 6 mi of shorefront and 268 family campsites. At Tahoe City, Hwy. 89 turns north to **Squaw Valley**, site of the 1960 Winter Olympics.

The Central Coast

From San Francisco south for several hundred miles, the California coastline shows off its beauty and power. Raging surf splashing rugged rocks, hidden tidal pools, and wind-warped trees mark the journey. Several towns provide entertainment, but the Pacific Ocean dominates. Coast-hugging Hwy. 1, sometimes precariously narrow, is the route of choice; it's slow and winding, but the surpassingly beautiful views make considerations of time seem unimportant.

Tourist Information

Monterey Peninsula: Chamber of Commerce (Box 1770, 380 Alvarado St., Monterey 93942, tel. 408/649–1770). Visitor Information Center (1 Santa Barbara St. at Cabrillo Blvd., Santa Barbara, tel. 805/965–3021).

Getting There

By Plane   **Monterey Peninsula Airport** (tel. 408/373–3731) and **Santa Barbara Municipal Airport** (tel. 805/683–4011) are served by regional airlines such as American Eagle, United Express, and Skywest.

By Train   **Amtrak**'s *Coast Starlight* makes stops in Santa Barbara, San Luis Obispo, and Salinas on its run from Los Angeles to Seattle.

By Car   Driving Hwy. 1 along the coast offers the richest rewards. U.S. 101 can be taken to Salinas, from which Hwy. 68 goes to Monterey. From San Francisco, I–280 connects with Hwy. 17 just south of San Jose and gets you to the coast near Santa Cruz.

Exploring the Central Coast

As you pick up Hwy. 1 heading south out of San Francisco, you'll be driving a clifftop past long beaches and coves on your right and artichoke and pumpkin fields on your left. About 75 mi south of the city is the seaside and college town of **Santa Cruz,** with an old-time boardwalk and an amusement park where one of the last clackety wooden roller coasters still dips and dives.

About an hour south of Santa Cruz, the Monterey Peninsula curves into the Pacific, with seaside forests of gnarled Monterey cypress. The town of **Monterey** is rich in California history. Its "Path of History" is a 2-mi self-guided tour through **Monterey State Historic Park** (tel. 408/649–7118). **Custom House,** built by the Mexican government in 1827 and believed to be the oldest government building west of the Rockies, is a logical starting place. The next stop along the path is the **Pacific House** (tel. 408/649–2907), a former hotel and saloon that is now a museum of early California life displaying gold-rush relics, historic photographs, and a costume gallery.

Inevitably, visitors are drawn toward Monterey's waterfront, if only because of the barking of sea lions. They're best seen along **Fisherman's Wharf,** an aging and touristy pier that children enjoy. From the wharf, a footpath leads to **Cannery Row,** where the old tin-roof canneries made famous by John Steinbeck's book have been converted into restaurants, art galleries, and minimalls. The **Monterey Bay Aquarium** (886 Cannery Row, tel. 408/649–6466) is a window on the sea waters beyond. Among standout exhibits are a three-story Kelp Forest, a bat-ray petting pool, a 55,000-gallon sea-otter tank, and an enormous outdoor artificial tide pool.

The celebrated **17-Mile Drive** offers a chance to explore an 8,400-acre microcosm of the coastal landscape around Monterey and neighboring Carmel. This is where you'll find the **Lone Cypress,** a weather-sculpted tree on a rocky outcrop above the waves. On **Seal Rock** and **Bird Rock,** just offshore, you can watch the creatures sunning themselves en masse. Also along the drive is the famous **Pebble Beach Golf Links.**

Carmel is a quaint village where buildings have no street numbers and live music is banned in the local watering holes. Before it became an art colony in the early 20th century and long before it became a shopping mecca, Carmel was an important religious center for Spanish California. Mission San Carlos Borromeo del Rio Carmelo, or the **Carmel Mission** (Rio Rd. and Lasuen Dr., tel. 408/624–3600), was founded in 1770 and served as headquarters for the mission system. Its stone buildings and tower dome have been beautifully restored, and a tranquil garden is nearby. Another example of Carmel's architectural heritage is the poet Robinson Jeffers's wondrous **Tor House** (26304 Ocean View Ave., tel. 408/624–1813). The stone cottage is handmade, as is the abutting Hawk tower, set with stones from the Great Wall of China and a Roman villa. The town's greatest beauty is in the rugged coastline and surrounding cypress forests, best seen at **Carmel River State Park** (off Scenic Rd., south of Carmel Beach, tel. 408/649–2836) and the larger **Point Lobos State Preserve** (tel. 408/624–4909), a 1,250-acre headland just south of Carmel. At the latter, the Sea Lion Point Trail lets you observe sea lions, otters, harbor seals, and seasonally migrating whales.

Another sort of migration takes place in the adjacent town of **Pacific Grove,** where each year (Oct.–Mar.) thousands of orange-and-black monarch butterflies take up residence in the pine and eucalyptus groves and hang from branches like fluttering veils.

Travel 13 mi south from Carmel for the quintessential view of California's coast from the elegant concrete arch of **Bixby Creek Bridge.** Just south of it, the **Point Sur Light Station,** atop a sandstone cliff, heralds the beginning of **Big Sur.** One of the few places where you can actually reach the water is at **Pfeiffer Beach** (follow the road just past the Big Sur Ranger Station for 2 mi); at the foot of the cliffs are huge, picturesque sea-washed rocks, one with a hole cut through it by the waves. On the ocean side of Hwy. 1, set high above the waves, is the restaurant **Nepenthe** (*see* Dining and Lodging, *below*). A few miles south, at the **Julia Pfeiffer Burns State Park** (tel. 408/667–2315), a trail leads up a small valley to a waterfall; the park also offers picnic and camping areas, as well as beach access.

About 30 mi south on Hwy. 1, the **San Simeon State Historical Monument,** or Hearst Castle, reigns in solitary splendor. Buses herd you up the hill, past grazing zebras (descendants of those in Hearst's private zoo), to newspaper magnate William Randolph Hearst's grandiose mansion, which has extravagant marble halls, lush swimming pools, and an extensive art collection. Begun in 1919 and never officially completed after work stopped in 1947, this grand place was meant not only as a residence but as a showcase for Hearst's magnificent collection of European art and antiquities. It will give you a new definition of the word *opulence. Reservations usually required: tel. 805/ 927–2020 or 800/444–7275. Admission: $14 adults, $8 children, plus $1.80 booking charge. Tours daily 8:20 AM–3 PM (later in summer). Closed Thanksgiving, Christmas, New Year's Day.*

The coastal ribbon of Hwy. 1 ends at **Morro Bay. Morro Rock,** with the sheltered harbor on one side and the Pacific surf on the other, is a preserve for peregrine falcons. At **San Luis Obispo,** just south, halfway between San Francisco and Los Angeles, are such historic sites as the 1772 **Mission San Luis Obispo de Tolosa** (tel. 805/543–6850) downtown. Drop by the garish, goofy **Madonna Inn** (100 Madonna Rd., off U.S. 101, tel. 805/ 543–3000) if only for a drink and a look at the bar's gilt cherubs and pink bar stools.

Santa Barbara has long been a weekend getaway and second-home retreat for the wealthy and celebrated from Los Angeles. Nestled between the hills and the ocean, the town is blessed with a temperate climate, is bursting with flowers, and seems like the most relaxed place in the world. It also retains its Spanish character, with wide tree-shaded streets, red-tile-roofed arcades downtown, and courtyards filled with upscale boutiques and restaurants. The landmark **Santa Barbara Mission** (Laguna St., tel. 805/682–4713), which inspired much of the downtown architecture, is set in the hills above town. Downtown are the Spanish-Moorish–style **Courthouse** (Anacapa St., tel. 805/962–6464), adorned with scenic murals from Hollywood's heyday; the Spanish-style **Public Library;** the **Santa Barbara Museum of Art** (1130 State St., tel. 805/963–4364), whose collections include Greek and Roman antiquities and paintings by Grandma Moses; **El Presidio State Historic Park** (123 E. Cañon Perdido St., tel. 805/966–9719), a military stronghold built by the Spanish in 1782; and **El Paseo,** a shopping arcade built around an old adobe home. Along the water-

front, not far from downtown, is **Stearns Wharf** (Cabrillo Blvd.
at State St.), a pier holding shops, eateries, and the Museum of
Natural History's **Sea Center,** which features a display of marine life. Also in Santa Barbara is the **Botanic Garden** (1212
Mission Canyon Rd., tel. 805/682–4726), just north of town,
with 60 acres of native plants.

What to See and Do with Children

The **Monterey Bay Aquarium** (*see* Exploring the Central Coast,
above) will entertain most children, as will the **boardwalk and
amusement park** in Santa Cruz. The **Santa Barbara Zoo** (500
Niños Dr., tel. 805/962–6310) has a scenic railroad and a barn-
yard petting zoo. At Santa Barbara's East Beach is an elaborate **jungle-gym play area.**

Shopping

In Monterey and Carmel you'll find many art galleries and
shops selling arts and crafts by local artists. Among the artists
whose work is shown at **Photography West Gallery** (Ocean Ave.
and Dolores St., Carmel, tel. 408/625–1587) is Ansel Adams,
who resided nearby for many years. In Santa Barbara, the **El
Paseo** shopping arcade houses some 32 galleries and shops, and
a dozen or more antiques and gift shops are clustered in Victorian buildings on **Brinkerhoff Avenue.**

Sports and Outdoor Activities

Biking The Monterey Peninsula is prime biking territory, with paths
following some of the choicest parts of the shoreline; rentals are
available from **Bay Bikes** (640 Wave St., Monterey, tel. 408/
646–9090). In Santa Barbara, the **Cabrillo Bike Lane** passes the
city zoo, a bird refuge, beaches, and the harbor; rent bikes from
Beach Rentals (8 W. Cabrillo Blvd., tel. 805/963–2524).

Fishing Charter boats leave from Monterey, Morro Bay, and Santa
Barbara. Most fishing trips—from such outfits as **Monterey
Sport Fishing** (96 Fisherman's Wharf, Monterey, tel. 408/372–
2203) or **SEA Landing** (Cabrillo Blvd. at Bath, Santa Barbara,
tel. 805/963–3564)—include equipment rental, bait, fish clean-
ing, and a one-day license.

Golf **Pebble Beach Golf Links** (17-Mile Dr., tel. 408/625–8518; reservations essential), with its sweeping ocean views, is one of the
world's most famous courses. At nearby **Spyglass Hill** (Spyglass
Hill Rd., tel. 408/624–3811), the holes are unforgiving, but the
views offer consolation. In Santa Barbara are the **Santa
Barbara Golf Club** (Las Positas Rd. and McCaw Ave., tel. 805/
687–7087) and **Sandpiper Golf Course** (7925 Hollister Ave.,
Goleta, tel. 805/968–1541).

Whale-watching On their annual migration between the Bering Sea and Baja
California, 45-foot gray whales can be spotted at many points
not far off the coast. The migration south takes place from December through February; the journey north, from late February to mid-May.

Beaches

In general, the shoreline north of San Luis Obispo is rocky and backed by cliffs, the water rough and often cold, and sunbathing limited to only the warmest hours of the early afternoon. Still, the boardwalk at **Santa Cruz, Point Lobos State Preserve** in lower Monterey Bay, **Big Sur,** and **Morro Bay** provide unparalleled beach experiences. **Pismo Beach** marks the first of the classic southern California beaches, with long, low stretches of sand. The shoreline from **Point Concepcion** down through Santa Barbara and into Ventura County contains some of the best beaches anywhere.

Near Santa Barbara, **East Beach** has lifeguards, volleyball courts, a jogging-and-biking trail, a jungle-gym play area, and a bathhouse with a gym, showers, and changing rooms. **Arroyo Burro Beach,** just west of Santa Barbara, is a state preserve, with a small grassy area with picnic tables and sandy beaches below the cliffs. West of Santa Barbara on Hwy. 1 are **El Capitan, Refugio,** and **Gaviota** state beaches, each with campsites, picnic tables, and fire pits. East of the city is the state beach at **Carpenteria,** a sheltered, sunny, and often crowded beach.

Dining and Lodging

For price ranges, see Charts 1 (B) and 2 (B) in Chapter 1.

Big Sur
Dining

Nepenthe. The 800-foot-high cliff site, overlooking lush meadows and the ocean, was once owned by Orson Welles. The food is adequate—from roast chicken with sage to sandwiches and hamburgers—but it's the location that warrants a stop. *Hwy. 1, south end of town, tel. 408/667–2345. Reservations for large parties only. AE, MC, V. Moderate.*

Lodging
★

Ventana Inn. Here you'll find California chic: restful *and* hip. The 12 cottagelike buildings are scattered in clusters on a hillside above the Pacific. Rooms are country-style, with quilts, natural wood interiors, and tile floors. Rates include Continental breakfast and afternoon wine and cheese. *Hwy. 1, 93920, tel. 408/667–2331; fax 408/667–2419. 59 rooms. Facilities: restaurant, 2 pools, spa. Minimum stay 2 nights on weekends, 3 on holidays. AE, D, DC, MC, V. Expensive.*

Big Sur Lodge. This lodge within Pfeiffer Big Sur State Park is the best place in Big Sur for families. Motel-style cottages—some with fireplaces or kitchens—are set around a meadow surrounded by redwood and oak trees. *Hwy. 1, Box 190, 93920, tel. 408/667–2171. 61 rooms. Facilities: pool, sauna. MC, V. Moderate.*

Cambria
Dining
★

The Hamlet at Moonstone Gardens. This patio in the middle of a plant nursery is perfect for lunch. An upstairs dining room overlooks the Pacific and the gardens. The fish of the day comes poached in white wine; other entrées range from hamburgers to rack of lamb. The extensive cellar has offerings from more than 50 wineries. *Hwy. 1, east side, tel. 805/927–3535. Reservations advised Fri.–Sun. MC, V. Closed Dec. Moderate.*

Carmel
Dining

Crème Carmel. This bright and airy small restaurant has a California-French menu that changes seasonally. Specialties include breast of duck with mushrooms and Zinfandel sauce and beef tenderloin with cabernet. A tasting menu is offered. *San*

Carlos St., near 7th Ave., tel. 408/624–0444. Reservations advised. AE, DC, MC, V. No lunch. Expensive.

Lodging **Highlands Inn.** The hotel's setting, on high cliffs above the Pa-
★ cific, gives it outstanding views in a region famous for them.
The plush condominium-style units feature wood-burning fireplaces and ocean-view decks; some have spa tubs and full kitchens. *Hwy. 1, Box 1700, 93921, tel. 408/624–3801, 800/538–9525,
or 800/682–4811 in CA; fax 408/626–1574. 142 rooms. Facilities: 2 restaurants, pool, entertainment. AE, D, DC, MC, V.
Expensive.*

Monterey **Fresh Cream.** Nine out of 10 locals' favorite spot for light, imag-
Dining inative California cuisine, this charming little restaurant in
★ Heritage Harbor serves such dishes as squab and quail from
nearby farms. *100 Pacific St., tel. 408/375–9798. Reservations
advised. AE, DC, MC, V. No lunch; closed Mon. Expensive.*
The Fishery. A mixture of Asian and Continental influences
characterizes both food and decor. Specialties include broiled
swordfish with saffron butter and fresh Hawaiian tuna
teriyaki. *21 Soledad Dr., tel. 408/373–6200. MC, V. No lunch;
closed Sun.–Mon. Moderate.*

Morro Bay **Margie's Diner.** This mom-and-pop diner-café serves generous
Dining portions of all-American favorites: ham or steak and eggs, omelets, chili, burgers, hot and cold sandwiches, fried chicken
steak, and deep-dish apple pie. The milkshakes are terrific.
*1698 N. Main St., tel. 805/772–2510. No credit cards. Inexpen-
sive.*

Pacific Grove **Asilomar Conference Center.** This camplike assortment of 28
Dining and Lodging rustic lodges sits in a 100-acre state park across from the beach.
★ The all-American menu features beef, chicken, and steak. Res-
ervations should be made at least a month in advance. *800
Asilomar Blvd., Box 537, 93950, tel. 408/372–8016. 313 rooms.
Facilities: restaurant, pool. No credit cards. Moderate.*

San Simeon **San Simeon Restaurant.** The imitation Greek columns, statues,
Dining and tapestries in the ocean-view dining room here are reminders of your proximity to Hearst Castle. The menu is standard
American; prime rib is the big draw. *Hwy. 1, east side, tel. 805/
927–4604. Reservations advised in summer. AE, MC, V. Moderate.*

Santa Barbara **Michael's Waterside.** Set in a Victorian house, Michael's serves
Dining haute-California cuisine, which is to say snazzier and more
★ elaborate dishes than what you might expect: mushroom
mousse with escargot, Gruyère soufflé, baked king salmon,
Santa Barbara prawns. Desserts are luscious and rich. *50 Los
Patos Way, tel. 805/969–0307. Reservations required. Jacket
and tie required. AE, DC, MC, V. No lunch (except Sun.
brunch); closed Mon.–Tues. Expensive.*
The Harbor Restaurant. Locals take out-of-town guests here
for fresh seafood; there's always catch of the day and Maine lobster. The lovely seascape makes the place especially pleasant
for breakfast or lunch. You can eat in the rather dressy Santa
Barbara Room (jacket required), in the more casual
Longboard's Bar and Grill upstairs, or on the grill's outdoor patio. *210 Stearns Wharf, tel. 805/963–3311. AE, MC, V. Moderate.*
East Beach Grill. The waves break right at the doorstep of this
outdoor café on the beach. A step above the usual beach stand,
it offers table service and real plates and cutlery. Basic break-

fast fare is followed by hot dogs and burgers for lunch. *At the Cabrillo Bath House, East Beach, tel. 805/965–8805. No credit cards. No dinner. Inexpensive.*

Lodging **Fess Parker's Red Lion Resort.** This sprawling waterfront complex has a lavishly appointed lobby, as well as spacious rooms—all with either private patio or balcony and many with ocean views. *633 E. Cabrillo Blvd., 93103, tel. 805/564–4333 or 800/ 879–2929; fax 805/564–4964. 360 rooms. Facilities: 2 restaurants, pool, tennis, health facilities. AE, D, DC, MC, V. Expensive.*

Four Seasons Biltmore. Muted pastels and bleached woods give the cabanas a light, airy touch while maintaining the main hotel building's reputation for understated elegance. This grande dame of Santa Barbara hostelries—more formal than other city accommodations, with lush gardens and palm trees galore—is a favorite hangout of local and visiting high society. *1260 Channel Dr., 93108, tel. 805/969–2261; fax 805/969–5715. 170 rooms, 12 cottages (4–6 rooms in each). Facilities: 2 restaurants, 2 pools, 2 health clubs, tennis courts. AE, DC, MC, V. Expensive.*

Ambassador by the Sea. Near the harbor and Stearns Wharf, this place has a real California beach feel. Sun decks overlook the ocean and bike path. *202 W. Cabrillo Blvd., 93101, tel. 805/ 965–4577; fax 805/965–9937. 32 rooms, 2 with kitchenettes. Facilities: pool. AE, D, DC, MC, V. Moderate.*

Pacific Crest Inn. A block from East Beach, this motel has clean and comfortable rooms, some with kitchens. *433 Corona Del Mar Dr., 93103, tel. 805/966–3103. 26 rooms. Facilities: laundromat. AE, D, DC, MC, V. Moderate.*

Motel 6. Low price and great location near the beach are the pluses for this no-frills place. Reserve well in advance all year. *443 Corona Del Mar Dr., 93103, tel. 805/564–1392 or 505/891– 6161. 52 rooms. Facilities: heated pool. AE, D, DC, MC, V. Inexpensive.*

The Arts

The famous **Monterey Jazz Festival** (Box JAZZ, Monterey 93942, tel. 408/373–3366) is a weekend of top jazz and blues in September; the **Monterey Bay Blues Festival** (tel. 408/394–2652) is in June. The **Arlington Theater** (tel. 805/963–4408) is home to the Santa Barbara Symphony.

Los Angeles

Los Angeles is a wholly 20th-century city, created, defined, dependent upon, and thrust into prominence only by the advances of the modern age: automobiles, airplanes, and the movies. It is a center of power and wealth, where the arts flourish and the rich and celebrated make their homes. Also a landing place for hundreds of thousands of immigrants, it is among the most ethnically diverse cities in the nation, with thriving Hispanic, Korean, Chinese, Japanese, and Middle Eastern cultures.

Tourist Information

Los Angeles: Visitors and Convention Bureau (633 W. 5th St., Suite 6000, 90071, tel. 213/624–7300).

Arriving and Departing

By Plane **Los Angeles International Airport** (LAX; tel. 310/646–5252), about 25 mi west of downtown and 10 mi from Beverly Hills, is served by most major airlines. Four smaller regional airports, in **Burbank, Long Beach, Orange County,** and **Ontario,** also serve the greater Los Angeles area. Taxis to downtown cost about $24 (request a flat fee—metered fares are more) and take 20–60 minutes, depending on traffic. The **SuperShuttle** (tel. 310/417–8988, 310/338–1111 for airport pickup) can get you from the airport to any of several downtown locations for about $12. **L.A. Top Shuttle** (tel. 310/670–6666) features door-to-door service from LAX to downtown hotels and Disneyland for $10.

By Car I–5 (called the Golden State or Santa Ana Freeway here) runs north–south. I–10 (Santa Monica Freeway) heads east cross-country. I–15 comes into the area from the northeast.

Train Station **Amtrak** serves Los Angeles's **Union Station** (800 N. Alameda St., tel. 213/624–6987).

Bus Station **Greyhound** (208 E. 6th St., tel. 213/620–1200).

Getting Around Los Angeles

Los Angeles was designed to be traversed by car. Freeways, whose names can change along the route, are the most efficient way to get from one end of the city to another.

By Public Transportation The **Southern California Metropolitan Transit Authority** (MTA; tel. 213/626–4455; fare $1.10) provides infrequent bus service and is expanding with the Blue Line, a commuter line that runs 22 mi between downtown and Long Beach, 5 AM to 10:15 PM daily, and the Red Line, a subway line still under construction that has 4.4 mi open between Union Station and MacArthur Park, 4:30 AM to 6:50 PM daily. **DASH** (Downtown Area Short Hop; tel. 213/689–8822) is a system of minibuses that serve the downtown area.

By Taxi Cabs must be ordered by phone, from such companies as **Independent Cab. Co.** (tel. 213/385–8294 or 213/385–8294) and **United Independent Taxi** (tel. 213/653–5050). The metered rate is $1.60 per mile.

Orientation Tours

Gray Line (1207 W. 3rd St., 90017, tel. 213/933–1475) offers tours to Disneyland, Universal Studios, the *Queen Mary*, Santa Catalina Island, and other attractions.

Exploring Los Angeles

Los Angeles is best approached as clusters of destinations, each to be explored separately.

Downtown Los Angeles Downtown's historic and ethnic neighborhoods can be explored on foot or by DASH minibuses. John Portman's 1974 **Westin Bonaventure Hotel** (404 S. Figueroa St., tel. 213/624–1000) projects five shimmering cylinders 35 stories into the sky, crowned by a revolving rooftop bar. Pyramidal skylights mark the **Museum of Contemporary Art** (250 S. Grand Ave., tel. 213/626–6222; admission charged), whose permanent collection in-

Los Angeles

TO VALENCIA

SAN FERNANDO

Foothill Fwy.

Hansen Dam Park

118

27

Topanga Canyon Blvd.

CANOGA PARK

RESEDA

Ventura Fwy

101

Sepulveda Dam Recreation Area

170

VAN NUYS

NORTH HOLLYWOOD

BURBANK

GLENDALE

Golden State Fwy.

210

5

SHERMAN OAKS

Mulholland Dr.

134

Universal Studios

Griffith Park

5

SANTA MONICA MTS.

Topanga State Park

405

101

Hollywood Bowl

Mann's Chinese Theater

WEST HOLLYWOOD

Santa Monica Blvd.

HOLLYWOOD

Dodger Stadium

27

Will Rogers State Historical Park

Sunset Blvd.

UCLA

BEVERLY HILLS

Rodeo Dr.

2

El Pueblo State Historic Park

Wilshire Blvd.

Museum of Contemporary Art

LAS FLORES

J. Paul Getty Museum

WESTWOOD

Santa Monica Blvd.

Los Angeles County Museum of Art

La Brea Tar Pits

Santa Monica Fwy.

10

1

← TO MALIBU

TOPANGA BEACH

San Diego Fwy.

Santa Monica Fwy.

La Cienega Blvd.

Exposition Park

SANTA MONICA

1

CULVER CITY

Museum of African American Art

Slauson Ave.

VENICE

MARINA DEL REY

Blvd.

INGLEWOOD

42

Los Angeles International Airport

Imperial Hwy.

Hawthorne Blvd.

Western Ave.

Harbor Fwy.

PACIFIC OCEAN

EL SEGUNDO

1

405

Sepulveda

MANHATTAN BEACH

HERMOSA BEACH

91

San Diego

REDONDO BEACH

Pacific

Coast Hwy.

TORRANCE

110

1

N

PALOS VERDES ESTATES

RANCHO PALOS VERDES

SAN PEDRO

0   5 miles

0   5 km

cludes works from the 1940s to the present; artists represented include Mark Rothko, Franz Kline, and Susan Rothenberg.

On weekends especially, **Chinatown's** colorful shops, exotic markets, and restaurants attract crowds of Asian shoppers. The southern edge of Chinatown merges with downtown Los Angeles's Spanish and Mexican history. The historic buildings of **El Pueblo State Historic Park** (visitor center, Sepulveda House, 622 N. Main St., tel. 213/628–1274) celebrate the birthplace of Los Angeles (no one knows exactly where the original 1781 settlement was). Fiestas are held nearly every weekend on **Olvera Street,** a Mexican-style marketplace with shops, stalls, restaurants, and the oldest downtown building (1818).

South of Olvera Street is the **Civic Center,** where **City Hall** (200 N. Spring St.) is recognizable from its roles as a backdrop on "Dragnet." South of the Civic Center, along 1st and San Pedro streets, stretches **Little Tokyo,** with Japanese shops, restaurants, and sushi bars. The **Japanese American Cultural and Community Center** (244 San Pedro St., tel. 213/628–2725) presents exhibits, theater, and concerts.

Amid shops and sidewalk vendors along Broadway catering to Hispanics, **Grand Central Market** (317 S. Broadway) has exotic produce, herbs, and meats. In contrast, the gentrified Victorian-era **Bradbury Building** (304 S. Broadway, tel. 213/626–1893) has a filigreed, glassed-in courtyard and open balconies.

In South-Central Los Angeles is **Exposition Park** (Figueroa St. at Exposition Blvd.), home of the **Memorial Coliseum,** the **Sports Arena,** and the **Swim Stadium** that were used in the 1984 Olympics, as well as two impressive museums: the **California Museum of Science and Industry** (tel. 213/744–7400; admission free) and the **Natural History Museum** (tel. 213/744–3466; admission charged).

Hollywood The cradle of the movie industry, Hollywood is rife with landmarks of its glamorous past. The **Capitol Records Building** (1756 N. Vine St.) was built in 1956 to resemble a stack of records. **The Palace** (1735 N. Vine St., tel. 213/467–4571) opened as the Hollywood Playhouse in 1927 and for years presented vaudeville shows; later a TV studio, it now hosts rock concerts and TV specials. The art deco **Pantages Theater** (6233 Hollywood Blvd.), originally a movie house, hosted the Oscars in the 1950s and now features traveling musicals. **Frederick's of Hollywood** (6608 Hollywood Blvd., tel. 213/466–8506) is the famous name in risqué lingerie, and also features a bra museum. **Mann's Chinese Theater** (6925 Hollywood Blvd., tel. 213/464–8111), originally Graumann's Chinese, invented the gala premier; its famous courtyard holds the footprints of more than 160 movie celebrities.

The **Hollywood Walk of Fame** immortalizes the names of movie and other greats on brass plaques embedded in pink stars along the city's sidewalks. Since the first stars were installed in 1960, nearly 2,000 have been added. Marlon Brando is at 1765 Vine Street, Clark Gable at 1608 Vine, John Wayne at 1541 Vine, and Marilyn Monroe at 6774 Hollywood Boulevard.

Five miles north of Hollywood, in the San Fernando Valley, off U.S. 101 (the Hollywood Freeway), **Universal Studios** shows off the (glamorized) inner workings of the film industry in its tremendously popular five- to seven-hour tram tours of the backlot, featuring special effects and stage shows. *100 Universal Pl., Universal City, tel. 818/508–9600. Admission: $26 adults, $20 children. AE, MC, V.*

Not far away, at **Burbank Studios,** you can observe the day-to-day action of movie making on a two-hour walking tour of whatever is being filmed at the time. *400 Warner Blvd., Burbank, tel. 818/954–1008. Admission: $25, no children under 10. Reserve 1 week in advance. Tours at 10 and 2. MC, V.*

Wilshire Boulevard Along 16-mi Wilshire Boulevard are many of the city's best museums and tallest office buildings, the heart of Beverly Hills and the opulent Westside, and the seaside cliffs of Santa Monica. Hispanic, Filipino, Korean, and Middle Eastern communities occupy the side streets from the Harbor Freeway west to Fairfax Avenue.

Some of the city's finer art deco architecture is preserved in such buildings as the recently restored **Wiltern Center,** a block-size building that now houses the **I. Magnin** department store (3050 Wilshire Blvd., tel. 213/382–6161) and the **Wiltern Theater** (corner of Western Ave., tel. 213/380–5005).

Hancock Park (Wilshire Blvd. at Curson Ave.) is built atop the **La Brea Tar Pits,** from which over 100 tons of fossils have been removed. Many are on view next door at the **George C. Page Museum** (5801 Wilshire Blvd., tel. 213/936–2230; admission charged). Also in the park is the **Los Angeles County Museum of Art** (5905 Wilshire Blvd., tel. 213/857–6111; admission charged), containing collections of paintings and decorative arts, a sculpture garden, and Japanese art. North of Hancock Park is the **Farmer's Market** (6333 W. 3rd St., tel. 213/933–9211), a partly covered marketplace, with vendors selling exotic and high-priced produce, food stalls, and a few boutiques.

The Westside L.A.'s Westside—encompassing West Hollywood, Beverly Hills, Bel Air, and UCLA—epitomizes what most people think of as the southern California good life: palatial hilltop homes, chic shops, and star-studded restaurants. **West Hollywood** is trendy, stylish, and home to both the bizarre and the beautiful. **Melrose Avenue** is a test kitchen for the avant-garde in quirky shops and a clutch of great eateries offering Thai, Mexican, yogurt, or burgers and fries. **Sunset Strip**—the stretch of Sunset Boulevard through West Hollywood—became a movie-star stomping ground in the 1930s, headquarters to the suave TV detectives of "77 Sunset Strip" in the 1950s, and today the center of a lively rock club scene. **Spago** (*see* Dining, *below*), the reigning champion of celebrity hangouts, is just off Sunset on Horn Avenue.

As it runs through **Beverly Hills,** Sunset Boulevard becomes a broad, tree-shaded avenue, with immaculately manicured lawns fronting mansions of every conceivable style. Perfectly coiffed and clad shoppers stroll among the chic shops of Rodeo, Camden, and Beverly drives. **Westwood,** home to the **University of California at Los Angeles,** straddles the hillsides between Wilshire and Sunset boulevards west of Beverly Hills. UCLA offers walking tours of the campus (tel. 310/206–8147), and on weekends the surrounding area offers lively nightlife.

Santa Monica and Wilshire Boulevard ends at Ocean Avenue in **Santa Monica,** a **the Beach Cities** mix of senior citizens, Yuppies, and the contingent of homeless people who hang out at **Palisades Park,** a palm-shaded stretch of green atop the cliffs above the beach. All are attracted to the **Santa Monica Pier** (tel. 310/394–7554), with its 46-horse antique carousel, gift shops, arcade, cafés, and psychic adviser.

To the south is **Venice,** known for the active scene on **Ocean Front Walk** and the **Venice Boardwalk.** Whatever the next craze in fashion or free time, you'll see it here first, along with street vendors and musicians and Californians seriously at play: rollerskating, pumping iron, playing volleyball, and tanning. Just south of Venice is **Marina del Rey,** the world's largest man-made small-boat harbor.

North from Santa Monica along the Pacific Coast Highway is **Malibu,** the beachfront home to many stars. The **J. Paul Getty Museum** (17985 Pacific Coast Hwy., tel. 310/394–7554) houses a collection of Greek and Roman antiquities, and paintings from the 13th to the 19th century. Admission is free, but parking reservations are required.

Long Beach To the south, in Long Beach, is the *Queen Mary* (Pier J, tel. 310/435–3511; admission charged). The famous ocean liner now houses shops and restaurants.

Pasadena The communities northeast of downtown L.A. were the first suburbs of the city, established by wealthy Angelenos in the 1880s. In **Highland Park** is the **Southwest Museum** (234 Museum Dr., tel. 213/221–2163; admission charged), with a collection of Native American art and artifacts. In **San Marino** is the **Huntington Library, Art Gallery and Botanical Gardens** (Oxford Rd., tel. 818/405–2100; donations), spread over 130 hilly acres. The complex's collections number more than 6 million items, including the Dead Sea Scrolls and the famous pair of English Romantic portraits known as *Blue Boy* and *Pinkie.*

In **Pasadena,** the **Norton Simon Museum** (411 W. Colorado Blvd., tel. 818/449–6840; admission charged) houses Impressionist paintings. The **Rose Bowl** (991 Rosemont Ave.) is the home of the New Year's Day game, as well as of the UCLA Bruins. Nearby **Gamble House** (4 Westmoreland Pl., tel. 818/793–3334; admission charged) is the ultimate in California Craftsman–style architecture.

In the Vicinity **Santa Catalina Island,** 26 mi offshore, is a good day trip or weekend getaway from L.A. From San Pedro and Long Beach, **Catalina Express** (tel. 310/519–1212) provides boat service and **Island Express** (tel. 310/491–5550) offers helicopter service. No private cars are permitted on the island (golf carts can be rented), but the main town of Avalon is easily explored on foot. The rest of the island is made up of rolling hills (on which buffalo roam), secluded beaches, and nature preserves. **Santa Catalina Island Co.** (tel. 310/510–2000 or 800/428–2566) offers escorted bus tours of the interior, coastal cruises, and glass-bottom-boat rides.

Parks and Gardens

Griffith Park (junction of Ventura and Golden State Fwys., tel. 213/666–4090) has acres of picnic areas, hiking and bridle trails, a carousel, and pony rides. Also in the park are the **Los Angeles Zoo** (tel. 213/666–4090), one of the major zoos in the United States, and noted for its breeding in captivity of endangered species, such as the California condor; **Travel Town** (5200 Zoo Dr., tel. 213/662–5874), with railcars, planes, and classic cars; and the **Planetarium and Observatory** (Los Feliz Blvd. and Vermont Ave., tel. 213/664–1191), offering planetarium and Laserium shows and an expansive view of the city below.

What to See and Do with Children

In Valencia, **Six Flags Magic Mountain** offers shows and 260 acres of rides, including the world's largest looping roller coaster and a simulated white-water wilderness adventure. *26101 Magic Mountain Pkwy., tel. 818/992–0884. Admission: $26 adults, $15 children. Hours vary seasonally.*

In San Pedro, the **Cabrillo Marine Museum** (3720 Stephen White Dr., tel. 310/548–7546) has seaquariums, a see-through tidal tank, and a touch tank. (*See also* Parks and Gardens, *above.*)

Shopping

You can find anything you want in Los Angeles's shops: brand names in department stores in any mall; one-of-a-kind items along Melrose Avenue; pricey designer originals on Rodeo Drive; art in galleries on La Cienega Boulevard; specialty foods at ethnic neighborhood shops and the Farmer's Market (*see* Exploring Los Angeles, *above*).

Shopping Districts **Rodeo Drive** in Beverly Hills is the world-famous street with such pricey shops as **Fred Hayman** (273 N. Rodeo Dr., tel. 310/271–3000) for designer men's and women's fashions; or **Bijan** (420 N. Rodeo Dr., tel. 310/273–6544), where you shop by appointment for designer men's fashions. The **Cooper Building** (860 S. Los Angeles St., tel. 213/622–1139) in downtown L.A. contains 82 discount outlet shops. For vintage styles or the weird, go to **Melrose Avenue** between La Brea and Crescent Heights. The stylish **Beverly Center** (Beverly Blvd. at La Cienega Blvd.) has more than 200 upscale stores and boutiques. **Santa Monica Promenade** and **Montana Avenue** feature boutique after boutique of quality goods.

Department Stores Los Angeles has branches of many national chains, including **Bloomingdale's, Neiman Marcus, I. Magnin, Saks Fifth Avenue,** and **Sears.** Most malls have such regional stores as **Nordstrom, Robinson's,** and **Bullocks** (all upscale), or the more middle-of-the-road **May Company** and **Broadway.**

Specialty Stores **French King Antiques** (135 S. Western Ave., tel. 213/383–4430)
Antiques has furniture, bronzes, and clocks.

Books **Book Soup** (8818 Sunset Blvd., West Hollywood, tel. 213/659–3110) has film and photography books, international magazines, and the occasional book-signing.

Gifts and Crafts **Tesoro** (319 S. Robertson Blvd., Beverly Hills, tel. 310/273–9890) stocks trendy ceramics, southwestern blankets, and contemporary art.

Music **Aron's Record** (1150 N. Highland Ave., Hollywood, tel. 213/469–4700) carries an extensive selection of old records.

Spectator Sports

Baseball **Dodgers** (Dodger Stadium, 1000 Elysian Park Ave., downtown, tel. 213/224–1400; Apr.–Oct.).

| Basketball | **Lakers** (Forum, 3900 West Manchester Ave., Inglewood, tel. 310/419–3182; Nov.–May). **Clippers** (L.A. Sports Arena, 3939 S. Figueroa St., downtown, tel. 213/748–6131; Nov.–May). |

Football **Raiders** (Memorial Coliseum, 3939 S. Figueroa St., tel. 213/747–7111; Sept.–Dec.).

Hockey **L.A. Kings** (Forum, tel. 213/419–3182; Nov.–Apr.).

Horse Racing **Santa Anita Race Track** (Arcadia, tel. 818/574–7223; Dec. 26–Apr. 27, Oct.–Nov.). **Hollywood Park** (near the Forum in Inglewood, tel. 213/419–1500; Apr.–mid-July).

Beaches

Los Angeles County beaches (and state beaches operated by the county) have lifeguards. Public parking (for a fee) is available at most. Most state beaches have picnic and rest-room facilities, and most city beaches are backed by a boardwalk with plenty of services.

Leo Carillo State Beach This beach is fun at low tide, when tide pools emerge. There are hiking trails, sea caves, and tunnels; whales, dolphins, and sea lions can often be seen. *36000 block of Pacific Coast Hwy. (PCH), Malibu, tel. 818/880–0350.*

Malibu Lagoon State Beach The steady 3- to 5-foot waves make this beach and the adjacent Surfrider Beach, both north of Malibu Pier, great long-board surfing spots. The lagoon is sanctuary for many birds. *23200 PCH, Malibu, tel. 310/880–0350.*

Manhattan State Beach Here are 44 acres of sandy beach for swimming, diving, surfing, and fishing, backed by a grassy park with duck pond and picnic facilities. *West of Strand, Manhattan Beach, tel. 310/372–2166.*

Paradise Cove With its pier and equipment rentals, this sandy beach is a mecca for sportfishing boats. *28128 PCH, Malibu, tel. 310/457–2511.*

Playa del Rey This underrated spot stretches almost 2 mi from Marina del Rey and attracts a young crowd. *660 Esplanade, Playa del Rey.*

Point Dume State Beach A favorite surfing spot, this sandy beach is ½ mi long, with tide pools and sandstone cliffs. *South end of Westward Beach Rd., Malibu, tel. 310/457–9891.*

Redondo State Beach This wide beach is usually packed in summer, and parking is limited. *Foot of Torrance Blvd., Redondo Beach, tel. 310/372–2166.*

Santa Monica Beach The widest stretch of beach on the Pacific coast, and one of the most popular, this spot offers bike paths, facilities for the disabled, playgrounds, and volleyball. *Santa Monica Blvd. and Ocean Ave., Santa Monica, tel. 310/394–3266.*

Topanga Canyon State Beach This great surfing spot is a rocky beach that stretches from the mouth of the canyon down to Coastline Drive. *18500 block of PCH, Malibu, tel. 310/394–3266.*

Will Rogers State Beach This wide, sandy beach is several miles long and has steady, even surf. Parking is limited, but there's plenty of beach, volleyball, and bodysurfing action parallel to the pedestrian bridge. *15800 PCH, Pacific Palisades, tel. 310/394–3266.*

Zuma Beach Malibu's largest and sandiest beach, this is a favorite surfing
County Park spot and teen hangout. *30050 PCH, Malibu, tel. 310/457–9891.*

Dining

Los Angeles's dining scene features foods influenced by the
city's myriad cultures, as well as cuisines haute, healthy, and
retro. Each ethnic neighborhood has its own wonderful restaurants: Chinese in Monterey Park, Mexican in East Los Angeles, Korean in Koreatown, Jewish in delis on Fairfax on the
Westside. Parking can be difficult; most restaurants listed here
offer valet parking except as noted. For price ranges, see Chart
1 (A) in Chapter 1.

Very Expensive **Rex Il Ristorante.** Two floors of a historic art deco building
★ were remodeled to resemble the dining salon of the 1930s Ital-
ian luxury liner *Rex.* The cuisine is the lightest of *cucina
nuovo,* in small portions at big prices. *617 S. Olive St. (Downtown), tel. 213/627–2300. Reservations required. Jacket and tie
required. AE, DC, MC, V. Closed Sun.*

Expensive **Chasen's.** Nostalgia fills these clublike rooms where the dishes
that Alfred Hitchcock, Gary Cooper, and Henry Fonda loved—
hobo steak, double-rib lamb chops, boiled beef with matzo
dumplings—continue to hold sway. *9039 Beverly Blvd. (West
Hollywood), tel. 310/271–2168. Reservations advised weekends. Jacket and tie required. AE, MC, V. No lunch weekends;
closed Mon.*

★ **Hotel Bel-Air.** The Bel-Air's restaurant is appealing not only
for the ambience of its country-garden setting but also for the
first-rate California-Continental cuisine. *701 Stone Canyon
Rd. (Bel Air), tel. 310/472–1211. Jacket and tie required. AE,
DC, MC, V.*

★ **L'Orangerie.** French specialties at this elegant restaurant include caviar-topped coddled eggs served in the shell, squab
with foie gras, pot-au-feu, and apple tart served with a jug of
double cream. *903 N. La Cienega Blvd. (West Hollywood), tel.
310/652–9770. Reservations required. Jacket and tie required.
AE, DC, MC, V. No lunch.*

Pacific Dining Car. Set in a 1920s railroad car is one of L.A.'s
oldest restaurants, known for well-aged steaks, rack of lamb,
and an extensive California wine list. It's a favorite haunt of
politicians, lawyers, and postgame Dodger fans. *1310 W. 6th
St. (Downtown), tel. 213/483–6000. MC, V.*

Moderate– **Spago.** At this restaurant that propelled Wolfgang Puck into
Expensive the culinary spotlight, the proof is in the tasting: grilled baby
★ Sonoma lamb, pizza with Santa Barbara shrimp, and baby
salmon. It's also "Entertainment Tonight" in person, but
noisy. *1114 Horn Ave. (West Hollywood), tel. 213/652–4025.
Reservations required 2 weeks in advance. Jacket required.
AE, DC, MC, V. No lunch.*

West Beach Cafe. At this first of Bruce Madder's string of innovative upscale restaurants, best bets are the filet mignon taco,
braised lamb shank, ravioli with port and radicchio, and possibly L.A.'s best hamburger and fries. *60 N. Venice Blvd. (Venice), tel. 310/823–5396. AE, DC, MC, V.*

Moderate **Border Grill.** At this very trendy, very loud storefront place,
the menu ranges from crab tacos to vinegared-and-peppered
grilled turkey to pickled pork sirloin. *1445 4th St. (Santa Monica), tel. 310/451–1655. AE, MC, V.*

★ **Gladstone's 4 Fish.** The view alone makes this the most popular restaurant along this section of the coast. Familiar seashore fare is prepared adequately and served in large portions. Best bets: crab chowder, steamed clams, and chili. *17300 Pacific Coast Hwy. (Pacific Palisades), tel. 310/454–3474. AE, DC, MC, V.*

Restaurant Katsu. This stark, simple, perfectly designed sushi bar serves the most exquisite sushi delicacies in all of southern California. *1972 N. Hillhurst Ave. (Hollywood), tel. 213/665–1891. Dinner reservations advised. AE, MC, V. No lunch Sat.*

Inexpensive– Moderate
California Pizza Kitchen. An immaculate, pleasingly modern dining room is supplemented with counter service by the open kitchen. Pizzas feature a wide choice of toppings; the pastas are equally interesting and carefully prepared. *207 S. Beverly Dr. (West Hollywood), tel. 310/272–7878. AE, MC, V.*

Mon Kee Seafood Restaurant. The place is crowded and messy, but the cooking is excellent and the ingredients are fresh. The garlic crab is addictive; the steamed catfish is a masterpiece of gentle flavors. *679 N. Spring St. (Downtown), tel. 213/628–6717. MC, V.*

Inexpensive
Chan Dara. In this Swiss chalet you'll find excellent Thai food. Try the noodle dishes, especially those with crab and shrimp. *310 N. Larchmont Blvd. (Hollywood), tel. 213/467–1052. AE, MC, V.*

El Cholo. This restaurant has been packing 'em in since the 1920s for good bathtub-size margaritas, a zesty assortment of tacos, make-your-own tortillas, and (June–Sept.) green-corn tamales. *1121 S. Western Ave. (Hollywood), tel. 213/734–2773. Reservations advised. AE, MC, V.*

Nate 'n Al's. This gathering place for Hollywood comedians, writers, and their agents serves first-rate matzo-ball soup, lox and scrambled eggs, cheese blintzes, potato pancakes, and the best deli sandwiches west of Manhattan. *414 N. Beverly Dr. (West Hollywood), tel. 310/274–0101. DC.*

Lodging

You can find almost any sort of accommodation in Los Angeles, from a motel room to a poolside bungalow. Because of L.A.'s sprawl, select a hotel that is close to where you want to be. For price ranges, see Chart 2 (A) in Chapter 1.

Very Expensive
Biltmore Hotel. Built in 1923 and renovated in 1985, this landmark hotel has hosted several U.S. presidents. The lobby ceiling was painted by Italian artist Giovanni Smeraldi; imported Italian marble and plum-color velvet adorn the Grand Avenue Bar, which features jazz nightly. Rooms, decorated with conservative contemporary furnishings, are painted in soft pink and white. *506 S. Grand Ave., 90071, tel. 213/624–1011 or 800/245–8673; fax 213/612–1545. 704 rooms. Facilities: 4 restaurants, health club (fee). AE, DC, MC, V.*

★ **Le Bel Age Hotel.** This all-suite, European-style hotel boasts such extravagant touches as multiple phones, original art, private terraces, and courtesy limousine service. South-facing suites have terrific views of the skyline. *1020 N. San Vicente Blvd., West Hollywood 90069, tel. 310/854–1111 or 800/424–4443; fax 310/854–0926. 190 suites. Facilities: 2 restaurants, lounge, pool. AE, DC, MC, V.*

Regent Beverly Wilshire. This famous hotel faces Rodeo Drive and the Hollywood Hills, and its clientele tends to be as glamorous as its surroundings. Style and service are emphasized, with limos to the airport, a multilingual staff, and a great restaurant. *9500 Wilshire Blvd., Beverly Hills 90212, tel. 310/275–5200 or 800/421–4354; fax 310/275–5986. 401 rooms. Facilities: restaurant, pool, health spa. AE, DC, MC, V.*

Expensive **Radisson Hollywood Roosevelt.** Across from Mann's Chinese Theater, and site of the first Academy Awards ceremony, the hotel was restored in 1985 right down to the art deco lobby, elegant courtyard, and pool decorated by David Hockney. The guest rooms' decor varies. *7000 Hollywood Blvd., Hollywood 90028, tel. 213/466–7000; fax 213/462–8056. 320 rooms, 90 poolside cabanas. Facilities: restaurant, valet parking. AE, DC, MC, V.*

★ **Westin Hotel LAX.** Rooms and suites at this airport hotel are decorated in muted earth tones and contemporary furnishings; many suites have private outdoor spas. The luxurious lobby is decorated in marble and brass, and the Trattoria Grande restaurant features pasta and seafood specialties. *5400 W. Century Blvd., 90045, tel. 310/216–5858 or 800/468–3571; fax 310/670–1948. 700 rooms, 47 suites. Facilities: 2 restaurants, lounge, pool, sauna, fitness center, pay parking. AE, DC, MC, V.*

Moderate **Barnaby's Hotel.** Modeled after a 19th-century English inn, with four-poster beds, lace curtains, and antiques, Barnaby's also has an enclosed greenhouse pool. *3501 Sepulveda Blvd. (at Rosecrans Ave., Manhattan Beach), 90266, tel. 310/545–8466 or 800/552–5285; fax 310/545–6691. 128 rooms. Facilities: 2 restaurants, lounge, pool. AE, DC, MC, V.*

Figueroa Hotel. This hotel has kept its charming Spanish style intact as it enters its second half-century. There's a poolside bar. *939 S. Figueroa St. (Downtown), 90015, tel. 213/627–8971, 800/421–9092, or 800/331–5151 in CA; fax 213/689–0305. 280 rooms. Facilities: restaurant, lounge, pool. AE, DC, MC, V.*

Holiday Inn–LAX. This hotel near the airport is in the chain's usual style, and offers such amenities as multilingual telephone operators and touring information. *9901 La Cienega Blvd., 90045, tel. 310/649–5151 or 800/238–8000; fax 310/670–3619. 403 rooms. Facilities: restaurant, pool, exercise room, pay parking. AE, DC, MC, V.*

Inexpensive **Best Western Royal Palace Hotel.** Suites at this small hotel just off I–405 have kitchenettes and are decorated with conservative blue-and-white prints that give the place a homey feel. *2528 S. Sepulveda Blvd. (West Los Angeles), 90064, tel. 310/477–9066; fax 310/478–4133. 23 rooms, 32 suites. Facilities: pool, exercise room, laundry. AE, DC, MC, V.*

Carmel Hotel. This hotel from the 1920s is a block from the beach, Santa Monica Shopping Plaza, movie theaters, and many fine restaurants. *201 Broadway, Santa Monica 90401, tel. 310/451–2469; fax 310/393–4180. 110 rooms. Facilities: restaurant, pay parking. AE, DC, MC, V.*

Orchid Hotel. One of the smaller downtown hotels, this offers clean, no-frills accommodations at a good price. *819 S. Flower St. (Downtown), 90017, tel. 213/624–5855; fax 213/624–8740. 66 rooms. Facilities: nearby pay parking, coin-operated laundry. AE, DC, MC, V.*

The Arts and Nightlife

The Calendar section of the *Los Angeles Times* is the best source of information for local events. Tickets can be purchased by phone from **TeleCharge** (tel. 800/762–7666), **Ticketmaster** (tel. 213/480–3232), or **Good Time Tickets** (tel. 213/464–7383).

The Arts

Theater Plays are presented at two of the three theaters at the Music Center (135 N. Grand Ave.): the **Ahmanson Theater** (tel. 213/972–7211) and the 742-seat **Mark Taper Forum** (tel. 213/972–7353). The **Center Theater Group at Mark Taper Forum** is a resident company but also books its shows into various theaters and mounts its own productions. The **James A. Doolittle Theater** (1615 N. Vine St., Hollywood, tel. 213/851–9750) presents dramas. **Westwood Playhouse** (10886 Le Conte Ave., Westwood, tel. 310/208–6500) offers musicals and comedies year-round.

Music The **Dorothy Chandler Pavilion** (135 N. Grand Ave., tel. 213/972–7211) is home to the Los Angeles Philharmonic Orchestra and offers other large-scale productions. **Ambassador Auditorium** (300 W. Green St., Pasadena, tel. 818/304–6161) presents a regular concert season. **Hollywood Bowl** (2301 Highland Ave., Hollywood, tel. 213/850–2000) offers an outdoor summer season of classical and popular music. The outdoor **Greek Theater** (2700 N. Vermont Ave., tel. 213/665–1927) offers a summer jazz/popular/pops schedule.

Nightlife

Comedy **The Comedy Store** (8433 Sunset Blvd., Hollywood, tel. 213/656–6225) showcases comedians, including the top names. The **Improvisation** (8162 Melrose Ave., West Hollywood, tel. 213/651–2583; 321 Santa Monica Blvd., Santa Monica, tel. 310/394–8664) features comedy and some music.

Discos **Bar One** (9229 Sunset Blvd., Beverly Hills, tel. 310/271–8355) is a hot and hip dance club. **Nucleus Nuance** (7267 Melrose Ave., Los Angeles, tel. 213/939–8666) is casual, cool, and swinging, with dancing until 2 AM.

Jazz Clubs Studio musicians often sit in at **The Baked Potato** (3787 Cahuenga Blvd. W, North Hollywood, tel. 818/980–1615), a club near Universal Studios. **The Lighthouse** (30 Pier Ave., Hermosa Beach, tel. 310/372–6911) offers a broad spectrum from reggae to big-band. **Vine Street Bar and Grill** (1610 N. Vine St., Hollywood, tel. 213/463–4375) presents top performers.

Rock Clubs The **Central** (8852 Sunset Blvd., West Hollywood, tel. 310/652–5937) is a musician's hangout. **Gazzarri's** (9039 Sunset Blvd., West Hollywood, tel. 310/273–6606) is a Sunset Strip landmark offering rock and roll to post-teens.

Orange County

Orange County sits between L.A. to the north and San Diego to the south. Though primarily suburban, it may be the entertainment capital of the state, what with Disneyland and the beaches within its borders.

Tourist Information

Anaheim Area: Convention and Visitors Bureau (Anaheim Convention Center, 800 W. Katella Ave., 92802, tel. 714/999–8999). **Guest Information Hot Line** (tel. 714/635–8900).

Getting There

By Plane **John Wayne Orange County Airport** (Santa Ana, tel. 714/252–5252) is served by a number of major carriers.

By Car I–405 (San Diego Fwy.) and I–5 (Santa Ana Fwy.) run north-south through Orange County, then merge into I–5 south of Laguna.

By Train **Amtrak** stops in Fullerton, Anaheim, Santa Ana, San Juan Capistrano, and San Clemente.

By Bus **Greyhound** (tel. 714/635–5060) serves Orange County.

Exploring Orange County

Inland Orange Anaheim is the home of **Disneyland.** Visitors enter the Magic
County Kingdom by way of Walt Disney's idealized turn-of-the-century **Main Street. Tomorrowland** is the site of the special-effects, sci-fi extravaganza Star Tours; *Captain Eo*, Michael Jackson's 3-D movie; the thrilling Space Mountain ride; and the Monorail. **Fantasyland** features rides based on children's stories. **Frontierland** depicts the Wild West. **Adventureland** has a cruise through a simulated jungle. **New Orleans Square** is the setting for Pirates of the Caribbean, a boat ride through a scene lavish with animated characters; and the Blue Bayou restaurant. **The Haunted Mansion** nearby is full of holographic ghosts. In **Critter Country** is Splash Mountain, a flume ride that drops 52 feet at 40 mph. **Mickey's Toontown,** a new "land" opened in 1993, is a child-size interactive community that's home to Mickey and other cartoon characters. Children can talk to manholes, sample Minnie's perfume, and bounce off the walls at Goofy's house. Along with the various thrill-rides and high-tech wizardry are the strolling Disney characters, a daily parade on Main Street, and fireworks nightly in summer. *1313 Harbor Blvd., tel. 714/999–4565. Admission: $28.75 adults, $23 children.*

Nearby in **Buena Park** is **Knott's Berry Farm,** a 150-acre complex of food, shops, rides, and other attractions. The park's thrill rides include the Boomerang, Bigfoot Rapids, the Corkscrew (an upside-down roller coaster with two 360-degree loops), and the Parachute Sky Jump. Areas of the park are themed: Camp Snoopy is especially for tiny tots and features a kid-size roller coaster, petting zoo, and playhouse; Fiesta Village features the Montezooma's Revenge roller coaster; Ghost Town, the park's original attraction, is a re-creation of an 1880s mining town, with a blacksmith shop, jail, and general store. Across Beach Boulevard from the main portion of Knott's is a replica of Philadelphia's Independence Hall. And don't miss Knott's Chicken Dinner restaurant (and the boysenberry pies) that started it all in 1934 and still serves thousands weekly. *8039 Beach Blvd., tel. 714/220–5200. Admission: $25.95 adults, $15.95 children.*

Just east of Knott's is the **Movieland Wax Museum,** which re-creates the famous in wax. *7711 Beach Blvd., tel. 714/522–1155. Admission: $12.95 adults, $6.95 children.*

Garden Grove is the site of the impressive **Crystal Cathedral** (12141 Lewis St., tel. 714/971–4013; donation), the domain of televangelist Robert Schuller.

The Coast Pacific Coast Highway is the main thoroughfare for all the beach towns along the coast. **Huntington Beach** is a popular surfer hangout; you can watch the action from the **Huntington Pier.** To the south is **Newport Beach,** a Beverly-Hills-by-the-sea; nearly 10,000 boats bob in the *U*-shape **Newport Harbor,** which arcs out into a peninsula sheltering eight small islands. A three-car ferry serves **Balboa Island,** with its **Victorian Balboa Pavilion,** a turn-of-the-century architectural gem. The **Newport Harbor Art Museum** (850 San Clemente Dr., tel. 714/759–1122; admission charged) holds a collection of works by California artists.

Farther south is the town of **Corona del Mar,** with an exceptional beach. In **Laguna Beach,** art galleries in town co-exist with the volleyball games and sun worship on nearby Main Beach; in July and August, the **Pageant of the Masters** (tel. 714/494–1147) features living models re-creating famous paintings. **San Clemente** is a popular surfing spot and the site of Richard Nixon's Western White House. In March, migrating swallows and spectacle-loving tourists flock to **San Juan Capistrano Mission** (Camino Capistrano and Ortega Hwy., tel. 714/248–2048; admission charged).

Sports and Outdoor Activities

Biking A **bike path** runs from Marina del Rey down to San Diego with only minor breaks. For rentals, try **Rainbow Bicycles** (Laguna, tel. 714/494–5806) or **Team Bicycle Rentals** (Huntington Beach, tel. 714/969–5480).

Water Sports Water-sports equipment rentals are near most piers. **Hobie Sports** has three rental locations (Dana Point, tel. 714/496–2366 and 714/496–1251; Laguna, tel. 714/497–3304). **Balboa Boat Rentals** in Newport Harbor (tel. 714/673–1320) and **Embarcadero Marina** at Dana Point (tel. 714/496–6177) rent sail and power boats.

Spectator Sports

Baseball **California Angels** (Anaheim Stadium, 2000 Gene Autry Way, tel. 714/634–2000; Apr.–Oct.).

Football **Los Angeles Rams** (Anaheim Stadium, tel. 714/937–6767; Aug.–Dec.).

Beaches

The Beaches in Orange County are among the finest and most varied in southern California, offering fine swimming and many services. Posted warnings about undertow should be taken seriously, as it can be quite strong.

Huntington Beach State Beach is a long stretch of flat, sandy beach with changing rooms, concessions, fire pits, and lifeguards. **Lower Newport Bay** is a sheltered enclave that includes a 740-acre preserve for ducks and geese. **Newport Dunes Aquatic Park** offers picnic facilities, changing rooms, and a boat launch. **Corona del Mar State Beach** has sandy beaches backed by rocky bluffs, and tide pools and caves. **Laguna** has the county's best spot for scuba diving in the **Marine Life Refuge,** from Seal Rock to Diver's Cove. **Main Beach,** a sandy arc just steps from downtown Laguna, is a popular picnic and volleyball venue. In South Laguna, **Aliso County Park** has recreational facilities and a fishing pier. **Doheny State Park,** near Dana Point Harbor, has food stands, camping, and a fishing pier. **San Clemente State Beach** has camping facilities and food stands and is renowned for its surf.

Dining and Lodging

For price ranges, see Charts 1 (A) and 2 (A) in Chapter 1.

Anaheim
Dining

JW's. This French-country dining room serves well-prepared classic fare, such as roast saddle of lamb, venison, and wild boar. *Marriott Hotel, 700 Convention Way, tel. 714/750–8000. Jacket required. AE, D, DC, MC, V. Expensive.*

Bessie Wall's. In this restored ranch house dating from 1927, you can get chicken and dumplings, as well as southern California/Mexican dishes. *1074 N. Tustin Blvd., tel. 714/630–2812. Jacket advised. AE, DC, MC, V. No lunch; closed Sat. Moderate.*

Lodging

Disneyland Hotel. This 60-acre resort is connected to the theme park by monorail. The towers and tropical village make for unique accommodations; rooms are decorated in soft pastel colors and have balconies with views of Disneyland or the hotel marina. *1150 W. Cerritos Ave., 92802, tel. 714/778–6600; fax 714/956–6597. 1,132 rooms. Facilities: 6 restaurants, pool, tennis. AE, DC, MC, V. Very Expensive.*

Inn at the Park. Mountains of all kinds can be seen from private balconies—the for-real Santa Anas as well as Disneyland's man-made Matterhorn. It is conveniently located for Disneyland and the convention center. *1855 S. Harbor Blvd., 92802, tel. 714/750–1811; fax 714/971–3626. 500 rooms. Facilities: restaurant, lounge, pool, exercise room. AE, DC, MC, V. Expensive.*

Ramada Hotel Maingate. This clean, reliable member of the chain is across the street from Disneyland and has a free shuttle. *1460 S. Harbor Blvd., 92802, tel. 714/772–6777; fax 714/999–1727. 467 rooms. Facilities: restaurant, pool. AE, MC, V. Moderate.*

Hampton Inn. Here you'll find basic lodging at a basic price a short drive from Disneyland. *300 E. Katella Way, 92802, tel. 714/772–8713; fax 714/778–1235. 136 rooms. Facilities: pool. AE, DC, MC, V. Inexpensive.*

Costa Mesa
Dining

Mandarin Gourmet. Dollar for bite, owner Michael Chang provides what the critics and locals consider the best Chinese cuisine in the area. *1500 Adams Ave., tel. 714/540–1937. AE, DC, MC, V. Inexpensive.*

Dana Point
Dining and Lodging
★

The Ritz-Carlton Laguna Niguel. One of California's most highly respected hotels, the Ritz offers beach access, a spectacular ocean view, the Dining Room restaurant, a lavishly decorated lobby, and spacious rooms with balconies, French doors, and some fireplaces. *33533 Ritz-Carlton Dr., 92677, tel. 714/240–2000; fax 714/240–0829. 393 rooms. Facilities: 3 restaurants, 3* *lounges, 2 pools, health club, tennis, golf course. AE, DC, MC, V. Very Expensive.*

Laguna Beach **Las Brisas.** A spectacular coastline view from the clifftop ter-
Dining race, great margaritas, irresistible guacamole, and nouvelle
Mexican dishes make this a local favorite. *361 Cliff Dr., tel. 714/
497–5434. AE, DC, MC, V. Moderate.*

Lodging **Surf and Sand Hotel.** At this hotel right on the beach, rooms
sport soft sand colors, wooden shutters, private balconies, and
honor bars. *15555 S. Coast Hwy., 92651, tel. 714/497–4477; fax
714/494–7653. 157 rooms. Facilities: 2 restaurants, pool, private beach. AE, DC, MC, V. Very Expensive.*

Newport Beach **Antoine's.** The lovely, candlelit dining room, made for romance
Dining and quiet conversation, serves the best French cuisine of any
★ hotel in southern California. *Hotel Meridien Newport Beach,
4500 MacArthur Blvd., tel. 714/476–2001. Jacket and tie required. AE, DC, MC, V. No lunch. Very Expensive.*
Crab Cooker. If you don't mind waiting in line, this shanty of a
place serves fresh fish grilled over mesquite at low, low prices.
*2200 Newport Blvd., tel. 714/673–0100. No credit cards. Inex-
pensive.*

Lodging **Four Seasons Hotel.** Marble and antiques fill the airy lobby. The
★ guest rooms, decorated in southwestern colors, have spectacular views. *690 Newport Dr., 92660, tel. 714/759–0808; fax 714/
720–1718. 285 rooms. Facilities: 2 restaurants, pool, tennis.
AE, DC, MC, V. Very Expensive.*
The Hyatt Newporter Resort. This elegant resort is a collection
of low buildings surrounded by lush gardens. Decor throughout is Mediterranean with marble and brass appointments.
*1107 Jamboree Rd., 92660, tel. 714/644–1700; fax 714/644–
1552. 410 rooms. Facilities: 2 restaurants, 3 pools, golf, exercise room. AE, DC, MC, V. Expensive.*

The Arts

Orange County Performing Arts Center (600 Town Center Dr.,
Costa Mesa, tel. 714/556–2787) presents symphony orchestras,
opera companies, and musicals. Summer concert series are
presented at **Irvine Meadows** (8800 Irvine Center Dr., tel. 714/
855–4515) and **Pacific Amphitheater** (Orange County Fairgrounds, Costa Mesa, tel. 714/740–2000).

San Diego

One of California's most attractive cities, San Diego is the
birthplace of Spanish California. Its combination of history,
pleasing climate, outdoor recreation and sports, and cultural
life make it a popular destination.

Tourist Information

San Diego: International Information Center (11 Horton Plaza,
92101, tel. 619/236–1212). Mission Bay Visitor Information
Center (2688 E. Mission Bay Dr., off I–5, tel. 619/276–8200).

Arriving and Departing

By Plane   **Lindbergh Field** is 3 mi northwest of downtown and is served by most domestic and many international air carriers. **The Super Shuttle Airport Limousine** (tel. 619/278–8877 or 800/948–8853) has door-to-door service. **San Diego Transit** Rte. 2 buses leave the airport every 20–30 minutes and cost $1.25. Taxi fare is $8 (plus tip) to most center-city hotels.

By Car   I–5 runs north–south. I–8 comes into San Diego from the east, I–15 from the northeast.

Train Station   **Amtrak** trains arrive at **Santa Fe Depot** (Kettner Blvd. and Broadway, tel. 619/239–9021).

Bus Station   **Greyhound** (120 W. Broadway and Los Angeles St., tel. 619/239–9171).

Getting Around San Diego

It's best to have a car, but avoid the freeways during rush hours. The **San Diego Trolley** (tel. 619/231–3004) travels the 20 mi from downtown to within 100 feet of the Mexican border; other trolleys on the line serve Seaport Village, the Convention Center, and inland areas. **Harbor Hopper** (tel. 619/488–5022) is a water-taxi service.

Exploring San Diego

Downtown   The **Embarcadero** is a waterfront walkway lined with restaurants and cruise-ship piers. The **Maritime Museum** (B St. Pier, tel. 619/234–9153; admission charged) has a collection of restored ships, including the windjammer *Star of India.*

Just south of the museum is the Seaport Village shopping mall; from here water taxis cross the bay to **Coronado,** a city of numerous Victorian houses whose most prominent landmark is the historic turreted and gingerbreaded **Hotel Del Coronado** (*see* Lodging, *below*)—the first electrically lighted hotel. Another Coronado landmark is the **North Island Naval Air Station** (tel. 619/545–8167), from which Charles Lindbergh took off on his flight around the world. You can drive to Coronado via the 2.2-mi San Diego–Coronado Bridge, which offers a stunning view of the San Diego skyline.

In downtown San Diego, the **Gaslamp Quarter** is a 16-block National Historic District containing most of the city's Victorian-era commercial buildings. The **Gaslamp Quarter Association** (William Heath Davis House, 410 Island Ave., tel. 619/233–5227) has walking-tour brochures and maps.

Balboa Park encompasses 1,400 acres of cultural, recreational, and environmental delights, including a theater complex and public gardens. Among the park's several museums are **The Museum of Man** (tel. 619/239–2001), one of the finest anthropological museums in the country; the **Hall of Champions** (tel. 619/234–2544), a sports museum; and the **Museum of Photographic Arts** (tel. 619/239–5262). Laserium and Omnimax shows are given in the **Reuben H. Fleet Space Theater and Science Center** (tel. 619/238–1168). All the above sights charge admission. The **Botanical Building** (no phone; admission free; closed Mon.) houses tropical and subtropical plant species and a stunning orchid collection.

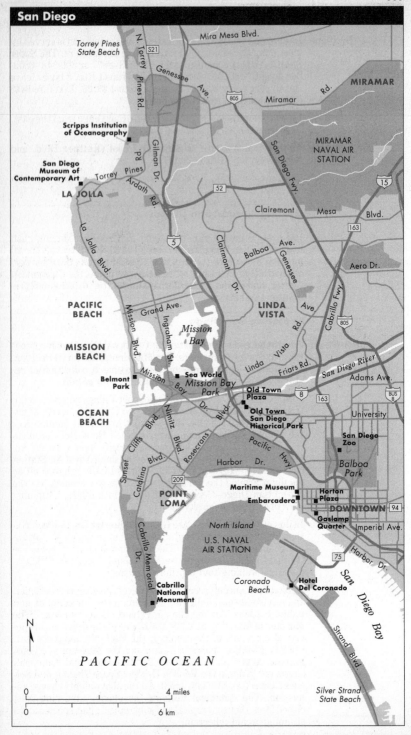

Balboa Park's most famous attraction is the **San Diego Zoo,** where over 3,200 animals roam in habitats built around natural canyons. The zoo is also an enormous botanical garden with a large collection of subtropical plants. *Tel. 619/234–3153. Admission: $12 adults, $4 children.*

San Diego's Spanish and Mexican history and heritage are on display in **Old Town** (San Diego Ave. and Mason St., tel. 619/237–6770). This state historic park is a six-block district of the city, clustered around **Old Town Plaza** and lined with shops and restaurants, some in historic buildings. **Bazaar del Mundo** is a colorful Mediterranean-style shopping complex with gardens, exotic shops, and outdoor restaurants. **Robinson-Rose House,** once the commercial center of old San Diego, is now park headquarters.

Mission Bay Park contains beaches, playgrounds, and the Giant Dipper roller coaster at **Belmont Park.**

At **Sea World's** ocean-oriented amusement park, the Shamu whale show, Penguin Encounter, shark exhibit, and tide pools are popular attractions. *Sea World Dr. at I–8, tel. 619/226–3901. Admission: $25.95 adults, $19.95 children.*

Thirteen miles north of downtown San Diego, in the upscale village of **La Jolla,** is the **San Diego Museum of Contemporary Art** (700 Prospect St., tel. 619/454–3541; admission charged) featuring post-1950 art. The **Stephen Birch Aquarium–Museum** (2300 Expedition Dr., tel. 619/534–3474; admission charged) at the **Scripps Institution of Oceanography** is the largest oceanographic exhibit in the country; tanks filled with colorful saltwater fish and a simulated submarine ride are among the attractions. North of La Jolla is **Torrey Pines State Beach and Reserve** (tel. 619/755–2063; admission charged), with a museum, hiking trails, and beaches. A short drive east of Oceanside along Hwy. 76 takes you to the 1798 **Mission San Luis Rey** (tel. 619/757–3651; admission charged), the largest and best-preserved mission in the area and still a working Catholic church.

Shopping

San Diego's shopping areas are a mélange of self-contained megamalls, historic districts, quaint villages, funky neighborhoods, and chic suburbs.

Horton Plaza, occupying six square blocks downtown (Broadway and G St., from 1st to 4th Aves.), is a multilevel postmodern mall with department stores, one-of-a-kind shops, fast-food counters, classy restaurants, a farmer's market, movies, and live theater.

The **Gaslamp Quarter** features art galleries, antiques shops, and other specialty stores. **La Jolla/Golden Triangle's** trendy boutiques line Girard Avenue and Prospect Street; and **Coast Walk,** along Prospect Street, offers shops, galleries, and restaurants. **Old Town** has **Bazaar del Mundo, La Esplanade,** and **Old Town Mercado,** with international goods, toys, souvenirs, and arts and crafts.

Spectator Sports

Baseball	**San Diego Padres** (Jack Murphy Stadium, 9449 Frials Rd., tel. 619/280–4636; Apr.–Oct.).
Football	**San Diego Chargers** (Jack Murphy Stadium, tel. 619/280–2111; Aug.–Dec.).
Horse Racing	**Del Mar Thoroughbred Club** (Del Mar Fairgrounds, tel. 619/755–1141; July–Sept.).

Beaches

Coronado Beach This wide stretch of uncrowded sandy beach is perfect for sunbathing or Frisbee throwing. There are rest rooms and fire rings; parking can be difficult on busy days. *From the bridge, turn left on Orange Ave., then follow signs.*

Imperial Beach Surfers and swimmers congregate at this beach, which offers lifeguards in summer, parking, rest rooms, and food vendors nearby. *Take Palm Ave. west from I–5 to the water.*

La Jolla Cove The cove is a favorite of rough-water swimmers, but Children's Pool, a shallow lagoon at the south end, is a safer haven. *Follow Coast Blvd. north to signs; or take the La Jolla Village Dr. exit from I–5, head west to Torrey Pines Rd., turn left and drive down the hill to Girard Ave., turn right and follow signs.*

Mission Beach/Pacific Beach The boardwalk is popular with strollers, roller skaters, and bicyclists. The south end is filled by surfers, swimmers, and volleyball players. Pacific Beach is a teen hangout; it's crowded in summer, and parking is a challenge. There are rest rooms and restaurants. *Exit I–5 at Garnet Ave. and head west to Mission Blvd.*

Silver Strand State Beach On Coronado, this beach has relatively calm water, an RV campground, and a wide array of other facilities. Parking is $6 per car. *Take the Palm Ave. exit off I–5 west to Hwy. 75; turn right and follow signs.*

Dining

San Diego's gastronomic reputation rests primarily on its seafood. A city that once stood solidly in the meat-and-potatoes camp now also boasts Afghani, Thai, Vietnamese, and other ethnic cuisines. For price ranges, see Chart 1 (A) in Chapter 1.

Very Expensive

★ **Dobson's.** The menu changes daily, beginning with the perennial mussel bisque and continuing with fish, veal, fowl, and beef entrées. *956 Broadway Circle, tel. 619/231–6771. Jacket advised. AE, MC, V. Closed Sun.*

★ **Issimo.** Beautifully arranged plates are served in grand style in an elegant soft green jewel box of a dining room. Start with a pasta or homemade pâté de foie gras, then move to osso buco, a plate of baby lamb chops, or a delicately sauced steak. *5634 La Jolla Blvd., La Jolla, tel. 619/454–7004. Jacket advised. MC, V. Closed Sun.*

Top O' the Cove. This romantic restaurant with a view of La Jolla Cove turns out beautifully garnished, luxury fare dressed with creamy and well-seasoned sauces. The extensive wine list has received countless awards. *1216 Prospect St., La Jolla, tel. 619/454–7779. Reservations advised. Jacket and tie advised. AE, DC, MC, V.*

Expensive **George's at the Cove.** An art-filled dining room, excellent ser-
★ vice, a view of La Jolla Cove, and an imaginative, well-prepared
menu featuring seafood, pasta, beef, and veal make this one of
the city's best restaurants. *1250 Prospect St., La Jolla, tel. 619/
454–4244. Dress: neat but casual. AE, DC, MC, V.*

Moderate **Cafe Pacifica.** The menu changes according to the day's catch.
Light, interesting sauces and imaginative garnishes are
teamed with simply cooked fillets of salmon, sea bass, and
swordfish. *2414 San Diego Ave., tel. 619/291–6666. Dress: neat
but casual. AE, DC, MC, V. No lunch weekends.*
El Crab Catcher. Its spectacular view of La Jolla Cove and casual Hawaiian atmosphere make this a favorite. Specialties include numerous crab dishes and simple beef and chicken dishes.
1298 Prospect St., La Jolla, tel. 619/454–9587. AE, DC, MC, V.
★ **McCormick's.** Seafood is served in a dining room of dark wood
and glass or on the ocean-view terrace. The menu changes daily; try the "singing scallops," served in their fluted pink shells,
or any of the grilled fish dishes. *4190 Mission Blvd., Pacific
Beach, tel. 619/581–3938. AE, D, DC, MC, V. Moderate.*

Inexpensive **Casa de Pico.** The centerpiece of the Bazaar del Mundo, this colorful eatery offers traditional American-Mexican foods, such
as burritos, enchiladas, quesadillas, and tostadas. *2754 Calhoun St., tel. 619/296–3267. AE, DC, MC, V.*
★ **Karinya.** At this casual and pretty Thai restaurant, try the
larb, a spicy salad; *mee krob,* a dish of noodles and shrimp; or
the tart, savory *tom yum gai* soup. *4475 Mission Blvd., tel. 619/
270–5050. AE, MC, V. No lunch weekends; closed Mon.*

Lodging

Most hotels have parking except as noted below. For price
ranges, see Chart 2 (A) in Chapter 1.

Very Expensive **Hotel Del Coronado.** Rooms and suites in the original Victorian
building, an 1888 historic landmark, are charmingly quirky.
More standardized accommodations are available in the newer
high rise. *1500 Orange Ave., Coronado 92118, tel. 619/435–
6611 or 800/468–3533; fax 619/522–8238. 660 rooms, 31 suites.
Facilities: restaurant, pool, tennis, beach. AE, DC, MC, V.*
★ **Westgate Hotel.** This elegant hotel offers European antiques,
hand-cut Baccarat chandeliers, Italian marble counters, oversize bathtubs, and brass fixtures with 14-karat-gold overlay.
*1055 2nd Ave., 92101, tel. 619/238–1818, 800/221–3802, or 800/
522–1564 in CA; fax 619/232–4526. 223 rooms. Facilities: 3 restaurants, lounge, exercise room. AE, DC, MC, V.*

Expensive **La Valencia.** This centrally located pink-stucco hotel is a La
★ Jolla landmark. It has a courtyard for patio dining and an elegant lobby where guests congregate to enjoy the spectacular
ocean view. Rooms have a romantic European ambience. *1132
Prospect St., La Jolla 92037, tel. 619/454–0771; fax 619/456–
3921. 100 rooms. Facilities: 3 restaurants, pool, fitness center,
lounge. AE, MC, V.*
San Diego Princess Resort. This family-oriented resort has
beautifully landscaped grounds, a marina, and beaches. Some
of the beach-style bungalows, which have white walls and
bright pastel furnishings, offer kitchens and bay views. *1404
W. Vacation Rd., 92109, tel. 619/274–4630 or 800/344–2626; fax
619/581–5929. 462 cottages. Facilities: 3 restaurants, 5 pools,
tennis, bike and boat rentals. AE, DC, MC, V.*

Moderate
★

Bahia Resort Hotel. This huge complex on a 14-acre peninsula in Mission Bay Park has tastefully furnished studios and suites with kitchens. *998 W. Mission Bay Dr., 92109, tel. 619/488–0551; fax 619/488–3328. 325 rooms. Facilities: pool, tennis, water-sports rentals. AE, DC, MC, V.*

Heritage Park Bed & Breakfast Inn. This romantic 1889 Queen Anne mansion in Heritage Park is decorated with 19th-century antiques. *2470 Heritage Park Row, 92110, tel. 619/295–7088. 8 rooms (4 share baths). MC, V.*

Torrey Pines Inn. Set on a bluff between La Jolla and DelMar, this contemporary-style hotel is adjacent to the Torrey Pines Golf Course and commands an expansive coastline view. *11480 Torrey Pines Rd., La Jolla 92037, tel. 619/453–4420; fax 619/453–0691. 75 rooms. Facilities: restaurant, lounge, pool. AE, DC, MC, V.*

Inexpensive
★

La Pensione. This budget hotel in a quiet downtown neighborhood has a pretty central courtyard and rooms with harbor views and some kitchenettes. *1546 2nd Ave., 92101, tel. 619/236–9292; fax 619/236–9988. 20 rooms. MC, V.*

Mission Bay Motel. A half-block from the beach, this motel offers modest units within walking distance of great restaurants and nightlife. *4221 Mission Blvd., 92109, tel. 619/483–6440. 50 rooms. Facilities: pool. MC, V.*

Padre Trail Inn. This family-style motel is within walking distance of Old Town, shopping, and dining. *4200 Taylor St., 92110, tel. 619/297–3291; fax 619/692–2080. 100 rooms. Facilities: restaurant, lounge, pool. AE, DC, MC, V.*

The Arts and Nightlife

San Diego enthusiastically supports opera, symphony, and a wide range of theaters. Book tickets well in advance through **Ticketmaster** (tel. 619/278–8497).

The Arts

Old Globe Theatre (Simon Edison Centre, Balboa Park, tel. 619/239–2255) presents classics, experimental works, and a summer Shakespeare Festival. **Copley Symphony Hall** (1245 7th Ave., tel. 619/699–4200) is home to the San Diego Symphony, whose season runs November–May. **Civic Theatre** (202 C St., tel. 619/236–6510) is where to catch the San Diego Opera.

Nightlife

San Diego's nightlife ranges from quiet piano bars to cutting-edge rock. **Casbah** (2812 Kettner Blvd., tel. 619/294–9033) showcases rock, reggae, and funk bands every night. **Humphrey's** (2241 Shelter Island Dr., tel. 619/224–3577) offers the city's best jazz and folk. **Leo's Little Bit O' Country** (680 W. San Marcos Blvd., San Marcos, tel. 619/744–4120) hosts country-western dancing. **The Comedy Store** (916 Pearl St., La Jolla, tel. 619/454–9176) hosts local and national touring talent. **Club Diego's** (860 Garnet Ave., Pacific Beach, tel. 619/272–1241) is a flashy disco by the beach.

Elsewhere in Southern California

Palm Springs

Getting There   Palm Springs is about a two-hour drive east of L.A. and a three-hour drive northeast of San Diego. From Los Angeles take the I–10E to Hwy. 111. From San Diego take I–15N to I–60E, then I–10E to Hwy. 111. **Palm Springs Municipal Airport** is served by national and regional airlines.

What to See and Do   A desert playground for Hollywood celebrities since the 1930s, Palm Springs has plenty of attractions: luxurious resorts, nearly year-round golf and tennis, shopping, celebrity watching, and top-name entertainment. The area's natural attractions include the desert landscape of **Joshua Tree National Monument** (I–10N to Hwy. 62 to the Oasis visitor center or I–10S to the Cottonwood Visitor Center, tel. 619/367–7511). The oddly shaped trees, with their branches raised like arms, and the sculptural outcroppings of rocks are entrancing. There are over 500 campsites within the park, and more in private campgrounds around it. The vast **Anza Borrego Desert State Park** (tel. 619/767–5311), in the southern portion of the region, explodes into color each spring when the wildflowers bloom. The **Palm Springs Chamber of Commerce** (190 W. Amato Rd., 92262, tel. 619/325–1577) and **Palm Springs Tourism** (2781 N. Palm Canyon, 92262, tel. 800/347–7746) can provide helpful information.

For an overview of the area, take a ride up the **Palm Springs Aerial Tramway** (1 Tramway Rd., tel. 619/325–1391). **Palm Canyon Drive** is the main shopping strip, with Saks Fifth Avenue as the centerpiece and shops offering jewelry, resort wear, and sportswear. **The Courtyard** at the Bank of Palm Springs Center features Paris fashion at Rodier and Yves St. Laurent.

As befits the home of the **Bob Hope Desert Classic** (Jan.) and the **Dinah Shore Championship** (Mar. or Apr.), golf courses abound in the area. The most famous are connected with resorts and private country clubs, but two open to the public are **Palm Springs Municipal Golf Course** (1885 Golf Club Dr., tel. 619/328–1005) and **Fairchilds Bel Aire Greens** (1001 El Cielo Rd., tel. 619/327–0332).

Dining and Lodging   The restaurant scene in Palm Springs benefits from so much L.A. influence. Full-service hotels and resorts are the city's strong suit, though there are plenty of basic lodging options. For price ranges, see Charts 1 (A) and 2 (A) in Chapter 1.

Dining   **Bono.** Palm Springs's former mayor, Sonny Bono, serves the southern Italian dishes his mother used to make. *1700 N. Indian Ave., tel. 619/322–6200. AE, DC, MC, V. No lunch weekends. Moderate.*

Lodging   **The Ritz-Carlton Rancho Mirage.** The poshest gem in the desert has all the amenities: restaurants, pools, bar, fitness center, and tennis. The rooms are comfortably furnished in 18th- to 19th-century style; they have marble baths and French doors opening onto a balcony or patio. *68-900 Frank Sinatra Dr.,*

Rancho Mirage 92270, tel. 619/321–8282; fax 619/321–6928.
240 rooms. AE, DC, MC, V. Very Expensive.

Death Valley

Getting There From the west (about 300 mi from Los Angeles), exit U.S. 395 at either Hwy. 190 or 178. From the southeast (about 140 mi from Las Vegas), take Hwy. 127 north from I–15 and Hwy. 178 past Funeral Peak, Badwater, Dante's View, and Zabriskie Point to Hwy. 190 at Furnace Creek. Reliable maps are a must; AAA is the best source.

What to See **Death Valley National Monument** (visitor center, Furnace
and Do Creek, tel. 619/786–2331), the lowest point in the country, is a desert wonderland, with 14 sq mi of sand dunes, 200 sq mi of crusty salt flats, 11,000-foot mountains, and hills and canyons of many hues. In the northwest section is **Scotty's Castle** (north on Hwy. 190), a $2.5 million Moorish-style mansion built by a onetime cowboy and performer in Buffalo Bill's Wild West Show. **Harmony Borax Works** (south on Hwy. 190) illustrates the mining history of the valley, from which the 20-mule teams hauled borax to the railroad at Mojave. **Dante's View,** 5,000 feet up in the Black Mountains, offers a view of both the lowest (Badwater) and highest (Mt. Whitney) points in the United States.

OREGON

By Jeff Kuechle

Updated by Tom Barr

Capital	Salem
Population	2,847,000
Motto	The Union
State Bird	Western meadowlark
State Flower	Oregon grape

Visitor Information

Oregon State Welcome Center (12348 N. Center Ave., Portland 97217, tel. 503/285–1631).

Scenic Drives

The **Crown Point Scenic Highway** twists and turns its way above I–84 through the heavily wooded, waterfall-laced fairyland east of Portland. U.S. 101 follows the unspoiled, monolith-studded Oregon coastline all the way from Washington to California. **Hwy. 138** from Roseburg to Crater Lake is a National Scenic Byway (*see* Elsewhere in the State, Ashland/The Rogue Valley, *below*).

National and State Parks

National Parks   **Crater Lake National Park** (Box 7, Crater Lake 97604, tel. 503/594–2511) began 6,800 years ago, when Mt. Mazama decapitated itself in a huge explosion. Rain and snowmelt eventually filled the caldera, creating a sapphire-blue lake so clear that sunlight penetrates to a depth of 400 feet. Visitors can drive or hike the park's 25-mi Rim Drive, explore a variety of nature trails, and (in summer) take guided boat trips around the lake itself. **Newberry National Volcanic Monument,** 25 mi southeast of Bend, contains over 50,000 acres of lakes, lava flows, and spectacular geological features administered by the Deschutes National Forest (1645 Hwy. 20E, Bend 97701, tel. 503/388–2715). **Oregon Caves National Monument** (19000 Caves Hwy., Cave Junction 97523, tel. 503/592–3400) offers guided tours of the "Marble Halls of Oregon." **Oregon Dunes National Recreation Area** (855 Highway Ave., Reedsport 97467, tel. 503/271–3611), a 47-mi swath of camel-colored sand, is popular with campers, hikers, mountain bikers, dune-buggy enthusiasts, and even dogsledders.

State Parks   Oregon's 225 state parks run the gamut from sage-scented desert to mountains to sea. The **Oregon State Parks and Recreation Department** (525 Trade St. SE, Salem 97310, tel. 503/238–7488) has information on the parks and facilities.

Portland

Portland has earned a reputation as one of the best-planned and most relaxing cities in America. Straddling the banks of the wide, salmon-filled Willamette River, it blends flower-filled parks, efficient mass transit, skyscrapers, and beautifully restored historic buildings. As one of the United States' most important gateways to the Pacific Rim, Portland has gained noticeable sophistication in recent decades.

Tourist Information

Portland/Oregon Visitors Association (World Trade Center 3, 26 S.W. Salmon St., 97204, tel. 503/222–2223 or 800/345–3214).

Arriving and Departing

By Plane **Portland International Airport** (tel. 503/335–1234) is in northeast Portland, about 12 mi from the city center, and is served by major domestic carriers. Taxi (**Portland Taxi,** tel. 503/256–5400; **Broadway Taxi,** tel. 503/227–1234), bus (**Raz Transportation,** tel. 503/246–3301), and hotel shuttle services connect the airport to downtown. A taxi ride downtown from the airport costs about $20, and the bus is $7.

By Car I–84 (Banfield Fwy.) and Hwy. 26 (the Sunset) run east–west; I–5 and I–205 run north–south.

By Train **Amtrak** serves Union Station (800 N.W. 6th Ave., tel. 503/273–4865).

By Bus **Greyhound** (550 N.W. 6th Ave., tel. 503/243–2310).

Getting Around Portland

The metro area is laid out in a logical grid system, with numbered avenues running north–south and named streets running east–west. The efficient **MAX light-rail line** links east Portland suburbs with the Lloyd Center district, the Convention Center, Memorial Coliseum, and the downtown core. The **Tri-Met bus system** covers the metro area extensively. Call 503/238–7433 for schedules and routes for both Tri-Met and MAX.

Exploring Portland

Start a tour downtown, with its lively shops, restaurants, galleries, museums, and theaters. In previous incarnations, the site of **Pioneer Courthouse Square** was the city's first school, an elegant hotel, and a parking lot. Now it's the city's main gathering place and people-watching venue. Nearby is the **Portland Center for the Performing Arts** (corner of S.W. Broadway and S.W. Main St., tel. 503/248–4496), the elegant hub of the city's arts community. Within its richly paneled confines are the 2,776-seat **Arlene Schnitzer Concert Hall,** the 916-seat **Intermediate Theater,** and the 292-seat **Delores Winningstad Theater.**

Pass westward through the tree-lined South Park Blocks, a series of city blocks that form a vast, green boulevard of statues and fountains, on your way to the **Portland Art Museum.** The Northwest's oldest arts facility, the museum contains 35 centuries of Asian, European, and Native American art. *1220 S.W. Park Ave., tel. 503/226–2811. Admission charged. Closed Mon.*

Across the South Park Blocks you'll note towering murals of Lewis and Clark and the Oregon Trail. The paintings frame the entrance to the **Oregon Historical Center,** where the state's history from prehistoric times to the present is documented. *1200 S.W. Park Ave., tel. 503/222–1741. Admission charged.*

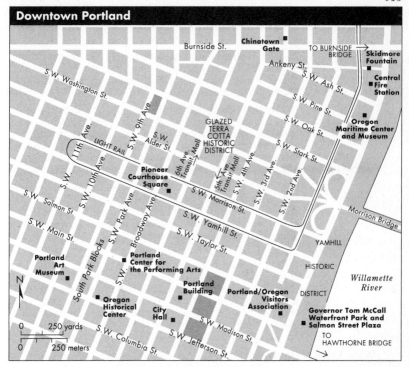

Downtown Portland

Southward on Madison Street is architect Michael Graves's **Portland Building** (1120 S.W. 5th Ave.), one of the country's first postmodern designs. *Portlandia*, a hammered-copper sculpture second in size only to the Statue of Liberty, kneels on the second-story balcony. Inside is the **Metropolitan Center for Public Art** (tel. 503/823–5111). Across Madison Avenue is the classically styled **City Hall,** built in 1895, with columns on two of its faces and high ceilings, marble hallways, and pillars inside.

The **World Trade Center** (26 S.W. Salmon St., tel. 503/222–2223) is a trio of buildings connected by sky bridges and designed by Portland architect Robert Frasca. Cross Front Avenue to **Governor Tom McCall Waterfront Park.** The grassy expanse, a former expressway, follows the curve of the Willamette north to Burnside Street; it's a popular venue for festivals, picnics, jogging, and biking.

Cross Front Avenue, and you're in the heart of the **Yamhill and Skidmore National Historic Districts,** which preserve many fine examples of 19th-century cast-iron architecture. The former commercial waterfront of Portland is now a district of galleries, fountains, and shops. Don't walk here at night.

The main mast of the battleship *Oregon,* which served in three wars, stands at the foot of Oak Street. Across Front Avenue is the **Oregon Maritime Center and Museum** (113 S.W. Front Ave., tel. 503/224–7724), whose exterior features prime street-level examples of cast-iron architecture. Inside are models of ships that once plied the Columbia River. Next door is the **Jeff**

Morris Memorial Fire Museum (111 S.W. Front Ave.) in the central Fire Station, which houses antique pumps and other equipment.

Nearby, **Portland Saturday Market** (100 S.W. Ankeny St., tel. 503/222–6072), also open on Sunday, features some 300 merchants selling an assortment of foods, art, and crafts from March through Christmas.

In the 1890s Portland's Chinese community was the second largest in the United States. Today it is compressed into several blocks in the northwest part of town, with fine restaurants, shops, and grocery stores. **Chinatown Gate** (N.W. 4th Ave. and Burnside St.) can be recognized by its five roofs, 64 dragons, and two huge lions; it is the official entrance to **Chinatown.**

The **Old Church,** built in 1882, is a prime example of Carpenter Gothic architecture, complete with rough-cut lumber, tall spires, and original stained-glass windows. Free concerts on one of the few operating Hook and Hastings pipe organs are presented on Wednesday at noon. *1422 S.W. 11th Ave., tel. 503/ 222–2031. Closed Sun.–Mon.*

Pittock Mansion, 1,000 feet above the city, offers superb views of the skyline, rivers, and Cascade Mountains. The 1909 mansion, which combines French Renaissance and Victorian decor, was built by Henry Pittock, former editor of *The Oregonian.* Set in its own park, the opulent manor has been restored and is filled with art and antiques of the 1880s. *3229 N.W. Pittock Dr., tel. 503/823–3624. Admission charged.*

In the Vicinity **Oregon City,** 13 mi south of Portland, was the western terminus of the Oregon Trail. The **End of The Trail Interpretive Center** highlights Oregon Trail travel with covered wagons, river rafts, firearms, and other artifacts, some of which were brought west by Trail travelers. *500 Washington St., tel. 503/ 657–9336. Admission charged.*

Here, also, is the **John McLoughlin House National Historic Site** (713 Center St., tel. 503/656–5146), commemorating the chief factor and superintendent of the Hudson's Bay Company, who built the house in 1846; his gaming table, china, bed, and other possessions remain. The **McLoughlin Historic District,** which surrounds the home, is part of his original plan and contains several blocks of picturesque dwellings and churches reflecting architectural styles from the 1840s to the 1930s.

Parks and Gardens

Portland is as famous for its parks as it is for its rain (37.81 in. per year on average). **Washington Park** covers 322 acres in the hills above downtown and contains the spectacular **International Rose Test Garden** and the **Japanese Gardens.** The fine **Washington Park Zoo** (4001 S.W. Canyon Rd., tel. 503/226–7627), established in 1887, has long been a prolific breeding ground for Asian elephants.

The 4,800-acre **Forest Park** (Box 2413, 97208, tel. 503/823–4492), in Portland's west hills, is America's largest urban wilderness, with more than 50 mi of trails and over 150 bird and animal species, including elk and bobcat.

What to See and Do with Children

Portland's Children's Museum (3037 S.W. 2nd Ave., tel. 503/823–2227) offers hands-on play with changing interactive exhibits. The **Oregon Museum of Science and Industry** (1945 S.E. Water Ave., tel. 503/797–4000), in a restored steam plant on the east bank of the Willamette, has touring exhibits and permanent displays.

Shopping

For local products, try the several **Made In Oregon** shops, at Portland International Airport, Lloyd Center, The Galleria, Old Town, Washington Square, or Clackamas Town Center. Merchandise ranges from books to distinctive myrtlewood, local wines, and woolen products.

Pioneer Place (700 S.W. 5th Ave., tel. 503/228–5800) is the jewel in the city's shopping crown. Its 66 specialty shops are anchored by a gleaming **Saks Fifth Avenue.** Next door is the original **Meier & Frank** (621 S.W. 5th Ave., tel. 503/223–0512) department store, a Portland landmark since 1857. **Nordstrom** (701 S.W. Broadway, tel. 503/224–6666), famous for personal service, features quality apparel and accessories and a large shoe department.

With more than 1 million new and used volumes, **Powell's City of Books** (1005 W. Burnside St., tel. 503/228–4651) is one of the largest bookstores in the world. **Norm Thompson** (1805 N.W. Thurman St., tel. 503/221–0764) features one-of-a-kind Northwest gifts. The **Portland Pendleton Shop** (900 S.W. 5th Ave., tel. 503/242–0037) carries men's and women's wear, including the Oregon mill's famous Pendleton shirts and blankets.

Spectator Sports

Basketball **Portland Trailblazers** (Memorial Coliseum, east end of Broadway Bridge, tel. 503/231–8000; Oct.–June).

Dining

Portland has more restaurants per capita than any other West Coast city. Bounteous local produce from land and sea receives star billing, but recent Pacific Rim immigrants have added depth and spice to the dining scene. For price ranges, see Chart 1 (B) in Chapter 1.

Expensive **Café des Amis.** At this romantic and unpretentious restaurant,
★ chef Dennis Baker puts a deft country-French spin on the superb local fish, game, and produce. The fresh-baked breads and desserts are among the city's best. *1987 N.W. Kearny St., tel. 503/295–6487. Reservations advised. AE, MC, V. No lunch; closed Sun.*

Genoa Restaurant. Small, crowded, and intimate, Genoa seats 35 people for sumptuous four- and seven-course northern Italian dinners. The menu changes to take advantage of seasonal bounty. *2832 S.E. Belmont St., tel. 503/238–1464. Reservations required. AE, D, DC, MC, V. No lunch; closed Sun.*

L'Auberge. At this French restaurant, you can dine simply beside the lounge fireplace or splurge on a six-course meal in the candlelit formal dining room. *2601 N.W. Vaughn St., tel. 503/*

223–3302. Reservations advised. Sun., bar menu only. AE, D, DC, MC, V.

Moderate **Chen's Dynasty.** The serene pastel interior of this downtown stalwart belies the flavorful Chinese regional cuisine. The 12-page menu ranges from the garlicky fire of Hunan to the delicate seafood of Canton, and includes such unusual items as peppered crunchy pig's ears. *622 S.W. Washington St., tel. 503/248–9491. Reservations advised. AE, DC, MC, V.*

★ **Indigine.** Owner-chef Millie Howe wows regulars with her original cuisine, which draws flavors from India, Latin America, Indonesia, and Italy. The surroundings are intimate, with a pleasing Japanese simplicity. *3725 S.E. Division St., tel. 503/238–1470. Reservations advised. MC, V. No lunch; closed Sun.–Mon.*

Jake's Famous Crawfish. Portland's best-known restaurant celebrated its 100th birthday in 1992. White-coated waiters serve up fresh Northwest seafood, selected from a lengthy sheet of daily specials, in a warren of old-fashioned wood-paneled dining rooms. *401 S.W. 12th Ave., tel. 503/226–1419. Reservations advised. AE, D, DC, MC, V. No lunch weekends.*

Inexpensive **Bangkok Kitchen.** Don't be daunted by the bland decor—the quality of the food makes up for it. Owner-chef Srichan Miller juggles lime, cilantro, coconut milk, lemongrass, curry, and (above all) hot peppers with great virtuosity. Order your dishes mild or medium-hot unless you have an asbestos tongue. *2534 S.E. Belmont St., tel. 503/236–7349. Reservations advised. No credit cards. No lunch Sat.; closed Sun.*

Yen Ha. The vibrant flavors of Vietnam find full expression at Yen Ha, thronged nightly with Asians and Caucasians alike. Superb rice-paper rolls (filled with shrimp, pungent bean threads, and fresh mint and dipped in peanut sauce) and exquisite noodle dishes are among the star attractions. *8640 S.W. Canyon Rd. (west Portland), tel. 503/292–0616; 6820 N.E. Sandy Blvd. (east Portland), tel. 503/287–3698. MC, V.*

Brew-pubs Portland's popular brew-pub scene offers both satisfying dining and good value. Among the standouts is the **B. Moloch Heathman Bakery and Pub** (901 S.W. Salmon St., tel. 503/227–5700), which offers a variety of local brews and inexpensive nouvelle pub cuisine. **The Bridgeport Brew Pub** (1313 N.W. Marshall St., tel. 503/241–7179) serves thick hand-thrown pizzas, washed down with creamy pints of Bridgeport real ale.

Lodging

There is a full array of national and regional chain offerings near the airport. The city center and waterfront support a variety of elegant new and historic hotels. B&Bs cluster in the West Hills and across the river in the Lloyd Center/Convention Center area. **Northwest Bed & Breakfast** (tel. 503/243–7616) is a good source of reservations for Portland and the entire coastal region. For price ranges, see Chart 2 (B) in Chapter 1.

Expensive **The Benson.** Portland's premier hotel, built in 1912, has received a $20 million face-lift, restoring it to its original turn-of-the-century grandeur. Elegance is everywhere, from walls paneled in Russian walnut to the muted tinkling of the lobby's grand piano to the opulent guest rooms. *309 S.W. Broadway, 97205, tel. 503/228–2000 or 800/426–0670; fax 503/226–4603.*

290 rooms. Facilities: 2 restaurants, 3 lounges, gift shop, air-port-shuttle service, concierge. AE, D, DC, MC, V.

★ **The Heathman.** Superior service, an award-winning restaurant, and a library of signed first editions by authors who have been guests here have earned The Heathman a reputation for quality. The guest rooms have original artwork by Northwest artists. *1009 S.W. Broadway, 97205, tel. 503/241-4100 or 800/551-0011; fax 503/790-7110. 152 rooms. Facilities: restaurant, bar, health club. AE, D, DC, MC, V.*

Hotel Vintage Plaza. This luxury hotel, built in 1991, takes its theme from the area's wine country. Suites feature full living areas appointed in hunter green, deep plum, cerise, and gold. *422 S.W. Broadway, 97205, tel. 503/228-1212 or 800/243-0555; fax 503/228-3598. 88 rooms, 19 suites. Facilities: restaurant, piano lounge, gym, business center, valet parking. AE, D, DC, MC, V.*

Red Lion/Lloyd Center. At Oregon's largest hotel, service runs like a well-oiled machine. Many large rooms with views of mountains or the city center have balconies. Lloyd Center shopping and MAX light rail are across the street. *1000 N.E. Multnomah St., 97232, tel. 503/281-6111 or 800/547-8010. 476 rooms, some handicapped accessible. Facilities: 3 restaurants, 3 lounges, entertainment, outdoor pool, weight room, airport shuttle, free parking. AE, D, DC, MC, V.*

Shilo Inn Suites Hotel. Each suite has three TVs, a VCR, a microwave, four phones, a refrigerator, a wet bar, and two over-size beds. *11707 N.E. Airport Way, 97220, tel. 503/252-7500 or 800/222-2244. 200 rooms, some handicapped accessible. Facilities: Continental breakfast, restaurant, lounge, indoor pool, spa, exercise room, steam room, business service center, airport shuttle. AE, D, DC, MC, V.*

Moderate **Best Western Inn at the Convention Center.** Rooms were redecorated in 1989 in pleasing creams and rusts at this property across the street from the convention center. *420 N.E. Holladay St., 97232, tel. 503/233-6331. 97 rooms. Facilities: restaurant (no dinner), whirlpool, free parking. AE, D, DC, MC, V.*

Portland Guest House. This northeast Portland "working-class Victorian," with its fresh coffee-and-cream exterior paint and original oak floors, was transformed into a cozy B&B in 1987. Rooms are done in white on white with Victorian walnut antique furniture and original Pacific Northwest art. *1720 N.E. 15th Ave., 97212, tel. 503/282-1402. 5 rooms (2 share bath). AE, DC, MC, V.*

Inexpensive **Downtown Portland YWCA.** The baths are down the hall, but the beds are new in this recently renovated Y for women 18 and older. At $6 to $30 a night, it's a rare lodging bargain. *1111 S.W. 10th Ave., 97205, tel. 503/223-6281. 23 rooms, plus an 8-bed hostel (all share baths). Facilities: full athletic club, laundry facilities, communal kitchenette, phones. MC, V.*

Mallory Hotel. This refurbished Portland stalwart is eight blocks from the city center. The rooms are on the small side but tastefully decorated in white and natural wood. *729 S.W. 15th Ave., 97205, tel. 503/223-6311 or 800/228-8657. 144 rooms. Facilities: restaurant, lounge, free parking. AE, DC, MC, V.*

Motels **Shilo Inn** (11707 N.E. Airport Way, 97220, tel. 503/252-7500), 200 suites, restaurant, pool, fitness center; expensive. **Portland Super 8** (11011 N.E. Holman St., 97220, tel. 503/257-

8988), 79 rooms, meeting rooms, guest laundry, copy machine, airport shuttle, free parking; moderate.

The Arts and Nightlife

The Oregonian (on newsstands) and *Willamette Week* (available free in the metro area) list arts and entertainment events. **Portland Area Theatre Alliance Hot Line** (tel. 503/241–4903) has current listings. **PDX-TIX** (921 S.W. Morrison St., tel. 503/241–4903), on the main floor of the Galleria downtown, offers half-price same-day tickets to many theatrical and musical events.

The Arts The Tony Award–winning **Oregon Shakespeare Festival,** from Ashland, performs from November to April at Portland's **Intermediate Theater** (1111 S.W. Broadway, tel. 503/248–6309). The **Portland Center for the Performing Arts** (tel. 503/248–4496) offers rock concerts, lectures, and Broadway musicals. The **Oregon Symphony** (tel. 503/228–1353) performs more than 40 concerts each season at the **Arlene Schnitzer Concert Hall. Portland Opera** performs September to June at the **Civic Auditorium** (S.W. 3rd Ave. and Clay St. downtown, tel. 503/241–1802).

Nightlife With its theaters, movie houses, bars, nightclubs, and comedy clubs, Portland's downtown core is the best bet for nightlife. **Dakota Cafe** (239 S.W. Broadway, tel. 503/241–4151) features top 40, dance, and alternative music for a young professional clientele. **Key Largo Restaurant and Bar** (31 N.W. 1st Ave., tel. 503/223–9919) is a romantic spot, with nightly live rock, jazz, and country music, in a historic building with brick walls and an outdoor courtyard. **The Dublin Pub** (6821 Beaverton/Hillsdale Hwy., tel. 503/297–2889) has a great selection of beers and Irish folk music. Jazz happens nightly at **Brasserie Montmartre** (626 S.W. Park Ave., tel. 503/224–5552). **Parchman Farm** (1204 S.E. Clay St., tel. 503/235–7831) offers prominent local jazz performers. For comedy try **The Last Laugh** (1130 S.W. Main St., tel. 503/295–2844), which presents headliners with a national reputation.

The Oregon Coast

Oregon has 300 mi of white-sand beaches, not a grain of which is privately owned. Hwy. 101 parallels the coast from Astoria south to California, past stunning monoliths of sea-tortured rock, brooding headlands, hidden beaches, haunted lighthouses, tiny ports, and, of course, the placid Pacific.

Tourist Information

Astoria: Chamber of Commerce (111 W. Marine Dr., 97103, tel. 503/325–6311). **Bay Area:** Chamber of Commerce (50 E. Central St., Coos Bay 97420, tel. 503/269–0215 or 800/824–8486). **Cannon Beach:** Chamber of Commerce (2nd and Spruce Sts., 97110, tel. 503/436–2623). **Florence Area:** Chamber of Commerce (270 Hwy. 101, 97439, tel. 503/997–3128). **Lincoln City:** Visitors Center (801 S.W. Hwy. 101, 97367, tel. 503/994–8378 or 800/452–2151).

Getting There

By Plane **Portland International** (*see* Portland, *above*) is the closest major airport.

By Car The best way to see the coast is by car, following twisting, slow-paced, two-lane Hwy. (U.S.) 101. Hwy. 26 (the Sunset) is the main link to Portland.

By Bus **Greyhound** (tel. 503/243–2323) serves coastal communities such as Coos Bay, Florence, and Lincoln City. **RAZ Transportation** (tel. 503/246–3301) serves Astoria and Seaside.

Exploring the Oregon Coast

Astoria, founded in 1811 where the mighty Columbia River meets the sea, is believed to be the oldest city west of the Mississippi. Here Lewis and Clark wept with joy at their first sight of the Pacific. The Victorian houses of fur, timber, and fishing magnates still dot the flanks of Coxcomb Hill; many are now inviting bed-and-breakfasts. **The Astoria Column,** a 125-foot-tall monolith atop Coxcomb Hill, patterned after Trajan's Column in Rome, rewards a climb up 164 spiral stairs with breathtaking views over Astoria, the Columbia, the Coast Range, and the sea.

The **Columbia River Maritime Museum** has exhibits ranging from the fully operational lightship *Columbia* to poignant personal belongings from some of the 2,000 ships that have been wrecked at the mouth of the river since 1811. *Foot of 17th St., tel. 503/325–2323. Admission charged.*

Nine mi south of Astoria is the **Ft. Clatsop National Memorial** (Hwy. 101, tel. 503/861–2471), a replica of the log stockade depicted in Clark's journal, commemorating the achievement of Lewis and Clark. Farther south are **Tillamook Head** and **Ecola State Park** (tel. 503/436–2844), a popular playground of sea-sculpted rock, sandy beach, tide pools, green headlands, and panoramic views.

Thirty miles south of Astoria is refined, artistic **Cannon Beach,** whose proximity to Portland has endowed it with a fabulous weathered-cedar shopping district, some of the coast's most beautiful beachfront homes, and a subtle, moneyed hauteur. It's a good place for shopping and eating, though expensive and pretentious by Oregon standards. **Haystack Rock,** a 235-foot offshore monolith a short walk across a sandy beach, is a bird sanctuary—and one of the most photographed sites on the coast.

South of Neahkahnie Mountain, **Tillamook** invites travelers to taste the cheese that has made the area world-famous, at the factory on U.S. 101. The **Three Capes Scenic Loop,** west of town, encompasses magnificent coastal scenery, a lighthouse, offshore wildlife refuges, sand dunes, camping areas, and hiking trails.

The bustling little towns of **Lincoln City** and **Newport,** united in spirit if a few miles apart geographically, are known for excellent seafood and lodgings.

Newport's charming old bayfront is a fine place for an afternoon stroll, with its fishing fleet, weathered buildings, art galleries, steaming crab kettles, and seafood markets. **Marina**

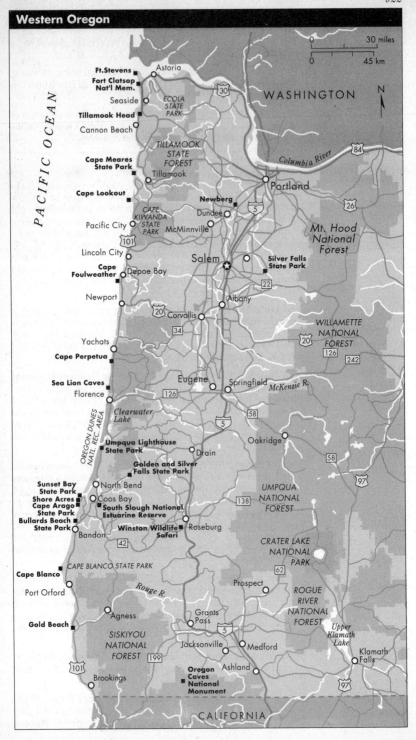

Western Oregon

WASHINGTON

PACIFIC OCEAN

30 miles
45 km

N

Ft. Stevens
Fort Clatsop
Nat'l Mem.
Astoria
Seaside
ECOLA STATE PARK
Tillamook Head
Cannon Beach

TILLAMOOK STATE FOREST

Columbia River

Portland

Cape Meares State Park
Tillamook

Cape Lookout
Newberg
Dundee
CAPE KIWANDA STATE PARK
McMinnville
Pacific City

Mt. Hood National Forest

Lincoln City
Cape Foulweather
Depoe Bay
Salem
Silver Falls State Park

Newport

Corvallis

Albany

WILLAMETTE NATIONAL FOREST

Yachats
Cape Perpetua

Eugene
Springfield
McKenzie R.

Sea Lion Caves
Florence

Clearwater Lake

OREGON DUNES NATL. REC. AREA

Oakridge

Umpqua Lighthouse State Park
Drain

Golden and Silver Falls State Park

UMPQUA NATIONAL FOREST

Sunset Bay State Park
North Bend
Shore Acres
Cape Arago State Park
Coos Bay
South Slough National Estuarine Reserve
Bullards Beach State Park
Winston Wildlife Safari
Roseburg
Bandon

CRATER LAKE NATIONAL PARK

CAPE BLANCO STATE PARK

Cape Blanco
Rouge R.
Port Orford
Prospect

ROGUE RIVER NATIONAL FOREST

Agness
Grants Pass
Gold Beach

SISKIYOU NATIONAL FOREST
Jacksonville
Medford

Upper Klamath Lake

Klamath Falls

Brookings
Oregon Caves National Monument
Ashland

CALIFORNIA

Square (250 S.W. Bay Blvd., tel. 503/265–2206; admission charged) includes undersea gardens and a wax museum. Across Yakina Bay is the **Oregon Coast Aquarium** (Ferry Slip Rd., tel. 503/867–3474; admission charged). New in 1992, it features 2.5 acres of pools, cliffs, and sandy shores; four indoor galleries; and a theater devoted to whales.

South of Newport, the coast takes on a very different character—slower-paced, less touristy, far less crowded, but just as rich in scenery and outdoor sporting activities. The peaceful coastal village of **Florence** is the northern gateway to the **Oregon Dunes National Recreation Area** (855 Highway Ave., Reedsport 97467, tel. 503/271–3611), a 47-mi swath of undulating lion-colored sand. The dunes, some more than 250 feet high, are a vast and exuberant playground for children, particularly the sandy slopes surrounding cool Cleawox Lake.

Umpqua River Lighthouse State Park (west of U.S. 101) adjoins an operating lighthouse and encompasses a small freshwater lake and campground. Next to it are a whale-watching station, 500-foot-high sand dunes, and the **Douglas County Coastal Visitors Center** (tel. 503/271–4631), which has local history exhibits.

Coos Bay is the Oregon coast's largest metropolitan area, and although its tourist amenities are somewhat rustic, it still makes a good home base for exploring the region. At lovely **Golden and Silver Falls State Park** (off U.S. 101, 24 mi northeast of Coos Bay, tel. 503/888–4902), Glenn Creek pours over a high rock ledge deep in the old-growth forest. West of Coos Bay, the Cape Arago Highway presents spectacular scenery at three state parks (tel. 503/888–4902): **Sunset Bay** with a white-sand beach, picnicking, and campgrounds; **Shore Acres,** once the estate of a timber baron, with a 7.5-acre formal garden and a glass-enclosed storm-watch viewpoint; and **Cape Arago,** a prime site for viewing sea lions and whales. At nearby **South Slough National Estuarine Reserve** (Seven Devils Rd., tel. 503/888–5558), rich tidal estuaries support life ranging from algae to bald eagles and black bears.

Bullards Beach State Park (tel. 503/347–2209), 1 mi north of Bandon, spreads over miles of shoreline and impressive sand dunes. It has a campground as well as the restored **Coquille River Lighthouse. Cape Blanco Lighthouse,** west of the community of Sixes, was built in 1878 and is still operating. It is the most westerly lighthouse in the contiguous 48 states. Adjacent **Cape Blanco State Park** (tel. 503/332–6774) offers sweeping views of rocks and beaches, plus a campground.

Many knowledgeable coastal travelers consider the 63-mi stretch of U.S. 101 between Port Orford and Gold Beach to be Oregon's most beautiful. The highway soars up green headlands, some hundreds of feet high, past awesome sea-sculpted scenery: caves, towering arches, natural and man-made bridges. One caution: Take time to admire the scenery, but make use of the many turnouts and viewpoints along the way—this close to California, traffic can be heavy, and rubbernecking dangerous.

Gold Beach, about 20 mi north of the California border, is notable mainly as the place where the wild Rogue River meets the ocean. Daily jet-boat excursions roar up the scenic, rapids-filled Rogue from Wedderburn, Gold Beach's sister city across the bay, from late spring to late fall. Gold Beach also marks the entrance to Oregon's banana belt, where milder temperatures encourage a blossoming trade in lilies and daffodils. You'll even see a few palm trees here—a rare sight in Oregon.

What to See and Do with Children

May brings the **Cannon Beach Sandcastle Contest,** when thousands throng the beach to view imaginative and often startling works in this most transient of art forms. **Indian Forest** (4 mi north of Florence on U.S. 101, tel. 503/997–3677) features buffalo, deer, and full-size Native American dwellings. **Sea Lion Caves** (tel. 503/547–3111), off U.S. 101 near Florence, is a huge vaulted chamber where kids can get a close view of hundreds of sea lions, the largest of which weigh 2,000 pounds or more. **West Coast Game Park Safari** (7 mi south of Brandon on U.S. 101, tel. 503/347–3106; closed weekdays) offers animals of more than 75 exotic species, some of which children can pet. At **Prehistoric Gardens** (13 mi south of Port Orford on U.S. 101, tel. 503/332–4463), kids come face-to-face with life-size dinosaurs.

Shopping

Hemlock Street, Cannon Beach's main drag, is the best place on the coast to browse for unusual clothing, souvenirs, picnic supplies, books, and gifts. Newport's **Bay Boulevard** is a good place to find local artwork, gifts, and foodstuffs. There are bargains galore at Lincoln City's **Manufacturer's Outlet Mall** (Hwy. 101, tel. 503/996–5000), which has elevated shopping to a sport along the central coast.

Sports and Outdoor Activities

Biking   The **Oregon Coast Bike Route** (tel. 503/378–3432) parallels Hwy. 101 and the coast from Astoria south to Brookings. For mountain bikers, the **Oregon Dunes National Recreation Area** (*see* Exploring the Oregon Coast, *above*) near Florence offers a unique challenge.

Fishing   Huge salmon (some weighing 50 pounds or more), delectable Dungeness crab, and dozens of species of bottom fish are the quarry here, accessible from jetties, docks, and riverbanks from Astoria to Brookings. Charter boats and guides are plentiful; contact local chambers of commerce (*see* Tourist Information, *above*) for information on seasons, rates, and schedules.

Golf   The Oregon coast has about 20 public and private courses, including (from north to south) **Salishan Golf Links** (Gleneden Beach, tel. 503/764–3632), the coast's most challenging course, with 18 holes; Newport's nine-hole **Agate Beach Golf Club** (tel. 503/265–7331); 18-hole **Ocean Dunes Golf Links** in Florence (tel. 503/997–3232); and Gold Beach's nine-hole **Cedar Bend Golf Course** (tel. 503/247–6911).

Beaches

Virtually the entire 300-mi coastline of Oregon is a clean, quiet white-sand beaches, accessible to all. Thanks to its sea-sculpted stone, **Face Rock Wayside,** just outside Bandon, is thought by many to have the most beautiful walking beach in the state. The placid semicircular lagoon at **Sunset Bay State**

Park on Cape Arago is Oregon's safest swimming beach. Fossils, clams, mussels, and other eons-old marine creatures embedded in soft sandstone cliffs make **Beverly Beach State Park** (5 mi north of Newport) a favorite with young beachcombers.

Dining and Lodging

For price ranges, see Charts 1 (B) and 2 (B) in Chapter 1.

Astoria
Dining

Dooley's West Texas Barbecue. You'll get tangy, lean barbecued and mesquite-grilled chicken, ribs, and beef at this riverfront restaurant. There are only about a dozen tables, so come early. *144 11th St., tel. 503/325–5534. Reservations advised. MC, V. Closed Sun. Moderate.*

Pier 11 Feed Store Restaurant & Lounge. This spacious restaurant, overlooking the Columbia from a renovated pier/warehouse, serves hearty and abundant fish, steaks, and prime rib. *Foot of 10th St., tel. 503/325–0279. MC, V. Moderate.*

Lodging
★

Franklin Street Station Bed & Breakfast. The ticking of clocks and mellow marine light shining through leaded-glass windows set the tone at this B&B, built in 1900. Breakfasts are huge, hot, and satisfying. *1140 Franklin Ave., 97103, tel. 503/325–4314. 5 rooms. MC, V. Moderate.*

Brookings
Dining

Mama's Authentic Italian Food. Home-style Italian food is served in this small, simply furnished, and always busy restaurant. *703 Chetco Ave., tel. 503/469–7611. MC, V. Inexpensive.*

Lodging
★

Chetco River Inn. Acres of private forest surround this remote but splendid modern fishing lodge B&B 15 mi up the turquoise river from Brookings. Fishing guides are available upon request, as are eclectic dinners cooked by the hosts. Quilts and fishing gear decorate the comfortable bedrooms. *21202 High Prairie Rd., 97415, tel. 503/469–8128 (radio phone) or 800/327–2688. 4 rooms (1 with shared bath). MC, V. Moderate.*

Cannon Beach
Dining

The Bistro. Cannon Beach's most romantic restaurant is small, candlelit, and intimate. The menu features imaginative, Continental-influenced renditions of fresh local seafood dishes in a four-course fixed-price menu. *263 N. Hemlock St., tel. 503/436–2661. MC, V. No lunch weekdays; closed Wed. Expensive.*

Dooger's. This comfortable family-style eatery's fresh, well-prepared seafood, exquisite clam chowder, and low prices keep 'em coming back for more. *1371 S. Hemlock St., tel. 503/436–2225. MC, V. Inexpensive–Moderate.*

Mo's. A half-dozen Mo's restaurants are scattered from Cannon Beach to Florence. The chowder is legendary—a creamy potion flavored with bacon and onion and studded with tender potatoes and clams. The menu glorifies fresh local seafood, simply prepared at family prices. Kids love this place. *4300 S. Hemlock St., tel. 503/436–1111. Other locations: Florence (1436 Bay St., tel. 503/997–2185); Newport (622 S.W. Bay Blvd., tel. 503/265–2979); and Otter Rock (925 1st St., tel. 503/765–2442). No reservations. No credit cards. Inexpensive.*

Lodging

Surfview Resort. The destination of choice on the north coast, this oceanfront resort offers cozy rooms, many with fireplaces, kitchens, and/or whirlpools; and the best views in Cannon Beach. *1400 S. Hemlock St., 97110, tel. 503/436–1566 or 800/345–5676. 33 units. Facilities: restaurant, lounge, indoor pool,* *sauna, whirlpool, weight room, kiddie pool, refrigerators, covered parking. AE, D, DC, MC, V. Expensive.*

Webb's Scenic Surf. This quiet beachfront hotel is a throwback to simpler times in Cannon Beach. The rooms, many with kitchens and fireplaces, are functional and clean, and the beds are comfortable. *255 N. Larch St., 97110, tel. 503/436–2706. 14 rooms. MC, V. Moderate.*

Coos Bay
Dining

The Blue Heron Bistro. You'll get subtle preparations of local seafood, chicken, and homemade pasta with an international flair at this busy bistro. There are no flat spots on the far-ranging menu; the innovative soups and desserts are also excellent. *100 Commercial St., tel. 503/267–3933. Reservations advised. MC, V. Moderate.*

The Portside Restaurant. This unpretentious spot with picture windows overlooking the busy Charleston boat basin buys directly from the fishermen moored outside. Try the steamed Dungeness crab with drawn butter, a local specialty, or the all-you-can-eat seafood buffet Friday night. *8001 Kingfisher Rd. (follow Cape Arago Hwy. from Coos Bay), tel. 503/888–5544. AE, D, DC, MC, V. No lunch weekends. Moderate.*

Lodging
★

This Olde House B&B. The charm and care that have gone into the renovation of this sprawling Victorian four blocks up the hill from downtown Coos Bay are matched only by the charm and warmth of its owners. *202 Alder Ave., 97420, tel. 503/267–5224. 4 rooms (3 share bath). Facilities: breakfast. No credit cards. Moderate.*

Florence
Dining

Bridgewater Seafood Restaurant. The venerably salty ambience of Florence's photogenic bayfront Old Town permeates this spacious fish house. Steaks, salads, and, of course, plenty of fresh seafood are the mainstays at this creaky-floored Victorian-era restaurant. *1297 Bay St., tel. 503/997–9405. AE, D, DC, MC, V. No lunch weekends. Moderate.*

Gleneden Beach
Dining and Lodging

Salishan Lodge. For most visitors, this is *the* resort on the Oregon coast. From the soothing, silvered-cedar ambience of its fireplaced guest rooms, nestled into a 750-acre hillside forest preserve, to its collections of wine (20,000 bottles at last count) and original art, Salishan embodies a uniquely Oregonian elegance. The dining room is famous for its seasonal Northwest cuisine. *Hwy. 101, 97388, tel. 503/764–2371 or 800/452–2300. 205 rooms. Facilities: 3 restaurants, bar, private beach access, indoor pool, spas and saunas, indoor and outdoor tennis courts, 18-hole golf course, men's and women's weight rooms, playground, conference facilities. AE, D, DC, MC, V. Expensive.*

Gold Beach
Dining and Lodging
★

Tu Tu Tun Lodge. This famous, richly appointed fishing resort perches above the clear blue Rogue River, 7 mi upstream from Gold Beach. The units are furnished with rustic charm; private decks overlook the river and the surrounding old-growth forest. Huge amounts of satisfying, straightforward American fare are served. *96550 North Bank Rogue, 97444, tel. 503/247–6664. 16 rooms, 2 suites, 1 3-bedroom house. Facilities: restaurant, bar, heated outdoor pool, hiking, boat dock and ramp, fishing (salmon, steelhead), jet-boat excursions. Closed Nov.–Apr. MC, V. Expensive.*

Lodging

Ireland's Rustic Lodges. Original one- and two-bedroom cabins filled with rough-and-tumble charm, plus newer motel rooms, are set amid spectacular landscaping. Each unit has a fireplace and a deck overlooking the sea. *1120 S. Ellensburg Ave. (just off Hwy. 101), 97444, tel. 503/247–7718. 3 cabins, 29 motel rooms. No-smoking rooms available. No credit cards. Inexpensive–Moderate.*

Lincoln City
Dining
★

The Bay House. This charming bungalow serves meals to linger over while you enjoy views across sunset-gilded Siletz Bay. The Northwest cuisine includes Dungeness crab cakes with roasted chile chutney, fresh halibut Parmesan, and roast duckling with fig-plum sauce. The wine list is extensive, the service impeccable. *5911 S.W. Hwy. 101, tel. 503/996–3222. Reservations advised. AE, D, MC, V. No lunch; closed Mon.–Tues. Nov.–Apr. Moderate–Expensive.*

Lighthouse Brew Pub. This westernmost outpost of the Portland-based McMenamins microbrewery empire features ales brewed on the premises, good food, and cheerfully eccentric decor. Families are welcome. *4157 N. Hwy. 101, (in the shopping center), tel. 503/994–7238. No reservations. MC, V. Inexpensive.*

Lodging

Ester Lee Motel. Perched on a seaside bluff, this small white-washed motel attracts a devoted repeat business through value and simplicity. For the price, there are some nice amenities, including wood-burning fireplaces, full kitchens, and cable TV in all rooms. *3803 S.W. Hwy. 101, 97367, tel. 503/996–3606. 54 units. D, MC, V. Moderate.*

Newport
Dining and Lodging
★

The Sylvia Beach Hotel. At this restored 1912 B&B, each of the antiques-filled guest rooms (some with decks) is named for a famous writer and decorated on that theme. In the Poe Room, for instance, a pendulum swings over the bed. Upstairs is a well-stocked library with fireplace, slumbering cats, and too-comfortable chairs. Breakfast is a hearty buffet. *267 N.W. Cliff St., 97365, tel. 503/265–5428. 20 rooms. Facilities: restaurant. No smoking. AE, MC, V. Moderate.*

Port Orford
Dining
★

The Whale Cove. The food here, such as broiled salmon with wasabi butter, is legendary—rich, subtle, and worth a drive from Portland. The interior is romantic, with flowers, classical music, and views of the Pacific. *190 6th St. (Hwy. 101), tel. 503/332–7575. Reservations advised. MC, V. Closed Mon.–Tues. Moderate.*

Campgrounds

Nineteen state parks along the coast include campgrounds. Most feature full hookups and tent sites. Many are near the shore, and some contain group facilities and hiker/biker or horse camps. The **Oregon State Parks and Recreation Department** (*see* National and State Parks, *above*) has details. **Honeyman State Park** (84505 Hwy. 101, Florence 97439, tel. 503/997–3641) adjoins the Oregon Dunes National Recreation Area. Reserve well ahead.

Elsewhere in the State

Mt. Hood and Bend

Getting There

Mt. Hood lies about an hour east of Portland on U.S. 26; the only way to get there is by car. Continue east on U.S. 26, then south on U.S. 97, for the resort town of Bend, two hours beyond

Mt. Hood. **Bend-Redmond Airport** (tel. 503/548–2148) is served by **Horizon Airlines** (tel. 800/547–9308) and **United Express** (tel. 800/241–6522).

What to See and Do Mt. Hood, 11,235 feet high and surrounded by the 1,079,169-acre **Mt. Hood National Forest** (2955 Northwest Division, Gresham 97030, tel. 503/666-0700), is an all-season playground that attracts more than 4 million visitors annually for skiing, camping, hiking, fishing, or day trips to breathe the resinous mountain air. Historic **Timberline Lodge** (off U.S. 26 a few miles east of Government Camp; Timberline 97028, tel. 503/272–3311 or 800/547–1406) has withstood howling winter storms on the mountain's flank for 60 years; it's a popular spot for romantic getaways. There is year-round skiing on the slopes above.

Hood River is the self-proclaimed sailboarding capital of the world. **Columbia Gorge Sailpark** (Port Marina, tel. 503/386–2000), on the river downtown, offers a boat basin, a swimming beach, jogging trails, and picnic tables.

The skiing is also excellent in **Bend,** which occupies a tawny high-desert plateau in the very center of Oregon, framed on the west by three 10,000-foot Cascade peaks. With its plentiful dining and lodging options, Bend makes a fine base camp for skiing at nearby Mt. Bachelor, white-water rafting on the Deschutes River, world-class rock-climbing at Smith Rocks State Park, and other outdoor activities. Don't miss the archaeological and wildlife displays at the **High Desert Museum** (59800 S. U.S. 97, 6 mi south of Bend, tel. 503/382–4754; admission charged). **Newberry Crater National Monument** (25 mi southeast of Bend, tel. 503/388–2715) provides recreation for cross-country skiers, snowmobilers, fishermen, and hikers.

Willamette Valley/Wine Country

Getting There I–5, the state's main north–south freeway, runs straight down the center of the Willamette Valley from Portland.

What to See and Do Oregon's wine country occupies the wet, temperate trough between the Coast Range to the west and the Cascades to the east. More than 40 wineries dot the hills between Portland and Salem, and dozens more are scattered from Newport as far south as Ashland, on the California border. Although tiny in comparison with California's, Oregon's wine industry is booming. Cool-climate varietals such as Pinot noir and Riesling have gained the esteem of international connoisseurs.

Most of the vineyards welcome visitors, and a day of touring, tasting, and picnicking is a popular local excursion. The best way to tour is by car. "Discover Oregon Wineries," an indispensable map and guide to the wine country, is available free at wineshops and wineries or by calling the **Oregon Winegrowers' Association** (tel. 503/228–8337). **Northwest Bed & Breakfast** (tel. 503/243–7616) is a good source of reservations for the area's extensive B&B network.

Newberg, a graceful old pioneer town at a broad bend in the Willamette River southwest of Portland, is the site of the **Hoover-Minthorne House** (115 S. River St., tel. 503/538–6629), the boyhood home of President Herbert Hoover. Built in 1881, the beautifully preserved and well-landscaped frame house includes many of the original furnishings. To the south, the idyllic orchardland around **Dundee** produces 90% of America's hazelnut crop.

Salem, the state capital, makes a good base of operations; in addition to its hotels, B&Bs, and restaurants, there are some fine gardens and museums. A brightly gilded 23-foot-high bronze statue of the Oregon Pioneer atop the 140-foot capitol dome is the centerpiece of Salem's **Capitol Mall** (900 Court St., tel. 503/378–4423), where Oregon's legislators convene every two years. Nearby are the tradition-steeped brick buildings of **Willamette University,** the oldest college in the West, founded in 1842. Just south of downtown, **Bush's Pasture Park** (600 Mission St. SE, tel. 503/363–4174) includes a Victorian mansion with 10 fireplaces and an art center with two exhibition galleries. **Deepwood Estate** (1116 Mission St. SE, tel. 503/363–1825), on the National Register of Historic Places, encompasses 105 acres of lawns, formal English gardens, and a fanciful 1894 Queen Anne mansion with splendid interior woodwork and original stained glass. **Silver Falls State Park** (26 mi east of Salem, tel. 503/873–8681) covers 8,300 acres and includes 14 waterfalls accessible to hikers.

At **Albany,** 24 mi south on I–5, visitors can take self-guided driving tours of three historic districts with 350 homes in every major architectural style popular in the United States since 1850. Tour maps are available at the **Albany Chamber of Commerce** (435 W. 1st St., 97321, tel. 503/926–1517).

Eugene, Oregon's second-largest city, is the home of the **University of Oregon** (the setting for *National Lampoon's Animal House*) and the **Willamette Science and Technology Center** (2300 Leo Harris Pkwy., tel. 503/687–3619), where imaginative hands-on scientific exhibits and a planetarium absorb children and adults alike.

To the south, the sleepy farming community of **Roseburg** is on the Umpqua River, famous among fishermen. West of town are eight of the region's wineries. The **Douglas County Museum** (Fairgrounds, I–5 Exit 123, tel. 503/440–4507) has an exceptional fossil collection. **Winston Wildlife Safari** (3 mi west of I–5, Winston, tel. 503/679–6761; admission charged) is a drive-through wildlife park with a petting zoo, elephant rides, a restaurant, and an RV park. **Hwy. 138** from Roseburg to Crater Lake is a National Scenic Byway. It takes you through rugged canyons and past several waterfalls, numerous camping areas, and some mountain lakes.

Ashland/The Rogue Valley

Getting There   Ashland is midway between Portland and San Francisco on I–5, about 15 mi north of the California border. **Jackson County Airport** (tel. 503/772–8068) in nearby Medford is served by **Horizon Airlines, United, United Express,** and **USAir.**

What to See   **Ashland** is home to the Tony Award–winning **Oregon Shake-**
and Do   **speare Festival** (tel. 503/482–4331), which annually attracts more than 400,000 visitors to this relaxing Rogue Valley town. The local arts scene, a warm climate, and a critical mass of opulent B&Bs and sumptuous restaurants make this an exceptionally pleasant place for a holiday. There is excellent downhill and Nordic skiing atop 7,523-foot-high **Mt. Ashland;** to the west, the famous Rogue River boils and churns through the rugged

and remote **Kalmiopsis Wilderness** in Siskiyou National Forest (tel. 503/479–5301). The local wineries are also worth a visit.

Nearby **Jacksonville** preserves the look and feel of an Old West pioneer settlement; the entire town is a National Historic Landmark. Each summer Jacksonville hosts the **Peter Britt Festival** (tel. 503/773–6077), a concert series featuring some of the world's best jazz and classical musicians. **Crater Lake National Park** (*see* National and State Parks, *above*) is about 80 mi northeast along Hwy. 62.

WASHINGTON

By Tom Gauntt
Updated by
Loralee Wenger

Capital	Olympia
Population	4.9 million
Motto	By-and-by
State Bird	Willow goldfinch
State Flower	Rhododendron

Visitor Information

Washington Tourism Development Division (101 General Administration Bldg., Olympia, 98504, tel. 206/586–2088).

Scenic Drives

About 90 mi north of Seattle, starting from just south of Bellingham on I–5, Hwy. 11 loops 25 mi around **Chuckanut Bay.** On one side of Hwy. 11 is the steep, heavily wooded Chuckanut Mountain, and on the other are sweeping views of Puget Sound and the San Juan Islands. The area is also dotted with fine restaurants. Hwy. 14 winds east from Vancouver, near the Oregon border, into the **Columbia River National Scenic Area.** The road clings to the steep slopes of the gorge most of the time and features several tunnels and picturesque towns such as Carson, known for its hot springs, and White Salmon, renowned for windsurfing.

National and State Parks

National Parks **Mt. Rainier National Park** (Superintendent's Office, Tahoma Woods, Star Rte., Ashford 98304, tel. 206/569–2211), about 85 mi southeast of Seattle, features 14,410-foot Mt. Rainier—the fifth-highest mountain in the lower 48 states—and nearly 400 sq mi of surrounding wilderness. The visitor center has exhibits, films, and a 360-degree view of the summit and surrounding peaks. For a vision of the apocalypse, head for the **Mt. St. Helens National Volcanic Monument** (3029 Spirit Lake Hwy., Castle Rock 98611, tel. 206/274-6644). The visitor center is on Hwy. 504, 3 mi east of the Castle Rock exit off I–5. The monument is 45 mi east of Castle Rock. Although the crater still steams and small earthquakes are common, excellent views are available within 10 mi of the mountain. **Olympic National Park** (3002 Mt. Angeles Rd., Port Angeles 98362, tel. 206/452–0330) is one of the most outstanding pieces of natural beauty in America, with such diversified areas as the wilderness coastline, the lush green of the temperate Hoh Rain Forest, some 60 active glaciers, and the alpine beauty of Hurricane Ridge. **North Cascades National Park** (2105 Hwy. 20, Sedro Woolley 98284, tel. 206/856–5700), a little-known park about 120 mi northeast of Seattle, holds some of the state's most rugged mountains, high, craggy peaks, and jewellike lakes.

For information about any of the national parks and monuments in Washington, contact the **U.S. Forest Service and National Park Service Outdoor Recreation and Information Center** (915 2nd Ave. #442, Seattle 98174, tel. 206/553–0170).

State Parks **Leadbetter State Park** (Robert Gray Dr., 2 mi south of Ilwaco, Box 488, 98624, tel. 206/642–3078), at the northernmost tip of the Long Beach Peninsula, is a wildlife refuge, good for bird-watching. The dunes at the very tip are closed April to August to protect the nesting snowy plover. Black brants, sandpipers, turnstones, yellowlegs, sanderlings, knots, and plovers are among the 100 species known to inhabit the point.

Seattle

Whether it's a double, tall, decaf nonfat latte with a dash of nutmeg or a standard cup of java, coffee has transformed Seattle's reputation from soggy and mossy to rich, dark, and steamy. Ever since three enterprising young men first started Starbucks, the city's premier coffee company, 15 years ago, Seattle has risen to claim its place as the nation's coffee capital. On nearly every block downtown and dotting Seattle neighborhoods, visitors will find espresso carts and coffee shops.

In the days when Starbucks began setting the stage for caffeine mania, Seattle was largely a city of Boeing employees who exited to the Olympic and Cascade mountains as often as possible to hike, backpack, and climb. Wearing corduroy slacks and a plaid wool shirt with a slide rule in the pocket was de rigueur.

Today Seattle has grown into a major cultural center, and its sophistication is evident in its architecture, food, fashion, and arts. The city is a magnet for people who are drawn by its blend of urban sophistication, easygoing charm, and ready access to spectacular outdoor recreation. The arts are strong and innovative, and the restaurants—from tiny International District dumpling stands to posh world-class dining rooms—serve a steady supply of visitors, longtime residents, and newcomers, all caught up in the act of simultaneously discovering and celebrating this place. Surrounding it all are still the old familiars, the mountains and the water.

Tourist Information

Seattle/King County: Visitor Information Center (666 Stewart St., 98101, tel. 206/461–5840). **Seattle/King County:** Convention and Visitors Bureau (800 Convention Pl., at the I–5 end of Pike St., 98101, tel. 206/461–5840).

Arriving and Departing

By Plane **Seattle-Tacoma International Airport (SeaTac)** is 20 mi south of downtown, and is served by major American and some foreign airlines. A cab ride to downtown takes about 30 to 45 minutes, and the fare is about $25. **Gray Line Airport Express** (tel. 206/626–6088) buses run to and from major downtown hotels. Fare: $7 one-way, $12 round-trip.

By Car I–5 enters Seattle from the north and south, I–90 from the east.

Bus Station **Greyhound** (8th Ave. and Stewart St., tel. 206/624–3456).

Train Station **Amtrak** (303 S. Jackson St., tel. 800/872–7245).

Getting Around Seattle

You need a car to cover metropolitan Seattle. Downtown, however, despite steep hills, is good for walking, as are several neighborhood areas.

By Car Driving can be a chore, with steep viaducts, tunnels, reversible express lanes, and frustrating rush hours. Main thoroughfares into downtown are Aurora Avenue (called the Alaskan Way Viaduct through town) and I–5.

By Public Transportation **Metropolitan Transit** (tel. 206/553–3000) provides a free-ride service in the downtown-waterfront area; fares to other destinations range from 75¢ to $1.50, depending on the zone and time of day. The elevated **Monorail**, a futuristic leftover from the 1962 Seattle World's Fair, runs the 2 mi from the Seattle Center to the edge of downtown; the fare is 60¢.

By Taxi Cab hailing is not a Seattle sport. Fare is $1.20 at the flag drop and $1.40 per mile. Major companies are **Farwest** (tel. 206/622–1717) and **Yellow Cab** (tel. 206/622–6500).

Orientation Tours *By Bus* **Gray Line** (Sheraton Hotel, 1400 6th Ave., tel. 206/626–5208) offers guided bus tours of the city and environs, from a daily 2½-hour spin to a six-hour "Grand City Tour," offered in spring, summer, and fall.

By Boat **Seattle Harbor Tours** (Pier 55, tel. 206/623–1445) offers one-hour tours of Elliott Bay and the port of Seattle.

Walking Tours The **Underground Tour** (tel. 206/682–4646 or 206/682–1511) explores the Pioneer Square area, including the now-below-ground sections that have been built over.

Exploring Seattle

Downtown Downtown Seattle is bounded by the Kingdome to the south, the Seattle Center to the north, I–5 to the east, and the waterfront to the west. You can reach most points of interest by foot, bus, or the Monorail. Remember, though, that Seattle is a city of hills, so wear your walking shoes.

The **Seattle Art Museum** (1320 2nd Ave., tel. 206/625–8900; admission charged) opened in 1991. The five-story building, designed by postmodern theorist Robert Venturi, is a work of art in itself, its limestone exterior with vertical fluting accented by terra-cotta, cut granite, and marble. Inside are extensive collections of Asian, Native American, African, Oceanic, and pre-Columbian art, a café, and a gift shop.

Pike Place Market (1st Ave. at Pike St., tel. 206/682–7453) is a Seattle institution, begun in 1907 when the city issued permits allowing farmers to sell produce from their wagons parked at Pike Place. Urban renewal almost closed the market, but citizens rallied and voted it a historical asset. Sold here are fresh seafood (which can be packed in dry ice for your flight home), produce, cheese, Northwest wines, bulk spices, teas, coffees, and arts and crafts.

At the base of the Pike Street Hillclimb at Pier 59 is the **Seattle Aquarium** (tel. 206/386–4320; admission charged), showcasing Northwest marine life. Sea otters and seals swim and dive in their pools, and the "State of the Sound" exhibit shows aquatic life and the ecology of Puget Sound.

Seattle

Green Lake

Woodland Park Zoo

3rd Ave.
Phinney Ave.
99

N.E. 65th St.
20th Ave. N.
N.E. 55th St.
N.E. 50th St.
N.E. 45th St.

Fremont Ave.
Stone Way
Meridian Ave.
Eastern Ave.

Lake Washington Ship Canal

Thomas Burke Memorial Washington State Museum
Henry Art Gallery
University of Washington

Union Bay

Portage Bay
Museum of History and Industry

520

Lake Union

10th Ave.
Boyer Ave.

Washington Park Arboretum

Queen Ann Ave.

E. Valley St.

W. Mercer St.
Seattle Center
99
5
12th Ave.
E. Thomas St.

Space Needle
Denny Hwy.
Westlake Center
Olive Way
Madison St.
E. Union St.
19th Ave.
23rd Ave.
E. Cherry St.

Western Ave.
Virginia St.
Pike Place Market
Seattle Art Museum
Aquarium
4th Ave.
2nd Ave.
Empire Way

Elliott Bay

Nippon Kan Theater
Wing Luke Museum
E. Yesler Way
Pioneer Square
International District
Jackson St.
S. Dearborn St.

N

Kingdome

0 500 yards
0 500 meters

S. Lake Way
90

S. Holgate St.

Harbor Island

1st Ave. S.
4th Ave.
E. Marginal Way S
17th Ave. S.
900
S. McClellan St.

5
TO BOEING FIELD

A couple blocks east of Pier 51, at the foot of Yesler Way, is **Pioneer Park,** where an ornate iron-and-glass pergola stands. This was the site of Henry Yesler's pier and sawmill and of Seattle's original business district. An 1889 fire destroyed many of the wood-frame buildings in the area now known as **Pioneer Square,** but the residents rebuilt them with brick and mortar. Also in the square is the **Klondike Gold Rush National Historical Park** (117 S. Main St., tel. 206/553–7220; admission free).

Southeast of Pioneer Square is the **International District** (ID), where a third of the residents are Chinese, a third Filipino, and the rest from elsewhere in Asia. The ID began as a haven for Chinese workers after they'd finished the Transcontinental Railroad. Today the district includes many Chinese, Japanese, and Korean restaurants, as well as herbalists, massage parlors, and acupuncturists. The **Nippon Kan Theater** (628 S. Washington St., tel. 206/467–6807) was historically the focal point for Japanese-American activities, including Kabuki theater. Renovated and reopened in 1981 as a national historic site, it presents many Asian-oriented productions.

North of Downtown From **Westlake Center** (*see* Shopping, *below*), a shopping complex completed in 1989, you can pick up the Monorail to **Seattle Center,** a 74-acre complex built for the 1962 Seattle World's Fair. It includes an amusement park, theaters, the Coliseum, exhibition halls, museums, and shops. Also here is the **Space Needle,** a Seattle landmark, which is visible from almost anywhere in the downtown area and looks like something from "The Jetsons." The glass elevator to the observation deck offers an impressive view of the city, and there's a popular restaurant.

From downtown or the Seattle Center, Hwy. 99 (Aurora Ave. N) heads north across the Aurora Bridge to the 50th Street exit, then to the **Woodland Park Zoo** (N. 50th St. and Fremont Ave., tel. 206/684–4800; admission charged), where many animals are free to roam within sections of the zoo's 92 acres.

A short drive east is the 33,500-student **University of Washington** (locals call it the U-Dub), founded in 1861. On the northwestern corner of the campus is the **Thomas Burke Memorial Washington State Museum** (17th Ave. NE and N.E. 45th St., tel. 206/543–5590; admission free), Washington's natural-history and anthropological museum. Near the university's Husky Stadium is the **Museum of History and Industry** (2700 24th Ave. E, tel. 206/324–1125; admission charged).

Parks and Gardens

Seattle's setting makes it a natural for parks and gardens. At **Washington Park Arboretum** (2300 Arboretum Dr. E, tel. 206/325–4510), near the university, Rhododendron Glen and Azalea Way are in full bloom from March through June. The Hiram M. Chittenden Locks, better known as the **Ballard Locks** (3015 N.W. 54th St., west of the Ballard Bridge, tel. 206/783–7059; closed Tues.–Wed. in winter), close the 8-mi-long Lake Washington Ship Canal connecting freshwater Lake Washington to Puget Sound; alongside the canal is a 7-acre **ornamental garden** of native and exotic plants, shrubs, and trees.

Seattle for Free

Gallery Walk (tel. 206/587–0260) is an open house hosted by Seattle's art galleries that explores new exhibits the first Thursday of every month. The **Out to Lunch Series** (tel. 206/623–0340) is outdoor concerts held weekdays at noon in various downtown parks, plazas, and atriums mid-June–early September.

What to See and Do with Children

Seattle Children's Museum (fountain level of Seattle Center, 305 Harrison St., tel. 206/441–1768) features an infant-toddler area with a giant, soft ferryboat for climbing and sliding and offers intergenerational programs, special exhibits, and workshops. **Seattle Children's Theater** (N. 50th St. and Fremont Ave. N, at south entrance to the Woodland Park Zoo, tel. 206/633–4567) presents six plays each year.

Shopping

Shopping Districts **Westlake Center** (1601 5th Ave., tel. 206/467–1600) is a three-story steel-and-glass building with 80 upscale shops and covered walkways connecting to Seattle's major department stores, **Nordstrom** and **The Bon.**

The **University District** (University Ave., north and south of 45th St., tel. 206/527–2567) has an eclectic mix of imports, a few upscale shops, and the city's largest concentration of bookstores.

Food Market **Pike Place Market** (*see* Exploring Seattle, *above*) offers a wide selection of fresh meat, seafood, and produce.

Specialty Stores **Antique Importers** (640 Alaskan Way [Aurora Ave.], tel. 206/
Antiques 628–8905) carries mostly English oak antiques.

Jewelry **Fourth & Pike Building** houses many retail-wholesale jewelers. **Turgeon-Raine Jewelers** (1407 5th Ave., tel. 206/447–9488) is an exceptional store with a sophisticated but friendly staff.

Men's Apparel **Jeffrey-Michael** (1318 4th Ave., tel. 206/625–9891) carries a fine line of traditional, business, and casual men's clothing.

Outdoor Wear **Eddie Bauer** (5th Ave. and Union St., tel. 206/622–2766) fea-
and Equipment tures sports and outdoor apparel. **REI** (1525 11th Ave., tel. 206/323–8333) sells clothing and outdoor equipment in a creaky, funky building on Capitol Hill.

Toys **Magic Mouse Toys** (603 1st Ave., tel. 206/682–8097) has two floors of toys, from small windups to giant stuffed animals.

Women's Apparel **Boutique Europa** (1015 1st Ave., tel. 206/624–5582) features sophisticated European clothing. **Local Brilliance** (1535 1st Ave., tel. 206/343–5864) showcases fashions by local designers.

Spectator Sports

Baseball **Seattle Mariners** (Kingdome, 201 S. King St., tel. 206/628–3555; Apr.–early Oct.).

Basketball **Seattle SuperSonics** (Seattle Center Coliseum, 1st Ave. N, tel. 206/281–5850; Oct.–Apr.).

Football **Seahawks** (Kingdome, tel. 206/827–9777; Aug.–Dec.).

Dining

For price ranges, see Chart 1 (A) in Chapter 1.

Very Expensive **Canlis.** This sumptuous restaurant is a Seattle institution. Its
★ famous steaks—and its equally famous oysters from Quilcene
Bay and fresh fish in season—are cooked to a turn. *2576 Aurora
Ave. N, tel. 206/283–3313. Reservations advised. Jacket required. AE, DC, MC, V. No lunch; closed Sun.*

Expensive **Campagne.** Overlooking Pike Place Market and Elliott Bay,
Campagne is intimate and urbane, with white walls, picture
windows, and colorful modern prints setting the tone. The flavors of Provence pervade the menu in such dishes as chicken
stuffed with goat cheese and fresh herbs, and salmon in a co-
gnac-and-champagne butter sauce. *Inn at the Market, 86 Pine
St., tel. 206/728–2800. Reservations advised. Jacket required.
AE, MC, V.*

Hunt Club. This very traditional, almost clubby restaurant
with dark wood and plush seats offers innovative cuisine. Besides perfectly prepared lamb with shiitake mushrooms in Madeira sauce, or seasonal king salmon with Pinot-noir butter,
you may happen upon such surprising fare as green cattail
spikes (the texture of asparagus, the flavor of artichokes). *Sor-
rento Hotel, 900 Madison St., tel. 206/622–6400. Reservations
advised. Jacket required. AE, DC, MC, V.*

Moderate **Place Pigalle.** Despite its French name, this is a very American
restaurant and popular with locals. Large windows look out
over Elliott Bay and, in good weather, are open to admit the
salt breeze. The menu features seasonal meals of seafood and
local ingredients. *Pike Place Market, tel. 206/624–1756. Reservations advised. Dress: casual but neat. MC, V. Closed Sun.*

★ **Wild Ginger.** The specialty is Pacific Rim cookery, including
tasty southern Chinese, Vietnamese, Thai, and Korean dishes
served in a warm, clubby dining room. Daily specials are based
on seasonally available products. *1400 Western Ave., tel. 206/
623–4450. Reservations advised. Dress: casual but neat. AE,
DC, MC, V. No lunch Sun.*

Inexpensive **Emmet Watson's Oyster Bar.** This small lunch place is hard to
★ find (it's in the back of Pike Place Market's Soames-Dunn
Building and fronts a small courtyard), but it's worth the effort. The oysters are fresh and offered in a number of varieties;
the beer list, too, is ample, featuring 50 or more selections from
local microbrews to fancy imports. *Pike Place Market, 1916
Pike Pl., tel. 206/448–7721. No reservations. No credit cards.
No dinner; closed Sun.*

Salvatore Ristorante Italiano. You'll wait for a table at this
small storefront, but regulars don't consider that much of a
drawback. Go for one of the specials—which always include individual pizzas, pasta dishes, and meat and fish courses—that
are chalked onto the blackboard above the kitchen window. The
wine list has some locally rare Italian bottlings. *6100 Roosevelt
Way NE, tel. 206/527–9301. No reservations. MC, V. No lunch
Sat.; closed Sun.*

Lodging

Seattle boasts an abundance of lodgings, from deluxe downtown hotels to smaller, less expensive digs in the University
District. For information on the ever-growing number of

B&Bs, contact the **Pacific Bed & Breakfast Agency** (701 N.W.
60th St., Seattle 98107, tel. 206/784–0539) or the **Washington
State Bed-and-Breakfast Guild** (2442 N.W. Market St., Seattle
98107, tel. 509/548–7171). For price ranges, see Chart 2 (A) in
Chapter 1.

Expensive–Very **Alexis.** At this intimate hotel in a restored 1901 building near
Expensive the waterfront, guest rooms are decorated in contemporary
★ subdued colors. Some suites feature whirlpools and wood-
burning fireplaces. *1007 1st Ave., 98104, tel. 206/624–4844 or
800/426–7033; fax 206/621–9009. 39 rooms, 15 suites. Facilities: restaurant, café, bar, access to health club. AE, MC, V.*

★ **Four Seasons Olympic Hotel.** Restored to its 1920s grandeur,
the Olympic is Seattle's most elegant hotel. Its public rooms
are furnished with marble, thick rugs, wood paneling, and potted plants. The less luxurious guest rooms feature a homey ambience with comfortable reading chairs and floral-print fabrics.
*411 University St., 98101, tel. 206/621–1700 or 800/223–8772;
fax 206/682–9633. 450 rooms. Facilities: 3 restaurants, health
club, indoor pool. AE, DC, MC, V.*

Moderate– **Edgewater.** The only hotel on Elliott Bay, the Edgewater was
Expensive famous for guests fishing from their waterside windows. In
1988 new ownership banned the fishing but remodeled and redecorated the rooms in a comfortably rustic style featuring
green-and-blue plaid fabrics, and unfinished wood furnishings.
*Pier 67, 2411 Alaskan Way, 98121, tel. 206/728–7000 or 800/
624–0670; fax 206/441–4119. 234 rooms. Facilities: restaurant,
bar, free parking. AE, DC, MC, V.*

★ **Inn at the Market.** This sophisticated but unpretentious hotel is
adjacent to the Pike Place Market. It combines the best aspects
of a small, deluxe hotel with the informality of the Pacific
Northwest, offering a lively setting that's perfect for travelers
who prefer personality over big-hotel amenities. Rooms are
spacious, have contemporary furnishings and ceramic sculptures, and offer views of the city, Elliott Bay, the Pike Place
Market, and the hotel courtyard. *86 Pine St., 98109, tel. 206/
443–3600; fax 206/448–0631. 65 rooms. Facilities: access to
health club and spa, room service, no-smoking rooms available. AE, D, DC, MC, V.*

Mayflower Park Hotel. This pleasant hotel built in 1927 is conveniently connected with Westlake Center and the Monorail
terminal to Seattle Center. Brass fixtures and antiques give
both the public and private spaces a muted Oriental feel. The
service is unobtrusive and smooth. *405 Olive Way, 98101, tel.
206/623–8700; fax 206/382–6997. 178 rooms, 17 suites. Facilities: restaurant, access to health club, no-smoking rooms
available. AE, DC, MC, V.*

Moderate **Meany Tower Hotel.** Built in 1931 and remodeled several times,
★ this pleasant hotel a few blocks from the University of Washington campus features a contemporary ambience, with a muted
peach–colored scheme and brass fixtures, and careful, attentive service. Nearly all the rooms have views of the Cascades or
the Olympic Mountains, the University of Washington, or Lake
Union. The tiled baths include old-fashioned pedestal sinks.
*4507 Brooklyn Ave. NE, 98105, tel. 206/634–2000; fax 206/634–
2000. 155 rooms. Facilities: restaurant, lounge, no-smoking
rooms available. AE, DC, MC, V.*

Inexpensive **Seattle YMCA.** A member of the American Youth Hostels Association, this Y offers rooms that are clean and plainly furnished

with a bed, phone, desk, and lamp. Single and double dorm units can accommodate four people each. *909 4th Ave., 98104, tel. 206/382–5000. 198 beds. Facilities: pool, health club. No credit cards.*

Motels

Doubletree Suites (16500 Southcenter Pkwy., Tukwila 98188, tel. 206/575–8220), 221 suites, restaurant, lounge, health club, indoor pool, whirlpool, sauna; expensive. **Doubletree Inn** (205 Strander Blvd., Tukwila 98188, tel. 206/246–8220), 200 rooms, dining room, coffee shop, lounge, outdoor pool; moderate. **University Plaza Hotel** (400 N.E. 45th St., 98105, tel. 206/634–0100), 135 rooms, restaurant, lounge, fitness room, outdoor heated pool; inexpensive.

The Arts and Nightlife

The Arts In recent years Seattle has gained a reputation as a world-class theater town; it also has a strong music and dance scene, with local, national, and international artists. The Friday *Seattle Times* and *Post-Intelligencer* detail the coming week's events. *Seattle Weekly*, which hits newsstands on Wednesday, has detailed coverage and arts reviews.

To charge tickets, call **Ticketmaster** (tel. 206/628–0888). **Ticket/Ticket,** with two locations (401 Broadway E, tel. 206/324–2744; 1st Ave. and Pike St., tel. 206/682–7453, ext. 26), sells half-price, same-day tickets for cash only.

Theater The **Seattle Repertory Theater** (Bagley Wright Theater, Seattle Center, 155 Mercer St., tel. 206/443–2222) presents high-quality programming from classics to new works. The **New City Arts Center** (1634 11th Ave., tel. 206/323–6800) features experimental performances by the resident company and in conjunction with national and international artists. The **Empty Space Theater** (107 Occidental Ave. S, tel. 206/587–3737) has a strong reputation for introducing new playwrights. The **Group Theatre** (Center House lower level, Seattle Center, tel. 206/441–1299) presents socially provocative works by old and new artists of varied cultures and colors. **A Contemporary Theater** (100 W. Roy St., tel. 206/285–5110) develops works by new playwrights, including at least one world premiere every year.

Music **Seattle Symphony** (Opera House, Seattle Center, tel. 206/443–4747) presents some 120 concerts September–June in and around town. **Northwest Chamber Orchestra** (tel. 206/343–0445), the Northwest's only professional chamber orchestra, presents a full spectrum of music, from Baroque to modern, at various venues.

Opera **Seattle Opera** (Opera House, Seattle Center, tel. 206/443–4711), considered one of the top companies in America, presents six productions during its August–May season.

Dance **Pacific Northwest Ballet** (Opera House, Seattle Center, tel. 206/547–5920) is a resident company and school that presents 60–70 performances annually.

Nightlife For a relatively small city, Seattle has a strong and diverse music scene. On any given night, you can hear high-quality sounds at a wide variety of night spots.

Bars and
Nightclubs
Bars with waterfront views are plentiful hereabouts. Among the best: on the Ship Canal, **Hiram's at the Locks** (5300 34th Ave. NW, tel. 206/784–1733); on Lake Union, **JC's on Lake Union** (2501 N. Northlake Way, tel. 206/634–2129) and **Arnie's Northshore Restaurant** (1900 N. Northlake Way, tel. 206/547–3242); and on Shilshole Bay, **Ray's Boathouse** (6049 Seaview Ave. NW, tel. 206/789–3770).

Blues/R&B Club
The **Ballard Firehouse** (5429 Russell St. NW, tel. 206/784–3516) is a music mecca in Ballard, with an emphasis on the blues.

Jazz Club
Dimitriou's Jazz Alley (2037 6th Ave., tel. 206/441–9729) is a downtown club with nationally known performers every night but Sunday. Excellent dinners are served before the first show.

Rock Clubs
Central Tavern (207 1st Ave. S, tel. 206/622–0209) is a crowded Pioneer Square tavern with an ever-changing roster of local and national rock acts. **Parker's** (17001 Aurora Ave. N, tel. 206/542–9491) is a sophisticated dinner-and-show venue for rock artists.

Grunge Clubs
Seattle has become a center for grunge music, producing such top bands as Nirvana, Pearl Jam, and Alice in Chains. Reminiscent of '70s acid rock, grunge was popularized in the movie *Singles*, which was filmed here. Grunge clubs include the **Off-Ramp Cafe & Lounge** (109 Eastlake Ave. E., tel. 206/628–0232), **OK Cafe/Gallery & Club** (212 Alaskan Way S., tel. 206/223–1721), and the **Re-Bar** (1114 Howell St., tel. 206/233–9873).

Comedy Club
Comedy Underground (2225 Main St., tel. 206/628–0303), a Pioneer Square club that's literally underground, beneath Swannie's, presents stand-up comedy and open-mike nights.

Dance Clubs
In Pioneer Square are several clubs featuring recorded dance music, including **Borderline** (608 1st Ave., tel. 206/624–3316), **Celebrity** (313 2nd Ave. S, tel. 206/467–1111), and **Hollywood Underground** (323 2nd Ave. S, tel. 206/628–8964).

Excursion to Whidbey and the San Juan Islands

What to See
and Do
Whidbey Island and the San Juan Islands are the jewels of Puget Sound. Because, except for Whidbey, they are reachable only by ferry, airplane, or private boat, the islands beckon souls longing for a quiet change of pace, whether it be kayaking in a cove, walking a deserted beach, or nestling by the fire in an old farmhouse. The islands are a popular weekend getaway spot for Seattleites. The **San Juan Tourism Cooperative** (Box 65, Lopez 98261, tel. 206/468–3663) can provide information.

Whidbey Island is mostly rural, with undulating hills, gentle beaches, and little coves. **Langley** is a quaint town that caters to locals and tourists with a handful of good restaurants, shops and galleries. It sits atop a 50-foot-high bluff overlooking the southeastern shore. About two-thirds of the way up this 50-mi-long island is **Coupeville**, site of many restored Victorian houses and one of the largest National Historic Districts in the state. The town was founded in 1852 by Captain Thomas Coupe; his house, built in 1853, is one of the state's oldest.

Ebey's Landing National Historic Reserve (tel. 206/678–4636), west of Coupeville, is a 22-acre area including Keystone, Coupeville, and Penn Cove. Established by Congress in 1980, the reserve is the first and largest of its kind, dotted with 91 nationally registered historic structures, farmland, parks, and trails. At **Deception Pass State Park** (tel. 206/675–2417), at the north end of the island, take in the spectacular view and stroll among the madrona trees, with their peeling reddish-brown bark.

The other major islands are **Lopez Island,** with old orchards, weathered barns, and sheep and cow pastures; **Shaw Island,** where Franciscan nuns in traditional habits run the ferry dock; **Orcas,** a large, mountainous, horseshoe-shaped island with marvelous hilltop views and a slew of good restaurants; and **San Juan Island,** with the colorful, active waterfront town of Friday Harbor.

Bicycling, boating, fishing, and camping are favored activities on the islands, but the small villages also teem with antiques shops and art galleries. There are a few restaurants not to miss: On Orcas, **Christina's** (North Beach Rd. and Horseshoe Hwy., tel. 206/376–4904; moderate–expensive) emphasizes fresh local seafood, with some of the best salmon entrées in the Northwest. On San Juan Island, **Duck Soup Inn** (3090 Roche Harbor Rd., tel. 206/378–4878; expensive) has a Mediterranean-inspired menu of fresh local fish. On Whidbey, **Garibyan Brothers Café Langley** (113 1st St., Langley, tel. 206/221–3090; moderate) offers Greek fare.

Getting There From Seattle-Tacoma International Airport (*see* Seattle, *above*), **West Isle Air** (tel. 800/874–4434) flies to San Juan Island from Anacortes and Bellingham. **Harbor Airlines** (tel. 800/521–3450) flies to San Juan Island and Whidbey Island. **Lake Union Air** (tel. 206/284–0300 or 800/826–1890) and **Kenmore Air** (tel. 206/486–8400 or 800/543–9595) fly floatplanes from Lake Union in Seattle to the San Juan Islands.

The **Washington State Ferry System** (tel. 206/464–6400 or 800/542–9052) provides car and passenger service from Mukilteo, on Hwy. 525, 30 mi north of Seattle, to Clinton on Whidbey Island and from Anacortes, about 90 mi north of Seattle, to the San Juan Islands. **A.I.T. Waterways** (tel. 206/671–1137) takes passengers from Bellingham to Orcas Island and San Juan Island's Friday Harbor.

By car from Seattle, drive north on I–5 to La Conner; go west on Rte. 536 to Rte. 20W and follow signs to Anacortes; then pick up the ferry for the San Juan Islands. Whidbey Island can be reached by ferry from Mukilteo, or you can drive from Seattle along I–5, then head west on Hwy. 20 and cross the dramatic Deception Pass via the bridge at the north end of the island.

Excursion to Tacoma

What to See and Do Because of a variety of industrial aromas emanating from **Tacoma,** Seattleites often make fun of the city. Nevertheless, Tacoma offers many good arts performances, wonderfully restored residential neighborhoods, fine bay views, and a world-class zoo. (**Tacoma-Pierce Visitors and Convention Bureau,** 906 Broadway, Tacoma 98402, tel. 206/627–2836.)

Union Station (1713 Pacific Ave., tel. 206/931–7884) is an heirloom from the golden age of railroads, when Tacoma was the western terminus for the transcontinental Northern Pacific Railroad. Built by Reed and Stem, architects of New York

City's Grand Central Station, the massive copper-domed, Beaux Arts–style depot was completed in 1908 and shows influences from the Roman Pantheon and the 16th-century Italian Baroque. Now housing federal courts, the building will eventually be home to the state historical society. The rotunda is open to the public.

The **Tacoma Art Museum** (12th St. and Pacific Ave., tel. 206/ 272–4258; admission free) contains a rich collection of American and French paintings, as well as Chinese jades and imperial robes. The nearby **Washington State Historical Society** (315 N. Stadium Way, tel. 206/593–2830; admission charged) houses exhibits on the natural, Native American, pioneer, maritime, and industrial history of the state. In **Wright Park** (6th and Division Sts., Yakima and Tacoma Aves., tel. 206/591–5331; admission free), a pleasant 30-acre park just north of downtown, is the **W. W. Seymour Botanical Conservatory**, a Victorian-style greenhouse with an extensive collection of exotic flora. While in town, try to catch a meal at the **Pacific Rim Restaurant** (100 S. 9th St., tel. 206/627–1009; expensive). This much-praised spot has an inventive seafood-and-Italian menu, genuinely friendly staff, and the atmosphere of an elegant Victorian club.

Northeast of Tacoma is the 700-acre **Point Defiance Park,** one of the largest urban parks in the country. Within it is the **Point Defiance Zoo and Aquarium,** founded in 1888 and now one of the top zoos in America. Using the Pacific Rim as its theme, it has blossomed (since an extensive renovation in 1986) into an impressive example of humane and innovative trends in zoo administration. *5400 N. Pearl St., tel. 206/591–5335. Zoo admission charged. Closed Thanksgiving, Christmas.*

Getting There Tacoma is about 35 mi south of Seattle via I–5. SeaTac airport is about a 30-minute drive away. The city is served by major bus, train, and air carriers.

Excursion to Olympia

What to See and Do The pace of life in **Olympia,** Washington's state capital, is largely determined by the legislative season: When they're in session, it's hopping; when they're not, it's fairly quiet. You can tour the stately **Legislative Building** (Capitol Way between 10th and 14th Aves., tel. 206/586–8687), a handsome Romanesque structure with a 287-foot dome that closely resembles the Capitol Building in "the other Washington." Behind it is the modern **State Library,** also worth a visit. If history and politics make you hungry, stop by **La Petite Maison** (2005 Ascension Way, tel. 206/943–8812; expensive), where imaginative French food is served in a converted 1890s farmhouse.

Getting There Olympia is on I–5, about 60 mi southwest of Seattle and 25 mi southwest of Tacoma.

The Olympic Peninsula

The rugged Olympic Peninsula is the northwestern corner of the continental United States. Much of it is wilderness, with the Olympic National Park and National Forest at its heart. The peninsula has tremendous variety: the wild Pacific shore, the sheltered waters along the Hood Canal and the Strait of

Juan de Fuca, the rivers of the Olympic's rain forests, and the towering Olympic Mountains.

Tourist Information

North Olympic Peninsula Visitor & Convention Bureau (Box 670, Port Angeles 98362, tel. 206/452–8552 or 800/942–4042). **Port Angeles:** Visitor Center (121 E. Railroad St., 98362, tel. 206/452–2363).

Getting There

By Plane Horizon Air (tel. 800/547–9308) flies into Port Angeles from Seattle-Tacoma airport. Private charter airlines fly into Port Angeles, Forks, and Hoquiam.

By Car U.S. 101 loops around the Olympic Peninsula, which can be reached from Olympia via Rtes. 8 and 101 and from Tacoma, 50 mi away, via Hwy. 16.

By Bus **Greyhound–Hardy's Jackpot** (tel. 206/452–8311) serves the Olympic Peninsula.

Exploring the Olympic Peninsula

From Olympia, go west along Hwy. 101 and Rtes. 8 and 12 to Gray's Harbor and the twin seaports of **Hoquiam** and **Aberdeen.** From Hoquiam, you can drive north on Rte. 109, which sticks to the coast and passes through resorts and ample beach areas such as **Copalis Beach, Pacific Beach,** and **Moclips** on its way to the Quinault Indian Reservation and the tribal center of **Taholah.** The town itself is rustic and offers little in the way of tourist attractions, the main draw here, as elsewhere on the peninsula, being the vast pristine scenery.

Hwy. 109 dead-ends at Taholah, and you must backtrack to return to U.S. 101. About 20 mi north of Aberdeen on Hwy. 101 is the Hoh Road, which goes east to the **Hoh Rain Forest,** part of the Olympic National Park. This complex and rich, temperate ecosystem of conifers, hardwoods, grasses, mosses, and other flora shelters such wildlife as elks, otters, beavers, salmon, and flying squirrels. The average rainfall here is 145 inches a year. The **Hoh Visitor Center,** at the campground and ranger center at road's end, has information, nature trails, and a museum. *Hoh Rd., 1.5 mi north of the Hoh River Bridge; visitor center is 20 mi farther. Tel. 206/374–6925. Admission charged. Visitor center open year-round but often unstaffed Sept.–May.*

North on U.S. 101 is the small logging town of **Forks,** renowned for its lavish three-day Fourth of July celebrations, which feature logging-truck parades, lots of fireworks, and a demolition derby. From here, La Push Road leads west about 15 mi to **La Push,** a coastal village and the tribal center of the Quileute Indians. Several points along this road have short trails with access to the ocean, fabulous views of offshore islands, and dramatic, stark rock formations.

Returning to U.S. 101, which swings to the east as you go north from Forks, you go through the **Sol Duc River Valley,** famous for its salmon fishing. The **Soleduck Fish Hatchery** (tel. 206/327–3246) has interpretive displays on fish breeding. A few miles past the tiny town of Sappho are the deep azure waters of **Lake**

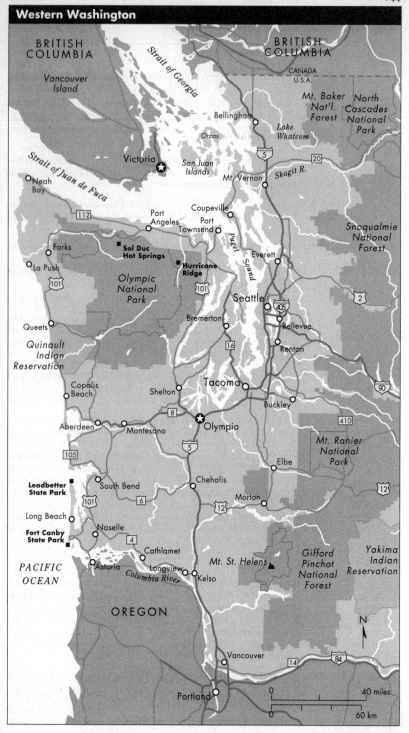

Western Washington

Crescent. The area has abundant campsites, resorts, trails, canoeing, and fishing. The original lodge buildings of 1915 (*see* Dining and Lodging, *below*)—well worn but comfortable—are still in use.

Twelve miles south on Soleduck Road (which meets U.S. 101 1 mi west of the western tip of Lake Crescent) is an entrance to Olympic National Park and to **Sol Duc Hot Springs,** where you can dip into three hot sulfur pools ranging from 98° to 104°. *Tel. 206/327–3583. Admission charged. Closed Oct.–mid-May.*

Back on U.S. 101 east, you will soon come to **Port Angeles,** a bustling commercial fishing port and an access route to Canada. The town hosts the visitor center for **Olympic National Park** (*see* National Parks, above), at 3002 Mt. Angeles Road. The road up to **Hurricane Ridge,** 17 mi south of Port Angeles, rises nearly a mile above sea level as it enters the park and offers spectacular views of the Olympics, the Strait of Juan de Fuca, and Vancouver Island.

A wide variety of animal life, present and past, can be found in the charming town of **Sequim** (pronounced "squim"), 17 mi east of Port Angeles on U.S. 101, at the **Sequim-Dungeness Museum** (175 W. Cedar St., tel. 206/683–8110; closed Dec.–mid-Feb.), where you can view the remains of an Ice Age mastodon and exhibits on the early Klallam Indians and the town's pioneer history. In the fertile plain at the mouth of the Dungeness River, 4 mi northwest of Sequim, the **Dungeness National Wildlife Refuge** (tel. 206/457–8451) is home to thousands of migratory waterfowl, as well as clams, oysters, and seals.

About 10 mi east of Sequim, Rte. 20 turns northward 12 mi to **Port Townsend.** Its waterfront is lined with handsome brick buildings from the 1870s that have been carefully restored and house a variety of attractive shops and restaurants. High up on the bluff are large gingerbread-trimmed Victorian homes, many of which have been turned into elegant B&Bs.

Driving south on Hwy. 101 through the sawmill town of **Shelton** will bring you back to Olympia.

Shopping

Confirmed shoppers head for the array of waterfront boutiques and stores in **Port Townsend,** all of which feature a good selection of Northwest arts and crafts.

Sports and Outdoor Activities

Biking   Biking is popular in the flatter parts of Port Townsend and within Olympic National Park. There are bike-rental shops in Port Townsend and other resort areas on the peninsula.

Fishing   Trout and salmon fishing are abundant in rivers throughout the peninsula. Contact the area tourist office (*see* Tourist Information, *above*) for details.

Hiking   Both ocean and mountain areas offer numerous hiking trails for all levels. Contact the **Olympic National Forest** (1835 Blacklake Blvd. SW, Olympia 98502, tel. 206/956–2400) or **Olympic National Park** (*see* National and State Parks, *above*).

Skiing   **Hurricane Ridge** (*see* Exploring the Olympic Peninsula, *above*)
offers 25 mi of cross-country ski trails.

Beaches

Beaches abound on the Olympic Peninsula, although many are
on tribal or private land and are not generally accessible. Remember that the North Pacific is not for swimming—unless
you wear a wet suit. For walking and exploring, the main
beaches are **Copalis** and **Pacific,** north of Hoquiam; a series of
scenic, unnamed beaches north of **Kalaloch;** and **Rialto Beach,**
near La Push.

Dining and Lodging

For price ranges, see Charts 1 (B) and 2 (B) in Chapter 1.

Copalis Beach   **Iron Springs Resort.** This string of cottages 3 mi north of town
Lodging   can accommodate from 2 to 10 people—perfect for families. The
decor in this older resort might be called well-kept funky. *Rte.
109, Box 207, 98535, tel. 206/276–4230. 25 units. Facilities:
heated and covered pool. AE, MC, V. Moderate.*

Gig Harbor   **Neville's Shoreline.** This pleasant, accommodating restaurant
Dining   at the marina specializes in seafood—try the simply but well-
★   prepared salmon and clams—and serves a Sunday brunch. *8827
N. Harborview Dr., tel. 206/851–9822. Reservations advised.
AE, D, MC, V. Moderate.*

Port Angeles   **C'est Si Bon.** This locally famous spot run by a French couple is
Dining   probably the most elegant restaurant on the decidedly informal
Olympic Peninsula. The walls are adorned with art, the tables
with fine linen, and windows offer a good view of the rose gar-
dens and the Olympic Mountains. The cuisine, of course, is
French. *2300 Hwy. 101E (4 mi east of town), tel. 206/452–8888.
Reservations advised. AE, DC, MC, V. No lunch; closed Mon.
Expensive.*

Lodging   **Lake Crescent Lodge.** This old but comfortable accommodation
with a big main lodge and small cabins overlooks the beautiful
deep-blue Lake Crescent. Units in the lodge are minimal—
bathrooms down the hall, dimly lit rooms—but the setting
makes up for sparse amenities. *HC–2, Box 11, 98362, tel. 206/
928–3211. Facilities: restaurant, fishing, boating. AE, DC,
MC, V. Closed mid-Nov.–Apr. Inexpensive.*

Port Townsend   **Fountain Café.** This small café off the main tourist drag is one of
Dining   the best restaurants in town. You can count on seafood and pas-
★   ta specialties with imaginative twists, such as smoked salmon
in black porter sauce. *920 Washington St., tel. 206/385–1364.
Reservations advised. MC, V. Moderate.*
Salal Café. Featuring home-style cooking and daily specials,
this cooperatively run restaurant shines among early morning
breakfast joints. Try one of many variations on the potato-egg
scramble for lunch. Seafood and regional American-style meals
are good, portions ample, and prices reasonable. *634 Water St.,
tel. 206/385–6532. No reservations. No credit cards. No dinner; closed Tues. Inexpensive.*

Lodging   **James House.** This splendid, antiques-filled Victorian B&B, on
the bluff overlooking downtown and the waterfront, presents a
homey atmosphere in a terrific location. *1238 Washington St.,
98368, tel. 206/385–1238. 12 rooms. MC, V. Expensive.*

Palace Hotel. A friendly B&B in the historic section of downtown, it is tastefully decorated to reflect its 1889 construction date and its onetime history as a bordello. *1004 Water St., 98368, tel. 206/385–0773. 15 units, 1 with kitchenette. AE, D, MC, V. Moderate.*

Quinault
Lodging

Lake Quinault Lodge. This deluxe lodge is set on a perfect glacial lake in the midst of the Olympic National Forest. Built in 1926 of cedar shingles, the lodge has delightfully decorated public rooms with antiques and a fireplace. *S. Shore Rd., Box 7, 98575, tel. 206/288–2571. 89 rooms. Facilities: restaurant, bar, whirlpool, indoor pool, sauna, golf course, games room. MC, V. Expensive.*

Sol Duc
Lodging

Sol Duc Hot Springs Resort. The comfortable, casual resort, featuring minimally outfitted cabins, dates from the turn of the century. It's recently been spiffed-up without becoming slick and soulless. *12 mi south of Hwy. 101 on Soleduck Rd. (Box 2168), 98362, tel. 206/327–3583. 32 units, camping and RV facilities. Facilities: restaurant (reservations required), hot springs, outdoor pool. MC, V. Closed mid-Oct.–mid-May. Moderate.*

Campgrounds

Camping areas abound on the Olympic Peninsula. Some of the best within the Olympic National Park are **Hoh River, Mora,** and **Fairholm** (tel. 206/452–0330). Elsewhere on the peninsula: **Bogachiel State Park** (tel. 206/374–6356; near Forks; and **Ft. Flagler State Park** (tel. 206/385–1259 near Port Townsend. Also see **Sol Duc Hot Springs Resort** (*see* Dining and Lodging, *above*).

Long Beach Peninsula

If the waters of the Pacific and the Columbia River met in a less turbulent manner, a huge seaport might sit at the river's mouth. Instead, the entrance to the Columbia is sparsely populated, dotted with fishing villages and cranberry bogs. Although only a 3½-hour drive southwest of Seattle and 2 hours northwest of Portland, the Long Beach Peninsula is worlds away from either city. Just north of the river's mouth, the peninsula separates the Pacific Ocean and Willapa Bay and is known for excellent bird-watching, beachcombing, hiking, history, and a handful of gourmet restaurants.

Tourist Information

Long Beach: Visitors Bureau (intersection of Hwys. 101 and 103, Seaview 98644, tel. 206/642–2400).

Getting There

By Plane
The only air service to the peninsula is provided by **Astoria Flight Center** (tel. 503/861–1222), whose charters serve Seattle and Ilwaco from Portland, Astoria, and Seaside in Oregon.

By Car
Long Beach is accessed from the east via Hwy. 4, which connects with I–5 near Longview; and from the north and south via U.S. 101.

Exploring Long Beach Peninsula

U.S. 101 crosses the broad Columbia River between Astoria, Oregon, and Megler, Washington, in a high, graceful span. Just beyond, on Hwy. 103, is **Ilwaco,** a small fishing community of about 600. The **Ilwaco Heritage Museum** (115 S.E. Lake St., tel. 206/642–3446; admission charged) uses dioramas to present the history of southwestern Washington, beginning with the Native Americans.

A couple of miles south is the **Cape Disappointment Lighthouse,** first used in 1856 and one of the oldest lighthouses on the West Coast. The cape was named by English fur trader Captain John Meares in 1788 in honor of his unsuccessful attempt to find the Northwest Passage.

Ft. Canby State Park (5 mi west of Ilwaco, off U.S. 101 (tel. 206/ 642–3078 or 800/562–0990) was an active military installation until 1957, when it was turned over to the Washington State Parks and Recreation Commission. Now it is best known for great views of the Columbia River Bar during winter storms. The **Lewis & Clark Interpretive Center** documents the 8,000-mi round-trip journey of the famous pair and their Corps of Volunteers for Northwest Discovery from Wood River, Illinois, to the mouth of the Columbia. *Tel. 206/642–3029 or 604/642–3078. Closed weekdays Labor Day–Memorial Day.*

The town of **Long Beach** caters to tourists with beach activities and an old-fashioned amusement park with go-carts and bumper cars. About halfway up the peninsula is **Ocean Park,** the area's commercial center. A few miles north is **Oysterville,** established as an oystering town in 1854. When the native shellfish were fished to extinction, a Japanese oyster was introduced, but the town never made a comeback. Tides have washed away homes, businesses, and a Methodist church, but the village still exists. Maps inside the vestibule of the restored **Oysterville Church** direct you through town, which is now on the National Register of Historic Places. At the northern tip of the peninsula is **Leadbetter State Park** (*see* National and State Parks, *above*).

Shopping

The Bookvendor (101 Pacific Ave., Long Beach, tel. 206/642–2702) stocks an extensive supply of children's books, classics, and travel books, as well as art supplies. **North Head Gallery** (600 S. Pacific Ave., Long Beach, tel. 206/642–8884) has the largest selection of Elton Bennett originals, plus Bennett reproductions and works from other Northwest artists.

Sports and Outdoor Activities

Biking Good areas for bicycling on the peninsula's 20 mi include Ft. Canby and North Head roads, Sandridge Road to Ocean Park and Oysterville, U.S. 101 from Naselle to Seaview, and Rte. 103 along Willapa Bay. There are rentals available in virtually every town.

Fishing Salmon, rock cod, lingcod, flounder, perch, sea bass, and sturgeon are popular and plentiful for fishing. A guide is available from the **Port of Ilwaco** (Box 307, 98624, tel. 206/642–3143). Clamming season varies depending on the supply; for details call the **Washington Department of Fisheries** (tel. 206/753–6552) or the **Fisheries' shellfish lab** (tel. 206/665–4166). There are tackle shops all over Long Beach Peninsula, and most sell the necessary fishing licenses.

Golf There are two nine-hole golf courses: the **Peninsula Golf Course** (tel. 206/642–2828), at the north end of Long Beach, and the **Surfside Golf and Country Club** (tel. 206/665–4148), 2 mi north of Ocean Park.

Hiking Hiking trails are available at **Ft. Canby** and **Leadbetter** state parks (*see* Exploring Long Beach Peninsula, *above*, and National and State Parks, *above*, respectively).

Dining and Lodging

For price ranges, see Charts 1 (B) and 2 (B) in Chapter 1.

Ilwaco **Inn at Ilwaco.** This B&B is set in a renovated New England–
Lodging style church, built in 1928. The guest rooms—most of them upstairs in the old Sunday-school rooms—are cozily furnished with some antiques, armoires, and eyelet or printed chintz curtains and coverlets. *120 Williams St. NE, 98624, tel. 206/642–8686. 9 rooms (2 share bath). MC, V. Expensive.*

Long Beach **My Mom's Pies.** Though this place in a mobile home keeps very
Dining irregular hours, it's worth dropping by for such specialty pies as banana whipped cream, chocolate almond, sour-cream raisin, and fresh raspberry. Also on the menu are clam chowder and quiche. *Hwy. 103 and 12th St. S, tel. 206/642–2342. No reservations. MC, V. No dinner; closed Mon. Inexpensive.*

Pacific Beach **Sandpiper Beach Resort.** This modern, four-story complex of-
Lodging fers clean, attractive suites; most have a sitting room, dining area, fireplace, small kitchen, porch, bedroom, and bath. This is definitely the place for a getaway: no in-room phones, no pool, no TV, no restaurant. *Rte. 109 (1½ mi south of Pacific Beach), Box A, 98571, tel. 206/276–4580. 30 rooms. MC, V. Moderate.*

Seaview **The Shoalwater Restaurant.** The dining room at the Shelburne
Dining Inn (*see* Lodging, *below*) has been acclaimed by *Gourmet* and
★ *Bon Appétit.* Seafood brought from the fishing boats to the restaurant's back door is as fresh as it can be; mushrooms and salad greens are gathered from the peninsula's woods and gardens. *Pacific Hwy. and N. 45th St., tel. 206/642–4142. Reservations advised. Dress: casual but neat. AE, MC, V. No lunch Fri.–Mon.; closed Wed. Oct.–May. Expensive.*
42nd Street Cafe. This middle-of-the-road restaurant is nestled comfortably between deep-fried seafood and expensive gourmet fare, emphasizing home-cooked food on a menu that changes daily. *Hwy. 103 and 42nd St., tel. 206/642–2323. V. Moderate.*

Lodging **Shelburne Inn.** This bright and cheerful, antiques-filled inn built in 1896 is on the National Register of Historic Places. It is also right on the highway, which can make it noisy, so the best picks are rooms on the west side. *Hwy. 103 and N. 45th St., 98644, tel. 206/542–2442. 16 rooms. Facilities: restaurant (see* Dining, *above*), pub. AE, MC, V. Expensive.*
Sou'wester. A stay here is a bohemian experience. Choose from rooms and apartments in a historic lodge, cabins, or classic mobile-home units on the surrounding property just behind the

beach. The lodge was built in 1892 as the summer retreat for Henry Winslow Corbett, a Portland banker, timber baron, shipping and railroad magnate, and U.S. senator. *Beach Access Rd., Box 102, 98644, tel. 206/642–2542. 3 rooms with shared bath and kitchen, 4 cabins, 6 trailers. MC, V. Inexpensive.*

Campgrounds

Camping is available at **Ft. Canby State Park** (Box 488, Ilwaco 98624; *see* Exploring Long Beach Peninsula, *above*), **Chinook County Park** (Box 261, Chinook 98614, tel. 206/777–8442); **Ocean City State Park** (148 State Rte. 115, Hoquiam 98550, tel. 206/289–3553); and **Pacific Beach State Park** (tel. 206/276–4297).

Elsewhere in the State

Yakima Valley

Getting There The valley is along I–82 between Yakima and the tri-city area of Richland, Kennewick, and Pasco. From Seattle, drive east on I–90 to Ellensburg and south on Hwy. 97 (about 180 mi). Yakima has a small airport with limited service from Seattle, Spokane, and Portland on United Airlines. There is no passenger train service, but the area is served by Greyhound buses, which stop in Yakima, Toppenish, Sunnyside, Wapato, and Prosser.

What to See and Do The attraction here, aside from the views of 12,688-foot Mt. Adams and 14,410-foot Mt. Rainier to the west, is an abundance of wineries. Dozens of small operations dot this fertile area, which is gaining a reputation for producing fine wines. Some of the best-known vineyards are **Hogue Cellars, Château Ste. Michelle,** and **Quail Run Winery.** The **Yakima Valley Wine Grower Association** (Box 39, Grandview 98930) publishes maps of the region and a brochure that lists local wineries with tasting-room tours.

Spokane

Getting There Spokane Airport is served by Horizon, Northwest, and United airlines. Amtrak and Greyhound both serve Spokane. By car, Spokane can be reached by I–90 (east–west) and Hwy. 195 (north–south).

What to See and Do Billed as the "Capital of the Inland Empire," Spokane (pronounced "Spo-CAN") seems like a bit of the Midwest dropped into the Far West. This city of about 350,000 doesn't necessarily accept Seattle as the state's cultural capital or Olympia as the seat of government. Wedged against the Idaho border (which residents cross regularly in search of outdoor recreation), Spokane is separated from Seattle by a good 300 mi and the formidable Cascade Range.

In town, the main attraction is **Riverfront Park,** 100 acres covering several islands in the Spokane River and including a spectacular falls. While Spokane has extensive historic areas, it may be best remembered for hosting the 1974 World's Fair. Ultramodern buildings from that exposition still remain, and today house an IMAX theater, a skating rink, and exhibition space. In sharp architectural contrast is the town's 1902 **Great Northern Railroad Station,** with its tall stone clock tower.

Just 30 mi east of town on I–90 is Idaho's **Lake Coeur d'Alene** (*see* Idaho), which features fishing, camping, hiking, water sports, and a wide variety of resort accommodations.

11 The Pacific

The Pacific Region

Barrow

Chukchi Sea

RUSSIA

Bering Strait

BROOKS

Noatak
National
Preserve

Gates of the Arctic
National Park
and Preserve

Cape Krusenstern
National
Monument

Kobuk Valley
National
Park

Kotzebue

Bettles

Bering
Land Bridge
National
Preserve

ARCTIC CIRCLE

Teller

Kanuti Flats
National
Wildlife
Refuge

Koyukuk
National
Wildlife
Refuge

Council

Nome

*Saint
Lawrence
Island*

Norton Sound

Yukon River

Baker

Nowitna National
Wildlife Refuge

INTER

*Bering
Sea*

Innoko
National
Wildlife
Refuge

Denali
National Park
and Preserve

ALASKA RR.

MOUNTAINS

Mt. McKinley

Cantwell

GEORGE PARKS
HWY.

RA

Yukon Delta
National
Wildlife
Refuge

KUSKOKWIM

SOUTH

*Nunivak
Island*

Bethel

ALASKA

Willow

Palm

Anchorage

Tyonek

Whittier

Kenai

Kuskokwim Bay

Togiak
National
Wildlife
Refuge

Lake Clark
National Park
and Preserve

Seward

Dillingham

Iliamna Lake

Homer

Cook

Inlet

Kenai
Fjords
Nationa
Park

Katmai
National Park
and Preserve

Kenai National
Wildlife Refuge

Bristol Bay

Port Lions

Chugach
National
Forest

Kodiak
National
Wildlife
Refuge

Kodiak

ALASKA PENINSULA

Aniakchak
National Monument
and Preserve

PAC

Beaufort Sea

Prudhoe Bay
Deadhorse

Arctic
National
Wildlife
RANGE Refuge

Yukon Flats
National Wildlife Refuge

Circle
Livengood
Chena
Hot Springs
Fairbanks
Yukon-
Charley Rivers
National
Preserve
Delta Jct.
Boundary
OR
GE
Tok
Paxson
Slano
ENTRAL
Glennallen
Wrangell-
St. Elias
Valdez National Park
Chugach and Preserve
National Forest
Prince Cordova
William
Sound Mt. St. Elias

Gulf of Alaska

Yukon River

Dawson City

CANADA

Whitehorse YUKON TERR.
BRITISH COLUMBIA

Skagway
Haines
Glacier Bay
National Park
and Preserve Juneau
Hoonah
SOUTHEAST
Petersburg
Sitka Tongass
National Wrangell
Forest
Ketchikan
Metlakatla

IC OCEAN

0   100 miles
0   150 km

Haena KAUAI
Lihue Wailua
Waimea Poipu HAWAII
NIIHAU Kauai Channel

Honolulu Waikiki MOLOKAI
OAHU MAUI
Kaiwi Lahaina Kahului
Lanai City Kihei Hana
LANAI Wailea
Wailea KAHOOLAWE Alenuihaha Channel

PACIFIC OCEAN Waimea
Mauna
Kea Hilo
Kailua-Kona
Mauna Kilauea
Loa
HAWAII Naalehu
(The Big Island)

0   50 miles
0   50 km   N

Introduction

*By Paula
Consolo and
Jillian
Magalaner*

The two youngest states in the union, Alaska and Hawaii, have more in common than first appears. Both are thousands of miles from the U.S. mainland, both have dramatic landscapes, and both have significant populations of indigenous people. The two states are also connected by their reliance on water—rivers, lakes, and the Pacific Ocean, which supply a means of transportation, a source of food, and a host of recreational possibilities. Humpback whales make a physical connection with both states, summering in Alaska's Bering Sea, then swimming the 4,000 mi to Hawaii to mate, calve, and nurse their young in the warm waters off Maui. Although Alaskan and Hawaiian stores are stocked with the same aspirin and the same cereal found in any mainland state, there is something of the exotic in both places—albeit in very different forms.

Alaska, with its vast, austere wilderness and extreme weather, is a demanding land, but it rewards exploration with temperate summers, a frontier atmosphere, and flora and fauna rarely accessible elsewhere on the planet. From the nation's highest mountain, Mt. McKinley, to the islands, glaciers, and fjords of the southeast, the state provides superb hiking, boating, and fishing—and scenery as majestic and unspoiled as any in North America.

Hawaii's gentle climate and tremendous diversity make it a welcoming and endlessly fascinating place. Each of the eight major volcanic islands has its own character; some offer lush tropical scenery and stunning white beaches, while others provide dramatic cliffs or beaches with black sand. If you enjoy rampant commercialism in a spotlessly clean, well-groomed environment, Oahu's Waikiki is the place for you. From pineapple plantations to active volcanoes in spectacular mountain ranges; from cheerful towns to remote, exquisite natural refuges, Hawaii's islands lure visitors with myriad delights.

Tour Groups

A tour of Alaska could mean a cruise through waters where seals cling to icebergs, a soaring flight over a mammoth glacier, or a visit to Mt. McKinley. Tours of Hawaii are equally diverse, ranging from rugged hikes through lush forests and along volcanic slopes to luxurious idling on white-sand beaches.

Gadabout Tours (700 E. Tahquitz Way, Palm Springs, CA 92262, tel. 619/325–5556 or 800/952–5068) offers six different itineraries to Alaska ranging from eight to 29 days. **Globus** (5301 S. Federal Circle, Littleton, CO 80123, tel. 303/797–2800 or 800/221–0090) offers 10- or 13-day escorted tours of Hawaii that include visits to Pearl Harbor and Volcanoes National Park, or eight to 14-day independent packages. For budget escorted tours to Hawaii contact Globus's affiliate, **Cosmos Tourama** (same address). Globus also offers a 12-day tour of Alaska and the Yukon, including Seattle, Anchorage, Fairbanks, and a cruise through the islands of British Columbia. **Maupintour** (Box 807, Lawrence, KS 66044, tel. 913/843–1211 or 800/255–4266) offers a nine-day visit to Oahu, Maui, and Kona, and a 12-day excursion to Hawaii, Maui, Kauai, and Oahu. **Tauck Tours** (Box 5027, Westport, CT 06881, tel. 203/226–6911 or 800/468–2825) has a 13-day tour of Alaska that includes Mt. McKinley, Anchorage, flights over glaciers, and a cruise through Glacier Bay back to Seattle. A daylong Arctic Circle option is also available. For Hawaii, Tauck has a nine-day/three-island tour or a 13-day/five-island trip.

For independent packages to Hawaii check out **America West Vacations** (1150 East University, Suite 101, Tempe, AZ 85281, tel. 800/247–0747) and **GoGo Tours** (69 Spring St., Ramsey, NJ 07446–0507, tel. 800/821–3731).

When to Go

Alaska Most visitors come to Alaska in **summer,** when mild temperatures and the midnight sun prevail. In fact, many tour operators, accommodations, and services are not open at any other time of year. Predictably, hotels and campgrounds are crowded, and prices are often higher than in the off-season: Advance planning is essential. The farther north you go in summer, the longer the days; Fairbanks in June is never really dark, although the sun does set for a couple of hours. In the Interior, temperatures can easily reach the 80s and 90s in June and July. The rest of the state is cooler, and rain is common in coastal areas. Mosquitoes are fierce in summer, especially in wilderness areas; never travel without repellent. **Fall** in Alaska is an abbreviated three weeks in September, when trees blaze with color and daytime temperatures are still pleasant. **Winters** are extremely cold (daytime temperatures of 0° or lower away from the coast), but many Alaskans prefer that season, because it opens up the country for travel by snowmobile and dogsled. **Spring** is often a month-long soggy period of thawing and freezing, starting at the beginning of April.

Hawaii Hawaii's long days of sunshine and fairly mild year-round temperatures allow for 12 months of pleasurable island travel. In resort areas near sea level, the average afternoon temperature during the coldest months of December and January is 80°F; during the hottest months of August through October, temperatures can reach the low 90s. The northern shores of each island usually receive more rain than those in the south. Mid-December through mid-April and July through August are peak travel times, which means accommodation rates can be 10%–15% higher.

Festivals and Seasonal Events

Alaska **Mid-Feb.: Anchorage Fur Rendezvous** includes the three-day world-championship sled-dog sprint through city streets, plus hundreds of other winter activities. *Tel. 907/277–8615.*

Early Mar.: Iditarod Trail Sled Dog Race is a 12-day run across more than 1,000 mi from Anchorage to Nome. Most people witness the start in Anchorage or the finish in Nome. *Tel. 907/376–5155.*

Late Aug.: Alaska State Fair in Palmer, north of Anchorage, is a traditional celebration complete with cooking, handicrafts, livestock, and brewing competitions. *Tel. 907/746–7157 or 907/745–4827.*

Hawaii **Feb.: Hawaiian Open Golf Tournament,** on Oahu, lures top golf pros with big prize money. *Tel. 808/526–1232.*

Mar. or Apr.: Merrie Monarch Festival in Hilo on the Big Island is a full week of ancient and modern hula competitions. Tickets must be purchased months in advance. *Tel. 808/935–9168.*

May–June: Festival of the Pacific is a three-week, statewide celebration of sports, music, songs, and dances highlighting regional ethnic culture. *Tel. 808/965–7060.*

Aug.: Hawaii International Billfish Tournament, spanning a week and taking place in Kailua-Kona on the Big Island, is the world's leading marlin-fishing contest. *Tel. 808/836–0974.*

Sept.–Oct.: Aloha Festivals are a state-wide celebration dating from 1946. *Tel. 808/944–8857.*

Getting Around

Alaska By Plane The majority of Alaska-bound flights touch down at **Anchorage International Airport** (tel. 907/266–2437). The other major gateways are Ketchikan, Juneau, and Fairbanks, with other destinations in the state reached by connecting flights. Alaska Airlines, MarkAir, and most major domestic carriers serve the state. Small carriers and charter aircraft that land on wheels, floats, or skis are a common means of transportation between small communities and to recreation sites in the bush.

By Car Alaska has few roads for its size. In Southeast Alaska, travel between communities is almost exclusively by boat or airplane. In South Central and the Interior, most highways have only two lanes, and a few are dirt roads. The following are paved highways that are open year-round: The Alaska Highway enters the state from Canada near Tok and continues west to Fairbanks. The Glenn Highway begins at Tok and travels south to Anchorage. The Richardson Highway runs north–south between Valdez and Delta Junction. The Seward Highway heads south from Anchorage through the Kenai Mountains to Seward, with the branch Sterling Highway heading southwest to Kenai and Homer. The George Parks Highway runs north from Anchorage, past Denali National Park to Fairbanks.

By Train The **Alaska Railroad** (tel. 907/265–2623 or 800/544–0552 outside AK) runs from Seward through Anchorage to Fairbanks. A spur of the railroad runs to Whittier, southeast of Anchorage on Prince William Sound. Travel to Seward is in the summer only; the rest of the route operates year-round, with reduced services September–May. The **White Pass and Yukon Route** operates round-trip summer sightseeing excursions between Skagway and Fraser, British Columbia, following the route that gold-seekers took into the Yukon. The **Alaska Pass** (tel. 800/248–7598 or 800/89–82–85 from the U.K.) offers discounted prices on train, bus, and boat travel throughout the state.

By Bus **Gray Line of Alaska** (300 Elliott Ave. W, Seattle, WA 98119, tel. 907/277–9581 or 800/544–2206) offers tours between and within Alaskan cities. **Alaska Direct Bus Lines** (Box 501, Anchorage, 99510, tel. 612/228–1009 or 800/328–9730) travels the Alaska and Glenn Highways to Anchorage; service is available most of the year.

By Boat The **Alaska Marine Highway System** (Box 25535, Juneau 99802, tel. 800/642–0066) is a state-operated ferry system that serves ports in the Southeast and South Central regions of the state.

You cannot get from Southeast to South Central by ferry; the boats do not cross the Gulf of Alaska. For information on cruise-ship travel in Alaska, *see* Alaska, Cruising, *below*.

Hawaii
By Plane
Honolulu International Airport (tel. 808/836–6411), on Oahu, is served by major domestic carriers and by Hawaiian Airlines. Aloha and Hawaiian airlines fly interisland from Honolulu and from the four major Neighbor Island airports: **Keahole** (Big Island, tel. 808/329–2484), also served by United; **Hilo International** (Big Island, tel. 808/933–4782); **Kahului** (Maui, tel. 808/877–0078), also served by Air America, Aloha IslandAir, American, Delta, and United; and **Lihue** (Kauai, tel. 808/246–1400), also served by United.

By Car
No Hawaiian island can be circumnavigated completely by car. The Big Island's roads are well maintained, although lava has closed the road from Kalapana to just east of Kamoamoa in Hawaii Volcanoes National Park. On Maui, highways are in good shape, although a four-wheel-drive vehicle is necessary for the road east of Hana. Kauai's main route runs south from Lihue and west to Polihale Beach; a narrower northern route runs to Haena, the beginning of the roadless Na Pali Coast. Molokai's main route becomes narrow and potholed as it nears Halawa Valley in the east. Lanai's few paved roads are fine, but a four-wheel-drive vehicle is essential for any adventurous exploring.

By Bus
Honolulu is the only island with a municipal service, **The Bus** (tel. 808/848–5555). A locally sponsored **Hele-On Bus** (tel. 808/935–8241) operates between Hilo and Kailua-Kona on the Big Island. The other islands have no public bus system, although shuttles run between the airports and major hotels.

By Boat
An expensive, extravagant way to tour the islands is with **American Hawaii Cruises** (550 Kearny St., San Francisco, CA 94108, tel. 800/765–7000), which offers week-long interisland excursions on two ships.

ALASKA

By Barbara Hodgin and Mary Engel

Capital	Juneau
Population	600,000
Motto	North to the Future
State Bird	Willow ptarmigan
State Flower	Forget-me-not

Visitor Information

Alaska Division of Tourism (Box 110801, Juneau 99811–0801, tel. 907/465–2010). The **Alaska Public Lands Information Center** (*see* National and State Parks, *below*) has information on recreation in the state.

Cruising

About one-third of Alaska's visitors arrive by cruise ship. Most cruises leave either from Seattle or from Vancouver, British Columbia, on a week-long itinerary up the Inside Passage of Alaska's Southeast panhandle, visiting Ketchikan, Petersburg, Juneau, and either Haines or Skagway. Most include a side trip into Glacier Bay National Park. The rewards of this sometimes soggy climate are misty views of giant forests and glacier-clad mountains.

The major cruise lines serving Alaska are **Princess Tours** (2815 2nd Ave., Suite 400, Seattle, WA 98121–9981, tel. 206/728–4202 or 800/835–8907) and **Holland America Line/Westours** (300 Elliott Ave. W, Seattle, WA 98119, tel. 800/426–0327). State ferries provide year-round budget service for passengers and vehicles (*see* Southeast, *below*) on similar routes.

National and State Parks

Alaska has more land in national parks, wilderness areas, and national wildlife refuges than all the other states combined. For information on these areas, contact the **Alaska Public Lands Information Center** (605 W. 4th Ave., Anchorage 99501, tel. 907/271–2737).

National Parks **Denali National Park and Preserve** (*see* The Interior, *below*) is among the state's most popular parks. **Glacier Bay National Park and Preserve** (Box 140, Gustavus 99826, tel. 907/697–2230), in the Southeast, is a marine preserve where spectacular glaciers meet tidewater and seals float on icebergs. **Katmai National Park and Preserve** (*see* Elsewhere in the State, *below*), a volcanic wonderland on the Alaska Peninsula, is home to huge coastal brown bears who share the Brooks River with trout fishermen. On the Kenai Peninsula south of Anchorage is **Kenai Fjords National Park** (*see* South Central, *below*). Virtually all of the backcountry in the Southeast is part of the **Tongass National Forest**.

State Parks Along with Tongass National Forest, **Chugach State Park** (HC 52 Box 8999, Indian 99540, tel. 907/694–2108) near Anchorage is the recreational backyard for most Southeast Alaskans, who

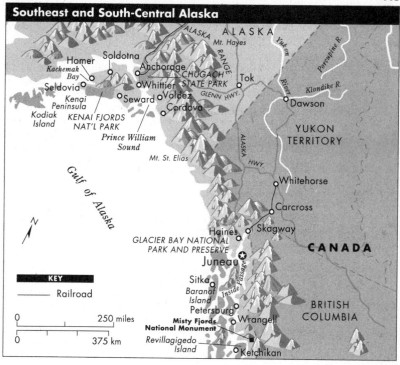

Southeast and South-Central Alaska

KEY
—— Railroad

0 ___ 250 miles
0 ___ 375 km

visit it for the scores of hiking trails, good fishing on lakes and
streams, and state-owned recreational cabins for rent.

Southeast

Southeast Alaska is a maritime region of thousands of islands
blanketed by old-growth spruce forest. The waters abound in
Pacific salmon (five species) and sea mammals. The shore is
home to deer, bears, and hamlets climbing mountainsides along
misty fjords. The wet climate inspires locals to call galoshes
"Juneau tennis shoes," although summer does bring some
breathtakingly beautiful sunny days. Tlingit, Haida, and
Tsimshian villages, as well as museums and cultural centers in
the region's larger communities, offer insights into Native
American cultures.

Getting There

Southeast Alaska is mainly accessible by air or water. The
mainland road system (south from Fairbanks through the Canadian Yukon) connects only with tiny northern communities
after hundreds of miles of wilderness road. Cruise ships (*see*
Cruising, *above*) or state ferries are the most common means of
transportation.

By Plane Regular jet service is available from dozens of Pacific Coast and
southwestern U.S. cities to Ketchikan, Wrangell, Petersburg,
Sitka, and Juneau (Juneau International Airport, tel. 907/789–
7821). The area is served by Alaska Airlines (tel. 800/426–0333)

and Delta Airlines (tel. 800/221–1212). Floatplane and wheel-plane service to the villages is available from the region's larger communities.

By Car Ferries to Southeast Alaska leave from Bellingham, Washington, or from Prince Rupert, British Columbia. From the north, the Alaska and Haines or Klondike highways lead to Skagway and Haines, and ferries continue south through the region.

By Ferry The **Alaska Marine Highway System** (Box 25535, Juneau 99802, tel. 800/642–0066) is an extensive network of large and small vessels that links most Southeast communities. All ferries take cars (reservations necessary in summer) and have restaurants; most also have staterooms, but many Alaskans camp out on deck in tents or on the lounges' floors.

Ketchikan

Tourist Information **Ketchikan:** Visitors Bureau (131 Front St., 99901, tel. 907/225–6166 or 800/770–2200).

Exploring Ketchikan Ketchikan is a fishing and logging town at the south end of the panhandle. Most of its attractions are within walking distance of the visitors' kiosk on the city dock near Main and Dock streets. Don't miss **Creek Street,** the historic red-light district now home to quaint shops built on stilts over Ketchikan Creek. Ten miles north of town, the **Totem Bight State Historical Park** (Rte. 1, tel. 907/247–8574) contains beautiful totems—many dating from the 1930s but replicating much older totems—as does the village of **Saxman,** 2 mi south of Ketchikan. The area, in fact, contains the largest collection of totems in the world.

Shopping **Silver Lining Seafoods** (1705 Tongass Ave., tel. 907/225–6664), north of the city dock, has excellent locally smoked seafoods. It also carries fish-motif cards and posters by local artist Ray Troll.

Dining For price ranges, see Chart 1 (B) in Chapter 1.

★ **Salmon Falls Resort.** Fresh local seafood is served in a lovely log building overlooking the ocean. Located 17 mi north of town, it's a good choice after a visit to Totem Bight park. *Mile 17, North Tongass Hwy., tel. 907/225–2752. Reservations advised. AE, MC, V. Expensive.*

Lodging For price ranges, see Chart 2 (B) in Chapter 1.

Ingersoll Hotel. Housed in a 1920s building downtown, the hotel features wainscoting and period etched glass. The rooms' predictable motel decor is brightened with Alaskan art. *303 Mission St., Box 6440, 99901, tel. 907/225–2124; fax 907/225–8530. 58 rooms. Facilities: conference room. AE, D, DC, MC, V. Expensive.*

B&B Reservations **Alaska Bed and Breakfast Association** (Box 21890, Juneau 99802, tel. 907/586–2959).

Sitka

Tourist Information **Sitka:** Visitors Bureau (Box 1226, 99835, tel. 907/747–5940) provides brochures and advice.

Exploring Sitka This historic town was the capital of Russian America before Alaska was sold to the United States in 1867. Russian cannons still crown **Castle Hill,** and the flagpole where the Stars and

Stripes replaced the czarist Russian standard still stands. **St. Michael's Cathedral** (Lincoln St., tel. 907/747–8120) is a 1976 replica of the 1848 church. During the 1966 fire that destroyed the original, townspeople entered the burning building to rescue precious icons and other religious objects; these are now on display.

Nearby is the **Russian Bishop's House** (Lincoln St.), a log structure built in 1842 and restored by the National Park Service. Farther east is **Sheldon Jackson College** (Lincoln St., tel. 907/747–8981), with its fine museum of priceless Native American, Aleut, and Eskimo items. In **Sitka National Historic Park** (tel. 907/747–6281), Tlingit carvers still work at the venerable craft of carving totems; a forest trail winds among old and new totems.

Dining For price ranges, see Chart 1 (B) in Chapter 1.

The Channel Club. Consistently fine steaks and seafood are served in nautical surroundings, including glass fishnet floats and whalebone carvings. *2906 Halibut Point Rd., tel. 907/747–9916. AE, MC, V. Expensive.*

Lodging For price ranges, see Chart 2 (B) in Chapter 1.

Westmark Shee Atika. The lobby and rooms are decorated with Tlingit artwork. Many rooms overlook Crescent Harbor and islands beyond; others have mountain and forest views. *330 Seward St., 99835, tel. 907/747–6241 or 800/544–0970; fax 907/747–5486. 100 rooms. Facilities: restaurant, bar. AE, D, DC, MC, V. Expensive.*

B&B Reservations See Ketchikan, *above.*

Juneau

The state capital clings to the mountainside along a narrow saltwater channel. It was born as a gold-rush town in 1880 and remained an active gold-mining center for the next 60 years. Today the number-one employer here is the state government, with transportation and tourism important runners-up.

Tourist Information **Juneau:** Convention and Visitors Bureau (369 S. Franklin St., Suite 201, 99801, tel. 907/586–1737). Information Center (134 3rd St., tel. 907/586–2201).

Exploring Juneau Although Juneau's hills are steep, most visitors can explore the charming town on foot. Houses downtown date from the gold rush. The **Alaska State Capitol** (4th and Seward Sts., tel. 907/465–2479), fronted by huge marble pillars, was built in 1930; it holds the governor's offices and other state agencies. The tiny, onion-domed **St. Nicholas Russian Orthodox Church** (5th and Gold Sts.), constructed in 1894, is the oldest Russian church in Alaska. The **Alaska State Museum** (395 Whittier St., tel. 907/465–2901), near the waterfront, highlights the state's rich cultural heritage, with Eskimo and Native American artifacts, gold-rush memorabilia, and natural-history displays.

Shopping The **Alaska Steam Laundry Building** (S. Franklin St.) has shops and a good coffeehouse downstairs. Across the street, the **Senate Building Mall** houses a charming Christmas store and other import shops. On the city dock, look for shops selling locally smoked seafoods.

Dining For price ranges see Chart 1 (B) in Chapter 1.

★ **The Silverbow Inn.** This small, antiques-filled former bakery serves a blend of classic and American cuisine, with an emphasis on local products and a well-chosen wine list. *120 2nd St., tel. 907/586–4146. AE, D, DC, MC, V. Expensive.*

The Summit. The funky frame exterior belies this restaurant's prestigious reputation. In the small, candlelit interior, diners have their choice of nearly two dozen excellent local fish and shellfish dishes. *455 S. Franklin St., tel. 907/586–2050. Reservations advised. AE, DC, MC, V. No lunch. Expensive.*

The Fiddlehead. Healthy, eclectic food ranging from black beans with rice to pasta with smoked salmon is served in a comfortable setting of light wood, stained glass, and hanging plants. The homemade bread is delicious. *429 Willoughby Ave., tel. 907/586–3150. Reservations advised. AE, MC, V. Moderate.*

Lodging For price ranges see Chart 2 (B) in Chapter 1.

The Baranof Hotel. This grande dame of Juneau hotels has been refurbished over the years to reflect the decor of its 1930s origins. *127 N. Franklin St., 99801, tel. 907/596–2660 or 800/544–0970; fax 907/586–8315. 193 rooms, 6 suites. Facilities: bar, coffee shop. AE, D, DC, MC, V. Expensive.*

Westmark Juneau. Across from the docks, the hotel features spacious rooms, modern decor, and wood-mural carvings in the dining room. *51 W. Egan Dr., 99801, tel. 907/586–6900 or 800/544–0970; fax 907/463–3567. 106 rooms. Facilities: restaurant, coffee shop. AE, D, DC, MC, V. Expensive.*

There are also three restored historic hotels in downtown Juneau: The 1890s **Silverbow Inn** (120 2nd St., 99801, tel. 907/586–4146; fax 907/586–4242), 6 rooms, restaurant; expensive. The 1913 **Alaskan Hotel** (167 S. Franklin St., 99801, tel. 907/586–1000; fax 907/463–3775), 40 rooms, lounge; moderate. The 1898 **Inn at the Waterfront** (455 S. Franklin St., 99801, tel. 907/586–2050), 22 rooms, restaurant, lounge, steam room; moderate.

B&B Reservations *See* Ketchikan, *above.*

Sports and Outdoor Activities

Fishing Southeast Alaskans are blessed with great salmon fishing off city docks and on beaches where creeks meet salt water. Fishing licenses are available in most grocery and sporting-goods stores. For more information, contact the **Department of Fish and Game**'s Southeast office (Box 240020, Juneau 99824, tel. 907/465–4112) or the **State Fish and Game Office** (Box 25526, Juneau 99802, tel. 907/463–4270). Another option is to take an air taxi to a hot spot for a day's fishing or an extended stay (*see* Wilderness Camps and Lodges, *below*).

Kayaking and Rafting You can bring your own kayak aboard state ferries or hire a local outfitter—such as **Alaska Discovery Wilderness Expeditions** (234 Gold St., Juneau 99801, tel. 907/586–1911)—for a guided Inside Passage or Glacier Bay excursion. For rafting on the Mendenhall River, contact **Alaska Travel Adventures** (9085 Glacier Hwy., Suite 204, Juneau 99801, tel. 907/789–0052). Tours of nearby Misty Fjords National Monument in Tongass National Forest are available from **Outdoor Alaska** (Box 7814, Ketchikan 99901, tel. 907/225–6044).

Ski Areas

The **Eaglecrest** ski area, across the channel from Juneau on Douglas Island, has 30 trails, two lifts, a ski school, and equipment rental. *155 S. Seward St., Juneau 99801, tel. 907/586–5284. Open Dec.–Apr.*

Cross-country skiing is popular in all Southeast communities. Check with local visitor centers for the location of trails groomed for diagonal and skate skiing.

Campgrounds

State and national forest campgrounds are available near all Southeast communities. For information, contact the Public Lands Information Center (*see* National and State Parks, *above*). *The Milepost*, available in most Alaska and Washington bookstores, lists campgrounds throughout the state.

Wilderness Camps and Lodges

Accommodations range from Spartan bunkhouses to luxury lodges where guests dress for candle-lit dinners. Among agencies that book area lodges are the **Alaska Sportfishing Lodge Association** (500 Wall St., Seattle, WA 98121, tel. 800/352–2003) and **Alaska Sportfishing Packages** (15375 S.E. 30th Pl. #350, Bellevue, WA 98007, tel. 800/426–0603).

South Central

South Central is home to most of the state's population and many of its most popular attractions. A visit starts in Anchorage, then continues south to the fishing communities of the Kenai Peninsula.

Getting There

By Plane **Anchorage International Airport** (tel. 907/266–2437), about 6 mi from downtown, is served by Alaska Airlines, Markair, Northwest, Delta Airlines, and Continental. Commuter-plane service is available to Denali National Park, Homer, and Kenai. **People Mover** buses (tel. 907/343–6543) will get you downtown for $1; a cab will cost between $10 and $15, including tip.

By Car To get to Anchorage from Tok, on the Alaska Highway near the Canadian border, head southwest on the Glenn Highway. From Fairbanks travel south on the George Parks Highway. From Anchorage, the Seward and Sterling highways lead south to the Kenai Peninsula.

By Ferry The South Central section of the **Alaska Marine Highway** ferry system (*see* Southeast, *above*) is not connected to the Southeast section. You can board at Valdez for a trip through Prince William Sound via Columbia Glacier to Whittier, the port 50 mi east of Anchorage. Ferries also serve Seward, Cordova, Homer, Port Graham, and Kodiak.

By Train The **Alaska Railroad** (tel. 907/265–2494 or 800/544–0552) offers service between Seward, Anchorage, Denali National Park, and Fairbanks.

<table>
<tr><td>**By Bus**</td><td>**Gray Line of Alaska** (tel. 907/277–5581 in season; 800/544–2206 off-season) serves Anchorage and Fairbanks.</td></tr>
</table>

Anchorage

Tourist Information Anchorage: Convention and Visitors Bureau (1600 A St., Suite 200, Anchorage 99501, tel. 907/276–4118). Log Cabin Information Center (W. 4th Ave. and F St., tel. 907/274–3531).

Exploring Anchorage Anchorage is a young, spirited city in a spectacular setting between mountains and sea. With nearly half the state's population residing here, it's home to everything from oil industry high rises to backwoods cabins with resident dogsled teams.

The **Anchorage Museum of History and Art** (W. 7th Ave. and A St., tel. 907/343–6173) has a fine collection of local art and an outstanding exhibit on Native Alaskan life. Just north of downtown, at **Ship Creek**, you can see salmon jump in summer as they head upstream to spawn; there's a platform for easy viewing.

At **Earthquake Park,** at the west end of Northern Lights Boulevard, you can survey the damage wrought by the 1964 quake, when houses tumbled into the ocean. Trees have reclaimed the earth mounds and ponds created by the quake's force. The nearby floatplane base at **Lake Hood** is the world's largest; in summer, planes bound for bush camps and lodges buzz along the coast of Anchorage.

The **Alaska Zoo** (tel. 907/346–3242), at Mile 2 on O'Malley Road, 6 mi south of downtown, is a popular destination for viewing wildlife native to Alaska, including polar bear and brown bear. A few miles farther down the Seward Highway is **Potter Marsh,** home in summer to Canada geese and other migratory birds. The boardwalk allows visitors to approach the birds without harming them. For more information, contact the **Chugach State Park headquarters** (*see* National and State Parks, *above*).

What to See and Do with Children The **Imaginarium** (725 W. 5th Ave., tel. 907/276–3179) is an experimental science museum with a shop selling educational toys.

Shopping If Alaska has a shopping mecca, Anchorage is it. The gift shops along 4th Avenue sell all manner of T-shirts and trinkets. The **Alaska Native Arts and Crafts Association** (333 W. 4th Ave., tel. 907/274–2932) offers genuine—if pricey—local baskets, carvings, and beadwork.

Spectator Sports Most Alaskans are doers rather than watchers of sports. One exception is the vastly popular sled-dog racing. On winter weekends, the **Anchorage Sled Dog Racing Association** (tel. 907/272–7333) hosts races. Check the *Anchorage Daily News* for times. The **Fur Rendezvous,** world-championship sled-dog races, are held in downtown Anchorage in mid-February.

Dining For price ranges, see Chart 1 (B) in Chapter 1.

★ **The Double Musky.** It's worth the 40-mi trip south of town and the wait once you arrive. The little building set among spruce trees is casually decorated with Mardi Gras memorabilia, the better to prepare you for the fine Cajun dishes and huge, tender steaks to come. *Crow Creek Rd., Girdwood, tel. 907/783–2822. No reservations. AE, D, MC, V. Expensive.*

★ **The Marx Brothers Cafe.** Innovative American cuisine, such as wild game and caramelized rack of lamb, is served in an inti-

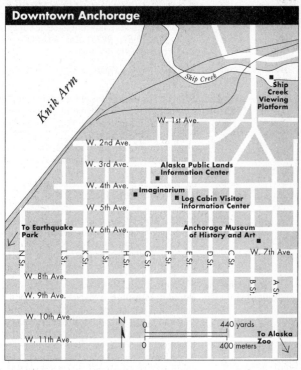

Downtown Anchorage

Knik Arm

Ship Creek

Ship Creek Viewing Platform

W. 1st Ave.

W. 2nd Ave.

W. 3rd Ave. — Alaska Public Lands Information Center

W. 4th Ave. — Imaginarium

Log Cabin Visitor Information Center

W. 5th Ave.

To Earthquake Park

W. 6th Ave. — Anchorage Museum of History and Art

N St.   L St.   K St.   I St.   H St.   G St.   F St.   E St.   D St.   C St.   W. 7th Ave.

W. 8th Ave.

W. 9th Ave.   B St.   A St.

W. 10th Ave.

N

0   440 yards

To Alaska Zoo

W. 11th Ave.

0   400 meters

mate downtown cottage. *627 W. 3rd Ave., tel. 907/258–6279. Reservations required. AE, DC, MC, V. Moderate–Expensive.*

Simon and Seafort's Saloon and Grill. Large windows overlook Cook Inlet at this brass-and-wood restaurant serving fine local seafood and innovative pastas and salads. *420 L St., tel. 907/ 274–3502. Reservations advised. AE, MC, V. No lunch Sun. Moderate.*

The Downtown Deli. This classic delicatessen offers sandwiches, salads, and local fish in a casual, woodsy atmosphere. *525 W. 4th Ave., tel. 907/276–7116. AE, D, MC, V. Inexpensive.*

Lodging For price ranges, see Chart 2 (B) in Chapter 1.

Anchorage Hotel. Many original details have been restored in this charming, centrally located small hotel, built in 1916. *330 E St., 99501, tel. 907/272–4553 or 800/544–0988; fax 907/277– 4483. 31 rooms. AE, DC, MC, V. Expensive.*

★ **Hotel Captain Cook.** This three-tower hotel takes up a full city block. The South Pacific decor includes teak paneling in public spaces and teak furniture in the rooms. *5th Ave. and K St., 99501, tel. 907/276–6000 or 800/843–1950; fax 907/278–5366. 499 rooms, 76 suites. Facilities: 4 restaurants, pool, health club, boutiques. AE, D, DC, MC, V. Expensive.*

Voyager Hotel. This small four-story hotel features full kitchens in all rooms. Some rooms have views of the Cook inlet. *501 K St., 99501, tel. 907/277–9501 or 800/247–9070; fax 907/274– 0333. 38 rooms. Facilities: restaurant. AE, D, DC, MC, V. Expensive.*

Anchorage International Hostel. In a cinder-block building downtown guests share dorm-style rooms and a kitchen on each floor. *700 H St., 99501, tel. 907/276–3635. Capacity: 95. No credit cards. Inexpensive.*

B&B Reservation Service
Alaska Private Lodgings (Box 200047, Anchorage 99520, tel. 907/248–2292).

The Arts and Nightlife
The **Alaska Center for the Performing Arts** (621 W. 6th Ave., tel. 907/263–2787) is home to a local opera company, concerts, plays, and other events. The Fly-by-Night Club's **Whale Fat Follies** (3300 Spenard Rd., tel. 907/279–7726) is a popular revue, with lots of good boogie-woogie music and tacky jokes. The Friday *Anchorage Daily News* includes a weekend activity guide.

The Kenai Peninsula

Tourist Information
Kenai Peninsula: Visitor Information Center (Box 236, Soldotna 99669, tel. 907/262–1337). **Homer:** Visitor Center (Box 541, Homer Spit Rd., 99603, tel. 907/235–5300 in season, 907/235–7740 off-season). **Seward:** Visitor Information Center (3rd and Jefferson Sts., Box 749, 99664, tel. 907/224–8051).

Exploring the Kenai Peninsula
Thrusting into the Gulf of Alaska south of Anchorage, the **Kenai Peninsula** is a glacier-hewn landscape offering magnificent wildlife viewing and fishing from its spectacular coastline. In summer, the Alaska Railroad runs a passenger train daily to **Seward,** a small fishing and timber town on Resurrection Bay, but most people drive the three hours from Anchorage. Tour boats leave Seward's busy downtown harbor for cruises that include visits to sea lions and bird rookeries and close-up visits to tidewater glaciers.

Seward is the jumping-off point for **Kenai Fjords National Park** (Box 1727, Seward 99664, tel. 907/224–3175), a dramatic coastal parkland of sheer cliffs, waterfalls, and deep-green spruce. **Mariah Charters** (tel. 907/224–8623 in season, 907/243–1238 off-season) has tours of the park.

At the southern terminus of the Seward Highway, 210 mi from Anchorage, lies **Homer,** in a breathtaking setting at the end of a sand spit that juts into Kachemak Bay. The town's buildings are picturesque, and you can comb the beach, fish off the docks, or charter a boat for halibut fishing (*see* Sports and Outdoor Activities, *below*). Wildlife abounds in the bay, and most fishing charters include a chance to view whales, seals, porpoises, and birds close up. If you walk along the docks at the end of the day, you can see fishermen unloading their catch. Across from the end of the Homer spit is **Halibut Cove,** a small community with several lodges that is removed from the summer crowds. **Seldovia,** on the other side of Kachemak Bay from Homer, has onion-domed Russian churches and excellent fishing.

Dining
For price ranges, see Chart 1 (B) in Chapter 1.

The Fresh Sourdough Express. The bakery has delicious goodies to go, and the dining room offers tasty local dishes. Try a "stuff" bread pouch filled with cheese and vegetables. *On Ocean Dr. en route to the spit, Homer, tel. 907/235–7571. AE. Moderate.*

★ **The Saltry.** This restaurant with a deck over the water has the best seafood, including fine sushi, in South Central. To get there, take the half-hour ride on the Kachemak Bay Ferry from Homer Harbor. *Halibut Cove (boat and dining reservations through Central Charter Booking Agency, tel. 907/235–7847 or 800/478–7847 in AK). AE, V. Moderate.*

Harbor Dinner Club. This rambling bungalow with several small dining rooms has good local halibut and salmon. *220 5th Ave., Seward, tel. 907/224–3012. DC, MC, V. Inexpensive.*

Lodging For price ranges, see Chart 2 (B) in Chapter 1. For information on wilderness camps and lodges, *see* Southeast, *above.*

Land's End. Decor is rustic in the original section of this hotel located at the end of the spit; a recently completed addition is more modern. Most rooms have small balconies from which to enjoy views of the bay—especially beautiful at sunset. *Box 273, Homer 99603, tel. 907/235–2500. 50 rooms, 12 suites. Facilities: restaurant. AE, D, MC, V. Expensive.*

Van Gilder Hotel. This aging but dignified three-story stucco building is listed on the National Register of Historic Places. Rooms are a bit shabby but serviceable; the staff is friendly. *308 Adams St., Seward 99664, tel. 907/224–3079; fax 907/224–3689. 26 rooms. Facilities: restaurant, lounge. AE, D, DC, MC, V. Moderate.*

Sports and Outdoor Activities

Biking Most South Central highways are suitable for biking on the shoulder. Anchorage has more than 125 mi of bike trails. The **Matanuska Valley** is an increasingly popular place for farm-road rides. Bikes are available for rent at many hotels and at **Downtown Bicycle Rental** (145 W. 6th Ave., Anchorage, tel. 907/279–5293).

Fishing All South Central coastal communities have fishing charters, outfitters, and guides. Although Anchorage does not have good saltwater fishing—glacial runoff makes the water too murky—the freshwater lakes are stocked. In Homer, **Central Charter Booking Agency** (4241 Homer Spit, 99603, tel. 907/235–7847 or 800/478–7847 in AK) books salmon and halibut charters. **Alaska Wildland Adventures** (Box 389, Girdwood 99587, tel. 800/344–8730 or 800/478–4100 in AK) offers a variety of float and fish packages on the Kenai River, world-famous for its huge salmon runs. Licenses are sold in most grocery and other retail stores. For further information, contact the **Department of Fish and Game**'s South Central office (333 Raspberry Rd., Anchorage 99518, tel. 907/267–2218 or 907/349–4687 for recorded information).

Hiking and Backpacking Many hiking trails in South Central have public cabins for rent along the way. For information on these and on the trails themselves, contact the Public Lands Information Center (*see* National and State Parks, *above*).

Kayaking and Rafting Floating is available on hundreds of rivers within a small area. **Nova Riverrunners** (Box 1129, Chickaloon 99674, tel. 907/745–5753) offers guided day trips on the Chickaloon and Matanuska. **Ketchum Air Service** (Box 190588, Anchorage 99519, tel. 907/243–5525 or 800/433–9114) provides drop-off and pick-up service and full outfitting for wilderness float trips.

Ski Areas

The **Alyeska Ski Resort** (Box 249, Girdwood 99587, tel. 907/783–2222), about 40 mi south of Anchorage, is the largest in the state, with 450 acres of skiable terrain, a 3,125-foot vertical drop, 60 trails, and six lifts, including a new 60-passenger tram. It also has a 300-room hotel and a ski school. **Hilltop Ski Area** (715 Abbot Rd., Anchorage 99516, tel. 907/346–1446), at the top of Abbott Road 10 mi from downtown Anchorage, has two lifts, eight trails, a vertical drop of 300 feet, downhill ski instruction, cross-country trails, and a national-grade half-pipe for snowboarders.

Campgrounds

In Anchorage, the city-operated **Centennial Camper Park** (Box 196650, 99519, tel. 907/333–9711) has 88 spaces and showers. For information on other campgrounds in the region, contact the Public Lands Information Center (*see* National and State Parks, *above*).

The Interior

The Alaska and George Parks highways offer access to this diverse area, a vast wilderness of birch and spruce forest, tundra valleys, and abundant wildlife. Its crown jewel is Denali National Park, 250 mi north of Anchorage. En route here from Anchorage, visitors travel through green Matanuska Valley farm country. North of Fairbanks, two hot springs retreats welcome visitors year-round.

Getting There

By Plane Daily scheduled air service between Anchorage, Juneau, and Fairbanks (Fairbanks International Airport, tel. 907/479–8700) is provided by Alaska Airlines, Delta, and Markair; Alaska Airlines also flies to Denali in summer. A number of bush carriers originate in Fairbanks and will take you to otherwise inaccessible destinations in the region.

By Car Much of the Interior is inaccessible by road. One exception is the George Parks Highway, which runs from Anchorage to Fairbanks. Hardy RV'ers and campers drive the Alaska Highway through British Columbia and the Yukon to Alaska; it takes at least a week.

By Train The **Alaska Railroad** (tel. 907/265–2494 or 800/544–0552) offers service between Anchorage and Fairbanks via Denali.

Denali National Park

Tourist Information **Denali National Park and Preserve** (Superintendent, Box 9, Denali National Park 99755, tel. 907/683–2686 or 907/683–2294; fax (May–Sept.) 907/683–1265). **Alaska Public Lands Information Center** (*see* National and State Parks, *above*).

Exploring Denali National Park Denali is 6 million acres of wilderness, including the majestic Mt. McKinley—at 20,320 feet the highest peak in North America. Along with unmatched vistas of mountains, glacial rivers, and alpine meadows, the park offers abundant wildlife—look for bears, wolves, moose, Dall sheep, and caribou. To enhance viewing opportunities, the park is closed to private vehicles, other than those with campground permits for sites inside the park. Visitors ride shuttle buses on the 10-hour tour to the **Eielson Visitor Center** and **Wonder Lake.** If you tire of the ride, you can get out and walk, then catch another bus (they leave every half hour) in either direction to continue your journey. The park also offers naturalist and sled-dog demonstrations; check with the **Riley Creek Information Center** near the park entrance for the day's schedule. Denali is open year-round, but services and accommodations are limited from September to May. For information on camping, *see* Campgrounds, *below.*

Dining   There's not a great variety of food available at the park. All hotels have their own restaurants. For price ranges, see Chart 1 (B) in Chapter 1.

Lynx Creek Campground Pizza Parlor. This funky frame building is popular with young park workers for after-work beer and pizza; try the reindeer-sausage topping. *Parks Hwy., 1½ mi north of park entrance, tel. 907/683–2548. No reservations. MC, V. Closed Sept.–May. Inexpensive.*

Lodging   For price ranges, see Chart 2 (B) in Chapter 1.

★ **Camp Denali.** This cabin compound in the heart of the park has shared bathrooms but no electricity. Many consider it the best place to stay in the park for its rustic charm and delicious home cooking. A knowledgeable staff will acquaint you with the wilderness that surrounds you. *Box 67, Denali National Park 99755, tel. and fax 907/683–2290 summer; tel. 603/675–2248, fax 603/675–9125 winter. 17 cabins. Closed early Sept.–mid-June. Expensive.*

Denali National Park Hotel. This spread-out complex includes some accommodations in old railroad Pullman cars. It's at the park entrance, across from the railroad station. *Box 87, Denali National Park 99755, tel. 907/276–7234 or 907/683–2215; fax 907/258–3668. 100 rooms. Facilities: restaurant, bar. MC, V. Closed Sept.–May. Expensive.*

Denali Princess Lodge. This large log complex above the Nenana River is the most luxurious hotel at the park; some suites have whirlpools. *Parks Hwy., 1 mi north of park entrance, Dept. VP, 2815 2nd Ave., Suite 400, Seattle, WA 98121, tel. 800/426–0500; fax 206/443–1979. Facilities: 2 restaurants, bar. AE, MC, V. Closed Sept.–May. Expensive.*

Denali Hostel. A wood-frame bunkhouse offers shared accommodations and bus service to and from the park. It's located 10 mi north, near Healy. *Box 801, Denali National Park 99755, tel. 907/683–1295. No credit cards. Closed Sept.–May. Inexpensive.*

Campgrounds   There are seven campgrounds in Denali. Three are open to private vehicles for tent and RV camping; three are reached by shuttle bus and are restricted to tent camping; and one is for backpackers only. For more information, contact the Park Superintendent (*see* Tourist Information, *above*). Several private campgrounds can be found outside the park along the highway, such as **Grizzly Bear Cabins and Campground** (Box 7, Denali National Park 99755, tel. 907/683–2696 or 907/488–3932 in winter). For information on public campgrounds outside Denali, contact the Public Lands Information Office (*see* National and State Parks, *above*).

Fairbanks

Tourist
Information
Fairbanks: Convention and Visitors Bureau (550 1st Ave., 99701, tel. 907/456–5774 or 800/327–5774).

Exploring
Fairbanks
Built on the banks of the Chena River, Fairbanks was founded by gold miners early in the century and later became a transportation center for all of the Interior. Today it's the state's second-largest city, although its atmosphere is more that of a frontier town. Its residents—who cope with incredible winter temperatures (lows reach –50°F), darkness or twilight almost around the clock in winter, and ice fog—consider themselves hardier and more truly Alaskan than people from elsewhere in the state.

One of Fairbanks's main attractions is the **University of Alaska** (tel. 907/474–7211), which offers a two-hour guided walking tour of the campus. On its grounds are the **Large Animal Research Station,** home to musk-ox and caribou, and the **University of Alaska Museum,** whose collection includes a 38,000-year-old mummified steppe bison. The west ridge of the campus affords an excellent view of the **Alaska Range** to the south.

Another big draw in Fairbanks is the **Alaskaland Park** (Airport Way and Peger Rd., tel. 907/459–1087; closed early Sept.–late May), on the Chena River near downtown. Among its numerous attractions are a museum, a theater, an art gallery, a native village, and a reconstructed gold-rush town. A tram offers free transportation to and from downtown and nearby hotels and motels.

Spectator Sports
The North American Open Sled Dog Championship is held in downtown Fairbanks in March. Check with the visitors bureau (*see* Tourist Information, *above*) for details. **Ice hockey** is a passion here: The professional **Gold Kings** (tel. 907/456–7825) and the University of Alaska **Nanooks** (tel. 907/474–6868) draw big crowds at their arenas October through March.

Dining
For price ranges, see Chart 1 (B) in Chapter 1.

★ **Pump House Restaurant.** A restored mining pump station is the setting for good seafood and other American dishes, as well as specials served family style. *Mile 1.3, Chena Pump Rd., tel. 907/479–8452. AE, MC, V. Moderate.*

Lodging
For hotel price ranges, see Chart 2 (B) in Chapter 1.

★ **Sophie Station.** At this spacious, modern hotel near Fairbanks International Airport, some rooms have kitchens. *1717 University Ave., 99701, tel. 907/479–3650; fax 907/479–7951. 147 rooms. AE, D, DC, MC, V. Expensive.*
Westmark Fairbanks. This full-service hotel, close to downtown, is built around a courtyard on a quiet street. *813 Noble St., tel. 907/456–7722; fax 907/451–7478. 240 rooms. Facilities: 2 restaurants, 2 lounges. AE, D, DC, MC, V. Expensive.*

B&B Reservations
Alaska Fairbanks B&B (Box 74573, 99701, tel. 907/452–4967; fax 907/451–6955).

Hot Springs Retreats

Their discovery of natural hot springs in the frozen wilderness just north of Fairbanks sent early miners scrambling to build communities around this heaven-sent phenomenon. Today the area is a popular excursion for Fairbanks residents, who come to soak in the pools filled with hot spring water and to enjoy excellent fishing, hiking, and cross-country skiing.

Chena Hot Springs Resort. This resort, just 60 mi from Fairbanks on Chena Hot Springs Road, is the closest and most popular destination among locals. There's a campground, as well as hotel rooms and cabins. Nonguests can pay to use the heated pool and eat in the restaurant. *Box 73440, Fairbanks 99707, tel. 907/452-7867 weekdays; fax 907/456-3122. 40 rooms. Facilities: restaurant, lounge, spring-heated pool, 2 Jacuzzis, hot tub. AE, DC, MC, V. Moderate-Expensive.*

Arctic Circle Hot Springs. A full day's drive from Fairbanks on the Steese Highway, this spa retains the original hotel dating from 1930. There's a campground nearby. *Box 254, Central 99730, tel. 907/520-5113. 68 rooms. Facilities: restaurant, lounge, spring-heated pool, indoor Jacuzzi. No credit cards. Moderate.*

Sports and Outdoor Activities

Canoeing The Chena River is popular for canoeing, both in Fairbanks and out in the wilderness. Entry points are marked along Chena Hot Springs Road. Avoid the Tanana River, with its swift and tricky current and hidden sandbars.

Fishing Char, grayling, and pike are abundant in the lakes and rivers of the Interior. The Chena River between Fairbanks and Chena Hot Springs is especially popular for grayling fishing. For more information, contact the **Fish and Game Department's** Interior office (1300 College Rd., Fairbanks 99701, tel. 907/456-8819 or 907/456-4665 for recorded information).

Hiking and Backpacking Skilled wilderness travelers can hike anywhere in Denali National Park, with the exception of areas occasionally closed because of bear-related dangers. There are well-marked beginner trails near the park entrance.

Rafting Several companies offer white-water trips on the thrilling **Nenana River,** which parallels the George Parks Highway near the Denali entrance. Try **Denali Raft Adventures** (Dept. VP, Drawer 190, Denali National Park 99755, tel. 907/683-2234 or 907/479-7822) or **McKinley Raft Tours** (Box 138, Denali National Park 99755, tel. 907/683-2392).

Wilderness Camps and Lodges

See Southeast, *above.*

Elsewhere in the State

The Arctic

Getting There You must travel to Nome and Kotzebue by plane, as no highway leads there. **Princess Tours** (2815 2nd Ave., Seattle, WA 98121-9981, tel. 800/426-0442) offers package tours; the road to Prudhoe Bay is closed to private traffic past Chandalar.

What to See and Do The gold-rush town of **Nome** sits just below the Arctic Circle. Colorful saloons and low-slung, ramshackle buildings help perpetuate its vintage gold-camp aura, present since ore was dis-

covered here in 1898. **Kotezebue,** on the other hand, is a proud
Eskimo community north of Nome that preserves its heritage
in the **Living Museum of the Arctic** (tel. 907/442–3301). In town,
salmon dries on wooden racks and Eskimo boats rest in yards.
At the top of the state, tours of the **Prudhoe Bay** area explore
the oil-industry life there, as well as the wildlife and tundra
surrounding it. For more information, contact the Alaska Division of Tourism (*see* Visitor Information, *above*).

Katmai National Park and Preserve

Getting There At the base of the Alaska Peninsula, 290 mi southwest of Anchorage, Katmai is accessible only by plane to King Salmon and
then float plane for the 20-minute hop to the park. The Alaska
Division of Tourism's vacation planner contains information on
air taxis and guide services (*see* Visitor Information, *above*).

What to See
and Do Katmai is a relatively primitive park compared with the likes of
Denali, but therein lies its charm. The peaceful valley became a
land of steaming fumaroles after the 1912 eruption of Mt. No-
varupta and the collapse of nearby Mt. Katmai's peak. The residents who fled the area, now dubbed the **Valley of Ten
Thousand Smokes,** have been replaced by sports lovers and
tourists. Fishermen flock here for trophy rainbow trout and
salmon. Hiking, boat tours, and wildlife viewing are other Katmai attractions. **Katmailand Inc.** (4700 Aircraft Dr., Suite 2,
Anchorage 99502, tel. 907/243–5448 or 800/544–0551) offers
tours; or contact **Katmai National Park and Preserve** (Box 7,
King Salmon 99613, tel. 907/246–3305).

The Aleutian and Pribilof Islands

Getting There About the only practical way to see these areas is through a
package tour. Schedules are flexible, as weather often delays
flights to and from the islands. Contact **Reeve Aleutian Airways**
(4700 International Airport Rd., Anchorage 99508, tel. 907/
243–4700 or 800/544–2248) for flight and package-tour information.

What to See
and Do The **Aleutian Islands** stretch 1,000 mi from the Alaska Peninsula toward Japan. This semivolcanic, treeless archipelago of 20
large and several hundred smaller islands makes Alaska the
westernmost point (as well as the *easternmost* point!) on the
continent. The Aleut natives who live in the tiny settlements
here work in canneries or as fishermen and guides. Out here,
where the wind blows constantly and fog is common, can be
found some of the most spectacular bird-watching in the country, with abundant terns, guillemots, murres, and puffins, as
well as species unique to the islands.

Each spring the largest northern fur-seal herd in the world
comes to the tiny green **Pribilof Islands,** in the Bering Sea
about 200 mi northwest of Cold Bay. Most tours fly to **St. Paul,**
one of the largest islands and home to the descendants of Aleut-
Russians, whose churches, names, and facial features reveal
their heritage.

HAWAII

By Marty
Wentzel

Capital	Honolulu
Population	1,209,000
Motto	The Life of the Land Is Perpetuated in Righteousness
State Bird	Nene (Hawaiian goose)
State Flower	Hibiscus

Visitor Information

Hawaii Visitors Bureau (2270 Kalakaua Ave., Suite 801, Honolulu 96815, tel. 808/923–1811 or 212/947–0717 in NYC).

Scenic Drives

On the eastern tip of Oahu, the 10-mi stretch of **Kalanianaole Highway** from Hanauma Bay to Waimanalo is a cliffside road resembling those of the California coast. On the Big Island, **Hwy. 19** north out of Hilo runs along the rugged Hamakua Coast to Waipio Valley, past sugarcane fields and spectacular ocean views. From Paia to Hana, Maui's **Hana Highway** (Hwy. 36) is a winding, 55-mi coastal route that spans numerous rivers and passes tropical waterfalls. From the town of Waimea, Kauai's **Waimea Canyon Drive** meanders upward past panoramas of Waimea Canyon, culminating at the 4,120-foot Kalalau Lookout.

National and State Parks

National Parks **Hawaii Volcanoes National Park, Puuhonua o Honaunau,** and **Puukohola** (*see* The Big Island of Hawaii, *below*), national historic sites. **Haleakala National Park** (*see* Maui, *below*). **Kalaupapa** (*see* Elsewhere in the State, *below*).

U.S.S. *Arizona* **Memorial** (1 Arizona Memorial Pl., Honolulu 96818–3145, tel. 808/422–0561), a 20-minute drive east from downtown Honolulu, shields the hulk of the U.S.S *Arizona*, which sank with 1,102 men aboard when the Japanese attacked Pearl Harbor on December 7, 1941.

State Parks **Hapuna State Recreation Area** (*see* The Big Island, *below*). **Kahana Valley** (52–290 Kamehameha Hwy., Kaneohe 96744, tel. 808/237–8858), an ancient valley on windward Oahu, includes 20 acres of hiking trails and picnic areas. **Kokee** (*see* Kauai, *below*). **Wailua River** (Wailua Marina, Kapaa 96746, tel. 808/822–5065) meanders past the sites of ancient villages and culminates in an enormous, fern-laced lava tube. For brochures and other information, write the **State Parks Office** (Box 621, Honolulu 96809, tel. 808/587–0300).

Honolulu and Waikiki

Honolulu, on the island of Oahu, is worlds apart from any other city in the country. Here the salad of cultures is artfully tossed in a blend that is harmonious yet allows each culture to retain its distinct flavor and texture. Its downtown sector combines a royal history with the modern-day action of a major metropolitan center. Just 3½ mi from downtown is Waikiki, a tourist mecca par excellence. Set on the sunny, dry side of Oahu, Waikiki touts the natural splendors of the islands while offering the glittering atmosphere that makes it a resort of international renown.

Tourist Information

Hawaii Visitors Bureau (*see* Visitor Information, *above*).

Arriving and Departing

By Plane A 30-minute drive west of Waikiki, **Honolulu International Airport** (tel. 808/836–6411) is undergoing a multimillion-dollar renovation scheduled for completion in the mid- to late 1990s. U.S. carriers serving Honolulu include American, America West, Continental, Delta, Hawaiian, Northwest, TWA, and United. A cab from the airport to downtown costs about $20 plus tip. **Terminal Transportation** (tel. 808/836–0317) runs a shuttle service to Waikiki ($6). Some hotels also provide shuttle service; ask when you make reservations.

Getting Around Honolulu and Waikiki

By Car There's no need to rent a car if you don't want to leave Waikiki. Driving in rush hour (6:30–8:30 AM and 3:30–5:30 PM) is frustrating because of traffic, parking limitations, and numerous one-way streets. If you do plan to rent, reservations are suggested year-round.

By Public Transportation You can ride **The Bus** (tel. 808/848–5555) all around Oahu for a mere 60¢.

By Taxi You can usually get a cab outside your hotel. The two biggest taxicab companies are **Charley's** (tel. 808/531–1333) and **SIDA of Hawaii** (tel. 808/836–0011).

Orientation Tours

The daylong **Circle Island Tour** from Akamai Tours (tel. 808/971–4545) takes you past highlights outside Honolulu. The **Pearl Harbor and Punchbowl Tour** offered by Polynesian Adventure Tours (tel. 808/922–0888) includes a boat tour to Pearl Harbor. In downtown Honolulu, the **Chinatown Walking Tour** (tel. 808/533–3181) provides a fascinating peek at Oahu's oldest neighborhood.

Exploring Honolulu and Waikiki

Directions are often given in terms of *mauka* (toward the mountains) and *makai* (toward the ocean), or they may refer to Diamond Head (east, toward the famous volcanic landmark) and *ewa* (west).

Honolulu Including Waikiki

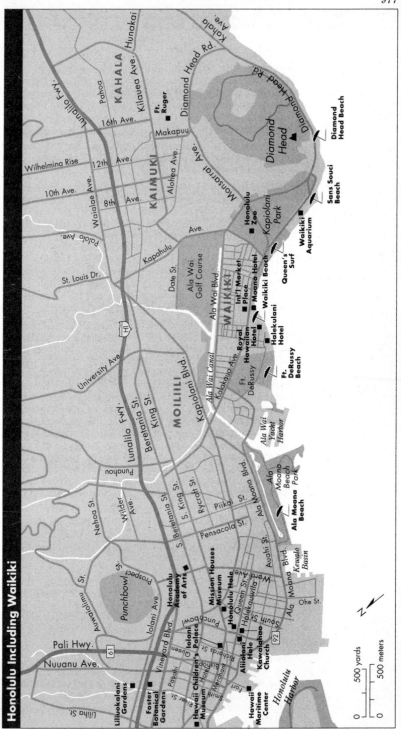

Downtown Honolulu

The **Hawaii Maritime Center,** across Ala Moana Boulevard from Alakea Street, features exhibits honoring Hawaii's relationship with the sea. *Pier 7, tel. 808/536–6373. Admission charged. Closed Christmas.*

Nearby, at King and Richard streets, is **Iolani Palace** (tel. 808/ 522–0832), built in 1882 and the only royal palace in America. The Victorian structure has been beautifully restored and is open for guided tours Wednesday–Saturday. Tickets should be reserved in advance.

Across King Street is **Aliiolani Hale,** the old judiciary building that served as the parliament hall during the monarchy era. In front is the gilded statue of Kamehameha I, the Hawaiian chief who unified the islands.

Honolulu Hale (530 S. King St. at Punchbowl St.), the city hall, is a Mediterranean/Renaissance–style building constructed in 1929. Across the street is **Kawaiahao Church** (957 Punchbowl St., tel. 808/522–1333), built in 1842 of massive blocks of solid coral. The church witnessed the coronations, weddings, and funerals of generations of Hawaiian royalty. Next door is the **Mission Houses Museum** (553 S. King St., tel. 808/531–0481), home of the first U.S. missionaries in Hawaii after their arrival in 1820. The mission's three main structures—the **Hale La'au** wood-frame house, the **Printing Office,** and the **Chamberlain House**—are among the oldest buildings on the islands.

Waikiki

The impressive **Halekulani Hotel** (2199 Kalia Rd., tel. 808/923– 2311) is built on the site of a 1917 hotel that was the setting for the first of the Charlie Chan detective novels, *The House Without a Key*. The hotel's modern version features a massive floral arrangement in the lobby and a pool with an orchid mosaic at the bottom. Follow the paved ocean walk to the pink **Royal Hawaiian Hotel** (2259 Kalakaua Ave., tel. 808/923–7311), built in 1921 when Waikiki was still a sleepy paradise. Cross the street and walk toward Diamond Head to the **International Market Place** (2330 Kalakaua Ave., tel. 808/923–9871), with its spreading banyan tree and dozens of souvenir stands. On the makai side of the street is the oldest hotel in Waikiki, the **Moana** (2365 Kalakaua Ave., tel. 808/922–3111), which underwent a major renovation in the late 1980s. The Beaux Arts–style building includes a Historical Room with hotel memorabilia dating from the turn of the century.

At the Diamond Head end of Waikiki, the **Honolulu Zoo** (151 Kapahulu Ave., tel. 808/971–7171) is home to thousands of furry and finned creatures. It's not the biggest zoo in the country, but its 40 lush acres certainly make it one of the prettiest. **Kapiolani Park,** a vast green playing field, is where you'll find the **Waikiki Shell** (2805 Monsarrat Ave., tel. 808/521–2911), Honolulu's outdoor concert arena. Next door, the **Kodak Hula Show** (tel. 808/833–1661) has been wowing crowds for more than 50 years. The **Waikiki Aquarium** (2777 Kalakaua Ave., tel. 808/923–9741), the third-oldest aquarium in America, harbors more than 300 species of marine life.

The hike to the summit of **Diamond Head** offers a marvelous view of Oahu's southern coastline. The entrance is about 1 mi above Kapiolani Park. Drive through the tunnel to the inside of the crater, park, and start walking. It's a half-hour jaunt to the top. *Monsarrat Ave. near 18th Ave., tel. 808/548–7455. Admission free.*

What to See and Do with Children

In addition to the creatures on display at the zoo and aquarium (*see* Exploring Honolulu and Waikiki, *above*), porpoises and penguins are on view in the lagoon at the **Kahala Hilton** (5000 Kahala Ave., tel. 808/734–2211). At the **Hawaii Children's Museum** (650 Iwilei Rd., tel. 808/522–0040), children can learn about the body and see a bug zoo.

Shopping

Just outside Waikiki is the **Ala Moana Center** (1450 Ala Moana Blvd., tel. 808/946–2811), a 50-acre open-air mall with major department stores, including **Liberty House** (tel. 808/941–2345). Eclectic boutiques and eateries populate **Ward Centre** (1200 Ala Moana Blvd.) and **Ward Warehouse** (1050 Ala Moana Blvd.; tel. 808/531–6411 for both). In Waikiki there's the **International Market Place** (*see* Exploring Honolulu and Waikiki, *above*), as well as the **Royal Hawaiian Shopping Center** (2201 Kalakaua Ave., tel. 808/922–0588)—three stories high and three blocks long, with 120 stores.

Beaches

Honolulu   **Ala Moana Beach Park,** across from Ala Moana Shopping Center, is the most popular beach for families because the protective reef keeps waters calm. Facilities include bathhouses, indoor and outdoor showers, lifeguards, concession stands, and tennis courts. **Hanauma Bay,** a 30-minute drive east of Waikiki, is a marine preserve with outstanding snorkeling, a snack bar, bathhouses, and gear rental.

Waikiki   **Ft. DeRussy Beach,** the widest part of Waikiki Beach, has volleyball courts, picnic tables, showers, and food stands. **Queen's Surf,** across from the Honolulu Zoo, is named for Queen Liliuokalani's beach house, which once stood here. Sand here is soft, and the beach slopes gently to the water; it attracts a mixture of families and gays. **Sans Souci,** across from Kapiolani Park, is a favorite of singles in skimpy bathing suits. Its shallow waters are safe for children.

Dining

The strength of Hawaii's tourist industry has attracted some of the finest chefs in the world to Oahu's hotels, where you'll find the best dining on the island. A variety of restaurants serve fine ethnic food, especially Chinese, Japanese, and Thai. No matter what or how you eat, you'll probably pay higher prices in Waikiki than in the rest of Hawaii. For price ranges, see Chart 1 (A) in Chapter 1.

Very Expensive   **Bali by the Sea.** An oceanside setting provides glorious views of
★   Waikiki Beach, outdone only by such upscale international entrées as roast duck with papaya puree and poached mahimahi and opakapaka, a pair of island fish served with two sauces. *Hilton Hawaiian Village, 2005 Kalia Rd., tel. 808/941–2254. Reservations advised. Dress: collared shirt. AE, D, DC, MC, V. No dinner Sun.*

★   **La Mer.** In the exotic atmosphere of a Mandalay mansion is served a unique blend of French and nouvelle Hawaiian cuisine. A standout among entrées is breast of duck with fresh pears and spiced apples in a light ginger sauce. *Halekulani Hotel, 2199 Kalia Rd., tel. 808/923–2311. Reservations required. Jacket required. AE, D, DC, MC, V. No lunch.*

Maile. The signature restaurant of the "hotel of the stars" is glamorous and glittering, despite the lack of views. Steaks and meats are the pride of the Maile, including roast duckling Waialae with fruit sauce. *Kahala Hilton, 5000 Kahala Ave., tel. 808/734–2211. Reservations required. Jacket advised. AE, D, DC, MC, V. No lunch.*

Michel's. With mirrors, piano music, chandeliers, and panoramas of the sea, this is easily the most romantic restaurant in town. The Continental fare includes pepper steak flamed with Jack Daniels whiskey. *Colony Surf Hotel, 2895 Kalakaua Ave., tel. 808/923–6552. Reservations required. Jacket required at dinner. AE, D, DC, MC, V.*

Expensive

Hy's Steak House. Things always seem to go well at Hy's, from the glazed New York peppercorn steak to the cherries jubilee. The atmosphere is snug, and you can watch the chef work behind glass. *Waikiki Park Heights Hotel, 2440 Kuhio Ave., tel. 808/922–5555. Reservations required. AE, D, DC, MC, V. No lunch.*

★ **Restaurant Suntory.** Here is Japanese dining at its most elegant. Choose from the sushi bar, rooms devoted to *teppanyaki* (food prepared on an iron grill) or *shabu-shabu* (thinly sliced beef boiled in broth), or a private room. *Royal Hawaiian Center, 2233 Kalakaua Ave., tel. 808/922–5511. Reservations advised. AE, DC, MC, V.*

The Secret. Formerly the Third Floor, this elegant restaurant has a European feel, with extravagant food displays, dim lights, and huge wicker chairs. Indian *naan* bread starts things off, followed by steaks and seafood. *Hawaiian Regent Hotel, 2552 Kalakaua Ave., tel. 808/922–6611. Reservations required. AE, DC, MC, V. No lunch.*

Moderate

Golden Dragon. Szechuan, Cantonese, and unconventional nouvelle Chinese cuisine is served in this dining room by the sea. Among the best items is the beggar's chicken (whole chicken baked in a clay pot). *Hilton Hawaiian Village, 2005 Kalia Rd., tel. 808/946–5336. Reservations advised. AE, D, DC, MC, V. No lunch.*

Keo's Thai Cuisine. Hollywood celebrities have discovered this orchid-filled nook, where the Evil Jungle Prince (chicken, shrimp, or scallops in a sauce of fresh basil, coconut milk, and red chile pepper) is tops. *625 Kapahulu Ave., tel. 808/737–8240. Reservations required. AE, DC, MC, V. No lunch.*

Rex's Black Orchid. Since restaurateur Rex Chandler took it over in 1992, the dark-wood art deco dining room has loosened up and lowered prices. Black-and-blue ahi (tuna) with Cajun spices, seared and left raw inside, is one of the understandably popular appetizers. *500 Ala Moana Blvd., tel. 808/521–3111. Reservations required. AE, DC, MC, V.*

Tripton's American Cafe. The spare Napa Valley ambience (a real change of pace from the relentless glitter of nearby Waikiki) and inventive American cuisine—including seasonal specialties and knockout desserts—make this a favorite of local residents as well as visitors. *Diamond Head Center, 449 Kapahulu Ave., tel. 808/737–3819. Reservations advised. AE, DC, MC, V.*

Inexpensive **California Pizza Kitchen.** A tiled and mirrored glass atrium
★ showcases designer pizzas with such toppings as Thai chicken,
Peking duck, and Caribbean shrimp. There's another branch
(tel. 808/955–5161) on Ala Moana Boulevard in Waikiki. *Kahala*
Mall, 4211 Waialae Ave., tel. 808/737–9446. No reservations.
AE, MC, V.

Compadres Mexican Bar and Grill. The outdoor terrace is fun
for margaritas and chips. Inside, lively photographs and colorful paintings create a festive setting for fajitas, chili rellenos,
and nachos. *Ward Centre, 1200 Ala Moana Blvd., tel. 808/523–*
1307. No reservations. AE, MC, V.

Hau Tree Lanai. Next to Sans Souci Beach and shaded by a
huge hau tree, this outdoor café provides relaxing ocean views
to accompany the American entrées. At breakfast try the Belgian waffle or salmon omelet. *New Otani Kaimana Beach Ho-*
tel, 2863 Kalakaua Ave., tel. 808/921–7066. Reservations
advised. AE, DC, MC, V.

Maple Garden. The fine reputation of this restaurant is founded
on the spicy Szechuan cuisine, not on the no-frills decor. A consistent favorite is the eggplant in hot garlic sauce. *909 Isenberg*
St., tel. 808/941–6641. Reservations advised. AE, DC, MC, V.

Lodging

Oahu's best accommodations are in or near Waikiki, with a few
places of note in Honolulu. Except for the peak months of January, February, and August, you'll have no trouble getting a
room if you call first. For B&Bs in the area contact **Hawaii's**
Best Bed and Breakfasts (Box 563, Kamuela 96743, tel. 808/
885–0550). (Note: All mailing addresses are in Honolulu.) For
price ranges, see Chart 2 (A) in Chapter 1.

Very Expensive **Halekulani Hotel.** This sleek, modern hotel boasts fresh mar-
★ ble-and-wood rooms, some with breathtaking ocean views. It
also offers two of the finest restaurants in Honolulu, and a pool
with a giant orchid mosaic. *2199 Kalia Rd., 96815, tel. 808/923–*
2311 or 800/367–2343; fax 808/926–8004. 456 rooms. Facilities:
3 restaurants, 3 lounges, fitness room, pool. AE, D, DC, MC,
V.

★ **Hilton Hawaiian Village.** The state's largest resort includes
four towers, botanical gardens, and a pond with penguins.
Rooms are done in raspberry or aqua, with rattan and bamboo
furnishings. A wide variety of rates is available. *2005 Kalia*
Rd., 96815, tel. 808/949–4321; fax 808/947–7898. 2,523 rooms.
Facilities: 22 restaurants, 11 lounges, 3 pools. AE, D, DC, MC,
V.

Kahala Hilton. In an elegant neighborhood minutes away from
Waikiki, this is the choice of stars, kings, and presidents. The
lobby features chandeliers, tropical-flower displays, and a musician playing a grand piano. Large rooms decorated in earth
tones have his-and-her dressing rooms and parquet floors.
Three distinguished restaurants are here. *5000 Kahala Ave.,*
96816, tel. 808/734–2211 or 800/367–2525; fax 808/737–2478.
309 rooms, 60 cottages. Facilities: 3 restaurants, 2 lounges,
health club, pool. AE, D, DC, MC, V.

Expensive **Colony Surf.** This is a small oceanside hotel with impeccable
★ personal service; each unit is equipped with a full kitchen. Location is a plus, on the quiet east end of Waikiki near Diamond
Head. *2895 Kalakaua Ave., 96815, tel. 808/923–5751 or 800/*

252–7873; fax 808/922–8433. 50 units. Facilities: 2 restaurants, 2 lounges. AE, D, DC, MC, V.

Outrigger Waikiki Hotel. A $35 million renovation has just been completed at this star beachfront property. Each room has a Polynesian motif and a lanai, and some have kitchenettes. *2335 Kalakaua Ave., 96815, tel. 808/923–0711 or 800/462–6262; fax 800/622–4852. 529 rooms. Facilities: 6 restaurants, 6 lounges, pool. AE, D, DC, MC, V.*

★ **Waikiki Joy.** In the heart of Waikiki, this gem has some rooms with refrigerators, others with kitchens, wet bars, or king-size beds. Every room has a whirlpool, a deluxe stereo system, and a bedside control panel. *320 Lewers St., 96815, tel. 808/923–2300 or 800/733–5569; fax 808/924–4010. 101 rooms. Facilities: restaurant, lounge, pool. AE, D, DC, MC, V.*

Waikiki Parc. Despite the main entrance down a narrow side street, this hotel's location just one block from Waikiki's beach is a real plus. Rooms have rattan furniture and blue-and-white decor. *2233 Helumoa Rd., 96815, tel. 808/921–7272 or 800/422–0450; fax 808/923–1336. 298 rooms. Facilities: 2 restaurants, pool. AE, D, DC, MC, V.*

Moderate **Hawaiiana Hotel.** The aloha spirit permeates this Waikiki old-timer, from the fresh pineapple when you arrive to the flower lei when you leave. The three-story property arranged around a tropical garden is only a short walk from Ft. DeRussy Beach. Rooms are decorated simply but include kitchens and electronic safes; many have lanais. Complimentary coffee and juice are served each morning. *260 Beach Walk, 96815, tel. 808/923–3811 or 800/367–5122; fax 808/926–5728. 95 rooms. Facilities: pool. AE, MC, V.*

★ **Manoa Valley Inn.** Tucked away in a lush valley 2 mi from Waikiki, this inn was built in 1919 and renovated when it was converted into a bed-and-breakfast 13 years ago. Rooms have antique four-poster beds, marble-top dressers, and patterned wallpaper. *2001 Vancouver Dr., 96822, tel. 808/947–6019 or 800/634–5115. 8 rooms (4 share baths), 1 cottage. AE, MC, V.*

New Otani Kaimana Beach. Polished to a shine, it sits right on the beach across from Kapiolani Park. Rooms are small but nicely renovated, with soothing pastels and off-white furnishings. *2863 Kalakaua Ave., 96815, tel. 808/923–1555 or 800/421–8795; fax 808/922–9404. 125 rooms. Facilities: 3 restaurants, lounge. AE, D, DC, MC, V.*

Outrigger Reef. A beachfront location and moderate rates are this hotel's selling points. Extensive renovations have improved the mauve-and-pink rooms, many of which have lanais. *2169 Kalia Rd., 96815, tel. 808/923–3111 or 800/462–6262; fax 800/622–4852. 883 rooms. Facilities: 2 restaurants, 4 lounges, nightclub, shops, pool. AE, D, DC, MC, V.*

Inexpensive **Continental Surf.** This budget Waikiki high rise is two blocks from the ocean and convenient to shopping and dining. Rooms, with standard modern decor and Polynesian hues, have limited views; some have kitchenettes. *2426 Kuhio Ave., 96815, tel. 808/922–2755 or 800/367–5004; fax 808/533–0472. 140 rooms. AE, DC, MC, V.*

Edmunds Hotel Apartments. This low-priced spot on the Ala Wai Canal has views of the mountains. The rooms are small and nondescript but include kitchenettes. *2411 Ala Wai Blvd., 96815, tel. 808/923–8381. 12 rooms. No credit cards.*

★ **Royal Grove Hotel.** A flamingo-pink Waikiki landmark, this hotel has a family atmosphere. Rooms have no real theme or views but do come with kitchens. *15 Uluniu Ave., 96815, tel. 808/923–7691. 87 rooms. Facilities: pool. AE, DC, MC, V.*

The Arts and Nightlife

The Arts
Theater The **Diamond Head Theater** (520 Makapuu Ave., Honolulu, tel. 808/734–0274) presents experimental, contemporary, and classic works, including musicals and dramas.

Music The **Honolulu Symphony** (1441 Kapiolani Blvd., Honolulu, tel. 808/942–2200) performs pops, classics, and summer "starlight" programs.

Nightlife
Cocktail and Dinner Shows The **Monarch Room** (Royal Hawaiian Hotel, 2259 Kalakaua Ave., Waikiki, tel. 808/923–7311) combines traditional and contemporary Hawaiian tunes in an oceanside setting.

Dinner Cruises Based on an ancient Hawaiian design, **Aikane Catamarans** (677 Ala Moana Blvd., Honolulu, tel. 808/522–1533) has cruises that include dinner and dancing. **Windjammer Cruises** (2222 Kalakaua Ave., Honolulu, tel. 808/922–1200) ferries you along Oahu's south shores on the 1,500-passenger *Rella Mae*, done up like a clipper ship.

Luaus The **Royal Luau** (2259 Kalakaua Ave., Waikiki, tel. 808/923–7311) takes place at the venerable Royal Hawaiian and is a notch above many others on the island.

Nightclubs **Rumours** (Ala Moana Hotel, 410 Atkinson St., Honolulu, tel. 808/955–4811) provides video and disco dancing with high-tech lights.

Rock Clubs A two-story, smoky dive called **Anna Bannana's** (2440 S. Beretania St., Waikiki, tel. 808/946–5190) has fresh, loud, and sometimes avant-garde live music.

Excursions from Honolulu and Waikiki

The **North Shore of Oahu** is the flip side of Honolulu. Instead of high rises there are old homes and stores, some converted into businesses catering to tourists, surfers, and beach bums. The area's wide, uncrowded beaches, rural countryside, and slower pace are reminiscent of Hawaii's other islands.

Getting There On the Diamond Head end of Waikiki, go toward the mountains on Kapahulu Avenue and follow the signs to the Lunalilo Freeway (H–1). Follow H–1 northwest to H–2 through Wahiawa, where the road becomes two-way. Follow the signs to Haleiwa, which marks the official beginning of the north shore.

Haleiwa is a sleepy plantation town that has come of age, with contemporary boutiques and galleries. Northeast of Haleiwa the road continues past such famous beaches as **Waimea Bay,** where winter waves can crest at 30 feet. Across the street is **Waimea Falls Park** (tel. 808/638–8511), a lush area for wildlife, walks, and cliff-diving shows.

East of here is the **Polynesian Cultural Center,** 40 acres containing lagoons and seven re-created South Pacific villages, where a spectacular evening luau and revue is offered. *55–370 Kamehameha Hwy., Laie, tel. 808/293–3333 or 808/923–1861. Admission to villages and demonstrations: $40.50 adults, $23.50 children. Closed Sun., major holidays.*

The Big Island of Hawaii

Nearly twice as large as all the other Hawaiian Islands combined, this youngest island of the chain is still growing: Since 1983, the lava spewed intermittently by Kilauea, the world's most active volcano, has added more than 70 acres to the island. A land of superlatives, the Big Island is also the most diverse island. You can hike into a crater, catch a marlin weighing hundreds of pounds, or simply sunbathe on 266 mi of coastline.

Tourist Information

Hawaii Visitors Bureau (180 Kinoole St., Suite 105, Hilo 96720, tel. 808/961–5797; 75–5719 W. Alii Dr., Kailua-Kona 96740, tel. 808/329–7787).

Getting There

Visitors to the west side of the island fly into Kona's **Keahole Airport** (tel. 808/329–2484). Those staying on the east side fly into **Hilo International Airport** (tel. 808/933–4782). Both airports are served by Aloha Airlines and Hawaiian Airlines; United flies into Kona.

Exploring the Big Island

The Big Island is so large and varied that it's best to split it up when exploring. Spend a night in the county seat of Hilo, visit the cowtown of Waimea, head to Volcanoes National Park for some hiking, then wind up on the west coast, home of the best beaches, weather, and nightlife.

Hilo and the Hamakua Coast Hilo is nicknamed the City of Rainbows because of its frequent showers, but rain or shine, this east-coast town is truly beautiful. In the last couple of years its old-timey buildings have been the focus of a refurbishment that has revitalized the downtown area.

The morning catch is auctioned at the **Suisan Fish Market** (85 Lihiwai, tel. 808/935–8051). Stop by at about 7:30 AM to see sellers hawking aku, ahi, and other fish.

Farther west is the **Lyman House,** built in 1839 by missionaries from Boston. The unique collection at the adjacent **Lyman Museum** ranges from carved wooden cuspidors to historical dress. *276 Haili St., tel. 808/935–5021. Admission charged. Closed Sun.*

About 10 mi north of Hilo and 5 mi inland is **Akaka Falls State Park,** where two waterfalls provide dramatic photo opportunities. Hwy. 19 continues through sleepy little towns to **Honokaa,** where the first macadamia trees were planted in Hawaii in 1881. Eight mi west of Honokaa is **Waipio,** where you can make arrangements for a four-wheel-drive tour of **Waipio Valley** (tel. 808/775–7121), where there are 2,000-foot cliffs and 1,200-foot waterfalls. Back on Hwy. 19, the top attraction in **Waimea** (also known by its older name, Kamuela) is the **Parker Ranch Visitor Center and Museum** (tel. 808/885–7655), which delves into the history of the island's ranching with life-size replicas and a slide show. Nearby is **Hale Kea** (tel. 808/885–6094), once the ranch of Laurance Rockefeller and now remodeled with shops, art galleries, and a restaurant.

Hawaii Volcanoes National Park Thirty miles southwest of Hilo is **Hawaii Volcanoes National Park,** a 344-sq-mi park established in 1916 that features an abundance of attractions inspired by Kilauea. Just beyond the park entrance is **Kilauea Visitor Center,** where displays and a movie focus on past eruptions. Next door is the **Volcano Art Center** (tel. 808/967–7511), built in 1877 as a lodge and featuring the work of local artists. Across the street is the **Volcano House** (tel. 808/967–7321), a charming old lodge dating from 1941, with a huge stone fireplace. Windows in the restaurant and bar boast picture-perfect views of Kilauea Caldera and its steaming fire pit, Halemaumau Crater. Drive around the caldera to see the **Thomas A. Jaggar Museum** (tel. 808/967–7643), with seismographs and filmstrips of current and previous eruptions. *Box 52, Volcano 96718, tel. 808/967–7311. Admission charged.*

Kailua-Kona Much of the action in this touristy seaside village on the island's west coast centers on **Kailua Pier,** where the fishing fleet arrives each evening. During the big-game tournaments each summer, daily catches are weighed in here. Nearby, the two-story **Hulihee Palace** (75–5718 Alii Dr., tel. 808/329–1877) served as King Kalakaua's summer residence in the 1880s. Across the street is **Mokuaikaua Church** (tel. 808/329–0655), built in 1836, though the original church was founded in 1820 by Hawaii's first missionaries. Toward the end of the mile-long strip is **Waterfront Row** (75–5770 Alii Dr., tel. 808/329–8502), a trendy assemblage of shops and restaurants.

Kohala Coast If you're staying in Kona, you can tour the Kohala Coast by driving north from Kailua-Kona on Hwy. 19 past luxury resorts and sweeping stretches of old lava flows. Stop at the **Puukohola National Historic Site** Visitor Center, which tells the story of the three stone temples (one of them is submerged just offshore) built here by King Kamehameha's men in 1791. *Box 44340, Kawaihae 96743, tel. 808/882–7218. Admission free.*

What to See and Do with Children

The 65-foot *Atlantis* submarine offers a 50-minute underwater ride from Kailua-Kona's pier. Sign up at the King Kamehameha Kona Beach Resort (75–5660 Palani Rd., tel. 808/329–6626). **Puuhonua o Honaunau** (Hwy. 160, Honaunau, tel. 808/328–2326), about 14 mi south of Kailua-Kona, is a 180-acre national historical park offering demonstrations of Hawaiian crafts, games, and canoe making; the park includes tidal pools and a picnic area.

Shopping

In Hilo, **Prince Kuhio Plaza** (111 E. Puainako, tel. 808/959–3555) offers specialty boutiques and larger stores. The upscale hotels of the **Kohala Coast** provide quality goods at high prices. In Waimea, the **Parker Ranch Shopping Center** (junction of Hwys. 19 and 190, tel. 808/885–7178) houses 35 shops, including the popular **Gallery of Great Things** (tel. 808/885–7706), which sells fine art and handicrafts.

Sports and Outdoor Activities

Camping and Hiking Popular areas are the 13,796-foot **Mauna Kea,** in the northeast, and Hawaii Volcanoes National Park. For more information, contact the **Department of Parks and Recreation** (25 Aupuni St., Hilo 96740, tel. 808/961–8311).

Diving The Kona coast has calm waters for diving. Outfitters include **Big Island Divers** (74–425 Kealakehe Pkwy. #7, Kailua-Kona, tel. 808/329–6068). Many Kohala Coast resorts, such as Waikoloa Resort, hold scuba-diving classes for guests.

Fishing More than 50 charter boats are available for hire, most of them out of Honokohau Harbor, just north of Kailua. For bookings call the **Kona Activities Center** (tel. 808/329–3171 or 800/367–5299).

Golf On the Kohala Coast, the **Mauna Kea Beach Resort** (1 Mauna Kea Dr., tel. 808/882–7222) has an 18-hole course, and the **Francis I'i Brown Golf Course** (Mauna Lani Resort, tel. 808/885–6655) is known for its two 18-hole courses.

Sailing/Snorkeling **Captain Zodiac Raft Expeditions** (Kailua, tel. 808/329–3199) offers a four-hour snorkel cruise off the Kona coast.

Skiing Skiing on 13,796-foot Mauna Kea is for experienced adventure skiers only; the best months are February and March. Currently the ski area has no lodge or lifts. **Ski Guides Hawaii** (64–5323 Puu Nanea, Kamuela, tel. 808/885–4188 or 808/889–6398) furnishes transportation, guides, and equipment.

Beaches

Onekahakaha Beach Park, a protected white-sand beach 3 mi south of Hilo, is a favorite of local families. Close to Kailua-Kona, the most popular beach is **Kahaluu Beach Park,** where the swimming, snorkeling, and fine facilities attract weekend crowds. Currents can pull swimmers away from the beach when the surf is high. On the Kohala Coast, **Anaehoomalu Beach** (Royal Waikoloan Resort) is an expanse perfect for water sports. Equipment rentals and instructors are on call at the north end. The long white **Kauna'oa Beach** (Mauna Kea Beach Resort) is one of the most beautiful on the island. Beware, though, of the high surf that pounds the shore during winter months. Amenities here are hotel-owned. Between the Mauna Kea Beach and Mauna Lani resorts, **Hapuna State Recreation Area** is a ½-mi crescent of sand flanked by rocky points. The surf can be hazardous in winter, but calmer summer water makes it ideal for swimming, snorkeling, and scuba diving.

Dining and Lodging

Choosing a place to eat in West Hawaii is difficult, with so many good restaurants on the scene. The Kohala Coast is somewhat pricey, while Hilo dining has remained fairly inexpensive and family-oriented. The same theme prevails for accommodations. The Kohala Coast costs more, while in Hilo there is only one expensive listing. You can find good deals on charming accommodations by calling **Hawaii's Best Bed and Breakfasts** (Box 563, Kamuela 96743, tel. 808/885–0550). For price ranges, see Charts 1 (B) and 2 (B) in Chapter 1.

Hawaii Volcanoes National Park
Dining

Ka Ohelo Room. What makes this restaurant so special is its mountain-lodge setting at the edge of Kilauea Crater. Try the mahi Florentine, followed by pie made from ohelo berries, unique to the area. *Volcano House, tel. 808/967–7321. Reservations advised. AE, D, DC, MC, V. Inexpensive.*

Hilo
Dining

Sandalwood Room. This is Hilo's most elegant restaurant, with one side open to a stretch of lawn overlooking the coastline. The menu features local items such as Hawaiian spiny-back lobster and a luau plate served in a monkeypod dish. *Hawaii Naniloa Hotel, 93 Banyan Dr., tel. 808/969–3333. Reservations advised. AE, D, DC, MC. Expensive.*

Roussel's. This Cajun-Creole eatery boasts arched doorways, high ceilings, and 16 tables with cane-back chairs. Recommended are shrimp Creole, with a piquant tomato sauce, and trout Alexander, which combines a boneless fish fillet with lobster, shrimp, mushrooms, and sherry. *60 Keawe St., tel. 808/ 935–5111. Reservations advised. AE, DC, MC, V. Closed major holidays. Moderate.*

★ **Pescatore's.** Lace curtains and a miniature waterfall provide a quaint backdrop to traditional Italian dishes such as eggplant parmigiana and seafood *fra diavolo* (shrimp, clams, and fish in marinara sauce). *235 Keawe St., tel. 808/969–9090. DC, MC, V. Inexpensive.*

Lodging

Hawaii Naniloa Hotel. Recent renovations have done wonders for this hotel, whose rooms are decorated in beige and rose. The seven- and 12-story towers are connected by a lobby to shops. *93 Banyan Dr., 96720, tel. 808/969–3333 or 800/367– 5360; fax 808/969–6622. 325 rooms. Facilities: 3 restaurants, bar, health club, pool. AE, D, DC, MC, V. Expensive.*

Arnott's Lodge. This plain, tidy dwelling in a wilderness setting has dorm rooms for up to four people—semiprivate, double, and private rooms, and suites. It's best for active visitors who don't mind sharing a kitchen and a TV room. *98 Apapane Rd., 96720, tel. 808/969–7097; fax 808/961–0649. 9 rooms. DC, MC, V. Inexpensive.*

Kailua-Kona
Dining

Phillip Paolo's. Portions are generous at this split-level Italian restaurant. Try *osso bucco* (veal) or *opakapaka* (pink snapper) with crab, shrimp, mushrooms, and capers served over pasta. *Waterfront Row, 75–5770 Alii Dr., tel. 808/329–4436. Reservations advised. AE, MC, V. Moderate.*

Lodging

King Kamehameha Kona Beach Resort. Though its rooms are not particularly special, this is the only centrally located Kailua-Kona hotel—right next to the pier—with a white-sand beach. There's a shopping mall in the lobby. *75–5660 Palani Rd., 96740, tel. 808/329–2911 or 800/367–2111; fax 808/329– 4602. 460 rooms. Facilities: 2 restaurants, 2 lounges, pool, shops. AE, D, DC, MC, V. Expensive.*

★ **Kona Islander Inn.** Turn-of-the-century plantation-style architecture in a setting of palms and torchlit paths makes this older apartment hotel across the street from Kailua Bay a good value. *75–5776 Kuakini Hwy., 96740, tel. 808/329–3181 or 800/ 922–7866; fax 808/326–9339. 82 units. Facilities: pool. AE, DC, MC, V. Moderate.*

Kohala Coast and Waimea
Dining
★

The Canoe House. This open-air beachfront restaurant surrounded by fish ponds serves Pacific Rim cuisine, such as wok-fried sesame shrimp on crisp noodles and steamed mahimahi with ginger-scallion salsa. *Mauna Lani Bay Hotel, 1 Mauna*

Lani Dr., tel. 808/885–6622. Reservations advised. Jacket advised. AE, D, DC, MC, V. Expensive.

★ **Merriman's.** Peter Merriman earns rave reviews for his imaginative Pacific Rim cuisine using fresh local ingredients, including vegetarian selections. Try opakapaka ravioli in orange-dill sauce, and tangy *lilikoi* (passion fruit) mousse. *Opelo Plaza, corner of Rte. 19 and Opelo Rd., Kamuela, tel. 808/885–6822. Reservations advised. AE, MC, V. Moderate.*

Lodging **Kona Village Resort.** Accommodations are in thatched-roof
★ huts by the sea or around fish ponds. The extra-large rooms have no phones, TVs, or radios but do come with ceiling fans and bright tropical prints. *Box 1299, Kaupulehu-Kona 96745, tel. 808/325–5555 or 800/367–5290; fax 808/325–5124. 125 units. Facilities: 2 dining rooms, 2 bars, 2 pools, shops. AE, D, DC, MC, V. Closed 1 week in Dec. Expensive.*

Mauna Kea Beach Hotel. Since 1965 this low-key, world-class resort has made a name for itself for its gently sloping white-sand beach and peaceful ambience. The rooms, which regrettably are in need of renovation, have tropical furnishings but no TVs. *1 Mauna Kea Dr., Kohala Coast 96743, tel. 808/882–7222 or 800/882–6060; fax 808/882–7757. 310 units. Facilities: 7 restaurants, 6 lounges, pool, shops. AE, D, MC, V. Expensive.*

Parker Ranch Lodge. In the cool upcountry, the lodge has rustic rooms that look out on green pastures. All units have heaters and some have kitchenettes. The lodge has no restaurant, but a number of good Waimea establishments are nearby. *Box 458, Kamuela 96743, tel. 808/885–4100. 20 rooms. AE, MC, V. Moderate.*

Nightlife

The hottest place on the island is **Spats** (1 Waikoloa Rd., Kohala Coast, tel. 808/885–1234) at the Hyatt Regency Waikoloa. In Hilo, **d'Angora's** (101 Apuni St., tel. 808/934–7888) offers dancing to live bands. Luaus and Polynesian revues are especially popular on the island's west side. **Kona Village Resort** (tel. 808/ 325–5555) offers the most authentic island entertainment.

Maui

Maui is known internationally for its perfect beaches, heady nightlife, and sophisticated resorts. The island offers a range of experiences, from the sun, fun, and nightlife of the West Maui "Gold Coast" to the laid-back lifestyle of Hana to the east. Maui also has outstanding restaurants and lavish landscapes, all of which are presided over by a 10,023-foot dormant volcano named Haleakala, where you can see a sunrise like none other on earth.

Tourist Information

Maui Visitors Bureau (250 Alamaha St., N–16, Kahului 96732, tel. 808/871–8691).

Getting There

Maui's major airport, **Kahului Airport** (tel. 808/872–3800 or 808/872–3830), at the center of the island, is served by United, American, Delta, Hawaiian Airlines, and Aloha Airlines. If you're staying in West Maui, you might be better off flying into **Kapalua-West Maui Airport** (tel. 808/669–0228), served by Hawaiian Airlines and Island Air. The landing strip at **Hana Airport** (tel. 808/248–8208) is served by Island Air.

Exploring Maui

West Maui   The road that follows the island's northwest coast passes through the beach towns of **Napili, Kahana,** and **Honokowai,** all packed with condos and a few restaurants. South of these is **Lahaina,** former capital of the islands and a 19th-century whaling town. On the ocean side of **Front Street,** where many old buildings have been renovated, is a **banyan tree** planted in 1873 and the largest of its kind in Hawaii. Docked nearby at Lahaina Harbor is the brig *Carthaginian II* (tel. 808/661–3262), built in Germany in the 1920s and now open as a museum. Also worth a visit is the **Baldwin Home** (696 Front St., tel. 808/661–3262), where missionary doctor Dwight Baldwin dwelled from 1836. The **Seamen's Hospital** (1024 Front St., tel. 808/661–3262) was built in the 1830s as a royal party house for King Kamehameha III and later turned into a hospital.

Central Maui   **Kahalui** is an industrial and commercial town that most tourists pass through on their way to and from the airport. Get on its main street, Kaahumanu Avenue (Hwy. 32), and take a right on Puunene Avenue (Hwy. 350). On the right is the **Alexander & Baldwin Sugar Museum,** which details the rise of sugarcane on the islands. *3957 Hansen Rd., Puunene, tel. 808/ 871–8058. Admission charged. Closed Sun.*

Back on Kaahumanu Avenue, follow signs toward **Wailuku** and take a right on Kahului Beach Road. Continue on the beach road until you reach Kanaloa Avenue, make a left, and soon you'll find **Maui Zoological Botanical Gardens** (tel. 808/243–7337), with a small children's zoo and native Hawaiian gardens. Follow Kaahumanu Avenue to **Wailuku's Historical District,** much of which is on the National Register of Historic Places. A right on Market Street off Main Street takes you to the **Iao Theater** (68 N. Market St., tel. 808/242–6969), dating from 1927. Follow Main Street toward the mountains to reach **Iao Valley State Park,** home of **Iao Needle,** a 1,200-foot rock spire rising from the valley floor.

Haleakala and   The western slopes leading up **Mt. Haleakala,** called Up-
Upcountry   country, encompass the fertile land responsible for much of Hawaii's produce and flowers. Starting in Kahului, drive on Haleakala Highway (Hwy. 37) toward Haleakala. At the fork, veer to the left on Hwy. 377. After about 6 mi, make a left onto Haleakala Crater Road. The switchback ascent begins here. At 7,000 feet is **Haleakala National Park Headquarters,** with a gift shop and rest rooms. *Tel. 808/572–9306. Park admission charged.*

At **Haleakala Visitor Center,** at about 9,800 feet, a ranger gives lectures on Haleakala geology each afternoon. The road ends at **Puu Ulaula Overlook,** where you'll find a glass-enclosed lookout with a 360-degree view from the summit. Sunrise begins between 5:45 and 7, depending on the time of year. On a clear day you can see the islands of Molokai, Lanai, Kahoolawe, and Hawaii.

Maui

Heading down on Hwy. 377, you'll see **Kula Botanical Gardens** (Upper Kula Rd., tel. 808/878–1715), home of bountiful flora. When you join up with Hwy. 37, follow it about 8 mi to **Tedeschi Vineyards and Winery** (Ulupalakua Ranch, Haleakala Hwy.,tel. 808/878–6058) and sample Hawaii's only homegrown wines.

East Maui   The road to Hana is 55 mi of hairpin turns and spectacular scenery. It begins in **Paia** on the north coast and passes **Hookipa Beach,** popular with windsurfers. At mile marker 11, stop at the bridge over **Puohokamoa Stream,** where there are pools, waterfalls, and picnic tables. Another mile takes you to **Kaumahina State Wayside Park,** which also has a picnic area and a lovely overlook to the Keanae Peninsula.

Past **Honomanu Valley,** with its 3,000-foot cliffs and a 1,000-foot waterfall, is the **Keanae Arboretum,** devoted to native plants and trees. Here you can stop and take a fairly rigorous hike. Near mile marker 17 is the **Keanae Overlook,** with views of taro farms and the ocean; it's an excellent spot for photos. As you continue on toward Hana, you'll pass **Waianapanapa State Park** (tel. 808/248–8061), with state-run cabins and picnic areas. Closer to Hana is **Helani Gardens** (tel. 808/248–8274), a 60-acre enclave of tropical plants and flowers, such as ginger and bird of paradise, grown by Hana native Howard Cooper.

The small town of **Hana** is just minutes from Helani Gardens. On the hill above town is **The Cross,** erected in memory of rancher Paul Fagan, who built the Hotel Hana-Maui and stocked the surrounding pastureland with cattle. Once past Hana, the next 10 mi of road are rutted, rocky, and twisting, but a dip in the pools at **Oheo Gulch** makes the drive worth it.

Shopping

You can have fun browsing through the stores of Front Street in Lahaina or the boutiques in the major hotels. Maui also has several major shopping malls. **Kaahumanu Center** (275 Kaahumanu Ave., Kahului, tel. 808/877–3369) has more than 60 shops and restaurants, including **Liberty House** (tel. 808/877–3361) and the Japanese retailer **Shirokiya** (tel. 808/877–5551). Also in Kahului is the **Maui Mall** (corner of Kaahumanu and Puunene Aves., tel. 808/877–5523), with 33 stores. The **Lahaina Cannery Mall** (1221 Honoapiilani Hwy., Lahaina, tel. 808/661–5304), resembling an old pineapple cannery, has some 50 shops, including **Dolphin Galleries** (tel. 808/661–5000), which offers sculpture, paintings, and other Maui artwork.

Sports and Outdoor Activities

Fishing   You can fish year-round here for such catch as tuna, bonefish, Pacific blue marlin, and wahoo. Plenty of fishing boats run out of Lahaina and Maalaea harbors, including *Finest Kind* (Lahaina Harbor, Slip 7, tel. 808/661–0338).

Golf   **Kapalua Golf Club** (300 Kapalua Dr., Lahaina, tel. 808/669–8044) has three 18-hole golf courses. The **Wailea Golf Club** (120 Kaukahi St., Wailea, tel. 808/879–2966) has two courses.

Sailing   Most companies combine their sailing tours with a meal, snorkeling, or whale-watching. Try **Genesis Charters** (Lahaina, tel. 808/667–5667).

Snorkeling and Scuba Diving Lahaina has numerous dive shops—including **Dive Maui** (Lahaina Market Place, tel. 808/667–2080)—which rent equipment and offer diving trips and lessons. Many dive companies offer snorkeling tours as well; the **Ocean Activities Center** (1325 S. Kihei Rd., Kihei, tel. 808/879–4485) offers an enjoyable trip to the nearby island of Molokini.

Tennis The finest facilities are at the **Wailea Tennis Club** (131 Wailea Ike Pl., Kihei, tel. 808/879–1958), often called "Wimbledon West" because of its grass courts.

Windsurfing Hookipa Bay, 10 mi east of Kahului, is the windsurfing capital of the world. Rent a board or get lessons from **Kaanapali Windsurfing School** (104 Wahikuli Rd., Lahaina, tel. 808/667–1964).

Beaches

If you start at the northern end of West Maui and work your way down the coast, you'll find the following beaches: **D.T. Fleming Beach,** 1 mi north of Kapalua, is a sandy cove better for sunbathing than swimming in its strong current. **Napili Beach,** a secluded crescent, is right outside the Napili Kai Beach Club. **Kaanapali Beach** is best for people-watching and plenty of action; cruises, windsurfers, and parasails launch from here. Farther south are **Wailea**'s five crescent beaches, which stretch for nearly 2 mi with little interruption. South of Wailea are **Big Beach,** a 3,000-foot-long, 100-foot-wide strand, and **Little Beach,** popular for nude sunbathing (officially illegal here).

Dining and Lodging

Maui cuisine consists of more than the *poi* (pounded taro root) and pineapple you'll find at a local luau. The island attracts fine chefs who combine unique Hawaiian produce with classic preparations. Some of the best restaurants are in hotels. The island boasts a large number of luxury hotels and condominiums. West Maui is the center of tourism, while central Maui's choices are limited; East Maui is a mixed bag of rates and comfort. For B&B accommodations contact **Bed & Breakfast Maui-Style** (Box 98, Kihei 96784, tel. 808/879–7865 or 800/848–5567). For price ranges, see Charts 1 (B) and 2 (B) in Chapter 1.

East Maui Dining **Haliimaile General Store.** It was a camp store in the 1920s, and now its white, green, and peach tin exterior looks a little out of place in an Upcountry pineapple field. This charmer serves a fine smoked duck with pineapple chutney and dynamite barbecued ribs. *900 Haliimaile Rd., tel. 808/572–2666. Reservations advised. AE, MC, V. Closed Mon. Expensive.*

Casanova. This Upcountry establishment with contemporary decor serves nouvelle Italian food. Try a wood-fired pizza with mozzarella, ham, and broccoli, followed by a delicious version of *tiramisu,* a creamy cake topped with powdered chocolate. *1188 Makawao Ave., Makawao, tel. 808/572–0200. Reservations advised. AE, D, MC, V. Moderate.*

★ **Polli's.** Stop by this Upcountry Mexican cantina for tacos, burritos, enchiladas (vegetarian versions, too), and some of the best margaritas in the state. *1202 Makawao Ave., Makawao, tel. 808/572–7808. AE, MC, V. Inexpensive.*

Lodging ★ **Four Seasons Resort.** Low-key elegance defines this stunning property with refined, open-air public areas and access to one of Maui's best beaches. Nearly all of the rooms have an ocean view and feature elegant marble bathrooms with high ceilings. *3900 Wailea Alanui, Wailea 96753, tel. 808/874–8000 or 800/ 334–6284; fax 808/874–2222. 380 rooms. Facilities: 3 restaurants, pool, health club, shops. AE, D, DC, MC, V. Expensive.*

★ **Hotel Hana-Maui.** Surrounded by lush ranch lands, the hotel's buildings have white plaster walls and trellised verandas. Rooms feature bleached-wood floors, overstuffed furniture in natural fabrics, and local art. *Box 8, Hana 96713, tel. 808/248– 8211 or 800/321–4262; fax 808/248–7202. 97 rooms. Facilities: restaurant, lounge, pool, shops. AE, D, DC, MC, V. Expensive.*

Hana Kai-Maui. This small condominium is the only true beachfront property in Hana. The large, simply furnished units are set on manicured grounds that include a spring-fed swimming pool on one side of the property. *Box 38, Hana 96713, tel. 808/248–8426 or 800/346–2772; fax 808/248–7482. 17 units. AE, MC, V. Moderate.*

Aloha Cottages. Two-bedroom units and one studio are sparsely furnished but clean and adequate. A special touch is the view of papaya, banana, and avocado trees on the neighboring property. *Hana 96713, tel. 808/248–8420. 4 cottages. No credit cards. Inexpensive.*

★ **Heavenly Hana Inn.** A Japanese gate flanked by lions guards this rustic inn, where interiors full of knickknacks verge on eccentric. Each unit has a kitchenette and is decorated with Japanese screens and antiques. *Box 146, Hana 96713, tel. 808/248– 8442. 4 rooms, 2 cottages. No credit cards. Inexpensive.*

West Maui
Dining
★ **Avalon.** This open-air restaurant combines ethnic influences for a Pacific Rim cuisine that features such dishes as giant prawns in a garlic-and-black-bean sauce. The only dessert, caramel Miranda, is made of fruit, caramel sauce, ice cream, and brown sugar. *Mariner's Alley, 844 Front St., Lahaina, tel. 808/667–5559. Reservations advised. AE, DC, MC, V. Expensive.*

★ **Gerard's.** This Victorian-style, indoor-outdoor restaurant is the creation of Gerard Reversade, who serves French dishes such as ravioli topped with medallions of veal. *Plantation Inn, 174 Lahainaluna Rd., Lahaina, tel. 808/661–8939. Reservations required. AE, D, DC, MC, V. Expensive.*

Lahaina Coolers. This surf bistro serves unusual dishes, such as pepper chicken linguine in a sauce of roasted bell peppers, and spinach-and-feta quesadilla. *180 Dickenson St., Lahaina, tel. 808/661–7082. Reservations advised. AE, MC, V. Inexpensive.*

Lodging **Kapalua Bay Hotel.** Isolated from the other hotels of West Maui, Kapalua has a California ambience, with exteriors of white and natural wood. The orchid-filled open lobby has a fine view of the ocean, and the rooms are spacious. *1 Bay Dr., Kapalua 96761, tel. 808/669–5656 or 800/367–8000; fax 808/ 669–4694. 194 rooms, 135 condo units. Facilities: 4 restaurants, lounges, pool, shops. AE, D, DC, MC, V. Expensive.*

Plantation Inn. Here is a place you won't find anywhere else; resembling a Victorian home, the newly constructed inn is centrally located on a quiet country street in the heart of Lahaina. Its European charm is expressed in wood floors, stained glass, ceiling fans, and brass beds. Downstairs is one of Hawaii's best French restaurants, Gerard's. *174 Lahainaluna Rd., Lahaina*

96761, tel. 808/667–9225 or 800/433–6815; fax 808/667–9293. 18 rooms. Facilities: restaurant, pool. AE, MC, V. Moderate.
Pioneer Inn. This plain hostelry retains a flavor of old Lahaina. Downstairs is a boisterous saloon. Rooms upstairs are small and rather dim, with ceiling fans and no air-conditioning—but lots of history. *658 Wharf St., Lahaina 96761, tel. 808/661–3636 or 800/457–5457; fax 808/667–5708. 48 rooms. Facilities: 2 restaurants, lounge, shops. AE, DC, MC, V. Inexpensive.*

Nightlife

The best options are in resort areas. **Moose McGillycuddy's** (844 Front St., Lahaina, tel. 808/667–7758) has dancing to recorded music. New on the scene is **Tsunami** (Grand Hyatt Wailea, tel. 808/875–1234), a high-tech, New York–style club with a dance floor that moves. The best luau on Maui is the small, personal, and authentic **Old Lahaina Luau** (505 Front St., Lahaina, tel. 808/667–1998).

Kauai

Many of the hotels and attractions closed due to the damage wrought by Hurricane Iniki in September 1992 are now re-opening, and Mother Nature has been quite busy doing repair work on the island's lush landscape.

Tourist Information

Hawaii Visitors Bureau (3016 Umi St., Suite 207, Lihue 96766, tel. 808/245–3971). For the latest information on conditions on Kauai, **Kauai Hotlines** (tel. 800/262–1400; fax 800/637–5762) are available between 6 AM and 6 PM Hawaii time.

Getting There

Lihue Airport (tel. 808/246–1400) handles most of Kauai's air traffic; 3 mi east of the county seat of Lihue, it is served by Aloha and Hawaiian. Island Air flies to **Princeville Airport** (tel. 808/826–3040), a tiny strip to the north.

Exploring Kauai

A coastal road runs around the rim of Kauai and dead-ends on either side of the rugged 15-mi coast called Na Pali ("the cliffs"). If you're looking for sunshine, head to the southern resort of Poipu; for greener scenery and a wetter climate, try Hanalei and Princeville to the north.

The Road North From **Wailua Marina** on the east coast, boats depart for **Fern Grotto,** a yawning lava tube with enormous ferns and an 80-foot waterfall. *Smith's Motor Boat Service, 174 Wailua Rd., Kapaa, tel. 808/822–4111. Admission charged.*

North of here on Hwy. 56 is the former plantation town of **Kilauea.** The **Kilauea Lighthouse** (tel. 808/828–1413), built in 1913, is now a wildlife refuge. The **Hanalei Valley Overlook** provides a panorama of more than ½ mi of taro, the staple plant of the Hawaiian diet, plus a 900-acre endangered waterfowl refuge. **Hanalei** is the site of the **Waioli Mission** (Kuhio Hwy., tel. 808/245–3202), founded by Christian missionaries in 1837.

| To the South and West | In the southern town of **Lihue,** visit the **Kauai Museum** (4428 Rice St., tel. 808/245–6931) to learn about the island's history. Nearby **Kilohana** (3–2087 Kaumualii Hwy., tel. 808/245–5608), a historic sugar-plantation house dating from 1935, is now a 35-acre visitor attraction with agricultural exhibits, local arts-and-crafts displays, and more. Farther south, Poipu Road (Hwy. 52) runs through the sunny resort of **Poipu** to **Spouting Horn,** a waterspout that shoots up through an ancient lava tube like Old Faithful. |

Head west to the sleepy town of **Waimea,** which first welcomed British captain James Cook to the Sandwich Islands in 1778. Drive mauka (toward the mountains) on Waimea Canyon Drive, which makes a steep climb past the spectacular panoramas of **Waimea Canyon.** Created by an ancient fault in the Earth's crust, the canyon measures 3,600 feet deep, 2 mi wide, and 10 mi long. At 4,000 feet the road passes through **Kokee State Park** (tel. 808/335–5871), a 4,345-acre wilderness. The road ends 4 mi above the park at the **Kalalau Lookout.** At 4,120 feet above sea level, it offers the best views on Kauai.

What to See and Do with Children

Kamokila (6060 Kuamoo Rd., Kapaa, tel. 808/822–1192) is a restored riverside Hawaiian village where families can learn ancient crafts and games. **Smith's Tropical Paradise** (174 Wailua Rd., Kapaa, tel. 808/822–4654) is 30 acres of jungle, exotic foliage, tropical birds, and lagoons.

Shopping

In Lihue is **Kukui Grove Center** (3–2600 Kaumualii Hwy., tel. 808/245–7784), Kauai's largest mall. **Kauai Lagoons** (Kalapaki Beach, tel. 808/245–5050) in Nawiliwili has designer boutiques, including **Louis Vuitton** (tel. 808/245–7025).

East-coast malls are highlighted by **Coconut Plantation Marketplace** (4–484 Kuhio Hwy., Kapaa, tel. 808/822–3641). **Kauai Village** (4–831 Kuhio Hwy., Kapaa, tel. 808/822–4904) boasts 19th-century plantation-style architecture and 25 shops. To the north, **Princeville Center** (5–4280 Kuhio Hwy., Kapaa, tel. 808/826–3320) has interesting shops, such as **Kauai Kite and Hobby Shop** (tel. 808/826–9144).

Sports and Outdoor Activities

Fishing	For deep-sea fishing, **Sportfishing Kauai** (Koloa, tel. 808/742–7013) has two six-passenger custom Bertram Sportfishers. For freshwater fishing, try **Bass Guides of Kauai** (Lihue, tel. 808/826–2566).
Golf	Best known are the Makai and Prince courses at **Princeville Resort** (Princeville, tel. 808/826–3580). **Kauai Lagoons Resort** has two courses (Kalapaki Beach, Lihue, tel. 808/246–5061).
Hiking	Kokee State Park has 45 mi of hiking trails. The **Department of Land and Natural Resources** (Lihue, tel. 808/241–3444) provides hiking information.
Snorkeling and Scuba Diving	Explore spectacular underwater reefs with **Dive Kauai** (4–976 Kuhio Hwy., Kapaa, tel. 808/822–0452). **Hanalei Sea Tours**

(Hanalei, tel. 800/733–7997) has a four-hour snorkeling cruise off the Na Pali coast.

Tennis **Coco Palms Resort** (Lihue, tel. 808/822–4921) is a standout for its three clay courts.

Beaches

The waters that hug Kauai are clean, clear, and inviting, but be careful where you go in: The south shore sees higher surf in the summer, while north-shore waters are treacherous in winter.

North Shore On the winding section of Hwy. 56 west of Hanalei is **Lumahai Beach,** flanked by high mountains and lava rocks. There are no lifeguards here, so swim only in summer. **Hanalei Beach Park** offers views of the Na Pali coast and shaded picnic tables. Near the end of Hwy. 56, **Haena State Park** is good for swimming when the surf is down in summer. Hwy. 56 dead-ends at **Ke'e Beach,** a fine swimming beach in summer.

South and West Shores **Kalapaki Beach,** a sheltered bay ideal for water sports, fronts the Kauai Lagoons Resort. Small to medium-size waves make **Brennecke's Beach** in Poipu a bodysurfer's heaven, and there are showers, rest rooms, and lifeguards. At the end of Hwy. 50W is **Polihale Beach Park,** a long, wide strand flanked by huge cliffs. Swim here only when the surf is small; there are no lifeguards.

Dining and Lodging

On Kauai you can enjoy almost any style of cuisine. Kauai's accommodations range from swanky resorts to bare-bones cabins. For an insider's look at Kauai, book with **Bed & Breakfast Hawaii** (Box 449, Kapaa 96746, tel. 808/822–7771 or 800/733–1632). For price ranges, see Charts 1 (B) and 2 (B) in Chapter 1. Some of the establishments listed below may have suffered damage from Hurricane Iniki; it is important to call before you plan a visit.

East and North Kauai *Dining* **La Cascata.** Terra-cotta floors and trompe l'oeil paintings give the restaurant the feel of an Italian villa. The Mediterranean-inspired dishes include ahi with tomatoes, olives, capers, and oregano; and roasted guinea-fowl breast with spinach, pine nuts, and raisins. *Princeville Hotel, Princeville, tel. 808/826–9644. Reservations required. Jacket advised. AE, D, DC, MC, V. Expensive.*

★ **A Pacific Cafe.** In this stylishly intimate restaurant with Oriental overtones, Asian cooking combines with homegrown ingredients. Try lamb with plum-tamarind sauce or sizzling squid salad with lime-ginger vinaigrette. *Kauai Village, 4–831 Kuhio Hwy., Kapaa, tel. 808/822–0013. Reservations advised. AE, D, MC, V. No lunch. Expensive.*

★ **Casa di Amici.** Dine on the porch of this "House of Friends" and choose your own combination of pasta with such sauces as pesto or *salsa di noci* (walnut-cream sauce with Romano cheese and marjoram). *2484 Keneke St. at Lighthouse Rd., Kilauea, tel. 808/828–1388. Reservations advised. AE, DC, MC, V. Moderate.*

Bull Shed. This A-frame restaurant is rustic, with exposed wood, ocean views, and family-style tables. Menu highlights include New Zealand rack of lamb and prime rib. *796 Kuhio Ave.,*

Waipouli, tel. 808/822–3791. Reservations advised. AE, MC, V. No lunch. Inexpensive.

Lodging **Princeville Hotel.** Reopened in 1991 after extensive remodel-
★ ing, this cliffside hotel, which has breathtaking views of Hanalei Bay, suffered extensive hurricane damage in 1992. It is scheduled to reopen early in 1994. Bathrooms have gold-plated fixtures and picture windows that cloud up for privacy at the flick of a switch. Box 3069, Princeville 96722, tel. 808/826–9644 or 800/826–4400; fax 808/826–1166. 242 rooms. Facilities: 3 restaurants, 3 lounges, pool, shops. AE, D, DC, MC, V. Expensive.

Kapaa Sands. Furnishings in this intimate condominium are bungalow-style, with rustic wood and ceiling fans. Ask for an oceanfront room with open-air lanai and Pacific views. 380 Papaloa Rd., Kapaa 96746, tel. 808/822–4901 or 800/222–4901. 22 units. Facilities: pool. AE, DC, MC, V. Moderate.

South and West **Tamarind.** The centerpiece of the Stouffer Waiohai Resort is
Kauai decorated in earth tones and chrome finishings. House specials
Dining include lamb marinated in mustard and garlic; duckling and
★ lobster are also excellent choices. 2249 Poipu Rd., Poipu, tel. 808/742–9511. Reservations advised. Jacket required. AE, D, DC, MC, V. No lunch. Expensive.

Brennecke's Beach Broiler. At this veteran restaurant with the names of local fish inscribed on its white walls, the chef specializes in mesquite-broiled foods and homemade desserts. Ho'one Rd., Poipu, tel. 808/742–7588. Reservations advised. MC, V. Moderate.

★ **Green Garden.** In business since 1948, this family-run restaurant has orchids on every table and a no-frills setting. Local fare includes breaded mahimahi fillet and passion-fruit chiffon pie. Hwy. 50, Hanapepe, tel. 808/335–5422. Reservations advised for dinner. AE, DC, MC, V. No dinner Tues. Inexpensive.

Lodging **Hyatt Regency Kauai.** Low-rise architecture, extensive gardens, and open-air courtyards make this the most Hawaiian Hyatt. Rooms have bamboo and wicker furnishings; most have ocean views. 1571 Poipu Rd., Koloa 96756, tel. 808/742–1234; fax 808/742–1577. 600 rooms. Facilities: 3 restaurants, 2 lounges, nightclub, pools, health club, shops. AE, D, DC, MC, V. Expensive.

Westin Kauai. This opulent, modern hotel in a rural setting appeals to those who like glitz. It boasts a $2.5 million art collection and rooms with floor-to-ceiling sliding doors affording ocean or mountain views. Kalapaki Beach, Lihue 96766, tel. 808/245–5050; fax 808/245–5049. 850 rooms. Facilities: 12 restaurants, spa, shops. AE, D, DC, MC, V. Expensive.

Kokee Lodge. Twelve mountaintop cabins are surrounded by pine trees and hiking trails. Furnishings are rustic (prices vary according to quality), but each is cozy with a wood-burning stove. Box 819, Waimea 96796, tel. 808/335–6061. 12 cabins. Facilities: restaurant, shop. DC, MC, V. Inexpensive.

Nightlife

Locals enjoy **Club Jetty** (Nawiliwili Harbor, Nawiliwili, tel. 808/245–4970), a disco by the sea. **Legends Nightclub** (Harbor Village, Nawiliwili, tel. 808/245–5775) delivers Top 40 tunes in a garden setting. Of Kauai's luaus, the local favorite is **Tahiti**

Nui Luau (Kuhio Hwy., Hanalei, tel. 808/826–6277), a family-style party.

Elsewhere in the State

Molokai

Getting There | Hoolehua Airport (tel. 808/567–6140), a tiny strip just west of central Molokai, is served by Hawaiian Airlines, **Island Air** (tel. 800/323–3345), and **Air Molokai** (tel. 808/521–0090).

What to See and Do | With its slow pace and emphasis on Hawaiiana, Molokai drowses in another era. There are no high rises, no traffic jams, and no stoplights on the 10- by 38-mi island. The fanciest hotels are bungalow style, and there's plenty of undeveloped countryside.

Among interesting sights here are the **Meyer Sugar Mill** (tel. 808/567–6436), built in 1878 and reconstructed to teach visitors about sugar's local importance; and **Purdy's All-Natural Macadamia Nut Farm** (tel. 808/567–6601 or 808/567–6495), a family business where you can learn all about the delectable nuts.

Rustic activities are popular on the island. **Damien Tours** (tel. 808/567–6171) will lead you on a fascinating tour of **Kalaupapa National Historic Park** (Box 222, Molokai 96742, tel. 808/567–6102). This pretty town, a leper's colony until 1888, is now a National Historic Landmark. The **Molokai Ranch Wildlife Safari** (tel. 808/552–2555, ext. 7553) is a tour through a 1,000-acre preserve, home to such animals as the ibex and the eland. The **Molokai Wagon Ride** (tel. 808/567–6773 or 808/558–8380) takes you on a scenic amble in a horse-drawn wagon, followed by a beach barbecue.

Down Kaluakoi Road, 2 mi beyond Kaluakoi Resort, is **Papohaku Beach,** a 3-mi strip of white-sand glory wide enough for relaxing in privacy.

For more information, including advice on accommodations, contact **Destination Molokai Association** (Box 960, Kaunakakai 96748, tel. 808/553–3876) or **Visitors Information** on Maui (tel. 808/877–4636).

Lanai

Getting There | Hawaiian Airlines and IslandAir serve this tiny island, whose airport (tel. 808/565–6757) is a 10-minute drive from Lanai City.

What to See and Do | Known as the Pineapple Island since Jim Dole bought it in 1922, Lanai is now being turned into the Private Island by developer David Murdock, who owns nearly all of its 140 sq mi. Lanai City, the only town on the island, has a 10-room hotel; visitors can also try one of Murdock's two new lavish resorts, geared to upscale guests, or opt for a house rental or B&B experience.

Lanai is for those who are happy to spend a lot of time outdoors, because the island has no commercial attractions other than those offered at the two resorts. Instead, you can visit such sights as the **Garden of the Gods,** where rocks and boulders are scattered across a crimson landscape; spend a leisurely day at **Hulopoe Beach,** where the waters are so clear that you can see fish in hues of turquoise and jade; hike or drive to the top of **Lanaihale,** a 3,370-foot perch from which you can see every inhabited Hawaiian island except Kauai and Niihau; or golf at **Experience at Koele Golf Course** (tel. 808/565–7300). **Oshiro U-Drive & Taxi** (tel. 808/565–6952) rents four-wheel-drive Jeeps for exploring an island where many roads are bumpy and unpaved.

For more information, contact **Destination Lanai** (Box 700, Lanai City 96763, tel. 808/565–7600).

Appendix

Special-Interest Travel

By Karen Cure   You can see the United States in many ways, but you'll have most fun seeing it in the company of like-minded travelers, doing what you like to do best. The following pages suggest what's available; contact state tourism departments for other ideas.

Group Trips   Want a vacation-immersion in archeobotany? How about studying the natural history of New York's Finger Lakes, or whooping cranes, or bald eagles? Have you always wanted someone to teach you kayaking? Or yearned to ride-and-roll the white water down the Colorado? Whatever your interest, you'll find a program or an organization sponsoring group trips in the field.

How to Choose   First pick a destination, then gather names of outfitters or resorts in the area you want to visit and contact them. For trips, ask about group size and composition (singles, couples, families, and so on), daily schedules, required gear, and any specifics of the activity. When looking into resorts, consider size, facilities, activities, and style. For courses and workshops, also find out about lodging arrangements, instructors' qualifications, and diversions for nonparticipating traveling companions. In every case, inquire about costs—what's included (meals, equipment), what's extra, how you pay, and how you get a refund if necessary. Check references.

Sports and the Outdoors

Sightseeing isn't always the best way to see the sights. Americans themselves may provide your most memorable travel experience; the nation's deep forests, mighty waters, and wide-open spaces are some of its most distinctive sights. The best way to experience the people and the land is in the great outdoors, pursuing one of the nation's favorite sports.

Group Trips   Knowledgeable leaders make group trips the safest way to develop or add to your wilderness experience. Because you overnight in campgrounds or simple accommodations, costs are often modest. Some trips are sponsored for members by conservation-minded nonprofit groups, such as the **American Forestry Association** (1516 P St. NW, Washington, DC 20005, tel. 202/667–3300 or 800/323–1560), the **Appalachian Mountain Club** (5 Joy St., Boston, MA 02108, tel. 617/523–0636), and the **Sierra Club** (730 Polk St., San Francisco, CA 94109, tel. 415/776–2211). On Sierra Club trips, members volunteer as leaders, participants do camp chores, and costs stay low. **American Youth Hostels** (Box 37613, Washington, DC 20013–7613, tel. 202/783–6161), strong on biking, also offers other trips, all open to travelers of all ages.

Private firms offering outdoors-oriented trips include **American Wilderness Experience** (Box 1486, Boulder, CO 80306, tel. 800/444–0099); adventure-travel pioneer **Mountain Travel Sobek** (6420 Fairmount Ave., El Cerrito, CA 94530–3606, tel. 800/227–2384); and for the Southeast, **Nantahala Outdoor Center** (13077 Hwy. 19W, NC 28713, tel. 704/488–6737).

Bookings and Information	Energetic **Pat Dickerman,** in business since 1949, matches travelers with congenial operators in her comprehensive books, *Adventure Travel North America* and *Farm, Ranch, and Country Vacations* ($19 and $12 respectively, plus postage, from Adventure Guides, Inc., or Farm & Ranch Vacations, Inc., 7550 E. McDonald Dr., Scottsdale, AZ 85250, tel. 800/252–7899). The quarterly *Specialty Travel Index* (305 San Anselmo Ave., Suite 313, San Anselmo, CA 94960; tel. 415/459–4900; $10 annually) has ads for everything from fishing and mountain-bike trips to gambling and shopping trips. Specialty magazines available on newsstands are full of ideas; the following sections suggest other resources.
Bicycling	Biking the nation's byways shows off its bewitching hodge-podge of farms and factories, antique mansions and trailer parks, forests and strip malls. The leisurely pace makes it easy to stop to inspect a cottage garden or get ice cream at a local stand.
Distinctively American Cycling	Clapboard houses, salty seacoasts, and pine-and-hardwood forests beckon cyclists to **New England,** particularly the Maine coast, Vermont's green and bucolic Northeast Kingdom, the forests and farms along New Hampshire's Connecticut River banks, Massachusetts's beach-ringed Martha's Vineyard and moor-covered Nantucket Island, northwest Connecticut (hilly but not killingly so, and scattered with old houses and charming inns), and mansion-laden Newport, Rhode Island.
	The flat to mildly rolling landscape yields a bounty of scenic nooks and crannies in corners of the **mid-Atlantic states,** such as Pennsylvania's Lancaster County, full of peaceful byroads and Amish farms; northern Virginia's manicured, emerald horse country; Maryland's Eastern Shore, with its long Atlantic beaches and marshy backwaters; and the woods-edged towpath of the old C & O Canal near Washington, D.C.
	In the **Rockies,** cyclists are mad for rugged, fat-tired mountain bikes—common sights in the piney-rugged high country near Durango, Colorado, and on the sandstone-clifftop Slickrock Trail near Moab, Utah, where the landscape is the color of sunset.
	In **California,** the pedaling is good on the roads through the vineyards of Napa Valley and on the rock-bound Monterey Peninsula, while Hwy. 1, teetering on the clifftops above the Pacific, is the trip of a lifetime. Traveling by bike is also a rewarding way to experience **Hawaii** in all its floral splendor.
	Some 50,000 mi of **abandoned railroad beds nationwide** are slated to become bike trails; contact American Trails (1400 16th St. NW, Suite 300, Washington, DC 20036, tel. 202/797–5418) for information on the 5,000 mi converted so far.
Mountain Biking	Climbing steep inclines, fording streams, and darting over dirt trails are all part of the exhilaration of mountain biking, now a subculture all its own. Look for designated trail systems in city, county, and state parks; in addition, many ski resorts open their slopes, trails, and chair lifts to mountain bikers during the off-season. *See* Resources, *below,* for organized tours.
With a Group	Bicycle-tour operators package basic-to-sumptuous lodging with escorts, "sag wagons" to carry luggage and weary pedalers, optional rental bikes and helmets, and sometimes meals. They also supply maps pinpointing easy-to-strenuous

routes between overnights—you choose the one that suits you and pedal at your own pace. **Bikecentennial** (Box 8308, Missoula, **MT** 59807, tel. 406/721–1776), the country's largest nonprofit recreational cycling organization, is as good a source as the **AYH** (*see* Sports and the Outdoors, Group Trips, *above*).

Resources **Bikecentennial** (*see above*) has helpful trip-planning information for members ($22 annually). *Bicycling* magazine (tel. 212/697–2040) lists specialist operators such as the active **Backroads Bicycle Touring** (1516 5th St., Berkeley, CA 94710, tel. 510/527–1555 or 800/462–2848); **Carolina Cycle Tours** (13077 Hwy. 19W, Bryson City, NC 28713, tel. 704/488–6737), which specializes in the Southeast; **Country Cycling Tours** (140 W. 83rd St., New York, NY 10024, tel. 212/874–5151), which roams up and down the East Coast and packages trips with transportation to and from Manhattan; **Timberline Bicycle Tours** (7975 E. Harvard St., # J, Denver, CO 80231, tel. 303/759–3804), which concentrates on the West; and **Vermont Bicycle Touring** (Bristol, VT 05443, tel. 802/453–4811), which has won many fans with its trips over country roads and overnight stops at local inns. For organized mountain-biking tours, contact **Backcountry Bicycle Tours** (Box 4029, Bozeman, MT 59772, tel. 406/586–3556) for trips in the national parks of the West; and **Vermont Mountain Bike Tours** (Box 685, Pittsfield, VT 05762, tel. 802/746–8580) for customized inn-to-inn and camping trips.

Canoeing and Kayaking Paddling along the ocean's edge, across freshwater lakes, or down free-flowing streams gives a traveler a view of the wilderness that's hard to come by any other way. Moving almost soundlessly, canoes and kayaks seldom disturb wildlife feeding at the water's edge, and paddlers encounter birds and animals alike, practically eye to eye. The choice of craft is up to you: Canoes are more comfortable and give you more room to carry gear (and easier access to it); kayaks are more stable—important when you're maneuvering between boulders on white water.

Distinctively American Canoeing You don't have to be an expert to tackle some of America's most beautiful paddling waters. Many are within the skills of even beginners—though that can be changed by wind, heavy rainfall, or spring runoff.

In the East, canoeists head for **Maine's wild Allagash River** and adjacent stream- and portage-connected lakes; or the island-flecked lakes in **New York's Adirondack Mountains,** where log lean-tos shelter campers on the mainland and on pristine islands. Lush hardwood forests edge white-water torrents in **West Virginia.** In the South, the still waters of **Florida's Everglades National Park** and **Georgia's Okefenokee National Wildlife Refuge** access water-based "prairies" and mangrove swamps. The water in parts of Okefenokee—stained black by leachings from vegetation—perfectly mirrors the verdant foliage overhead.

In the Midwest, Voyageurs National Park and the Superior National Forest and its Boundary Waters Canoe Area Wilderness showcase the mighty woods of **northern Minnesota,** crossed by rivers and streams and scattered with lakes; in some areas, no motorized vehicles are permitted, and you could explore for months without backtracking. **Missouri's Ozark National Scenic Riverways** and **Arkansas's Buffalo National River**—bluff-edged blends of rapids, fast water, and still pools—are just two of six National Rivers administered by the National Park Service (Box 37127, Washington, DC 20013–7127, tel. 202/208–4747); the service also administers nine National Wild and Scenic Rivers.

Resources The century-old **American Canoe Association** (7432 Alban Station Blvd., Suite B226, Springfield, VA 22150, tel. 703/451–0141) has lists of canoeing clubs, schools, books, and trips. Consult *Canoe* (tel. 206/827–6363) and *Paddler* (tel. 619/630–2293) magazines for other ideas.

River Rafting The spray soaks your clothes and stings your face, the roar drowns out your screams, and every roll and drop leaves your heart somewhere back *there:* Nothing reveals nature's power like roller-coaster white water. By comparison, the quiet stretches are all the more peaceful, the campfires more glowing, the air fresher, the picnic lunches and steak-and-potatoes dinners more savory. It's no wonder river rafting is so popular.

Distinctively American Rafting Rafting the **Colorado** through the Grand Canyon may be the ultimate American river experience, with the hundred-odd devilishly named rapids and the glowing canyon scenery on both sides. However, it gets a run for its money from the river's demanding **Cataract Canyon** section, in Utah's Canyonlands National Park; Idaho's **Salmon** (both the Main Fork, the stream that Lewis and Clark called the River of No Return, and its Middle Fork, with 80 stretches of white water); and Idaho's sometimes-hellish **Selway**. Long, smooth stretches between rapids make Oregon's **Rogue**, a National Wild and Scenic River (*see* Canoeing and Kayaking, *above*), especially good for families.

In the East, the most famous white-water rafting stream may be Georgia's **Chattooga,** where *Deliverance* was filmed. But river rats know West Virginia as the country's most concentrated area of challenging and diverse white water. One case in point is the powerhouse **New River** (actually the oldest river on the Continent), which roars through a gorge so deep it's known as the Grand Canyon of the East.

Raft Trips Commercial outfitters make even the rowdiest white water accessible to the inexperienced. They also supply gear, food, and appropriate permits—all you have to do is show up (and hold on!). Every outfitter has a different style. Some use motorized rafts, some only oar power; some request paddling help, others prohibit it. Find out what's expected before you book.

Resources State tourism offices and **America Outdoors** (Box 1348, Knoxville, TN 37901, tel. 615/524–4814) have names of outfitters. **OARS** (Outdoor Adventure River Specialists; Box 67, Angels Camp, CA 95222, tel. 209/736–4677), established in 1972, and the nonprofit **American River Touring Association** (Star Rte. 73, Groveland, CA 95321, tel. 209/962–7873 or 800/323–2782) have extensive programs, as does **Dvořák Kayak & Rafting Expeditions** (17921 U.S. 285, Nathrop, CO 81236, tel. 719/539–6851 or 800/824–3795), the outfitter that introduced you-paddle trips. *Paddler* magazine (tel. 619/630–2293) covers guided trips and paddling schools.

Climbing and Mountaineering Even the average hiker understands why climbers are drawn to a mountain peak: "Because it's there." Every year scores of hardy walkers visit the nation's highest peaks and leave invigorated by the view and exhilarated by their accomplishment. Rock-climbing skills put just that many more summits within reach on longer mountaineering expeditions. Mastering climbing techniques makes vertical planes seem suddenly more horizontal.

Distinctively American Climbs

Routes on Colorado's 14,255-foot **Longs Peak,** Maine's 5,267-foot **Mt. Katahdin,** New Hampshire's 6,288-foot **Mt. Washington,** and New York's 5,344-foot **Mt. Marcy** are within the abilities of well-conditioned hikers. Many other peaks require rock-climbing skills—or expert guiding. In the West, the most famous of these may be 20,320-foot **Mt. McKinley,** "The Great One," in Alaska's Denali National Park; but the 13,770-foot hunk of granite known as the **Grand Teton,** in Wyoming's eponymous national park, and the granite walls and domes of California's **Yosemite** have comparable charisma. Easterners find challenges in New York's **Adirondacks** and **Shawangunks.**

Schools and Guided Ascents

For extra excitement in national parks, try a day at the **Colorado Mountain School** (Box 2062, Estes Park, CO 80517, tel. 303/586–5758) in Rocky Mountain National Park, the **School of American Mountaineering** (Box 56, Moose, WY 83012, tel. 307/733–2297) in the Tetons, and **Yosemite Mountaineering School** (Yosemite National Park, Yosemite, CA 95389, tel. 209/372–1244 or 209/372–1335 in summer). Offering a good mix of guided climbs and lessons at beginner-to-advanced levels are the **American Alpine Institute** (1515 12th St., Bellingham, WA 98225, tel. 206/671–1505); **Fantasy Ridge Mountain Guides** (Box 1679, Telluride, CO 81435, tel. 303/728–3546); **Sierra Wilderness Seminars** (Box 707, Arcata, CA 95521, tel. 707/822–8066); and, in the East, **Adirondack Alpine Adventures** (Box 179, Keene, NY 12942, tel. 518/576–9881), the southern Appalachians' **Nantahala Outdoor Center** (13077 Hwy. 19W, Bryson City, NC 28713, tel. 704/488–6737), and the White Mountains' **Eastern Mountain Sports** (Main St., Box 514, North Conway, NH 03860, tel. 603/356–5433).

Resources

Contact the **American Alpine Club** (113 E. 90th St., New York, NY 10128, tel. 212/722–1628) for more information on climbing schools.

Fishing

The challenge of filling up a stringer isn't the only reason angling is the country's single most popular sport. There's also the prospect of a fresh-fish dinner. And the quiet hours spent by the water are their own reward.

Distinctively American Angling

Surf-casting on Atlantic-pounded beaches and jetties yields good sport from Cape Cod to south Florida. **Deep-sea fishing** gives you a good dose of the local culture. You can charter anything from a creaky wooden boat to a state-of-the-art yacht, or join the often rough-and-ready crowd aboard party boats, where anglers pay by the head. Ocean City, Maryland, thinks of itself as the world's white-marlin capital, but marlin is prime quarry in Hawaii, too, where a whole fleet of boats leave Kona every morning. There are huge sportfishing fleets in the Florida Panhandle at small towns such as Destin and Fort Walton Beach, and in the Florida Keys, particularly Islamorada, Marathon, and Key West, where you might catch a long, gleaming, needle-nosed tarpon. **Fishing for snook,** a wily, scrappy, bony fish, is great sport—the Florida west coast town of Naples is a hotbed—as is **casting for bonefish** in shallow saltwater flats.

In fresh water, **trout fishing** is a whole angling subculture on such celebrated streams as Vermont's Battenkill, New York's Beaverkill, Arkansas's White River, and many rivers in Michigan and the northern Rockies. In Missouri, **river fishing** is for bass in clear, slow, bluff- and forest-edged streams; in Idaho, it's for steelhead and chinook in waters like the Salmon, Snake, and Clearwater; in Oregon, it's for steelhead, with huge runs in winter.

Other anglers prefer **lake fishing** and take motorboats or canoes in search of their quarry: lake trout and landlocked salmon in deep waters such as Maine's Moosehead and New Hampshire's Winnepesaukee; crappie and largemouth bass on such man-made lakes in the South and Midwest as Kentucky's Lake Barkley and Kentucky Lake, and South Carolina's Lakes Marion and Moultrie. Northern Minnesota woodlands are as famous for yielding creels of scrappy walleye and northern pike, and large and smallmouth bass, as for canoeing.

In a class by itself, **fishing in Alaska** is legendary: in the Southeast Panhandle for salmon (including sockeye, humpback, calico, king, and coho), and in the interior and the south-central part of the state for grayling. Good fishing is often right beside a highway; but fly-in trips to remote lakes and streams are common.

To plan a trip, decide what kind of fishing you want to do, then pick a destination. A letter to appropriate state fish and wildlife departments and a follow-up phone call are the first steps to a good creel. (Or choose a fishing lodge in an area you want to visit, and let the pros find the fish.) Bait-and-tackle shops or sporting-goods stores, thriving wherever there are waters to fish, can tell what's biting where and sell necessary licenses (usually required only by states and necessary only for freshwater fishing).

Schools To hone your skills, spend time at the **Joan and Lee Wulff Fishing Schools** (Lew Beach, NY 12758, tel. 914/439–4060) or **Bud Lilly's Trout Shop** (Box 698, 39 Madison Ave., West Yellowstone, MT 59758, tel. 406/646–7801), both founded by veteran anglers; or at **Orvis Fly Fishing Schools** (Rte. 7A, Manchester, VT 05255, tel. 802/362–3622), sponsored by the noted equipment maker.

Resources Fishing lodges—establishments dedicated to the care and feeding of anglers—advertise in *Field & Stream* (tel. 212/779–5000), *Fishing World* (tel. 516/352–9700), and *Fly Fisherman* (tel. 717/657–9555).

Golf Although most top courses are at private clubs, U.S. resorts offer challenges for itinerant players, not to mention the chance to enjoy some of country's lushest scenery.

Distinctively The Masters Tournament, held annually at the **Augusta National Golf Club** in Augusta, Georgia, has made the Southeast *Golfing* famous among golfers. Although that course is not open to the public, golfers can enjoy southern graciousness along with equally verdant, beautifully tended layouts at another American golf center—**Pinehurst, North Carolina,** home of the PGA Hall of Fame, the Pinehurst Hotel (Box 4000, Pinehurst, NC 28374, tel. 800/487–4653), and no less than seven golf courses. Two old-line southeastern mountain resorts offer an equally sharp picture of golfing America: the **Homestead** (U.S. 220,

Hot Springs, VA 24445, tel. 703/839–5500) and **The Greenbrier Hotel** (White Sulphur Springs, WV 24986, tel. 304/536–1110). On **Hilton Head Island, South Carolina,** the beach scene meets the golf culture, and the hybrid attracts golfers from all over the country.

The golf-loving Japanese bought the world-class **Pebble Beach Golf Links** (17-Mile Dr., Pebble Beach, CA 93953, tel. 408/624–3811), with a view to making a virtually private enclave of this California institution flung along the ragged edge of the rocky Monterey Peninsula; but public outcry has ensured that it will continue to show off the best side of U.S. golfing to itinerant players. For sheer numbers, golf enthusiasts look south to **San Diego,** home of six dozen courses. Courses like the Gold at the posh **Wigwam Resort** (Box 278, 300 Indian School La., Litchfield Park, AZ 85340, tel. 602/935–3811) have brought Arizona the fame once reserved for California. Meanwhile, elegant Hawaii resorts such as **Mauna Kea** (1 Mauna Kea Beach Dr., Kohala Coast, HI 96743, tel. 808/882–7222), **Mauna Lani** (Box 4959, Kohala Coast, HI 96743, tel. 808/885–6655), and **Princeville at Hanalei** (Box 3040, Princeville, HI 96722, tel. 808/826–3040) mix challenges with verdant coastline scenery and attract a golf-loving crowd from all over the country.

Golf Clinics Most resort pros also teach. Then there are golf clinics, where golfers spend whole vacations working on their swing: the **Golf Digest Instruction Schools** (5520 Park Ave., Box 395, Trumbull, CT 06611, tel. 203/373–7130 or 800/243–6121), with programs year-round at resorts nationwide, and the **Craft-Zavichas Golf School** (600 Dittmer Ave., Pueblo, CO 81005, tel. 719/564–4449).

Hiking and Backpacking From sea to shining sea, the United States has forests and trails to wear out a lifetime of hiking boots. If you've graduated from short walks in local parks, you're ready to tackle the wide-open spaces of national parks and forests.

Distinctively American Backpacking The Rockies showcase snowcapped mountains, high-country lakes, and mixed conifer-hardwood forests. Key destinations include national forests such as the huge, wild, and varied **Nez Perce** (Rte. 2, Box 475, Grangeville, ID 83530, tel. 208/983–1950), and trail-crossed national parks such as Colorado's **Rocky Mountain National Park** (Estes Park, CO 80517, tel. 303/586–2371), northern Wyoming's **Grand Teton National Park** (Drawer 170, Moose, WY 83012, tel. 307/733–2880), and **Yellowstone National Park** (Box 168, Yellowstone National Park, WY 82190, tel. 307/344–7381) to the north. For a unique experience in **Glacier National Park** (Belton Chalets, Box 188, West Glacier, MT 59936, tel. 406/888–5511), book a night in one of its spartan pair of World War I–era chalets, accessible only by trail. The Sierras have an entirely different mountain landscape, with granite peaks, lichen-splotched granite boulders, and pine and fir forests; in **Yosemite National Park,** you don't even have to carry camping gear if you stay in one of the five High Sierra Camps ($72.88 per night, by reservation from Yosemite Park & Curry Co., 5410 E. Home Ave., Fresno, CA 93727, tel. 209/252–4848).

In the East, backpackers tramp the Appalachians, ancient mountains with rounded summits, hardwood forests, and many a killer grade. In the Appalachians' bare, windswept **White Mountains' Presidential Range,** the Appalachian Mountain

Club runs no-frills hikers' huts ($50 nightly by reservation through the AMC, Box 298, Gorham, NH 03581, tel. 603/466–2727). The **Great Smoky Mountains National Park** (Gatlinburg, TN 37738, tel. 615/436–1200), which preserves another range of the Appalachians and is crossed by some 800 mi of trails, shows off a gentler side of these old mountains, splendid in spring when the dogwood is in bloom and in fall when the foliage is at its peak.

Backpacking is less common in the Midwest, except in Arkansas reserves such as the **Ouachita National Forest** (Box 1270, Hot Springs, AR 71902, tel. 501/321–5202) and the **Ozark National Forest** (Box 1008, Russellville, AR 72801, tel. 501/968–2354). For hikers in **northern Michigan and Minnesota,** the draw is often the superior fishing in waters that are accessible only on foot. **Isle Royale National Park** (87 N. Ripley St., Houghton, MI 49931, tel. 906/482–0984) and **Superior National Forest** (Box 338, Duluth, MN 55801, tel. 218/720–5324) are popular.

Long Trails   Veteran hikers aspire to walk the length of the 2,147-mi, Maine-to-Georgia **Appalachian Trail** (Appalachian Trail Conference, Box 807, Harpers Ferry, WV 25425, tel. 304/535–6331); Vermont's 265-mi **Long Trail** (Green Mountain Club, RR1, Box 650, Waterbury Center, VT 05677, tel. 802/244–7037); the 2,700-mi **Continental Divide Trail** (Box 30002, Bethesda, MD 20824, no phone), and the 2,638-mi **Pacific Crest Trail** (Box 2040, Lynnwood, WA 98036, tel. 206/771–7208).

Offbeat   If you don't have the experience to tackle a long backpacking
Guided   trip on your own, go with a group. In the West you have the op-
Trips   tion of llama treks; **Shasta Llamas, Ltd.** (Box 1137, Mt. Shasta, CA 96067, tel. 916/926–3959), the first in the nation to use these sturdy, gentle animals to carry gear, now has many imitators. In the East, inn-to-inn trips put country comfort at trail's end—and innkeepers transport your gear between stops. Contact **Country Inns Along the Trail** (RD3, Box 3115, Brandon, VT 05733, tel. 802/247–3300) or **Knapsack Tours** (5961 Zinn Dr., Oakland, CA 94611, tel. 510/339–0160). **Vermont Walking Tours** (Box 31, Craftsbury Common, VT 05827, tel. 802/586–7767) specializes in backroads walks in the Green Mountain State's unspoiled Northeast Kingdom.

Resources   *Fodor's Sports: Hiking* ($12) covers other trips and trails. Magazines such as *Outside* (tel. 312/951–0990) and *Walking* (tel. 617/266–3322) list many group trips.

On Horseback: Seeing the country from the back of a horse has more than a few
Pack Trips and   advantages—not the least of them that you don't have to carry
Dude Ranch   your gear and can cover more ground than on foot yet still pene-
Vacations   trate deep into the wilderness.

Pack Trips   The horse fancier's version of guided backpacking trips, pack trips mix days of traveling between base camps and layover days filled with hiking, fishing, loafing, and eating. Western hospitality prevails, and experience is seldom required. Some outfitters schedule trips in advance, while others do custom trips; daily cost is $85–$175. When choosing, ask about the ratio of traveling to layover days, daily distances covered, and the extent of horse care you're expected to provide.

If this appeals to you, look into the American Forestry Association's **Trail Riders of the Wilderness** program (*see* Group Trips, *above*) or contact local specialists; for names, consult state tourism offices or Pat Dickerman's *Adventure Travel* (*see* Bookings and Information, *above*).

Inn-to-Inn Rides Eastern horse-lovers relish the inn-to-inn rides of **Kedron Valley Stables** (Box 368, South Woodstock, VT 05071, tel. 802/457–2734) and **Vermont Icelandic Horse Farm** (RR 376-1, Waitsfield, VT 05673, tel. 802/496–7141).

Dude Ranches Some are spiffy, upscale resorts, such as **Rancho de los Caballeros** (Box 1148, Wickenburg, AZ 85358, tel. 602/684–5484), where riding is combined with top-notch tennis and golf. Others, such as **Lone Mountain** (Box 69, Big Sky, MT 59716, tel. 406/995–4644), also offer rafting trips, fishing excursions, and other outdoor activities. At working ranches like **C Bar M** (Box AE, Clyde Park, MT 59018, tel. 406/686–4687), pitching in is part of the fun. All offer a healthy dose of horse-related activities, such as pack trips, breakfast cookout rides, and horseback picnics. Rates range from $500 to more than twice that weekly.

Pat Dickerman's *Farm, Ranch & Country Vacations* (*see* Bookings and Information, *above*) is a good source; for other listings, contact the **Colorado Dude and Guest Ranch Association** (Box 300, Tabernash, CO 80478, tel. 303/887–3128), the **Dude Ranchers Association** (Box 471, LaPorte, CO 80535, tel. 303/223–8440), and **Old West Dude Ranch Vacations** (c/o American Wilderness Experiences, Box 1486, Boulder, CO 80306, tel. 800/444–3833), as well as state tourism offices.

Nature Education and Wildlife Watching Spotting moose and seals and focusing your binoculars on trumpeter swans are among the pleasures of outdoor activities. Specialized programs and tours help you understand what you see.

Nature Camps Naturalists on hikes, in classrooms, and around evening campfires offer insights into nature and its interdependencies at several summer programs. The half-century-old **Audubon Ecology Camps** (613 Riversville Rd., Greenwich, CT 06831, tel. 203/869–2017) attract people of all ages to one- and two-week summer sessions held in Wyoming's Wind River Range, on a 300-acre Maine island, and at a Greenwich, Connecticut, nature sanctuary. Accommodations are simple but comfortable. These are almost as well known among outdoors lovers as the **Sierra Club Base Camps** (730 Polk St., San Francisco, CA 94109, tel. 415/776–2211), wilderness camps in the Sierras, the Rockies, the Smokies, and other wild places where club members spend a week or two among similarly conservation-minded vacationers, day-hiking into the surrounding countryside, helping with camp tasks under staff supervision, and paying relatively modest fees. Also look into **National Wildlife Federation Conservation Summits** (1400 16th St. NW, Washington, DC 20036, tel. 703/790–4363), which mix nature, outdoor skills, and folk culture; the **University of the Wilderness** (Box 1687, Evergreen, CO 80439, tel. 303/674–9724), which sponsors trips and classes on environmental topics at a Laramie, Wyoming, campus and in the mountains and deserts of the West and Southwest; and the **Chewonki Foundation** (RR2, Box 1200, Wicasset, ME 04578, tel. 207/882–7323), an environmentally oriented group with the twin objectives of nature education and personal growth that numbers naturalist Roger Tory Peters among its alumni.

In the National Parks Participants learn more about the environment through lectures, field courses, and photography and writing workshops at **Canyonlands Field Institute** (Box 68, Moab, UT 84532, tel.

801/259–7750) in Canyonlands National Park; the **Glacier Institute** (Box 7457, Kalispell, MT 59904, tel. 406/756–3911); the **Olympic Park Institute** (Port Angeles, WA 98362, tel. 206/928–3720); **Point Reyes Field Seminars** (Bear Valley Rd., Point Reyes Station, CA 94956, tel. 415/663–1200), at the Point Reyes National Seashore; and the **Yellowstone Institute** (Box 117, Yellowstone National Park, WY 82190, tel. 307/344–7923).

Naturalist-Led Tours and Cruises
Guided by university professors, botanists, or zoologists, wildlife tours reveal dimensions of the American landscape that most vacationers never even suspect. Hiking and camping may be involved, but often accommodations are comfortable or even luxurious and travel is by small cruise boat or van. Whale-watching is often a feature. **Biological Journeys** (1696 Ocean Dr., McKinleyville, CA 95521, tel. 707/839–0178) and **Nature Expeditions International** (474 Willamette Ave., Box 11496, Eugene, OR 97440, tel. 503/484–6529) are typical.

Wilderness Skills Programs
Here you might learn winter camping, sea kayaking, rock-climbing, minimum-impact camping, or river rafting; but it's the personal growth that comes from mastering something new that attracts participants to the rigorous mental and physical challenges of **Outward Bound** (384 Field Point Rd., Greenwich, CT 06830, tel. 203/661–0797 or 800/243–8520), the granddaddy of such programs, or the **National Outdoor Leadership School** (288 Main St., Lander, WY 82520, tel. 307/332–6973), originally founded to train trip leaders.

Sailing
The mighty U.S. coastline ranks among the nation's most stirring sights, and while roads provide access to much of it, seeing it from the water gives an undeniably better view.

Distinctively American Sailing
Nothing says United States quite like **Maine's rocky coast,** known to sailors all over the world for its scenery, good moorings, and abundant facilities. But there's comparable variety among the islands, coves, and shoreside towns of **Chesapeake Bay** and **Long Island Sound.** The waters off **Newport, Rhode Island,** home of the Museum of Yachting, are light-years away from landlubber gridlock; the crowd is well-heeled and tony. In the **Florida Keys,** the winds are good, the waters teeming with marine life, and the shoreside life casual and laid-back. In the Midwest, sailors relish the challenging **Great Lakes,** inland seas. **California** is sail-crazed; Sausalito, near San Francisco Bay, and Marina del Rey and Newport Beach, in the south, are boating centers. In northwest Washington State, the **San Juan Islands** offer their own barefoot life amid coves and beaches teeming with birds and animals. For the adventurous side of the sport, consider **Alaska**—extraordinary with its fjords, shoreline peaks and waterfalls, good fishing, and abundant wildlife.

Charters
You can book craft either crewed (staffed to handle cooking and navigation) or bareboat (for experienced sailors only). Contact state tourism offices for lists of charter operators.

Schools
The pleasures of the sea mix with the satisfaction of acquiring a new skill at the nation's two principal sailing programs: the **Annapolis Sailing School** (Box 3334, Annapolis, MD 21403, tel. 410/267–7205 or 800/638–9192), which has a branch in the U.S. Virgin Islands, and the **Offshore Sailing School** (16731 McGregor Blvd., Suite 110, Fort Myers, FL 33908, tel. 813/454–1700 or 800/221–4326), founded by former Olympian Steve Colgate and now offering programs on Florida's Captiva Is-

land, in Newport, Rhode Island, and in Port Washington, New York.

Resources   Consult *Fodor's Sports: Sailing* ($12) for more on great sailing destinations. Ads and information on charter operators can be found in *Sail* (tel. 617/964–3030), *Cruising World* (tel. 401/847–1588), and *Yachting* (tel. 401/849–4644).

Windjammer   The beating of sails in the wind, good food, the smell of the sea,
Cruises   and the excitement of calling at scenic ports create unbeatable camaraderie on cruises aboard the nation's fleet of tall ships—restorations or reconstructions of 19th-century craft that accommodate under 30 passengers. Per-person fares of $75–$100 a day, much lower than on larger cruise ships, are a plus, and most people don't mind the spartan cabins and cold showers (or absence thereof), since it's easy to clean up at local marinas.

In the East, Rockland, Camden, and Rockport, Maine, are base for a dozen ships, mostly members of the **Maine Windjammer Association** (Box 317, Rockport, ME 04856, tel. 800/624–6380). Also contact Maine's state tourism office. In the Midwest, look into the **Traverse Tall Ship Company** (13390 S.W. Bay Shore Dr., Traverse City, MI 49684, tel. 616/941–2000).

Skiing   Ski areas can be found even in such unlikely states as Indiana, but the best skiing in the country—and some of the best in the world—is in the Rockies.

True, the typical ski area in the Alps has a greater vertical drop (as skiers call the altitude difference between lift base and the highest lift-served point). But no other ski areas boast comparable snow quality. Not only is snowfall (usually) abundant, but it is also dry and feather-light, and snow quality is consistent from top to bottom—a fact that dazzles skiers from Europe, where this is seldom the case. To enjoy it all, you don't have to be a hot-dog mogul skier or one of the manic daredevils dubbed "extreme skiers," who like to drop onto mountaintops from helicopters. U.S. mountains have slopes you can ski no matter what your ability.

Distinctively   Every resort has its own style and ambience. In the Rockies
American   you'll find an affluent crowd in **Sun Valley,** Idaho; a certain for-
Skiing   mer Colorado mining town known as **Aspen;** faux-Alpine **Vail** not far away; and perhaps **Deer Valley,** Utah, a relative newcomer that's relentlessly tasteful right down to the marble in the base lodge rest rooms. For mellow western charm in addition to abundant facilities, it's hard to beat **Breckenridge, Copper Mountain, Keystone,** and **Steamboat,** Colorado, or even **Park City,** Utah; or friendly, low-key spots like **Big Mountain,** near Whitefish, Montana, practically unknown outside the West. The same can't be said of New Mexico's challenging **Taos;** Wyoming's one-of-a-kind **Jackson Hole;** Utah's cozy, rustic **Alta,** the sine qua non among powder skiers, and its mod cousin, **Snowbird.** But even then, by comparison to the big Colorado resorts, their fame is limited.

Elsewhere in the West, California's Sierras get massive amounts of snow, and skiers come by the thousands to the resorts around crystal-clear Lake Tahoe, including **Squaw, Heavenly, Northstar,** and **Kirkwood.**

In the East, narrow trails and icy conditions magnify the challenges, although slope grooming and snowmaking ease the sting at Vermont's **Stowe** and its Vermont cousins closer to the big cities: huge **Killington** and **Mt. Snow,** genteel **Stratton** and **Sugarbush.** New Hampshire resorts such as **Waterville Valley** are even more relaxed.

To choose, consider area personality, terrain, and convenience. Are there slopeside accommodations or do you need a car? Can you find the lodgings you want (motel, inn, B&B, dorm, resort) at a price you can afford? Are there programs for kids? Families appreciate areas with centralized lift layouts, which make it easy to rendezvous for lunch or at day's end.

Ski Schools and Packages Most ski areas offer instruction and packages. Some offer deals on multiday lift tickets; others add lessons, lodging, meals, or other perks. The best deals are midweek, particularly in areas with heavy weekend traffic.

Resources *Ski* (tel. 212/779–5000), *Skiing* (tel. 212/779–5000), *Snow Country* (tel. 203/373–7000), and *Powder* (tel. 714/496–5922) magazines cover the field.

Ski Touring Heavy snows that otherwise make the nation's meadows and forests inaccessible are no problem for those who can cross-country ski.

Distinctively American Ski Touring You can cross-country ski almost anywhere there's snow. National and state park and forest trails are sometimes suitable for cross-country skiing, although rental equipment is not always available. At ski areas, valleys at the base and high ski-touring ridges and plateaus often offer excellent sport.

For a once-in-a-lifetime experience there's nothing like **Yellowstone National Park.** In winter, waterfalls freeze into bizarre sculptures; steam billowing from the thermal features turns trees into hoary ghosts; and icicles glitter everywhere. Lodging, equipment, and instruction are available.

Elsewhere in the West there's abundant ski touring at several areas in and around Wyoming's **Grand Teton National Park** and California's **Yosemite National Park.** Idaho's **Sun Valley** has hundreds of skiable acres, and you can even helicopter up to the high country. Communities of cross-country fanatics flourish in Colorado at **Steamboat Springs** and **Vail,** and the trail system in **Aspen** is one of the nation's most extensive. Minnesota's **Superior National Forest** enjoys abundant snowfall and hundreds of miles of trails.

In the East, prime areas include Massachusetts's **Berkshire Mountains,** full of parks, forests, and inns; New Hampshire's **Mt. Washington Valley;** and Vermont's **Stowe,** where dozens of miles of trails link restaurants, inns, and shops.

Group Trips Rock-climbing schools (*see* Climbing and Mountaineering, *above*) often have cross-country skiing programs. For inn-to-inn tours, contact **Country Inns Along the Trail** (RD3, Box 3115, Brandon, VT 05733, tel. 802/247–3300). A bit more rugged, hut-to-hut tours of Colorado's spectacular Tenth Mountain Trail are offered by **Paragon Guides** (Box 130, Vail, CO 81658, tel. 303/926–5922).

Resources The **USIA Cross-Country Ski Areas Association** (259 Bolton Rd., Winchester, NH 03470, tel. 603/239–4341) publishes a book detailing more than 500 cross-country areas and can send a list of those sponsoring overnight cross-country trips. Also read *Cross Country Skier* magazine (tel. 612/377–0312).

Tennis You can easily lob and volley away several lifetimes of vacations on U.S. courts. If you have nonplaying companions, consider a full-scale resort with a heavy tennis program; otherwise consider tennis camps or clinics, where tennis is the only activity. Rather than trying to remake your game, most build on what you have to send you home a better player.

Camps and Clinics Staged at resorts nationwide year-round and at private schools in summer, these provide the most intense tennis experience, with up to five hours of play every day. Established in 1968, **Tennis Camps, Ltd.** (444 E. 82nd St., New York, NY 10028, tel. 212/879–0225 or 800/223–2442) is a major player. **Nick Bollettieri Tennis Academy** (5500 34th St. W, Bradenton, FL 34210, tel. 813/755–1000 or 800/872–6425) and **Harry Hopman/ Saddlebrook International Tennis** (5700 Saddlebrook Way, Wesley Chapel, FL 33543, tel. 813/973–1111 or 800/729–8383) are both famed for turning prodigies into pros. For off-court luxury the last word is **John Gardiner's**—both the exclusive California ranch (Box 228, Carmel Valley, CA 93924, tel. 408/659–2207) and its even posher desert cousin (5700 E. McDonald Dr., Scottsdale, AZ 85253, tel. 602/948–2100). Former top players mastermind the friendly **John Newcombe's Tennis Ranch** (Box 310–469, New Braunfels, TX 78131, tel. 512/625–9105 or 800/ 444–6204), the **Van Der Meer Tennis Center Camps** (Box 5902, Hilton Head Island, SC 29938, tel. 800/845–6138), and the high-tech **Vic Braden Tennis College** (23335 Avenida la Caza, Coto de Caza, CA 92679, tel. 714/581–2990 or 800/422–6878).

Resorts Planned resort developments almost always have extensive facilities. At **Hilton Head Island, South Carolina,** two resorts alone offer more than five dozen courts—Sea Pines Plantation (Box 7000, Hilton Head Island, SC 29938, tel. 800/845–6131) and Palmetto Dunes (Box 5606, Hilton Head Island, SC 29938, tel. 803/785–7300 or 800/845–6130). Ski resorts usually have extensive tennis programs—among them Bolton Valley, Killington, Stratton, and Sugarbush. So do large resort hotels. A special case is the elegant Gulf Coast **Colony Beach & Tennis Resort** (1620 Gulf of Mexico Dr., Longboat Key, FL 34228, tel. 813/383–6464 or 800/237–9443), devoted exclusively to tennis.

To choose, ask the pro shop about court fees, reservations procedures and availability, game-matching services, night play, guest tourneys, court-time limits, instruction, and the resort's court-to-room ratio (one to 10 is fine; half that if there are many other activities).

Resources See *Tennis* magazine (tel. 212/789–3000) for listings of tennis resorts, camps, and clinics.

Spiritual and Physical Fitness Vacations

Providing meaningful recreation for both mind and body is the objective of hundreds of establishments across the United States. Far from being spas in the old, European sense—grand hotels that cosset those who come to sip the waters—American spas reflect current attitudes on diet and health: *Fodor's Healthy Escapes* ($15) lists 240 fitness-oriented camps, resorts, and programs costing $30–$250 a day, some all-inclusive packages and some à la carte.

Holistic Centers Exemplifying what's available are destinations such as the verdant Catskills' **New Age Health Spa** (Rte. 55, Neversink, NY

12765, tel. 914/985–7601 or 800/682–4348), which helps guests balance body, soul, and mind via programs ranging from astrological consultations and aerobics to Zen meditation. Flotation tanks and massages supplement nutrition and counseling at such old-timers as the **Omega Institute** (260 Lake Dr., Rhinebeck, NY 12572, tel. 914/266–4301 or 800/862–8890).

Spas for Luxury and Pampering To those who say "No pain, no gain," others reply, "No frills, no thrills," and seek out deluxe establishments for regimens of body wraps, saunas, Swiss showers, massages, manicures, and maybe a yoga class or two. On the cutting edge is **Canyon Ranch** (Belle Fontaine, Kemble St., Lenox, MA 01240, tel. 413/637–4100 or 800/726–9900; 8600 E. Rock Cliff Rd., Tucson, AZ 85715, tel. 602/749–9000 or 800/726–9900), where up-to-the-minute treatments are combined with such outdoor activities as hiking, biking, and tennis, as well as sophisticated spa cuisine. Two for-women-only establishments set the standards: **Maine Chance,** Elizabeth Arden's rose garden of a retreat (5830 E. Jean Ave., Phoenix, AZ 85018, tel. 602/947–6365) and **The Greenhouse** (107th St., Box 1144, Arlington, TX 76004, tel. 817/640–4000), a study in elegant Texan style. More typically, luxury spas take the more active approach of the serene **Golden Door** (Deer Springs Rd., Box 463077, Escondido, CA 92046, tel. 619/744–5777), where individually planned programs include 6 AM hikes and exercise classes. **La Costa Hotel & Spa** (Costa del Mar Rd., Carlsbad, CA 92009, tel. 619/438–9111 or 800/426–5483) is the megaresort of the breed. The **Doral Saturnia International Spa Resort** (8755 N.W. 36th St., Miami, FL 33178, tel. 305/593–6030 or 800/331–7768), a vision of Tuscany with its red-tile roof, fuses a typically American program involving exercise and stress-management training with European treatments, such as warm mud packs for muscular problems.

Weight Management and Preventive Medicine Centers Another group of American spas involves extensive medical supervision. Typifying these are the well-rounded **Duke University Diet and Fitness Center** (804 W. Trinity Ave., Durham, NC 27701, tel. 919/684–6331); the **Aerobics Center** (12230 Preston Rd., Dallas, TX 75230, tel. 214/386–4777 or 800/444–5192), inspired by aerobics pioneer Dr. Kenneth H. Cooper; and the **Pritikin Longevity Centers** (1910 Ocean Front Walk, Santa Monica, CA 90405, tel. 310/450–5433 or 800/421–9911; 5875 Collins Ave., Miami Beach, FL 33140, tel. 305/866–2237 or 800/327–4914), which focus on the late Nathan Pritikin's belief that diet can reverse atherosclerosis.

Volunteer Vacations Although fees for the nation's hundreds of vacation volunteer programs may be partly tax-deductible, their allure has less to do with money than with the satisfaction that comes from giving something back to society, the excitement of an entirely new activity, the intensity of the group experience. Will you enjoy it? Yes, if you're flexible and independent, can take the initiative and cope with the unexpected, have a sense of humor, and like to be a team player.

When choosing a program, be sure to ask about insurance, the number of participants and staff, and the standards by which project and leader were chosen.

Field Research How about tagging dolphins, mapping mammoth bones, or collecting subtropical plants? Scientists in need of enthusiastic, inexpensive labor for projects like these are happy to enlist help from vacationers, who pay a stipend to cover their own expenses and defray expedition costs. Matching up scientists and vacationers are such organizations as **Earthwatch** (680 Mt. Auburn St., Watertown, MA 02272, tel. 617/926–8200), the oldest in the field; the **Foundation for Field Research** (787 S. Grade Rd., Box 2010, Alpine, CA 91903, tel. 619/445–9264); **Smithsonian Research Expeditions Program** (490 L'Enfant Plaza SW, Room 4210, Washington, DC 20560, tel. 202/287–3210); and the **University Research Expeditions Program** (UREP, c/o University of California, Berkeley, CA 94720, tel. 510/642–6586), with University of California scientists.

Archaeological Research
It's hot, dirty, and strenuous—but you don't have to be an archaeologist to catch the excitement. Earthwatch, FFR, and UREP often list digs among their fieldwork opportunities. For other ideas, consult the lists in the Archaeological Institute of America's *Fieldwork Opportunities Bulletin* ($13.50 from the Kendall Hunt Publishing Co., Order Dept., 2460 Kerper Blvd., Dubuque, IA 52001, tel. 800/338–5578).

Trail Building and Maintenance
Helping state and national parks and forests maintain old trails, build new ones, and clean up and replant campgrounds is the mission of several private groups that welcome volunteers—among them the active **Sierra Club** (*see* Sports and the Outdoors, Group Trips, *above*) and the **Appalachian Mountain Club** (Trails Conservation Corps, Box 298, Gorham, NH 03581, tel. 603/466–2721). Many state parks or conservation departments use volunteers, as do the National Park Service, U.S. Fish and Wildlife Service, and U.S. Forest Service.

Social Service
Building community centers, repairing churches, setting up youth programs, and serving in group homes are just a few activities of volunteer work camps. Contact clearinghouses such as the **Volunteers for Peace International Workcamps** (43 Tiffany Rd., Belmont, VT 05730, tel. 802/259–2759) and **Council on International Educational Exchange** (205 E. 42nd St., New York, NY 10017, tel. 212/661–1414).

Resources
Volunteer—the National Center (736 Jackson Pl. NW, Washington, DC 20503, tel. 202/408–5162) and **Volunteers for Peace** (*see* Social Service, *above*) have listings of other volunteer opportunities.

Education and Culture

All travel stretches the observant voyager's mind. A number of programs—university-sponsored tours and continuing-education courses, as well as workshops in the arts—institutionalize that process.

Academic Tours and Programs
Once upon a time, **Chautauqua** (Box 1098, Chautauqua, NY 14722, tel. 716/357–6200) was unique among travel destinations in offering language, history, crafts, hobbies, music, and other arts programs. Established in 1874, it now crams over 170 courses into the nine-week July–August program on its lakeside campus.

Vacations on College Campuses
At these you can expand your intellectual horizons in the company of university professors and other inquisitive spirits, in the spirit of Chautauqua, at summer colleges sponsored by continuing-education divisions at major colleges and universities. Typically, these programs require no tests, give no grades, admit nonalumni as well as alumni, keep costs low with simple

dormitory lodging and cafeteria meals, and explore such themes as Victorian England or capitalism in China. They also fill up fast.

Summer schools for adults are currently offered in the East at **Cornell** (626 Thurston Ave., Ithaca, NY 14850, tel. 607/255–6260); **Dartmouth** (308 Blunt Alumni Center, Hanover, NH 03755, tel. 603/646–2454); **Johns Hopkins** (3211 N. Charles St., Baltimore, MD 21218, tel. 410/516–0363), which has programs in Snowmass, Colorado, as well as on campus; and **Penn State** (409 Keller Conference Center, University Park, PA 16802, tel. 814/863–1743). Comparable programs have recently been mounted in the South at the **University of North Carolina at Chapel Hill** (Vacation College Humanities Program, 209 Abernethy Hall, Chapel Hill, NC 27599, tel. 919/962–1544) and at **Washington and Lee University** (Office of Special Programs, Lexington, VA 24450, tel. 703/463–8723); and in the Midwest at **Indiana University** (Mini University, Indiana Memorial Union, Suite 400, Bloomington, IN 47405, tel. 812/855–4670) and the **College of Wooster** (Alumni Relations, Wooster, OH 44691, tel. 216/263–2263).

Programs come and go, however, so it's best to pick a university you'd like to attend, then call its alumni office or its continuing education or adult-education department to inquire about what's being offered.

Academic and Other Cultural Tours Major U.S. museums sponsor dozens of study tours every year, most escorted by museum personnel, university professors, and other experts. Another option is the programs of independent operators; for extensive listings, consult *The Guide to Academic Travel* ($19.95 postpaid from Shaw Guides Publishers, 625 Biltmore Way, Coral Gables, FL 33134, tel. 305/446–8888).

History Tours American architecture, social history, and culture are emphasized on tours led by the **National Trust for Historic Preservation** (1785 Massachusetts Ave., Washington, DC 20036, tel. 202/683–4000). Four- to seven-day trips have explored Virginia's grand houses and plantations, the heritage of the Maine coast, and Rte. 66.

Cooking Schools Those who love to cook, eat well, and enjoy fine wines have few travel options better than to sign up for an intensive multiday cooking course at a hotel or cooking school. When choosing, be sure to find out about the demonstration-to-participation ratio—an important consideration if you're interested in donning an apron and learning to debone a chicken.

Intensive Courses at Cooking Schools Two- to five-day programs are widely available. Some are through professional schools such as the **Culinary Institute of America** (Hyde Park, NY 12538, tel. 800/888–7850), the nation's major professional school; the **California Culinary Academy** (625 Polk St., San Francisco, CA 94102, tel. 415/771–3536); and **Johnson and Wales University** (Abbot Park Pl., Providence, RI 02903, tel. 401/456–1000 or 800/343–2565).

Well-known chefs and cookbook authors sponsor other programs, notably **Julie Sahni's Indian Cooking** (101 Clark St., Brooklyn Heights, NY 11201, tel. 718/625–3958) and **Karen Lee Chinese Cooking Classes** (142 West End Ave., New York, NY 10023, tel. 212/787–2227). Other options are at such vineyards as the **Robert Mondavi Winery** (Box 106, Oakville, CA 94562, tel. 707/944–2866) and **Beringer Vineyards** (Box 111, St. Helena, CA 94574, tel. 707/963–7115), where Madeleine Kamman runs the school for American chefs.

Programs at Hotels, Inns, and Resorts If your traveling companions would rather play golf or tennis than slave over a hot stove, look into short programs at such inns as the Delmarva Peninsula's elegant **Channel Bass Inn** (6228 Church St., Chincoteague, VA 23336, tel. 804/336–6148), or at such grand resorts as **The Greenbrier Hotel** (White Sulphur Springs, WV 24986, tel. 304/536–1110 or 800/624–6070), where La Varenne's Anne Willan directs.

Resources For extensive listings of both short- and long-term programs, as well as information on gourmet and wine tours, consult *The Guide to Cooking Schools* ($19.95 postpaid from Shaw Guides Publishers, 625 Biltmore Way, Coral Gables, FL 33134, tel. 305/446–8888).

Crafts Workshops Short workshops in the crafts and fine arts are staged by major museums and at national parks such as Glacier, Yosemite, and Olympic. More extensive programs lasting from one to several weeks and focusing on a range of crafts—from metal, wood, and ceramics to indigenous regional and Native American crafts—are held at colleges, crafts centers, and individual studios.

Interdisciplinary Crafts Centers Dozens of weekend and week-long courses in basketry, bookmaking, ceramics, woodworking, and other topics draw pros as well as beginners and intermediates to such crafts centers as **Anderson Ranch Arts Center** (Box 5598, Snowmass Village, CO 81615, tel. 303/923–3181), on a Rocky Mountains ranch near Aspen; the **Arrowmont School of Arts and Crafts** (Box 567, Gatlinburg, TN 37738, tel. 615/436–5860), founded in 1945 on 70 acres a mile from the Great Smoky Mountains National Park; and the **Haystack Mountain School of Crafts** (Deer Isle, ME 04627–0518, tel. 207/348–2306), occupying a shingled, Atlantic-view studio complex on a Maine island. Several focus on traditional folk crafts; the oldest and most active are the **John C. Campbell Folk School** (Rte. 1, Box 14A, Brasstown, NC 28902, tel. 704/837–2775), whose campus is a National Historic District, and the **Penland School of Crafts** (Penland, NC 28765, tel. 704/765–2359), on 500 acres in the Blue Ridge Mountains.

Specialized Programs You can study everything from basketry and wooden boatbuilding to papermaking, couture sewing, and weaving. For extensive listings of what's available, consult *The Guide to Art & Craft Workshops* ($19.95 postpaid from Shaw Guides Publishers, 625 Biltmore Way, Coral Gables, FL 33134, tel. 305/446–8888).

Painting and Other Fine-Arts Workshops Amateurs can get professional tutelage at intensive programs at inns, resorts, museums, fine-arts centers, and even crafts schools nationwide (*see* Crafts Workshops, *above*).

Varied Programs Diverse programs that embrace disciplines ranging from printmaking, watercolor, portraiture, and still life to landscape painting are available at such schools as **The Art Institute of Boston** (Continuing Education, 700 Beacon St., Boston, MA 02215, tel. 617/262–1223) and **Dillman's Sand Lake Lodge** (Box 98, Lac du Flambeau, WI 54538, tel. 715/588–3143 or 800/359–2511), an old family summer resort in northern Wisconsin. Programs abound in Maine, among them the **Maine Coast Art Workshops** (c/o Merle Donovan, Box 236, Port Clyde, ME 04855, tel. 207/372–8200).

Specialized Programs   Some workshops concentrate on a specific medium, such as pastels or watercolors, or a specific style or theme—realism, western motifs, or seascapes, for instance. A comprehensive listing is in *The Guide to Art & Craft Workshops* (*see* Crafts Workshops, *above*).

Resources   *American Artist* (tel. 212/764–7300) magazine lists a wide array of summer programs such as those in its March issue.

Photography Workshops and Tours   Throughout the year amateurs and professionals sign up for workshops and tours designed to polish their techniques and take them to photogenic spots at the best possible times.

Workshops   Each workshop has a distinctive focus. Some cover theory and practice through fieldwork and seminars in black-and-white and color, looking at photography as both a fine and an applied art, in fields ranging from fashion to reportage. The active, well-established **Maine Photographic Workshops** (2 Central St., Rockport, ME 04856, tel. 207/236–8581) explores most aspects of photography, as do the well-respected if less picturesquely situated **International Center of Photography** (1130 5th Ave., New York, NY 10128, tel. 212/860–1776) and **Visual Studies Workshop** (31 Prince St., Rochester, NY 14607, tel. 716/442–8676). The **Friends of Photography Workshops** (250 4th St., San Francisco, CA 94103, tel. 415/495–7000) carries on the tradition of the venerable Ansel Adams Workshop, founded in 1940, which it now encompasses.

Guided Tours   Specialist tours, accompanied by professional photographers and scheduled to catch photogenic spots at optimal times, are offered by many organizations, including **Close-Up Expeditions** (1031 Ardmore Ave., Oakland, CA 94610, tel. 510/465–8955), the official Photographic Society of America tour operator; **Photo Adventure Tours** (2035 Park St., Atlantic Beach, NY 11509, tel. 516/371–0067); and **Thru the Lens Tours** (5855 Green Valley Circle, Culver City, CA 90230, tel. 310/645–8480 or 800/521–5367).

Resources   *American Photo* (tel. 212/767–6000) and *Popular Photography* (tel. 212/767–6000) magazines advertise tours and workshops. *The Guide to Photography Workshops & Schools* ($19.95 postpaid from Shaw Guides Publishers, 625 Biltmore Way, Coral Gables, FL 33134, tel. 305/446–8888) has extensive listings of programs.

Special Priorities

Traveling with Physical Limitations   Current legislation will mean more accessibility for people with disabilities. Many state tourism offices have special publications for disabled travelers. However, the quality of this information varies, and it falls to individual travelers to research destinations' accessibility. The **Information Center for Individuals with Disabilities** (Fort Point Pl., 27–43 Wormwood St., Boston, MA 02210, tel. 617/727–5540 or TDD 617/345–9743) has lists of travel agents specializing in tours for the disabled. The **Moss Rehabilitation Hospital Travel Information Service** (1200 W. Tabor Rd., Philadelphia, PA 19141, tel. 215/456–9600 or TDD 215/456–9602) maintains files on the accessibility of tourist sites, transportation, and accommodations, and can put you in touch with local organizations that will provide further information. The **Travel Industry and Disabled Exchange** (5435 Donna Ave., Tarzana, CA 91356, tel. 818/368–5648) has a quarterly newsletter for members ($15 annually). **Amtrak** (60 Massachusetts Ave. NE, Washington, DC 20001) outlines services for the disabled in the free, annually published book *Amtrak's America;* call 800/872–7245 for a copy. **Greyhound** (tel. 800/ 231–2222 or TDD 800/345–3109) will carry a disabled person and companion for the price of a single fare.

Other Resources Twin Peaks Press publishes three useful books: *Wheelchair Vagabond* ($16.95 postpaid) and *Travel for the Disabled* and the *Directory of Travel Agencies for the Disabled* (both $21.95 postpaid; all from Box 129, Vancouver, WA 98666, tel. 206/694–2462).

Traveling with Children A vacation with the kids presents a major quandary. Will you go for family togetherness or for time alone with your significant other? The answer is a destination with something for everyone or an activity that everyone likes.

For some families, **resorts with children's programs** are ideal because they attract other families—and potential playmates. Of these resorts, many offer simple two-hours-a-day programs, while others have their own day camps, complete with counselors. Among the many good bets is friendly, informal **Tyler Place** (Box 1, Highgate Springs, VT 05460, tel. 802/868–3301), whose programs were developed with families in mind. Like New York State's grand **Mohonk Mountain House** (New Paltz, NY 12561, tel. 914/255–1000), it offers age-segregated activity groups as well as a huge roster of indoor and outdoor activities. Youngsters also like **dude ranches,** and dude ranches like families, tailoring their activities to their needs. When choosing a resort for your family, don't forget to ask about baby-sitting, cribs, and high chairs if you need them.

If you want to get around a bit more, look into **cruises** geared toward families. **American Hawaii Cruises** (550 Kearny St., San Francisco, CA 94108, tel. 415/392–9400 or 800/765–7000), for example, offers substantial discounts and plenty of activities for kids on board. For other lines, ask your travel agent. Or try **houseboating** on the nation's mighty man-made lakes; it allows you to travel at your own pace, carrying all your paraphernalia aboard, and stop for fishing, swimming, and picnicking as the mood strikes. **RV travel** also minimizes the time you'll spend loading and unloading every night yet doesn't force you to stay in one place.

Opportunities for Senior Citizens Crossing the half-century mark opens up a whole new world of travel discounts and opportunities.

Programs for Seniors **Elderhostel** (75 Federal St., Boston, MA 02110, tel. 617/426–8056) programs cover everything from basket-weaving and bridge to contra dancing; they're open to over-60s only. Escorted tours especially for seniors are offered by **Saga Holidays** (222 Berkeley St., Boston, MA 02116, tel. 617/262–2262 or 800/ 343–0273) and the **AARP Travel Service** (400 Pinnacle Way, Bldg. 400, Norcross, GA 30071, tel. 800/927–0111).

Travel Partners **Saga Holidays Club** (120 Boylston St., Boston, MA 02116–9804, tel. 800/343–0273) has a membership program that matches up solo seniors.

Tips for Singles Your options extend as far as your sense of adventure—and may well put you in social situations with both other singles and married folk traveling alone on a vacation that their spouse wouldn't enjoy. You might learn a sport, sign up for an outdoor survival school, take an adventure trip, pursue a hobby such as art or photography, or even take a campus vacation. Many resorts are hospitable to singles—dude ranches being just one example.

For tours, contact **Singleworld** (401 Theodore Fremd Ave., Rye, NY 10580, tel. 914/967–3334 or 800/223–6490), founded in 1957. Or look into travel-companion matchmakers such as the large **Travel Companion Exchange** (Box 833, Amityville, NY 11701, tel. 516/454–0880).

State-Name Abbreviations

The following abbreviations are used for names of states in the United States:

Alabama AL	Nebraska NE
Alaska AK	Nevada NV
Arizona AZ	New Hampshire NH
Arkansas AR	New Jersey NJ
California CA	New Mexico NM
Colorado CO	New York NY
Connecticut CT	North Carolina NC
Delaware DE	North Dakota ND
Florida FL	Ohio OH
Georgia GA	Oklahoma OK
Hawaii HI	Oregon OR
Idaho ID	Pennsylvania PA
Illinois IL	Rhode Island RI
Indiana IN	South Carolina SC
Iowa IA	South Dakota SD
Kansas KS	Tennessee TN
Kentucky KY	Texas TX
Louisiana LA	Utah UT
Maine ME	Vermont VT
Maryland MD	Virginia VA
Massachusetts MA	Washington WA
Michigan MI	West Virginia WV
Minnesota MN	Wisconsin WI
Mississippi MS	Wyoming WY
Missouri MO	District of Columbia DC
Montana MT	

Toll-Free Numbers

Airlines

Air Canada (tel. 800/776–3000)
Alaska (tel. 800/426–0333)
Aloha (tel. 800/367–5250)
American (tel. 800/433–7300)
America West (tel. 800/247–5692)
British Airways (tel. 800/247–9297)
Canadian (tel. 800/426–7000)
Continental (tel. 800/525–0280)
Delta (tel. 800/221–1212)
Hawaiian (tel. 800/367–5320)
IslandAir (tel. 800/323–3345)
MarkAir (tel. 800/426–6784)
Mesa (tel. 800/637–2247)
Northwest (tel. 800/225–2525)
SkyWest (tel. 800/453–9417)
Southwest (tel. 800/435–9792)
TWA (tel. 800/221–2000)
United (tel. 800/241–6522)
USAir (tel. 800/428–4322)

Trains

Amtrak (tel. 800/872–7245)

Buses

Greyhound (tel. 800/231–2222)

Car Rentals

Alamo (tel. 800/327–9633)
Avis (tel. 800/331–1212)
Budget (tel. 800/527–0700)
Courtesy (tel. 800/252–9756)
Dollar (tel. 800/800–4000)
Enterprise (tel. 800/325–8007)
General (tel. 800/327–7607)
Hertz (tel. 800/654–3131)
National (tel. 800/328–4567)
Rent-A-Wreck (tel. 800/522–5436)
Sears (tel. 800/527–0770)
Thrifty (tel. 800/367–2277)
Ugly Duckling (tel. 800/843–3825)

Hotels

Adam's Mark (tel. 800/444–2326)
Best Western (tel. 800/528–1234)
Clarion (tel. 800/252–7466)

See state sections in the regional chapters above for state tourist office numbers that are not toll-free.

Colony (tel. 800/777–1700)
Comfort (tel. 800/228–5150)
Days Inn (tel. 800/325–2525)
Doubletree (tel. 800/528–0444)
Embassy Suites (tel. 800/362–2779)
Fairfield Inn (tel. 800/228–2800)
Forte (tel. 800/225–5843)
Four Seasons (tel. 800/332–3442)
Guest Quarters Suites (tel. 800/424–2900)
Hilton (tel. 800/445–8667)
Holiday Inn (tel. 800/465–4329)
Howard Johnson (tel. 800/654–4656)
Hyatt & Resorts (tel. 800/233–1234)
Inter-Continental (tel. 800/327–0200)
La Quinta (tel. 800/531–5900)
Leading Hotels of the World (tel. 800/223–6800)
Marriott (tel. 800/228–9290)
Meridien (tel. 800/543–4300)
Nikko International (tel. 800/645–5687)
Omni (tel. 800/843–6664)
Quality Inn (tel. 800/228–5151)
Radisson (tel. 800/333–3333)
Ramada (tel. 800/228–2828)
Red Lion (tel. 800/547–8010)
Ritz-Carlton (tel. 800/241–3333)
Sheraton (tel. 800/325–3535)
Sleep Inn (tel. 800/221–2222)
Stouffer (tel. 800/468–3571)
Westin Hotels & Resorts (tel. 800/228–3000)
Wyndham Hotels & Resorts (tel. 800/822–4200)

Motels

Budget Hosts Inns (tel. 800/283–4678)
Econo Lodge (tel. 800/553–2666)
Friendship Inns (tel. 800/453–4511)
Motel 6 (tel. 800/437–7486)
Rodeway (tel. 800/228–2000)
Super 8 (tel. 800/848–8888)

State Tourist Information

Alabama (tel. 800/252-2262)
Alaska*
Arkansas (tel. 800/643–8383)
California (tel. 800/862–2543)
Colorado (tel. 800/433–2656)
Connecticut (tel. 800/282–6863)
Delaware (tel. 800/441–8846)
Florida*
Georgia (tel. 800/847–4842)
Hawaii*
Idaho (tel. 800/847–4843)
Illinois (tel. 800/223–0121)
Indiana (tel. 800/289–6646)
Iowa (tel. 800/345–4692)
Kansas (tel. 800/252–6727)
Kentucky (tel. 800/225–8747)
Louisiana (tel. 800/334–8626)
Maine (tel. 800–533–9595)

Maryland (tel. 800/543–1036)
Massachusetts (tel. 800/447–6277)
Michigan (tel. 800/543–2937)
Minnesota (tel. 800/657–3700)
Mississippi (tel. 800/647–2290)
Missouri (tel. 800/877–1234)
Montana (tel. 800/541–1447)
Nebraska (tel. 800/228–4307)
Nevada (tel. 800/237–0774)
New Hampshire (tel. 800/258–3608)
New Jersey (tel. 800/537–7397)
New Mexico (tel. 800/545–2040)
New York (tel. 800/225–5697)
North Carolina (tel. 800/847–4862)
North Dakota (tel. 800/435–5063 or 800/437–2077)
Ohio (tel. 800/282–5393)
Oklahoma (tel. 800/652–6552)
Oregon (tel. 800/547–7842)
Pennsylvania (tel. 800/847–4872)
Rhode Island (tel. 800/556–2484)
South Dakota (tel. 800/843–1930)
South Carolina*
Tennessee*
Texas (tel. 800/888–8839)
Utah*
Vermont*
Virginia (tel. 800/847–4882)
Washington (tel. 800/544–1800)
Washington, DC (tel. 800/422–8644)
West Virginia (tel. 800/225–5982)
Wisconsin (tel. 800/432–8747)
Wyoming (tel. 800/225–5996)

Mileages between Major U.S. Cities

	Albuquerque	Atlanta	Billings	Boston	Chicago	Cincinnati	Cleveland	Dallas	Denver	Houston	Kansas City
Albuquerque	-	1409	990	2237	1327	1508	1605	649	447	864	773
Atlanta	1409	-	1833	1108	712	446	751	802	1418	790	807
Billings	990	1833	-	2189	1257	1562	1619	1395	553	1580	1045
Boston	2237	1108	2189	-	995	872	659	1774	1994	1848	1482
Chicago	1327	712	1257	995	-	288	346	929	1022	1096	541
Cincinnati	1508	446	1562	872	288	-	250	929	1190	1061	592
Cleveland	1605	751	1619	659	346	250	-	1190	1351	1340	745
Dallas	649	802	1395	1774	929	929	1190	-	789	244	508
Denver	447	1418	553	1994	1022	1190	1351	789	-	1035	611
Houston	864	790	1580	1848	1096	1061	1340	244	1035	-	697
Kansas City	773	807	1045	1482	541	592	745	508	611	697	-
Los Angeles	807	2278	1252	3017	2048	2115	2389	1424	1028	1546	1524
Memphis	1013	388	1538	1337	543	479	732	459	1045	580	467
Miami	2018	668	2536	1526	1317	1119	1260	1332	2076	1179	1456
New Orleans	1158	478	1880	1525	924	804	1056	512	1309	349	840
New York	2066	870	2065	208	808	675	476	1567	1790	1632	1230
Orlando	1795	437	2257	1320	1162	897	1059	1142	1863	976	1238
Philadelphia	1948	763	2021	324	776	584	434	1451	1749	1540	1152
Phoenix	464	1845	1264	2684	1766	1845	2047	954	802	1175	1247
Portland, OR	2334	2692	896	3179	2122	2358	2438	2042	1265	2260	1836
St. Louis	1038	572	1350	1198	295	359	578	642	871	842	250
Salt Lake	614	1927	604	2377	1416	1701	1747	1292	535	1503	1121
San Francisco	1100	2488	1242	3120	2159	2394	2472	1746	1261	1947	1865
Seattle	1447	2662	822	3060	2080	2375	2421	2121	1327	2362	1882
Washington, D.C.	1866	726	2047	456	705	527	367	1317	1648	1385	1054

Los Angeles	Memphis	Miami	New Orleans	New York	Orlando	Philadelphia	Phoenix	Portland, OR	St. Louis	Salt Lake	San Francisco	Seattle	Washington, D.C.
807	1013	2018	1158	2066	1795	1948	464	2334	1038	614	1100	1447	1866
2278	388	668	478	870	437	763	1845	2692	572	1927	2488	2662	726
1252	1538	2536	1880	2065	2257	2021	1264	896	1350	604	1242	822	2047
3017	1337	1526	1525	208	1320	324	2684	3119	1198	2377	3120	3060	456
2048	543	1317	924	808	1142	776	1766	2122	295	1416	2159	2080	705
2115	479	1119	804	675	897	584	1845	2358	359	1701	2394	2375	527
2389	732	1260	1056	476	1059	434	2047	2438	578	1747	2472	2421	367
1424	459	1332	512	1567	1112	1451	954	2042	642	1292	1746	2121	1317
1028	1045	2076	1309	1790	1863	1749	802	1265	871	535	1261	1327	1648
1546	580	1179	349	1632	976	1540	1175	2260	842	1503	1947	2362	1385
1524	467	1456	841	1230	1238	1152	1247	1836	250	1121	1865	1882	1054
-	1815	2749	1930	2791	2507	2713	374	387	1836	696	375	1137	2666
1815	-	997	410	1094	787	1025	1474	2330	285	1574	2109	2315	870
2749	997	-	858	1340	230	1222	2358	3277	1212	2555	3089	3335	1064
1930	410	858	-	1334	650	1238	1515	2552	687	1815	2304	2615	1091
2791	1094	1340	1334	-	1114	102	2518	2909	988	2191	2926	2876	236
2507	787	230	650	1114	-	997	2123	3078	998	2337	2875	3125	860
2713	1025	1222	1238	102	997	-	2442	2862	904	2153	2892	2844	138
374	1474	2358	1515	2518	2123	2442	-	1305	1492	650	757	1487	2326
387	2330	3277	2552	2909	3078	2862	1305	-	2076	760	639	174	2978
1836	285	1212	687	988	998	904	1492	2079	-	1371	2115	2137	846
696	1574	2555	1815	2191	2337	2153	650	760	1371	-	743	834	2126
375	2109	3089	2304	2926	2875	2892	757	639	2115	746	-	808	2889
1137	2315	3335	2615	2876	3125	2844	1487	174	2137	834	808	-	2763
2666	870	1064	1091	236	860	138	2326	2978	846	2126	2889	2763	-

Frequent Flyer Affiliations: Hotels and Car Rentals

	Hotels														Car Rental						
	Adam's Mark	Doubletree	Hilton	Hyatt	Inter-Continental	Marriott	Omni	Radisson	Red Lion	Sheraton	Stouffer	Westin	West Mark	Wyndham	Alamo	Avis	Budget	Dollar	Hertz	National	Thrifty
Alaska Mileage Plan				●					●			●	●		●		●				
American AAdvantage		●	●		●	●				●				●	●	●			●		
America West Flight Fund			●					●				●					●				●
British Airways						●															
Canadian Canadian Plus					●								●								●
Continental		●				●		●							●			●		●	●
Delta Frequent Flyers			●	●		●										●					
Northwest World Perks				●		●		●				●					●		●	●	
TWA Frequent Flyers	●	●																●			
United Mileage Plus			●	●	●					●		●			●			●	●	●	
USAir Frequent Traveler			●	●		●	●	●			●	●			●				●	●	

Conversion Tables

Distance

Kilometers/Miles To change kilometers to miles, multiply kilometers by .621.
To change miles to kilometers, multiply miles by 1.61.

Km to Mi	Mi to Km
1 = .62	1 = 1.6
2 = 1.2	2 = 3.2
3 = 1.9	3 = 4.8
4 = 2.5	4 = 6.4
5 = 3.1	5 = 8.1
6 = 3.7	6 = 9.7
7 = 4.3	7 = 11.3
8 = 5.0	8 = 12.9
9 = 5.6	9 = 14.5

Meters/Feet To change meters to feet, multiply meters by 3.28.
To change feet to meters, multiply feet by .305.

Meters to Feet	Feet to Meters
1 = 3.3	1 = .31
2 = 6.6	2 = .61
3 = 9.8	3 = .92
4 = 13.1	4 = 1.2
5 = 16.4	5 = 1.5
6 = 19.7	6 = 1.8
7 = 23.0	7 = 2.1
8 = 26.2	8 = 2.4
9 = 29.5	9 = 2.7

Weight

Kilograms/Pounds To change kilograms to pounds, multiply kilos by 2.20.
To change pounds to kilograms, multiply pounds by .453.

Kilo to Pound	Pound to Kilo
1 = 2.2	1 = .45
2 = 4.4	2 = .91
3 = 6.6	3 = 1.4
4 = 8.8	4 = 1.8
5 = 11.0	5 = 2.3

6 = 13.2	6 = 2.7
7 = 15.4	7 = 3.2
8 = 17.6	8 = 3.6
9 = 19.8	9 = 4.1

Grams/Ounces To change grams to ounces, multiply grams by .035.
To change ounces to grams, multiply ounces by 28.4.

Grams to Ounces	Ounces to Grams
1 = .04	1 = 28
2 = .07	2 = 57
3 = .11	3 = 85
4 = .14	4 = 114
5 = .18	5 = 142
6 = .21	6 = 170
7 = .25	7 = 199
8 = .28	8 = 227
9 = .32	9 = 256

Liquid Volume

Liters/U.S. Gallons To change liters to U.S. gallons, multiply liters by .264.
To change U.S. gallons to liters, multiply gallons by 3.79.

Liters to U.S. Gallons	U.S. Gallons to Liters
1 = .26	1 = 3.8
2 = .53	2 = 7.6
3 = .79	3 = 11.4
4 = 1.1	4 = 15.1
5 = 1.3	5 = 18.9
6 = 1.6	6 = 22.7
7 = 1.8	7 = 26.5
8 = 2.1	8 = 30.3
9 = 2.4	9 = 34.1

Escape to ancient cities and exotic

islands *with CNN Travel Guide, a*

wealth of valuable advice. Host Valerie Voss will take you

to all of your favorite destinations,

including those off the beaten path.

Tune into your passport to the world.

CNN TRAVEL GUIDE

SATURDAY 10:00 PMᴘᴛ   SUNDAY 8:30 AMᴇᴛ

WHEREVER YOU TRAVEL, *H*ELP IS NEVER FAR AWAY.

From planning your trip to

providing travel assistance along

the way, American Express®

Travel Service Offices* are

always there to help.

1-800-YES-AMEX

**American Express Travel Service Offices are
found in central locations throughout the
United States.**

INTRODUCING

AT LAST, YOUR OWN PERSONALIZED LIST OF WHAT'S GOING ON IN THE CITIES YOU'RE VISITING.

KEYED TO THE DAYS WHEN YOU'RE THERE, CUSTOMIZED FOR YOUR INTERESTS, AND SENT TO YOU BEFORE YOU LEAVE HOME.

EXCLUSIVE FOR PURCHASERS OF FODOR'S GUIDES...

Introducing a revolutionary way to get customized, time-sensitive travel information just before your trip.

Now you can obtain detailed information about what's going on in each city you'll be visiting <u>before</u> you leave home—up-to-the-minute, objective information about the events and activities that interest you most.

This is a special offer for purchasers of Fodor's guides – a customized Travel Update to fit your specific interests and your itinerary.

Travel Updates contain the kind of time-sensitive insider information you can get only from local contacts – or from city magazines and newspapers once you arrive. But now you can have the same information before you leave for your trip.

The choice is yours: current art exhibits, theater, music festivals and special concerts, sporting events, antiques and flower shows, shopping, fitness, and more.

The information comes from hundreds of correspondents and thousands of sources worldwide. Updated continuously, it's like having your own personal concierge or friend in the city.

You specify the cities and when you'll be there. We'll do the rest — personalizing the information for you the way no guidebook can.

It's the perfect extension to your Fodor's guide and the best way to make the most of your valuable travel time.

Your Itinerary:
Customized reports available for 160 destinations

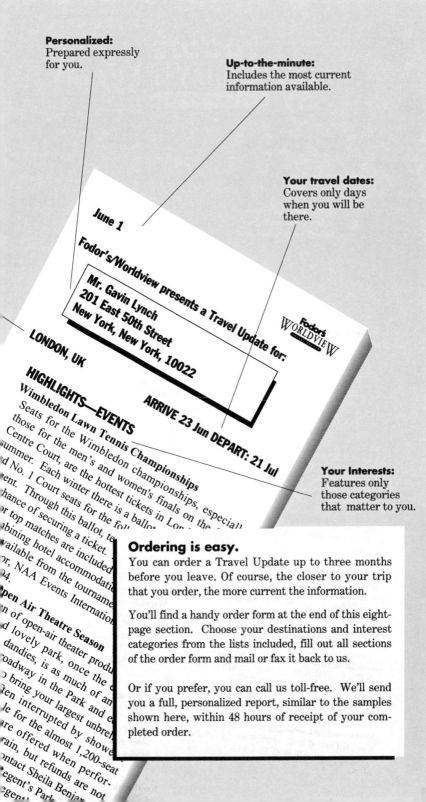

Personalized:
Prepared expressly for you.

Up-to-the-minute:
Includes the most current information available.

Your travel dates:
Covers only days when you will be there.

June 1

Fodor's/Worldview presents a Travel Update for:

Mr. Gavin Lynch
201 East 50th Street
New York, New York, 10022

WORLDVIEW

LONDON, UK

ARRIVE 23 Jun DEPART: 21 Jul

Your Interests:
Features only those categories that matter to you.

HIGHLIGHTS—EVENTS

Wimbledon Lawn Tennis Championships

Seats for the Wimbledon championships, especially
those for the men's and women's finals on the
Centre Court, are the hottest tickets in Lon
summer. Each winter there is a ballo
d No. 1 Court seats for the fol
ent. Through this ballot, te
hance of securing a ticket.
or top matches are included
bining hotel accommodat
vailable from the tourname
or, NAA Events Internation
4.

Open Air Theatre Season
n of open-air theater produ
d lovely park, once the
dandies, is as much of an
roadway in the Park and e
o bring your largest unbre
en interrupted by showe
le for the almost 1,200-seat
are offered when perfor-
rain, but refunds are not
ontact Sheila Benja
egent's Park
egen

Ordering is easy.

You can order a Travel Update up to three months
before you leave. Of course, the closer to your trip
that you order, the more current the information.

You'll find a handy order form at the end of this eight-
page section. Choose your destinations and interest
categories from the lists included, fill out all sections
of the order form and mail or fax it back to us.

Or if you prefer, you can call us toll-free. We'll send
you a full, personalized report, similar to the samples
shown here, within 48 hours of receipt of your completed order.

**Special concerts—
who's performing
what and where**

**One-of-a-kind,
one-time-only events**

**Special interest,
in-depth listings**

Children — Events

Angel Canal Festival
The festivities include a children's funfair, entertainers, a boat rally and displays on the water. Regent's Canal. Islington. N1. Tube: Angel. Tel: 267 9100. 11:30am-5:30pm. 7/04.

Blackheath Summer Kite Festival
Stunt kite displays with parachuting teddy bears and trade stands. Free admission. SE3. BR: Blackheath. 10am. 6/27.

Megabugs
Children will delight in this infestation of giant robotic insects, including a praying mantic 60 times life size. Mon-Sat 10am-6pm; Sun 11am-6pm. Admission 4.50 pounds. Natural History Museum, Cromwell Road. SW7. Tube: South Kensington. Tel: 938 9123. Ends 10/01.

Childminders
This establishment employs only women, providing nurses and qualified nannies to

Music — Jazz & Blues

Tito Puente's Golden Men of Latin Jazz
The father of mambo and Cuban rumba king comes to town. Royal Festival Hall. South Bank. SE1. Tube: Waterloo. Tel: 928 8800. 8pm. 7/15.

Georgie Fame and The New York Band
Riding a popular tide with his latest album, the smoky-voiced Fame and his keyboard are on a tour yet again. The Grand. Clapham Junction. SW11. BR: Clapham Junction. Tel: 738 9000. 7:30pm. 7/07.

Jacques Loussier Play Bach Trio
The French jazz classicist and colleagues. Kenwood Lakeside. Hampstead Lane. Kenwood. NW3. Tube: Golders Green, then bus 210. Tel: 413 1443. 7pm. 7/10.

Tony Bennett and Ronnie Scott
Royal Festival Hall. South Bank. SE1. Tube: Waterloo. Tel: 928 8800. 8pm. 7/11.

Santana
Royal Festival Hall. South Bank. SE1. Tube: Waterloo. Tel: 928 8800. 8pm. 7/12.

Count Basie Orchestra and Nancy Wilson Trio
Royal Festival Hall. South Bank. SE1. Tube: Waterloo. Tel: 928 8800. 8pm. 7/14.

King Pleasure and the Biscuit Boys
Royal Festival Hall. South Bank. SE1. Tube: Waterloo. Tel: 928 8800. 6:30 and 9pm. 7/16.

Al Green and the London Community Gospel Choir
Royal Festival Hall. South Bank. SE1. Tube: Waterloo. Tel: 928 8800. 8pm. 7/13.

BB King and Linda Hopkins
Mother of the blues and successor to Bessie Smith, Hopkins meets up with "Blues Boy" ... Festival Hall. South Bank. SE

Music — Classical

Marylebone Sinfonia
Kenneth Gowen conducts music by Puc and Rossini. Queen Elizabeth Hall. So Bank. SE1. Tube: Waterloo. Tel: 928 8 7:45pm. 7/16.

London Philharmonic
Franz Welser-Moest and George Benja conduct selections by Alexander Go Messiaen, and some of Benjamin's own positions. Queen Elizabeth Hall. South SE1. Tube: Waterloo. Tel: 928 8800. 8pr

London Pro Arte Orchestra and Forest C
Murray Stewart conducts selectio Rossini, Haydn and Jonathan Willcocks. Queen Elizabeth Hall. South Bank. Tube: Waterloo. Tel: 928 8800. 7:45pm.

Kensington Symphony Orchestra
Russell Keable conducts Dvorak's D

Here's what you get . . .

Detailed information about what's going on — precisely when you'll be there.

Show openings during your visit

Reviews by local critics

Exhibitions & Shows—Antique & Flower

Westminster Antiques Fair

Over 50 stands with pre-1830 furniture and other Victorian and earlier items. Thu-Fri 11am-8pm; Sat-Sun 11am-6pm. Admission 4 pounds, children free. Old Royal Horticultural Hall. Vincent Square. SW1. Tel: 0444/48 25 14. 6-24 thru 6/27.

Royal Horticultural Society Flower Show

The show includes displays of carnations, summer fruit and vegetables. Tue 11am-7pm; Wed 10am-5pm. Admission Tue 4 pounds, Wed 2 pounds. Royal Horticultural Halls. Greycoat Street and Vincent Square. SW1. Tube: Victoria. 7/20 thru 7/21.

[Ha]mpton Court Palace International Flower Show

[M]ajor international garden and flower show [ta]king place in conjunction with the British

Theater — Musical

Sunset Boulevard

In June, the four Andrew Lloyd Webber musicals which dominated London's stages in the 1980s (Cats, Starlight Express, Phantom of the Opera and Aspects of Love) are joined by the composer's latest work, a show rumored to have his best music to date. The 1950 Billy Wilder film about a helpless young writer who is drawn into the world of a possessive, aging silent screen star offers rich opportunities for Webber's evolving style. Soaring, aching melodies, lush technical effects and psychological thrills are all expected. Patti Lupone stars. Mon-Sat at 8pm; matinee Thu-Sat at 3pm. In-person bookings only at the box office; credit card bookings, Tel: 344 0055. Admission 15-32.50 pounds. Adelphi Theatre. The Strand. WC2. Tube: Charing Cross. Tel: 836 7611. Starts: 6/21

Leonardo A Portrait of Love

A new musical about the great Renaissance arti[st] and inventor comes in for a London premier[e] tested by a brief run at Oxford's Old Fire Stati[on] [in] autumn. The work explores the relations[hip] [of Da] Vinci and the woman '

Alberquerque • Atlanta • Atlantic City • N
Baltimore • Boston • Chicago • Cincinnati
Cleveland • Dallas/Ft.Worth • Denver • De[troit]
• Houston • Kansas City • Las Vegas • Los
[Los] Angeles • Memphis • Miami • Milwaukee •
New Orleans • New York City • Orlando •
[Colorado] Springs • Philadelphia • Phoenix • Pittsburg[h]
Portland • Salt Lake • San Antonio • San Di[ego]
• San Franc[isco] • Sea[ttle] • [St.] Louis • Tamp[a]
Oslo • Was[hington] • [Honolul]u • Island •
Hawaii • Kauai • Maui • Abacos • Bimini
Exu[ma] • [Free]port • [Har]bour Island •
Ber[muda] Countryside • [Ham]ilton • [Is]lan[d]
Antigua & B[arbuda] • [Ar]uba [Ne]vis • [T]orto[la]
[Virgin] Gorda • Barbados • Dominica • Gren[ada]
[Cura]cia • St. Vincent • Trinidad &Tobago •
[Cay]mans • Puerto Plata • Santo Doming[o]
• Aruba • Bonaire • Curacao • St. Ma[arten]
[Queb]ec City • Montreal • Ottawa • Toro[nto]
[Van]couver • Guadeloupe • Martiniqu[e]
[St. B]arthelemy • St. Martin • Kingston • Ixta[pa]
[Montego] Bay • Negril • Ocho Rios • Ponce •
[Sa]n • Grand Turk • Providenciales • S[t.]
[St.] John • St. Thomas • Acapulco •
[Cancun] & Isla Mujeres • Cozumel • Guadal[ajara]
• Los Cabos • Manzanillo • Mazatl[an]
[Mexico] City • Monterrey • Oaxaca • Puerto [Escondido]
[Lare]do • Puerto Vallarta • Veracruz • Ix[tapa]
[ban] • Athens • B[arcelona]

Spectator Sports — Other Sports

Greyhound Racing: Wembley Stadium

This dog track offers good views of greyhound racing held on Mon, Wed and Fri. No credit cards. Stadium Way. Wembley. HA9. Tube: Wembley Park. Tel: 902 8833.

Benson & Hedges Cricket Cup Final

Lord's Cricket Ground. St. John's Wood Road. NW8. Tube: St. John's Wood. Tel: 289 1611. 11am. 7/10.

Business-Fax & Overnight Mail

Post Office, Trafalgar Square Branch

Offers a network of fax services, the Intelpost system, throughout the country and abroad. Mon-Sat 8am-8pm, Sun 9am-5pm. William IV Street. WC2. Tube: Ch[aring]

Fodor's WORLDVIEW TRAVEL UPDATE

Interest Categories

For <u>your</u> personalized Travel Update, choose the categories you're most interested in from this list. Every Travel Update automatically provides you with *Event Highlights* – the best of what's happening during the dates of your trip.

| 1. | **Business Services** | Fax & Overnight Mail, Computer Rentals, Photocopying, Secretarial , Messenger, Translation Services |

Dining

2.	**All Day Dining**	Breakfast & Brunch, Cafes & Tea Rooms, Late-Night Dining
3.	**Local Cuisine**	In Every Price Range—from Budget Restaurants to the Special Splurge
4.	**European Cuisine**	Continental, French, Italian
5.	**Asian Cuisine**	Chinese, Far Eastern, Japanese, Indian
6.	**Americas Cuisine**	American, Mexican & Latin
7.	**Nightlife**	Bars, Dance Clubs, Comedy Clubs, Pubs & Beer Halls
8.	**Entertainment**	Theater—Drama, Musicals, Dance, Ticket Agencies
9.	**Music**	Classical, Traditional & Ethnic, Jazz & Blues, Pop, Rock
10.	**Children's Activities**	Events, Attractions
11.	**Tours**	Local Tours, Day Trips, Overnight Excursions, Cruises
12.	**Exhibitions, Festivals & Shows**	Antiques & Flower, History & Cultural, Art Exhibitions, Fairs & Craft Shows, Music & Art Festivals
13.	**Shopping**	Districts & Malls, Markets, Regional Specialities
14.	**Fitness**	Bicycling, Health Clubs, Hiking, Jogging
15.	**Recreational Sports**	Boating/Sailing, Fishing, Ice Skating, Skiing, Snorkeling/Scuba, Swimming
16.	**Spectator Sports**	Auto Racing, Baseball, Basketball, Football, Horse Racing, Ice Hockey, Soccer

Please note that interest category content will vary by season, destination, and length of stay.

Destinations

The Fodor's/Worldview Travel Update covers more than 160 destinations worldwide. Choose the destinations that match your itinerary from this list. (Choose bulleted destinations only.)

United States (Mainland)
- Albuquerque
- Atlanta
- Atlantic City
- Baltimore
- Boston
- Chicago
- Cincinnati
- Cleveland
- Dallas/Ft. Worth
- Denver
- Detroit
- Houston
- Kansas City
- Las Vegas
- Los Angeles
- Memphis
- Miami
- Milwaukee
- Minneapolis/St. Paul
- New Orleans
- New York City
- Orlando
- Palm Springs
- Philadelphia
- Phoenix
- Pittsburgh
- Portland
- St. Louis
- Salt Lake City
- San Antonio
- San Diego
- San Francisco
- Seattle
- Tampa
- Washington, DC

Alaska
- Anchorage/Fairbanks/Juneau

Hawaii
- Honolulu
- Island of Hawaii
- Kauai
- Maui

Canada
- Quebec City
- Montreal
- Ottawa
- Toronto
- Vancouver

Bahamas
- Abacos
- Eleuthera/Harbour Island
- Exumas
- Freeport
- Nassau & Paradise Island

Bermuda
- Bermuda Countryside
- Hamilton

British Leeward Islands
- Anguilla
- Antigua & Barbuda
- Montserrat
- St. Kitts & Nevis

British Virgin Islands
- Tortola & Virgin Gorda

British Windward Islands
- Barbados
- Dominica
- Grenada
- St. Lucia
- St. Vincent
- Trinidad & Tobago

Cayman Islands
- The Caymans

Dominican Republic
- Puerto Plata
- Santo Domingo

Dutch Leeward Islands
- Aruba
- Bonaire
- Curacao

Dutch Windward Islands
- St. Maarten

French West Indies
- Guadeloupe
- Martinique
- St. Barthelemy
- St. Martin

Jamaica
- Kingston
- Montego Bay
- Negril
- Ocho Rios

Puerto Rico
- Ponce
- San Juan

Turks & Caicos
- Grand Turk
- Providenciales

U.S. Virgin Islands
- St. Croix
- St. John
- St. Thomas

Mexico
- Acapulco
- Cancun & Isla Mujeres
- Cozumel
- Guadalajara
- Ixtapa & Zihuatanejo
- Los Cabos
- Manzanillo
- Mazatlan
- Mexico City
- Monterrey
- Oaxaca
- Puerto Escondido
- Puerto Vallarta
- Veracruz

Europe
- Amsterdam
- Athens
- Barcelona
- Berlin
- Brussels
- Budapest
- Copenhagen
- Dublin
- Edinburgh
- Florence
- Frankfurt
- French Riviera
- Geneva
- Glasgow
- Interlaken
- Istanbul
- Lausanne
- Lisbon
- London
- Madrid
- Milan
- Moscow
- Munich
- Oslo
- Paris
- Prague
- Provence
- Rome
- Salzburg
- St. Petersburg
- Stockholm
- Venice
- Vienna
- Zurich

Pacific Rim Australia & New Zealand
- Auckland
- Melbourne
- Sydney

China
- Beijing
- Guangzhou
- Shanghai

Japan
- Kyoto
- Nagoya
- Osaka
- Tokyo
- Yokohama

Other
- Bangkok
- Hong Kong & Macau
- Manila
- Seoul
- Singapore
- Taipei

Fodor's
WORLDVIEW **Order Form**
TRAVEL UPDATE

THIS TRAVEL UPDATE IS FOR (Please print):

Name

Address

City	State	ZIP
Country	Tel # ( ) -	

Title of this Fodor's guide:

Store and location where guide was purchased:

INDICATE YOUR DESTINATIONS/DATES: Write in below the destinations you want to order. Then fill in your arrival and departure dates for each destination.

		Month	Day		Month	Day
(Sample) LONDON	From:	6 /	21	To: 6	/	30
1	From:	/		To:	/	
2	From:	/		To:	/	
3	From:	/		To:	/	

You can order up to three destinations per Travel Update. Only destinations listed on the previous page are applicable. Maximum amount of time covered by a Travel Update cannot exceed 30 days.

CHOOSE YOUR INTERESTS: Select up to eight categories from the list of interest categories shown on the previous page and circle the numbers below:

1 2 3 4 5 6 7 8 9 10 11 12 13 14 15 16

CHOOSE HOW YOU WANT YOUR TRAVEL UPDATE DELIVERED (Check one):

❑ Please mail my Travel Update to the address above **OR**

❑ Fax it to me at **Fax #** ( ) -

DELIVERY CHARGE (Check one)

	Within U.S. & Canada	Outside U.S. & Canada
First Class Mail	❑ $2.50	❑ $5.00
Fax	❑ $5.00	❑ $10.00
Priority Delivery	❑ $15.00	❑ $27.00

All orders will be sent within 48 hours of receipt of a completed order form.

ADD UP YOUR ORDER HERE. *SPECIAL OFFER FOR FODOR'S PURCHASERS ONLY!*

	Suggested Retail Price	Your Price	This Order
First destination ordered	$13.95	$ 7.95	$ 7.95
Second destination (if applicable)	$ 9.95	$ 4.95	+
Third destination (if applicable)	$ 9.95	$ 4.95	+
Plus delivery charge from above			+
		TOTAL:	$

METHOD OF PAYMENT (Check one): ❑ AmEx ❑ MC ❑ Visa ❑ Discover
❑ Personal Check ❑ Money Order

Make check or money order payable to: Fodor's Worldview Travel Update

Credit Card #   **Expiration Date:**

Authorized Signature

SEND THIS COMPLETED FORM TO:
Fodor's Worldview Travel Update, 114 Sansome Street, Suite 700, San Francisco, CA 94104

OR CALL OR FAX US 24-HOURS A DAY
Telephone **1-800-799-9609** • Fax **1-800-799-9619** (From within the U.S. & Canada)
(Outside the U.S. & Canada: Telephone 415-616-9988 • Fax 415-616-9989)

(Please have this guide in front of you when you call so we can verify purchase.)

Offer valid until 12/31/94.